D1871061

The Natural History of Animals

DIANA MONKEYS (*Cercopithecus Diana*)

These pretty little animals are characteristic members of the West African fauna, and belong to the group of Guenons (*Cercopithecus*). The white beard and white crescent on the forehead are distinctive features, the latter having been fancifully compared to " Dian's bow ", hence the popular and specific names. Diana monkeys are typical tree-forms, living in communities and, being gentle easily-tamed creatures, have alwavs been favourite pets.

1

DIANA MONKEYS (CERCOPITHECUS DIANA)

The Natural History of Animals

The animal life of the world in its various aspects and relations

IN FOUR VOLUMES

BY

J.R. AINSWORTH DAVIS

Volume I

GIAN PUBLISHING HOUSE

New Delhi-110002

Gian Publishing House
4348, Madan Mohan Street
4C, Ansari Road, Darya Ganj.
New Delhi - 110002

First Indian Edition 1989
First Printed 1905

ISBN 81 - 212 - 0253 - 1 Set
ISBN 81 - 212 - 0256 - 6

Printed In India
at
Goyal Offset Printers, Delhi.

PREFACE

Signs are not wanting that at the present time a revival of interest in Zoology is taking place, and this book is an attempt to help on the movement by pointing out the various lines of study and explaining in simple language the views of modern specialists. Every effort has been made to treat the subject-matter in such a way as to interest the general reader, while at the same time the needs of junior students, amateur naturalists, and teachers of elementary Zoology (including "Nature Study") have been steadily borne in mind.

All the larger popular books on Zoology which have so far appeared in English take the various animal groups seriatim, a time-honoured plan which is in many ways valuable and useful, but which fails to bring out the complex interrelations that exist between the different groups, the interdependence of animals and plants, and the bearing upon life of chemical and physical conditions. A due appreciation of the great complexity of the struggle for existence, and a realization of our comparative ignorance regarding adaptation of structure to habit, should open innumerable fascinating lines of really scientific study to many amateurs who are at present mere collectors of insects, birds' eggs, or shells. It may, however, be noted that Half-Vols. I and II to some extent meet the needs of those who prefer the old plan, for they review in brief the entire animal kingdom, as a necessary preliminary to the study of the Food of Animals, Animal Defences, &c., which constitute the subject-matter of the remaining volumes. Even in the first two half-volumes, however, comparisons are constantly instituted between different animals and different groups, in illustration of general principles.

The Introduction fully explains the plan of the work, and the lines which have been adopted in writing it, and books to which the Author is specially indebted are mentioned in the text. It is both mentally and physically impossible for one zoologist to know at first hand more than a small part of his subject, and for this reason full quotations, in preference to mere paraphrases, have been taken from the writings of many distinguished specialists, the sources in such cases being always indicated.

Many of the coloured plates have been drawn expressly for this book by Mr. A. Fairfax Muckley and Mr. William Kühnert, and others are by Specht, the distinguished delineator of animal life. Some of the black-and-white plates, and many of the text illustrations are also new, and the remainder have been taken or re-drawn from acknowledged sources. Mr. R. A. L. Van Someren has been so good as to place at my disposal a number of his interesting photographs of birds and birds' nests, while Prof. D'Arcy W. Thompson and Mr. W. H. Reeves have obligingly supplied me with other original photographs.

Special acknowledgment is also due to the authors and publishers of *Das Tierreich*, *Die Schöpfung der Tierwelt*, *Das Leben des Meeres*, and *Tierische Schädlinge und Nützlinge* for their courteous permission to make use of other illustrations. My friend and colleague, Dr. H. J. Fleure, was so kind as to undertake the arduous task of editing the Index.

J. R. AINSWORTH DAVIS.

ABERYSTWYTH, *October*, 1904.

CONTENTS

VOL. I.

INTRODUCTION

CHAPTER I

CLASSIFICATION—STRUCTURE OF MAN TAKEN AS A TYPE

CHAPTER II

ESSENTIAL CHARACTERS OF VERTEBRATE ANIMALS. STRUCTURE AND CLASSIFICATION OF MAMMALS (Mammalia)

MAMMALS (Mammalia)

A. Eutheria

CHAPTER III

STRUCTURE AND CLASSIFICATION OF BIRDS (AVES)

CHAPTER IV

STRUCTURE AND CLASSIFICATION OF REPTILES (REPTILIA)

CHAPTER V

STRUCTURE AND CLASSIFICATION OF AMPHIBIANS (AMPHIBIA)

LIST OF ILLUSTRATIONS

VOL. I

PLATES

ILLUSTRATIONS

NATURAL HISTORY

INTRODUCTION

ON SCIENTIFIC METHOD

There are so many things to study in this world of ours, and outside it too, that it is no easy task to draw up a complete list of subjects. And supposing this done, it is a still harder task to determine the connection between the various subjects. This is not the place to attempt such a labour, and it will suffice for our present purpose to point out that in universities and other seats of learning it is customary to draw a distinction between "Arts" and "Science" courses, though the boundary line is indefinite. The Arts student is chiefly concerned with language, literature, mathematics, and philosophy; while the Science student, as such, is especially distinguished by the fact that he must work in the laboratory as well as in the lecture-room, at chemistry, physics, and biology, besides attending mathematical and, it may be, philosophical classes. It will thus be seen that mathematics and philosophy are considered common ground.

As this book deals with a branch of science, it may be well to enquire more particularly what "science" actually is. And here we have to distinguish between "pure" and "natural" science. "Pure" mathematics, the fringe of which is touched by all of us when we study arithmetic, algebra, and geometry, is an example of the former. It starts with certain self-evident truths, and makes deductions from these. The "natural" sciences, on the other hand, such as chemistry, physics, and biology, involve the study of facts by observation and experiment, these facts being afterwards used as a means of determining the laws which regulate the universe. It is this special mode of procedure, the "*scientific method*", which distinguishes the natural sciences. The mode itself is known to everyone, though comparatively few could explain its exact nature. Huxley says (in his well-known address "On the Educational Value of the Natural History Sciences"): "Science is, I believe, nothing but *trained and organized common sense*, differing from the latter only as a veteran may differ from a raw recruit; and its methods differ from those of common sense only so far as the guardsman's cut and thrust differ from the manner in which a savage wields his club". The essence of the method consists in first ascertaining facts, resorting when necessary to experiment, then coming to some general conclusion based on the facts, and finally testing that conclusion by appeal to some case not previously investigated. Take, for example, the discovery of coal-seams by sinking a shaft through the chalk rocks at Dover. Prior to 1826 numerous observations had been made on the coal-bearing rocks in Somerset on the one hand and the north of France on the other hand, the conclusion being drawn that the two sets of rocks are practically identical. Twenty-nine years later, from these and many other additional facts regarding the distribution and arrangement of the coal-bearing rocks, Godwin Austen came to the conclusion that coal-fields exist far below the surface in the south-east of England. One such fact, the existence of coal below the surface-rocks of Oxfordshire, was determined by an experimental boring at Burford. Various considerations ultimately led to the selection of Dover as a suitable place for making a trial boring, which was begun in 1886 and completed in 1892. This boring proved the existence of a coal-field containing twelve seams of coal, the top of which is 1113 feet below high-water mark.[1]

Steps in above example of scientific method:—

1. The collection and arrangement of facts relating to the coal-fields of Somerset, north of France, and Belgium, some of the facts being determined by experiment.

2. Arrival at the following conclusion or generalization based on the said facts:—" Buried coal-fields exist in the area between

[1] The barest outline of the facts is here given. Details may be found in a pamphlet "On the Relation of Geology and Engineering," by Professor Boyd Dawkins, F.R.S.; being the "James Forrest" Lecture delivered at the Institution of Civil Engineers, Session 1897–98.—Published by the Institution, Great George Street, Westminster, London, S.W.

Somerset and north of France, the most likely locality being the neighbourhood of Dover".

3. Verification of the generalization. A shaft is sunk at Dover and a buried coal-field is actually discovered.

Among other striking examples of the scientific method may be mentioned the discovery of the Laws of Gravitation by Newton, and the discovery of the planet Neptune by Galle in the position where Adams and Leverrier independently prophesied a new planet would be found. It may be stated generally that when a theory or generalization enables us correctly to prophesy future events, that theory may be regarded as embodying one or more Laws of Nature. Thus, from calculations based on the theory of gravity, the position of the heavenly bodies at a given time can be predicted. Such calculations are to be found in the *Nautical Almanac*, published every three years, and these have always been found correct. Hence the Laws of Gravitation are regarded as Laws of Nature.

The scientific method is essentially experimental, and thus requires further illustration. Much can be done by observation only, but the progress of science would be exceedingly slow if it were not for *experiment*, *i.e.* the observation of facts under controlled conditions, enabling us to determine points which the mere watching of nature might never allow us to elucidate. Very good instances are found in the history of the "germ theory", which explains infectious diseases as only the action of microscopic organisms found within the body. Cattle, for example, are liable to be attacked by a most virulent complaint of the sort known as *anthrax* or *splenic fever*. It was noticed that the blood of animals which had died from this disease always swarmed with rod-shaped microscopic organisms, members of the large group of *bacteria* (microbes), the lowest subdivision of the vegetable kingdom. Mainly on the strength of this fact was founded the generalization—"Anthrax is due to rod-like bacteria in the blood". Then followed experiments designed to test the truth of this proposition. It was found that if healthy animals were inoculated with infected blood they quickly developed all the symptoms of anthrax, and died in the same manner and after the same time as in naturally occurring cases of the disease. A certain support was thus given to the generalization, but the possibility that the rods might be the consequence and not the cause of anthrax was not excluded, and further experiments of more elaborate and painstaking nature became necessary. By well-known methods, "pure cultures" were made of the rod-shaped microbes, *i.e.* they were grown in an artificially-prepared medium, free from all other germs, in such a way that such other germs continued to be excluded. Healthy animals were then inoculated from these pure cultures, with the result that typical anthrax at once manifested itself. In this way the original generalization was experimentally verified. By similar methods of procedure many other diseases have been proved to be due to the noxious action of specific microbes. Other instances of the experimental method will be given in the course of this work.

In all such cases the value of the *imagination* can hardly be overestimated. To frame a reasonable generalization from a mere collection of facts requires a mental jump, so to speak, and the man of real genius in the scientific world—the "epoch-making" man—is he who can make such leaps in the dark with the best prospect of alighting on solid ground.

THE STUDY OF ANIMALS

Subject-matter of Biology.—All material objects are composed of what is known as "matter", about which all that can positively be stated is that it occupies space, takes up room, as we may say. Matter is liable to undergo change, and these changes are dealt with by chemistry and physics; by the former if they involve modification in composition; by the latter if they do not. One particular kind of matter is distinguished by the possession of life, which is recognized by its effects, though we are profoundly ignorant of its real nature. *Biology*, the science of life (Greek *bios*, life; *logos*, a discourse), deals with living matter, that is to say, with plants and animals, from all possible points of view. As organisms are constantly undergoing both chemical and physical changes, it is obvious that a knowledge of physics and chemistry is, to say the least, of immense value to the biologist. It has even been suggested that life will some day be explained by chemical and physical laws; but, even if such mechanical explanation be possible, that day is far distant, for at present our knowledge of the composition of living substance is exceedingly crude and imperfect.

SUBDIVISIONS OF BIOLOGY.—So vast a subject as that dealing with life obviously needs subdivision for purposes of convenience, and it is customary to recognize two main branches, *Botany* and *Zoology*, dealing with plants and animals respectively (Greek *botanē*, a plant; *zōŏn*, an animal). This does not mean, however, that there is any sharp boundary between the animal and plant worlds. No doubt it is easy to tell the difference between a higher plant and a higher animal, though it might not be so simple to point out in exactly what the difference consists; but when we come to microscopic organisms, difficulties soon arise, and the usual tests break down. Well-defined lines of division but rarely occur in the organic world.

In this book we shall confine ourself in the main to *Zoology*, or *Natural History* as it is often called, but reference to the vegetable kingdom will have to be made in many connections, owing to the obvious fact that there is a very intimate relation between plants and animals.

WAYS OF STUDYING ZOOLOGY.—Animals, of course, can be studied from various stand-points, some of which will here be mentioned, as they form a basis for the splitting up of the subject. The accumulated observations of thousands of observers constitute such a mass of knowledge (one, too, that is ever growing), that it is a hopeless task for any individual to acquaint himself with what is already known, and even the professional zoologist can do no more than acquire a general knowledge of his subject, with special knowledge of some limited branch. And when we reflect that, after all, the known is very small, while the unknown is stupendously large, in amount, the present tendency to specialization becomes fully intelligible. It is nevertheless quite easy for anyone of average intelligence to acquire sound general ideas regarding the various possible modes of attacking the subject.

1. *The Stand-point of the Naturalist.*—Zoology to the naturalist is essentially an open-air study. He delights in watching living animals with the view of finding out all he can about their habits, naturally learning at the same time a great deal about their external features, and also finding it necessary to know something

about classification. Nearly every country child is a naturalist in this sense, not to mention many older persons, though for some decades there has been an unfortunate tendency to ignore habit and pay overmuch attention to what we may call laboratory zoology. The most admirable type of English naturalist is undoubtedly Gilbert White, author of the well-known book, *The Natural History of Selborne*, in which he records observations made by him during his residence there. Selborne was his native place. Born in 1720, he later on filled a curacy in the neighbouring parish of Faringdon (1755–84), ending his life as curate of Selborne (1784–93). The late Richard Jefferies, himself an ardent naturalist, speaks of White in a preface written to the Camelot edition of the *Natural History*. After quoting an observation as to the way the garden warbler sips honey from the Crown Imperial, Jefferies remarks:—"Here we . . . see how different minds may trace out the bearing of the same fact. The old naturalist at Selborne simply records it in language which could not be better chosen, highly delighted evidently, and taking a deep interest in it for its own sake. In the same manner, anyone who has a taste for out-of-door observations may study natural history without any previous scientific learning. . . . Part of his (White's) success was owing to his coming to the field with a mind unoccupied. He was not full of evolution when he walked out, or devolution, or degeneration. He did not look for microbes everywhere. His mind was free and his eye open. To many it would do much good to read this work, if only with the object of getting rid of some of the spiders' webs that have been so industriously spun over the eyesight of those who would like to think for themselves." Fortunately a reaction has been setting in of late in favour of natural history, and we are beginning to realize that far less is known about the habits than about the structure of animals.

Among charming books of the kind the following may well be mentioned:—

Bates—*Naturalist on the Amazons.*
Belt—*Naturalist in Nicaragua.*
Brehm—*From North Pole to Equator.*
Buckland—*Logbook of a Fisherman and Naturalist*, and *Curiosities of Natural History.*
Darwin—*A Naturalist's Voyage.*
Forbes—*A Naturalist's Wanderings in the Eastern Archipelago.*
Fowler—*Tales of the Birds*, and *A Year with the Birds.*

Gosse—*A Year at the Shore*, and other works.
Hickson—*A Naturalist in North Celebes.*
Hudson—*The Naturalist in La Plata.*
Jefferies—*Red Deer*, and other works.
Lloyd Morgan—*Animal Sketches.*
Moseley—*Naturalist on the "Challenger"*
Semon—*In the Australian Bush.*
Fred Smith—*Boyhood of a Naturalist.* A little book which breathes the spirit of Gilbert White in every page.
Wyville Thomson—*The Depths of the Sea*, and *Voyage of the "Challenger"*.
Thoreau—*Walden.*
Wallace—*Malay Archipelago*, and *Tropical Nature.*
Waterton—*A Naturalist's Wanderings in South America.*

The camera has lately with great success been pressed by the brothers C. and R. Kearton into the service of outdoor zoology, but this has not been done without untiring patience and the expenditure of a very large amount of time. Their books, *With Nature and a Camera*, *British Birds' Nests*, and *Wild Life at Home*, are ideally illustrated.

2. *The Stand-point of Classification.*—Such an enormous number of animals exist (considerably more than a million kinds being now known to science) that as a matter of convenience it is found necessary to classify them, that is, to arrange them into groups according to their likenesses and differences. Animals have always played such an important part in the lives of human beings, as sources of food, clothing, ornament, &c., and as objects of interest, that even the most primitive languages contain words for different kinds of animal. The names of those animals which have been longest domesticated, such as ox and sheep, are thus found to be of extremely ancient origin, and the same is true in the case of certain widely distributed and conspicuous wild forms, such as mouse, midge, beaver, and eel. But in addition to this we have class-names, such as bird, fish, snake, &c., which constitute the unconscious beginning of a rough classification, as they embody the fact that many kinds of animal collectively form a larger group, *e.g.* that of birds. But besides this we learn from the literature of many cultured peoples that even in early times deliberate attempts at classification were made. An example of this may be found in Genesis, i. 26, where we read, ". . . let them have dominion over the fish of the sea, and over the fowl of the air, and over the cattle, . . . and over every creeping thing

that creepeth upon the earth". Solomon is represented (1 Kings iv. 33) as using the same fourfold division, except that the word "beast" is used instead of "cattle". The creatures included under the former term are evidently those which are popularly called "quadrupeds" at the present day, while scientifically they are known as "mammals". The lower terrestrial forms of life are embraced by the comprehensive term "creeping things". The word "insect" was used in English till comparatively recently much in the same way. This crude classification is clearly based on the nature of the media in which the various animals live, *i.e.* it is a division into animals living respectively on the land, in the water, and in the air, land animals being further subdivided into higher and lower forms. Such a grouping is of necessity very superficial, for habitat is a very misleading guide to affinity or likeness. Whales, porpoises, and seals are as much "beasts" as cows and sheep, though to this day we speak of whale and seal "fisheries". And further, such a group as "creeping things" or "insects" (in the old sense) contains such a miscellaneous assortment of creatures that it may be looked upon as a mere receptacle for forms finding no place in the other three subdivisions.

The first man to place zoology on a scientific basis was the Greek philosopher Aristotle (384–322 B.C.), "perhaps the greatest and most truly scientific man in the highest sense of the word that the world has ever known" (Milnes Marshall), who, though the study of animals was not the one to which most of his time was devoted, has nevertheless been styled the "Father of Natural History". Aristotle had a very considerable knowledge of the habits and structure of the animals known to him, about 500 in number; he was impressed by the fact that the animal kingdom exhibits a transition from lower to higher, and devised a scientific system of classification based on structure. His great merit here lies in the fact that he divided the animal kingdom into two groups,—(A) Animals with red blood and a backbone, and (B) Animals without red blood and no backbone, a division which corresponds precisely with the modern one into Vertebrata (Backboned animals) and Invertebrata (Backboneless animals), though we now know that the distinction as to blood is not quite so absolute as Aristotle supposed. He further recognized five classes among the backboned animals (viviparous quadrupeds producing living young, egg-laying or oviparous quadrupeds, birds, fishes, and whales), and four among the backboneless (molluscs, scaly animals, animals with soft scales, and insects).

Unfortunately, after the time of Aristotle zoology progressed in a backward direction, and during the Middle Ages all sorts of absurd ideas gathered around it. A fresh start was made by Wotton (1492–1555), a native of Oxford who afterwards became a London physician. He went back to the classification of Aristotle, and from his own observations enlarged upon it. Further work in the same direction was afterwards done by the Swiss professor, Gesner (1516–65), and by the Englishman, John Ray (1628–1705), work which led up to the better known and more extensive labours of Karl von Linné, usually known by the name of Linnæus (1707–78). As professor of Natural History in the Swedish university of Upsala, he wrote his *System of Nature*, which must ever remain a classical work, and in which are laid down the foundations of our modern classification. Comparing the plant and animal worlds to armies, he instituted a series of subdivisions named, beginning with the largest, class, order, genus, and species, metaphorically equivalent to the legions, cohorts, maniples, and contubernia of a Roman host. His animal classes were six in number. Linnæus also introduced the system of giving each kind of animal a double name, the first being that of the genus, the second that of the species. We find living in Britain, for example, three kinds or species of hare-like animals, all belonging to the genus *Lepus*, and called in popular language rabbit, hare, and Alpine or Irish hare. The double scientific names of these are respectively, *Lepus cuniculus*, *Lepus timidus*, and *Lepus variabilis*. The utility of such names is obvious, for if in recording observations on, say, the rabbit, we speak of it as *Lepus cuniculus*, a zoologist of any nationality whatsoever will know to what animal we are referring, while merely to employ the popular name might lead to great confusion. It will be noticed that the first or generic name is comparable to a surname, while the second or specific name may similarly be compared to a Christian name. The generic name is placed first merely as a matter of convenience, just as in an official list of human beings, such as a list of voters, it is found more convenient to give first place to the surname. By universal consent, scientific names are almost entirely taken from the dead languages, Latin and Greek, as these are studied by all civilized nations. Unfortunately many such names are clumsy, and some are barbarous mixtures of Latin and Greek; but in spite of this the system is a good one.

The classification of Linnæus, like that of Aristotle, is a "classification by definition". As a result of observation, certain groups are *defined*, *i.e.* their essential characters are given, and newly-discovered animals are placed in this or that group according as they are found to possess or lack certain features. Such a classification assumes the existence of sharp boundary lines in nature, and is really based on the idea that the different kinds or species of animal were created separately and independently. The Linnean Class of *Mammals*, for instance, is defined as being a group of viviparous animals, possessing a four-chambered heart and hot red blood. Any newly-found kind of animal possessing these features would be considered a mammal. In framing such a classification comparatively few prominent features are selected, and more attention is paid to the boundary lines than to the resemblances between the animals constituting a group. This particular method of subdivision is by no means confined to natural history; an example from another province is afforded by the classification of Britons according to income for income-tax purposes. Those individuals falling well within a subdivision are of no special interest, but those only just coming up to the amount of a particular class are objects of commiseration to themselves as paying a particular percentage with the least reason, while on the other hand those who only just escape falling within a more highly-taxed section have a special interest for the assessors.

After the time of Linnæus the rapid progress of more accurate observation, now aided by fairly good microscopes, gradually led to the conviction that classification by definition is far from satisfactory, and to a reaction against the current idea that the different groups of the animal kingdom form a linear series, a gradual ascent from low to high in, so to speak, a straight line. The next important scheme of classification, which we owe to the great French anatomist Cuvier (1769–1832), is one by "type". This system lays stress upon the resemblances between the members of a group rather than on the boundary lines between different groups, or, in other words, "The class is steadily fixed, though not precisely limited; it is given, though not circumscribed; it is determined, not by a boundary line without, but by a central point within; not by what it strictly excludes, but by what it eminently includes; by an example, not by a precept; in short, instead of a definition we have a type for our director" (Whewell). Cuvier was the first to recognize the fact that the different groups of animals are related to one another like the branches of a tree, and not like successive portions of a straight line. He recognized four great branches—Vertebrates, Molluscs, Articulates, and Radiates, each distinguished by its special type of structure.

Since Cuvier's time it has come to be more and more recognized that in a "natural" classification, *i.e.* one having regard to as many distinctive features as possible, in contradistinction to an "artificial" system which regards only one or a few arbitrarily chosen characters, the groups of animals must be represented diagrammatically by a tree, in which the large branches represent the large groups, their subdivisions the smaller groups, and the leaves individuals. This conclusion has been greatly supported and extended this century by the study of extinct animals, placed on a scientific basis by Cuvier himself; and by the teachings of development or embryology, a zoological branch of which the foundations were firmly laid by von Baer (1792–1876).

The real meaning of this tree-like arrangement of organisms was at first a mystery, but, thanks more particularly to Charles Darwin and his contemporary Alfred Russell Wallace, who is fortunately yet among us, we now understand it to be an expression of an actual blood-relationship—to be, in fact, a veritable genealogical tree, the outcome of a process of evolution. And hence classification at the present time is a "classification by pedigree", and is perfect, in so far as we are successful in arranging animals according to their actual affinities.

3. *Zoology as regarded by the Morphologist or Student of Animal Form.*—One of the main subdivisions of modern zoology is the branch dealing with the shape or form of animals, using these words in their broadest sense. This part of the subject is *Animal Morphology* (Gk. *morphe*, form; *logos*, a discourse); and it deals not only with the external characters, the outward form, but also with the structure or inward form, as revealed by dissection and by the use of the microscope. The external characters of animals were naturally those first noticed; then came the study

of their anatomy, to which Cuvier gave an immense impetus; and lastly, the investigation of minute structure or histology (Gk. *histŏs*, a texture), which, though the compound microscope was invented near the end of the sixteenth century, practically began as a serious study with Malpighi and others nearly a hundred years later, and has rapidly advanced up to the present time, every successive improvement of the microscope leading to the acquisition of more extended and more accurate knowledge. The microscope, too, besides vastly increasing our knowledge regarding the structure of well-known animals, has thrown open to investigation a once unsuspected world of minute forms, just as the telescope has extended our field of observation in the other direction.

Morphology, however, is not content with merely cataloguing facts regarding the structure of different sorts of animals. It compares and classifies these facts, and endeavours, as far as may be, to explain them in the light of the evolution theory. Innumerable problems are met with, many being of the most fascinating description, and the solution of these constantly engages the attention of numerous expert workers. Some of these questions are naturally very abstruse, but many of them, when properly presented, are certain to excite the interest and arrest the attention of almost any intelligent person. As a good example of such a problem and its solution we may take the nature and origin of teeth.

Teeth, as seen, for example, in a dog or cat, are hard bodies having a certain complex structure, and developed by the lining of the mouth-cavity. The question may be asked—"How have teeth been evolved, and are any other parts of the animal body comparable with them?" No answer can be given to this unless the comparative method be adopted (a method we owe to the illustrious German biologist, Johannes Müller, and which is of supreme importance in zoological matters) and a general survey taken of the backboned animals generally. Mammals, birds, and amphibians do not afford a solution of the problem; but on coming to fishes we find that many of them possess numerous hard defensive bodies in the skin known as "placoid scales", which vary greatly in shape in different cases. Now these scales greatly resemble teeth in structure, and if in a dogfish we closely examine the neighbourhood of the mouth, it will be found that the placoid scales gradually become more and more tooth-like as regards shape, all the intermediate stages being found. To this it may be added that the mouth-cavity develops as a pit or depression in the surface of the body, so that its lining is really specialized skin, and might be expected to produce similar structures to those characteristic of skin. Piecing together these various facts we arrive at the conclusion—"Teeth have resulted from the modification of scales belonging to the mouth-cavity", a conclusion which is rendered still more probable when we find that teeth are by no means limited to the edges of the jaws, but may also be found (in some fishes, reptiles, &c.) on the roof and other parts of the mouth-cavity. That teeth should persist in animals like mammals, which have long since lost the original scaly covering of remote ancestral forms, is explained by the principle of "change of function", often exemplified by organs which are out of work from having lost their original job. This is a case of primarily defensive structures which have been pressed into the service of the digestive system, though they may also, in certain instances, again be modified for defence and offence on new lines.

4. *The Physiologist's Stand-point.*—Students of physiology are, like naturalists, interested in the life-manifestations of animals, but their enquiries are more subtle, and aim at determining the uses or functions of the various parts revealed by anatomy and histology. To determine the nature of life is the final aim of the physiologist. The several departments of zoology are so intimately related that they are briefly described here under separate headings merely as a matter of convenience. This is particularly true of physiology and morphology, which are so closely interwined that it is impossible to separate them. The study of form would be extremely dull and largely profitless without some knowledge of function, and the study of function presupposes a preliminary knowledge of form. For example, a far more vivid interest is imparted to a description of the structure of the eye if the uses of its various parts are kept in view, while any explanation of vision would obviously be impossible were the related anatomical facts ignored. A very good example is afforded by the tooth problem, dealt with in the last section, where questions both of morphology and physiology are involved.

5. *The Embryologist's Stand-point.*—The study of form and

function when applied to animals before they reach the adult condition is known as Embryology or Development. From very early times it attracted a considerable amount of attention, but was first placed on a really scientific footing by von Baer (1792–1876), and as the result of the labours of many specialists, notably Francis Maitland Balfour (1851–82), formerly Professor of Animal Morphology in the University of Cambridge, and the Russian zoologist Kowalewsky, is now an important, perhaps even an overestimated, branch of the subject. As in so many other cases, the interest of the facts has been enormously increased as a result of the influence of the theory of evolution. Consisting as the subject-matter does of the life-histories of animals, it has always formed part of the work of the field naturalist, who has delighted in the mysterious growth of frog from tadpole, or the passage of caterpillar into chrysalis, and that again into the butterfly. Such interest had quite a new turn imparted to it when the evolutionist formulated the "Law of Recapitulation", according to which, in the words of Milnes Marshall, "every animal in its own development repeats its history, climbs up its own genealogical tree". Thus interpreted, the fish-like tadpole points to the descent of frogs from ancestors which in many respects possessed those characters which we now associate with fishes. There has been, however, a tendency to exaggerate the importance of this law.

6. *The Stand-point of Distribution.*—Under this heading two things call for consideration—(*a*) Distribution in Space and (*b*) Distribution in Time.

(*a*) *Distribution in Space.*—Everyone knows that different countries are inhabited by different sorts of animals, *e.g.* that kangaroos are to be found in Australia, ostriches in Africa, and sloths in South America. Until the rise of the evolution theory no explanation was given of such facts, except that animals have been created separately where we now find them. This was the doctrine of "special creation", and if we adopt it, the study of distribution can be little more than a recording of facts. Admitting however, the truth of the evolution theory, it becomes possible to give a reasonable explanation of many curious and at first sight anomalous instances of the sort. We have, for example, the well-known case of the tapir, an animal somewhat resembling the pig in appearance but possessing a short proboscis. These creatures are only found in South America and the Malay region. We know, however, from geological evidence, that animals of the kind formerly existed in North America, Europe, and Asia, and their present occurrence in two widely isolated areas is thus explained, extinction (dying out) having taken place in the intervening tracts owing to the competition of other forms of life.

(*b*) *Distribution in Time.*—As will be fully explained in the sequel the study of geology enables us to some extent to carry back the study of animal life to periods immensely remote from the present, and to construct a history of animals in chronological order. As, from an evolutionary stand-point, we might expect, there has been on the whole a progress from low to high, and it is even possible to work out with some approach to accuracy the pedigrees of certain existing groups. We learn that some forms, including Man himself, are of comparatively recent origin, while, on the other hand, there are many groups of animals which have no living representatives. Much light is also thrown, as indicated above in the case of the tapirs, upon problems of distribution in space.

7. *The Utilitarian Stand-point.*—We may include under this heading not only economic zoology, dealing with the animal kingdom as a source of food, clothing, ornament, &c., but also facts regarding animals as they appeal to the sportsman, the keeper of pets, and the lover of the beautiful.

Economic zoology, though largely statistical, also involves issues of more general interest, such as the improvement of farm stock, fish-hatching, oyster culture, and bee-keeping. Facts observed from a purely practical stand-point in these and other departments of applied zoology have often proved invaluable to theorists, as appears abundantly in the pages of Darwin's great work, *Plants and Animals under Domestication*; while, on the other hand, researches conducted by theorists have repeatedly borne practical fruit.

As regards animals in a sporting connection, it commonly happens that sportsman and naturalist are combined in the same individual, and our knowledge of the habits of many animals is largely derived from this source. Such books as Sir Samuel Baker's *Wild Beasts and their Ways*, Shield's *The Big Game of North America*, and Chapman's *Wild Norway*, *Wild Spain*, and *Bird-life of the Borders*, among innumerable others, illustrate this point.

Animal Æsthetics, dealing with animals as objects of beauty, is a branch of zoology which can scarcely be said to be organized, but it is a commonplace to say that animal form and colour have always proved more or less attractive to painters, sculptors, and human beings in general. The uses of animals, parts of animals, or animal products for ornamental purposes fall to be treated of by economic zoology. The old idea was that the beautiful or striking forms and colours of plants and animals were intended solely for the gratification of human tastes. Modern theory interprets them as playing some part with reference to the organisms themselves. Predatory animals are often coloured so as to render them inconspicuous to their prey, while, on the other hand, many creatures are thus protected to some extent from their enemies. Conspicuous colours and markings, such as those of the wasp, may be of "warning" nature, acting as danger-signals, while some of the most beautiful tintings are plausibly explained as "courtship colours", *e.g.* the brilliant scarlet hues assumed by the male stickleback during the nesting season.

8. *The Philosophic Stand-point.*—The groundwork of zoology undoubtedly depends on observation of the various classes of facts enumerated under the preceding headings, but this is not the highest development of the subject. Here the palm must be given to zoology considered as a branch of philosophy, aiming at the explanation of the facts relating to animal form, function, and distribution by means of theories founded on such facts. Thus we see an otherwise chaotic mass of material falling under general laws, and assuming orderly proportions, as in the sister sciences of astronomy, chemistry, physics, and geology. All intelligent workers in the zoological field, whatever may be their special branch—form, function, development, classification, or what not,—adopt the philosophic stand-point more or less, for without a reasonable admixture of theory the subject-matter of zoology is but as bread without leaven, or meat without salt.

Although speculation, often crude, it is true, has always been more or less associated with the study of living beings, its influence as a revolutionary and stimulating agent undoubtedly dates from 1859, the year in which Darwin and Wallace formulated their theory of evolution. And it is the especial glory of zoology that the theory then propounded has had the most wide-reaching influence, not upon biology alone, but upon every branch of learning. For biology connects on the one hand with subjects such as chemistry, physics, and geology, and on the other with the study of mankind and the works of man. From morphology and physiology we pass, though not without huge gaps in knowledge, to the study of mind (psychology), sociology, political economy, law, ethics, and history, while even linguistic students are nowadays confronted with problems best explained on an evolutionary basis.

THE PLAN OF PRESENT WORK

Most popular modern books on zoology written in English deal with the various groups seriatim, beginning with the highest forms and ending with the less familiar creatures, our knowledge of which is mainly due to the microscope. Of such books Cassell's *Popular Natural History* and Lydekker's *Royal Natural History* may be mentioned as admirable types.

This plan is not here followed, but an attempt is made to treat the subject in a comparative manner, taking function as the basis, and illustrating the various points as they occur by examples taken from all or many of the animal groups. It is believed that this plan is better adapted than the other for bringing into relief the most interesting facts and theories of modern zoology. Such a mode of treatment was once much in vogue, both in lecture courses and in books like the late Dr. Carpenter's *Animal Physiology*.

A sketch of *Classification* will first be given, so as to familiarize the reader with the chief groups of animals and the range in form presented by the animal kingdom, especially as regards external characters. Special attention will be given to familiar forms, particularly such as are native, and those which may be commonly seen in zoological gardens. This will be followed by a section on the *Food and Feeding of Animals*, with special reference to interesting modifications and adaptations resulting from the various ways in which animals get their livelihood, if one may use the expression. *Animal Defences* will next be treated, and this section is closely connected with the preceding, as means of defence are mainly necessary to protect animals from the attempts of other animals to eat them. *Breathing and Movement*, as two primary functions, will form the subject of the next two sections, under which will be fully treated adaptations for breathing in air and in water, and modes of movement above-ground, underground, in water, and in air.

The subject of *Development* will next be dealt with, and typical life-histories will be given, after which such subjects as *Care of Eggs and Young* and *Animal Homes and Dwellings* will receive attention.

The lower functions of animals having been dealt with in the earlier sections of the book, the higher functions will next be considered, and some of the more important details regarding the structure and function of *Nervous System* and *Sense Organs* will be presented. This will be followed by a section on *Instinct* and *Intelligence*, activities involving the operation of the organs described in the preceding section. Such matters as the migration of mammals and birds, the habits of social insects (ants, bees, wasps, &c.), and the "homing instinct" of certain forms, will here receive treatment.

In the remaining part of the book considerable space will be devoted to the wide and interesting questions connected with the *Association of Organisms.* The first thing here to be dealt with will be the various kinds of association obtaining between plants and animals, such as the relation of insects to flowers, ants to various plants, insectivorous plants, and galls produced by insects. Next will follow an account of the chief kinds of association between animals of the same species, including chapters on Mating and Courtship, and on Animal Communities, in so far as the last subject was not treated of in relation to instinct. Different kinds of association between organisms of different species will be the last heading under this section, and will include all the various sorts of relation known to biologists, among these being *Commensalism*, where messmates are associated; *Mutualism*, where there is an intimate beneficial union; and *Parasitism*, in which unwelcome guests prey upon a "host".

The concluding sections of the book will be devoted to Utilitarian Zoology, Distribution in Space and Time, and Philosophical Zoology.

Under *Utilitarian Zoology* we shall have occasion to deal with animals as the foes and friends of man, and this will naturally involve some description of the chief ways of coping with foes, *e.g.* agricultural pests, and some of the methods, *e.g.* pisciculture, by which the usefulness of animals is enhanced. Some space will also be devoted to domestic animals, animal pets, sporting zoology, and animal æsthetics.

Distribution in Space will be illustrated by typical cases, involving a brief exposition of leading principles. A short account of life as modified by various surroundings will follow, and such subjects as deep-sea, fresh-water, and underground faunas will here receive treatment.

Distribution in Time will involve a sketch of the ancient life-history of the earth, under which the most interesting extinct forms will, of course, be described.

The section on *Philosophical Zoology* will of necessity be chiefly occupied by some account of the Theory of Evolution, and of related matters, such as the question of Heredity.

CHAPTER I

CLASSIFICATION—STRUCTURE OF MAN TAKEN AS A TYPE

GENERAL CONSIDERATIONS

In considering any scheme of classification, and in subsequently dealing with the various functions of animals, reference will constantly have to be made to external characters and to various sets of organs and their mode of action. It would therefore appear desirable, in order to clear the ground, to give some account of certain points of fundamental importance, and this can perhaps best be done by fixing our attention at start upon some familiar organism. It is undoubtedly the best plan to begin with the known, and from this to proceed to matters regarding which the majority of readers are more or less ignorant, though throughout this book no technical knowledge will be assumed. And for various reasons, such, *e.g.*, as that a very large number of persons have some elementary acquaintance with Human Anatomy and Physiology, it is deemed advisable to begin this chapter by a brief account of the structure and life-functions of man himself.

SYMMETRY.—The body of a human being, and the same is true for the common domestic animals, is built with a certain sort of regularity to which the name of two-sided or *bilateral symmetry* is applied. And to fully appreciate what is meant by this we must suppose the body to be placed with its front surface downwards, as is permanently the case in a dog, rabbit, or frog. This is clearly necessary, for if we are to compare man with the lower animals the same relative positions must be assumed for purposes of description.

Bilateral symmetry means, then, that the body can be divided into two corresponding halves in one way and one way only. Simple examples of this kind of regularity are afforded by an isosceles (or equal-sided) triangle, many leaves, and most of the so-called irregular flowers. The two halves, conveniently termed right and left, are not exact counterparts, but are what has been termed mirror-images. That is to say, if one half be placed with its cut surface against a mirror its reflection will correspond to the missing half. But bilateral symmetry in an animal involves more than a distinction between right and left, it means also, or the terms right and left could not be properly used, a distinction between front (anterior) and back (posterior) ends. Not only so, but we further perceive that an upper (dorsal) surface can be recognized as distinct from an under (ventral) surface. These points come out somewhat more clearly in lower animals

Fig. 1.—Cod-fish (*Gadus morrhua*)

The pelvic fins are seen under the throat and a pectoral fin on side of body above them.

than in man. Take, for instance, a fish, say a cod (fig. 1). The anterior end is clearly the head-end, the end which under ordinary circumstances goes first, and which, therefore, naturally bears the mouth, and is provided with the most important sense organs, such as those of smell, sight, and hearing—here most conveniently situated, as organs by which the presence of food, or it may be of enemies, is mainly perceived. The posterior or tail end bears in this animal a powerful propeller in the form of a fin. We also see marked differences as regards the dorsal and ventral surfaces, having an obvious relation to the needs of the animal. These differences are partly of form and partly of colour. Nothing need here be said on the former head, but as to the latter we note that the dorsal surface is dark while the ventral is pale, an arrangement which, as will be fully explained elsewhere, makes the animal match its surroundings much better than would otherwise be the case. Bilateral symmetry, therefore, is essentially a distinction between right and left, anterior and posterior, dorsal and ventral. It may be taken as an expression of the fact that the external influences which act upon the body are different in different directions, and we must seek in this fact an explanation of the origin of such symmetry. Were external influences the same in all directions we might expect the body to be spherical, but as this obviously can rarely or never be the case, we are prepared for the fact that absolutely spherical animals scarcely exist. In certain fixed forms, however, as coral polypes (fig. 2) and the like, we do get radial or star-like symmetry, where there is a distinction between upper and lower, but none between right and left, or posterior and anterior. In such a case the part of the animal facing upwards is exposed to the light, while the part facing downwards is shaded. All parts of the margin, however, are, on the whole, liable to be acted on in much the same kind of way—by light and other external influences.

Fig. 2.—Red Coral (*Corallium rubrum*) magnified. A, Polypes; B and C, Embryos.

LIMBS.—We further notice, as regards a fish, that, in addition to the unpaired expansions or fins, which project from the middle line of the body, there are four paired fins, which may with propriety be termed limbs, *i.e.* a pair of anterior or pectoral fins and a pair of posterior or pelvic fins. These are all unjointed, paddle-shaped expansions, with quite continuous margins. Let us now turn to the Frog, which begins life as a fish-like tadpole. Fixing our attention upon an individual which is beginning to turn into a frog, we shall distinguish all the features which belong to the bilateral state; but the limbs, instead of being fin-like, are divided transversely into certain regions, and are also provided with digits. Both of these features have relation to the semi-terrestrial life which the adult is destined to lead. Taking next an adult frog, we find the limbs well-developed, while the long swimming tail which was so conspicuous a feature in the tadpole has entirely disappeared. Nevertheless the trunk clearly possesses anterior and posterior ends, while the distinction between dark dorsal and light ventral surface is equally clear. Suppose the frog now to stand on its hind-legs in the erect attitude commonly attributed to it in illustrated books of fables and the like, and we shall see that the anterior and posterior ends of the trunk become upper and lower, while the ventral surface faces to the front, and the dorsal surface faces, if one may so speak, to the back. A frog thus disposed has a comic resemblance to a human being, and the reason is clear—the erect attitude in both cases brings about the same relative positions of ends and surfaces.

Let us next examine the two pairs of limbs possessed by Man. A very cursory inspection will show that they are divided into similar regions, and this is best expressed in tabular form—

Anterior or Fore Limbs.	*Posterior or Hind Limbs.*
1. Upper arm.	1. Thigh.
2. Forearm.	2. Lower leg.
3. Hand.	3. Foot.
(*a*) Wrist.	(*a*) Ankle.
(*b*) Palm region.	(*b*) Sole region.
(*c*) Thumb and four fingers.	(*c*) Great-toe and four others.

STRUCTURE OF THE HUMAN BODY

It was long ago pointed out by Huxley that the body, apart from the limbs, may be looked upon as a double tube. When halved longitudinally, and the internal organs removed, this can be very clearly seen (fig. 3), and the same thing is obvious in the similarly divided carcasses of sheep and other animals to be seen hanging up in a butcher's shop. The two tubes may also be clearly seen in a cross section. One of them is dorsal, the other ventral. The latter forms in the trunk the large cavity of the chest and abdomen, being divided into two parts corresponding to these two regions by a partition, the mid-riff or diaphragm, which is partly fleshy, partly fibrous. The thoracic part contains the heart, lungs, most of the gullet, and part of the large blood-vessels; while the abdominal part contains the bulk of the digestive organs, the kidneys, and various other structures. The dorsal tube in the trunk is comparatively small, and consists of a narrow canal running down within the backbone and enclosing the spinal marrow. It is continued through the neck, and in the head expands greatly into the large cavity of the cranium or brain-case, in which the brain is situated. The brain and spinal marrow are continuous with one another. One can scarcely say that the ventral cavity is represented at all in the neck or head.

N.B.—In the following account of the human body it is supposed to be placed with the front (ventral) surface directed downwards and the back (dorsal) surface directed upwards, as in a quadruped. The "upper" and "lower" parts, commonly so called, will be termed anterior and posterior respectively, unless the ordinary words happen to be specially convenient, as *e.g.* when the arrangement for supporting the weight of the body are described.

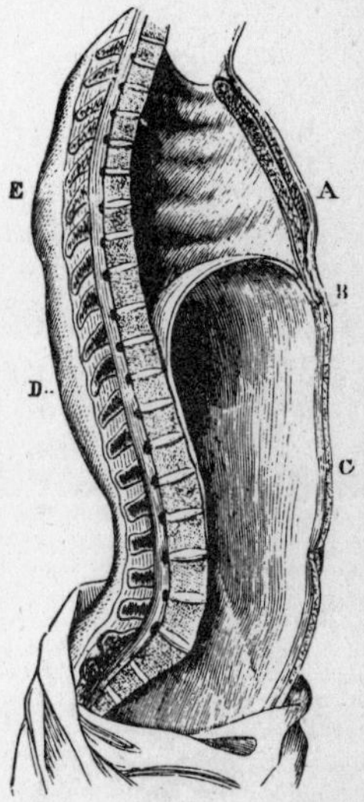

Fig. 3.—Trunk in Longitudinal Section. A, Ventral wall of thorax; B, Diaphragm; C, Ventral wall of abdomen. To right of E and D is seen backbone in section with spinal canal.

The body of a large and complicated animal such as a human being requires hard parts to serve as a protection to the delicate internal organs, to act as a stiffening or support, and to furnish points of attachment to the bands or masses of flesh (muscles) by means of which movements are effected. Such hard parts constitute the *skeleton*, which may be either external (*exoskeleton*) or internal (*endoskeleton*), both being present in many animals. In Man the *exoskeleton* is not so well developed as in many other cases, but it is present in the form of the horny outer layer of the skin (epidermis), and the hairs and nails which grow out from this. Without epidermis the numerous blood-vessels in the deeper part of the skin (dermis) would constantly be wounded, while the many nerves there ending would be the source of constant pain. Any bald-headed person can testify to the value of hair as a protection from extremes of temperature and damp, while nails help to protect the sensitive ends of the fingers and toes, though this, of course, is not their only or even their chief use.

THE ENDOSKELETON.

The endoskeleton (figs. 3–7) is built up from bone, gristle (cartilage), and tough fibrous material (connective tissue). We may conveniently distinguish between the *axial skeleton* (supporting the head, neck, and trunk) and the *skeleton of the limbs*. The former consists of *backbone*, *skull*, *ribs*, and *breast-bone*. It will be perhaps best to begin with the first of these.

THE AXIAL SKELETON.

1. *The Backbone.*—A glance at the backbone, or, as it is often called, the *vertebral column* (fig. 4), shows that it is thrown into a series of curves, which converts it into a kind of spring for breaking the shocks to which the body is constantly liable, and which if transmitted to the brain would often result in stunning, or it might be even more serious injury. A further obvious fact is that we have not here to deal with a single bone, but a large number of them, piled on top of one another. Each of these vertebræ (fig. 5) is irregular in shape, consisting of a bung-shaped *body* (centrum) and a curved *arch* from which several projections or processes grow out. The successive bodies are placed one above the other on the ventral side of the backbone, and are separated from one another by pads of gristle which act as buffers, allowing at the same time as much flexibility as is consistent with a proper degree of firmness. Successive arches are further linked together by the overlapping of their processes. It will further be noted that in this way a kind of tunnel is formed in which the spinal marrow is lodged and efficiently protected. This is essential, for it is an exceedingly delicate organ, and any severe injury inflicted upon it would result either in death or else in paralysis of the parts posterior to the damaged region. The vertebræ differ among themselves in size and shape, and are divisible into groups belonging to different regions of the body. The first seven, beginning at the head end, are the *neck-vertebræ*, and of these the first and second have a special interest (fig. 6). The first, or *atlas*, supports the rounded skull, just as, to compare

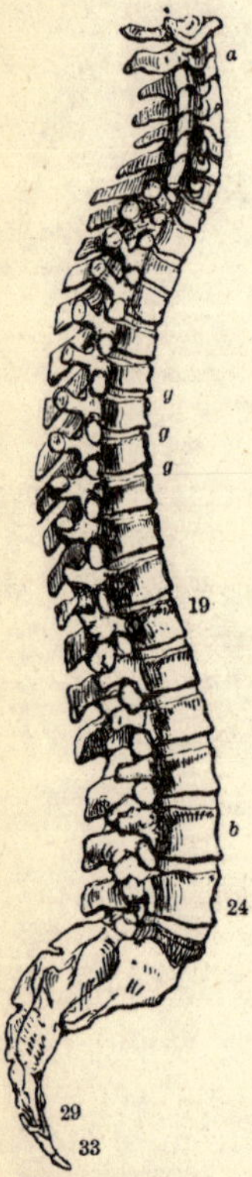

Fig. 4.—Backbone

7, 19, 24, 29, 33, Last vertebræ of neck, chest, loin, sacral, and tail regions; *a b*, ventral curvatures; *g g g*, pads of gristle between bodies of vertebræ.

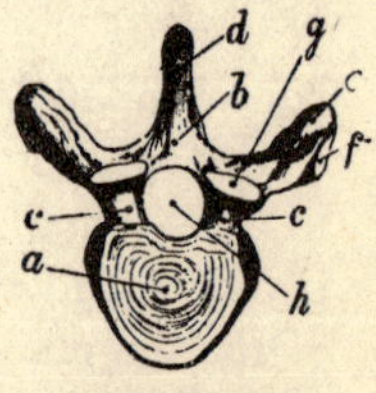

Fig. 5.—A Dorsal Vertebra

a, body; *b c*, arch; *d g*, processes; *h*, spinal canal.

small things with great, the giant Atlas was supposed to bear the globe on his shoulders. This vertebra presents two shallow cups on the side facing the skull, from which project two corresponding rounded projections. A hinge-joint is thus constituted, as a result of which we are able to nod our heads backwards and forwards. Movement from side to side would, however, be restricted by this arrangement if it were not for another one which exists to compensate it. The second vertebra, or *axis*, bears a firm bony peg, which projects through the ring-like atlas towards its ventral side and forms, as its name indicates, a pivot round which the head with the atlas can turn, too great freedom of movement being prevented by firm fibrous bands or ligaments which run from the peg to the skull. Following the neck-vertebræ come twelve rib-bearing *chest-vertebræ*, which form part of the dorsal wall of the chest-cavity. Next come five large *loin-vertebræ*, the size of which is due to the necessity for a firm support to the very considerable weight of the parts of the body coming above them. Still lower down this necessity becomes still greater, and the demand is met by a complicated basin-shaped mass of bone, the *pelvis*, the numerous arch-like curves of which are so arranged as to confer immense strength. The pelvis consists of three bones firmly fused together in the adult, the dorsal one, which alone belongs to the backbone, being the *sacrum*, made up of five broad flat sacral vertebræ immovably fused together. The last section of the backbone is a small curved structure termed the *coccyx* (Gk. for cuckoo), so named from its supposed resemblance to a cuckoo's beak, and resulting from the intimate union of four small tail vertebræ. It is chiefly interesting as being the useless representative of the tail, which is such a useful appendage in many of the lower forms.

Fig. 6.—A, Atlas vertebra, anterior view, ventral surface upwards: *a e*, body; *g*, cup for reception of occipital condyle: *f*, process; *k*, position of a ligament; *l*, spinal canal. B, Axis vertebra, ventral view, anterior end upwards: *bed*, parts of peg; *c*, anterior end of body; *gg*, processes.

2. *The Skull.*—The hard parts of the head together constitute the *skull* (see fig. 7), which consists of a brain-case, of relatively enormous size in Man, and the bony framework of the face. The *brain-case* is made up of a number of flat bones, firmly united by interlocking edges and also in part by overlapping surfaces, the net result being an arched box of very

great resisting power—a very necessary arrangement, since the contained brain, the most important organ in the whole body, is soft and pulpy. A further point of interest is found in the fact that the skull-bones possess three layers, a compact outer layer, a spongy middle layer, and a compact inner layer. Here again is another arrangement for breaking shocks.

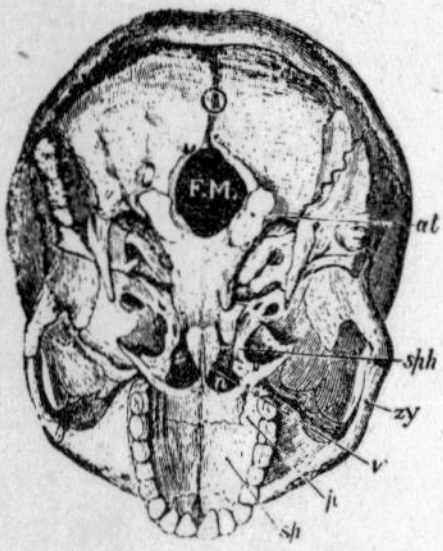

Fig. 7.—Base of Skull

FM, Foramen magnum surrounded by occipital bone; *a t*, an occipital condyle; *p*, *sp*, bony palate with teeth in a curve round margin; *n*, opening of nasal cavities; other letters refer to various bones

As previously stated, the spinal marrow is continuous with the brain, and this continuity is rendered possible by the presence of a round hole (*foramen magnum*) in the back of the cranium bounded by the occipital bone, which is really made up of four bones fused together (fig. 7). On each side of this hole is a smooth rounded prominence, or occipital condyle, which fits into a corresponding cup in the atlas vertebra. The presence of *two* condyles is an important point to notice from the classificatory stand-point.

The skeleton of face (fig. 7) is constituted by numerous bones arranged in a very complicated manner, and including as their largest elements the framework of the jaws. The two upper jawbones are the biggest, and they are firmly united together in the middle line, presenting also on the side facing the mouth a curved margin carrying the sockets for the upper teeth. The lower jawbone, or mandible, really consists of two firmly-united bones bearing the sockets for the lower teeth. It is united with the main skull by a hinge-joint, formed by two rounded projections (condyles) of the mandible, which fit into corresponding pits above. This joint varies in character in different animals in accordance with the kind of movement which the lower jaw has to execute, and this again depends upon the nature of the food and the manner of feeding. In a flesh-eating animal, such as the cat, the condyles are transversely elongated, so as to give a very perfect hinge-joint, only permitting a series of snaps. Anyone who has watched a cat or dog feeding is familiar with the kind of action indicated. A large number of familiar animals, such as rat, mouse, squirrel, and rabbit, constantly gnaw various things with their chisel-shaped front teeth, and in them the condyles are elongated from before backwards, allowing of a corresponding movement. Those forms again which "chew the cud", *e.g.* cow, sheep, goat, are obliged to move their jaws from side to side, a kind of movement which is rendered possible by flattish condyles. In human beings the lower jaw can be moved in all three ways, and the condyles are not only convex from side to side, and from before backwards, but are set on obliquely, an arrangement which permits all varieties of movement.

The skeleton of the face is also reckoned to include another loose bone, the hyoid (so named from its resemblance to the Greek letter Ypsilon, Υ, corresponding to our U), which supports the root of the tongue, and keeps the top of the windpipe open. It possesses two pairs of horn-like projections, and is interesting as representing what is a very elaborate apparatus in such lower forms as fishes.

In the skeleton of the face there are also properly included the minute bones or ossicles which belong to the organs of hearing, and regarding which more will be said elsewhere.

3. *The Ribs*, and 4. *The Breast-bone.*—The ribs and breast-bone (sternum) complete the axial endoskeleton. These, with the thoracic part of the backbone, form a firm framework by which the heart, lungs, and other delicate structures contained in the chest are protected from injury. There are twelve pairs of ribs, jointed on to the backbone dorsally, and, except the two last pairs, connected by pieces of gristle (costal cartilages) with the breast-bone.

Skeleton of the Limbs.—Turning to the skeleton of the limbs (see p. 196), we find that, both as regards the arm and leg, we can distinguish between (*a*) a firm bony girdle by which the base of the limb is connected with the trunk, and (*b*) the hard parts within the free or movable portion of the limb. In the case of the arm we have a ***shoulder-girdle*** consisting of two bones, the broad triangular shoulder-blade (scapula), placed dorsally and firmly bound by muscles to the trunk skeleton, and the collar-bone (clavicle), which runs across from scapula to sternum. One corner of the triangular scapula is provided with a shallow cup, the *glenoid cavity*, into which the rounded end of the upper-arm bone fits so as to form a ball-and-socket joint, which allows of very free movement. It is important to notice a bony projection which overhangs the glenoid cavity, and which, from a supposed resemblance to the beak of a raven (Gk. *kŏrax*, a raven), has been named the *coracoid process*. Here again we have a vestige of what is an important structure elsewhere, representing as it does the coracoid bone, which, in such a creature as a bird, is as large as the scapula and quite distinct from it.

1. *Arm.*—The arm itself is supported by a number of bones, many of which belong to the class of long bones, and of which we may take the *humerus*, or upper-arm bone, as a typical example. This consists of a hollow marrow-containing shaft, and swollen extremities presenting smooth gristle-covered surfaces well adapted for entering into the formation of joints. The shaft is a good example of the mechanical device of the hollow column, presenting the advantages of lightness and economy of material without loss of strength. The thickened ends are made for the most part of spongy bone, consisting of layers arranged in such a way as to combine great strength with lightness, while at the same time the transmission of shocks is very largely hindered. As already mentioned, the upper end of the humerus helps to form the ball-and-socket-like shoulder-joint. At its lower end is a pulley-shaped surface, which, in combination with the two long bones of the forearm, gives the hinge-like character to the elbow-joint. These bones are known as the radius and ulna, the former being on the thumb-side, and the latter on the little finger side. The upper end of the ulna is large, projecting behind the elbow as what is popularly called the "funny bone", but is in reality not a separate bone at all. The lower end of the ulna is comparatively small. Exactly the reverse is true of the radius, which is small at its upper end, but large at its lower end, where it has to support the hand. And here we find a point of great interest. The forearm is capable, as is known to everyone, of a rotatory movement whereby the hand can be turned with its back upwards, the position of *pronation*, as contrasted with the position of *supination*, in which the palm is upwards. In the latter position the ulna and radius are parallel, but in the former the radius, carrying with it the hand, crosses obliquely over the ulna. Such an arrangement obviously adds vastly to the use of the hand and arm, and is absent in those animals where the fore-limbs are used mainly for locomotor purposes.

The *wrist* is supported by eight small irregular bones, arranged so as to combine strength with flexibility, as well as to break the shocks to which the hand is especially liable. They are succeeded

THE HUMAN SKELETON

1. Parietal bone.
2. Frontal bone.
3. Temporal bone.
4. Orbit.
5. Side of occipital bone.
6. Malar, or cheek-bone.
7. Nasal bone.
8. Upper jaw-bone.
9. Lower jaw.
10. Four lower neck (cervical) Vertebræ.
11. Two upper chest (thoracic) Vertebræ.
12. Two lowest chest (thoracic) Vertebræ.
13. Loin (lumbar) Vertebræ.
14. Sacrum.
15. Coccyx.
16. Ribs.
17. Breast-bone (Sternum).
18. Shoulder-blade (Scapula) } Shoulder
19. Collar-bone (Clavicle) } Girdle.
20. Humerus.
21. Radius.
22. Ulna.
23. Wrist-bones (Carpus).
24. Palm-bones (Metacarpus).
25. Finger-bones (Phalanges).
26. Hip-bones, Hip Girdle.
27. Thigh-bone (Femur).
28. Knee-cap (Patella).
29. Shin-bone (Tibia).
30. Clasp-bone (Fibula).
31. Ankle-bones (Tarsus).
32. Instep-bones (Metatarsus).
33. Toe-bones (Phalanges).

2

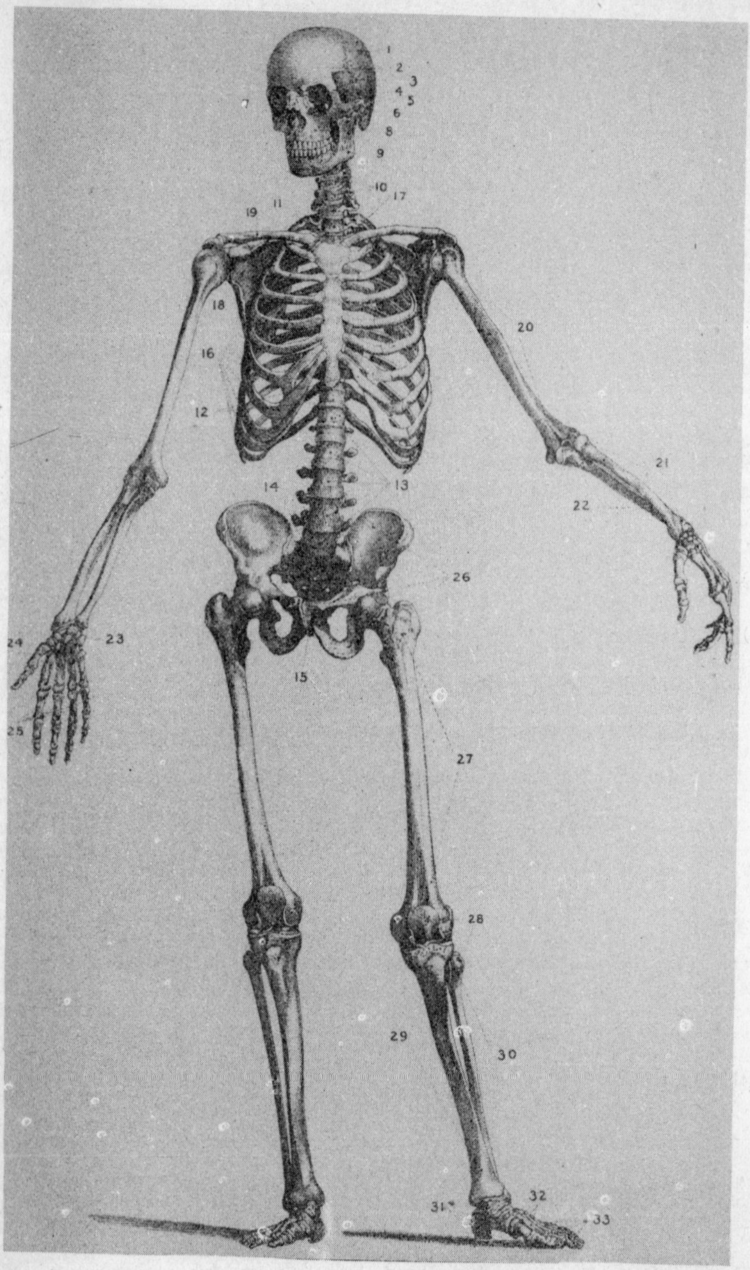

THE HUMAN SKELETON

by five elongated bones, which support the palm, and from their shape are classed with the long bones. Fourteen small phalanges of similar shape complete the skeleton of *the hand*, each finger possessing three, while the thumb has only two. Each end-phalanx is broadened out and roughened at its tip to afford a support to a nail.

Two further points of interest deserve mention in regard to the hand. One is the unequal lengths of the *digits* (or fingers), a device which renders them much more efficient in delicate manipulations, enabling their tips to be brought together with great ease. The other point is the opposability of the thumb, *i.e.* it can be bent over so as to directly oppose any one of the fingers. How important a matter this is may be realized by trying to pick up a small object, say a pin, by means of the fingers alone. The arrangement is rendered possible by the peculiar nature of the joint between the base of the thumb and the wrist. The opposing surfaces are here saddle-shaped, allowing a much larger range of movement than any other combination of curves. The same kind of jointing is found in a bird's neck, which is well known to be exceedingly flexible.

2. *The Leg.*—Here we find in the first place a *hip-girdle*, comparable to the shoulder-girdle of the upper limb. But the necessity for supporting the very considerable weight of the body has in this case brought about an intimate union with the skeleton of the trunk, and the two girdles are firmly united with one another and with the *sacrum* to form the basin-like *pelvis* mentioned above (see p. 27). Each girdle is constituted by an irregular hip-bone, consisting of three elements fused together, and corresponding to what in many animals are clearly to be distinguished as three separate bones. The pelvis is arched so as the better to support the weight of the body transmitted to it, and thence to the thigh-bones, by means of the sacrum, which may be compared to the keystone of the arch. A further use of the pelvis is to protect certain delicate internal organs placed within its cavity.

On the outer side of each hip-bone is a deep cup for receiving the globular upper end of the large *femur*, or thigh-bone, which is comparable to the humerus in the upper arm. The joint at the thigh, like that at the shoulder, is of the ball-and-socket kind, but here greater firmness is necessary, and consequently less freedom of movement is permitted, the cup being much deeper and the union by fibrous bands more intimate.

The lower end of the femur helps to form the hinge-like knee-joint in conjunction with the shin-bone (*tibia*) of the lower leg, which corresponds to the radius in the forearm. The front of this joint is protected by a round and somewhat flattened bone, the *patella* or knee-pan. There is nothing corresponding to this in the elbow.

The chief bone of the lower leg is the *tibia*; but there is also a second much slenderer one, the *fibula*, corresponding to the ulna in the forearm, but not helping to form the knee-joint. Just as the wrist is supported by a number of irregular bones, so is the *ankle*, but as these have to support the weight of the body they are relatively much larger and stronger. Following them come five sole-bones, corresponding to palm-bones; while the toes, like the fingers, are completed by fourteen phalanges, which, however, are relatively short. The great toe is not opposable and is very much larger than the others, since it plays an important share in supporting the weight of the body. It may be remarked that the skeleton of the foot presents an arch from before backwards, and another from side to side, an arrangement which combines great strength with a large amount of springiness. The weight of the body falls mainly on the heel, toes, and outer side of the foot

NUTRITION.

The body is constantly undergoing waste, and also, in the earlier part of life, increasing in volume, or growing. This waste must be counterbalanced and materials for growth provided; hence the necessity for food, which may be compared to the materials used for repairing a machine and, it may be, making additions to it. And just as the original nature of a machine determines the material to be employed, so also in the case of the body. In other words, if we are to understand the nature of the food, we must have some knowledge of the composition of the body.

Chemical Composition of the Body.—When the body of an animal is acted upon by intense heat most of it is dissipated in the form of gas, the comparatively small remainder, or ash, consisting of various mineral matters. The gaseous portion, when further analysed, is found to contain the four elements, Carbon, Hydrogen, Oxygen, and Nitrogen. It is therefore to be expected that our food should consist in the main of compounds of the same four chemical elements[1], and this is actually the case. Obviously this must be so for the fleshy part of the food, and it is also true for the vegetable portion. The different kinds of food may be classified as follows:—

1. *Nitrogenous Food*, consisting, in ultimate analysis, of carbon, hydrogen, oxygen, and nitrogen, together with sulphur, and in some cases phosphorus. Such foods are of exceedingly complex chemical nature, and may broadly be called *proteids* or *albuminoids*[2]. The last name is taken from albumin, of which white of egg may be considered as a type; while egg-yolk, lean meat, blood, gelatin, and cheese are of the same nature in whole or part. An example from the vegetable kingdom is gluten, the sticky constituent of flour, to which the tenacious character of dough is chiefly due.

2. *Non-nitrogenous Food*, as the name indicates, contains no nitrogen. Its various kinds are:—

(*a*) *Carbohydrates*, containing carbon, hydrogen, and oxygen, and including starch, sugar, gum, &c.

(*b*) *Hydrocarbons*, or fats and oils, consisting of the same three elements, arranged, however, in different proportions.

(*c*) *Mineral Salts*, including compounds of lime and iron, as well as common salt (sodium chloride). The more complicated foods enumerated under the preceding headings contain a varying amount of such mineral compounds, which have, however, to be supplemented in Man and various other animals by common salt. The importance of salts of lime becomes apparent when we remember that the hard part of bones and teeth consists of them.

(*d*) *Water*, consisting of hydrogen and oxygen, and generally containing mineral salts dissolved in it. Water is not only taken in the form of drink, but also forms an important constituent of albuminous, starchy, and fatty foods.

This complex food, unlike the food of plants, which is entirely gaseous or liquid, is largely taken into the body in the form of

[1] A chemical element is a substance which cannot, so far as we know, be resolved into components of different nature.

[2] The term *albuminoid* is often used in a narrower sense than this.

solid or semi-solid fragments, hence the necessity for an internal digestive cavity, the possession of which is characteristic of a higher animal as contrasted with a higher plant. In Man, for example, we have a set of digestive organs, the function of which is to deal with this crude food and reduce it to such a condition that it can be utilized for repair and growth, or, in other words, to digest it.

DIGESTIVE ORGANS.—These consist essentially of a long digestive tube, more briefly termed the gut, into which a number of structures known as digestive glands pour fluids.

1. *The Gut.*—The gut (figs. 8 and 9) is of very unequal width in different parts of its course, and, being very much longer than the body, is only able to pursue a straight course from the mouth

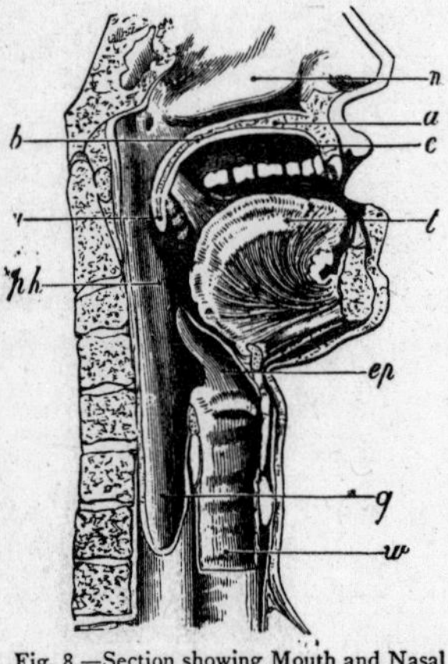

Fig. 8.—Section showing Mouth and Nasal Cavities, Gullet, Windpipe, &c.

a, Hard palate; *b* to *u*, soft palate; *c*, mucous membrane; *n*, cavity of nose; *t*, tongue; *ph*, pharynx; *g*, gullet; *ep*, epiglottis; *w*, windpipe.

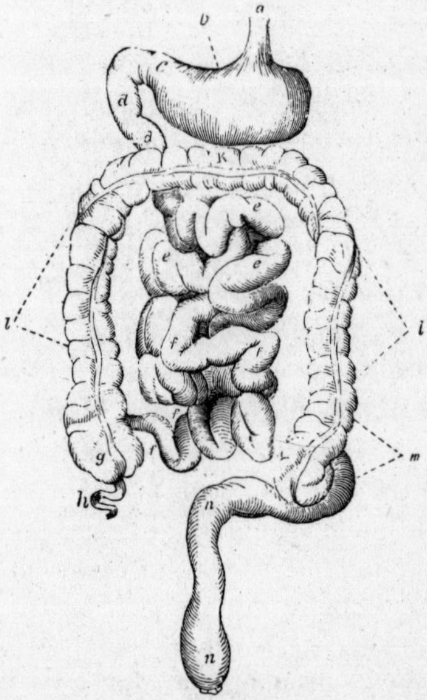

Fig. 9.—The Gut

a, Gullet; *bc*, stomach; *def*, small intestine; remaining letters indicate parts of large intestine.

to the end of the thorax, while in the abdomen it is largely coiled. The mouth, bounded by fleshy lips, leads into the fairly large mouth-cavity, marked features of which are the teeth and muscular tongue. At the back of this cavity is the pharynx, communicating with the cavities of the nose and ear; while on its floor is an opening, the glottis, leading into the breathing organs. The pharynx may be looked upon as the dilated front end of a narrow muscular tube, the gullet, which succeeds it, and, running along the neck and through the thorax, pierces the midriff, to become continuous with the large transversely-placed stomach, which has thick muscular walls. This in its turn is succeeded by a very long thin-walled tube, the small intestine, followed by a shorter but broader large intestine, which ultimately opens to the exterior.

The whole of the gut is lined by the mucous membrane, a soft reddish skin richly provided with blood-vessels.

2. *The Teeth* (figs. 10 and 11).—These deserve further mention, as they present interesting adaptations to the food and mode of feeding, while their number and form furnish important characters for purposes of classification.

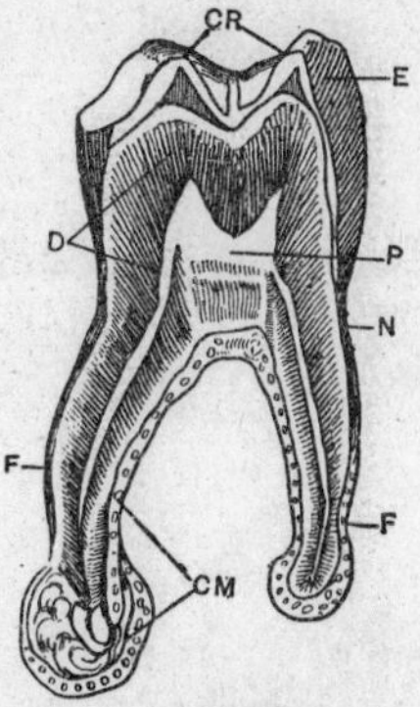

Fig. 10.—Section of a Tooth

Cr., Crown; N, neck; FF, fangs; P, pulp cavity; E, enamel; D, dentine; Cm., cement.

All the teeth are imbedded in sockets, the imbedded part being the fang, while the projecting portion constitutes the

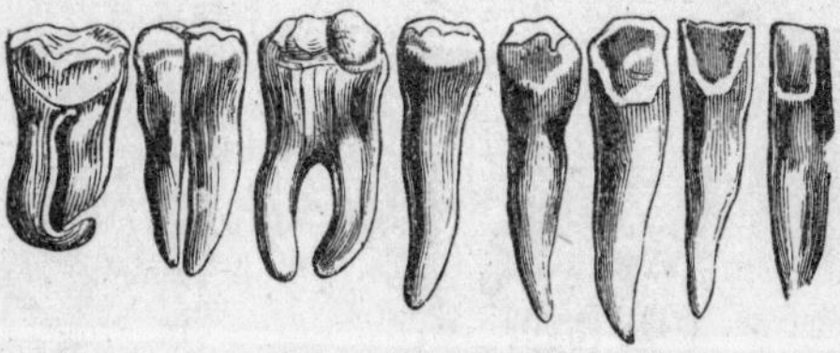

Fig. 11.—Kinds of Teeth

This figure shows the eight teeth in one half of a jaw.

crown. The greater part of a human tooth is composed of a very hard substance, dentine, within which is hollowed out a cavity for the sensitive pulp, richly provided with blood-vessels and nerves. The fang is covered by a layer of bony material, cement, while the crown is invested by an intensely hard substance, the enamel. It is a matter of common knowledge that there are two sets of teeth, the first or milk set consisting of twenty teeth, which are replaced by the thirty-two teeth making up the permanent set. Beginning with the latter, we find in the front of the jaws eight chisel-edged incisors adapted for dividing food. Outside these are the four pointed eye-teeth or canines, which in such creatures as cats and dogs play an important part as weapons and holdfasts. Lastly come the broad-crowned cheek-teeth, twenty in number, of which the first eight are known as bicuspids or premolars, while the remainder are called molars. All this may be expressed by a dental formula as follows:—

$$i. = \frac{2-2}{2-2},\quad c. = \frac{1-1}{1-1},\quad p.m. = \frac{2-2}{2-2},\quad m. = \frac{3-3}{3-3} = 32.$$

[*i.* = incisor, *c.* = canine, *p.m.* = premolar, *m.* = molar.]

Each fraction corresponds to one kind of teeth, the numerator representing upper and the denominator lower ones, while the dashes above and below mark the distinction between teeth on the right and left side. Since these structures are symmetrically arranged it is only necessary to represent those of one side, and so it is convenient to shorten the formula to—

$$\frac{2.1.2.3}{2.1.2.3} \times 2 = 32.$$

In the first or milk set the incisors, canines, and premolars are represented respectively by milk incisors, milk canines, and milk molars, while the molars of the permanent set have no predecessors.

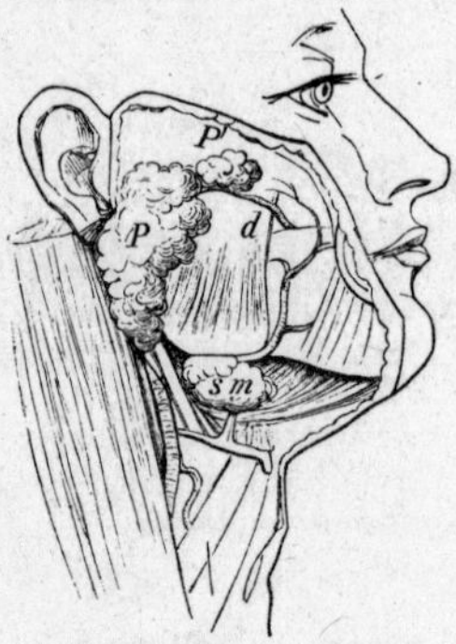

Fig. 12.—The Salivary Glands

P P′, Parotid; *sm*, sub-maxillary. *d* is placed below the duct of the parotid.

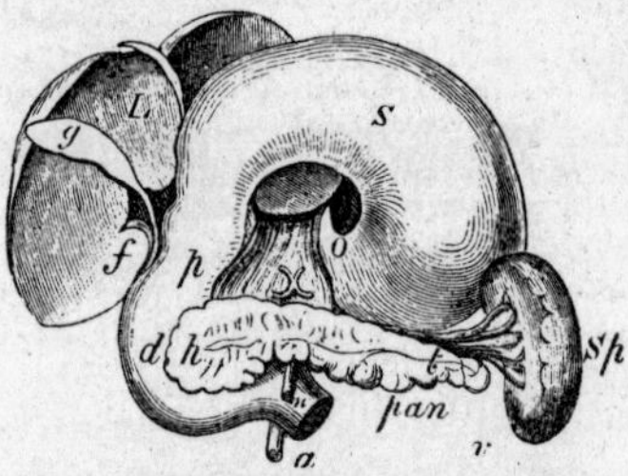

Fig. 13.—Relations of the Stomach to the Liver, Pancreas, and Spleen

osp, Stomach; *d*, small intestine; L, liver; *g*, gall-bladder; *f*, placed to left of bile-duct; *h*, *t*, pancreas; *sp*, spleen; *v*, placed below blood-vessels of spleen; *a* and *n*, blood-vessels.

3. *Digestive Glands* (figs. 12 and 13).—These elaborate or secrete different fluids, which act chemically upon the food. Opening into the mouth-cavity are three pairs of soft masses, the *salivary glands*, which secrete the spittle or saliva. One pair is placed in front of the ear (parotid), and it is these structures which swell up and become painful in cases of mumps. A second pair (sub-maxillary) are placed between the halves of the lower jaw, while the third and much smaller pair (sub-lingual) are imbedded in the deeper part of the tongue.

Other very important organs of the kind, the *peptic* or *gastric glands*, are found as innumerable minute branching tubes opening into the stomach, in the lining of which they are imbedded. The fluid secreted by these glands is the gastric juice.

The *liver*, which is the largest organ of the body, is, among other things, a digestive gland. It is a bulky reddish-brown mass placed in the upper part of the abdominal cavity, and its secretion, the bile or gall, passes into the beginning of the small intestine through a small thick-walled tube, the bile-duct. Connected with this is a pear-shaped bag, the gall-bladder, in which bile can be temporarily stored up.

The last digestive gland of importance is the *pancreas*, popularly known as the sweetbread, which lies in the first loop made by the small intestine, and pours its secretion, the pancreatic juice, through a short tube into the bile-duct.

PROCESS OF DIGESTION.—The process of *Digestion* essentially consists in the conversion of food into a dissolved or else a very finely-divided state. It is effected partly in a *mechanical*, partly in a *chemical* manner.

1. *Mechanical Digestion.*—As regards mechanical digestion an important part is played by the teeth, which reduce the food to small fragments, this being rendered more easy by the pouring out of saliva, which acts as a moistening and softening agent. The muscular tongue and cheeks are also of importance here, because they help to keep the fragments between the grinding teeth. In gullet, stomach, and intestines a further division is brought about as the result of a squeezing action exerted by the muscle-containing walls of these organs.

2. *Chemical digestion* is even more important. Within the stomach abundant gastric juice is poured on to the digesting food and acts more particularly upon the albuminoids, converting some of them into a soluble form known as peptone.

The *saliva* is concerned with starchy foods, which it converts into a kind of sugar.

Chemical digestion is completed in the small intestine by the *bile* and *pancreatic juice.* The latter finishes the work on the starchy and albuminous matters begun by saliva and gastric juice, besides which it acts on fats, converting them into a milky state or emulsion, where minute globules of the fat are suspended in fluid. The bile helps in the digestion of fats, and is of importance in several other ways, *e.g.* it prevents the digesting food from becoming putrid.

The digested foods are now absorbed into the minute blood-vessels which branch in the mucous membrane, the digested fats, however, passing into other minute tubes called lacteals, which ultimately communicate with the blood-system. It must, of course, be understood that blood-vessels and lacteals do not open into the cavity of the gut, but the digested materials, so to speak, soak into them. Those parts of the food which are not digested pass out of the body altogether.

CIRCULATORY ORGANS

Branching elaborately within the body, and sending its twigs into almost all its different parts, is a closed set of tubes constituting the blood-system. Propelled by the heart or central pump the red fluid known as blood is constantly circulated through this system. Supplementary to the blood-system we have a set of spaces and tubes (of which the lacteals mentioned above form a part) making up the lymph-system. This contains a pale fluid, the lymph, which it pours into certain of the great blood-tubes. The two fluids, blood and lymph, especially the former, may be regarded as a sort of medium of exchange as regards the various parts of the body. Certain things are taken out of them to meet local requirements, and certain other things pass into them.

Speaking more precisely, the functions of the circulatory system are as follows:—(1) It distributes the digested food, *i.e.* the materials for repairing waste and providing for growth; (2) It removes waste matters from all parts of the body, and carries these to organs which can get rid of them; (3) It carries oxygen to promote this waste; and (4) It distributes heat and equalizes the temperature of different parts.

THE BLOOD (figs. 14 and 15).—When examined under the compound microscope a drop of blood is found to consist of colourless liquid (plasma) in which float a vast number of minute bodies, the *blood-corpuscles.* These are of two kinds—red, and colourless or white. The former are biconcave discs not more than $^1/_{3200}$ of an inch in diameter, and they owe their colour to the presence of a peculiar pigment (hæmoglobin) that, as we shall presently see, is of great importance in respiration. The white or colourless corpuscles are less numerous but somewhat larger ($^1/_{2300}$ of an inch in diameter), and possess the power of spontaneous movement by thrusting out lobes of the semi-fluid substance (protoplasm) which composes them. They are thus enabled to slowly crawl, as it were, along the walls of the blood-vessels. In the middle of each such colourless corpuscle is a particle of somewhat different chemical nature, the nucleus, and this is probably to be regarded as a modification of the substance composing the rest of the corpuscle. No such particle can be discerned in a human red corpuscle, which is therefore said to be non-nucleated, a character which happens to be one of classificatory importance.

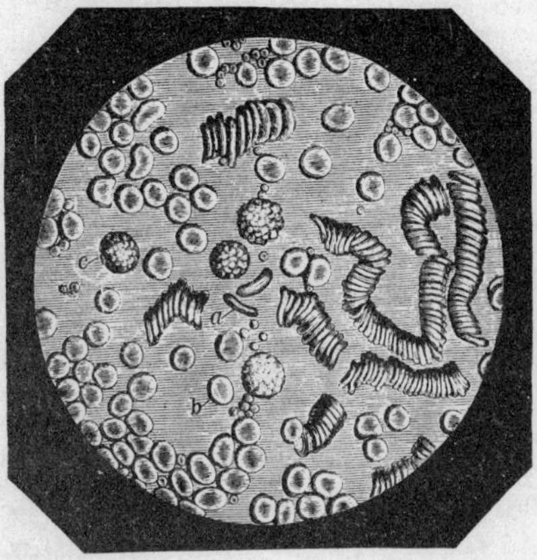

Fig. 14.—A Drop of Blood, seen under a microscope magnifying by 350 diameters

a and *b*, red corpuscles. *c*, white corpuscle.

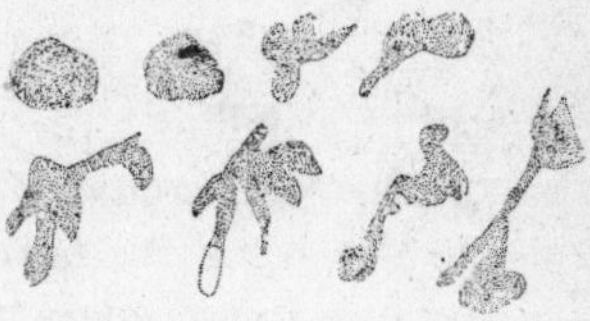

Fig. 15.—White Blood Corpuscle. Its successive changes of shape.

The Heart and Blood-System.—This very complicated organ is in principle a force-pump possessing an internal set of valves which only permit fluid to pass in certain directions. The blood-vessels which carry blood to it are veins, while those which carry it away are arteries. To understand the heart's action it is necessary to consider the simplest case, that of a heart with only one chamber or cavity (fig. 16). We may represent such a heart by an india-rubber syringe with a tube at each end, one for carrying fluid in and the other for carrying it out. There must also be, at least at one end, an internal valve consisting of a flap which readily permits fluid to pass in one direction but resists its passage in the other. In such a simple model the central swelling will represent the heart, while the tube conveying fluid into it will play the part of a vein, and the other tube the part of an artery. Propulsion of fluid will be brought about by squeezing with the hand. An actual heart requires, of course, no squeezing from outside, its walls moving in such a way that the internal cavity is alternately diminished and increased in size. This is due to the fact that its substance is made up of slender muscular fibres arranged in a very complicated fashion. Each fibre possesses the power of contraction, *i.e.* it is able to shorten itself, becoming at the same time thicker. It is clear, therefore, that if a large number of such fibres arranged transversely and obliquely to make up the wall of a hollow structure contract at the same time, the result will be that the contained cavity becomes smaller, regaining its original size when the fibres again relax. This is what happens in the case of a heart, enabling it to do pumping work.

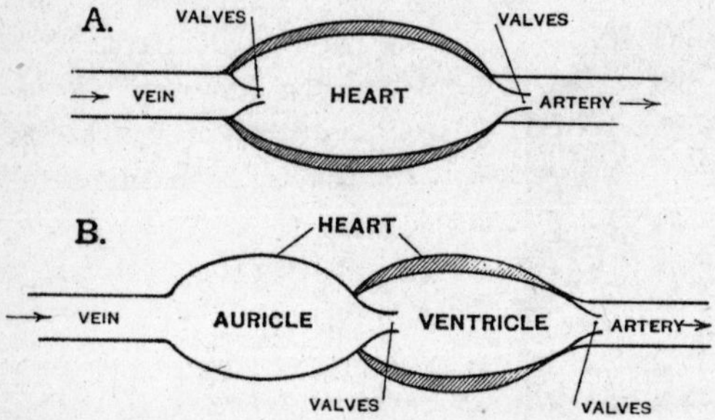

Fig. 16.—Diagrammatic Hearts. A, One-chambered; B, two-chambered.

An advance upon the simple one-chambered heart as just described is found in such a case as the common garden snail, where there are two chambers (fig. 16), one a thin-walled *auricle*, receiving blood from the vein, and squeezing it on into a thick-walled *ventricle*, which does the pumping work.

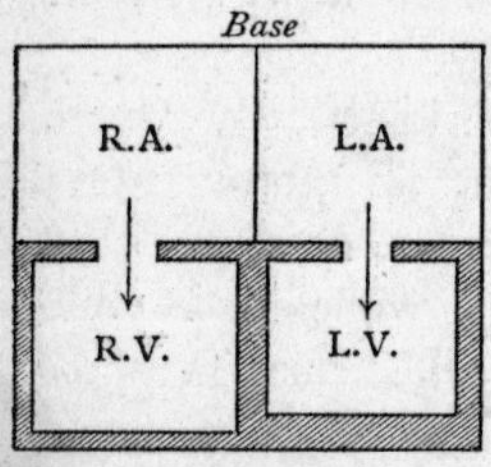

Fig. 17.—Diagram of Auricles and Ventricles

R A and L A, Right and left auricles; R V and L V, right and left ventricles.

The heart of a human being, however, has two sets of pumping work to do—(1) it forces pure blood all over the body, and (2) it drives impure blood to the lungs for purification. It is therefore not surprising that in such a heart there are four chambers, right and left auricles, and right and left ventricles, disposed as shown in the accompanying diagram (fig. 17). The right side of the heart contains only impure blood which it receives from the great veins, which open into the right auricle. This chamber passes the blood on to the right ventricle, which pumps it through a large vessel (pulmonary artery) to the lungs. These purify the blood, and from them it is conducted through pulmonary veins to the left auricle, from which it enters the left ventricle in order to be pumped through a great artery to the body at large. This artery is known as the *aorta* (Gk. *aĕirō*, I carry), and it is characteristic for the group of animals to which Man belongs, *i.e.* the Mammalia, that the curved part or arch with which the aorta begins should turn to the left. In a Bird it would be found curving round to the right.

If the *aorta* be traced, its arch will be found to give off large branches to the anterior part of the body, after which it bends into the middle line, and (as the dorsal aorta) runs just ventral to the backbone, supplying the parts it passes, and ending posteriorly by forking into two great vessels for the lower limbs. Any branch artery farther traced will be found to divide, tree-like, into smaller and smaller twigs, which at last pass into a close net-work of excessively minute thin-walled tubes, the *capillaries*. The same thing will be observed on tracing the pulmonary artery. It may, in fact, be said that almost all parts of the body are traversed by a dense net-work of capillaries, and from these the smallest veins arise, uniting, river-like, into larger and larger trunks till the great veins opening into the heart are constituted. We may therefore say that the heart and blood-vessels form a closed set of tubes, as the capillaries intervene between the smallest arteries and the smallest veins. This may be clearly seen in the web of a frog's foot.

Capillaries are of enormous importance, because their thin walls permit exchanges between the blood they contain and the body-substance they traverse.

The veins of the stomach, intestine, and certain other parts unite into a large portal vein, which enters *the liver*, and there divides up into smaller and smaller branches. The blood in this vein contains most of the digested food which has been absorbed from the gut, and the object of passing it through the liver is to let that organ take up some of these products, and store them for distribution as needed. The impure blood from the liver itself is poured by several blood-vessels into one of the great veins running to the right auricle. The arrangement just described for supplying the liver with impure blood, in addition to the pure blood which it gets from a branch of the aorta, is called the portal circulation.

THE LYMPH-SYSTEM.—The circulatory organs include a *lymph-system* as well as a blood-system. The *lymph* is a clear, colourless fluid, consisting of plasma and colourless corpuscles. It is contained in the large internal cavities of the body, in minute crevices which exist in the substance of the various organs, and in delicate *lymphatic vessels* which ramify in most

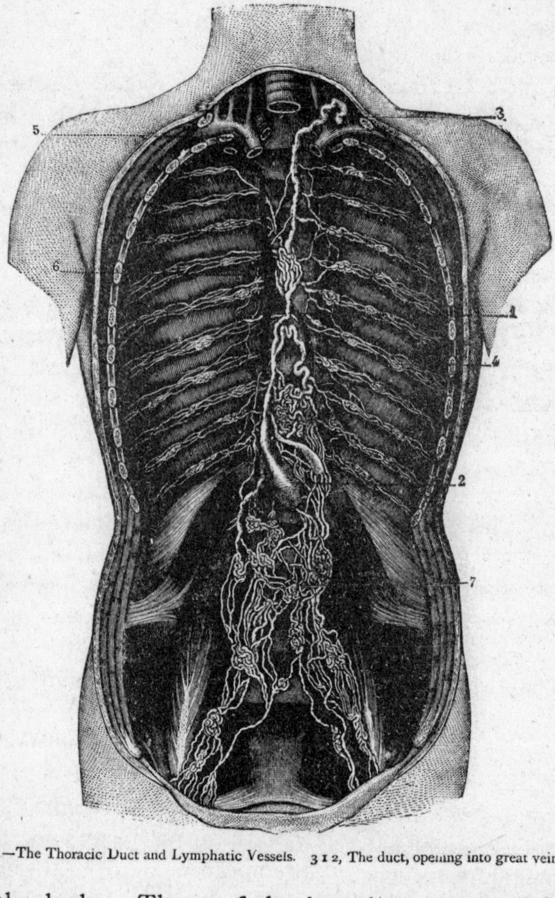

Fig. 18.—The Thoracic Duct and Lymphatic Vessels. 3 1 2, The duct, opening into great veins at 3.

parts of the body. Those of the intestines are termed *lacteals*, and receive the digested fats. Most of the lymphatics ultimately open into the thoracic duct (fig. 18), a narrow tube lying ventral to the backbone, and opening on the left-hand side into the great veins at the base of the neck. In this way the blood receives the digested fats, and a constant supply of colourless corpuscles.

The so-called *ductless glands* are related to the lymph-system. The largest of them is the dark-red milt or *spleen* (fig. 13), situated close to the stomach. It has to do with the destruction of worn-out red corpuscles. The *thyroid gland* is closely applied to the ventral side of the larynx, and is notorious as the organ which swells up in cases of Derbyshire neck (goître). It has been proved to be of importance in regulating the nutrition of the body. The *thymus gland* is a fatty-looking mass wrapped round the base of the heart, and much larger in infants than in adults. In the early stages of life it is one of the chief sources of colourless corpuscles.

Lymphatic glands are little swellings placed here and there in the course of lymphatics (fig. 19). New colourless corpuscles are constantly being formed in them.

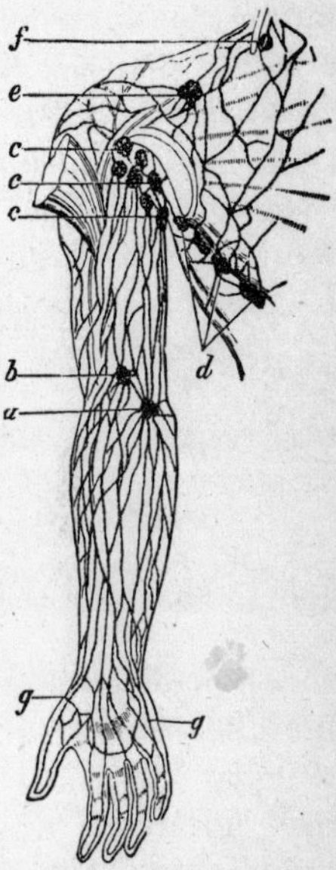

Fig. 19.—Lymphatics of the Arm and Arm-pit

Glands at the inner side of the elbow, *a b*; in the arm-pit, *c c c*; on the chest in front of the arm-pit, *d*; above the collar-bone and communicating with the arm-pit, *e f*. *gg* point to lymphatic vessels forming an arch round the hand. The dark lines are lymphatic vessels.

WASTE-REMOVING ORGANS

The living substance making up the body of an animal is constantly undergoing a process of change, whereby it breaks down into simpler compounds. We have, in fact, two sets of chemical changes constantly going on within the body:—

(*a*) A series of upbuilding or constructive processes whereby the food is gradually converted, step by step, into the substances which constitute the body, and of which the most complex is the living material known as protoplasm. This series of chemical changes is comprised under the head of *assimilation* (L. *adsimilo*, I make like), *i.e.* processes whereby the body makes the material taken in as food into fresh substance like itself. Assimilation is most naturally dealt with under the head of Nutrition.

(*b*) The other set of chemical changes within the body are destructive in nature, involving the down-breaking of material, partly of protoplasm itself, and partly of other less complex compounds. These changes have been called "local death", and are absolutely essential to life, for without them life would be impossible. Every manifestation of vitality by an organism, such as movement, production of digestive or other secretions, sensations, and mental operations, involve the breaking down or waste of material, without which the necessary energy would not be available. Broadly speaking, energy is the power of doing work, and a distinction is drawn between potential or stored energy and actual or kinetic energy. Complex chemical substances, such as high explosives, represent a store of energy, and when these break down into simpler substances, *i.e.* explode, a large amount of actual energy is liberated, which, in the case of the explosives alluded to, can be made to do various kinds of useful work. Protoplasm and the other complex body-substances are, so to speak, of explosive nature. The final results of these down-breaking changes are waste products, which have to be eliminated or excreted from the system. The accompanying diagram (fig. 20) illustrates the matter. It represents a double staircase, with a shorter ascending stair on the left, and a longer descending stair on the right. Food is represented as being on the level of the lowest step of the left-hand stair, the successive steps of which represent the stages by which more and more complex substances are built, till the most complex of all, protoplasm, is produced. The breaking down of this into simpler and simpler substances is represented by the successive steps of the descending stair, at the bottom of which are the waste products. These are represented at a lower level than the food, because they are of simpler chemical constitution. They are mainly—water (H_2O), carbonic acid gas. (CO_2), and compounds of nitrogen.

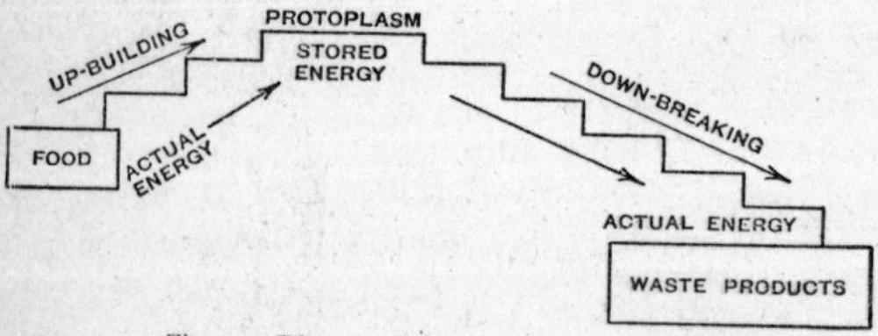

Fig. 20.—Diagram of chemical changes in Body

The organs which get rid of waste are (1) skin, (2) lungs, (3) kidneys, and (4) liver.

1. The Skin, among its other functions, eliminates a large amount of water and small quantities of the other kinds of waste, here constituting the excretion called sweat or perspiration. Imbedded in it are innumerable sweat-glands, in the form of

minute coiled tubes, each opening by a very small pore on the surface. The coiled part of each such gland is sunk deeply in the dermis, and is surrounded by capillary blood-vessels, from the blood contained in which the materials making up sweat are separated.

2. THE LUNGS (fig. 21) are two spongy bodies contained in the thorax, and their function as breathing or respiratory organs is twofold—(1) to excrete or get rid of the waste carbonic acid gas, together with a large quantity of water, and (2) to supply the blood with free oxygen, which is necessary as the agent by which the waste constantly going on in the body is rendered possible. This waste is in fact a process of oxidation, *i.e.* a conversion of protoplasm, &c., into simpler bodies containing a larger proportion of oxygen. The lungs are spongy in character because they are made up of innumerable little air-tubes, ending blindly in groups of minute air-sacs, with walls invested by a close network of capillaries, the blood contained in which is so near to

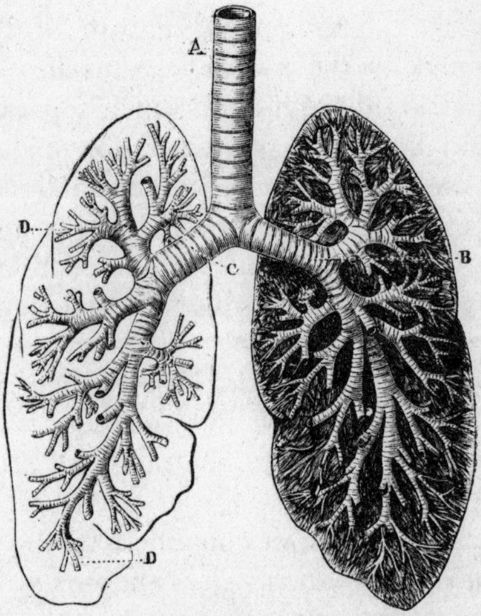

Fig. 21.—Lungs and Air-passages
A, Windpipe; B C, bronchi; D D, smaller air-passages.

the air in the air-cells that an exchange of materials is possible. On the one hand, a large amount of the carbonic acid gas with which the impure blood is highly charged is able to diffuse into the air-sacs, from which, on the other hand, the oxygen of the air is able to diffuse into the blood. The *hæmoglobin* of the red corpuscles plays an important part as an oxygen-carrier, taking it up from the air in the lungs and readily parting with it to the substance of the body. A large amount of water in the form of vapour also diffuses out of the blood into the air-sacs. As a result of this, the air breathed out contains far more carbonic acid gas and water-vapour, but much less oxygen, than the air breathed in. This exchange of gases constitutes the essential part of breathing; but the mechanical part has also to be considered, *i.e.* the arrangements by which the air-passages of the lungs are continually provided with fresh pure air, and get rid of impure air. Without going into unnecessary detail, it may be pointed out that the walls of the chest are movable, so that the size of that region is alternately increased (when air is breathed in) and diminished (when air is breathed out). During the former process, the breast-bone and ribs are moved on the joints by which the latter are hinged to the backbone, in such a way as to increase the volume of the chest from side to side and from front to back. The general nature of these movements can be easily noted by the reader in himself. At the same time the muscular midriff or diaphragm, which separates the chest from the abdomen, and in a state of rest is convex towards the former, flattens out as a result of its own contraction, and thus increases the size of the chest in the direction of its length. As the thorax is, so to speak, an air-tight box, the contained lungs are obliged to expand as it increases in volume, the result being that air passes into their larger air-passages. The reverse process to the one described, whereby diminution of volume is effected, is largely due to the elasticity of the thoracic walls, while at the time the diaphragm ceases to contract, and resumes its normal curved shape. Air consequently passes out from the larger air-passages. Purification of the air contained in the smaller air-passages (bronchial tubes) and their blind endings is brought about by diffusion. A few words are necessary on the direction taken by the air. The proper course for this (fig. 8) is through the nostrils, into the nasal cavities, and thence by a special aperture (posterior nares) into the pharynx, on the floor of which is a slit-like opening, the glottis, leading into the windpipe. Of course breathing can also be effected through the mouth, but the primary use of this is as a food-passage.

In front of the glottis there is an elastic flap, the *epiglottis* (fig. 8), which, when food is swallowed, folds back over the glottis and forms a sort of bridge to the gullet. The windpipe (trachea), into which the glottis leads, is a good-sized tube (fig. 22), with its walls stiffened by hoop-like pieces of gristle and so prevented from collapse. It can easily be felt in the front of the neck, from which it runs into the thorax, there bifurcating into a bronchus for each of the lungs. Either bronchus when traced is found to divide repeatedly to form smaller and smaller air-passages, the smallest of which end, as already described, in delicate air-sacs. The advantage of this arrangement is to provide a very large surface over which the blood can be purified without taking up a large amount of room.

It is interesting to notice that the lungs are developed as outgrowths from the pharynx, which are at first simple pouches, but gradually become more complicated.

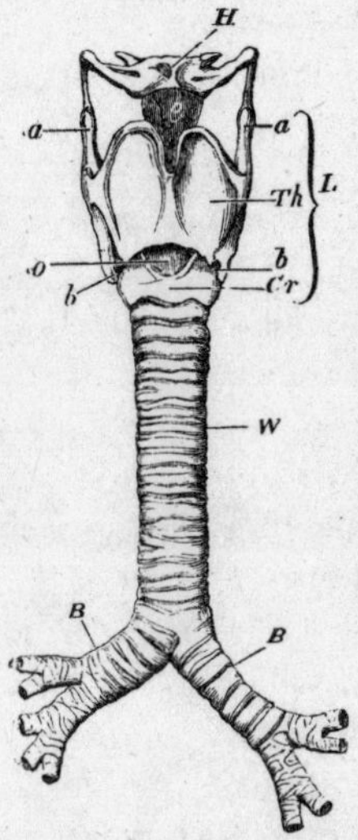

Fig. 22.—The Larynx and Windpipe

L, Larynx, formed of *Th* and *Cr*, thyroid and cricoid cartilages; *a a b b*, parts of thyroid; H, hyoid bone; *e*, epiglottis; W, windpipe; B B, bronchi.

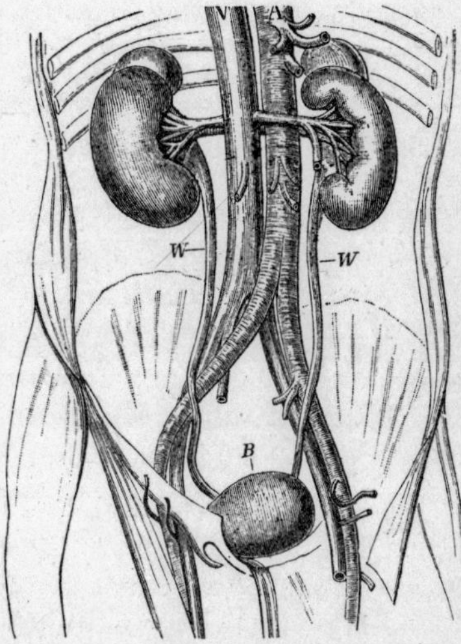

Fig. 23.—The Situation of the Kidneys

A, Dorsal aorta; V, vena cava; B, bladder; W, ureters. Branches of the aorta are seen going to the kidney, and veins from it are shown joining the vena cava.

The *organ of voice* falls to be mentioned here, since it is intimately associated with the air-passages. The beginning of the windpipe is dilated into a voice-box or *larynx* (fig. 22), supported by various pieces of gristle, of which the largest (thyroid cartilage) can be felt in the swelling known as "Adam's apple". Projecting into the cavity of the larynx are two narrow elastic cushions with sharp edges, which can be brought parallel to one another by appropriate muscles. If, when this has been done, air is sharply breathed in or out, a musical note results, and the cushions in question, commonly but rather inappropriately called the *vocal chords*, can be stretched to different extents, so that the resulting note varies in pitch, a low note being produced when they are slackened, and the opposite when they are pulled tight. Vowel sounds of various kinds are produced by altering the shape of the mouth-cavity through which the air breathed out is passed, while consonants result from momentarily blocking the air-current in different ways. The entire mechanism is extremely complicated, and this is not the place to describe it more fully.

3. The Kidneys.—The kidneys are generally described as the excretory organs *par excellence*, the useless matter here being nitrogenous waste and mineral salts dissolved in a large bulk of water. They are two characteristically-shaped structures placed in the abdominal cavity (fig. 23) close to the ventral

side of the backbone, and from each of them a tube, the ureter, conducts the products of waste to a good-sized bag, the urinary bladder, which is sheltered in the cavity of the pelvis and opens to the exterior.

4. The Liver.—Nitrogenous waste is got rid of chiefly by the liver and kidneys. The liver, which has already been described as a digestive gland, is also a waste-eliminating organ, for bile is a waste product as well as a digestive juice.

ORGANS OF MOVEMENT.

1. Muscular Action.—The obvious movements of the body are brought about by the masses of flesh technically known as *muscles*, which make up a large proportion of its weight. These muscles are of various shapes, in accordance with the differences in their uses; but they all agree in being composed of vast numbers of microscopic fibres which, under the control of the nerves, are able to contract, *i.e.* to shorten, while at the same time they become broader. The result is, that the parts to which the ends of an elongated muscle are fixed are brought nearer together. Such a muscle is generally attached at one end (the origin) to a relatively fixed part, and at the other (the insertion) to a relatively movable part. This is the case, for example, with the biceps muscle, easily felt as a mass of flesh on the front of the forearm (fig. 24). This takes origin from the scapula and is inserted into the radius, the result being that when it contracts, the forearm, being the relatively movable part, is drawn up.

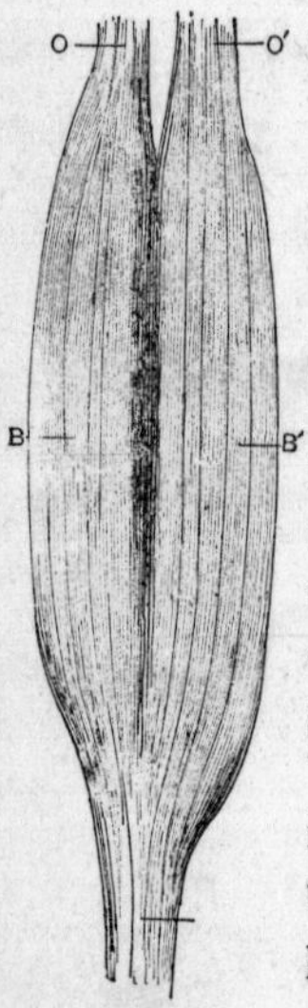

Fig. 24.—Biceps Muscle of the Arm

B B′, Fleshy part; O O′, origin; I, insertion.

Muscles are commonly attached by means of firm fibrous cords, the *tendons*, an arrangement which permits a large number of muscles to be attached to a small part, such as a finger-bone, and further permits such muscles to act from a considerable distance. The use of skeletal parts in giving attachment to muscles is obvious, and the numerous ridges and projections seen on bones are largely related to this function.

Muscle is also important in relation to the movements of

internal organs, as has already been seen in the case of the heart. It also enters into the walls of the blood-vessels, serving to regulate their size, and the walls of the food-tube are also largely composed of the same substance, which here exerts a kind of squeezing action by which the digesting food is gradually passed on. The muscle, however, making up the flesh of the body is different in structure from that found in internal organs, and is termed voluntary, being under the direct control of the will; while the muscle of the heart, &c., is involuntary, because it cannot be regulated in this way.

2. Ciliary Action.—Movement in the human body is, however, not all due to muscular action, but can be brought about in two other ways. One of these is *ciliary action*, of which a good example is afforded by the lining of the windpipe. If this is examined under a compound microscope it will be found to be lined with fragments of protoplasm (cells), covered thickly with short protoplasmic threads known as *cilia* (fig. 25). Each cilium is able to alternately bend and straighten itself, and when numerous cilia work together, as is usually the case, they are able to move along small particles placed upon the surface they beset. Their action in the case mentioned is to sweep particles of dust, &c., towards the exterior, thus keeping the ciliated surface clean. The last kind of movement is the peculiar creeping motion exemplified by the colourless corpuscles of blood and lymph (fig. 15). It is said to be *amœboid.*

Fig. 25.—Cells of Ciliated Epithelium, much magnified

The two kinds of movement just described are much more primitive than muscular action, and, as might be expected, play a much more leading part in the lower forms of life than they do in such a complicated organism as a human being.

NERVOUS SYSTEM AND SENSE ORGANS.

The great complexity of the body, with its numerous subtly interwoven functions, demands some means of controlling and correlating these, and of keeping the body as a whole in touch with the outer world. The means is found in those organs to which the terms nervous system and sense organs are applied.

The Nervous System.—The nervous system essentially consists of certain central organs, which may be regarded as the head-quarters of the life of the individual; and of numerous branching cords, the *nerves,* which connect up the central organs with all parts of the body. The central organs consist of brain and spinal cord, elaborately sheltered within the axial skeleton (fig. 26), and of a more subsidiary part lodged in the body cavity close against the backbone, and known as the sympathetic nervous system.

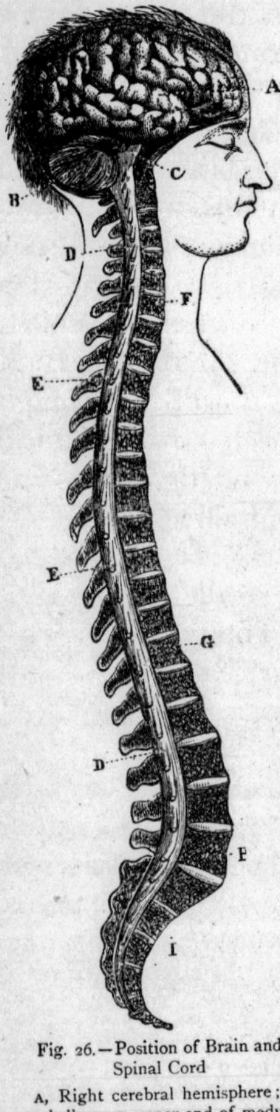

Fig. 26.—Position of Brain and Spinal Cord

A, Right cerebral hemisphere; B, cerebellum; C, upper end of medulla oblongata D D, spinal cord with beginnings of spinal nerves; E E, processes of vertebræ; F G H, last vertebræ of neck, chest, and loin regions; I, sacrum.

The Spinal Cord.—It is best to begin a consideration of these organs with the spinal cord or marrow, a soft cylindrical mass contained in the backbone, and continuous at one end with the brain, while at the other it tapers to a thread. This cord is protected by investing membranes, and in a cross-section (fig. 27) presents a somewhat singular appearance, due to its being made up of two sorts of nervous matter, white and grey, the former being external while the latter constitutes a sort of core, which in the section looks like a couple of cres-

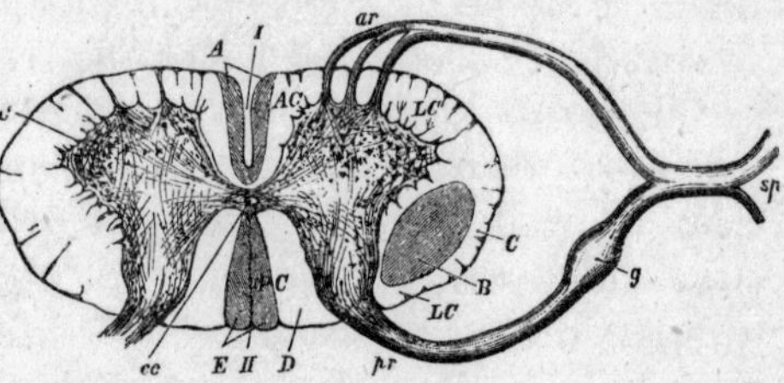

Fig. 27.—Cross section of the Spinal Cord, dorsal side below. Partly diagrammatic. Magnified

N C, Groups of nerve-cells in grey matter; remaining capital letters indicate regions of white matter; *sp*, a spinal nerve, formed by union of dorsal (posterior) and ventral (anterior) roots, *pr* and *ar*; *g*, ganglion on dorsal root.

cents placed back to back. A further point of importance is the presence of a minute central canal, so that the cord can be regarded as a tube with small bore and very thick walls, somewhat as is the case with the stem of a thermometer. The *grey matter* is mainly made up of angular or star-shaped structures of very small size, each of these being a *nerve-* or *ganglion-cell* (fig. 28). It is these cells which collectively make up the essential part of the central organs, while the *white matter* and the nerves consist of an infinite number of slender *nerve-fibres* which have a conducting function. To take an electrical analogy, the nerve-cells may be looked upon as batteries, while the nerve-fibres are comparable to wires. The analogy, however, is a very rough one, for here batteries and wires alike are alive, and there does not appear to be the same coupling up of nerve cells and fibres that exists between batteries and wires in an ordinary electric system. There is indeed a certain amount of connection, but how much is a matter of doubt. Not improbably the cells, to some extent, are able to act independently of fibres, recalling the wireless telegraphy which is now being developed.

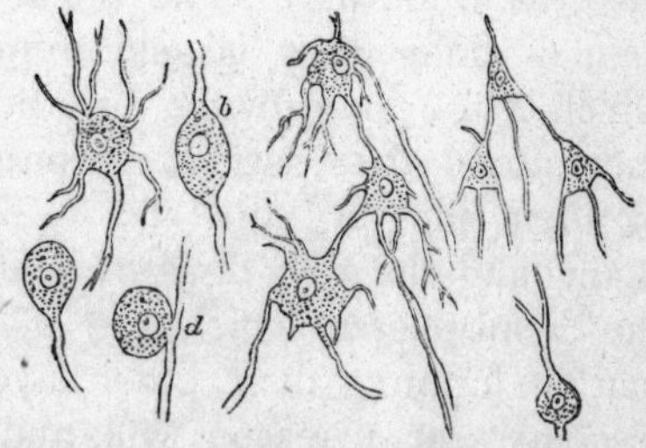

Fig. 28.—Various Forms of Nerve-cells. *b* and *d* from ganglia on dorsal roots of spinal nerves. Observe nucleus in centre of each.

Subject to the brain, a large amount of control over the neck, trunk, and limbs is exerted by the spinal cord, and in accordance with this the parts in question are supplied by numerous pairs of *spinal nerves* which arise from the cord. The examination of any particular spinal nerve (fig. 27) will show that it takes origin in a couple of bundles of fibres which, from their position, are respectively known as the dorsal and ventral roots. It has been shown that, broadly speaking, the fibres of the dorsal root are carrying nerve impulses—telegraphic messages, as it were—to the central organs, while those of the ventral root carry such impulses away from them. To express this, the names afferent and efferent fibres (L. *affĕro*, I carry to; *effĕro*, I carry out) are respectively given. The *afferent fibres* convey information to the central organs about what is going on in the body or outside it, while the *efferent fibres* carry impulses from the central organs to the other parts of the body, with the result that certain actions take place, or it may be that actions in progress are modified or stopped.

The Brain.—The brain is an exceedingly complex organ, and is the centre of sensations and voluntary actions, besides, like the spinal cord, carrying on operations not dependent on the will. It consists of a central axis, which may be regarded as a forward extension of the spinal cord, and of various outgrowths from this. The brains of different kinds of backboned animals differ very largely from one another in the extent to which these outgrowths are developed. In the human brain they attain their largest proportions, and the most noteworthy of them (fig. 26) are the *cerebellum* in the hinder part of the brain, and the two *cerebral hemispheres* in front of these. It is the hemispheres which are of greatest interest, for the grey matter forming their outer layer, or *cortex*, appears to be the ultimate seat of reason, will, and intelligence. It can be mapped out into small areas or centres, which are partly motor, controlling special muscles, and partly sensory, concerned with the special sensations. We have, for example, a special motor area concerned with the muscles of the arm, and if this centre be injured, paralysis of the arm follows. Again, a special centre of vision has been recognized, and if this be damaged, the sight is more or less impaired. In fact, what are termed sensations of sight, hearing, taste, &c., depend on changes taking place in these centres consequent on nerve impulses which are conveyed to the brain along afferent nerve-fibres. The hemispheres are connected together by a broad band of nerve-fibres (corpus callosum), the presence of which is important as regards classification.

The spinal cord is not only a central organ capable of doing certain regulative work on its own account, but also serves as a channel of communication between the brain and those parts of the body supplied by the spinal nerves. The brain, however, communicates directly with the head and some other parts of the body by means of twelve pairs of *cranial nerves* which take origin from it. These differ in many ways from spinal nerves. Some of them are composed entirely of afferent fibres, which place sense organs in communication with the brain, *e.g.* the optic nerve connected with the eye, and the auditory nerve with the internal organs of hearing. Others are entirely composed of efferent fibres, *e.g.* three pairs of small nerves which do nothing but supply the muscles moving the eyeballs. Others, again, contain both efferent and afferent fibres, as is the case with the remarkable tenth pair of cranial nerves, named vagus on account of their wandering course. Running along the neck, these nerves pass into the thorax, where they send branches to both heart and lungs, and, piercing the midriff, end in branches supplying the stomach.

The Sympathetic System.—This brief survey of the nervous system may be completed by referring to the *sympathetic system*, which consists in the main of a couple of slender cords running ventral to the backbone, and dilating at intervals into small swellings known as the sympathetic ganglia, containing nerve-cells, and therefore considered as collectively constituting a part of the central nervous system. They are connected with the spinal and some of the cranial nerves, and largely control the internal organs and blood-vessels, to which they send numerous branches. The working of the sympathetic system is entirely involuntary, a fortunate circumstance to which we owe the fact that we are very largely unconscious of the internal movements of the body.

Sense Organs.—The sense organs have been described as the implements of the nervous system, gaining, as it does, information about the external world by their means. A sense organ may broadly be regarded as a more or less modified piece of skin adapted to receive impressions from some external agent (contact, heat, light, sound, &c.) or *stimulus* (L. *stimulus*, an ox-goad), and connected up with the central nervous system by a sensory nerve.

Fig. 29. — Magnified View of a Papilla of Skin, with a Touch Corpuscle

The Skin as a Sense Organ.—The skin of the neck, trunk, and limbs is richly supplied with sensory nerves derived from the spinal cord, while the skin of the head and the linings of the mouth- and nose-cavities receive branches from the fifth cranial nerve. Connected with many of the smallest twigs of these nerves are microscopic bodies which are known as *touch-corpuscles* (fig. 29), because they are believed to have to do with the sense of *touch*. A finger-tip furnishes the best example. Upon it will readily be seen a series of fine ridges arranged in a characteristic manner, differing largely, however, in different individuals, and thus affording an important means of identification. Under these ridges, imbedded in the deeper layer of the skin (dermis) are to be seen rows of touch-corpuscles. The sense of touch proper gives us information about bodies which actually come into contact with the skin, and how extensive such information may be is seen in the case of blind persons. The sequence of events before we feel a sensation when, say, a finger-tip touches any object, is somewhat as follows:—The first effect of contact is to cause some kind of to-and-fro movement in the minute particles (molecules) of which the touch-corpuscles are made up, or, to use more technical language, a "molecular vibration". The corpuscles may be called the "end-organs of touch", because they form the external end of the set of structures concerned with touch. Next follows a "nerve impulse" (which is another kind of molecular vibration) along the sensory nerve to the spinal cord and thence to the brain. Lastly, a part of the grey matter composing the external coat or cortex of a brain hemisphere is affected, a third variety of molecular vibration being set up in it. Then, and not till then, is a sensation of touch experienced, by which we know that something has happened in the finger-tip. What that something may be is judged by comparison with past happenings of a like nature. The sequence of events here very roughly described for touch applies, *mutatis mutandis,* to any other sense, and therefore will not be spoken of again; but it is important to bear in mind that all the various sensations—touch, taste, smell, hearing, and sight—are, so to speak, manufactured in the brain, and it is only as the result of long practice that we learn to recognize them as resulting from changes set up in end-organs by different external agents (stimuli), enabling us to form judgments about what is happening outside the body altogether.

The skin is not merely concerned with touch proper, but is also the organ of the *temperature-sense,* by which we learn something about the condition of external bodies as regards their condition with reference to heat or cold.

The Sense of Taste (fig. 30).—The object of this sense being to give us information about food, it is not surprising to find its end-organs limited to the lining of the mouth-cavity. The most obvious of these are contained in the mucous membrane of the tongue, upon the upper side of which organ, at the back, are to be noted a number of small projections or *papillæ,* in the sides of which are imbedded minute ovoid taste-buds containing slender *taste-cells.* These cells are connected with nerve-fibres which have been usually regarded as coming from the ninth cranial nerve, though there is reason to believe that they really belong to the fifth. However that may be, there are only two sensations of taste proper, *i.e.* sweetness and bitterness, and the stimulus which initiates either of these must be something in a dissolved condition. Many so-called tastes are partly smells, and that such "flavours" are of this mixed nature is practically demonstrated by a cold in the head, which largely destroys what we popularly call taste, although only the nose is affected. We are able to smell the food in the mouth by reason of the fact that mouth-cavity and nasal cavities alike communicate with the pharynx (see p. 34). It must also be borne in mind that the lining of the mouth, especially that part of it covering the tongue, also ministers to the sense of touch. The tip of the tongue is even more sensitive in this respect than a finger-tip, and there is also good reason for thinking that what we call "acid tastes" are more properly to be regarded as varieties of touch.

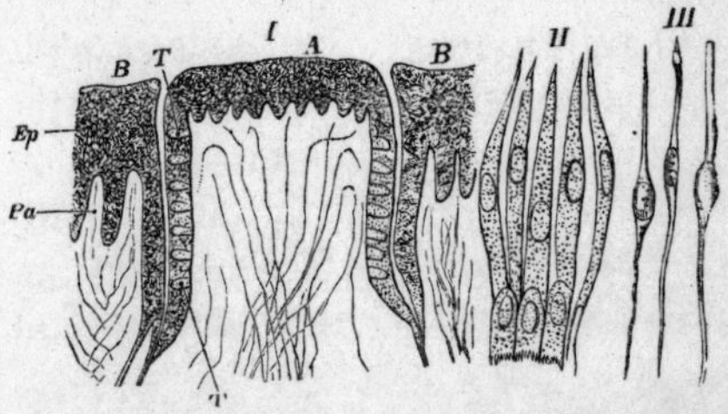

Fig. 30.—Section of Papillæ of the Tongue—highly magnified

I A, Section of the central papilla; B B, section of the surrounding elevation; *Pa*, papilla of the dermis; *Ep*, layer of epithelium; T, taste buds; II and III represent very highly magnified views of cells of the taste buds. Note their oval nuclei.

The Sense of Smell (fig. 31).—The organs of smell have to do with testing the quality of the air taken into the lungs, and it is therefore natural that they should be situated at the beginning of the breathing passages. They consist of the two cavities of the nose, opening behind into the pharynx. The mucous membrane which lines the upper part of these cavities contains numerous slender *olfactory cells,* which are the end-organs of

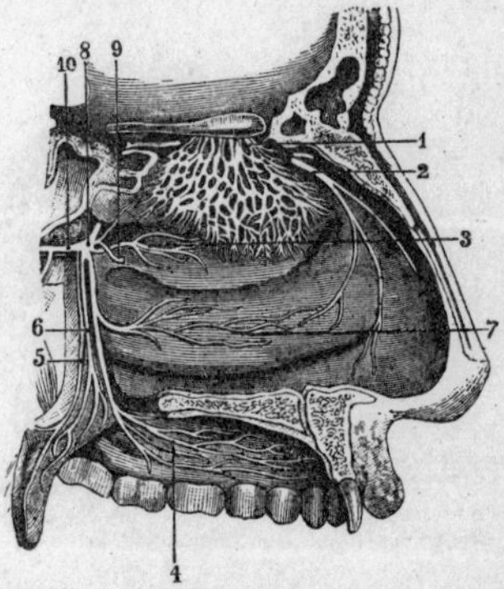

Fig. 31.—Distribution of Nerves over interior of Nasal Cavity, outer wall

1, Branches of nerves of smell—olfactory nerve; 2, nerves of touch to the nostril; 4, 5, 6, nerves to the palate springing from a ganglion at 8; 3, 7, 9, branches from one of the palate nerves to nostrils.

smell, and are acted upon by gases and vapours. Fragrance and its contrary are the only smells to which the name can strictly be applied, as some so-called "odours", such as those of a pungent nature, are due to the delicate sense of touch connected with the nasal cavities. The first cranial or olfactory nerves are those of smell proper, and they supply the end-organs alluded to. As already mentioned, certain sensations which we are accustomed to call tastes are partly of the nature of smells.

The Organs of Hearing (fig. 32).—These complicated structures consist of two subdivisions—(1) the essential parts containing the end-organs, and (2) certain sound-conducting arrangements. (1) The essential parts constituting what is known as the *internal ear* are imbedded in the firm side-wall of the skull, and consist of a complicated bag, the *membranous labyrinth*, on each side. This bag is really a small portion of the skin, which has been folded in so as to reach a sheltered position and escape injury. If the head of an embryo chick be examined, a small pit will be seen on either side of it. This is the commencing internal ear, and later on the mouth of the pit closes, converting it into a minute vesicle lying just below the surface. This vesicle sinks inwards, and gradually assumes the complex shape characteristic of the labyrinth in the adult, while at the same time bony matter is formed round it. The lining of the labyrinth is made up in several places of slender *auditory cells*, which are the end-organs for hearing, and are supplied by the eighth or auditory cranial nerves. (2) The end-organs of hearing are stimulated by those vibrations of the air which are known as sound-waves, but, owing to the deep position of the

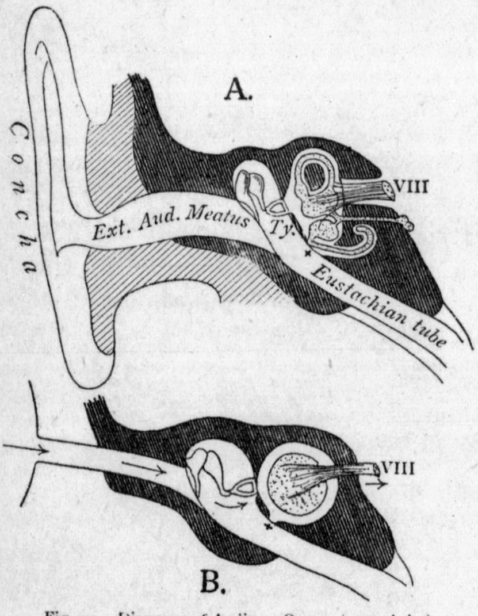

Fig. 32.—Diagrams of Auditory Organs (natural size)

Parts cut through are shaded, the close shading indicating the temporal bone. Membranous labyrinth dotted. *Ty*, Tympanic cavity; VIII, auditory nerve. Arrows indicate direction in which sound-waves and resultant nerve impulses pass. A is after Schwalbe, and B is a still simpler diagram.

labyrinth, a special conducting apparatus, consisting of middle and external ears, is necessary. The *external ear* consists of the flap to which the name "ear" is applied in ordinary language, that of *concha* or *pinna* scientifically, and of a short auditory tube leading down into the head. Stretched across the inner end of this tube is a firm tympanic membrane. The *middle ear* consists of a tympanic cavity ("drum" of the ear) internal to the tympanic membrane, and communicating with the pharynx by a tube-like prolongation (Eustachian tube). The internal ear is situated close to the inner side of the tympanic cavity, and at one place the protecting bone is absent, leaving a little oval space, the oval window (fenestra ovalis), filled by membrane only. If this were perforated, the fluid which surrounds the labyrinth would escape into the tympanic cavity. Stretching across the cavity from tympanic membrane to oval window is a chain of minute bones, the auditory ossicles, called, from their shape, hammer, anvil, and stirrup. The handle of the first is fixed to the tympanic membrane, while the foot-plate of the last fits into the oval window. Sound-waves enter the auditory tube, throw the tympanic membrane into vibrations, like those of a drum-head, and this moves the chain of ossicles backwards and forwards, thus acting upon the membrane of the oval window, thereby affecting the fluid surrounding the labyrinth. The wall of the labyrinth itself is thus jolted, and the fluid it contains agitated. So far the vibrations (except the sound-waves themselves) are not molecular, but now begins the first part of hearing proper, for the auditory cells of the labyrinth are thrown into molecular vibration, followed by the transmission of impulses along the auditory nerve to the brain.

The Organs of Sight (fig. 33).—The eyes, which to a very large extent act together, are sheltered in bony depressions of the face known as the orbits, and are provided with muscles for moving them in different directions, which obviously largely adds to their efficiency. There are also other accessory structures, such as eyelids and tear-glands, the former protective, and the latter secreting a fluid which washes the front of the eye, and as it is done with passing down a narrow tube into the nose-cavity.

The eyeball is covered by three coats, of which the outermost, the *sclerotic*, is very tough, and forms what is called "the white" of the eye. A circular external area of this is the transparent *cornea*, which permits light rays to enter. Within the sclerotic is a much softer *choroid coat* containing numerous blood-vessels; this, however, does not line the cornea and its immediate neighbourhood, but runs transversely across the front part of the eye to form the coloured part we call the *iris*, in the centre of which is a hole, the *pupil*. Optically speaking the iris is a diaphragm for regulating the amount of light entering the eye, and the size of its central aperture, the pupil, varies in size according to circumstances, becoming very small in a bright light and very large in a dim light. Lining the choroid is a third eye-coat, pulpy in consistency, and known as the *retina*. It contains the end-organs for sight (rods and cones), and acts as a sensitive screen upon which light falls. The second cranial or optic nerves run into the retina, branching within it to supply the rods and cones.

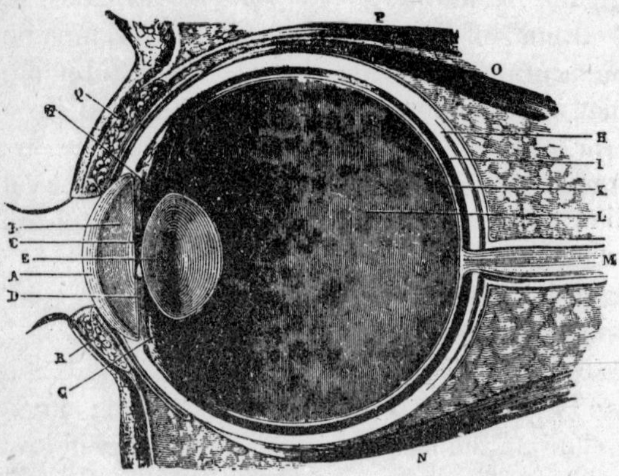

Fig. 33.—Representation of a vertical cut through the Eyeball in its Socket

A, Cornea; B, aqueous humour; C, pupil; D, iris; E, lens; H, sclerotic; I, choroid; K, retina; L, vitreous humour; M, optic nerve; N, an eye-muscle; P, an eyelid-muscle, with an eye-muscle (O) below it; Q R, eyelids.

The eye is filled with refracting structures, of which the most important is the biconvex *lens*, placed just behind the iris. The small space in front of the lens is filled by a clear fluid, the *aqueous humour*, and the much larger space at its back by the jelly-like *vitreous humour*. Just as the lens of a photographer's camera forms a picture of surrounding objects upon the sensitive plate at the back of the apparatus, so do the refracting substances within the eye act with reference to the retina.

A study of the development of the eye shows that its sensitive part, the retina, is formed from an outgrowth of the brain, and as this organ is in reality a piece of skin folded in and much modified, the retina must be looked upon as of the same nature.

Common Origin of Sense Organs.—We have seen that all the sense organs agree with one another in the important point that their essential parts, *i.e.* those containing end-organs, are really modifications of part of the skin, though this is not apparent at first sight, and reference must be made to the facts of development in order to prove it. But as the different sense organs are adapted to respond to very different agents, it is only natural that they should be modified for the purpose, so that the ear, for example, possesses an elaborate sound-conducting apparatus, while the eye consists largely of refracting structures.

CHAPTER II

ESSENTIAL CHARACTERS OF VERTEBRATE ANIMALS. STRUCTURE AND CLASSIFICATION OF MAMMALS

VERTEBRATES AND INVERTEBRATES. — It has already been pointed out (p. 8) that Aristotle in his natural history drew what is perhaps the most important boundary line in zoology, *i.e.* the one dividing Backboned or Vertebrate Animals from Backboneless or Invertebrate ones.

The description which has just been given of the structure and functions of the human body will have given a rough idea of the leading characters of the Vertebrates, and it is now necessary to indicate those features which characterize the group as a whole. The following classes are here included:—

I. MAMMALS, or ordinary warm-blooded quadrupeds.—*Exs.*: Lion, Horse, Rabbit, Bats, Monkeys, Human Beings.
II. BIRDS.—*Exs.*: Fowl, Parrot, Ostrich.
III. REPTILES.—*Exs.*: Crocodiles, Lizards, Turtles, Snakes.
IV. AMPHIBIANS.—*Exs.*: Frogs, Toads, Newts, Salamanders.
V. FISHES.—*Exs.*: Herring, Salmon, Shark, Lamprey.
VI. PROTOCHORDATES, including various low forms, none of which are familiar to most persons.

Essential Characters of Vertebrates. — The body is nearly always bilaterally symmetrical, though cases are known where this is only true for the very young animal while the adult is more or less asymmetrical. A good case in point is that of Flat-fishes, such as turbot, sole, and plaice, in which the young fry closely resemble those of other fish, but as development advances one eye is shifted round to the other side of the head. In a turbot (fig. 34), for example, the dark and light sides are not dorsal and ventral, as might at first sight be supposed, but left and right, both the eyes being situated on the former side, which is kept turned upwards during life.

Segmentation, or division of the body into a number of similar parts or *segments* from before backwards, is another characteristic of Vertebrates; but is not equally obvious in all of them. It is particularly well seen in the lancelet (Amphioxus), a small somewhat fish-like animal classed with the Protochordates (fig. 293).

The body of an average Vertebrate is divisible into *head*, *trunk*, and *tail*, though the last may be entirely absent in some terrestrial forms, as, *e.g.*, the frog, which, however, possesses a large tail in its tadpole stage. When *limbs* are present they are never more than four in number, in which case the fore- and hind-limbs may be much alike, as in a pig, lizard, or newt, or else they may be widely dissimilar, as in a bat or bird, where the fore-limbs are modified for the purposes of flight. One pair of limbs may be entirely absent, as in whales, which possess no hinder extremities, though there can be no doubt that such were present in the ancestral forms from which whales are descended. The complete absence of limbs in certain cases may be due to the fact that they never have been present, as in Protochordates; or it may be a case of the dwindling away and disappearance of members once possessed, as in snakes, which occasionally retain small and imperfect hind-limbs.

Fig. 34.—Left side (apparent dorsal side) of a Turbot

The *double-tube arrangement*, which has been described as characteristic of the human body, is found among Vertebrates generally, and running along the axis of the trunk between the two tubes is either a backbone proper, or at any rate a firm supporting rod which answers the same purpose. A rod of this sort, the *notochord*, is found throughout life in the lancelet, for example. It is not composed of bone or gristle, but of an elastic substance. Such a rod is found in the embryos of all Vertebrates, but as development proceeds it is usually more or less replaced by a *vertebral column* made of cartilage or bone, or both. The presence of a notochord at some period or other of life is one of the most distinctive characters of Vertebrates, which for this reason are often termed CHORDATA.

In the vast majority of Vertebrates we find, at the beginning of the digestive tube, *jaws* having an up-and-down movement. Certain of the higher Invertebrates, *e.g.* lobster, scorpion, cockroach, also possess parts which are called jaws, but they are really limbs which move from side to side, are placed entirely outside the mouth, and do not form, as in a Vertebrate, a part of the head.

In all groups of Vertebrates we find that at some period or other of life there are certain slit-like openings on the side of the throat, by means of which the cavity of the pharynx communicates with the exterior (fig. 35). These openings in aquatic forms, such as fishes, become the *gill-slits* of the adult. Probably everyone has lifted up the flap or gill-cover, which is found on each side of the head in such a fish as a salmon or herring, and seen the red comb-like gills attached to the bars between these slits. And those who have not done this are likely to have noticed gold-fish or the like in an aquarium, and if so, will have observed that the animals continually open and shut their mouths, taking in water, which passes out again through these gill-slits in the process of breathing. In such terrestrial forms as Mammals, Reptiles, and Birds such slits are present in the embryo only (fig. 35), but they never perform any function, and ultimately close up altogether, only serving as a token that in the remote past the ancestors of these groups were aquatic forms, possessing gill-slits and breathing by means of gills. Such a statement as the last might appear very far-fetched, were it not that in the life-history of the frog, and other Amphibia, we can actually see a gill-possessing fish-like creature gradually turn before our eyes into a terrestrial animal,

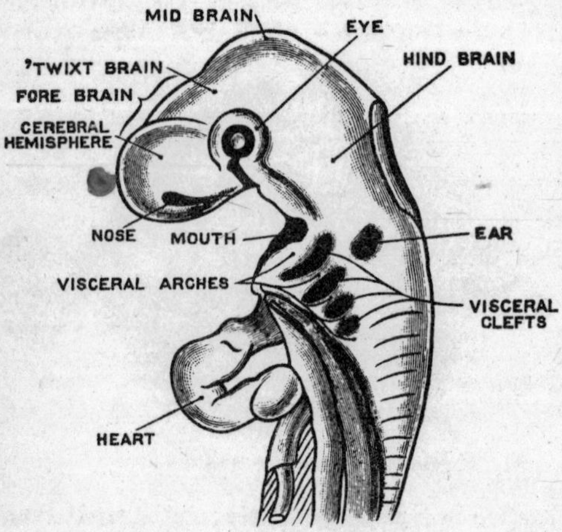

Fig. 35.—Front part of Chick Embryo

breathing air by means of lungs and quite devoid of gills and gill-slits. For it is a familiar commonplace that the frog starts life as a "pollywog" or tadpole, which to all intents and purposes is a fish, and would be classed as such if it developed no further. In due course, however, the tadpole grows lungs, while at the same time its gills shrivel up and its gill-slits close, changes which are accompanied by growth of limbs and loss of tail, the ultimate product of these revolutionary proceedings being a frog.

All Vertebrates possess a *blood system*, consisting of a set of tubes in which blood is circulated, usually by the pumping action of a *heart* placed near the under or ventral side of the animal. In the higher groups the heart is much more complicated in structure than in the lower ones.

The chief part of the *central nervous system* in a Vertebrate is a thick-walled tube, the front part of which is larger than the rest and is termed the *brain*, while the rest is the *spinal cord*. This tube has a dorsal position. The sensitive parts of the characteristic *eyes* are developed as outgrowths of the brain.

A brief survey of the Vertebrate groups, with their subdivisions, may now be appropriately entered into, beginning with the Mammals and ending with the Protochordates.

MAMMALS

Mammals are justly regarded as being the highest group of Backboned animals, and a number of characters mark them off pretty sharply from the remaining groups. These characters, as well as others of less importance, have been for the most part dealt with in the sketch already given of Man, the highest member of the group.

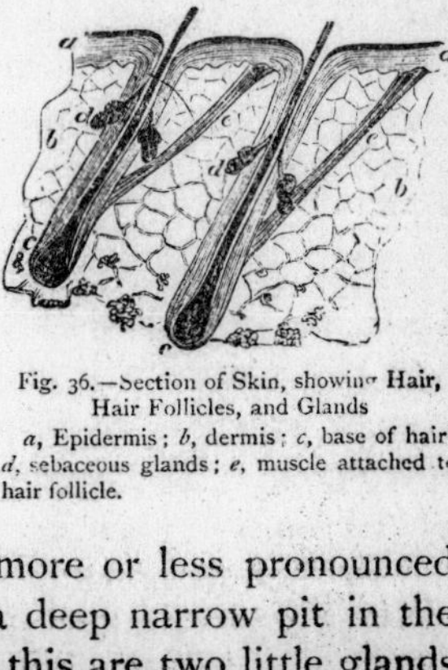

Fig. 36.—Section of Skin, showing Hair, Hair Follicles, and Glands
a, Epidermis; *b*, dermis; *c*, base of hair; *d*, sebaceous glands; *e*, muscle attached to hair follicle.

Probably the two most striking features which characterize a Mammal are the possession of (1) hair and (2) milk-glands, both of which belong to the skin.

(1) *Hair* (fig. 36).—In all cases we find that the epidermis gives rise to a more or less pronounced hairy covering, each hair growing from a deep narrow pit in the skin, called a hair-follicle. Opening into this are two little glands

(sebaceous glands), secreting an oily substance that may be regarded as a sort of natural pomatum. After a hair has attained a certain length it falls out, and is succeeded by another hair growing from the same follicle. Many animals at stated periods of the year undergo a sort of moult in preparation for the growth of a new coat. This is the case, for example, with horses, which lose their hair on the approach of winter and develop a thicker covering.

There is very great variation as to the amount of hair present, some aquatic forms, such as whales, being almost devoid of any such covering, which on the other hand is extraordinarily well developed in such creatures as sheep and goats. There may also be a localization of well-developed hair, as in the mane of horse or lion, and the beard of man and many apes. Not only are there these differences in amount of hair, but also in kind and colour. Both these points are illustrated by the races of mankind, which present such differing types as the fair wavy hair of many Europeans, the black straight hair of the Chinese, and the frizzly wool of negroes. These differences are not merely ones of colour, but shape, for the hairs of a Chinaman are almost perfectly cylindrical, while the wavy hairs are flattened to some extent, and the wool is much flattened, as in curling wood-shavings. In the last case, too, the hairs are set obliquely in the skin. Even in a human being we can distinguish between the coarser hair of the head and the fine downy hair covering most parts of the body; but in many mammals such a distinction is much better marked, as in the fur-seal, which possesses coarse comparatively long hair, together with the soft close-set finer sort which makes the skin valuable commercially. A more violent contrast is seen in a hedgehog (fig. 52), where we find not only ordinary hair, but also spines, which are simply very large strong protective hairs, and this is carried a step further in porcupines.

The epidermis of Mammals also produces other structures, which are more or less allied to hairs. The horn of a rhinoceros is of this nature, and may be considered as a mass of fused hairs, a view which is confirmed by examination of sections under the microscope. The fringed scales of some armadilloes are to be looked upon in a similar light, while such structures as claws, nails, and the hollow horns of cattle are more remotely related.

Mammals exhibit the greatest variety in the *coloration* of the hairy covering of the body, and some of the colour-schemes are of great beauty, as, for example, in tigers and leopards. As a general rule, the under side of the body is paler than the rest (see p. 22). In the inhabitants of cold climates it frequently happens that there is a well-marked distinction between summer and winter coats in the matter of colour. All these different arrangements are not haphazard, but bear a definite relation to the habits of the animal, commonly rendering them inconspicuous to foes or prey, &c. Such uses will be fully dealt with elsewhere, when the colours of animals in general will be considered.

(2) *Milk.*—One of the most noteworthy features regarding Mammals is the care taken by them of their young, a character which has much to do with the dominant position in the struggle for existence which has been gained by this group of animals. The word "gained" is used advisedly, for geological study shows us that this leading place was in earlier periods occupied by types of very different kind; *e.g.* the Reptiles constituted what may be called the last reigning Vertebrate dynasty prior to the Age of Mammals in which we now live. Just as in that age Man, the newest comer, has, in virtue of his intellectual qualities, dethroned his lower relatives and taken first place.

It is a matter of common knowledge that in the early part of their existence the young of Mammals are nourished by milk, a substance which also plays, in various forms, a most important part in the economy of human adults. As might be expected, milk is an exceedingly nutritious substance, and may be taken as the type of a perfect food. The composition of cow's milk is approximately as follows:—

Water, ...		87·0
Solids, consisting of—		
1. Albuminoids (chiefly casein), ...	4·0	
2. Carbohydrates (milk-sugar), ...	4·6	
3. Fats, ...	3·7	
4. Inorganic salts, ...	0·7	
		13·0
		100·0

It will be seen (see p. 33) that all the necessary constituents of animal food are present, and it may be added that they are in the most advantageous proportions.

A Mammal possesses one or more pairs of *milk-glands*, and their position varies considerably in different species, but in all cases such a gland consists of an aggregate of blindly-ending tubes which are ingrowths of the epidermis. As a general rule, these tubes open externally upon a *teat*, but in the two lowest known Mammals this is not the case, there being a simple depression of the skin, within which milk-pores are seen.

Besides the two important characters just dealt with, the Mammalia are distinguished by others of scarcely less value, which may be conveniently dealt with under the headings employed when describing the anatomy of the human subject.

Endoskeleton (see pp. 25–32).—Two very noteworthy features enable one to distinguish the *skull* of a Mammal from that of other Vertebrates. One is the presence of two occipital condyles at the back, and the other is the fact that the lower jaw is made up of only two pieces united together in front. Birds and Reptiles possess only one such condyle, and this, in cases where a well-developed neck is present, allows the head a very free motion, as may be observed in a bird, though in this particular case the large range of movement is also in part due to the existence of very perfect joints in the neck itself. Amphibia, *e.g.* the frog, also have two occipital condyles, but their skulls differ from those of Mammalia in so many other ways that no one is likely to be led into error thereby. As to the nature of the lower jaw, it is made up of a considerable number of pieces in Vertebrates lower than Mammals.

The *backbone* of a Man is typically Mammalian in its main features, except that the tail region is much more reduced than is usually the case. We note that the individual joints are flat-ended, and that in the young state the body or centrum of each is made up of a central piece, to which a bony disc is united at each end. This character applies to all but the very lowest members of the group. A further typical feature, to which but very few exceptions are known, is found in the fact that the vertebræ of the neck are seven in number, even in a giraffe.

The skeleton of the human *limbs* is typical in many ways, the chief modifications of a special nature being seen in the structure of the lower limbs, especially as regards the peculiar arches of the pelvis. Such peculiarities are adaptations to the requirements of the erect attitude. But the various bones recognizable in Man are recognizable also in most Mammals, and it may in particular be remarked that the possession of five fingers and five toes is the typical condition, though all sorts of reductions in number may take place, by which a fitness for special kinds of locomotion, &c., is brought about. The most extreme case is that of the horse, which possesses but one well-developed digit in each limb.

Digestive Organs (see pp. 34–38).—In most respects the digestive organs of Man may be taken as typical, especially as regards the fact that there are two sets of teeth, and that these teeth are of several kinds. The total of thirty-two for the permanent set is not, however, typical, a much nearer approach to this being found in the pig, which possesses forty-four teeth in all, arranged according to the following dental formula:—

$$i. = \frac{3-3}{3-3},\quad c. = \frac{1-1}{1-1},\quad p.m. = \frac{4-4}{4-4},\quad m. = \frac{3-3}{3-3} = 44.$$

Many Mammals, however, have undergone much greater reduction in the number of teeth than human beings, and in some species these structures have been lost altogether, as in the Great Ant-eater of South America. Porpoises and the like, on the other hand, have a very large number of teeth not divided into distinct kinds. The nature of the teeth, which is determined by the kind of food, is of great classificatory importance.

Circulatory Organs (see pp. 38–43).—Hot blood (about 98° F.), a four-chambered heart, with impure blood on its right and pure blood on its left side, and an aorta with its arch curving to the left, are the most characteristic features, and have all been dealt with in the preliminary sketch.

The necessity of maintaining the blood at a temperature often higher than that of the surrounding medium appears to be one reason for the possession of a thick coating of hair.

Respiratory Organs (see pp. 45–47).—No Mammal at any time possesses gills, though gill-slits are found in the embryo (see p. 62), but breathing is always effected by a pair of spongy *lungs* situated in the cavity of the thorax. There is present, as in Man, a partly muscular partition, the midriff or *diaphragm*, separating the cavity of the thorax from that of the abdomen, and materially assisting in the movements of breathing by which the air in the lungs is renewed.

Nervous System (see pp. 49–53).—The arrangements described in Man may be taken as fairly typical for Mammals in general, except as regards the *brain*, which is proportionately very much larger than in any other form.

It is characteristic that the cerebral hemispheres should be large, and united by a corpus callosum, while their surface is usually marked by more or less distinct convolutions. There is a relation between the intelligence of a Mammal and the size and complexity as regards convolutions of its hemispheres.

CLASSIFICATION OF MAMMALS

Existing Mammals fall into three natural groups, which are again subdivided into Orders, the arrangement being as follows:—

A. EUTHERIA.—This group embraces the vast majority of Mammals, including all the highest forms and those with which we are most familiar in this country. The distinctive characters mostly require a specialist knowledge of anatomy to be appreciated, and it may suffice to state that the hemispheres of the brain are large and convoluted, and that the young are born in a comparatively perfect condition, never being sheltered in a pouch after birth, as is the case with the second group of Mammals.

The orders are as follows:—

1. *Primates.—Exs.*: Man, Apes, Monkeys.
2. *Lemurs* (Lemuroidea).
3. *Bats* (Chiroptera).
4. *Insect-eaters* (Insectivora).—*Exs.*: Hedgehog, Mole, Shrew.
5. *Flesh-eaters* (Carnivora).—*Exs.*: Dog, Cat, Bear, Otter, Seal.
6. *Cetacea.—Exs.*: Whale, Porpoise.
7. *Sea-cows* (Sirenia).—*Exs.*: Dugong, Manatee.
8. *Elephants* (Proboscidea).
9. *Conies* (Hyracoidea).—*Ex.*: Syrian Hyrax.
10. *Hoofed Mammals* (Ungulata).—*Exs.*: Tapir, Rhinoceros, Horse, Hippopotamus, Pig, Deer, Cattle, Giraffe, Camel.
11. *Gnawers* (Rodentia).—*Exs.*: Squirrel, Rat, Porcupine, Rabbit.
12. *Edentates* (Edentata).—*Exs.*: Sloth, Armadillo, Ant-Eater, Pangolin.

B. METATHERIA.—The forms embraced by this group have smooth and relatively small cerebral hemispheres. The young are born in a very immature condition, and are usually sheltered for a time in a pouch ventral to the abdominal region of the mother. Within this pouch are situated the long teats, to which the young remain attached for some time, and these are so immature as to be at first incapable of sucking, the milk being squeezed into their mouths. Under such conditions they would be in imminent danger of choking were it not that the top of the

THE HIPPOPOTAMUS (*Hippopotamus amphibius*)

The Hippopotamus is closely related to the members of the Pig family, and, like them, does not chew the cud. It lives for the most part in water, inhabiting some of the great African rivers. A closely allied species inhabited Britain during prehistoric times. The Hippopotamus is a remarkably bulky animal, and weighs from three to four tons when adult.

THE HIPPOPOTAMUS (HIPPOPOTAMUS AMPHIBIUS)

windpipe projects into the back of the nasal passages, so that the feeding and breathing tracts are kept separate.

There are also two well-marked features of the skeleton, one concerning the lower jaw and the other the pelvis. The hinder corners or angles of the former are bent (inflected) inwards (fig. 37), while the latter possesses two extra bones (epipubic bones) which are at most represented by vestiges in members of the Eutheria.

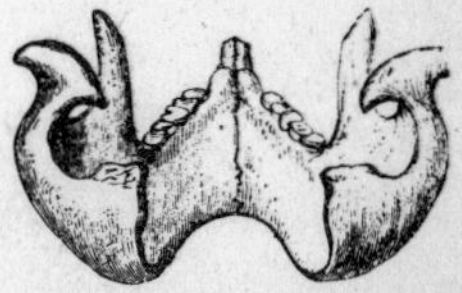

Fig. 37.—Lower Jaw of a Wombat from behind. Note inwardly bent angles.

There is only one order, *i.e.*:

13. *Pouched Mammals* (Marsupials), of which all the existing types are limited to Australia and its adjacent islands, with a few exceptions found in America.—*Exs.*: Kangaroo, Wombat, American Opossums.

C. Prototheria.—A very small number of Mammals constitute this group, and they are marked off from the higher forms by the possession of very remarkable characters. Agreeing with Marsupials in the characters of the brain, which is, however, of a still lower type, and the presence of epipubic bones, they differ from them and all other Mammals in the fact that they lay tough-shelled eggs. The young, when hatched, are nourished by milk, as in other cases, but the milk-glands possess no teats, simply opening upon a bare patch of skin. The Prototheria are also distinguished by the comparatively low temperature of the blood, the peculiar structure of the shoulder-girdles, and the fact that the intestine ends by opening into a chamber, the *cloaca*, which also receives the products of nitrogenous waste. As to the shoulder-girdle, it was mentioned in describing the human scapula (p. 30) that a coracoid process is present on that bone, and that the process in question must be regarded as the vestige of what in ancestral forms was a distinct bone. Prototheria possess a distinct coracoid bone (fig. 38), and also certain other bony elements in the shoulder-girdle, approximating in this respect to what is found in lizards among the Reptiles. It may indeed be noted generally that the peculiar characteristics of these lowest Mammals point to reptilian affinities.

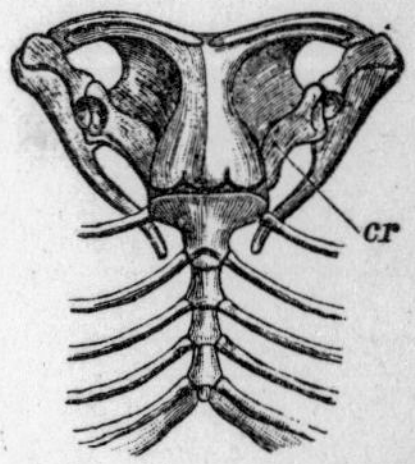

Fig. 38.—Sternum and Shoulder-girdles of Duck-Mole, from below *cr*, Coracoid bone, just above which is the cup (glenoid cavity) for attachment of upper-arm bone.

There is only one order of Prototheria, *i.e.*:

14. *Monotremes* (Monotremata), including only three living genera—the Duck-Mole (*Ornithorhynchus*), found in Australia and Tasmania (fig. 39); the Spiny Ant-Eater (*Echidna*) of Australia, Tasmania, and New Guinea; and the Spiny-tongued Ant-Eater (*Proechidna*), limited to the last-named island.

Fig. 39.—Duck-billed Platypus or Duck-Mole (*Ornithorhynchus paradoxus*).

Order I.—Man and Monkeys (Primates)

I. *Man.*—Human beings are distinguished from all other Primates by the possession of vastly superior mental powers, but when structural features are regarded there is no marked difference, and every organ found in a man exists equally in an ape. The human brain, however, in correlation with the human intellect, is very much larger than that of any ape, and the convolutions of its hemispheres are much more complex. This is true for the lowest savage equally with the genius. Man, again, is the only Mammal to which the erect posture is easy and habitual, and we accordingly find that the lower limbs are specially modified with a view to the maintenance of this position. And as compared with the highest apes, the human upper limbs are comparatively short, and adapted to perform the most delicate manipulations.

Although the differences between the different races of mankind are well marked, all are now regarded as having sprung from a common stock, and as belonging to the same genus, Homo, and the same species, sapiens. The scientific name for Man, regarded as an animal, is therefore *Homo sapiens.*

II. *Apes and Monkeys.*—These are tropical mammals closely approximating to Man in structure, with opposable thumbs, eyes

Fig. 40.—Anthropoid Apes

1, Gorilla (*Gorilla Savagei*); 2, Chimpanzee (*Anthropopithecus niger*); 3, Silver Gibbon (*Hylobates leuciscus*); 4, Orang-utan (*Simia satyrus*).

placed in orbits which are complete bony cups, teeth of the four typical kinds, and agreeing pretty closely in number with those of Man, and a pair of milk-glands situated on the chest. A point, related to the habit of climbing, in which these animals differ from Man, is found in the possession of opposable great toes.

Monkeys may be divided into three groups, corresponding largely to their geographical distribution: (1) Old World Monkeys, (2) New World Monkeys, and (3) Marmosets.

(1) *Old World Monkeys.*—These agree with Man in the number of the teeth, so that the dental formula is the same. They do not possess a well-formed projecting nose, but the nostrils are forwardly directed and close together, being separated by a narrow partition.

The *man-like* or *anthropoid apes* (fig. 40), come nearest to Man in structure. They include the Gorilla and Chimpanzee,

Fig. 41.—Entellus Monkeys (*Semnopithecus entellus*).

which are limited to the dense tropical forests of West and Central Africa, the Orang-utan, of Borneo and Sumatra, and the Gibbons of the East Indian Islands, further India, and South China.

The *tailed monkeys* constitute the remainder of the Old World section of ape-like forms. They are provided with hard patches (callosities) on the hind-quarters, and many of them possess cheek-pouches in which, as known to all visitors of zoological gardens and menageries, food can be temporarily stored.

Of these tailed monkeys, one group includes tree-inhabiting forms of comparatively slight build, a good example of which is the Entellus Monkey, or Hunuman (*Semnopithecus entellus*) (fig. 41). It is held sacred by the natives of India, and is therefore allowed to commit serious depredations without let or hindrance. Another species of the same genus (*S. roxellanus*), found in the north of Thibet, has a well-developed pug nose; and in a Bornean form, the Proboscis Monkey (*S. nasica*), that

Fig. 42.—The Barbary Ape (*Inuus ecaudatus*).

part of the anatomy has a more classic outline, and confers upon the animal an expression of comic wisdom.

The *Colobi* of tropical Africa are comparable to the members of the preceding genus, from which they are distinguished by stronger jaws and a greatly reduced condition of the thumb. A typical species is the Guereza (*Colobus guereza*), of the Abyssinian highlands.

The *Guenons* are representatives of another African genus (*Cercopithecus*) closely related to Semnopithecus, but differing in the possession of cheek-pouches, and a relatively large thumb. The members of the different species live together in large communities, and on account of their thievish habits are regarded with far from friendly feelings by the natives. One of the prettiest species is the West African Diana Monkey (*Cercopithecus diana*), in which the face is surrounded by a quaint-looking border of white fur drawn out below into a pointed beard. Another example is the Green Guenon (*C. sabæus*), which is among the common inhabitants of the monkey-house at the Zoo. The Moustache Monkey (*C. cephus*) is a handsome species of the same genus.

Fig. 43.—The Wanderoo (*Macacus silenus*).

Macaques, belonging to the genus *Macacus*, are of stouter build than the preceding species, and their tails at most do not exceed the body in length. Cheek-pouches are present. One species, the Magot, or Barbary Ape (*Macacus* or *Inuus ecaudatus*) (fig. 42), is of special interest, as being the only monkey with a range extending into Europe; for though its head-quarters are to be found in North Africa, it also occurs on the rock of Gibraltar, an interesting fact of distribution which has led to the popular belief that there is a submarine passage between Africa and Europe. The Boonder, or Rhesus Monkey (*Macacus rhesus*) of the East Indies, which is particularly common in the basin of the Ganges, has the same reverence extended to it by the natives as in the case of the Hunuman. Very similar in character is the Java Monkey (*M. cynomolgus*), but the Wanderoo (*M. silenus*) of Malabar is much more like a baboon (fig. 43). It is endowed with white beard and whiskers of ample proportions, and, being the happy possessor of a wide range of mental characteristics, has been variously described as "a comedian" and "the philosopher among the monkeys". It should be noted that all the Macaques, with the exception of the Barbary Ape, are Asiatic forms.

The familiar *Baboons*, which live chiefly on the ground and have dog-like heads, are for the most part natives of Africa.

Fig. 44.—The Mandrill (*Papio mormon*)

The Arabian Baboon (*Papio hamadryas*), which once lived in Egypt also, was the prototype of Thoth, the old Egyptian God of Letters, and in this capacity, as well as in the humbler one of a simple ape, is often represented upon the ancient monuments of that country. It is a large and powerful creature of greyish colour, and the adult male, with his pinkish face, large mane on neck and shoulders, and bright-red swellings of large size on the hind-quarters, is by no means a prepossessing object. The West African Mandrill (*Papio mormon*) (fig. 44), however, is even more hideous. Its adornments are of a vivid nature, for there are blue swellings on the face, and the large bare projections on the hinder regions are blue and red. The Yellow Baboon (*Papio babuin*) of West Africa is handsome by comparison with the two last species.

(2) *New World Monkeys* are a stage lower in development than those of the Old World, and consequently less human in appearance and structure. They always possess a tail, which is commonly used as a grasping orga i, and may also serve as

Fig. 45.—Red Howling Monkeys (*Mycetes seniculus*)

a delicate organ of touch. The total number of permanent teeth is thirty-six, four more than in Man and the Old World apes, the excess being due to the presence of an extra premolar on each side of each jaw. There is also a difference in the nose, which has nostrils facing somewhat sideways, and separated by a broad partition.

Three distinct sections are recognized:—Naked-tailed Monkeys, Sajous, and Sakis.

In the *Naked-tailed Monkeys*, at least part of the long and powerful tail is devoid of hair on the under side, and is used as a tactile and grasping organ. Among the noisiest of these forms are the *Howlers* of South America, such, for example, as the Red Howler (*Mycetes seniculus*) (fig. 45), in which the vocal organs are provided with peculiar resonating structures that greatly add to the volume of sound produced in the dismal concerts to which these animals are addicted. Other illustrative species are the Barrigudo (*Lagothrix Humboldti*), with woolly fur, and the slender *Spider-*

Fig. 46.—The Miriki or Woolly Spider-Monkey (*Eriodes arachnoides*).

Monkeys, such as the Miriki (*Eriodes arachnoides*) (fig. 46), which are distinguished by the reduced condition of the thumb.

The most familiar New World monkeys are probably the *Sajous* or *Capuchin Monkeys*, belonging to the genus *Cebus*. The face is bare and wrinkled, and there are generally peculiar adornments of the nature of whiskers, &c. The long prehensile tail is completely covered with hair, and does not serve as an organ of touch. An example is the Weeper Capuchin (*Cebus capucinus*).

Lastly, in the *Sakis* the tail is not modified as a grasping organ. Examples are the Black Saki (*Pithecia Satanas*), with bushy tail and ample beard, found in the basins of the Orinoco and Amazons, and the Squirrel Monkey (*Chrysothrix sciurea*) of Guiana.

(3) The *Marmosets* or *Clawed Monkeys* of America are the lowest and least intelligent forms to which the name "monkey"

Fig. 47.—The Ouistiti or Common Marmoset (*Hapale Jacchus*)

can properly be applied. These small creatures, of which the Common Marmoset (*Hapale Jacchus*) may be taken as type (fig. 47), have claws on all the digits except the great toe, which is provided with a flat tail, and is opposable. The thumb, unlike that of an ordinary monkey, is non-opposable. The teeth are thirty-two in number, as in Man and the Old World forms, but the dental formula is different, for whereas these possess eight premolars and twelve molars, a Marmoset has twelve premolars and eight molars, agreeing in the former particular with the New World monkeys proper.

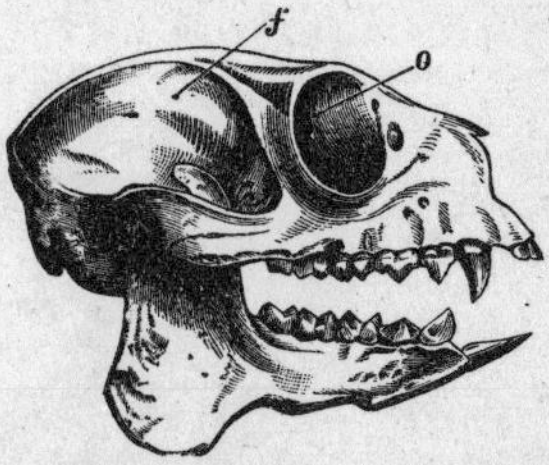

Fig. 48.—Skull of Black Indris Lemur
f, Temporal fossa; *o*, orbit. In this case the orbit is open behind and thus communicates with the temporal fossa.

Order 2.—Lemurs (Lemuroidea)

This order includes a somewhat heterogeneous collection of tropical climbing mammals, of which the large majority are limited to Madagascar, while a smaller number are found in South-east Asia and in tropical West Africa. They have usually been included in the Primates, but on insufficient grounds, the chief common peculiarity being the possession of opposable thumb

Fig. 49.—Ring-tailed Lemur (*Lemur catta*)

and great toe, a character associated with the climbing habit. The brain-case is relatively smaller than in a monkey, and the orbits are not completely walled in at the back by bone (fig. 48). In accordance with their nocturnal habits these animals have

Fig. 50.—The Spectre-Tarsier (*Tarsius spectrum*)

large and sometimes even enormous eyes. There are generally more than one pair of mammary glands.

The Ring-tailed Lemur (*Lemur catta*) of South-west Madagascar may be taken as an average member of the order (fig. 49), while the little Spectre-Tarsier (*Tarsius spectrum*), with a body of only about 6 inches long, will serve as an example of the forms with especially large eyes (fig. 50). It is an East Indian and Philippine species.

Order 3.—Bats (Chiroptera)

Bats or "flittermice" differ from all other mammals in the possession of efficient flying-organs, differing entirely in structure, however, from the wings of a bird. A tough membrane extends between the body, limbs, and commonly the tail as well (fig 51). The thumb is free, or partly so, and is provided with a strong curved claw, but the fingers are exceedingly long and slender, their use being to keep the membrane extended, thus

Fig. 51.—The Long-eared Bat (*Plecotus auritus*)

acting pretty much like the ribs of an umbrella. Bats, though nocturnal, have very small eyes, whence the expression "blind as a bat", but this is compensated by their long sensitive ears, and in many cases there are also curious leaf-like outgrowths on the nose. All our native bats, like the majority of forms included in the order, live on insects, and in accordance with this habit have numerous sharply-pointed teeth. A pair of mammary glands are present, situated on the breast. Although the general appearance of a bat's body enables us to understand why it should have received the old English name of flitter-*mouse*, these animals are in reality much more closely allied to hedgehogs and moles.

The order is divided into the two sections of Fruit-eating Bats and Insect-eating Bats.

The comparatively small section of *Fruit-eating Bats* only

includes the so-called Flying-foxes, which are natives of the Old World, Australia, and the South Sea Islands. The cheek-teeth have flattened crowns adapted for chewing, and there is generally a claw on the first finger as well as on the thumb. A typical species is the Kalong (*Pteropus edulis*) of the East Indies.

The *Insect-eating Bats* are by far the larger section, and include all our undoubted native species, twelve in number. All the cheek-teeth have sharp-pointed crowns, there is a claw on the thumb only, and the snout is shorter than in the fruit-eating forms. There are two families:—The True Bats (Vespertilionidæ) and the Leaf-nosed Bats (Phyllostomata).

In the *True Bats* (Vespertilionidæ), which are cosmopolite, the nose is simple in form, but there is a sensitive pointed projection from inside the ear to which the name of "earlet" (tragus) has been given.

A common British kind is the Long-eared Bat (*Plecotus auritus*) (fig. 51), abundant in the wooded regions of Europe, and ranging as far as India.

The European kinds which possess the greatest powers of flight belong to the genus *Vesperugo*, and include the Noctule (*V. noctula*) and the Pipistrelle (*V. pipistrellus*), which are respectively the largest and smallest of our native species.[1]

The *Leaf-nosed Bats* (Phyllostomata) are for the most part natives of the tropics, and differ from the preceding family in the possession of outgrowths from the nose, which serve apparently as special organs of touch. The food is not limited to insects, but may also include fruit, and some of them attack birds and mammals of other groups. A comparatively small and simple nose-leaf is found in the cave-inhabiting form to which reference is frequently made in works on Egyptian exploration (*Rhinopoma microphyllum*). A larger nose-leaf is present in the South American *Vampires*, which have earned an unenviable notoriety on account of their blood-sucking propensities, though an enormous grain of salt must be added to the numerous legends and stories which are current. The largest species is the True Vampire (*Phyllostoma spectrum*), which with its sharp front teeth is able to inflict a small wound

[1] The remaining British members of the family, omitting doubtful cases, are:—Hairy-armed Bat (*Vesperugo Leisleri*), Serotine Bat (*V. serotinus*), Bechstein's Bat (*Vespertilio Bechsteini*), Natterer's Bat (*V. Nattereri*), Daubentin's Bat (*V. Daubentini*), Whiskered Bat (*V. mystacinus*), and the Barbastelle (*Synotus barbastellus*).

in the body of a sleeping animal, the toes being the region favoured in the case of human beings. It is, however, only fair to add, that insects, or even fruit, are the favourite articles of diet.

A very complicated nose-leaf is found in the Old World forms belonging to the genus Rhinolophus, which are known as *Horse-shoe Bats.* Though these range from England to Tasmania, their head-quarters are in the southern parts of Asia. Only two forms, both of which occur in Britain, are found in Europe north of the Alps. These are the Lesser Horse-shoe Bat (*Rhinolophus hipposideros*) and the Greater Horse-shoe Bat (*R. ferrumequinum*).

Order 4.—Insect-Eaters (Insectivora)

Insectivores (fig. 52) are small nocturnal mammals of low organization, adapted for preying upon insects, worms, snails, and other small creatures, for the seizing and holding of which their sharp-pointed teeth are peculiarly well adapted. There is generally a long pointed snout, suited for poking into the small corners and crevices inhabited by their prey. As might be expected in a primitive group like this, there are the typical number of digits, *i.e.* five on each hand and foot, and all are provided with claws. Several pairs of mammary glands are found in the abdominal region. Six groups of the Insectivora may be distinguished:—Banxrings, Jumping-Shrews, Desmans, Shrews, Hedgehogs, and Moles.

Banxrings or *Tree-Shrews* are arboreal forms which somewhat resemble squirrels in appearance, chiefly owing to the presence of a large bushy tail; but the long pointed snout is characteristically insectivore. A typical form is the Bornean Tree-Shrew (*Tupaia tana*).

The African group of *Jumping-Shrews* includes small long-snouted creatures common in desert regions, and distinguished by the relative length of their hind-limbs, upon which they spring actively about. The Elephant-Shrew (*Macroscelides typicus*) of South Africa is a good example.

Desmans are swimming forms found in Thibet, West Africa, South Russia, and North Spain. One of the best-known species is the Musk-Shrew (*Myogale moschata*) of the Volga and other Russian rivers.

All the preceding are small groups, but the mouse-like *Shrews* include a large number of species, and are found in all parts of the world except South America and Australia with its related

Fig. 52.—Insectivores

1, Hedgehog (*Erinaceus*); 2, Mole (*Talpa*); 3, Elephant-Shrew (*Macroscelides*); 4, Shrew (*Crocidura*); 5, Tanrec (*Centetes*); 6, Banxring (*Tupaia*).

islands. There are three British species, the Common Shrew (*Sorex vulgaris*), the Lesser Shrew (*Sorex minutus*), and the Water Shrew (*Crossopus fodiens*). The two first are the smallest British mammals, and indeed the group includes the smallest known mammals found in any part of the world, one species, the Tuscan Shrew (*Crocidura Etrusca*), being under an inch and a half long, with a tail one inch in length.

The Common Shrew was an object of superstition in the Middle Ages, being looked upon as an enemy to domestic animals,

Fig. 53.—The Colugo or Flying-Lemur (*Galeopithecus*)

and by way of antidote it was often immured alive in a hole cut in the trunk of an ash-tree.

The Common Hedgehog (*Erinaceus Europæus*) is a well-known type of a fairly large Old World group, which may broadly be taken to include hedgehogs proper, the spineless Agouta (*Solenodon*) of Cuba and Hayti, and the Tanrecs (*Centetes*, &c.) of Madagascar, some of which are spiny. The last are adapted to very various habits.

The Common Mole (*Talpa Europæa*) is our British representative of a large group mainly distributed through the temperate parts of the northern hemisphere, and structurally modified so as to fit them for a burrowing habit. Related to them are the *Golden Moles* of the Cape, in which, however, the digits of the hand are reduced to three, and the fur has a beautiful iridescent sheen.

A remarkable animal, native to the East Indies, known as the Colugo, or Flying-Lemur (*Galeopithecus*), is probably best regarded as constituting a specialized group of the Insectivora. On each side of the body (fig. 53) there is a fold of skin which connects together the limbs and tail, and acts as a parachute, facilitating progress from one branch to another.

Order 5.—Flesh-Eaters (Carnivora)

This large, dominant, and widely distributed order of mammals includes a great diversity of widely differing forms, nearly all of which, however, are adapted for preying on weaker animals. In accordance with this the digits generally possess sharp claws, and the strong lower jaw, moved by very powerful muscles, is united to the skull by a well-marked hinge-joint (see p. 28), while large canines and cheek-teeth with cutting crowns are also characteristic. Carnivores possess considerable intelligence, particularly so in the domestic forms, such as cat and dog, and some, at least, of their senses are very acute.

The group is divided into two sub-orders—I, the true Carnivora, or Fissipedia; and II, the aquatic forms, or Pinnipedia. The former include most of the species, and Cat, Dog, and Bear may be taken as the leading types, of which the first is most specialized for flesh-eating, while the last is least so.

I. Fissipedia.—It is customary to divide the forms of this sub-order into Cats, Dogs, and Bears, using these words in a very wide sense.

CATS

These Carnivores have their feet lifted off the ground (fig. 54) so as to walk upon the digits (digitigrade), and their teeth are fewer in number and more specialized than is the case in the other two groups. There are four families:—1. Cats Proper (Felidæ);

THE TIGER (*Felis tigris*)

The Tiger is a typical member of the Cat family (*Felidæ*), which includes the most specialized forms belonging to the order of flesh-eating mammals. Tigers have a wide range, from India to south-east and east Asia, and the variety which lives in the more northerly part of the last area is possessed of a thick almost woolly coat. The animal figured is one of the familiar Indian kind, sometimes distinguished by the name of Royal or Bengal tiger.

The striped skin of this creature is a typical case of *aggressive general coloration*, harmonizing with the colour-scheme and confused light and shade of his native haunts, and thereby preventing the contemplated prey from taking premature alarm.

THE BENGAL TIGER—(FELIS TIGRIS)

2. Viverrines (Viverridæ); 3. Hyænas (Hyænidæ); and 4. Earth-wolves (Protelidæ).

1. *Cats Proper* (Felidæ) include a vast variety of forms, among which are the most highly specialized and the most rapacious of Carnivores. The teeth are fewer than in the other families and adapted to an exclusively animal diet, and the claws are usually prevented from getting blunt by being withdrawable into special sheaths, as everyone must have noticed in the domestic cat (fig. 55). Members of the family are to be found in all the continents except Australia, and they include: (1) the True Felines, (2) the Lynxes, and (3) the Hunting Leopards.

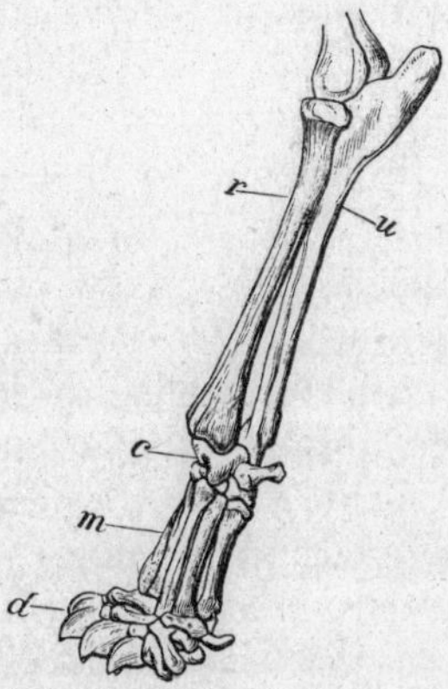

Fig. 54.—Lower part of the Fore-limb of a Lion, to illustrate the digitigrade structure. *r*, Radius; *u*, ulna; *c*, wrist-bones; *m* and *d*, bones of digits.

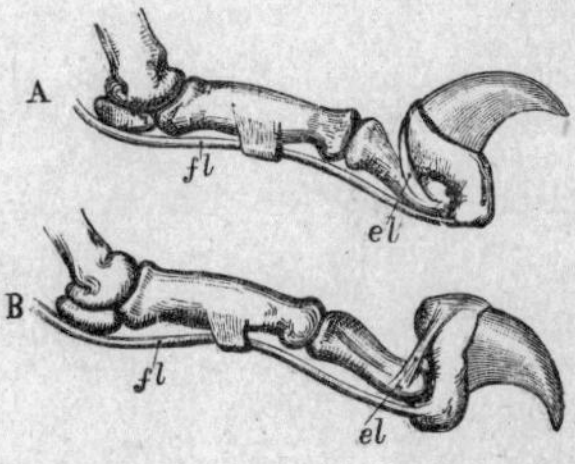

Fig. 55.—One of the Digits of a Cat, (A) with the claw in its ordinary position, (B) with the claw pulled down. *fl*, Tendon of the flexor muscle, or muscle that pulls down the claw; *el*, elastic ligament, which pulls back the claw.

(1) *True Felines* (genus *Felis*) have comparatively short strong legs, and differ among themselves chiefly in the matter of size and in the coloration and markings of the skin. The Lion (*Felis leo*) is the only species which, fortunately for the natives, does not possess the power of climbing trees, and the absence of stripes or spots may be noted. The mane of the male is also a characteristic feature. Lions are chiefly found in Africa, but also range into the south-west of Asia. The Tiger (*Felis tigris*) is the equal of the lion as regards both size and strength, and its stealthy habits render it much more dangerous. The dark stripes on the skin are very characteristic, and their presence makes the animal very inconspicuous in its natural surroundings. Both in Africa and Asia spotted felines are to be found, to which the names Leopard and Panther are indifferently applied. We have, for

example, the African Leopard (*Felis leopardus*) and the Asiatic Panther (*Felis panthera*), which closely resemble one another. Various small felines are native to Asia and Africa, one of them, the Fallow Cat (*Felis maniculata*), being probably the form from which the domestic animal is descended. It was venerated and embalmed by the ancient Egyptians, and its present range includes North-east Africa and part of South-west Asia. An European species, the Wild Cat *par excellence* (*Felis catus*), is probably native to Britain but is now practically limited to the more remote parts of Scotland.

All the true felines so far mentioned belong to the New World, but forms of similar kind are also found on the American continent. Of these the Jaguar (*Felis onca*), resembling a large leopard in its characters, is distributed through the whole of South America to the southern part of North America, while the Puma (*Felis concolor*), a much less dangerous form, ranges from Canada to Patagonia. There are also smaller species, *e.g.* the Pampas Cat (*Felis pajeros*), which is a native of Patagonia, and is not unlike the European Wild Cat.

(2) *Lynxes* (genus Lynx) have longer legs than the true felines, and a smaller number of teeth, indeed their dentition is more specialized than in any other carnivorous genus. They are further distinguished by tufts of hair on the tips of the ears and by the shortness of the tail. Most of them are restricted to the northern hemisphere. There are two European species, of which the smaller, the Spanish Lynx (*L. pardinus*) is only found in the Peninsula, while the Polar Lynx (*L. vulgaris*) is now chiefly found in Scandinavia and Russia (fig. 56).

(3) The third genus (Cynailurus) of the Felidæ includes the *Hunting Leopards*, which look something like ordinary leopards, but have slender limbs and non-retractile claws. Their range includes Africa and South-west Asia, and the best-known form is the Cheetah (*C. jubatus*) of the latter region, which is trained for hunting purposes.

A ferocious cat-like animal, the Foussa (*Cryptoprocta ferox*), found only in Madagascar, and sometimes considered as constituting a distinct family, may be mentioned here as a form intermediate in some respects between the present family and the one next to be described.

2. The *Viverrines* (Viverridæ) are small carnivores represented

by numerous species in the warmer parts of the Old World. The long slender body is provided with short legs, the long bushy tail tapers to a point, and the snout is somewhat long. The teeth are more numerous and not so typically carnivorous in type as in the Felidæ. Two sub-families are distinguished which differ in the

Fig. 56.—The Polar Lynx (*Lynx vulgaris*)

structure of the feet and in other ways. These are: (1) the Civets and (2) the Mangoustis.

(1) *Civets* are not unlike cats in their general appearance, and like them are digitigrade and able to retract their claws. One species, the Common Genet (*Genetta vulgaris*), is found in Spain and South France, its range also including those parts of Morocco and Algeria which are north of the Atlas Mountains. Well-known on account of the disgusting odour which they emit are the African Civet-Cat (*Viverra civetta*) and the Indian Civet-Cat (*V. zibetha*) (fig. 57)

(2) *Mangoustis* are smaller than civets, and somewhat weasel-like in appearance. The long toes are provided with non-retractile claws, and the animal does not walk in the same tiptoe fashion as the cats or civets. Most of the species are African, but some

Fig. 57.—The Indian Civet-Cat (*Viverra zibetha*)

are characteristic of South Asia, and one ranges into Europe. A common type is the Egyptian Ichneumon (*Herpestes ichneumon*), venerated by the ancient Egyptians probably on account of the services rendered by it in the destruction of snakes and the eggs of the crocodile. All sorts of wonderful stories were once current about this animal's supposed habit of entering the crocodile's mouth for the purpose of preying upon its vitals, and its imagined knowledge of herbs acting as antidotes to the bite of a poisonous serpent. A smaller species (fig. 58), the Mungoose (*Herpestes griseus*), is undoubtedly of great use to the inhabitants of India, on account of its propensity for destroying snakes and rats. Here again natives believe that the animal is acquainted with antidotes

Fig. 58.—The Mungoose or Grey Ichneumon (*Herpestes griseus*)

to snake-bites. One species of Mangousti (*Herpestes Widdringtoni*) is found in the south of Spain.

3. The family of *Hyænas* (Hyænidæ) includes only three species of powerfully-built though not very large carnivores, two of which are limited to Africa south of the Sahara. A rather peculiar appearance is given by the greater length of the fore-limbs and the presence of an incipient mane. Hyænas are digitigrade, and the four toes of each foot, both fore and hind, are provided with non-retractile claws. The excessively strong jaws are provided with teeth of marked carnivorous type, and the biting apparatus is powerful enough to successfully negotiate the hardest bones. Carrion is the chief food. The Spotted Hyæna (*Hyæna crocuta*) and Brown Hyæna (*H. brunnea*) are limited to South Africa, while the Striped Hyæna (*H. striata*) has a much wider distribution, inhabiting the temperate and warm parts of both Africa and Asia.

4. The family of *Earth-Wolves* (Protelidæ) is instituted for the reception of a single species, the Earth-Wolf (*Aardwolf*) of

the Cape (*Proteles Lalandii*), which is a burrowing form looking much like a small hyæna (fig. 59). It is, however, a distinct type,

Fig. 59.—The Earth-Wolf or Aardwolf (*Proteles Lalandii*)

as shown by the insignificant cheek teeth and other anatomical characters.

DOGS

Dogs, if one includes under that term not only the species commonly so called, but also wolves, foxes, and other similar forms, are a large group of carnivores distributed over the greater part of the world. They are not so highly specialized as the cats, this being shown, for example, by the fact that their teeth are more numerous and not of so highly developed carnivorous type. The legs are long and adapted for running, and there are five toes on each fore-foot and four on each hind-foot, all provided with blunt non-retractile claws. Nearly all the members of the group belong to the genus *Canis*, and the more robust species, with a rounded pupil to the eye, are known as *Wolves*. Of these the largest species is the Common Wolf (*Canis lupus*), which has a wide distribution through the cold and temperate parts of the northern hemisphere, and was at no very remote period a native of Britain.

Fig. 60.—The Sahara Fox or Fennec (*Canis zerda*)

As is well known, it hunts in packs, like many other dog-like animals, and this habit at times renders it formidable even to man. Few animals play a larger part in legend and fable, from the time of Æsop down to Uncle Remus. The Coyote or Prairie Wolf (*Canis latrans*) is a smaller North American species. Closely related to the wolf is the Jackal (*Canis aureus*), a much smaller animal, with a fox-like appearance. It ranges from India to Central Africa, and is also found in Greece and Dalmatia.

It has been pointed out that the domestic cat is probably the descendant of one particular wild species, but this is not the case with dogs, these seeming to have a more varied origin. It is possible that the Dingo or Native Dog (*Canis dingo*) of Australia, which is especially interesting from the paucity of higher mammals in that continent, ought not, properly speaking, to be regarded as a wild form in the ordinary sense, but as the descendant of domesticated dogs introduced by man.

Foxes, as represented by their more characteristic species, are distinguished from wolves by a narrower snout, larger ears, shorter legs, and more bushy tail. The pupil of the eye, instead of being circular, is a vertical oval. A good type is our native species, the Common Fox (*Canis vulpes*), which is as widely distributed as the wolf, and represented by many different varieties. No animal figures more prominently in fable and legend, a somewhat exaggerated estimate being usually taken of its wisdom. Among related species the smallest and prettiest is undoubtedly the Fennec or Sahara Fox (*Canis zerda*), distinguished by the very great size of its ears (fig. 60).

BEARS

These are carnivores which walk upon the soles of the feet, or in other words are plantigrade (fig. 61), and their teeth are not so specialized as in cats and dogs, some of the molars possessing crowns adapted for crushing food instead of merely dividing it. This is in accordance with the diet, which commonly includes both animal and vegetable items.

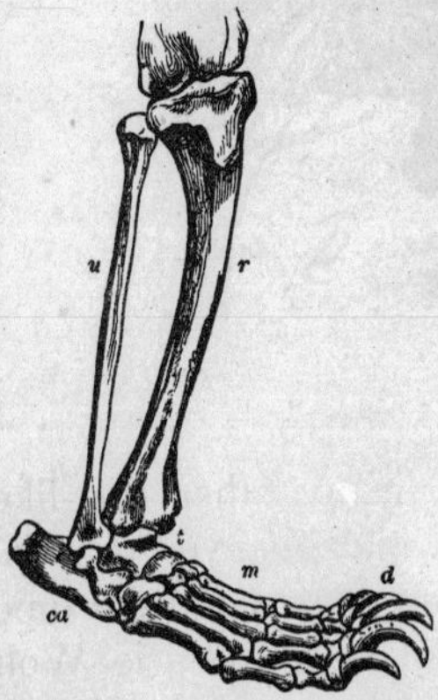

Fig. 61.—Skeleton of Hind-limb of Bear, to illustrate the Plantigrade Structure. *r*, Radius; *u*, ulna; *t*, ankle-bones; *m* and *d*, bones of digits; *ca*, heel-bone.

The group is divided into three families:—1. Small Bears (Procyonidæ); 2. Large Bears (Ursidæ); 3. Badgers, Weasels, and Otters (Mustelidæ).

1. The *Small Bears* (Procyonidæ) are probably best known in the person of the Common Raccoon (*Procyon lotor*), a very active and inquisitive creature native to the forests of North America. As the specific name indicates (Lat. *lotor*, a washer), it has the curious habit of washing its food (fig. 62).

2. *Bears* (Ursidæ) are much larger and clumsier animals, familiar to all from menagerie and zoo specimens. Though pretty

widely distributed, they are not found in Africa south of the Sahara, nor in the Australian region, and are but scantily represented in South America. The Common or Brown Bear (*Ursus arctos*) (fig. 63), which is the species once native to Britain, is

Fig. 62.—The Common Raccoon (*Procyon lotor*)

found in suitable localities throughout the whole extent of the Old World north of the Atlas and Himalaya ranges. He figures as the companion of wolf and fox in many fables and stories. Although the Brown Bear is no mean antagonist, it is surpassed both in size and fierceness by the Grizzly Bear (*Ursus ferox*) of the Rocky Mountains. The Polar Bear (*Ursus maritimus*) is of even greater size, and is indeed the largest living carnivore.

Fig. 63.—Brown Bears (*Ursus arctos*). (From an instantaneous photograph)

3. *Badgers*, *Weasels*, and *Otters* (Mustelidæ) together make up a family of which the majority of members are small in size, and

Fig. 64.—The Common Badger (*Meles taxus*)

which is of considerable economic importance since it is the source of many valuable furs.

Badgers are plantigrade forms with stoutly-built body and strong, short legs, armed with powerful claws used for burrowing. There are stink-glands opening near the root of the tail. The Common Badger (*Meles taxus*) (fig. 64) is commoner in some parts of Britain than generally supposed, for as a nocturnal and burrowing animal it is naturally seldom seen. The colour presents a reversal of the usual condition of things among animals, for the upper side of the body is light and the under side dark, instead of the opposite. Our native form ranges right across the temperate parts of Europe and Asia, from Britain to Japan. Other genera are found in Africa, South Asia, and North America. Closely related to the badgers are the *Skunks*, which range throughout both North and South America. Undoubtedly the most graceful creatures of the kind, they are at the same time the most offensive, possessing as they do the power of ejecting to a considerable distance a fluid of indescribably disgusting odour secreted by their well-developed stink-glands.

Fig. 65.—The Weasel (*Putorius vulgaris*)

Martens and *Weasels* constitute a group, of which the most typical members are small lithe animals with an elongated narrow body and a long bushy tail. Most of them are digitigrade, and the claws may be retractile. The largest British species is the Pole-cat (*Putorius fœtidus*), found in rapidly diminishing numbers in various districts of Great Britain. Its local name of "foumart" (*i.e.* foul marten) has reference to the evil odour which it possesses, due to the same cause as in the badgers. The ferret is simply a domesticated variety of this animal. There are three other native species of marten: (1) the Stoat (*Putorius erminea*), which in its winter coat is known as the Ermine; (2) the Pine Marten (*Mustela martes*); and (3) the Weasel (*Putorius vulgaris*), which is smaller than the rest (fig. 65). The Stoat and Pine Marten are found in Ireland as well as in Great Britain.

The Sable (*Mustela zibellina*) of Russia-in-Asia is the most valuable fur-yielding member of the group, while the Glutton (*Gulo borealis*) of the Arctic regions has earned an unenviable reputation for voracity, though this has been much exaggerated.

Otters are Mustelines adapted for an aquatic life, as seen in the flattened tail and webbed feet. Our native species, the Common Otter (*Lutra vulgaris*), is found both in Europe and in Asia north of the Himalayas, including Japan.

II. Pinnipedes (fig. 66) include sea-lions, walruses, and ordinary seals, in all of which the limbs are converted into flippers. In the first two groups the hind-limbs can be turned forward to assist in a clumsy sort of progression on land, but in the seals proper they are permanently turned backwards and bound up by folds of skin with the tail so as to form a fin.

The *Walrus* (*Trichechus rosmarus*) of the Arctic regions is remarkable not only for its flipper-like limbs but also in the reduced and specialized nature of its dentition, which is adapted for obtaining and crushing shell-fish and sea-urchins. Front teeth are altogether absent in the adult, and the upper canines are great tusks with which the food is dug up, and which also serve as weapons. There are ten cheek teeth with flattened crowns, three on each side above, and two on each side below.

The *Sea-Lions* or *Eared Seals*, so named from the presence of a small pinna, range all round the world in the colder parts of the southern hemisphere, and are also found in the North Pacific. A good type of the group is Steller's Sea-lion (*Otaria Stelleri*), which is most abundant in the neighbourhood of Behring's Straits, from which it ranges south to California and Japan. Its sharp-pointed teeth are well suited for the capture of fish.

The *True Seals* are more thoroughly adapted to an aquatic life than the two other groups of Pinnipedes, and have a much wider distribution, being absent only from the shores of the East Indies and Africa. They are also found in some inland seas, as the Caspian, the Sea of Aral, and Lake Baikal, which is one of the proofs that these were formerly connected with the Arctic

Fig. 66.—Pinnipedes. 1, Eared Seals (*Otaria*). 2, Common Seal (*Phoca*)

Ocean. Like the sea-lions, they are adapted for preying upon fish. Five species of seal are known to British waters, of which the Common Seal (*Phoca vitulina*) may be mentioned. The commonest sort in the seas of the far north is the Greenland Seal (*Phoca Grœnlandica*), one of the chief victims to seal-fishers.

Order 6.—Whales and Porpoises (Cetacea)

The Cetaceans are mammals which are completely adapted for an aquatic life, being so much modified for that purpose as to be commonly mistaken for fishes, which they superficially resemble in the general form of the body. Hair is practically absent in the adult, though there may be a few stiff bristles in the neigh-

Fig. 67.—The Porpoise (*Phocæna communis*)

bourhood of the mouth, but the lack of a protective external covering is fully compensated by the thickness of the skin and by the presence of a thick layer of fat (blubber) underneath it. A tail fin is present, but this, instead of being flattened from side to side, as in a fish, is flattened from above downwards. The fore-limbs have been converted into paddles, presenting externally no trace of digits, and the hind-limbs have disappeared, though traces of them are to be found on dissection. There may be one or two nostrils, situated, for convenience in breathing, on the top of the head. Cetacea feed on other animals, ranging from comparatively large forms to small creatures which are found in huge shoals.

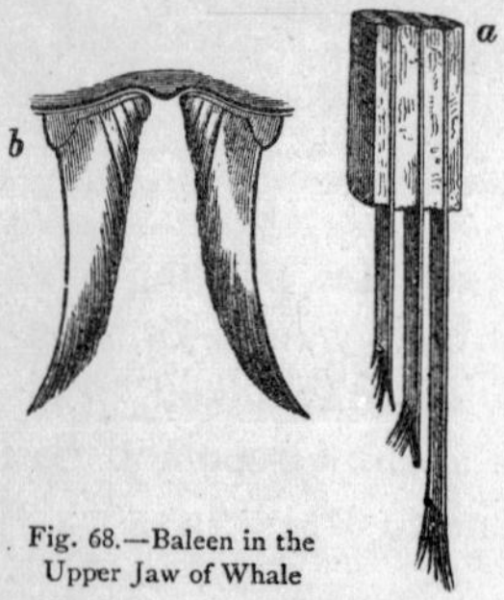

Fig. 68.—Baleen in the Upper Jaw of Whale

a, Section of a portion of the palate of a whalebone whale, showing three baleen plates. *b*, The arrangement of the baleen plates on opposite sides of the jaw.

The Porpoise (*Phocæna communis*) (fig. 67), which possesses numerous simple teeth, is a familiar British species, while the Greenland or Right Whale (*Balæna mysticetus*) is an example of the large toothless forms, which feed on shoals of minute marine organisms, from which the water is strained by numerous plates of whalebone (baleen) projecting downwards from the palate (fig. 68).

Order 7.—Sea-Cows (Sirenia)

This small order includes only two living genera of aquatic mammals, inhabiting the shores of the Atlantic and Indian Oceans,

Fig. 69.—The Manatee (*Manatus*)

and also making their way up some of the large rivers. As might be expected, considering their mode of life, they are shaped not unlike Cetaceans, with which they agree in the general shape of the body, absence of hind-limbs, and possession of a horizontally-flattened tail fin and flipper-like fore-limbs. They are not, however, quite so much specialized, for there is a fairly-well-marked neck, and the nostrils are situated at the end of a broad muzzle, provided with thick fleshy lips beset with moustache hairs. There are also eyelashes, and the thick skin is covered with short stiff hairs. They subsist entirely on vegetable food, and simple grinding teeth are present in both genera. A pair of mammary glands are found on the breast.

The Dugong (*Halicore Dugong*) is 16 or 17 feet long, and frequents the shores of the Indian Ocean, while the somewhat smaller Manatee (*Manatus*) (fig. 69) is found on the west coast of Africa and the east coast of America, from the Gulf of Mexico southwards. A certain interest attaches to these creatures from the fact that they appear to be the chief foundation for legends of mermaids and mermen. It requires a pretty vivid imagination, however, to see any resemblance in these uncouth animals to the golden-haired conventionalities which have gradually been evolved from the inner consciousness of artist and poet.

Order 8.—Elephants (Proboscidea)

These familiar mammals, the largest of existing land animals, are in many respects primitive in structure, particularly as regards the limbs, which possess five digits, united together into flat rounded feet, provided with a varying number of small hoofs. The limbs are very thick and pillar-like, being thus enabled to support the enormous weight of the body. Elephants, however, are very highly specialized as regards the structure of the head, of which the most striking feature is the trunk, or prolonged snout, at the end of which the nostrils are situated. The uses of this remarkable organ are innumerable, and there can be no doubt that its development has led to a corresponding growth of intelligence. The teeth are highly peculiar, only two kinds, incisors and molars, being present. Of the former only an upper pair exists, modified in the male, or it may be in both sexes, into the well-known tusks, which are composed entirely of ivory or dentine (see p. 35). The molars are enormous, and possess broad grinding crowns, provided with numerous transverse ridges (fig. 70). For the most part only four are in place at once, one on each side

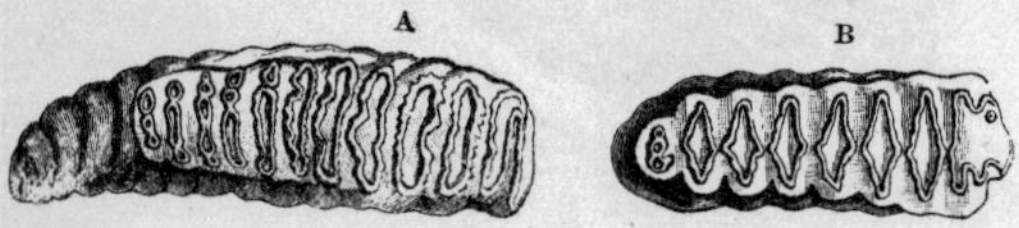

Fig. 70.—A, Last Lower Tooth (molar) of Indian Elephant. B, Last Lower Tooth (molar) of African Elephant.

of either jaw, and they are replaced by others which grow from behind and gradually push out their predecessors as these get worn away. It is scarcely necessary to remark that in the vast majority of mammals teeth are succeeded by others which grow up vertically below them. The skull of an adult elephant is of remarkable form, and the cranium is much larger than the brain

Fig. 71.—African Elephant (*Elephas Africanus*). (From an instantaneous photograph)

which it contains, owing to the excessive development in its roof of air-chambers separated by complex bony plates. It may lastly be noted that the thick skin is but sparsely covered with hairs, and that the mammary glands are situated between the fore-limbs. The food consists exclusively of vegetable matter.

Elephants are now represented by only two species, one the Indian form (*Elephas Indicus*), found also in Ceylon, Borneo, and Sumatra, while the other (*Elephas Africanus*) is limited to Africa south of the Sahara (fig. 71).

Order 9.—Conies (Hyracoidea)

This small order includes only certain little creatures about the size of a rabbit, which inhabit the deserts of Africa and Syria. The general resemblance to a rabbit is seen chiefly in the cleft upper lip, and the presence of two long upper incisors which grow continuously, while canine teeth are entirely absent. In the character of the cheek teeth, however, and in the nature of the digits they are much more like the tapir and rhinoceros. Each fore-foot has four toes, and each hind-foot three, all of which, except the innermost toe of the hind-foot, which is clawed, possess small rounded hoofs.

The "coney" of the English Bible, otherwise known as the Syrian Hyrax (*Procavia Syriaca*) may be taken as a type. "The

Fig. 72.—The Abyssinian Hyrax (*Procavia Abyssinica*)

conies are but a feeble folk, yet make they their houses in the rocks" (Prov. xxx. 26). The illustration (fig. 72) represents a similar species, the Abyssinian Hyrax (*P. Abyssinica*).

Order 10.—Hoofed Mammals (Ungulata)

This very large and important order includes animals in which the limbs are modified for the sole purpose of terrestrial progression, while the organization generally is adapted to the herbivorous habit, as more particularly seen in the grinding crowns possessed by the cheek teeth.

Two sub-orders are recognized: I. the Odd-toed Ungulates (Perissodactyla); and II. the Even-toed Ungulates (Artiodactyla)

I. Odd-toed Ungulates (Perissodactyla).—This sub-order embraces the three families of: 1. Tapirs, 2. Rhinoceroses, and 3. Horses, in all of which there is an odd number of toes on the hind-foot, and generally on the fore-foot as well. A much more important distinction, however, is found in the fact that the third digit dominates over the rest and is symmetrical in itself, continuing the direction of the limb-axis.

1. The *Tapirs* in general appearance are not unlike large pigs, but the symmetry of the feet is quite different, and so is the number of the toes, there being four on the front, and three on the hind foot, all provided with hoofs. A pig has four toes on every foot. The snout is drawn out into a short proboscis, which

Fig. 73.—The Brazilian Tapir or Anta (*Tapirus Americanus*)

suggests what the incipient proboscis of the ancestors of elephants was probably like. Tapirs present a remarkable case of the phenomenon known as "discontinuous distribution", where a species or some larger group inhabits two or more areas more or less remote from one another, while it is absent from the intermediate space. In this instance the disconnected areas are South and Central America on the one hand, and the Malay region on the other. The species commonly seen in zoological gardens is the Brazilian Tapir (*Tapirus Americanus*) (fig. 73).

2. *Rhinoceroses* are huge clumsy-looking animals of little intelligence and surly disposition. The massive head, borne on a short thick neck, is characterized by its small eyes, oval erect ears, and one or two unpaired horns on the upper side of the snout. It is indeed the possession of such a horn which is the most

striking feature, giving the common name of the animal (Gk. *rhīnós,* of the nose; *kéras,* a horn), and it is probably responsible for the creation of the legendary unicorn. This defensive structure, when examined microscopically, is seen to be made up of innumerable horny fibres cemented together, and it has been aptly compared to a big wart, for there is no connection between it and the underlying bone. The African natives have a curious superstition that cups made from this horny material destroy the potency of any poisoned drink which may be poured into them.

Each one of the four extremities ends in three toes, provided with strong hoofs, there being thus a reduction in the fore-foot as compared with tapirs. The skin is exceedingly thick and but scantily provided with hair, though there is a well-marked tuft on the end of the short tail. The snout is not produced into a proboscis, but the upper lip is extremely flexible. The teeth are well adapted to a vegetable diet, for the grinders have broad crushing crowns of peculiar and characteristic pattern. Upper canines are absent, and sometimes lower ones too. There is much variability in regard to the front teeth, and in the adult these may be absent altogether.

The group is at the present time confined to South Asia and Tropical Africa, and typical species are the one-horned Indian Rhinoceros (*Rhinoceros Indicus*), in which the thick skin is disposed in remarkable armour-like folds, and the Common Rhinoceros (*Atelodus bicornis*) of Africa, the skin of which is relatively thin and devoid of folds, while there are two well-developed horns placed close together.

3. *Horses* and their immediate allies are decidedly the most highly specialized of the odd-toed Ungulates. All the living species belong to the single genus *Equus*, the external characters of which are too well known to need description. It may, however, be noted that the long legs, well suited for swift running, possess but one externally visible toe, corresponding to the middle one of five-toed forms, and provided with a rounded hoof. The front teeth are well developed, and each of them has a deep indentation in the crown, which gets filled up with fragments of the food, and is the cause of the black central area commonly known as the "mark". The canines are reduced and often absent in the female, but the cheek teeth are numerous, and their flattened crowns exhibit an exceedingly complex pattern.

THE INDIAN RHINOCEROS (*Rhinoceros Indicus*)

The living species of Rhinoceros are native only to Africa and South Asia, although, as shown by geological evidence, animals of the kind were once very widely distributed, and some of them inhabited prehistoric Britain. The group is known to have originated in North America. The common Indian species represented ranges from Bengal to Cochin-China, and is the kind which figured in the gladiatorial displays of the ancient Romans. It is distinguished by the possession of a single horn upon the nose, and armour-like folds in the thick skin.

THE INDIAN RHINOCEROS (RHINÓCEROS INDICUS)

A STUDY FROM THE LIFE

The domesticated Horse (*Equus caballus*) has such a long history of captivity that its ancestry is obscure, and it is by no means certain that all horses have descended from one stock. It is, however, generally believed that one original stock was Asiatic, and perhaps the Tarpan or Wild Horse (*Equus tarpan*) of Central Asia comes nearest to this stock, though even that is far from being certain. *Wild Asses* are found both in Africa and Asia, and the domesticated form familiar to us comes nearest to an Asiatic species, the Onager (*Equus onager*), which ranges from Asia Minor to India. The domestic asses of Egypt and Abyssinia, however, more closely resemble the African Wild Ass (*Equus tæniopus*), native to the region between the Red Sea and Nile. The remaining living equines are those striped African species known as *Zebras* or *Tiger Horses.* The kind most commonly seen in zoological gardens is Burchell's Zebra (*Equus Burchelli*), herds of which are still to be found in the grassy plains to the north of the Orange River.

II. Even-toed Ungulates (Artiodactyla).—This large and important group of Ungulates includes not only many valuable domesticated forms, such as swine, oxen, goats, sheep, and camels, but such familiar types as hippopotamus, antelopes, llama, and giraffe. The even number of the toes is a character of far less importance than the symmetry of the foot, there being no single digit which is symmetrical in itself, like the third or middle one in the preceding group.

Two sections are recognized:—A. Non-ruminating forms; and B. Ruminants.

A. *Non-Ruminating Forms*

This includes: 1. the Hippopotamus Family, and 2. the Pig Family, in neither of which are the digestive organs modified for the purpose of ruminating or "chewing the cud". They belong, therefore, to the "unclean animals" of the Levitical law, despite their cloven feet (Lev. xi).

1. The *Hippopotamus Family* is entirely confined to the rivers of Africa, with the adjacent swampy ground, and is represented by two living species, *i.e.* the small Liberian Hippopotamus (*Hippopotamus Liberiensis*), limited, so far as known, to Liberia, and the Common Hippopotamus (*H. amphibius*), the large form frequently seen in captivity, which has a much wider range. The appearance

of this huge lumbering creature, which weighs about $2\frac{1}{2}$ tons, suggests a parody on the pig, or a large barrel mounted on four stout ungainly legs. Each foot possesses four toes provided with rounded hoofs. The head is enormous, and the snout greatly swollen. The thick skin is almost devoid of hair, and is thrown into folds above the limbs. Those who have noticed a captive hippo open its tremendously wide mouth will have seen a truly terrific dentition displayed. Above are four peg-like incisors flanked by large canines, while below there are two huge cylindrical incisors, two smaller incisors, and formidable tusk-like canines (fig. 74). A full complement of grinding teeth is present, and the large molars, when their crowns are worn, exhibit a pattern resembling a double trefoil. The hippopotamus was well known to the ancients, and is the behemoth of Scripture.

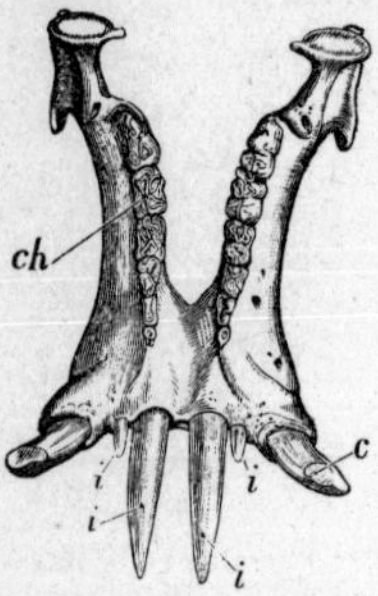

Fig. 74.—Lower Jaw of Hippopotamus

ch, The cheek teeth, originally tubercled, but worn down by use so as to present the appearance of clover-leaves bordered by bands of enamel; *i*, incisors; *c*, canines.

2. The *Pig Family* has a wide distribution both in the Old and the New World. Well-marked features are the bristly skin, flexible snout tipped by a fleshy disc within which the nostrils open, teats extending right along the under side of the body, and legs of moderate length and thickness. There are four toes on each foot, the two central ones only reaching the ground, and being of relatively large size. The most illustrative type is the Wild Boar (*Sus scrofa*), once a native of Britain, and which at the present time ranges throughout Europe, Asia, and North Africa. It appears to be the original stock from which the domestic pig has been derived. The teeth are numerous and of primitive type, the points of greatest interest being the tusk-like canines, all four of which are upwardly directed, and the grinding teeth, which possess tuberculated crowns.

In Africa south of the Sahara the Wild Boar type is replaced by forms in which there are swellings on the face caused by underlying bony projections. These are comparatively small in the Red River-Hog (*Potamochœrus penicillatus*) of Guinea, which is further distinguished by a tuft of hair at the tip of each ear; but in the *Wart-Hogs* they are of large size, and give the enormous head a particularly forbidding appearance. There are two species, one (*Phacochœrus Æthiopicus*) being found at the Cape, while the other (*Ph. Africanus*) is much more widely distributed.

In Celebes and the adjacent islands a remarkable pig is found known as the Babirussa (*Porcus babirussa*), in which the lower tusks are like curved daggers in shape, while the upper tusks curve back over the face almost like horns. The natives say that the animal hangs itself up by these when it wishes to sleep peacefully.

In America, from Mexico southwards, the pigs are represented by small forms called *Peccaries*, one species being the Collared Peccary (*Dicotyles torquatus*).

B. *Ruminants*

The members of this section agree with the pigs in possessing on each foot only two toes which reach the ground, in addition to which there may or may not be two smaller digits, but they differ markedly from pigs in the greater length of their limbs, which are eminently adapted for rapid progression. The most characteristic feature, however, is to be found in the possession of a very complex stomach, adapted for ruminating; *i.e.* the food is first swallowed without chewing, and then returned to the mouth in successive portions for leisurely mastication in a safe place. The cheek teeth have grinding crowns, provided with crescentic ridges, and (except in camels) the upper incisors are replaced by a hard pad. The following families together constitute the section:—1. Chevrotains; 2. Deer; 3. Prongbucks; 4. Oxen and their allies; 5. Giraffes; and 6. Camels.

1. The *Chevrotains* are a restricted group, including the smallest and least specialized ruminants, approaching the peccaries in some structural features. In appearance they suggest diminutive hornless deer, and on this account are sometimes called Mouse-Deer. There are no upper incisors, and the upper canines of the male are slender, downwardly-directed tusks. Of the six existing species five belong to the genus *Tragulus*, and are distributed through South Asia from India eastwards. The smallest species is the Malay Kanchil (*Tragulus Javanicus*) (fig. 75), than which only one other Ungulate, *i.e.* the Royal Antelope, is of less size. The sixth species of this family is the Water Chevrotain (*Dorcatherium aquaticum*), which is only found on the west coast of Africa.

2. The *Deer Family* includes a large number of species, widely distributed throughout both hemispheres, though absent from Africa south of the Sahara. There are four toes to each foot, all being provided with hoofs, but the supporting bones of the extremities are rather more specialized than in the Chevrotains. The leading characteristic of the family is undoubtedly the possession of antlers

Fig. 75.—The Kanchil (*Tragulus Javanicus*)

by the male in nearly all cases. These structures are essentially bony outgrowths from the skull, which are annually shed, and in many cases become more complex in shape each successive year so as to be an indication of age. The young antlers are composed of living bone and are covered by a continuation of the skin ("the velvet"). When their full size is attained the base of the antler grows out into a ring-like projection (the "burr"), cutting off the blood-supply from the skin, which consequently peels off from the underlying bone, causing this to become dead and hard. A further characteristic of deer is the presence of a pit in front of each eye, within which certain glands open.

It is convenient to first mention the Musk Deer (*Moschus moschiferus*, because it differs considerably in structure from all other members of the group, having, *e.g.*, a less complex brain, and possessing a gall-bladder, which organ is absent in other deer. There are no antlers, and the upper canines of the male resemble those present in Chevrotains. Most of the musk of commerce is obtained from a pouch situated pretty far back on the under side of the body in the male. Musk Deer are active creatures inhabiting the high land of Central Asia.

The Chinese Water Deer (*Hydropotes inermis*), which lives on the banks of the Yang-tse-Kiang, shares with the preceding species the two primitive characters of tusk-like upper canines and absence of antlers in the male. This does not, however, indicate any special relationship between the two forms.

The Red Deer (*Cervus elaphus*) is still numbered among British mammals, though in the wild state it is now restricted to the remoter parts of Scotland and Ireland, with isolated patches in England. It is characterized by the complex antlers (fig. 76), which have a brow-tine projecting over the forehead, a bez-tine above this, and, in mature specimens, a terminal cluster of twelve or more points. Outside Britain this species has a wide distribution through the temperate parts of Europe and Asia.

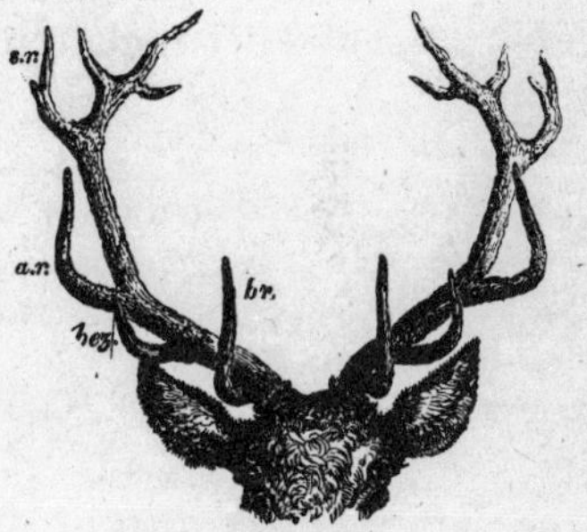

Fig. 76.—Antlers of Red Deer
br. Brow-tine; *bez.* bez-tine; *a.r.* antler royal; *s.r.* sur-royal.

The large Wapiti (so-called "Elk") of North America (*Cervus Canadensis*) is closely allied to the Red Deer. Ranging at one time over most of North America, it is now restricted to the mountainous parts of the Western States and to British territory in the north.

The familiar Fallow Deer (*Cervus dama*) is not a native of these islands, though introduced at an early date, but is indigenous to the Mediterranean countries. It is much smaller than the Red Deer, and the antlers are of different formation. They are said to be "palmated", *i.e.* ending in a broad expansion divided into points, and compared to a hand with its fingers. Below this expanded portion is a branch called the trez-tine, and a good way below this a prominent brow-tine juts out.

Great interest attaches to the Reindeer (*Rangifer tarandus*) for several reasons, one being their great importance to certain primitive peoples as domestic animals. At the present time they are limited to the northern parts of both hemispheres, but in prehistoric times, when the climate of the northern hemisphere was much more rigorous than now, their range extended much farther south, as evidenced by remains found in the caves of Britain and other countries. Indeed they were so characteristic of a stage in human history, when carefully-chipped stone weapons and implements had replaced the cruder attempts in this direction, that the term "Reindeer Age" is often applied to the period in question. A marked peculiarity is the presence of antlers in both sexes, these structures being of great length and set on far back. There is a brow-tine, greatly developed and branched in the male, just above this a bez-tine, and then a long beam, the end of which is palmated. The two antlers are commonly markedly unlike one another. The main hoofs are very broad and flat, and separate when the feet are brought to the ground, afterwards clapping together in a curious way when the feet are raised.

The largest living species of deer is the Elk or Moose (*Alces machlis*), the distribution of which roughly corresponds to that of the reindeer, though it does not range into those extreme northerly regions from which trees are absent. The long head terminates in a muzzle of curious humped appearance, suggesting a Roman nose; the neck is short, and the body slopes markedly from front to rear. The long legs are provided with broad hoofs. Many peculiarities are presented by the massive antlers, which, beginning with short beams devoid of tines, expand laterally into broad palmated portions. A curious feature of the male is the presence of a flap of skin hanging down from the under side of the neck.

The remaining species of which space permits a mention is the little Roe Deer (*Capreolus caprea*), our second native form, though now only found in Scotland as a truly wild animal. From Britain it ranges east through Europe into Persia. The rough antlers are of simple conformation. The beam rises vertically from the top of the head, gives off a front tine about the middle of its length, and then curves back to end in a simple fork.

3. The *Prongbuck Family* contains only the single species (*Antilocapra Americana*), to which it owes its name (fig. 77). It is a small active animal found in the temperate parts of western North America. Although in appearance suggesting a deer, its affinities are rather with the antelope section of the family of oxen. The horns, however, present a remarkable peculiarity, for though they consist of bony cores covered by horny sheaths, as in an

antelope, they are shed annually, which is not the case with the last-named form, and a further difference is seen in the presence of a small front branch. The two peculiarities mentioned

Fig. 77.—The Prongbuck (*Antilocapra Americana*)

suggest antlers, but otherwise there is no reason for classifying Prongbucks with the deer

4. The *Ox Family* is an exceedingly large one, including those forms which are commonly known as hollow-horned ruminants (Cavicornia), because the unbranched horns, which are never shed, consist of hollow horny sheaths borne upon bony outgrowths from the skull. They may be present in both sexes, or else restricted to the male. The upper incisors and also the canines are absent, their place being taken by a horny pad, against which the lower front teeth bite, as in deer, prong-bucks, and giraffes. The feet are much like those of deer, each possessing two large toes shod

with hoofs, two other toes being commonly represented by small hoofs, though these may be in this case absent altogether. The family not only includes (1) oxen in the widest sense, but also (2) sheep, (3) goats, and (4) antelopes. With but few exceptions, these are found only in the Old World.

(1) As in the case of so many other domesticated forms, there is considerable doubt as to the ancestry of European *oxen* (*Bos taurus*), but there can be little doubt that these are largely descended from the Auroch or Urus (*Bos primigenius*), which was hunted by prehistoric man and existed as a wild species so late as the twelfth century, though they are now known only as half-wild cattle of comparatively small size, the best known of these being the herd preserved at Chillingham in Northumberland. In this case the muzzles and ears are red (though at an earlier date they were black), while the rest of the body is white.

A different origin must be sought for the *humped cattle* of Africa and India, the latter often receiving the name of Zebu (*Bos indicus*). It has been claimed that these are descended from an African stock, though this is only conjectural, and it may be observed that there are several wild species of Asiatic oxen which exhibit the humped character to a greater or less degree. This is the case, for example, with the Gaur (*Bos gaurus*) of India and Further India, to which the name "bison" is often misapplied, and the Yak (*Bos grunniens*) of Thibet, distinguished by its long hair and horse-like tail.

The group of *Bisons*, to which in some respects the Yak approximates, are distinguished by several special features, among the most striking of which are the great disproportionate height of the front part of the body and the projection of the back of the head above the origin of the horns. The European Bison (*Bos bonassus*), once abundant, is now practically restricted to Lithuania and the Caucasus, and appears doomed to extinction, like the American Bison (*Bos Americanus*) (fig. 78), which existed in countless herds at no very remote period. Under the name of "buffalo" this animal plays a large part in various kinds of literature dealing with North America.

Buffaloes, using the term in the strict sense, are stoutly-built oxen with broad snout, strong thick horns, and large fringed ears set on rather far down. The hair is comparatively coarse and scanty, and the long tail is tufted. The group is characteristic of the warmer parts of the Old World, and the most powerful species is the Cape Buffalo (*Bos caffer*), which has a wide distribution in Africa. While in this form the broad bases of the horns meet together in the middle, the long backwardly-directed horns of the much smaller Indian Buffalo (*Bos bubalus*) are separated by a wide interspace. As a wild animal it is confined to

Fig. 78.—The American Bison (*Bos Americanus*). (From an instantaneous photograph)

India, but in the domesticated condition has a wide distribution through south-east Asia, and has also been introduced into Asia Minor, Egypt, and Italy.

The Musk Ox (*Ovibos moschatus*) (fig. 79) with its ram-like horns is more of the nature of a sheep than an ox. At the present time it is restricted to the arctic parts of the western hemisphere, and it is remarkable that so large a creature is able to find a sufficiency of vegetable food in such inhospitable wilds. Its name is due to the peculiar musky flavour which the flesh possesses

(2) *Sheep* resemble oxen in many respects but are much smaller animals, and the neck bends sharply up, so that the head

is carried comparatively high. Although in many wild forms horns are present in both sexes, those of the male are specially characteristic. Their form is more or less spiral, with the tips turned outwards; they are triangular in section, and marked by numerous transverse wrinklings. The snout is pointed, and there is usually a glandular pit below the eye, the tail is short, and a

Fig. 79.—The Musk-Ox (*Ovibos moschatus*)

bottle-shaped gland opens between the central toes of each foot. Of the eleven existing wild species nine inhabit the mountainous parts of Europe and Asia north of the Himalayas, while the remaining three belong respectively to North-west India, North Africa, and North America. The Bighorn (*Ovis Canadensis*) and Mouflon (*O. musimon*) may be taken as illustrations. The former ranges through the mountains of western North America from Alaska to Mexico, while the latter is at the present time only found in Corsica and Sardinia.

The same doubt attaches to the origin of tame sheep, which

have been domesticated from prehistoric times, as to that of most other farm-animals.

(3) *Goats* agree with sheep in many respects, but in typical cases are distinguished by the concavity of the face, peculiar hard patches on the knees, absence of glandular pits below the eye, and lack of hoof-glands in the hind-feet. The male is characterized by a peculiarly unpleasant odour, strong backwardly-curved horns, often with a corrugated surface, and a tuft of hair on the chin. The group is essentially characteristic of the mountainous axis of the Old World, from Spain eastwards to Thibet and North China, but outlying species occur in South India, Africa, and North America. The species known as the Bezoar Goat or Grecian Ibex (*Capra œgagra*), which ranges from some of the Greek islands eastwards to Persia, where it is called the pasang, is interesting as being probably the chief stock from which the Domestic Goat (*Capra hirca*) is derived. Goats are known to have been tamed from very early times, and Homer, in describing those of the Cyclops, was no doubt alluding to this particular species, which formerly had a much wider range in Greece.

Among other species may be mentioned the Spanish Ibex or Wild Goat (*Capra Pyrenaica*), the almost extinct Alpine Ibex (*C. ibex*), the Himalayan Ibex (*C. Sibirica*), and the Arabian Ibex (*C. Sinaitica*). The solitary American species is the Rocky Mountain Goat (*Haploceros montanus*), which ranges through the Rocky Mountains from California to Canada. It is not a very typical goat, and forms one of a small group of genera intermediate in character between goats and antelopes.

(4) *Antelopes* constitute a large group of hollow-horned ruminants difficult, if not impossible, to define, but including those members of the family which are obviously neither oxen, sheep, nor goats. There are, however, many transitional forms, such as the one last mentioned under the heading of goats. The group is now characteristic of Africa, Syria, and Arabia, though there are a number of outlying species. A typical antelope is elegant in form, with head carried well above the body and bearing graceful horns, prominently ringed, and straight, simply curved, or twisted. The bony horn-cores are of more solid nature than in the other divisions of the ox family, and there is frequently, as in sheep, a glandular pit below the eye.

The Chamois (*Rupicapra tragus*) is one of the transition forms between goats and antelopes, so that it may be placed indifferently in either of them. It ranges from the Pyrenees to the Caucasus, and is the only animal in West Europe which has any claim to the name of antelope. A characteristic feature is seen in the sharp hook-like termination of the short black horns.

Among the most graceful members of the group are the small desert forms which, under the name of *Gazelles*, have been immor-

Fig. 80.—The Saiga Antelope (*Colus Tartaricus*)

talized by various poets. The Dorcas Gazelle (*Gazella dorcas*), which inhabits North Africa, Syria, and Asia Minor, is perhaps the best-known kind. Other species are the Persian Gazelle (*G. subgutturosa*), the Indian Gazelle (*G. Bennetti*), and the Arabian Gazelle (*G. Arabica*).

Probably the most remarkable looking antelopes are the Saiga Antelope (*Colus Tartaricus*) and the Wildebeest or Gnu (*Catoblepas gnu*). The former, which looks as if it suffered from badly-swollen face (fig. 80), ranges from the steppes of Russia-in-Europe to the Altai Mountains. Apart from the Chamois it is the only European antelope. The Gnu (fig. 81) is an inhabitant of South Africa, and looks like a mixture of buffalo and horse, being endowed with the head of the one and the tail of the other.

5. The *Giraffe Family* includes the Okapi (*Okapia Johnstoni*, see vol. ii, p. 170), and the Giraffe (*Giraffa camelopardalis*). The latter is found in desert and semi-desert regions to the south of the Sahara. The more familiar South African variety (fig. 82) is marked with conspicuous brown blotches upon a tawny back-

Fig. 81.—The Wildebeest or White-tailed Gnu (*Catoblepas gnu*)

ground, and this, suggesting the markings of a leopard, has given rise to the alternative name of Camelopard by which the animal is often known. In the variety living farther north the colours are reversed, so to speak, the background being brown, but the tawny hue is disposed not in patches but a close network of lines. Unfortunately, it appears to be one of the many species doomed to complete extinction at no distant date.

The giraffe rejoices in the distinction of being the tallest living mammal, adult bulls sometimes measuring as much 19 feet from the top of the head downwards. This unusual height is partly due to the great length of the neck, and partly to the relatively greater height of the front part of the body. The head is decidedly graceful, the long tail is tufted, and there is no trace of accessory hoofs at the sides of the feet. As in sheep, &c., the upper incisors and canines are replaced by a horny pad. A very distinctive external feature consists in the possession of two short rounded horns, consisting of a bony core covered by soft skin. There is also a rounded skin-covered knob between the eyes.

Fig. 82.—The Giraffe (*Giraffa camelopardalis*). (From an instantaneous photograph)

The protrusible tongue is extremely flexible, and serves as a grasping organ for seizing the twigs of trees.

6. The *Camel Family* is the last to be mentioned under the heading of Ruminants. The head is devoid of horns and placed at the end of a long curved neck. The limbs are elongated, and each of them terminates in two toes only, while the hoofs are replaced by pad-like swellings on the under side of the foot. Further characteristics are the split upper lip, incisors in the upper jaw, and well-developed canines both above and below. The family includes the camels of the Old World, and the llamas, with allied forms, in the New World.

Camels, which are now unknown as wild animals, though admittedly invaluable domestic forms, are decidedly ugly if measured by our standards of good looks; nor do they make up by amiability what they lack in beauty. Kipling's faithful delineation of the "gawd-forsaken oont" is too well known to need quotation, but the following vivid account of the purchase of a camel given by Conan Doyle (*Daily News* of April 21, 1896) is probably less familiar.

"There are camels to be bought, and it is a study in Eastern ways to see the *Daily News* buying them. Some men have the gift of pantomime, and some have not. I know by experience that I have not. On the occasion of an eclipse of the moon I endeavoured to explain the cause of it by gesture to an Arab. I pointed to the moon and to the earth. Then I pointed to a horse and to his shadow. Presently the Arab rose and began to examine the horse's hind-legs, and I found that I had convinced him that the creature was ill. I have given up gestures since then. But the *Daily News* has all the Arab's energy of movement, with a good command of abuse, and some powers as a pedestrian. With these gifts, one may buy camels.

"Having looked depreciatingly at the beast—and you cannot take a better model than the creature's own expression as it looks at you—you ask how much is wanted for it. The owner says sixteen pounds. You then give a shriek of derision, sweep your arm across as if to wave him and his camel out of your sight for ever, and, turning with a whisk, you set off rapidly in the other direction. How far you go depends upon the price asked. If it is really very high, you may not get back for your dinner. But as a rule, a hundred yards or so meet the case, and you shape your course so as to reach the camel and its owner. You stop in front of them and look at them with a disinterested and surprised expression, to intimate that you wonder that they should still be loitering there. The Arab asks how much you will give. You answer eight pounds. Then it is his turn to scream, whisk round, and do his hundred yards, his absurd chattel with his hornpipe legs trotting along behind him. But he returns to say that he will take fourteen, and off you go again with a howl and a wave. So the bargaining goes on, the circles continually shortening, until you have settled upon the middle price. But it is only when you have bought your camel that your troubles begin. It is the strangest and most deceptive creature in the world. Its appearance is so staid and respectable that you cannot give it credit for the black villainy that lurks within. It approaches you with a mildly interested but superior expression, like a patrician lady in a Sunday-school. You feel that a pair of glasses at the end of a fan is the one thing lacking. Then it puts its lips gently forward, with a far-away look in its eyes, and you have just time to say 'The pretty dear is going to kiss me', when two rows of frightful green teeth clash in front of you, and you give such a backward jump as you could never have hoped at your age to accomplish. When once the veil is dropped, anything more demoniacal than the face of a camel cannot be conceived. No kindness and no length of ownership seems to make them friendly. And yet you must make allowances for a creature which can carry 600 lbs. for twenty miles a day, and ask for no water and little food at the end of it."

The Arabian Camel (*Camelus dromedarius*) is the common one-humped form of Africa and Asia, while the two-humped Bactrian Camel (*C. bactrianus*), a smaller animal, is characteristic of the desert regions of Central Asia.

The American members of the Camel Family consist of two wild species, conveniently grouped under the head of *Llamas*, a term also including the two domesticated forms. These animals are smaller than camels and more gracefully built; they are also devoid of a hump. The ears are pointed and comparatively long, instead of being short and rounded, the tail is very short, and the feet are relatively small as compared with the camel.

Of the two wild species the animal known as the Guanaco (*Lama guanacus*) is larger and more heavily built. It ranges from the mountains of Ecuador southwards to Tierra del Fuego. It is probably from this species that the two domestic forms, known as the Llama (*L. lama*) and the Alpaca (*L. pacos*), are descended.

The second wild species is the comparatively small and graceful Vicunia (*L. vicunia*), which ranges through the mountains of South America from Bolivia to Ecuador.

Order 11.—Gnawers (Rodentia)

This widely-distributed order includes a larger number of forms than any other, all of which feed largely, and the majority entirely, upon vegetable food. The largest species does not exceed the size of a small pig, while some are extremely small. Most of

THE LLAMA (*Lama lama*)

This animal was domesticated in very remote times by the ancient Peruvians, and even now is an important beast of burden in the high Andes of Peru and Bolivia, though the original breed has been replaced to a great extent by domesticated forms introduced from the Old World. In former times it was used in great numbers for the transport of silver ore from the famous mines of Potosi in Bolivia, more than 13,000 feet above the sea.

The Llama may be described as an American cousin of the Camel, belonging, as it does, to the same group (*Tylopoda*) of Ruminants or Cud-chewers. The earliest known members of this group were, however, native to North America, from which area the stock spread on the one hand into South America, and on the other into the Old World, having since become extinct elsewhere.

PERUVIAN LLAMAS (LAMA LAMA)

A STUDY FROM THE LIFE

them live upon the surface of the ground, but some burrow and some climb, while others have taken to the water. The general organization is of rather a low type, but there is much specialization in the most characteristic structures, *i. e.* the teeth. Rodents walk entirely or partly upon the soles of the feet, and the digits are usually provided with claws, though more rarely they possess small hoofs. The most striking feature regarding the teeth is the character of the incisors, of which in the adult never more than four are developed to a useful extent. These are large chisel-ended structures, growing continuously throughout life, as they are worn away by the constant gnawing which is so characteristic of the order. This is strikingly seen in the cases of unfortunate animals which have lost one incisor, as a result of which the corresponding tooth has nothing to bite against, and not being therefore subjected to wear, grows to an enormous length, ultimately killing its unlucky owner. A similar state of things may result from malformation or accident, if thereby the upper and lower teeth are prevented from coming together. Canine teeth are always absent, and the cheek teeth are commonly reduced in number, and more or less adapted to act as grinders. There is an interesting feature, already alluded to (p. 28), regarding the jaw-joint, which permits of the free backward-and-forward movement necessary for gnawing. This is due to the fact that the condyles of the lower jaw are elongated from front to back, and fit into sockets of corresponding shape.

There are four great groups of existing Rodents, which may broadly be called: 1. Rabbits; 2. Squirrels; 3. Mice; and 4. Porcupines.

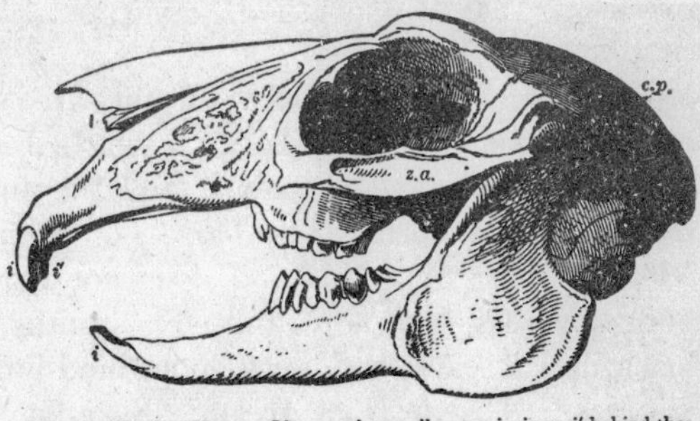

Fig. 83.—Skull of Hare. Observe the small upper incisors *i'* behind the large functional ones *i*; *c.p.* coronoid process; *z.a.* zygomatic arch.

1. The group of RABBITS, including also Hares and Pikas, is distinguished by the presence of two small upper incisor teeth, situated immediately behind the two large teeth of the same kind present here as in all Rodents (fig. 83). It may also be added that the two bones of the lower

leg (tibia and fibula) are united together at their lower ends. Three animals common in Britain may be taken as illustrations, *i.e.* the Rabbit, Hare, and Alpine Hare.

The Rabbit (*Lepus cuniculus*) (fig. 84), though so common in the British area, is believed not to be indigenous, and the same may be said of many other countries where it now abounds. Its

Fig. 84.—The Rabbit (*Lepus cuniculus*)

original home was probably in the area adjoining either shore of the western Mediterranean. Marked characteristics are gregariousness, burrowing habits, and the immature state in which the young are born. The Hare (*L. timidus*) is a larger animal which is not gregarious and does not burrow, while the newly-born leverets can see, and are scantily clad with fur. The black-tipped ears and very long hind-limbs are also noticeable features. Absent from Ireland, Scandinavia, and North Russia, the hare has a wide distribution over the rest of Europe from Great Britain to the Caucasus. The Alpine Hare (*L. variabilis*) assumes a white or light-coloured winter coat. In the British area it is found in Scotland and the northern parts of England, while it replaces the common species in Ireland. From our islands it ranges across the northern part of the Old World to

Japan, and also from the Pyrenees to the Caucasus. Other species of hare are found in various parts of Asia, Africa, North America, and South America.

Pikas, or *Calling Hares*, are small creatures somewhat resembling guinea-pigs, apparently devoid of tail, and with rounded ears of small dimensions. They are gregarious, and, failing fissures in the rocks, excavate burrows. Most of the species inhabit the north and central parts of Asia, one of these, the Siberian Pika (*Lagomys Alpinus*) (fig. 85), ranging into Eastern Europe. There is also one species in North America.

Fig. 85.—The Siberian Pika (*Lagomys Alpinus*)

The three remaining groups of Rodents—Squirrels, Mice, and Porcupines—agree with one another, and differ from rabbits and their allies, in the number of the incisor teeth, these being only four in number, two above and two below.

2. The SQUIRRELS include forms in which the bones of the lower leg (tibia and fibula) are not united together. Squirrels, Marmots, and Beavers are the representative types.

SQUIRRELS, as well seen in the Common Squirrel (*Sciurus vulgaris*), our native species, have a rounded head, from which large tufted ears project, a large bushy tail, and extremities provided with sharp claws. The thumb is of very small size. The range of this species includes the greater part of Europe, North and Central Asia, and North Africa. Squirrels of one sort or another are found in almost all hot and temperate countries, Madagascar and Australia excepted. *Ground-Squirrels*, which, as the name indicates, live upon the ground, are common in the colder parts of the northern hemisphere. Much resembling ordinary squirrels in appearance, they differ in the smaller size of the tail, the absence of tufts to the ears, and the possession of large cheek-pouches. They excavate burrows in the ground. The Common Chipmunk (*Tamias striata*) of North America is a good example. *Flying-Squirrels* possess a parachute-like fold of skin on either side, much as in the Flying-Lemur (cp. p. 86). They mostly range from India to Japan, but are also represented in North America, Siberia, and East Europe. The Brown Flying-Squirrel (*Pteromys petaurista*) is the largest species. The African Flying-Squirrels (*Anomalurus*), mostly natives of West Africa, differ from the preceding chiefly in the structure of the tail and flying-membrane.

Fig. 86.—The Common Suslik (*Spermophilus citillus*)

Least squirrel-like of the squirrel sub-group are the *Susliks* or *Gophers*, found in much the same regions as the ground-squirrels. They are burrowing forms with large cheek-pouches. The Common Suslik (*Spermophilus citillus*), which ranges from Central Europe to Siberia, has a short tail and very small ears (fig. 86). The Striped Gopher (*S. tridecemlineatus*) of North America is somewhat better off as regards ears and tail, and is prettily marked with stripes and rows of dots.

Marmots are more stoutly built than squirrels, their ears being smaller and their tails shorter, while cheek-pouches are present. They are burrowing social forms, and their area of distribution includes the colder parts of the northern hemisphere. A familiar European type is the Alpine Marmot (*Arctomys marmotta*) of the Pyrenees, Alps, and Carpathians. A common North American form is the Woodchuck (*Arctomys monax*).

The *Prairie Marmots* of North America are closely related to the preceding. The best-known species is the Common Prairie Marmot, often called "prairie-dog" (*Cynomys ludovicianus*), large numbers of which inhabit the plains on the east of the Rocky Mountains (fig. 87).

BEAVERS are comparatively large Rodents which spend a large part of their time in the water and are modified accordingly, the hind-feet being webbed, and the rudder-like tail flattened and scaly. There are only two living species, one in Eurasia and the other in North America. The former, or European Beaver

Fig. 87.—Prairie-Dogs (*Cynomys Ludovicianus*)

(*Castor fiber*), at present ranges from France to Siberia, but was once distributed much more widely, and in remoter times was a member of the British fauna, as attested by numerous remains. The American Beaver (*Castor Canadensis*) is now practically limited to Canada, though it once extended over the greater part of North America.

3. MICE include a very large number of species, and are represented in all parts of the world. A characteristic anatomical feature is found in the union of the two bones of the lower leg (tibia and fibula). The group includes the following families:—(1) Mice and Rats; (2) Mole-Rats; (3) Pouched Rats; (4) Jumping-Mice; and (5) Dormice.

(1) The *Mouse and Rat Family* includes more species than the others, and unlike them is cosmopolitan, being represented

even in Australia, from which all the other groups are absent. The tail is bare and scaly, the incisor teeth narrow, and the fore- and hind-limbs of about the same length. The thumb is much reduced. No less than eight species are found in Britain including rats, mice, and voles. The largest of these is the Common or Brown Rat (*Mus decumanus*), which, like all members of the same genus, has a long tail, and projecting tubercles on the crowns of the grinding teeth. It is supposed to have been introduced in the year 1730, and has largely ousted the smaller Black Rat (*M. rattus*), which is also an introduced form, though the date of its first arrival was much more remote. The most familiar of our mice is the House-Mouse (*M. musculus*), distinguished by the large size of its delicate ears. The Wood-Mouse, also called the Long-tailed Field-Mouse (*M. sylvaticus*), is very similar in appearance, but can be distinguished by its white under-surface. The little Harvest-Mouse (*M. minutus*), the nests of which are often found suspended from corn-stalks, is the most diminutive of our native mammals, the smallest shrew alone excepted. *Voles,* of which three species are native to Britain (but not Ireland), are distinguished from rats and mice by their clumsier proportions, shorter limbs and tail, and blunter snouts. They feed entirely upon vegetable matter, their back teeth being adapted to this kind of food, and having crowns of peculiar

Fig. 88.—The Water-Vole (*Microtus amphibius*)

pattern, suggesting a double series of opposed triangles alternating with one another. The largest of our three species is the Water-Vole (*Microtus amphibius*), often miscalled the Water "Rat". It is brown in colour and about the same size as an ordinary brown rat (fig. 88). The Bank-Vole (*M. glareolus*) is less stoutly built, with redder fur and longer tail. Much smaller and more abundant than these two species is the Field-Vole (*M. agrestis*), which sometimes multiplies to such an extent as to become a serious agricultural pest. It is often called the Short-tailed Field-Mouse, but is at once distinguished from a mouse by its shorter tail, and by the other features already enumerated as characteristic of voles generally.

Fig. 89.—The Lemming (*Myodes lemmus*)

Other examples of the Mouse family are afforded by the *Hamsters*, *Lemmings*, and *Musquashes*. The Common Hamster (*Cricetus frumentarius*) of Europe and North Asia is a comparatively large rodent, being as much as a foot in length inclusive of the short tail, the abbreviated nature of which at once shows that the creature is not a rat, which animal it otherwise somewhat resembles in external appearance. There are very large cheek-pouches. Hamsters are burrowing forms, and they store up large quantities of grain, seed, and other vegetable matter. They increase very rapidly in number and often do serious damage to crops. "A South American relative (*Ichthyomys*) of the Hamster lives in streams, and feeds on fish. The edges of the upper incisors are slanted towards each other to give a Λ-shaped notch. This is an adaptation for holding the slippery prey."

Lemmings resemble voles in many respects, but their tails are even shorter, while their claws are better developed and the fur is much thicker. The best-known species is the Norwegian Lemming (*Myodes lemmus*) (fig. 89), which inhabits the mountain regions of Scandinavia, and from time to time migrates in vast numbers, travelling in a straight line despite all obstacles, and ultimately plunging into the sea, where it soon perishes, as might be anticipated.

Fig. 90.—Kangaroo-Rat (*Dipodomys Phillipsi*)

The Musquash or Musk-Rat (*Fiber zibethicus*), which has a wide range in North America, may be regarded as a very large vole, thoroughly adapted to an aquatic life, as may be seen by its partly-webbed feet and strong flattened tail. It is largely hunted for the sake of its fur.

(2) The *Mole-Rat Family* includes Old World rodents which have taken to a burrowing life, with the result that their structure has undergone modifications of much the same kind as those exemplified by ordinary moles. A typical species is the Great Mole-Rat (*Spalax typhlus*), the range of which includes South-east Europe, South-west Asia, and lower Egypt.

(3) The North American *Pouched-Rat Family* includes a

number of forms which, though they differ greatly among themselves in appearance, all possess large hair-lined cheek-pouches. The Common Pocket-Gopher (*Geomys bursarius*) looks something like a compromise between a rat and a mole. It is a burrowing form inhabiting the central plains watered by the Mississippi and its tributaries. The Common Kangaroo-Rat (*Dipodomys Phillipsi*) is a desert animal with long hind-limbs and tail (fig. 90), enabling it to adopt the mode of progression characteristic of the kangaroo. The Banded Pocket-Mouse (*Perognathus fasciatus*) of the States resembles the last-named form on a small scale.

Fig. 91.—The Jerboa (*Alactaga decumana*)

(4) The *Jumping-Mouse* or *Jerboa Family* includes species which, like the Kangaroo-Rat and Pocket-Mouse of the last family, are specialized in relation to a springing mode of progression. They are, however, devoid of cheek-pouches. The species are chiefly found in Africa and Asia, though the family is also represented in South Europe and North America. A good illustrative species is the Siberian Jerboa (*Alactaga decumana*) (fig. 91).

(5) The *Dormouse Family* embraces small mouse-like animals which have adopted an arboreal life, and in some respects have become specialized in much the same way as squirrels. Species are found in Europe, Asia, and Africa, and there is one British form, the Common Dormouse (*Muscardinus avellanarius*), abundant in the south of England, but absent from Ireland and the northern part of Great Britain (fig. 92).

4. The PORCUPINE group of Rodents takes in a large number of forms, of which one common character is the separateness of the two bones (tibia and fibula) of the lower leg. The group is predominatingly American, and specially characteristic of South America. The following five families are included:—(1) Octodons; (2) Porcupines; (3) Chinchillas; (4) Agoutis; and (5) Cavie

(1) *Octodons* are somewhat rat-like forms mostly found in

South America, but also represented in the West Indies and in Africa. A typical form is the Degu (*Octodon degus*) of Peru and Chili (fig. 93). The enamel folds on the crowns of the grinding teeth have a characteristic figure-of-eight pattern.

Fig. 92.—The Common Dormouse (*Muscardinus avellanarius*)

(2) The *Porcupine Family*, distinguished by the possession of quills, is very widely distributed, Australia being the only continent from which its members are absent. All the Old World forms live on the ground, as is, for example, the case with the Common Porcupine (*Hystrix cristata*), which inhabits the Mediterranean countries, though comparatively scarce in those of them which are European. The Brush-tailed Porcupine (*Atherura Africana*) of West and Central Africa looks like a spiny rat. The New World forms are distinguished by being climbers. A common example is the Canadian Porcupine (*Erethizon dorsatus*).

None of the remaining families of the Porcupine group are

found outside South America, Central America, and the West Indies.

(3) The family made up of the *Chinchillas* and their allies is distinguished by the soft fur, well-developed tail, elongated hind-legs, and transversely-ridged crowns to the grinding teeth. The Common Chinchilla (*Chinchilla lanigera*) (fig. 94), a valuable

Fig. 93.—The Degu (*Octodon degus*)

fur-bearing animal inhabiting the mountains of Chili and Bolivia, is a very active squirrel-like creature in which there are five toes on the fore- and four toes on the hind-foot. The allied Viscacha (*Lagostomus trichodactylus*) is a stoutly-built burrowing form, of which the communities are common in the pampas of South America.

(4) The *Agoutis* and *Pacas* together constitute a South American family of which the members attain a considerable size. The claws are blunt and hoof-like. The short-tailed Common Agouti (*Dasyprocta agouti*) inhabits the forest regions of South America, and the tailless Paca (*Cœlogenys paca*), distinguished

by the presence of five rows of yellow spots on the fur, has a wide range through the same continent, east of the Andes and to as far south as Paraguay. It is also a native of the islands of Trinadad and Tobago.

(5) The family of *Cavies* resembles the preceding in the hoof-like nature of the claws, and are further characterized by the

Fig. 94.—The Common Chinchilla (*Chinchilla lanigera*)

extreme brevity of the tail. The grinding teeth are complex, and their crowns present numerous transverse ridges. A common example is the domestic Guinea-Pig (? *Guiana pig*), introduced into Europe in the sixteenth century. The Restless Cavy (*Cavius porcellus*) of Uruguay and Brazil has been claimed as the ancestral stock, though the view is now held that this distinction rests with Cutler's Cavy (*Cavia Cutleri*), a Peruvian form supposed to have been domesticated by the Incas. The largest known Rodent, the Capybara (*Hydrochœrus capybara*), is simply an exaggerated Cavy specialized for an aquatic life, as testified by its webbed feet. It inhabits the great rivers of South America, and is not unlike a small pig in general appearance and

Fig. 95.—The Unau or Two-toed Sloth (*Cholæpus didactylus*)

size. The writer well remembers seeing a tame specimen, which had escaped from the grounds of its owner and swum down the Teign estuary to Teignmouth, being exhibited in the lifeboat-house there as "a pigfacious hippopotamus".

Order 12.—Edentates (Edentata)

This very remarkable group includes a number of both Old and New World forms, which are rather low in the scale, and have had to adopt various expedients in order to avoid being exterminated by the active competition of more highly organized forms. It is very doubtful whether the Old World forms have any special relation to the New World ones, or in other words the order is a very artificial one. This comes out strikingly when an attempt is made to discover common characters. About all that can be said is, that the teeth are highly peculiar in character, and that the digits are provided with curiously modified curved hoofs. As to the former structures the term "edentate", *i.e.* toothless, is somewhat misleading, for though this is the case with some forms, it is not generally true, though the front teeth are always more or less deficient. A further point is that the teeth are always devoid of enamel.

Most of the Edentates are found only in South America, and of these the following are representative species:—The Two-toed Sloth (*Cholœpus didactylus*) (fig. 95) of Guiana and Surinam; the Six-banded Armadillo (*Dasypus sexcinctus*) (fig. 96) of the South American pampas; and the Ant-Bear (*Myrmecophaga jubata*) of Paraguay. Old World forms are: The Cape Ant-Eater or Aard-Vark (*Orycteropus Capensis*) (fig. 97) of South Africa, and the Long-tailed Pangolin (*Manis pentadactyla*) (fig. 98) of West Africa.

Order 13.—Pouched Mammals (Marsupialia)

This is the only order in the Mammalian sub-class Metatheria, under which heading its leading characters have already been given (p. 68).

The great bulk of existing Marsupials are confined to Australia and its adjacent islands, as far as Celebes, though the order is also represented in America. The great interest attached to the Australian forms is found in the way they have become specialized in various directions to fill the most varying places in the economy of nature. Other more highly organized mammals having been absent, they have had the field to themselves without other serious competition, and the places occupied in most parts of the world

POUCHED MAMMALS (*Marsupialia*)

1. Tree-Kangaroo of New Guinea (*Dendrolagus ursinus*).
2. Koala (*Phascolarctos cinereus*).
3. Water Opossum (*Chironectes minima*).
4. Pig-footed Bandicoot (*Chœropus castanotis*).
5. Tasmanian Devil (*Sarcophilus ursinus*).
6. Squirrel-like Flying Phalanger (*Petaurus sciureus*).
7. Jerboa Pouched-mouse (*Antechinomys laniger*).
8. Philander Opossum (*Didelphys philander*).
9. Great Grey Kangaroo (*Macropus giganteus*).
10. Tasmanian Wolf (*Thylacinus cynocephalus*).
11. Hairy-nosed Wombat (*Phascolomys latifrons*).
12. Gunn's Bandicoot (*Perameles Gunni*).
13. Common Dasyure (*Dasyurus viverrinus*).

Numbers 3 and 8 are American forms, the remainder belong to the Australian region.

GROUP OF POUCHED MAMMALS (MARSUPIALIA)

Fig. 96.—The Six-banded Armadillo or Poyou (*Dasypus sexcinctus*)

by such groups as Carnivora, Insectivora, &c., are here filled by marsupial sub-orders.

The American marsupials have had to compete with forms

Fig. 97.—The Aard-Vark or Cape Ant-Eater (*Orycteropus Capensis*)

better adapted to struggle for existence, and play but a subordinate part in the fauna of that continent. They consist of the Opossums, found both in North and South America, and of a small creature Cœnolestes recently discovered in the latter continent. The Common Opossum (*Didelphys Virginiana*) has

Fig. 98.—The Long-tailed Pangolin (*Manis pentadactyla*)

a wide distribution in North America, from Canada to Mexico. It is the well-known "'possum" of American story and verse.

Order 14.—Egg-laying Mammals (Monotremata)

Like the preceding one, this order is the only one in its subclass (Prototheria), of which the leading characters have already been given (p. 69). It will suffice to remark here that its members are only found in the Australian region, like the majority of Marsupials, and having had to compete with these comparatively more powerful forms, have been prevented from occupying more than a subordinate position in the fauna of that region.

CHAPTER III

STRUCTURE AND CLASSIFICATION OF BIRDS

Though Birds are familiar objects to all, and obviously characterized by the possession of wings and feathers, these are not the only essential features distinguishing them, and it will clear the ground to briefly describe some well-known and typical example of the class. This is the better worth doing since the great bulk of existing birds resemble one another to a much greater extent than is the case with mammals.

As convenient a type as any, and one possessing special interest from the fact that Darwin devoted a very large amount of attention to it from the evolutionary stand-point, is the Pigeon (*Columba livia*). Of this there are a large number of domestic varieties, some very peculiar in appearance, but for our purpose the best is the one known to fanciers as the "Blue Rock", which best represents the central form from which the different varieties have sprung, and which is found wild in Europe, North Africa, and West Asia as far as India.

The wild Blue Rock nests in caves or clefts of the rock, and is of common occurrence round the northern coasts of Ireland and Scotland. Its prevailing hue is grey, but the rump is white, and the neck and upper part of the breast green and purple, with a metallic sheen. There is a characteristic broad black bar running across the end of the tail, while the wing is crossed by two similar but narrower bands.

External Characters (fig. 99).—The outlines of a bird are mainly determined by the feathers, as is strikingly seen on comparing a living bird with a plucked specimen, the latter presenting a very comical appearance. The head is well rounded behind, in correspondence with the presence of a large brain, while the face is produced in front into a somewhat conical horny beak, at the base of which are situated the two slit-like nostrils, overhung by a bare patch of swollen skin, the *cere*. The large eyes are provided not only with upper and lower eyelids, but also with a translucent *nictitating* membrane, or third eyelid, which can be rapidly twitched over the front of the eye by special muscles. A narrow bare area of skin surrounds each eye, and in such breeds as the Carrier, this area and the cere are highly developed into peculiar fleshy outgrowths. Below and behind the eye is the

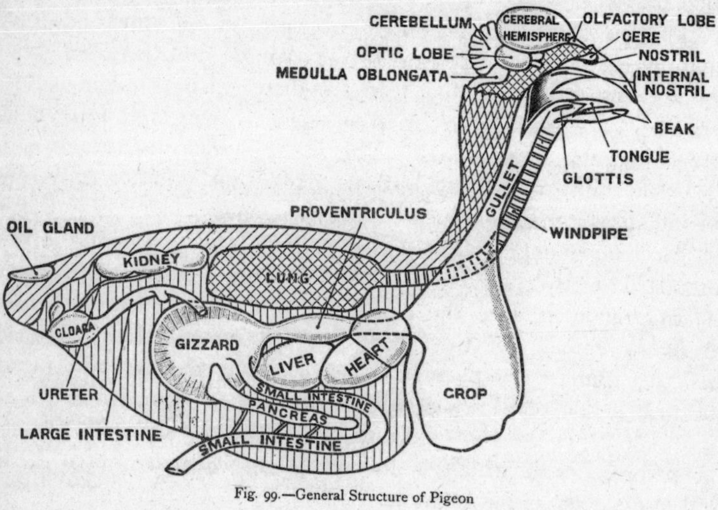

Fig. 99.—General Structure of Pigeon

small round auditory aperture, which is not provided with a pinna as in most mammals.

The long and exceedingly mobile neck is sharply marked off from the stout boat-shaped trunk, which is terminated by a stumpy tail, on the upper surface of which is a prominent papilla carrying the aperture of the large oil-gland. On the under side of the trunk, near its hinder end, is the opening of the cloaca, a small chamber into which open the intestine, the kidney-ducts, and the ducts of the reproductive organs.

The body of a bird exhibits innumerable adaptations to an aerial life, and this is seen very strikingly in the fore-limbs, which are modified into wings, quite different, however, in structure from those of a bat (see p. 81). The same sections are present as in a mammal, *i.e.* upper arm, fore-arm, and hand, but there are considerable differences in detail. In so far as folds of skin connect upper arm and fore-arm in front, and upper arm and trunk behind, there is a certain resemblance to the bat's wing, but we do not find in the bird long slender fingers supporting a well-developed membrane, but a reduced hand possessing only three modified digits. The efficient part of the wing consists of feathers, and the limb is specialized so as to serve as a firm support for these.

When a bird is not flying it is supported by the hind-limbs, but the problem of bipedal progression is not solved here in the same way as in a human being (see p. 66), where the trunk is raised into a vertical position and brought into the same line as the legs. The hind-limbs of a bird are, as it were, shifted forwards so that the body is balanced somewhat obliquely between them. There are, however, some forms, such as Penguins (fig. 127), in which the trunk is raised into an approximately upright position, but even then the resemblance to the attitude of an erect human being is remote, for not only is the thigh attached as in other birds, but it points slantingly upwards instead of being directed downwards. It would not indeed be possible for a bird to completely straighten out its leg, for the thigh is more or less enclosed in the boundaries of the trunk, and is not entirely free, as in ourselves.

It is also noticeable that the regions of a bird's leg, with the exception of the uppermost one, or thigh, do not exactly correspond with the subdivisions found in a mammal. The other two sections may be called, for convenience, lower leg and foot, but the ankle-joint between them is not in exactly the same position as in the last-named group. This will be more fully explained in dealing with the endoskeleton. The digits are four in number, instead of five as in a typical mammal, the digit corresponding to the little toe of which being absent. The great toe is turned backwards, and, since the body is supported upon the digits while the metatarsus and tarsus are raised from the ground, the bird may be termed digitigrade.

Skin and Exoskeleton.—The thin skin is made up, as in a mammal, of epidermis and dermis, and the former gives rise to a well-marked exoskeleton, consisting of beak, claws, scales, and feathers. The *beak* comes under this heading in so far as the horny sheaths which cover both upper and lower jaws are concerned, while the toes are provided with *claws*, and the feet are covered by overlapping *scales.* The characteristic parts of the skeleton, however, are the *feathers* (fig. 100), structures which are possessed by all birds, but by no other animals. They do not cover the entire surface of the body, but are limited to certain feather tracts (*pterylæ*), between which are bare patches (*apteria*). Feathers, like hairs, spring from pits in the skin, and are renewed from time to time, during a moulting season. They are of three kinds: 1. small downy *filoplumes*, consisting of a stalk with a tuft

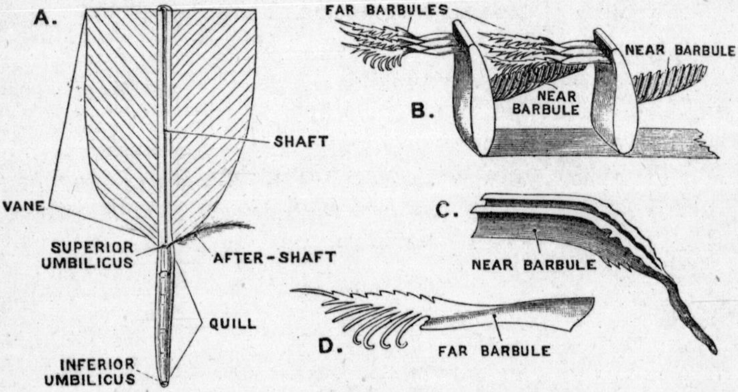

Fig. 100.—Structure of a Feather (there is no after-shaft in the Pigeon)

A, Base of quill-feather; B, barbs and barbules (much enlarged); C and D, separate barbules (still further enlarged).

of filaments at the end; 2. *contour* feathers, which cover most of the body, and, as the name indicates, determine its shape; and 3. large *quill-feathers* used in flight, and attached to the wings and tail. The last two kinds closely resemble one another in structure, and it may suffice to describe one of the quills, which are the most specialized and characteristic of feathers. Both light and strong, with a large surface for opposing to the air, they are exquisitely adapted to their purpose, even in the minutest details of their structure. We can distinguish between a central shaft, consisting of a hollow *quill* continued into a solid *rachis*, and oblique filaments or *barbs* projecting from each side of the rachis and constituting with it the *vane.* Each barb is provided with an oblique set of *barbules* on its far or distal side, facing the end of the feather, and a similar set on its near or proximal side, facing towards the base of the feather. The barbules of the distal row are provided with hooklets, which catch on to ridges possessed by the row of proximal barbules immediately in front of them.

Twenty-three quills (remiges) are attached to the hinder margin of each wing, eleven of them being *primaries* fixed to the hand, while the twelve others are *secondaries* borne by the fore-arm. The bases of these quills are covered above and below by other feathers known respectively as upper and lower *wing-coverts*. There is also a tuft of feathers, the *bastard wing* (ala spuria), upon the thumb.

Twelve *tail-quills* (rectrices) are attached in the form of a fan to the stumpy tail, and the bases of these are covered by upper and lower *tail-coverts*.

The *contour feathers*, including the coverts and the bastard wing, resemble quill-feathers on a small scale, but when they are plucked away a number of *filoplumes* are found among them, each consisting of a stalk bearing a loose tuft of barbules at its end. The *down-feathers* with which the nestling is covered closely resemble these.

Endoskeleton (fig. 101).—The same regions and parts can be recognized as in a mammal, but there are very considerable differences in detail, most, if not all, of which are related to the mode of life. The bones are particularly light and spongy, while many of them contain air instead of marrow, one of the arrangements whereby the specific gravity of the body is reduced as an adaptation to flight.

A number of features distinguish the *skull* from that of a mammal, one being that in the adult the bones are fused together so as to obliterate the junctions between them. This feature, however, is also seen in the lowest mammals, *i.e.* the Spiny Ant-Eater and Duck-billed Platypus, and is not the only point in which these creatures show a resemblance to birds. We have seen that at the back of a mammal's skull (p. 28) there are two rounded occipital condyles which fit into corresponding cups in the first joint of the backbone, but in the pigeon only one such condyle is to be seen, and as a result of this the head can be turned very freely about from side to side. There is also a remarkable peculiarity in the attachment of the lower jaw to the skull, as this takes place by the intervention of a special bone, the *quadrate*, there being thus a double jaw joint, permitting the mouth to be opened very widely, a capacity which must have struck anyone who has ever examined a nest of young pigeons, sparrows, or canaries. It may also be noted in a young skull that each half of the lower jaw is made up of several pieces instead of only one as in a mammal.

The *backbone* is very long and there are remarkable contrasts between its several regions, for whereas the neck vertebræ are united together by saddle-shaped surfaces so as to give extraordinary flexibility, the vertebræ of the trunk are largely fused

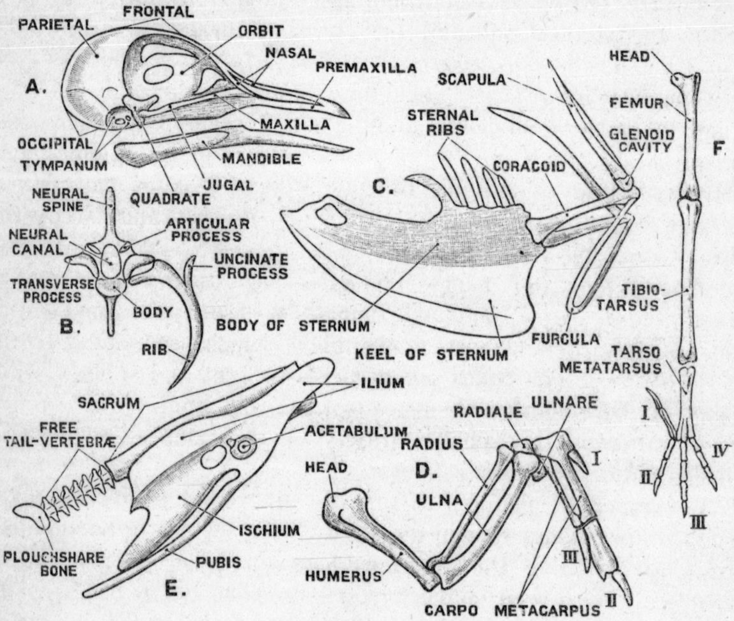

Fig. 101.—Skeleton of Pigeon

A, Skull; B, vertebra and rib (front view); C, sternum and shoulder-girdles; D, wing; E. pelvis and tail; F, leg.

together so as to confer great rigidity, an important matter in connection with the requirements of flight. What is called the "sacrum" in a pigeon is made up by the union of vertebræ belonging to very different regions, including one thoracic, six lumbar, two sacral proper, and five caudal. The remaining vertebræ of the abbreviated tail are ten in number, and the last four of them are fused into a laterally-flattened *ploughshare bone*, which supports the tail-quills.

Since the walls of the thorax are fairly mobile in a bird, and by their movement help in breathing, the breastbone and ribs are hinged on to the backbone so as to permit of this.

All the five thoracic vertebræ bear *ribs* which unite with the breastbone, and each rib in its upper section possesses a backward projection, the *uncinate process*, absent in all mammals. It should also be noted that the posterior neck vertebræ bear small free ribs.

The *breastbone* or sternum of a pigeon is exceedingly large, and is in particular distinguished by the presence of a very prominent vertical plate or keel on its under side. The use of this is to give a large surface to which the powerful muscles of flight are attached. A bat's sternum possesses a small keel for a similar reason.

Skeleton of Fore-Limb.—The special function of this being to serve as a firm support for the wing-quills, it is not surprising to find that the bones of the hand have undergone a good deal of reduction in number, and also of fusion, the digits being only three, corresponding to the thumb and first two fingers of a mammal. Such a hand skeleton as that described for Man (p. 31), made up of numerous small bones flexibly united together, is very suitable for a limb capable of performing all sorts of complicated movements, but much too elaborate for a mere support, as in the case of a wing.

The upper part of the limb skeleton, or *shoulder-girdle*, includes three bones: the dorsal narrow *scapula*, the rod-shaped ventral *coracoid* which unites with the sternum, and a collar-bone or *clavicle*. In the possession of a distinct coracoid, Birds and Monotreme Mammals agree (p. 138). The two narrow curved clavicles are firmly fused together into the familiar "merry-thought" or *furcula*, which acts as a spring and keeps the two wings well separated.

Skeleton of Hind-Limb.—The *hip-girdle* is made up of the same three elements as in a mammal, *i.e. ilium*, *ischium*, and *pubis*. The ilium is very large and runs both fore and aft, uniting by its inner surface with the long "sacrum", thus affording a very firm support to the body when the bird rests or walks. Both ischium and pubis, especially the latter, are narrow and backwardly-directed, and do not unite with one another in the mid-ventral line as in a mammal (see p. 31).

The chief peculiarity in the bones of the free part of the leg is found in the ankle, for the *tarsus*, instead of being made up of a number of small irregular bones, as in the mammal (see p. 32), consists, in the very young bird, of two elements only, of which one fuses with the tibia to form a tibio-tarsus, while the other fuses with three of the metatarsals, these also uniting with one another, the compound product being known as the "tarso-metatarsus". It will thus be seen that what corresponds to the ankle-joint of the human foot (p. 32) comes in the middle of the tarsus, and not between it and the bones of the lower leg. The great toe possesses a metatarsal which is distinct from the others, and this digit therefore has a greater power of movement. The remaining point deserving mention here is in regard to the number of phalanges in the various toes. It will be remembered that in Man (p. 31), and the same thing is true for mammals generally, the great toe has two and the remaining toes three phalanges each. A bird has similarly two phalanges in the great toe and three phalanges in the second toe, but the third toe possesses four, and the fourth five, thus giving the regular succession two, three, four, five, each digit possessing one more phalanx than its number in the series.

Digestive Organs (fig. 99).—The pigeon, like all existing birds, is entirely devoid of teeth, and its beak is only useful for picking up food, not being capable of breaking up the hard grain on which the animal largely feeds. A temporary receptacle for food is therefore necessary, and this is found in the large *crop* into which the gullet swells. A further peculiarity, common to all birds, is found in the nature of the stomach, which consists of two parts, chemical stomach (proventriculus) and gizzard. The former looks like a swelling at the end of the gullet, but is distinguished by the presence of numerous *gastric* or *peptic glands* (see p. 37) imbedded in its mucous membrane, and secreting gastric juice. The *gizzard* is a rounded and somewhat flattened structure with a tough lining and exceedingly thick muscular walls. As is well known, it serves to grind up the food, its action being assisted by small stones and other hard bodies which are swallowed for the purpose. The stomach is followed by a long *small intestine* into which the *liver* and *pancreas* pour their secretions; and a much shorter *large intestine*, opening into a *cloaca*, which communicates with the exterior by a cloacal aperture.

Circulatory Organs (fig. 102).—As in a mammal, both blood

and lymph systems are present, but we need only consider a few points concerning the former.

The blood is much hotter than that of a mammal, maintaining a temperature of about 103° F. on the average as against 98° F., a fact which has relation to the extreme activity of birds, and the intensity, so to speak, of all their life processes. The well-developed investment of feathers by which the body is covered, and which entangles a large amount of air, is of great importance as a non-conducting coat, which prevents the too rapid dissipation of the heat of the body without checking ventilation of the body surface. A drop of pigeon's blood examined under the microscope shows the same constituents as are seen in a mammal (see p. 39), *i.e.* a liquid *plasma* in which are suspended *white* and *red corpuscles.* The latter, however, though discs, are of a pointed oval shape instead of being circular, and each of them encloses a firmer particle or nucleus.

The pigeon's *heart* and *blood-vessels* agree in essential respects with those of a mammal (see p. 39), but there are numerous differences in detail. Thus, though the heart is four-chambered and the impure blood of the right side is thus completely separated from the pure blood of the left side, there are differences as regards the valves, especially the one between right auricle and ventricle, which is a muscular flap instead of consisting of three membranous pieces. The great artery of the body, the *aorta*, where it arises from the heart, curves round to the right and not to the left. The enormously large muscles of flight, which make up the flesh of the breast, are provided with large blood-vessels.

Breathing Organs and *Organs of Voice* (fig. 102).—The separation between food-tract and breathing-tract is less complete here than in a mammal (see p. 34), for the hinder openings of the nasal cavities (*posterior nares*) are situated on the roof of the mouth instead of farther back. Upon the floor of the pharynx the slit-like glottis is situated, but this is not guarded in front by an epiglottis. It leads into the larynx, which is *not* in birds the organ of voice, and is continued into the very long windpipe (trachea) that divides into two branches (*bronchi*) for the lungs. These air-passages are not supported by hoops of cartilage, as in mammals (p. 46), but by bony rings. From this point onwards a number of striking peculiarities are encountered, for the lungs do not constitute the only goal of the in-breathed air, but communicate with a number of thin-walled *air-sacs*, and these again with the air-filled cavities in the bones. The only other animals which are so thoroughly permeated by air are insects, and in them, as in birds, one end to be gained is the reduction of the specific gravity of the body as an aid to flight. The small *lungs*, though spongy, are not freely movable in the thoracic cavity, but are firmly fixed to its roof,

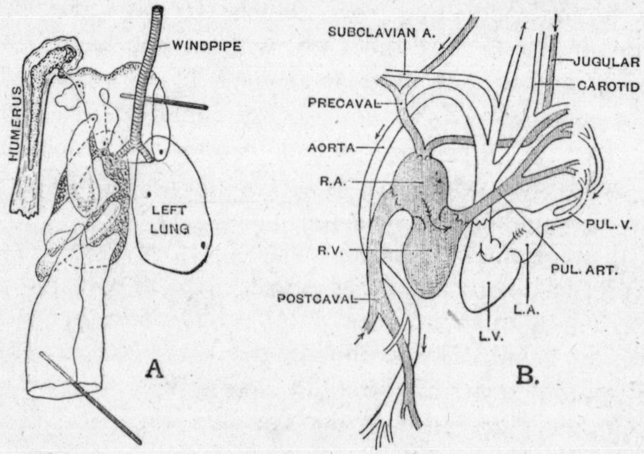

Fig. 102.—Structure of Pigeon

A, Respiratory organs, seen from vertical side. Air-sacs connected with right lung are drawn in outline. Rods are inserted into two cut air-sacs. B, Diagrams of heart and great blood-vessels, from ventral side. Two halves of heart shown as if separated, and direction of blood-flow indicated by arrows. R.A. and L.A., right and left auricles; R.V. and L.V., right and left ventricles; Pul. Art. and Pul. V., pulmonary artery and vein; A. and V. elsewhere mean artery and vein.

and there being no midriff as in a mammal (see p. 46), there is no sharp boundary between thoracic and abdominal regions. The bronchi branch out in their respective lungs, and their larger branches run to the lung surface, where they open into the large thin-walled air-sacs, which are placed in various positions. Some of the anterior air-sacs communicate with the air-spaces contained in certain bones, as, *e.g.*, the humerus and sternum. The mechanical part of breathing is brought about by the movement of the ribs and sternum, much as in a mammal (p. 46), but here there is, of course, no diaphragmatic breathing. The entering air rushes into all the air-sacs, and the work to be done by diffusion is not so great as in a mammal. The reason for this is, to keep the process of blood oxygenation going very rapidly, as, if this were not the case, the high temperature of the body could not be maintained.

Voice.—Although the pigeon possesses a larynx, this is not the organ of voice, which consists of a structure known as the *song-box* or *syrinx*, formed by the modification of the extreme end of the windpipe and the beginning of the two bronchi to form a small resonant chamber (*tympanum*) into which an elastic fold projects. The sound is produced by vibration of this fold, and it can be stretched to various extents so as to alter the pitch of the note.

Organs of Movement.—As in the human subject, the *white corpuscles* of blood and lymph are able to creep about by means of amœboid movement (p. 39), and the windpipe and certain other structures are lined by *ciliated membranes* (p. 49); but, as before, the chief movements of the body are brought about by *muscular action.* The most interesting peculiarities in the muscular system are connected with flight and with perching. The large fleshy mass covering the breast is made up of the pectoral muscles, which are attached to the wings in such a manner as to pull them alternately up and down; but this is not the place to furnish details, which will be given farther on in connection with locomotion.

The *perching mechanism* is an arrangement by which the toes can be all brought together at the same time by a pull exerted upon a single tendon connected with two muscles of the leg. When a bird is roosting, the weight of the body bends the limb in such a way as to pull on this tendon and bring all the toes firmly against the branch or other supporting object, the danger of falling off during sleep being thus averted.

Nervous System (fig. 103).—The *brain* of the pigeon is extremely short and broad, and is distinguished by several peculiarities. The cerebral hemispheres are large and rounded, but are quite smooth externally, and are not, as in mammals, united across the middle line by a fibrous band or corpus callosum (see p. 52). Both these points are related to the comparatively small intelligence of the animal. The organs of smell are not well developed, and therefore, as might be expected, the olfactory lobes are of small size; but on the other hand, in accordance with the unusually acute vision, the optic nerves, optic tracts, and optic lobes are very large.

These last are two rounded elevations situated one on each side, while the corresponding parts in a mammal are four in number, and have a dorsal situation. The cerebellum is very large, and marked by deep transverse furrows.

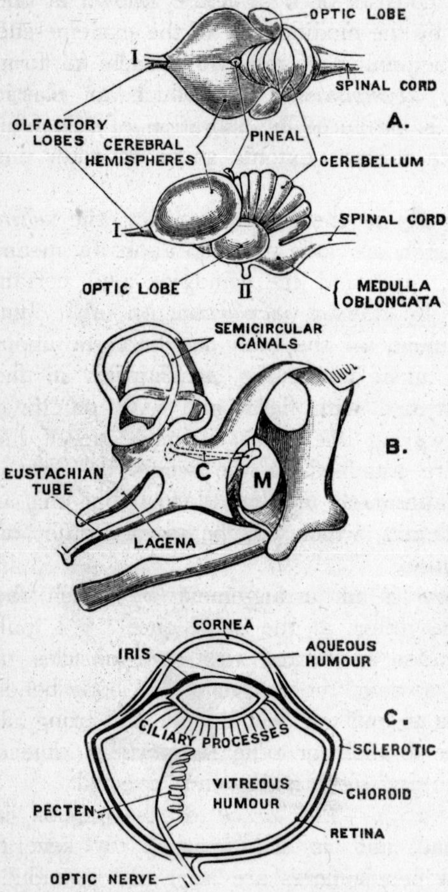

Fig. 103.—Structure of Pigeon

A, Brain from above and from left side: I, olfactory nerve; II, optic nerve. B, Organs of hearing (much enlarged); C, columella: M, position of tympanic membrane; C, Diagrammatic section of eye (enlarged).

Sense Organs (fig. 103).—Only the ear and eye deserve special mention under this heading. The *organs of hearing* consist, as in a mammal (see p. 56), of internal, middle, and external ears, but there are a number of differences in detail. The internal ear or membranous labyrinth differs most as regards the *cochlea*, which is a slightly-curved tube (lagena) instead of being spirally coiled. In the middle ear it may be noted that instead of a chain of auditory ossicles there is a minute rod, the *columella*, which runs across the tympanic cavity from its external membrane to the *fenestra ovalis*. The external ear consists simply of a passage leading down from the outside of the head to the tympanic membrane, there being no external flap or pinna. It will be remembered, however, that the pinna is also absent in certain aquatic mammals, such as the whales and the true seal.

The *eye* of a bird is not, as in a mammal, approximately spherical, but consists of outer and inner halves possessing very different degrees of curvature, the former almost resembling a cone with its apex rounded off instead of being pointed. Within the outer part of the sclerotic, or firm white external eye-coating, there is a circlet of small overlapping bony plates. The remaining most striking difference is seen in the presence of a *pecten*, a folded structure which projects into the vitreous humour close to the point where the optic nerve pierces the eyeball to branch up in the retina or sensitive innermost eye-coating.

It was noticed under external characters that there is a third eyelid in addition to the usual upper and lower ones. Some mammals, as the rabbit, possess such an eyelid, though it is not so mobile.

Development (fig. 104)—All birds lay eggs, protected externally by a firm limy *shell*, and the lowest mammals agree with them

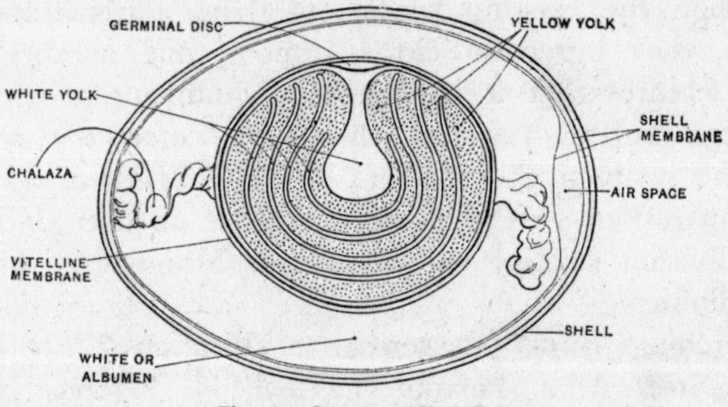

Fig. 104.—Structure of Hen's Egg

in this respect. One or both parents in turn sit upon or incubate the eggs, thus providing the necessary warmth without which the young bird cannot develop. Most of the egg consists of material which will serve for the nourishment of the embryo, the body of which is evolved from a very small patch (*germinal disc*), to be seen on one side of the yellow part known as the *yolk*. The part of the yolk on which the germinal disc rests is lighter than the rest, and this side therefore floats upwards in the glairy matter termed the "white", or more properly speaking the *albumen*. Hence the embryonic part of the egg is kept constantly turned towards the source of heat, *i.e.* the incubating parent. Young pigeons are hatched in a very imperfect state, and have to be fed for some time by the parents, part of their food consisting of a whitish material, the so-called "pigeon's milk", secreted by the lining of the crop. The helpless nestling is very imperfectly clad with feathers, and these down-feathers are much simpler in nature than the ordinary feathers of the adult bird.

CLASSIFICATION OF BIRDS

Excluding fossil forms, birds are divided into two sub-classes of very unequal size: I. Flying Birds (Carinatæ), of which the Pigeon is an example; and II. Running Birds (Ratitæ), of which the best-known kind is the Ostrich.

I. FLYING BIRDS (Carinatæ) are more or less perfectly adapted for flight, as will have been seen from the typical example just described. The most striking characters are found in the structure of the wings and the keeled sternum, in reference to which latter feature the group is technically called Carinatæ (L. *carina*, a keel).

Although the existing species of flying birds are extremely numerous, they agree so closely among one another in most essential features that it is exceedingly difficult to divide them into orders, but eighteen of these are commonly recognized, though the distinctive characters of many of them are founded upon comparatively trivial matters, and we do not get the broad lines of division existing in the case of Mammals. The orders are as follows:—

1. Perching Birds (Passeres); 2. Picarian Birds (Picariæ); 3. Owls (Striges); 4. Parrots (Psittaci); 5. Pigeons and Sand-Grouse (Columbæ); 6. Gulls (Gaviæ); 7. Plovers (Limicolæ); 8. Bustards and Cranes (Alectorides); 9. Rails (Grallæ); 10. Game-Birds (Gallinæ); 11. Tinamous (Crypturi); 12. Eagles and Vultures (Accipitres); 13. Ducks, Geese, and Flamingoes (Anseres); 14. Herons and Storks (Herodiones); 15. Pelicans and Cormorants (Steganopodes); 16. Petrels and Albatrosses (Tubinares); 17. Divers and Grebes (Pygopodes); 18. Penguins (Impennes).

Order 1.—PERCHING BIRDS (Passeres).

This order is regarded as the highest of the sub-divisions of birds, and the large majority of them are included in it, more particularly those which are familiarly known as "song-birds". The first toe can be moved independently of the others, which is not the case in other birds, and possesses a larger claw than they do. In most cases the back of the metatarsus is protected by two narrow elongated plates, instead of by scales. There are generally ten, or it may be nine, primary quills in the wing, which is covered by only a few small contour feathers. The tail-quills are usually twelve in number. The young are helpless and almost destitute of feathers.

Among the enormous number of birds included in this order are the following representatives of important families:—1. Crows; 2. Birds of Paradise; 3. Bower-Birds; 4. Starlings; 5. Orioles;

Fig. 105.—Rook (*Corvus frugilegus*)

6. Finches; 7. Weaver-Birds; 8. Buntings; 9. Larks; 10. Wagtails; 11. Creepers; 12. Nuthatches; 13. Sun-Birds; 14. Tits; 15. Shrikes; 16. Thrushes and Warblers; 17. Wrens; 18. Swallows; and 19. Lyre-Birds. The British species belonging to these families, if any, will be enumerated, except in the case of rare stragglers.

1. *Crows* and their allies are large birds with strong beaks, and nostrils protected by bristles. Many of them are black or black and white, and they are practically cosmopolitan, being absent, however, from New Zealand, Among British forms the Raven (*Corvus corax*) is entirely black, as are the Carrion Crow (*Corvus corone*) and the Rook (*Corvus frugilegus*) (fig. 105), there being, however, in the latter a bare patch extending round the base of the beak. The Jackdaw (*Corvus monedula*) has a grey neck, while the long-tailed Magpie (*Pica rustica*) is black and white, as the name indicates. The Jay (*Garrulus glandarius*) is a much more brightly-coloured member of the same family, its

plumage exhibiting white, black, brown, and blue, while there is a handsome crest upon the head.

The remaining British species are: Hooded Crow (*Corvus cornix*), Nutcracker (*Nucifraga caryocatactes*), Chough (*Pyrrhocorax graculus*).

Fig. 106.—Great Paradise Bird (*Paradisea apoda*)

2. The *Birds of Paradise* are closely related to the crows in structure, but are remarkable for the gorgeous and varied plumage of the males, certain of the feathers being prolonged and modified in various ways. The region from which such feathers spring differs in different species. Birds of Paradise are for the most

part limited to New Guinea and the neighbouring islands, though they also range into the north of Australia. The Great Paradise Bird (*Paradisea apoda*) of the Aru Islands is depicted in fig. 106.

3. *Bower-Birds* constitute a small family mainly confined to Australia, though also found in New Guinea, and are chiefly interesting because they construct and decorate so-called "bowers", which appear to be solely used for the purpose of amusement. A well-known form is the Satin Bower-Bird of New South Wales (*Ptilonorhynchus holosericeus*).

Fig. 107.—Starlings
Common Starling (*Sturnus vulgaris*).

4. *Starlings* (fig. 107) constitute a well-known family with a wide distribution in the Eastern hemisphere, being absent only from Australia. They do not, however, occur in America. The beak is fairly long and often slightly curved, while its base is free from bristles. Flocks of these birds can often be seen in meadows hunting for insects and worms. Another characteristic feature is that of the ten primary wing-quills; the first is less than half the length of the second.

The Common Starling (*Sturnus vulgaris*), immortalized in Sterne's *Sentimental Journey*, is a refreshing exception to the general rule for British birds, its numbers being on the increase. The black plumage, shot with green and blue, and tipped with buff, is extremely handsome. There is one other British species, the Rose-coloured Starling (*Pastor roseus*).

5. *Orioles* or Golden Thrushes are characteristic of Africa and South Asia, though they are represented in Australia and Europe. The beak is slender and almost straight, the legs short, and the plumage brilliant.

The Golden Oriole (*Oriolus galbula*) of continental Europe

and South-west Asia is known as a visitor in this country. In colour it is golden-yellow, with black on the wings and tail, and the call-notes of the male are flute-like in tone.

6. *Finches* make up a very large family, absent only from the Australian region, and characterized by strong conical beaks adapted for feeding upon seeds and grain, while there are only nine primary wing-quills instead of ten. The food is by no means limited to seeds and the like.

The following small British birds belong here:—Sparrow (*Passer domesticus*); Tree-Sparrow (*P. montanus*); Bullfinch (*Pyrrhula Europæa*); Chaffinch (*Fringilla cælebs*); Brambling (*F. montifringillina*); Linnet (*F. cannabina*); Mealy Redpole (*Cannabina linaria*); Lesser Redpole (*C. rufes*); Twite (*C. flavirostris*); Greenfinch (*Ligurinus chloris*); Goldfinch (*Carduelis elegans*); Hawfinch (*Coccothraustes vulgaris*); Siskin (*Chrysomitus spinus*); Crossbill (*Loxia curvirostra*).

7. *Weaver-Birds*, remarkable for the way in which they intertwine fibres to form their nests, resemble finches in appearance and in their stout conical beaks, but possess ten instead of nine primary wing-quills as in the latter. The family is more particularly characteristic of Africa south of the Sahara, but is also well represented in South Asia and in Australia. The Java Sparrow or Rice-Bird (*Munia oryzivora*) is familiar in this country as a cage-bird.

8. *Buntings* are finch-like forms inhabiting the colder parts of the Old World. They differ from the true finches in minor features, one of which is that when the beak is shut its edges do not come into contact except at the base and tip.

There are several British species, of which the most familiar is the Yellow Bunting (*Emberiza citrinella*), better known as the Yellow Hammer.

The remaining British species are:—Cirl Bunting (*Emberiza cirlus*); Corn Bunting (*E. miliaria*); Reed Bunting (*E. schœniclus*); Snow Bunting (*Plectrophenax nivalis*).

9. *Larks* constitute a tolerably large group, limited with but few exceptions to Europe, Asia, and Africa, where they are most abundant in plains and deserts. Their powers of song are known to everyone. The first toe is provided with a very long straight claw.

The Skylark (*Alauda arvensis*) and Woodlark (*A. arborea*) are well known in Britain. The Shore Lark (*Otocorys alpestris*) is a visitor.

BRITISH PERCHING BIRDS (*Passeres*)

The species figured are Finches (1, 2, 5), a Bunting (4), and a Tit (3). Finches (*Fringillidæ*) live in wooded districts, and their short stout conical beaks are adapted to seed-eating. Buntings (*Emberizidæ*) inhabit open grassy localities, and are easily distinguished from Finches by a notch in the side of the beak. Tits (*Paridæ*) are chiefly found among trees, and feed for the most part on insects.

1. Bullfinch (*Pyrrhula Europæa*).
2. Chaffinch (*Fringilla cœlebs*).
3. Blue Tit (*Parus cœruleus*).
4. Yellow-hammer (*Emberiza citrinella*).
5. Goldfinch (*Carduelis elegans*).

8

BRITISH PERCHING BIRDS (PASSERES)

1. Bullfinch.
2. Chaffinch.
3. Blue-Tit.
4. Yellow-Hammer.
5. Goldfinch.

10. *Wagtails*, with their allies the *Pipits*, make up a small family which, though found in all parts of the world, except the Pacific Islands, is especially characteristic of the northern parts of Europe and Asia. The body is slender and the tail long. The narrow-pointed beak is well suited for the capture of insects, and the feet are somewhat like those of larks, except that the claw of the first toe is more curved. Most of the birds here included are found chiefly on the ground, and run very quickly.

Common British species are the following:—Pied Wagtail (*Motacilla lugubris*); Meadow Pipit or Titlark (*Anthus pratensis*).

The other native species are the following:—White Wagtail (*Motacilla alba*); Blue-headed Wagtail (*M. flava*); Grey Wagtail (*M. melanope*); Yellow Wagtail (*M. Raii*); Rock Pipit (*Anthus obscurus*); Richard's Pipit (*A. Richardi*); Tree Pipit (*A. trivialis*).

11. *Creepers* are a small family of wide distribution, with long curved beak and sharp claws. They are adapted for the pursuit of insects upon the trunks of trees, walls, and similar places.

The only resident British species is the Tree Creeper (*Certhia familiaris*), which has a wide range in the Northern hemisphere. Though fairly common, its plumage harmonizes so well with the surroundings that it often escapes observation. The tail is stiffened, and its pointed quills are of great assistance in climbing.

12. *Nuthatches* constitute another small family of climbing birds, somewhat more widely distributed than the Creepers, being absent only from South America, Africa south of the Sahara, and the Pacific Islands. They differ in no very important respect from the Creepers. Their food consists not merely of insects, but also of nuts.

Our only native species is the Nuthatch (*Sitta cæsia*), common in the wooded parts of Central and South Europe, and also found in North Africa. It also ranges into South-west Asia, but, unlike the Creeper, is unknown in North America.

13. The *Sun-Birds* are small, brilliantly-coloured forms ranging through the tropics of the Old World, and often confounded with the humming-birds, which they resemble in appearance and habits, though there is no close relationship between the two groups.

14. *Tits* or *Titmice* are small active birds, the general appearance of which is well known to everyone, and which, though

specially characteristic of the northern hemisphere, are found in most parts of the world. The beak is short and conical, and the first wing-quill is never more than half the length of the second one. These birds inhabit trees, and chiefly feed on insects, though vegetable food is by no means disdained. A meat-bone or partly-opened cocoa-nut placed outside the window of a house is almost certain to attract any tits which may be in the neighbourhood.

The best-known British species is the Blue Titmouse (*Parus cœruleus*), which possesses extremely beautiful plumage, exhibiting shades of blue, yellow, yellowish-green, and white. It ranges throughout most of Europe, and is abundant in Asia Minor.

Other typical native forms are:—Coal-Tit (*Parus ater*); Crested Tit (*P. cristatus*); Great Tit (*P. major*); Marsh Tit (*P. palustris*); Long-tailed Tit (*Acredula caudata*).

15. *Shrikes* make up a fairly large family of tree-inhabiting birds which have their head-quarters in Africa, though they are found in all parts of the world, except South America and New Zealand. Their food consists of insects, and also in some cases of small vertebrates, and in accordance with this the beak is strong and often somewhat hooked.

The most abundant British species is the Red-backed Shrike (*Lanius collurio*), the plumage of which is mainly chestnut above and buff on the under side. Like other "butcher-birds", as these forms are often called, this form has the habit of impaling its victims upon sharp thorns. Its range includes most of Europe, South-west and Central Asia, and in winter it is found as far south as the Cape. Another native form is the great Grey Shrike (*L. excubitor*).

16. *Thrushes* and *Warblers* together constitute an enormous group of cosmopolitan birds distinguished for their powers of song. The beak is slender and bent a little at the end, and the first wing-quill is very short. Some feed entirely on insects, but others eat berries and the like as well. The plumage is quiet in colour, and there is not much difference in this respect between the sexes.

Thrushes are stoutly-built omnivorous birds, in which the young differ from the adults in their spotted plumage. They are commonest in South America, but are found in all parts of the world, except Madagascar and New Zealand.

Fig. 108.—Warblers

1. Barred Warbler (*Sylvia nisoria*). 2. Lesser Whitethroat (*S. curruca*). 3. Garden Warbler (*S. hortensis*). Whitethroat (*S. cinerea*). 5. Blackcap (*S. atricapilla*).

Common British forms are the Song-Thrush (*Turdus musicus*), Fieldfare (*T. pilaris*), and Blackbird (*T. merula*), all of which are widely distributed in Europe, Asia, and North Africa.

The remaining native thrushes and thrush-like birds are:—Redwing (*Turdus iliacus*); Ring-Ousel (*T. torquata*); Missel-Thrush (*T. viscivorus*); Red-spotted Bluethroat (*Cyanecula suecica*); Nightingale (*Daulias luscinia*); Robin Redbreast (*Erithacus rubecula*); Whinchat (*Pratincola rubetra*); Stonechat (*P. rubicola*); Wheatear (*Saxicola œnanthe*); Redstart (*Ruticilla phœnicurus*); Black Redstart (*R. tithys*).

Warblers (fig. 108) are smaller and slenderer birds than thrushes, and more insectivorous in their habits. There is not the same difference of plumage between young and adult birds as in thrushes. Though the group is cosmopolitan, it is essentially characteristic of the Old World.

Fig. 109.—Golden-crested Wren (*Regulus cristatus*) below; Fire-crested Wren (*R. ignicapillus*) above.

Among the numerous British species may be mentioned:—Whitethroat (*Sylvia cinerea*); Golden - crested Wren (*Regulus cristatus*), the smallest of European birds) (fig. 109); Sedge Warbler (*Acrocephalus phragmitis*); and Hedge-Sparrow (*Accentor modularis*).

Our remaining species of warblers are:—Lesser Whitethroat (*Sylvia curruca*); Blackcap Warbler (*S. atricapilla*); Garden Warbler (*S. hortensis*); Dartford Warbler (*S. undata*); Marsh Warbler (*Acrocephalus palustris*); Reed Warbler (*A. streperus*); Grasshopper Warbler (*Locustella nœvia*); Chiffchaff (*Phylloscopus rufus*); Wood-Wren (*P. sibilatrix*); Willow-Wren (*P. trochilus*); Fire-crested Wren (*Regulus ignicapillis*) (fig. 109).

17. *Wrens*, properly so called, are small birds with fairly long, straight, or nearly straight, beaks and rounded wings. The tail is usually carried bent up over the back. Commonest in South America, these birds are also found in North America, Europe and some parts of Asia.

The Common Wren (*Troglodytes parvulus*) of Britain is

essentially an European bird, but is also found in South-west Asia and parts of North Africa.

18. *Swallows* are cosmopolitan birds with remarkable powers of flight. The beak is short and broad at the base, the feet weak, the wings very long and pointed, and the tail generally forked. The food consists of insects, which, as is well known, are caught on the wing.

The three British species are the Swallow (*Hirundo rustica*), the House-Martin (*Chelidon urbica*), and the Sand-Martin (*Cotile riparia*). All three have a wide distribution in Europe, Asia, and Africa, while the Sand-Martin also ranges from the north of North America as far south as the Amazon valley.

19. *Lyre-Birds*, remarkable for the shape assumed by the tail of the male, have no very near allies. They are only found in South and East Australia.

Order 2.—Picarian Birds (*Picariæ*)

This large order resembles that of the perching birds in many respects, but is distinguished by slight anatomical differences of too technical a nature to be given here. Most members of the group lay white eggs in holes or other places likely to escape observation.

Among other families, those of 1. Woodpeckers, 2. Toucans, 3. Cuckoos, 4. Humming-Birds, 5. Swifts, 6. Night-Jars, 7. Hoopoes, 8. Hornbills, and 9. Kingfishers, may be more especially noticed.

1. *Woodpeckers.*—These are tree-climbing birds, in which the fourth toe is turned back parallel to the first (zygodactyle type of foot), while the strong chisel-shaped beak is used both in the pursuit of insects and to dig out holes for nesting purposes. The long worm-like tongue, which, covered by a sticky secretion, is used to capture insects, can be protruded to a considerable distance, and the related muscles and bones are specially modified, as will be described elsewhere. The young are helpless. Woodpeckers range over the entire globe, with the exception of Australasia.

There are three British species, of which the best known is the Green Woodpecker (*Gecinus viridis*), a form which is distributed over most of Europe, and also ranges into Asia Minor and Persia. The other two are the Great Spotted Woodpecker (*Dendrocopus major*) and the Lesser Spotted Woodpecker (*D. minor*).

2. *Toucans* are South American birds, distinguished by exceedingly gay plumage and an enormous flattened bill, which also is brightly coloured. Their feet are zygodactyle.

3. *Cuckoos* are long-tailed birds, with feet like those of woodpeckers, the fourth and first toes being turned backwards.

Fig. 110.—Cuckoo (*Cuculus canorus*)

They range over most of the globe, but their head-quarters are in tropical regions. Most of the Old World species lay their eggs in the nests of other birds, but the New World species build nests of their own.

The Common Cuckoo (*Cuculus canorus*) (fig. 110), which is a British resident from April to August (though the young birds may stay later), somewhat resembles a hawk in appearance, and is often taken for such not only by human beings but also by small birds. The familiar cry is uttered by the male only, the note of the female being quite different. It may be interesting to remark that the "cuckoo" call is only possessed by this species and by a South African form (*Cuculus gularis*). The common cuckoo ranges over most of Europe, Africa, and Asia.

4. *Humming-Birds*, remarkable for their small size, remarkable powers of flight, and, as a rule, the metallic brilliancy of their plumage, range from Mexico to the extreme south of South America. The beak in the adult is long and slender, and the tongue has an elaborate mechanism for pushing it out and pulling it back, much as in woodpeckers. Only the first toe is turned backwards.

5. *Swifts* are swallow-like birds with very long pointed wings, conferring considerable powers of flight. The short beak is broad at its base, and the mouth is consequently wide. A swift can easily be distinguished from a swallow by counting the tail-quills, which are ten in number instead of twelve. The distribution is world-wide, if New Zealand be excepted.

The Common Swift (*Cypselus apus*) of the British Isles is a summer visitor which nests in holes in roofs, walls, &c. With the exception of a light patch under the chin, it is of a blackish colour, the tail is forked, and the exceedingly small feet have all four toes directed forwards. This species ranges over the greater part of the Old World.

Fig. 111.—Hoopoe (*Upupa epops*)

6. *Night-Jars* or *Goat-Suckers* are mottled forms with broad beaks like those of swifts, and hair-like feathers in the neighbourhood of the mouth. The spotted eggs are laid in open places, and the young are thickly covered with down. Members of the group are found in all parts of the world, except New Zealand and some of the islands of the Pacific.

The European Night-Jar (*Caprimulgus Europæus*) is found in these islands from mid-May till September, or it may be later. Its range includes most of Europe and Africa and South-west Asia.

7. *Hoopoes* in many respects resemble the perching birds,

with which they are often included. The well-developed first toe is turned backwards. They are essentially desert forms, and their beautiful plumage is coloured so as to largely harmonize with surroundings of the kind. The head is distinguished by its long slender curved beak and handsome crest of features, which can be raised or depressed at will.

Fig. 112.—Rhinoceros Hornbill (*Buceros rhinoceros*)

The European Hoopoe (*Upupa epops*) (fig. 111) is a fairly common visitor to Britain.

8. *Hornbills* (fig. 112) are large tropical birds, ranging from Africa to the Solomon Islands, and distinguished by the possession of enormous beaks, which in some cases have a large projection or casque on the upper side at the base.

9. *Kingfishers* are distinguished by the structure of their feet, in which the great toe is backwardly directed, and the two outer toes united together. The beak is strong and pointed, varying in shape according to the food, which in one group consists of fish, in the other of reptiles and small mammals. Kingfishers have a world-wide distribution, but are most abundant in the Australian half of the East Indies, from Celebes to New Guinea, to which area the majority of the genera are confined.

The European Kingfisher (*Alcedo ispida*), which is a well-known British resident, is distinguished by its beautiful plumage, in which various shades of blue predominate above while the under surface is chestnut-coloured. As in the fish-eating species generally, the beak is long and pointed, while the tail is short. As an example of the reptile-eating kingfishers, the Laughing

Jackass (*Dacelo gigantea*) (fig. 113) of Australia and New Guinea may be taken. Here the beak is broader and stronger, and the tail is longer than in fish-eating forms.

Order 3.—Owls (*Striges*)

Here are included birds of prey, which are mostly nocturnal, and of characteristic appearance mainly due to the large forwardly-directed eyes surrounded by discs of radiating feathers. The four toes of the strong feet are all provided with sharp claws, and the fourth toe is reversible, being turned forwards or backwards at will. In flight these birds are peculiarly noiseless, their plumage being extremely soft. The young are helpless. Owls are universally distributed, and in all countries are regarded with awe by the superstitious, which is no doubt the result of their peculiar appearance and habits, aggravated by a most unearthly voice.

Fig. 113.—Laughing Jackass (*Dacelo gigantea*)

The most familiar British form is undoubtedly the Barn-Owl (*Strix flammea*), which is almost as universally distributed as the order to which it belongs. Other well-known native forms are the Tawny or Wood-Owl (*Syrnium aluco*), the "hoot" of which is a familiar country sound, the Long-eared Owl (*Asio otus*), and the Short-eared Owl (*Asio accipitrinus*). The "ears" of the last two kinds are tufts of feathers on the top of the head. The large Snowy Owl (*Nyctea Scandiaca*) regularly visits North Scotland during the winter.

The largest members of the group are the Great Horned or Eagle-Owls, of which the Great Eagle-Owl (*Bubo ignavus*) is sometimes caught in Great Britain, while the Pigmy-Owls are the smallest, being little more than half the size of the Barn-Owl. Interesting modifications of habit are found in the Hawk-Owl (*Surnia ulula*) of North Europe and Asia, which hunts its prey during the day; the Fish-Owls of Africa and South Asia, which frequent the neighbourhood of streams and lakes; and the little Burrowing-Owl (*Speotito cunicularia*) of America, which lives in the burrows excavated by rodents.

Order 4.—PARROTS (*Psittaci*)

Parrots and the like constitute a large and well-marked group, the characters of which are familiar to almost everybody. The beak is short, stout, and hooked, a remarkable feature being that the upper jaw can be moved up and down as well as the lower jaw. A prominent cere is present. The legs are short and strong, while the feet are modified to serve as climbing organs, the fourth as well as the first toe being turned permanently backwards. The hooked beak is also used in climbing. The young birds are hatched in a helpless condition. The group is essentially tropical and sub-tropical, and is most abundantly represented, as regards number of species, in Australasia, from Celebes eastwards; while in abundance of individuals South America stands pre-eminent.

Probably the most familiar form is the common Grey Parrot (*Psittacus erithacus*) of Equatorial Africa. Its short square-ended red tail is distinctive. The *Cockatoos*, distinguished by their crests, are natives of Australia and the eastern Malay Islands, ranging also into the Philippines. The gorgeous long-tailed *Macaws* range from South America into Mexico, while the little *Love-Birds* are limited to Madagascar and Africa south of the Sahara. The *Parrotlets* are diminutive South American forms. Two small and peculiar families of parrots are confined to New Zealand and the neighbouring islands. One of these includes the Nestor-Parrots, of which the form known as the Kea (*Nestor notabilis*) has earned an evil reputation by its acquired habit of preying on sheep. The other family is constituted solely for the reception of the Kakapo or Owl-Parrot (*Stringops habroptilus*),

LEADBEATER'S COCKATOO (*Cacatua Leadbeateri*)

Cockatoos (*Cacatuidæ*) are among the most typical birds of the Australasian region, from Celebes to the Solomon Islands, and also ranging north to the Philippines. They are absent from New Zealand. The erectile crest and short broad tail are characteristic features.

The beautiful species figured is native to South Australia, and is of unusually large size, attaining the length of 16 inches.

LEADBEATER'S COCKATOO (CACATUA LEADBEATERI)

which has lost the power of flight and lives on the ground. The owl-like appearance is due to slender radiating feathers round the eye.

Order 5.—Pigeons and Sand-Grouse (Columbæ)

The description already given of a pigeon (p. 139) will give a good idea of the appearance and structure of the birds of this order.

Pigeons and *Doves* are distributed over the entire globe, but the largest number of peculiar genera and species are found in the southern land masses, especially Australia.

Fig. 114.—Crowned Pigeon (*Goura*)

British species are the Rock-Dove or Blue-Rock (*Columba livia*), the Ring-Dove, Wood-Pigeon, or Cushat (*C. palumbus*), the Stock-Dove (*C. œnas*), and, as a summer visitor, the Turtle-Dove (*Turtur communis*). Probably the most striking of exotic forms, and the largest members of the group, are the Crowned Pigeons of Australasia (fig. 114).

Sand-Grouse are essentially desert birds, and are quietly coloured to harmonize with their surroundings. Their head-quarters are Africa and Central Asia, also extending into South-west Europe and into India. Their unusually short legs and toes prevent them from perching, but the wings are long and pointed, conferring great powers of flight. The tail is also pointed. Some naturalists place these birds in a special order, and they have affinities with game-birds as well as pigeons, as shown by the structure of their digestive organs and the fact that their young are precocious.

Pallas's Sand-Grouse (*Syrrhaptes paradoxus*) inhabits, during summer, the steppes between the Caspian and Lake Baikal, migrating farther east in winter, and from time to time invades Europe in smaller or larger flocks, penetrating as far west as the British Isles.

Order 6.—Gulls (Gaviæ)

In many respects these birds resemble the plovers, and like them are cosmopolitan, and have precocious young. They differ, however, in being adapted to a marine life, as seen especially in the fact that the three front toes are connected by a web. It may also be noted that the plumage is entirely or largely light in colour.

Fig. 115.—Herring-Gull (*Larus argentatus*)

Well-known British types are the Common Tern (*Sterna fluviatilis*), the Common Gull (*Larus canus*), the Herring-Gull (*Larus argentatus*) (fig. 115), and the Kittiwake (*Rissa tridactyla*).

The other British gulls, &c., are:—Lesser Black-backed Gull (*Larus fuscus*); Great Black-backed Gull (*L. marinus*); Glaucous Gull (*L. glaucus*); Iceland Gull (*L. leucopterus*); Little Gull (*L. minutus*); Black-headed Gull (*L. ridibundus*); Sandwich Tern (*Sterna Cantiaca*); Roseate Tern (*S. Dougalli*); Arctic Tern (*S. macrura*); Little Tern (*S. minuta*); Black Tern (*Hydrochelidon nigra*); Common Skua (*Stercorarius catarrhactes*) (fig. 117); Richardson's Skua (*S. crepidatus*); Long-tailed Skua (*S. parasiticus*); Pomatorhine Skua (*S. pomatorhinus*).

Order 7.—Plovers (Limicolæ)

Here are included birds with long pointed wings and long legs. The toes are not as a rule webbed, and the first toe is very small. Young precocious. The distribution is world-wide.

They include Plovers, Curlews, Phalaropes, Sandpipers (fig. 116), Woodcock, Snipe, &c.

British types are the Golden Plover (*Charadrius pluvialis*) (fig. 117), the Lapwing or Peewit (*Vanellus cristatus*), distinguished by its handsome crest and peculiar wailing cry, the

Fig. 116.—Sandpipers (*Totanus*)

Woodcock (*Scolopax rusticula*), and the Common Snipe (*Gallinago cœlestis*), both these last possessing long, straight, slender beaks.

The remaining British species are:—Stone Curlew (*Œdicnemus scolopax*); Pratincole (*Glareolus pratincola*); Ringed Plover (*Ægialitis hiaticula*); Kentish Plover (*Æ. Cantiana*); Dotterel (*Eudromias morinellus*); Oyster-Catcher (*Hæmatopus ostralegus*); Grey Plover (*Squatarola Helvetica*); Turnstone (*Strepsilus interpres*); Sanderling (*Calidris arenaria*); Bar-tailed Godwit (*Limosa Lapponica*); Black-tailed Godwit (*L. Belgica*); Great Snipe (*Gallinago major*); Jack Snipe (*G. gallinula*); Ruff (*Machetes pugnax*); Curlew (*Numenius arquata*); Whimbrel (*N. phæopus*); Grey Phalarope (*Phalaropus fulicarius*) (fig. 117); Red-necked Phalarope (*P. hyperboreus*); Common Sandpiper (*Totanus hypoleucus*); Wood Sandpiper (*T. glareolus*); Green Sandpiper (*T. ochropus*); Dunlin (*Tringa alpina*); Knot (*T. canutus*); Little Stint (*T. minuta*); Sharp-tailed Sandpiper (*T. acuminata*); Purple Sandpiper (*T. striata*); Curlew Sandpiper (*T. subarquata*); Temminck's Sandpiper (*T. Temmincki*).

Order 8.—Bustards and Cranes (Alectorides)

This is a somewhat artificial assemblage of forms which agree in many respects with the game-birds, differing, however, in minor anatomical characters. The young are precocious.

Bustards are thick-set birds common in the open parts of

Fig. 117.—Skuas (*Stercorarius*), Phalarope (*Phalaropus*), and Golden Plovers (*Charadrius*) (from left to right)

the Old World, including Australia. The Great Bustard (*Otis tarda*) was formerly abundant in Britain, but is now only an occasional visitor. The male possesses curious white "whiskers" made up of hair-like feathers.

Cranes resemble herons and storks in their general appearance, but are distinguished from them by a number of characters, one being that the short first toe is raised a little off the ground. Further, the young are precocious instead of being helpless. The Common Crane (*Grus cinerea*) (fig. 118) is now only seen wild in Britain as a rare visitor, but 300 years ago was common. It ranges over most of Europe, North Africa, and Asia.

Order 9.—Rails (Grallæ)

These cosmopolitan birds are closely allied to those of the following order, but are of more slender build, with feebler wings, shorter tail, and less compact plumage. Many of the species have lost the power of flight.

Common British examples are the Land-Rail or Corn-Crake (*Crex pratensis*), the peculiar creaking call of the male being a

Fig. 118.—Common Crane (*Grus cinerea*). (From an instantaneous photograph)

familiar sound on summer evenings, the Water-Rail (*Rallus aquaticus*), the Moor-Hen (*Gallinula chloropus*), and the Coot (*Fulica atra*). The toes of the last-named species are lobed. The Spotted Crake (*Porgana marnetta*) also occurs in this country.

Order 10.—GAME-BIRDS (Gallinæ)

One has only to think of the appearance of ordinary fowls to realize the leading characteristics of this order. The body is plump and supported on strong legs adapted for rapid progression, and provided with strong claws suitable for scratching up the ground. The neck is fairly long, and the rounded head is provided with a strong beak, the upper half of which projects beyond the lower. The young are precocious, and soon able to look after themselves.

All the various domestic breeds of fowls, despite their extreme diversity in appearance, would appear to be descendants of the Red Jungle-Fowl (*Gallus Bankiva*), a species which ranges across North India from Kashmir to Assam, and also extends farther east as far as the Philippines. In general appearance these birds much resemble game-fowls, and, like their tame relatives, possess a notched fleshy comb, and a pair of wattles hanging from the throat.

Jungle-fowl are closely related to the *Pheasants*, which have a wide range in the Old World. The common Pheasant (*Phasianus Colchicus*) is not a native of this country, but of Asia Minor and South-east Europe. Other species extend the distribution of the group to East Asia, which must be considered its head-quarters. The male bird, as in so many other cases, is much more brightly coloured than the female, and this difference is emphasized in many exotic forms, as particularly in the Gold and Silver Pheasants (*Chrysolophus pictus* and *Gennœus nycthemerus*), both of which are natives of Eastern Europe.

Conspicuous among domesticated game-birds in this country are the Peacock (*Pavo cristatus*), found native in India and Ceylon, Guinea-Fowl (*Numida meleagris*), belonging, as the name indicates, to West Africa, and the Turkey (*Meleagris gallopavo*), from the southern parts of North America.

Other well-known inhabitants of Britain are: Partridge (*Perdix cinerea*); Red-legged or French Partridge (*Caccabis rufa*), intro duced about a century ago; Quail (*Coturnix communis*); Capercailzie (*Tetrao urogallus*); Black Grouse (*Lyrurus tetrix*); Red Grouse (*Lagopus Scoticus*); and Ptarmigan (*L. mutus*), the last being remarkable for the changes of plumage exhibited at different seasons of the year.

The Red Grouse deserves special mention, for, with the exception of certain fresh-water fishes, it is the only vertebrate species peculiar to Britain.

Order 11.—Tinamous (Crypturi)

This is a small group of South American birds which are locally called "partridges", a name which at once suggests their general appearance and size. Though, however, appearing to have certain points in common with game-birds, they are also allied to flightless birds (ostriches, &c.), as is evidenced by the structure of the skull and by the much-reduced tail, the quills of which are not supported by a ploughshare-bone resulting from the fusion of the last few vertebræ (see p. 144).

Fig. 119.—Peregrine Falcon (*Falco peregrinus*)

Order 12.—Eagles and Vultures (Accipitres)

It has been a frequent practice to associate together as "birds of prey" eagles, vultures, owls, and their allies; but the association, like many others founded mainly on habit, is an artificial one, and it is now considered better to make two groups of such birds. The one under consideration includes those forms which hunt their prey in the daytime. The beak is hooked and the toes are furnished with formidable talons, but the great toe is not reversible as in owls, being permanently directed backwards. The plumage is compact, and the eyes face to the side.

Four groups are here included—Falcons, vultures, American vultures, and secretary-birds.

Falcons.—Most of these forms pursue living prey, while both head and neck are as well provided with feathers as the other parts of the body.

As a type of the true falcons, the Peregrine Falcon (*Falco peregrinus*) may be taken, and this form is of particular interest on account of its former use in hawking. The head and upper side of the body are dark, and the under side light with black barrings (fig. 119). The short beak is notched at the sides, and the legs and cere are yellow. It ranges through Europe and away to Japan in the east and North-east Africa in the south.

The Kestrel or Windhover (*Falco tinnunculus*) is a familiar species closely related to the preceding, but much smaller. Its range is similar.

The remaining British Falcons are:—Merlin (*Falco æsalon*); Hobby (*F. subbuteo*); Red-footed Falcon (*F. vespertinus*).

Another group closely related to the true falcons is that of eagle-like birds, including not only eagles, but also kites, buzzards, hawks, and harriers. The eagle par excellence is the Golden Eagle (*Aquila chrysaëtus*), of which the eyries are still to be found in the Highlands and along the west and north of Scotland, while a few are to be seen on the west coast of Ireland. Its geographical range is very considerable, including Europe, North Asia, North Africa, and the greater part of North America. We have also the White-tailed Eagle (*Haliaëtus albicilla*). The Crowned Harpy (*Harpyhaliaëtus coronatus*) is a crested eagle, widely distributed in South America.

A familiar example of the smaller eagle-like birds is the rapacious Sparrow-Hawk (*Accipiter nisus*), which is common in the well-wooded parts of Britain. Long-legged and slender in its proportions (fig. 120), this bird is otherwise not unlike a falcon as regards the character and markings of the plumage, but is distinguished by shorter wings, more gently curving beak devoid of notches at the side, and a peculiarly dashing flight. The female Sparrow-Hawk destroys more game than any other native bird of prey. As to range, this form extends throughout Europe, North Asia, and North Africa, while allied species are found in most parts of the globe.

The other eagle-like birds of Britain are:—Common Buzzard (*Buteo vulgaris*); Rough-legged Buzzard (*B. lagopus*); Marsh Harrier (*Circus æruginosus*); Montagu's

RÜPPEL'S VULTURE (*Gyps Rüppeli*)

This powerful bird is an inhabitant of the Western Soudan. Its strong hooked beak and well-developed talons show it to be a bird of prey, while the bare neck is characteristic of the group of Vultures to which it belongs. In tropical countries dead animals begin to putrefy very rapidly, and would constitute a serious nuisance were there not some natural provision for their speedy removal. Vultures are typical scavengers; the bare necks of these creatures are an obvious adaptation to their nauseous but useful habits.

10

RÜPPEL'S VULTURE (GYPS RÜPPELI)

A STUDY FROM THE LIFE

Harrier (*C. cineraceus*); Hen Harrier (*C. cyaneus*); Kite (*Milvus ictinus*); Osprey (*Pandion haliaëtus*); Honey Buzzard (*Pernis apivorus*).

Vultures.—Here are included large birds which for the most part feed on carrion, and therefore play an important part in nature as scavengers, in accordance with which habit the head and neck are as a rule devoid of plumage, or only provided with short stiff feathers. The long beak is sharply bent down at the tip, and there is a large cere. These birds are common in the warm parts of the Old World.

A well-known species is the Black Vulture (*Vultur monachus*), which ranges from the European and African shores of the Mediterranean to India and China in the east. Its beak is black, like its plumage, while the bare head and neck are flesh-coloured, the latter being further distinguished by a peculiar ruff of feathers, as commonly is the case in birds of the group. Another typical form is Rüppel's Vulture (*Gyps Rüppeli*), a native of North Africa.

Fig. 120.—Sparrow-Hawk (*Accipiter nisus*)

American Vultures differ in a number of respects from those of the Old World, as particularly in the absence of a syrinx (the organ of voice specially characteristic of birds), and the lack of a partition between the right and left nostrils. To this group belongs the largest of living flying birds, the Condor (*Sarcorhampus gryphus*) of the Andes, in which the spread of the wings may be as much as 9 feet. The shining black plumage is relieved by a white neck-ruff, and by white and grey shading on the wings. In the male there is a fleshy outgrowth or wattle on the top of the head. These birds, though mainly carrion feeders, also prey on living animals.

Secretary-Birds.—The only representative of the last group of diurnal birds of prey is the well-known Secretary-Bird (*Serpentarius secretarius*), which ranges from South Africa far north along both sides of the continent. In general appearance it looks like a modified eagle mounted on stilts, and may exceed 4 feet in height. The naturally long tail is made still longer by the great extension of its middle pair of quills, and projecting backward from the head on each side is a loose crest which suggesting a bundle of quill pens carried above the ear, has given rise to the popular name. The plumage on the head, neck, and front part of the body and wings is mostly light-grey, but the top of the head, with the crests, the quills (except the middle pair of the tail), the abdomen, and the tops of the legs, are much darker in hue.

Secretary-Birds feed on reptiles, small mammals, and game birds.

Order 13.—Ducks, Geese, and Flamingoes (Anseres)

In this large order the large bill is usually broad and flattened, and the three front toes are united by a web. The young are "precocious", *i.e.* able to run about and feed themselves almost at once, as is familiarly illustrated by the case of the duckling. Species belonging to the order are found in all parts of the world.

Ducks and *Geese.*—These are short-legged birds with broad straight bills and smooth plumage which easily sheds the water. They are essentially adapted to an aquatic life, and their clumsy movements on land are familiar to all. A common type is the British Wild Duck (*Anas boschas*), from which our domesticated varieties are derived. The brilliant colouring of the drake is too familiar to need description. This species ranges over the whole of the Northern Hemisphere. *Shoveller Ducks* are distinguished from other ducks by the peculiar shape of their unusually large bills. The Common Shoveller (*Spatula clypeata*) is a winter visitor in Britain. Among other British ducks, Teal (*Querquedula quetta*), Widgeon (*Mareca penelope*), and Eider Ducks (*Somateria mollissima*) may be mentioned here.

The remaining native ducks are:—Pintail (*Dafila acuta*); Tufted Duck (*Fuligula cristata*); Pochard (*F. ferina*); Golden-eye Duck (*F. glaucion*); Scaup (*F. marila*); Ferruginous Duck (*F. myroca*); Long-tailed Duck (*Harelda glacialis*);

Smew (*Mergus albellus*); Goosander (*M. merganser*); Red-breasted Merganser (*M. serrator*); Velvet Scoter (*Œdemia fusca*); Black Scoter (*Œ. nigra*); Sheldrake (*Tadorna cornuta*).

Geese are heavier and clumsier birds than ducks, and there is a curious knob on the tip of the bill. The domestic form is in all probability descended from the Grey-lag Goose (*Anser cinereus*) (fig. 121), which breeds only in Britain, and ranges from our islands throughout Europe and as far east as China. The Egyptian Goose (*Chenalopex Ægyptiacus*) was domesticated by the ancient Egyptians, who much appreciated it as an article of diet, as is attested by sculptures.

Fig. 121.—Grey-lag Goose (*Anser cinereus*)

Other British geese besides the Grey-lag are:—White-fronted Geese (*Anser albifrons*); Pink-footed Geese (*A. brachyrhynchus*); Bean Geese (*A. segetum*); Brent Geese (*Bernicla brenta*); Bernicle Geese (*B. leucopsis*).

Swans are large birds related to the geese, but distinguished by their long slender necks and shorter bills. The common White or Mute Swan (*Cygnus olor*) is distributed through Europe, and also ranges into Asia and North Africa. We have also Bewick's Swan (*C. Bewicki*) and the Whooper (*C. musicus*). Remarkable species as regards colour are the Black Swan (*Cygnus atratus*) of Australia and the Black-necked Swan (*Cygnus nigricollis*) of the southern parts of South America.

Flamingoes are large birds which give a general impression of swans mounted on storks' legs, but are peculiar in regard to the beak, which is very large and bent sharply downwards for the greater part of its extent. The species are not very numerous, but have a wide distribution, being absent, however, from the colder regions of the globe and from Australia. The Common

Flamingo (*Phœnicopterus roseus*), like all its allies, is distinguished by the prevailing red colour of the plumage, the predominant shade in this case being rose-pink relieved by the black wing-quills and scarlet wing-coverts. The black-tipped beak is otherwise rose-coloured, as are the legs and feet. This particular species ranges from the south of France and Spain eastwards to Siberia and India, and southward to the Cape.

Order 14.—HERONS and STORKS (Herodiones)

The birds of this order are long-legged waders with powerful wings and long strong pointed beaks. The feet are either not

Fig. 122.—Herons and their Nests

webbed at all or only partially so, and in the latter case the great toe is always free. The order includes the groups of herons, storks, and ibises.

Herons (fig. 122).—These are slenderly-built birds with narrow beak, and in most cases a slender neck. The wings are large but blunt-tipped, and there is a curious patch of "powder down" feathers on each side of the rump, *i.e.* of downy feathers the tips of which readily crumble into powder. The plumage is somewhat loose, and the head or adjacent parts are often crested. Herons are mostly found in marshy places, preying upon fish, or it may be other small animals. Though commonest in tropical and subtropical regions, they are also widely distributed elsewhere, and are best known in Britain as represented by the Common Grey Heron (*Ardea cinerea*), the unfortunate bird which was the chief victim of the ancient sport of falconry. This species ranges eastwards to Japan, and southwards to the Cape. Bitterns and Boat-billed Herons are other members of the group.

Besides the Grey Heron, we have in Britain:—Common Bittern (*Botaurus stellaris*); Little Bittern (*Ardetta minuta*); Night Heron (*Nycticorax griseus*).

Storks.—These are not so slenderly built as herons, and do not possess the patches of powder-down feathers. The three front toes are connected together at their bases by a small web. Like herons, they haunt swamps and inland waters, feeding largely on frogs, and their distribution is equally wide.

The White Stork (*Ciconia alba*) is found in most parts of Europe, from which it ranges into North Africa, Central Asia, and India. This bird is a familiar object on the Continent, enjoying for the most part immunity from human attack, and nesting on chimneys, the gable-ends of buildings, &c. It plays a large part in fairy tales and stories, as everyone knows who has read "Andersen's Fairy Stories", and who has not? All will remember that the Stork is supposed to bring the new brothers and sisters, as witness the story of the irreproachable Peter, whose invocations to this invaluable bird were rewarded by the appearance of a brother and sister at the same time. Closely related to ordinary storks are the large, ungainly Adjutants or Marabout Storks of Africa and India, with enormous bills. They feed not only upon small living animals, but also on carrion, and in accordance with this habit the head is destitute of ordinary feathers.

Ibises.—Smaller than the average members of the preceding groups, these birds possess beaks which are only hard at the tip. Their wings are pointed and their tails abbreviated. In habits and distribution they are very similar. The best-known species is the African Ibis (*Ibis Æthiopica*) (fig. 123), which was venerated and embalmed by the ancient Egyptians, and which, with its long curved beak and bald black head and neck contrasting with the generally white plumage, is a striking object. Its head-quarters are now the upper waters of the Nile, from which it ranges with diminishing numbers to Cape Colony. A beautifully - coloured form is the Scarlet Ibis (*Guara rubra*) of tropical America and the West Indies, in which the plumage is bright scarlet except the wing-tips, which are black.

Fig. 123.—African Ibis (*Ibis Æthiopica*)

The widely distributed *Spoonbills* are closely related to the Ibises, but are distinguished by the peculiar form of the broad straight beak, which widens out into a rounded end. The White Spoonbill (*Platalea leucolodia*) is a common European bird which also ranges into North Africa and eastward to India and North China. It is but rarely seen in our own country. The beak and legs are black and the plumage prevailingly white

Order 15.—PELICANS and CORMORANTS (Steganopodes)

This order of swimming birds includes short-legged forms in which all four toes are well developed and connected together by a web. The wings and tail are large, and the organization is adapted for the pursuit of fish. Four groups are here included: Pelicans, Cormorants, Frigate-Birds, and Tropic-Birds.

Pelicans.—These well-known birds are distinguished by their enormous flattened beaks, to the lower half of which is attached a large pouch in which fish can be stored. "Feeding time" with the Pelicans is one of the favourite spectacles of interest at the Zoo. The group is widely distributed in the warmer parts of the globe, and its members haunt the banks of rivers and the neighbourhood of swamps. The best-known species is the European Pelican (*Pelecanus onocrotalus*), which is found not only in South Europe, but North Africa, and also in parts of West Africa.

Cormorants.—These are smaller birds than the pelicans, and are characterized by their long bodies and necks and the possession of a moderately long beak, rather narrow, and hooked at its tip. Both face and throat are bare of feathers. Cormorants are excellent divers and swimmers, and their greediness is extreme. Two species are well known in British seas. One, the Black Cormorant (*Phalacrocorax carbo*), has an extraordinarily wide range, including all Europe, North Africa, most of Asia, and the Atlantic shores of North America. The other British species is the Green Cormorant or Shag (*P. graculus*). The Chinese and Japanese train cormorants to fish for them, and, until properly trained, a ring is put round the neck to prevent the captures from being swallowed.

Other birds related to the cormorants are *Gannets* and *Darters*. Of the former the most familiar type is the Common Gannet (*Sula bassana*), found on the coasts of the northern seas, and breeding in vast numbers at one locality on the east coast of Britain, the Bass Rock. The Scottish name for this bird is the Solan Goose, a name which suggests its general appearance, though about the neck and head it is much more like a cormorant. The head and neck are buff-coloured and the wing-tips black, but otherwise the plumage is white. The "boobies", so named from their fearlessness, of which we read in accounts of voyages to southern seas, are closely allied to gannets.

Darters or *Snake-Birds* are a small group with exceedingly long flexible neck, small head, and long, extremely sharp-pointed beak. The legs are attached far back to the elongated body. These forms haunt the inland waters of South America, Africa, India and Further India, and Australia.

Frigate and *Tropic Birds* are both distinguished by their pelagic habits, *i.e.* they are commonly found in the open sea at great distances from land. Each group contains but a single genus, and the distribution is similar, as both of them are found in the warmer parts of the Atlantic, Pacific, and Indian Oceans.

The Great Frigate-Bird (*Fregatus aquila*) is a striking object, with its long, hooked beak, powerful wings, and forked, swallow-like tail. The legs are extremely short, and feathered to the toes, which have but an imperfect web. The dark plumage of the male is relieved by a bright-reddish throat. Tropic-Birds are well known from their habit of following ships. They are

Fig. 124.—Albatross (*Diomedea exulans*)

small and light-hued, differing from Frigate-Birds in the shape of the beak, the complete webbing of the toes, and the nature of the tail, of which the two middle quills are much elongated. The commonest species is the Red-beaked Tropic-Bird (*Phæthon æthereus*), prevailingly white in colour, but with a coral-red beak.

Order 16.—Petrels and Albatrosses (Tubinares)

The birds of this order are good swimmers, and have webbed feet not unlike those of the next two orders. They are essentially marine, and have a wide distribution, being commonest, however, in the seas of the southern hemisphere. The members of the group are distinguished by being "tube-nosed", *i.e.* the nostrils open upon a pair of forwardly-directed tubes. All are powerful flyers, and their food consists of fish, various small marine animals, and refuse of various kinds. The strong beak, with sharp, hooked tip, is well adapted to the carnivorous habit.

The Wandering Albatross (*Diomedea exulans*) (fig, 124), distinguished by its enormous spread of wing (10 to 12 feet), and

Fig. 125.—Great Auk (*Alca impennis*)

found chiefly in southern seas, is immortalized in Coleridge's *Ancient Mariner*. Almost as well known is the Storm Petrel (*Procellaria pelagica*) of the North Atlantic, called "Mother Carey's Chicken" by sailors. It is only 6 inches long, and is the smallest web-footed bird found in British seas.

Order 17.—Divers and Grebes (Pygopodes)

The diving birds are distinguished by the modifications they have undergone to enable them to pursue fish. In accordance with this, the short legs are attached to the body extremely far back, and the feet are either webbed or the toes are broadened out into lobes. As in a pigeon, there are three forwardly-directed digits, but the great toe, instead of being well-developed, is either small or absent, not being required in birds which are not in the habit of perching on branches and the like. The wings are comparatively short, and are useful not only as organs of flight, but to assist the animal in swimming. The straight beak is more or less flattened from side to side. Auks, Divers, and Grebes are included in this order. Of the first group perhaps the most interesting is the Great Auk, or Gare-Fowl (*Alca impennis*) (fig. 125), which is unfortunately extinct, the last specimens having been shot in 1844. It formerly occurred in great numbers on some small Icelandic islands, and Funk Island, near Newfoundland, to which localities it largely resorted for breeding purposes. Its small wings were useless for the purposes of flight, a fact which had much to do with its extinction. All the remaining flightless birds are limited to the southern hemisphere. The nearest living relative of the Great Auk is the Common Razorbill (*Alca torda*) (fig. 126), which is common in British seas and has a wide range along both shores of the North Atlantic. Near the Auks come the *Guillemots*, with narrower and straighter beaks. The type form is the Common Guillemot (*Uria troile*), which has a similar distribution to the Razorbill. Much more peculiar forms are the *Puffins*, called "sea parrots" from the shape of their exceedingly large and laterally-compressed bills. The Common Puffin (*Fratercula arctica*) is the only kind found in British waters, and has a winter range from the Arctic regions to the Tagus on the eastern shore, and to New York on the western shore, of the Atlantic. The orange-coloured beak, shading into red at the tip, and the white plumage covering the breast and sides of the head, make this bird a conspicuous object.

Other British Auks are:—Little Auk (*Mergulus alle*); Black Guillemot (*Uria grylle*).

The *Divers* differ from the auks in several particulars, the most obvious of which is found in the greater length and sharpness of the beak. The Great Northern Diver (*Colymbus glacialis*), which ranges from the Arctic regions to the Mediterranean and is not infrequent on British coasts, is distinguished by its black head, throat shaded with black and white, and dark back crossed by rows of white flecks. The under side is white, as in so many birds and other animals.

There are two other British Divers:—Black-throated Diver (*Colymbus arcticus*); Red-throated Diver (*C. septentrionalis*).

Grebes resemble the preceding groups in many respects, but their toes are expanded into lobes instead of being webbed, and

Fig. 126.—Razorbills (*Alca torda*)

the tail is very small, and provided with a downy tuft instead of the usual quills. The plumage of Grebes is much used for ornamental purposes, and its beauty is mainly due to the silky white feathers which cover the breast.

The most familiar member of the group in Britain is the Dabchick or Little Grebe (*Podicipes fluviatilis*), a bird which has a very wide range and is common on rivers and ponds.

Other Grebes which occur in British waters are:—Slavonian Grebe (*Podicipes auritus*); Great Crested Grebe (*P. cristatus*), Red-necked Grebe (*P. griseigena*); Eared Grebe (*P. nigricollis*).

Order 18.—Penguins (Impennes)

Penguins are web-footed birds with reduced great toe, resembling the divers in a number of particulars, but still better adapted to an aquatic life, as is seen especially in the wings, which are useless for the purpose of flight and are transformed into flippers covered with very numerous scale-like feathers. The hind-limbs, in which the tarso-metatarsal region is unusually short, are fixed to the body very far back, and the small tail, unprovided with efficient quills, serves as a prop by which the body is steadied in the upright position which is habitual on land. The long, straight beak, somewhat flattened laterally and with a sharp point, is well adapted for seizing and holding the fish which constitute the chief food. Penguins have a very wide range along the shores of the continents and islands south of the equator, flocks of them being abundant even on the desolate Antarctic coast. Few birds, if any, are so remarkable in appearance, and they have attracted the attention of all travellers in southern seas.

As examples may be taken the Emperor Penguin (*Aptenodytes Forsteri*) of the Antarctic regions, which is about 3½ feet high; the King Penguin (*Aptenodytes Pennanti*) (fig. 127) of Kerguelen Land; and the Blue Penguin (*Eudyptula minor*) of South Australia and New Zealand, which is less than half that size.

II. Running Birds (Ratitæ).—These birds, of which the most familiar form is the African ostrich, are mostly large, while all are flightless, this being to some extent compensated by the possession of unusual powers of rapid progression on the ground. The group is essentially one belonging to the southern hemisphere.

Inability to fly is associated with a number of structural features, foremost among which is a great reduction in the size of the wings. There are also a number of characteristic features about the plumage, which is not arranged in definite tracts as in flying birds (see p. 142). The quills, which in ordinary birds play such an important part in flight, are here much reduced, and the barbules of the feathers are not connected together by hooklets. The vertebræ of the tail are not fused together into a ploughshare-bone as in flying birds, there being no efficient tail-quills to support. The name of the group (Lat. *rates*, a raft) has reference to the absence of a keel on the broad sternum. It will be remembered that the keel in an ordinary bird (p. 145) serves for the attachment of the large muscles of flight. There is no "merry-thought", while the scapula and coracoid are in the same line with one another instead of being at an angle. The overlap-

Fig. 127.—King Penguin (*Aptenodytes*)

ping uncinate processes, which in a flying bird help to strengthen the chest, are here absent or few in number.

The strong legs are well adapted for running, and in nearly all cases there is a reduction in the number of toes.

The structure of these birds is best explained on the assumption that they are descended from carinate birds in which the power of flight has been lost, and their nearest relatives are probably the Tinamous.

The Ratitæ which are now living may be divided into African Ostriches American Ostriches, Cassowaries and Emeus, and Kiwis.

African Ostriches are distributed through the deserts of Africa, and also range into Arabia and Syria. The small flat head is provided with a strong, broad beak, capable of being opened very widely, and large eyes surrounded with small bristly feathers resembling eyelashes. Both the head and the long neck are covered with long fluffy feathers. The legs are immensely powerful, and are used as weapons as well as for locomotion. Only two toes are present—the third and fourth, the former being much the larger, and there is a soft pad on the under side of each, much as in a camel. The plumage of the female is grey, that of the male black, except the wings and tail, which are pure white. There are no after-shafts to the feathers. The nest is simply a hollow made in the sand, and several hens lay their yellowish-white eggs in it. The work of incubation is almost entirely done by the male.

There are apparently several species of ostrich, the most familiar one (*Struthio camelus*) being distinguished by its red neck, while an East African form has a bluish neck, and this region is grey in a smaller kind from South Africa.

American Ostriches or *Rheas* are only found in South America, and can be distinguished at once by the presence of three toes, less modified than those of the African form, feather-covered head and neck, larger wings, and no tail. In structure (including the absence of after-shaft) and habits they resemble in most points the African forms, and their eggs are of similar colour. The plumage is grey, and both sexes closely resemble one another in this respect.

Three species are recognized, of which the Common Rhea (*Rhea Americana*) is largest and best known. It is commonest in the pampas region of the Argentine Republic, ranging north to Bolivia and south to the Rio Negro. Darwin's Rhea (*Rhea Darwini*) is found from the east of Patagonia to some distance north of the above-named river, while the Long-billed Rhea (*Rhea macrorhynca*) is limited to North-east Brazil.

Cassowaries and *Emeus* are to be regarded as the ostriches of the Australian region. They agree with the rheas in possessing three toes, but the wings are much reduced, the feathers appear double from the presence of very large after-shafts, and the eggs are green and rough.

The Emeu (*Dromæus*), found only on the Australian continent

THE AFRICAN OSTRICH (*Struthio camelus*)

African Ostriches are the largest living members of the group of Running Birds (Ratitæ), all of which are restricted to the Southern Hemisphere. The South African variety represented is the one domesticated for the sake of its feathers, and is somewhat smaller than a variety which lives farther north. African Ostriches possess but two toes, and this reduction is related to the specialization of the legs for the purpose of rapid locomotion. The extinct Æpyornis, of which bones and eggs are found in Madagascar, was an immense form related to the Ostrich, and possibly the prototype of the "Roc" which figures largely in Eastern tale and legend.

SOUTH AFRICAN OSTRICHES (STRUTHIO CAMELUS)

A STUDY FROM THE LIFE

and some of its islands, resembles an ostrich in appearance, but is shorter-necked and has a slenderer body. The feathers of the head and upper part of the neck are very small, and the plumage generally is very loose, the feather barbules being widely separated. Unlike ostriches, these birds are monogamous, but, as in them, incubation is carried on by the male. The young birds are striped.

Cassowaries (*Casuarius*) (fig. 128) are restricted to North

Fig. 128.—Cassowary (*Casuarius*)

Australia, Ceram, New Guinea, and adjacent islands. Their appearance is very striking, and in some respects they are the most modified of all the running birds. The head and upper part of the neck are bare and brilliantly coloured—blue, red, green, or yellow, according to the species. In some cases there are fleshy outgrowths or wattles on the neck. The beak is not unlike that of an ordinary fowl in shape, and there is a peculiar "casque" on the top of the head, formed by an outgrowth from the skull. The shining plumage is bluish-black, and resembles hair in texture rather than feathers. The small wing bears four or five quills, represented, however, only by their shafts. Feathers extend down to the ankle-joints of the legs, which are characterized by the further feature that the innermost toe bears a claw twice as long as those on the other toes.

Unlike the other ostrich-like birds, they inhabit forest-regions. The nesting habits, so far as known, resemble those of the emeu.

The *Kiwis* (*Apteryx*) (fig. 129) are New Zealand birds of remarkable appearance, and much smaller than the preceding forms, being about the size of a hen. The reduction of wings and tail is greater than in the other running birds, and their plumage is more hair-like, peculiarities which confer a certain grotesque resemblance to a man with his hands in his pockets. Two marked characters at once distinguish them from the ostrich-like forms of the same group. One is the slender snipe-like beak at the end of which the nostrils are situated. The other is found in the presence of the first toe. The legs are very strong, and all four toes are provided with powerful claws. At the base of the beak are a number of long whisker-like feathers. Kiwis are nocturnal birds, and resemble the emeu and cassowary in their nesting habits. The cream-coloured eggs are of relatively enormous size, being about 5 inches in length.

Fig. 129.—Kiwi (*Apteryx*)

CHAPTER IV

STRUCTURE AND CLASSIFICATION OF REPTILES

The two great groups of Backboned Animals so far considered, *i.e.* Mammals and Birds, are both characterized as "warm-blooded", for the animals included possess hot blood which is maintained at a practically constant temperature independently of external conditions. This peculiarity is associated of necessity with very perfect breathing arrangements (see pp. 45 and 147), and results in great activity and high intelligence.

Contrasted with these two high groups we have the Reptiles and still lower forms, which are "cold-blooded", in the sense that the blood is of the same approximate temperature as the surrounding medium—air or water, as the case may be—and is therefore hot in hot weather and cold in cold weather. Such animals, as compared with Mammals or Birds, are in the main sluggish, and not remarkable for intelligence.

Reptiles are a very ancient group, and probably form the stock from which both Mammals and Birds have been derived, on which subject more will be said in another section of the book. Reptiles preceded Mammals as the dominant Vertebrates both on sea and land, and many remarkable groups once existed which are now entirely extinct. Recent Reptiles include crocodiles, lizards, turtles, and snakes, with their respective allies. The most average forms are probably *Lizards*, of which there are three British species, and a brief description of the most typical of these will be an appropriate introduction to the study of Reptiles in general.

The Sand Lizard (*Lacerta agilis*) is commonly to be found on sunny slopes in this country, and appears to be especially abundant where the soil is of a sandy nature. When thoroughly warmed by basking, it is capable of moving with considerable rapidity, hence the specific name *agilis*. Average specimens are not more than 5 or 6 inches long, but this length is sometimes exceeded by 2 or 3 inches.

External Characters.—The flattened triangular head, with blunt forwardly-directed apex, is separated by a short ill-marked neck from the long rounded trunk, and this again passes into a very long slender tail. The shape is well adapted to the darting movements by which the animal makes its way through heather and grass. The limbs are short and primitive-looking: they are divided into the same regions which we have found to be typical for Mammals (p. 24) and Birds (p. 140); *i.e.* upper arm, fore-arm, and hand for the front-limb, corresponding to the thigh, lower leg, and foot in the hind-limb. There are five fingers and five toes, all ending in claws, and the shortest digits in their respective limbs are the thumb and great toe. The body is not lifted well off the ground by the limbs, and this is not because these are short, but owing to their "sprawling" arrangement, knee and elbow projecting outward, instead of being brought well below the trunk, as in a dog, cat, or other Mammal.

Returning to the head, the flatness of which as compared with a Bird is due to the relatively small brain, we note a large mouth extending far back from the front end of the snout, near the tip of which can be seen the two small nostrils. Further back come the good-sized eyes, which, as in a Bird, are provided with a nictitating membrane (p. 140), as well as with upper and lower eyelids. Some little distance behind either eye, not far from the angle of the mouth, is an auditory aperture, devoid, as in Birds, of an external flap or pinna. Here, however, the external passage of the ear (external auditory meatus), which leads down to the tympanic membrane, is excessively short, so that the membrane is brought close to the surface, and can readily be seen without dissection.

The only other aperture of importance is that of the cloaca (p. 146), a transverse cleft on the under side of the trunk where it passes into the tail.

While Mammals are distinguished by the possession of hair, and Birds by their feathers, Reptiles have an exoskeleton of scales, which, like hairs and feathers, are products of the outer layer of the skin, or epidermis. Bony plates, or bony scutes formed in the deeper part of the skin (dermis), may be present as well. The scales of the Sand Lizard are very obvious structures with a definite arrangement. Those on the head are comparatively large, and it has been found convenient to give some of them special names, as their arrangement is constant for a given species, and is therefore an important aid to classification. The scales on the upper side of the trunk are small, but those on its under side are much larger, and arranged in longitudinal rows, while those of the tail are also of a good size, and arranged in regular encircling rings.

The colour of the Lizard harmonizes with its surroundings, and this "general resemblance" is both "protective" and "aggressive", as it renders the animal inconspicuous as well to its own foes as to the insects upon which it preys. The ground colour of the male is greenish on the upper side, shading into lighter colour below; but in the female duller tints of grey or brown predominate. Both sexes are darkly marked on the upper side, there being an especially well-marked stripe running down the middle of the trunk.

Endoskeleton (fig. 130).—The same regions are present as in a bird, but though there are many points of agreement there are numerous differences, partly due to the great peculiarity of the bird. The lizard's bones do not contain the air-cavities which are so often found in birds.

In the *skull* the brain-case is much smaller in proportion than in a bird, a fact directly related to the relative size of the brain in the two animals. With few exceptions the bones of the skull are the same as in the bird, but the boundaries between them remain fairly distinct in the adult, instead of fusing together so as to obliterate all boundaries. There is one occipital condyle (see p. 28), or rounded prominence for union with the backbone, each half of the lower jaw is made up of several pieces, and the presence of a movable quadrate bone enables the mouth to be opened very widely (see p. 143): all points of agreement with Birds and difference from Mammals. An interesting peculiarity is found in the presence of a small hole, the *parietal foramen*, in the top of the brain-case. Imbedded in the floor of the mouth, and giving attachment to the muscles of the extremely mobile tongue, is the gristly "hyoid apparatus", made up of a central pointed portion, from which three slender rods run out on each side.

The *backbone* consists of a large number of vertebræ, and is fairly flexible throughout, exhibiting neither of the extremes which characterize the Pigeon (see p. 144). The usual regions can be made out, except that it is not possible to say where the thoracic vertebræ end and the lumbar ones begin, and the numbers are as follows:—Cervical, 8; thoracic and lumbar together, 22; sacral, 2; caudal, very numerous, but of no constant number. The ends of the centra or bodies of the vertebræ are neither flat as in Mammals nor saddle-shaped as in Birds, but concave in front and convex behind, or, technically speaking, *procœlous.* This is the commonest arrangement among recent reptiles. The first two joints of the neck are constituted by atlas and axis as in a Mammal (see p. 26) or Bird; but the odontoid peg which projects forwards from the front end of the latter is never fused with, though firmly fixed to, it. The peg is in reality a bit of the atlas centrum which has been appropriated by the axis for the purpose of making a pivot. There are two interesting peculiarities about the tail, one of which consists in the presence of small Y-shaped bones united to the under sides of many of the caudal vertebræ, the stem of the Y being directed downwards. In this way a canal is formed in which the great blood-vessels of the tail are sheltered, an arrangement which is found in various groups of backboned animals. Another and more interesting peculiarity is found in the fact that the body of almost every vertebra in this region remains unossified, *i.e.* is not of bony nature, across a narrow central strip. The tail of a lizard is extremely brittle, partly as a result of the arrangement described, and this would appear to be a defensive provision, whereby, supposing the animal to have been attacked in the rear by an enemy, a part is sacrificed to save the rest.

Slender curved *ribs* are attached from the fourth neck-vertebra right back to the sacrum, and, as elsewhere, the first thoracic vertebra is taken to be the one bearing the first rib that is connected with the sternum. Only five pairs are so connected in the Sand Lizard, the means of union being slender gristly *sternal ribs,* by which the bony *vertebral ribs* are continued in the downward direction (see p. 29). Each of the two sacral vertebræ possesses a strong transverse process on each side, by which attachment to the hip-girdle is effected, and it has been shown that these processes ossify or become bone independently of the bodies of these vertebræ, fusing with them subsequently. On this account the processes are looked upon as ribs which have united with the vertebræ to which they belong—a phenomenon which is paralleled elsewhere.

The *sternum* is an insignificant lozenge-shaped piece of cartilage, running back behind into a couple of slender rods, with which the hinder sternal ribs are united, while the others connect with the two posterior sides of the lozenge.

Skeleton of Limbs.—This is in many ways interesting, being to a large extent of what is called "generalized type", an expression which deserves a little examination, as it embodies an important idea constantly recurring in biological works. It often happens that in examining a series of human contrivances designed to meet the same or a similar end, a kind of general plan or similarity will be found to run through all of them. Under such circumstances it would very likely be possible to pick out some one of the series which might be looked upon as embodying the ideas involved in a general kind of way, and from which, by modification, the other members of the series might be derived. This case would form a *generalized type* of the entire series. A good instance is that of various kinds of habitation, of which the moderate-sized houses which make up a formal row may be taken as generalized types. In such a house would probably be found, among other apartments, breakfast-room, dining-room, drawing-room, study, and a certain number of bedrooms, all these, let us suppose, of reasonable size, and square or rectangular shape. Modifications of such an average plan might be effected in one or more of the following ways:—(1) Variation in *shape*: the dining-room, for example, might be oval or polygonal. (2) Variation in relative *size*: the drawing-room, say, might be the same size as the dining-room, or smaller, or it might be larger. (3) Variation in *number*, either on the side of increase, as by addition of a second drawing-room, or on the side of decrease, as by reducing the number of bedrooms. In the latter case a particular sort of room, perhaps the study, might be made so small as to deserve the name of a "vestige", and the next step would be its complete suppression. (4) Coalescence, or fusion of rooms, as, for instance, by complete or partial removal of the party-wall separating two adjoining rooms. By application of these principles of alteration, a small cottage on the one hand, or a castle on the other, might be referred to the same type as the average house, and it is obvious that dwellings of all styles and sizes are, after all, neither more nor less than houses or places of human habitation, and must fulfil certain average requirements. It may also be noted, in passing, that the house illustration may be made to illustrate very well another biological principle, *i.e.* "change of function", already alluded to in the Introduction (p. 13). A room intended for a particular purpose may be, of course, used for some other purpose, as when what should be a study is converted into a nursery. An amusing case is known to the writer of a small tradesman, who, on retiring, thought of taking a house of more ambitious nature than the one that had been connected with his shop. Seeing a bath-room for the first time, he remarked that he had no use for it, and would make it a lumber-room.

Some meaning will now be attached to the expression "generalized type" as applied to the limbs of a lizard. But we may go a step further, and speak of a "theoretical type", by which is meant an arrangement so generalized that it is rarely, if ever, found in existing animals. The endoskeleton of the limbs of terrestrial vertebrates is best understood by reference to such theoretical types, which may here be conveniently explained.

As has already been pointed out (see pp. 29 and 145), the skeleton of either fore- or hind-limb consists of a girdle by which attachment to the trunk is brought about, and the skeleton of the free limb, and it has also been indicated (p. 24) that there is a correspondence or *serial homology* between fore- and hind-limb.

Girdles.—The theoretical type of *shoulder-girdle* consists of a dorsal piece, *scapula*, and two ventral pieces, the larger, *coracoid*, behind, and the smaller, *precoracoid*, in front. At the junction of the scapula with the other elements is a shallow *glenoid cavity*, to which the bone of the upper arm is attached. The *hip-girdle* consists similarly of three pieces—a dorsal *ilium*, uniting below with a ventral and anterior *pubis*, and a ventral and posterior ischium. Corresponding in position to the glenoid cavity is a somewhat deeper cup, the *acetabulum*, for the attachment of the thigh-bone.

Free Limb.—If the limb of a lizard be spread out at right angles to the body, in what is usually called the *primitive position*, and a line or axis drawn down its centre, an anterior or *preaxial* edge can be distinguished from a posterior or *post-axial* edge, and an upper or *dorsal surface* from an under or *ventral surface*. Taking first the fore-limb, we find an upper-arm bone or *humerus*, down the centre of which the axis runs, and succeeding this in the fore-arm, two bones, a preaxial *radius*, a post-axial *ulna*. Next

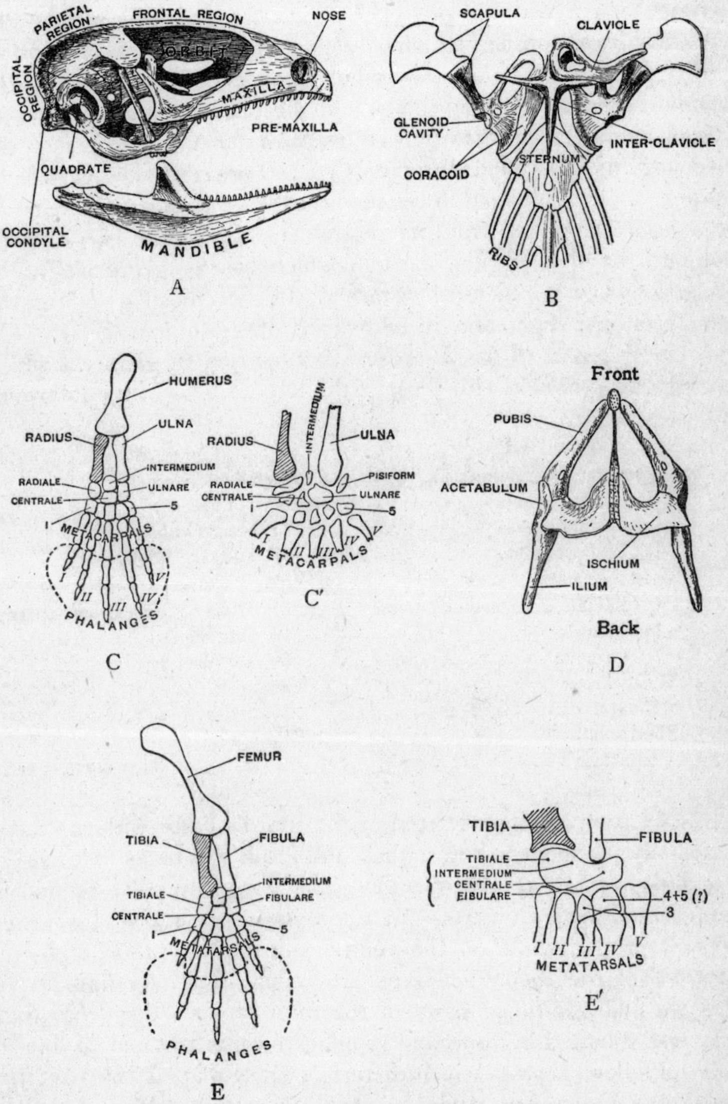

Fig. 130.—Skeleton of Lizard

A, Skull. B, Sternum and Shoulder-Girdles. C, Pattern Fore-Limb; 1 and 5, first and fifth carpalia. C, Wrist of Lizard. D, Hip-Girdles. E, Pattern Hind-Limb; 1, first tarsale, 4+5, fourth and (?) fifth tarsalia. E′, Ankle of Lizard.

comes the wrist (*carpus*), made up of a number of small elements, arranged in a near or proximal and a far or distal row. The proximal row consists of three elements—a preaxial *radiale,* so called because it is on the radial side, an *intermedium* in the middle, and an *ulnare* on the side of the ulna. The distal row of carpal elements consists of five *carpalia* for the support of the five fingers, and called, beginning on the preaxial side, carpale 1, carpale 2, &c. Wedged in between the two rows of carpal elements is a *centrale,* named from its central position. The five carpalia support the five fingers, each of which has a *metacarpal* at its base, followed by slender *phalanges,* two of these going to the thumb or first digit, and three to each of the others.

The free part of the *hind-limb* is supported by elements which correspond precisely with those of the fore-limb, as in the following table:—

Fore-Limb.	*Hind-Limb.*
1. Upper-arm bone (humerus).	1. Thigh-bone (femur).
2. Bones of fore-arm:	2. Bones of lower leg:
(*a*) Preaxial radius.	(*a*) Preaxial tibia.
(*b*) Postaxial ulna.	(*b*) Postaxial fibula.
3. Wrist (carpus):	3. Ankle (tarsus):
(*a*) Radiale, intermedium, ulnare	(*a*) Tibiale, intermedium, fibulare.
(*b*) Centrale.	(*b*) Centrale.
(*c*) Carpalia: 1, 2, 3, 4, 5.	(*c*) Tarsalia: 1, 2, 3, 4, 5.
4. Metacarpus:	4. Metatarsus:
Metacarpalia: 1, 2, 3, 4, 5.	Metatarsalia: 1, 2, 3, 4, 5.
5. Phalanges:	5. Phalanges:
Thumb, 2; other digits, 3 each.	Great toe, 2; other digits, 3 each.

If we compare the skeleton of the lizard's limbs with the theoretical arrangement just described, the result will be as follows:—

Fore-Limb—Shoulder-Girdle.—The dorsal scapular section is represented by two parts—an upper *supra-scapula* and a lower *scapula* proper, while on the ventral side both *coracoid* and *pre-coracoid* of the theoretical type are seen. But over and above this we find additional parts in the form of a slender *collar-bone* (clavicle) situated in front, and running towards the middle line to join its fellow, besides which there is a cross-shaped *inter-clavicle,* belonging to neither girdle, but coming between them, and also attached to the sternum. *Free Limb.*—Here there is a very close correspondence with the theoretical type, differences being chiefly seen in the presence of an accessory bone in the carpus coming just outside the ulnare, and the presence of an extra phalanx in the third digit, and two extra phalanges in the fourth digit. The extra carpal bone is known as a *pisiform*, and is of different nature from the rest, for it has been developed in the course of a tendon (see p. 48), the muscle belonging to which acquires thereby a greater leverage.

Hind-Limb—Hip-Girdle.—Except in unimportant particulars we get a very close agreement with the theoretical type, all three elements—*ilium*, *pubis*, and *ischium* being present. *Free Limb.*—There is considerable departure from the simple type as regards the tarsus, the proximal part of which is represented by one element, probably representing tibiale, intermedium, fibulare, and centrale, all fused together. Only two distal elements can be seen in the tarsus; one of these is probably tarsale 3, for the third digit is united with it, while, since digits 4 and 5 both unite with the other distal elements, it perhaps may be regarded as equivalent to the two corresponding tarsalia fused together. It is not clear what has become of the first and second tarsalia. The digits are supported by the same number of phalanges as in the hand. One point is specially worthy of remark, *i.e.* the ankle-joint comes in the *middle* of the tarsus, not, as in Mammals, between the tarsus and bones of the lower leg. Such a mesotarsal ankle-joint is characteristic of both Reptiles and Birds (see p. 146).

Digestive Organs (fig. 131).—Lizards feed on insects, small worms, and the like, and possess numerous small conical teeth, and a very mobile forked tongue. The teeth are not lodged in sockets as in a Mammal, but are fixed on to the inner sides of the bones which form the margin of the upper and lower jaws. There are also two small groups of teeth on the palate. It is particularly worthy of notice that reptilian teeth, as compared with those of ordinary Mammals, are not only extremely numerous, but not divided into different kinds—incisors, canines, &c. And while a Mammal develops two sets of teeth, a Reptile has, as a rule, an indefinite succession of them, a worn-out tooth being replaced by a new one, which grows up at its base. The tongue can be protruded to some distance, and is worked by a well-developed set of muscles attached to the hyoid apparatus, the large size of which is thus accounted for.

The *digestive tube* or *gut* into which the mouth-cavity is continued consists of a *gullet*, wide slightly curved *stomach*, fairly long coiled *small intestine*, and short wide *large intestine*, terminating in a *cloaca*. A large *liver*, provided with a *gall-bladder*, and a small *pancreas*, open into the beginning of the small intestine.

Circulatory Organs (fig. 131).—As in Mammals and Birds, we can distinguish between blood system and lymph system, of which only the former need here be considered.

Blood System.—This is a closed system of tubes, consisting of heart, arteries, veins, and capillaries, in which the cold blood circulates. Seen under the microscope, a drop of lizard's *blood*

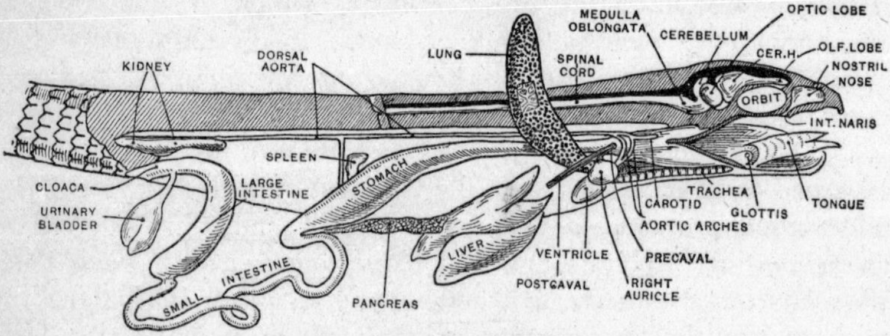

Fig. 131.—General Structure of Lizard. CER.H., cerebral hemisphere

presents much the same appearance as a drop of bird's blood, and is made up of a clear liquid plasma, in which float irregular white corpuscles capable of executing creeping movements, and oval red corpuscles, each of which is a nucleated cell.

The *heart* is enclosed in a double-walled pericardial sac, and is distinctly a more imperfect organ than in the Mammal or Bird, as, though there are two auricles, there is only one ventricle, and therefore the impure blood received by the right auricle from the body mixes to some extent with the pure blood received from the lungs by the left auricle. As will be seen, however, there are several devices by means of which the mixture of the two sorts is partly prevented.

The three great *caval veins*, two in front and one behind, bring back the impure blood to the heart, as in a Mammal or Bird (see fig. 102), but, instead of opening directly into the right auricle, they pour their blood into a thin-walled pouch, the *venous sinus*, which communicates by a valvular opening with the right auricle. As usual, the purified blood from the lungs is poured by pulmonary veins into the left auricle. The two auricles squeeze their blood through a single valvular opening into the thick-walled ventricle, but the two kinds of blood do not mix here, for the party-wall between the auricles projects into the opening, and divides it into a right half and a left half. Although the cavity of the ventricle is single, there is a well-marked ridge protruding into it which must be regarded as an incipient partition, and actually divides the ventricle when it contracts into a right half, mostly receiving impure blood, and a left half, mainly containing pure blood. Impure blood is pumped to the lungs through a *pulmonary artery* arising from the right half of the ventricle, just as the same artery is given off from the right ventricle in a Mammal or Bird (see p. 40 and fig. 102).

A notable peculiarity here deserves mention. In a Mammal (see p. 41) the great body-artery, known as the *aorta*, starts from the left ventricle in an *aortic arch*, which curves round to the left, while in a Bird there is a similar arrangement, except that the aortic arch curves round to the right. In the Lizard there is, as it were, a combination of both conditions. There is a *right aortic arch*, resembling a Bird's in that it arises from the left half of the ventricle and curves over to the right. Since this arch starts from that side of the ventricle which receives pure blood from the left auricle, it has blood of that sort pumped into it. And since the arteries supplying the head and fore-limbs are branches of the right aortic arch, these parts of the body are necessarily supplied with pure blood. And it is natural that the brain above all organs should get a pure blood supply, which it does in this way.

But there is also a *left aortic arch*, curving as in the Mammal, and conducting away some of the impure blood from the right half of the ventricle. The *dorsal aorta* is formed by the union of right and left arches, receiving pure blood from one, and impure blood from the other, and therefore supplying what may be called *mixed* blood to the trunk, tail, hind-limbs, and most of the internal organs. Yet another point deserves attention. Each of the aortic arches is *double* for part of its extent, and really represents a pair of arches fused together. The presence of one or more arches at the beginning of the great arteries of the body in terrestrial Vertebrates strikes one as peculiar, and without reference to Fishes is inexplicable. As will later be explained, however, it is an indication of descent from gill-bearing ancestors (see p. 244), for the circulatory organs of lung-bearing forms are not constructed on a brand-new pattern especially suited to their requirements, but are simply a modification of the more ancient arrangement found in fish-like animals. In both Mammals and Birds the modification is very perfect, and there is a complete separation of pure and impure blood; but in Reptiles and Amphibia the separation is less complete, and the relative sluggishness of these creatures is partly due to the fact that their bodies are to a large extent supplied with mixed blood, *i.e.* with blood which, being a mixture of pure and impure blood, is only imperfectly oxidized.

Not only does the Lizard possess an *hepatic portal system* (see p. 41), by which the blood of the digestive organs is carried to the liver, but there is also a *renal portal system* in connection with the kidneys, by which some of the impure blood from the hinder part of the body is supplied to those organs, the function of which is, as elsewhere, to get rid of nitrogenous waste.

Breathing Organs and Organs of Voice (fig. 131).—The arrangements connected with respiration are here much simpler than in either Mammals or Birds, which is what might be expected, as cold-blooded animals have not the same need for thorough and rapid oxygenation of the blood, though at the same time it must be remarked that Lizards exhibit less complication than is usual among Reptiles.

On the floor of the mouth behind the tongue there is a slit-like *glottis* leading into the organ of voice or *larynx* that forms the beginning of the *wind-pipe*, which runs back and forks into two bronchi, one for each lung (see p. 46). These air-tubes are supported by gristly rings, and thus prevented from collapsing. Nothing is present equivalent to the syrinx or song-box of a Bird (see p. 149). The *lungs* are spindle-shaped bags, the linings of which are raised into a honey-combing of ridges, by which the surface exposed to the air is considerably increased.

Nervous System and Sense Organs (fig. 131).—Only a few points call for special attention. As previously remarked (p. 192), the flatness of the head is an indication of the relatively small size of the *brain*. At the front end of this organ are the club-shaped *olfactory lobes*, which supply the fairly well developed organs of smell, and pass back into the smooth *cerebral hemispheres*, the relatively small size of which as compared with a Bird (see p. 149) is an index of inferior intelligence. Still farther back are two large *optic lobes*, much like those of a Bird (see p. 150), but placed side by side on the upper side of the brain instead of being separated from one another. Lastly comes the *medulla oblongata*, which passes gradually back into the *spinal cord*, and exhibits on its upper side, just behind the optic lobes, a small smooth lobe which corresponds to the complicated *cerebellum* found in a Mammal or Bird (see pp. 52 and 150). A side view of the brain shows clearly a sharp downward bend (cranial flexure) in the region of the medulla oblongata.

The same *sense organs* are present as in a bird, though there are many differences in detail; and it may be particularly mentioned that the complex bag or membranous labyrinth (see p. 150), which is imbedded in the side wall of the skull and constitutes the inner ear, is rather less complex.

In dealing with the skull it was mentioned that there is a small hole, the parietal foramen, in the roof of the brain-case. This hole is occupied by a rounded structure, which in some Lizards has clearly the structure of an eye, so much so that it is usually called the *pineal eye*. It is connected with a sort of stalk which runs upwards from that part of the brain-axis of which the cerebral hemispheres are outgrowths. Even in Lizards this unpaired eye is more or less degenerate, and it is only represented in most of the Vertebrates by the stalk just mentioned, to which the name of "pineal body" is usually given. Even in the human brain a pineal body can be distinguished, and the fact that the philosopher Descartes regarded it as the seat of the soul has invested it with a certain curious interest. It is clearly to be regarded as one of those "vestigial organs" or "vestiges" which are of common occurrence in the animal body, and represent the dwindling remains of structures which were of importance in ancestral forms.

Development.—The Sand-Lizard lays eggs much like those of a bird, but with softer shells.

Classification of Reptiles. — Leaving the numerous extinct groups out of consideration, as these will be dealt with elsewhere, Reptiles may be divided into five orders, as follows:—

1. Crocodilia: Crocodiles, Alligators, &c.
2. Chelonia: Turtles and Tortoises.
3. Lacertilia: Lizards.
4. Ophidia: Snakes.
5. Rhynchocephala: Hatteria, a lizard-like New Zealand form.

It may be well at this point to summarize the chief features, all of which have been illustrated in the foregoing description of a Lizard, in which these five groups agree, or, in other words, to give a definition of the Reptilia.

Reptiles are cold-blooded Vertebrates defended by an exoskeleton composed of either epidermic scales, or bony dermal scutes, or it may be of both. In those forms which possess well-developed extremities, there are always more than three digits in the fore-limb, and commonly five in the hind. *The skull is jointed on to the backbone by a single occipital condyle, each half of the lower jaw consists of several bones,* and the surfaces of the vertebral centra are not saddle-shaped. The sacrum is made up of two vertebræ. The interclavicle, when present, does not fuse with surrounding parts, and in existing forms the ilia do not extend far in front of the acetabula, both pubes and ischia unite together ventrally, and the tarsus fuses neither with the tibia nor with the metatarsus. *The ankle-joint is in the middle of the tarsus.* Conical teeth are usually present (except in Chelonia) and *the gut ends in a cloaca.* The heart possesses two auricles but (except in Crocodilia) only one ventricle, and in all cases the body is partly supplied with mixed blood. There is never less than one pair of aortic arches. The brain is small, and the optic lobes are placed close together on its upper side. *Breathing is in no case effected by means of gills.*

There are many points of agreement between Reptiles and Birds, and this is especially striking if extinct forms are taken into consideration. Those characters which are printed in *italics* in the above definition are common to both groups, which are often associated together into a larger division, the Sauropsida, contrasting with Mammals on the one hand and Ichthyopsida (Amphibia plus Fishes) on the other.

Order I.—Crocodiles (Crocodilia)

Crocodiles and Alligators (fig. 133) much resemble gigantic lizards in appearance, and agree with these in many particulars of structure, though decidedly of higher type. As is well known, these animals spend a large part of their time in water, and some of their peculiarities of structure are related to the aquatic habit. The large and hideous head provided with formidable jaws is separated by an ill-marked neck from a long body, and this again passes into a long and powerful tail, which is the chief swimming organ. The body is flattened from above downwards, and the tail, in correspondence with its function, from side to side. The sprawling lizard-like limbs do not lift the trunk well off the ground, the feet are webbed to some extent, and there are five digits in the fore- but only four in the hind-limb, the little toe being represented only by a small bone visible in the prepared skeleton.

Returning to the head, we find several arrangements that are of special use to an aquatic form. The slit-like nostrils are situated on the tip of the snout, and can be closed by muscular action so as to prevent entry of water when the animal is submerged, while their position enables breathing to go on when only a very small part of the body is above the surface. As in birds and lizards (as well as some mammals), the eye possesses not only upper and lower eyelids but also a third eyelid which can be drawn over it for protection, and the tympanic membrane, corresponding in position to that of the lizard (see p. 192), is provided with a little protective flap or "ear-lid" which can be folded over it.

The chief peculiarity of the *skin* (fig. 133) is found in the fact that it develops a very complete exoskeleton, composed externally of rectangular horny scales, which on the tail and upper and lower sides of the trunk are disposed in regular longitudinal and transverse rows. Some of these scales project upwards from the upper side of the tail, forming a jagged crest. This, however, is not all. Underlying the scales of the upper and sometimes of the under surface are sculptured bony plates (scutes), which are developed in the deeper part of the skin (dermis). The arrangement of the scales and scutes differs in different species, and affords characters which are of use in classification. The strong musky odour which distinguishes crocodiles is due to the secretion of musk-glands, some of which open on the edge of the upper jaw, others into the cloaca, and the remainder on the dorsal surface of the trunk.

The *endoskeleton* of the crocodile can be compared point for point with that of the lizard, though it presents a number of interesting peculiarities. In the large and massive *skull* the boundaries between the separate bones can be always made out, and the upper surface is sculptured something like the scutes. It is, indeed, almost certain that some of the flat bones which help to cover in the skull in those vertebrates possessing a bony skeleton are in reality scutes which have sunk inwards and attached themselves firmly to underlying parts.

The bones of the jaw are very long, and their margins present a large number of sockets, arranged in a single row, for the reception of the formidable pointed teeth. As in a bird or lizard, the lower jaw hinges on behind to an elongated bone known as the quadrate (see p. 143); but whereas in those forms the bone in question is more or less movable so that a sort of double jaw-joint is constituted, here it is firmly fixed to the skull. Such a double joint detracts somewhat from firmness, which is very necessary to an animal that, like a crocodile, has to overcome prey possessing considerable muscular strength. And further, the long jaws enable the mouth to be opened widely enough without the presence of a joint of the kind. A notable peculiarity is found in the very great length of the bony palate which supports the roof of the mouth, and above which runs a passage into which the cavities of the nose open, and along which air is conducted to and from the glottis, or aperture of the windpipe. In a bird or lizard the internal openings of the nasal cavities are situated on the roof of the mouth fairly far forwards, but in the crocodile the arrangement described throws them very far back, and as the top of the windpipe projects into them a distinct air-passage from the external nostrils backwards is constituted, so that breathing can take place when the tip of the snout is above water, even if the mouth be open, without any danger of water getting down into the lungs. Similar anti-choking arrangements are found in other air-breathing aquatic vertebrates, and will be described in another chapter.

The thoracic *ribs* exhibit one feature which is characteristic of birds, each of them having a backwardly-directed plate on its margin not very far from the backbone (see p. 145). These uncinate processes add to the firmness of the wall of the chest. Not only are ordinary ribs present, but also "abdominal ribs", situated behind the sternum and developed in connection with the muscles. It is interesting to note that ribs of the kind are also present in the oldest known fossil bird (*Archæopteryx*), which also approached reptiles in other more important particulars, such as the possession of teeth and a long jointed tail.

In the skeleton of the *limbs* the absence of clavicles may be noted (see p. 145), and also the fact that both tarsus and carpus are considerably modified. One of the bones of the former (calcaneum) has a heel-like projection, and this is the only case outside the Mammalia where anything of the kind is present.

The *digestive organs* (fig. 132) are interesting in a number of ways. The strong conical teeth which form an irregular row along the margin of each jaw are, as already mentioned, imbedded in distinct sockets, and, as in lizards, are replaced to an indefinite extent by successors which grow up from below and push them out as they get worn down with wear. When the jaws are

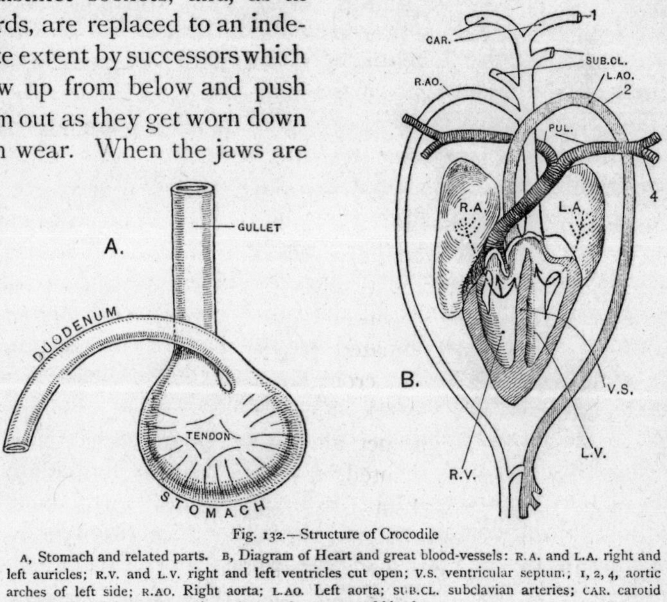

Fig. 132.—Structure of Crocodile

A, Stomach and related parts. B, Diagram of Heart and great blood-vessels: R.A. and L.A. right and left auricles; R.V. and L.V. right and left ventricles cut open; V.S. ventricular septum; 1, 2, 4, aortic arches of left side; R.AO. Right aorta; L.AO. Left aorta; SUB.CL. subclavian arteries; CAR. carotid arteries; PUL, Pulmonary arteries. Arrows show course of blood.

brought together the upper and lower teeth interlock, forming a very efficient arrangement for seizing and holding. There are no teeth on the roof of the mouth as in a lizard (see p. 199), and the tongue is a flat rounded organ devoid of any great mobility. Crocodiles are in the habit of pulling their prey under water and holding it there till drowned, during which operation a good deal of water must get into the mouth of the aggressor. In the way already explained this water is prevented from getting down into the lungs, and there are soft projections at the back of the mouth-cavity which can be brought together so as to keep it out of the gullet. In other words, the hinder part of the mouth-cavity is partitioned into a *pharynx* (see p. 34), which passes back into the wide *gullet*. This in its turn communicates with a *stomach* which is singularly bird-like, since part of it is modified into a muscular gizzard (see p. 146). The resemblance is strengthened by the crocodile's habit of swallowing stones, which presumably help, as in a bird, to grind up the food. This is the more necessary since the teeth are not suited for chewing, and the prey is either swallowed whole or in large pieces, according to its size. As in Birds and Lizards (see pp. 146 and 200) the *large intestine* terminates in a *cloaca*, which opens to the exterior by a longitudinally oval aperture situated on the under side of the root of the tail.

The *blood*, *heart*, and *blood-vessels* (fig. 132) are much like the corresponding parts in the lizard (see p. 200), the most important difference being that there are two ventricles, a feature possessed by no other known reptile. This limits the impure blood to the right side of the heart and the pure blood to the left, as in mammals and birds, but the advantage gained is less than at first sight appears, for the two kinds of blood mix *outside* the heart. This is so because we still have, as in the Lizard (see p. 201), two aortic arches, a right which takes origin in the left ventricle and carries off pure blood from it, and a left which conducts away impure blood from the right ventricle. It is clear, therefore, that the dorsal aorta, which is formed by the union of the two arches and which supplies the body behind the fore-limbs, must contain mixed blood, and the two arches also communicate by a small hole just where they leave the heart. A reduction of the aortic arches has taken place as compared with the Sand Lizard (see p. 191), for each of them is here single instead of being formed by the partial union of two. If the left arch were entirely done away with we should have a condition closely resembling that found in the bird (see fig. 102), and all parts of the body would be supplied by pure blood. There can be little doubt that some of the remote reptile-like ancestors of birds possessed circulatory organs much like those of the crocodile, and that in them part of the body was consequently supplied with mixed blood.

The *breathing organs* and parts connected with them differ from those of the lizard not only in the arrangement of the air-passages as already described, but also in the structure of the lungs themselves, which have relatively thick spongy walls. A similar arrangement, however, is found in some large lizards, and, speaking generally, it is only small reptiles which have very simple lungs. Crocodiles also possess an imperfectly-developed representative of the muscular partition known as midriff or diaphragm, which plays such an important part in the breathing movements of Mammals (see p. 46).

The *brain* of a crocodile is of higher type than a lizard's, both cerebral hemispheres and cerebellum being much larger in proportion. The *sense organs* are also more complex, especially those connected with smell and hearing. In the latter case it is interesting to note that the complex bag known as the membranous labyrinth (fig. 103), which constitutes the essential part of the inner ear, is shaped very much as in a bird, there being a well-developed curved tube to represent the coiled cochlea of Mammals.

Crocodiles are hatched out from eggs much resembling those of birds, and laid in holes or imperfect nests scooped out in the sand, where they get the benefit of the sun's heat. The young reptile has a horny wart on the tip of its snout, which helps it to break through the firm egg-shell.

The existing members of the order Crocodilia (fig. 133) are found in tropical and sub-tropical regions both in the New and Old Worlds. Three groups are commonly recognized:—(1) Alligators; (2) Crocodiles proper; and (3) Garials.

Alligators, with the exception of a Chinese species, are confined to the tropical parts of America. The snout is relatively short and broad, and the different teeth are of very unequal size, among the large ones being the first and fourth in the lower jaw, which bite into pits in the upper jaw in such a way that they are hidden from view when the mouth is shut. There are several special features in the skull, of which perhaps the most striking is the shortness of the region where the two halves of the lower jaw unite together in front. Some members of the Alligator group possess scutes on the under side of the body as well as on the upper. The hind-limbs have a rounded outline and the toes are only half-webbed.

Three species are known of the Alligator proper, one being found in China, and the others in the south-east part of North America, of which two by far the best known is the Pike-headed or Mississippi Alligator (*Alligator Mississippiensis*), which may attain the length of about 15 feet. The first name given to this creature expresses a resemblance to the fresh-water fish well known as the Pike.

The remaining members of the Alligator group, the *Caimans* or *Jacares*, are limited to Central America and the tropical parts of South America. The different species vary greatly in size; all but one, however, being much smaller than the Mississippi Alligator. Unlike the Alligators proper the Caimans possess ventral scutes, and those which make up the dorsal armour are firmly united with one another.

Crocodiles proper have a very wide distribution throughout the tropics, being found in America, Africa, South Asia, and North Australia. The head is somewhat narrower and longer than in alligators, and the teeth are not so markedly unequal. Although, as before, the large first lower tooth bites into a pit, this is not the case with the large fourth lower tooth, which merely bites into a groove and is partly visible when the mouth is shut. The united part of the lower jaw is rather longer than in alligators, as might be expected from the shape of the head, and there is no ventral bony armour as in caimans. The hind-limbs have a jagged posterior fringe, and the feet are more completely webbed than in alligators.

Probably the most familiar species is the Nile Crocodile (*Crocodilus Niloticus*), which was regarded as sacred by the ancient Egyptians, and like other animals which figured in their religion was considered worthy of embalmment. It has now been exterminated in the lower Nile, where it was formerly very abundant, and its range includes South Africa, Senegal, Madagascar, and Syria. Large specimens may considerably exceed the Mississippi Alligator in size.

The Indian Crocodile (*Crocodilus palustris*) ranges from Baluchistan to the Malay region, and avoids the tidal parts of rivers. Another Indian species, the Estuarine Crocodile (*C. porosus*), has exactly the contrary habit, as the name indicates, and is not only common in estuaries, but swims out to sea for a considerable distance. This fact is interesting, for the vast

Fig. 133.—Crocodilia

1. Chinese Alligator (*Alligator Sinensis*). 2. Spectacled Caiman (*Caiman sclerops*). 3. Nile Crocodile (*Crocodilus Niloticus*). 4. Ganges Garial (*Garialis Gangetica*).

majority of existing reptiles are confined to land or fresh water, though some of the extinct groups were exclusively marine. The Estuarine Crocodile is one of the fiercest and most dreaded species, and at the same time probably the largest, for a specimen has been recorded as having the great length of 33 feet. It ranges from the east of India to South China, North Australia, and the Solomon and Fiji Islands.

American Crocodiles have slender snouts, a feature possessed in an exaggerated form by a West African Crocodile (*C. cataphractus*).

Garials form a small group of crocodilian reptiles, distinguished by extremely slender snouts, and jaws armed with a large number of comparatively small teeth, all fairly equal in size and arranged with greater regularity than in the other forms. These special modifications convert the jaws into a very perfect fish-catching arrangement, which is paralleled in some of the aquatic Mammals (Cetacea). The first and fourth lower teeth bite into grooves above, and, as is but natural, the united part of the lower jaw is extremely long. The feet are more completely webbed than in other crocodilians, and both fore- and hind-limbs have a posterior ragged fringe. There are only two existing genera, both confined to the south of Asia.

Schlegel's Garial (*Rhynchosuchus Schlegeli*) is found in Borneo, and may attain the length of 14 feet. The better-known Gangetic Garial (*Garialis Gangetica*) is confined to the Ganges, Indus, Brahmaputra, and some smaller Indian rivers. It is of larger size than the Bornean Garial (20 feet), and the snout is longer and more slender. By the natives they are regarded as sacred.

Order 2.—Toothless Reptiles (Chelonia)

This order includes the Turtles and Tortoises, toothless Reptiles provided with a remarkable defensive exoskeleton.

The most familiar member of the group is the small Grecian Tortoise (*Testudo Græca*), common as a pet in this country, and indigenous to the south of Europe (fig. 134). The short broad trunk is enclosed in a strongly arched shell, forming a sort of box with an opening in front into which the head, neck, and fore-limbs can be withdrawn, and a similar opening behind for the benefit of the hind-limbs and stumpy tail. The head is rounded, and the toothless jaws, covered as in birds with firm horny sheaths, give it a very characteristic appearance. Two small rounded nostrils are seen close together on the front of the head, the fairly large eyes are provided, as in lizards, with three eyelids, and behind each of them is a depression in which the tympanic membrane is visible. Protection is afforded by a number of horny plates united by their edges. The immobility of the trunk is largely made up for by a fairly long and exceedingly

Fig. 134.—Grecian Tortoise (*Testudo Græca*)

flexible neck, covered by soft skin. When retracted it is thrown into an S-shaped curve. The stumpy limbs are adapted for terrestrial locomotion, and can lift the body well off the ground. As, however, the movements are extremely slow, defensive armour is a necessity, and on the slightest alarm the animal withdraws head, neck, tail, and limbs into the cover of the shell, when the protective arrangements are completed by the horny plates on the head and strong overlapping scales which are present on the limbs.

The usual limb-regions are present, though not well marked externally, and the existence of five digits in either extremity is indicated by a corresponding number of blunt claws.

The *exoskeleton* resembles that of caimans, in that there are not only horny plates and scales of epidermal nature, but also bony pieces developed in the deeper part of the skin both above and below. Here, however, these pieces cannot be stripped off with the skin, but are to a great extent intimately welded to parts of the internal skeleton. The arched upper or dorsal half of the shell is termed the *carapace*, and the flat under or ventral piece with which it is firmly united at the edges is the *plastron*. It will be convenient first to deal with the superficial horny shields and then with the underlying bony plates. Beginning with the carapace, there is a series of *neural shields* running down the centre, and these are flanked on either side by broad transverse *costals*, outside which again are more numerous *marginals*, forming a right and left series separated in the extreme front by a median *neck-shield* (nuchal) and behind by a pair of *caudals*. Some of the marginals on either side bend sharply round to the under surface and help to cover the bones of the plastron. The greater part of this, however, is veneered by six pairs of horny shields, of which those in front (gulars) and behind (anals) are smaller than the rest, which have received the names of humerals, pectorals, abdominals, and femorals.

When these horny shields are stripped off, a number of bony plates are exposed which have a very similar arrangement, though their number is not the same, and therefore, of course, their edges do not correspond with those of the overlying plates, as is the case with the armour of caimans. Running down the middle of the carapace are eight *neural plates*, which may be regarded as the flattened tops of vertebræ, and which are continuous on each side with a similar number of *costal plates* fused with the underlying ribs. The carapace is completed by a *nuchal plate* in the middle of its front margin and *pygal plates* similarly placed behind, while a series of eleven *marginal plates* are disposed on either side. The plastron is made up of one unpaired plate, and four others arranged in pairs. The former is possibly to be compared with the interclavicle of a lizard (see p. 198), while the others are in all probability to be regarded as equivalent to the abdominal ribs of the crocodile.

As will have been gathered from the foregoing description, there is intimate union between bony plates belonging to the external skeleton and parts of the *internal skeleton*, *i.e.* the ribs and trunk vertebræ, and we see here that the girdles of the limbs are brought within the shelter of the ribs, a remarkable and unique arrangement. The immobility of the trunk is largely made up for by the great flexibility of the neck, which is supported by eight vertebræ, of which the centra exhibit great variety in the shape of their ends. There is no breast-bone, the presence of the plastron rendering it quite unnecessary.

As regards the *skull*, it need only be noted here that the jaws possess a continuous sharp bony edge for the support of the horny sheaths which do duty as teeth. The lower jaw is jointed on to a massive quadrate bone which, as in a crocodile, is firmly fused with the rest of the skull.

The skeleton of the *fore-limb* corresponds pretty closely to the theoretical type, except that some of the bones have fused, as radiale with centrale, and carpale four with carpale five. In the *hind-limb* there is a fair correspondence with the type, but, as in Reptiles generally, there is a good deal of fusion in the ankle-bones and a tendency for the ankle-joint to come between the two rows of these.

The *food* of the Grecian Tortoise consists mainly of vegetable matter, but it also devours sundry small animals, such as worms, insects, and snails. The *digestive organs* present no points of very special interest, but it may be noted that the tongue is comparatively immobile, as in the crocodile, and, as in that animal, the large intestine ends in a cloaca which opens externally by a longitudinal slit.

Except as regards its flattened shape, the *heart* of a tortoise closely resembles that of the Sand Lizard (p. 191), and there is also agreement in reference to the great blood-vessels which enter and leave it, each of the two aortic arches, however, as in crocodiles and the larger lizards, being single instead of double for a part of its course. The body is therefore, as in other Reptiles, largely nourished by imperfectly-purified blood, and a tortoise is a particularly good example of the sluggishness and cold-blooded condition entailed by this arrangement. It also exhibits in a very marked way the great tenacity of life which distinguishes cold-blooded vertebrates when compared with birds and mammals.

The *breathing-organs* agree in most respects with those of

the crocodile, but the internal nostrils open on the roof of the mouth, as the habits of the animal do not require any special provision to be made for a distinct breathing tract as distinct from the cavity of the mouth. It may also be remarked that the immobility of the trunk presents a certain obstacle to the rapid renewal of the air in the lungs, and this is probably the chief reason for the sluggishness of chelonians.

The *brain* presents the usual parts, and is, for a reptile, of comparatively high type, being only inferior to that of the crocodile.

Tortoises are developed from hard-shelled eggs much like those of a bird. About a dozen of these are deposited together in a hole scooped out in the earth, and are afterwards carefully covered up. A warm spot is selected for the purpose, and the eggs, which are laid in early summer, are hatched out by the heat of the sun.

The following groups are recognized among the Chelonia, and in dealing with them space will only permit of allusion to some of the more interesting forms:—

(1) Leathery Turtles.
(2) S-necked Chelonia.
  (*a*) Land and Fresh-water Tortoises.
  (*b*) Turtles.
(3) Side-necked Tortoises.
(4) Soft Tortoises.

(1) *Leathery Turtles.* — This group contains but a single species, the Leathery Turtle or Luth (*Sphargis* or *Dermatochelys coriacea*) (fig. 135), which differs in many important particulars from other Chelonia, not only from the terrestrial and fresh-water forms, but also from the Turtles proper, which, like it, are marine. It is the only living representative of an important extinct group, some members of which attained a very considerable size, and is the largest existing marine species, being when full-grown over 6 feet long. The limbs are modified into large nailless flippers, which are very efficient swimming organs. These, however, are not its special peculiarity, for similarly modified limbs are found in ordinary turtles, but this is found in the nature of the "shell". The carapace is made up of numerous bony pieces united together in a tesselated manner and quite free from the

underlying ribs and vertebræ, besides which there is a complete absence of overlying horny plates, the place of these being taken by leathery skin raised into a small number of prominent longitudinal ridges. The plastron is not so well developed as in

Fig. 135.—Leathery Turtle (*Dermatochelys coriacea*)

ordinary turtles, and is covered by ridged skin resembling that on the upper surface. These creatures are found in the tropical parts of all the great oceans.

(2) The *S-necked Chelonia* include the large majority of existing species, and are so called because the head, when retracted, is drawn straight back into the shell, being at the time thrown into an S-shaped curve.

(*a*) *Land and Fresh-water Tortoises.*—The genus *Testudo* (figs. 134 and 136), to which the Grecian Tortoise (*Testudo Græca*) belongs, is a representative of the largest family of Land Tortoises, or indeed of Chelonia generally, including a score of genera which embrace between them some 113 species. The family is found in all parts of the world except Australia, New Guinea, and the related islands. Among the most interesting forms included in the same genus with the Grecian Tortoise are fourteen giant species, which either are or have been within the last 300 years inhabitants of some of the islands in the Indian and South Pacific Oceans. Of these probably the best known are those found in the Galapagos Islands off the north-east coast of South America. Several species have been described, one of which (*Testudo nigrita*) was described by Darwin as reaching such large dimensions that large specimens could only be lifted by from six to eight men.

The European Pond-Tortoise (*Emys orbicularis*) may be mentioned as a good example of a fresh-water form. In accordance with its aquatic habits, the shell is much flatter than in a land tortoise, and the feet are webbed. It is a native of South Europe, South-west Asia, and parts of North Africa. Specimens, mostly of small size, are often exhibited for sale in this country.

(*b*) *Turtles* are marine Chelonia obviously adapted for aquatic life, as may be seen from their flattened shells and paddle-like limbs, the digits of which have for the most part lost their claws. The front end of the carapace is notched, and the head can be only partly retracted. The true turtles somewhat resemble the Leathery Turtles (see p. 217) in form, a result of adaptation to the same sort of life, but, unlike the latter, the shell is covered by horny plates, and some of the digits have retained their claws. There are also important differences as regards the plastron and carapace. The former, though not so complete as in the Grecian Tortoise, is more so than in the Leathery Turtle, while the carapace is made up of the same elements as in the tortoise and is firmly connected with the internal skeleton. Two species may be noted here—the Green Turtle and the Hawk's-bill Turtle.

The Green Turtle (*Chelone midas*), found in all the warmer parts of the ocean, is the species which has attained a doubtful sort of fame in connection with aldermanic feasts. Its short beak devoid of a hook is well adapted for biting off the pieces of sea-weed which constitute the food. The horny plates which cover the carapace are united by their edges.

The Hawk's-bill Turtle (*Chelone imbricata*) has the same wide distribution as the preceding species, but is somewhat smaller. Its strongly-hooked beak accords with a carnivorous habit, and the overlapping horny plates covering the carapace are the source of "tortoise-shell".

(3) The *Side-necked Tortoises* are a rather remarkable assemblage of fresh-water form, owing their name to the fact that

Fig. 136.—Tortoise (*Testudo sulcata*) and Green Turtle (*Chelone midas*)

the head and neck cannot be drawn straight back into the hollow of the shell, but the same end is effected by bending back the head sideways. These tortoises are all restricted to the southern land-masses, and range right round the globe, being represented in South America, Africa, Madagascar, Australia, and New Guinea.

(4) *Soft Tortoises.*—These are found in the rivers of the

hotter parts of Asia, Africa, and North America, their name being derived from the fact that the shell is entirely devoid of any horny plates. Not only so, but the carapace is deficient as regards bony elements, the marginals being either absent or largely so, and it is not united to the plastron, which is still more deficient. The shape of the body and limbs accords with the thoroughly aquatic habit, but the latter are not so completely

Fig. 137.—Nilotic Soft Tortoise (*Trionyx triunguis*)

converted into flippers as in the turtles. The head is provided with a curious tapering snout, and is situated upon a very long mobile neck, which on the one hand can be retracted as in the S-necked forms, and on the other can be shot out with extreme rapidity. This is, no doubt, a useful acquisition to the large carnivorous members of the group, but is at the same time a very unpleasant one, for these large species are very fierce, and the natives are often badly bitten by them. The skin is of a greenish colour as a rule, with yellow spots.

Of the six genera included among the Soft Tortoises, *Trionyx* is by far the most important and also the most widely distributed, being the only one which extends into the New World as well as the Old. Typical species are the Gangetic Soft Tortoise (*Trionyx Gangeticus*), the Nilotic Soft Tortoise (*T. triunguis*) (fig. 137), which feeds largely on the eggs and young of the crocodile, and the common American Soft Tortoise (*T. ferox*), a native of the North American streams which flow into the Gulf of Mexico, and noted as a destroyer of the alligator's eggs and young.

Fig. 138.—Wall Gecko (*Tarentola Mauritanica*)

Order 3.—Lizards (Lacertilia)

The large Lizard order, of which a fair average sample has already been described at some length, embraces representatives in all parts of the globe except the polar regions, and includes no less than twenty families, containing about 1700 species. It will only be possible here to mention a few of the more interesting forms, included in the families of—1. Geckos; 2. Scale-footed Lizards; 3. Agamoids; 4. Iguanas; 5. Snake Lizards; 6. Venomous Lizards; 7. Monitor; 8. Common Lizards; 9. Skinks; and 10. Chameleons.

1. *Geckos* are small nocturnal lizards, with large eyes, and lobed feet adapted for climbing. They are found in all the warmer parts of the earth, and the Wall Gecko (*Tarentola Mauritanica*) (fig. 138) of the Mediterranean shores is the most familiar example. One structural feature of the family deserves notice here, *i.e.* the shape of the centra of the vertebræ. These are biconcave, a very primitive feature specially

characteristic of fish and low types of other vertebrate groups. In Reptiles generally it is most commonly the case that the centra are concave in front but convex behind.

2. *Scale-footed Lizards* make up a small family of snake-like forms found in Australia, Tasmania, and New Guinea. The fore-limbs are entirely wanting, though the hind-limbs are represented by lobe-like projections, but for which these creatures might well be mistaken for serpents. An examination of their structure, however, clearly shows that they are true lizards.

The Common Scale-foot (*Pygopus lepidopus*) of Australia and Tasmania may be mentioned as an example.

3. The family of *Agamoid Lizards* is a very large one, limited to the southern and eastern parts of the Old World. A typical form is the Black-lipped Tree-Lizard (*Calotes nigrilabris*) of Ceylon. Its body is of a metallic green tint, except the lips and sides of the head, which are black. Among the more remarkable members of the family are the so-called *Flying Lizards* or *Dragons* of South Asia, small forms which certainly do not live up to the latter name. These animals do not fly in the proper sense of the word, but there is a parachute-like expansion on each side of the body, supported by extensions of some of the ribs, and capable of being folded up or extended. The Malayan species (*Draco volans*) is well known. The *Thorny-tailed Lizards* of Africa and Asia have the tail covered with rings of spiny scales, and one species, the Dabb (*Uromastix spinipes*), is common in Arabia, Egypt, and Crete. Australia furnishes two remarkable species in the Frilled Lizard (*Chlamydosaurus Kingi*), which has the habit of walking about on its hind-legs, and the Moloch (*Moloch horridus*), covered with large thorny spines.

4. The *Iguanas* are, with few exceptions, found in the warmer parts of America and the West Indies. The Common Iguana (*Iguana tuberculata*) is a good type of the family, and the prominent toothed ridge running down the middle of the back is a characteristic feature. It is a vegetarian and lives mostly in trees, but is also a very active swimmer. It may attain a length of over 4 feet, which includes, however, the exceedingly long tail. One of the most interesting members of the family is the Galapagos Sea-Lizard (*Amblyrhynchus cristatus*), the only known marine member of its order. In size it rather exceeds the

Common Iguana, which it resembles in the presence of a dorsal-toothed ridge. The head, however, is smaller and rounder, and there is a group of conical scales on the upper surface, while the powerful tail is flattened from side to side and thus rendered an efficient swimming organ, there being also an indication of webbing between the digits. The food consists of sea-weeds. Among the most bizarre species related to the Iguanas are the Helmeted Basilisk (*Basiliscus Americanus*) of Central America and Costa Rica, which perhaps suggested one of the fabulous animals of mediæval zoologists, the somewhat similar Capuchin Lizard (*Corythophanes cristatus*) of Costa Rica, and the Californian Horned "Toad" (*Phrynosoma cornutum*), the general appearance of which certainly does suggest a spiny sort of toad, possessed, however, of a tail.

5. The *Snake-Lizards*, of which the name suggests the external appearance, have their head-quarters in Central America and the West Indies, but also occur north and south of this in the New World, and are represented in Europe, North Africa, and India. They not only possess horny scales but also underlying bony scutes, which on the top of the head attain a relatively large size.

The most familiar species is the Blind-Worm or Slow-Worm (*Anguis fragilis*), common in Britain, and having a wide range in Europe, occurring also in North Africa and in Asia. It is

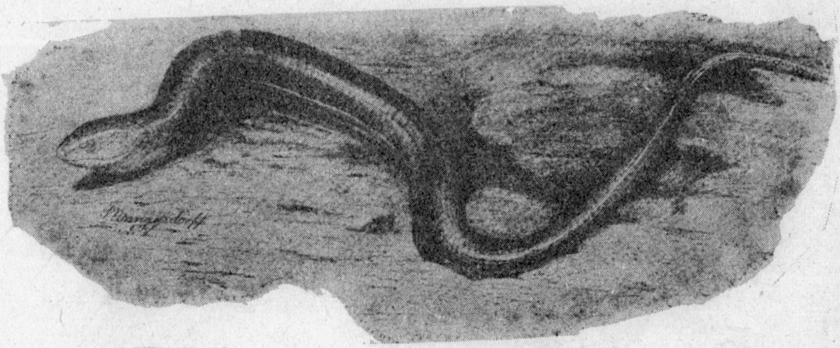

Fig. 139.—The Scheltopusik (*Ophisaurus apus*), a blind-worm native to S. Europe and S.W. Asia

often mistaken for a snake, and erroneously regarded as exceedingly poisonous. Its popular name dates back to the times when the word "worm" was applied to serpents, and a survival of this old usage appears to remain in some place-names, such as "Worms" Heath, in Surrey. The Blind-Worm exhibits no external trace of limbs, though vestiges of these are present in some of its relatives (see fig. 139), and its teeth are slender and fang-like. Its food consists of slugs, worms, insects, and the like. The specific name "fragilis" has reference to the readiness with which the tail breaks off when the animal is handled or struck, a protective arrangement not uncommon among lizards (p. 194).

6. *Venomous Lizards* are represented only by one genus containing two species, both North American, one being from Mexico (*Heloderma horrida*) and the other from Arizona (*H. suspecta*). They are carnivorous forms of considerable size, coloured and mottled in such a way as to make them conspicuous objects when seen apart from their natural surroundings. The poison arrangement is something like that found in snakes, there being slender fang-like teeth grooved to conduct a poisonous fluid from glands at their bases.

7. *Monitors* are the largest living lizards, and are distributed over the warmer parts of the Old World. In general proportions

Fig. 140.—The Nile Monitor (*Varanus Niloticus*)

they are not unlike the typical form previously described, with which also they agree in the possession of a well-developed forked tongue capable of being thrust far out of the mouth. A common species is the Nile Monitor (*Varanus Niloticus*), which ranges over most of Africa (fig. 140). The food consists of small vertebrates and various kinds of eggs, including those of the crocodile. The name Monitor embodies an erroneous idea that this creature hisses in a peculiar way when a crocodile approaches, and so gives a "warning" of its presence.

8. What may perhaps be called the *Common Lizards* (Lacertidæ) include some 100 species, distributed over Europe, Africa, and Asia. The Sand Lizard (*Lacerta agilis*) of Britain is one example, and the only other British member of the order (except the Blind-Worm), the Common Lizard (*Zootoca vivipara*), is another. Among the larger and handsomer forms may be noted the Green Lizard (*Lacerta viridis*), ranging from Portugal to Persia, and found abundantly as far north as Germany, and the Wall Lizard (*Lacerta muralis*), which is specially characteristic of the countries bordering the Mediterranean.

9. The *Skinks*, or *Burrowing Lizards*, constitute a family of which the distribution is world-wide. The Common Skink (*Scincus officinalis*), found on both sides of the Red Sea and on the north side of the Sahara, suggests in appearance a fish mounted on legs. The shape and smoothness of the scales are apparently features related to the burrowing habit, and the animal also possesses the useful power of seeing with its eyes shut, for the lower eyelid is provided with a transparent area which answers the purpose of a window.

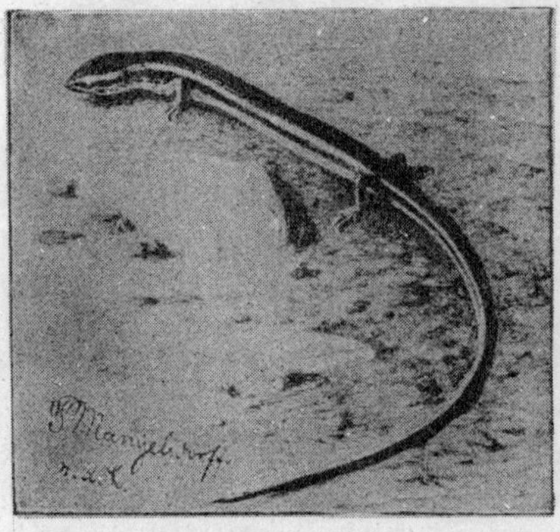

Fig. 141.—Snake-eyed Lizard (*Ablepharus pannonicus*)

The European Snake-eyed Lizard (*Ablepharus pannonicus*) (fig. 141) of South-east Europe and parts of South-west Asia is a slender creature with very small five-toed limbs.

The Three-toed Bronze Lizard (*Chalcides tridactylus*) of Italy, Sicily, Sardinia, and the opposite part of Africa, is snake-like in form, with small reduced limbs. From Roman times to the present day it has been groundlessly regarded as extremely venomous.

The most extraordinary member of the family, however, is the Stump-tailed Lizard (*Trachysaurus rugosus*) (fig. 142) of Australia, with short flattened tail, strong limbs provided with well-developed claws, and very prominent regularly-arranged scales.

10. *Chameleons* are small tree-inhabiting reptiles, familiarly known as possessing the power of changing the colour of their skins to harmonize with the surroundings for the time being.

Fig 142.—Stump-tailed Lizard (*Trachysaurus rugosus*)

They exhibit many remarkable peculiarities of structure related to climbing and the capture of their prey, which consists of insects. They form a well-marked group, differing so much from the other subdivisions of lizards that it would probably be better to consider them as a distinct order. The scales are very small and granular, and the remarkable head is possessed of enormous eyes which can be moved independently of one another, while each is provided with a circular eyelid, in the middle of which is a small round hole. There is no external trace of organs of hearing. Both limbs and tail are modified for climbing. The tongue is club-ended and worm-like, and can be rapidly protuded to a distance equalling the length of the body (exclusive of the tail). Being rendered sticky by a special secretion, it forms a very efficient insect-catching apparatus. The lungs of Chameleons are of interesting structure, there being an approach to the air-sacs of Birds (see p. 148), for each lung, though fairly spongy and thick-walled in front, is produced behind into a number of thin-walled slender processes which extend between the various internal organs. It does not appear however that these outgrowths are of much use in breathing, but they can be distended with air so as to swell out the body. This may be a protective arrangement.

Nearly fifty species of Chameleon are known, of which the vast majority are natives of Africa and Madagascar, though

Fig. 143.—Common Chameleon (*Chamæleo vulgaris*)

outlying members of the group are found in Arabia, India, and Ceylon, while one species, the Common Chameleon (*Chamæleo vulgaris*) (fig. 143), ranges round the eastern and southern shores of the Mediterranean, and also extends into the south of Spain.

Order 4.—SNAKES (Ophidia)

Although at first sight there seems to be a great deal of difference between snakes and lizards, careful examination shows that there are important points of resemblance, and some zoologists include the two groups in a single order, *Squamata*, among the distinctive features of which are the possession of well-marked overlapping scales, a transverse cloacal opening, quadrate bone movably attached to the skull so as to give a double jaw-joint, and simple lungs.

The elongated cylindrical form is well suited for gliding through thick undergrowth or herbage, and it may be for climbing, while some snakes are modified for swimming and others for burrowing. The resemblance to the limbless lizards is striking, but here as elsewhere too much importance must not be attached to similarity of shape, as this may result from the same or similar habits in animals which are not closely related. No snake ever possesses the least trace of fore-limbs, even their girdles being entirely absent, as also is the sternum. Snake-like lizards, on the other hand, may have very small fore-limbs or external traces of the same; and if not, as in the blind-worm, dissection shows that the girdles are represented, nor is the sternum ever absent. As regards hind-limbs, these are generally entirely absent in snakes, but vestiges are in some cases to be found one on each side of the cloacal aperture.

The head is small and flattened, passing without any perceptible neck into the trunk, and that again into a gradually-tapering tail. In nearly all cases the mouth is a wide slit, and a small rounded nostril can be seen on each side of the snout at or near its tip. The stony stare which is so characteristic of a snake is due to a very peculiar arrangement. Instead of upper and lower eyelids, there is a circular area of transparent skin by which the eye is protected, and occupying the space between this and the front of the eyeball is a tear-chamber always full of the secretion of the tear-gland.

Numerous overlapping *scales* cover the body, these being replaced on the head and under surface of the body by horny plates. *Ventral shields*, as those in the latter position are termed, are never to be seen in the limbless lizards. Snakes exhibit a great variety of colouring and marking, by which protection or other purposes are served, as will be seen elsewhere. One very characteristic habit, not peculiar to this group, however, is the periodical shedding of the outer part of the skin. The snake wriggles out of this slough, turning it inside out in the process.

The internal organs of snakes (fig. 144) exhibit a number of peculiarities, dependent partly on the elongated shape of the body, partly on the way in which prey is secured and swallowed, and partly on the manner of locomotion. The first factor, for example, influences the number of the vertebræ, and the way in which the internal organs are packed into the long but narrow space available for the purpose.

The *skull* is made up of very hard and polished bones, its most notable features being the loose union between the various bones connected with the jaws. The two halves of the lower jaw, for instance, are not firmly united at their tip, as is the case of most reptiles, but are only connected by an elastic ligament which permits of a good deal of stretching. Not only so, but the upper jaw also is capable of a good deal of movement. This flexibility has to do with the necessity for great expansion in the act of swallowing large prey, and also plays a large part in enabling poisonous forms to use their poison-fangs effectively. It may also be noticed that the hyoid apparatus is extremely small. The long *backbone* is made up of some two or three hundred vertebræ, the centra of which have the usual reptilian shape, *i.e.* concave in front and convex behind. Such a large number of ball-and-socket joints give a very large amount of flexibility, but some provision is necessary to impose a limit to this, as otherwise dislocation would be liable to occur when complicated curvings were being described. This is partly provided for by overlapping articular processes on the arches of the vertebræ, as in most Vertebrates with well-ossified backbones (see p. 26), but in addition to these a pair of wedge-shaped projections stick out from the front of each arch and fit into corresponding pits at the back of the preceding one. It should be mentioned that similar processes are found in some other reptiles, as, for example, Iguanas, where, however, they are not so well developed.

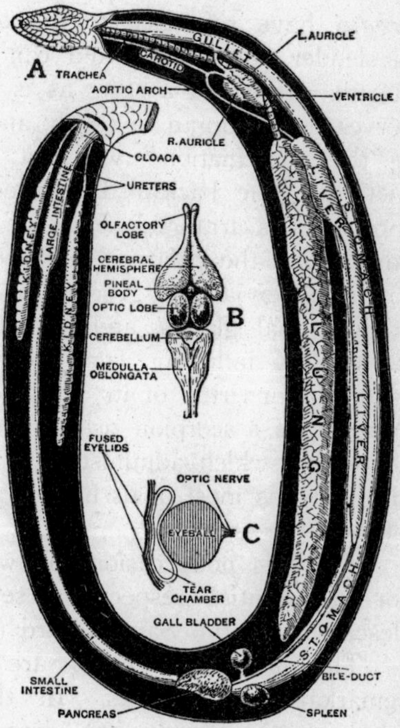

Fig. 144.—Structure of a Snake

A, General dissection. B, Upper side of brain. C, Diagrammatic vertical section to show tear-chamber in front of eye.

In the absence of both sternum and pelvis, means of distinguishing between regions of the backbone largely fail, and though the first two vertebræ are undoubtedly cervical, it is best to speak of the rest as divided into two kinds only—trunk vertebræ and tail vertebræ. Each of the former kind bears a pair of simple curved *ribs*, the free ends of which are firmly connected to a pair of the ventral epidermal shields.

The most interesting features connected with the *digestive organs* have reference to the tongue and teeth. The former is slender and forked, and can be drawn back into a kind of sheath. It is not a sting as is popularly believed, but probably serves as an organ of touch, and may perhaps also play a part in the "fascination" which a snake seems to exert over its victims. The backwardly-curved, sharply-pointed teeth are in most snakes arranged along the margins of the jaws and in two rows along the palate. In poisonous forms the two front teeth in the upper jaw are grooved or channelled for conducting poison from special glands, and it is these "poison fangs" which are capable of inflicting fatal wounds. Such a snake, therefore, is deadly in virtue of its power of giving a poisoned bite. The "sting" of a scorpion or wasp is an entirely different thing, and the organ which administers it is situated at the hinder end of the body, as most of us have practical cause to know in the case of the latter animal.

There is no occasion to dwell upon the *circulatory organs*, for in essential respects these are constructed on the plan described for the Sand Lizard (see p. 191).

The *breathing organs* are distinguished by one or two remarkable peculiarities. In the first place, the top of the windpipe is drawn out into a tube, the end of which protrudes from the mouth when prey is being swallowed, an operation that would otherwise stop the breathing altogether. The two lungs are very unequally developed, for whereas the left one is reduced to a mere vestige, the other is correspondingly large and extends far back in the body, the arrangement being convenient in a body so elongated and narrow. The hinder part of this right lung is thin-walled, and appears to chiefly serve as a reservoir of air.

The *brain* agrees in the main with the type described for the Sand Lizard, and in regard to *sense organs* one peculiarity

Fig. 145.—Pythons and Boas

1. Indian Python (*Python molurus*). 2. West African Python (*P. sebæ*). 3. Anaconda (*Eunectes murinus*). 4. Boa Constrictor (*Boa constrictor*).

has already been dealt with, *i.e.* the tear-chamber of the eye. The organs of hearing consist solely of the membranous labyrinth, the sound-conducting middle ear being entirely absent. The tongue appears to be used as an organ of touch.

As at least a thousand species of snakes are known, it will only be possible here to mention a few of the more important forms. The following groups can be recognized:—1. Simple-toothed Snakes; 2. Whip-Snakes; 3. Cobras and Coral Snakes; 4. Sea-Snakes; 5. Vipers; and 6. Blind-Snakes.

1. *Simple-toothed Snakes* are non-poisonous forms, in which both upper and lower jaws are provided with rows of solid, hook-like teeth. Here are included the giant snakes known as *Pythons* and *Boas* (fig. 145), which are found in the tropical regions all round the world, but are especially abundant in South America. Among the species may be mentioned the Indian Python (*Python molurus*), which may attain a length of 30 feet, the somewhat longer West African Python (*P. sebæ*), the Anaconda (*Euneces murinus*) of tropical South America, which is credited with being the largest of living snakes, and the much smaller Boa Constrictor (*Boa constrictor*) from the same region. All these forms kill their prey by crushing, and it may also be noted that their skins are very beautifully marked with elaborate patterns. They are the only snakes which possess externally visible remains of the hind-limbs.

Not very distantly related to the giant snakes are the two harmless forms (fig. 146) which are found in Britain, *i.e.* the Grass Snake (*Tropidonotus natrix*) and the Smooth Snake (*Coronella lævis*). The former is commonly met with in the neighbourhood of fresh water, and it is a good swimmer. The frog is the favourite article of diet, but small mammals, birds, and fish are also eaten. This snake can readily be distinguished from the poisonous Adder by its colour and markings. The darker upper surface is usually brownish or greenish, marked by darker spots or narrow transverse bands, while at the back of the head is a good-sized yellow or orange patch on each side, behind these again being a broad dark "collar". The underside of the body is mottled, and of much lighter hue.

The Smooth Snake is not common in Britain, but is sometimes found in dry places in the southern English counties. It is smaller than the Grass Snake, and may readily be distinguished by the markings on its upper side, consisting of a dark blotch on the neck and a double series of brown spots running down the body. It feeds on other reptiles.

Both these British species, especially the Grass Snake, have a wide distribution outside of Great Britain.

Fig. 146
1. Grass Snake (*Tropidonotus natrix*). 2. Smooth Snake (*Coronella lævis*). 3. Adder (*Pelias berus*).

2. *Whip-Snakes* and their allies are green tree-inhabiting forms, native to the tropical regions of Asia, Africa, and America. The head is small and pointed, the body extremely slender. But the most remarkable peculiarity is seen in a varying number of the hinder teeth of the upper jaw, each of which has a groove in front. Such grooves on the upper teeth of serpents generally

serve the purpose of conducting poison from a poison-gland into wounds made by the teeth, and it has been asserted that this is the case in some members of this group.

3. *Cobras* and *Coral-Snakes* are tropical forms in which the front upper teeth are grooved poison-fangs, conducting venom from poison-glands. Cobras are found in South Asia and Africa. Examples are the Common Cobra of India (*Naia tripudians*), called "cobra de capello" (hooded snake) by the Portuguese settlers on account of its power, characteristic of the genus, of inflating the skin of the neck when irritated.

The Coral-Snake (*Elaps corallinus*) of South America and the West Indies is a small form, in which the body is beautifully marked by broad scarlet rings alternating with much narrower black rings with greenish edges.

4. *Sea-Snakes* are venomous forms ranging from the Persian Gulf eastwards as far as New Guinea and North Australia. Their poison-fangs are of the same kind as described for cobras, &c., and the hinder part of the body is flattened from side to side so as to constitute a powerful swimming organ. Unlike land snakes they cast their skins in pieces, and not in a continuous slough.

5. *Vipers* of all snakes are the most specialized as regards the mechanism of the poison-fangs. Of these, two are present, and they are the only teeth in the upper jaw. The groove seen on the front of the fangs of other poisonous forms is here converted into a canal, open above to receive the fluid from the large poison-gland, and below so that this may be introduced into the wound. Hook-like teeth of the ordinary solid kind are present on the roof of the mouth and along the margin of the lower jaw, The head of a viper is flat and triangular, possessing more than in any other kind of poisonous snake the shape of the conventional "spade" on a playing-card, which is so often quoted as characteristic of venomous species. It is, however, a fallacy to suppose that all the dangerous reptiles of the order can be easily distinguished in this way.

Two species may be taken as examples, the Adder (*Pelias berus*) (fig. 146) and the Common Rattle-Snake (*Crotalus durissimus*). The former is the only poisonous British snake, and it has a very wide distribution in both Europe and Asia. Smaller than the Grass Snake, it may be distinguished from that species not only by the shape of the head but also by the presence of a dark zigzag stripe running down the back, and it is especially common in dry localities, such as sandy heaths.

The Common Rattle-Snake (fig. 147) is a representative of the "Pit" Vipers, a group characteristic of South Asia and the New World, and so called because they possess a deep pit in front of each eye. This particular kind is a large species

Fig. 147.—Common Rattle-Snake (*Crotalus durissimus*)

(length up to 6 feet) which inhabits North America, and, like five other allied American species, is distinguished by the peculiar organ known as a "rattle". This consists of a number of interlocked horny rings at the tip of the tail, generally supposed to be the remains of successive cast skins, though this is denied by some authorities. The rings are at any rate more numerous in old forms, while to begin with, the rattle is only represented by a button-like knob.

6. *Blind-Snakes* are small animals adapted to a burrowing life, and differing in many ways from other members of the order. The small head merges insensibly into a worm-like trunk, and that again into a very short tail. The body is uniformly covered with rounded scales, the large ventral horny

shields so characteristic of an ordinary snake being absent. The small mouth is on the under side of the head, and cannot be opened widely; nor is this necessary, as the food consists of ants and other small creatures. Strong horny plates protect the front of the head, and each of the vestigial eyes is covered by one of these.

Blind-Snakes are widely distributed through the hotter parts of both Old and New Worlds, one species, the European Blind-Snake (*Typhlops vermicularis*), ranging from Western Asia into Greece.

Order 5.—Tuataras (Rhynchocephala)

This order, which is of great age geologically, is of very special interest, because it probably comes near the ancestral stock from which all the groups of Reptiles have sprung, and

Fig. 148.—The Tuatara (*Hatteria punctata*)

also, more indirectly, the Birds and Mammals. It is represented at the present day by a solitary species, the lizard-like Tuatara (*Hatteria punctata*) (fig. 148), now unfortunately on the verge of extinction, and mainly found on, if not indeed absolutely limited to, some small islands off the north-east coast of New Zealand. In length it is about 20 inches, and, judging from external characters only, would no doubt be classified with lizards, as was formerly the practice. The large head is fairly well marked off from the stoutish body, which again passes into a large flattened tail. The short limbs present the usual regions, and each of the extremities possesses five clawed digits. The eyes are large, but there is no external trace of organs of hearing. The scales of the upper surface are in the form of small granules, with the exception of a series of sharp spiny ones which make up a crest running down the middle line. A number of squarish horny plates arranged in transverse rows cover the under surface.

As regards its internal structure the Tuatara differs in many important points from typical lizards, but as the distinctions are largely of a technical nature, only a few of them can be mentioned here.

The *quadrate bone*, to which the lower jaw is hinged, is not movable as in a lizard (see p. 206), but firmly fixed to the skull as in the crocodile, and the two halves of the lower jaw are united together in front only by fibrous tissue. The centra of the *vertebræ* are biconcave in shape (see p. 221), and exhibit other primitive characters. The *ribs* possess uncinate processes as in Birds and Crocodiles (see p. 145), and there are *abdominal ribs* as in the latter (see p. 206). The *teeth* are also peculiarly arranged, there being two rows above, one on the upper jaw and the other on the roof of the mouth, and into the groove between these the teeth of the lower jaw bite, getting in course of time ground to a sharp edge. In the front of the upper jaw are two wedge-shaped teeth, almost reminding one of those present in a rabbit. All these teeth are firmly fused with the edges of the firm bones, and in old animals may be so much ground down that the bones themselves act as biting organs.

CHAPTER V

STRUCTURE AND CLASSIFICATION OF AMPHIBIANS

This class of cold-blooded vertebrates is often confounded with Reptiles, from which, however, its members differ in many important respects, being altogether of simpler type. They are, in fact, more closely related to Fishes, with which they are sometimes associated to form a larger group, the Ichthyopsida, or Fish-like Animals (Gk. *ichthus*, fish; *opsis*, appearance), as has already been stated. A typical species will here be briefly described, and a comparison with what has been said about the Sand Lizard (p. 191) will illustrate the points of agreement as well as of difference between Amphibians and Reptiles.

The Spotted Salamander (*Salamandra maculosa*) (fig. 152) is a European animal from 6 to 9 inches long which has long attracted attention, mainly perhaps on account of its supposed power of withstanding fire. The flattened rounded head is not separated by any appreciable neck from the somewhat clumsy trunk, which passes gradually back into a long thick tail. The four sprawling limbs are directed a good deal outwards, and scarcely lift the body from the ground: the fore-limb possesses four digits, the hind-limb five. The mouth is a wide slit, and the two small valvular nostrils are placed near the tip of the blunt snout. Large eyes, provided with upper and lower eyelids, are present, but no trace of auditory organs can be seen externally. There is a longitudinal slit, the opening of the cloaca, on the under side of the body near the root of the tail.

The animal is rendered very conspicuous by its colouring, which consists of a ground of black, upon which are arranged broad patches of orange-yellow. The skin differs markedly from that of a reptile, for it is soft, moist, and smooth, being entirely devoid of scales, plates, or claws. Its damp feel is due to the secretion of very numerous skin-glands, some of which secrete a poisonous fluid. Of these the most conspicuous are grouped so as to form a swelling behind either eye.

The *internal skeleton* (fig. 149) is not so bony as in a reptile, consisting largely of tough membrane and gristle. The *skull*, like that of a mammal, has a pair of condyles at the back for joining on to the backbone. There is no quadrate bone, but the lower jaw is hinged on to a cartilaginous projection of the skull which represents it. The "hyoid apparatus" (see p. 29) in the floor of the mouth consists of a small unpaired cartilage in the middle line and other pieces of cartilage at the sides, of which three pairs are the most conspicuous. These, as we shall see later, are vestiges of structures which were once more important.

The *backbone* consists of a considerable number of fairly bony vertebræ, the centra of which are for the most part convex in front and concave behind, just the reverse of what is true for most reptiles. This is only characteristic for some of the Amphibia, however. The following regions can be distinguished: neck, trunk, sacral, and tail. Only the first vertebra, the ring-shaped *atlas*, can be considered as definitely belonging to the neck region. It, and the hinder vertebræ of the tail, bear no *ribs*, which are present, however, as short slender bones in all the others. There is a single sacral vertebra united to the pelvis by means of its ribs, and forming a division between the trunk vertebræ in front and the caudal vertebræ behind. A *sternum* is present in the form of a small plate of cartilage on the under side, but this, from the way in which it is developed, appears to be equivalent to two small abdominal ribs fused together, and is not, therefore, of the same nature as the part so called in the higher vertebrates.

The *limbs* are supported by an internal skeleton, which corresponds very closely with the patterns described on pp. 196–198. Indeed it ought to be stated that these patterns are very largely founded on what is seen in the Amphibia, these being the simplest backboned animals possessing limbs suited for progression on the ground. Two deviations from the pattern may, however, be noted, one being that in the fore-limb the little finger is entirely absent, while the other is that in the pelvic girdle there is no clear boundary between pubis and ischium, the two being represented by a plate of cartilage with the hinder part of which a bony plate is connected.

There are not many points which need detain us in the structure of the *digestive organs* (fig. 150). A considerable number of small *teeth*, with forked crowns, are fused with the bones which form the margins of the jaws, and there are two longitudinal rows of similar teeth on the roof of the mouth. Gullet, stomach, small intestine, and large intestine are present, the last being very short and opening behind into a cloacal chamber. The Salamander is found in damp places, where it lurks in crevices, coming out in the evening or during rain to feed upon worms, snails, and slugs.

Very special interest attaches to the *circulatory organs* (fig. 150), especially as regards the structure of the heart and the arrangement of the large arteries. There is a certain agreement with the Sand Lizard (see p. 191) in so far that the great veins open into a thin-walled *venous sinus*, that pours the impure blood it receives from them into a *right auricle*, which is separated by a party-wall from a *left auricle* receiving pure blood from the lungs. Both auricles open into the single *ventricle*. But there is here not even an internally projecting ridge for partial division of the ventricle into right and left halves, and there is an additional region to the heart, the *arterial cone*, a tube which is in communication with the cavity of the ventricle on the right-hand side, and from which the great arteries take origin in the form of four pairs of arterial arches. It is now time to consider more fully the actual meaning of such arches, which have been seen to be present, though in a much less pronounced form, in Reptile, Bird, and Mammal (see p. 201).

A Salamander when starting an independent existence is unlike the adult in many important respects, and is therefore called a *larva*. In this particular case, though a pair of small lungs are present, they are, to begin with, of little or no use for breathing purposes. The efficient organs of respiration are three pairs of feathery gills growing from the sides of the throat, and containing a net-work of delicate blood-vessels. Floating freely in the surrounding water, these gills present a large surface through which the dissolved oxygen can diffuse into the blood and the waste carbon dioxide diffuse out of it. Close inspection reveals the presence of four small *gill-slits* on each side of the throat, by which the back part of the mouth-cavity communicates with the exterior, and each slit is in front of a corresponding

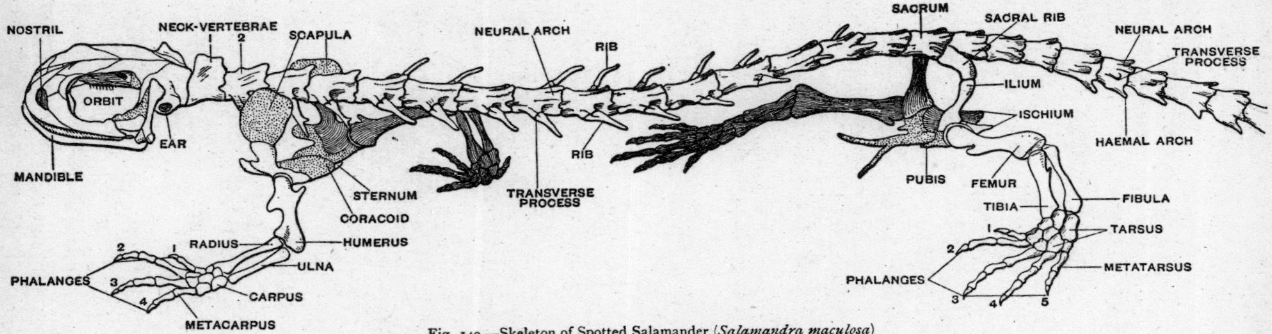

Fig. 149.—Skeleton of Spotted Salamander (*Salamandra maculosa*)

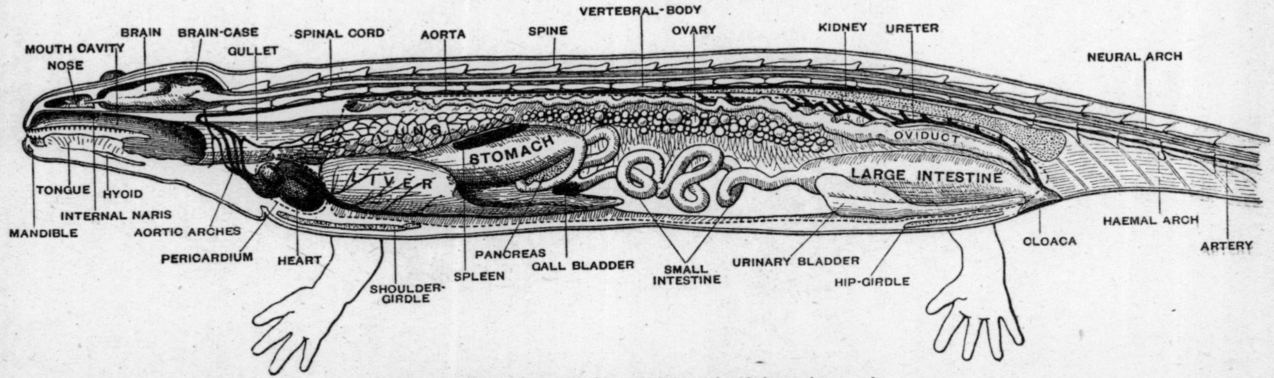

Fig. 150.—General Structure of Spotted Salamander (*Salamandra maculosa*)

bar-like thickening or *gill-arch*. These bars and slits are good examples of visceral arches and clefts, the presence of which at some period of life or other is one of the primary characteristics of a Vertebrate (see p. 62). The three gills on each side grow out from the tops of the three first gill-arches. The heart of the larva contains impure blood only, returned from all parts of the body, and its function is to pump this blood to the gills for purification through paired afferent branchial vessels which run within the gill-arches. The purified blood is collected up from the gills and distributed to the body by efferent branchial vessels which unite above to form a dorsal aorta. Each afferent vessel, with the corresponding efferent one, constitutes what may be called an *aortic arch*. As the larva gradually assumes the structure of the adult all the gill-slits close, the gills at the same time shrivelling up. Meanwhile the lungs have increased in size, and take on the work of purifying the blood, and the aquatic gill-bearing larva is thus converted into a terrestrial air-breathing Salamander. The heart now receives not only impure blood from the body, but also purified blood from the lungs, and it becomes necessary to solve the problem of how to keep these two sorts of blood separate by modifying an arrangement specially adapted for pumping impure blood to the gills. To use an illustration, it is as if a pumping apparatus made for distributing cold water were to be also connected with a warm-water supply, and one were then called upon to modify the apparatus so as to keep the two kinds of water as distinct as possible. The problem is only partially solved in the Salamander, for the separation of the two kinds of blood is incomplete, the result being that some of the blood distributed by the heart is impure, some pure, and the rest mixed. Just as if, in modifying the supposed pumping apparatus, we succeeded to a certain extent, part of the warm and cold supplies mixing, however, to give tepid water. In such an event the pump would distribute three kinds of water as regards temperature, *i.e.* cold, warm, and tepid, these corresponding to the impure, pure, and mixed blood of the Salamander.

It would take too much space to fully describe how the circulatory organs of the Salamander are modified during the change from larva to adult, but some of the leading features may be noted. To begin with, the originally single auricle is divided into two, a right half to receive the impure blood and a left to receive the pure, and although these two halves possess a common opening into the undivided ventricle, yet the prolongation of the party-wall between them into that opening prevents the blood from mixing there. Arrived in the cavity of the ventricle, which is transversely elongated, mixture does not take place so much as would be anticipated, for there is a system of ingrowths from the ventricular wall which largely prevents this, so that the blood passed into the right side of the ventricle remains impure and that on the left pure, while between the two comes a zone of mixed blood. The arterial cone to which blood from the ventricle passes on is placed on the right, and when the ventricle contracts it receives first *impure*, then *mixed* and lastly *pure* blood, as the result of the arrangement just described. Next, as to the way in which the four pairs of aortic arches coming off from the arterial cone are modified for their new purpose. The first pair, which supplied the first gills, are converted into *carotid arches* running to the head; the second and third pairs, which supplied the corresponding gills, unite to form the *dorsal aorta*, and supply most of the body except the head; while the fourth aortic arches, branches of which have all along supplied the lungs, continue to do so, having, however, enlarged. And it is interesting to notice that the parts of the fourth arches which connect them with those in front become converted into fibrous cords through which blood is not able to pass. It is clear, therefore, that the blood received by the cone must go either to the head, general body, or to the lungs, its course for any given moment being in the direction of least resistance. Now, when the ventricle begins to contract, forcing out blood which is quite impure, the easiest course is to the lungs, and this impure blood takes that course and flows to the lungs for purification. As that is being accomplished mixed blood begins to flow into the cone, and by this time the easiest course is through the second and third arches to the general body, since the fourth arches have just been filled and can take no more. Meanwhile the ventricle has begun to squeeze out its remaining blood, which is pure, and the easiest course this can take is through the first arches to the head. Containing as it does the brain and highest sense organs, it is important for the head to receive, as in fact it does, the purest blood-supply.

Two things will now have become apparent if the foregoing description has been carefully followed: (1) That the aortic arches found in higher Vertebrates, which always breathe by lungs, point to descent from ancestors which were aquatic and breathed by means of gills growing from gill-arches between which there were gill-slits; (2) the Amphibians and Reptiles are, so to speak, still grappling with the problem of adapting a circulatory system originally suited for pumping impure blood to gills, to the new conditions brought about by the adoption of a terrestrial life.

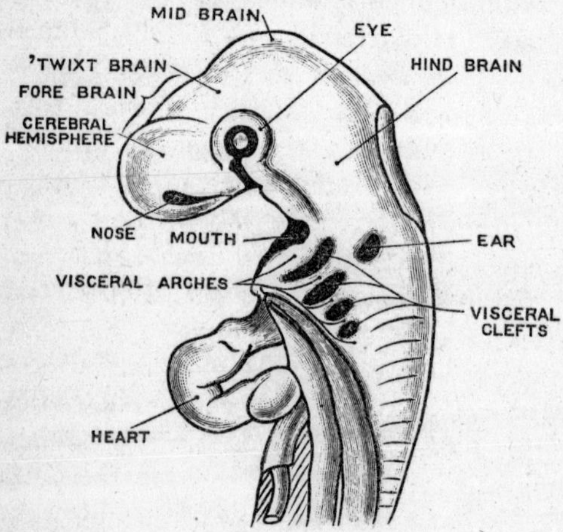

Fig. 151.—Front part of Chick Embryo

Even in crocodiles, which by development of two ventricles have succeeded in preventing the two sorts of blood from mixing in the heart itself, have not been successful in preventing them from mixing outside the heart (see p. 208). These facts become clearer still when the development of the higher Vertebrates is studied, and in, say, an embryo chick (fig. 151) gill-arches and clefts are clearly to be seen with their aortic arches, although no true traces of actual gills have been discovered. It may also be pointed out that gill-arches are supported by parts of the internal skeleton in the form of jointed rods which unite with unpaired pieces in the floor of the throat, and the "hyoid apparatus", which has been described in various animals, is largely made up of bits of this gill-arch skeleton, now turned to further uses. The cartilages which support the larynx or voice-box of terrestrial Vertebrates are also derived from this source, in part at least. These are admirable examples of "change of function" (p. 13).

The *breathing-organs* (fig. 150) of the adult Salamander have already been spoken of in the foregoing, but it may be added that the lungs and air-passages agree fairly well with what has been described for the Sand Lizard (see p. 191). The provision for renewal of air in the lungs is, however, different, for there is here no means of altering the capacity of the chest by movements of ribs and sternum, air being in this case renewed in the lungs by the upward and downward movement of the floor of the mouth-cavity. During this process the mouth is kept shut, air passing from and to the exterior through the nose, which opens externally by valvular nostrils and internally by small apertures on the roof of the mouth.

The Salamander, too, is not altogether dependent on the lungs for the purification of its blood, as the moist skin also serves as an accessory breathing-organ, the blood which it purifies entering the great veins which pour impure blood into the sinus venosus. This blood is therefore less impure than would otherwise be the case.

The *brain* (fig. 150) is much like that of the Sand Lizard, but is of lower type, it being especially noticeable that both cerebral hemispheres and cerebellum are smaller in proportion. As regards the chief *sense organs*, the eye is not provided with a third eyelid, and its crystalline lens is spheroidal instead of being biconvex as in animals better adapted for a terrestrial life. The ear on each side consists essentially of a membranous labyrinth not unlike that found in a Lizard (see p. 203). There are, however, no special arrangements, for conducting sound-waves. This, however, is not a feature which characterizes all Amphibia; the frog, for example, having a tympanic cavity and tympanic membrane, and a small rod, the columella or ear-bone, running from that membrane to the part of the skull in which the membranous labyrinth is lodged.

The Amphibia now living are divided into three orders:—1. Urodela, or Tailed Amphibia; 2. Anura, or Tailless Amphibia; and 3. Gymnophiona, or Limbless Amphibia.

Order 1.—Tailed Amphibians (Urodela)

Salamanders, Newts, and allied forms are here included (fig. 152). The Spotted Salamander (*Salamandra maculosa*), just described, is a good example of the Urodela. Its relative, the Black Salamander (*S. atra*), is a smaller Alpine form, and other allied species inhabit the Peninsula and the Caucasus.

Newts or *Efts* differ from Salamanders proper in the possession of a tail flattened from side to side and used as a swimming organ. Running round the margin of the tail is a fin-like expansion, which, however, is not supported by hard parts as in a fish. Three kinds are native to Britain, and constitute our only representatives of the tailed Amphibia. Of these the

Fig. 152.—Tailed Amphibia.—Spotted Salamander (*Salamandra maculosa*), below. Crested Newt (*Triton cristatus*), above.

commonest is the Small Newt (*Triton tæniatus*), which is only a little more than 3 inches long. The upper surface and sides are olive-coloured, with dark spots and streaks, while the paler under side is marked by a longitudinal orange-coloured band. The male has a fin-like crest running down the middle line on the upper side of the trunk, and continued into a similar fold which margins the tail: the colouring and marking are not quite the same as in the female. Another British species, the Crested Newt (*Triton cristatus*), may be more than 5 inches long, and the crest on the back of the male is much better developed. The only other species found in this country, and that less frequently, is the Webbed Newt (*Molge palmata*), which is not more than 3 inches long. There are no spots on the under surface, and the hind-feet of the male are webbed.

The largest living Amphibian is the Giant Salamander (*Megalobatrachus maximus*) from Japan and China, which is commonly 3 feet long, and is said to attain a still greater size.

Fig. 153.—The Olm (*Proteus anguineus*)

It is a clumsy-looking creature, with a huge flattened head, broad rudder-like tail, and short, unfinished-looking limbs. The body is covered with a dark leathery skin, raised into numerous warts, and exhibiting a thick wavy fold on each side. This creature is a representative of a group of forms known as "Fish Newts", in which the trunk is long and the limbs weak, while other primitive characters are present, such as biconcave centra to the vertebræ, eyelids represented by a circular fold, and (except in the Giant Salamander itself) persistent remains of a gill-breathing condition, seen, it may be, in the actual retention of gills along with the lungs, or of a pair of gill-slits in the throat.

Fig. 154.—The Axolotl
Adult or salamander stage (*Amblystoma tigrinum*), above; larval or axolotl stage (*Siredon Mexicanus*), below.

The Hell-Bender, or Salamander of the Mississippi (*Cryptobranchus lateralis*), has a pair of gill-clefts, or sometimes one on the left side only. The Three-toed Salamander (*Amphiuma means*), from the same river, is eel-like in shape, with very small weak limbs, terminating in three or it may be only two digits. A pair of gill-slits are present.

The flesh-coloured Olm (*Proteus anguineus*) (fig. 153) is a remarkable eel-like form, about 10 inches long, which inhabits the underground lakes and streams of certain caves in Dalmatia, Carniola, and Carinthia. Both fore- and hind-limbs are very small, and furnished respectively with three and two digits. Coral-coloured external gills are present as well as two pairs of gill-slits. The eyes are small and concealed beneath the skin. Much longer (28 inches) than the Olm is the Siren (*Siren lacertina*) of the south-east part of the United States. The dark-coloured body is extremely eel-like and the hind-limbs are entirely absent, while the four-toed fore-limbs are very small. External gills and three pairs of gill-slits are present.

One of the most interesting Urodeles is the Mexican Axolotl (fig. 154), which in what must be called the adult state is a thorough-going Salamander, known as *Amblystoma tigrinum*, and in the United States, to which the range of the animal extends, this adult condition is reached. In the lake surrounding the city of Mexico, however, this is not the case, and the Axolotl permanently remains in the larval state, resembling an enormous newt tadpole. Gill-slits and external gills are present, and eggs are laid just as by adults. We have here the astonishing phenomenon of an animal which, so to speak, is dropping the adult stage out of its life-history, the conditions being unfavourable for its development. We only know this by accident, and the precocious tadpoles were, when first described, thought to be adult, receiving the name of *Siredon Mexicanus*. There are doubtless other still undetected cases of this remarkable phenomenon in the animal kingdom.

Order 2.—Tailless Amphibians (Anura)

While the Tailed Amphibia are confined to the Northern Hemisphere, the Frogs and Toads, which constitute the group of Tailless Amphibia, are cosmopolitan. The Grass Frog (*Rana temporaria*), which is one of the most familiar British Vertebrates, is a good type of one of the most widely-distributed families of the order, and a brief description of its more obvious external characters (fig. 155) will illustrate the differences which distinguish animals of the sort from Salamanders and their allies.

The flattened triangular head, with rounded snout, passes

into a short plump body without any intervening neck-region. In the adult animal there is absolutely no trace of a tail, though this is well-developed in the larval form or tadpole, a fact which no doubt points to the descent of Frogs from tailed ancestors. The limbs are much better developed than in the Salamander, but the hind-limbs, which serve both as leaping and swimming

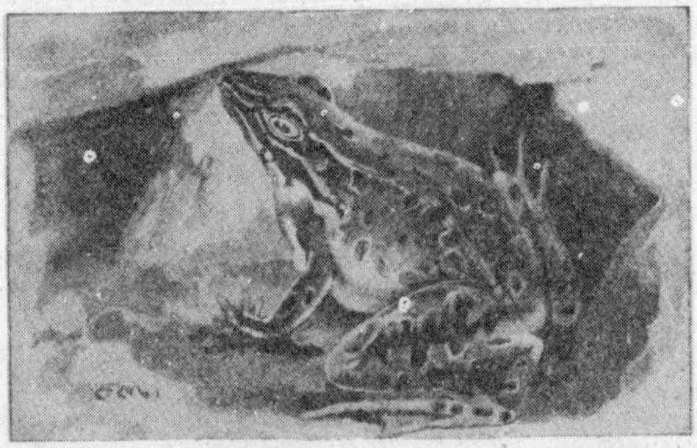

Fig. 155.—Tailless Amphibia
Grass Frog (*Rana temporaria*), above; Common Toad (*Bufo vulgaris*), below.

organs, are out of all proportion large as compared with the fore-limbs. Four digits only are externally visible in the latter, there being no apparent trace of a thumb, but the hind-limb possesses five well-developed toes, between which a delicate web extends. A very curious feature is the presence of a little horny spur, the *calcar*, on the inner side of the foot, and examination of the skeleton shows that this is really an extra digit, though in a much-reduced condition.

Nostrils and eyes are present closely resembling those of a Salamander, but behind either eye may be seen a well-marked rounded area corresponding to the tympanic membrane covered over by skin. A small rounded cloacal aperture is present at the hinder end of the trunk. The skin is soft and moist, as in Amphibians generally, and is entirely devoid of hard parts, with the trifling exception of the horny spur on the foot. The upper surface is mottled and the under surface pale, and, as in the Chameleons, though not quite to the same extent, the animal has the power to adjust its colour so as to match the surroundings for the time being. A frog which has been kept for some time in a dark place becomes almost black in colour, but if the same animal is transferred to grass it will gradually assume a greenish tint.

Endoskeleton (fig. 156). The peculiarities of the *skull* cannot be entered into here, but as regards the *backbone*, it may be said that the number of vertebræ is reduced to ten, their centra, too, being concave in front and convex behind, as in Reptiles. The first vertebra is a ring-like *atlas*, and the last fulfils the function of a *sacrum*, being connected with the hip-girdles supporting the hind-limbs. The hinder end of the backbone is completed by a bony rod, the *urostyle*. No separate *ribs* can be distinguished, but there is reason to believe that the prominent transverse processes which project from the sides of the vertebræ are partly equivalent to these. It is quite a common thing for ribs to fuse with vertebræ, at least in certain regions, *e.g.* in the human skeleton short neck-ribs have undoubtedly been soldered, so to speak, with the vertebræ which support the neck.

The *sternum* is much better developed here than in the Salamander, and is closely connected with the *shoulder-girdles*. These present the typical regions, but it may be noted that the precoracoid bar is covered over by a collar-bone or clavicle. The skeleton of the rest of the *fore-limb* corresponds fairly well with the pattern limb (see pp. 196–198), and a vestige of the thumb can be made out. The forearm, however, presents a very interesting case of fusion, for its two typical bones, the radius and ulna, are here closely united together. In the *hind-limb* a number of instructive variations on the pattern form are to be seen. The *hip-girdles* are quite unlike the corresponding parts in a

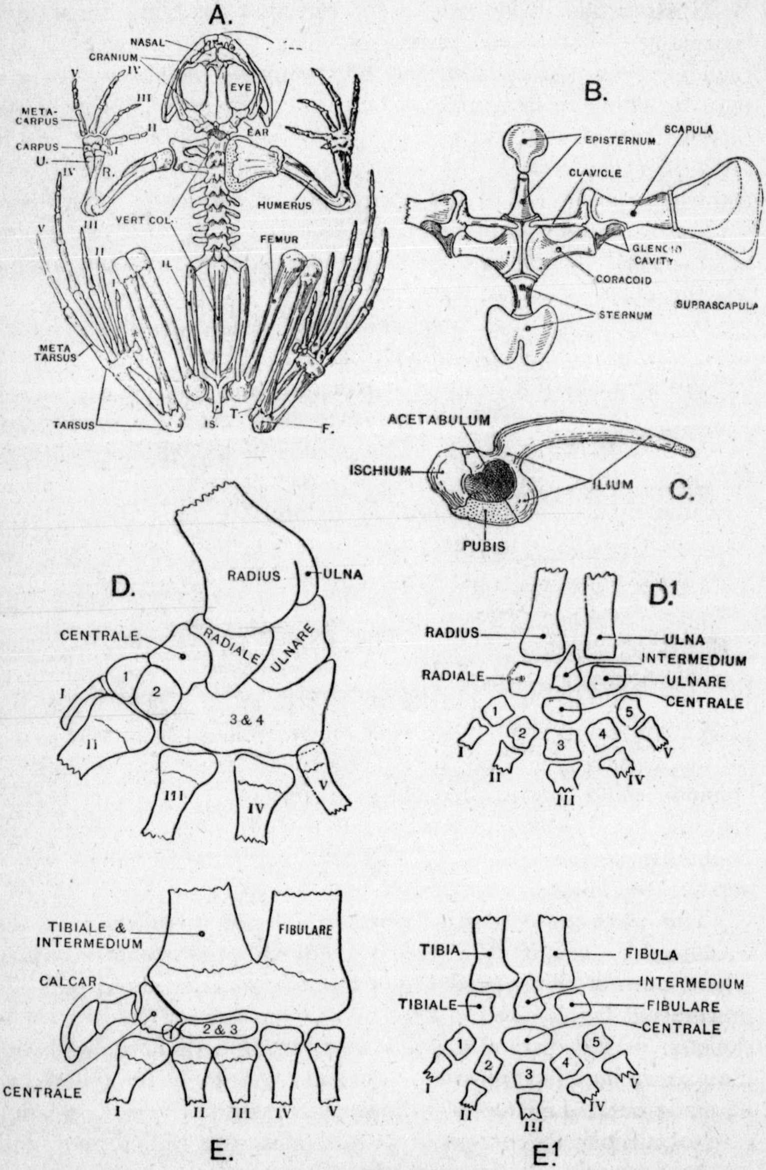

Fig. 156.—Skeleton of Frog

A, Skeleton seen from above (R, radius; U, ulna; IL, ilium; IS, ischium; T, tibia; F, fibula; *, calcar). B, Sternum and shoulder-girdles. C, Right hip girdle, from side. D, Wrist. D', Pattern wrist. E, Ankle. E', Pattern ankle.

Salamander. They are very intimately united into a forked bone, of which the forwardly-directed prongs are the ilia. The bones of the free limb are longer in proportion than in the fore-limb, and the bones of the lower leg, tibia and fibula, are fused together just like the radius and ulna in the fore-limb. Great specialization has taken place in the *tarsus*, for while that part of it next the fused tibia and fibula is represented by two elongated bones (= tibiale and fibulare) the rest has dwindled

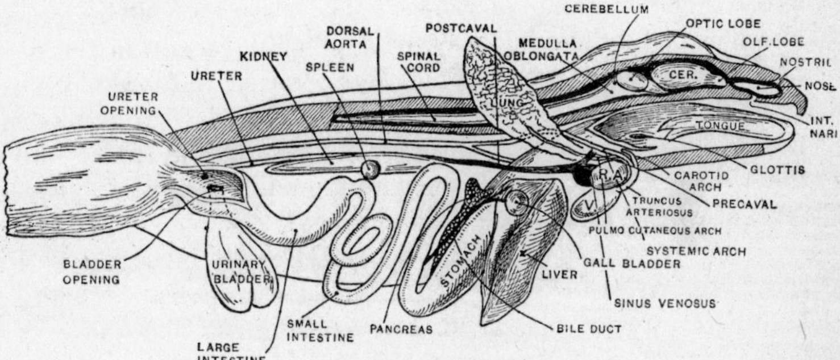

Fig. 157.—General Structure of Frog

away to insignificant vestiges. All this is to fit the limb for its use as a leaping organ, and changes of similar kind are seen in certain Mammals which use the hind-limbs in the same way. It is another illustration of the close connection which exists between form and function, though much space would be required to work it out in detail, even had we all the necessary data, which does not appear to be the case.

Broadly speaking, the *digestive organs* (fig. 157) agree with those of the Salamander except as regards the teeth and tongue. The *teeth* are entirely absent from the lower jaw, though they fringe the upper jaw, and occur in two small groups on the roof of the mouth. The long forked *tongue* has the remarkable peculiarity of being attached to the front of the mouth-floor, with its tip pointing backwards when not in use. It is an insect-catching organ of no mean order of perfection, which can be whipped out of the mouth with great rapidity and as rapidly drawn back, generally carrying with it the desired booty.

The *circulatory organs* are built on the same type as those of the Salamander (see p. 240), and keep the impure and pure blood separate to the same extent, supplying the former to lungs and skin for purification and the latter to the head, while the greater part of the body has to put up with mixed blood. There are, however, numerous minor differences, one of the most striking being the presence of three pairs of aortic arches as against four, those corresponding to the third pair in the Salamander having disappeared.

The *lungs* are similar in nature to those in the Salamander (see p. 244), being a pair of bags, the linings of which are raised into a honeycombing of ridges. The supply of air of the lungs is renewed in the same way, by a pumping action in the mouth-cavity, the floor of which is alternately raised and lowered.

The only points in the *nervous system* and *sense organs* which need be noticed are the extreme shortness of the spinal cord and the presence of a sound-conducting middle ear not unlike that present in the Sand Lizard (see p. 192).

The *life-history* of the Frog is extremely interesting. From the eggs are hatched fish-like limbless tadpoles, in which the breathing organs are at first *external gills*, like those of the larval Salamander (see p. 240). After a time, however, these begin to shrivel and are replaced by the so-called *internal gills*, consisting of folds on the walls of the four pairs of gill-clefts, quite unlike anything found in the Tailed Amphibia but closely resembling the gills of some fishes. As these gills develop, a fold of skin grows backwards over the gill-slits and unites to the body behind them, leaving only a small round hole on the left side through which is expelled the water that has been taken in at the mouth and passed through the gill-slits. The adult form is reached by growth of limbs, accompanied by loss of tail and closure of the gill-slits, the lungs assuming their adult function. There is also a change in the nature of the food, for a tadpole is a vegetarian while the adult frog lives on insects and other small animals.

The Grass Frog has a wide distribution through Europe and non-tropical Asia, while the family (Ranidæ) to which it belongs is represented in all parts of the world except New Zealand and Polynesia. The well-known Edible Frog of the Continent (*Rana esculenta*) is common in the east of England, but has most likely been introduced. Much larger species of the same family are the Bull Frog (*Rana Catesbyana*), inhabiting the east of North America and attaining a length of over 7 inches, while Guppy's Frog (*Rana Guppyi*) from the Solomon Islands is nearly a foot long.

The Common Toad (*Bufo vulgaris*) is a more sluggish animal than the Grass Frog, and better adapted to a terrestrial life (fig. 155). Its skin is dull and warty, and prominent neck-glands like those of the Salamander are present. Teeth are entirely absent. The range of this species is even wider than that of the Grass Frog, for it is found in North-west Africa as well as in Europe and Asia.

Another species of toad found in Britain, though less frequently than the ordinary kind, is the Natterjack (*Bufo calamitata*), readily distinguished by a yellow or whitish streak down the middle of the back. The family to which both these toads belong (Bufonidæ) is almost as widely distributed as the Ranidæ, but is absent from Madagascar and rare in the Australian region.

There are thirteen other families of the Tailless Amphibia besides those mentioned, but none of them are so widely distributed, and some have a very restricted range.

Order 3.—Limbless Amphibians (Gymnophiona)

The remarkable modifications which have taken place in the bodies of some Fish-Newts, such as the Siren (see p. 248), are carried a step further here, for the tropical worm-like creatures (fig. 158) which make up the order are entirely limbless, tailless, and modified in other ways for a burrowing life. The body of a Cæcilian is encircled by grooves, and in some species small bony plates are imbedded in the skin. The small mouth is provided with sharp backwardly-curved teeth suited for the capture of earth-worms, insects, and other small creatures. The

Fig. 158.—A Cæcilian (*Siphonops annulata*) from tropical America

vertebræ exhibit the primitive feature of biconcave centra, and small movable ribs are attached to them. There is no sternum, and even the limb-girdles are absent. As in Snakes, some of the internal organs are modified to suit the narrow shape of the body, and it may be mentioned in particular that the right lung is much larger than the left. In regard to the sense organs, it may be noticed that the small eyes are hidden under the skin and the sound-conducting middle ear is absent. The development of an East Indian form (*Epicrium glutinosum*) has been studied, and presents some curious points. When the embryo is hatched it possesses three pair of external gills, a pair of gill-slits, a short tail, and traces of hind-limbs. Immediately hatching takes place, however, these gills are lost; but in spite of this the larva takes to the water and lives there for some time.

BUTTERFLIES (*Rhopalocera*)

Butterflies and Moths together constitute the order of Scale-winged Insects (*Lepidoptera*), in which the four wings are opaque and coloured, owing to the presence of minute dust-like scales. Typical Butterflies are diurnal in habit, their antennæ are club-shaped, and they bring the wings together above the back when they settle. Those figured are among the most attractive of tropical and British species, belonging to the Fritillaries (1-4) and Swallow-tails (5, 6).

1. Giant Blue (*Morpho cypris*). } Tropical America.
2. Resplendent Ptolemy (*M. neoptolemus*). } Tropical America.
3. Purple Emperor (*Apatura Iris*), oakwoods in the southern English counties.
4. Peacock Butterfly (*Vanessa Io*), Europe (including Britain) and N. Asia to Japan.
5. Common Swallow-tail (*Papilio machaon*), ranges from Britain to the Himalayas.
6. Imperial Swallow-tail (*Tinopalpus imperialis*), male; in the female each hind-wing has two tails. Sikkim.

BUTTERFLIES (RHOPALOCERA)

1. Giant Blue. 2. Resplendent Ptolemy. 3. Purple Emperor. 4. Peacock Butterfly. 5. Common Swallow-tail. 6. Imperial Swallow-tail.

CONTENTS

CHAPTER VI

STRUCTURE AND CLASSIFICATION OF FISHES (PISCES) AND PRIMITIVE VERTEBRATES (PROTOCHORDATA)

FISHES (PISCES)

PRIMITIVE VERTEBRATES (PROTOCHORDATA)

CHAPTER VII

BACKBONELESS ANIMALS (INVERTEBRATA). STRUCTURE AND CLASSIFICATION OF NEMERTINES AND MOLLUSCS

CHAPTER VIII

STRUCTURE AND CLASSIFICATION OF JOINTED-LIMBED ANIMALS (ARTHROPODA)

A, *Air-breathing Arthropods* (Tracheata).

B, *Aquatic Arthropods* (Branchiata).

CHAPTER IX

STRUCTURE AND CLASSIFICATION OF SEGMENTED WORMS, SIPHON-WORMS, WHEEL-ANIMALCULES, MOSS-POLYPES, AND LAMP-SHELLS

SEGMENTED WORMS (ANNELIDA)

SIPHON-WORMS (GEPHYREA)

WHEEL-ANIMALCULES (ROTIFERA)

MOSS-POLYPES AND LAMP-SHELLS (MOLLUSCOIDA)

CHAPTER X

STRUCTURE AND CLASSIFICATION OF FLAT-WORMS (PLATYHELMIA) AND THREAD-WORMS (NEMATHELMIA)

FLAT-WORMS (PLATYHELMIA)

THREAD-WORMS (NEMATHELMIA)

CHAPTER XI

STRUCTURE AND CLASSIFICATION OF ECHINODERMS (ECHINODERMATA)

CHAPTER XII

STRUCTURE AND CLASSIFICATION OF ZOOPHYTES (CŒLENTERATA), SPONGES (PORIFERA), AND ANIMALCULES (PROTOZOA)

ZOOPHYTES (CŒLENTERATA)

SPONGES (PORIFERA)

ANIMALCULES (PROTOZOA)

LIST OF ILLUSTRATIONS

PLATES

ILLUSTRATIONS

CHAPTER VI

STRUCTURE AND CLASSIFICATION OF FISHES AND PRIMITIVE VERTEBRATES

The 7300 odd species of existing fishes known to science are divided into the following five sub-classes:—

I. Lung-Fishes (Dipnoi).
II. Bony Fishes (Teleostomi).
III. Sharks and Rays (Elasmobranchii).
IV. Chimæras (Holocephali).
V. Round-Mouths (Cyclostomata).

Probably the best idea of the general structure of the group will be obtained by briefly describing such a common example of the Shark kind (Elasmobranchs) as the Spotted Dog-Fish (*Scyllium canicula*), abundant on our shores, especially during the herring season. It may to all intents and purposes be regarded as a small shark.

External Characters (fig. 166).—The spindle-shaped body is well suited for progression through the water, and its outline is continuous, there being no sharp boundary between head and trunk, or trunk and tail. We have seen that in tadpoles and some adult Amphibia (see p. 246) there is a membranous fringe bordering the tail above and below and running forwards on the upper side of the trunk. Such a longitudinal fringe running in the middle line is known as an *unpaired fin*, and is especially characteristic of Fishes, where, however, it is not a mere soft membrane as in Amphibia, but is supported by firm rod-like structures, the *fin-rays*. We find that in the Dog-Fish, as in most fishes, this membrane is not continuous, but is represented by a number of separate pieces, each of which is named with reference to its position. Here, for example, there is a *caudal fin* bordering the tail, two *dorsal fins* in front of this above, and an *anal* or *ventral fin* in front of it on the under side. Special attention may be called to the tail-fin, which is unsymmetrical, consisting of a large upper lobe into which the slender end of the body is continued, and a smaller lower lobe. Such unequal or *heterocercal* (Gk. *heteros*, diverse; *kerkos*, tail) tails are shown by reference to fossil forms to be of very ancient type. There is good reason to believe that remote fish-ancestors had a continuous unpaired fin, of which the existing ones are fragments which have been retained and enlarged to suit special purposes. The Dog-Fish, however, also possesses *paired fins*, consisting of two large *pectorals* in front and two smaller *pelvics* placed close together farther back. These are the equivalents of the fore- and hind-limbs of the terrestrial vertebrates so far described, but differ in important respects in accordance with differences in use. The limbs of a Salamander, for instance, have to support the weight of the body and are the means of progression. The presence of digits is of obvious advantage as regards the former, while locomotion would be difficult and awkward were the limbs not transversely divided into regions capable of being moved upon one another. But the limbs of an ordinary fish do not support the body, and their chief use seems to be that of steadying it in the water and directing its movements. For these purposes the undivided paddle-like shape which we associate with the paired fins of a fish appears best adapted.

The large curved *mouth* is situated on the under side of the head, and not far in front of it are the rounded *nostrils*, each of which is connected by a groove with the corresponding corner of the mouth. Far back on the under surface of the body, and marking the junction of trunk and tail, is a rounded *cloacal aperture* situated between the pelvic fins. On each side of this opening is a small aperture known as an *abdominal pore*, of unknown use, but commonly found in more than one group of fishes. The oblique cat-like *eyes* are provided with imperfectly movable upper and lower eyelids. A tadpole, it will be remembered, has four gill-slits on each side of the throat, the cavity of which is thus placed in communication with the exterior. Here there are five *gill-slits*, and also a superseded gill-slit known as the *spiracular cleft* and opening behind the eye by a small round hole, the *spiracle*.

The *skin* is of a brownish hue, much darker above than below, and marked with good-sized roundish spots. Projecting from the surface are the sharp points of innumerable small hard structures, closely resembling teeth in structure and usually known as *placoid scales.* The presence of these causes a peculiar roughness suggestive of sand-paper. Numerous sense organs are present in the skin, some of which will be alluded to farther on.

The first point of general interest to note with regard to the *internal skeleton* (fig. 159) is that it is entirely made up of

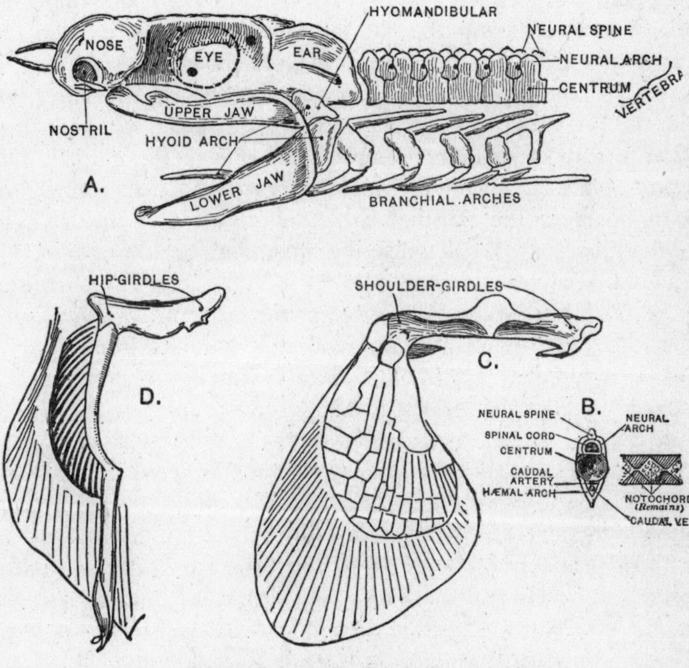

Fig. 159.—Skeleton of Dog-Fish (*Scyllium canicula*)

A, Skull and part of vertebral column. B, End view of a caudal vertebra, and longitudinal section through centra of two vertebræ. C, Pectoral fin (from below). D, Pelvic fin (from below).

cartilage and fibrous tissue, as generally in what are called "cartilaginous fishes", while in ordinary "bony fishes", including all the common edible forms, a great deal of bone is present as well as more or less cartilage.

The *skull* is extremely simple compared with that of the higher animals so far considered, and consists of a brain-case to which are attached protective capsules for nose and internal ear, the framework of the jaws, and what is known as the "visceral skeleton". Regarding the last two a little more may be said, as they have much to do with the visceral arches and clefts which are so characteristic of Vertebrates, and have been so often alluded to in the foregoing pages (see pp. 62 and 242).

Examination of a young embryo of the Dog-Fish will show that on each side of the head there are seven oblique bar-like thickenings and six slits occupying the interspaces between them. These are respectively termed *visceral arches* and *clefts*, the hindermost five having the special name of gill arches and clefts because the gills are developed in connection with them. The first arch is the *mandibular arch* and the second the *hyoid arch*, while the slit between them is naturally called the *hyo-mandibular cleft* and is no other than the spiracular cleft of the adult. These various arches are traversed and supported by firm jointed rods forming part of the internal skeleton. The mandibular arch is so called because it becomes the mandible or lower jaw, while the upper jaw is a forward outgrowth from it. The skeleton of the rest of the arches constitutes the *visceral skeleton*, which stiffens the gill region and prevents the gill-slits from becoming closed, giving also firm points of attachment to many muscles. A special function is performed by the upper joint of the skeleton of the second or hyoid arch, this being a stout piece of cartilage (hyomandibular cartilage) which slings the jaws to the main skull. In Vertebrates higher than Fishes this cartilage loses its original function, for the jaws are directly attached to the skull, and most probably some or all of the little ear-bones, which help to conduct sound-waves across the drum of the ear in such higher Vertebrates, correspond to this cartilage. This is one of the best examples known of a change of function. The rest of the visceral skeleton, here so important in connection with the gill-clefts, dwindles in air-breathing Vertebrates to the "hyoid apparatus", which has been so often mentioned (see pp. 29, 193, and 239) as supporting the base of the tongue in these forms, and to the cartilages which support the voice-box or larynx. In the life-history of the frog the passage from a well-developed visceral skeleton in the gill-bearing tadpole to such remnants in the adult lung-possessing animal can be traced step by step.

In the *vertebral column* it is only possible to distinguish between trunk-vertebræ and tail-vertebræ, and all these possess biconcave centra, which may be regarded as the most primitive kind. Short *ribs* can be distinguished in the trunk, but there is no trace of any sternum.

The skeleton of the *paired fins* exhibits many differences from the supporting parts of the limbs of terrestrial Vertebrates, and comparison between the two is extremely difficult. In the pectoral fin there is a very simple *shoulder-girdle*, consisting of a curved piece of cartilage running transversely and fusing with its fellow in the middle line below. At the base of the free part of the fin are three cartilages, followed by a number of others, and these again by jointed *fin-rays*. In the pelvic fins the two *hip-girdles* are represented by a simple transverse bar, while the free fin is supported by a stout rod bearing a large number of fin rays.

Digestive Organs (fig. 160).—The jaws are bordered by numerous rows of small pointed *teeth*, all much alike, and replaced by fresh ones during life as often as necessitated by wear and tear. These teeth are not suited for chewing, but for seizing such prey as small fish, crustaceans, &c., and afterwards preventing their escape. Around the margins of the mouth we find all gradations between ordinary placoid scales and teeth, which is intelligible when we recollect that the cavity of the mouth is developed as a pit on the surface of the body. The lining of such a pit, or inpushing of the general surface, so to speak, is evidently equivalent to skin, and teeth here and elsewhere are simply more or less modified scales, developed within the margins of the mouth. The *tongue* is merely an immobile fold on the floor of the mouth. The nasal organs do not possess internal nostrils as in the lunged vertebrates. The cavity of the mouth passes behind into a wide *pharynx*, out of which the spiracular cleft and gill-clefts open; and then follow gullet, U-shaped stomach, and intestine opening into a cloaca. There is no clear distinction, as in forms so far considered, between small and large intestine. Within this intestinal part of the gut is a so-called *spiral valve*, which is simply a projecting shelf winding round and round and presenting a large surface for the absorption of digested food. A large *liver* pours bile into the beginning of the intestine, and there is also a *pancreas* opening not far from it.

Circulatory Organs (fig. 160).—Here we have the same conditions as in the Tadpole before the lungs begin to be of use, and the conditions are consequently comparatively simple, the problem of separating two kinds of blood not having yet arisen. The *heart* consists of a thin-walled venous sinus, which receives the impure blood of the body and passes it on to a single auricle, by which it is squeezed into a thick-walled ventricle, continued again into a muscular tube, the arterial cone. Valves to prevent the blood from running back the wrong way are placed at the points of junction between sinus,

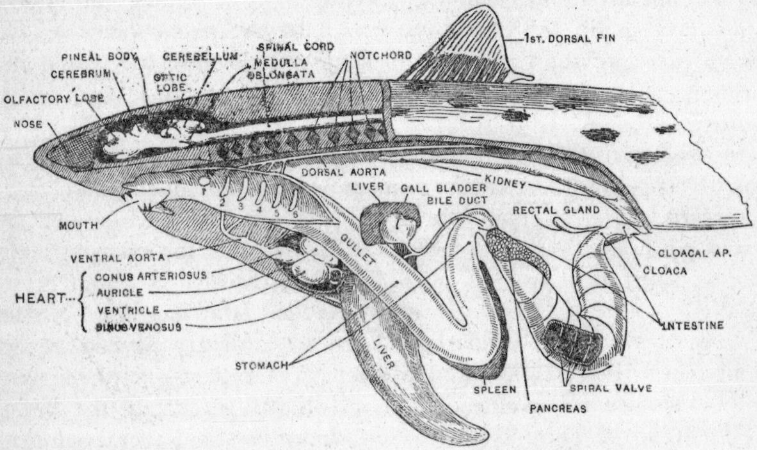

Fig. 160.—Side-dissection of Dog-Fish (*Scyllium canicula*). Left half of liver has been removed 1, Internal opening of spiracular cleft. 2, 3, 4, 5, 6, Internal openings of gill-clefts.

auricle, and ventricle, and several transverse rows of valves are present in the arterial cone. From the *ventral aorta*, which runs forward from the cone, five pairs of *afferent* gill-arteries run out and carry impure blood to the gills, from which five pairs of *efferent* gill-arteries conduct the purified blood, uniting above to form the *dorsal aorta* that runs back to the end of the tail, giving off numerous vessels by which the various organs and regions receive their pure blood-supply. Each afferent artery, with its corresponding efferent one, may be looked upon as constituting an *aortic arch* (see p. 242).

Breathing-organs (fig. 160).—Upon the walls of the five pairs of gill-slits, or pouches, to speak more correctly, numerous closely-set gill-folds are placed, and in these folds there are very numerous capillary blood-vessels, with which the gill-arteries are in communication. Water is constantly taken in at the mouth, and, passing back, streams outwards through the gill-pouches—thus passing over these folds, which collectively present a large surface over which the oxygen dissolved in the water can diffuse into the blood, while the waste carbon dioxide of the blood can diffuse outward into the water and be carried away to the exterior.

In this connection great interest attaches to the spiracular cleft, which looks very much like a narrow gill-pouch, and on close examination is seen to have a number of small folds on its front wall. These are so gill-like that they have been collectively called a *false gill* (pseudobranch), and when it is added that some few fishes possess a properly-developed set of gill-folds in this place, it will be clearly seen that the spiracular cleft is really a gill-cleft which is losing its function. There is every reason to believe that the cavity of the middle ear in higher Vertebrates, together with the Eustachian tube, is equivalent to the spiracular cleft. Here, then, is a structure which once had to do with breathing and is now concerned with sound-conduction—another excellent example of change of function.

Nervous System and Sense Organs (fig. 160).—The *brain* is pretty well developed, a peculiar feature being that the two cerebral hemispheres are represented by an unpaired swelling, while the olfactory lobes are placed on stalks. The cerebellum is much larger than in Amphibia.

The *eyeball* is flattened on the outside and its crystalline lens is approximately spherical, as in aquatic animals generally. Probably everyone has noticed, some time or other, the lens in the eye of a cooked bony fish, such as salmon or herring, looking, as it does, like a sugar-coated pill. Needless to say, the opacity is the result of cooking. Here, too, the lens is spheroidal. The *organs of hearing* consist simply of the internal ear or membranous labyrinth, contained in a gristly capsule on either side of the back end of the brain-case. In shape the labyrinth is somewhat simpler than in the Amphibia. The *skin* contains a large number of sense-organs, some of which are sunk in a tube which runs along each side of the body and opens to the exterior at intervals. An external streak, the *lateral line*, marks the position of either tube, but this is much better seen in a bony fish than in the Dog-Fish. There are also peculiar *jelly-tubes* which open by regularly arranged pores on the under side of the head, and undoubtedly have to do with sensation. Little is known of the use of these organs, but they no doubt respond to certain vibrations in the surrounding water. It is important to avoid the common error, made when dealing with the sense-organs and sensations of lower animals, of trying to explain them by reference to ourselves.

Development.—The Dog-Fish is developed from an egg, which looks almost like the "yolk" of a fair-sized bird's egg were it not for its greenish tint. This egg is enclosed in a horny "purse", the corners of which are drawn out into tendril-like threads which curl round sea-weeds and other firm objects.

We may now proceed to the consideration of the chief groups of Fishes.

Sub-class I.—LUNG-FISHES (Dipnoi)

Of all known fishes these come nearest to the Amphibia, and some zoologists place them in a class of their own, distinct from that containing more ordinary fishes. They are a very ancient group, now represented by only three genera, all of which are found in fresh water. They are the Barramunda or Burnett Salmon (*Ceratodus*) from the Burnett and Mary rivers in Queensland; the African Lung-Fish (*Protopterus*), native to some of the rivers of tropical Africa; and the South American Lung-Fish (*Lepidosiren*), found in the Amazon and upper part of the Paraguay rivers and their tributaries (fig. 161).

There are certain characters common to all three forms. Taking first the *external characters*, the head is somewhat amphibian-like, and has been compared to that of a salamander, while the tail tapers considerably and is symmetrically margined by a fin which is not expanded into lobes (protocercal or diphycercal caudal fin). There is no spiracle, but gill-clefts are present, protected by a flap or *gill-cover*. The paired fins are much elongated, and the body is covered by thin overlapping scales.

The most characteristic feature of the internal organs is the presence of one or two bag-like *lungs* opening on the under side of the pharynx, so that these animals possess, like some adult Amphibia, both gills and lungs at the same time, and it is from this circumstance that they derive the name of Dipnoi (Gk. *dis*, twice; *pnoe*, breath).

Since the heart receives pure blood from the lung or lungs, as well as impure blood from the general body, the problem of separating the two kinds demands solution; but this is only effected in an imperfect manner, for there is not even, as in Amphibia (see p. 240), a complete separation of the two auricles which are here present.

These are the only fishes in which there are *internal nostrils* as well as external ones. They open just within the margin of

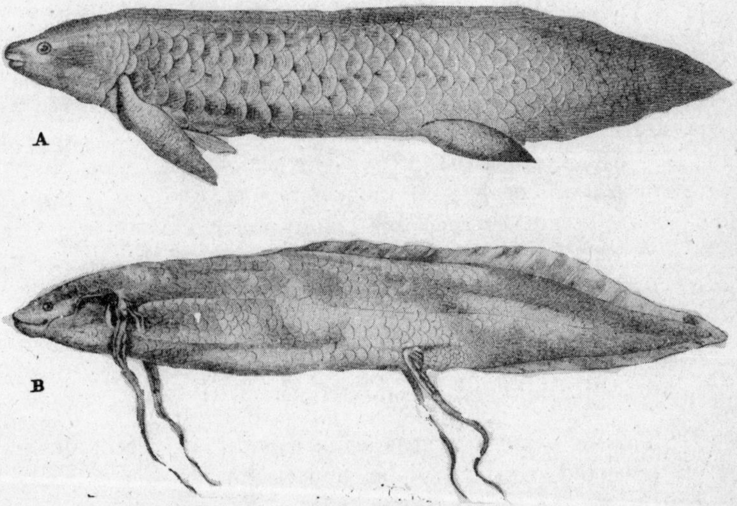

A

B

Fig. 161.—Dipnoi

A, Australian Lung-Fish (*Ceratodus*), $\times \frac{1}{7}$. B, African Lung-Fish (*Protopterus*), $\times \frac{1}{4}$.

the upper lip. The mouth is provided with large dental plates of peculiar form.

Ceratodus is a large broad fish, attaining the length of 4 or 5 feet, and with its body covered by very large scales. The paired fins are broad and paddle-shaped, and each of them is supported by a central axis made up of numerous joints, and of a series of fin-rays attached to the axis in front and behind in a feather-like way. *Protopterus* is much more slender in form and its paired fins are extremely narrow, the fin-rays on the central axis being largely suppressed. Some specimens are said to reach a length of 6 feet. There are small external gills as well as the gill-folds on the walls of the gill-clefts. *Lepidosiren* is an eel-like form which may be as much as 6 feet long. Its paired fins are even narrower than those of Protopterus, and supported only by a central jointed axis.

Sub-class II.—BONY FISHES (Teleostomi)

This large group of fishes includes a vast number of recent and fossil forms which present such varying characters that it is difficult to give a satisfactory definition. There is, however, a good deal of bone in the skeleton, and the jaws, instead of being mere bars of gristle, as in a Dog-Fish, are ensheathed by tooth-bearing bones in the same way as in higher forms. The gill-clefts are very near together, and the gill-arches between them are comparatively narrow, so that the gill-folds as seen in a Dog-Fish are not supported along the whole of their length, but project more or less to the exterior as free *gill filaments.* The gill-clefts are covered over and protected by a flap, the gill-cover or *operculum,* which is supported by bones. Two orders may be distinguished:—1. Ganoids, and 2. Bony Fishes proper or Teleosts.

Order 1.—Ganoids (Ganoidei)

Under this name are included a number of recent genera, widely scattered over the globe, and for the most part limited to fresh water (fig. 162). They are the last surviving remnants of groups which were once of great importance, but which have been unable to compete with more highly-organized fishes, and have greatly declined in consequence. Of recent forms the two most primitive are the Bichir (*Polypterus*) of the Nile and some other African rivers, and the Reed-Fish (*Calamoichthys*) from the rivers of Old Calabar. The former is a remarkable-looking creature of respectable size, being as much as 4 feet long. Running along the back are a considerable number of little dorsal fins, each with a strong spine in front, while the last of them abuts against the rounded protocercal fin of the tail, close to which, on the under side, is an anal fin. The paired fins consist of a thickened basal part, supported by cartilages something like those described for Dog-Fish (see p. 261), and fringed by a thinner region supported by radiating fin-rays. The body is covered by thick lozenge-shaped bony plates (ganoid

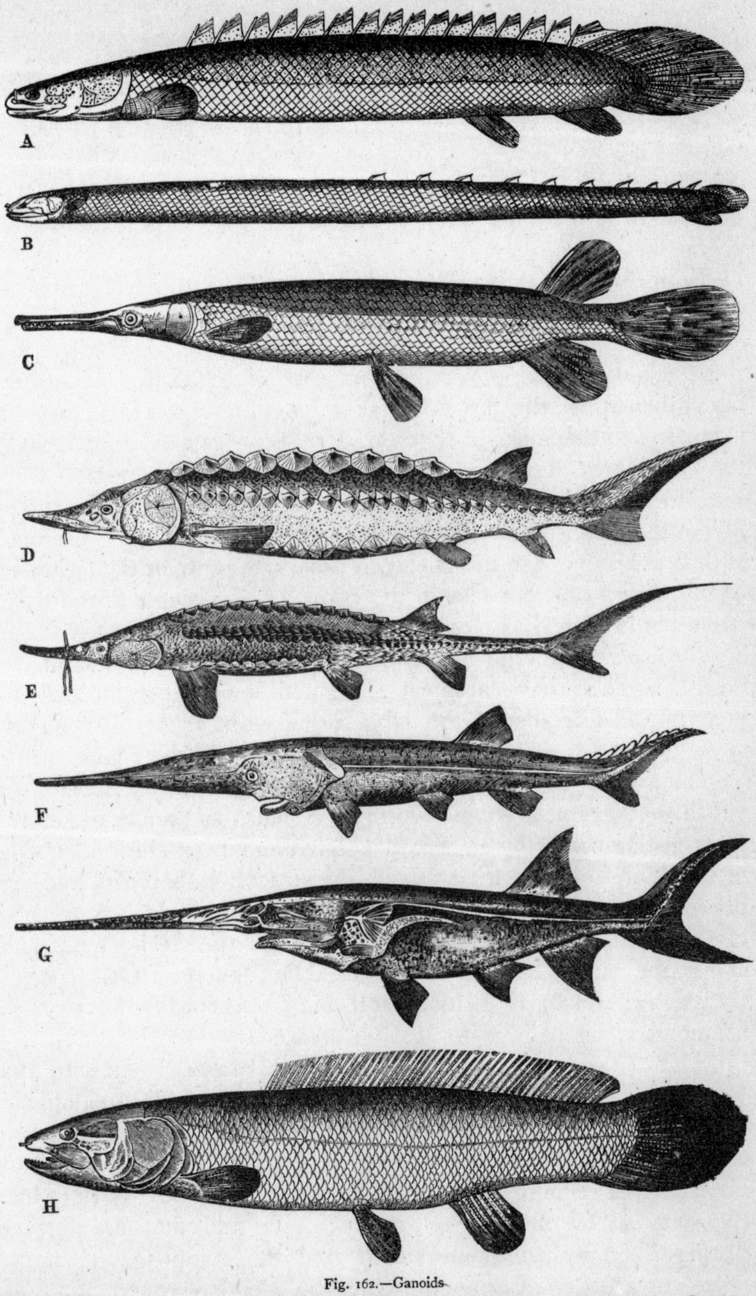

Fig. 162.—Ganoids

A, Bichir (*Polypterus*), $\times\frac{1}{4}$. B, Reed-Fish (*Calamoichthys*), $\times\frac{3}{7}$. C, Gar-Pike (*Lepidosteus*), $\times\frac{1}{7}$. D, Common Sturgeon (*Acipenser*), $\times\frac{1}{24}$. E, Shovel-nose Sturgeon (*Scaphirhynchus*), $\times\frac{1}{7}$. F, Slender-beaked Sturgeon (*Psephurus*), $\times\frac{1}{8}$. G, Spoonbill Sturgeon (*Spatularia* or *Polyodon*), $\times\frac{3}{8}$. H, Bow-Fin (*Amia*), $\times\frac{3}{10}$.

scales), united firmly by their edges and having a very regular arrangement in oblique rows, while the head is covered by paired bony plates.

The Reed-Fish is what a small Bichir might be imagined to become if it were pulled out into an eel-like form and lost its pelvic fins.

Both these forms are distinguished as "Fringe-finned" Ganoids on account of the structure of the paired fins; while the remaining recent Ganoids are "Ray-finned", *i.e.* the paired fins have lost the thickened basal portion and consist of a fan-like expansion strengthened by the numerous diverging fin-rays, which may be compared to the sticks of the fan. These ray-finned forms include the Gar-Pikes, Sturgeons, and Bow-Fins of the present day.

The Gar-Pike (*Lepidosteus*) is common in the fresh waters of North America, and may be as much as 6 feet long. Covered with firm armour like the Bichir, it differs not only in the structure of the paired fins, but also in the presence of a single dorsal only, while the head is drawn out into long but powerful jaws.

Sturgeons are large fishes which have lost more or less of the dermal armour, have a much elongated snout, and an unsymmetrical tail like that of the Dog-Fish (see p. 258). The mouth is on the under side of the body, at the base of the snout. The Common Sturgeon (*Acipenser*) includes some twenty species, of which the largest, a Russian form, is as much as 30 feet in length. It is distinguished by its broad pointed snout, on the under side of which are four sensitive thread-like structures (barbels), and the presence of rows of broad keeled plates in the skin. Sturgeons of this kind are widely distributed through the fresh waters and along the coasts of the Northern Hemisphere. One species (*Acipenser sturio*) is British, and may occasionally be seen in fishmongers' shops.

The Shovel-nose Sturgeon (*Scaphirhynchus*), native to the Mississippi and the rivers of Central Asia, is of more elongated form than the common form, and its dermal armour is more complete, especially in the hinder part of the body.

The two remaining kinds of Sturgeon both have teeth, while the sorts so far mentioned are toothless; and they are further distinguished by enormous snouts and the complete, or almost complete, absence of armour. One, the Slender-beaked Sturgeon (*Psephurus*) of the Yang-tse-Kiang and Hoang-ho rivers has a conical snout, and the other a broad flattened one, as is indicated by the name of Paddle-Fish or Spoon-bill Sturgeon (*Spatularia*). It is found in the Mississippi.

The last remaining recent Ganoid, the Bow-Fin (*Amia*), resembles the ordinary bony fishes in many respects, and was for long confused with them. Its body is covered by thin overlapping flexible scales. In distribution it corresponds to the Gar-Pike.

One structural feature in which all these Ganoids differ from the Dog-Fish is the possession of an elongated air-containing sac, the swim-bladder or *air-bladder*, which opens into the pharynx, usually on the upper side. In the Bichir, however, the air-bladder, like the lungs of terrestrial Vertebrates, is paired, and opens into the under side of that region. The original use of the swim-bladder is apparently that of a balancing organ, but in some Ganoids (Bichir, Gar-Pike, Bow-Fin) it assists in breathing, and in the Dipnoi has been converted into a lung. It is highly probable that the lungs of the higher Vertebrates are simply to be regarded as modified swim-bladders, and if so, an extremely interesting example of change of function is afforded.

Order 2.—Ordinary Bony Fishes (Teleostei)

Here are included the ordinary bony fishes of the present day, which include some three thousand existing species. The most important features of the group may be understood by briefly describing an average form, such as the common fresh-water Perch, and noting the differences between it and the Dog-Fish (see pp. 257–264).

The Common Perch (*Perca fluviatilis*) (fig. 163) is widely distributed through the fresh waters of Europe and North Asia, and is very beautifully coloured. The upper parts are of a warm reddish-brown, passing into golden on the sides and again into white below. Several broad dark bands run across the body, tapering off on the sides. Well-grown specimens in this country attain a length of 9 or 10 inches, or even a foot, but much larger specimens have been recorded.

The body is much flattened from side to side and the outline is spindle-shaped. It has been compared to a rounded wedge, eminently adapted for rapid progression through the water by means of the powerful lateral strokes of the large tail-fin, while the remaining fins act as balancers and steerers. The fairly large mouth, its jaws supported by bones bearing small teeth, is placed at the end of the pointed head, and above it may be seen two external nostrils, one on either side of the snout. Farther back still come the large, round, expressionless eyes,

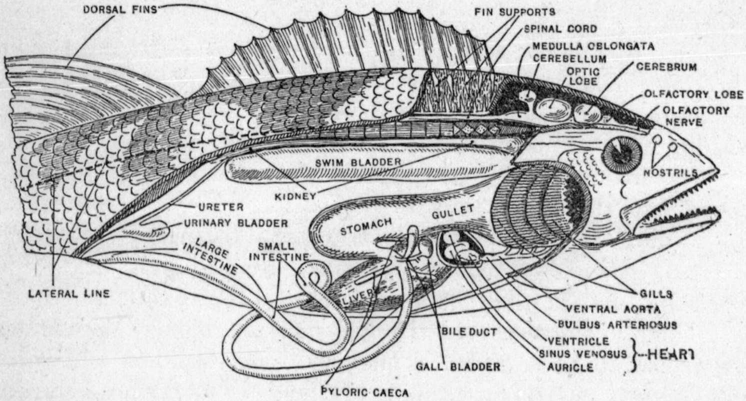

Fig. 163.—Side-dissection of Perch (*Perca fluviatilis*)

devoid of eyelids, but there are no spiracles behind them. No gill-slits are externally visible, but these may be seen by lifting up the firm gill-cover or *operculum* placed at the side of the head as in a Ganoid. Four such slits are present, instead of five as in the Dog-Fish (see p. 258), with four narrow bar-like gill-arches bearing the red, comb-like gills the separate teeth of the combs being the gill-filaments The gill-openings here are really slit-like, and not pouches as in Dog-Fish, and their existence is practically demonstrated by every school-boy who strings his small catches on a piece of grass, which he threads through the mouth and gill-slits under the gill-cover to the exterior. It is further of great interest to notice that on the inner side of the gill-cover, close to the first gill-slit, there is a small reddish projection. This *false gill* (pseudobranch) is the vestige of the first gill present in a Dog-Fish, and must not be confused with the false gill of that animal (see p. 263), which is on the front wall of the spiracular cleft, here entirely absent.

The *unpaired fins* consist of two large dorsals, of which the first is supported by exceedingly sharp spines, of an externally symmetrical (homocercal) caudal fin shaped like a fan, and an anal fin, quite close to which is the external opening of the intestine, for there is here no cloaca. Fan-shaped *pectoral* and *pelvic fins* are present, of the rayed type found in living Ganoids except the Bichir and Reed-Fish, and it may be noted that the latter are placed very far forward, much more so than in many other Teleosts. The *lateral line*, marking the position of important sense-organs (see p. 263), is indicated by a dark streak running along either side of the body about the level of the eye. The body is covered by thin overlapping scales.

The *internal skeleton* is complicated by the presence of a large number of bones, and contrasts strongly with the comparatively simple cartilaginous skeleton in Dog-Fish (see p. 259). The *skull* is particularly elaborate, and it must suffice to mention once more the presence of tooth-bearing bones bordering the jaws, which are attached at the back to the main skull by a hyo-mandibular bone equivalent to the cartilage of the same name in Dog-Fish (see p. 260). And as the Dog-Fish possesses no operculum, it has nothing corresponding to the bones which support that structure here.

The skeleton by which the base of the tail is supported presents some points of great interest. It will be remembered that in the Dog-Fish the tail is unsymmetrical (heterocercal), the vertebral column bending upwards and running into its upper lobe. Here, on the contrary, the expanded tail is externally symmetrical (homocercal), and the backbone apparently stops short at its base. Examination of certain very young Teleosts, however, shows that in them the tail is unsymmetrical, the backbone bending up in the characteristic way, and close examination of the apparently symmetrical tail of the adult shows that behind the last joint of the backbone is a little bony rod which turns upwards, and marks what is really the posterior end of the body. The homocercal tail, therefore, is really a modification of the old-fashioned heterocercal one, and may be looked upon as an improved type which has arisen from it.

Digestive Organs (fig. 103).—Small pointed teeth are present on the roof of the mouth-cavity as well as on the margins of the jaws, and the usual regions of the gut are present, *i.e.* mouth-cavity itself, pharynx out of which the gill-slits open, gullet, stomach, and intestine, the last not opening into a cloaca as in Dog-Fish, nor provided with a spiral valve (see p. 261). A large liver is present, but the pancreas appears to be represented physiologically by some blindly-ending tubes (*pyloric cæca*) which open into the beginning of the small intestine.

The *Circulatory Organs*, broadly speaking, are constructed on the same type as in Dog-Fish (see p. 261), though important differences are seen in the *heart*, which no longer possesses an arterial cone with numerous rows of valves, but presents a new structure, the arterial bulb (fig. 163), which succeeds the ventricle, and is really the swollen beginning of the ventral aorta, which, as before, runs forwards on the floor of the gill-region, and gives off the afferent branchial arteries that carry the impure blood to the gills to be purified.

The only *organs of respiration* are the gills, of which enough has been said to give an idea of their arrangement.

Nervous System and Sense Organs (fig. 163).—The *brain* presents the same regions as in a Dog-Fish (see p. 263), but is shorter and broader. The olfactory lobes are not placed on stalks, and there are two cerebral hemispheres instead of an unpaired projection, while the cerebellum is smooth and tongue-shaped.

Two obvious points as regards the *sense-organs* may be mentioned. One is that the nasal sacs have no internal openings into the mouth-cavity as in Dipnoi, but are distinguished by the possession of double external nostrils; while the other peculiarity is a negative one and consists in the absence of the numerous jelly-tubes so characteristic of the Dog-Fish (see p. 263).

A membranous *swim-bladder* (fig. 163) is present, situated above the other internal organs, close to the under surface of the backbone, but though it contains air, it has lost in the adult all connection with the gullet, and therefore cannot play even a subsidiary part in respiration.

Little more can be done here than briefly mention some of the more important or interesting types of bony fishes, but even so, it will make things clearer to indicate the chief groups. which are as follows:—

A.—Teleosts in which the swim-bladder when present has lost its connection with the gullet.

Sub-order 1.—Spine-finned Fishes (Acanthopterygii).
Sub-order 2.—Tuft-gilled Fishes (Lophobranchii).
Sub-order 3.—Firm-jawed Fishes (Plectognathi).
Sub-order 4.—Soft-finned Fishes (Anacanthini).

B.—Teleosts in which the swim-bladder retains its connection with the gullet by a pneumatic duct or tube.

Sub-order 5.—Tube-bladdered Fishes (Physostomi).

Sub-order 1.—Spine-finned Fishes (Acanthopterygii)

Here as in the Perch, which is a type of the sub-order, some or all of the fin-rays which support the dorsal, anal, and pelvic fins are sharp unjointed spines. Some 3650 different species are here included, divided into about 60 families, of which only a few can be mentioned.

1. *Perch Family* (fig. 163).—This is a group of carnivorous fishes, almost entirely confined to fresh water and distributed through the northern hemisphere.

2. *Bass Family.*—This is a large group of fishes, which are for the most part marine though some inhabit fresh water, and which have a very wide distribution. A well-known British species is the Common Bass (*Morone labrax*), which is much like the Perch, but more slender in build and not so brilliantly coloured, being bluish-grey above, gradually shading off to white on the under surface.

3. *Sword-Fish Family.*—The members of this family are large fishes, mostly found in the open sea, and deriving their name from the formidable sword-like weapon into which the upper jaw is produced. The Common Sword-Fish (*Xiphias gladius*) is sometimes taken in British seas, and occurs on both sides of the Atlantic. Other species are found in the Atlantic and Pacific. These fishes have become notorious from the fact that their swords have been found broken off in the timbers of ships, penetrating to a depth of as much as 22 inches (in a specimen exhibited in the British Museum). The force with which such blows have been given may be imagined.

4. *Dory Family.*—This includes marine fishes of extraordinary form, found in the East Atlantic, Mediterranean, and the seas of Australia and New Zealand. The John Dory (*Zeus faber*) is not uncommonly found in British seas. The body is much flattened, and with the head has a broad oval outline.

From behind each of the sharp spines of the large first dorsal fin projects a long filament. A small part of the upper side is dark-brown, which shades into golden-yellow farther down, and again into brownish white. On each side of the body there is a large round blotch, dark in colour with a lighter margin. By the ancient Romans it was regarded as sacred to Neptune.

5. *Mackerel Family.*—This is an important group of carnivorous food-fishes, abundant in the temperate and tropical seas of both hemispheres. They are remarkable for their powers of swimming. The Common Mackerel (*Scomber vernalis*) suggests the lines of a racing-boat in the beautifully graduated curves of its rather slender body, terminated behind by a well-developed caudal fin shaped like the head of a broad arrow. Rows of pointed finlets fringe the body in the spaces between the tail and the anal and second dorsal fins.

Another member of the family, sometimes taken off the south of England, and the object of an important Mediterranean fishery, is the Tunny (*Orcynus thynnus*), which may attain the length of 10 feet and a weight of more than 1000 pounds. Smaller species of the same genus are the Bonito (*Thynnus pelamys*) and Albicore (*Thynnus albicora*), which prey largely on Flying-Fishes, and, being rendered conspicuous by this habit, are often mentioned in accounts of voyages.

6. *Angler-Fish Family.*—This embraces widely-distributed fishes of extraordinary form, some of which frequent shallow water, while others drift with sea-weed in the open ocean, and still others live at great depths. A well-known British species is the Fishing-Frog (*Lophius piscatorius*), with its body dwarfed by an enormous head, the wide gaping mouth of which, armed with numerous teeth, is a regular death-trap for unwary little fishes of all sorts. The first dorsal is reduced to its long spines, the foremost of which terminates in a soft flap. The upper side is of a blackish brown and the under side white.

7. *Bull-Head Family.*—These are small ground fishes of wide distribution, and mostly found near to land, while there are also fresh-water forms. A common British species is the Bull-head or Miller's Thumb (*Cottus gobio*), common in brooks, as every school-boy knows; while just as common along our shores is the Sea-Scorpion (*Cottus scorpius*), which has much the same appearance.

8. The *Gurnards* are larger relatives of the preceding and are distinguished by their curiously-shaped bony heads, and by the fact that the first three rays of the pectoral fin have become distinct and form "fingers" used as organs of touch and in progression along the sea-bottom. They are fishes of wide distribution and often of bright coloration. The commonest British species is the Red Gurnard (*Trigla pini*), which is bright red in colour above and gleaming white below and on the sides.

9. *Goby Family.*—Gobies and their allies are small fishes common along the coasts of both tropical and temperate seas, while some are estuarine and a few inhabit fresh water. There are nearly a dozen British species, of which the largest and probably on that account best known is the Rock Goby (*Gobius niger*). In these fishes the pelvic fins are united into a funnel-shaped sucker.

10. *Blenny Family.*—The fishes of this family are mostly small and have the same wide distribution as the Gobies. The pelvic fins are very much reduced, and there is a single dorsal running along the whole length of the back, and equivalent to the two dorsals of perch fused together. A common British species is the Smooth Blenny or Shanny (*Blennius pholis*), in which the long, low dorsal fin is not broken into sections. The Wolf-Fish (*Anarrhichas lupus*), common on the north British coasts and ranging to Norway and Greenland, may be over 6 feet long, and resembles the Shanny on a large scale. The margins of its jaws and the roof of the mouth are studded with blunt teeth, adapted for breaking the coverings of molluscs and crustacea.

11. *Grey Mullet Family.*—Grey Mullets are common along the coasts of tropical and temperate regions, frequenting estuaries. The first dorsal fin is small, with only four spines, and the lateral line is absent. The best-known British species is the Common Grey Mullet (*Mugil capito*).

12. *Mackerel-Pike Family.*—Here are included Gar-Fishes and Flying-Fishes. The former are distributed throughout tropical and temperate seas, and the Common Gar-Fish (*Belone vulgaris*) is common on the British coasts. The body is much elongated and the snout is lengthened into a narrow pointed beak, well suited for seizing small fish. *Flying-Fishes* include a considerable number of species limited to the warmer parts of the ocean. The

Common Flying-Fish (*Exocœtus volitans*), found in all tropical seas, has immensely elongated pectoral fins, which constitute the so-called wings.

13. *Stickleback Family.*—The familiar little fishes constituting this family are mainly, but not entirely, inhabitants of fresh water, and are only found in the Arctic and North Temperate zones. The name is derived from the fact that the first dorsal fin is represented only by its spines, of which there are a variable number. There are three common British species, all of them nest-builders. Of these the largest is the Sea Stickleback (*Gastrosteus spinachia*), with fifteen spines. It also frequents brackish water. The other two kinds live in fresh or brackish water, the smaller being the Ten-spined Stickleback (*Gastrosteus pungitius*) or "Tinker", while the other is the Three-spined Stickleback (*Gastrosteus aculeatus*).

14. *Wrasse Family.*—Wrasses are widely-distributed shore fishes, being absent, however, from the polar regions, and are especially numerous on rocky coasts and coral reefs. Most of them are handsomely coloured, and some are pre-eminent among fishes in this respect. The bones which constitute the bases of the skeleton supporting the gill-arches (lower pharyngeal bones) are fused together into a single tooth-bearing piece. Many members of the group are distinguished by the possession of thickened lips, and all have blunt conical teeth suitable for crushing the shells of molluscs and crustacea, of which the food consists. There are a number of British species, of which one of the commonest is the Ballan Wrasse (*Labrus maculatus*), a stoutly-built fish of some 15 inches long. The colour is of a bright brown with numerous whitish spots, and touches of green on the fore-part of the head and the bases of the fins. Some individuals, however, are of a greenish colour all over. The spiny first dorsal is long and low, while the soft second dorsal is much shorter and higher.

Sub-order 2.—Tuft-gilled Fishes (Lophobranchii)

This small sub-order includes about 120 species of curiously modified fishes, in which pelvic fins usually, and anal and caudal fins commonly, have disappeared. The snout is drawn out into a tube, at the end of which the small rounded toothless mouth

WRASSES (*Labridæ*)

Wrasses are tropical and temperate shore fishes, possessed of thick lips and crushing teeth well suited to the food, which consists of molluscs. Many of them are beautifully coloured. All four of the species figured are native to the seas of Britain. Their names are:—

1. Rainbow Wrasse (*Coris julis*).
2. Ballan Wrasse (*Labrus maculatus*).
3. Cuckoo Wrasse (*L. mixtus*), male.
4. Corkwing (*Crenilabrus melops*).

WRASSES (LABRIDAE)

1. Rainbow Wrasse. 2. Ballan Wrasse. 3. Cuckoo Wrasse. 4. Corkwing.

is situated. Scales are absent, but their place is taken by bony plates developed in the deeper part of the skin and arranged in regular transverse rings. The name of the group (Gk. *lophos*, a tuft; *branchia*, gills) has reference to the gill-filaments, which are arranged in tufts and not in combs as in ordinary Teleosts. The male fish usually has a pouch in the skin on the under side of the body in which the eggs are developed and the young protected.

The Great Pipe-Fish (*Syngnathus acus*) is a common British species, with much-elongated cylindrical body and a small caudal fin. A much more extraordinary looking species is the Short-snouted Sea-Horse (*Hippocampus antiquorum*) (fig. 164), which has a very wide range and is sometimes found off the British coast. The name is suggested by the shape of the head, which is sharply bent on the trunk and separated from it by a sort of neck. The animal maintains a vertical position in the water, both when swimming and also when attached to sea-weed by means of its prehensile tail, which is devoid of a caudal fin.

Fig. 164.—Sea-Horse (*Hippocampus*)

Sub-order 3.—Firm-jawed Fishes (Plectognathi)

This also is a small group, embodying about 180 species, most of which have a well-developed external skeleton. There is as a rule nothing to correspond to the spiny first dorsal and pelvic fins of a perch, except, perhaps, a few spines. The gill-cover is not a large free flap, but is united with the surrounding parts so as to leave only a small aperture through which the water which has passed over the gills can flow out to the exterior. The internal skeleton is deficient in bony matter, but the bones of the upper jaw are very firm and fused to the main mass of the skull, a feature which the name of the sub-order suggests (Gk. *plektos*, woven together; *gnathos*, jaw). The included species are characteristic of tropical seas, though not confined to them, and include: 1. File-Fishes; 2. Coffer-Fishes; 3. Globe-Fishes; and 4. Sun-Fishes.

1. *File-Fishes* constitute a widely distributed family, in which

the skin is rough and there is a small spiny first dorsal fin, of which the first spine is ridged like a file on its front surface. The firm jaws, provided with strong teeth, are well adapted for breaking open the shells of molluscs, or nipping off pieces of coral. The Mediterranean File-Fish (*Balistes capriscus*) has occasionally been taken in British seas.

2. *Coffer-Fishes* are curious-looking creatures in which the body is almost entirely protected by numerous six-sided plates united by their edges. The Four-horned Coffer-Fish (*Ostracion quadricornis*) has been taken off the coast of Cornwall.

3. *Globe-Fishes* mostly have their bodies covered with strong spines, and possess the power of dilating the gullet with air, when the body swells out into a globe-like form and the spines are erected, furnishing a formidable protection. In this condition they are unable to swim, but are drifted along with the under side turned upwards. In the genus *Diodon* there is a bony plate in the front of each jaw, while in the allied genus *Tetrodon* each of these plates is divided into two, giving the appearance of four large front teeth.

4. *Sun-Fishes* are remarkable for the shortness and depth of the body, the caudal fin forming a border to the hinder end, which does not taper as in an ordinary fish. Adjoining the caudal fin is a long pointed dorsal above and a similar anal below.

Sub-order 4.—Soft-finned Fishes (Anacanthini)

In these fishes the rays which support the various fins are all soft and jointed, and the pelvic fins are situated very far forwards. There are some 370 species, of which many are of great economic importance. Only two of the included families need be mentioned here, *i.e.*: 1. the Cod Family, and 2. that in which the Flat-Fishes are included.

1. *Cod Family.*—The Common Cod (*Gadus morrhua*) (fig. 1) is the most important representative of a genus distinguished by the possession of three dorsal and two anal fins, while in this and some of the other species of the genus there is a filament or barbel attached to the lower jaw. The Cod abounds on both sides of the northern part of the North Atlantic, the most famous fishery being on the banks of Newfoundland. The Haddock (*Gadus æglefinus*) is another important species with a

similar range. It can easily be distinguished from the Cod by the black colour of the lateral line, and the presence of a rounded black patch just behind the gill cover. A third allied but smaller species is the Whiting (*Gadus merlangus*), the range of which is restricted to the seas of Northern Europe. It has a dark patch at the root of each pectoral fin and lacks the barbel of the two preceding species.

A small number of the species included in the Cod Family are fresh-water, and the best known of these is the Burbot or Eel-pout (*Lota vulgaris*), abundant in many of the rivers of North America and North and Central Europe. In England it is found in some of the rivers which flow into the North Sea. There are two dorsal fins, of which the second is very long and low, while on the under side of the body there is an anal fin of similar character. A barbel is present as in the Cod.

2. *Flat-Fish Family.*—The familiar food-fishes which make up this family are distinguished by a remarkable want of symmetry, which has no parallel among Vertebrates. One might at first sight imagine that the dark and light surfaces of the body were respectively upper and lower. A little closer inspection, however, would show that a long dorsal fin ran along one edge of the body and a long anal fin along the other; and further, that each surface had a lateral line running along it, and possessed both gill-cover and paired fins, thus conclusively proving the broad surfaces to be the sides. In some cases the dark upper side is the right one and in others the left. A flat-fish starts life with the same kind of symmetry as an ordinary fish, one eye being on the right and the other on the left, while the body is maintained in the usual position; but as development proceeds, and the body gets more flattened, one side becomes pigmented, and the eye of the contrary side is displaced so as to be near its fellow. We may take as well-known examples, Turbot, Plaice, and Sole.

The Turbot (*Rhombus maximus*) (fig. 34) is a large broad fish limited to European seas, and with the eyes on the *left* side. In the Plaice (*Pleuronectes platessa*), which though broad is a much smaller fish, the dark, eye-bearing surface is the *right* side. It is marked by large orange spots. This species ranges along the west coast of Europe and extends as far north as Iceland. The Common Sole (*Solea vulgaris*) also has the eyes on the *right* side, but its shape is an elongated oval. It is confined to European seas.

Sub-order 5.—Tube-bladdered Fishes (Physostomi)

This large group (some 2500 species) includes many important food-fishes, and includes both marine and fresh-water forms as well as forms which, like the Salmon, live partly in the one and partly in the other. The fins are supported by soft jointed rays, except, in some cases, the first ray in the dorsal and pectoral, which may be transformed into spines. The pelvic fins are situated far back in what must be considered as the primitive position, judging by other orders of fishes. The air-bladder, which, as previously stated, is an outgrowth from the gut, always retains a connection with it by means of a tube, whence the name of the sub-order. Only the more important families can be mentioned here.

1. *Cat-Fish Family.*—The Cat-Fishes or Siluroids include a large number of species inhabiting the fresh waters of tropical and temperate regions, while some of them are estuarine or even marine, though in the latter case they do not go far from shore. The name "Cat-Fish" has reference to the presence of long barbels, suggesting to a lively imagination the "whiskers" of a cat. The scaleless body is sometimes protected by bony plates. There is only one European species, the Wels (*Silurus glanis*) (fig. 165), and this is limited to the rivers east of the Rhine. Excepting only the Giant Sturgeon, it is the largest of European fresh-water fishes, attaining a maximum length of 13 feet and weight of 400 pounds, though average specimens are very much smaller. In this species the skin is soft, and there are six barbels, two very long ones above and four much smaller ones below.

2. *Salmon Family.*—The members of this group are in the main either purely fresh-water in habit, or ascend rivers to spawn, and, with the exception of a New Zealand genus, are confined to the northern hemisphere. There are, however, a few purely marine species. The body is of the typical fish-form, and covered with scales, except in the head region. A fairly-large first dorsal is situated about the middle of the back, and much farther back there is a small second dorsal, which, on

Fig. 165.—Group of Fishes reduced to various scales.

1, Salmon (*Salmo salar*). 2, Common Sturgeon (*Acipenser sturio*). 3, Wels (*Silurus glanis.*) 4, Eel (*Anguilla* account of its fatty texture, is generally called the adipose fin. An anal fin is placed opposite or nearly opposite this.

The Salmon (*Salmo salar*) (fig. 165) ranges right round the northern hemisphere as far south as latitude 41° in the New World and 43° in the old. It is well known as one of the fishes that live partly in the sea and partly in fresh water, while the Common Trout (*Salmo fario*) is limited to the latter.

The Common Smelt (*Osmerus eperlanus*) is an example of the smaller members of the Salmon family. It is found in the seas of both Northern and Central Europe, as well as in some of the lakes and rivers of the same regions.

3. *Pike Family.*—This is a small group of predatory fresh-water fishes, including only seven species, of which six are confined to the United States, while the Common Pike (*Esox lucius*) has a wide distribution through the temperate regions of the northern hemisphere. There is no fatty fin, and the single dorsal is placed far back near the tail. The shape of the head, with its flattened snout and projecting lower jaw, is very characteristic.

4. *Carp Family.*—This is a large group of fresh-water fishes distributed through all the great land masses except South America and Australia. There is no fatty fin, and the mouth is entirely devoid of teeth, though these structures are present in the pharynx, attached to the bones which support the gill-arches. The Common Carp (*Cyprinus carpio*) is a stoutly-built fish with a long dorsal fin and two pairs of small barbels. It is a native of Asia, but, being much esteemed as food, was introduced into Europe at an early date, and is supposed to have been naturalized in this country by the monks during the Middle Ages. The well-known Gold-Fish (*Carassius auratus*) is a domesticated species of a genus of carps in which barbels are absent. It is a native of China and Japan, and the bright colouring is the result of artificial surroundings. Remarkable varieties of form have also been produced, as in other animals which have come under the influence of man.

Among native members of the family may be mentioned the Gudgeon (*Gobio fluviatilis*), a small fish with a pair of short barbels; the much larger Barbel (*Barbus vulgaris*), with four barbels; the Common Bream (*Abramis brama*); the Bleak (*Alburnus lucidus*), Roach (*Leuciscus rutilus*), Chubb (*L.*

GROUP OF FRESHWATER FISH

1. The Carp (*Cyprinus carpio*) inhabits ponds, lakes, and sluggish streams, living upon worms, insect larvæ, &c., and vegetable matter, to which food its thick-lipped mouth, provided with four sensitive barbels, is well adapted. It is very tenacious of life, and exceedingly long-lived (100 years or more). 2. The Crucian Carp (*Carassius vulgaris*) is a small fish common in the lakes and ponds of Central and Northern Europe. It is often kept in captivity, together with its near relative, the Gold-Fish, which is a domesticated variety of the Golden Carp (*C. auratus*). 3. The Tench (*Tinca vulgaris*) is a well-known ground-fish of the carp kind, and its food is of the same mixed nature. It lives in stagnant water, which may be so foul that no other fishes can maintain themselves in it. 4. The Pike (*Esox lucius*) is an exceedingly voracious fish, widely distributed through temperate North America, Europe, and Asia. It attains a very considerable size.

GROUP OF FRESHWATER FISH

1. The Carp (Cyprinus carpio).
2. The Crucian Carp (Carassius vulgaris).
3. The Tench (Tinca vulgaris).
4. The Pike (Esox lucius).

cephalus), Dace (*L. vulgaris*), and Minnow (*L. phoxinus*); Tench (*Tinca vulgaris*); and the Common Loach (*Nemachilus barbatulus*), a small elongated slimy fish, with mouth on the under side of the head and a fringe of six barbels round the edge of the upper jaw.

5. *Herring Family.*—The fishes of this family are mostly marine, and are found in the shallower parts of the sea all the world over in tropical and temperate regions. Although not distinguished by number of species, they are unsurpassed among fishes in the number of individuals, these often swimming together in vast shoals, which partly accounts for their very great commercial value. The body is of the typical fish-shape, and much laterally flattened, especially on the under side, which may form a sharp edge, often with a saw-like margin and sometimes supported by small bony plates. Fatty fin and barbels are absent. The head is naked, but the rest of the body is covered by thin glittering scales, which are easily detached.

The Herring (*Clupea harengus*) abounds in the North Atlantic, North Sea, and Baltic, and is also found in the Black Sea. The Pilchard (*C. pilchardus*) ranges from the Mediterranean round to the English Channel, and when young is the familiar Sardine. The Sprat (*C. sprattus*) abounds on the west coast of Europe and extends into the Baltic and part of the Mediterranean.

6. *Eel Family.*—The snake-shaped fishes belonging to this family have a wide distribution through both the seas and fresh waters of tropical and temperate regions. The pelvic and sometimes the pectoral fins also are absent, and the dorsal, caudal, and anal fins all form a continuous fringe. The skin is either entirely devoid of scales, or numerous very minute scales are imbedded in it.

The Common Eel (*Anguilla vulgaris*) (fig. 165) has pectoral fins and minute scales. It has a wide distribution throughout Europe, the countries bordering the Mediterranean, and North America. The large marine eel known as the Conger (*Conger vulgaris*) is found in almost all parts of the world, and is distinguished from the Common Eel by the entire absence of scales, and its large mouth armed with formidable teeth. The maximum length appears to be about 8 feet. The Mediterranean Muræna (*Muræna helena*) is the typical representative of a widely-distributed section of marine eels. It attains the size of the Conger and was well known to the ancient Romans, who not only esteemed it as a delicacy but kept it as a pet. The skin is scaleless, as in the Conger, and is brilliantly coloured. The front end of the body is very thick, and the large mouth is armed with powerful teeth. Pectoral fins are entirely absent.

Sub-class III.—SHARKS AND RAYS (Elasmobranchii)

The Spotted Dog-Fish (*Scyllium canicula*) is a good type of this sub-class, and the description already given of it (pp. 257–264) will serve to give an idea of the essential features in the structure of the group. The most important of those features are the following:—The unsymmetrical tail, and position of the mouth and nasal openings on the under surface of the head. The possession of spiracular clefts and at least five pairs of gill-pouches, the external openings of which are not protected by a gill-cover. A cartilaginous skeleton, with comparatively simple skull and well-developed visceral skeleton, and paired-fin skeleton on the Dog-Fish type. Numerous rows of teeth on the margins of the jaws, constantly being renewed during life. A spiral valve in the intestine, and a cloaca. Well-developed arterial cone in the heart. A thick skin with placoid scales. No swim-bladder, or at most a small tubular outgrowth from the upper side of the gullet to represent it. Eggs large, containing much food-yolk.

It is convenient to divide these fishes into two orders, one containing the Sharks and Dog-Fishes (Selachoidei), the other Skates and Rays (Batoidei).

Order I.—Sharks and Dog-Fishes (Selachoidei) (fig. 166)

The shark-like fishes of this order comprise about 150 species, distinguished by spindle-shaped bodies gradually tapering to the tail-end, which is sharply bent up. The gill-slits open on the side of the body, and the eyes possess lids. There are nine families, of which only seven need be mentioned.

1. *Blue Sharks.*—The type of this family is the Blue Shark (*Carcharias glaucus*), which often reaches the length of 15 feet. Though not uncommon in British seas during the warmer part of the year they are specially abundant in the tropics, like most

of the larger sharks. The Common Tope (*Galeus canis*) is a small shark with a very wide distribution, and is a well-known British species. It may attain a length of 6 feet or more, and in colour is dark grey above and white below. The body is slender and the snout prolonged and pointed. A somewhat

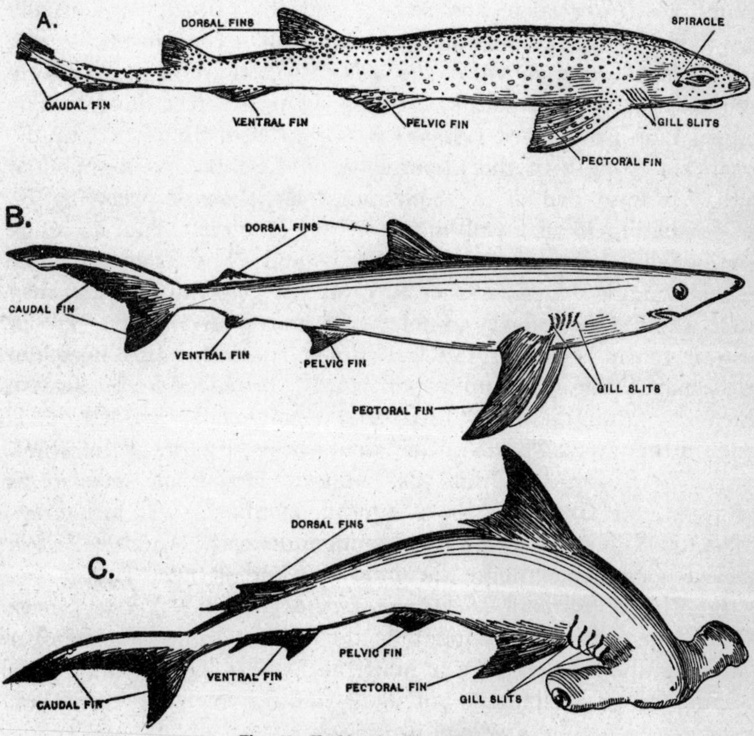

Fig. 166.—Sharks, reduced to various scales

A, Spotted Dog-Fish (*Scyllium canicula*). B, Blue Shark (*Carcharias glaucus*). C, Hammer-headed Shark (*Zygæna malleus*).

smaller form, common in British seas and widely distributed over the world, is the Smooth Hound (*Mustelus lævis*), which can easily be distinguished from the Tope by its blunter snout, and the presence of whitish spots on the back. The most remarkable-looking member of this family is undoubtedly the Hammer-headed Shark (*Zygæna malleus*), in which, as the name indicates, the head is broadened out like a T by the presence of projections upon which the eyes are situated. It has occasionally been taken in

British seas, but cannot be considered as a native species, its habitat being the warmer parts of the ocean in almost all parts of the world.

2. *Porbeagles.*—This includes sharks, which are most abundant in the open ocean and are often of very large size. The pointed teeth are large and strong, and the gill-slits are usually very wide, while the spiracle is small or even absent. The Porbeagle (*Lamna cornubica*) is a North Atlantic form and fairly common on British coasts. It is about 10 feet long. The Thresher or Fox-Shark (*Alopecias vulpes*) is distinguished by the remarkable length of the upper lobe of the tail. It is abundant in the Atlantic and is the commonest large shark occurring on our coasts, but is also well-known in the Mediterranean, its range also including the coasts of California and New Zealand. The Basking-Shark (*Selache maxima*) of the North Atlantic may reach a length of over 30 feet. It is not uncommon on our western coasts. Unlike the last-named species, which does not attack man, the huge Rondeletian Shark (*Carcharodon Rondeletii*), which may attain the length of 40 feet, is universally dreaded. It is found in the warmer parts of the open sea in all parts of the world.

3. *Dog-Fishes.*—Of this the Spotted Dog-Fish, selected as our type (pp. 257–264), is a typical member. All are coast-fishes, found in most tropical and temperate seas. Another British species, closely resembling the preceding but of much larger size, is the Nurse Hound (*Scyllium catulus*). The Zebra Shark (*Stegostoma tigrinum*), common in the Indian Ocean, is a member of this family. It may be as much as 15 feet long, and receives its name from the characters of its markings, which consist of dark transverse bands on a yellowish ground.

4. *Spiny Dog-Fishes.*—The species belonging here are mostly of small size and are devoid of an anal fin. The gill-slits are small and a spiracle is present. The Piked Dog-Fish (*Acanthias vulgaris*) is common on the British coasts, and is characterized by the presence of a sharp spine in front of each dorsal fin. A much larger species is the Greenland Shark (*Læmargus borealis*), which inhabits the seas of the Arctic region, and is one of the worst enemies of the Greenland Whale, from the tail of which it bites large pieces. It sometimes strays as far south as Britain, and, though it may be as much as 15 feet long, is harmless to man.

5. *Angel-Fishes.*—This contains a single species, the Angel- or

Monk-Fish (*Rhina squatina*), found all over the world in tropical and temperate seas, and not uncommon on our western coasts. Its chief interest lies in its flattened shape, in which respect it may be regarded as an intermediate stage between the sharks and skates, and in the extremely large pectoral fins (the "wings" of the imaginary angel) which also afford a point of resemblance to the latter group.

6. *Port Jackson Shark Family.*—This is a small group of comparatively small forms, including only one genus of four species, of which two are found on either side of the Pacific. The best known is the Port Jackson Shark (*Cestracion Philippi*) which ranges from Japan south to Australia and New Zealand. The head is short and blunt, and there is a sharp spine in front of each dorsal fin; but the chief peculiarity is found in the teeth. Those in front are sharp-pointed, but the rest have blunt rounded crowns, and, being arranged in several closely adjacent rows, form a surface well adapted to crush the molluscs upon which the shark feeds.

7. *Comb-toothed Sharks.*—This is a small group of tropical and sub-tropical species possessing certain primitive characters. There is only one dorsal fin, and the gill-slits, instead of being five in number on each side, as in other members of the sub-class, are either six or seven. Four of the five known species belong to one genus (*Notidanus*), and one of them, the Grey Six-gilled Shark (*N. griseus*), an Atlantic and Mediterranean form, is sometimes taken in British waters. The teeth are elongated, and each of them consists of a series of slanting cusps diminishing in size from one end of the tooth to the other. The other three species of this genus have seven gill-slits on each side. The Japanese Frill-gilled Shark (*Chlamydoselache anguineus*), which inhabits very deep water, resembles an eel in shape, and its mouth is at the front end of the body instead of upon its under surface. There are six gill-slits on either side, and each of them is protected by a backwardly-directed fold of skin, pleated in a frill-like manner.

Order 2.—Skates and Rays (Batoidei) (fig. 167)

The Skates and Rays which constitute this group are much flattened from above downwards, just the reverse of what obtains in an ordinary flat-fish, the breadth being increased by the enormous development of the pectoral fins, which form great wings extending from the head to the pelvic fins. As a result of this depressed shape, the gill-slits, of which the typical five pairs are present, are situated on the under side. The tail is narrow and forms a mere appendage, upon the upper side of which the small dorsal fins are placed, while the anal fin is absent. There are six families, of which five may be specially mentioned.

1. *True Rays.*—The numerous species of the rhomboidal-shaped fishes belonging to this family have a wide distribution, but are chiefly temperate forms more abundant in the northern than in the southern hemisphere. The numerous small teeth are closely packed in a considerable number of rows, arranged so as to form two roller-like surfaces which bite against one another. There are about twelve British species, of which the commonest are the Skate (*Raia batis*), in which the skin is comparatively smooth, and the Thornback (*Raia clavata*), which has the dorsal surface irregularly studded with large placoid scales of curious shape, each consisting of a circular disc from which a thorn-like spine projects, while a row of similar scales runs down the middle of the back.

2. *Saw-Fishes.*—This includes five species of fishes especially characteristic of tropical regions, and one of which (*Pristis antiquorum*) is common in the Atlantic and Mediterranean. The body is not broadened out to the same extent as in Rays, and in this respect is, so to speak, half-way between them and the Sharks. A remarkable peculiarity is found in the prolongation of the snout into a long flattened rostrum, in the sides of which are imbedded sharp teeth. These fishes may exceed 20 feet in length, as much as six of this being taken up by the "saw".

3. *Eagle-Rays.*—These are found both in tropical and temperate zones, one species, the Whip-Ray (*Myliobatis aquila*) being occasionally taken in British seas. The extremely slender tail is armed above with a strong spine, while the teeth, instead of being pointed, have flattened crowns, and are in contact with one another at the edges, so as to constitute a very perfect crushing surface, shaped like a roller.

4. *Sting-Rays.*—This group includes much-modified Rays, commonest in the tropics. The body is excessively broad, and the pectoral fins run forwards so as to surround the front of the

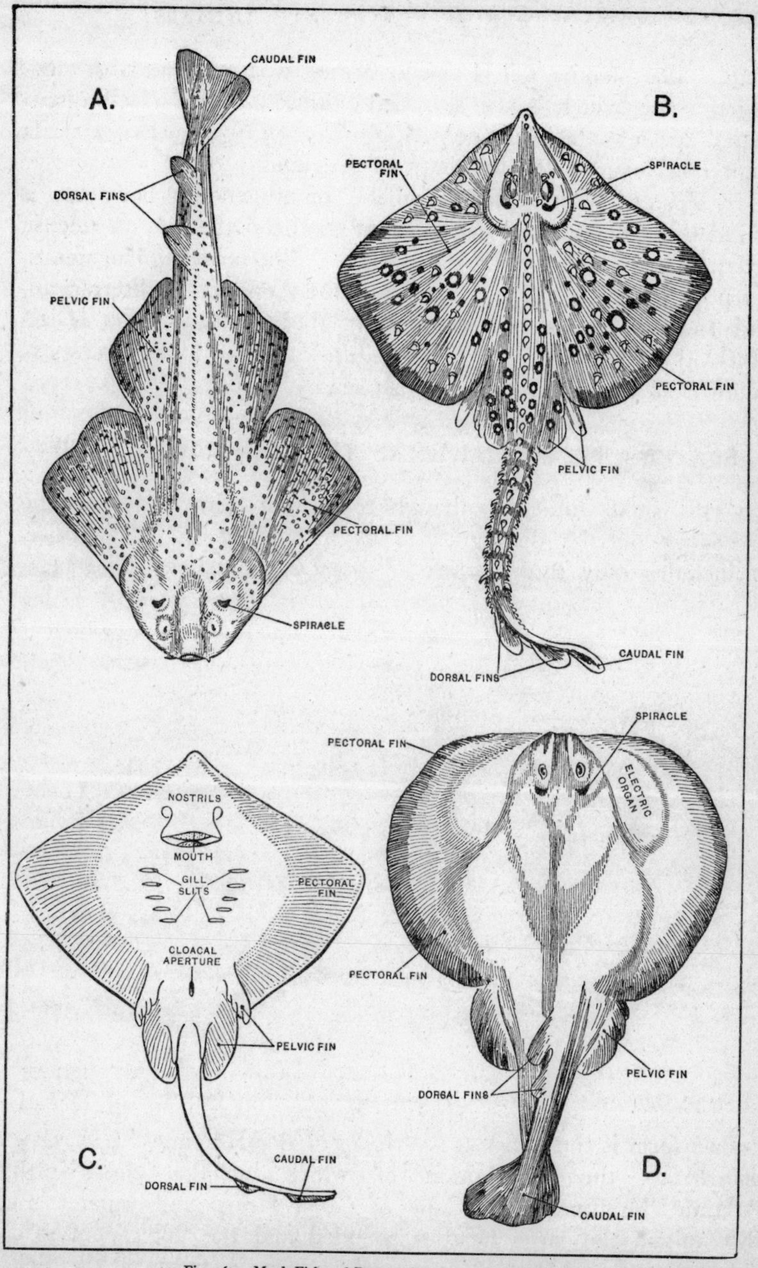

Fig. 167.—Monk-Fish and Rays, reduced to various scales

A, Monk-Fish (*Rhina squatina*). B, Thornback (*Raia clavata*). C, Under Side of young Skate (*Raia batis*) Electric Ray (*Torpedo nobiliana*).

head. The slender tail is usually armed with a formidable saw-edged spine, which is the so-called "sting". One widely distributed species, the Common Sting-Ray (*Trygon pastinaca*), is sometimes caught off the south of England.

5. *Electric Rays.*—In these the broad smooth body has a rounded outline, and on each side of the head there is an electric organ, capable of giving severe shocks. The most familiar genus, Torpedo, is represented by species in the Atlantic, Mediterranean, and Indian Oceans. A well-known Mediterranean form is the Marbled Torpedo (*Torpedo marmorata*), and an allied species is taken from time to time in British seas.

SUB-CLASS IV.—CHIMÆRAS (HOLOCEPHALI) (fig. 168)

This small sub-class, though related in many ways to the preceding one, is distinguished by a number of peculiarities. It includes only three genera of deep-water fishes. The best-

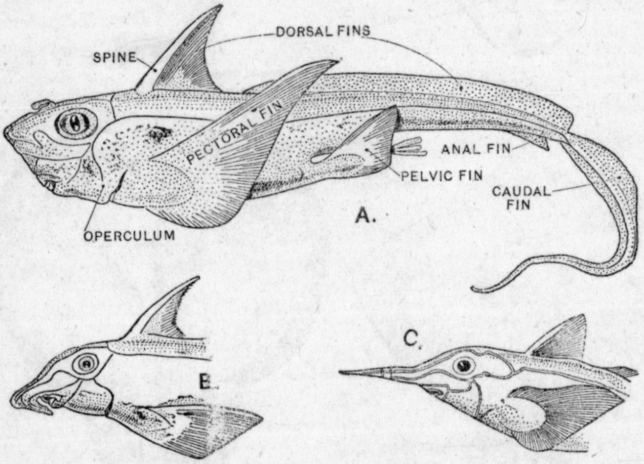

Fig. 168.—Chimæroids, reduced to various scales
A, Sea-Cat (*Chimæra monstrosa*), male. B, Bottle-nosed Chimæra (*Callorhynchus antarcticus*). C. *Harriotta.*

known form is the Sea-Cat or "King of the Herrings" (*Chimæra monstrosa*), the distribution of which includes the North Atlantic, Mediterranean, Cape of Good Hope, and Japan. In this animal the large head is rounded and the tail tapers to a mere thread. There is a powerful spine in front of the first dorsal fin, while in the male there is a peculiar tentacle-like structure on the top of the head, armed with curved spines and capable of being drawn back into a pit. The eyes are very large and the skin is smooth. Only four gill-slits are present on each side, and they are covered over by a membranous flap or gill-cover. There is no spiracle. Another species of Chimæra is taken off the coast of Portugal, and the third is found on the Pacific coast of North America.

The Bottle-nosed Chimæra (*Callorhynchus antarcticus*) of the southern seas is more shark-like in form, and its name is derived from the curious thickened form of the snout. A third genus (*Harriotta*), recently discovered in very deep water both in the Atlantic and Pacific, is comparatively small and is distinguished by its slender-pointed snout.

SUB-CLASS V.—ROUND-MOUTHS (CYCLOSTOMATA)

The Lampreys and Hags which make up this sub-class are so unlike other fishes in many respects that many zoologists place them in a class of their own. They have a wide distribution

Fig. 169.—Lampern (*Petromyzon fluviatilis*)

in the temperate regions of both hemispheres, and the lampreys occur in fresh as well as in salt water. There are four British species, three of these being lampreys, any one of which will serve to illustrate the chief characters of the sub-class. They are the Sea-Lamprey (*Petromyzon marinus*), the River-Lamprey or Lampern (*P. fluviatilis*) (fig. 169), and the Small Lamprey (*P. branchialis*). The eel-like body is bordered by three narrow unpaired fins, two dorsals and a caudal, but all traces of paired fins are absent. Instead of possessing a slit-like mouth bounded by jaws, as in all the backboned forms so far considered, a rounded sucker-like concavity is present on the under surface of the head, and the small mouth opens within this. The scientific name of the group is derived from this peculiarity (Gk. *kuklos*, a circle; *stoma*, a mouth). The skin is devoid of scales, but there are numerous little horny structures lining the mouth-sucker, and a muscular tongue armed with similar bodies can be protruded from the mouth and used as a rasping organ. A single nostril opens on the top of the head, behind this is the eye, and then come seven small round holes, which are the external openings of as many gill-pouches. The egg of the Lamprey develops into a larva which is so unlike the adult that it was formerly thought to be a distinct kind of fish and received the name of *Ammocœtes*.

The Common Hag-Fish (*Myxine glutinosa*) is shaped like a Lamprey, but the dorsal fin is absent, and the imperfect eyes are covered by the skin. The suctorial mouth is margined by eight barbels. At first sight there appear to be no gill-openings, but there are in reality six pairs of gill-pouches, the outer ends of which are drawn out below the skin into backwardly directed tubes, those on the same side uniting together and having a common opening pretty far back on the under surface of the body. The skin is very glandular, possessing the power of producing vast quantities of slime which sets into a firm jelly.

PRIMITIVE VERTEBRATES (Protochordata)

We now come to a number of very primitive forms, most of which were classified with the backboneless animals till comparatively recently. The characters of the backboned animals or Vertebrates have been enumerated and explained in an earlier part of this volume (pp. 60–63), to which reference must be made for details. It may, however, be remarked here that there are three chief characters by which a Vertebrate, or, to use a wider and better term, a Chordate, may be distinguished.

1. The possession at some period of life of a firm gelatinous rod, the *notochord*, running longitudinally below the central nervous system. Such a supporting rod can be made out in the embryos of all the forms hitherto described, but in most of them it is sooner or later squeezed out of existence, partly or entirely, by the development of a vertebral column. In some few instances,

however, as Lung-Fishes, Chimæra, Lamprey, and Hag, it persists throughout life, though invested in a firm sheath and supplemented by the development of cartilage. Ordinary bony fishes are a good instance of partial persistence of the notochord. Almost everyone must have noticed, in the pursuit of breakfast-table anatomy, that a gelatinous substance occupies the spaces between the doubly-cupped ends of the vertebræ in such fish as salmon and cod. This substance represents the part of the notochord which has not been nipped out of existence by the ingrowth of hard material to make up the joints of the backbone. In a Protochordate there never is a vertebral column or a backbone in the proper sense of the word, but only a more or less developed notochord.

2. It is scarcely less distinctive of Chordate animals that in them the pharynx should be perforated by visceral clefts in the embryo if not in the adult.

3. It is typical for a Chordate to possess a central nervous system (brain and spinal cord) situated *dorsally* above the notochord, and having the nature of a thick-walled *tube*.

We will apply these tests to the three recognized orders of Protochordates, *i.e.*: 1. Lancelets (Cephalochorda); 2. Sea-Squirts (Urochorda); and 3. certain still simpler forms grouped provisionally as Hemichorda. Very great theoretical interest attaches to the study of these forms, and much attention has been bestowed upon them, largely with a view of finding out how far they throw light upon the obscure problem having for its goal a determination of the characters of the simplest and earliest Vertebrates which appeared upon the globe.

SUB-CLASS I.—LANCELETS (CEPHALOCHORDA)

Lancelets are small fish-like creatures widely distributed round the coasts of the globe where the two conditions of sand and shallow water are combined. There are about 8 species, popularly referred to one genus *Amphioxus* (Gk. *amphi*, both; *oxus*, sharp), which, like the ordinary name, has reference to the fact that the flattened body is pointed at both ends. The common European species (*Amphioxus lanceolatus*) (fig. 170) is found on the Mediterranean and both Atlantic coasts, including our own islands. It is particularly abundant at Naples, where the fishermen use it as bait. The translucent body varies in length from about 1½ inch to rather more than double that size, and at first glance one might be puzzled to say which was the front end of the body, as no distinct head is present. On closer inspection, however, a little hood-like structure, fringed by slender

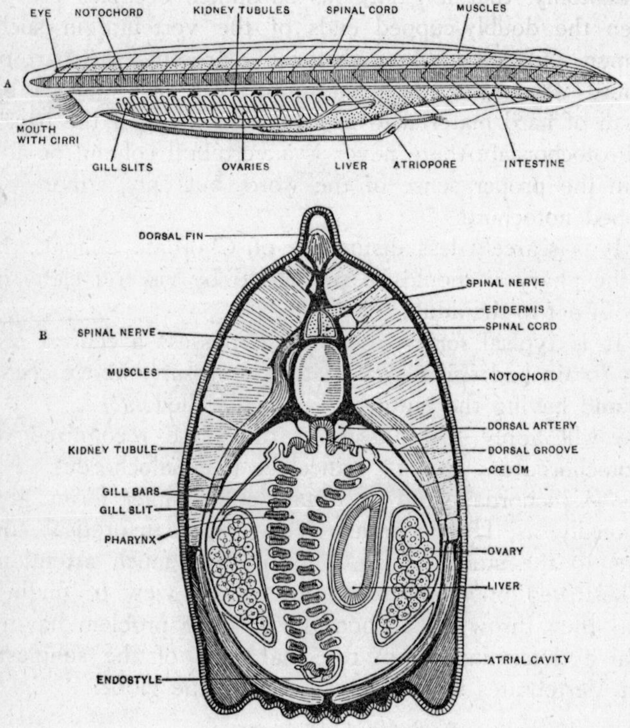

Fig. 170.—Lancelet (*Amphioxus lanceolatus*)

A, Side View, with internal organs seen by transparency. Semidiagrammatic. B, Transverse section. Much enlarged and semidiagrammatic.

tentacles, can be seen near one extremity. This marks the under side of the head end, and, since it leads to the mouth, has been called the *oral hood*, which has a certain resemblance to the mouth sucker of a Lamprey. Here as there jaws are absent, and the Lancelet is further devoid of the tooth-like projections and powerful rasping tongue which distinguish the Lamprey. Running along the upper margin of the body is a narrow *dorsal fin*, passing behind into a slightly expanded *caudal fin*, which again is in one piece with a narrow *anal fin* running forward for a short distance. In front of this the under side of the body is broad, convex, marked by longitudinal pleats, and bounded on each side by a prominent fold which runs forwards to the oral hood. These two lateral folds converge behind and end where the anal fin begins. In the description of the Dog-Fish it was stated (p. 258) that the various unpaired fins are probably expanded surviving fragments of a continuous fin which, in ancestral forms, ran along the middle of the back, round the tail, and forwards for some distance along the under surface. Such a condition is actually represented by the Lancelet, for, as just stated, its unpaired fins constitute a continuous fringe to the body. But further, it is by no means improbable that the pectoral and pelvic fins of an ordinary fish represent the front and back ends of a continuous *lateral fin* which once existed on either side. There are no paired fins in the Lancelet, but the lateral ridges in front of the anal fin are perhaps equivalent to such continuous lateral fins.

The Lancelet is obviously segmented, *i.e.* divided into a number of similar successive parts from before backwards, and this segmentation is well seen in the muscles which make up a great part of the side of the body, these being divided up into >-shaped sections. At first view the animal looks as if it were bilaterally symmetrical, but this is not the case, for the muscle-segments do not correspond on the two sides of the body; and further, the external opening of the intestine (there is no cloaca) is placed on the left side of the body near the base of the tail-fin. There is also a lack of symmetry in other respects which need not be mentioned here.

A well-developed *notochord* is present, and like many of the other internal organs can be made out without dissection by examination of small specimens mounted whole as microscopic objects. There is, however, one peculiarity about it. Instead of stopping short about the middle of the brain, as it does in the higher Vertebrates, it runs to the extreme front, and the scientific name of the sub-class alludes to this (Gk. *cephalon*, head; *chordē*, string).

No *gill-slits* are visible on the exterior, but dissection shows that a very large number are present as oblique openings in the wall of the large pharynx. They do not, however, open directly to the outside, but into a large *atrial cavity* which surrounds the pharynx, and which itself opens to the exterior by a rounded hole, the *atriopore*, on the under side of the body just in front of the anal fin. The state of things may be more clearly understood by reference to the development of the tadpole (p. 254), where the gill-slits at first open directly to the exterior but are

Fig. 171.—Two Simple Ascidians. 1, *Ciona intestinalis*. 2, *Phallusia mammillata*

later on covered over by the backward growth of a fold of the body-wall, the upshot of this being the formation of a branchial chamber into which the gill-slits open, and which opens to the exterior itself by a small hole on the left-hand side of the body. If this hole were in the middle line below, instead of on the left side, it might be compared to the Lancelet's atriopore, while the branchial cavity has much the same relations as the atrial cavity. It would probably be incorrect to consider the two cavities as closely equivalent, for they develop in very different manners.

The Lancelet will also stand the third test of a Vertebrate, for it possesses a tubular *nerve-cord*, situated above the notochord, but not extending so far forwards. There is, however, no distinct brain.

It is usual to find this animal buried in the sand in a vertical position, with the head end projecting; but it can also swim, and is able to burrow in the sand with great rapidity.

SUB-CLASS II.—SEA-SQUIRTS (UROCHORDA)

Among the objects cast up by the tide on the sea-shore, or found attached to rocks which are uncovered at low-water, are certain leathery-looking objects which when touched emit a jet of water, a habit which has earned for them the name of *Sea-Squirts.* On account of the firm cover or tunic with which they are invested the name of Tunicates has also been widely used. They are the first fixed or sedentary animals with which we have had to deal, and this mode of life has had a profound influence upon their structure. A common British species, *Ascidia mentula*, may be taken as an example.

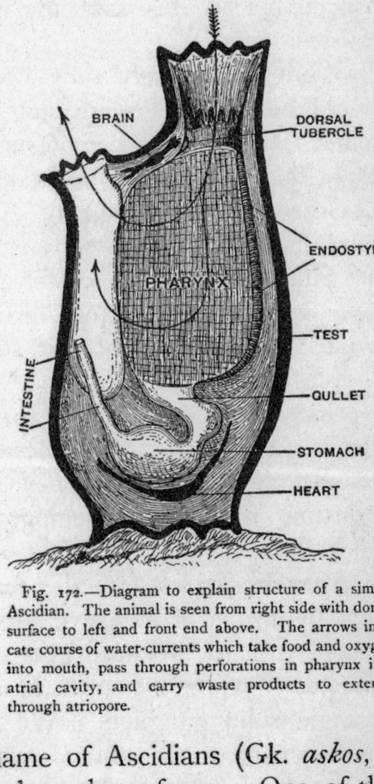

Fig. 172.—Diagram to explain structure of a simple Ascidian. The animal is seen from right side with dorsal surface to left and front end above. The arrows indicate course of water-currents which take food and oxygen into mouth, pass through perforations in pharynx into atrial cavity, and carry waste products to exterior through atriopore.

The plump rounded body is attached by one end to some foreign object, while at the other end may be seen two orifices (see p. 296, fig. 171), each placed on a projection, so as to give a distant resemblance to the skin bottles used in the East, and which is embodied in the name of Ascidians (Gk. *askos*, a wine-skin; *eidos*, like) often applied to these forms. One of the openings is situated at the extreme end and the other somewhat on one side. The former is the *mouth* and the latter the *atriopore*, and observation of a living specimen placed under water will show that currents set into one and out of the other. The protective tunic or *test*, which is thick and gristly in texture, is interesting on account of its chemical composition, as it is largely made up of a substance, cellulose, which is almost entirely confined to plants. Dissection (fig. 172) fails to show the presence of a notochord, and the central nervous system merely consists of an elongated thickening or *ganglion*, placed about half-way between the two apertures, but the pharynx is perforated for breathing purposes as in ordinary Vertebrates. The mouth, in fact, leads into a large branchial sac or *pharynx*, perforated by innumerable small holes and suspended in an atrial cavity which opens by the atriopore already mentioned. There is therefore a general resemblance to the Lancelet in this respect, but in this case the intestine also opens into the atrial cavity.

Were we to rely only upon the anatomy of the adult we should hesitate before placing the Sea-Squirt among the Vertebrates, seeing that it conforms to only one of the three chief tests; but the matter is set definitely at rest by a study of the development. The egg of Ascidia becomes a tadpole-shaped *larva* in which a *notochord* is present, though it is confined to the tail, and for that reason is often called a urochord (Gk. *oura*, tail; *chordē*, string), which gives the name Urochorda, adopted at the head of this section as the name for the group of Sea-Squirts generally. And further, the ascidian tadpole is possessed of a hollow brain and spinal cord situated on the dorsal side of the body, besides which it may be noted that the perforations in the pharynx are at first of simple character, consisting of paired openings suggestive of the gill-clefts of fishes, &c.

After leading a free life for some time the tadpole attaches itself by means of adhesive projections situated at the head end, the tail with its urochord gets smaller and smaller and ultimately disappears, while the central nervous system is simplified into a single solid ganglion. We have, therefore, the remarkable phenomenon of an animal which, when young, possesses the distinctive vertebrate characters, but loses most of them in the adult condition, becoming, so to speak, of lower grade. This is a good example of biological *degeneration*.

It is a singularly interesting fact that one or two small free-swimming Ascidians, of which the best known (*Appendicularia*) (fig. 173) occurs in British seas, retain throughout life the tadpole form and the typical Vertebrate characters. It is possible that these are primitive forms which retain the features distinctive of the ancestral Ascidians, but it is also possible that we have a case of animals which have dropped the adult stage out of their life-history, just as the Mexican Axolotls appear to be doing (see p. 249).

Ascidians may be divided into Fixed and Free-swimming forms, each of which groups can be again split up into Simple

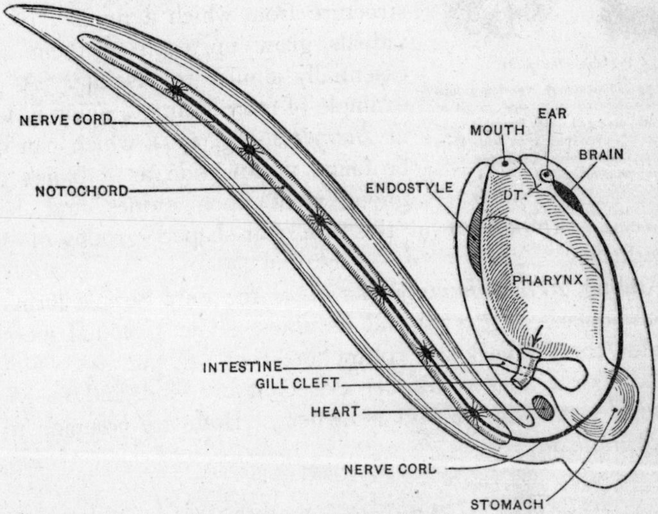

Fig. 173.—Diagrammatic drawing of Appendicularia (much enlarged), as seen from left side, with dorsal surface to right. D T, Dorsal tubercle.

and Colonial species. The last expression needs explanation, as it involves a phenomenon of which no instance is furnished by the animals previously considered. All these are propagated solely by means of eggs, but in Ascidians and many of the lower Invertebrates there may be increase by means of outgrowth of buds (gemmation) or by the bodily splitting (fission) of individuals to form others. As this suggests similar processes among plants, it is commonly known as *vegetative propagation.* A collection of animals which have been formed in this way, and which remain united together, constitute a *colony*, or are said to be colonial. In Ascidians colonies may be formed by means of budding.

The individuals of *Fixed Ascidians* are of comparatively large size in the Simple forms (fig. 171), of which the example taken is a typical one. The Colonial forms are made up of smaller individuals, and the colonies produced may be of the most varying form and size, while the degree of union between the members of the colony is more or less complete. In such a native genus, for instance, as *Clavellina*, we find a creeping stalk-like structure from which a number of individuals grow up, each of them being essentially similar to Ascidia. A good example of more intimate union is found in *Botryllus* (fig. 174), which can often be found at low tide as a bluish gelatinous crust upon stones and brown sea-weed. Imbedded in this are star-shaped groups of small individuals.

Fig. 174.—*Botryllus*

To left, a small colony, showing groups of individuals. To right, two groups of individuals, enlarged. The lower group is made up of seven members, with their mouths at outer ends. In centre is an atriopore common to all of them.

Among *Free-swimming Ascidians* the only Simple forms are Appendicularia (fig. 173) and its allies. The Colonial members include the remarkable phosphorescent *Pyrosoma*, which is shaped like a hollow cylinder closed at one end, and the *Salps*, of which more will be said elsewhere. Both are common in the Mediterranean.

Sub-class III.—WORM-LIKE PROTOCHORDATES (Hemichorda)

Here are massed together a small number of forms about which there has been endless discussion, and of which the one with most certain tenure of Chordate rank is a worm-like creature which has no common name, but which may perhaps be called the Acorn-headed Worm (*Balanoglossus*) (fig. 175). It is found at low-tide mark in many parts of the world, living in mud or sand which it glues together into a sort of temporary tube by means of a slimy fluid poured out from the skin. One species is found in the Channel Islands. The front of the body is made up of a swollen *proboscis*, yellow or orange in colour, and capable of altering its shape to a very great degree. It is attached behind by a narrow stalk, and the general outline in some species suggests the term "acorn-headed". The *mouth* is situated on the under side, at the base of this proboscis. Next comes a comparatively short region, named from its appearance the *collar*, while the rest, and by far the longest part, of the animal may be termed the *trunk*. On the upper side of the trunk, behind the collar, are a considerable number of *gill-slits* arranged in pairs, and forming the external apertures of *gill-pouches* which communicate internally with the digestive tube. They resemble in many respects the corresponding structures in the Lancelet. A small *notochord* has also been identified, but here we have the opposite extreme from what is found in an Ascidian tadpole, for the structure in question is a small rod which projects into and supports the base of the proboscis. It is in reality a thickened forward outgrowth from the digestive tube, and has a peculiar microscopic structure which is distinctive of notochords wherever they are found. The fact that it grows out of the gut is also a point in support of its notochordal nature, for in more typical cases, as, *e.g.*, Lancelet or Frog, the notochord arises as a thickening in the wall of the digestive tube. The remaining test of a Vertebrate is also answered in a fairly satisfactory way, for what may be described as the *central nervous system* in this creature is a more or less hollow thickening running along the dorsal part of the body in the collar region.

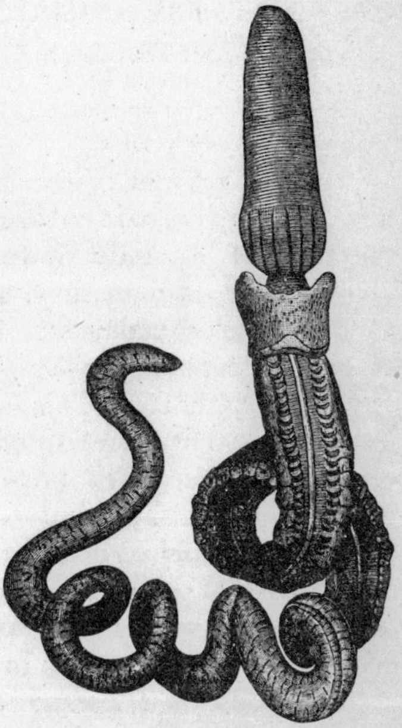

Fig. 175.—Acorn-headed Worm (*Balanoglossus*)

There are certain other more doubtful claimants to a place in the Hemichorda, but a discussion of their characters would be out of place in a preliminary sketch of the animal kingdom.

CHAPTER VII

BACKBONELESS ANIMALS (INVERTEBRATA). STRUCTURE AND CLASSIFICATION OF NEMERTINES AND MOLLUSCS

A brief account of the Backboned or Vertebrate animals has now been given, and in accordance with the usual custom from the time of Aristotle downwards all the remaining forms, far more numerous than they, may be conveniently lumped together as Backboneless animals or Invertebrates, divisible into a number of great groups or phyla, each of which is on a footing with the phylum Vertebrata. The lower Invertebrates are so unlike the Vertebrates that close comparison is not possible, but there are certain features which broadly serve to mark off a higher Invertebrate from a typical backboned animal. These are, to a large extent, implied in the summary given previously (pp. 60–63) of the chief Vertebrate characters, but it may be useful at this point to take such a form as a Cray-Fish or Lobster and point out the distinctive features in question (fig. 176).

The body of a *Lobster* has the same two-sided or bilateral symmetry as that of a Vertebrate, and there is a clear distinction between front (anterior) and back (posterior) ends, upper (dorsal) and lower (ventral) surfaces, and right and left sides. The body, too, is segmented, or divided into a number of similar parts from before backwards, as in, say, a Lancelet. This is evident in the Lobster's tail. It must not, however, be hastily assumed that a segment of a Lobster is the exact equivalent either of a Vertebrate segment or a segment in an Invertebrate from another group.

Now come a number of important differences. A large number of jointed *limbs* are present, arranged in pairs, while a Vertebrate has at most two pairs of limbs, though these may differ in nature in different animals, and in the simplest case, that of fishes, are unjointed fins. The limbs are modified for various purposes. The most obvious are those which end in the large pincers, behind which four large pairs of walking-legs are apparent. Under the head are a number of overlapping limbs, turned somewhat forwards, which guard the mouth and act as jaws. In a Vertebrate the jaws are part of the bony framework of the head, helping to bound the mouth-cavity, and the lower jaw works up and down. But the limb-jaws of the Lobster are outside the opening of the mouth, and from the nature of the case work against one another from side to side. To realize this, raise your hands to your mouth and "clap" them together, which will give an idea of the way in which one pair of the Lobster's jaws are worked. Six pairs, however, are present in all.

By combining the knowledge obtained by dissecting one Lobster from the side and making a cross-section through another, the following distinctive characters of higher Invertebrates can be easily verified:—

1. There is a protective *external skeleton* (exoskeleton) but no internal skeleton (endoskeleton), *i.e.* nothing can be discovered equivalent to the skull, backbone, &c., of, say, a Perch, or to the notochord of a Lancelet. The absence of endoskeleton modifies the structure in many ways, as, *e.g.*, in regard to the attachment of muscles. In such a limb as the human arm the numerous muscles are attached to the bones, but in a Lobster's leg they are attached to the firm exo-skeleton.

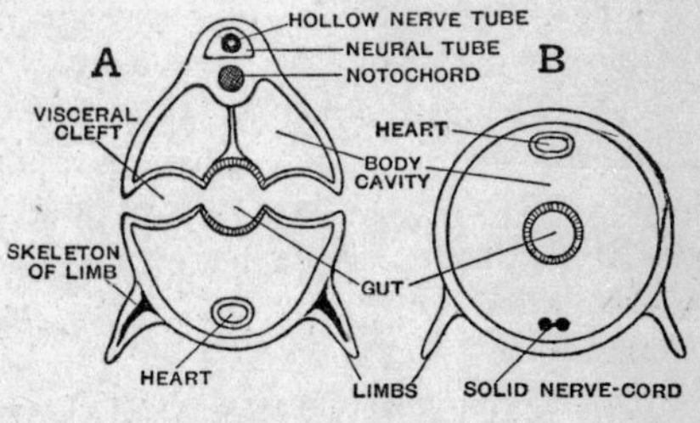

Fig. 176.—Diagrammatic Cross-sections through, A, a Vertebrate; B, a higher Invertebrate

2. The body is not a double but a *single tube* in structure.

3. The side-walls of the digestive tube are not perforated by gill-slits.

4. The *heart* is situated *dorsally*, the exact opposite of the Vertebrate condition.

5. The *nervous system* consists of a *ring* surrounding the gullet, and continued backwards into a *ventral nerve-cord*. The dorsal side of the ring is thickened into a double *brain* or *cerebral ganglion*. A very large number of Invertebrates possess such a nerve-ring and ventral cord, while many more have the ring

though not the cord. In no Invertebrate does the central nervous system consist, as in Vertebrates, of a hollow cord running along the dorsal side of the body.

The contrasts between a Vertebrate and a higher Invertebrate are illustrated by the accompanying diagrams (fig. 176).

The following groups or *phyla* of the Invertebrata are recognized. It must not be imagined, however, that they are anything like of equal size, for some are exceedingly large, while others are relatively small.

I. Nemertines (NEMERTEA).—Worm-like marine forms, which in some respects approach the Chordata in structure.

II. Molluscs (MOLLUSCA), including such forms as Cuttle-Fishes, Snails, Slugs, Oysters, and Mussels.

III. Jointed-limbed Animals (ARTHROPODA), the largest group of the animal kingdom, comprising such creatures as Insects, Scorpions, Spiders, and Mites; Centipedes and Millipedes; Shrimps, Lobsters, and Crabs.

IV. Segmented Worms (ANNELIDA).—A large group of forms, including innumerable Marine Worms (free-living and tube-inhabiting), Earth-Worms, Fresh-water Worms, and Leeches.

V. Siphon-Worms (GEPHYREA).

VI. Wheel Animalcules (ROTIFERA).

VII. Moss-Polypes and Lamp-Shells (MOLLUSCOIDA).—The great bulk of these are fixed marine animals, and those belonging to the first group are nearly all colonial.

VIII. Flat-Worms (PLATYHELMIA).—The most familiar of the forms grouped here are the Flukes and Tape-Worms, which are found as parasites within the bodies of other animals.

IX. Thread-Worms (NEMATHELMIA).—The name of the group indicates the shape of these creatures, most of which are parasites, either in plants or else within the bodies of other animals.

X. Echinoderms (ECHINODERMATA).—This phylum is constituted by such marine forms as Star-Fishes, Sea-Urchins, Sea-Lilies, and Sea-Cucumbers.

XI. Zoophytes (CŒLENTERATA).—Mostly marine animals, which may be either simple or colonial, fixed or free-swimming. Familiar examples are Jelly-Fishes, Sea-Anemones, and Corals.

XII. Sponges (PORIFERA).—Mostly marine, colonial, and fixed.

XIII. Animalcules (PROTOZOA).—This lowest phylum includes an immense number of simply-constructed animals, which are nearly always very small or microscopic in size. They are found almost everywhere, but are unfamiliar to those who are not in the habit of using the compound microscope.

A brief survey will now be made of these thirteen phyla, but many particulars regarding them will be found in other parts of this work.

NEMERTINES (NEMERTEA)

Although the worm-like forms which belong here have a wide distribution, and are particularly common between tide-marks on almost all coasts, they are nevertheless practically unknown except to the professed naturalist, and have received no common names. There are some forty British species. The vast majority are marine, and either shore or shallow-water forms, but they are also represented in fresh water and even on land. They have been given here the first place among Invertebrates, in deference to the views of many zoologists, in whose opinion they come near to the Protochordates.

The body of a typical Nemertine (fig. 177) is cylindrical, and presents no trace of segmentation. It may be only a small fraction of an inch in length, or in other cases many yards long. A common British form (*Lineus marinus*) is one of the species which are extremely elongated, and it may not infrequently be found under stones, with its slimy black body twisted up into a complicated coil. Other species may be more or less brightly coloured.

The *mouth* is a small oval opening on the under side of the head end, while the aperture of the intestine is at the extreme tip of the tail. Close examination will show that above the mouth on the front end of the body there is a small pore, and in a living specimen a narrow thread may sometimes be seen to shoot out from this pore, through which it can again be drawn back into the body. This thread is known as the *proboscis*, and, as described elsewhere, it is used as a means of killing or paralysing the marine worms upon which a Nemertine chiefly feeds. When within the body it is enclosed in a special sheath which overlies the digestive tube. The proboscis is hollow, and the way in which it is protruded and again drawn back may be understood by taking the somewhat hackneyed illustration of a glove with one finger. If this finger be pulled back into the main glove by turning it outside inwards, we shall have a rough model of the proboscis when lying within the body.

If now the finger be pushed out, it will represent the extended proboscis. The pulling in is effected by means of a muscle band which runs along the interior of the thread and is attached to its tip, while the pushing out is the result of fluid being squeezed into the thread from its sheath. This kind of principle is utilized elsewhere in the animal kingdom, and a very familiar example

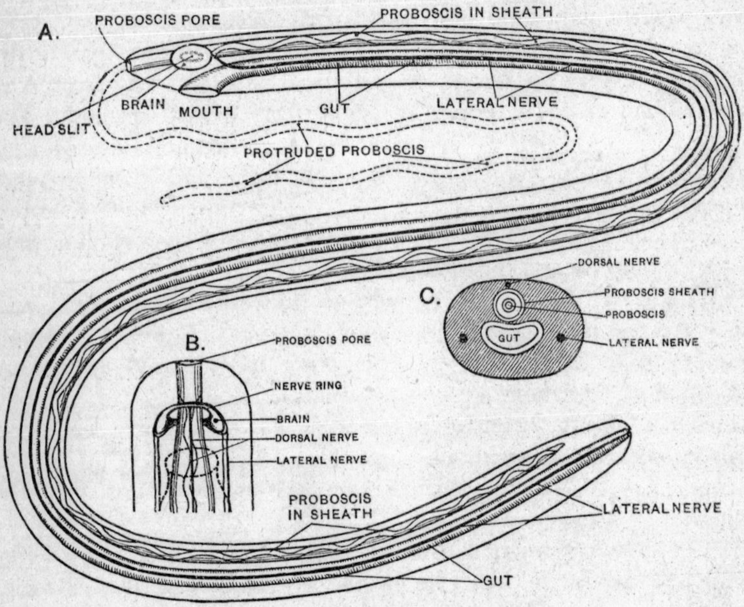

Fig. 177.—Structure of a Nemertine (diagrammatic)

A, Side view, internal organs seen by transparency. B, View from above of front end; position of mouth and beginning of gut indicated by the dotted line. C, Cross-section.

is found in the "horns" of the common Snail, which can either be stretched out (as immortalized in the nursery rhyme wherein the adventures of certain snail-hunting tailors are set forth) or withdrawn into the body at will.

Reasons have been adduced for thinking that the proboscis-sheath is comparable to a notochord, and the proboscis to a curious little structure attached to the under side of the brain in Vertebrates, and known as the pituitary body.

The *central nervous system* of a Nemertine is interesting in many ways. It consists of a *nerve-ring*, which encircles the front end of the proboscis, and not the digestive tube as is usual among

Invertebrates. Each side of the ring is thickened into a ganglion, from which a lateral nerve-cord runs along the corresponding side of the body, while there is a much more slender nerve running back in the middle line above from the upper side of the ring. This *dorsal nerve* has attracted a great deal of attention, for it has been compared to the spinal cord of a Vertebrate, though, unlike this, it is solid.

MOLLUSCS (Mollusca)

Molluscs include such familiar shell-fish as Periwinkles, Oysters, Cockles, and Mussels, as well as soft-bodied animals like Cuttle-Fishes, to which the term Mollusca (Lat. *mollis*, soft) was originally applied.

Examination of such a typical form as the Ormer or Sea-Ear (*Haliotis tuberculata*), which is common in the Channel Isles, will give some idea of the characters of Mollusca in general, and of the special subdivision to which this particular sea-snail belongs (fig. 178).

External Characters.—The most obvious feature is the presence of a large external *shell* covering the upper side of the body, from which it cannot be detached without cutting through a large rounded fleshy mass, the *shell-muscle.* The shell is not symmetrical, for a row of holes can be seen running along near its left margin, and on the right side at the back a spiral twist can be made out. Turning the animal over, a huge fleshy mass with a flattened surface is seen projecting from the under side of the body. By means of this *foot* the Ormer is able to adhere to rocks like a Limpet, and to crawl about like an ordinary Snail. A foot in some form or other is characteristic of all Mollusca, and it must be understood that the word is here employed with a special meaning of its own. Projecting in front from above the foot a short *head* can be seen bearing a blunt snout, at the end of which the *mouth* is placed, and a pair of pointed feelers or *tentacles*, which are solid, and cannot therefore, like those of a common Snail, be withdrawn into the body. Seen from below, the body of the Ormer is bilaterally symmetrical, and the twisted condition of its upper part is a special condition characteristic of snail-like forms in general.

On removal of the shell by cutting through the shell-muscle the soft upper part of the body in which a large part of the viscera are contained will be exposed, and it will be noticed that this *visceral hump*, as it has been called, is twisted behind in correspondence with the twist in the shell. Skirting the visceral hump is a flap, produced by a pulling out, so to speak, of the body wall, and known as the *mantle*. In the Ormer it is narrow for most of its extent, but is very well developed in the part underlying the row of holes in the shell, where it roofs in a large *mantle-cavity*, which has a long slit-like aperture above and a wide opening in front about the head. That this mantle-cavity should freely communicate with the exterior is very necessary, for not only does it contain the breathing organs, but the intestine and the kidneys open into it. A very small amount of dissection reveals the presence of the breathing organs in the form of two plume-like *gills* attached along their sides, and having their tips pointing forwards. The projecting end of the intestine will also be seen, and right at the back of the cavity two small holes by which the kidneys open.

Just behind the mantle-cavity the *heart* is situated, consisting of a central *ventricle*, which pumps purified blood from the gills through *arteries* which come off from it fore and aft, and of a thin-walled *auricle* on either side. The ventricle is folded round the intestine, a noteworthy peculiarity, though one not known to have any physiological meaning. A heart like this, which contains pure blood only, is said to be *systemic*, and it should be noted how markedly it differs from the heart of an ordinary fish, which contains impure blood only. The complex heart of a Bird or Mammal is physiologically equivalent to both these varieties of heart, for its right half receives impure blood and pumps it to the breathing organs, while its left half is concerned with the reception of pure blood from those organs, and the distribution of the same to the general system.

The *digestive organs* of the Ormer consist of a long digestive tube with large glands opening into it, and including pharynx, gullet, stomach, and intestine, the last, as already noted, ending in the mantle-cavity. Particular interest attaches to the *pharynx*, or buccal mass, which is partly modified into a complex *rasping organ* (odontophore), characteristic of two great groups of the Mollusca. It essentially consists of a rounded cushion rising from the floor of the pharynx, over which is stretched from front to

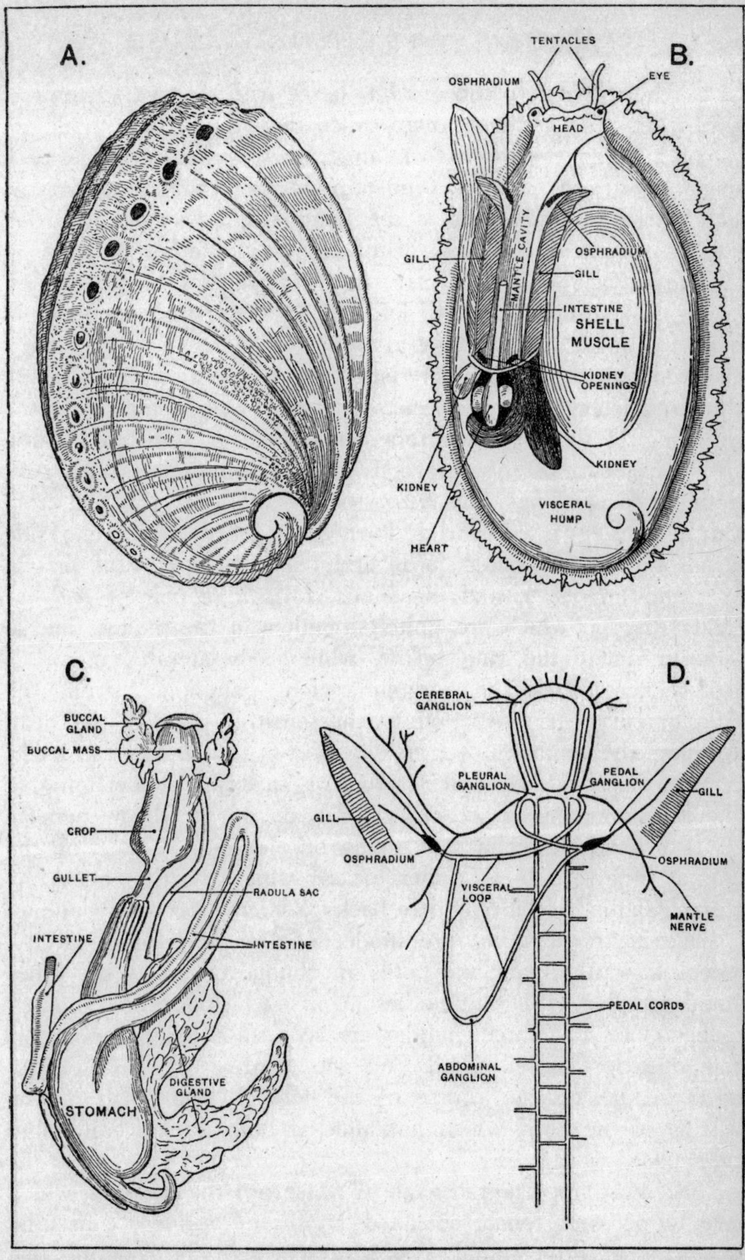

Fig. 178.—Structure of the Ormer (*Haliotis*)

A, Shell from above. B, Semidiagrammatic view from above after removal of shell. The roof of the mantle-cavity has been cut away and the heart exposed. The small left kidney (unshaded) and hinder part of large right kidney (shaded) shown by transparency. C, Digestive organs. D, Diagram of nervous system.

back a horny ribbon, the *radula*, beset with transverse rows of flinty teeth. This ribbon, often called the "tongue" or "palate", has often been compared to a finger-nail, and as worn away it constantly grows forwards from a projection (radula sac) at the back of the pharynx, just as the finger-nail does from its root. A fuller account of this organ will be given in another place.

The *kidneys* of the Ormer are two irregular brown bodies, opening as described. The left one is very small, and would seem not to act as a kidney at all.

There are certain characteristic features of the *nervous system* which require notice. It consists of a *nerve-ring* surrounding the beginning of the digestive tube, and of other connected parts. The upper part of the ring consists of a transverse band connecting two swellings, the *brain* (or cerebral) *ganglia*, and from each of these two cords run downwards to constitute one side of the ring. The outer cords end below in a pair of *lateral* (or pleural) *ganglia*, and the inner cords in a pair of *foot* (or pedal) *ganglia*, which are united together in the middle line so as to complete the ring below, while each lateral ganglion is also connected with the adjoining foot ganglion. From the brain ganglia, nerves run off to the sensitive parts of the head including the tentacles, and strong nerves to the foot run backwards through the substance of that organ from the foot ganglia. There still remains to be described a *nerve-loop*, which connects the two lateral ganglia and gives off nerves to some of the internal organs. It is a nerve-cord which, starting from one lateral ganglion, runs obliquely backwards, and, turning round in a curve at the level of the hinder end of the mantle-cavity, sweeps forwards again and takes an oblique course to the other lateral ganglion, taking altogether a course which may be compared to the figure 8. Three ganglia are seen as swellings upon this loop, one close to each gill, and the third at the back end of the 8. The curious course of the loop is one result of the twisting of the body which has affected both the visceral hump and shell.

The most important organs of sense are the *tentacles*, which have to do with touch, so-called *organs of hearing*, consisting of a pair of little rounded sacs attached to the foot ganglia, and two small cup-shaped *eyes*, one at the base of each tentacle. There is also a special sense-organ connected with each gill, which is generally considered a kind of organ of smell, entrusted with the duty of testing the quality of the water which enters the pallial cavity. It is termed the *osphradium.*

The preceding account of the Ormer illustrates the most prominent characters of Mollusca generally, which are: (1) the absence of segmentation, (2) the presence of a *mantle,* (3) the muscular *foot,* (4) the systemic *heart,* (5) plume-like *gills,* and (6) a *nerve-ring* surrounding the first part of the digestive tube. The vast majority of Molluscs either possess all these characters or else a sufficient number of them to leave no doubt as to how they should be classified. Other very common, though by no means universal, characters of the group are the presence of a *shell* and development of a *rasping organ* (odontophore). Large numbers of Molluscs are also distinguished by the bilateral symmetry of their bodies, and though the Ormer is not one of these, it is, as already pointed out, symmetrical so far as the lower half of the body is concerned.

Five classes are recognized among Mollusca, as follows:—

1. Head-footed Molluscs (CEPHALOPODA), including the Pearly Nautilus, Cuttle-Fishes, Squids, and Octopi.
2. Snails and Slugs (GASTROPODA).
3. Bivalve Molluscs (LAMELLIBRANCHIA), including forms with the shell in two pieces, *e.g.* Oyster, Mussel, and Cockle.
4. Tusk-shells (SCAPHOPODA).
5. Proto-Molluscs (AMPHINEURA), a small group of which the only common member is Chiton, distinguished by the possession of eight overlapping shelly plates on the upper surface of the body.

CLASS I.—HEAD-FOOTED MOLLUSCS (CEPHALOPODA)

As a good type for description we may select the Common Cuttle-Fish (*Sepia officinalis*), one of our native species, which preys upon fishes and crustacea in shallow water, and is a free-swimming form (fig. 179).

External Characters.—The body is bilaterally symmetrical, and at one end of it the *mouth* may be seen, provided with a pair of horny *jaws* resembling those of a parrot, and surrounded by ten arms or *tentacles,* of which two are very long and can be drawn back into special pouches. The inner sides of the eight short arms are studded with adhesive *suckers,* and each long arm swells at its end into an oval pad, one side of which is similarly provided. Outside the circlet of arms a large *eye* can be seen on either side, covered by a circular eyelid perforated by a small hole. The presence of mouth and eyes shows that we are dealing with the head end of the animal. In comparing the body with that of the Ormer we must place this end downwards and slant the rest of the animal, which is mostly visceral

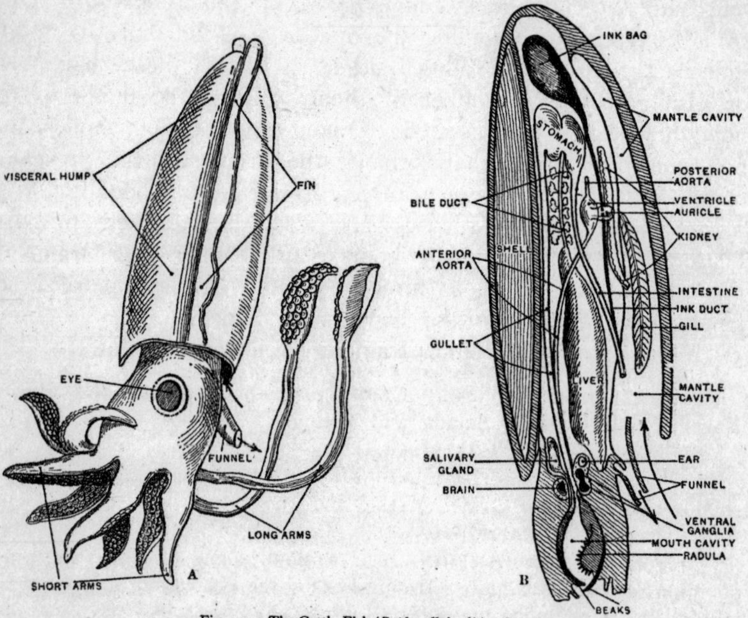

Fig. 179.—The Cuttle-Fish (*Sepia officinalis*) reduced

A, View from left side. B, Side-dissection. Arrows show course of water into and out of mantle cavity.

hump, upwards and backwards as shown in the diagram (A). It will then be clear that the long axis of the body is pretty nearly at right angles to the direction corresponding to the long axis in the Ormer. The long *visceral hump* will possess two gently-curved sides facing respectively forwards and backwards, and two sharp edges placed right and left and margined by a fin-like expansion. The next point will be to find mantle and foot. The former is readily made out running round the edge of the large visceral hump at its lower end, just above a narrowed "neck" indicating the boundary of the head. Most of it is at the back, where it constitutes the hinder wall of a large *mantle-cavity*, into which a large slit-like opening leads. The *foot* has grown round the head, and chiefly consists of the ten arms or tentacles. It is from this peculiarity the name of the class is derived (Gk. *kephalon*, a head; *pous*, a foot). Just above the back of the head, and projecting from the opening into the mantle-cavity, will be noticed a muscular conical tube, the *funnel*, by the ejection of water through which the Cuttle-Fish is able to swim rapidly backwards. It will be observed that the mantle-cavity is here at the back, while in the Ormer it is in front, one result of the twisting which the visceral hump of that animal has undergone. In its natural position, whether resting on the sea-bottom or swimming, the front side of the head and visceral hump is directed upwards, and this side is much darker than the other. It may be taken as a general rule that the surface of an animal habitually facing in this direction is the darkest part of the body, though its actual nature varies in different animals. Here it is the front side, but in a Dog-Fish it is the true upper or dorsal side, and in a flat-fish either the right or left side according to the species (see p. 279). One peculiarity of the Cuttle-Fish's skin is especially noteworthy. If a living specimen is watched, it will be seen that beautiful purplish flushes of colour sweep over the body from time to time, leaving it comparatively pale in the interval. The cause of this is to be sought in the presence of innumerable little rounded *colour-bodies* (chromatophores), which, under the control of the nervous system, vary in size. When reduced to their smallest dimensions the skin is pale, but when fully expanded it is dark. A similar phenomenon has been described for the Frog (p. 251), where, however, the colour changes are comparatively slow.

Cutting open the mantle-cavity, we shall find similar parts and openings to those described for the Ormer (p. 308). In the middle line there is the projecting end of the intestine, and on either side of this a kidney aperture, while a plume-like *gill* is to be seen on either side. As is well known, the Cuttle-Fish and many of its allies are able to eject an inky substance into the surrounding water as a means of protection. This ink is formed within a rounded *ink-bag*, and carried off through a slender tube which has a common external opening with the intestine.

The front side of the visceral hump has imbedded in it a broad "cuttle-bone", composed of overlapping layers of calcareous material. This is to be regarded as a *shell*, and is not internal in the same sense as the internal skeleton of a Vertebrate, for it is inclosed in a pouch of the skin which has lost the opening to the exterior probably possessed by ancestral forms. Some Molluscs still exist in which the shell is almost but not quite covered by folds of the skin which have grown over it.

As regards the internal structure of the Cuttle-Fish, it need only be remarked that there is a very large *rasping organ* (odontophore); a systemic *heart*, consisting of a ventricle and two auricles; and a *nerve-ring*, swollen into very large ganglia and protected by a cartilaginous case.

The eggs are enclosed in oval cases which are united together into masses, that have been compared to bunches of grapes in appearance, and which are among the common objects cast up on the sea-shore.

Cephalopods are divided into two sub-classes, named, according to the number of gills: 1. Dibranchiata (Gk. *dis*, twice; *branchia*, gills), of which the Cuttle-Fish is an example; and 2. Tetrabranchiata (Gk. *tetra*, four; *branchia*), of which the only living representative is the Pearly Nautilus.

Sub-class 1.—CUTTLE-FISHES (Dibranchiata)

This sub-class is again divided into two groups, *Decapoda* with ten arms, and *Octopoda* with eight. The former includes the Cuttle-Fishes, of which Sepia is a type, the Squids, and Spirula. Squids, or, as they are sometimes termed, Calamaries, have an even wider distribution than Cuttle-Fishes, for they are not only found in coastal waters, but are also pelagic, *i.e.* living in the open sea, where shoals of them are met with. A common Atlantic and Mediterranean species which abounds on our shores is the Common Squid (*Loligo vulgaris*). This animal is of more slender build than the Cuttle-Fish, and a large triangular fin projects from each side. The shell or "pen" is a narrow horny structure, shaped like a lance-head. The old name Calamary for creatures of the kind was given in allusion to this "pen" (L. *calamus*, a quill), its shape being compared to a short quill.

Some of the Squid family attain gigantic dimensions, and there can be little doubt that specimens of the kind are largely responsible for the numerous tales and legends which exist regarding a supposed marine monster, the Great Sea Serpent, or Kraken. Actual measurements which have been made from time to time of bodies or portions of the bodies of such creatures leave no doubt that a total length of over 50 feet may be attained, the greater part of this, however, being taken up by the long arms. Gigantic Squids of the kind are sometimes cast ashore on the western coasts of Britain among other localities.

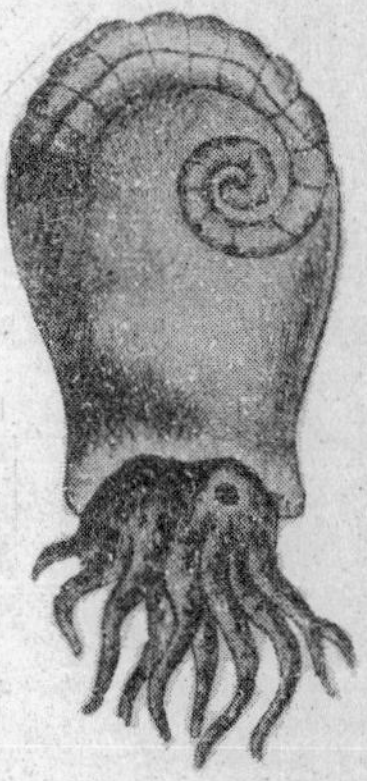

Fig. 180.—Spirula

Spirula (Fig. 180) is a small animal in which the shell is spiral and divided into numerous chambers by transverse partitions. It is partly enclosed in folds of the skin. The animal itself is but rarely met with, though its shells are common on Pacific shores and may be seen in most museums.

The *Octopods*, or 8-armed Cephalopods, differ from the Cuttle-Fishes and Squids in the absence of the two long arms, besides which they are entirely devoid of an internal shell. The visceral hump is short and rounded, and the suckers on the arms are unstalked. The group includes the Octopi and their allies, and the Paper Nautilus or Argonaut.

The Common Octopus (*Octopus vulgaris*) is common on rocky shores on the margins of both Atlantic and Mediterranean, lurking in crevices, crawling by means of its sucker-studded arms, or swimming swiftly backwards like the Squids. Each arm is provided with two rows of suckers, while in an Octopod, common on British coasts, *Eledone moschata*, there is only one. The specific name of this particular species, which is eaten by the Italians, has reference to the strong musky odour of the animal.

Some Octopods attain a very large size, though they are inferior to Squids in this respect. Large specimens are reputed to be common on the shores of the island of Sark in the Channel group, and a well-known description of an imaginary combat with one of these is given in Victor Hugo's *Toilers of the Sea.*

The Argonaut or Paper Nautilus (*Argonauta argo*) is a pelagic form, common in the Mediterranean, in which the female is provided with a thin cap-shaped shell, which is symmetrical, and large enough to contain the entire body of the animal. It is mainly secreted by the inner surfaces of two of the arms, which are dilated at their ends into large lappets. By means of these the animal holds on to the shell, which is not attached to it by any muscular or fibrous tissue.

Sub-class 2—Pearly Nautilus (Tetrabranchiata)

The only living representative of this is the Pearly Nautilus, of which the best-known species (*Nautilus pompilius*) (fig. 181) has a wide distribution in the Indian and Pacific Oceans. The animal is enclosed in a large spiral shell, of which the coiled-up portion projects forwards towards the animal's front end. The body does not occupy all the shell, for a considerable part of this is divided into a series of gas-containing chambers by means of curved partitions, concave towards the external aperture. The last and broadest part forms a body-chamber in which the animal is contained, the rounded end of its visceral hump resting against the concave surface of the last partition. The shell grows in size by successive additions to its aperture or mouth in accordance with the growth of the animal, and at the same time the older part of it is from time to time cut off by formation of a new partition, the body slipping forwards, as it were, so as to permit of this. The old chambered part of the shell is not, however, entirely devoid of soft parts, for each partition is perforated in the middle by a hole continuous with a short tube directed away from the body-chamber, and in this way a hollow structure know as the *siphuncle* is constituted,

Fig. 181.—Pearly Nautilus (*Nautilus pompilius*). The left half of its shell has been removed

which is traversed by a fleshy cord, continuous almost like a tail with the rounded end of the visceral hump. This is also connected with either side of the body-chamber by means of a broad shell-muscle. The shell consists of an external membrane exhibiting brown and white marking, a white porcelain-like layer, and an internal layer possessing a beautiful pearly lustre, the appearance of which has suggested the ordinary name of the animal.

The *foot* is not constituted by long tentacles or arms as in the Cuttle-Fishes, &c., but consists of a number of lobes upon which are borne a large number of slender adhesive tentacles, the tips of which can be drawn back into sheaths. A *funnel* is present as before, but instead of being a complete tube it is made up of two halves which are rolled upon each other. Within the mantle-cavity, which occupies the same relative position as in a Cuttle-Fish, there are four instead of two plume-like gills, and in correspondence with this the heart has four auricles, one for receiving the purified blood from each gill, and there are four instead of two kidneys. The *eye* is of extremely simple structure, and has been compared to a pin-hole camera, consisting as it does of a deep cup, which would be closed externally were it not for the presence of an extremely small rounded aperture like a pin-hole.

CLASS 2.—SNAILS AND SLUGS (GASTROPODA)

The Ormer already described (pp. 307–311) belongs to this class, that includes a very large number of species, of which the vast majority are distinguished by the presence of a head bearing tentacles, a flattened creeping foot, and a shell which consists of only one valve or piece, and is therefore said to be *univalve.* The class is split up into smaller divisions as follows:—

Sub-class 1.—Streptoneura (Prosobranchia).

Order (1). Comb-gilled Snails (Ctenobranchia).

Order (2). Shield-gilled Snails (Aspidobranchia).

Sub-class 2.—Euthyneura.

Order (1). Hind-gilled Snails (Opisthobranchia).

Order (2). Lung Snails and Slugs (Pulmonata).

Sub-class 1.—STREPTONEURA (Prosobranchia)

This subdivision of Gastropods is partly founded on the course taken by the nerve-loop which is attached to the nerve-ring. It is here twisted, as, *e.g.*, in the Ormer (see p. 310), into a shape resembling the figure 8. Another important feature is afforded by the gill or gills which, when present, are in front of the heart, as again in the Ormer (see p. 308). These Molluscs may therefore be termed "fore-gilled" or *prosobranch* (Gk. *pro*, in front of; *branchia*, gills). They include most of the marine snails which are to be found on the sea-shore. On the shape of the gills, among other characters, the two orders of the sub-class are marked off from one another, *i.e.* (1) *Comb-gilled Snails*, with a single gill consisting of an axis bearing a series of small flattened plates, comparable to the teeth of a comb; and (2) *Shield-gilled Snails*, in which there are two series of such plates, one on each side of the gill-axis. In some members of the second order two gills are present.

Order (1). *Comb-gilled Snails* (Ctenobranchia).—This order is divided into no less than fifty-nine families, so that space will prevent more than a brief notice of a few common forms.

Probably no sea-snail is more familiar than the Periwinkle (*Littorina littorea*), common on the rocks between tide-marks, and illustrating a number of points in which the members of the order differ from the Ormer and related forms. The thick rounded shell is obviously spiral, and the visceral hump it covers is of the same shape. The spiral, as in most snails, is a right-handed one, *i.e.* with its turns running in the same direction as an ordinary screw or corkscrew, so that if the shell be placed on end with apex above, its turns or whorls will be seen to slope up from left to right. The most primitive Molluscs known are bilaterally symmetrical, devoid of a prominent visceral hump, and with a posterior mantle-cavity into which the intestine, &c., open. Such spirally-twisted forms as Periwinkle have apparently arisen from simple forms of the kind by development of a visceral hump, together with a strong shell to cover it, and also to serve as a shelter into which the animal might withdraw itself. At the same time twisting took place, perhaps as a result of the weight of the parts, and the result has been that mantle-cavity, end of intestine, gills, heart, and kidneys have been brought round to the front (fig. 182). It is at any rate pretty clear that a spiral hump and shell are more compact and convenient than a much elongated hump covered by an extinguisher-shaped shell. In most cases the twisting, as viewed from above, has taken place in a direction opposed to the hands of a watch, but in some few snails the opposite has been the case, so that the spiral shell is left-handed.

A little observation at the sea-side will show that Periwinkles are in the habit of creeping about on the rocks, feeding on sea-weed, from which they are able to scrape small pieces by means of the rasping organ. The part of such an animal which protrudes from the shell will be seen to be bilaterally symmetrical, and to mainly consist of a foot much smaller than that of the Ormer (see p. 307), and a head provided with a prominent snout and two tentacles, each of which bears a small eye at its base in the form of a black spot. The projecting hind-end of the foot bears upon its upper side a horny plate, the *operculum*, which when the animal is completely withdrawn into the shell by means of the shell-muscle stops up the aperture, thus guarding the only weak point in the defences. The operculum corresponds in shape with the aperture or mouth of the shell, which here, as in vegetarian snails generally, possesses a continuous margin devoid of any notch.

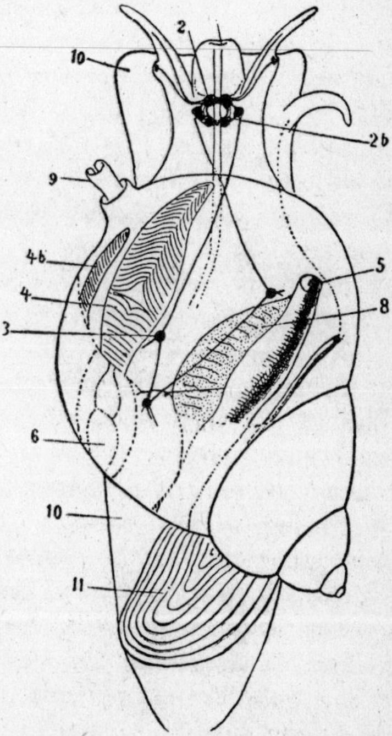

Fig. 182.—Diagram of a Comb-gilled Snail, seen from above. The roof of mantle-cavity and overlying shell supposed transparent.

1, Mouth; 2, brain-ganglion; 2*b*, nerve-cord connecting side-ganglion (above) with foot-ganglion (below); 3, one of the three ganglia on the twisted nerve-loop; 4, gill; 4*b*, osphradium; 5, opening of intestine; 6, heart in pericardium; 8, a gland (purple-gland in Purpura); 9, siphon; 10, 10, foot; 11, operculum.

Examination of the mantle-cavity and the related organs will show several important points of difference from the Ormer (see p. 308). As before, the last part of the intestine can be seen, lying, however, well over on the right side, while on the left there is a single *gill* with the comb-like shape characteristic of the order, and running alongside it a projecting ridge, the *water-testing organ* (osphradium). The *heart* is placed immediately behind the gill, and has but one auricle, placed in front of the ventricle, which is not folded round the intestine as in the Ormer. It is indeed exceptional for the intestine of a snail to run through the heart, though it is characteristic of bivalve molluscs. There is but one *kidney* in the Periwinkle, opening into the back of the mantle-cavity, on the left-hand side. The suppression of one gill, auricle, and kidney is believed to be one result of the twisting of the body, though exactly why is uncertain. They have perhaps been subjected to pressure, and so to speak squeezed out of existence. The twisting of the visceral loop in the nervous system is another result of the coiling of the body, and this is easily understood.

Two species closely related to the Periwinkle are common on British coasts. In one (*Littorina rudis*) the coiled apex or spire of the shell is very short. The other (*L. obtusāta*) is a small form, varying in colour from greenish-brown to orange-yellow, and entirely devoid of a projecting spire, the apex of the shell being rounded off so as to make the general outline of the shell spheroidal. It is common on the brown sea-weed (*Fucus*) with which 'tween-tide rocks are often thickly covered.

The River-Snail (*Paludina*), common in the streams of this country, is something like the Periwinkle in general shape, but it is a good deal larger and the shell is much thinner.

Living side by side with the Periwinkle on our rocks will be found the Purple Snail (*Purpura lapillus*), with a dense angular white shell extremely unlike the rounded covering of the former species. It belongs to a different family, and is a good example of a carnivorous sea-snail. The mouth of the shell is notched at its front end, *i.e.* the end away from the spire, for the transmission of the *siphon*, a spout-like prolongation of the mantle by means of which water enters the mantle-cavity. The Purple is one of the forms in which the pharynx with its rasping organ is situated in the end of a long *proboscis*, that is retracted when not in use. The typical genus of this particular family is *Murex*, many of the tropical species of which possess extremely beautiful shells, covered with long spines and having the front angle of the mouth drawn out into a long canal for the reception of the siphon. Tyrian purple was obtained from species of Murex and Purpura, the organ yielding it being a gland in the roof of

Fig. 183.—Whelk (*Buccinum*). *a a*, Tentacles; *b*, siphon; *c*, operculum

the mantle-cavity, of which the juice turns purple on exposure to sunlight.

The Common Whelk (*Buccinum undatum*) (fig. 183), inhabiting both shallow and deep water around our coasts, closely resembles the Purple in structure, but is very much larger.

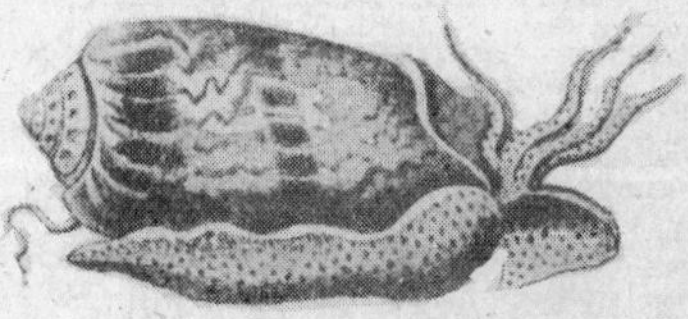

Fig. 184.—Olive (*Oliva*)

As examples of other families may be mentioned:—Mitre-Shells (*Mitra*), Volutes (*Voluta*), Olive-Shells (*Oliva*) (fig. 184), Harp-Shells (*Harpa*), Cone-Shells (*Conus*), Turret-Shells (*Turritella*), Wing-Shells (*Strombus*) (fig. 185), Helmet-Shells (*Cassis*), and Cowries (*Cypræa*) (fig. 186). In many of these the shells are extremely handsome, and occupy a prominent place in museums and private collections.

Special mention must be made of the *Heteropods*, a group of comb-gilled snails which swim freely in the open sea. The body in these pelagic forms is transparent, and the foot is a laterally-flattened fin-like structure, by means of which the animal swims back downwards. The shell may be spiral (*Atlanta*) or cap-shaped (*Carinaria*), but in some cases (*Pterotrachea*) is entirely absent.

Order (2). *Shield-gilled Snails* (Aspidobranchia).—As already mentioned, these forms possess a gill or gills in which the axis has a series of plates on either side. The primitive bilateral

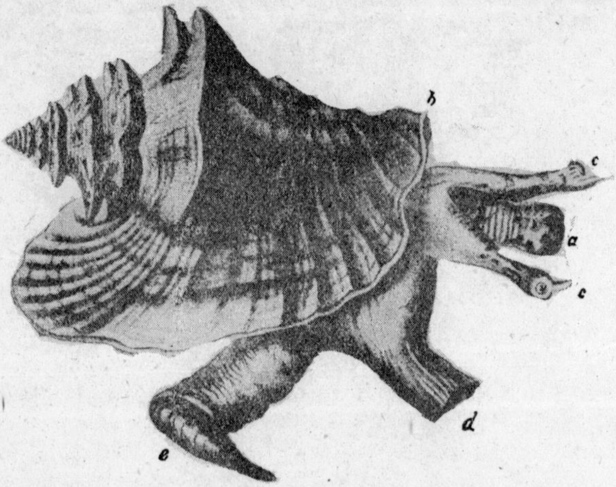

Fig. 185.—Strombus

a, Proboscis; *b*, notch in shell-mouth; *c*, eye-bearing tentacles; *d*, foot; *e*, operculum.

symmetry of the body has not been disturbed to the same extent, for both right and left gills, auricles, and kidneys may be present.

There are fifteen families, of which one, the *Trochidæ*, represented by twenty British species, may be taken as representing forms with well-coiled shell, the colours and markings of which are often of extreme beauty. Two auricles and kidneys are present, but only one gill.

Fig. 186.—Cowry (*Cypræa*)

The Ormer (*Haliotis tuberculata*), already described (pp. 307–311), is the type of another family, and, as we have seen, it possesses two auricles, gills, and kidneys. There is good reason to believe that it is descended from forms possessing a well-coiled visceral hump, covered by a shell of corresponding shape, and large enough to serve as a retreat into which the animal could withdraw itself at the approach of danger. Although the hump and shell still retain a certain amount of twisting they have been flattened out to a large extent, and the shell no longer serves as a refuge. This, however, is made up for by the immense size of the foot, by which the animal can adhere firmly to the rock, at the same time pulling the shell down so as to cover the exposed parts.

In the much smaller Key-hole Limpet (*Fissurella Græca*) of the Mediterranean the visceral hump is completely flattened out, and the shell is conical, with a hole at the apex communicating with the mantle-cavity. It possesses two gills, &c., like the Ormer.

In John Knox's Limpet (*Acmæa testudinalis*), not uncommon on certain parts of the British coast, still further changes have taken place, for there is only one auricle and a single gill. Nor does the intestine pass through the heart, as is the case in the shield-gilled forms so far mentioned. The Common Limpet (*Patella vulgata*) agrees with this species in most respects, but has lost both the gills, at least as functional breathing-organs. If the small mantle-cavity lying above the neck be cut open the end of the intestine will be seen projecting into it, and on each side of this the opening of a kidney. On the floor of the cavity are two little orange-coloured projections, examination of which as to structure and nerve-supply shows that each represents the vestige of a gill covered by its water-testing organ (osphradium). The Limpet, however, does possess *gills*, though of another kind, which are seen as a large number of flattened plates running right round the body well above the foot and overhung by the mantle skirt, which is a well-developed continuous flap. Since these gills are not the equivalents of the ordinary plume-like gills characteristic of Molluscs they are termed *secondary* gills. This use for the word secondary is a common one in zoology.

At first sight a Limpet, with its simple conical shell, might be taken for a very primitive animal. If it were so, however, the mantle-cavity, with its related organs, would be at the hind end of the body instead of in front, and the nerve-loop of the nervous system would not be, as it is, 8-shaped. These considerations, and comparison with other forms, would lead to the conclusion that the apparent simplicity is secondary, and that the Limpet's ancestors were forms with spirally coiled visceral hump and shell. A very interesting confirmation of this conclusion is afforded by the life-history, for at an early period of its existence, when it is a free-swimming larva, it actually does posses. spirally twisted visceral hump and shell. This is another example of the law of recapitulation previously exemplified (see p. 14).

Sub-class 2.—EUTHYNEURA

These are forms in which the nerve-loop of the nervous system is not twisted (except in one family), but it would appear that this is not, as might at first sight be supposed, a primitive feature, but the result of an untwisting process. A further character is the possession of two pairs of tentacles by the head. There are two orders: 1. Hind-gilled Snails (Opisthobranchia), with the auricle of the heart behind the ventricle, and the gill in a corresponding situation; and 2. Lung Snails (Pulmonata), in which the gills are entirely absent and the mantle-cavity has been converted into a lung.

Order 1.—HIND-GILLED SNAILS (Opisthobranchia)

A very great variety of marine forms are placed in this order, some snail-like in appearance, others slug-like, and others again of modified shape and adapted for swimming in the open sea. A distinction is drawn between species in which there is typically a gill sheltered in the mantle-cavity (Tectibranchs), and the Sea-Slugs (Nudibranchs), devoid of mantle and shell.

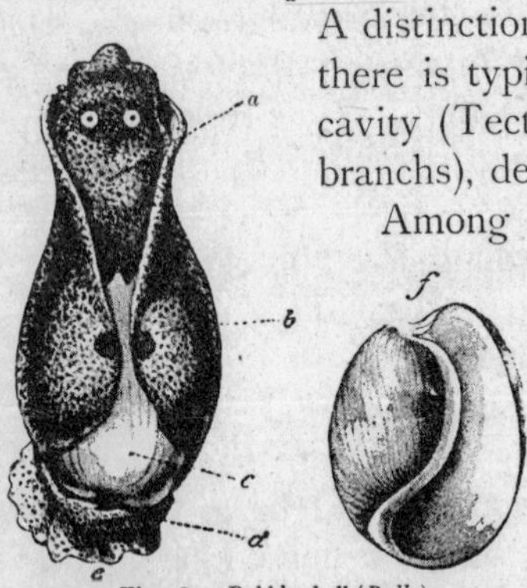

Fig. 187.—Bubble-shell (*Bulla*)
a, Head-lappets; *b*, right epipodium; *c*, shell; *d*, mantle-lobe; *e*, hind-end of foot; *f*, shell.

Among the *Tectibranchs* the Bubble-Shells possess a thin translucent spiral shell (fig. 187), overlapped by a body-fold (epipodium) each side.

Another related family is exemplified by a small white mollusc, *Philine aperta*, very common in shallow water round the British coast. The shell is something like that of a bubble-shell, but is not visible externally, as folds of the mantle have grown completely over it. In the Sea-Hare (*Aplysia*) the shell is still further reduced, being a thin oval plate situated on the upper side of the body and almost entirely covered over. A large *gill* is present, protected in a *mantle-cavity* which opens on the right-hand side (see fig. 188). The external opening of the single *kidney* is at the root of the gill, and the intestine terminates still further back outside the mantle-cavity altogether. The Sea-Hare was at one time pointed to as a good example of a form in which the twisting process had begun, carrying the mantle-cavity with its organs on to the right side. If this were so, however, we should expect to find two auricles to the heart, two gills, and two kidneys, which is not the case. A more adequate explanation is that the Sea-Hare is descended from forms in which coiled visceral hump and shell were present, and which had lost an auricle, a gill, and a kidney; forms, in fact, resembling such a species as the Periwinkle in structure (see p. 318). We must suppose that in these the visceral hump gradually flattened out and the shell gradually became reduced, while at the same time a certain amount of untwisting took place, bringing back the mantle-cavity to the right-hand side of the body. In this way a secondary or spurious simplicity has been acquired. The non-twisted nerve-loop (fig. 188) is characteristic of Euthyneura generally.

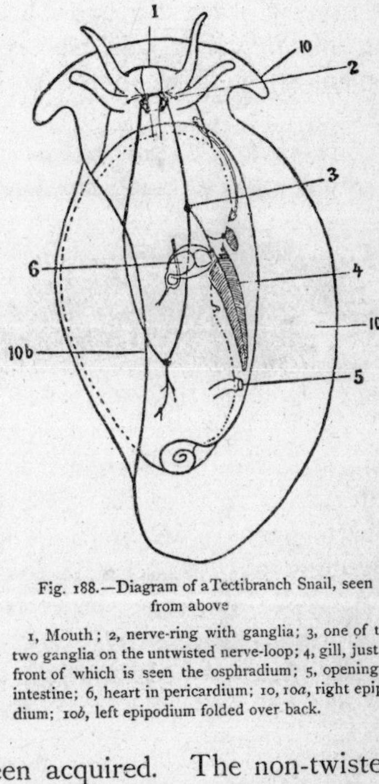

Fig. 188.—Diagram of a Tectibranch Snail, seen from above

1, Mouth; 2, nerve-ring with ganglia; 3, one of the two ganglia on the untwisted nerve-loop; 4, gill, just in front of which is seen the osphradium; 5, opening of intestine; 6, heart in pericardium; 10, 10*a*, right epipodium; 10*b*, left epipodium folded over back.

Eight out of the twenty families embraced by the Tectibranchs are collectively known as the *Wing-footed Snails* or *Pteropods* (Gk. *pteron*, a wing; *pous*, a foot), formerly regarded as a distinct class of the Mollusca. They are small pelagic creatures, vast shoals of which are to be found swimming in the open sea. Some of them possess a mantle-cavity and a transparent shell either spiral or conical in shape. In these the foot is transformed into a pair of fin-like structures. Others again have no mantle and shell, and though they possess fins, these are not formed from the foot, but from the region of the body immediately above it, and equivalent to flaps found in this position in the Sea-Hare (epipodia) or to the halves of the funnel in a Pearly Nautilus (see p. 317).

Sea-Slugs (Nudibranchs).—These are beautifully coloured creatures with a large creeping foot. Their symmetrical form is not a primitive character, but due to the untwisting process just described for the Sea-Hare. Here, however, modification has gone a stage further, for not only is there no shell, but both mantle-cavity and the typical plume-like gill are absent. The intestine opens in the middle line on the posterior part of the body.

A common British genus is *Doris*, in which the absence of plume-gills is made up for by the presence of a circlet of branched *secondary gills* situated on the upper side of the body around the opening of the intestine. If the expanded gills of a living specimen be touched they are immediately drawn in, being sheltered in a ring-like groove when so retracted. Another common genus is *Eolis* (fig. 189), in which the back is studded with numerous slender club-like processes.

Fig. 189.—Eolis

A very interesting little Nudibranch is the free-swimming Mediterranean form *Phyllirhoë*, which possess a transparent laterally-flattened body and is devoid of foot. There are numerous little phosphorescent bodies in the skin.

Order 2.—Lung Snails (Pulmonata)

The seventeen families of this order are mostly inhabitants of the land or of fresh-water, and familiar examples are furnished by the land-snails and slugs. The common Garden Snail (*Helix aspersa*) may be taken as an illustrative type (fig. 190).

The part of the body which is protruded from the shell when the animal crawls is symmetrical, and its under part is made up of the well-developed *foot*, which has a rounded front end and ends in a point behind. The head is fairly distinct, and bears two pairs of *tentacles*, which are hollow and can be drawn back into the body. The front pair are short, while the others are long, and each of them bears an eye at its tip. There is a well-coiled *visceral hump* covered by a *shell* of corresponding shape, into which the animal can be withdrawn, though there is no operculum to guard the entrance. During the winter the snail

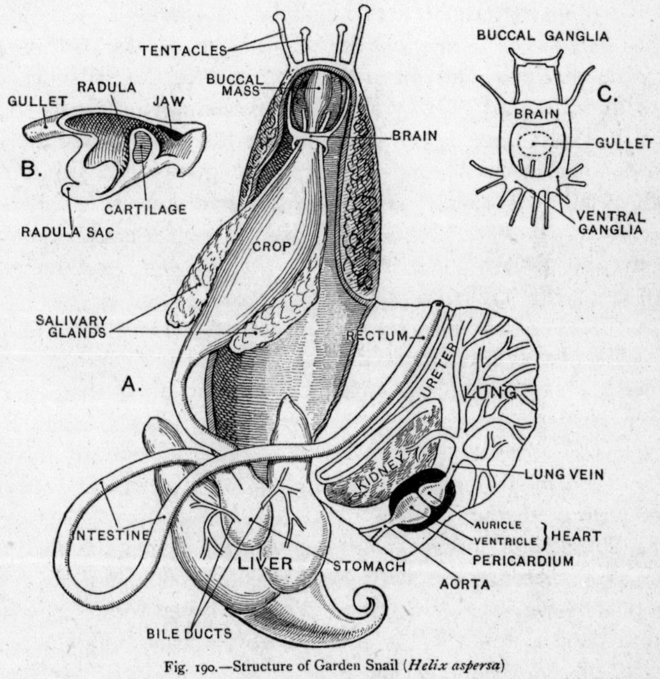

Fig. 190.—Structure of Garden Snail (*Helix aspersa*)
A, General dissection, from upper side; roof of lung spread out to right. B, Buccal mass, right half removed. C, Nerve-ring, from back.

remains in a torpid condition within its shell, or in other words *hibernates*, under which condition the want of operculum is compensated for by the formation of a limy partition across the mouth of the shell, leaving, however, a small aperture for breathing purposes.

As would be expected in a form so twisted, the *mantle-cavity* is in front, but no longer has a wide opening to the exterior, as this would lead to its delicate lining being dried up. There is, instead, a small aperture on the right-hand side, easily seen just within the margin of the shell. When the mantle-cavity is opened no trace of a gill can be seen, but the thin *mantle* which forms its roof is raised up into a net-work of ridges traversed by blood-vessels and acting as a lung. The intestine runs down the right side of the mantle-cavity to its termination close by the lung-opening, and by its side runs the slender tube which carries off the waste matter from the single *kidney*, abutting against which is the pericardium containing a two-chambered *heart*.

The *nerve-ring* encircles the beginning of the gullet just behind the pharynx, and the nerve-loop is exceedingly short, and fused with it in such a way as to be exceedingly difficult to recognize. About 6000 species are included in the Pulmonata, and of these some 3500 belong to the same genus (*Helix*) as the Garden Snail. A much larger species than this is the Roman Snail (*Helix pomatia*), common abroad, and on the chalk downs of Kent and Surrey. It is said to have been introduced in Roman times for culinary purposes.

Land-Slugs may be regarded as derived from snail-like forms which have been more or less flattened out, and in which the shell is reduced or, it may be, absent altogether. Two common British species may be mentioned as examples, the small grey Field-Slug (*Limax agrestis*) with a reduced internal shell, and the much larger Black Slug (*Arion ater*) in which the shell is entirely absent.

The Pulmonate forms so far mentioned all agree in the possession of four tentacles, with eyes situated on the tips of the larger posterior ones. But there are still other forms in which only one pair of tentacles is present, at the bases of which the eyes are placed. Among these may be mentioned the Pond-Snail (*Limnæa stagnalis*) with a thin, pointed shell, and the Trumpet-Shell (*Planorbis corneus*), also an inhabitant of fresh water, and possessing a flat spiral shell.

CLASS 3.—BIVALVE MOLLUSCS (LAMELLIBRANCHIA)

The shell of a Gastropod, when it possesses one, always consists of one piece or valve, *i.e.* is *univalve*; but in the class now to be considered there is a *bivalve* shell consisting of a right and a left valve. The *Fresh-water Mussels*, abundant in many of our streams, canals, and ponds, furnish a convenient type. They belong to two genera, *Anodon* and *Unio*, which agree in their main features, though there are certain differences, especially as regards the shell.

External Characters.—The animal is completely invested by the two elongated oval pieces which make up the shell, and are right and left respectively (fig. 191). They are united together above, along what is called the *hinge-line*, and can either be brought close together elsewhere so as entirely to cover the soft parts, or may be separated so as to "gape" more or less, which is always the case in dead specimens.

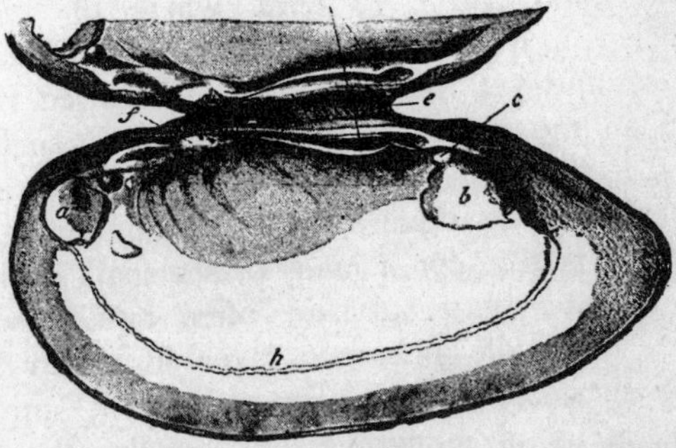

Fig. 191.—Shells of Fresh-water Mussel (*Unio*), seen from within
a b, Impressions of anterior and posterior adductors; *d f*, hinge-teeth; *e*, ligament; *h*, pallial line.

A series of closely-set lines following the curve of the shell can be seen on the outside, and it will be found that these "lines of growth", which mark successive additions of material, have as their centre a pointed projection near the straight upper edge of the valve, known as the *beak* or *umbo*. This clearly marks the oldest part, and, as in bivalves, usually projects forwards, and is nearer the front than the back end. When the shell is removed from the soft parts by cutting through certain muscles, it will be found that each valve covers a soft flap which lines it during life, and is really half the *mantle* (fig. 192), here clearly divided into right and left halves, which may be compared to the flaps of a man's coat, if the further assumption be made that the coat is a part of the body and its flaps are big enough to entirely cover the occupant.

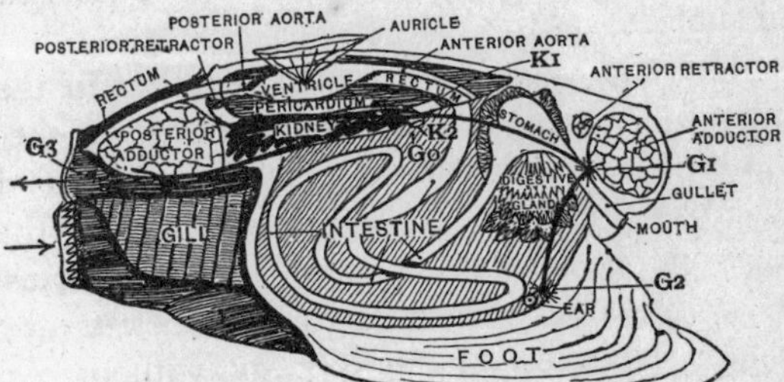

Fig. 192.—Structure of Fresh-water Mussel (*Anodonta*)
G1–G3, ganglia: Go, opening of oviduct; K1 and K2, internal and external kidney-openings

Structure and Formation of the Shell.—The shell is a horny structure largely impregnated by salts of lime. It is produced by the underlying epidermis, from which a sticky substance exudes which afterwards becomes hard. In all classes of Molluscs the mantle has a great deal to do with the formation of the shell, but even here, where the mantle is very well developed, it does not line the part of the shell near the hinge-line, and yet that part can be repaired if broken. In a Garden Snail the mantle is of comparatively small extent, the chief part of it being the roof of the lung, yet all parts of the snail's shell can be repaired. The shell of the Mussel, and the same thing is true for a land- or sea-snail, consists of three layers: (1) a greenish external skin, often called incorrectly the epidermis; (2) a middle prismatic layer in which the calcareous material consists of oblique prisms; and (3) an internal pearly layer, made up of numerous thin lamellæ, the edges of which form a series of minute wavy ridges on the inner side of the shell, which are the agents to which the rainbow tints of the pearly layer are due. The edge of the mantle is thickened, and, both here and in most Mollusca, plays a very important part in the formation of the shell, the two outer layers originating from it alone. Repairs, therefore, except at the edge of the shell, are carried out in pearly material only, though further observations are wanted on the subject.

The two valves are united together in the region behind the umbo by a horny elastic band known as the *ligament*, which is kept on the stretch when the shell is closed. In the shell of Unio (fig. 191) there are projecting *teeth* along the inner side of the hinge-line in each valve, which fit into corresponding sockets in the other valve. Such teeth and sockets are entirely absent in Anodon, whence its name (Gk. *an*, without; *odous*, a tooth). The inner side presents a number of markings due to the attachment of muscles, and therefore called *muscular impressions*. The two largest of these are oval, and situated respectively near the front and back ends. They correspond (see fig. 192) to a couple of large muscles, the fibres of which run transversely across from valve to valve, and which, since their contraction serves to adduct or pull the valves together, are termed the anterior and posterior *adductor muscles* (L. *adduco*, I lead to). When they cease to contract, the elasticity of the stretched ligament comes into play and pulls the shell open. Running from one adductor scar to the other is a curved *pallial line*, marking the attachment of the pallium or mantle to the shell. In a case like this, where the line is unbroken by any indentation, it is *integropalliate*, a point which will be referred to later when other bivalves are considered.

Both shell and contained animal are bilaterally symmetrical, a fact which is expressed as regarding the former by using the term equivalve. Each valve is in fact a mirror-image of the other, but in itself does not exhibit bilateral symmetry, *i.e.* is *inequilateral.*

The Mussel is in the habit of remaining obliquely buried in the mud with its hinder end projecting, and examination of an aquarium specimen in this position will show two openings, one above the other, between the mantle lobes (fig. 192). Water-currents continually set into the lower or *inhalent aperture*, serving the double purpose of carrying food to the mouth and oxygen to the breathing-organs, while other currents as constantly flow out of the upper or *exhalent aperture*, taking with them the various forms of waste matter. The inhalent aperture is fringed with sensitive tentacles, and if these are touched the shell at once closes, an arrangement which is obviously protective. The Mussel, therefore, is able to feed, breathe, and get rid of waste, with most of its body concealed from observation.

After removal of the shell (fig. 192) it will be found that the mantle-lobes are not united together except between the two apertures just described. If one of them be turned back other parts come into view, and the first thing to determine is which is front and which back end. A distinct head will be looked for in vain, and its absence is one of the characters of this class, which sometimes receive the name of "headless" Molluscs (*Acephala*, from Gk. *a*, without; *kephalon*, a head). This cannot be regarded as a primitive feature, and there is good reason to believe that the bivalves are descended from forms which possessed a distinct head, the dwindling of which has been brought about by a sluggish mode of life and dependence as regards food upon minute organisms brought to the mouth by water currents. The *mouth* will be seen in the Mussel as a wide slit just behind one of the adductor muscles, at the end further from the inhalent and exhalent apertures, which thus mark the hinder end of the animal. There is a complete absence of anything in the way of jaws, but a pair of soft leaf-shaped bodies, the *labial palps*, may be seen on either side of the mouth. The body hangs down between the mantle-lobes, and its ventral part is modified into the orange-coloured *foot*, which, instead of presenting a creeping under surface, as in a snail, is flattened from side to side and projects forwards as a muscular body which has been variously compared, as regards its shape, to an axe or ploughshare. It can be protruded from between the valves of the shell, and serves as a pushing-organ, by which the animal can slowly plough its way through the mud with its front end first.

Very conspicuous are the plate-like *gills*, which have suggested the scientific name of the class (Lat. *lamella*, a plate; Gk. *branchia*, gills), and which are not only breathing-organs but are also largely concerned with setting up the currents of water which play such an important part in the life of the animal, being largely aided, however, in both these duties by the lobes of the mantle. The water-currents are a result of ciliary action (see p. 49). Each gill consists of an outer and an inner plate, and, despite its specialized form, has been produced by the modification of a gill-plume similar in kind to those found in the Ormer (see p. 308). The stem of the gill runs fairly parallel to the long axis of the body, and is attached to the body-wall above. The *mantle-cavity* is here the huge space between the mantle-lobes into which the gills and lower part of the body hang down, and, by the attachment of the former to adjacent parts, it is divided into a large lower section into which the inhalent aperture leads and a much narrower upper portion, above the gills, and communicating with the exterior by the exhalent aperture. This is most clearly seen behind the posterior adductor muscle, where the inner plate of one gill is seen to be fused along the middle line with the corresponding plate of the other gill, thus forming a partition between the upper and lower sections of the mantle-cavity.

Digestive Organs (fig. 192).—The most striking feature is a negative one, consisting in the entire absence of the characteristic rasping organ (odontophore) possessed by the other molluscan classes. It is believed that bivalves are descended from ancestors which were provided with this structure, which has been lost as a result of the same conditions which led to the dwindling of the head, and which have already been alluded to. The mouth leads into a short gullet, which opens into a stomach, that again continues into a coiled intestine, the last part of which runs up to the dorsal side, traverses the heart (see below), and runs back over the posterior adductor to its termination in the upper section of the mantle-cavity.

Circulatory Organs (fig. 192). — The *heart*, situated in a pericardial cavity, has the dorsal situation characteristic of Invertebrates, and is essentially similar to the heart of the Ormer (see p. 308), consisting as it does of a central ventricle to which a thin-walled auricle is attached on either side. Purified blood is received by the auricles from the mantle-lobes and gills, and then passes into the ventricle, which distributes it to the body.

Respiratory and Excretory Organs (fig. 192).—As already mentioned, the function of breathing is carried out by mantle-lobes and gills. As to excretion of nitrogenous waste, this is effected by two elongated brown *kidneys* underlying the pericardium, with which they communicate on the one hand, while they open to the exterior on the other.

Nervous System and Sense Organs (fig. 192).—The *central nervous system* consists, as in the Ormer (see p. 310), of a nerve-ring and a nerve-loop. The former presents a ganglion on each side of the mouth (equivalent to one of the brain ganglia of the Ormer with a lateral ganglion fused with it) connected with one another above and with a pair of foot-ganglia embedded in the body close to the muscular foot. The nerve-loop is connected in front with the upper ganglia of the ring, and its posterior end lies just below the posterior adductor, where it is thickened into a pair of visceral ganglia. The three pairs of ganglia send out nerves to the parts of the body in their neighbourhood.

The Mussel undoubtedly possesses the sense of *touch*, especially as regards the edge of the mantle. It is also probable, though not absolutely certain, that it is endowed with *smell* and *taste*, and *water-testing organs* (osphradia) can be recognized near the visceral ganglia, though there is some doubt about their function, for they lie in the upper section of the mantle-cavity in the course of the outgoing currents of water, which is not in accordance with their supposed function. So-called *organs of hearing* are present, as in the Ormer (see p. 310), in the form of two little vesicles connected with the foot-ganglia and containing particles of carbonate of lime. They are probably concerned with the sense of equilibrium. Eyes are altogether absent.

Lamellibranchs are divided into five orders based on the

characters of the gills, and embrace between them some forty families. It will be enough for our present purpose to mention a few common species in illustration of the range of characters found within the class.

The *Cockle Family* includes a large number of shallow-water forms found along coasts and estuaries in most parts of the world. They are especially characteristic of places where sand is abundant. The best-known British form is the Edible Cockle (*Cardium edule*) of the Atlantic and Mediterranean areas. The shell is rounded in outline, and marked by prominent ribs which radiate from the beak. The edges of the mantle-lobes are much more extensively united than is the case with the Fresh-water Mussel, but an orifice is left in front through which the foot can be protruded, and at the back inhalent and exhalent apertures are seen as before, a striking difference being that they are here placed at the ends of two short tubes or *siphons*, both fringed by tentacles. The narrow bent *foot* is able not only to push the animal through the sand, but also by its sudden contraction to bring about springing movements in the water. The siphons can be drawn back within the shell by means of a special *retractor muscle*, and the attachment of this to the shell causes the pallial line to be indented at its posterior end, just as, to use a somewhat fanciful comparison that has been employed, a coast-line is broken by a bay or, to use the Latin word, *sinus*. By examination of the shell only we are therefore able to say in a given case (fig. 193) whether siphons of any size were present, the extent of the bay being roughly proportional to their development. This *sinupalliate* condition is contrasted with the integropalliate one described for the Mussel (p. 331), but it must not be forgotten that small siphons may be present devoid of muscles sufficiently powerful to indent the pallial line perceptibly.

Fig. 193.—Inside of right valve of a sinupalliate shell. The bay (sinus) in the pallial line is seen on the right

The *Gaper Family* presents a certain amount of resemblance to the preceding as regards habit, and a common British form, the Sand Gaper (*Mya arenaria*) (fig. 194), is found both in mud and sand off many parts of our coast, and also on the opposite side of the North Atlantic. The thick oval shell is not ribbed like the Cockle, and the name "Gaper" has reference to the fact that the valves cannot be brought together behind owing to the presence of enormous *siphons* that can only be drawn back into the shell to a limited extent. The two siphons are united into a single fleshy mass with two orifices at its tip, and protected by a brown wrinkled layer continuous with the outer horny layer of the shell. The protective arrangement suggested in the Mussel (see p. 331) is here carried to a much greater extent, for when the animal is buried in the mud, with only the tip of the siphon-tube projecting, it is singularly inconspicuous, though feeding and breathing can go on without interruption. The foot of the Gaper is small, and is of no use for springing.

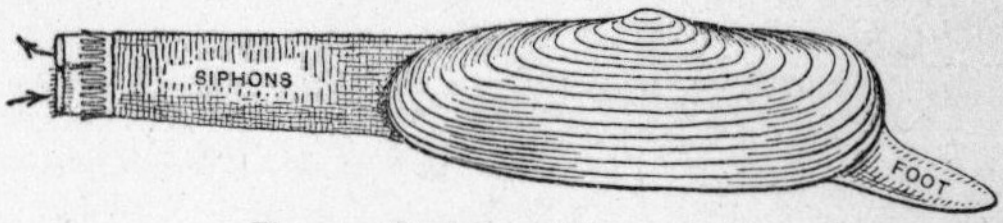

Fig. 194.—Sand-Gaper (*Mya arenaria*)

Fig. 195.—Razor-Shell (*Solen*). Foot seen on left, siphons on right

A closely-related family is that of the *Razor-shells* (fig. 195), of which two British species are very common, *i.e. Solen siliqua* and *Solen ensis*. In both cases the shell is very long and narrow, and gapes at both ends, but in the former species it is straight and in the latter curved.

Some very interesting boring molluscs come fairly close in affinity to the Gapers. The *Rock-borers* (*Saxicava*) and *Piddocks* (*Pholas*) (fig. 196), both of which can excavate burrows in hard rock, include a number of British species belonging to two families, while a third family is represented in the Atlantic and Mediterranean by the so-called "Ship-worm" (*Teredo navalis*) that often completely riddles timber with its burrows, which are lined by a smooth shelly layer secreted by the surface of the long siphonal tubes.

All the preceding families belong to one, and that the largest, of the five orders of bivalves. We may take the *Sea Mussel Family* as representing another order, and of the forms included by far the most familiar, largely on account of its economic importance, is the Edible Mussel (*Mytilus edulis*) (fig. 197), of which vast numbers are found together attached to stones, wooden piles, or other firm objects, by means of strong blackish threads constituting the *byssus*. The dark bluish shell is somewhat wedge-shaped, and the sharp beaks are placed at the extreme front end. There are no siphons, but merely two apertures, as in the Fresh-water Mussel, the inhalent one being very large and fringed. The small dark *foot*, though capable of being used as a locomotor organ, is not in constant employment as in free bivalves, which probably accounts for its relatively small size. The byssus arises from a deep pit behind the foot, and though it is commonly found

Fig. 196.—Piddocks (*Pholas dactylus*) in their Burrows

mooring the animal, it can be cast off if necessary, enabling the animal to creep away to some more desirable spot. The anterior adductor muscle is much smaller than the other, and this point is of special interest, because it foreshadows cases where only the posterior adductor is present in the adult. This is a tendency to specialization, but the gills on the other hand are simpler in structure than those of a Fresh-water Mussel, for though they consist of two plates on each side, yet each of these can easily be broken up into distinct filaments. The gill is, in fact, a somewhat modified plume-gill in which the separate side-branches of the plume have not yet firmly united into plates, as in the fresh-water mussel.

The *Ark-Shells* constitute a family belonging to the same

order as the Marine Mussels, and agree with them in the character of the gills. The shell is somewhat rectangular in form, with a long hinge-line possessing many small similar teeth. The foot has a flattened under-surface, an exception to the general rule among bivalves. The group is represented by species in all parts of the world, and some of the individual species have a very wide distribution, as in the case of the British species *Arca lactea.*

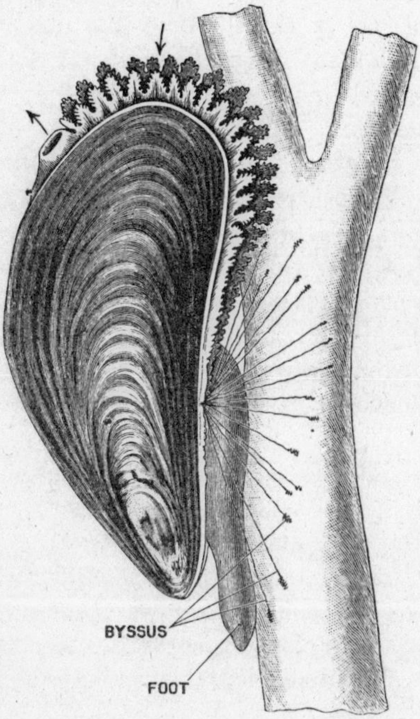

Fig. 197.—Edible Mussel (*Mytilus edulis*)

In the *Scallop Family* we have represented a third order of bivalves which possess gills more complicated than those of Ark-Shells and Edible Mussels, but less so than in the Fresh-water Mussel and associated families. There are several

Fig. 198.—Pilgrim Scallop (*Pecten Jacobæus*)

species of British Scallops belonging to the genus *Pecten*, in which the shells are fan-shaped. The Pilgrim Scallop (*Pecten Jacobæus*) (fig. 198) is interesting as the source of the "cockle-shell" which the mediæval pilgrim to the Holy Land wore in his hat. Only one adductor muscle is present, the equivalent of the posterior one in the families so far mentioned. In some of the species the valves of the shell are equal according to the general rule, and in these the animal is able to swim by flapping them. In other cases, of which the edible Scallop commonly seen in fishmongers' shops furnishes an example, the animal is sedentary, and during life rests with its right valve below, this being well curved, while the upper or left valve forms a flat lid. A byssus is present, serving to attach the creature to some firm object. There is in this genus an interesting variation on the mode of opening the shell described for the Fresh-water Mussel (see p. 330). There is no external ligament but what is called an *internal ligament* or cartilage, placed in a deep pit at the hinge and kept compressed when the shell is shut. When therefore the adductor muscle ceases to contract, the elasticity of this body will come into play, causing the shell to gape, just as a door might be made to fly open by the expansion of a piece of india-rubber shut into its hinge and thereby strongly compressed. The mantle-lobes of Pecten are quite free from one another, so that not only are siphons absent but also special inhalent and exhalent openings. The long plate-like *gills* follow the curve of the body, and water has ready access to them through the wide cleft between the mantle-lobes exposed when the animal opens its shell. The edge of the mantle is fringed by long tentacles, and bears quite a number of spherical eyes of a beautiful green colour. These have a very complicated structure, approaching in some respects to the eyes of Vertebrates.

The *Oyster Family* is closely allied to the preceding, but its members are still more modified. The shell is very irregular, and the animal is attached by the substance of the left valve, which in the Common Oyster (*Ostrea edulis*) of British seas is hollowed out while the right valve is lid-like, just the opposite to what is the case in a Scallop. The foot is entirely absent, and though the mantle-edges bear short tentacles, they are devoid of eyes.

Brief mention may be made of the *Nucula Family* as representing a comparatively small order of bivalves in which the gills present primitive characters. In the type genus *Nucula*, for example, the gill on each side is small and obviously like one of the gill-plumes of the Ormer, and a further primitive character is found in the possession of a foot with flattened creeping surface.

CLASS 4.—TUSK-SHELLS (SCAPHOPODA)

This small class includes the typical genus Dentalium and its allies. A British form, the Common Tusk-Shell (*Dentalium vulgare*) (fig. 199), may be taken as a type. It is found burrowing in the sandy parts of the sea-floor. The curved body is bilaterally symmetrical, with the upper side concave, and it is covered by a tubular *shell* shaped something like an elephant's tusk, whence its name. This shell has an aperture at each end, the larger one being in front, and its formation may be understood if we suppose the presence of two long mantle-flaps which have fused together in the middle line below, and that shelly matter has been secreted continuously all round. This view is justified by the development. So far there would appear to be affinity with the bivalve molluscs, and this is confirmed by the shape of the *foot*—which, however, has a lobe each side as well as a central portion—and by the character of the *nervous system*. In other respects there is an approach to Gastropods, for though the head is much reduced it is not entirely absent, the mouth being placed on the end of a short non-retractile *proboscis*, behind which is a pharynx provided with the typical *rasping-organ*.

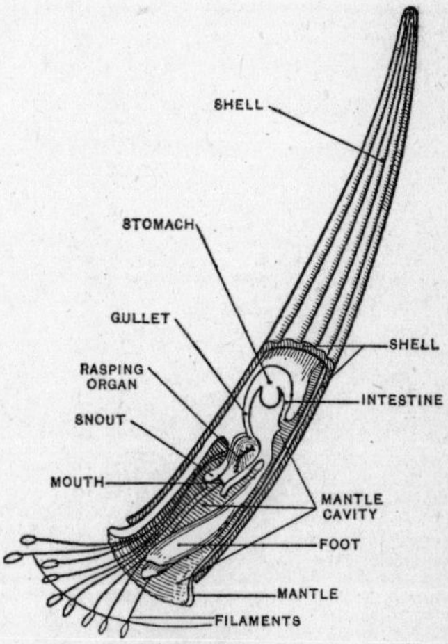

Fig. 199.—Tusk-shell (*Dentalium*). Shell partly removed

Springing from the base of the proboscis are two bunches of long filaments dilated at their ends, and capable of protrusion for some distance from the mouth of the shell. These are supposed to be of use in capturing small organisms as food, and it is possible that they represent the gills of other forms, though this is by no means certain.

CLASS 5.—PROTO-MOLLUSCS (AMPHINEURA)

The different classes of Molluscs are all supposed to have sprung from bilaterally symmetrical forms with fairly distinct head, a rasping-organ, and a creeping foot. There was probably a continuous mantle-flap sheltering in the hinder-part of the body a pair of plume-like gills, near which would open the paired kidneys, one on each side of the intestinal aperture. The heart would be dorsal and posterior in position, and would most likely consist of a muscular ventricle with a thin-walled auricle on each side. From creatures of this kind we can imagine Cephalopods, Gastropods, Lamellibranchs, and Scaphopods derived by specialization along different lines, the nature of which has been already indicated in the description of these classes. The small number of forms which make up the present class have probably retained to a higher degree than any other living forms the characters

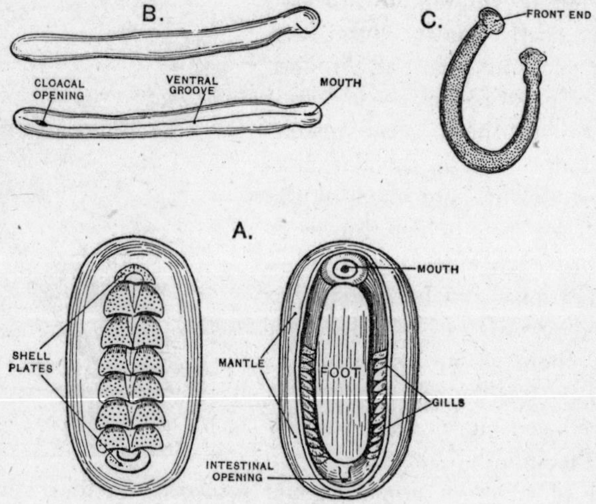

Fig. 200.—Proto-molluscs

A, Mail-Shell (*Chiton*), seen from above and below.
B, Proneomenia, right side and under surface. C, Chætoderma.

of these hypothetical ancestors, though they also have undergone modifications of their own, and it is often a difficult problem to determine which of their characteristics are primitive and which not.

The most abundant and familiar of these animals are the *Mail-Shells* or *Chitons* (fig. 200), most of which live under stones near low-water mark. A common British form is *Chiton marginatus*. In the bilateral symmetry, the presence of a fairly well-marked *head*, a broad, creeping *foot*, and a continuous *mantle-flap*, the Chitons are probably primitive. The same thing may be said regarding the dorsal *heart*, which is placed posteriorly and possesses the three typical chambers, and the *kidneys*, which are paired and open far back. The *rasping-organ*, however, is highly complex, and the *gills* are arranged in a row on each side, instead of being two in number. Quite possibly, however, the many-gilled is more primitive than the two-gilled condition, and there are some Chitons which have a limited number of gills far back on each side. As to the *shell*, we find eight overlapping plates situated on the dorsal side.

The remaining Proto-molluscs (fig. 200) are unfamiliar marine forms inhabiting moderately or very deep water. They possess no *shell*, but the skin is beset with calcareous spicules, and they are more or less worm-like in appearance. The *foot* is either a narrow ridge placed in a longitudinal groove (*Neomenia*, *Proneomenia*), or may be entirely absent (*Chætoderma*). There is a small posterior *mantle-cavity* into which the intestine and paired kidneys open, while it may shelter a pair of plume-like *gills* (*Chætoderma*), or these may be represented by a tuft of filaments (*Neomenia*) or merely by folds (*Proneomenia*). Though at first sight the view is tempting that these genera are more primitive than Chiton, and give an indication of how Molluscs might arise from worm-like forms, it is more probable that they are simplified animals which have lost some of the typical molluscan characters, and are, so to speak, going downhill rather than uphill.

CHAPTER VIII

STRUCTURE AND CLASSIFICATION OF JOINTED-LIMBED ANIMALS (ARTHROPODA)

This is by far the largest of the great groups of the animal kingdom, including, as it does, Insects; Scorpions, Spiders, and Mites; Centipedes and Millipedes; Lobsters, Crabs, Shrimps, and a host of other Crustacea.

The Lobster, a typical member of the phylum, has already been briefly described in illustration of the characters of the higher Invertebrates (see pp. 302–304). It may be convenient to point out the respects in which it is typical of the group Arthropoda. These are: *bilateral symmetry*, the division of the body into a series of *segments* grouped into regions and bearing a series of paired *jointed limbs*, and the presence of a central nervous system consisting of a *nerve-ring* and a *ventral cord*. It may also be noted that the so-called *body-cavity* consists of a set of blood-containing spaces situated between the internal organs and the wall of the body. They form, therefore, a part of the blood-system, while the body-cavity of a Vertebrate (see p. 42) belongs to the lymph-system. Molluscs agree with Arthropods in this respect, except that in them the pericardial cavity does not contain blood, but is comparable to the corresponding cavity in a Vertebrate so far as that particular feature is concerned. In Arthropods, however, the heart is situated in a blood-containing space from which blood passes into it.

The phylum is divided into the following classes, which will be considered in the same order:—

A.—Air-breathing Forms (Tracheata).

Class 1. Insects (INSECTA).
Class 2. Spider-like Animals (ARACHNIDA).—Scorpions, Spiders, Mites
Class 3. Centipedes and Millipedes (MYRIAPODA).
Class 4. Peripatus (PROTOTRACHEATA).

B.—Aquatic Forms (Branchiata).

Class 5. Crustaceans (CRUSTACEA).—Lobsters, Crabs, Shrimps, &c.
Class 6. King-Crabs (XIPHOSURA).
Class 7. Sea-Spiders (PYCNOGONIDA).

A.—AIR-BREATHING ARTHROPODS (TRACHEATA)

CLASS I.—INSECTS (INSECTA)

This class embraces an astonishing number of species, more numerous, in fact, than those of all other groups of land animals put together. Yet, in spite of this, they do not exhibit so wide a range of characters as might be expected, so that the study of a carefully-chosen type forms an intelligible key to the entire class. The too-familiar Cockroach or Black "Beetle" (*Periplaneta orientalis*) furnishes just such a type, though the American species (*P. Americana*) obtainable in many seaports, is decidedly better on account of its larger size.

External Characters (fig. 201).—The body is obviously divided into three regions—head, thorax, and abdomen—the distinction between the first two being emphasized by the presence of a narrow neck. In such an insect as a wasp the demarcation between thorax and abdomen is equally sharp, while in many insects, on the other hand, the three regions are bounded by a continuous curved outline unbroken by constrictions.

Each one of these three regions of the body is made up of rings or *segments*, which differ very much among themselves in character, and in some places are so closely fused together that their exact number cannot be definitely made out. Arthropods, in fact, or any large group of them, furnish innumerable instances of the phenomena described elsewhere (see p. 195) in reference to the skeleton of the limbs, where all sorts of modification of a common plan may arise by unequal development of parts, fusion, and reduction. One of the lower Arthropods, for example, such as a Centipede or Peripatus, consists of a large number of similar segments which have only undergone great specialization at the head end, while in such highly specialized forms as Insects the segments have been much reduced in number, and are grouped into regions which, in correspondence with special uses, have acquired special characters.

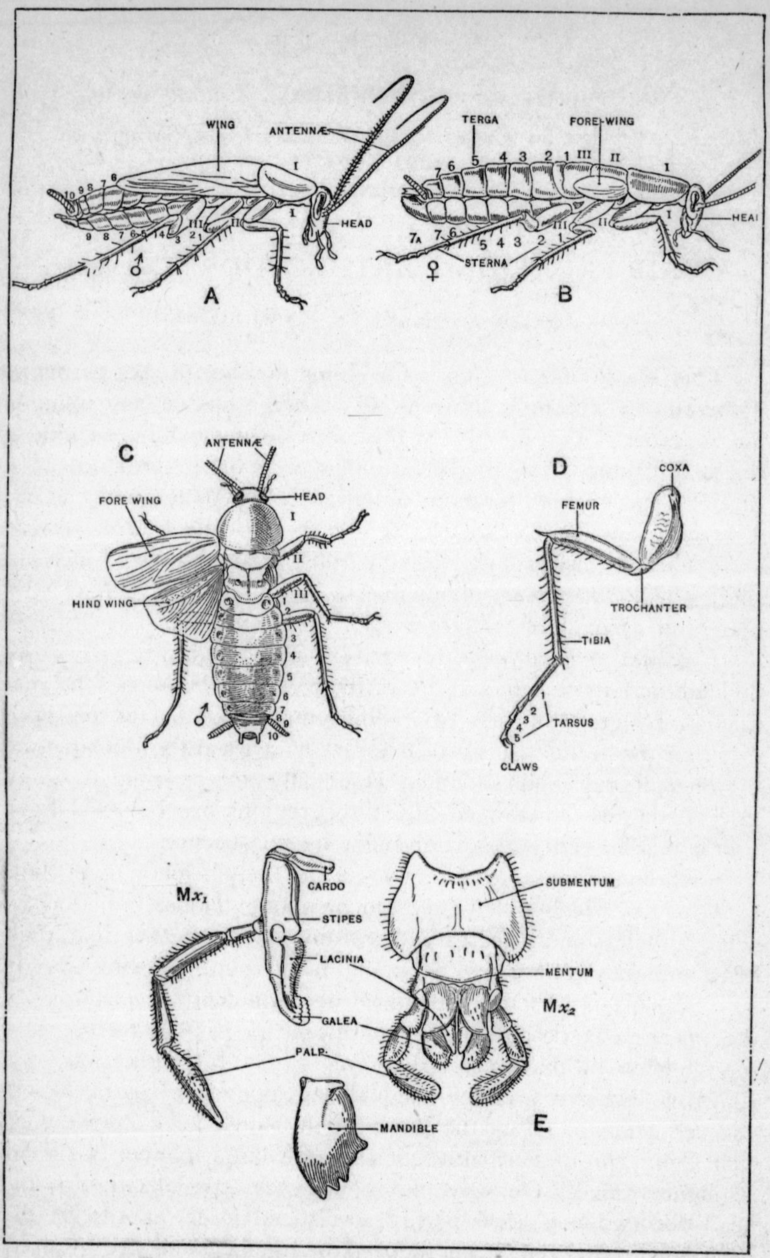

Fig. 201.—External Characters of Cockroach (*Periplaneta orientalis*)

A, B, C, Side views of male and female, and top view of male; I, II, III, segments of thorax; 1–10, segments of abdomen. D, A leg (enlarged). E, Jaws (much enlarged). Mx_1, First maxilla; Mx_2, second maxilla.

Among Insects the Cockroach is a fairly central type, and the least modified part of it is the *abdomen*, in which ten segments can clearly be distinguished. A pair of flattened jointed rods, the *cerci*, spring from the last segment, and are probably to be regarded as limbs, which are otherwise absent in this region, if certain doubtful structures be excepted. This practically limbless condition of the abdomen is characteristic of insects, and has been brought about by reduction. The *thorax* is commonly regarded as made up of three segments, and each of these bears a pair of jointed limbs or appendages in the shape of *walking-legs*. Each leg is composed of several pieces (10) movably jointed together, a character which is common to all Arthropod limbs, and has given the name to the phylum (Gk. *arthros*, jointed; *pous*, a foot). The parts of the leg differ much among themselves in respect of size and shape. The thorax also bears a pair of flattened expansions, forming the wings, attached to its second and third segments, which in the male of the common Cockroach, and both sexes in the American species, extend far backwards and overlap the abdomen. The fore-wings are horny structures, and may be termed the *wing-covers*, since they cover and protect the delicate membranous hind-wings, or wings proper. In the female of the ordinary Cockroach the fore-wings are very small and the hind-wings absent, reduction having taken place in both cases.

The *head* consists of a number of segments which have fused so intimately together that the boundaries between them cannot be made out. As, however, in the higher Arthropods the presence of pairs of jointed limbs is taken to indicate the existence of a corresponding number of segments, a certain clue is afforded, though, as all segments do not bear limbs, such evidence is only partial. In this case, as in Insects generally, there are four pairs of appendages, so that the head possesses at least four segments. The first of these are two slender jointed feelers or *antennæ*, serving as organs of touch, and probably also having to do with other senses. The remaining appendages are three pairs of jaws, named, from before backwards, mandibles, first maxillæ, and second maxillæ. As in all Invertebrates they are quite outside the opening of the mouth, and those of them which are used for biting work from side to side. Each *mandible* consists of a single broad horny piece, toothed on its inner edge, where it bites against its fellow. The *first maxilla* on either side has a two-jointed stalk, upon the end of which are borne a slender outer and a shorter inner branch. The former is made up of a number of narrow joints, and is known as a *palp*, while the inner branch consists of two parts, a cutting blade next the middle line and a soft piece adjacent to the palp. The smaller *second maxillæ* are built on the same lines, but are fused together to form what is commonly called the "under lip" or *labium*. It is the united stalks which have so fused, and though these particular appendages are considered as jaws, the union has of course taken away any power of biting against each other. Projecting from the front of the mouth is a broad horny plate, the "upper lip" or *labrum*, and in the narrow space between this and the labium the mandibles and cutting parts of the first maxillæ work against one another. The Cockroach is clearly an example of Insects with biting mouth-parts, but in other cases we find the corresponding appendages adapted to very different uses, furnishing one of the best examples known of modifications of a common type.

A large kidney-shaped *eye* will be seen on each side of the head, and a good lens will show that each of these possesses a large number of six-sided facets. An eye like this is generally known as a "compound eye", each of the facets having been formerly regarded as equivalent to an independent simple eye. Some of the other external characters are mentioned elsewhere.

Skin and Exoskeleton.—The body is invested in a strong horny covering secreted by the underlying epidermis. Movement is rendered possible by the presence of softer areas between the firmer tracts, so that the head is not immovably fixed, the segments of the abdomen can move one upon the other, and the joints of the limbs can be bent in various directions. In fact the same problem has had to be solved as that involved in the construction of a suit of armour, *i.e.* the combination of efficient protecting power without undue sacrifice of flexibility. It is of especial importance to notice that the narrow side of the body is for the most part provided with a softer investment than the broad upper and lower surfaces.

Digestive Organs (fig. 202).—The head of the Cockroach is bent downwards at right angles to the long axis of the body, so that the mouth-opening at its end faces downwards. It leads

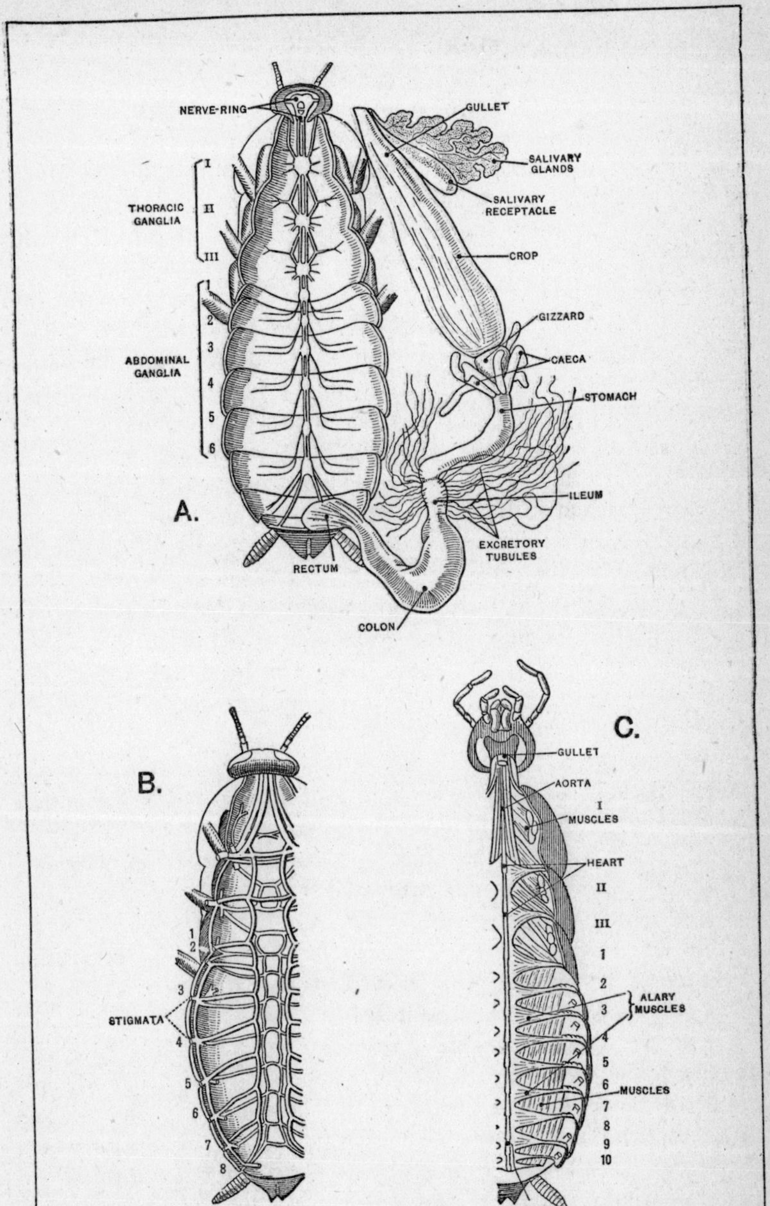

Fig. 202.—Structure of Cockroach (*Periplaneta orientalis*) (enlarged)

A, Digestive organs and nervous system. B, Air-tubes (tracheæ). C, Heart and muscles. I–III, Segments of thorax; 1–10, segments of abdomen.

into a small *mouth-cavity*, from the back of which projects a pointed *tongue*, and which passes into a narrow *gullet* continuous with a large thin-walled *crop*, and that again with a smaller thick-walled *gizzard*, from which a fairly long *intestine* runs to its termination between the cerci. The gizzard is provided with an internal chewing arrangement, such as is not uncommon among Arthropods. It consists of a firm lining raised into horny teeth and bristly ridges. Digestive fluids are poured into the digestive tube by a pair of branching *salivary glands* which open into the mouth-cavity, and a number of club-shaped "*liver*" *tubes* (digestive cæca) which encircle the beginning of the intestine.

Circulatory Organs (fig. 202).—This is not very highly specialized, for a reason to be mentioned later. The whole of the body is traversed by irregular blood-spaces of various sizes, but the only definite tubular structure is the *heart*, a long narrow blood-vessel running through the thorax and abdomen close to the upper surface. Along its sides are numerous pairs of valvular openings, through which blood passes in from the surrounding blood-space (pericardial sinus) to be pumped forwards. The heart is systemic, as it contains pure blood.

Respiratory Organs (fig. 202).—These organs present a very interesting and remarkable arrangement, for instead of the impure blood being sent to a localized lung for purification, air is conveyed to all parts of the body by means of branching *tracheal tubes.* These communicate with the exterior by means of ten pairs of small openings or *stigmata* on the sides of the body, all but the first two pairs being in the abdomen. Observation of a living Cockroach will show that the abdomen alternately dilates and contracts, the result being that air is drawn into and expelled from the stigmata. It is therefore possible to choke an insect by smearing the sides of the body with oil or some other substance which will block up these openings. The tracheal tubes appear silvery under the microscope, owing to the air which they contain, and they are lined by an elastic membrane thickened into a continuous spiral thread, so as to render them very flexible and non-collapsible. Just within each spiracle is a kind of valve, formed as a projection of the lining membrane and helping to prevent the intrusion of foreign particles.

As a result of this very thorough system of aeration, the blood never has the opportunity of remaining impure, a fact which accounts to some extent for the imperfect condition of the circulatory organs. The restless activity of insects, and their great muscular powers, are also no doubt related to the unusually perfect state of the breathing apparatus.

Excretory Organs.—These also are very unlike anything so far described in the animal groups reviewed. They consist of a large number of very slender *Malpighian tubes*, which open into the intestine not far from its commencement.

Nervous System and Sense Organs (fig. 202).—The *nervous system* consists of a narrow and much-thickened *nerve-ring* closely encircling the gullet, and of a ventral double *nerve-cord.* The upper part of the ring is formed by a pair of large brain-ganglia, sending nerves to the eyes and antennæ, while its lower part is made up of another pair of ganglia, supplying the upper lip and three pairs of jaws. The ventral cord dilates within the thorax into three pairs of ganglia which innervate the three thoracic segments, and within the abdomen into six smaller pairs of ganglia, of which the first five belong to the corresponding abdominal segments, while the last and largest pair provide for the nerve-supply of the last five segments. Segmentation of the body as exhibited by Vertebrates, Arthropods, and some other phyla of the animal kingdom, means the existence of a number of successive rings or segments, containing sections of the various internal organs. Where the segmentation is very well marked, many structures are affected by it, and the more primitive the animal the more closely do the segments resemble one another. As regards the nervous system of Arthropods, there can be no doubt that the simplest condition is found in the presence of a distinct pair of ganglia for each segment, but Insects especially present considerable modifications of this primitive arrangement. Where a segment is relatively large, its ganglia will be so too, as seen in the thorax of the Cockroach, while fusion of segments will be accompanied by fusion of ganglia, as in the case of the jaw-bearing segments. The ganglia, further, may be among the first parts to fuse together, as seen in the last pair of the abdominal chain in the Cockroach, which represent the ganglia for the last five segments all united together, though the segments themselves are still more or less distinct.

The chief *sense organs* are those of *touch*—including the

antennæ, maxillary palps, labial palps, and cerci—and those of *vision*, as represented by the large compound eyes. There is good reason to believe that the antennæ are organs of *smell* as well as of touch, and it is probable that some of the mouth parts, perhaps the second maxillæ, have to do with *taste*. It may be further remarked that great difficulty attaches to the interpretation of many of the sense organs possessed by animals (see p. 264), and Insects, among others, are undoubtedly endowed with special senses of which it is difficult, if not impossible, for us to form any idea, our only definite standards being our own sense organs, which are those of much specialized land animals. In a subsequent chapter this interesting subject will be more fully discussed.

Life-history.—An insect such as a Butterfly or Moth goes through widely different stages in its life-history. Hatching from the egg as a caterpillar, it grows to a considerable size, and then becomes a motionless chrysalis, from which the adult insect later on escapes, its body having been formed by a series of revolutionary changes from the substance of the chrysalis body. This life-history, familiar to all who have kept silkworms, and furnishing a useful metaphor to moralists of all centuries, is one which exhibits complete change of form, or *metamorphosis*, to use the technical expression. The life-history of the Frog (see p. 254) is an example of the same kind of thing, the essence of which consists in considerable modification in form and structure after the animal has been hatched out and has started a free independent existence. Insects differ very much among themselves as to the amount of metamorphosis, and the Cockroach exemplifies an order in which it is so slight as to be practically absent. The eggs are laid in horny capsules, each containing sixteen, and the just-hatched Cockroach closely resembles the adult, from which it chiefly differs in its smaller size and the absence of wings. As growth proceeds, the firm exoskeleton is not increased in size to suit the enlarging body as in a Mollusc, but is bodily thrown off or "moulted", a very common phenomenon among Arthropods. After some seven moults the adult size is attained.

Classification of Insects.—Considering that some 250,000 distinct species have been described, and that at least ten times this number are believed to exist, it will be realized that the classification of insects is likely to present some difficulties, especially as there are not the same obvious distinctions as are found in some other groups, *e.g.* Molluscs. Various subdivisions have been proposed, some of the modern ones being complex, but it will be the simplest plan to adopt here the comparatively old-fashioned grouping into nine orders, primarily based upon the characters of the wings, and which is mainly due to Linnæus. It will be enough for the present purpose if some of the commonest insects are mentioned, and sufficient detail given to enable the reader to refer an insect to its proper order.

Order 1. Bugs (HEMIPTERA).—Four wings, of which the front pair are often only membranous at the tips.

Order 2. Fringe-winged Insects (THYSANOPTERA).—Four wings, all very narrow and fringed.

Order 3. Flies (DIPTERA).—A single pair of membranous wings equivalent to the front pair of other insects.

Order 4. Moths and Butterflies (LEPIDOPTERA).—Four wings present, covered with scales.

Order 5. Beetles (COLEOPTERA).—Four wings, of which the front ones are converted into hard wing-cases, covering the membranous hind-wings, which during repose are folded transversely.

Order 6. Membrane-winged Insects (HYMENOPTERA). — Four membranous wings possessing but few nervures, and which cannot be folded up. Fore-wing larger than the hind.

Order 7. Net-winged Insects (NEUROPTERA). — Four membranous wings, with an elaborate net-work of nervures.

Order 8. Straight-winged Insects (ORTHOPTERA).—Four wings, of which the front pair are horny wing-cases, while the others are membranous and fold up in a fan-like manner when at rest.

Order 9. Wingless Insects (APTERA). — Primitive wingless insects. Insects belonging to other orders may have lost their wings by a process of reduction affecting one or both sexes.

Order 1.—BUGS (Hemiptera)

The English name given to the order is somewhat libellous, for though a number of repulsive forms are included here, others again are beautifully coloured and attractive objects. A typical species is outlined in fig. 203. There is considerable variation in the matter of *wings*, as both pairs may be much alike, or the fore-wings may be wing-cases, or again both pairs may be absent. In all cases the mouth-parts are converted into piercing and sucking organs, which, though much unlike the corresponding parts of the Cockroach both in appearance and use, can be compared with them part for part. The narrow *upper lip* is pointed, and below it are the *mandibles*, but these, instead of being cutting-jaws, are long piercing stylets, grooved along their inner sides in such a way as, when applied together, to form a double tube down the lower half of which saliva can pass to the object pierced, while juices can travel along its upper half to the mouth. Outside, and close to the mandibles, are the *first maxillæ* in the form of two more stylets devoid of palps. The four stylets to-

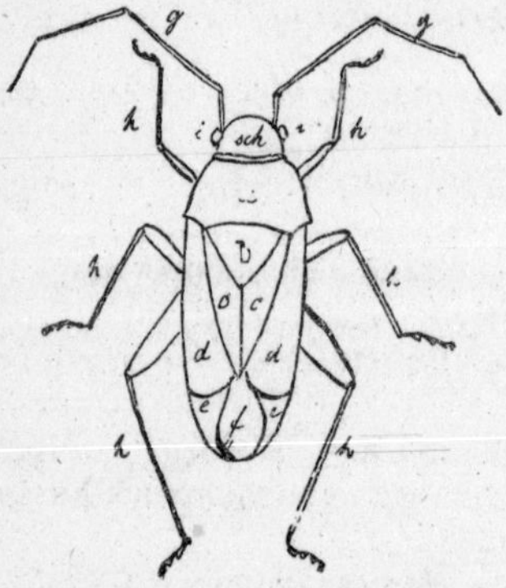

Fig. 203.—A typical Bug (*Capsus*)
a, *b*, First two segments of thorax; *c*, *d*, horny part of wing-covers; *e*, *f*, membranous part of wing-covers; *g*, antennæ; *h*, *h*, *h*, legs; *i*, eyes; *sch*, top of head

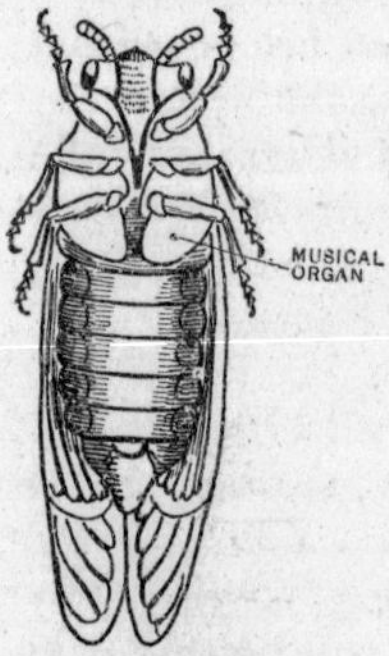

Fig. 204.—Cicada, seen from below

gether constitute an efficient piercing organ which can be protruded or drawn back at will by the action of special muscles, and it also forms a channel along which fluids can be conducted to the mouth, as just explained. The *second maxillæ*, including their palps, are fused together into a sheath for the piercing mouth-parts. In most cases the adult condition is attained without any large amount of metamorphosis.

The order is conveniently divided into two sub-orders; *i.e.* 1. Homoptera, in which the two pairs of wings are similar; and 2. Heteroptera, in which they are unlike.

1. *Homoptera.* — These all live upon the juices of plants, and their fore-wings are of uniform texture. *Cicadas* (fig. 204) are large, broad insects with membranous wings of considerable size, which may be opaque and brightly coloured. The antennæ are very small, and the head not only bears large lateral eyes, but also three simple eyes or *ocelli* placed in front and often gem-

like in appearance. The males are provided with musical organs on the under-side of the thorax, by which they are enabled to make a chirping sound, the well-known "song of the Cicada". The eggs are deposited in the branches of trees by means of a piercing organ with which the tail of the female is provided, and from them are hatched wingless larvæ, which dig into the ground by means of their fore-legs and subsist on the juices of roots, ultimately making their way up again and becoming adult. The larvæ may remain as such for a long period, in one North American species for seventeen years. Cicadas, of which there are very numerous species, inhabit the warmer parts of the earth, some of them being natives of South Europe.

Lantern-Flies and their allies make up a closely-related family, many members of which are beautifully coloured, but the species found in Europe (including Britain) are not highly endowed in this respect. The name "lantern-fly" has not been so far justified.

Most persons have seen, during the summer months, those frothy masses on plants to which the name "cuckoo spit" is vulgarly given. These enclose the larvæ of small insects belonging to this sub-order, and known as *Frog-Hoppers* on account of their leaping powers.

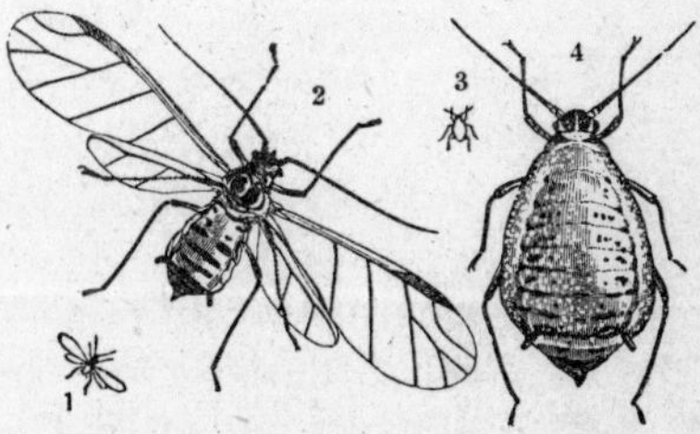

Fig. 205.—Cabbage Aphis (*Aphis brassicæ*)

1, 2, Male (natural size and enlarged); 3, 4, female (natural size and enlarged)

Plant-Lice, or *Green-Flies*, furnish other examples (fig. 205). The best-known forms are the little green aphides common on geraniums and other garden plants, and which, like their immediate allies, are distinguished by a complex life-history. The Vine-Louse (*Phylloxera vastatrix*) is a creature of the kind which does immense damage in vineyards.

The Cochineal Insect (*Coccus cacti*), on the other hand, is of economic importance. It is a native of Mexico and Central America, where it feeds upon cacti.

2. *Heteroptera.*—To the insects of this sub-order the name "bug" is properly applied. When wings are present, the front pair are transformed into wing-covers, the tips of which, however, remain membranous. Many of the species are distinguished by

a disagreeable odour, due to the secretion of certain glands which open on the under-side of the third segment of the thorax. Some are terrestrial and others aquatic. Many of the land bugs are not among the personal enemies of man, but feed on the juices of plants. These forms mostly escape the observation of those who are not entomologists, but the wingless blood-sucking bed-bug (*Cimex lectularius*) has an effective way of compelling attention that has rendered it the most widely known among its order. Even more odious are the small wingless forms known as *lice* which infest the bodies of human beings and many other animals, multiplying with astonishing rapidity. They are regarded as bugs which have become degenerate as a result of their parasitic habit. A typical example is the Head-Louse (*Pediculus capitis*), which feeds on the blood of the scalp, and lays its eggs on the hairs, to which they are firmly attached.

The *water-bugs* comprise a number of forms familiar to the student of fresh-water life, and to some extent known even to the casual observer. The *skaters*, which are often seen gliding about on the surface of the water, are of this kind, or, to speak more accurately, constitute a family allied both to land- and water-bugs. The Needle-Bug (*Limnobates stagnorum*), with long attenuated body and deliberate movements, is conspicuous among them. The Pond-Skater (*Gerris paludum*) has a stouter body and moves very rapidly. One genus (*Halobates*) is especially interesting in being a marine form living upon the surface of the sea even at great distances from land. This is remarkable, for though insects are exceedingly dominant as terrestrial forms, and are far from uncommon in fresh water, they are almost unrepresented in the marine fauna.

Water-bugs proper are inconspicuous insects distinguishable from their terrestrial allies by their extremely-reduced antennæ, and by the fact that they actually live in the water and not merely on it like the skaters. The *Water-Scorpions* are rapacious narrow-headed forms, in which the fore-legs are used for seizing their prey. The narrow tail-like prolongation which has suggested the common name is an arrangement connected with breathing, as will elsewhere be described. In some species there is a broad flat body (*e.g. Nepa cinerea*), while in others it is long and narrow (*Ranatra linearis*). Equally common are the broad-bodied *Water-Boatmen* (*Notonecta*), which, by means of their long hair-fringed hind-legs, row themselves along upon their backs. Like the forms already mentioned, they prey upon small flies and the like.

Order 2.—FRINGE-WINGED INSECTS (Thysanoptera)

This is a very restricted order, including minute insects with suctorial mouth, long narrow body, well-developed slender antennæ, and four narrow wings with a fringe of hairs. The male is wingless. There is also a peculiarity about the feet, which end in bladder-like lobes.

Some of the species infest flowers, *e.g.* those of Elder; and the Corn Thrips (*Thrips cerealium*) (fig. 206) does a good deal of damage to crops.

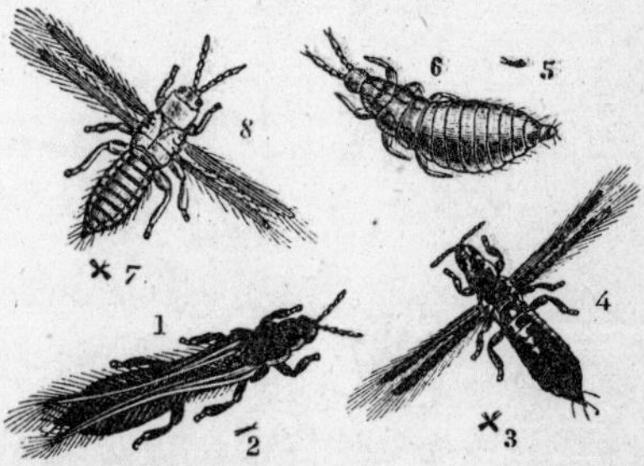

Fig. 206.—Corn Thrips (*Thrips cerealium*); 1, 2, female walking; 3, 4, female flying. Potato Thrips (*Thrips minutissima*); 5, 6, larva; 7, 8, female flying; 2, 3, 5, 7, natural size; 1, 4, 6, 8, enlarged.

Order 3.—FLIES (Diptera)

This is one of the largest orders of Insects, and includes not only innumerable *Flies*, but also those modified forms which are known as *Fleas*. As the scientific name indicates (Gk. *dis*, twice; *pteron*, a wing), only two wings are present (fig. 207). These are membranous, with comparatively few nervures, most of which run longitudinally, and they correspond to the fore-wings of other Insects. The hind-wings, however, have not entirely disappeared, but are represented by two club-shaped vestiges, which from their function are known as *balancers* (*halteres*).

The *mouth-parts* (fig. 207) are adapted for sucking, and often for piercing as well, but there are considerable differences from the arrangements which serve similar purposes in the Hemiptera. These structures are best developed in the females of such forms as Gnats, Mosquitoes, and Gad-Flies, where mandibles, maxillæ, and tongue are in the form of five piercing stylets, ensheathed in an imperfect tube formed by the labium and partly covered over by the long sharp labrum. Maxillary palps can be seen at the base of the proboscis. In the males of these forms, and both sexes of some members of the group, *e.g.* House-Fly (*Musca domestica*), the piercing parts are much reduced and the mouth is purely suctorial.

Diptera undergo a complete *metamorphosis*. From the egg a limbless *larva* (maggot) is hatched, which becomes a *pupa*,

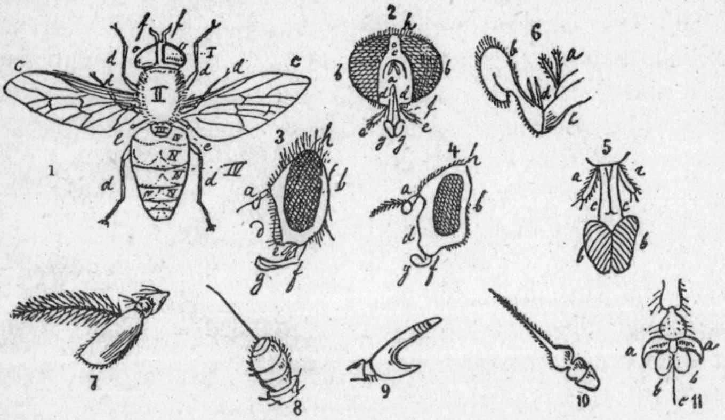

Fig. 207.—Structure of Flies (*Diptera*), enlarged to various scales

1, Parts of body: I, head; *o*, *o*, eyes; *f*, *f*, antennæ; II and III, thorax; *c*, *c*, wings; *e*, *e*, balancers; *d*, *d*, *d*, legs; IV, abdomen, with segments indicated. 2, Head (front view): *a*, antennæ; *b*, *b*, eyes; *c*, forehead; *d*, *d*, upper lip; *e*, *e*, palps; *f*, body of proboscis; *g*, *g*, suctorial flaps of proboscis. 3, 4, Head (side view): *a*, antennæ; *b*, eyes; *d*, lower part of face; *e*, palp; *f*, proboscis; *g*, suctorial flaps of proboscis; *h*, crown of head. 5, Proboscis (front view); *a*, *a*, palps; *b*, *b*, suctorial flaps; *c*, *c*, stalk. 6, Proboscis (side view): *a*, palps; *b*, suctorial flaps; *c*, stalk; *d*, mandibles. 7–10, Antennæ of various flies. 11, Foot: *a*, *a*, claws; *b*, *b*, adhesive lappets; *c*, bristles.

that may or may not possess the power of movement, and from which the adult insect or *imago* is developed. As the adult does not grow in size, the various-sized Flies which are often to be seen on windows and elsewhere are different species, and not, as often supposed, different stages in the growth of the same species.

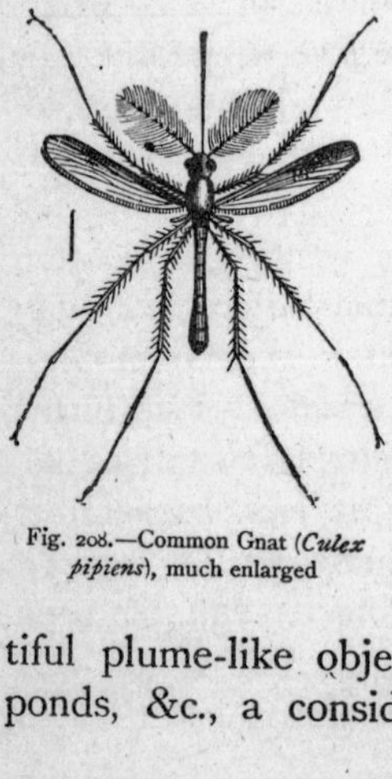

Fig. 208.—Common Gnat (*Culex pipiens*), much enlarged

The Common Gnat (*Culex pipiens*) (fig. 208) is a representative of a very large family in which the females are distinguished by their blood-sucking propensities, while the males are supposed to live upon the juices of plants. The body is slender, the legs long, and the antennæ are well-developed, those of the male being beautiful plume-like objects. The eggs are laid on the surface of ponds, &c., a considerable number being agglutinated together into a sort of raft. The *larvæ* which hatch out from them (fig. 209) look something like little red worms with large heads, and they possess a special breathing arrangement in the form of two tubes, each with a stigma at its tip, projecting from the hinder end of the body. The favourite position of the larva is suspended head downwards close to the surface, with the ends of these tubes just projecting above water, and so enabling breathing to

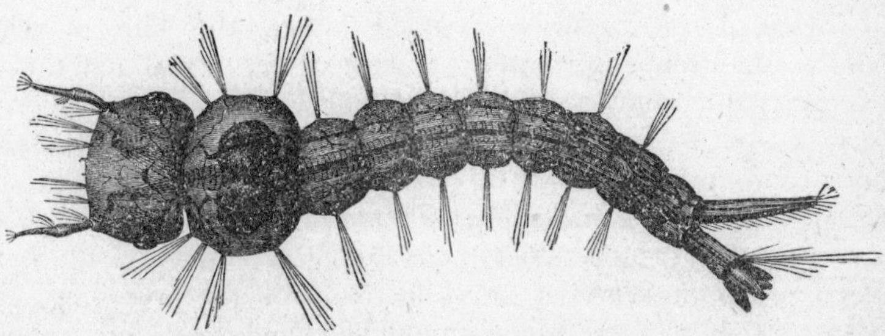

Fig. 209.—Larva of Common Gnat (*Culex pipiens*), greatly enlarged

be carried on. After several moults, the larva becomes a *pupa*, at the front end of which the wings, legs, and antennæ of the adult can be dimly made out under the skin. From each side of the thorax a breathing-tube projects, and these are used like those of the larva, except that owing to their position the animal is suspended tail downwards. The pupa is active, and swims by jerking its tail. Examination from time to time of almost any old rain-water butt will enable one to trace the successive stages of the life-history of the Gnat, the final one of which is reached by the splitting of the pupal skin down the middle of the back, making a rent from which the adult Gnat makes its exit, being floated up meanwhile by the buoyancy of its investments.

Midges resemble Gnats in many particulars, and pass through a somewhat similar life-history; but they are much smaller, and it is only the females of some species which possess mouth-parts adapted for blood-sucking. The small black Midge (*Ceratopogon*) which is so troublesome in the summer months is one of these forms. The Plumed Midge (*Chironomus plumosus*), of which hosts may be seen dancing together any summer evening, is a well-known species, distinguished by the great beauty of the antennæ in the male.

The *Crane-Flies* are much larger insects, of which the Daddy-Long-Legs (*Tipula oleracea* and other species) is known to all. The peculiarly long legs are especially useful in enabling the animal to progress rapidly through grass. The eggs are laid in meadows, and the larvæ feed upon the roots of grasses.

All the preceding are distinguished by comparatively long antennæ, but in numerous families these appendages are very short. Well-known examples are the Horse-Stinger or Cleg (*Tabanus bovis*), a large speckled insect, the bite of whose female has been experienced by most of us in walking through woods; the notorious cattle pests called *Bot-Flies* (*Hypoderma bovis*, ox-bot; *Œstrus ovis*, sheep-bot; *Gastrophilus equi*, horse-bot); and the Tsetse-Fly (*Glossina morsitans*). Here, too, belong the Blue-Bottle (*Musca vomitoria*), House-Fly (*Musca domestica*), and their allies, constituting a family in which the piercing mouth-parts, as found in many of the preceding, have been reduced to mere vestiges, while a complex sucking proboscis is present, formed chiefly by the labium. The Fly's tongue is one of the commonest, most beautiful, and at the same time most complicated, of microscopic objects.

The *Fleas* are doubtfully associated with the Diptera as degraded forms living parasitically on the bodies of warm-blooded animals. The mouth-parts are modified for piercing and sucking, but present considerable differences from the arrangement described for the Gnats, &c. (p. 355). Wings are absent, and so are compound eyes, the organs of vision consisting only of a simple eye on each side. The long strong hind-legs are associated with great powers of leaping. The Common Flea (*Pulex irritans*) is not, as often imagined, the same species as those infesting cats, dogs, and other domestic animals. It appears, indeed, that there are very numerous sorts of Fleas associated with different Mammalia, even Bats being attended by their own peculiar species.

Order 4.—Moths and Butterflies (Lepidoptera)

The insects of this order are, in the vast majority of cases, so characteristic-looking that they can be recognized at first sight mainly because they possess two large pairs of wings covered with minute variously-shaped scales (fig. 210), easily rubbed off as what is popularly called the "dust" of the wing. The presence of these scales gives rises to all sorts and combinations of colours, often of extreme beauty. The male and female of the same species are often very different in appearance.

The *head*, which is well-marked off from the thorax, bears long antennæ and prominent compound eyes, while its mouth-parts are converted into a long *proboscis*, carried rolled up into a spiral when not in use (fig. 211). This organ is used to suck up the nectar of flowers or, in some cases, liquid matter of a less savoury kind, but differs entirely in structure from the corresponding organ of a Fly. The *upper lip* is inconspicuous, and the *mandibles* have disappeared altogether, while the *second maxillæ* are fused into a small plate bearing two conspicuous palps. The sucking part is formed entirely from the much-elongated *first maxillæ*, each of which is a long jointed structure grooved deeply on its inner side, so that when approximated to its fellow a tube is formed, the firmness of which is often enhanced by a series of interlocking hooks.

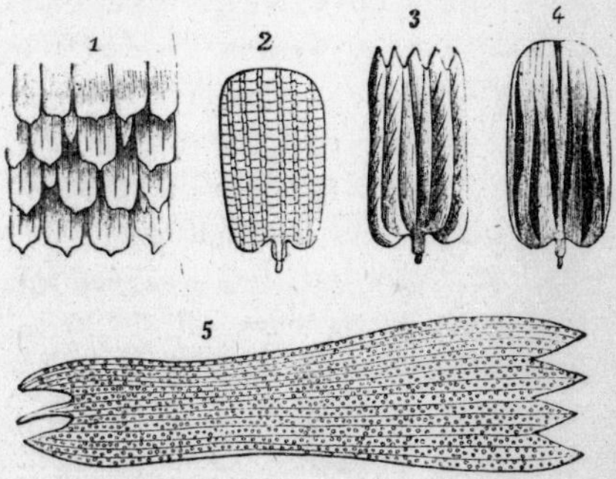

Fig. 210.—Scales from Wings of various Butterflies (greatly enlarged)

The *thorax* bears not only the wings, but three pairs of weak legs, and is fairly well marked off from the *abdomen*, which is generally elongated, but may either be very slender or else broad according to the species.

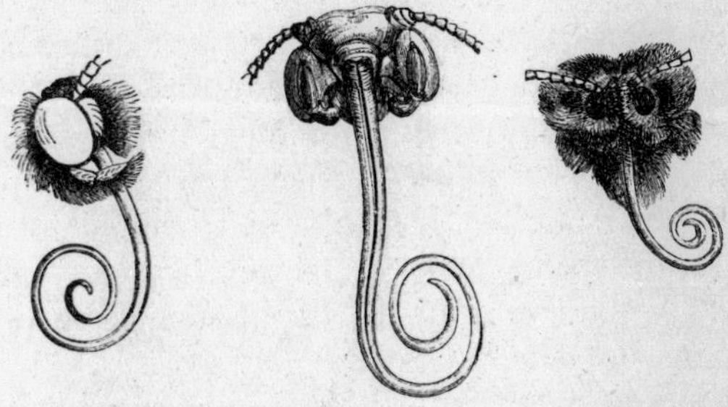
Fig. 211.—Heads and Proboscides of various Butterflies (enlarged)

The *life-history* of a Moth or Butterfly furnishes a good example of complete *metamorphosis*. The eggs are laid upon some special food-plant, and the larvæ which hatch out from them are ravenous *caterpillars* which feed upon vegetable matter or, more rarely, other substances. The head is provided with an extremely short pair of antennæ, a group of simple eyes on each side, and biting mouth-parts. The cylindrical trunk is composed of eleven segments, the first three of which bear jointed legs corresponding to those of the adult; and besides this, from one to five of the other segments possess stumpy pro-legs which have sucker-like ends. Those at the posterior end of the body are often modified in various ways.

Caterpillars vary much in size, colour, and other characters, among which may be mentioned presence or absence of hairs, some being smooth and hairless, and others so hirsute as to have earned the popular name of "woolly bears". After leading a life entirely devoted to continuous feeding for a period varying from weeks to years, during which time the skin is frequently moulted as the body increases in size, the caterpillar becomes lethargic and passes into the quiescent pupa stage, constituting what is generally called a *chrysalis.* A continuous horny covering invests body and limbs alike, beneath which the parts of the perfect insect can be dimly traced. Innumerable methods of concealment and protection ward off to some extent the attacks of enemies during this helpless period. In some cases the chrysalis is to be found above-ground suspended by a silken cord, or fastened to some object by a girdle of the same material, in which cases its colour commonly harmonizes with the surroundings and renders it inconspicuous. Other chrysalides are sheltered underground, and others again are to be found within cocoons, of which the silkworm is the most familiar illustration.

The last stage is reached when the perfect insect or *imago* issues from the chrysalis at a time dependent upon favourable conditions of temperature and various other factors, such, *e.g.*, as a suitable state of the particular food-plant upon which the eggs are laid.

The most convenient way of subdividing Lepidoptera is into the two groups of (1) Butterflies (Rhopalocera) and (2) Moths (Heterocera), of which the latter include a very much greater number of species, there being in Britain, for example, over 1900 sorts of Moths as against between sixty and seventy species of Butterflies.

1. *Butterflies* (Rhopalocera).—Butterflies for the most part are active in the daytime, especially during sunny weather. They can readily be distinguished from Moths by the antennæ,

which are club-shaped, and in most cases by their habit of shutting the wings together over the back when they alight. As the wings are far less brilliantly coloured on their under sides, which are then the only surfaces visible, a very efficient means of protection is afforded. The body is comparatively slender, and the demarcation between thorax and abdomen well-marked. The eggs are often sculptured in a way which renders them extremely beautiful microscopic objects, and the caterpillars may be naked, slightly hairy, or covered with branching spines. They posses five pairs of pro-legs. The angular chrysalis is sometimes simply suspended by the tail, or it may be fixed head upwards both by the tail and by a silken girdle round the thoracic region. It is frequently marked with metallic patches, to which the name chrysalis is due (Gk. *chrysos*, gold).

Butterflies are found in all parts of the world, and some common examples may here be mentioned.

The *Fritillary Family* is at once the largest and most widely distributed group of Butterflies. They are distinguished by the remarkable fact that their fore-legs are so much reduced as to be useless for walking purposes. Among British species are the Great Tortoiseshell (*Vanessa polychloros*) (fig. 212), the Small Tortoiseshell (*V. urticæ*), the Peacock Butterfly (*V. Io*), and the Red Admiral (*V. Atlanta*), in all of which the larvæ feed on nettles: the Painted Lady (*V. cardui*), an almost cosmopolitan species, of which the larvæ feed on thistles; and the Purple Emperor (*Apatura Iris*), a much rarer and finer insect, with a predilection for carrion. Closely related to these is the Resplendent Ptolemy (*Morpho Neoptolemus*), a gorgeous tropical Butterfly. *Morpho cypris* is brilliant blue, streaked with white.

Fig. 212.—Great Tortoiseshell Butterfly (*Vanessa polychloros*)

The family of *Whites* includes several British species which are perhaps more familiar than any other, partly on account of their conspicuous colour and partly owing to the ravages which their larvæ perpetrate in the kitchen-garden. The abdomen is enveloped by the basal part of the hind-wings. This family is almost universally distributed, and British species are:—the Black-veined White (*Aporia cratægi*), the Large White or Cabbage Butterfly (*Pieris brassicæ*), the Small White or Garden White (*P. rapæ*), and the less common Green-veined White (*P. napi*); the beautiful little Orange Tip (*Anthocharis cardamines*), so named from the markings on the wings of the male; and the handsome Brimstone Butterfly (*Gonopteryx rhamni*), with angular outlines to the wings.

The *Swallow-tailed Butterflies*, which rival the Whites in their range of distribution, include numerous gorgeous tropical species, and the common name has reference to the slender "tail" into which the posterior margin of each hind-wing is often produced. The type genus, *Papilio*, comprises over 300 species, including our largest British form (*Papilo machaon*), now limited to the fen district. The huge Bird-winged Butterflies (*Ornithoptera*) of the Malay region belong to the same family, though they are without tails.

The family of *Blues* and *Coppers* is represented in all parts of the world, many of the tropical species being exceedingly beautiful. Two common British species of small size may be mentioned in illustration: the Common Blue (*Polyommatus alexis*) and the Small Copper (*Chrysophanus phlœas*).

2. *Moths* (Heterocera).—Moths are mostly nocturnal forms, differing from Butterflies in many particulars, among which may be mentioned the absence of knobs on the ends of the antennæ, and the habit of reposing with the wings spread out horizontally or folded round the body. The body is often much thickened, and the demarcation between thorax and abdomen is not well marked. In most cases there is a special "hook-and-eye" arrangement for uniting the wings during flight, and consisting of one or more bristles at the root of the hind-wings, which fit into a socket on the under side of the adjoining part of the fore-wings. The larvæ are either naked or more or less hairy, and may possess as many pro-legs as those of Butterflies, or fewer. The pupæ are rounded in outline, usually enclosed in a cocoon, and in many cases concealed underground.

The group may be divided into (I) Large Moths, including Hawk-Moths, Clear-Wings, Spinners, Owlets, and Loopers; and (II) Small Moths, embracing Leaf-Rollers, Leaf-Miners, Plume-Moths, and many others.

I. *Large Moths*, as the name indicates, are usually of considerable size, and agree with the Butterflies in the following characters:—The wings are elaborately veined, and the larvæ, which feed upon leaves, have downwardly-directed heads, and, usually, a curved line of horny bristles near the tip of each pro-leg. The abdomen of the pupa is devoid of transverse rows of spines.

Hawk-Moths are large swiftly-flying insects with a very long proboscis, suited for draining honey from flowers (such as honeysuckle) possessing a very long tubular spur. The caterpillars have smooth brightly-coloured skins, and are provided with five pairs of pro-legs, while a horn-like projection is found on the upper surface, near the hinder end of the body. The pupæ are found underground, enclosed in cocoons of earth. British examples are the Death's-Head Moth (*Acherontia Atropos*), with markings on the upper side of the thorax looking like a skull and cross-bones, and the Privet Moth (*Sphinx ligustri*). The larva of a common European species, the Pine Hawk-Moth (*Sphinx pinastri*), is very destructive to pine-trees.

The *Clear-Wings* are remarkable from the absence of scales on the wings, owing to which, and the nature of their markings, they resemble wasps, &c., this being no doubt a protective arrangement. The Hornet Clear-Wing (*Trochilium apiforme*) is a typical native species.

Spinners are large clumsy moths, clothed with abundant hair, and provided with a short proboscis. The colours are dull, and the two sexes differ considerably in appearance, *e.g.* in the character of the antennæ, which are plume-like in the male, and thread-like in the female. The caterpillars are more or less hairy, and before becoming pupæ spin cocoons, which may be entirely of silk, or contain a number of cast hairs in addition. One of the most beautiful British species belongs here, the Emperor Moth (*Saturnia carpini*), with an eye-like marking on each wing, and the caterpillar, abundant on heather, of emerald-green with pink tubercles. The spread of wing may be as much as 3 inches, but this appears small by comparison with exotic species, especially the Atlas Moth (*Attacus atlas*), in which the wings measure about a foot across. Among other native species may be mentioned the large Goat Moth (*Cossus ligniperda*), with wood-boring larva; the Tiger Moth (*Arctia caja*); the Puss Moth (*Cerura vinula*), with an extraordinary-looking caterpillar; the Buff-Tip (*Pygæra *bucephala*); the Pale Tussock-Moth (*Dasychira pudibunda*); the Lackey (*Clisiocampa neustria*); and the Oak Eggar (*Lasiocampa quercus*). Spinner Moths, however, are best known from the Silkworm Moth (*Bombyx mori*), a native of China introduced into many countries for the sake of its silk.

Owlets form the largest group of the Lepidoptera, and include dull-coloured species, with comparatively small fore-wings, each of which is characteristically marked with a couple of spots, one round and the other somewhat kidney-shaped. The larvæ of many species, as "surface caterpillars", do much harm to crops, and the pupæ are found underground, enclosed in earthen cocoons. Common British species are: the Common Wainscot Moth (*Leucania pallens*), Yellow Underwing (*Triphæna pronuba*, fig 213), the Heart-and-Dart Moth (*Agrotis exclamationis*), and the Silver Y (*Plusia gamma*).

Fig. 213.—Yellow Underwing (*Triphæna pronuba*) 1, Caterpillar; 2, chrysalis; 3, adult.

Loopers are moths of slender build, with broad thin wings and small antennæ. The caterpillar has but two pairs of pro-legs, placed right at the posterior end of the body, and this necessitates a curious mode of locomotion, which gives the name to the group. The body is stretched out to its full length, and then, while holding firmly by means of its three ordinary legs, the pro-legs are brought up and fixed close behind them, the body being thus thrown into a loop. Now, holding firmly by the pro-legs, the body is stretched forwards, and the ordinary legs attach themselves again. By repeating these manœuvres the caterpillar can move rapidly along in a curious looping fashion. When at rest the larva has a curious habit of attaching itself by the pro-legs, and stretching out the body at an angle to the surface of attachment, at the same time stiffening itself. This position can be retained for hours, and the caterpillar looks so like a short bare twig that it is rendered extremely inconspicuous to its enemies. Common British species are: the Brimstone Moth (*Rumia cratægata*), the Magpie or Currant Moth (*Abraxas grossulariata*), the Winter Moth (*Cheimatobia brumata*), and the Chimney Sweeper (*Tanagra chærophyllata*).

II. The *Small Moths*, as their name indicates, differ from the members of the other group in size, and usually possess long slender antennæ. The caterpillars, which burrow in vegetable substances or conceal themselves by rolling leaves together, have their heads forwardly directed, and a circlet of spines near the tip of each pro-leg, of which there are five pairs. The pupæ are generally distinguished by the presence of transverse rows of spines on the upper side of the abdomen. Among the groups may be mentioned Leaf-Rollers, Leaf-Miners, and Plume-Moths.

Leaf-Rollers are so named from the habit many of the larvæ have of feeding either between leaves which they have glued together with silk, or else inside individual leaves which have been rolled up and fixed in a similar way. Common British species are: the Green Oak Moth (*Tortrix viridana*), and the Codlin Moth (*Carpocapsa pomonella*), of which the caterpillar tunnels within the fruit of apples and pears.

The *Leaf-Miners* constitute a large group of small and very small moths with narrow hair-fringed wings. One of the prettiest species is the Little Ermine-Moth (*Hyponomeuta padella*), the larvæ of which keep together in companies as hatched out, and spin a considerable amount of web. They devastate the leaves of hawthorn, sloe, &c. Another beautiful but extremely small form is the Brown Dolly (*Lithocolletis corylella*), the caterpillars of which mine in hazel leaves. Unfortunately, however, the best-known are the different species of Clothes Moth (*Tinea pellionella*, *Trichophaga tapetzella*) (figs. 214 and 215).

Fig. 214.—Adult stage of a Clothes Moth (enlarged)

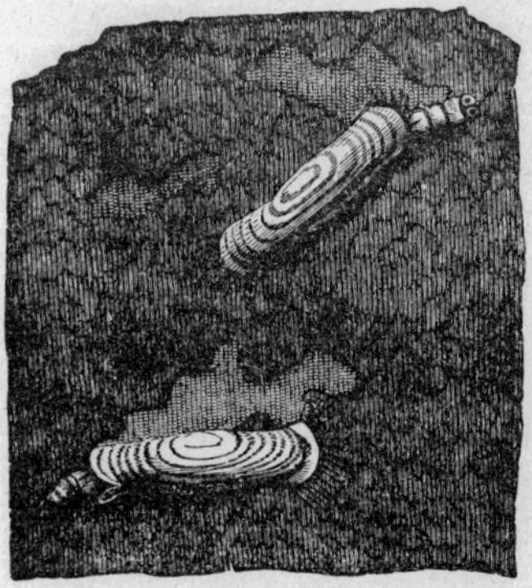

Fig. 215.—Larvæ of a Clothes Moth (enlarged)

The *Plume-Moths* are a comparatively small group of pretty little long-legged moths with wings split up into a varying number of plume-like portions. Common British species are: the Common Plume-Moth (*Pterophorus pterodactylus*) and the Twenty-Plume Moth (*Alucita polydactyla*).

Order 5.—BEETLES (Coleoptera)

This is by far the largest order of insects, and includes forms which are for the most part easily recognizable, though the name of "beetle" is popularly but erroneously given to members of other groups, *e.g.* to the Cockroach. The wings of an average beetle are of very characteristic appearance and nature, as may be seen by examining such a typical example as the little Lady-Bird (*Coccinella*), which is at once known by its conspicuous colouring of black spots on a red ground (fig. 216). At first sight such an insect appears to have no wings at all, but every child who has induced a lady-bird to "fly away home", by persuasive shoves added to an alarming story of domestic calamity, knows better than that. The fore-wings are not, however, organs of flight, but horny wing-covers or *elytra* (see p. 345) stretching back over the abdomen and abutting against one another in the middle line. They protect the membranous hind-wings (fig. 217), which, when not in use, are hidden beneath them, and are not only folded longitudinally, as in a Cockroach, but also transversely, a very characteristic feature for beetles. The *head* is large, and bears a pair of compound eyes, and two antennæ varying greatly in shape according to the

Fig. 216.—Lady-Birds

1, Cluster of eggs; 2, egg (greatly magnified); 3, larva (magnified); 4, actual length of same; 5, 6, pupæ; 7, 8, varieties of Two-spotted Lady-Bird (*Coccinella bipunctata*); 9, Seven-spotted Lady-Bird (*C. septempunctata*).

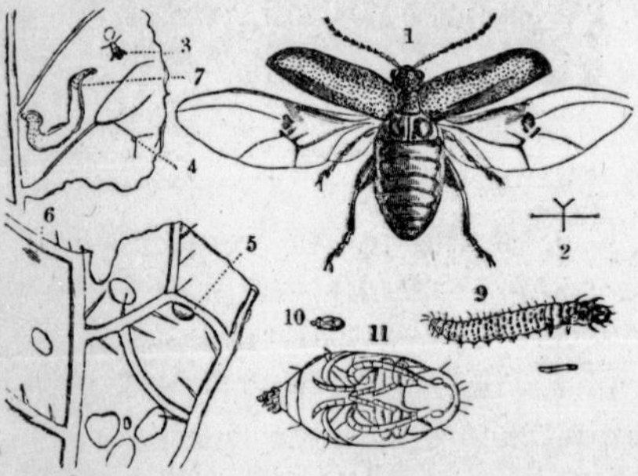

Fig. 217.—Stages of Turnip Flea-Beetle (*Haltica nemorum*)

1, Adult (enlarged), showing wing-covers and wings spread out; 2, 3, natural size of same; 4, 5, eggs (enlarged); 6, 7, burrows of larvæ (enlarged); 8, 9, larva (natural size and enlarged); 10, 11, pupa (natural size and enlarged).

species. The *mouth-parts* are adapted for biting, and are built on the same plan as in the Cockroach (see p. 345), but with many differences in detail, as seen, for example, in the more complete fusion which has taken place between the two second maxillæ, and in the fact that these jaws are much reduced. The *life-history* of a beetle (figs. 216 and 217) exhibits a complete *metamorphosis*, the larva being a grub possessed, in most cases, of three pairs of legs corresponding with those of the adult, and becoming a pupa differing from that of a moth or butterfly as regards the limbs and wings, which form prominent projections instead of being merely indicated beneath the continuous horny covering.

Fig. 218.—Green Tiger-Beetle (*Cicindela campestris*)

Only a few common species, representing important families, can be mentioned here.

Tiger-Beetles are very active, predaceous insects, including somewhere about a thousand species, and distributed generally throughout the world, though most abundant in the tropics. A common British form is the Green Tiger-Beetle (*Cicindela campestris*) (fig. 218), common on sandy banks, and distinguished by the beautiful golden-green colour of its upper surface. The larva is provided with enormous curved mandibles, and excavates a vertical burrow in which it lies in wait for prey.

Ground-Beetles are also predaceous, and even more widely distributed than the Tiger-Beetles, though much more numerous, there being some eleven thousand species. They are least abundant in the tropics. A large and well-known British species, the Violet Ground-Beetle (*Carabus violaceus*), so named on account of the dark violet sheen exhibited by its upper surface, is common in fields and gardens, and may also be found in houses, where it preys upon cockroaches and crickets.

Water-Beetles include ravenous forms which resemble ground-beetles in many respects, but are adapted to an aquatic life. The largest British form is the Great Water-Beetle (*Dytiscus marginalis*) (fig. 219), and here may also be included the Whirligig Beetle (*Gyrinus natator*), which almost everyone must have noticed twirling round and round at the surface of the water in ponds and ditches.

Rovė-Beetles, possessing broad heads, narrow bodies, and short elytra, agree with the preceding families in their carnivorous habits. Most familiar perhaps in Britain is the Devil's Coach-Horse (*Ocypus olens*), which has the curious habit of turning up its tail when molested (fig. 220).

Fig. 219.—Great Water-Beetle (*Dytiscus marginalis*)

Male to left, and female to right. Part of the fore-foot of male (enlarged) is represented in centre to show the pad and suckers with which it is provided.

The *Scarabs* rival the ground-beetles in number of species and include many large and handsome forms, distinguished by characteristic antennæ, of which the last few joints are so broadened out that when expanded they look like a small fan. The adults and larvæ feed either upon vegetable substances or on dung. Here belongs the largest British species, the Stag-Beetle (*Lucanus cervus*), in which the mandibles of the male resemble antlers. The largest-known beetles are not very distantly related, and forms commonly seen in museums are the Hercules-Beetle (*Dynastes hercules*) from tropical America, and the Goliath-Beetle (*Goliathus Drurei*), the male of the former species sometimes exceeding 5 inches in length, as against the 3 inches of our Stag-Beetle. One of the commonest British dung-beetles is the Dumble-Dor (*Geotrupes stercorarius*), a sluggish insect of bluish-black colour, often seen crawling slowly along country roads. An allied genus includes the Sacred Scarab (*Scarabæus sacer*) of the Egyptians.

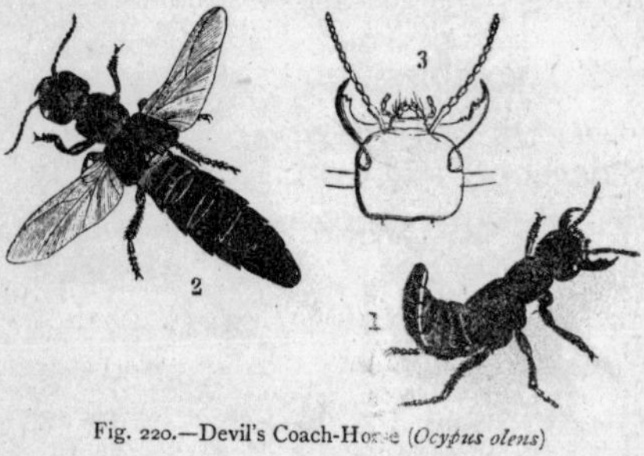

Fig. 220.—Devil's Coach-Horse (*Ocypus olens*)

1, Standing with turned-up tail; 2, flying; 3, head enlarged, to show eyes, antennæ, and jaws.

The *Chafers* constitute a large and well-known group of the Scarab Beetles. Common British species are the Cockchafer (*Melolontha vulgaris*), the green-and-brown Garden Chafer (*Phyllopertha horticola*), and the beautiful golden-green Rose Chafer (*Cetonia aurata*) (fig. 221).

Weevils are small beetles with long snouts which do great damage to timber, fruit, and grain. Some ten thousand species are known. A common British form is the Nut Weevil (*Balaninus glandium*), which lays its eggs in hazel-nuts and acorns, upon the kernels of which the larvæ feed when they have hatched out. Two species of Weevil are represented in fig. 222.

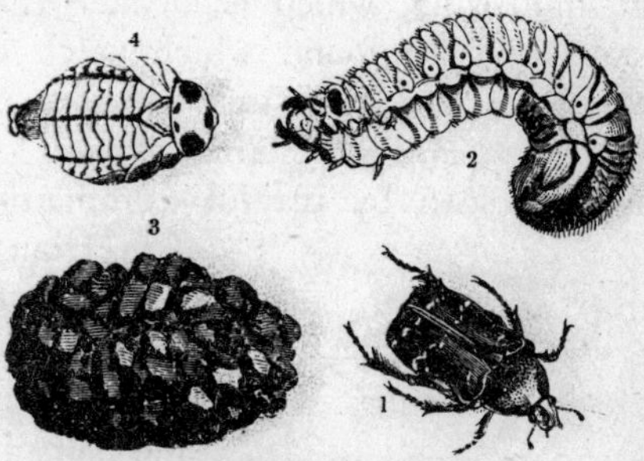

Fig. 221.—Rose Chafer (*Cetonia aurata*)
1, Adult; 2, larva; 3, cocoon; 4, pupa.

Lady-Birds (fig. 216) are among the insects which are of great use to man, as they prey upon plant-lice, to which their larvæ are a veritable terror. Over a thousand species are known distributed throughout most regions of the globe. The commonest British species are the Seven-spotted Lady-Bird (*Coccinella septempunctata*) and the Two-spotted Lady-Bird (*C. bipunctata*), distinguishable by the number of black spots upon the red elytra.

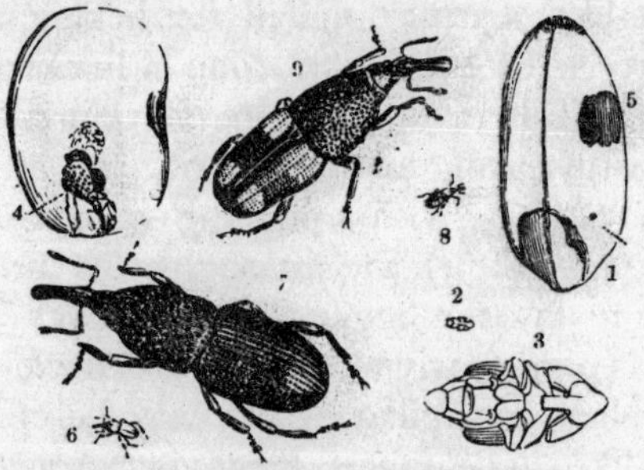

Fig. 222.—Corn-Weevil
1, Grain of wheat, showing the punctured hole; and 5, the exit of the perfect weevil. 2, Pupa (natural size); 3, magnified. 4, Grain of Indian corn, with weevil inside. 6, 7, Corn-Weevil (*Calandra granaria*), natural size and magnified; 8, 9, Rice-Weevil (*C. oryzæ*), natural size and magnified.

Order 6.—Membrane-winged Insects (Hymenoptera)

This very large order contains many thousand described species, including among many others the different kinds of bee, wasp, and ant. Not a few live in communities of exceedingly complex organization, and these display so much intelligence that there is much to be said for the view that the order is the highest among insects. Four membranous wings (fig. 223) are present, whence the technical name (Gk. *hymēn*, membrane; *pteron*, wing); they possess comparatively few nervures, and are not folded during repose. It will be remembered that in most Moths there is a "hook-and-eye" arrangement for coupling the wings together during flight. In the present order the same end is brought about by a more perfect contrivance. On the front margin of the hind-wing, which is smaller than the fore-wing, a series of hooks will be found which catch on to a fold on the hinder margin of the latter, and due to a curling up of the edge. The complex *mouth-parts* are adapted for both biting and licking, as may be seen by careful examination of a hive-bee (fig. 223). The triangular *upper lip* will here be seen to overlap a pair of powerful *mandibles*, under which come the long *first maxillæ*, provided with cutting-blades and palps (in this species very small), and lastly follow the fused *second maxillæ*. These are drawn out into a slender tongue-like structure suited for licking, and grooved for the conduction of liquid.

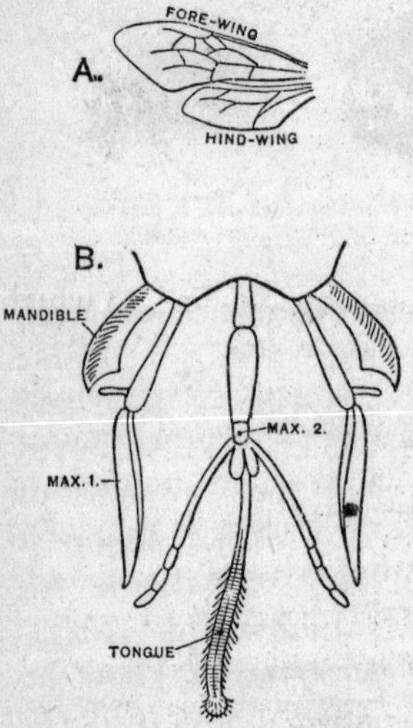

Fig. 223.—Structure of Hymenoptera

A, Wings of a bee. B, Diagram of mouth-parts of Honey-Bee (*Apis mellifica*), much enlarged and widely separated.

Female Hymenoptera are either provided with a sting at the posterior end of the body, or else with a piercing arrangement (ovipositor) for making holes in which to lay the eggs. The *metamorphosis* is particularly well-marked. Larvæ resembling caterpillars, or it may be of worm-like appearance, hatch out from the eggs, which have previously been deposited in plants, the bodies of other insects, or sometimes in specially-constructed chambers (as in bees). The pupæ are generally enclosed in a cocoon of silk, and, as in beetles (see p. 366), their limbs project freely.

Three sub-orders are recognized:—1. Plant-Eaters, 2. Insect-Eaters, and 3. Stinging Hymenoptera.

1. *Plant-Eating Hymenoptera* include the *Saw-Flies* and *Wood-borers*, of which some thousand species have been described. The ovipositor of the female is adapted for boring holes in plants, and the abdomen does not in either sex narrow to a stalk at its base, as in a wasp or ant. The mouth-parts are not so specialized as in the example taken above. The larvæ resemble caterpillars, for which indeed they are often mistaken, but may easily be distinguished by the presence of more than five pairs of pro-legs in

addition to the three pairs of legs proper, while a caterpillar never has more than five pairs of pro-legs, and often fewer. Nor do these pro-legs possess, like those of most caterpillars, a curved row or circlet of minute bristles near their tips. Further, a "false" caterpillar has a rounded instead of a flattened head, moves its abdomen vertically up and down when disturbed, and curls it up in a state of rest.

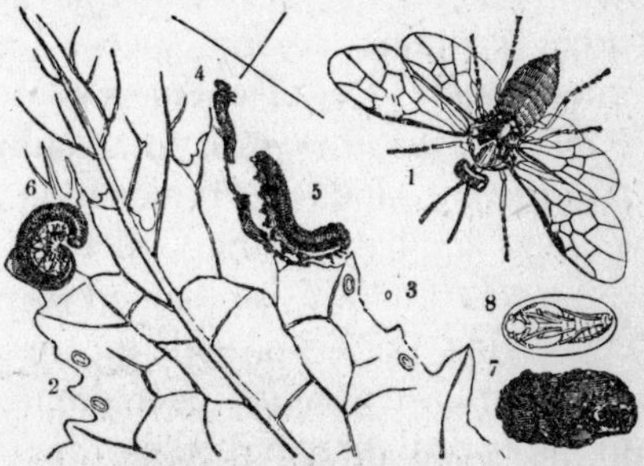

Fig. 224.—Turnip Saw-Fly (*Athalia spinarum*

1, Adult female, enlarged (natural size represented to left of it); 3, 2, Eggs (natural size and enlarged); 4, 5, 6, larvæ; 7, cocoon; 8, pupa in cocoon.

The "saw" of a saw-fly consists of two curved saw-like blades protected by sheaths when not in use. The blades are worked alternately backwards and forwards, and the eggs slip down between them into the incision formed. A common species is the Turnip Saw-Fly (*Athalia spinarum*) (fig. 224), the larvæ of which ravage the crop after which the insect is named.

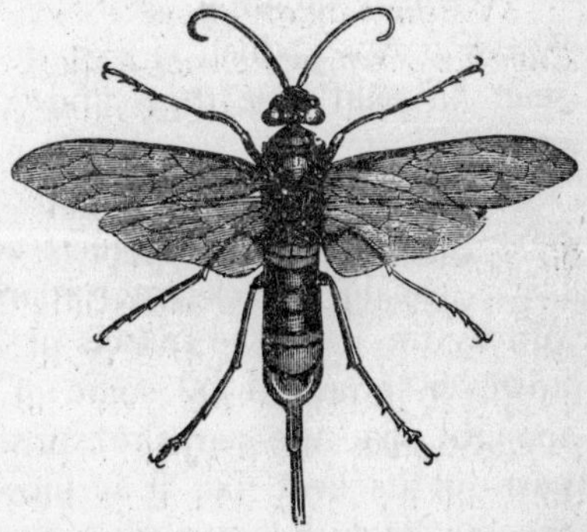

Fig. 225.—Large Wood-Borer or Wood-Wasp (*Sirex gigas*)

In a *Wood-Borer* the blades corresponding to the saws of a saw-fly are fused together into a boring spine, which is used like an auger. A conspicuous species, not infrequently seen in this country, is the Large Wood-Borer (*Sirex gigas*) (fig. 225), also called Wood-Wasp from the transverse black and yellow bandings of its body. The female bores holes in pine-trees in which to lay her eggs, and from these, eyeless grubs hatch out which only possess the three pairs of ordinary legs. These larvæ burrow in the timber by means of their strong mandibles, and later on become pupæ enclosed in cocoons formed from silk mixed with fragments of wood.

2. The *Insect-Eating Hymenoptera* are so named because the larvæ are commonly parasitic within the larvæ of other insects,

though to this there are many exceptions. The abdomen is stalked, and the female is provided with a piercing ovipositor by which punctures are made for the reception of eggs. The larvæ are pale legless grubs. It is stated as probable that the sub-order contains 20,000 species or even more, which means an innumerable host of enemies to other insects. The Winter Moth (*Cheimatobia brumata*), for example, is attacked by no less than 63 different kinds of Hymenoptera belonging to this group. Two leading families are the Gall-Flies and Ichneumon-Flies.

Gall-Flies are so named because they puncture plants for egg-laying purposes, with the result that the wounded parts give rise to those peculiar excrescences known as "galls", of which the spherical brown bodies called "King Charles's oak-apples", common on the oak, are known to everyone who has been in the country. This tree indeed is peculiarly liable to the attacks of different species of gall-fly, which lead to the production of galls of totally different appearance, some resembling currants, others looking like little cones, and others again being in the form of circular scales ("oak spangles") on the backs of the leaves.

We may mention, as a specific example of a gall-fly, the form *Rhodites rosæ*, which is responsible for the tufted red galls often seen on wild rose-trees and known as rose-bedeguars or "old man's beard".

Ichneumon-Flies constitute a family of which nearly 6000 species have been described, over 1200 of these being British. The larvæ usually attack caterpillars, in or on which the eggs were laid by the parent. Insects of other kinds, and even spiders, are, however, attacked by some of the species. It was till recently thought that the parasite subsisted by devouring the non-vital parts of its host, but it is more probable that it simply absorbs the blood of the caterpillar through its skin.

One common ichneumon-fly (*Microgaster glomeratus*) lays its eggs in the caterpillar of the common white Cabbage Butterfly, within which they hatch out. When the unfortunate host has reached its full term of growth, and should be ready to turn into a chrysalis, it is too much enfeebled to do so. The unwelcome guests now bite their way out of the caterpillar and become pupæ on their own account, and it is no uncommon thing to find a dead caterpillar which has fallen a victim to ichneumon larvæ side by side with a little heap of pupæ belonging to these foes. Another species (*Hemiteles melanarius*) (fig. 226) lays its eggs in the chrysalis of the Green-veined White.

3. *Stinging Hymenoptera* are generally distinguished by the presence of a sting in the female, which takes the place of the ovipositor found in the forms so far mentioned. Special cells are usually constructed in which the helpless larvæ are reared. As in the last sub-order, the abdomen is attached by a stalk, which may be extremely slender. Ants, Wasps, and Bees are here included, many of which live in social communities, the politics of which will be dealt with in another part of this book, and which in itself would require an entire volume to do it justice.

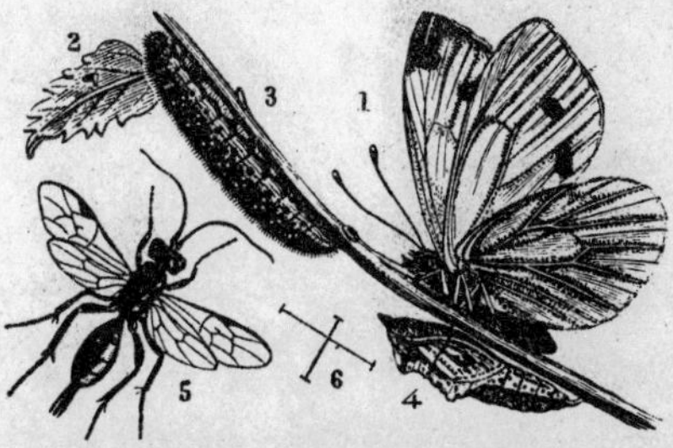

Fig. 226.—The Green-veined White (*Pieris napi*), and an Ichneumon-Fly (*Hemiteles melanarius*), which lays its eggs in the chrysalis of the same. 1, 2, 3, 4, Adult female, eggs, caterpillar, and chrysalis of the butterfly; 5, adult female of the ichneumon-fly, of which natural size is shown by 6.

More than a thousand species of *Ants* have been described, of which over thirty are British. Among these are the large red Wood Ant (*Formica rufa*), the large "ant-hills" of which may be seen in fir-woods, the Slave Ant (*Formica fusca*), the Slave-making Ant (*Polyergus rufescens*), the Black Ant (*Lasius niger*), the Yellow Ant (*Lasius flavus*), and the Solitary Ant (*Mutilla Europæa*).

Sand-Wasps dig tunnels in the ground, at the end of which their eggs are laid. Many of them make a curious provision for their larvæ in the shape of insects, caterpillars, grubs, or it may be spiders, which they have stung in the nerve-cord so as to render them powerless without actually killing them. Among British forms may be mentioned the Path-Wasp (*Pompilius exaltatus*), which stores up spiders; the Common Sand-Wasp (*Ammophila sabulosa*), which buries caterpillars; and the Fly-storing Sand-Wasp (*Mellinus arvensis*), which does the same to flies.

Wasps are either solitary or social, the most familiar example of the latter kind being the Common Wasp (*Vespa vulgaris*), which, as is well known, constructs nests in banks and other places. The combs which these contain are constructed of a kind of paper formed by working up bark and decayed wood to a sort of pulp. Another and larger social wasp is the Common Hornet (*Vespa crabro*), in which the front part of the body is of a reddish colour. Of solitary species the Mud-Wasps (*Odynerus parietum* and others) may be mentioned, which construct their cells of mud in the crevices of walls, the hollow stems of plants, and other places.

Fig. 227.—Bees and Flowers of Broad-Bean

1, Wood-Bee (*B. leucorum*). 2, 2, Holes cut by bee in bases of flowers. 4, Humble-Bee (*Bombus terrestris*) extracting nectar through one of the holes.

Bees, like Wasps, include social and solitary species, the Hive-Bee (*Apis mellifica*) furnishing a good example of the former sort, that also includes the Humble-Bee (*Bombus terrestris*) (fig. 227), which makes its nests in the ground. In solitary bees the labium is much shorter than in the Hive-Bee. They belong to numerous genera, and include Leaf-Cutter Bees, which make their cells from pieces of leaf, Carpenter-Bees (*Xylocopa*), which cut out cells one above another in the trunks of trees, and Flower-Bees (*Anthophora*), forms which look something like humble-bees.

Order 7.—Net-winged Insects (Neuroptera) (fig. 228)

This order, which is much smaller than some of those already dealt with, contains a great variety of forms which differ very widely in appearance. The most typical members of the order possess four membranous wings exhibiting an elaborate net-work of nervures, quite unlike the simple arrangement characteristic of Hymenoptera. The mouth-parts are usually adapted for biting. Eleven families are recognized, arranged in five groups; *i.e.*—1. Dragon-Flies, May-Flies, and Stone-Flies; 2. Flat-winged Neuroptera; 3. Caddis-Flies; 4. White Ants and Book-Lice; 5. Biting-Lice.

1. *Dragon-Flies*, *May-Flies*, and *Stone-Flies* all possess the four typical wings and pass through an aquatic larval stage. *Dragon-Flies* are among the most beautiful objects to be seen in the course of a summer walk in the country. The four large wings are of

Fig. 228.—Net-winged Insects (*Neuroptera*)

1, 1*a*, 1*b*, Stages of common May-Fly (*Ephemera vulgata*); 2, another species of May-Fly (*Palingenia horaria*); 3, 3*a*, adult and larva of Horse-Stinger (*Libellula depressa*); 4, 5, Common Scorpion-Fly (*Panorpa communis*); 6, 6*a*, Alder-Fly (*Sialis lutaria*); 7, Large Caddis-Fly *Phryganea grandis*); 8, Diamond-spotted Caddis-Fly (*Limnophilus rhombicus*).

about equal size, and the long body is handsomely marked and coloured. The freely movable head is provided with very small antennæ, a pair of huge compound eyes, three simple eyes (ocelli), and biting mouth-parts. Dragon-Flies catch other insects on the wing, and their flight is exceedingly rapid, making them the swallows of the insect world. The eggs are laid either in water or attached to water-plants, and from them extremely voracious aquatic larvæ hatch out, which are distinguished by the possession of an extremely long transversely-jointed lower lip. This is usually known as the "mask", because when not in use it is folded up in front of the face, from which position it can be suddenly shot out for the capture of small animals. The action has been compared to that of an old-fashioned carriage-step. The larval condition is maintained for about a year or rather less, during which time a number of moults occur, while towards the end of the period the rudiments of wings make their appearance. There is no motionless pupa stage, but the full-grown larva climbs up the stem of some plant till it is above water, when its skin splits longitudinally along the dorsal surface, and the adult dragon-fly, which has been meanwhile forming within, gradually works its way out. Over forty species of British dragon-flies are known, of which the following may be mentioned:—The Great Dragon-Fly (*Æschna grandis*), a large reddish-brown insect, with lighter markings; the Horse-Stinger (*Libellula depressa*) (fig. 228), with broad abdomen, light brown, with yellow spots in the female and violet in the male; and the little Demoiselle Dragon-Fly (*Agrion puella*), with T-shaped head, and slender abdomen, black in the female and banded with light-blue in the male.

The *May-Flies* or *Day-Flies* are fragile insects in which the hind-wings are much smaller than the others, and the abdomen has two or three slender tails attached to it. The adult only lives a short time, though the traditional day may in some cases be extended to a fortnight. The life-history broadly resembles that of the dragon-flies, and the larva of some forms appears to live three years, an unusually long time, contrasting sharply with the brief existence of the imago. Something like 300 species have been described, and common British forms are the Common May-Fly or Gray Drake (*Ephemera vulgata*) (fig. 228) and the Green Drake (*E. Danica*). Some of the most successful lures of the fly-fisher are copies of various may-flies, of which the two drakes are examples, as are also many of the "duns" and "spinners".

Stone-Flies are dull-coloured flattened insects with four membranous wings which, when at rest, are disposed so as to overlap the back and sides of the body. The antennæ are long, and there are usually two filaments of similar appearance attached to the tip of the abdomen. The life-history resembles that of the preceding two groups. Stone-Flies are widely distributed, and include a large number of species. The best-known British form is the Common Stone-Fly (*Perla bicaudata*), well known to anglers as a good bait for trout.

2. *Flat-winged Neuroptera* include Alder-Flies, Snake-Flies, Scorpion-Flies, Ant-lions, Lace-wing Flies, and other forms, in all of which there are four similar wings, not capable of being folded, but turned back when at rest so as to lie either flat, or sloping like the roof of a house. The adult possesses well-developed mandibles, contrasting in this respect with the last group of Neuroptera, in which the mouth-parts are much reduced. There is a terrestrial or aquatic larva, which becomes a quiescent pupa.

The Alder-Fly (*Sialis lutaria*) (fig. 228), which figures on the angler's list, is a brown insect with brownish wings, clumsy body, and long antennæ. The wings in repose cover the thorax and abdomen in a roof-like manner. It is common on river-banks in Britain. The cylindrical greyish eggs are deposited in patches on the stems of grasses or rushes near the water, into which the rapacious larvæ that hatch out from them find their way. Later on, they come out of the water and bury themselves in the soil, where they become pupæ.

Snake-Flies, of which there are several British species (*e.g. Raphidia ophiopsis*), are more slenderly built insects, sometimes found in woods. They are distinguished by the presence of a sort of neck, and there is an ovipositor in the female. The rapacious larva is found in rotten wood, where it passes into a pupa stage.

Scorpion-Flies are much more abundant in this country than Snake-Flies, and the Common Scorpion-Fly (*Panorpa communis*) (fig. 228) may be taken as a type. The name is due to the fact that the abdomen in the male ends in a pair of pincers, and its hinder part can be curled up over the back like a scorpion's tail. The wings are narrow, and when at rest are held in a horizontal position. The head is of characteristic shape, for it is prolonged into a downwardly-directed beak, which has been compared in appearance to the face of a horse. Though the insect is small (about ½ inch long), its black body, yellow legs and beak, and wings speckled with white and brown make it a striking and beautiful object. The larva is predatory and terrestrial, being not unlike the false caterpillar of a saw-fly in appearance, possessing as it does three pairs of legs proper, followed by eight pairs of pro-legs. Later on, it passes into a quiescent pupa stage.

Ant-Lions are insects with slender body, four equal membranous wings, and antennæ clubbed like those of butterflies. They do not occur in this country, but are common on the Continent, where they have long attracted attention from the peculiar habits of the larvæ in the type-genus (*Myrmeleo*). It is these to which the name ant-lion was originally applied on account of the devastations they commit among those and other insects, their mode of operation being to dig pit-falls in the sand, at the bottom of which they remain buried, with only the enormous mandibles projecting.

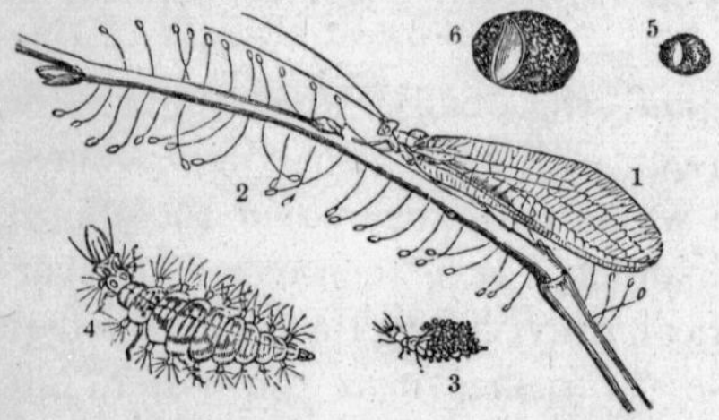

Fig. 229.—Golden-eyed Fly (*Chrysopa vulgaris*)
1. Adult female; 2, stalked eggs; 3, 4, larva (natural size and enlarged); 5, 6, cocoon (natural size and enlarged).

Lacewing-Flies are represented by about fifteen native species, a common example being the Golden-eyed Fly (*Chrysopa vulgaris*) (fig. 229), an extremely fragile green insect with four gauzy wings, long slender antennæ, and brilliant eyes gleaming like gold. The eggs are attached to leaves by long stalks, and the voracious larvæ which hatch out from them are known as "aphis lions", a name fully justified by the effective manner in which they keep plant-lice in check.

3. *Caddis-Flies* (fig. 228) in the adult condition look rather like moths, but their wings are hairy instead of scaly, and their larvæ are aquatic "caddis-worms", remarkable for the habit of forming protective cases from sand-grains, bits of stick, or other foreign matters. A caddis-worm is something like a caterpillar,

devoid, however, of pro-legs, while at the end of its tail is a pair of pincers by which it can attach itself firmly to the case. The food is mainly of vegetable nature. After from seven to ten months the larva closes the opening of the tube with silk and passes into the pupa stage, which, after remaining quiescent for two or three weeks, bites its way out of the case and swims on its back to some plant or other object up which it can climb out of the water. The pupal skin then splits, and the caddis-fly emerges.

4. *White Ants*, more correctly called *Termites*, since they have nothing whatever to do with ants proper, are but too well known to the inhabitants of tropical countries on account of the havoc they work with wooden furniture and the like. They are social insects, living in communities organized in an extraordinarily complex manner, about which particulars will be given in the sequel. In every community both winged and wingless individuals may be found, the former possessing four very long narrow wings of the kind characteristic of the order, which are held flat on the back when at rest. There is but a slight metamorphosis. Two species are found in South Europe (*Calotermes flavicollis* and *Termes lucifugus*), but the most remarkable forms are natives of tropical Africa, and some of these (*e.g. Termes bellicosus*) construct nests of earth which may be as much as 14 feet high.

Book-Lice are minute forms of somewhat doubtful affinities, and most familiarly known by the wingless species giving the name to the group, but also including the "death watches" (*Atropos divinatoria* and others), commonly reputed by the superstitious to herald death by a ticking noise, though the sound is more probably produced by a wood-eating beetle (*Anobium*). The winged species, which are the most numerous, are to be found feeding on lichens, fungi, and other plants. Of the four membranous wings, which are provided with but few nervures, the hind ones are much the smaller. The antennæ are very long. There is but a slight metamorphosis. Among the British winged species may be mentioned *Psocus fasciatus*.

5. *Biting-Lice* are small wingless, large-headed creatures which live on the skins of birds and mammals, and must carefully be distinguished from ordinary lice (p. 354), in which the mouth-parts are adapted for piercing and sucking. The common

fowl is infested by no less than five species (*Menopon pallidum* and others), and the "dust baths" in which this bird indulges are no doubt taken with a view of getting rid of these and other parasites. Mammals are less troubled with attacks of the kind, the dog being an example of animals which are thus attended. *Trichodectes latus* is the name of its unwelcome guest.

Order 8.—STRAIGHT-WINGED INSECTS (Orthoptera)

The Cockroach, of which an account has already been given, may be taken as a type of this order, which also includes such familiar forms as locusts, grasshoppers, earwigs, and crickets. The *mouth-parts* are adapted for biting, and it is particularly to be noticed that the second maxillæ are not so closely fused together to form a lower lip or labium as in most other insects. The *fore-wings* are modified into leathery wing-covers, and the large membranous hind ones are usually traversed by nervures radiating from the point of attachment, and are thus enabled to fold up in a fan-like manner when not in use. There can scarcely be said to be a metamorphosis, for the young insects when just hatched differ from the adult mainly in size and in the absence of wings, while there is no quiescent pupa stage. It is supposed that at least 10,000 species of recent Orthoptera exist, including the largest known insects, but of this large number less than forty are native to Britain. A distinction is drawn between: 1. Running Orthoptera, including Earwigs, Cockroaches, Soothsayers, Stick-Insects, and Leaf-Insects; 2. Leaping Orthoptera, embracing Grasshoppers, Locusts, and Crickets.

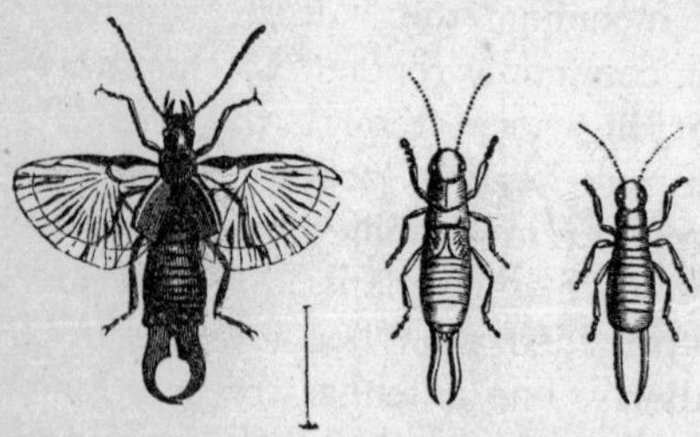

Fig. 230.—Common Earwig (*Forficula auricularia*) Adult (line indicates actual size) and earlier stages

1. In *Running Orthoptera* all three pairs of legs are pretty much alike. The Common Earwig (*Forficula auricularia*) (fig. 230) may be taken as a type of a family in which the wings are folded up in a remarkably complex manner under the short wing-covers, and the tail is provided with curved forceps. No satisfactory explanation has been given of the curious

popular notion that these insects are in the habit of entering the human ear, for this does not appear to be the case, and though it is true that the hind-wings are strikingly ear-shaped, they are so rarely seen unfolded that it may be doubted whether this has to do with the name "earwig".

Cockroaches are widely distributed insects, especially common in tropical regions. Only three small species appear to be indigenous to Britain, for the familiar "black beetle" is undoubtedly an importation. Some of the exotic species are brightly coloured, while others are wingless.

Soothsayers or *Praying-Insects* form a remarkable group dependent upon a warm climate, and often assuming the most extraordinary forms, calculated in many cases to harmonize with the surroundings, being thus rendered inconspicuous to their prey, which consists of other insects. The front-legs are modified into seizing-organs, and it is the curious way in which these are extended that has given rise to the common names, as, *e.g.*, that of Praying Mantis (*Mantis religiosa*) applied to a French species, the only European one found at any great distance from the Mediterranean shores. A Mantis in such an attitude is, however, merely on the look-out for insects, and not in a prophetic or devout frame of mind.

Stick- and *Leaf-Insects* assume even more remarkable forms than the members of the preceding family, and mostly have a close resemblance to sticks, leaves, pieces of bark, and other parts of plants, which in this case may be looked upon as a protective arrangement, for, unlike the Soothsayers, they affect a vegetable diet. They are widely distributed through the warmer parts of the globe, and some of them may be as much as 9 inches long.

2. *Leaping Orthoptera*, in accordance with their habit of springing, possess very large hind-legs. Remarkable structures related to hearing are usually present, and the males generally possess musical organs as well. Three families are recognized—Locusts and Grasshoppers, Green Grasshoppers, and Crickets.

Locusts and *Grasshoppers* are distinguished by the shortness of their antennæ and the presence of auditory organs in the first segment of the abdomen. The familiar little grasshoppers of British fields represent a number of species of varying size, some of the larger belonging to the genera *Stenobothrus* and *Gomphocerus*.

while the very smallest are included in the genus *Tettix.* The characteristic chirping is produced by rubbing the inner side of the hind-legs against the outer surface of the front wings, the former being provided with a ridge made up of small peg-like projections. The sounds audible to human ears are produced only by the male.

What are popularly known as "locusts" are simply species of grasshopper, which from time to time appear in swarms

Fig. 231.—Migratory Grasshopper—"Locust" (*Acridium peregrinum*)

which migrate from place to place and do a vast amount of damage. The best-known species is the European migratory locust, which ranges from China to the Atlantic. A large species (*Acridium peregrinum*) (fig. 231), common in North Africa, is probably the locust mentioned in the book of Exodus.

Green Grasshoppers are easily distinguished from the members of the preceding group by their extremely long and slender antennæ. There are generally auditory organs situated in the front legs just below the knee. Chirping organs, when present, are placed on the bases of the fore-wings, the left carrying a roughened edge (file) and the latter a sharp edge. In most species the female possesses a long egg-laying tube or ovipositor.

The most conspicuous British species is the Large Green Grasshopper (*Locusta viridissima*) which, despite its generic name, is not a locust at all. Other examples are the North American Katydids.

Crickets agree in many essential particulars with the members of the preceding group, possessing as they do long, slender antennæ and similarly situated musical and vocal organs, while the female is usually provided with an ovipositor. There are, however, differences in detail; *e.g.* the tarsus is usually three-jointed instead of four-jointed, and the musical organs involve a larger part of the wing. There are four different kinds of cricket in the British area, of which by far the most familiar is the House-Cricket (*Gryllus domesticus*), which is one of the animals most constantly associated with human dwellings, and is not unconnected with superstitious ideas. Habit has rendered its chirpings agreeable to our ears, and Dickens's ever-popular story, *The Cricket on the Hearth*, gives it an interest which few Orthoptera can boast. It is perhaps rather unromantic to add that in dramatic presentments of the tale the all-important chirp is imitated by using a glass-stoppered bottle, the stopper of which is twisted round so as to produce a creaking sound. This particular insect ranges over a large part of the Old World, and also occurs in North America. Its distribution has probably been extended by human agency. Of the two British species of Field-Cricket, one (*Nemobius sylvestris*) is small in size, while the other (*Gryllus campestris*) is a good deal larger than the Common Cricket, and usually black in colour. The Mole-Cricket (*Gryllotalpa vulgaris*) (fig. 232) is a remarkable form, practically limited to the south of England with us, though common on the Continent. It burrows underground by means of its remarkably modified fore-feet, and its habits will be dealt with elsewhere.

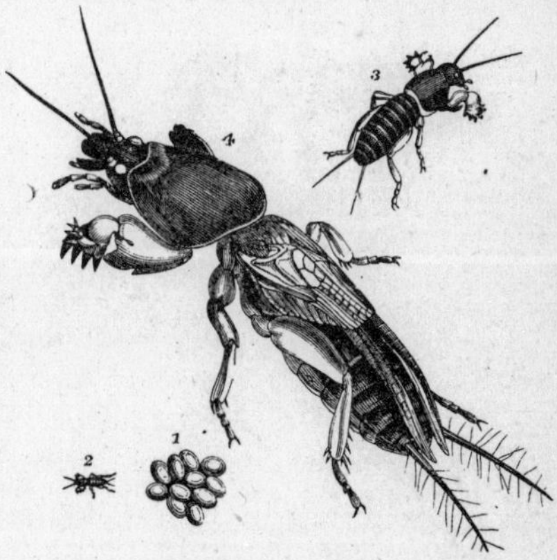

Fig. 232.—Mole-Cricket (*Gryllotalpa vulgaris*)
1, Eggs; 2, 3, larvæ; 4, adult.

Order 9.—WINGLESS INSECTS (Aptera)

This is a group of small inconspicuous insects which are of great interest theoretically, as they are probably to be regarded as insects in their simplest form, *i.e.* are of "primitive" nature. They never possess any traces of wings, nor do they appear to be descendants of winged ancestors, as is the case with the numerous wingless insects placed in other groups. The segmentation of the body is more clearly marked than in other insect orders, and the segments are not so specialized, besides which small abdominal appendages are not uncommon. The horny covering of the body is comparatively delicate. Two sub-orders are recognized:— 1. Tassel-Tails (*Thysanura*) and 2. Springers (*Collembola*).

1. *Thysanura.*—The most marked feature of the sub-order consists in the presence of two or three long styles projecting from the hind end of the body. Probably the commonest British species is the Silver-Fish (*Lepisma saccharina*) (fig. 233), found in brown sugar and old books. It possesses three tail-filaments, and its silvery lustre is due to the presence of peculiar scales, which make beautiful microscopic objects. Another species, common in the crevices of rocks at the sea-side, is *Machilis maritima*, which is not unlike the preceding, but grey in colour instead of silvery.

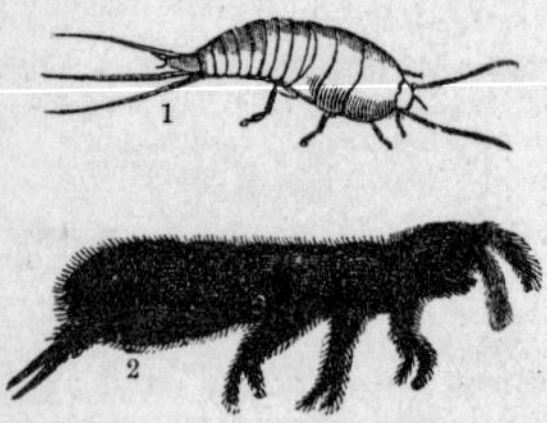

Fig. 233.—Aptera (magnified)
1, Silver-Fish (*Lepisma saccharina*); 2, Glacier-"Flea" (*Desoria glacilis*).

2. *Collembola.*—Many, but by no means all, of these possess a curious springing apparatus in the form of two stiff bristles which can be folded under the body and secured by a sort of catch projecting from the third segment. When released the animal is thrown into the air much like the "jack-jumper" children are so fond of fabricating from the "merrythought" of a goose. They are common under bark, dead leaves, stones, &c., and one species (*Podura aquatica*) may often be seen floating on the surface of stagnant pools. Some kinds are abundant in Alpine regions, on the surface of snow or ice, and among these may be mentioned the Glacier-"Flea" (*Desoria glacialis*) (fig. 233). The Collembola are not all provided with a springing

apparatus, and of these special interest attaches to *Anurida maritima*, remarkable for its habit of floating on the surface of rock-pools along certain parts of the coast. As remarked elsewhere, insects as a rule are very intolerant of salt water.

CLASS 2.—SPIDER-LIKE ANIMALS (ARACHNIDA)

This class is constituted by Scorpions, Spiders, Mites, and other allied forms, though the affinities of some of these is more than doubtful. The majority of species live upon animal matter, and many of them pursue living prey. Arachnids are popularly confused with insects, from which, however, they differ in many

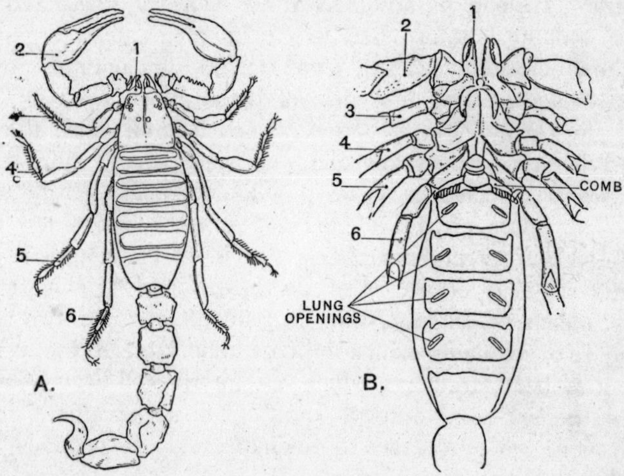

Fig. 234.—Scorpion, seen from above (A) and below (B). 1, Chelicerae; 2, pedipalps; 3–6, walking legs.

important particulars. These differences, as well as the points of agreement, will be best understood by briefly describing a Scorpion as a type (fig. 234). Spiders are more familiar to us in this country, but as they are much specialized it will be better to take them later. In dealing with the Scorpion, comparison may well be made with the account of a typical insect given on pp. 343–350.

The obviously segmented body is protected by a firm horny coating, which is very thick and hard in some places, while in others it is comparatively soft and flexible, so as to permit of a certain amount of movement. The body is not divided, as in an insect, into well-defined head, thorax, and abdomen, for the parts commonly considered as equivalent to the first two of these are fused together into one mass known as the *cephalo-thorax*, which consists of at least six segments, for it bears six pairs of appendages. The remainder of the body is made up of twelve rings or segments, the last five forming a narrow *tail* which is carried bent up over the body, and bears at its tip a pear-shaped spine on the sharp end of which open two poison-glands. Here we have an example of a true "sting", like that of a bee or wasp, as contrasted with the biting arrangements found in serpents, bugs, and gnats.

The *appendages* of a Scorpion differ strikingly from those of an insect. Instead of antennæ, three pairs of jaws, and three pairs of walking-legs, we find two pairs of grasping organs and four pairs of walking-legs, while feelers or antennæ are not present as such. The first pair of these appendages are short, strong, forwardly-directed *nippers* (cheliceræ), and they are followed by a very large second pair (pedipalps), which end in strong *pincers* much like those of a lobster and used for seizing prey. The bases of these appendages are adapted for biting. The possession of eight *walking-legs* is as characteristic of an Arachnid as that of six is of an insect, and this affords the simplest means of distinguishing the members of the two classes.

The two segments which immediately succeed the cephalo-thorax also bear structures which are interpreted as appendages, the first being fused into a small plate (operculum) notched behind, while the others are comb-shaped organs (pectines), which probably have a tactile function.

An ordinary insect breathes by means of air-tubes which open to the exterior by a series of pores on each side of the body, but the respiratory organs of a Scorpion consist of four pairs of "lung-books" which open by a corresponding number of oblique slits placed on the under side of the segments following the one upon which the comb-shaped organs are borne. Each of these breathing organs consists of a cavity into which a large number of thin plates project, these being packed together in a way which suggests the leaves of a book, hence the name lung-"book". An insect, again, typically possesses a pair of large compound eyes, and simple eyes may be present in addition. Here the eyes are all simple and are arranged on the upper side of the cephalo-thorax, two of them being close together near the middle line, while the remainder form a couple of groups, one on each side, near the front end of the body. Each of these groups contains from two to five separate eyes. The development takes place without metamorphosis.

The class is divided into the following orders:—

1. Scorpions (SCORPIONIDÆ).
2. False Spiders (SOLPUGIDÆ).
3. False Scorpions (PSEUDOSCORPIONIDÆ).
4. Whip-Scorpions (PEDIPALPI).
5. Harvestmen (PHALANGIDÆ).
6. Spiders (ARANEIDÆ).
7. Mites (ACARINA).

To these are usually added two small groups of doubtful affinities, *i.e.*—

8. Tongue-Worms (LINGUATULIDÆ).
9. Bear-Animalcules (TARDIGRADA).

Order 1.—SCORPIONS (Scorpionidæ)

Scorpions, all of which conform to the description already given, are widely distributed throughout the warmer parts of the globe. Two common South European species are the little House-Scorpion (*Euscorpius Europæus*), which ranges as far as the Tyrol and Carpathians; and the much larger Field-Scorpion (*Buthus Europæus*), common in the Mediterranean countries. The largest and most poisonous forms are the black *Rock-Scorpions* of Africa and India, which may be as much as 9 inches in length. These belong to the type-genus *Scorpio.*

Order 2.—FALSE SPIDERS (Solpugidæ)

The order of False Spiders includes a small number of species having a wide distribution, and mostly limited to warm countries. A well-known type is the Common False-Spider (*Galeodes araneoides*) (fig. 235), found in South Russia, Persia, Arabia, and Egypt, and much feared on account of its poisonous bite. The Kalmucks, Kirghiz, and other nomad tribes avoid regions where it abounds, for its attacks are not limited to human beings, but extend also to domestic animals, such as sheep, and camels. This creature resembles a large spider in appearance: its body is about 2 inches long and its legs long and hairy. There are great differences of structure and proportion as compared with a Scorpion. The body is unique among Arachnids in being distinctly divided into *head*, *thorax*, and *abdomen*, much as in an insect, and the last region is composed of ten segments and cylindrical in shape, there being no sting-provided tail. A further resemblance to insects is found in the breathing organs, which consist of *air-tubes*, opening to the exterior by three pairs of stigmata situated on the under surface, the first at the bases of the second legs, and the others on the abdomen. As in a Scorpion, the first appendages are *nippers*, here of very large size, and constituting the chief offensive weapons, since poison glands open upon them. The *pedipalps*, however, are not, as in a Scorpion, stout and pincer-bearing, but slender leg-shaped structures having a forward direction and acting as tactile organs. The first pair of legs closely resemble the pedipalps in appearance and function, and it may be noted that these four similar appendages are provided at their bases with cutting projections, situated at the sides of the mouth and serving as jaws. The remaining legs are attached to the thorax, as in an insect, the resemblance being emphasized by the fact that each ends in a claw-bearing tarsus. There is nothing to correspond to either the operculum or the combs of a Scorpion, and only two *simple eyes* are present, placed on the front of the head close to the middle line.

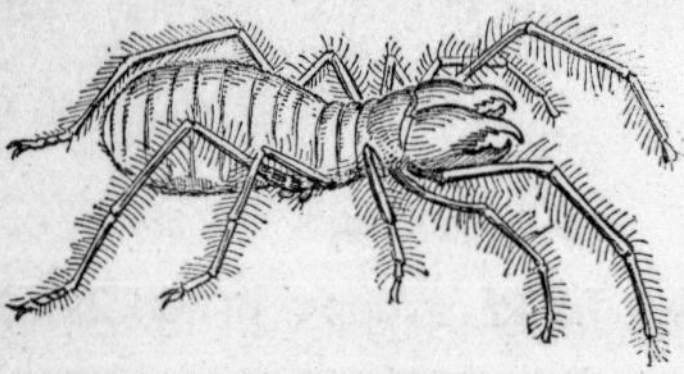

Fig. 235.—Common False-Spider (*Galeodes araneoides*)

Order 3.—FALSE SCORPIONS (Pseudoscorpionidæ)

False Scorpions are minute widely-distributed animals not unlike Scorpions in appearance, the resemblance being due to similarity in the appearance and structure of the chelicerae, pedipalps, and walking-legs. There are, however, no poison-glands, and the broad flat abdomen does not narrow into a tail. Breathing is effected by means of *air-tubes*, which open on the under side of the abdomen by two pairs of stigmata. *Spinning glands* open on the chelicerae, and the *simple eyes*, two or four in number, are situated on either side of the front of the head.

A common European species is the little Book-Scorpion (*Chelifer cancroides*) (fig. 236), often found in old books and similar dark places.

Fig. 236.—Book-Scorpion (*Chelifer cancroides*), enlarged. Natural size indicated by line.

Order 4.—WHIP-SCORPIONS (Pedipalpi)

The Whip-Scorpions make up a small but widely-distributed order, the members of which are fairly large in size. They are found in the warmer parts of both hemispheres, and considerable interest attaches to them, owing to the fact that they are in some respects intermediate between Scorpions and Spiders, on which account they are sometimes called Scorpion-Spiders. A typical Whip-Scorpion (*Thelyphonus*) looks not unlike a real Scorpion, the pedipalps being large and provided with pincers, and the abdomen narrowed into a sort of tail, reduced, however, to a mere filament. The breathing organs are lung-books (two pairs), and the eyes are arranged in a central and two lateral groups. Among the important differences from Scorpions may be noted—chelicerae provided with claws, not nippers, modification of the first pair of legs into tactile organs, and distinct marking off of the abdomen.

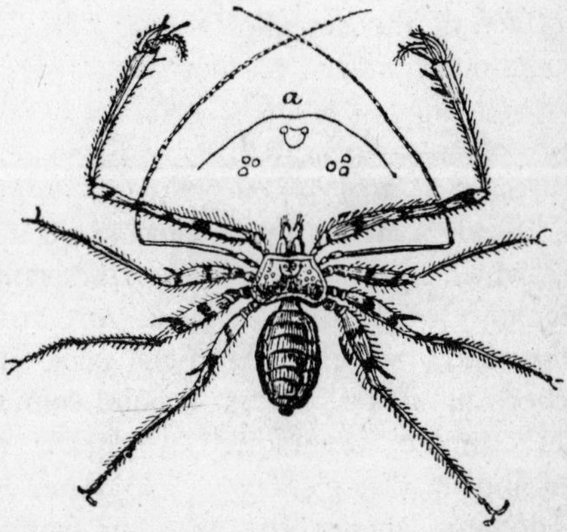

Fig. 237.—A Whip-Scorpion (*Phrynus*). *a*, Front of cephalo-thorax, enlarged to show eyes.

Some of the other genera (as *Phrynus*) (fig. 237) approximate more closely to the Spiders, for the pedipalps possess claws instead of pincers, and the abdomen is joined to the rest of the body by a narrow waist. The tail filament is only represented by a button-like knob.

Order 5.—HARVESTMEN (Phalangidæ)

Harvestmen constitute a large and almost universally-distributed order, represented in this country by some two dozen species. They are common in our fields and are generally mistaken for spiders, from which, however, the native species can at once be distinguished by the great length and slenderness of the four pairs of legs, and the fact that the small oval body is not marked off distinctly into regions. The chelicerae are provided with relatively large pincers, but the pedipalps are usually short and leg-like. The breathing organs are air-tubes which open by a pair of stigmata on a forward prolongation of the abdomen, just behind the bases of the first legs. A pair of simple eyes is borne on the upper surface of the cephalo-thorax. *Phalangium opilio* is one of the commonest native species (fig. 238).

Fig. 238.—A Harvestman (*Phalangium opilio*)

Order 6.—SPIDERS (Araneidæ)

Spiders make up a very large and widely-distributed order, of which there are several thousand known species. A well-known British form is the large Garden-Spider (*Epeira diadema*) (fig. 239), which constructs large regular webs resembling a wheel in shape. The ground-colour varies from yellowish to dark brown, diversified by darker markings, and usually presenting a conspicuous white mark on the upper side of the abdomen, whence the German name of "cross-spider" (*Kreuzspinner*), and the French name "cross-carrier" (*porte croix*). As in a scorpion, the head and thorax are closely fused together, but the large egg-shaped abdomen is connected by a narrow wasp-waist to the rest of the body, and the segments of which it is made up are so intimately united together that the boundaries between them cannot be made out.

The first pair of appendages (*chelicerœ*) are two-jointed, and of very characteristic construction, for the sharp curved end-joint, at the tip of which a pair of poison-glands open, can be folded down on the basal joint, much as the blade of a pocket-knife folds down on the handle. In this way an efficient grasping and holding organ is formed. The *pedipalps* are slender forwardly-directed structures, looking something like antennæ. As in

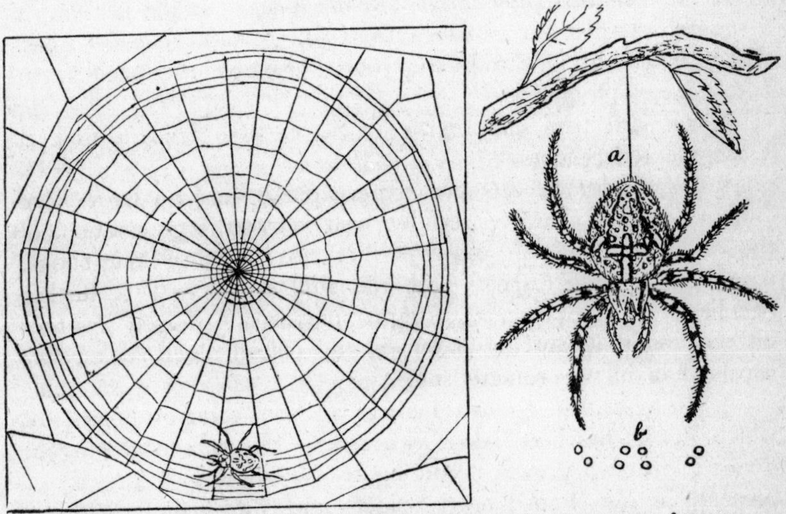

Fig. 239.—Garden-Spider (*Epeira diadema*) and Web. *a*, Female spider; *b*, arrangement of eyes.

Scorpion their basal joints are provided with cutting edges, which work against one another and act as jaws. The tips of the pedipalps are curiously modified in the male. The four pairs of *legs* are strong and of considerable length. Each of them is provided at its tip with several toothed claws, serving as efficient grasping organs.

As regards *breathing organs*, the Garden-Spider combines the arrangements characteristic of Scorpions on the one hand and Insects on the other. There are two lung-books, which open by a pair of slits on the under-side of the abdomen, near its base, while farther back there is a single aperture, situated in the middle, and opening into a set of air-tubes.

One of the most striking peculiarities of an ordinary spider is its power of spinning webs; indeed the word spider probably means "spinner". The silk is made by a large number of spinning-glands situated in the hinder part of the body, and opening upon conical "spinnerets", of which there are six in the Garden-Spider, four large and two small. They will be found as conical projections on the under side of the abdomen near its tip.

The Garden-Spider possesses eight *simple eyes*, situated on the upper side of the cephalo-thorax, at its front end. Four of them are comparatively large and are placed at the corners of a square, on each side of which are a pair of rather smaller ones. As in Arachnids generally the young resemble the adult when hatched, except in size.

There are two sub-orders: 1. Segmented Spiders, and 2. Unsegmented Spiders.

1. *Segmented Spiders* are represented by certain large East Indian species, characterized by well-marked segmentation of the abdomen and the possession of two pairs of lung-books, agreeing in these respects with the whip-scorpions. A further peculiarity is the presence of eight spinnerets, grouped together on the under-side of the abdomen, and placed much farther forwards than in an ordinary spider.

2. *Unsegmented Spiders* include all the common forms, of which Epeira has been taken as a type. The sub-order is again divided into two groups according to the number of lung-books present, *i.e.* into Four-lunged Spiders and Two-lunged Spiders.

Four-lunged Spiders include the largest members of the order, which excavate burrows in the ground and line them with silk, but do not construct snaring-webs. Some of these prey upon small birds, *e.g.* the Bird-eating Spider (*Mygale avicularia*), a gigantic South American form often seen in collections. Here also are included the *Trap-door Spiders* (*Cteniza* and *Nemesia*) of South Europe and elsewhere, which make hinged lids to their burrows. There is only one British species (*Atypus Sulzeri*), which burrows in damp earth.

Two-lunged Spiders, of which *Epeira diadema* is a typical example, embrace the large majority of species, and all the British forms except Atypus. Only some of the kinds construct snaring-webs, and among these may be mentioned, in addition to the Garden-Spider, the common House-Spiders (*Tegenaria domestica* and *T. civilis*), and the Hedge-Spider (*Agalena labyrinthica*), which constructs strong horizontal webs on bushes, hedges, &c. A very interesting aquatic form is the Water-Spider (*Argyroneta aquatica*), which constructs a thimble-shaped nest under water, attaching it to surrounding objects by mooring-strands which also serve to snare prey. The nest is filled with air, which the spider brings down in the form of bubbles adhering to its hairy abdomen.

Examples of common British spiders which do not construct webs are the Wolf-Spiders (*Lycosidæ*), and the handsomely-striped Harlequin-Spider (*Salticus scenicus*), distinguished by its leaping powers.

Order 7.—MITES (Acarina)

Mites, as their name indicates, are minute forms, and they embrace an exceedingly large number of species, some of which are found almost everywhere. A typical example is the Cheese-Mite (*Tyroglyphus siro*) (fig. 240). The abdomen is unsegmented and closely fused with the cephalo-thorax, the entire body being oval in shape. The small chelicerae are provided with pincers, and the pedipalps are short and slender. The usual four pairs of walking-legs are present, two directed forwards and two backwards. Respiratory organs are absent. Another well-known species is the "Red-Spider" or "Money-Spinner", which lives on the juices of leaves and spins a protective web. One of the chief features in which it differs from the Cheese-Mite is in the possession of breathing organs, which are in the form of air-tubes. Other examples of the group are Ticks, Mange-Mites, and similar pests, which will be dealt with in another section.

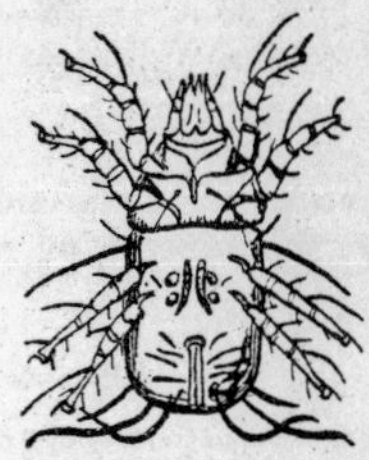

Fig. 240.—Cheese-Mite (*Tyroglyphus siro*), seen from below. Enlarged forty times.

Fig. 241.—Tongue-Worm (*Pentastomum tænioides*)

Order 8.—TONGUE-WORMS (Linguatulidæ)

Tongue-Worms are worm-like forms which in the adult condition are found as parasites in the nasal cavities of Dog and Wolf. The only appendages are two pairs of hook-like structures in the neighbourhood of the mouth. *Pentastomum tænioides* is the type (fig. 241).

Order 9.—Bear-Animalcules (Tardigrada)

Bear-Animalcules are minute creatures found in damp moss, or sometimes in salt or fresh water. The shape of the body ludicrously suggests an unlicked bear-cub (fig. 242). There are four pairs of stump-like legs, each provided with a pair of claws at its tip. The only representatives of jaws are to be found in a pair of sharp stylets which can be protruded from the mouth.

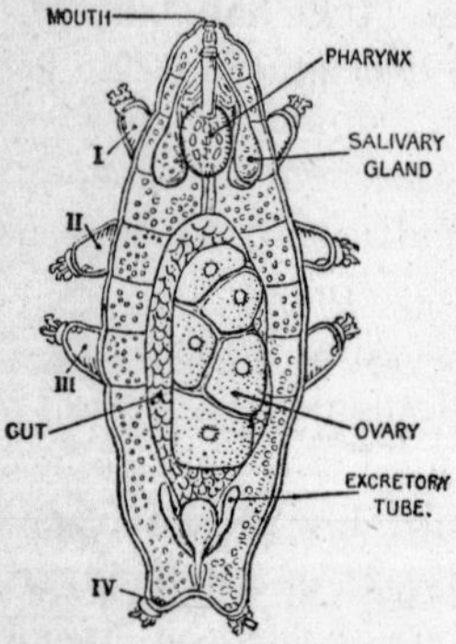

Fig. 242.—A Bear-Animalcule (*Macrobiotus*), much enlarged and seen from above; I-IV, walking legs.

Class 3.—Centipedes and Millipedes (Myriapoda)

Centipedes and Millipedes, which make up the third class of Jointed-limbed Invertebrates, are of simpler structure than the average members of the preceding classes, Insecta and Arachnida, contrasting strongly with them in regard to the legs, of which numerous similar pairs are present, though by no means so many as the names "centipede" and "millipede" would seem to imply. A common British centipede, the Thirty-Foot (*Lithobius forficatus*) (fig. 243), may be taken as a type. This is a small chestnut-coloured creature which lurks under stones or among loose earth, and glides rapidly away when disturbed. The body is flattened from above downwards, and is made up of a head and trunk, the latter consisting of sixteen segments, of which the first is extremely narrow, while each of the remainder bears a pair of jointed legs ending in pointed claws. The last two legs are much larger than the others, and turn sharply backwards. The narrow first segment of the trunk is provided with a pair of modified limbs, the bases of which are fused together, while each of them ends in a strong curved claw, near the end of which a poison gland opens.

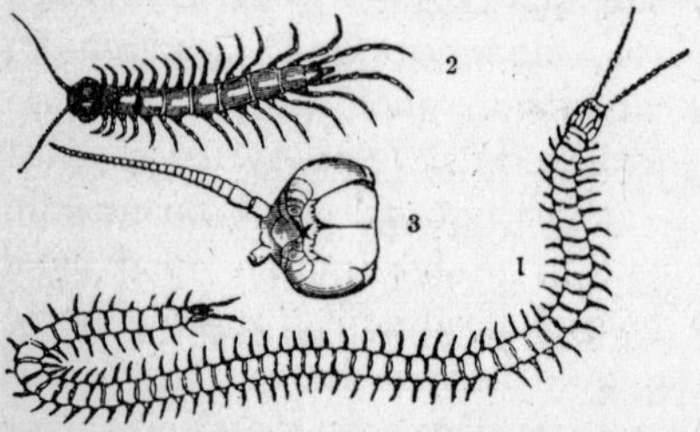

Fig. 243.—British Centipedes: 1, (*Geophilus longicornis*); 2, 3, the Thirty-Foot (*Lithobius forficatus*); 3 is under side of head enlarged.

The most obvious appendages of the head (fig. 244) are two long-jointed antennæ, while the remainder consist of three pairs of *jaws* guarding the opening of the mouth, and overlapped by the poison-claws. There is also a plate-like upper lip. The jaws, which are comparable in some respects to those of a cockroach (see p. 345), consist of a pair of hard-biting *mandibles*, followed by delicate flattened 1*st maxillæ*, and these again by leg-like 2*nd maxillæ*.

As in an insect, the breathing organs are *air-tubes* ramifying throughout the body, opening to the exterior on the sides by small holes (stigmata), of which the 3rd, 5th, 8th, 10th, 12th, and 14th leg-bearing segments each bears a pair. A group of *simple eyes* is to be seen on each side of the top of the head.

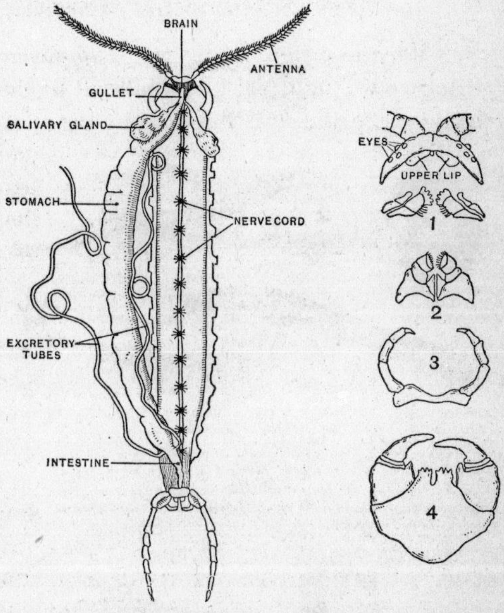

Fig. 244:—Structure of Centipede

1, Mandibles; 2, first maxillæ; 3, second maxillæ; 4, first limbs of trunk, with poison claws

It will be seen from the above description that a Myriapod is decidedly simpler in structure than an Insect or average Arachnid, only the front part being clearly marked off as a head, while there is no distinction between thorax and abdomen, though the first segment of the trunk is specialized. The presence of numerous pairs of legs, extending right to the posterior end of the body, is also characteristic, there being no restriction of walking-legs to the front part of the trunk, as in a scorpion or cockroach, where there are no legs on the abdominal region. As in many other cases of animals with unspecialized trunk, there is considerable variation within the limits of the class as to the number of segments, and another noteworthy point is the similarity these segments exhibit among one another.

Myriapods are divided into the following five orders:—

1. Millipedes (CHILOGNATHA or DIPLOPODA).
2. Centipedes (SYNGNATHA or CHILOPODA).
3. Spider-legged Myriapods (SCHIZOTARSIA).
4. Insect-like Myriapods (SYMPHYLA).
5. Larva-like Myriapods (PAUROPODA).

Order 1.—MILLIPEDES (Chilognatha or Diplopoda)

Millipedes (fig. 245) are vegetarian Myriapods, devoid of poison-claws, and with cylindrical bodies. The legs are comparatively weak, and throughout the greater part of the trunk two pairs of them are borne by each segment, their bases being close together instead of wide apart, as in a Centipede. The antennæ are short and club-shaped, while each of them is made up of seven somewhat bell-shaped joints. The mouth is provided with a plate-shaped upper lip, strong mandibles, and two pairs of maxillæ fused together into a broad plate. There are two pairs of stigmata on each trunk-segment, and also two small pores (*foramina repugnatoria*), which are the openings of defensive stink-glands. The eyes resemble those of a Centipede in structure and position.

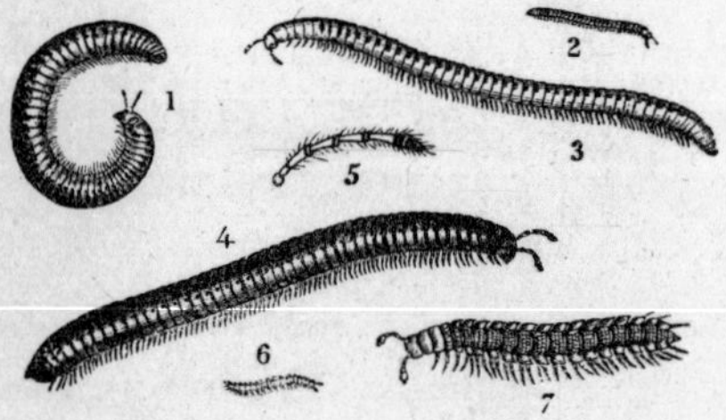

Fig. 245.—British Millipedes

1, London Snake-Millipede (*Iulus Londinensis*); 2, 3, Spotted Snake-Millipede (*Iulus guttatus*), natural size and enlarged; 4, 5, Earth Snake-Millipede (*Iulus terrestris*) and antennæ of same, both enlarged, 6, 7, Flattened Millipede (*Polydesmus complanatus*), natural size and enlarged.

Millipedes differ very much in length. A common British species of average length is the Earth Snake-Millipede (*Iulus terrestris*), a sluggish creature about an inch in length, commonly found under loose bark, &c., and with the habit of curling itself up when alarmed. The *Pill-Millipedes* are short forms which roll themselves into compact balls under similar circumstances. The genus *Glomeris* is represented by British species.

Order 2.—CENTIPEDES (Syngnatha or Chilopoda)

Centipedes conform in the main to the description already given of the common British form (*Lithobius*). The large Centipedes of tropical countries, feared on account of their painful bite, constitute a widely-distributed family, including larger and longer forms, provided with twenty-one pairs of legs. Some of them may be as much as a foot in length. A well-known species is *Scolopendra morsitans.* Another family of Centipedes, found all over the world except in the coldest regions, includes slender elongated forms, which are devoid of eyes, and burrow underground in pursuit of earth-worms. Some of them are phosphorescent (fig. 243), as, *e.g.*, the common British species (*Geophilus longicornis*).

Order 3.—SPIDER-LEGGED MYRIAPODS (Schizotarsia)

Spider-legged Myriapods include the species of a genus (*Scutigera*) which is widely distributed through the warmer parts of the globe. The body is comparatively short, but antennæ and legs are very much elongated. The eyes are compound, a unique peculiarity in the class. The breathing organs differ considerably from those of ordinary Myriapods, and open to the exterior by a single row of stigmata placed in the middle line on the upper side of the trunk. They are very active creatures, and most of them pursue their prey in broad daylight, even when the sun is strong.

Order 4.—INSECT-LIKE MYRIAPODS (Symphyla)

Insect-like Myriapods include but one genus (*Scolopendrella*), of very small size, and represented by a number of widely-distributed species, of which two are British. The adjective "insect-like" is used on account of the very strong resemblance which exists to the primitive insects of the order Thysanura (p. 384), and some zoologists go so far as to state that we should look upon these forms as coming very near to the ancestral stock from which insects have been derived. There is at any rate a close relationship.

Order 5.—LARVA-LIKE MYRIAPODS (Pauropoda)

The order of Larva-like Myriapods includes certain exceedingly small creatures first discovered in Britain, and thought at first by their discoverer (Sir John Lubbock) to be larvæ.

The most remarkable character is found in the antennæ, which are branched. No breathing organs have, so far, been discovered. The type-genus is *Pauropus*.

CLASS 4.—PRIMITIVE TRACHEATES (PROTOTRACHEATA)

There are certain small groups of animals to which special interest attaches on account of the speculations regarding genealogy and origin of organs to which they have given rise. One such group is the Hemichorda, already briefly described (p. 300); another is the class now to be dealt with. It includes but a single genus, *Peripatus*, a primitive type which appears to be of great antiquity, and as the name of the class indicates, is supposed to represent the ancestral stock from which the air-breathing arthropods already described have been derived. The word "represent" must, however, as in such cases generally, be taken with some qualification, for Peripatus can only be regarded as representing that stock in a general sort of way, as no doubt it has to some extent specialized on lines of its own, acquiring peculiarities which adapt it to a special mode of life. To those who are not professed zoologists it may appear that specialists make an unnecessary fuss about an obscure creature that may briefly be described as a "permanent caterpillar"; but the marvel is explained when we remember that this lowly animal enables us to throw light upon the origin and relationships of Myriapods, Arachnids, and Insects, the last of which, taken by themselves, include the majority of terrestrial species.

Like many archaic forms, Peripatus has an extremely wide geographical distribution, and its included species are found in South Africa, the Malay Peninsula, East Australia, New Zealand, South America, Central America, and the West Indies. Yet all these widely-separated species resemble one another with sufficient closeness to be placed in the same genus.

Peripatus was first described (in 1826) as a Mollusc, later as a Myriapod and as an Annelid (segmented worm). The late Professor Moseley, in 1874, proved it to be an Arthropod, and our detailed knowledge of its structure and development is mainly due to the investigations of the late Professor F. Maitland Balfour and Mr. Adam Sedgwick. It is now a widely-accepted view that Arthropods have been derived from Annelids, and the special interest attached to Peripatus centres in the fact that it, to use the words of Sedgwick, "stands absolutely alone as a kind of half-way animal between the Arthropoda and Annelida".

Peripatus (fig. 246) is a small cylindrical animal, found among rotting wood or the like, and comparable in appearance either to a well-nourished caterpillar or a segmented worm. The velvety *skin* is beautifully coloured, the tint varying according to the species. The front part of the body, called by courtesy the *head*, is not sharply marked off from the *trunk*, and this again is not clearly segmented, though its segmentation is indicated by the fact that it bears numerous pairs of stumpy *legs*, the exact number depending upon the species. These legs are hollow, conical projections (much like the appendages of some Annelids), and only exhibit in an imperfect way the jointing that characterizes Arthropods generally. Each of them is provided with a couple of sharp claws at its tip. Upon the under side of the head there is a swollen circular *lip* surrounding a depression within which the *mouth* opens. On each side of the head, outside this lip, is a short cylindrical projection known as *oral papilla*, and equivalent to a pair of modified limbs. Upon the tip of each of these is the opening of a large *slime-gland*, which secretes a sticky substance that can be forcibly ejected either as a defensive measure or else (in the New Zealand species at any rate) as a means of capturing prey. Within the circular lip are a pair of muscular *jaws*, each armed with two claw-like projections used for chewing the food. These jaws, again, are to be looked on as modified limbs, and the presence of such limb-jaws is an Arthropod character, though the limitation to a single pair is a peculiarity of Peripatus. A pair of cylindrical imperfectly-ringed *antennæ* project from the front of the head, and near the base of each of them there is a simple *eye*.

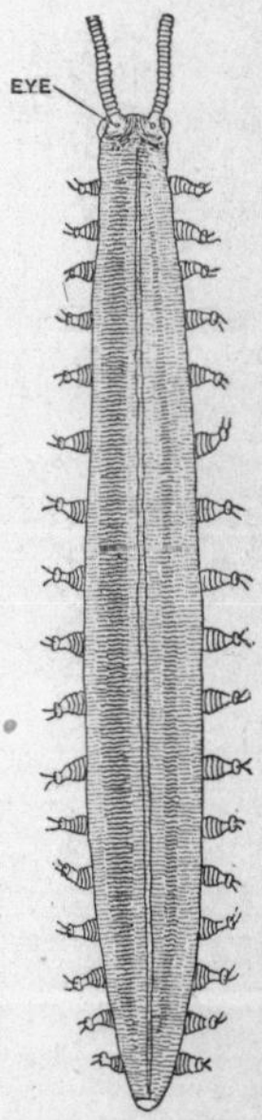

Fig. 246. — Cape Peripatus (*Peripatus Capensis*), enlarged

Only a few of the more important details regarding the *internal structure* (fig. 247) can be mentioned here, and these may be conveniently grouped into: 1. Arthropod characters, and 2. Annelid characters.

1. *Arthropod characters.* — The organs of *circulation* con-

form in the main to the type which has been described for the Cockroach (p. 348). The *heart* is a slender tube placed close to the upper surface of the body and suspended in a blood-containing pericardial space, from which blood passes into it through numerous pairs of valvular apertures. The rest of the blood-system consists of larger and smaller spaces which, together with the heart and pericardial cavity, make up a circulatory arrangement of which the parts communicate with one another.

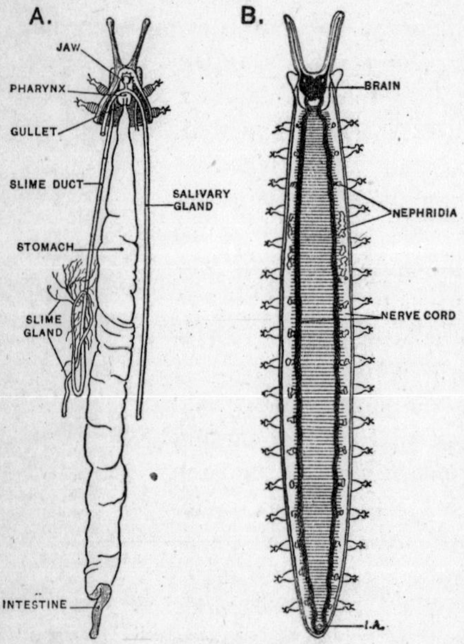

Fig. 247.—Structure of Peripatus

A, Digestive organs (from below). B, Nervous system and excretory organs (from above). I.A. Position of intestinal aperture (on under side).

This appears to be a suitable place in which to speak more fully of the nature of the Arthropod heart, which is essentially a blood-tube within a blood-space with which it communicates by paired apertures. In a Vertebrate (p. 40) or a Mollusc (p. 308) the heart possesses one or more *auricles*, into which blood is poured by veins, and the pericardial space surrounding it does not contain blood at all. Professor Ray Lankester explains the arthropod condition by supposing that the heart was originally a tube receiving blood by several pairs of lateral vessels which later on dilated into auricles where they joined the central tube. The fusion of these auricles into a large space round the heart would give the state of things now existing. The pericardial space of, say, Peripatus is therefore to be regarded, if the theory be well founded, as equivalent to a big auricle surrounding the heart; the physiological problem solved in this case being the evolution of an arrangement for storing blood about to enter the heart.

Peripatus further agrees with typical air-breathing Arthropods in the character of its *breathing organs*, which are air-tubes. These are, however of very simple character, and open by very numerous stigmata scattered over the surface of the body and even present on the legs. The arrangement is not entirely irregular, for some of these apertures are placed in a double longitudinal row on the upper surface, while others are similarly disposed on the under surface. We have, on the whole, what may be considered a primitive or undifferentiated condition of these organs, from which it is easy to imagine the derivation of the more complex arrangements found in Myriapods, Arachnids, and Insects.

2. *Annelid characters.*—These will naturally be better appreciated after the Annelids have been considered, and will only be briefly enumerated.

The *body-wall*, like that of an ordinary segmented worm, consists of a thin skin covered by a delicate cuticle, and underlain by a muscular coat, consisting of an external layer of transversely-running fibres and an internal layer of fibres having a longitudinal direction. In regard to minute structure, the muscle-fibres differ from those of Arthropods in being devoid of transverse striations.

The mouth of Peripatus leads into a muscular *pharynx*, like that of many Annelids, but quite unlike what is to be found in Arthropods. A much more striking feature is to be found in the *excretory organs*. These consist of a series of tubes known as *nephridia*, one of which opens at the base of almost every leg, on its under surface. Such segmentally-arranged renal organs are extremely characteristic of segmented worms.

The *central nervous system* consists of a double brain- or cerebral-ganglion above the pharynx, and two ventral cords connected with these. A remarkable character is seen in the fact that these cords are widely separated except at the extreme posterior end of the body, where they unite together above the gut. Very numerous slender transverse nerves connect these two cords, much as the rungs of a ladder connect its sides, though the "rungs" of the nervous system differ in being much more narrow and numerous. The nerve cords are dilated at regular intervals into ill-marked ganglia. This nervous system agrees with that of various Annelids, and is also much like that characteristic of the Proto-Molluscs.

Lastly, it may be noted that the eyes of Peripatus agree more closely with those of Annelids than with those of Arthropods.

B.—AQUATIC ARTHROPODS (BRANCHIATA)

The four Arthropod classes which have so far been reviewed, *i.e.* Insects, Arachnids, Myriapods, and Prototracheates, together make up the air-breathing or Tracheate division of Arthropoda; and we now come to the aquatic division, including the two classes of Crustaceans (Crustacea) and King-Crabs (Xiphosura), to which the Sea-Spiders (Pycnogonida) are doubtfully appended.

CLASS 5.—CRUSTACEANS (CRUSTACEA)

This very large class, of which a typical member, the Lobster, has already been partly described in contrasting Vertebrates with higher Invertebrates (p. 302), includes animals which are for the most part marine, though many, of the minute forms especially, inhabit fresh water, and some few are terrestrial.

So great is the diversity of structure within the limits of the class that no single type fully illustrates it; but it may be as well to enlarge somewhat upon the description already given of the Lobster (*Homarus vulgaris*), taking it as a good average example of the higher Crustacea. To those desirous of seeing how a single type may be made to illustrate the whole of the class in question, and at the same time give a sound knowledge of the principles of zoology generally, a perusal of Huxley's classic work, *The Crayfish*, is recommended.

External Characters of the Lobster (fig. 248).—The body is *bilaterally symmetrical*, and the hinder part of it, or tail, is clearly divided into *segments*. The front part of the body is a *cephalo-thorax*, consisting of head and thorax closely fused together, though segments are present here too, as shown by the numerous paired appendages. The *head* is marked off from the *thorax* by means of a distinct groove (cervical groove). The number of segments appear to be as follows:—head, 5; thorax, 8; tail or abdomen, 7. All the segments, and the appendages they bear, are constructed on the same common plan (see p. 195), but there are many differences in detail, to serve various physiological ends.

Appendages.—The letter Y may be taken as a diagram of the type on which the appendages are constructed, the stem of the letter corresponding to a basal stalk by which the appendage is attached to the body, while its two forks represent outer and inner branches. The same thing may be expressed in another way, by saying that the typical limb in a higher Crustacean is cleft or forked. We will now see how far the appendages of the Lobster conform to this Y diagram, and in doing so it will be convenient to start with the *abdomen*, as this is the least modified region. Of the seven segments here present only the first six bear appendages, while the last, usually known as the *telson*, forms the middle portion of the tail-fin. An average abdominal segment, say the fourth, bears two small forked appendages somewhat inappropriately termed *swimmerets*, and it will be seen from the diagram that these conform to the Y type. The appendages of the sixth abdominal segment are relatively large, and form the side-parts of the great tail-fin. Each of them, however, may be compared to a Y in which the main stem is shortened and broadened, while the two branches are flattened out into oval plates. It may further be noted that the first two pairs of abdominal appendages in the male are curiously modified, while in the female the appendages of the first abdominal segment are either absent or very much reduced.

Thoracic appendages.—The four hindermost segments of the thorax are stout *walking-legs*, of which the two first pairs end in small pincers. At first sight they deviate entirely from the Y type, for they are obviously not forked. This is a case where the facts of development are of use in throwing light on a problem, for we find that in a very young Lobster these walking-legs are forked, but their outer branches are comparatively feeble and ultimately disappear altogether. There is a further peculiarity about the three first pairs of these legs to which attention must be called, but before doing so it is necessary to speak of the nature and position of the breathing organs or *gills*. These are delicate plume-like outgrowths of the body, limited to the thoracic region, and sheltered in a gill-cavity on either side, the outer wall of which is formed by a firm gill-cover that constitutes the side of the *carapace* or hard shield covering the greater part of head and thorax. When this gill-cover is cut away the gills will be seen, and it can readily be shown that they are of three kinds, attached to different regions of the body. It need only be mentioned here that some of them are *limb-gills*, so called because they are borne by the bases of certain limbs, among which are the three first pairs of legs. When one of these is carefully detached it will be seen that a thin plate (gill-plate) projects from its base, and that to that plate a feathery gill is attached. The fourth thoracic segment bears the most conspicuous appendages of all, *i.e.* the great *pincers*, which are constructed on the same lines as the nipper-bearing walking-legs, and like them are provided with gill-plates and limb-gills.

The three first segments of the thorax bear appendages modified for chewing, and called *foot-jaws*, the name suggesting the idea that they were once locomotor in function but have acquired new duties. The last or third pair of foot-jaws are decidedly leg-like, but are provided with stiff bristles where they bite against one another. An outer branch is present, though small, and gill-plate with limb-gill will be readily recognized. The middle or second foot-jaws are like the preceding, but a good deal smaller, while the first foot-jaws are very delicate, with broad biting basal stalk, small outer and inner branches, and gill-plate devoid of gill.

Head Appendages.—These consist of three pairs of jaws behind and two pairs of feelers in front. The jaws, beginning with the last pair, are named, as in an insect, second maxillæ, first maxillæ, and mandibles. The *second maxillæ* somewhat resemble the first foot-jaws, but gill-plate and gill are absent, while the outer branch is broadened into an oval "baler", which lies in the front of the gill-chamber, and by its constant scooping movement brings about a forward movement of water over the gills. The *first maxillæ* are still more delicate, and are reduced to a two-jointed basal stem and an insignificant inner branch.

The same parts are present in the first jaws or *mandibles*, but their proportions and texture are very different. The basal joint of the stalk is broadened into a hard biting-piece, strongly toothed on its inner margin, while the second joint of the stalk together with the inner branch make up a small three-jointed "palp" which probably has sensory functions.

Owing to an upward bend of the region in front of the

mouth, the two pairs of feelers are directed forwards, an advantageous position for sense organs of the kind. The second or smaller pair, the *antennules*, conform markedly to the Y-diagram, and consist of a basal stalk and slender outer and inner branches. But it is by no means certain that we are justified in comparing the parts of this appendage with those

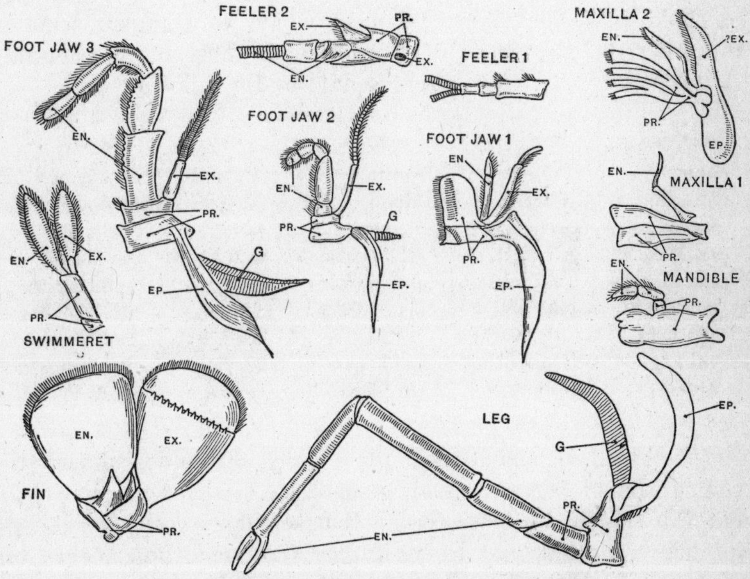

Fig. 248.—Appendages of Lobster (*Homarus vulgaris*)

PR. Base of appendage (protopodite); EN. inner branch (endopodite); EX. outer branch (exopodite), (the right-hand EX. in feeler 2 indicates excretory aperture; EP. gill-plate (epipodite); G, gill.

of the other ones, for it must be noted that the basal stem is here three-jointed instead of two-jointed as in all the other cases. The large feelers or *antennæ* conform to the type, for they consist of a two-jointed stalk, to which are attached a scale-shaped outer branch, and an excedingly long inner branch, which can be swept round so as to explore a considerable area in the neighbourhood of the body.

We have in the Lobster appendages an excellent example of the principles enumerated on p. 195, whereby structures of generalized type are modified in various ways to bring about special ends. These principles are: 1. variations in *shape*:

compare, *e.g.*, the antennæ, great pincers, and swimmerets; 2. variation in relative *size*: compare outer and inner branches in an average swimmeret and the side-pieces of the tail-fin; 3. variation in *number*: taking the Y-shape as the generalized type, the gill-plate is an addition in some cases, while in others the outer branch is much reduced or even absent; 4. *fusion* of parts: seen in the first abdominal appendages of the male.

This is a convenient point at which to compare some of the anterior appendages of Lobster with those of air-breathing Arthropods. One view is represented by the following table:—

Cockroach.	*Scorpion.*	*Centipede.*	*Peripatus.*	*Lobster.*
Antennæ	Absent.	Antennæ	Antennæ	Antennules
Absent	Cheliceræ	Absent	Absent	Antennæ
Mandibles	Pedipalpi	Mandibles	Jaws	Mandibles
1st Maxillæ	1st Legs	1st Maxillæ	Oral Papilla	1st Maxillæ
2nd Maxillæ	2nd Legs	2nd Maxillæ	1st Legs	2nd Maxillæ
1st Legs	3rd Legs	Poison Claw	2nd Legs	1st Foot-jaws
2nd Legs	4th Legs	1st Claw	3rd Legs	2nd Foot-jaws
3rd Legs	Operculum	2nd Legs	4th Legs	3rd Foot-jaws
Absent	Combs	3rd Legs	5th Legs	Great Pincers

It should be mentioned that many difficulties attend the comparison of segments and appendages in different groups, for one can seldom be quite certain that segments really correspond in different cases, and, even if they did, some appendages are apt to shift their position in the course of development.

The Lobster is protected by a firm shelly *exoskeleton* in the form of a horny layer which is thin where mobility is required, while elsewhere it is thick and hardened by the deposit of salts of lime. This strong suit of armour cannot increase in size as the animal grows, and the exigencies of the case are met by a process of moulting, which takes place frequently in young animals and at longer intervals later on. At the commencement of the operation a transverse split appears along the back, where the carapace joins the tail, and through this opening the animal painfully makes its way out. A sheltered corner is chosen for moulting purposes, and here the soft and defenceless creature remains till its new armour is properly developed and hardened.

The chief external characters have now been reviewed, and

the remainder may be taken in connection with the various systems of organs which are concerned, and which will be considered seriatim.

Digestive Organs (fig. 249).—These consist of (1) a symmetrical food-tube or *gut*, which runs back from the oval mouth situated on the under side of the head to the vent placed below the telson, and (2) of *digestive glands*. It will be noted that, as in Arthropods generally, the jaws are modified limbs, which work against one another from side to side and are entirely outside the mouth,

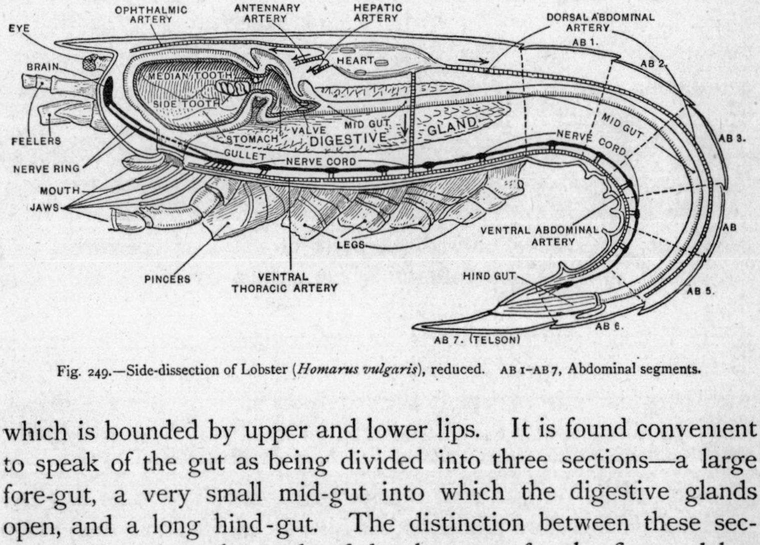

Fig. 249.—Side-dissection of Lobster (*Homarus vulgaris*), reduced. AB 1–AB 7, Abdominal segments.

which is bounded by upper and lower lips. It is found convenient to speak of the gut as being divided into three sections—a large fore-gut, a very small mid-gut into which the digestive glands open, and a long hind-gut. The distinction between these sections is based on the mode of development, for the first and last of them begin as pits which extend farther and farther inwards till they join the developing mid-gut, and form with it a continuous tube. It is not therefore surprising to find that the fore- and hind-guts, since they are formed by inpushing of the body-wall (see p. 261), are lined by a firm horny layer continuous with the exoskeleton, and that this layer is shed and replaced every time the animal moults. The *fore-gut* consists of a short *gullet* dilating into a very large *stomach*, divided into a cardiac section in front and a pyloric part behind. The stomach is said to be a "masticatory" one, for it contains a chewing apparatus or *gastric mill*, consisting of a number of hard pieces formed by thickening and calcification of the horny lining. These pieces make up an elastic framework on which are borne two large lateral and one median tooth, and by the action of appropriate muscles these can be brought together so as to effectually chew anything that happens to be between them. The cavity of the pyloric part of the stomach is narrowed, and numerous interlacing bristles project from its walls, constituting a very effective "strainer", which prevents any but finely-divided particles from passing back into the short *mid-gut*. The lining of this part of the food-tube is soft, and a pair of large *digestive glands*, commonly called the liver, open into it. These organs are physiologically equivalent to liver and pancreas of a Vertebrate (see pp. 37 and 38). The *hind-gut* or intestine is a narrow tube continuous with the mid-gut, and possessing a firm lining raised up into longitudinal ridges.

The *Circulatory Organs* (fig. 350) conform to the Arthropod type already described in dealing with the Cockroach (p. 348), but the *heart*, instead of being a long slender tube, is a short broad sac, possessing only three pairs of valvular apertures, and suspended in the blood-containing pericardial cavity by means of fibrous cords. It is systemic (see pp. 308 and 348), *i.e.* contains purified blood, which it pumps through delicate branching arteries to the body at large. Sooner or later these arteries communicate with irregular spaces which ultimately open into a large *sternal sinus* running along the lower part of the body just within the body-wall. Meanwhile the blood has become impure by loss of much of its oxygen and receipt of carbon dioxide as a waste product. It therefore passes to the gills for purification, and, when this has been effected, is carried to the pericardial cavity, whence it passes into the heart through the valvular openings with which that organ is provided.

The *Excretory Organs*, by which nitrogenous waste is removed from the blood, consist of a pair of *antennary-* or *green-glands*, situated in the front part of the head and opening on the bases of the antennæ. Each is essentially a coiled tube, possibly equivalent to a nephridium (see p. 401).

The *Muscular System* is complex. The largest muscles are to be found in the tail, which is the organ by means of which the lobster is able to swim backwards through the water with great rapidity. Powerful *flexor muscles*, lying below the gut, bend the tail down and enable it to give its effective stroke, while less powerful *extensor muscles*, lying above the gut, straighten it for another downward movement.

The Central Nervous System (fig. 249) consists of a *nerve-ring* surrounding the gullet, and a double *ventral cord* upon which numerous pairs of ganglia are developed. The upper part of the nerve-loop is thickened into a pair of brain or cerebral ganglia, by which the important sense organs of the head are supplied. The general arrangement conforms to that described in the Cockroach (see p. 349).

Organs of Sense are well developed, and many of them are in the form of specialized bristles or *setæ*, the soft axes of which are in communication with the skin by means of vertical canals which perforate the hard exoskeleton. Many of these setæ minister to the sense of *touch*, and this is especially true of those found on the antennules and antennæ. Organs of taste are not definitely recognized, though they probably exist on some of the appendages of the mouth. Certain peculiar spatula-shaped setæ present on the external branches of the antennules have to do with *smell.*

The extremely interesting *auditory organs* consist of two pear-shaped sacs, one of which is lodged in the basal joint of each antennule, and opens by a slit to the exterior. These sacs are really in-pushings of the skin, and they contain numerous specialized auditory setæ, and also grains of sand which have been introduced from the exterior. The chief interest attaching to these organs lies in the fact that they correspond to a stage in the development of more complex structures, such, *e.g.*, as the membranous labyrinths of Vertebrates, which start as pits in the skin (see p. 56).

The *visual organs* are in the form of two compound eyes situated on the front of the head near the antennules, and borne on stalks.

Development.—The Lobster passes through a *metamorphosis* in the course of its life-history, for it hatches out as a *larva*, which differs in many ways from the adult.

Crustacea, of which the Lobster has been described as a type, may be defined as aquatic Arthropods possessing two pairs of feelers (antennules and antennæ), and breathing organs (when such are present) in the form of gills. The appendages are typically forked. The class is subdivided in the following way:—

Sub-class 1.—Higher Crustacea (MALACOSTRACA).

Order 1. Stalk-eyed Crustacea (THORACOSTRACA).—Lobster, Cray-fish, Crab, Locust-Shrimp, Opossum-Shrimp, &c.

Order 2. Sessile-eyed Crustacea (ARTHROSTRACA).—Sand-Hoppers, Wood-Lice, &c.

Order 3. Intermediate Crustacea (LEPTOSTRACA).—Mud-Shrimps (Nebalia and its allies).

Sub-class 2.—Lower Crustacea (ENTOMOSTRACA).

Order 1. Barnacles (CIRRIPEDIA).—Ship-Barnacle, &c.

Order 2. Bivalve Crustacea (OSTRACODA):—Cypris, &c.

Order 3. Fork-footed Crustacea (COPEPODA).—Cyclops, Fish-Lice.

Order 4. Leaf-footed Crustacea (PHYLLOPODA).—Apus, Water-Fleas, &c.

Sub-class 1.—HIGHER CRUSTACEA (Malacostraca)

The following features, illustrated by the Lobster, are characteristic of the sub-class:—The body is made up of a constant and limited number of segments, each of which, with the exception of the last (or telson), bears a pair of appendages. In nearly all cases the segments are twenty in number, distributed as follows:—head, 5; thorax, 8; Abdomen, 7. The excretory organs typically present are antennary glands. The development is complex, and in most cases there is a larval form, differing markedly in appearance from the adult.

Order 1.—STALK-EYED CRUSTACEA (Thoracostraca)

In this order the head and thorax are fused together, and the eyes are usually situated on stalks. There are four sub-orders:—1. Ten-legged Crustacea (*Decapoda*), 2. Opossum-Shrimps (*Schizopoda*), 3. Locust-Shrimps (*Stomatopoda*), and 4. the Cumacea.

1. The *Decapoda* are so named because the last five pairs of thoracic limbs are seven-jointed locomotor organs, in which the outer branches are absent in the adult.

One large section of the sub-order is distinguished by the presence of a long and powerful tail, provided with a well-developed tail-fin. Among the British species here included are the following:—Lobster (*Homarus vulgaris*) (fig. 250), Rock-

Fig. 250.—Mediterranean Crustacea

1, Lobster (*Homarus vulgaris*); 2, Bear-Crab (*Scyllarus arctus*); 3, Dromia Crab (*Dromia*); 4, Spider-Crab (*Maia squinando*); 5, Locust-Shrimp (*Squilla mantis*).

Lobster (*Palinurus vulgaris*) (fig. 251), Norway Lobster (*Nephrops Norvegicus*), Prawn (*Palæmon serratus*), Shrimp (*Crangon vulgaris*). The Crayfish (*Astacus fluviatilis*) is a fresh-water form.

Fig. 251.—Rock-Lobster (*Palinurus vulgaris*)

Another section, including forms intermediate between the above and Crab, is formed by the *Hermit-Crabs* (fig. 252), which take up their abode in the empty shells of various sea-snails, and possess a soft unsymmetrical tail that has lost most of its appendages except the last pair. These have lost their original function of acting as swimming organs, and are modified into hook-like structures, by which the hermit-crab holds on to its house.

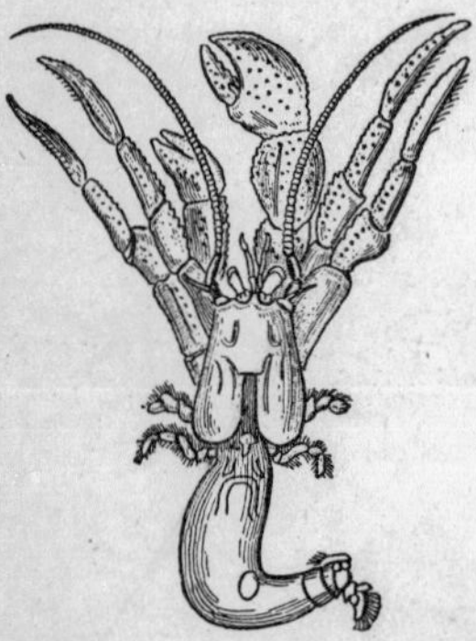

Fig. 252.—A Hermit-Crab (*Pagurus Bernhardus*), removed from its dwelling

The last section of the Decapods includes the true *Crabs* (fig. 250), in which the cephalo-thorax is very broad, and the tail so much reduced as to be useless as a swimming organ. Among British species may be noted the Edible Crab (*Cancer pagurus*) and the Shore Crab (*Carcinus mœnas*).

2. The *Opossum-Shrimps* (Schizopoda) are small marine forms

often found swimming in large shoals, and superficially resembling ordinary shrimps, though of much smaller size. They differ, however, from these in many important particulars, among which may be mentioned the delicate nature of the shield covering the cephalo-thorax, to which at least one thoracic segment is not united. There are, further, eight pairs of closely similar thoracic legs, provided both with outer and inner branches. The commonest British genus is *Mysis* (fig. 253), which so closely resembles a

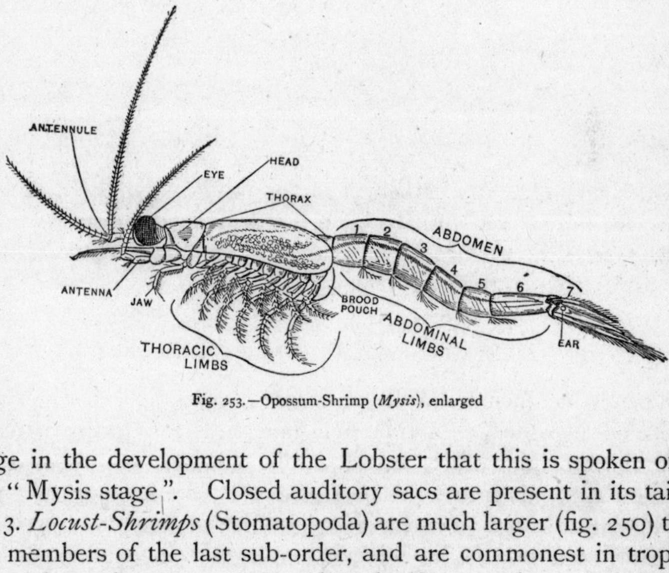

Fig. 253.—Opossum-Shrimp (*Mysis*), enlarged

stage in the development of the Lobster that this is spoken of as the "Mysis stage". Closed auditory sacs are present in its tail.

3. *Locust-Shrimps* (Stomatopoda) are much larger (fig. 250) than the members of the last sub-order, and are commonest in tropical seas, where they may attain a length of as much as 8 inches or more. The cephalo-thorax is small, for not only does it not include the last three thoracic segments, but it does not have to shelter the gills, as these are attached to the appendages of the broad well-developed abdomen. The thoracic appendages are remarkable, for the first five pairs of them are modified into foot-jaws, of which the second are extremely large and modified as seizing-limbs (fig. 250). So strikingly do they resemble the first pair of legs of the Praying Mantis (see p. 381), which have a similar function, that these Crustacea are often known as "Mantis-Shrimps". The last three pairs of thoracic appendages are leg-like, and possessed of both outer and inner branches. Two species are not uncommon in the Channel Islands (*Squilla Desmaresti* and *Squilla mantis*). Like

the other members of the sub-order, they are burrowing forms found in shallow water.

4. The sub-order *Cumacea* includes small shrimp-like forms (fig. 255) which live in shoals, and inhabit fairly deep parts of the sea where the bottom is of sand. The cephalo-thorax is even more

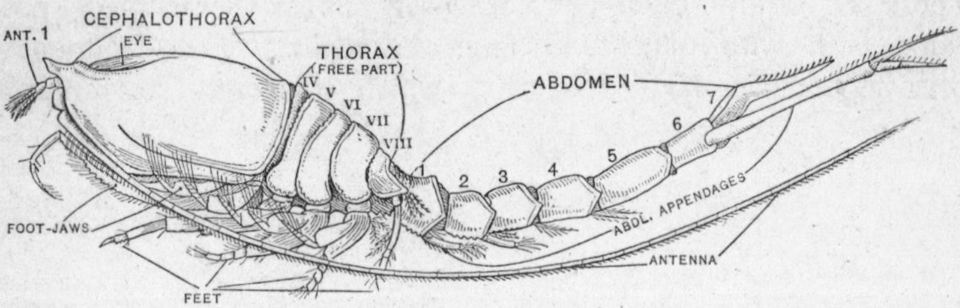

Fig. 254.—*Cuma* (enlarged). ANT. 1, Antennule IV-VIII, posterior thoracic segments; 1-7, abdominal segments.

limited than in the Locust-Shrimps, for the last five thoracic segments are not united with it. Some at least of the thoracic limbs possess outer as well as inner branches, and the two compound eyes are stalkless and sometimes fused together.

Order 2.—Sessile-eyed Crustacea (Arthrostraca)

The order includes a large number of comparatively small Crustacea, in which, as a rule, only one thoracic segment is fused to the head, and there is consequently no great armour-covered cephalo-thorax, as in a Crab or Lobster. The head-appendages correspond to those of a Lobster, but the thorax possesses only one pair of foot-jaws, its other appendages being seven pairs of legs, none of which are provided with pincers. There are usually six pairs of limbs on the abdomen. The eyes are devoid of stalks, *i.e.* are sessile

Two sub-orders are recognized, one containing laterally-flattened animals (Amphipoda), and the other forms which are flattened from above downwards (Isopoda).

1. The most typical members of the Amphipoda (fig. 255) are springing forms, of which the Sand-Hopper (*Talitrus locusta*) is a good example. During the summer months this may often be seen in leaping myriads between tide-marks on sandy shores. Its appearance suggests a strongly-curved flattened shrimp. Very similar in character are the species of the genus *Gammarus*, common in shallow water, both salt and fresh. The curious

Whale-Louse (*Cyamus ceti*) is exceptional among the members of the sub-order in having its body flattened from above downwards, and it is found parasitic on the skin of whales, to which it is enabled to hold fast by means of strongly-hooked legs. The abdomen is reduced to a mere stump entirely devoid of appendages. The weird-looking Skeleton Shrimps (*Caprella*) are also distinguished by the presence of a much-reduced abdomen. They are found climbing like monkeys among the branching colonies of various zoophytes.

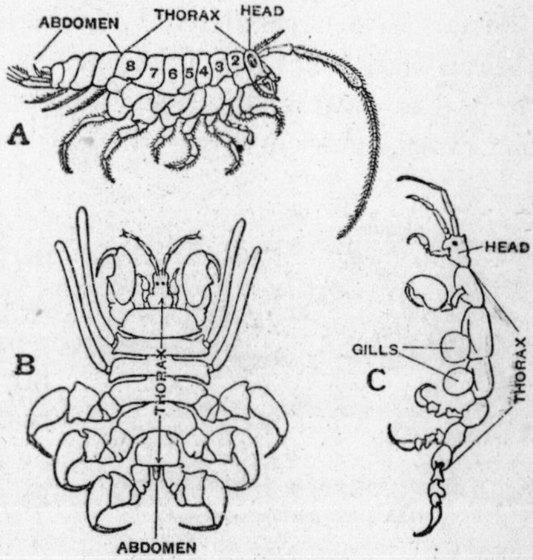

Fig. 255.—Amphipods (enlarged)

A, Sand-Hopper (*Talitrus locusta*); 2-8, last seven segments of thorax, the first is fused with the head. B, Whale-Louse (*Cyamus ceti*). C, Skeleton Shrimp (*Caprella*).

2. *Isopods* (fig. 256) differ from Amphipods in being flattened from above downwards, while the abdomen is shortened and bears plate-like appendages. Most of the species are marine, and of these *Cirolana*, *Idotea*, and *Sphæroma* may be taken as typical British genera. Some, however, are fresh-water, as, *e.g.*, the common native Fresh-water Shrimp (*Asellus aquaticus*), distinguished by its long limbs; and still others are terrestrial, of which the most familiar is the Wood-Louse (*Oniscus murarius*), commonly found under damp stones and in similar places. Some of the Isopods are curiously modified to fit them for a parasitic life, and these will be mentioned elsewhere.

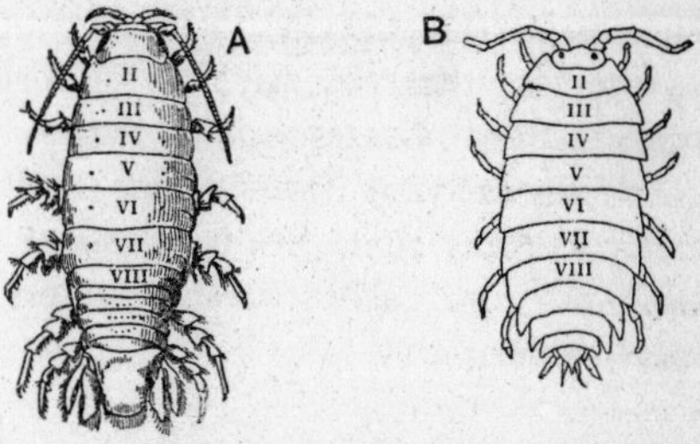

Fig. 256.—Isopods (enlarged)

II–VIII, Free segments of thorax, the first is fused with the head. A, *Cirolana borealis*; B, Wood-Louse (*Oniscus murarius*).

Order 3.—Intermediate Crustacea (Leptostraca)

The *Mud-Shrimps*, including *Nebalia* (fig. 257) and allied genera, form a restricted but interesting group of small marine shrimp-like creatures found in all parts of the world. These forms have attracted a good deal of attention, because they are a connecting-link between the higher and lower Crustacea, and some zoologists place them in a separate sub-class. Like the higher Crustacea they are composed of a definite and limited number of segments, in this case, however, twenty-one instead of twenty, for the abdomen has an extra segment, and the excretory organs include antennary glands. They also agree with stalk-eyed forms as regards their visual organs. But on the other hand all the segments of the thorax are free, though it and part of the abdomen are covered by a bivalve *shield* which grows back from the head, and the eight pairs of thoracic appendages are leaf-like, as in some of the lower Crustacea. The first four segments of the abdomen bear forked appendages as in certain other of the lower Crustacea (Copepoda), a further agreement with which is found in the fact that the tail also is forked. In addition to antennary glands they possess other excretory structures (shell-glands) resembling those of lower forms. On the whole it may be taken as fairly certain that the Leptostraca resemble in many points the ancestral stock from which the various groups of higher Crustacea have diverged.

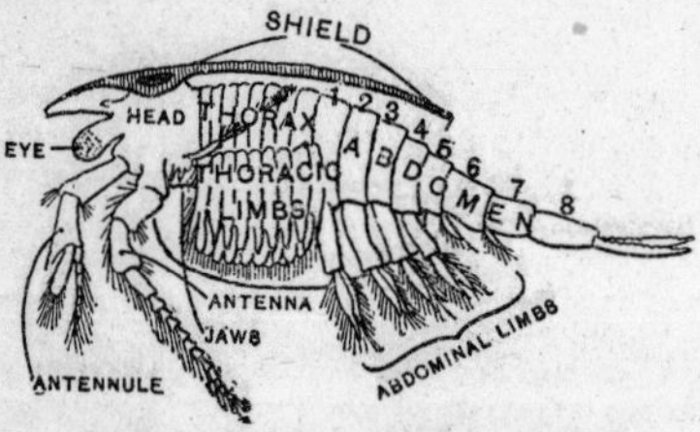

Fig. 257.—Mud-Shrimp (*Nebalia*), enlarged
Left half of shield cut away.

Sub-class 2.—Lower Crustacea (Entomostraca)

This is an exceedingly large and greatly diversified group, including both marine and fresh-water forms, of which the large majority are very small, and which play a very important part in nature as the food of higher animals. There is a very large amount of variation as regards the number of segments, and a similar wide range in the nature of the appendages, which are often flattened and leaf-like, though in other cases they may exhibit the bifurcated type which we have found to be characteristic of higher forms. There is no gastric mill, and it is common to find three functional eyes present in the adult, two compound and one simple. As a general rule the embryo hatches out as a *Nauplius larva* (fig. 258), which typically possesses an unsegmented ovoid body and three pairs of appendages by means of which it swims, these corresponding to the antennules, antennæ, and mandibles of the adult. A larva of this kind is rarely found among higher Crustacea.

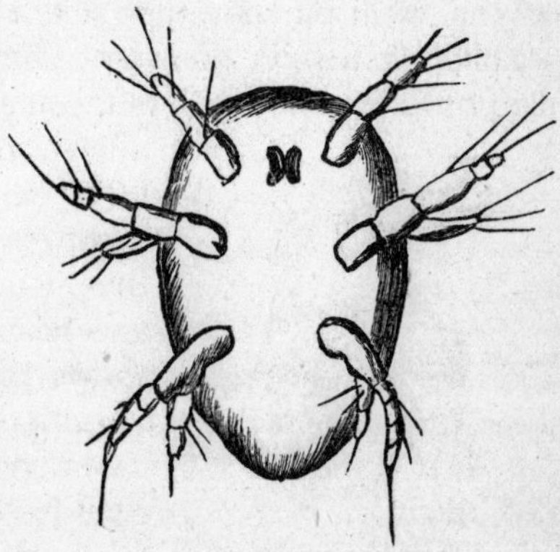

Fig. 258.—A Nauplius larva (seen from below and greatly enlarged). Note unpaired eye and three pairs of appendages

The four included orders have already been enumerated; *i.e.* 1. Barnacles (*Cirripedia*); 2. Bivalve Crustacea (*Ostracoda*); 3. Fork-footed Crustacea (*Copepoda*); and 4. Leaf-footed Crustacea (*Phyllopoda*).

Order 1.—BARNACLES (Cirripedia)

This is a remarkable group of marine Crustacea, all of which are either fixed or parasitic, and have undergone considerable, or, it may be, profound modifications resulting from their mode of life. Leaving out of consideration the degenerate parasitic forms, which will be dealt with elsewhere, there remain the widely-distributed group of Barnacles, of which the best known are the Ship-Barnacle (*Lepas anatifera*), and the Acorn-Barnacles (species of *Balanus*), which encrust the rocks between tide-marks on the coasts of Britain.

The characters of the group will best be understood by briefly describing the Ship-Barnacle (*Lepas anatifera*), large numbers of which are often found attached to floating objects which have been cast up on our shores, and which in old days were a serious nuisance to sailors, as they attached themselves to the wooden bottoms of ships in such vast numbers as to impede movement.

The *Ship-Barnacle* (fig. 259) is attached by means of a long soft *stalk* covered with corrugated skin, and upon this is borne a flattened oval swelling, covered by a number of shelly pieces, suggesting at first sight that the animal is a kind of Mollusc. A closer examination will show that these pieces are attached to a couple of soft flaps united together on one side, but leaving between them on the other side a slit through which, in a living specimen, a bundle of hairy-jointed filaments will from time to time protrude and spread out, being drawn back again immediately afterwards. These tendril-like structures, or *cirri*, which act as a kind of casting-net, whereby food is swept into the mouth, are six pairs of bifurcated appendages, and their jointed nature shows that we are dealing, not with a Mollusc, but with an Arthropod. To a strong imagination they might suggest feathers in a vague way, and they are probably responsible for the well-known natural-history legend, according to which the Solan Goose ("Barnacle" Goose) develops from a barnacle, the chicks falling into the water when sufficiently grown to look after themselves. The specific name of the barnacle, "anatifera" (L. *anser*, a goose; *fero*, I bear), has reference to this old belief. On removing the shell, and the flaps to which it is attached, the soft body of the animal will be found, consisting mainly of *thorax*, to which the tendril-like appendages are attached. The *abdomen* is reduced to a limbless process ending in a long filament. The under (ventral) side of the thorax is turned upwards, and at its front end will be found the *mouth*, provided with upper lip, mandibles, and two pairs of maxillæ. No eyes or feelers are visible, but study of the development shows that the animal is fixed by its head, which has grown into a long stalk, at the end of which were situated the short antennules, that served as organs of attachment from which the sticky secretion of special "cement glands" was poured out. The antennæ, present in the larva, entirely disappear in the adult. Huxley has graphically compared a barnacle to a man lying upon his back and kicking his food into his mouth.

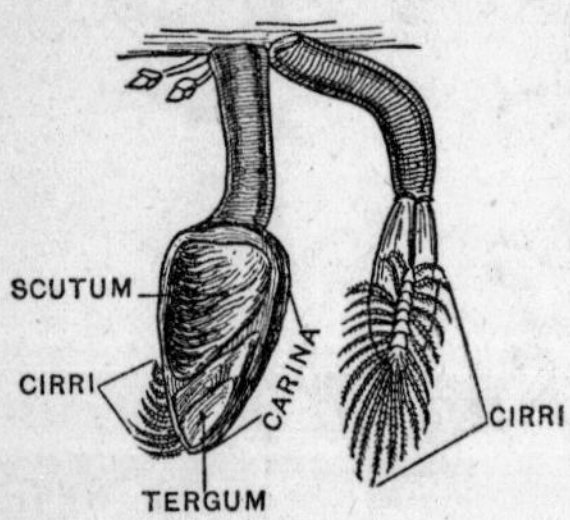

Fig. 259.—Ship-Barnacles (*Lepas anatifera*), reduced

Acorn-Barnacles agree essentially in structure with the ship-barnacle, but do not possess a stalk, and there is an extra protection to the body in the form of a sort of shelly cup made up of a number of pieces fused together. The appearance of the body within the cup has no doubt suggested the name "acorn"-barnacle, but the resemblance is remote.

Order 2.—Bivalve Crustacea (Ostracoda)

These are small Crustacea common both in salt and fresh water, especially where the bottom is muddy. Examination of the mud from almost any pond will often reveal the presence of

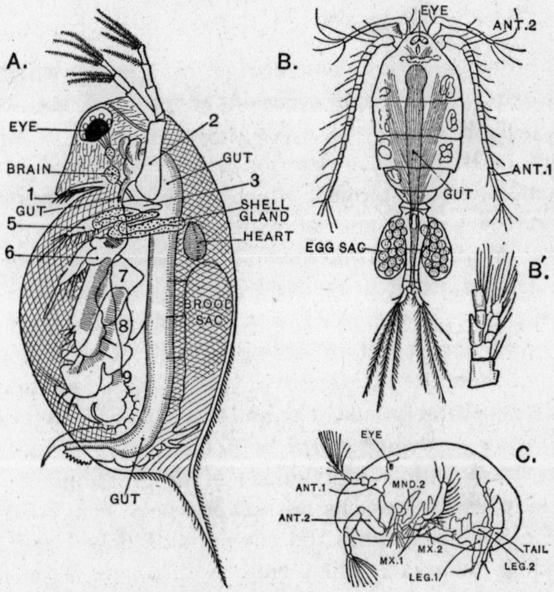

Fig. 260.—Small Fresh-water Crustacea (much enlarged to various scales)

A, Water-Flea (*Daphnia*): 1, antennule; 2, antenna; 3, mandible; 5–9, flattened thoracic appendages. B, Cyclops (seen from above): ANT.1, antennule; ANT.2, antenna. B′, Swimming-foot of Cyclops, showing the typical forked shape. C, Mussel-Shrimp (*Cypris*): ANT.1, antennule; ANT.2, antenna; MND., mandible; MX.1, first maxilla; MX.2, second maxilla.

one or more *Mussel-Shrimps*, species of the typical genus *Cypris* (fig. 260), which therefore furnishes a convenient type. The most striking feature is the presence of a *bivalve shell*, comparable to the carapace of other forms and entirely enclosing the body, reminding one of the arrangement characteristic of bivalve Molluscs (p. 311). The resemblance is enhanced by the fact that the two valves of the shell can be closed by the contraction of an adductor muscle and opened by the action of an elastic ligament. The body of the animal is extremely short, and the abdomen is a mere vestige. Segmentation is only indicated by the appendages, of which there are but seven pairs, five belonging to the head (two pairs of feelers and three pairs of jaws), and the remainder, in the form of narrow pointed legs, to the *thorax*. These legs can be protruded from the shell, and so can the well-developed feelers which are used as organs of locomotion, as in a nauplius larva. There is an unpaired eye on the front of the head.

Order 3.—FORK-FOOTED CRUSTACEA (Copepoda)

This order is a vast assemblage of species which are for the most part minute, and occur in all parts of the world both in salt and fresh water. Many of them are found in huge shoals at the surface of the open sea, forming a variety of ***plankton***, as such assemblages are termed, which furnishes an important item in the food of whales and of many fishes, such as the herring. The fishes, however, do not have it all their own way with the Copepods, for attached to their eyes and gills may often be found parasitic members of the order, which are often strangely modified. Leaving such forms out of consideration for the present, and turning our attention to free-living Copepods, we may take a common fresh-water genus, *Cyclops* (fig. 260), as a type of the order. It can be distinguished with the naked eye as an active whitish creature with a jerky mode of progression.

The body of Cyclops has not unaptly been compared in shape to half of a split pear, with the convex side dorsal and the stalk corresponding to a tail. The body is distinctly segmented, and the five *head-segments* are fused with one another and with the first thoracic segment. Then follow the five free segments of the *thorax* and the four narrow segments of the *tail*, the last of which bears a *tail-fork* provided with two bunches of bristles. Upon the front of the head is a single reddish *eye*, which has suggested the generic name of Cyclops; and there are the usual five pairs of head appendages, of which the first, *i.e.* the *antennæ*, are very large and employed as oars. The thorax bears four large pairs of forked *swimming-feet*, and the abdomen is limbless. The female, which is the sex commonly seen, usually has a pair of large *egg-sacs* attached at the base of the abdomen.

Order 4.—LEAF-FOOTED CRUSTACEA (Phyllopoda)

These are Crustacea of varying size, though none are very large, which are for the most part inhabitants of fresh water. The segments and appendages differ greatly in number in different cases, but those of the latter situated farther back than the head are characterized by their flattened leaf-like form. There are two sub-orders—1. Gill-footed Phyllopods (Branchiopoda), and 2. Water-Fleas (Cladocera).

1. *Gill-footed Phyllopods* possess a special interest, since they not improbably present many of the characters distinguishing the ancestral stock from which all the different groups of Crustacea are descended.

A typical genus is *Apus* (fig. 261), species of which are sometimes found in great abundance at various localities on the Continent, especially in flooded meadows. For the sub-order this form reaches a considerable size, being as much as 2 inches in length. It is of a greenish-brown colour, and though segmentation is not apparent in the head, the rest of the body is composed of a large number of obvious segments. The most striking feature is the presence of a broad thin *carapace*, which, arising from the head, extends backwards so as to cover the back and sides of the greater part of the body. The narrow posterior end of the abdomen remains uncovered by the carapace, and terminates in a pair of long jointed filaments. The *head* bears a minute pair of antennules, vestiges of antennæ, strong mandibles, and two pairs of maxillæ. A very large number of flattened lobed swimming-feet are attached to the *thorax* and front part of the *abdomen*. They are not limited in number to one pair per body-segment, as is the case with the majority of Crustacea. A typical *swimming-foot* consists of a number of small pointed inner lobes, and two larger outer lobes, of which one is a soft

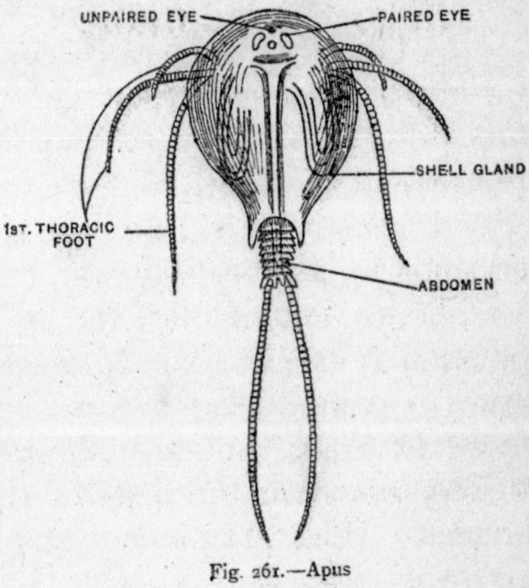

Fig. 261.—Apus

pear-shaped *gill.* Such a limb is regarded by many as the generalized type from which the varied kinds of appendages found within the class have been derived by modifications of different kinds (see p. 403). This may perhaps be so, but it is not always easy to recognize with certainty the equivalent parts in different Crustacean groups. All these swimming-feet in Apus are by no means exactly alike; *e.g.* some of the inner lobes of the first thoracic pair are drawn out into long filaments, liable at first glance to be mistaken for antennules and antennæ, while in the female the eleventh thoracic pair are partly modified into *brood-capsules* within which the eggs develop.

The *excretory organs* of Apus are not, as in the higher Crustacea, antennary glands, but coiled tubular *shell-glands* which open to the exterior upon the second maxillæ. Three *eyes* are placed close together on the top of the head—a small unpaired "nauplius eye" in the middle line, and a pair of compound eyes.

2. The *Water-Fleas* (Cladocera) are small active Crustacea, mostly inhabiting fresh water. The characters of the sub-order are well seen in the very common form *Daphnia* (fig. 260). The thorax and shortened abdomen are enclosed in a bivalve *carapace* which grows back from the head. The usual five pairs of appendages are borne by the head (except second maxillæ, which are absent), and of these the most remarkable are the large forked plume-like *antennæ* which are used as swimming organs. There are five pairs of flattened thoracic *swimming-feet*, something like those of Apus, but the short abdomen is limbless. It bends sharply round to the under surface and ends in a pair of curved bristles. When Daphnia is examined alive under the microscope, an oval pulsating sac will be noticed near the dorsal surface. This is the *heart.* The coiled *shell-gland* is also easily seen, and the large *compound eye* is a conspicuous object. It lies in the front of the head, and has been formed by the fusion of two lateral eyes. It is constantly in a state of trembling movement. A small *nauplius eye* is present a little farther back.

CLASS 6.—KING-CRABS (XIPHOSURA)

This small but interesting class includes only the *King-Crab* (*Limulus*), a large marine Arthropod living in shallow water in the East Indies and the warmer parts of the West Atlantic and

West Pacific. There has been much discussion as to its classificatory position, some authorities including it in the Crustacea and others in the Arachnida. In support of the latter view it has been shown that, allowing for the fact that one is a marine and the other a terrestrial animal, there is a very remarkable agreement between King-Crab and Scorpion. As, however, the matter is by no means settled, it appears better for the present to assign Limulus a class of its own.

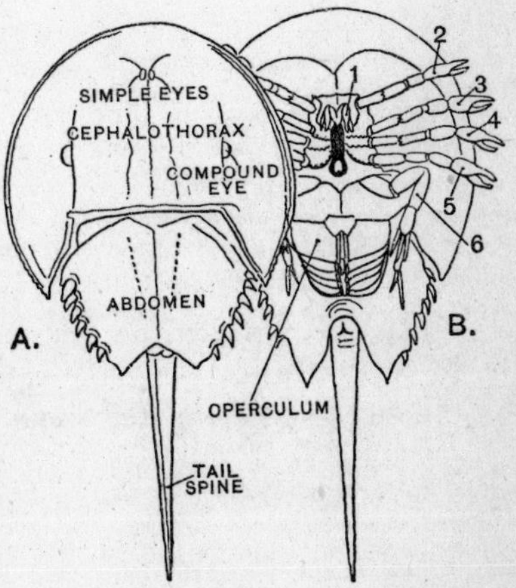

Fig. 262.—King-Crab (*Limulus*), reduced. A, From above; B, from below. 1, Chelicerae; 2–6, legs. The mouth is seen in B as a darkly-shaded slit between the bases of the legs.

The body of a King-Crab (fig. 262) is divided into two regions, a *cephalo-thorax* covered above by a large horse-shoe-shaped shield, and a similarly protected *abdomen* to which a long movable *spine* is attached behind. A pair of *simple eyes* are situated on the top of the front shield towards the anterior end, and farther back there are a pair of large *compound eyes*, placed at a greater distance from each other.

Upon the under side the appendages can be seen, the first of which are the small *chelicerœ*, provided with pincers and situated in front of the mouth. Then follow five pairs of *legs* apparently equivalent to the pedipalps and legs of the Scorpion. The first of them are provided with pincers in the female, and the next three pairs are similarly provided in both sexes. The ends of the last pair are curiously modified so as to fit them for digging. The bases of these leg-like appendages are provided with biting projections, which between them almost surround the elongated *mouth*. The remaining appendages are six plates, obviously formed by the fusion of pairs of appendages and borne by the abdomen. The first of them is equivalent apparently to the operculum of Scorpion (p. 386), and the second to the combs of that animal. All but the first bear numerous gill-folds.

CLASS 7.—SEA-SPIDERS (PYCNOGONIDA)

These are widely distributed marine Arthropods, mostly of small size. Some zoologists associate them with Arachnida, but their real affinities are as yet undetermined. Taking such a typical form as the Shore Pycnogon (*Pycnogonum littorale*), we see (fig. 263) that the spider-like appearance is due to the presence of four slender pairs of thoracic limbs, in front of which are three pairs of smaller appendages, of which the first bear pincers and the last are used by the males for carrying the eggs about. The mouth is situated on the end of an elongated snout, and there are four simple eyes.

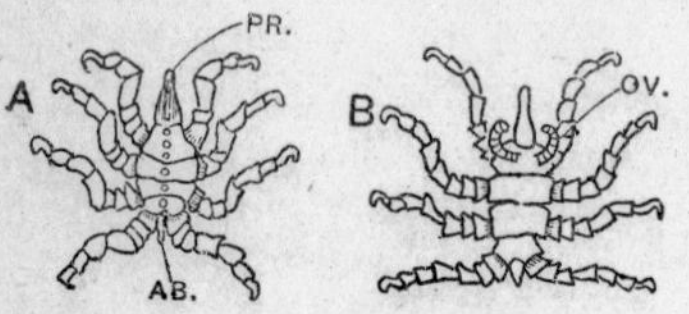

Fig. 263.—Shore Pycnogon (*Pycnogonum littorale*)
A, From above; B, from below. AB. Abdomen; OV. egg-bearing appendages; PR. snout.

CHAPTER IX

STRUCTURE AND CLASSIFICATION OF SEGMENTED WORMS, SIPHON-WORMS, WHEEL-ANIMALCULES, MOSS-POLYPES, AND LAMP-SHELLS

SEGMENTED WORMS (ANNELIDA)

This phylum is a vast assemblage of marine, fresh-water, and terrestrial worms and leeches, which agree with one another in the possession of a bilaterally symmetrical body divided into numerous similar segments, and in the absence of jointed appendages like those of the Arthropoda. The body-wall consists of skin with underlying layers of muscle; there is a muscular pharynx; and the excretory organs are in the form of numerous pairs of convoluted tubes (nephridia), each of which, in typical cases, opens on the one hand to the exterior, and on the other into a body-cavity of the same nature as that found in Vertebrates (see p. 42). The phylum is divided into two classes: 1. Bristle-Worms (Chætopoda), and 2. Leeches (Discophora).

CLASS I.—BRISTLE-WORMS (CHÆTOPODA)

A good typical example of this group is the so-called *Sea-Centipede* (fig. 264), a name popularly applied to several species of the genus *Nereis* which are found upon our coasts. The body is bilaterally symmetrical and obviously divided into a large number of *segments*, all very similar to one another except those at the extreme ends. There are clearly none of the jointed lateral appendages which are so characteristic of Arthropods, their place being taken by hollow "foot-stumps" (parapodia), of which each segment bears a pair. The nearest approach to such foot-stumps among the Arthropoda are the legs of Peripatus (p. 399). Examination by means of a lens will show that each *foot-stump* is divided into an upper lobe and a lower lobe near each of which is a short feeler or cirrus. Imbedded in each lobe is a bundle of bristles or *setæ*, of which one is much larger and stronger than the rest, though it only just projects from the surface of the body. These setæ are of great use in locomotion, acting as holdfasts by means of which the body gets a purchase on sand or the like. They exhibit all sorts of variations in shape. The *head*, upon the under side of which is the mouth, consists of a mouth-segment, and a projection in front of the mouth which may conveniently be called the head-lobe. From the upper side of this lobe, near the front, spring two short tentacles, and there are two much larger "palps" which arise from the under side of the same region rather farther back. Not only do these last-named structures act as sensory organs, but they also serve as lips to some extent. Upon the upper side of the head-lobe are four simple *eyes*, looking like black specks. The mouth-segment is provided with four pairs of slender feelers, which are apparently of the same nature as the cirri of the trunk-segments. None of the appendages are converted into jaws, a feature which is so characteristic of Arthropods, though it may be remembered that in the member of that group which comes nearest to the Annelida, *i.e.* Peripatus, there is only one pair of these structures (see p. 399). Turning now to the last tail segment, which is perforated by the opening of the intestine, we shall find that it is comparatively small and devoid of foot-stumps, though it possesses one pair of long backwardly-directed cirri.

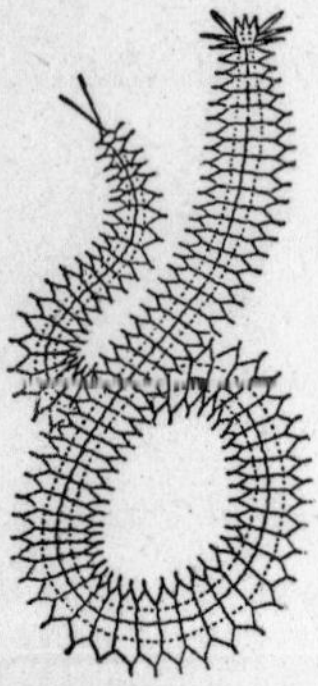

Fig. 264.—A Sea-Centipede (*Nereis*), diagrammatic

Internal Structure of Nereis (fig. 265). The *body-wall* presents very primitive features, reminding one of Peripatus (see p. 401). It consists of the *skin*, which is practically little more than a thin epidermis covered by a tough cuticle, and two underlying *muscle-layers*, of which the outer is composed of fibres which run transversely, while the other consists of four prominent bands in which the fibres have a longitudinal direction. Closely connected with the body-wall, though scarcely perhaps forming part of it, is an oblique sheet of muscle on each side, made up of numerous fan-shaped sections, which take origin near the sides of the ventral nerve-cord and spread out in the foot-stumps, to which they are attached and serve to move.

Digestive organs.—On cutting open the body of Nereis we find that it is traversed by a straight *food-tube*, between which and the body-wall is a large *body-cavity* which corresponds with that of Vertebrates in being a cœlom, *i.e.* a body-cavity which contains a lymph-like fluid and communicates with the exterior by excretory tubes (see p. 428). The segmentation prominent externally is emphasized internally by the division of the body into a series of compartments by transverse partitions attached

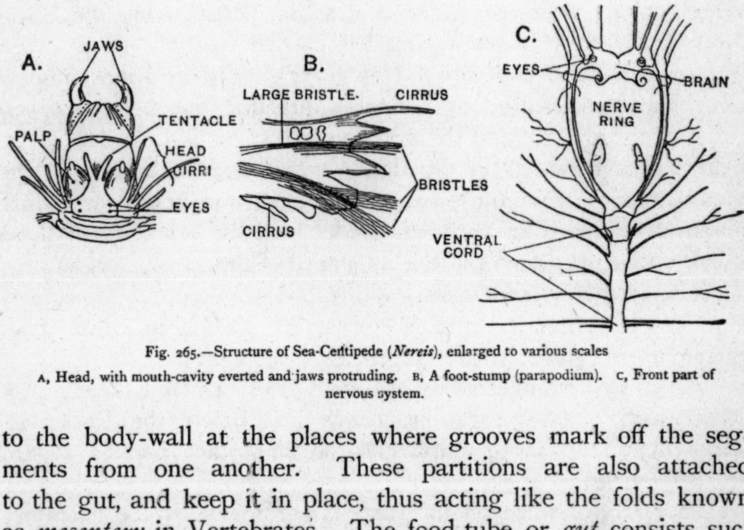

Fig. 265.—Structure of Sea-Centipede (*Nereis*), enlarged to various scales

A, Head, with mouth-cavity everted and jaws protruding. B, A foot-stump (parapodium). C, Front part of nervous system.

to the body-wall at the places where grooves mark off the segments from one another. These partitions are also attached to the gut, and keep it in place, thus acting like the folds known as *mesentery* in Vertebrates. The food-tube or *gut* consists successively of mouth-cavity, pharynx, gullet, and intestine. An interesting peculiarity of the short mouth-cavity is found in the fact that it can be everted, or turned inside out, by means of appropriate muscles, and under those circumstances the absence of limb-jaws is made up for by the protrusion of a pair of hard horny jaws carried on the inner side of the pharynx and acting as a very efficient pair of pincers for seizing food. The everted mouth-cavity is restored to its normal position by certain muscles attached to its wall which draw it back. The pharynx has extremely thick walls, another point in which one is reminded of Peripatus (see p. 401). The gullet is short and narrow, and a pair of glands open into it. The intestine, which makes up the greater part of the gut, is thin-walled.

Circulatory Organs.—We can here distinguish, as in a Vertebrate (see p. 38), between a blood-system and a lymph-system. The *blood-system* contains red blood, the colour being due to the presence of the same pigment (hæmoglobin) as that found in Vertebrates (see p. 265), though here it is dissolved in the plasma, or liquid part of the blood, and is not contained in corpuscles. The vessels which carry the blood form a closed system, the smaller branches of which break up into capillary net-works. No heart is present, and the pumping is effected by the larger vessels, along which waves of contraction pass, forcing the blood onwards, much as digesting food is carried onwards in an intestine by peristaltic contraction (see p. 37). The two most important blood-vessels are longitudinal in direction, one being a *dorsal vessel* above the gut and the other a *ventral vessel* below it. The blood flows forwards in the dorsal vessel and backwards in the ventral one. From these two chief trunks transverse vessels are given off regularly in segmental order, and the branches of these break up into net-works in the substance of the various organs.

The *lymph system* consists of the body-cavity, and the colourless lymph which it contains consists of plasma in which float numerous irregular lymph corpuscles (see p. 42).

Respiration is effected in the body-wall, which is richly provided with blood-vessels branching just below the epidermis. Most likely the foot-stumps play an important part in regard to this function.

Excretion of nitrogenous waste is performed by the excretory tubes or nephridia, of which a pair are present in almost every segment. Each of these organs is essentially a ciliated tube which begins by a small funnel placed just in front of one of the partitions which cross the body-cavity, runs back to pierce this, and ultimately opens to the exterior on the under surface of the body close to the base of a foot-stump.

The *Central Nervous System* consists of a *nerve-ring* encircling the commencement of the gut and a *ventral nerve-cord*, resembling, therefore, the corresponding organs of a lobster. The nerve-ring is thickened dorsally into a closely-fused pair of brain- or cerebral-ganglia, and the ventral cord, which is of double nature, swells into a pair of closely approximated ganglia in each segment.

Sense Organs.—The cirri and head-tentacles are presumably organs of *touch*. It is likely that the palps borne on the head have to do either with *taste* or *smell*, or it may be with both.

There are no auditory organs, and the four simple *eyes* have already been mentioned.

The Bristle-Worms are subdivided into three orders:—1. Many-bristled Worms (Polychæta); 2. Few-bristled Worms (Oligochæta); and 3. Simple Segmented Worms (Archiannelida).

Order 1.—Many-bristled Worms (Polychæta)

This order embraces an enormous number of marine worms, possessing a considerable number of setæ and agreeing in many other particulars with Nereis, which is a type of the order. Over thirty families are recognized, grouped into seven sub-orders, but it will be sufficient for our purpose to divide the order into two groups:—1. Free-living Polychætes (Errantia), and 2. Sedentary Polychætes (Sedentaria).

1. *Free-living Polychætes* (Errantia), of which Nereis is a good example, are carnivorous forms which move actively about in pursuit of their prey, swimming, crawling, or burrowing. To this habit their structure corresponds, for the locomotor organs (foot-stumps) are well-developed, as also is the head-lobe, with its eyes and feelers. The pharynx can be protruded in the way described for Nereis and is usually armed with horny jaws.

Only one or two British forms can be mentioned here in addition to Nereis. Species of *Polynoe* are common on our shores, and these can readily be identified by their elongated oval form and the presence of a double series of scales (elytra) on the upper surface, which appear to be organs of respiration. Built on somewhat the same lines is the conspicuous "Sea-Mouse" (*Aphrodite*), the plump body of which attains a considerable size. The setæ are of several kinds, and very numerous: some of those arising from the upper divisions of the foot-stumps are much elongated and beautifully iridescent. As in Polynoe, there is a double row of elytra, but they are here covered by a tough membrane consisting of numerous small setæ matted together.

2. *Sedentary Polychætes* (Sedentaria) either have limited powers of movement, and inhabit permanent tubes, or else are burrowing forms, which pour out a sticky fluid from the skin that glues together the sand or mud surrounding them into a sort of temporary case. They live upon vegetable matter. The head-

region may either be much reduced and devoid of appendages, or else, in the forms inhabiting firm permanent tubes, provided with numerous tactile filaments and large branching gills. The foot-stumps are not so well developed as in the free-living forms, and the pharynx is not armed with horny jaws or teeth.

The *Lugworm* (*Arenicola piscatorum*) (fig. 266) is well known as a burrowing form highly esteemed as bait. It makes U-shaped passages in the mud or sand, near which may be seen coiled "worm-castings" made up of sand and undigested food, which have been voided from the body. The most striking external feature consists in the presence of branching *gills* projecting from the middle region of the body. *Cirratulus* is a long cylindrical worm often to be found buried in the sand underneath stones. Its locomotor organs are much reduced, and the dorsal cirri are slender elongated filaments which project above the surface of the sand and act as gills, the active wriggling movements which they constantly execute giving them a resemblance to small red worms, for which they are often mistaken. Another common shore form is *Sabellaria*, which glues sand-grains together into a tube. Large numbers of these animals live associated together, and their tubes often form compact masses of considerable extent. Every-one must have noticed at the sea-side small convoluted limy tubes encrusting oyster-shells or stones. These belong to *Serpula*, a particularly beautiful form, in which the head bears two brightly-coloured bunches of gill-filaments. One of these is converted into a conical horny stopper, which closes the opening of the tube when the worm has withdrawn itself. *Spirorbis* is a related but much smaller form, in which the tube is coiled into a flat spiral. Large numbers of these may often be found adhering to brown sea-weeds.

Fig. 266. Lugworm (*Arenicola piscatorum*)

Order 2.—Few-bristled Worms (Oligochæta)

These are segmented worms which for the most part live in fresh water or burrow in the earth. They lack feelers and foot-stumps, while gills are but rarely present. Locomotion is effected by the contractions of the muscular body-wall aided by the setæ, which are comparatively few in number. The pharynx is not armed with horny jaws.

A common fresh-water form is the Red River-Worm (*Tubifex rivulorum*), a small creature often to be seen in ponds, partially imbedded in the mud. Large numbers often occur together, making up conspicuous red patches, that disappear when the mud is disturbed, which means that the worms have withdrawn themselves into it.

Earth-Worms are found in almost all parts of the world, and there are a number of British species, of which the Common Earth-Worm (*Lumbricus herculeus*) is usually taken as a type. The *head* consists of a mouth-segment and a head-lobe, and is entirely devoid of eyes or feelers. The *trunk* is divided into a large number of clearly-defined segments, and not very far from its front end is a band-like thickening, the *girdle* (clitellum), which has to do with the formation of capsules in which the eggs are enclosed. The popular notion is that it is the result of injury by the spade. If an earth-worm be passed, tail first, between the finger and thumb, a distinct feeling of roughness will be experienced, due to the presence of four double rows of setæ, the tips of which just project above the skin.

Order 3.—Simple Segmented Worms (Archiannelida)

A small number of simple marine worms constitute this order, and it is probable that to some extent at least they possess the characters of the ancestral stock from which all segmented worms are descended. It must not be forgotten, however, in this connection, that simplicity of structure is often the result of degeneration, and it is possible that some of these creatures may be on the down-grade. There is a small head-lobe, and most of them have a fairly long trunk. The segmentation of the body is well marked by the presence of encircling grooves, and also by rings of cilia, which serve as locomotor organs in place of setæ and foot-stumps, here entirely absent. Probably the most primitive of the Archiannelids is the minute *Dinophilus*, of which more than one species occur on our coasts. It presents certain points of affinity to the unsegmented worms, which will be considered later. *Polygordius* is a slender cylindrical red worm found, among other places, in the Mediterranean, and also recorded from the British coasts. It is more complex in structure than Dinophilus.

A word of explanation may be here necessary of the statement that the simplicity of these creatures is possibly not primitive, but the result of degeneration. Take, for example, the absence of setæ as a character to be criticised from the two points of view. This negative character may mean that the ancestors of the group did not possess setæ, and, if so, the character is a primitive one. To maintain, on the other hand, that the absence of setæ is due to degeneration is to suppose that the ancestral forms did possess setæ, which have been lost in the course of evolution. That such a thing is possible becomes clear if we compare Nereis with some of the sedentary Polychætes and with earth-worms. In the first case well-developed foot-stumps provided with setæ are present; in the second, these structures are reduced; while ordinary earthworms possess setæ but no parapodia. A further reduction would give the condition found in Polygordius (and some Oligochætes).

Class II.—LEECHES (Discophora)

Leeches are typically fresh-water or terrestrial forms, though some of them are marine. Most of them are blood-sucking parasites. The average characters of the group are conveniently exemplified by the common Medicinal Leech (*Hirudo medicinalis*). The elongated body, capable of considerable variation in form, is flattened from above downwards, and is provided with a *sucker* at each end, by alternate attachment of which looping movements can be performed, much as in a looper caterpillar (see p. 364). Both the suckers face downwards, and the mouth is in the middle of the front one, while the intestine opens outside and just above the hinder one. Encircling grooves divide the body into a large number of narrow rings, several of which go to a segment. Feelers, foot-stumps, and setæ are entirely absent. Ten simple *eyes* may be seen as black specks on the front end of the body, placed close to the margin of the upper surface. The well-known three-rayed bite of the leech is made by the finely-toothed margins of three horny jaws with which the muscular pharynx is provided.

Although the Medicinal Leech does occur in this country, a

much commoner native form is the Horse-Leech (*Aulastomum gulo*), which has smaller jaws and does not attack animals, preying only upon small aquatic animals. Some of the Leeches do not possess jaws, and these are grouped in a special subdivision of the class. Many of them are parasitic upon fish.

SIPHON-WORMS (GEPHYREA)

This group is retained as a matter of convenience to include a number of worm-like animals, little known except to professed naturalists, and some of which appear to be related to Annelida. None of them exhibit other than feeble traces of segmentation.

The *Bristle-Tail* (*Echiurus*) (fig. 267) has a stout cylindrical body covered by tough skin. The *mouth* is situated on the under surface at the base of a narrow forward projection known as the *proboscis*, which must be regarded as a head-lobe. It is used both as an organ of locomotion and in procuring food, a deep groove running along its under side to the mouth. Among the characters which show affinity to the Bristle-Worms may be mentioned the possession of *setæ*, one or two rings of which encircle the hinder end of the body, while there are a pair of hook-like bristles imbedded in the skin not far behind the mouth. Behind them are the openings of two pairs of excretory tubes (brown tubes) comparable to the nephridia of segmented worms.

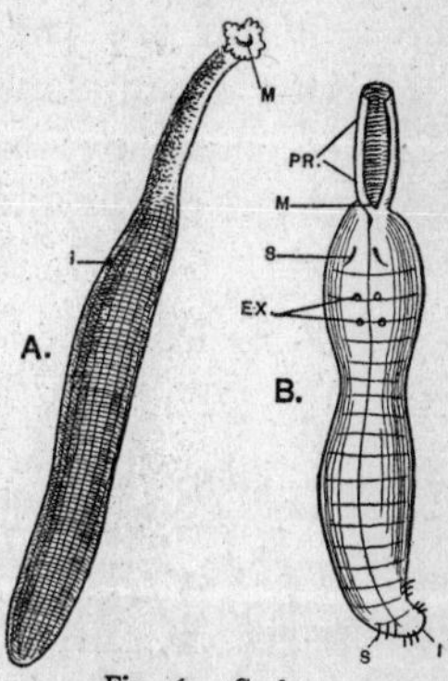

Fig. 267.—Gephyrea
Siphon-Worm (*Sipunculus*): M, mouth; I, intestinal aperture. B, Bristle-tail (*Echiurus*): PR., proboscis; M, mouth; S, S, setæ; EX, excretory apertures; I, intestinal aperture.

The *Siphon-Worm* (*Sipunculus*) (fig. 267), numbers of which are sometimes cast up on the shore by storms, burrows in the sand, which it swallows for the sake of the contained organic debris, in this respect reminding one of the earth-worm, to which also our native species have a slight external resemblance, though they differ markedly in the absence of setæ and body-segments. Examination of a living Sipunculus shows that the animal possesses the peculiar power of turning the narrow front part of its body outside in (introverting it), this and the reverse process often being rapidly repeated for a considerable number of times. When the body is fully extended the *mouth* will be seen at its tip surrounded by a series of short, grooved *tentacles*. This creature departs further than Echiurus from the typical segmented worms, for it is entirely destitute of setæ, and the convoluted intestine opens to the exterior not far from the front end of the body on the upper surface.

WHEEL-ANIMALCULES (ROTIFERA OR ROTATORIA)

The Wheel-Animalcules are minute transparent animals mostly found in fresh water, though some are marine, and others are to be found on damp earth and vegetation. They present great diversity in form and structure, and as microscopic objects are unsurpassed for beauty and interest. Unfortunately their true affinities are yet to seek, but as likely as not they are the degenerate descendants of higher worms, and are to be looked upon as permanent larvæ, the original adult form having been dropped out of the life-history. That such a thing is possible is shown by the case of the Axolotl among Amphibia, to which reference has already been made (p. 249).

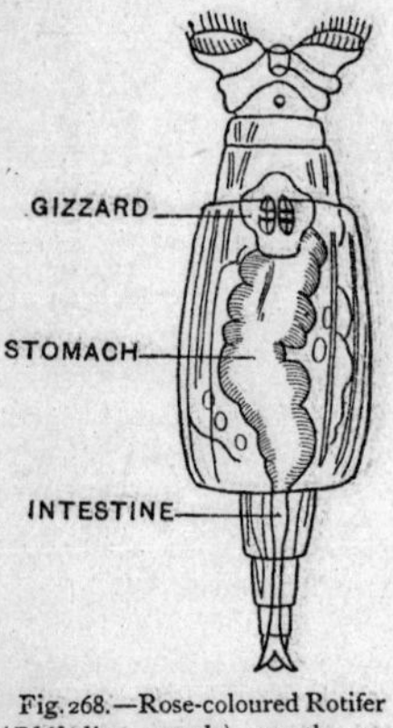

Fig. 268.—Rose-coloured Rotifer (*Philodina roseola*), greatly enlarged

A common and beautiful fresh-water form, which will serve as a type, is the *Rose-coloured Rotifer* (*Philodina roseola*) (fig. 268). The elongated body is covered by a firm cuticle, and this is marked by transverse furrows so as to give a deceptive appearance of segmentation. The posterior end of the body tapers into a jointed tail ending in a pair of forceps, and by means of this region the animal is able to progress somewhat like a leech. When the rotifer is fully extended, a couple of prominences are seen at the front end which together constitute the *wheel-organ*. Each of them is fringed with a circlet of cilia, and as these move one after another in a very regular way a deceptive appearance of rotation is produced, suggesting the movement of a wheel. By means of this organ the animal is able to swim and it also sets up currents by which food particles are brought to the mouth, lying in a depression at the front end of the body. The *mouth* opens into a mouth-cavity and this again into a muscular pharynx, which is continued by a short gullet into a wide stomach, this narrowing into an intestine which opens to the exterior on the upper surface of the body. Special interest attaches to the *pharynx*, usually known as the mastax, for the lining of this is thickened into a complicated set of hard pieces which work upon one another to crush the food. The transparency of the animal permits this process to be clearly seen, and it presents a curious and interesting spectacle, reminding one of the gastric mill in a lobster or the gizzard of a bird. The last section of the intestine is a *cloaca*, into which opens a thin-walled bladder (contractile vesicle) receiving nitrogenous waste matter from a couple of branched excretory tubes, which in some respects resemble the corresponding structures of the unsegmented worms. There are no specialized organs of circulation, these being represented simply by a fluid-containing body-cavity. *Respiration* takes place by the general surface of the body, as is very commonly the case with minute animals of all grades. The *nervous system* consists of a comparatively large brain, placed in the front part of the body above the mouth. A red *eye-spot* is imbedded in its upper surface, and it is also connected with a stiff *dorsal tentacle* (calcar) which ends in a bunch of stiff hairs and is probably an organ of touch

Rotifers differ from one another in many respects. The general outline of the body varies largely, and the wheel-organ in particular may be very variously shaped. Sometimes the cuticle is thickened into a firm protecting carapace. Many members of the group are fixed, and in this case a cement-gland opens on the tip of the tail. Such forms often live in a cup or "house" of various nature. Some of these will be described later on, when the defences of animals are dealt with in detail.

MOSS-POLYPES AND LAMP-SHELLS (Molluscoida)

Considerable doubt attaches to the affinities of the two aquatic groups here associated together for convenience sake. They were originally included in the Mollusca. Milne-Edwards established "Molluscoidea" for Moss-Polypes and Tunicates, to which Huxley added Lamp-Shells. When, however, it was proved beyond doubt that the last group should without doubt be associated with the Vertebrata (pp. 297–300), the term Molluscoida gradually fell into disuse, and the Moss-Polypes and Lamp-Shells were cut adrift. There is good reason for thinking that they are distantly related to the segmented worms, but their relationships to that group and to one another are very obscure. Perhaps the simplest plan will be to retain the old division Molluscoida for their reception, provided the derivation of the word (=mollusc-like) be ignored. As Huxley himself has remarked, it is often necessary to retain terms, the derivations of which have reference to obsolete views. The two included classes —1. Moss-Polypes (Polyzoa) and 2. Lamp-Shells (Brachiopoda)— are best considered separately.

Class I.—MOSS-POLYPES (Polyzoa)

These are small aquatic animals which are for the most part inhabitants of the sea, though some of them are found in fresh water. They present a peculiarity which so far we have only met with in some Tunicates (p. 300), *i.e.* they are *colonial.* From the egg a free-swimming embryo is hatched, which after a time becomes fixed and founds a colony by means of budding, in a way suggestive of what takes place in plants. The shape of the colony naturally depends upon the manner in which the buds arise, and it may be compact, flattened, or branched in a more or less elaborate way. There is a firm external skeleton for the support of the colony, sometimes of gelatinous nature, but more frequently of horny or calcareous consistency. Each member of the community (zooid) is lodged in a special depression or cup, and within the protective investment the bodies of the different zooids are connected together. The Polyzoa are among those animals included in the old group of "zoophytes" (Gk. *zōŏn*, an animal; *phyto*, a plant), so named from the exploded idea that they partook of the nature both of plants and animals, a notion largely due to the fixed nature and plant-like appearance of many kinds. Even yet some of them are popularly confounded with sea-weeds, and of such one of the most abundant is the Sea-Mat (*Flustra*) (fig. 269), the flattened branching skeletons of which are among the common objects thrown up on the shore by the action of the waves. Examination of one of these with a lens reveals the presence of innumerable closely-packed little cups, the homes of the constituent zooids. Another common form is the Lace-Coralline (*Membranipora*), seen at low tide as a delicate lace-like encrustation upon the large brown sea-weeds.

Fig. 269.—Polyzoa. 1, Sea-Mat (*Flustra*); 2, Sea-Net (*Retepora*)

The structure of the group is most conveniently studied in one of the fresh-water Polyzoa, the *Plume Coralline* (*Plumatella repens*) (fig. 270), the branched creeping colonies of which are

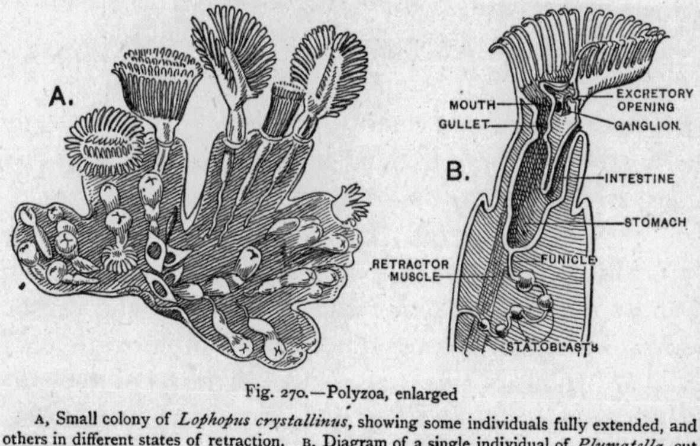

Fig. 270.—Polyzoa, enlarged

A, Small colony of *Lophopus crystallinus*, showing some individuals fully extended, and others in different states of retraction. B, Diagram of a single individual of *Plumatella*, cut through centre of body.

found creeping upon stones and other objects. The *skeleton* is horny, and from the tip of each branch a zooid can be protruded, the free end bearing the *mouth* surrounded by a double crown of ciliated *tentacles* in the form of a double horse-shoe, within the concavity of which is the external opening of the intestine. This protrusible part of the body is drawn back or introverted by a retractor muscle at the approach of danger, reminding one of the arrangement which obtains in Sipunculus (p. 433), a further resemblance to which animal is found in the approximation of the two openings of the gut, an obvious convenience in a tube-inhabiting animal. Within the translucent body the U-shaped *food-tube* can be clearly seen, consisting of gullet, stomach, and intestine. There are two small excretory tubes opening near the tentacular crown. The *nervous system* consists of a nerve-ring closely surrounding the beginning of the gullet, and thickened on the side next the intestine into a bilobed brain- or cerebral ganglion. The stomach is connected with the body-wall by a fibrous cord (*funicle*) in which are developed buds known as *statoblasts.* In winter the colony dies down, to be replaced in the following spring by fresh colonies to which these buds give rise.

Another very beautiful fresh-water form, the transparency of which makes it an attractive object under the microscope, is *Lophopus crystallinus* (fig. 270), in which the skeleton is gelatinous, and the entire colony, instead of being fixed, is able to creep slowly along the surface of water-plants.

Class II.—LAMP-SHELLS (Brachiopoda)

These are exclusively marine forms, including only about 120 recent species, though their area of distribution (which includes the British seas) is extremely wide. In some of the geological periods, however, they were extremely abundant, but have gradually declined in importance from very early times.

The most striking characteristic is found in the presence of a *bivalve shell,* which for a long time caused them to be confounded with bivalve Molluscs (pp. 328–338). Taking a typical *Lamp-Shell* (*Waldheimia* or *Terebratula*) (fig. 271) as an illustration, we shall find many well-marked differences from the members of the last-named group. To begin with, the two valves are not right and left, but upper and lower, and they are of unequal size, the upper being the smaller. In side view the shell resembles in outline an ancient lamp, a fact which has given the popular name to the class. The projecting beak of the lower valve is perforated by a rounded hole from which projects a cylindrical stalk by which the animal is attached, and which occupies the same relative position as the wick of the imaginary lamp. The fixed sedentary habit of this and most other forms is another point of contrast with the bulk of bivalve molluscs, which possess a marked power of locomotion. We shall further find that either valve is bilaterally symmetrical, which is not the case with a shell of cockle, mussel, or the like, while the two valves of such a mollusc are typically equal in size. There are also great differences in the minute structure of the shell.

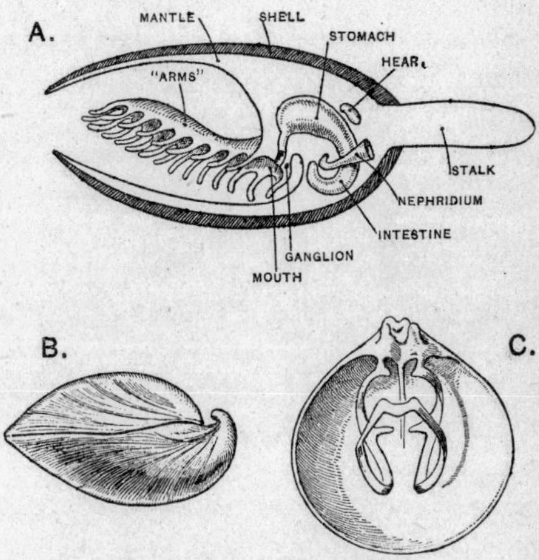

Fig. 271.—Lamp-Shell (*Waldheimia*)

A, Diagram of structure; body cut through centre. B, Shell, seen from left side. C, Interior of dorsal valve, to show "carriage-spring" support for arms.

Upon opening the shell of a Waldheimia, the animal will be found to occupy but a very small proportion of the space within, but there are two large coiled "arms", one on either side ot the mouth, fringed with a double set of *tentacles* and suggesting the tentacular crown of Plumatella, if one supposes the halves of this to be much elongated and coiled up. The so-called arms are supported by a curved loop, shaped like a carriage-spring and projecting from the upper valve. A mantle-lobe lines either shell.

In a bivalve mollusc the two halves of the shell are drawn together by adductor muscles and opened by an elastic ligament (p. 330). In a Lamp-Shell both processes are effected by muscles, and the hinge along which movements take place runs transversely and is placed close to the beak. The *gut* is a bent tube placed in the middle plane and consisting of gullet, stomach, and intestine, the last ending blindly. A good-sized digestive gland opens into the stomach. The *excretory organs* are in the form of a pair of funnel-shaped tubes, which, like the nephridia of a segmented worm (p. 425), place a spacious body-cavity in communication with the exterior. The *central nervous system* essentially consists of a ring surrounding the gullet, and thickened above into brain- and below into other ganglia. (The upper part of the ring is not shown in fig. 271, A.)

CHAPTER X

STRUCTURE AND CLASSIFICATION OF FLAT-WORMS (PLATYHELMIA) AND THREAD-WORMS (NEMATHELMIA)

FLAT-WORMS (PLATYHELMIA)

The animals included in this phylum are unsegmented worm-like creatures which in most cases are markedly flattened from above downwards, hence the name of the group. They are divided into three classes:—1. Tape-Worms (Cestoda); 2. Flukes (Trematoda); 3. Planarian Worms (Turbellaria).

CLASS I.—TAPE-WORMS (CESTODA)

Tape-Worms are all internal parasites, and in the adult stage are almost without exception inhabitants of the food-tube in various Vertebrate animals, from Man downwards. The structure has undergone profound modification as a result of the parasitic habit, and the life-history is often complicated for the same reason. Details must be deferred till the phenomenon of parasitism is fully discussed, it being sufficient for the present purpose to briefly consider an average example of the group, the *Common Tape-Worm* (*Tænia solium*) (fig. 272), the adult stage of which is found in the human intestine. The long flattened whitish body has earned the name of "tape"-worm for the animal, which may be as much as 3 yards in length. It consists of a very small *head* and *neck* followed by the *trunk*, which gets broader and broader as we pass back to the hinder end, and is divided into a very large number of *joints*, which must not be mistaken for true segments such as have been described for annelids. It is indeed doubtful whether a tape-worm should be regarded as a single individual. An alternative view is that the head and neck together represent what may be called the primary individual, from which a long series of secondary individuals, the joints, has been originated.

Close examination of the minute *head* by means of a lens

shows that at its front end there is a double circlet of horny *hooks*, behind which four large *suckers* are arranged at equal distances. By means of these hooks and suckers the head is attached to the mucous membrane lining the intestine of the host. Such organs of attachment are common among parasites, and another example is given further on in the case of the Thorn-headed Worm (p. 449). No trace of a mouth can be seen, and indeed *digestive organs* are entirely absent, for the parasite lives at the expense of its host, absorbing through the general surface of its body the digested food with which, in the small intestine, it is surrounded. Nor are there any special *circulatory* or *respiratory organs*. The *excretory organs* are well developed and quite unlike the paired nephridia of segmented worms. They consist essentially of a narrow tube on each side, running not far from the edge of the body, and connected with elaborate branching canals which ramify in the soft substance filling up the spaces between all the internal organs. The *nervous system* is feebly developed, and its central parts consist of a longitudinal cord on either side, these being connected in the head by a transverse band, which may be regarded as equivalent to a pair of brain-ganglia.

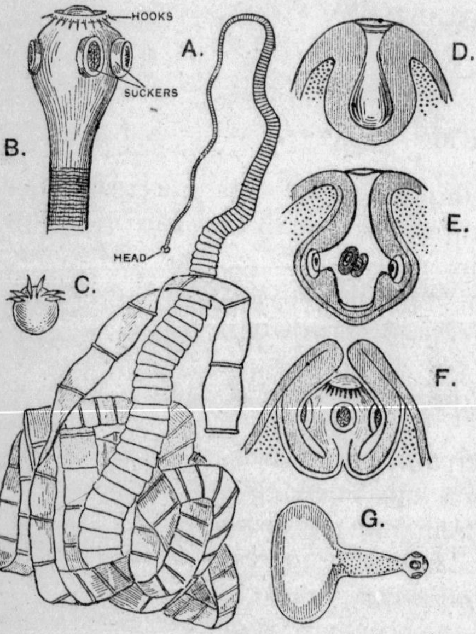

Fig. 272.—Common Tape-Worm (*Tænia solium*)

A, slightly reduced; B–G, enlarged to various scales. A, Adult, showing head and chain of joints (proglottides), the ripest of which have been broken off. B, Head. C, Six-hooked embryo. D–F, Stages in development of head. G, Bladder-Worm stage (cysticercus), with head protruded.

The *joints* which make up the trunk are largely filled with *egg-producing organs*, and, at the hind-end, joints full of ripe eggs are from time to time detached, passing out of the body of the host to the exterior. If any of these joints are devoured by a pig, the eggs hatch out in its stomach and the spherical embryos, each of which is provided with three pairs of hooks, bore their way into the blood-vessels and are carried to the muscles, where they pass into a quiescent stage (pork "measles"). If a pig so infested is slaughtered, and some of the "measly" pork eaten in an imperfectly cooked condition by a human being, the life-history of the parasite is continued a step further, for the "measles" develop in the intestine of the new host into adult tape-worms.

CLASS II.—FLUKES (TREMATODA)

Flukes, like Tape-Worms, are parasitic forms, but they present a wider range in the nature of their parasitism, some being found attached to the exterior of other animals, while some live within various organs of the host. Here again it will, for the present, suffice to describe a single member of the group, and the type which is most commonly taken as a sample is the *Liver-Fluke* (*Fasciola hepatica*) (fig. 273), a much-dreaded agricultural pest which gives rise to the disease of sheep known as "liver rot".

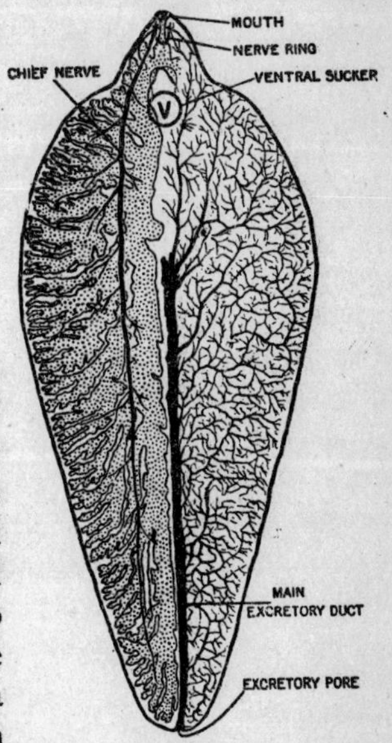

Fig. 273.--Liver-Fluke (*Fasciola hepatica*), diagrammatic

The adult Liver-Fluke is found often in large numbers in the liver of the sheep, or, in some cases, of other animals, among which Man must be included. The body is leaf-shaped and about an inch long. At the front end there is a conical projection on the tip of which is a *sucker* surrounding the opening of the mouth. There is a second sucker placed farther back on the under surface of the body, and the excretory organs open by a minute pore at the tip of the hinder end. The animal is covered by a thick *cuticle* beset with minute backwardly-directed spines, which facilitate an onward wriggling through the substance of the diseased liver, which gradually becomes more and more degenerated and broken down, till at last, in bad cases, the sheep dies.

The *internal structure* of the Fluke is extremely complex, and only a few of the more salient features can be mentioned. The *body-wall* consists of the cuticle with underlying epidermis and muscular layers, within which the spaces between the various organs is filled up by a soft packing material, much as in a tape-worm. Here, however, though special *circulatory* and *respiratory organs* are absent, the *digestive system* is well developed, for the surrounding food, consisting of blood and broken-down liver substance, requires to be digested. The mouth leads into a muscular pharynx, acting as a suction-pump, this into an extremely short gullet, and this again into a forked intestine, the halves of which are much branched and end blindly. The *excretory organs* are much of the same kind as in the Tape-Worm, and the *nervous system* is not much better developed. It consists of a ring round the front part of the gut, thickened above into ill-defined cerebral ganglia, and giving off a number of nerves, of which the most important take a backward direction.

The *life-history* is more complex than that of the Tape-Worm, and of a remarkable character, including a number of stages. The ripe *eggs* produced by the adult Fluke may be taken as the point of departure. These pass down into the intestine of the sheep and thence to the exterior. If they happen to fall into water or on to damp grass, and fluke-disease is commonest in wet fields, an elongated *ciliated embryo* hatches out from each of them. This swims actively about for some time, and if it happens to come across a certain small water-snail (*Limnæa truncatula*), further stages in its life-history become possible. The larva makes its way into the lung of the snail and becomes a shapeless bag (*sporocyst*) within which are developed a number of cylindrical rediæ, constituting the next stage. The *redia* makes its way out of the sporocyst and travels to the liver of the snail, upon which it preys. The last stage in the life-history is the tadpole-like *cercaria*, which is really an immature fluke, and this is produced within the redia much as that took origin within the sporocyst. The cercaria leaves the snail, and, swimming through the water by means of its tail, reaches a piece of grass or some other plant, to which it becomes attached. The tail is lost and the body becomes invested in a firm limy coat or cyst. If now a sheep should happen to swallow one of these encysted forms, the limy covering is dissolved by the action of the gastric juice, and the young fluke, escaping, passes on into the small intestine, whence it travels up the bile-duct into the liver, there becoming adult.

Class III.—PLANARIAN WORMS (Turbellaria)

These are widely-distributed flat-worms, differing from the members of the two preceding classes in being as a rule free-living, though a few are parasitic. All are carnivorous. Planarians are found abundantly in the shallower parts of the sea and in fresh water, while others are terrestrial, and are to be seen on damp earth and vegetation. One of the commonest British species is a fresh-water form, *Planaria lactea* (fig. 274). It is a flattened whitish creature of elongated oval shape, and an inch or less in length, which may be found gliding along over water-plants and stones. These movements are effected by a uniform covering of *cilia* with which the soft skin is clothed, and the presence of which constitutes one of the important differences from the Tape-Worms and Flukes. The ciliary action sets up minute currents and whirlpools in the surrounding water, which can easily be seen with a lens, and have given rise to the name Turbellaria, from the Latin *turbellæ*, a word vulgarly employed to denote the bustling of a crowd.

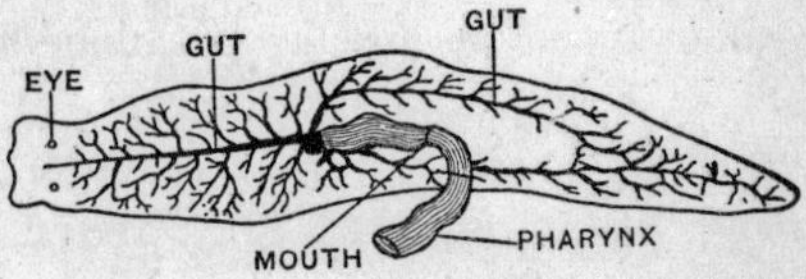

Fig. 274.—*Planaria lactea* (enlarged), with pharynx protruded to exterior

The front end of the body is comparatively broad, while the hind end is pointed. Upon the under side of the body, nearer the hind than the front end, is situated the *mouth*, which leads into a muscular *pharynx* continuous with a three-branched *intestine*, of which one section is directed forwards and the others backwards, while all three are beset with numerous branches that end blindly, reminding one of the condition of the digestive organs in a Liver-Fluke (p. 444). When the animal is in pursuit of prey, the pharynx is protruded from the mouth and used as an organ of capture, the food being taken directly into it, so, paradoxical as it seems, the mouth is not used as a mouth. As in Flukes and Tape-Worms there are muscular layers beneath the skin, and the spaces between the complex internal organs are filled up with packing material. As, too, in those forms there are no *circulatory* or *respiratory organs*, and the *excretory structures* are much of the same kind. The *central nervous system* consists of a pair of brain-ganglia in the front part of the body, giving off various nerves, of which the two longest take a backward course. Upon the upper side of the head region are two simple *eyes*, each of which is provided with a lens and supplied by a special optic nerve.

The *Land Planarians* largely agree with the preceding in structure, but are much more worm-like in appearance, though equally unsegmented. Some of the tropical forms attain a large size (up to 18 inches when extended), and are brilliantly marked with longitudinal streaks of colour, but our few native species are dull in colour and insignificant in size. An example is *Rhynchodemus terrestris*, which is under an inch in length, whitish in colour below and dark-grey above.

The commonest example of the *marine Turbellaria* native to Britain is probably *Leptoplana tremellaris* (fig. 275), which is frequently to be found adhering to the under surface of stones between tide-marks. It belongs to a group which is exclusively marine, and differs in a number of important particulars from *Planaria lactea.* The flattened oval body is rounded at either end but considerably broader in front. Not only is the animal able to progress in the gliding manner already described, but it can also swim with considerable rapidity by flapping the sides of the body up and down. It then looks curiously like a minute Skate. The *mouth* is situated about the middle of the under surface, and the *pharynx*, when protruded from it, resembles a wide funnel with plaited sides. This region of the gut leads into an elongated oval *stomach* from which branching, blindly-ending tubes radiate in all directions. The bilobed *brain* is situated fairly far back, and gives origin to a number of radiating nerves. There are four groups of simple *eyes* situated on the upper side of the body, in the neighbourhood of the brain.

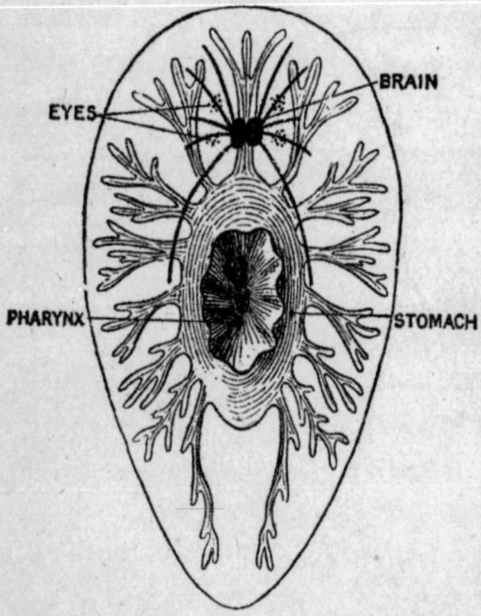

Fig. 275.—*Leptoplana tremellaris* (enlarged), as seen from under surface, with pharynx protruded to exterior

Certain Turbellarians belonging to the same group as the

species just described are brightly coloured, and some of them attain a large size, one recorded specimen being six inches long and four broad.

Speaking generally, the class of Turbellaria is one of extreme interest, for it contains the simplest animals exhibiting bilateral symmetry, and this is obviously associated with the creeping habit (p. 22).

THREAD-WORMS (NEMATHELMIA)

This phylum comprises an enormous number of unsegmented worm-like forms in which both ends of the body are usually pointed. The large majority of them are parasitic in the bodies of plants or animals, and various modifications in structure have taken place in consequence of this habit. A common and large type is the *Round-Worm*, one species of which (*Ascaris lumbricoides*) infests the human intestine, while a much larger species (*Ascaris megalocephala*) often abounds in the corresponding part of the horse.

The body of a Round-Worm (fig. 276), though cylindrical, exhibits bilateral symmetry, but not in so marked a manner as in the higher worms. Jaws and paired appendages of all kinds are entirely absent. The *mouth* is placed at the front end, and is guarded by three flap-like *lips*, of which one is dorsal, while the interspace between the other two is in the mid-ventral line. Each side-lip bears a small papilla which probably has to do with touch, and two of these are to be found on the dorsal lip. The intestine opens on the under side, not far from the hinder end, which in the male is sharply bent round. Close examination shows the presence of four streaks running longitudinally along the body and corresponding to special modifications of the body-wall. Two of these streaks are the *lateral lines*, one on each side, and the others are *dorsal* and *ventral lines*, running in the median plane above and below respectively.

The *body-wall* resembles that of a Nereis (p. 426) in so far that it consists of external cuticle with underlying epidermis and muscle, but the differences in detail are very considerable. The cuticle is very firm and strong, probably serving to protect the animal from the digestive juices of its host, while the epidermis is indistinct and projects inwards to form the lateral and median lines. As a result of this, the underlying muscle, which constitutes a sort of longitudinal layer, is broken up into four sections.

The *digestive organs* (fig. 276) consist of a narrow tube running straight through the body, beginning with a thick-walled gullet which passes into a thin-walled intestine. Between the gut and body-wall is a body-cavity containing fluid, but there is nothing else to which the name of circulatory system can be applied. There are no special breathing organs, and the *excretory organs* are quite unlike those of a segmented worm (p. 428), consisting as they do of a narrow tube running in each lateral line, and joining with its fellow in front to open by a minute pore on the under surface. The *nervous system* again is in many respects unlike that of a segmented worm (p. 428). It is closely connected with the skin, and its most conspicuous portions consist of a ring not far behind the mouth, from which nerves are given off both fore and aft. Those in front supply the lips, and of the others the largest are a dorsal and a ventral nerve which traverse respectively the dorsal and ventral lines.

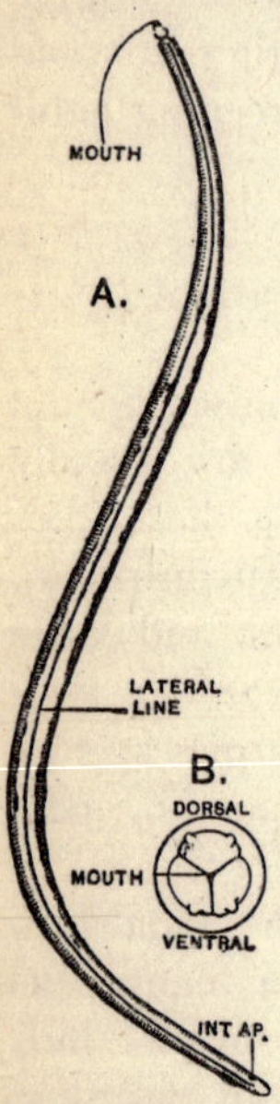

Fig. 276.—Round-Worm (*Ascaris*)

A, Side view; B, front end of body, much enlarged to show mouth and lips; INT. AP., intestinal aperture.

A common example of free-living Thread-Worms is the little Vinegar Eel (*Anguillula aceti*), common in paste and weak vinegar. Another curious creature, representing a group differing in many respects from the one containing Ascaris and Anguillula, is the Gordian-Worm (*Gordius*). This is a very slender black worm, often to be seen in pools or puddles, and the name has reference to the fact that a number of them may often be found twined together into a complicated tangle. In early life the Gordian-Worm is parasitic in an insect, leaving its host, however, when it becomes adult, and as large numbers do this about the same time, their appearance in public is somewhat sudden. Hence the rustic belief, once prevalent, that they have been rained down from the sky, a common explanation of the rapid appearance in any quantity of all sorts of small animals. Another curious popular idea, suggested by the appearance of the worms, is that they are horse-hairs into which the breath of life has mysteriously entered.

A small group, provisionally placed in the Thread-Worms, is that represented by a curious parasite the Thorn-headed Worm (*Echinorhynchus*), the front end of which is provided with a hook-studded projection, by means of which attachment to the lining of its host's intestine is effected. There are very many structural differences from such a typical form as the Round-Worm, the most remarkable being the absence of digestive organs, and it is more than doubtful whether the group should be included in the Thread-Worms at all. A typical species (*Echinorhynchus gigas*) lives, when adult, within the digestive organs of the pig, while its larval life is spent within the body of a Rose-Chafer or other related beetle.

CHAPTER XI

STRUCTURE AND CLASSIFICATION OF ECHINODERMS (ECHINODERMATA)

This is one of the most sharply-marked phyla in the animal kingdom, having specialized on very distinctive lines. Though considered after the flat-worms, it must not be imagined that it occupies a lower place in the scale. Indeed, as explained earlier (p. 11), it is impossible to place the various groups of animals in a linear series, each member of the series higher than the one next below it, and lower than the one next above it. But it is clearly necessary to describe the groups one after the other, just as if they actually formed such a series, and this is apt to give misleading ideas.

The phylum contains marine animals only, and probably the most familiar of these is the Common Star-Fish (*Uraster rubens*), found in abundance on many parts of our coast. It will serve very well as our illustrative example.

The body of a Star-Fish (fig. 277) is built on a plan quite different from those exhibited by the bilaterally symmetrical animals with which we have so far been concerned. As in a very large number of marine Invertebrates, there is a free-swimming larva, known in this case as a Bipinnaria, which is markedly bilateral. It is converted into the adult stage by a very complicated series of changes, constituting a true *metamorphosis*, one result of which is that the original bilateral symmetry becomes obscured, being replaced by a simpler kind of regularity to which the name of *radial symmetry* has been given, and which is well exemplified by the flower of a primrose, a cart-wheel, or a regular pentagon. In one kind of Star-Fish, indeed (*Goniaster*), the body is a pentagonal disc, but in the form selected for description, the corners of the pentagon have, so to speak, been drawn out so that a distinction can be drawn between a central *disc* and five radiating *arms*, which are continuations of it. In a Vertebrate, Arthropod, or Worm, the body can be divided into corresponding halves in one way only, *i.e.* by a median plane which separates the right side from the left, but here this can be done in five different ways. Another way of putting it is to say that the body is regularly built up around a series of axes which radiate from a common central point. Any part or organ which is cut by one of these axes may be said to occupy a *radial* position, while *interradial* structures

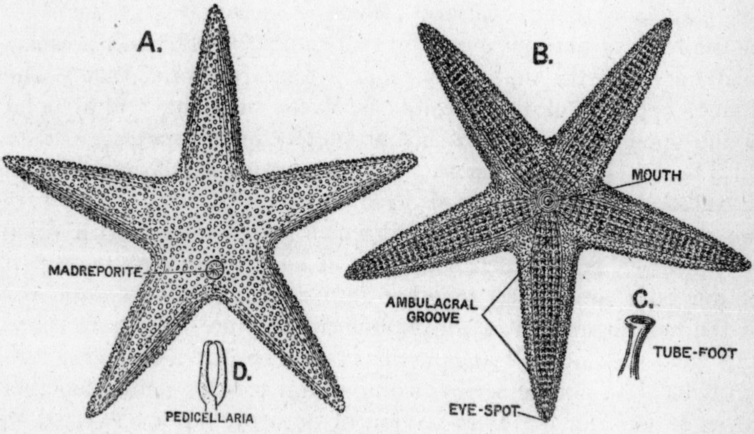

Fig. 277.—Common Star-Fish (*Uraster rubens*)
A and B, Upper and under surfaces, reduced; C and D, much enlarged.

fall between adjacent axes. There is, it is true, a distinction between upper and lower surfaces, as in vertebrates, &c., but it is by no means clear that we are justified in considering these to be truly dorsal and ventral.

Turning our attention to the pale under surface, we shall see, in its centre, the *mouth*, entirely devoid of jaws and placed in the middle of a soft area from which a deep groove runs along each arm to its tip. Occupying these five grooves are a large number of slender cylindrical structures which observation of a living star-fish shows to be used in locomotion, and which have consequently been termed *tube-feet*. Each groove has fancifully been termed an *ambulacrum*, because, together with its tube-feet. it suggested to the giver of the name a little pleasure grove or tree-lined avenue (Lat. *ambulacrum*). The tips of the arms are commonly seen to curl upwards, and each of them bears a reddish *eye-spot*.

The most conspicuous feature of the upper surface of the disc is found in the presence of a rounded plate in one of the interradial areas. The meandering grooves which mark its surface look like the markings upon certain corals (madrepores), and have suggested the name of madreporic plate or *madreporite.* As there is only one of these structures, the radial symmetry of the body is interfered with, and, strictly speaking, it is bilaterally symmetrical, the median plane passing through the plate and along one arm, which is generally considered to be the front or anterior one. So that the Star-Fish really presents bilateral symmetry masked by radial symmetry, so to speak. The minute aperture of the intestine is placed near the central point of the upper surface, but is not absolutely in the centre.

The Star-Fish is firm to the touch, owing to the presence of a well-developed system of hard *calcareous plates*, present in the deeper part of the skin, and which are best seen in a dried specimen. Those which support and strengthen the upper part of the body are united together into an irregular net-work, but in the neighbourhood of the ambulacra they are regular in shape and have a definite arrangement. Of these plates the most conspicuous are a double series of ambulacral ossicles united together so as to look, in the cross section of an arm, like an inverted V. The edges of the ambulacra are fringed with *spines*, and it is the presence of these in typical Echinoderms which has given the name to the phylum (Gk. *echinos*, a hedgehog; *derma*, skin). Spines, however, are much more numerous and conspicuous in the members of some of the other sorts of Echinoderm, notably in the Sea-Urchins, which is expressed in the name for "urchin", an old English word for a hedgehog. Among these spines, especially in the neighbourhood of the mouth, are some which have been peculiarly modified to form snapping jaw-like structures, known as *pedicellariæ.* One use of these is probably to assist in cleaning the surface of the animal.

Internal Structure (fig. 278).—Several points of interest are presented by the *digestive organs.* The *mouth* leads into a large *stomach* with folded walls, capable of being protruded outside of the body so as to engulf prey of comparatively large size. Star-fishes are extremely rapacious animals, and are among the worst enemies of the oyster. The stomach, after protrusion, is drawn back into the body by special muscles. It is continued into a five-angled *pyloric sac*, and this into a short thin-walled *intestine*. The cavity of each arm is largely occupied by a pair of large saccular tubes which open into one of the corners of the pyloric sac, and secrete a digestive juice. The *circulatory organs* chiefly consist of an ill-developed blood-system devoid of heart, and of a spacious body-cavity. Special *respiratory organs* are evidently necessary in a creature furnished with a firm exo-skeleton, and in this case the function is discharged in part by delicate branched gills which can be protruded through the interstices of the calcareous net-work which strengthens the upper

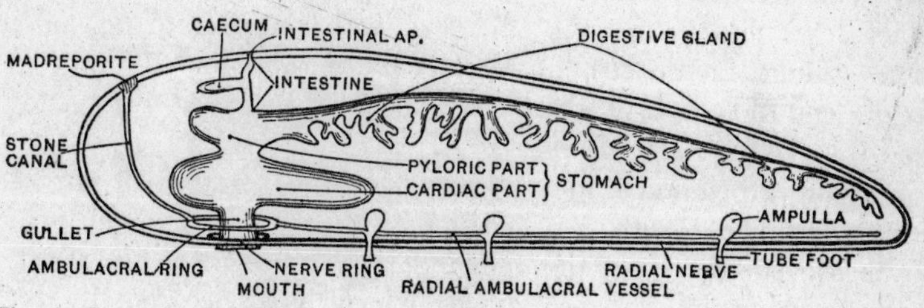

Fig. 278.—Common Star-Fish (*Uraster rubens*); cut through disc and one arm to show structure. Diagrammatic

surface. The tube-feet most likely help in breathing, and some of them in the neighbourhood of the mouth appear to be specially concerned with this function.

Great interest attaches to what is known as the *water-vascular system*, a set of organs to which the tube-feet belong, and which is quite unlike anything existing in other subdivisions of the animal kingdom. It consists of a tubular *ring* surrounding the beginning of the food-tube, and sending a *radial vessel* along each arm, just below the union of the two rows of ambulacral ossicles. The *tube-feet* are branches of the radial vessels, but they are also connected with little transparent bladders (ampullæ) placed within the cavities of the arms. The fluid filling the water-vascular system is largely sea-water, which is able to get in from the exterior by a *stone-canal* that runs from the madreporite to the central ring, the grooves in the former being perforated by numerous minute holes. The ampullæ, by their contraction, force fluid into the tube-feet, thus causing their protrusion. This method of working a set of locomotor organs is quite unlike anything we have so far met with, and it compensates for the comparative feebleness of the *muscular system*, correlated, it would seem, with the marked development of a continuous exoskeleton, between the parts of which there are not, as in Arthropods, well-marked joints permitting of free movement.

The *nervous system* is of very primitive type, and arranged, like the other internal organs, in accordance with the radial symmetry of the animal. It is intimately connected with the skin, of which, in fact, it may simply be regarded as a thickening, and its best-marked portions consist of a *ring* round the mouth, and five *radial nerves*, one of which runs along each arm. But the entire body is invested in a nervous sheath, consisting of a delicate net-work lying in the deeper part of the skin. The chief *sense organs* are the tube-feet, which appear to be, among other things, tactile structures—indeed there is an odd tube-foot at the end of each arm which may definitely be called a tentacle,—and the *eye-spots* already noted.

What are known as "comet" forms of Star-Fish are not infrequently met with, *i.e.* specimens in which from one to four arms are smaller than the remainder. The small arms are new ones growing in place of others which have accidentally been lost. Lower animals often possess considerable powers of regenerating mutilated parts, and this is to a limited degree the case even among some of the Vertebrates.

Living Echinoderms are arranged in five classes:—1. Star-Fishes (Asteroidea); 2. Brittle-Stars (Ophiuroidea); 3. Sea-Urchins (Echinoidea); 4. Sea-Lilies and Feather-Stars (Crinoidea); Sea-Cucumbers (Holothuroidea).

Class I.—STAR-FISHES (Asteroidea)

These conform in character to the described type in many at least of the particulars. They are found in all seas, and the majority are inhabitants of shallow water, though some, including the largest species, are found at considerable depths. There are generally five arms, but this is by no means a universal rule. A common British species, for instance, the Sun-Star (*Solaster papposus*), possesses no less than thirteen. The name has been given on account of its resemblance to the conventional symbol by which the sun is usually represented, *i.e.* a circle with a number of radiating lines.

ECHINODERMS

The animals here included constitute a well-marked group of marine animals, in which the body is typically star-shaped or spheroidal, or less commonly cylindrical. There is a more or less perfect calcareous skeleton developed in the skin, and part of it may consist of fixed or movable spines, hence the name of the group (Gk. *echinos*, a hedgehog; *derma*, skin: *i.e.* hedgehog-skinned). A peculiar system of tubes is present, containing sea-water and communicating with the exterior. In three of the constituent classes (star-fish, sea-urchins, and sea-cucumbers) part of this "water-vascular" system consists of sucker-like *tube-feet*, which are used for executing crawling movements.

Four common British forms are figured as types of the four classes now dominant, *i.e.* Star-fish (*Asteroidea*), Brittle Stars (*Ophiuroidea*), Sea-urchins (*Echinoidea*), and Sea-cucumbers (*Holothuroidea*).

1. Purple-tipped Sea-urchin (*Echinus miliaris*). Body covered by numerous spines attached by ball-and-socket joints to little knobs. ("*Urchin*" is an old name for the hedgehog.)
2. Black Sea-cucumber (*Holothuria nigra*). Leathery skin, in which scattered calcareous plates are embedded.
3. Brittle Star (*Ophiura*). Disc-like body with five flexible limb-like arms.
4. Common Star-fish (*Uraster rubens*). With five arms which are extensions of the central body. (The large specimen figured has more than the usual number of arms.)

ECHINODERMS

1. Sea-urchin. 2. Black Sea-cucumber. 3. Brittle Star. 4. Common Starfish.

Class II.—BRITTLE-STARS (Ophiuroidea)

The members of this class, though to some extent they resemble ordinary star-fishes, and are by some naturalists included with them in a common section of the phylum, differ in a number of important particulars. There are a number of British species, of which one of the commonest (*Amphiura squamata*) is a little creature found on the under sides of stones near low-tide mark (fig. 279). It is at once evident that the five *arms* are sharply marked off from the *central disc*. They are indeed more of the nature of appendages, and are here the organs of locomotion, for which their extreme flexibility eminently fits them. Upon the under side of the disc, as in an ordinary star-fish, is situated the *mouth* in the form of a five-rayed slit. There are no ambulacral grooves, and the under side of each arm is covered by a regular series of flat plates, at the sides of which the *tube-feet* project. They are not, however, used as feet, but serve as organs of touch and respiration. There are no eye-spots on the tips of the arms. Turning to the upper surface, no trace of a madreporite can be seen; it is represented by one of the plates situated interradially on the under side. There is no intestinal opening at all. Each arm is covered by a single series of plates, and a similar series runs along each of its sides. The margins of the arms are spiny, but there are no pedicellariæ.

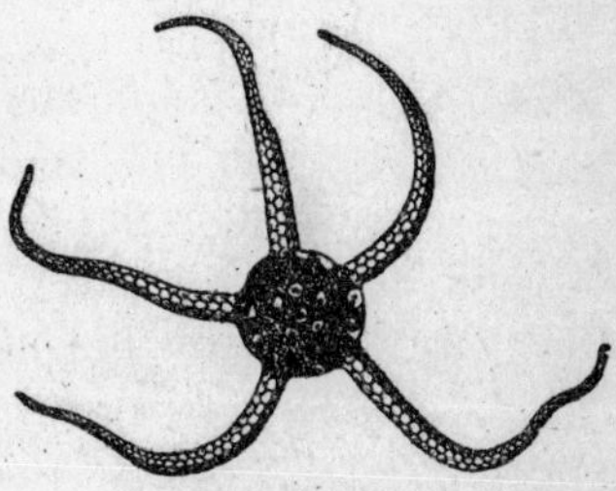

Fig. 279.—Brittle-Star (*Amphiura squamata*), seen from above. Enlarged

There are important differences as to internal structure between a brittle-star and an ordinary star-fish. The *mouth*, for example, is armed by a number of modified plates, and it leads into a spacious *stomach*, which bulges out into ten very short pouches. But there is no intestine and no digestive structures in the arms. Indeed each of these is traversed by a special series of ossicles, which have been called vertebral, because they are jointed together something like the successive vertebræ making up a backbone. Each of them is formed by the fusion of two ossicles, which are equivalent to a pair of the ambulacral ossicles of an ordinary star-fish. The stomach is not capable of being protruded as in one of the ordinary Stars.

Class III.—SEA-URCHINS (Echinoidea)

Among the animals commonly brought up by the dredge in British seas, and sometimes thrown up on the beach by storms is the Edible Sea-Urchin (*Echinus esculentus*) (fig. 280), which,

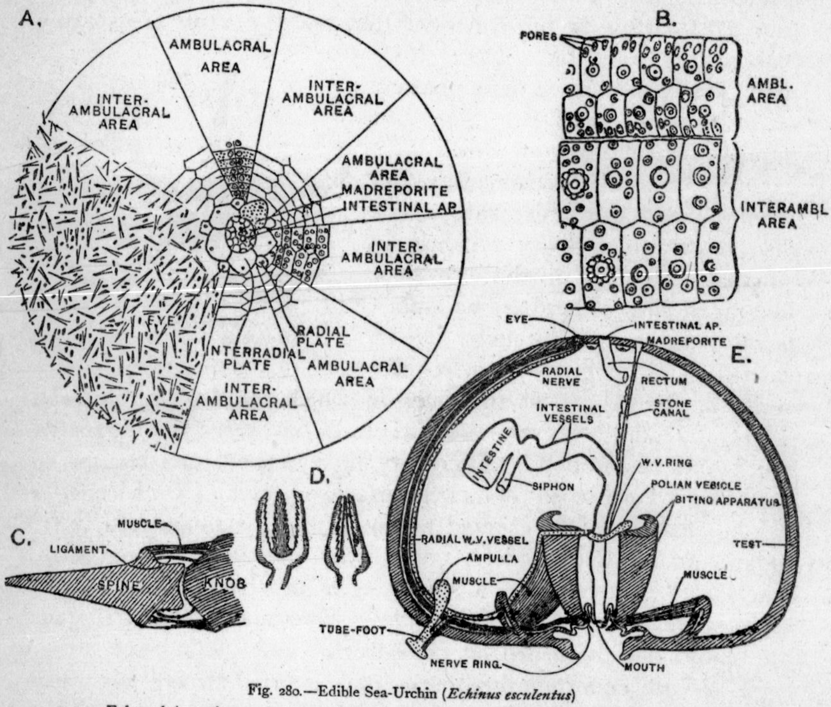

Fig. 280.—Edible Sea-Urchin (*Echinus esculentus*)

B, C, D, Enlarged to various scales. A, Diagram of upper surface, with most of spines removed. B, Plates of small part of an ambulacral and an interambulacral area, with spines removed. Pores for tube-feet and knobs for spines are shown. C, Diagrammatic section through spine and knob, to show mode of attachment. D, Pedicellariæ. E, Diagram of side-dissection, most of gut having been removed. W.V. is an abbreviation for "water vascular".

though it differs very much in appearance from a star-fish, is really constructed on much the same type. The spheroidal body suggests in appearance a curled-up hedgehog, whence, as previously explained, the name "sea-urchin", the appearance being due to the presence of an enormous number of *spines*, movably jointed to the underlying calcareous plates which, united firmly at their edges, constitute a firm protective "test". The base of each spine is hollowed out into a cup which fits over a corresponding knob on the test, so that there is a ball-and-socket joint arrangement, and by means of special strands of muscle the spine can be moved in any direction. This is an adaptation to locomotion as well as to protection. Effective *tube-feet* are, however, present, and in a living sea-urchin these may be seen protruding between the spines, and if we compare the animal to a globe with upper and lower poles, their distribution is expressed by saying that they are arranged in five meridional bands.

As in a star-fish, the *mouth* is situated in the centre of the under surface, but in this case there are five pointed structures to be seen projecting from it, these being the tips of hard *jaws* shaped something like the front teeth of a rabbit. The opening of the intestine is placed almost in the middle of the upper surface.

On scraping away the spines, the characters of the *test* may be studied in detail, and it is found to be made up of twenty regularly-arranged sets of plates arranged in ten strips, which are broad in the middle but narrow at either end, like the "gores" which make up a balloon, or are sewn together to cover a child's cloth-covered ball. Two meridional rows of plates are united to make up each of these bands. Five of these differ in one important particular from the others which alternate with them, the distinction resting in the presence of a series of *pores* arranged in pairs, and placed near either edge of the band to which they belong, Each pair of these pores belongs to a tube-foot, which is thereby placed in communication with a radial water-vascular vessel, and with an ampulla (see p. 453), both of these being situated within the test. The presence of these pores enables us to distinguish between five *ambulacral areas*, bearing tube-feet, and five intervening *inter-ambulacral areas.* The former correspond to the radii about which the body is symmetrically built, and the others are consequently interradial. It may be useful to institute a comparison with the star-fish, taking for the purpose, not the common form, but the kind (*Goniaster*) shaped like a pentagonal disc. If we suppose the body of such a form to gradually swell so as to become spheroidal, while at the same time the original upper surface gets smaller and smaller, the lower surface (bearing the tube-feet), becoming correspondingly extended, the sea-urchin type will be produced. For the five ambulacral grooves will be converted into the five ambulacral areas, and the regions between them into the five interambulacral areas.

There yet remain one or two other points to be noticed in the sea-urchin test. The plates at the upper pole, in the neighbourhood of the intestinal aperture, are somewhat specialized, and constitute an *apical disc*, the most important elements in which are ten plates, of which the five smaller ones are situated radially, and therefore correspond with the upper ends of the ambulacral areas. Each of them is called an "ocular", because it bears an eye-spot. The five interradial plates are somewhat larger, and one of them is modified into the *madreporite*, which has the same function as in an ordinary star-fish (see p. 452). Like that animal, too, the sea-urchin possesses those modified jaw-spines to which the name of *pedicellariæ* has been given, but in this case the jaws are three, and not two in number (fig. 281). Some possess poison-glands (fig. 281, right).

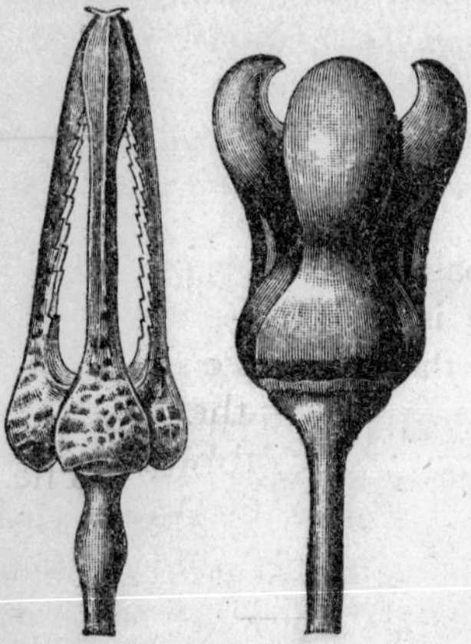

Fig. 281.—Three-jawed Pedicellariæ of Sea-Urchins; greatly enlarged

The *digestive organs* consist of gullet and intestine, the latter taking a spiral course, while the former traverses a complicated chewing apparatus fancifully called "Aristotle's lantern", and made up of the five jaws, together with many other hard parts. By means of special muscles the jaws can alternately be brought together and separated. As in the other groups of Echinoderms so far dealt with, there is a *blood system* of rather obscure nature, and the rest of the circulatory organs consist of a particularly spacious body-cavity in which the various internal organs are placed. *Breathing* is effected by the tube-feet, and also by ten branching *gills* placed in the neighbourhood of the mouth, and resembling the structures which project between the interstices of the skeleton in a star-fish (p. 453). This function is also possibly assisted by a narrow tube (siphon) running parallel to the gut and opening into it at either end. The *water-vascular system* is arranged on the same general plan as in a star-fish (p. 453), consisting of a ring round the gullet connected with the madreporite by a stone-canal, and giving origin to five radial vessels of which the tube-feet are branches, these vessels, however, running within the test. The *nervous system*, too, is of the same general kind, but there are two nervous net-works, one outside the test and the other within it.

Sea-Urchins are grouped in two divisions: I. *Regular forms*, of which the just-described species is typical, and II. *Irregular forms*, in which there is a strongly-marked bilateral symmetry, and the body is often flattened, while the upper parts of the ambulacra are broadened out so as to collectively make up a flower-shaped figure, the tube-feet of which are definitely specialized into *gills*. These irregular forms again are divided into Shield-Urchins and Heart-Urchins.

Shield-Urchins are sometimes very much flattened, as the name implies, and though the mouth has the normal position, the aperture of the intestine is shifted back into an interradial position.

Heart-Urchins are distinguished by the shape under which the heart is conventionally represented, the notch of the heart being in front. The opening of the intestine is displaced to the edge of the disc, and the mouth, instead of being central, is shifted forwards. The Heart-Urchins are devoid of the special chewing apparatus known as "Aristotle's lantern". A common British species is the Purple Heart-Urchin (*Spatangus purpureus*).

Class IV.—SEA-LILIES AND FEATHER-STARS (Crinoidea)

This is a decadent group, once of great luxuriance, but of which the most typical modern representatives are rare, and confined to the very deep sea. Taking such a typical Sea-Lily, for example, as *Pentacrinus* (fig. 282), it may roughly be compared to a star-fish with branching arms placed on the top of a long stalk, and having its mouth surface turned upwards. A certain vague sort of resemblance to a flower upon its stem has suggested the name.

Examining Pentacrinus more closely, there will be seen a relatively small central disc, or *cup*, as it is usually termed, from which five arms project. These are of the nature of appendages, and begin almost at once to branch in a forking manner. Each branch bears a double series of short filaments termed *pinnules*, the name having reference to the arrangement seen in some plants, *e.g.* in many ferns, where a central axis supports a row of leaflets on each side in a feather-like way. The *mouth* is in the centre of the upturned disc, and from it radiate five *ambulacral grooves*, corresponding to the similarly-named structures in a star-fish (p. 451). As the arms branch, so do these grooves, and their smallest subdivisions run along the pinnules. Projecting from each side of an ambulacral groove and its branches are a series of delicate pointed structures representing the tube-feet of a star-fish, but here no longer having anything to do with locomotion. The intestine opens near the mouth upon a projection situated in one of the interradial spaces. The under side of the cup is supported by regularly-arranged circlets of calcareous plates, some of which are comparable, it would appear, with the apical disc of a sea-urchin. There is, however, no madreporite. The under side of each arm, arm-branch, and pinnule is also supported by a series of hard parts, jointed together, however, so as to permit of a certain amount of movement. The stalk upon which the animal is supported is five-sided, and it is supported by a series of calcareous pieces, in the form of prisms

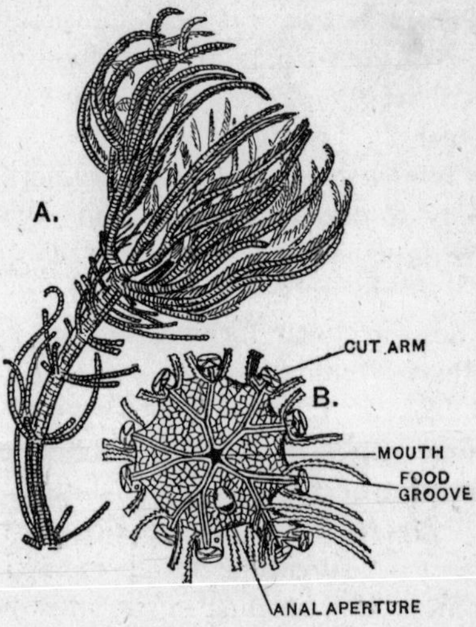

Fig. 282.—Sea-Lily (*Pentacrinus*)

A, Calyx and part of stalk (reduced). B, Upper side of calyx, with arms cut off.

Fig. 283.—Feather-Star (*Comatula*), climbing

joined end to end. At regular intervals the stalk bears circlets of jointed filaments (*cirri*) which also are strengthened by a deposit of lime.

The *internal structure* is very complex, and it need only be said that the gut does not extend into the arms, and that apart from it the chief organs have the radial arrangement described for other types.

Although Sea-Lilies are distinctly scarce animals, the same can scarcely be said for the Feather-Stars, of which one kind (*Antedon* or *Comatula rosacea*) (fig. 283) is not uncommon in British seas. Its *life-history* is one of peculiar interest, for the eggs develop into a stalked *larva* which is found attached to sea-weed, and looks like a minute Sea-Lily (fig. 284). Later on, the stalk disappears and the animal takes to a free life, though it is possessed throughout its existence of a circlet of cirri, corresponding to the top circlet of those structures in a stalked form, and used to anchor the creature, and also in climbing. The life-history is interesting, chiefly because it is one of the best-known examples of a case where the development of the individual is a compressed presentment of the genealogy of the species. If the Feather-Star were the only known Crinoid there would be a strong presumption that its remote ancestors were stalked, and this conclusion is fully borne out by a study of recent and fossil forms.

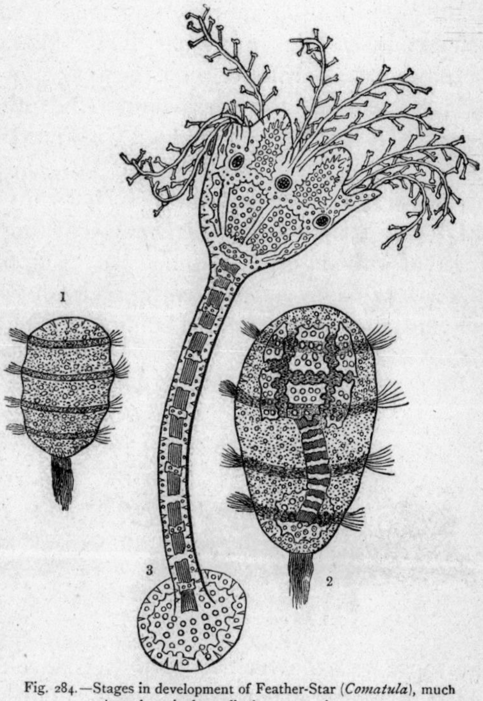

Fig. 284.—Stages in development of Feather-Star (*Comatula*), much enlarged. 3 is the stalked or pentacrinus stage

Class V.—SEA-CUCUMBERS (Holothuroidea)

These are for the most part leathery elongated forms, some of which look uncommonly like cucumbers, a similarity which has suggested the name of the group. They are regarded by some authorities as representing most nearly of living animals the ancestral stock from which all Echinoderms must be supposed to have taken origin. This, however, is extremely doubtful; but as unfortunately the class, unlike the other ones included in the phylum, is but poorly provided with hard parts, fossil remains are infrequent, and throw but little light upon the question.

In a typical Holothurian (such as the genus *Cucumaria*) (fig. 285) the elongated body is somewhat angular, and the two openings of the digestive organs are at opposite ends of the body, the *mouth* being surrounded by a circlet of ten branching *tentacles*, which can be retracted. The *ambulacral areas* are marked by five double rows of *tube-feet* protruding along the side of the body. No trace of a madreporite can be discerned. The body-wall consists of skin and underlying muscles, the latter being as well developed here as they are scanty in those forms which have a well-developed exoskeleton. The *hard parts* of a Holothurian are comparatively insignificant, the most important of them making up a calcareous ring round the gullet; and there are, besides, minute calcareous spicules scattered through the skin.

Fig. 285.—A Sea-Cucumber (*Cucumaria*), reduced

The *mouth*, as already stated, is placed in the middle of the crown of *tentacles*, and these are arranged in five pairs, one for each ambulacral area. One pair is smaller than the rest, and is used in shovelling food into the mouth. They correspond to the under surface of the body, which in some other members of the group is very sharply defined, though here the radial symmetry is not much interfered with. The mouth leads into a mouth-cavity, which opens into a gullet, and this again into a looped intestine, which dilates near its termination into a section which is known as the *cloaca*, though it can scarcely be said to correspond to the similarly-named cavity found in many of the vertebrate animals (see pp. 69, 146, 200, 240, 261).

The *circulatory organs* consist, as in a star-fish or sea-urchin, of a blood system and a lymph system. The former is chiefly made up of a ring round the beginning of the gut, of five radial vessels, and of branches to the digestive and some of the other internal organs. The lymph system consists of the spacious body-cavity filled with fluid, in which float both colourless and red corpuscles, reminding us of the blood of a typical vertebrate (see p. 38).

Breathing is no doubt partly effected, as in other cases, by the tentacles and tube-feet, but there are also other structures which probably have to do with the same function, in the form of two large branching *respiratory trees* that open into the cloaca. The branches of these organs are beset with innumerable minute ciliated funnels, by which the body-cavity is placed in communication with the exterior. It is extremely likely that these trees also have to do with getting rid of the nitrogenous waste of the body, and if so, they are *excretory* as well as respiratory organs.

The *water-vascular system* is constructed on the same plan as in a star-fish. There is a ring round the beginning of the gut from which a radial vessel runs along each ambulacrum to give off the double row of tube-feet. Branches of these vessels supply the tentacles, which are to be regarded as much-modified tube-feet, and there is a stone-canal with a madreporite which, instead of opening to the exterior, hangs down into the body-cavity. In a very young Holothurian, the stone-canal opens directly to the exterior, as in a star-fish or sea-urchin, but this connection is lost in the typical forms, though there are some deep-sea species in which it persists throughout life.

The *nervous system* is of the type already described for other subdivisions of the class (p. 454). *Sense Organs* are chiefly represented by the tentacles and tube-feet, which no doubt have to do with the sense of touch.

Within the limits of the class there are numerous variations in many respects. Certain deep-sea forms present a well-marked bilateral symmetry, and the body is produced into pairs of projecting processes. In such forms, a well-marked flattened lower surface upon which the animal creeps presents a sharp contrast with the curved upper surface. This is also the case with some of the species inhabiting much shallower water, and in these bilateral forms, three of the ambulacra are turned downwards, and bear tube-feet used in locomotion, while the other two face upwards, and their tube-feet are modified into pointed structures useful only as organs of breathing and touch. The tentacles also present a considerable variety in size and shape. Some common forms have the tube-feet irregularly scattered over the body instead of being arranged in rows, while in yet others the tube-feet, and even the radial branches of the water-vascular system, are absent altogether. This is the case, for example, in the genus *Synapta*, species of which are found in British seas. Here the translucent body is worm-like, and the small tentacles are feather-shaped, a further character of interest being found in the shape of the calcareous plates embedded in the skin, which are in the form of anchors with associated oval perforated plates (anchor plates). It also possesses ten minute *auditory sacs* in close connection with the nerve-ring.

CHAPTER X

STRUCTURE AND CLASSIFICATION OF ZOOPHYTES (CŒLENTERATA), SPONGES (PORIFERA), AND ANIMALCULES (PROTOZOA)

ZOOPHYTES (CŒLENTERATA)

The old expression "zoophyte" was applied to branching colonies of organisms regarding the animal nature of which doubt existed, and which were looked upon as being intermediate between animals and plants. Here were included the forms already briefly dealt with under the heading of Polyzoa (p. 436), but these are of much higher structure than the bulk of zoophytes, which may conveniently be grouped together under the phylum now to be considered. This embraces the Corals, Jelly-Fish, Sea-Anemones, and other creatures less familiar to the ordinary observer. As a simple and easily obtained type, it is customary to take the *Fresh-water Polype* (*Hydra*) (fig. 286), which is often found attached to pond-weeds, or sticking to the glass of a freshwater aquarium. By leaving such an aquarium in a brightly-lit window for some time, one may often secure a supply of these animals, which collect on the side next the light. As they are not more than about $\frac{1}{4}$ of an inch long, the naked eye alone is not sufficient for their proper examination. Much can be made out with a simple lens, but a compound microscope is necessary to determine details. This is one of the numerous cases where important results are to be obtained by means of cutting thin slices with a razor, an operation which requires that the animal

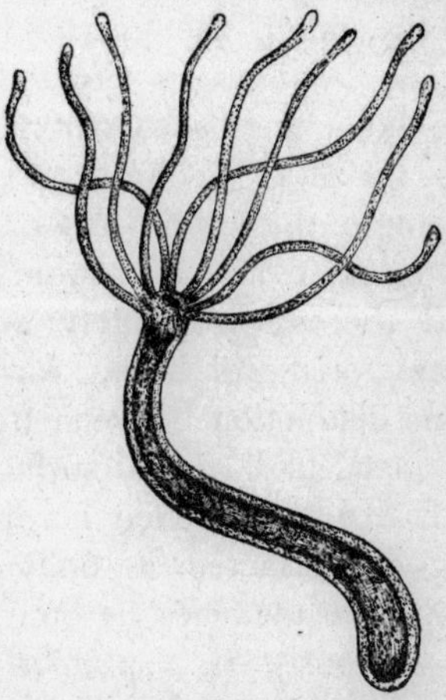

Fig. 286.—Green Hydra (*Hydra viridis*), enlarged

should be killed, stained, and imbedded in paraffin wax or some similar substance. Extremely delicate slices of known thickness can be cut by means of the instrument known as a *microtome*, in which a sharp razor is mechanically drawn across the imbedded specimen, this being held firmly by a suitable device. The slices, when prepared, have to be cleared from paraffin and mounted on a glass slide, in some transparent medium, such as glycerine or Canada balsam.

Specimens of Hydra are brown (*e.g. Hydra fusca*) or green (*Hydra viridis*) (fig. 286) according to the species, but in any case the form and structure are much the same. The colour of the green kind is particularly interesting, since it is due to the presence of a pigment (chlorophyll) which is characteristic of ordinary plants, and, as we shall see later, plays a leading part in their nutrition. The body of a fully-extended individual is a hollow cylinder closed at one end, the *foot*, by which attachment to a firm object is effected, while it is narrowed and open at the other, the aperture being the *mouth*. A circlet of long slender *tentacles* is situated quite close to the mouth, just where the body begins to narrow. The large internal *digestive cavity* has no other opening to the exterior. We find here a perfect example of the star-like or *radial symmetry* which is exemplified in a less complete manner by a star-fish or regular sea-urchin, and there is absolutely no trace of the bilateral symmetry so characteristic of higher forms (see p. 21). In other words, there is no distinction between front and back ends, right and left sides, or dorsal and ventral surfaces.

If a fully-extended Hydra be touched or shaken it will at once become retracted, its body shortening into a little rounded lump, while the tentacles become minute knobs. Such an arrangement is obviously of a protective character. When in an extended position the animal is on the look-out for prey, if such an expression may be used in the absence of visual organs. Its food consists of small aquatic animals such as Water-Fleas (see p. 422), which are much higher in the scale, and would at first sight appear to have every chance of escaping capture. This, however, is not the case, for if one of these active creatures happens to come into contact with one of the tentacles of the Hydra it stops dead as if paralysed, and is then by the help of the other tentacles drawn down to the dilatable mouth and passes out of view into the digestive cavity. The sudden arrest of activity on the part of the unfortunate water-flea is brought about by means of minute "thread-cells" or "nettling-cells", which, as will be explained elsewhere, are poisoned weapons of considerable virulence. Numerous groups or "batteries" of these are present upon the tentacles, on which they confer a roughened appearance, and they are also present, though less abundantly, upon other parts of the body. *Nettling-cells* are very characteristic of the Cœlenterates, a fact which has been painfully brought home to many bathers in the case of some of the larger jelly-fish, while even the innocent-looking sea-anemones have been known to seriously inconvenience persons who happened to touch them. Even, therefore, if Hydra, like many of its brethren, were condemned to remain fixed in the same spot it would not necessarily be starved, but, as already hinted, it possesses considerable powers of *locomotion.* It can, for example, slowly shuffle along upon the attached end of the body, and can also execute looping movements by alternately attaching the two ends of its body to the surface of a stone or water-weed, reminding one of what happens in the case of a leech (p. 432) or a looper caterpillar (p. 364). Specimens may also be found floating freely in the water, mouth downwards, with the foot close to the surface and held in place by what is known as surface tension.

Structure of the Body (fig. 287).—Most of the external characters of Hydra have now been dealt with, and it remains to consider the minute structure of the body as determined by means of the microscope. Much can be learnt by examination of a thin cross-section, which may instructively be compared with a similar section through the body of an earth-worm. There is a central space corresponding to the digestive cavity, and outside this the body-wall, which is clearly made up of an outer layer and a much thicker inner layer, the two being separated by a thin membrane (supporting lamella). These two layers are respectively known as the *ectoderm* (Gk. *ektos*, outside; *derma*, a skin) and *endoderm* (Gk. *endon*, within; *derma*, a skin), and a double body-wall made up in this way is eminently characteristic of Cœlenterates and Sponges, especially in embryonic stages, on which account these two phyla are often grouped together as the "*Diploblastica*" (Gk. *diplous*, double; *blastos*, germ or bud). Turning now to the section of earth-worm, we see in the middle a space corresponding to the digestive cavity or gut which, however, is not bounded directly by the wall of the body but by a wall of its own separated by a considerable space, the *body-cavity*, from the body-wall. Hydra is absolutely devoid of a body-cavity in this sense. If we attempt a comparison between the two animals, the epidermis of the worm may be looked upon as *ectoderm* and the innermost layer of the wall of the gut would appear to be equivalent to *endoderm*. But the greater part of body-wall and gut-wall in the worm, together making up what is called the middle layer or *mesoderm*, has no distinct representative in Hydra, unless, perhaps, it is represented in an inadequate manner by the thin membrane between ectoderm and endoderm. The presence of a distinct third layer coming between ectoderm and endoderm is characteristic of all the phyla above the Zoophytes, and this comes out very clearly and simply in embryo stages. Hence all these phyla are collectively grouped together as *Triploblastica*, *i.e.* three-layered animals, as contrasted with the two-layered forms or Diploblastica. The body-cavity is simply a split in the mesoderm, dividing it into an outer sheet lining the ectoderm and an inner sheet investing the endoderm.

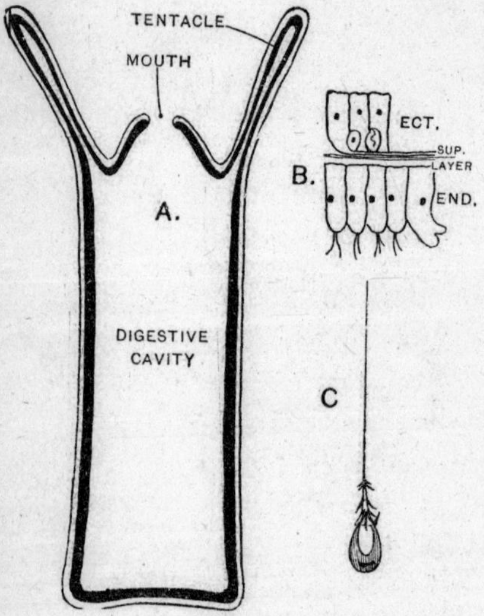

Fig. 287.—Diagrams, enlarged to various scales, illustrating the structure of Hydra

A, Longitudinal section: ectoderm left white, endoderm represented in black. B, Small part of longitudinal section through body-wall (the black dots are nuclei); ECT., three large cells and two packing cells are seen; SUP. LAYER, supporting layer or lamella; END., endoderm, showing four cells with flagella, and one with pseudopodia. C, A nettling-cell, with thread protruded—note barbs at the base of this, and the trigger hair on the right side; the protoplasm investing cell is shaded, and the nucleus represented in black.

Allusion has already been made to the fact that the body of a higher animal is made up of a number of different sorts of material having specific purposes and known as *tissues*, which are in effect the building materials from which the various organs are constructed. They are as follows:—1. *Epithelium*, consisting of membranes which line internal cavities and cover the external surface, having in the latter case the name of epidermis; 2. *Supporting tissues*, such as bone, gristle (cartilage), and connective tissue which makes up tendons and ligaments, while it is also found as a sort of supporting framework in almost all parts of the body; 3. *Muscle*, constituting the flesh or meat, and also entering largely into the construction of the walls of various internal organs, such as heart and stomach; 4. *Nervous tissue*, constituting the essential part of the nervous system; and 5. *Blood* and *Lymph*, which must be looked upon as liquid tissues, serving as media of exchange. In a higher animal these various tissues are highly specialized so as to fit them for particular kinds of work; *e.g.*, muscle has as its province the bringing about of active movements. Indeed it may be said that animals are "high" or "low" in proportion as the division of physiological work is completely or incompletely carried out. In a high animal there is great complexity of structure associated with this perfect division of function, while exactly the reverse is true for a low animal. And in degenerate forms, such as the Ascidians (p. 297), animals derived from relatively complex ancestors have become simplified so as to suit them for simpler conditions of life. The loss of digestive organs by tape-worms (p. 441) is a further example of the principle.

Careful examination of any one kind of tissue shows that it is entirely or largely composed of structural units known as *cells*, comparable to the bricks and stones, &c., which make up the building materials of a house, if we pursue a comparison which has elsewhere been made use of. It is these cells that consist of the actual living substance, *protoplasm*, with which vital actions are associated. Each cell contains a particle of specially modified protoplasm known as the *nucleus*, which appears to be a regulative centre. These cells differ largely in shape according to the nature of the tissue. A simple case is that of lymph (p. 41), which consists of a clear fluid (plasma) in which are suspended innumerable irregular lymph corpuscles, which in this instance are the constituent cells. *Epithelium* (fig. 288) again consists of one or more layers of cells closely packed together and possessing various shapes in different cases. There is, for example, simple *scaly epithelium*, made up of flattened cells united by their edges and only one cell thick; this is comparable to a tessellated pavement, each separate bit corresponding to a cell. The lining of heart and blood-vessels is of this nature. *Stratified scaly epithelium* resembles the preceding, but is several cells thick. Examples are to be found in the lining of the human mouth, and the epidermis of Frog. *Simple columnar epithelium* consists of prismatic cells packed together in a single layer, and is very characteristic of stomach and intestines. Other examples will be noted elsewhere. In many cases the surface cells of epithelium are provided

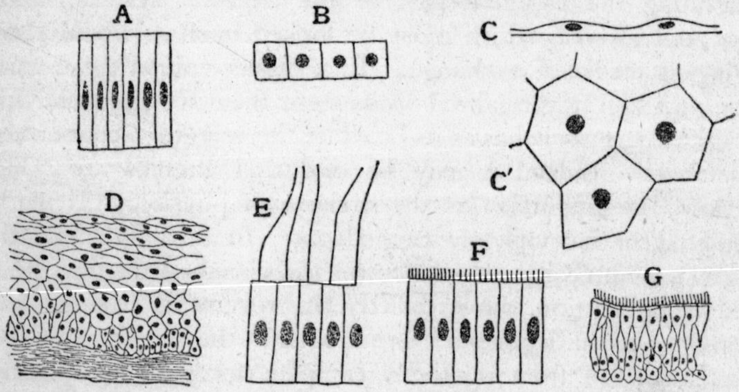

Fig. 288.—Different kinds of Epithelium, enlarged to various scales. All except C are in vertical section. Nuclei represented in black

A, Simple columnar; B, simple glandular; C, simple scaly; C′, simple scaly, surface view; D, stratified scaly; E, simple columnar, with flagella; F, simple columnar, with cilia; G, stratified, with cilia.

with numerous slender threads of protoplasm, cilia, which by their united action can set up currents. An individual *cilium* possesses the power of alternately bending and straightening itself. Various examples have already been given of the presence of such structures (pp. 49, 428, 445).

The *ectoderm* and *endoderm* of Hydra are to be regarded as tissues, but do not exhibit the high degree of specialization found in the phyla so far dealt with. They are more of the nature of epithelium than anything else, and this form of tissue is justly regarded as a comparatively primitive one. Beginning with the *ectoderm* (fig. 287), we find that the largest elements contained in this are what may be termed *tailed-cells*, since each of them is drawn out at its inner end into a fibre which appears to be of muscular nature. These tails all take a longitudinal direction, and collectively constitute a muscular layer by means of which the body can be shortened, supposing the fibres to contract or shorten simultaneously. Filling up the spaces between these large cells are much smaller *packing-cells* with indistinct outlines, some of which become transformed into the *nettling-cells* already noticed, and force their way to the surface. Deep down in the ectoderm are also to be found scattered *nerve-cells* of star-shaped outline, collectively representing an extremely primitive form of nervous system.

The *endoderm cells* of Hydra are much larger than those of the ectoderm, and are provided with muscular tails running in this case transversely, so that collectively they make up a circular muscle layer, by the contraction of which the body can be extended. These cells also have digestive functions, and their free ends, which are directed towards the digestive cavity, can be protruded into lobes by which food particles are bodily engulfed, or, to speak more technically, ingested. Many of the cells are also provided with groups of protoplasmic filaments, which execute lashing movements by means of which the contents of the digestive cavity are kept circulating. These are called flagella (L. *flagellum*, a whip), and though they are in some respects allied to cilia, differ from them in the relative complexity of their movements, their larger size, and the fact that but a small number of them are to be found on the same cell. In the green Hydra, the endoderm cells contain numerous spheres in which the characteristic pigment is contained, while in other species similar spheres are present, differing, however, in the nature of the colouring matter.

From what has been said concerning Hydra it will be seen that in this animal there is but little specialization or division of the work of the body. As to *digestive organs*, the animal is little more than an animated stomach, food being procured by the action of the tentacles, and digested by the endoderm. *Circulatory organs* are entirely absent, and, indeed, they are not necessary, for the digested food can easily diffuse to all parts of the body. Waste products are similarly easily got rid of, and there are therefore no special organs of *respiration* or *excretion*. Both *nervous system* and *sense organs* are in a very undifferentiated condition, the latter being chiefly represented by sensitive "trigger hairs", with one of which each thread-cell is provided.

Development (fig. 289).—New Hydræ are produced either by a process of *budding* or from eggs. In the former case, a little knob is seen to make its appearance on the body-wall, and, becoming gradually larger and larger, is shaped by degrees into a fresh individual, which ultimately becomes detached. This process goes on very vigorously in summer, and a Hydra may often be found bearing several mature buds, which, in their turn, are giving rise to a third generation. A temporary form of branching tree-like form is thus produced. Late in the summer, when external conditions as regards temperature and food become unfavourable, one or more rounded projections make their appearance near the foot, each of them containing an *egg*. After developing to a certain

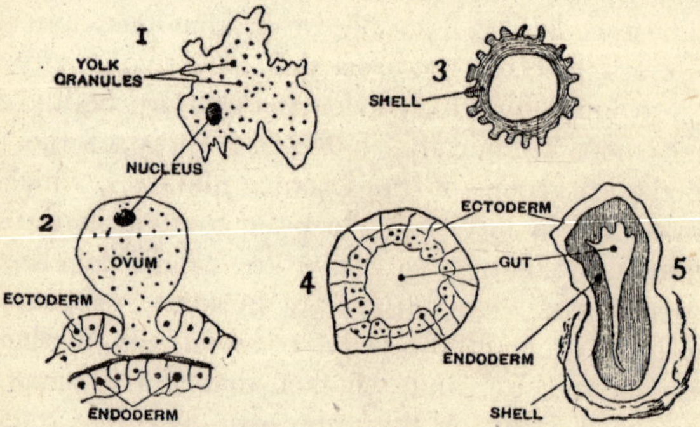

Fig. 289.—Development of Hydra, greatly magnified

1, Ovum. 2, Ovum, projecting from body-wall of parent. 3, Section through young embryo, to show protective egg-shell. 4, Cross-section of older stage. 5, Longitudinal section through embryo after rupture of egg-shell.

extent, the egg surrounds itself with a firm horny coating, serving as an efficient protection, and, invested in this, falls from the parent animal into the mud at the bottom of the pond or stream, where, in a dormant state, it is able to survive the winter, which is not usually the case with the Hydra itself. The development is completed in the following spring, when the egg-shell splits and the young animal makes its way out. In many groups of the animal kingdom, it is a common phenomenon for "winter eggs" of this kind to be produced, and the extinction of the species during the cold season is thereby prevented. A comparison may well be drawn with the seeds of higher plants, in which dormant embryos are contained that are able to resume growth with the advent of warmer weather.

An interesting property possessed by Hydra is its power of regenerating parts which have been injured or removed. To such an extent is this carried, that if an individual is cut into several pieces, each of them becomes a fresh Hydra. Powers of this kind are common among lower animals, and, as might be expected, are greatest where the body is but little specialized, as in the case now under consideration. Another case was mentioned when dealing with the Star-Fish (p. 454). The absence of specialization in Hydra is not so great, however, as supposed by the older zoologists, who imagined that the animal was so little discomposed when turned inside out that it lived on with the functions of the layers reversed.

Zoophytes are conveniently divided into the following three classes:—1. Sea-Flowers (Anthozoa or Actinozoa); 2. Hydroids (Hydrozoa); and 3. Comb Jelly-Fish (Ctenophora),

CLASS I.—SEA-FLOWERS (ANTHOZOA OR ACTINOZOA)

The brilliantly-coloured Sea-Anemones, Corals, Sea-Pens, and the like, which are grouped together in this class, justify its name (Gk. *anthos*, a flower; *zōŏn*, an animal), for, when expanded, they look not unlike chrysanthemums or double dahlias, to the individual florets of which the numerous tentacles bear a certain resemblance. Many of them are colonial, while others live singly, and of these we may take the common *Beadlet* (*Actinia mesembryanthemum*) as an example (compare fig. 290). It is abundant on rocks between tide-marks all round our coasts, looking, when expanded, like a scarlet flower, but shrinking to a rounded jelly-like mass when contracted. In the former condition, it may be compared to a short broad Hydra, but the mouth is in the centre of a wide disc, and is surrounded by several rows of comparatively short pointed tentacles. There are, however, important differences in structure. The *mouth* leads, not into a widely-continuous digestive cavity, but into a tubular *gullet*, which hangs down within the body, and ends abruptly below. This may be roughly represented by taking a piece of wide india-rubber tubing, and tucking in one end of it. The space between the lower end of the gullet and the base is called the *stomach*, and performs the function of a digestive organ. But this is not all, for running across in a radiating way from the body-wall to or towards the gullet are a large number of fleshy partitions, which divide the space external to gullet and stomach into a number of compartments. These partitions, or *mesenteries*, are, however, perforated above, so as to put adjoining compartments into communication. The stomach, which is bounded by the thickened free edges of the septa, is of necessity continuous with the various compartments, except when digestion is going on, at which time the edges of the septa are brought close together, a digestive juice being poured out from them upon the food. These points will be made clear by examination of the accompanying diagram. It may further be noted that the sides of the gullet are furrowed by two grooves placed opposite to each, and this organ can be collapsed in such a way as to convert these grooves into narrow tubes, these being lined by long cilia, which work in such a way that a current of water runs inwards in one tube, and outwards in the other.

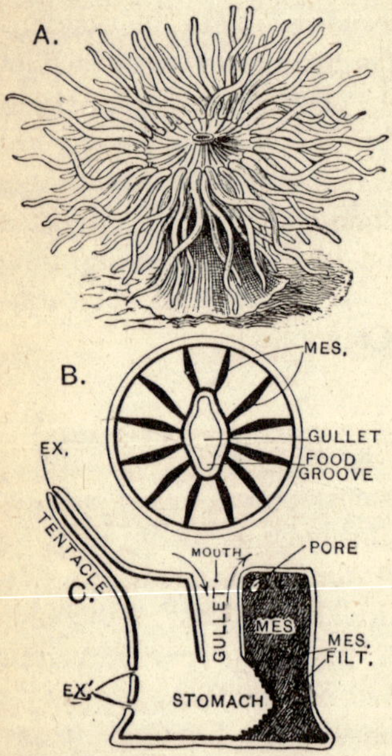

Fig. 290.—Sea-Anemone

A, External view of a Sea-Anemone (*Anemonia*). B, Diagrammatic cross-section; MES., mesenteries: only one of the two food-grooves is lettered. C, Diagrammatic longitudinal section, showing a mesentery (MES.), with mesenteric filaments (MES. FILT.) on the right, and one of the spaces between two mesenteries on the left; EX., EX'., excretory pores: the arrows indicate the course of currents into and out of the gullet along the food-grooves.

The *minute structure* corresponds in many ways to that of Hydra, there being ectoderm, endoderm, and a supporting lamella between them. Nettling-cells are abundantly present, but are more complex in pattern than those possessed by Hydra. There is further a greater amount of specialization, as seen especially in the muscular and nervous systems.

The Anthozoa include two orders:—1. Six-rayed Sea-Flowers (Hexactinia); and 2. Eight-rayed Sea-Flowers (Octactinia).

Order 1.—Six-rayed Sea-Flowers (Hexactinia)

These are distinguished by the fact that the tentacles are simple, while they and the mesenteries are usually arranged in multiples of six, and though this is often difficult to easily make out in the adult, it is clearly shown during the development. The Sea-Anemone just described is a good type of the order. Among

Fig. 291.—Skeletons of Arabian Corals, all reduced

1, Tuft-Coral (*Pocillopora favosa*); 2, Clove-Coral (*Trachyphyllia Geoffroyi*); 3, Antler-Coral (*Seriatopora subulata*); 4, Madrepore-Coral (*Madrepora laxa*); 5, Shrub-Coral (*Heteropora Hemprichii*); 6, Hedgehog-Coral (*Echinopora gemmacea*); 7, Sun-Coral (*Heliastræa Forskaliana*); 8, Mushroom-Coral (*Fungia scutaria*); 9, Brain-Coral (*Cœlaria labyrinthiformis*).

other British anemones may be mentioned: *Tealia crassicornis*, a large red form in which the outside of the body is studded with warts, to which fragments of sand or shells may be found adhering; and the brownish or greenish Opelet (*Anthea cereus*), which can only partially draw in its tentacles.

The majority of forms known as "corals" (fig. 291) are also members of the six-rayed order, and they include both simple and colonial species. Of the former may be mentioned a British species (*Caryophyllia Smithii*) found in the English Channel. In structure it is comparable to a sea-anemone, but a hard calcareous skeleton has been secreted by the ectoderm in the basal part of the animal. When the soft parts are removed this is seen to consist of a conical cup, from which calcareous plates project inward. A simple coral attaining a much larger size is the familiar Mushroom-Coral (*Fungia*), the flattened cup of which has some resemblance to the top of a mushroom, the gills being represented by the calcareous partitions or septa. Most corals, however, form colonies by budding (gemmation) or splitting (fission), and it is these which chiefly build up the coral-reefs so characteristic of the warmer parts of the ocean where the water is free from sand or mud. All sorts of different shapes may be assumed by the colonies, according to the species, some being encrusting or massive, while others branch in a tree-like way (fig. 291). The individual polypes may be separated by a larger or smaller interspace, so that their separate cups can be clearly made out, either imbedded in or else projecting from a *common skeleton* secreted by the common or colonial body (cœnosarc) which unites the different members together. In other cases the polypes are closely packed together, and it even happens in some cases that there is no proper division between them, it being only possible to determine the number of individuals by counting the mouths which are present.

Order 2.—Eight-rayed Sea-Flowers (Octactinia)

Although these forms agree in general plan of structure with corals and sea-anemones they also present striking differences, among which the most obvious are the possession of not more than eight feather-shaped tentacles and the same number of mesenteries. Nearly all the included species are colonial.

One of the commonest British members of the group is the organism to which the unpleasant name of *Dead-Man's Fingers* (*Alcyonium digitatum*) is applied, a name justified to some extent by the thick branches of the colony that look something like the swollen fingers of a clumsy hand (fig. 292). In a specimen cast up on the beach the individual polypes will have been drawn back into the fleshy substance of the colony, their position being indicated only by small depressions situated at a little distance from one another. Quite another appearance is presented by a living specimen with all the polypes protruded, these having a distinctly flower-like appearance, with eight feathery tentacles suggesting petals. As in an anemone, the mouth leads into a gullet, provided in this case, however (as also in some of the anemones), with but one ciliated groove, and united to the body-wall by only eight septa. The digestive cavities of the polypes are continuous with canals which traverse the common flesh. At first there appears to be no skeleton; but microscopic examination reveals the presence of numerous *calcareous spicules* of characteristic shape, scattered through the comparatively thick supporting layer which comes between the ectoderm and endoderm (see p. 474). There is reason to believe, however, that the spicules have been formed by the activity of ectodermic cells which have become detached from their own layer.

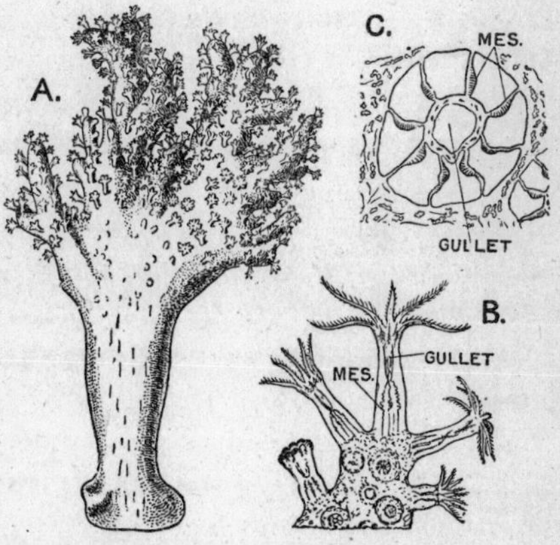

Fig. 292.—Dead-Man's Fingers (*Alcyonium*)

A, A colony, reduced. B, Tip of a branch, magnified, showing polypes in different stages of expansion and retraction; MES., a mesentery. C, Cross-section through body of a polype, magnified; MES., mesenteries (8 in all are present): note the single food-groove in lower side of gullet.

Another familiar example of the group is the *Organ-pipe Coral* (*Tubipora musica*), in a dried specimen of which may be seen numerous red tubes connected together by "platforms" of similar material at different levels. From these platforms new individuals grow up, and so the coral increases in breadth as it gets older. As in colonial corals generally the individuals are limited to the surface-layer, while the deeper part of the mass is cut off by partitions and merely consists of dead material. In a living specimen of Tubipora the upper end of each tube is occupied by a polype of similar character to those found in Alcyonium, and adjacent members of the colony are connected by living matter which extends along the uppermost platforms. Microscopic examination of the skeleton shows that it is formed by the intimate union of innumerable minute spicules comparable in nature though not in shape to those of Dead-Man's Fingers.

Other examples are *Red Coral* (*Corallium rubrum*) (fig. 2), where there is a compact branching skeleton (composed of united spicules) covered by the common flesh (cœnosarc) of the colony from which the polypes project at intervals; *Sea-Pens* (*Pennatula*, &c.), where the colony is feather-shaped with a series of individuals on each side, while the axis is supported by a firm rod; and the *Sea-Mats* (*Gorgonia*, &c.), where the flat upright colony is variously branched and supported by a horny skeleton, which is covered by common flesh with polypes much as in the Red Coral.

Class II.—HYDROIDS (Hydrozoa)

The Fresh-water Polype, Hydra, has already been described as a simple type of this class (pp. 465–471), which is predominatingly marine. The apparent simplicity of Hydra, it should be noted, is in all probability the result of reduction, and a much better idea of the group is to be obtained by briefly considering one of those marine forms to which at different stages of the life-history the terms "hydroid zoophyte" and "medusa" are applied. The horny skeletons of zoophytes of this sort are cast up on the shore in abundance by storms, and some may be found growing near low-tide mark in rock-pools. They are often confused with sea-weeds in amateur collections, in which their branching skeletons are frequently to be found. A very common British genus is *Obelia* (fig. 293), for which there is no popular name. It will be remembered that in dealing with Hydra it was pointed out (p. 472) that during summer, when that animal is actively budding, two or three generations of individuals may be temporarily connected together. If these buds were to remain united, and the budding process were carried further, a permanent branching colony would be the result. Obelia is a colony of this kind, and for its support some sort of skeleton is necessary, as is the case in the corals already described. Here, however, it is in the form of a horny investment, which covers the common body (cœnosarc) and expands at the tip of each branch into a little cup in which is lodged a hydra-like polype. There is, however, a further arrangement in the form of much larger cups (gonangia) within which are produced groups of special buds, the function of which is to produce eggs. When these buds are mature they are liberated in the form of small *jelly-fish* or *medusæ*, which lead an independent life for some time and possess active powers of movement. The jelly-like consistence in cases of the kind is due to the excessive development of the lamella between ectoderm and endoderm, which becomes thick and gelatinous, while cells from the two layers in question make their way into it. The little medusa may be compared to an umbrella with a very short handle (manubrium), and around its margin is a fringe of tentacles, eight of which have minute auditory vesicles at their bases, one to each. The *mouth* is situated at the end of the handle, and leads into a *stomach*, from which four tubes radiate to the edge of the umbrella, where they are continuous with a circular ring-canal. It may further be added that a little shelf or *velum* projects inwards from

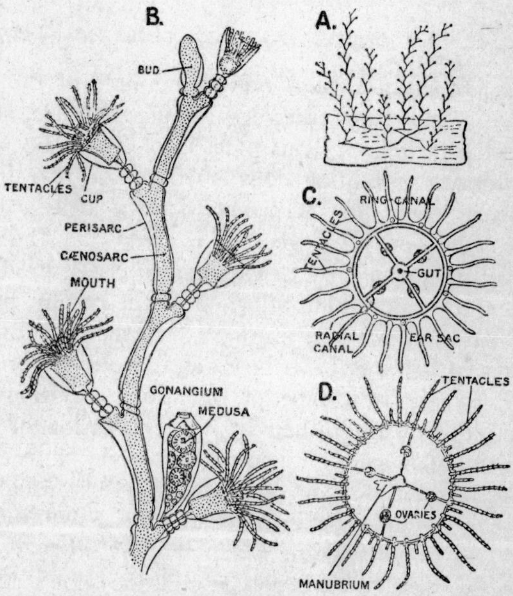

Fig. 293.—Fixed and Free-swimming Stages of a Hydroid Zoophyte (*Obelia*). A, Natural size; B–D, enlarged

A, A colony of the fixed (hydroid) stage, attached to a piece of sea-weed. B, End of a branch of same. C, Upper side, and D, under side of the free-swimming stage (jelly-fish or medusa).

the margin of the umbrella. The eggs give rise to hydra-like individuals, each of which develops a fresh colony by means of budding.

The Hydrozoa may conveniently be divided into two orders: 1. Budding Hydroids (Hydromedusæ); and 2. Splitting Hydroids (Scyphomedusæ).

Order 1.—Budding Hydroids (Hydromedusæ)

Obelia is a good typical example of the order, but in by no means all cases are egg-producing buds set free as medusæ, and a complete series of examples may be selected which range from that condition down to the state of things found in Hydra, where each egg is produced in a little swelling which has no resemblance whatever to a medusa. The intermediate stages are represented by cases where the egg-producing buds resemble medusæ but remain attached to the colony, and other cases where such buds may be compared to medusæ in which some of the typical features have been, as it were, suppressed.

Obelia is a type of one large division in which the fixed stage is distinguished by the possession of *cups* into which the individuals can be withdrawn, while if free-swimming jelly-fish are produced their sense organs are usually auditory vesicles. Other common British genera are *Sertularia* and *Plumularia.*

In another large group the investing skeleton ends abruptly at the base of each polype and does not expand into a cup, while the medusæ, if liberated as free-swimming individuals, usually possess eye-spots instead of auditory vesicles round the margin of the umbrella. *Tubularia* is a typical British genus, in which the polypes are comparatively large, and free-swimming medusæ are not developed. It is also customary to place Hydra in this group, as well as a very interesting marine genus, *Protohydra*, of somewhat similar character, though it has no tentacles, and is to be regarded as the simplest known member of the Hydrozoa.

Although most corals belong to the Anthozoa, there are a few cases of species belonging to the Hydrozoa which, instead of secreting a horny investment, develop a firm calcareous skeleton, and superficially resemble the true corals, though in reality sharply marked off from them by the structure of the soft parts. Representative genera are *Millepora* and *Stylaster*, in which there are hydra-like *nutritive individuals*, without well-developed tentacles, and reduced *prehensile individuals* devoid of mouths, and looking like large tentacles richly provided with nettle-cells, and branched in the case of Millepora. Each nutritive polype is surrounded by a number of these modified individuals, the function of which is to secure food. There are also egg-producing members of the colony, comparable in function, though not in form, to the medusa-stage of Obelia.

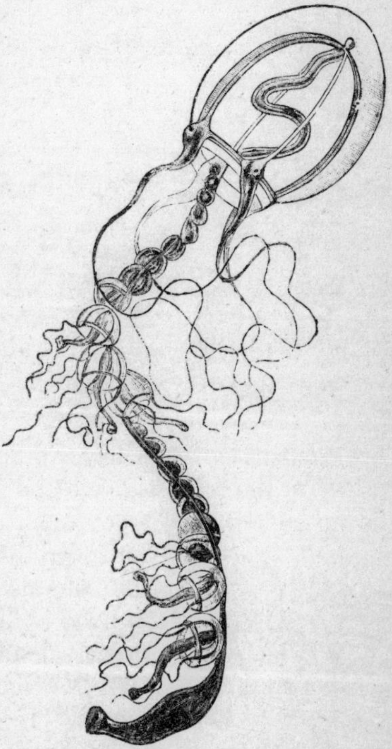

Fig. 294.—A Compound Jelly-Fish (*Sarsia*)

This may be regarded as a medusa (of which the large bell or umbrella is seen at upper end of figure) with a very long mouth-stalk (manubrium), on which smaller individuals are formed as buds.

It will have been gathered from the preceding that there is often a division of physiological work between the different members of a hydrozoan colony, just as in the complex body of a higher animal there is a similar division between the various tissues. This phenomenon is carried to an extreme in the free-swimming marine forms which are grouped together under the name of *Compound Jelly-Fish* (*Siphonophora*) (fig. 294). Each colony comprises individuals of the most various nature, and just as a hydroid zoophyte arises by the budding of a fixed hydra-like individual, so here we must suppose that buds of different kinds have been produced on a modified jelly-fish or medusa, in some cases upon the under side of the umbrella and in others upon the elongated mouth-stalk, which has been compared to the handle of the umbrella.

Order 2.—Splitting Hydroids (Scyphomedusæ)

To this order belong the large jelly-fish which are often seen in great numbers in British seas during the warmer parts of the year. The edge of the umbrella is lobed, the notches between the lobes sheltering peculiar sense organs formed by the modification of tentacles and covered by little lappets. Hence the term "covered-eyed medusæ" sometimes applied to these forms, to distinguish them from the "naked-eyed medusæ" of the preceding class, in which the marginal sense organs are not covered by such lappets. These terms, however, were not happily chosen, for it is only in certain cases that the sense organs have to do with sight. A negative characteristic of the jelly-fish included in this division is to be found in the absence of the true velum (see p. 479). The most typical members of the group present two stages in the life-history, as in Obelia (p. 480), *i.e.* (1) a fixed hydroid stage, and (2) the free-swimming medusa. The common British form *Aurelia* may be taken as an example (fig. 295). Here the fixed stage is what is called a *Hydra-tuba*, somewhat resembling a short, broad Hydra in shape, though internally it presents a difference in the presence of four longitudinal folds which project into the digestive cavity. Medusæ are developed from it, not by budding, but by a process of transverse splitting, and when the process is far advanced, the incipient medusæ may be compared to a pile of saucers. Sooner or later these become detached and grow into the mature jelly-fish, by which eggs are produced which complete the cycle of development by becoming hydra-tubæ.

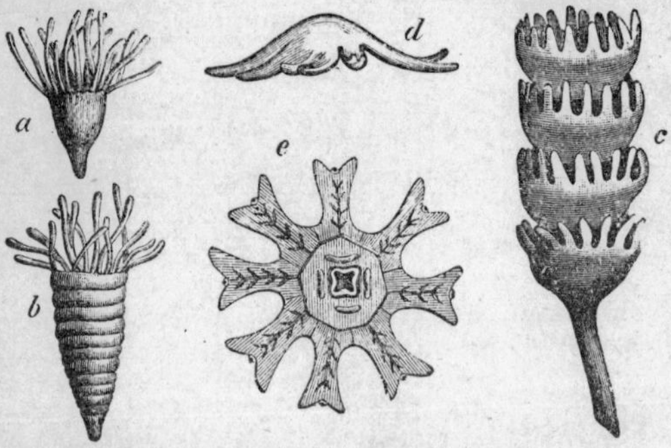

Fig. 295.—Development of Aurelia, enlarged

a, The fixed stage (hydra-tuba). *b* and *c*, Transverse splitting of *a* to form medusæ. *d* and *e*, Young medusa, seen from the side and from below.

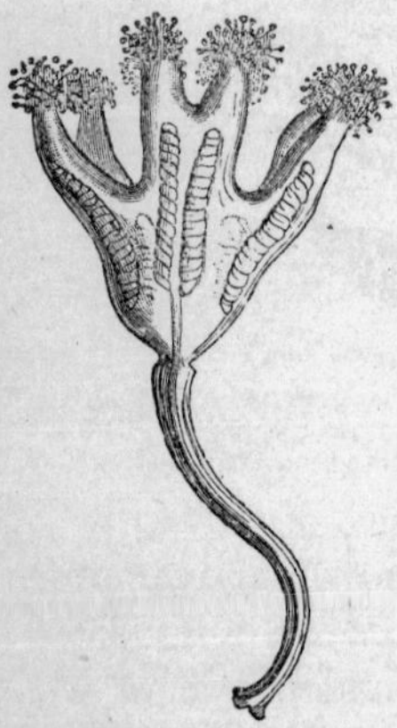

Fig. 296.—Lucernaria, enlarged

Some of the medusæ belonging to the order have no fixed stage, and in the case of certain other species (*Haliclystus*,

Lucernaria, &c.) there is, on the contrary, no medusa stage (fig. 296).

CLASS III.—COMB JELLY-FISH (CTENOPHORA)

These are small, transparent, free-swimming forms occurring in vast numbers in the open sea. When alive they are of extreme beauty. A common British genus, *Cydippe*, typically exhibits the features of the class (fig. 297).

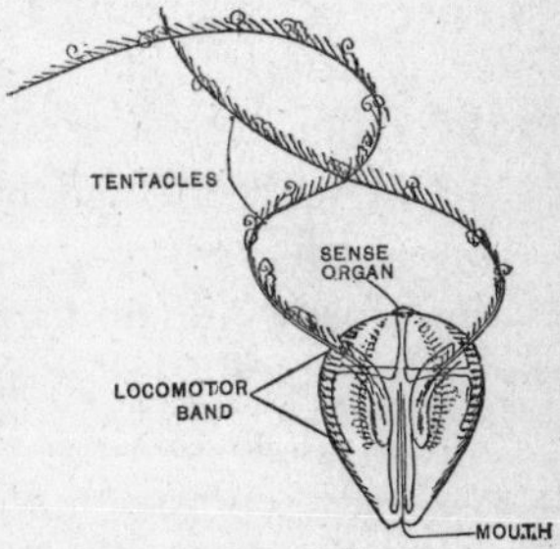

Fig. 297.—Cydippe

Here the body may be compared in shape to a minute melon, with the *mouth-opening* at one pole and a complex *sense organ* at the other. Locomotion is brought about by eight longitudinal bands of little paddles which suggest the teeth of a comb. Each *paddle* is apparently made up of a number of cilia which have fused together. From each side of the body a long feathery *tentacle* can be protruded, which is used for the capture of food. These tentacles, when not in use, are drawn back into pouches. The *mouth* leads into a gullet, and that into a complex system of canals, which communicate with the exterior by two pores at the opposite end of the body. Nettling-cells are absent, but the tentacles are provided with glutincus adhesive cells by which particles of food are secured. There is no fixed stage in the life-history.

Among other genera may be mentioned *Venus's Girdle* (*Cestus*), in which the body is band-shaped and may be as much as a foot in length; and *Beroë*, a cap-shaped form devoid of tentacles. There are also two very interesting creeping genera (*Ctenoplana* and *Cœloplana*), which, as a result of their mode of life (see p. 23), present an approach to bilateral symmetry, and have been compared to some of the Turbellarian worms (p. 445), it even being suggested that the Turbellaria have been derived from ancestral forms closely related to the Ctenophores.

SPONGES (Porifera)

Sponges were long considered to be of vegetable nature, an idea that was only finally upset by the study of their minute structure. Except to a naturalist the word "sponge" merely suggests a bath-sponge, which is in reality the horny skeleton of a colonial species. To gain a clear idea of the structure of the group it is necessary to consider the simpler cases presented by some of the solitary forms. In the simplest of these the body is shaped like a cup or vase, fixed at one end and open at the other. It is tempting to draw a comparison with Hydra, or better with Protohydra (p. 480), which is simply a tube open at one end. Such a comparison, however, is beset with difficulties, for while in Protohydra the aperture is clearly a mouth through which food is introduced, it will be found by watching the living sponge that currents of water are constantly flowing out of the corresponding opening, here technically known as the *osculum* (L. for little mouth). And, further, the body-wall of the sponge is perforated by numerous small holes through which water-currents set into the central digestive cavity. These currents are the result of ciliary action, and by their means the animal is provided with the food and oxygen it requires, while the various products of waste are swept out to the exterior through the osculum. This mode of life is associated with the sedentary or fixed habit of sponges, which is the chief reason for the old mistake of considering these creatures of vegetable nature.

Microscopic examination shows that the thin body-wall of the simple sponge consists of an external ectoderm made up of a layer of flattened cells, a middle supporting layer, and an internal layer of entoderm composed of *collar-cells*. Each of these cells is provided with a whip-like projection of protoplasm (*flagellum*) (see p. 471), at the base of which is a collar-like projection. By the lashing movements which these threads execute the water-currents upon which the life of the animal depends are produced. The middle supporting layer is comparable to the similarly-placed gelatinous layer of a jelly-fish, and it contains numerous cells of various kinds which have been derived from the ectoderm and entoderm. Some of these cells produce three-rayed calcareous spicules which form a very characteristic skeleton (fig. 298).

The majority of sponges, like corals (p. 476), are able to produce colonies of the most varied shape by processes of budding or splitting, and in such cases the boundaries between the individuals are usually very ill-marked, though the number of these

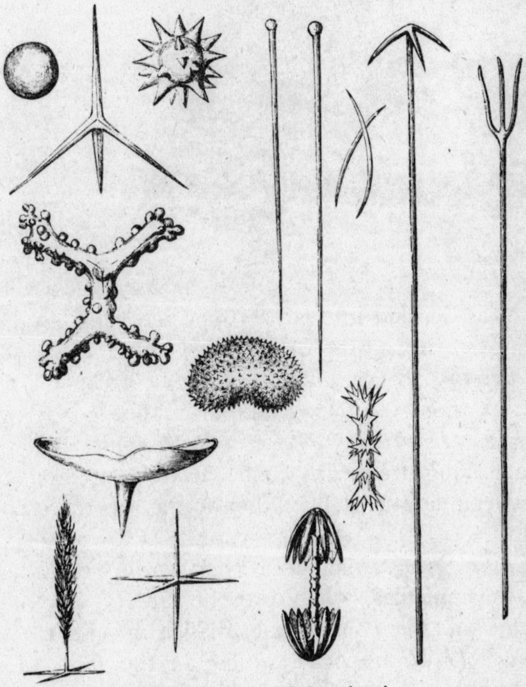

Fig. 298.—Sponge Spicules, enlarged

is generally to be told by counting the number of larger openings or oscula which are present. There is also a very large amount of variation in the nature of the skeleton and the extent to which it is developed. It may, as in the simple case described, be made up of scattered spicules, and these may either be calcareous or siliceous. Such spicules are of many different shapes (fig. 298), and they may be compacted into a firm, continuous mass, while they may further be associated with, or replaced by, a complex horny net-work. It should further be remarked that in the large majority of cases the body-wall is much more complicated than in the case described, and the collar-cells are restricted to small rounded chambers situated in the thickness of the wall and communicating by narrow canals with the exterior on the one hand and the central cavity on the other. The canal system may be exceedingly complex, as may be realized by looking at the labyrinth of spaces present in an ordinary bath-sponge.

Fig. 299.—Bath-Sponge (*Euspongia*), reduced

It will be sufficient for the present purpose to consider the Sponges as divided into two groups according to the nature of the skeleton; *i.e.*: 1. Calcareous Sponges, and 2. Siliceous Sponges.

1. *Calcareous Sponges*, when simple, correspond to the type described. A more complex example is afforded by the common British species *Grantia compressa*, a small white flattened sponge about an inch long, frequently found attached to stones and other objects between tide-marks. Other forms are represented in fig. 300.

2. *Siliceous Sponges* include a great variety of forms in which the supporting spicules, when present, are of siliceous or flinty nature. One of the commonest British species is the *Bread-crumb Sponge* (*Halichondria*), which, in the form of yellowish-brown or orange-coloured masses, may be found encrusting rocks near low-tide mark. On the surface of the sponge a number of little conical elevations may be seen, and on the end of each an *osculum* is situated. The *pores* by which currents enter are placed in the part of the sponge between these projections. For beauty of form nothing can surpass *Venus's Flower-Basket* (*Euplectella*), a deep-water form in which the skeleton may be compared to a cornucopia with a wall of lace-like appearance and a perforated lid. Another very interesting kind is the *Glass-rope Sponge* (*Hyalonema*) dredged in deep water off Japan. Here the ovoid body is anchored in the mud by bundles of long twisted spicules which have suggested the name.

The *Bath-Sponge* (*Euspongia*) possesses a horny skeleton, the texture of which makes it useful for a variety of purposes.

One small group of sponges is found in *fresh water*, and of

Fig. 300.—Group of Calcareous Sponges 1, *Leucandra aspera*. 2, *Sycandra raphanus*

these the commonest British genus (*Spongilla*) is found as a greenish crust upon various objects.

ANIMALCULES (Protozoa)

The innumerable host of simple animals which constitute this phylum are nearly all minute, while many of them can only be studied by the highest powers of the microscope, so that every improvement in the construction of that instrument has been followed by the acquisition of fresh knowledge concerning this group. Very great interest attaches to the study of the Protozoa, for here we have to deal with life under the simplest conditions, and find the actual living substance, *protoplasm*, which constitutes the essential part of all organisms, in a comparatively pure form, and not obscured to the same extent as in higher animals by the products of its own activity. It has become a tradition to take as a first type one of the simplest members of the group, *i.e.* the *Proteus Animalcule* or *Amœba*, which is commonly found creeping on the mud of ponds.

Reference has frequently been made to the microscopic bodies known as white or colourless corpuscles which abound in the blood and lymph of higher animals (see p. 41). These crawl through the body in all directions and perform various functions of no mean importance, one being that of destroying disease germs which have entered the organism from the exterior. These corpuscles may almost be said to lead an existence independent of the rest of the body, and indeed it is possible to keep them alive outside the organism to which they belong for some time, especially in the case of cold-blooded creatures such as the Frog. An Amœba resembles in many essential respects one of these corpuscles, so much so that when it cannot be obtained for study in the laboratory a white corpuscle is often taken as the best substitute. The body (fig. 301) consists of a particle of semi-fluid protoplasm possessing the power of active locomotion, employed in the search for *food*, which consists of microscopic plants and other solid bodies of organic nature. The complex and solid nature of the food, or part of it, is, as will be elsewhere shown, a characteristic of average animals as compared with average plants, and the powers of locomotion with which most animals are endowed has an obvious relation to this. In such a *fixed animal* as a sponge there is, as we have seen, a special arrangement by which food is brought to the body, compensating for the absence of locomotor powers. An ordinary *green plant*, feeding as it does upon gaseous and liquid food extracted from air and soil, has no need for powers of locomotion, and its branching form gives a very large surface through which the simple food can diffuse. An active *animal*, on the other hand, such as Amœba, has a compact body which is clearly more convenient for locomotor purposes and less exposed than a branching form would be to the attacks of enemies. When tree-like organisms, such as zoophytes, are of animal nature, they usually represent fixed colonies to which food is brought by currents.

The body of a living Amœba is seen to be constantly changing

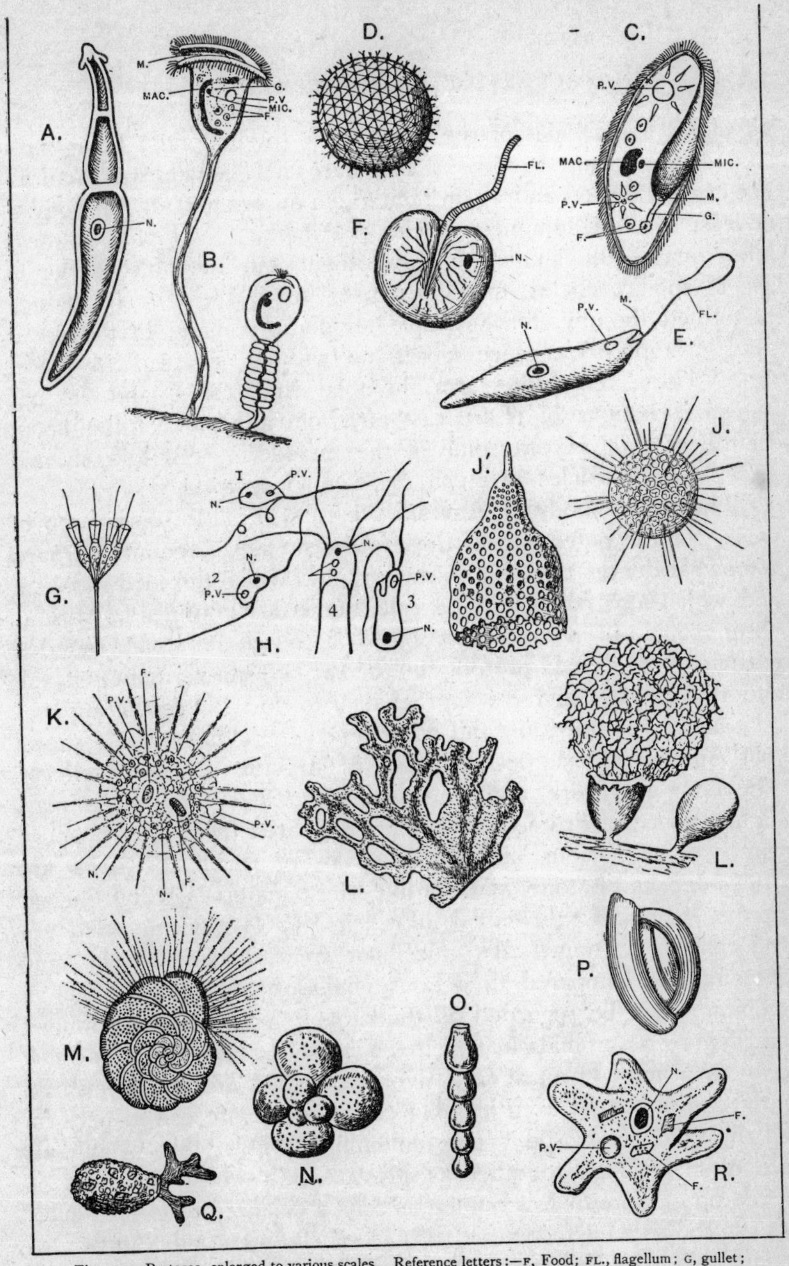

Fig. 301.—Protozoa, enlarged to various scales. Reference letters:—F, Food; FL., flagellum; G, gullet; M, mouth; MAC., macronucleus; MIC., micronucleus; N, nucleus; P.V., pulsating vacuole

A, Cockroach Gregarine (*Clepsidrina blattarum*). B, Bell-Animalcule (*Vorticella*), extended and retracted. C, Slipper-Animalcule (*Paramœcium*). D, Volvox. E. Euglena. F, Noctiluca. G, Codonocladium. H, Monads: I and 2, Springing Monad (*Heteromita*); 3, *Chilomonas*; 4, *Hexamita*. J and J′, Skeletons of Radiolaria (*Heliosphæra* and *Eucyrtidium*). K, A Sun-Animalcule (*Actinosphærium*). L and L′, Small piece of a Mycetozoon and two capsules (one ruptured) of same. M, A Foraminifer (*Rotalia*), with protruded threads of protoplasm. N, O, P, Shells of Foraminifera (*Globigerina*, *Nodosaria*, and *Miliola*). Q, A shell-bearing Rhizopod (*Difflugia*), allied to Amœba. R, Proteus Animalcule (*Amœba*).

its shape, blunt lobes of the protoplasm (pseudopods) being protruded from time to time. They are not constant structures, but can be formed and again obliterated at any part of the body—at least in the commonest species of Amœba. Not only do these lobes enable the animal to crawl about, but they also serve to secure food particles, engulfing them, so to speak. No breach is formed thereby, for any hole temporarily made in the semi-fluid protoplasm at once closes up without leaving any trace. Once within the protoplasm the food is digested, and the undigested portions of it are cast out from any part of the body. In the case of Hydra some of the endoderm cells take in and digest solid particles in much the same way (p. 471).

The simple body of Amœba presents but little distinction of parts, but the outer part of the protoplasm is clearer and perhaps somewhat denser than the inner part into which the food is taken, and which also contains, as a rule, numerous granules of various nature. As in a colourless blood corpuscle a small rounded particle of specialized protoplasm, the *nucleus*, can be distinguished, and this appears to have a great deal to do with regulating and controlling the nutrition and other functions. Its presence shows that Amœba is a single *cell* or unit of structure, *i.e.* is unicellular. The body of Hydra, and the same thing is true for all animals higher than the Protozoa, has been compared (p. 469) to a house composed of various building materials of which the units are bricks, blocks of stone, and the like, these materials being likened to the *tissues* of the animal in which *cells* of differing kind are the constituent units. An unicellular creature like Amœba may therefore be compared to a house built of one brick, if such a metaphor can be regarded as thinkable. The PROTOZOA indeed are defined as animals in which the body is made up of one cell only, or at most of an aggregate of cells which are not specialized into tissues, so that each member of the aggregate has to perform all the functions of life. The remaining thirteen phyla of animals are often grouped together as METAZOA, in which the body is made up of more or less numerous cells specialized to form tissues. It may be as well to express this in tabular form, advantage also being taken of the opportunity to show the limits of Vertebrata and Invertebrata, of Diploblastica and Triploblastica.

There can be no doubt that the Metazoa are descended from unicellular forms, which must have resembled some of the

	I.	VERTEBRATA	Triploblastica	METAZOA.
INVERTEBRATA	II.	Nemertea	Triploblastica	METAZOA.
INVERTEBRATA	III.	Mollusca	Triploblastica	METAZOA.
INVERTEBRATA	IV.	Arthropoda	Triploblastica	METAZOA.
INVERTEBRATA	V.	Annelida	Triploblastica	METAZOA.
INVERTEBRATA	VI.	Gephyrea	Triploblastica	METAZOA.
INVERTEBRATA	VII.	Rotifera	Triploblastica	METAZOA.
INVERTEBRATA	VIII.	Molluscoida	Triploblastica	METAZOA.
INVERTEBRATA	IX.	Platyhelmia	Triploblastica	METAZOA.
INVERTEBRATA	X.	Nemathelmia	Triploblastica	METAZOA.
INVERTEBRATA	XI.	Echinodermata	Triploblastica	METAZOA.
INVERTEBRATA	XII.	Cœlenterata	Diploblastica	METAZOA.
INVERTEBRATA	XIII.	Porifera	Diploblastica	METAZOA.
INVERTEBRATA	XIV.	PROTOZOA		

Protozoa, and consequently great interest attaches to the study of those members of the latter group which are aggregates of cells, since some of these may, in some respects, be like the transitional forms.

Returning to the consideration of Amœba, we find that this differs from a colourless corpuscle in possessing a liquid-filled space within the protoplasm which is constantly changing its size in a regular manner, and is therefore termed a *pulsating vacuole.* If carefully watched in a living specimen placed under the microscope, this will be found to slowly expand to a certain size and then to suddenly contract so as to be entirely lost to view, soon reappearing, however, at the same spot. It appears to communicate with the exterior, and probably has to do with getting rid of waste products (*excretion*) and perhaps also with the introduction of dissolved oxygen into the body for the purpose of *respiration.*

Amœba is *sensitive* to external influences, being affected, for example, by changes of temperature, but it also appears to be able to execute movements, apart from the direct action of such influences. Otherwise expressed, the minute fragment of protoplasm which constitutes the body of this animal, performs those functions which, in higher forms, are relegated to a *nervous system,* and its connected *sense organs.*

Careful observation has shown that Amœba multiplies itself by a process of splitting or *fission,* as observed in some animals higher in the scale (pp. 476). The nucleus elongates, and becomes divided into two parts, and at the same time the rest of the body is halved, the result being that the parent animal disappears altogether as an individual, being replaced by two new animals which subsequently increase in size.

It therefore appears that all the functions of life can be, and are, performed by a single cell, this having to discharge the duties which in higher organisms are distributed between different complex organs and tissues.

It is convenient to divide the Protozoa into three groups:—1. Infusorians (Infusoria); 2. Amœba-like Protozoa (Rhizopoda); and 3. Gregarines (Sporozoa).

Group 1.—Infusorians (Infusoria)

If boiling water is added to chopped hay or other vegetable matter, and the infusion so procured allowed to stand for some time, it will begin to putrefy, and a large number of minute active creatures will make their appearance in it. The same thing would happen if the infusion were of animal nature. The term *Infusoria* was first applied to the minute forms noted in various decomposing substances of the kind just mentioned, but they are by no means invariably associated with putridity, and abound both in salt and fresh water, or even on damp soil and vegetation.

A very common form is the *Slipper Animalcule* (*Paramœcium*) (fig. 301), which is readily obtained by making an infusion of hay as described. It is an active whitish creature, just visible to the naked eye. Placed under the microscope, it will be found to possess an elongated body, which, unlike Amœba, has a definite shape owing to the fact that the outer layer of the protoplasm (ectosarc) is firmer than the rest (endosarc), and covered by a thin elastic membrane or *cuticle*. As another consequence of this, food cannot be taken into, or solid waste ejected from, any part of the body, but there is on one side a depression which leads to a *mouth*, and this again into a very short *gullet*, that ends abruptly in the soft internal protoplasm (endosarc). Not far from this depression there is a spot where the cuticle is absent, and the solid refuse from the food can pass out to the exterior.

The presence of a cuticle, and the firm nature of the outer protoplasm, prevent the formation of the blunt lobes (pseudopods), which, as we have seen, serve in Amœba as organs for obtaining food and effecting locomotion. Their place is here taken by a uniform covering of *cilia*, which are protruded through minute holes in the cuticle. By them the animalcule is rowed about from place to place, and they also set up currents by which food particles are conducted into the mouth. Within the body two *pulsating vacuoles* can be seen, one at each end, and there are also two bodies of nuclear nature, which are placed close together. One of them is large (macronucleus), and the other small (micronucleus). They pass through a series of very complicated changes before the animal undergoes transverse splitting or *fission*, which is here the characteristic method of multiplication.

A very large section of the Infusoria are characterized by the presence of cilia, the arrangement of which differs in different species, and these constitute the group of *Ciliata*. We may take as a second example of this division the *Bell Animalcule* (*Vorticella*) (fig. 301), which is commonly found attached to water-weeds, or it may be to aquatic animals, such as the little red worm Tubifex (p. 431). Here the body is of bluntly conical form, with the narrow end drawn out into a long *stalk*, firmly fixed to the object upon which the animal lives. When fully expanded, it can be seen that the cilia are limited to the broad end of the body, on which they are arranged in a short spiral, while smaller cilia are continued down into a depression, which may be compared to that seen in the Slipper Animalcule, for it leads into a short gullet of the same kind. Within this depression there is a soft spot through which the undigested remains of the food are ejected. The wreath of cilia produces currents, which set into and out of the mouth-depression, carrying food and dissolved oxygen inwards and waste matters outwards. As in a Slipper Animalcule, the protoplasm is divided into a softer central *endosarc* and a firm external *ectosarc*, the latter being continued into a fibre which runs in a wavy manner through the stalk. If Vorticella is alarmed in any way, the free end of the body is folded in, and, at the same time, the elastic stalk is thrown into the form of a spiral by the shortening or contraction of the fibre it encloses.

Within the body one *pulsating vacuole* can be seen, and also two *nuclei*, the big one having a very characteristic horse-shoe form. Multiplication is effected by longitudinal splitting, one of the two new individuals remaining on the stalk, while the other becomes detached, being rowed about by the cilia till a suitable spot is reached, when it becomes attached, and develops a new stalk.

Some of the near relatives of the Bell Animalcule form colonies by means of fission, the new individuals remaining attached instead of at once becoming separated, as in Vorticella. All the members of the colony are of exactly similar nature.

Another large section of Infusorians, the *Flagellata*, is characterized by the presence of those protoplasmic threads known as *flagella* (p. 471), which, though allied to cilia, are capable of executing much more complex movements, and are not present in large numbers on the same cell. A common example is *Euglena* (fig. 301), a minute green form with worm-like body, found, sometimes very abundantly, in stagnant water. At the front end there is one long *flagellum*, which acts as a swimming organ, pulling the body after it through the water. At its base there is a minute *mouth* leading into an exceedingly short *gullet*, near which is a *pulsating vacuole*, and a red *pigment-spot*. The nucleus is central, and the green colouring matter (chlorophyll), which is of the same nature as that found in ordinary plants, is contained in specialized parts of the protoplasm. The body is constantly altering its shape in a peculiar manner, but the presence of a firm *cuticle* prevents the formation of pseudopods.

Putrefying infusions contain vast numbers of very minute flagellates, commonly known as *monads* (fig. 301). A well-known form is the *Springing Monad* (*Heteromita*), so named from the character of its movements. It is shaped like a bean, and possesses two long *flagella*, attached near the notched side. One of these is extended forward during locomotion like the single flagellum of Euglena, while the other is trailed behind.

A very interesting section of the present group contains simple and colonial forms, in which the individuals closely resemble the *collar-cells* of sponges (see p. 484). *Codonocladium* (fig. 301) may be taken as an example. The interest chiefly lies in the fact that such forms perhaps give a hint as to the ancestry of the sponges.

It has been mentioned that Euglena is like a green plant, inasmuch as it contains chlorophyll, but the presence of a mouth proves it to be an animal. There are, however, certain flagellates which are coloured green by this pigment, and at the same time are devoid of any mouth-opening. Indeed, many botanists claim them as plants. Some are simple, others colonial, and of the latter, one genus is particularly well known on account of its great beauty as a microscopic object. This is *Volvox*, a form shaped like a hollow sphere (fig. 301), and about the size of a very small pin's head. At regular intervals in the wall of the sphere are imbedded the green pear-shaped individuals, each of which is provided with a pair of *flagella*, and is connected by threads of protoplasm with its neighbours. The colony swims about by means of the flagella, slowly revolving as it does so. We have here an example of the most perfect type of symmetry known, that of the sphere, a shape which is only possible when external influences act on all parts alike, as can only be the case with a revolving aquatic form. At times, however, the symmetry of Volvox is disturbed by the specialization of certain cells for the purpose of propagation.

A small marine group of flagellates is represented by the remarkable form *Noctiluca* (L. *nox*, night; *lux*, light), countless myriads of which are sometimes found floating together in the sea (fig. 301), and are one of the causes of the phosphorescence common in the summer months. Each individual is of comparatively large size ($\frac{1}{25}$ of an inch in diameter) and is shaped like a peach, a very large *flagellum* being attached at one end of the groove. The *mouth* is situated at the base of this structure and leads into a short *gullet* into which a second but smaller flagellum projects.

Group 2.—Amœba-like Protozoa (Rhizopoda)

A description has already been given of the Proteus Animalcule (Amœba), which may be taken as a type of the group, all the members of which are provided with those projections of the body which are called pseudopods, though it is only in some cases that these are broad lobes, as in many species of Amœba.

There are a number of common fresh-water members of this group (fig. 301), which essentially resemble Amœba except that they possess a shell of varied nature and shape. Sometimes it consists of foreign particles cemented together, and at other times it is entirely made up of material presumably of horny nature formed by the activity of the protoplasm.

Cases like those just mentioned lead on to a large and important group found both in salt and fresh water, and characterized by the presence of a shell that is often riddled with minute pores or *foramina*, on which account the name of *Foraminifera* has been given (fig. 301). The shell may be either tough and membranous, composed of foreign particles agglutinated together, or, and usually, of calcareous nature. It either consists of a single chamber or of a number of chambers associated in various manners and presenting the utmost variety in form. One of the most abundant forms is *Globigerina*, the shell of which consists of several rounded chambers united together, and which occurs in such profusion in a calcareous deposit covering large tracts of the ocean floor that this has received the name of Globigerina ooze. Globigerina and other forms have also lived in earlier epochs of the earth's history, playing a very important part as rock-builders. The pure form of limestone called chalk is, for example, mainly composed of such remains. Most of the Foraminifera are of small size, but *Nummulina*, so called from its coin-like shape (L. *nummus*, a coin), reaches the size of a shilling piece. Its shells chiefly make up the important nummulitic limestone by which mountain ranges in the Mediterranean region are to a large extent built up.

The *pseudopods* of the Foraminifera are slender threads which often unite together into a sort of net-work. More than one *nucleus* is commonly present in the protoplasm of which the soft body consists.

The *Sun-Animalcules* (*Heliozoa*) (fig. 301) are a group of mainly fresh-water forms in which the body is spherical, and stiff pointed pseudopods radiate from it in a way which suggests the rays seen in the conventional representation of the sun; hence the name. There may be more than one nucleus and pulsating vacuole. *Actinophrys* and *Actinosphærium* are typical genera. In some members of the group the surface of the body is covered by loose flinty *spicules*, and in the stalked genus *Clathrulina* there is a continuous shell in the form of a perforated hollow sphere. This leads on to the condition found in most of the marine group of *Ray-Animalcules* (Radiolaria) (fig. 301), where there is a siliceous shell of extreme beauty and of the most varied shape. Some parts of the sea-floor are covered by Radiolarian ooze, mainly composed of such shells; and there are also fossil forms making up certain rocks, notably in the Barbados. Almost every microscopic cabinet contains a slide of this "Barbados earth".

The Amœba group may be reckoned to include certain problematic organisms called Myxomycetes or *Mycetozoa*, the latter name indicating the doubt which has existed as to whether

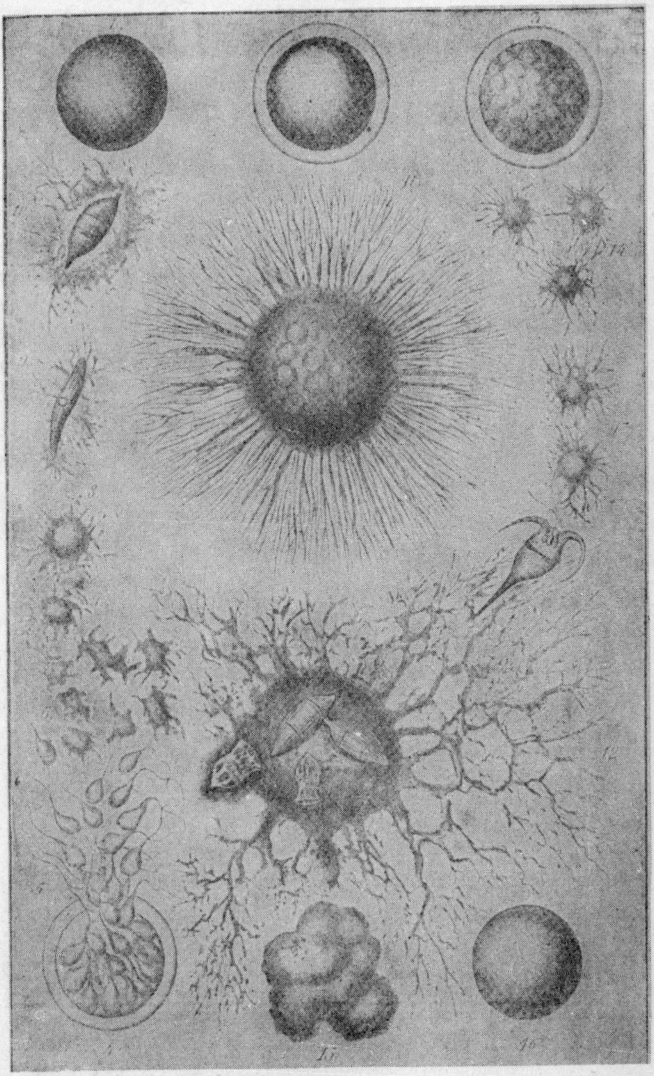

Fig. 302.—Stages in Life-History of *Protomyxa*, enlarged

1, Spherical resting stage; 2, the same invested with firm coat; 3, contents of same dividing into spores; 4, escape of spores (5), which assume amœba-like shape, feed (9 and 10), and fuse together (13, 14) to form adult stage, which is shown in hungry stage (11), and feeding (12). This ultimately contracts (15), and becomes round (16), after which the life-cycle recommences as before.

they are plants or animals (Gk. *mykēs*, a fungus; *zōon*, an animal). Indeed, like Volvox and its allies, they will be found described in most text-books, both of botany and zoology. A good example is the so-called "flowers of tan" (*Æthalium*) (fig. 301), which is to be found in the form of sulphur-coloured net-works of protoplasm creeping slowly over heaps of spent tan, and attaining a considerable size. At a certain time this organism produces little capsules in which a number of small hard-coated reproductive bodies known as *spores* are formed. From these escape little fragments of protoplasm, which are at first something like flagellate protozoans, for each of them possesses a single flagellum, while later on they assume the shape of minute amœbæ. A number of these fuse together to form a creeping net-work.

In the Amœba group we may also include one of the simplest known kinds of Protozoa, a minute marine animal—*Protomyxa aurantiaca* (fig. 302)—found on the coast of the Canary Islands. In colour and appearance it resembles a small individual of the tan-flower organism, but no trace of a nucleus was observed by its discoverer. After leading an active life for some time the body contracts into a spherical form and becomes surrounded by a firm investment. The protoplasm then divides up into a number of fragments, each of which possesses a single flagellum. These are liberated by the rupture of the protecting investment, soon assuming the shape of little amœbæ, of which numbers fuse together to form an adult.

Group 3.—Gregarines (Sporozoa)

This third and last group of the Protozoa has been modified by the parasitic habit. The body is covered by a firm cuticle, but cilia as well as pseudopods are absent. A good example is a form (*Clepsidrina blattarum*) (fig. 301), found within the alimentary canal of the Cockroach. The elongated body, when very young, is attached by a hooked narrower end to the lining of the cockroach's intestine. Later on, the hooked end is shed, the animal becoming free. A *nucleus* is discernible within the protoplasm, but no pulsating vacuole. As the name indicates, the group is characterized by the presence of those specialized reproductive cells called *spores*, which are more commonly met with in plants than in animals. Before these can be formed two individuals must together be surrounded by a firm coating or *cyst*, and they then break up into a multitude of little spores surrounded by firm coats. The spores become free by a somewhat complex process, the firm coat of each then ruptures, and the contained protoplasm emerges, ultimately growing into an adult Gregarine, which is at first imbedded in and nourished by one of the cells lining the intestine of the cockroach.

The Sporozoa not only include many forms more or less similar to the one described, but also a large number of much simpler species, parasitic in the cells of Vertebrates and other higher animals.

The Natural History of Animals

THE COMMON MACKEREL *(Scomber vernalis)*

This well-known fish inhabits the Atlantic and Mediterranean, and approaches our shores in large shoals in pursuit of herrings. It is remarkable for beautiful coloration, and also for its graceful shape, which is an adaptation to rapid swimming, offering but little resistance to the surrounding water. The symmetrical, deeply-forked tail serves as a propeller ot unusual power, and the lateral muscles are of a reddish colour, owing to the abundant blood-supply, which is associated with the power of prolonged and swift movement. The upper and lower rows of "finlets" on the hinder part of the body are characteristic.

THE COMMON MACKEREL (SCOMBER VERNALIS)

The Natural History of Animals

The animal life of the world in its various aspects and relations

IN FOUR VOLUMES

BY

J.R. AINSWORTH DAVIS

Volume III

GIAN PUBLISHING HOUSE

New Delhi-110002

GIAN PUBLISHING HOUSE
4348, Madan Mohan Street
4C, Ansari Road, Darya Ganj.
New Delhi - 110002

First Indian Edition 1989
First Printed 1905

ISBN 81 - 212 - 0253 - 1 Set
ISBN 81 - 212 - 0258 - 2

Printed In India
at
Goyal Offset Printers, Delhi.

CONTENTS

Vol III

ANIMAL MOVEMENT

CHAPTER XL.—ANIMAL MOVEMENT—FIRST PRINCIPLES

CHAPTER XLI.—MUSCULAR LOCOMOTION—SWIMMING OF LOWER INVERTEBRATES

CHAPTER XLII.—MUSCULAR LOCOMOTION—SWIMMING OF HIGHER INVERTEBRATES

SWIMMING MOLLUSCS (MOLLUSCA)

CHAPTER XLIII.—MUSCULAR LOCOMOTION—PRIMITIVE VERTEBRATES AND FISHES AS SWIMMERS

CHAPTER XLIV.—MUSCULAR LOCOMOTION—AMPHIBIANS, REPTILES, BIRDS, AND MAMMALS AS SWIMMERS

SURFACE-SWIMMING BIRDS

BIRDS WHICH SWIM UNDER WATER AND DIVE

MAMMALS (MAMMALIA) AS SWIMMERS

CHAPTER XLV.—MUSCULAR LOCOMOTION—CREEPING ANIMALS

CHAPTER XLVI.—MUSCULAR LOCOMOTION—WALKING, RUNNING, &c.

MAMMALS (Mammalia) AS WALKERS AND RUNNERS

CHAPTER L.—MUSCULAR LOCOMOTION—CLIMBING

MAMMALS (MAMMALIA) AS CLIMBERS

LIST OF ILLUSTRATIONS

Vol III

PLATES

ILLUSTRATIONS

NATURAL HISTORY

ANIMAL MOVEMENT

CHAPTER XL

ANIMAL MOVEMENT—FIRST PRINCIPLES

The living substance (protoplasm) which constitutes the essential part of the bodies of animals is endowed with a number of powers which characterize life as we know it. Ability to feed and breathe are two of these, and have been considered at considerable length in preceding sections. Living substance is also *contractile*, *i.e.* it is capable of changing its shape without diminution of volume, and this is the cause of all animal movements. Such movements lead to many results, some of which have already been dealt with, and of these results one of the most interesting is locomotion, in water, on the land, and in the air. Marked powers in this respect are characteristic of average animals as compared with average plants, and their purpose is sufficiently obvious. It is clear, for instance, that since animals require food of complex character, they must, as a rule, either move about in search of it, or else be possessed of arrangements whereby it is brought to them. The former state of things is the more usual, but in either case the contractile power of living substance is the primary motive power, and it may be desirable in the first instance to inquire more narrowly into the nature of this power. Most of the space in this section will, however, be given to the different kinds of Animal Locomotion.

As briefly explained in volume i, pp. 48, 49, there are three kinds of movement exemplified among animals, *i.e.* (1) Amœboid.

Movement, (2) Ciliary Movement, and (3) Muscular Movement, the first of these being the most primitive, and the last the most complex.

AMŒBOID MOVEMENT

This derives its name from the Proteus Animalcule or Amœba (see vol. i, p. 488), one of the simplest of existing animals, consisting as it does of a mere speck of comparatively pure living matter or protoplasm, devoid of any firm investment. It is, in fact, a mere unit-mass of such material, technically known as a *cell.* Constant change of shape here takes place (fig. 577), the result being that the protoplasm is thrust out into bluntish lobes termed *pseudopods*, by means of which the animal is able to crawl along, flowing after them, as it were, as they are protruded in a given direction. The pseudopods also serve, as we have elsewhere seen (vol. ii, p. 268), to engulf small plants and other bodies which are used as food. They are not in any sense permanent structures, but can be, and are, withdrawn from time to time, so as to be merged in the general substance of the body. We may take amœboid movement also to include stream-like flowings within the body of the Amœba, by which the food is carried round and round during the process of digestion. Movements of the kind are also clearly visible in the bodies of higher Animalcules, such as the Bell-Animalcule (*Vorticella*), where the presence of a firm external membrane or cuticle prevents pseudopods from being formed (see fig. 577).

The leading distinction between Animalcules (*Protozoa*) and animals higher in the scale (*Metazoa*) is that the former are unit-masses of protoplasm, *i.e.* are *single-celled* (unicellular), while the latter are more or less complex aggregates of such units, *i.e.* are *many-celled* (multicellular). It is the rule that some of the cells which make up the bodies of animals other than Animalcules should retain their powers of amœboid movement, as manifested not only by streamings within their substance, but also by the thrusting out of pseudopods. In the Freshwater Polype (*Hydra*), for example, a creature which is practically a living stomach with a double wall (see vol. i, p. 465), the digestive cavity is lined by large cells which possess the power of protruding pseudopods for the purpose of seizing food. And many other cases of the same kind might be mentioned.

Among the cells which build up the bodies of such forms as Worms, Star-Fishes, Arthropods, Molluscs, and Backboned Animals, are many which may be called "wandering cells", since they are not connected together like the constituents of muscle, nerve, &c., but move about by means of pseudopods. These abound in the circulatory fluids, and to them belong the colourless corpuscles of human blood and lymph (fig. 575), though it must not be supposed that they exist in the blood of all animals. An earth-worm, for example, possesses an elaborate system of blood-vessels, but there are no colourless corpuscles in the contained fluid, though such are abundantly present in the lymph which fills the large space (body-cavity) between the internal organs and the wall of the body. Plenty of wandering cells are also found in the "jelly" of jelly-fishes and the soft substance of sponges, though in these cases blood-system and lymph-system are both absent.

Fig. 575.—Colourless Corpuscle, greatly magnified, showing successive changes of shape, and protrusion of pseudopods

It is very interesting to find that the higher (compared to animalcules) animals of which mention has just been made, though they no longer use amœboid movement as a means of locomotion, employ it for other and very important purposes. Their wandering cells resemble amœba not only in structure and way of moving, but also in their method of feeding, by taking in solid particles bodily. So great is their independence that under suitable treatment they retain their vitality a long time after being removed from the body to which they belong, and can even be fed.

To do full justice to these curiously independent wandering cells would require a very considerable space, and it is only possible here to indicate some of their spheres of usefulness. They have metaphorically been called the scavengers, police, and defensive army of the body, and all these terms are more than justifiable. A remarkable instance of their scavenging function is exemplified by Star-Fishes. Although these animals possess specialized breathing organs, they are badly off as regards structures which perform the work of kidneys, *i.e.* get rid of nitrogenous waste products. The wandering cells make good this deficiency, for they take up granules consisting of this kind of waste, and then make their way to the exterior through thin places existing between the hard limy deposits in the wall of the body. Whether or no they get rid of the waste and then re-enter the body is not known, but such an occurrence is not impossible.

Wandering cells play an important part during development, when the various organs of the body are being, as it were, modelled out of plastic material, and also in cases where more or less remodelling is required in the course of the life-history. Of the latter phenomenon a good instance is afforded by the way a tadpole's tail disappears, as a part of the modifications necessary to produce a fully-formed frog. Many persons suppose that the tail simply drops off, but this is not so, for the material of which it is made up is too valuable to be thrown away. What really happens is that its substance gradually breaks down and is carried by wandering cells into the main body, there to be utilized for other purposes.

But by far the most interesting use of such cells is that of combating disease-germs which make their way into the system, eating them up amœba fashion. Were it not for the constant activity of these minute guardians of the body, infectious diseases would be able to do infinitely more mischief than is the case at present. And it is quite likely that the protection from disease afforded by inoculation may be due to the fact that this process has, so to speak, trained the wandering cells of the body to deal with some particular sort of invader.

CILIARY MOVEMENT

It is clear that only a naked mass of living matter (protoplasm) is able to protrude pseudopods, and in the case of cells covered by a firm membrane they are often replaced by the delicate protoplasmic threads known as *cilia* and *flagella* (fig. 576). These are protruded through little holes in the membrane covering the cell to which they belong, and in typical cases differ from pseudopods in being permanent structures which cannot be pushed out and again withdrawn at pleasure. In some animalcules we find slender thread-like pseudopods, which may be regarded as a stage in the evolution of the more specialized structures now under consideration. It may be as well to note here that a *flagellum* is a comparatively long thread of which only one, two, or at most a few, are borne on the same cell. It is capable of complex lashing movements. A *cilium*, on the other hand, is a relatively short thread, of which large numbers project from a single cell, and which is only capable of alternate bending and straightening. But in either case the result is something more definite than amœboid movement, as might be expected from the fact that the motile structures are of higher grade than pseudopods.

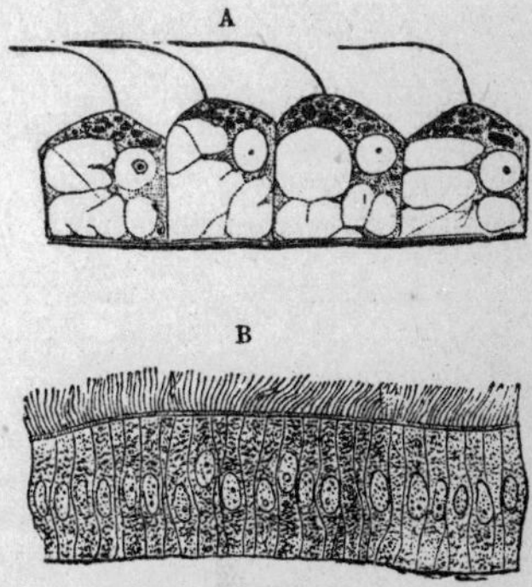

Fig. 576.

A, Four flagellated cells. B, Ciliated epithelium. Sections (greatly enlarged)

Cilia.—It is a very remarkable fact that numerous cilia are able to work together for a given end, numerous examples of this being furnished by different animalcules, one group of these being called "Ciliata", because they are provided with structures of the kind.

Ciliary action, for example, is quite competent to serve as a means of swimming, as seen in the Slipper-Animalcule (*Paramœcium*) and many other forms (fig. 577 c). In such animals the mouth is placed in a depression lined by special cilia, the working of which sets up currents by means of which food is procured. In fixed forms the latter is the chief use of the cilia which are present, the currents of water produced also bringing a supply of fresh oxygen for breathing purposes, while there are counter-currents which carry away the various products of waste. An excellent instance of this is presented by the Bell-Animalcule (*Vorticella*), in which the body is in the shape of a rounded cone, tapering at its narrow end into a stalk that is fixed to a plant or other firm body (fig. 577 B). The broad end is furnished with a short spiral of cilia, by which the necessary currents are set up. Bell-Animalcules may also be seen in which the stalk is absent, and in this case the cilia are the swimming organs. Some of these free individuals are the same in structure as the stalked ones, but others are both smaller and simpler, except that they possess a special band of cilia round the narrow end of the body, and this is related to the method of locomotion.

Cilia may also be used for creeping, as, for instance, in one or two small flattened Comb-Jellies (*Cœloplana* and *Ctenoplana*),

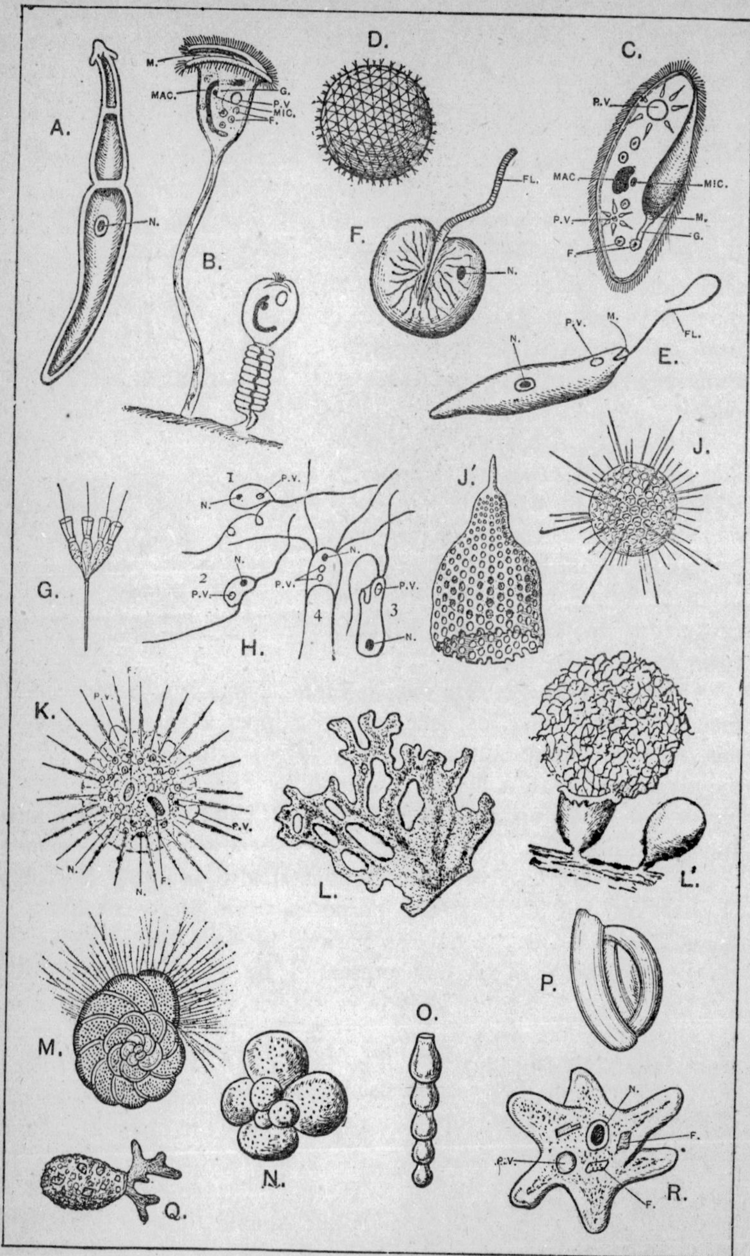

Fig. 577.—Protozoa, enlarged to various scales. Reference letters:—F, Food; FL., flagellum; G, gullet; M, mouth; MAC., macronucleus; MIC., micronucleus; N, nucleus; P.V., pulsating vacuole

A, Cockroach Gregarine (*Clepsidrina blattarum*). B, Bell-Animalcule (*Vorticella*), extended and retracted. C, Slipper-Animalcule (*Paramæcium*). D, Volvox. E, Euglena. F, Noctiluca. G, Codonocladium. H, Monads: 1 and 2, Springing Monad (*Heteromita*); 3, *Chilomonas*; 4, *Hexamita*. J and J′, Skeletons of Radiolaria (*Heliosphæra* and *Eucyrtidium*). K, A Sun-Animalcule (*Actinosphærium*). L and L′, Small piece of a Mycetozoon and two capsules (one ruptured) of same. M, A Foraminifer (*Rotalia*) with protruded threads of protoplasm. N, O, P, Shells of Foraminifera (*Globigerina*, *Nodosaria*, and *Miliola*). Q, A shell-bearing Rhizopod (*Difflugia*), allied to Amœba. R, Proteus Animalcule (*Amœba*) and in the Planarian Worms (*Turbellaria*) (fig. 578). These worms are mostly of flattened shape, and clothed with a uniform covering of short cilia, by which a sort of gliding movement is effected, greatly aided by the fact that the skin secretes and pours out a kind of slime. Land Planarians, although they live in damp places, would have a difficulty in moving by means of their cilia were it not for the presence of this secretion.

Fig. 578.—A Freshwater Planarian Worm (*Planaria gonocephala*), enlarged

Locomotion by means of cilia is of uncommon occurrence in the adults of animals higher in the scale than Planarian Worms, but is abundantly exemplified by aquatic embryos of such animals,

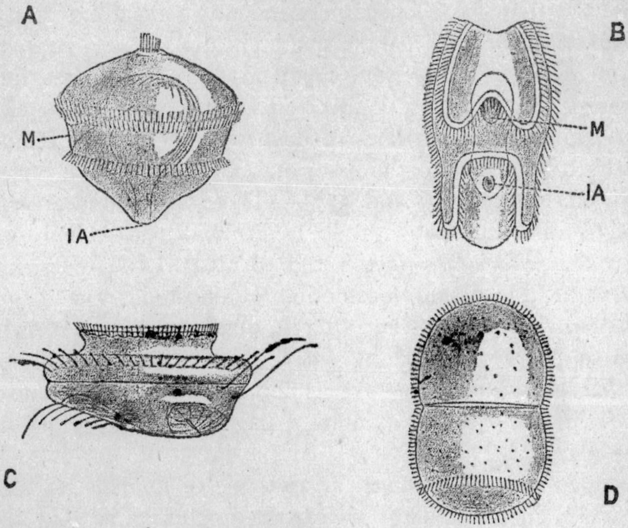

Fig. 579.—Ciliated Larvæ, enlarged to various scales

A, Annelid. B, Sea-Cucumber. C, Moss-Polype. D, Acorn-headed Worm (very young stage)
M, Mouth. I A, Intestinal aperture.

especially when these are *larvæ*, which, though they lead an independent existence, are very different from the adults into which they later on develop. Among larvæ which swim in this fashion are those of marine Annelids (*Trochospheres*), Echinoderms, Moss-Polypes, and the Acorn-headed Worm (*Balanoglossus*) (fig. 579).

In the adult animals of certain groups higher than Protozoa ciliary currents play a very important part in procuring food, bringing fresh supplies of oxygen, and carrying away the various kinds of waste. Mention may here be especially made of Sea-Lilies and Feather-Stars (*Crinoidea*), Moss-Polypes (*Polyzoa*), Lamp-Shells (*Brachiopoda*), Bivalve Molluscs (*Lamellibranchia*), Sea-Squirts (*Urochorda*), and the Lancelet (*Amphioxus*). A curious negative character of the great phylum of Arthropods is found in the complete absence of cilia.

Cilia are also of use in helping to carry onwards the contents of various tubular structures in animals of the most diverse nature. We find them lining the digestive tube of certain low Annelids, and they clothe the mouth-cavity and part of the gullet in Frogs. They are also commonly present in excretory tubules, whether these open independently to the exterior, as in an earth-worm, or form part of a complicated kidney, as in a frog. Even in Man himself a use is found for these structures, for they are present on the lining of the air-passages, working together in such a manner that particles of dust or other foreign bodies are gradually carried out to the exterior.

FLAGELLA (figs. 576 and 577).—These structures are characteristic of one important group of Animalcules, called on this account the *Flagellata* (see vol. i, p. 494). In free-swimming members of this group locomotion is effected by a flagellum, which drags along its owner after it, much as an expert swimmer is able to propel himself by means of one arm while his legs and other arm remain passive. The life-history of some other Animalcules (*Mycetozoa*) exhibits a flagellate stage, which swims in a similar way.

Sponges may be taken as an example of animals higher than Animalcules in which flagella play an important part in the life processes. For a Sponge is traversed by more or less elaborate canals, which are partly lined by flagellate cells. The movements of the flagella which these bear set up currents that answer the same purposes as the ciliary currents of the forms mentioned above.

MUSCULAR MOVEMENT

Strands of living matter are specialized into muscle-fibres in all the groups of animals, from Animalcules upwards. A good and simple example is afforded by the Bell-Animalcule (*Vorti-*

cella), one end of which is fixed by a hollow elastic stalk to some firm body. Running through the stalk, and forming a specialized part of the single cell of which the animal consists, is a muscle-fibre, which takes a wavy course from side to side (fig. 577 B). When it contracts, *i.e.* shortens and broadens, the stalk is thrown into a spiral, and the animal is able in this way to draw itself back from any object that threatens danger. When the fibre ceases to contract, the elasticity of the stalk straightens it out again.

All animals except Animalcules possess more or less complex bodies made up of numerous unit-masses of living substance, or *cells*; whereas an Animalcule consists of but a single cell, though the parts of this may be extremely specialized, *e.g.* a Bell-Animalcule possesses a muscle-fibre, a short spiral of cilia, a mouth, and a gullet. In other words, there is a *division of physiological labour* between the parts of the single cell in such a case, and these parts are more or less different from one another, *i.e.* are *differentiated.* But it is clear that when an animal is made up of many cells the possibilities of division of labour, with accompanying differentiation, are very great.

The amount of specialization in the way indicated is the real criterion as to whether a given kind of animal is "higher" or "lower" in the scale than some other sort of animal. As judged by this standard, for instance, an Insect is "higher" than a Centipede, and this again higher than Peripatus. Or we may say that an Amphibian is "lower" than a Reptile, and this again "lower" than a Mammal. Annelids are to be ranked above Zoophytes, and so on. Such comparisons are most fruitful when members of the same great animal group (*phylum*), or of a still smaller subdivision, are in question. For each group is specialized on lines of its own, being a distinct branch of the animal genealogical tree, and it would be difficult to say, for instance, whether an Insect is higher than a Cuttle-fish, or the contrary, for the two animals are adapted to a totally different set of external conditions, one being eminently marine, and the other eminently terrestrial, or indeed aerial. But we can hold with justice that a Bee is higher than a Cockroach, or that an Oyster is inferior to a Whelk.

If we consider the structure of a highly complex form, say a backboned animal, it will be found that its cells are divisible into several groups, or *tissues*, which are modified in different ways to fit them for the work which they perform (see vol. i, pp. 468–469). There is, for instance, nerve-tissue, which correlates the activities of the animal, and by aid of sense-organs keeps it in touch with its surroundings; and there is muscular-tissue, or muscle, with which we are here specially concerned. This is the agent of the most specialized form of movement, *i.e.* muscular movement. In muscle of all kinds the component elements are more or less converted into fibres, possessing the characteristic property of contraction, which means the power of shortening and at the same time of becoming broader.

The tissues are not much specialized in the lower groups of animals, and this is especially true of muscle. In such a creature as the Freshwater Polype (*Hydra*), the body is essentially a tube of which the wall consists of an outer and an inner layer of cells. Most of these cells are drawn out into muscle-fibres, those of the outer layer taking a longitudinal direction, and those of the inner layer a transverse or rather circular direction (fig. 580). Suppose that the fibres of the outer layer contract simultaneously, the body of the animal will obviously be shortened. If now they relax, and the fibres of the inner layer contract, it is equally clear that the body will lengthen out again, at the same time becoming narrower. Upon this simple principle are to be explained many of the internal movements which are continually going on within the bodies of animals higher in the scale than Hydra and its allies.

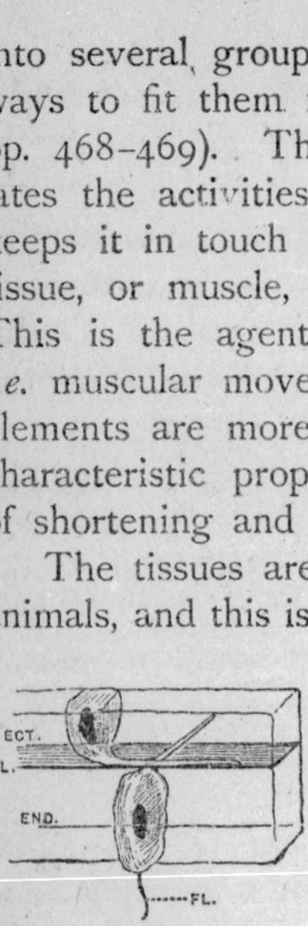

Fig. 580.—Small piece of Body-wall of Hydra (diagrammatic and greatly enlarged). ECT., Ectoderm. S.L., Supporting layer. END., Endoderm. FL., Flagellum. One ectodermic and one endodermic cell drawn, to show their muscle-fibres.

It would take up too much space, and be wearisome to the general reader, were the evolution of muscle-fibres traced throughout the animal kingdom. It will be sufficient to consider the nature and mode of action of such fibres in some of the higher forms, such as backboned animals and insects. In these cases we can distinguish between (1) unstriated muscle and (2) striated muscle, which are present in both cases, and represent two distinct grades of efficiency.

UNSTRIATED MUSCLE (fig. 581).—This consists of spindle-shaped cells which are united together by their tapering ends so as to form layers in the walls of various internal organs, including the large blood-vessels known as veins and arteries. This kind of muscle is not under the control of the will, and is therefore commonly known as "involuntary". In the intestine of a rabbit, for instance, there are two layers of such muscle, external to the mucous membrane, which forms a lining. The inner layer (or coat) is made up of fibres circularly disposed, while the fibres of the outer layer run longitudinally (compare Hydra, described above). This arrangement is adapted for squeezing the digesting food gradually onwards, for waves of contraction (peristaltic movements) pass along the layer of circular muscle, causing the cavity of the intestine to be narrowed, and thus forcing the food on. The contractions of the longitudinal layer enlarge the cavity of the tube, and at the same time pull its wall back over the food, which also assists onward progress. Regarding this Sir Michael Foster (in his *Text-book of Physiology*) says:—"A contraction of the longitudinal coat taking place in any segment of the tube would tend to draw the tube over the contents lying immediately above, or below, the segment, very much as a glove is drawn over a finger. And a succession of such contractions travelling along the tube would lead to a movement of the contents in the same direction. Were the circular coat absent a longitudinal coat might by itself possibly suffice to propel the contents along the tube."

Fig. 581.—An unstriated muscle-fibre (greatly enlarged). The dark band in the middle is the nucleus.

The wall of an artery (or vein) possesses a coat of circular muscle (fig. 582), the thickness of which depends upon the size of the vessel. It is also better developed in arteries than in veins. This coat, working under the control of the nervous system, is an important means of regulating the blood-flow. Take the case of an artery supplying a muscle with pure blood. Under average circumstances the fibres of its muscular coat are in a semi-contracted or "tonic" condition. If now the muscle supplied has need of more blood, these muscle-fibres relax, and the artery consequently enlarges. If, however, *less* blood is required, the muscle-fibres contract more strongly, and the size of the artery

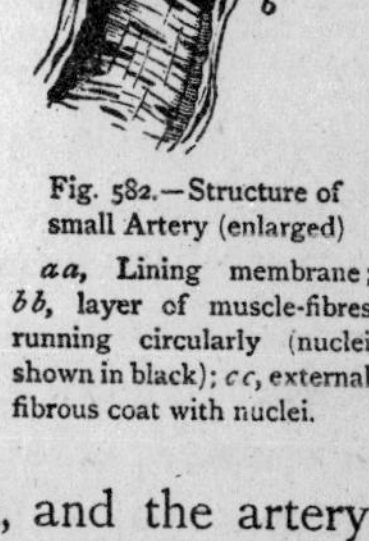

Fig. 582.—Structure of small Artery (enlarged) *aa*, Lining membrane; *bb*, layer of muscle-fibres running circularly (nuclei shown in black); *cc*, external fibrous coat with nuclei.

is correspondingly diminished. It may be well to add that the arteries also help in the propulsion of blood. Not, however, by means of the muscular coat, but by the action of an elastic layer which they contain. The contracting ventricles of the heart force blood into the arteries. Part of the force is expended in propelling the blood onwards, and part in dilating the arteries. When the ventricles of the heart cease to contract, the elasticity of the arteries comes into play, for as a result of this they become reduced to their usual size, and thus exert a squeezing action on their contents, which keeps the circulation going till the ventricles once more contract. The heart, from the nature of the case, is an intermittent pump, and were the arteries rigid the blood would be forced onwards in a series of jerks, which would be exceedingly uncomfortable, to say the least of it, and would probably be very injurious to the more delicate organs, such as the brain. The periodic swelling of an important artery in the wrist can readily be seen and felt, and is familiarly known as the "pulse". Being a result of the pumping action of the heart, it serves as an indication of whether or no that organ is working with vigour and regularity.

Fig. 583.—Striated Muscle of Heart (greatly enlarged)

The boundaries and nuclei of some of the cells shown on the right.

Heart Muscle (fig. 583).—The heart of a backboned animal, *e.g.* a rabbit, is chiefly made up of muscle-fibre, which, when it contracts, diminishes the contained cavities, forcing the blood onwards into the arteries, complicated valves preventing it from running back into the veins. But here the muscle-fibre is striated, though it is not so specialized as striated muscle proper, and, unlike this, it is involuntary. A little bit of it, looked at under the microscope, is seen to be made up of short broad cells united together, and markedly "striated", *i.e.* marked by numerous parallel transverse lines, and also by parallel longitudinal lines. It is not known for certain what the striations represent; perhaps they may be the expression of a specialized net-work within the cells; but, however that may be, it is a fact that striation is associated with vigorous powers of contraction, and such are required by the heart, which is essentially a force-pump.

The examples just given may serve as examples of the uses to which unstriated muscle and involuntary striated muscle are put in the bodies of higher animals, and the nature and mode of action of striated muscle proper falls next to be considered.

STRIATED MUSCLE (fig. 584).—This makes up what is popularly called the "flesh" of ordinary backboned animals, and the corresponding parts of Insects, Crustaceans, &c. Under the microscope it is seen to be composed of aggregates of slender well-striated fibres, produced by the activity of cells, though the boundaries of these are not clearly visible as in the tissue of the heart. It further differs from heart-muscle in the fact that each fibre is invested in a special membrane, and also because it is "voluntary", *i.e.* under the control of the will. Animal movements are very largely due to the action of this sort of muscle. It is the agent of the movements of breathing (see vol. i, p. 46), and is also the chief factor of muscular locomotion, though this is effected in many lower animals, such as jelly-fish and annelids, by unstriated fibres. It may also be stated generally that all the obvious movements of backboned animals and arthropods, whether they have to do with breathing and locomotion or not, result from the contractions of muscles belonging to the striated variety. This is the case, for instance, with movements of offence and defence, and those connected with securing and chewing food.

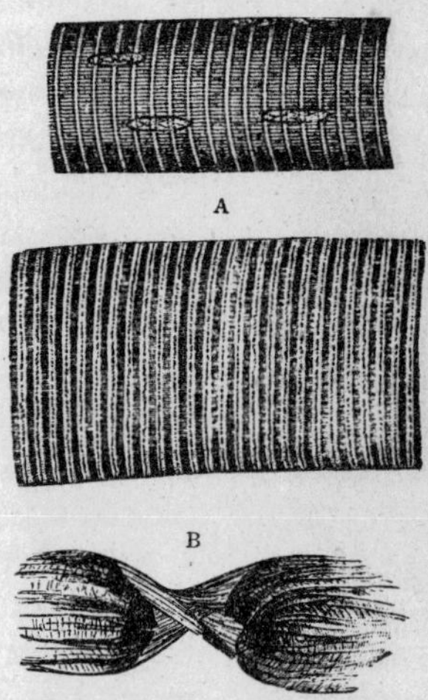

Fig. 584.—Voluntary Striated Muscle (greatly enlarged)

A, Parts of two fibres showing striations and (in upper piece) nuclei. B, Fibre torn across to show investing membrane (sarcolemma).

MUSCULAR LOCOMOTION.—The rest of the present section will deal with this alone, and before considering its different varieties a few points need elucidation. One of the most obvious facts requiring notice is that the muscular tissue of, say, a limb, is not one continuous mass, but is divided into a large number of separate parts, each of which is termed a *muscle*. In a typical case such a muscle is found to be a flat or spindle-shaped mass which has definite work to do. Walking, for example, is effected by the combined action of a large number of muscles, some of which move the leg on the trunk, while others move the various parts of the leg on one another. The motive power is precisely the same as that by which the stalk of a Bell-Animalcule is shortened (see p. 9), *i.e.* the property of contractility, briefly termed contraction, which the fibres making up a muscle individually possess. And, as already stated, this means a shortening accompanied by a corresponding broadening, effected under the control of the nervous system, and amenable to the influence of the will. It must be premised that ordinary muscles are, when at rest, kept in a partially contracted or "tonic" condition, like the muscular coat in the wall of an artery (see p. 11). The contraction of many muscles in the human body can be observed very readily. Take, for example, the great "calf-muscle" on the back of the leg (fig. 585). Raise yourself on tiptoe, grasping one of these muscles as you do so. It will be found to swell up, or pass into a state of contraction. This is an expression of greater breadth, and careful measurement will show that there has also been a decrease in length, its two ends being brought nearer together. This is the chief principle of all muscular action, and a contracting muscle obviously exerts a pull upon the parts to which its ends are attached, and this brings about a movement, the nature of which depends upon circumstances. One important use of a skeleton is to afford surfaces and projections for the attachment of muscles, and the different parts of a skeleton are jointed together in various ways, so as to determine the character of the movement brought about by muscular action. We find, for example, in the human skeleton, that there are hinge-joints at the elbow and knee, ball-and-socket joints at the shoulder and hip, and a pivot-joint between the first and second bones of the neck (see vol. i, p. 27). The fact that the skeleton is external in such a creature as an Insect naturally leads to the muscles being attached in quite a different way from those of a backboned animal, where the skeleton is internal, but the principle of action is precisely the same.

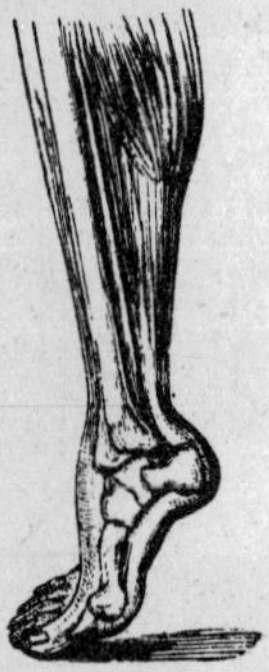

Fig. 585.

Leg raised on tiptoe by contraction of calf-muscle, of which lower end is shown, with the tendon by which it is inserted into the heel-bone.

TENDONS.—The muscle-fibres which make up a muscle are bound together by fibrous tissue, and the muscle is covered by a sheath of the same material. It commonly happens that a muscle is attached by one end (the *origin*) to a relatively fixed part, and by the other end (the *insertion*) to a relatively movable part. And in the case of the muscles which move the limbs the fibrous sheath passes at one or both ends into a firm inelastic cord, or *tendon*, which is attached to part of the skeleton. In this way a number of muscles can easily be fixed to a small bone (such as a finger-bone), and the tendons may be of considerable length, so that the corresponding muscles can be placed at a distance from the part moved. This is of great advantage in the case of hands and feet, for they need only contain the tendons of many of their muscles, and are thus prevented from becoming unnecessarily bulky and clumsy.

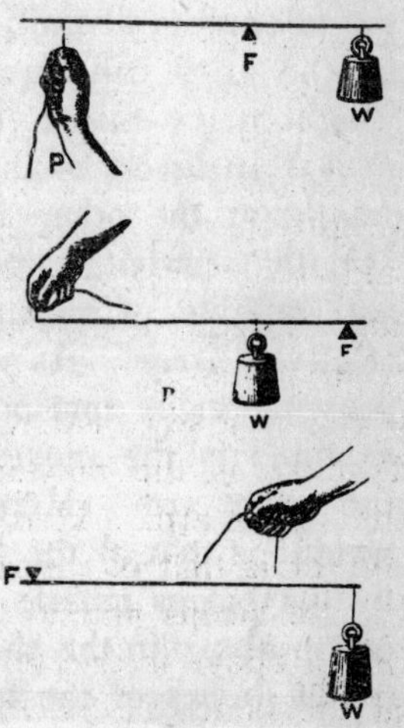

Fig. 586.—Levers of First (A), Second (B), and Third (C) Class

P, Power; F, fulcrum; W, weight or resistance

LEVERS (fig. 586).—One other mechanical principle of muscular action needs mention here, because it is of special importance with reference to locomotion. In many groups of animals swift progression is indispensable, it may be for the purpose of obtaining food, as in a tiger, or as a means of escape from enemies, as in antelopes. Each of the long bones of a limb may be regarded mechanically as a *lever*, *i.e.* a firm rod capable of being moved about a relatively fixed point known as the *fulcrum*. The work to be done may be called the *weight*, and the force doing it may be termed the *power*, this being furnished by muscular contraction in the case of animals. Levers are divisible into three classes, as follows:—(1) Levers of the *first class*, where the fulcrum is between weight and power and nearer the former, as in the case of a crowbar used to raise a block of stone. (2) Levers of the *second class*, where the fulcrum is at one end and the power at the other, the weight being between the two and nearer the fulcrum. This is exemplified by a crowbar with one end resting on the ground, and used for lifting a weight.

The value of the first and second classes of levers is that they give a mechanical advantage, enabling a relatively small power to overcome a large resistance, though the movement is of small extent, for "what is gained in power is lost in speed". Valuable ends are served by both these varieties of lever in the body of an animal, such as a human being. When the head is bent back the first kind is exemplified, for the fulcrum is at the joint between head and backbone, the weight is that of the head, lying chiefly in front of the fulcrum, and the power is supplied by muscles attached to the back of the head. A good example of the second class is the act of raising the body on tiptoe, for in the case of either leg the fulcrum is at the front end of the foot, the power is supplied by the great calf-muscle fixed by a tendon to the heel, and the weight to be raised (that of the body) comes between.

(3) In levers of the *third class* the fulcrum is at one end, the weight at the other, and the power between. Here it may be said that "what is lost in power is gained in speed", for range and rapidity of movement result, though the power has to be relatively large. As we might expect, therefore, the animal body presents many instances of this kind of lever action. A good example is the movement by which the forearm is bent upon the upper arm. Here the fulcrum is at the elbow-joint, and the weight is that of the hand and forearm. The power is supplied by the biceps muscle on the front of the upper arm. This takes origin above in the shoulder-blade, and is inserted below into one of the bones of the forearm (radius) a little way in front of the fulcrum at the elbow-joint.

CHAPTER XLI

MUSCULAR LOCOMOTION—SWIMMING OF LOWER INVERTEBRATES

Having considered the principles of muscular action, some of which apply only to higher animals possessed of a firm skeleton, external or internal, we may next inquire into the nature of the different kinds of locomotion brought about by muscular action. In the case of many animals various forms of progression can be resorted to by the same individual, according to circumstances. A Leech can creep or swim, a Bird fly or walk, and so on. Following the plan already adopted in the earlier part of this book, it may be necessary to allude several times to the same animal or kind of animal under different subdivisions of the present section. Considering that the sea is in all probability the original home of life, it will be convenient first to consider swimming as a typical method of aquatic locomotion, though not necessarily the most primitive form of progression among marine animals. Next will come creeping upon a firm surface, whether this be covered by water or not; and after that walking, running, leaping, and the like, exemplified most familiarly by land animals, though not by them alone. Burrowing of various kinds will afford material for a sub-section, climbing for another, while flight, and simpler arrangements leading up to it, will form a fitting conclusion to this part of the book.

SWIMMING OF LOWER INVERTEBRATES

In dealing with the various kinds of swimming we are, of course, concerned with aquatic animals, and these may be either *primarily* aquatic, or *secondarily* so. Primarily aquatic forms are of purely aquatic descent, there being no reason to think that any of their ancestors ever lived on land. Jelly-Fishes, Cuttle-Fishes, and ordinary Fishes may serve as examples. Secondarily aquatic animals, on the other hand, are those which are descended from land forms, illustrative cases being Whales and Water-insects.

Certain marine animals are able not only to swim actively, but also to drift passively along, guided by currents or blown by the wind. This reminds us of the fact that hosts of creatures chiefly or entirely depend upon the latter method of progression, to facilitate which organs of the nature of floats have been evolved in many cases. As, however, we are here concerned with muscular progression, consideration of drifting and floating organisms will be dealt with later in connection with Distribution in Space.

SWIMMING OF JELLY-FISH (*Hydrozoa*).—In most kinds of swimming part of the body is broadened out so as to get sufficient purchase upon the resisting medium, for the purpose of propulsion. In products of human ingenuity the same principle is necessarily followed, and may be illustrated by the broad ends of oars or the blades of a screw propeller. A simple Jelly-Fish or Medusa shows us how an extremely soft animal, devoid of any skeleton, is able to bring a sufficiently large surface to bear upon the water for the purpose of progression. Such an animal may be roughly compared to an umbrella, the mouth being placed at the end of the "handle". But the medusa differs from an umbrella in the fact that the curved part is of considerable thickness (like the top of a mushroom), owing to the presence of a large amount of jelly-like substance. This is bounded by firmer membranes both on the upper convex side and the lower concave side. The latter region, *i.e.* the inside of the umbrella, is generally called the sub-umbrella, and here are disposed muscle-fibres arranged in a circular way, parallel, that is, to the thin edge of the animal. When this layer of muscle contracts, the opening of the umbrella is thereby narrowed, and the sub-umbrella pushes against the water behind it, propelling the medusa with its convex side forwards, and in the direction of the long axis of its handle. Next follows a relaxation of the muscle-layer, causing the umbrella to expand, ready for another stroke. If you can imagine an actual umbrella possessed of the power of spontaneously opening and shutting, it is clear that it would be able to swim through the water in the same fashion as a Jelly-Fish. Medusæ vary greatly in shape and size, but they always swim in the same manner, and the movements are of very regular kind, which suggests that they

SWIMMING INVERTEBRATES

The plate illustrates typical ways of swimming as exemplified by various Invertebrates. At the top are two simple Jelly-Fish or Medusæ (3 and 4), where progression is effected by the opening and shutting of the rounded "umbrella", the under side of which possesses a thin muscular layer.

The Poulpe or Octopus (*Octopus vulgaris*, 2) swims backwards with great rapidity by forcibly ejecting the water from its mantle-cavity, in which the two gills are sheltered. Cuttle-Fishes and Squids move still more rapidly in the same way. This is an interesting example of adaptation, whereby the getting rid of water used for breathing purposes is turned to account in locomotion.

The Prawn (*Palæmon serratus*, 1), like Lobsters and Crayfishes, is also a swift backward swimmer, its movements being effected by downward strokes of the powerful tail, the end of which bears a lobed fin. It can also paddle itself along more slowly, either forwards or backwards, by means of the forked "swimmerets" situated between the walking-legs and the tail-fin.

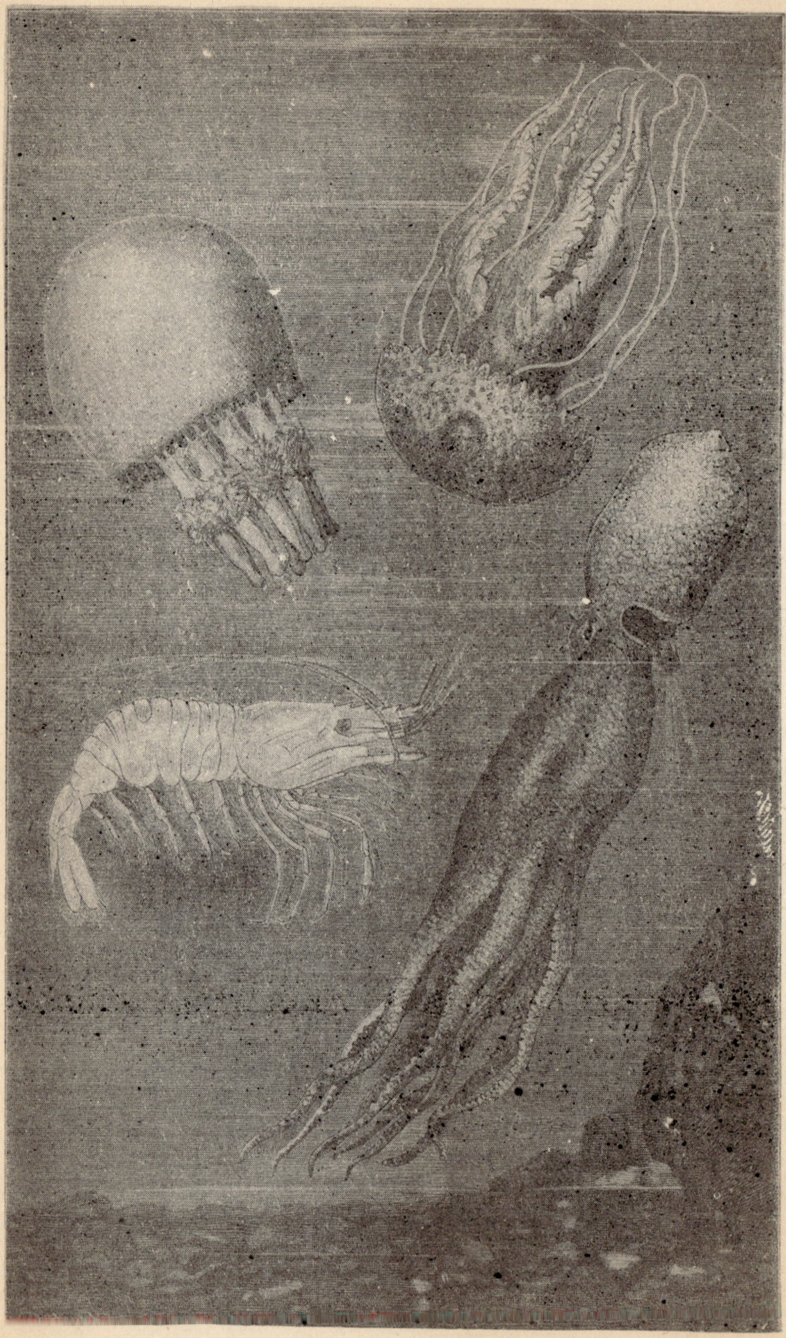

SWIMMING INVERTEBRATES

are carried out under the direction and control of a nervous system, and this has proved to be actually the case. It is interesting to note that the muscular layer forms but an insignificant part of the animal so far as mere bulk is concerned. Romanes (in *Jelly-Fish, Star-Fish, and Sea-Urchins*) states that "This tissue constitutes the earliest appearance in the animal kingdom of true muscular fibres, and its thickness, which is pretty uniform, is nowhere greater than that of very thin paper".

In many of the free-swimming colonies to which the name of COMPOUND JELLY-FISH (*Siphonophora*) has elsewhere been applied (see vol. i, p. 481), the work of the community is shared between different members of the community, which are consequently specialized in various directions, according to their particular duties. Here we have displayed in another form the principle of division of physiological labour, which largely determines the structure of the bodies of individual animals (see p. 9). In this particular case the individuals which propel the colony are known as swimming-bells, and each of them resembles a simple medusa devoid of handle. Of such locomotor individuals there may be one, two, or many, according to the species (see vol. i, p. 481, and vol. ii, p. 162).

The remarkable forms known as COMB-JELLIES (*Ctenophora*), which have probably been evolved as an offshoot from the class (*Hydrozoa*) to which Jelly-Fishes belong, may swim in the same way, as in the case of Beroë, which is a cap-shaped creature of great voracity

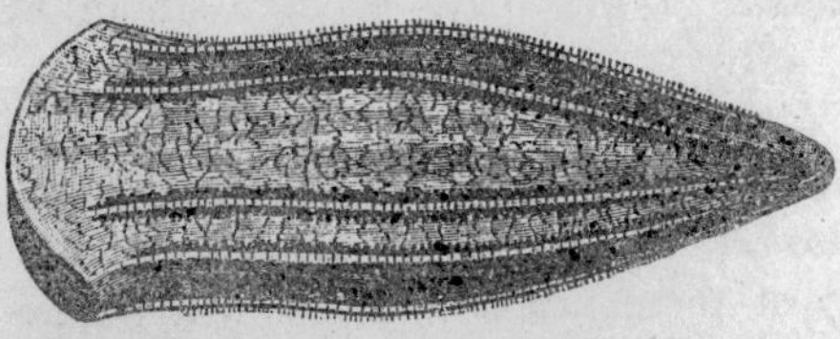

Fig. 587.—Beroë

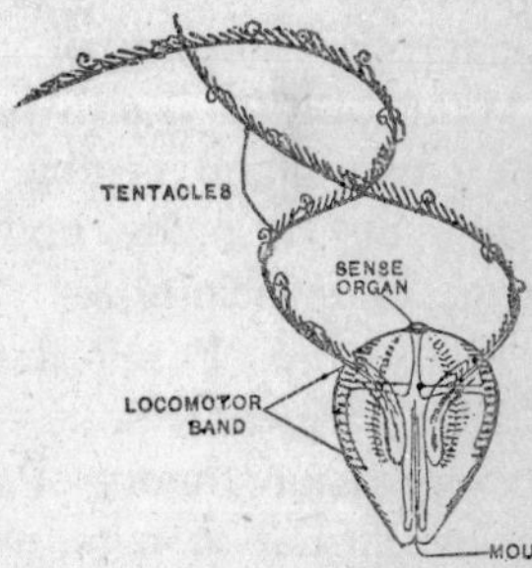

Fig. 588.—Cydippe

(fig. 587). But the typical method of swimming which is pursued by these creatures, and which is well exemplified by the melon-shaped form Cydippe, is dependent upon the presence of a number of longitudinal bands running from one pole of the body to the other (fig. 588). Each of these bands consists of a series of little swimming-plates, which can be moved to and fro under the control of the nervous system, and act like so many paddles, causing their owner to move onwards with the mouth-end at the back. It is particularly interesting to note that each little rowing-plate has been formed by the fusion of a number of those structures we have learnt to know as cilia (see p. 5). In this way mechanical efficiency is gained, for the continuous surface of the plate so constituted is able to bring a more effective stroke to bear upon the water than a series of thread-like structures. In Cydippe and many of its allies there is a long, branched fishing-line on either side of the body, which

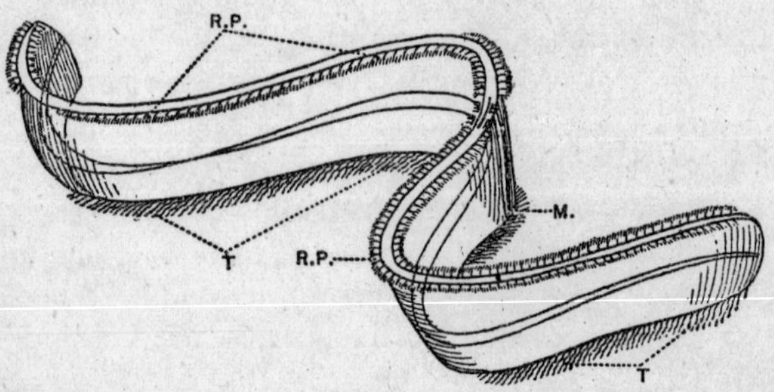

Fig. 589.—Venus's Girdle (*Cestus Veneris*), much reduced. M, Mouth; R.P. rowing-plates; T, fringe of tentacles

can either be stretched out to a considerable length or else withdrawn into a sort of pocket. These organs are probably also of use for the purpose of steering.

One of the Comb-Jellies, Venus's Girdle (*Cestus*), is shaped like a band, and is able to swim not only by means of rowing-plates, but also by undulations of the body brought about by means of muscle-fibres (fig. 589).

Swimming Planarian Worms (*Turbellaria*) and Thread-Worms (*Nemathelmia*).—Although the most characteristic mode of progression among Planarian Worms (*Turbellaria*) is creeping by means of cilia, many of them are able to swim by undulating their bodies. A more definite way of moving through the water is practised by the flattened leaf-shaped form, *Leptoplana tremellaris*, described elsewhere (vol. i, p. 446). The sides of the body are here used as paddles, being alternately bent upwards and downwards, and, being extremely flexible, are curved right over the back in the former case and right under the body in the latter. The comparatively swift movements thus brought about are effected by thin layers of muscle-fibre in the body-wall, and the creature when swimming looks very much like a miniature copy of one of those fishes known as Skates (fig. 590).

Some of the THREAD-WORMS (*Nemathelmia*) live in water and are able to swim by means of wriggling movements of the body, produced by a peculiar muscular layer below the skin. Most persons have seen such movements in the little creature popularly known as the Vinegar-Eel (*Anguillula aceti*).

ARROW-WORMS (*Chætognatha*).—There is a small class of marine animals (*Chætognatha*) containing certain little flattened spindle-shaped creatures called ARROW-WORMS (*Sagitta*, &c.), on account of their shape (fig. 591). They live in vast numbers in the surface-layer of the sea, and swim by bending their bodies to either side alternately. These movements are executed by the agency of a longitudinal layer of muscle-fibres in the body-wall, the part of this on one side first contracting, and then the part on the other side. These contractions are vigorous, and in correspondence with this the muscle-fibres are striated, an uncommon thing among lower forms. The powers of rapid locomotion which Arrow-Worms possess are related to their highly carnivorous habits, small crustaceans and larval fishes constituting a large part of their food. It remains to be mentioned that the tail and sides of the body are provided with fin-like expansions, supported by firm rods. These fins are not themselves swimming organs, but probably have to do with balancing and steering.

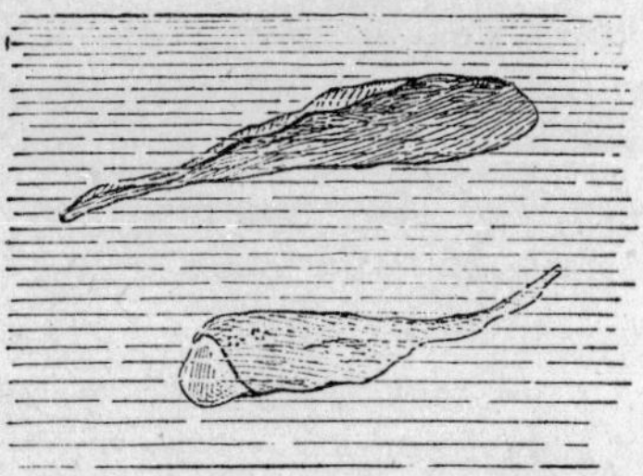

Fig. 590.—A Marine Planarian Worm (*Leptoplana tremellaris*), swimming

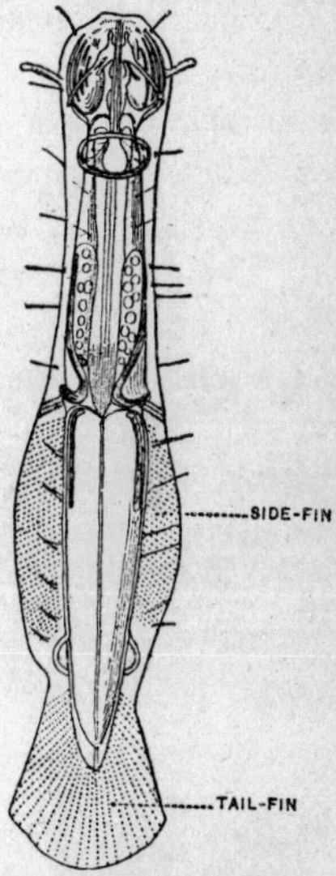

Fig. 591.—An Arrow-Worm (*Sagitta*), enlarged

SWIMMING ANNELIDS (*Annelida*).—Annelids are segmented worms, *i.e.* the body is made up of a series of rings or segments from before backwards. They include Leeches (*Discophora*) and Bristle-Worms (*Chætopoda*), many of which are able to swim.

In a common Medicinal Leech (*Hirudo medicinalis*) swimming is effected by graceful undulations of the somewhat flattened body. The movements are brought about by three layers of muscle in the body-wall, of which the most external is circular, the middle one oblique, and the internal one longitudinal. There are also bundles of fibres running from the upper side of the body to the lower, and these by their contraction are able to flatten the body so that it presents a larger surface for the strokes taken in swimming.

The BRISTLE-WORMS (*Chætopoda*) are in the main a group of creeping, burrowing, and tube-dwelling forms; but many of the free-living marine species are capable of swimming, and some few are highly specialized for the purpose. The body-wall of one of these animals contains an external circular layer and an internal longitudinal layer of muscle-fibres, besides which bundles of muscle run to the hollow "foot-stumps", of which a series is present on each side of the body, and in which the characteristic bristles are embedded. When one of the forms, not specially adapted for the purpose, takes to swimming, it simply wriggles through the water by contraction of the muscle-layers mentioned. The most specialized swimmers in the group (species of *Tomopteris*) are surface animals living in the open sea (fig. 592). The short body is provided with enormously large flattened foot-stumps, which serve as paddles, and have lost their bristles. Two long filaments which act as sense organs project backwards from the head, and look almost like the feelers of an insect. They have possibly been produced by modification of the first pair of foot-stumps, and

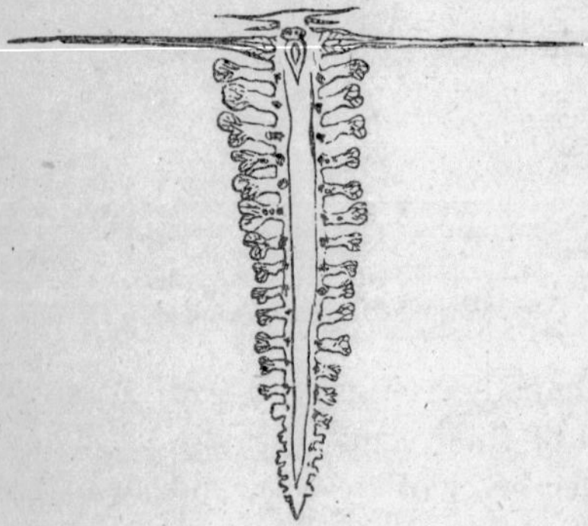

Fig. 592.—A Free-swimming Marine Bristle-Worm (*Tomopteris*)

as each is stiffened by a long slender bristle which runs right through it, they very likely help to balance the worm while it swims. Some other Bristle-Worms are specialized on the same lines as Tomopteris, but not nearly to the same extent.

SWIMMING ECHINODERMS (*Echinodermata*).—The animals of this phylum usually hatch out as active larvæ, which are often of remarkable shape, and swim by means of ciliated bands variously disposed in different cases. In the adult condition, however, most of them are specialized for creeping, and the members of one group (Sea-Lilies) are fixed. But a few forms have widened their sphere of activity by becoming adapted to the swimming habit, moving through the water somewhat after the fashion of jelly-fishes, though the parts of the body employed for the purpose are quite different. We find, for instance, that the ancient and declining group of CRINOIDS includes animals of quite different modes of life, *i.e.* Sea-Lilies and Feather-Stars. Sea-Lilies are fixed animals living in the deep sea, and broadly comparable to much-branched star-fishes fixed mouth upwards on the end of a long flexible stalk. They are the surviving remnants of a once numerous host of dominant marine creatures, the remains of which build up certain beds of limestone in the geological series. Feather-Stars, on the other hand, are exceedingly abundant all over the world, and may be regarded as sea-lilies which have given up the sedentary mode of life and abandoned their stalks (fig. 593). They are able to swim moderately well by alternately bending and straightening their branched arms, which collectively present a sufficient surface for striking on the surrounding water. But this arrangement is necessarily less efficient than in jelly-fishes, where an unbroken expansion is employed for the purpose.

Fig. 593.—A Feather-Star (*Comatula*)

The cylindrical creeping SEA-CUCUMBERS (*Holothuroidea*) would hardly be expected to swell the list of swimmers. Yet a member of the group has been discovered (*Pelagothuria*) which is much specialized in accordance with this mode of progression (fig. 594).

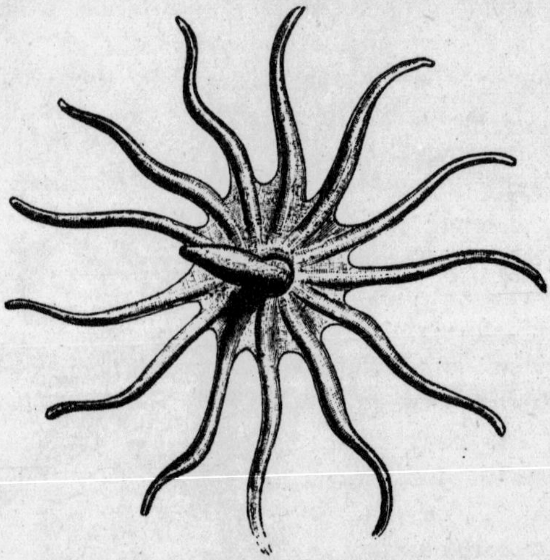

Fig. 594.—Free-swimming Sea-Cucumber (*Pelagothuria*), reduced

As in all Sea-Cucumbers the mouth is surrounded by a circlet of tentacles, which in this case are elongated, and connected together by a web, together constituting a swimming apparatus which acts much like the umbrella of a Jelly-Fish (see p. 18), and by alternately contracting and relaxing propels its owner backwards through the water. Its efficiency is increased by the fact that the body has become comparatively short.

SWIMMING NEMERTINE WORMS (*Nemertea*).—These curious unsegmented marine worms are in the main creeping forms, but some are specialized for swimming, the tail end being moved from side to side. The presence of a fin-like edge gives an increased surface. One species (*Pelagonemertes*) which lives in the open sea is short and leaf-shaped, tapering to a blunt point behind.

CHAPTER XLII

MUSCULAR LOCOMOTION—SWIMMING OF HIGHER INVERTEBRATES

In this chapter we are chiefly concerned with swimming Crustaceans, Insects, and Molluscs, which exhibit a great variety of specializations that attain the same end by different methods.

SWIMMERS AMONG LOWER CRUSTACEANS (ENTOMOSTRACA)

It is usual for lower (and much more rarely higher) crustaceans to hatch out of the egg in the condition of an active free-swimming larva known as a Nauplius (fig. 595). This has an oval body not divided into rings or segments, and provided with three pairs of jointed limbs, corresponding to the first and second feelers, and the first pair of jaws (mandibles) of the adult head. These limbs are of relatively large size, and are used as so many oars by which the animal is propelled.

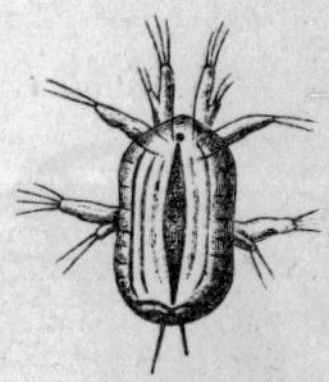

Fig. 595.—A Nauplius (enlarged)

In the adult stage of lower crustaceans (fig. 596) two other pairs of jaws (maxillæ) sprout out from the head, and a limb-bearing trunk is developed. Sometimes both pairs of feelers are used for swimming, as in the Nauplius, a case in point being that of the little MUSSEL-SHRIMPS (*Ostracoda*), in which the body is protected by a bivalve shell (fig. 596). A similar arrangement is found in the free-living members of the group of FORK-FOOTED CRUSTACEANS (*Copepoda*), of which Cyclops (fig. 596) is a common freshwater form, while many marine species are found living together in vast shoals. Here the animal can propel itself by means of the large first pair of feelers, much after the fashion of a man swimming by means of his arms alone, though the

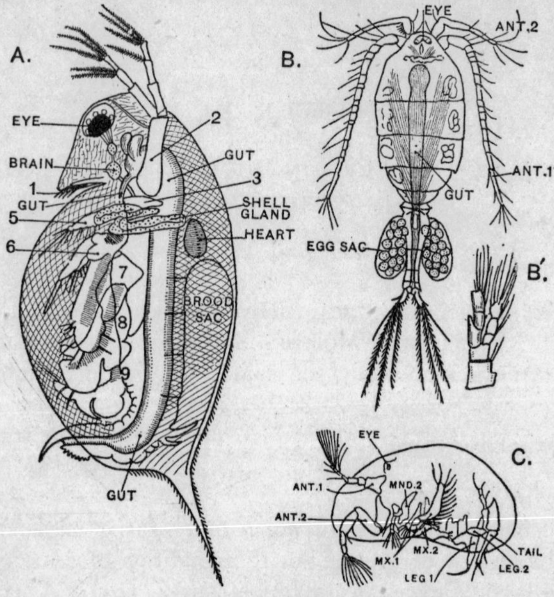

Fig. 596.—Lower Crustaceans (enlarged to various scales)

A, A Water-Flea (*Daphnia*); 1–9, appendages (2 is one of the large rowing feelers). B, Cyclops; ANT. 1, rowing-feeler; ANT. 2, small second feeler. B′, A forked rowing limb of Cyclops. C, A Mussel-Shrimp (*Cypris*); ANT. 1 and ANT. 2, first and second rowing-feelers; MND, MX. 1, and MX. 2, jaws.

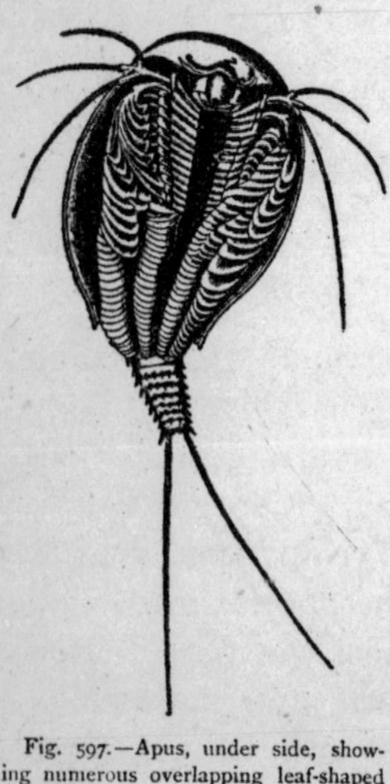

Fig. 597.—Apus, under side, showing numerous overlapping leaf-shaped paddles.

much smaller second feelers perhaps also give some assistance. This is not, however, the only possibility, for the trunk bears four pairs of forked rowing-limbs which are able to swing together in unison, so as to paddle the animal rapidly along.

In WATER-FLEAS (*Cladocera*), such as Daphnia (fig. 596), the first feelers are very small and only useful as sense-organs, but the second pair are of relatively enormous size, and forked at their ends into a pair of branches bearing long feathery bristles. By means of these organs Water-Fleas are able to swim rapidly on their backs in a jerky sort of way. Such larger forms as Apus (fig. 597), with which the Water-Fleas make up the group of LEAF-

FOOTED CRUSTACEANS (*Phyllopods*), also swim on their backs, paddling themselves along by means of the numerous pairs of flattened limbs attached to the trunk.

SWIMMERS AMONG THE HIGHER CRUSTACEA (MALACOSTRACA)

The most characteristic swimming organ in all but the Crabs is the long muscular tail, which acts as a fin, the effective stroke being made by a vigorous bending in the downward direction, after which follows a straightening in preparation for the next stroke. In this way a rapid backward movement is brought about, as may be seen in captive specimens of such animals as Prawns, Shrimps, Lobsters, and Cray-Fish. The forked and more or less flattened limbs of this region of the body are known as "swimmerets", and in smaller forms, *e.g.* Prawns and Shrimps, they may be used as paddles for propelling the animal either forwards or backwards, though not so rapidly as in the ordinary backward swimming. It is particularly interesting to note that the last pair of swimmerets are comparatively large and broad, making up with the last joint of the body a "tail-fin" which plays an important part in tail-swimming. When this region is moved upwards in the straightening which precedes every stroke, the broad last pair of swimmerets is folded up so as to present as small a surface as possible to the water, thus reducing the resistance to the upward movement.

Fig. 598.—A Crab Zoæa (enlarged), showing the well-developed rowing foot-jaws, behind which other limbs are beginning to sprout.

Higher Crustaceans but rarely begin life in the Nauplius form, though they exhibit a great variety of different larval stages, one of these being a Zoæa, characteristically present in the life-history of Crabs (fig. 598). The front part of the body is here covered by a carapace which is often provided with long spines, supposed to balance the body and determine the direction of the swimming movements. The limbs develop from before backwards, none, for example, being at first present in the tail-region. Swimming is chiefly effected in a way of which no example has so far been given, for the first two pairs of foot-jaws are broad-forked appendages, which do the same work as the feelers of a Nauplius, *i.e.* they are used as oars. Later on, the Crab-zoæa passes into what is termed the Megalopa stage, which possesses a full complement of limbs, swims by its tail, and resembles a minute lobster. The adult Crab in ordinary cases has given up swimming altogether, and its relatively small tail is carried folded up out of harm's way under the front part of the body, which is large and broad.

Fig. 599.—A Swimming or Fiddler Crab (*Thalamita natator*). Note at back the oar-shaped fourth pair of legs.

What are known as Swimming or Fiddler Crabs (fig. 599) have re-acquired the power of swimming possessed by their remote ancestors, which were long-tailed forms, of which the Megalopa stage in the life-history is a reminiscence. They do not, however, swim by means of their tails, as did those ancestors, but have broadened out their last pair of walking-legs into flattened oars.

SWIMMING INSECTS (Insecta)

We have had occasion to note (see vol. i, pp. 354, 357, 376) that although the class of Insects includes for the most part animals eminently adapted to life on land, there are some forms which, either in the adult or larval condition, or in both, live in the water. In such cases characteristic ways of swimming have been developed.

It is but seldom that an aquatic insect swims by means of its wings, but such appears to be the case in a small British species (*Polynema natans*) belonging to the family of membrane-winged insects (*Hymenoptera*), not distantly related to that which includes the gall-flies. We are reminded here of the Penguins among birds, which employ their wings as fins.

As in the case of the Fiddler Crabs, the chief swimming organs of most aquatic adult insects are the hind-legs, which are well-developed, more or less broadened, and fringed with

Fig. 600.—Freshwater Insects

1, Great Water-Beetle (*Dytiscus marginalis*); 2, Water Boatman (*Notonecta*); 3, Whirligig-Beetle (*Gyrinus*); 4, Pond-Skater (*Gerris*)

bristles (fig. 600). A good instance is afforded by the Great Water-Beetle (*Dytiscus marginalis*) of our ponds, and similar arrangements are found in some of the aquatic bugs, among which the Water-Boatmen (species of *Notonecta* and *Corixa*) swim on their backs (see fig. 600), and when resting keep the oar-like hind-legs stretched out, as is the case under the same circumstances with the sculls of a man using an outrigger boat. The shape of the body facilitates rapid progress.

Some small insects (species of *Scelimena*) belonging to the grasshopper family, and native to India and Ceylon, partly live and feed under water, their swimming-organs being the hind-legs, upon which are broad outgrowths for giving an increased rowing surface.

The little Whirligig-Beetles (*Gyrinidæ*) (fig. 600), often seen performing complicated curving movements upon the surface of ponds, swim on their backs like water-boatmen, but in this case not only the hind-legs but also the pair in front of them are specialized propulsive organs. Regarding these limbs Sharp (in *The Cambridge Natural History*) remarks:—"Their two hind pairs of legs are beautifully constructed as paddles, expanding mechanically when moved in the backward direction, and collapsing into an extremely small space directly the resistance they meet with is in the other direction".

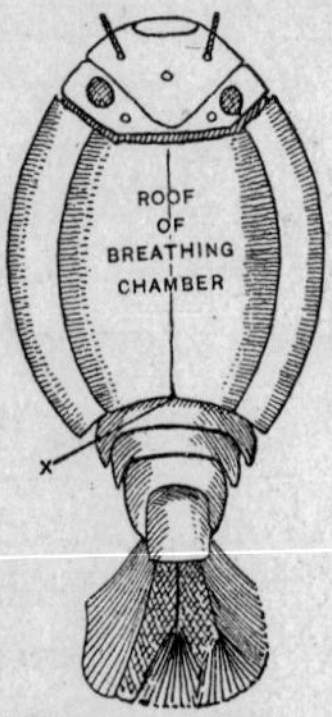

Fig. 601.—Crustacean-like Nymph of a May-Fly (*Prosopistoma*), enlarged. Note the paddling-bristles on the tail.

It is not necessary to say much about the swimming movements of aquatic insect-larvæ. The worm-like young of Gnats and the like simply wriggle through the water. A more specialized method of swimming is exemplified by the early stages of some net-winged insects (*Neuroptera*). This is especially the case with the nymphs of certain May-Flies (such as *Cloëon*), where the three rods which project from the tip of the tail are fringed with especially long bristles, and are supposed to act as paddles. This arrangement is exaggerated in the curious-looking nymph of another kind of May-Fly (*Prosopistoma*) (fig. 601).

SWIMMING MOLLUSCS (MOLLUSCA)

Swimming Molluscs belong to one or other of the three great groups of Cuttle-Fishes, &c. (*Cephalopoda*), Snails and Slugs (*Gastropoda*), and Bivalves (*Lamellibranchia*), especially to the first.

CUTTLE-FISHES, SQUIDS, &C. (CEPHALOPODA)

The body of a Cuttle-Fish or Squid is symmetrically disposed about a swimming axis, and well adapted by its shape for rapid progression through the water. It is flattened from front to back, the former being kept upwards during the swimming movements, and there is a fin-like expansion round the edge, where the flat surfaces pass into one another, which appears to be concerned with maintaining the proper balance. The method of propulsion is somewhat remarkable. A large gill-containing cavity is placed on the side of the body which is kept downwards during swimming, and water passes into this by a wide opening at the head-end, making its exit through a muscular tube or funnel. The wall of the gill-cavity is extremely muscular, and by its rhythmic contraction forces water out through the funnel with considerable force, so that the outcoming jet reacts on the surrounding medium and propels the animal backwards with great velocity. Comparison may here be made with a certain kind of toy steam-boat, provided with a small boiler, from which a tube passes out through the stern, conducting steam, that reacts against the water so as to propel the boat with considerable speed. If the tube opened at the bows the miniature craft would move stern first, and the resemblance to a Cuttle-Fish would be still greater. It further remains to be mentioned that a Cuttle-Fish possesses a kind of internal plate-like shell (and a Squid a horn-like "pen") lying close to the surface directed upwards during swimming, and this stiffens the body so as to prevent "wobbling", which would reduce the rapidity of movement. And were there nothing to obviate it, the water would be forced out of the gill-cavity through the wide slit by which it enters; but this is prevented by the existence of two knobs on the wall of the cavity, which, by fitting into corresponding pits, may almost be said to button up this aperture, so that the expelled water is bound to pass through the funnel. The most interesting feature of the Cuttle-Fish's mode of swimming consists in the fact that it is an adaptation of an arrangement of which the primary use is to renew the water in the gill-cavity, as an accessory to breathing.

What has so far been said about the Cephalopods refers more especially to the ten-armed forms (*Decapoda*), which possess eight relatively short sucker-studded "arms" and a pair of longer "tentacles", each of which is broadened out at its end into a sort of sucker-bearing pad. Another group is constituted by eight-armed forms (*Octopoda*), in which there are no long tentacles, but simply the eight short arms. In such a type as Octopus the body is plump and rounded, and not so well adapted for swimming as in an ordinary Cuttle-Fish, while the internal shell is absent. Although the animal is able to swim like a Cuttle-Fish, but not so perfectly, it has taken to a creeping mode of life, which has led to a corresponding change in shape and general proportions. A long flattened body would obviously be inconvenient under such conditions, for which a short rounded shape is much more suitable.

There are, however, certain eight-armed species which have, so to speak, taken once more to swimming (compare p. 28), and are possessed of new arrangements related to that kind of locomotion. One of the most interesting of these is the Argonaut, or Paper Nautilus (*Argonauta argo*), in which the female is remarkable as being the owner of a thin external shell, into which the greater part of the body can be withdrawn (fig. 602). This elegant structure is beautifully ribbed, and provided with a sharp keel. It has been formed or secreted by the first pair of arms, which are large, backwardly directed, and broadened out at their ends into broad lappets. During life these expansions clasp the shell firmly on the outside. It was formerly thought that they could be raised above the water and used as sails, but this would appear to be pure imagination, though the animal has often been figured in accordance with this erroneous idea. Regarding this interesting creature Rymer Jones (in *The Animal Creation*) makes the following comment:—"It was, indeed, to this Cephalopod that the ancients assigned the honour of having first suggested to mankind the possibility of traversing the sea in ships; and nothing could be more elegant than the frail bark in which the Argonaut was supposed to skim over the waves, hoisting sails to the breeze, and steering its course by the assistance of oars provided for the purpose. It is almost a thankless office to dispel so pretty a fiction: modern researches, however, serve to show that its sailing capabilities have been much exaggerated." In fact, a Paper Nautilus swims precisely like a Cuttle-Fish, by the ejection of water through the funnel,

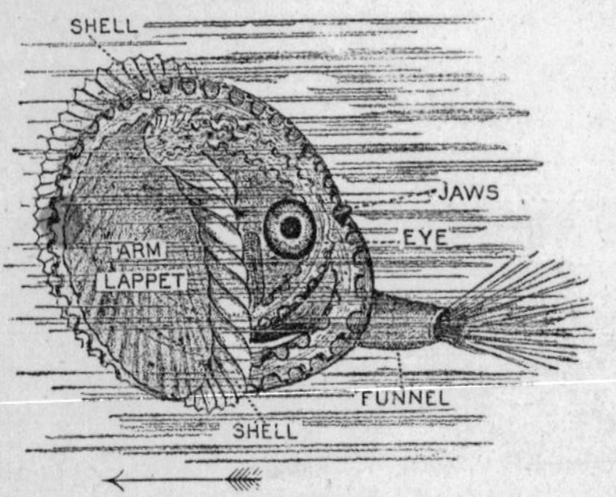

Fig. 602.—Female Argonaut (*Argonauta argo*), reduced, swimming backwards by ejection of water through the funnel. The arrow indicates direction of movement.

having previously drawn back into her shell and snugly coiled up the slender arms. Swift backward movement is facilitated by the sharp keel on the shell, which acts as a cut-water. Although better adapted for swimming than the Octopus, this creature spends much of its time in crawling upon the sea-floor.

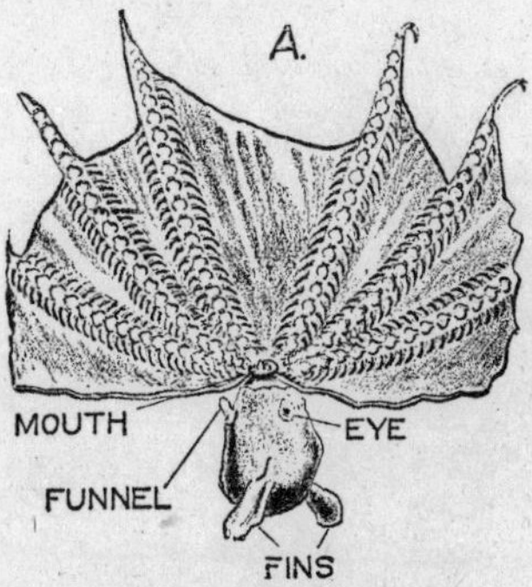

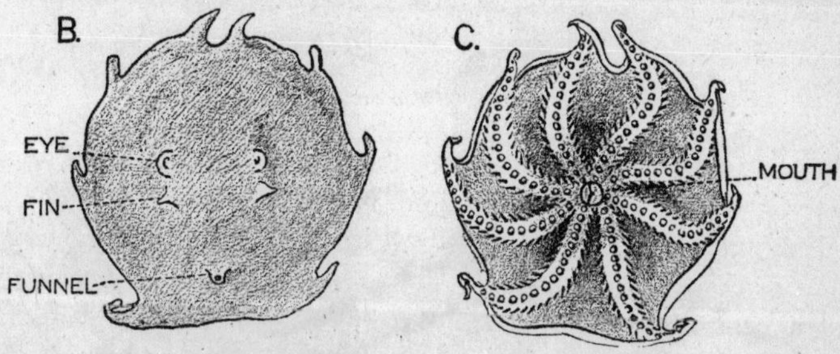

Fig. 603.—Specialized Swimming Octopods (reduced)

A, Cirroteuthis; the swimming-bell has been partly cut away. B and C, Upper and under sides of Opisthoteuthis. In both cases each of the eight arms bears a central row of suckers, flanked by hooks on either side.

In other animals related to the Octopus we find that the eight arms which are arranged in a circle round the mouth are more or less connected by a web-like membrane, and thus collectively form a muscular hollow expansion, which by alternate contraction and relaxation acts very much like the umbrella of a medusa (see p. 18), and forms an auxiliary, or in extreme cases the chief, swimming organ (fig. 603). There is one family (*Cirroteuthidæ*) where this line of evolution has greatly modified the proportions of the body. In one such form (*Cirroteuthis*) the swimming umbrella is of relatively enormous size, and the small body is provided with a well-marked pair of fins. Modification is carried still further in a related deep-sea form (*Opisthoteuthis*), where the animal is entirely converted into a flattish swimming-disc.

SWIMMING SNAILS AND SLUGS (GASTROPODA)

The most typical members of this group creep upon the broad muscular expansion of the under side of the body to which the name *foot* is applied, and this method of progression is familiarly illustrated by ordinary land snails and slugs. None of the members of the order (*Pulmonata*) to which these belong are able to swim, though some of the freshwater forms, such as the Pond Snail (*Lymnæus*); are often met with floating at the surface

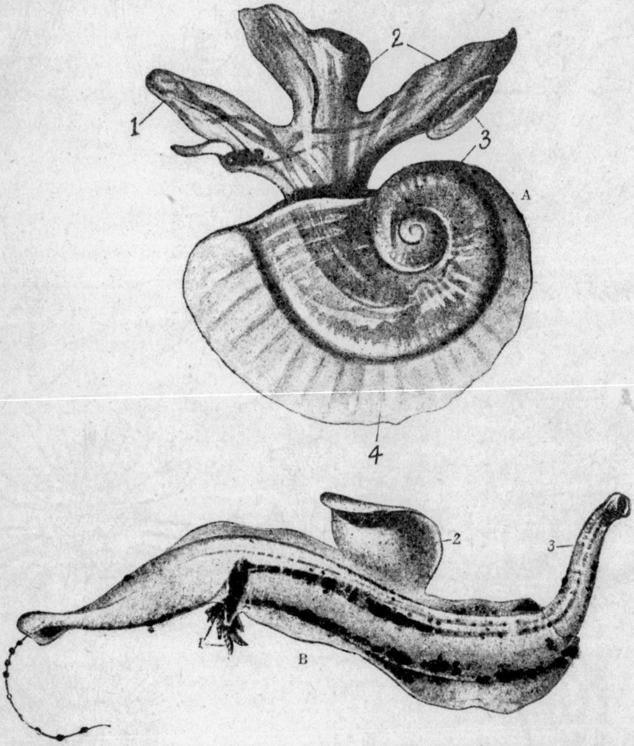

Fig. 604.—Heteropods (drawn in the swimming position, with under surface directed upwards)
A, Atlanta; 1, snout; 2, swimming foot; 3, operculum. B, Pterotrachea; 1, gills; 2, swimming foot; 3, snout.

of the water, foot upwards, and holding on to the surface film. But both in the order of Fore-gilled Snails (*Prosobranchia*) and that of Hind-gilled Snails (*Opisthobranchia*) species are included in which the foot, or part of it, is more or less completely converted into one or more fins, which are sometimes very perfectly adapted for swimming.

FORE-GILLED SWIMMERS (*Prosobranchia*).—These include a remarkable group (*Heteropods*), which lead a pelagic existence, *i.e.* live in the open sea, having entirely abandoned the creeping habit for a free-swimming mode of life. Their bodies are translucent, and present a great variety in shape, according to the species (fig. 604). Those which are least modified are provided with a spiral shell: in a further stage of specialization the shell has been reduced to a small cap-shaped structure, and in the most modified forms the shell has disappeared altogether, and the animal is much elongated. But in all these cases the foot is more or less converted into a flattened fin, the owner of which swims with its upper surface directed downwards.

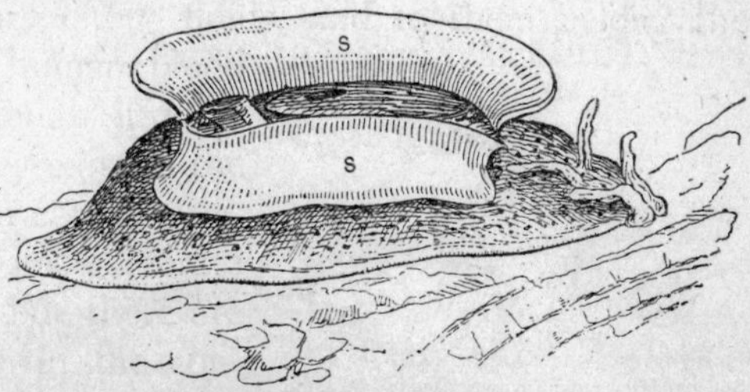

Fig. 605.—Sea-Hare (*Aplysia*), creeping. s s, Swimming flaps (parapods) turned back

Hind-gilled Swimmers (*Opisthobranchia*).—The hind-gilled Gastropods are divided into those which typically possess a shell (*Tectibranchs*), and the shell-less animals known as Sea-Slugs (*Nudibranchs*). It is among the former that most of the swimming forms are found. In some of them creeping is the chief means of progression, but each side of the foot is provided with a muscular flap (*parapod*), and these two expansions can be moved up and down so as to produce swimming movements. A common example of this sort of arrangement is found in the Sea-Hare (*Aplysia*) (fig. 605).

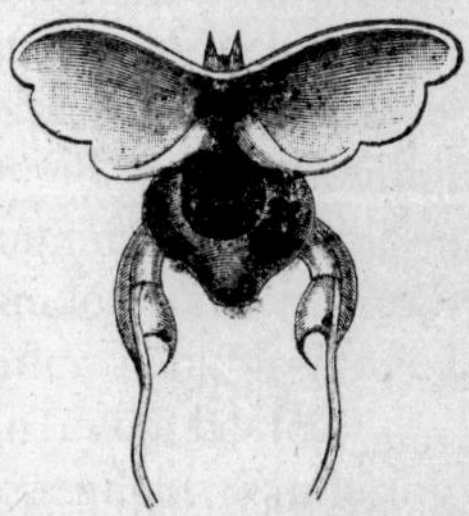

Fig. 606.—A Wing-footed Snail (*Hyalea*) or Sea-Butterfly (somewhat enlarged), showing swimming lobes.

Specialization for swimming is carried very much further in the *Wing-footed Snails* (Pteropods), formerly believed to constitute a distinct order of Molluscs (fig. 606). These little translucent creatures are of thoroughly pelagic habit, living in vast shoals at the surface of the ocean, and forming an important part of the food of whales and other animals. Some of them possess a glassy shell of various shape, while others again are quite shell-less. In either case the main part of the foot has been reduced to very small dimensions, while a pair of muscular flaps, growing out from its sides, look almost like wings, and serve as efficient fins. By means of these organs Pteropods may almost be said to flit through the water, and are sometimes metaphorically called "sea-butterflies".

The shell-less SEA-SLUGS (*Nudibranchia*) are even more characteristically creeping forms than their shell-bearing hind-

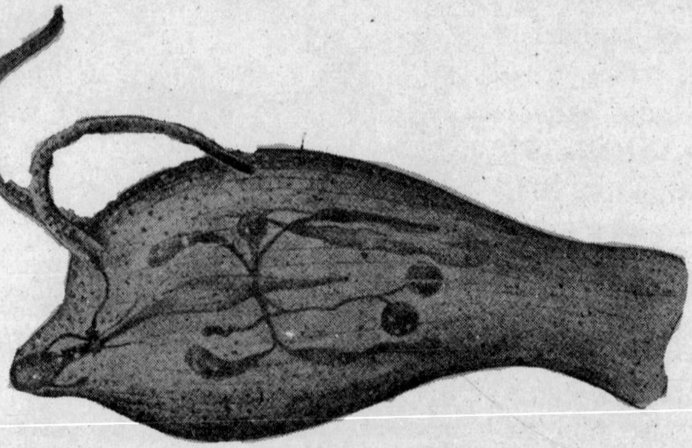

Fig. 607.—A Swimming Sea-Slug (*Phyllirhoë*) × 4

gilled relatives, but some of them are able to swim. The most remarkable instance of this is presented by a small pelagic creature, *Phyllirhoë*, in which the body is strongly compressed from side to side, while the foot is altogether absent, a very unusual character among molluscs. Swimming is effected by undulating movements of the body, the hinder end of which is rounded into a sort of tail-fin (fig. 607).

SWIMMING BIVALVE MOLLUSCS (LAMELLIBRANCHIA)

Bivalve Molluscs are mostly adapted to a burrowing life, while some of them, such as Oysters, are fixed when adult. The shell is primarily a protective organ, but in a few cases it has acquired a new use, having become a means of swimming. This is the case, for instance, in many of the Scallops (*Pecten*) and File-Shells (*Lima*). It has been explained elsewhere (vol. i, p. 330) that the two pieces or valves of the shell are movably united together by a sort of hinge. One or two strong bands of muscle (adductor muscles) run across from one valve to the other, and it is obvious that when these contract the shell is closed. When they relax the shell opens or "gapes" as a result of the elasticity of a fibrous band (ligament), or it may be a compressible pad (cartilage), placed in the region of the hinge. File-Shells may often be observed lying on the sea-floor in shallow water, with the shell widely gaping, and as the edge of the mantle, a fold of the body-wall which lines the valves, is brightly coloured and bears a fringe of sensitive tentacles, the appearance of the animal is both striking and beautiful. When disturbed these molluscs swim in a jerky way by means of the shell, which is alternately opened and closed with considerable rapidity (fig. 608). Closure is effected by the powerful adductor muscle (for only one is present here), and opening by elasticity. Scallops are closely related and swim in the same manner, but their hues are even brighter, for the mantle edge not only bears a fringe of tentacles, but possesses numerous small red eyes.

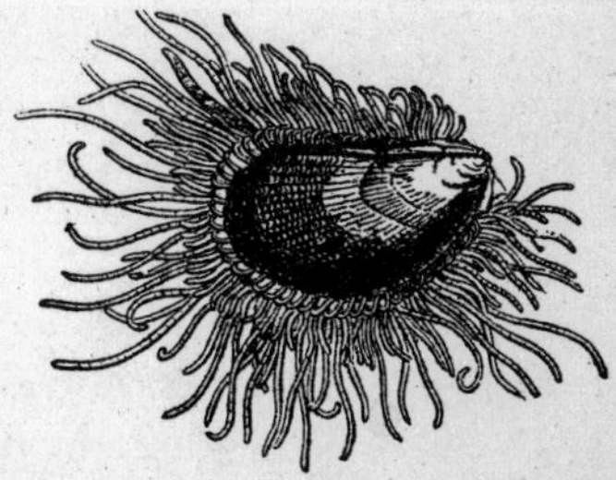

Fig. 608.—A File-Shell (*Lima*) with fringed mantle fully expanded (reduced).

A bivalve which when adult burrows in mud may swim in the manner just described during an early period of its existence. This is the case in the Freshwater Mussels (*Unio* and *Anodon*), which begin their independent existence as free-swimming larvæ (*glochidia*), propelled through the water by the agency of their triangular shells, which are quite unlike the shells of the adult (fig. 609).

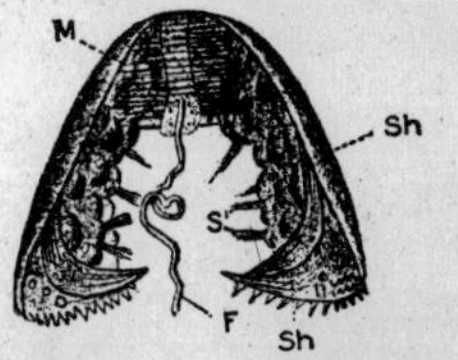

Fig. 609.—Larva (*Glochidium*) of Freshwater Mussel (much enlarged). F, Sticky thread (byssus) cut short; M, adductor muscle for closing shell Sh; S, sense organs.

CHAPTER XLIII

MUSCULAR LOCOMOTION—PRIMITIVE VERTEBRATES AND FISHES AS SWIMMERS

Some of the Primitive Vertebrates (*Protochordates*) swim when adult, or during the early part of their lives, and Fishes are for the most part eminently adapted for this kind of locomotion. They are best considered under separate headings.

PRIMITIVE VERTEBRATES (PROTOCHORDATA) AS SWIMMERS

SEA-SQUIRTS, TUNICATES, OR ASCIDIANS (*Urochorda*).—It is scarcely possible to imagine a creature more completely adapted to a fixed mode of life than an ordinary Sea-Squirt, such as Ascidia (fig. 610), which, as to its shape, resembles nothing so much as one of the skin bottles used in the East. One end is attached, and at the other are two apertures, into one of which, the mouth, currents of sea-water constantly stream as the result of ciliary action, making their exit through the second opening, which is somewhat on one side. There is no trace of that characteristic vertebrate structure, the notochord, which has been aptly called "the forerunner of a backbone". But if we follow the life-history of this animal we shall find that it hatches from the egg as a free-swimming larva, not unlike a tadpole in appearance. This propels itself by means of a muscular tail, that is stiffened

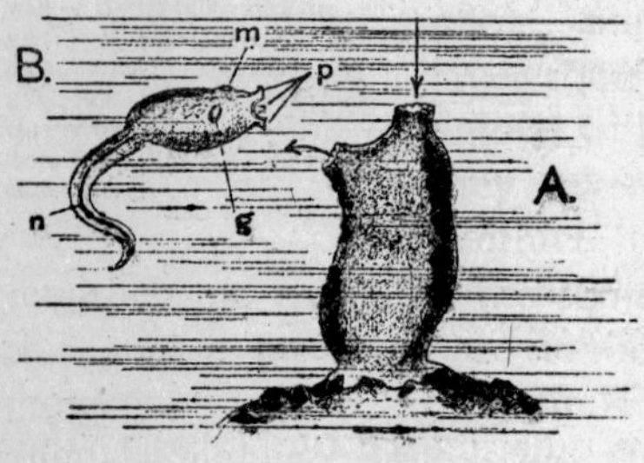

Fig. 610.—A Sea-Squirt (*Ascidia*)

A, Adult (reduced) attached to rock; arrows show course of food-supplying and waste-removing currents. B, Free-swimming tadpole larva (enlarged); g, gill-slit; m, mouth; n, notochord in tail; p, sticky knobs by which the larva later on fixes itself.

by a gelatinous notochord, to which the muscles are attached, these constituting a flattened mass on each side, by the agency of which the tail is drawn alternately to right and left. Later on, the larva fixes itself by the head-end, and its tail gradually diminishes and ultimately disappears entirely. This is a good instance of economy, for to keep the tail would be to maintain an organ no longer serving any useful purpose.

In one small group of pelagic Ascidians (*Appendicularia*, &c.) the tail is retained throughout life as the means of locomotion, and probably these forms resemble in many respects the ancestors from which the ordinary fixed Sea-Squirts have taken origin.

We have not yet exhausted the possibilities of locomotion among the Tunicates, for many of them, besides the members of the small group just mentioned, are free-swimming, translucent pelagic forms, some of which are colonial. These propel themselves by ejection of a stream of water, somewhat after the cuttle-fish manner. We may take as a type the Barrel Ascidian (*Doliolum*), in which the mouth and atrial aperture, instead of being close together, are wide openings at opposite ends of the body (fig. 611). Partly by means of ciliary action currents of water flow into the mouth and out at the atrial aperture. These are related not only to breathing (as in Cuttle-Fishes), but also carry into the body the small organisms and organic particles which constitute the food. So far as respiration and feeding are concerned, ciliary action would suffice, as it does in the fixed forms, but it is not vigorous enough for swimming purposes. To effect this kind of movement by reaction against the water of the outwardly-flowing current, the body of the animal is encircled by a number of muscle-bands, comparable to the hoops of a barrel. These contract and relax, causing water to alternately enter and leave the body, the outward flow taking place with sufficient force to propel the animal in a forward direction.

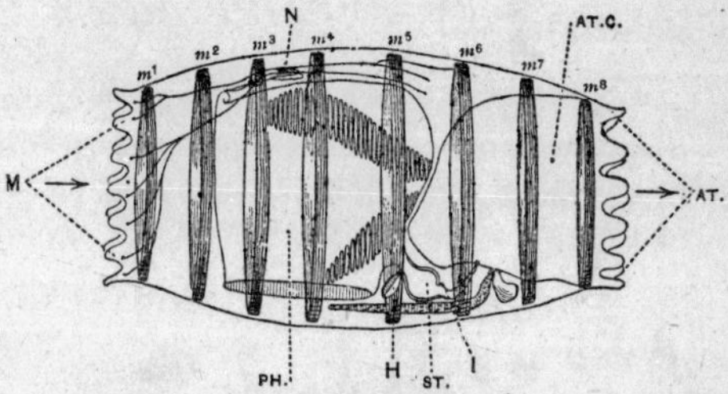

Fig. 611.—Barrel Ascidian (*Doliolum*)

M, Mouth; PH., pharynx, showing two rows of gill-slits of one side. ST., stomach; I, intestine; AT.C., atrial cavity; AT., atrial aperture; H, heart; m^1–m^8, muscle-bands; N, central nervous system, from which nerves are seen running off. Course of water currents indicated by arrows.

The Lancelet (*Amphioxus*).—The chief features of the anatomy of this small, somewhat fish-like creature have elsewhere been given (see vol. i, p. 293). It may be repeated here that the body is greatly flattened from side to side, and stiffened by a gelatinous notochord which runs from one end of the animal to the other underneath the nerve-cord. This supporting rod is covered by a firm fibrous sheath, continuous with partitions of a similar nature which run between the angular segments into which the muscles of each side are divided. The muscle-fibres are disposed longitudinally, and by their alternate contraction on the two sides of the body are able to bring about undulating swimming movements. The notochord is elastic, and straightens the body after it has been bent on one side by muscular action.

FISHES (Pisces) AS SWIMMERS

The fishes which are least specialized for swimming, such as Lampreys and Eels, may be said to "wriggle" through the water by undulating the body from side to side. In such instances the firm axis of the body, though presenting a great advance in complexity upon the simple notochord of the Lancelet, is still very flexible and elastic, lending itself readily to the sinuous swimming movements. As in all fishes, the smooth and slimy skin presents but little resistance to passage through the water.

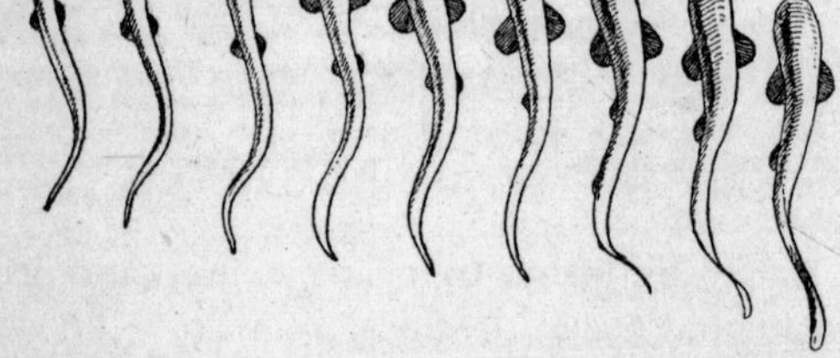

Fig. 612.—Phases of Movement in a Swimming Shark, seen from above (diagrammatic)

Advancing upwards in the scale we find that the fins, especially the tail-fin, are largely concerned with locomotion. In Sharks and Dog-Fishes (*Elasmobranchii*), for instance, although the body still describes undulating movements from side to side (fig. 612), the chief agent of propulsion is the powerful tail-fin, which in this case is markedly unsymmetrical (heterocercal), there being a large upper lobe, into which the spine is continued, and a small under lobe (fig. 613). Although these forms can swim at all levels, they are in the main "ground-fishes", and, being heavier than water, naturally sink to the bottom unless this is obviated by active contractions of the muscles. Indeed, the working of this sort of tail-fin, if left to itself, brings about a downward movement, for it causes the hinder region of the body to rise up and the head to be correspondingly depressed, so that the animal is enabled to propel itself with great rapidity to its favourite haunts far below the surface. If, however, the fish

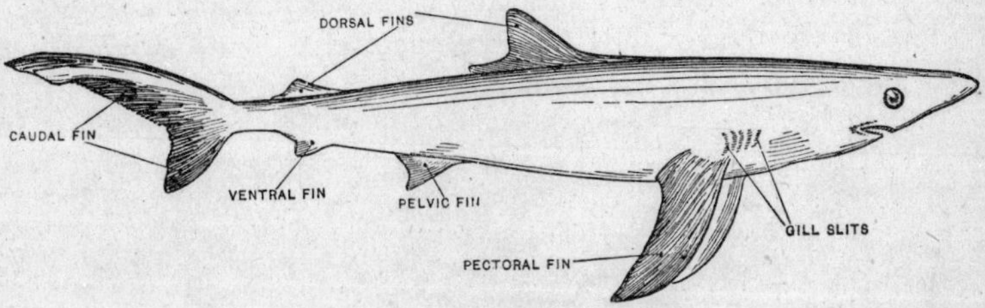

Fig. 613.—Blue Shark (*Carcharias glaucus*)

wishes to move horizontally or upwards, it is enabled to do so by adjusting the broad pectoral fin so as to steer the animal in the required direction. The higher the front edges of these fins as compared to their back edges, so much the more is a tendency to an upward path developed, and the downward bias resulting from the peculiar shape of the tail-fin is either just counterbalanced, when horizontal movement is the net result, or more than compensated, when an oblique upward movement is brought about.

The dominance of ORDINARY BONY FISHES (*Teleostei*) at the present time is largely due to the fact that in average cases they have become adapted to rapid swimming as regards both shape and structure. The most notable character is the possession of an outwardly symmetrical (homocercal) tail-fin, which propels the fish straight forwards, while the presence of a swim-bladder has reduced the specific gravity. Dean (in *Fishes, Living and Fossil*) thus describes a case where the adaptations to rapid progression have reached their maximum:—"In an example of a swift-swimming fish some of the most striking peculiarities of the aquatic form may be seen. The Spanish Mackerel [*Scomber colias*] shows admirably a stout, spindle-like outline; its entire surface is accurately rounded, and there appear no irregular points which could retard the forward motion of the fish. Even in the wedge-shaped head the conical surface has been made more perfect by the tightly-fitting rims of the jaws, by the smoothly-closed gill-shields, and by the eyes' accurate adjustment to the head's curvature. Viewed from in front, the fish's outline appears as a perfect ellipse, and seems surprisingly small in size: the fins, which appear so prominent a feature in profile, can now be hardly distinguished; above and below they form keels, sharp and thin. In side view the vertical or unpaired fins are seen surrounding the hinder region of the body: they resolve themselves into *dorsal*, *anal*, and *caudal* elements; the former are low and stout, elastic in their

Fig. 614.—Common Mackerel (*Scomber vernalis*)

firm cut-water margin, deeply notched and interrupted posteriorly, where useless elements have been discarded; the caudal is broadly forked, stout in its supporting rays, strong in power of propulsion. At its sides a remarkable ridge has been developed, functioning as a horizontal keel, and preventing the stroke of the caudal from varying from the vertical plane. The lateral or paired fins, *pectoral* and [*pelvic*], may rotate outward and arrange themselves in the line of the fish's motion, so that in a somewhat horizontal plane they may, like the unpaired fins, function as keels. When thus erected, the paired fins present a firm anterior margin, which serves as a cut-water. While thus somewhat similar in function to the vertical fins, the [pelvics], and especially the pectorals, may acquire additional uses: they may serve as delicate balancers, or may aid in guiding or arresting the fish's motions. In further conformity to aquatic needs, the entire surface of the fish is notably slime-covered, and although perfectly armoured by plates and scales, yet presents no point of resistance to forward motion." These remarks are equally applicable to the Common Mackerel (*Scomber vernalis*, fig. 614). It has been shown by mathematical calculation that the shapes of fishes such as the one just described are of the kind best suited to rapid movement in water.

Some bony fishes have evolved on different lines from those indicated above, in accordance with special modes of life. Many ground-fishes, for instance, are creatures of comparatively sluggish habits, and naturally differ in many respects from their swift-swimming cousins. An extreme case is that of Flat-Fishes, which are greatly flattened from side to side, and are incapable of swimming in the vertical position. During the whole adult life they both rest and move with one side of the body downwards, and when they swim, do so with an undulating movement of the body. Yet for some time after hatching, these fishes are of normal appearance and swim in the usual way, a fact which helps to prove that these highly-specialized forms have descended from ancestors of more average attributes. It is not surprising to find that Flat-Fishes never possess a swim-bladder.

Eels, again, though they have been mentioned in illustration of a simple mode of swimming (see p. 40), are not primitive forms, but have been evolved from fishes endowed with greater powers of swimming, and their peculiar characters are adaptations to life in the mud of ponds and streams.

Fig. 615.—Sea-Horse (*Hippocampus*)

An unique method of swimming is practised by the little Sea Horse (*Hippocampus*), which spends most of its time attached by its curly tail to sea-weed. Here all the fins have been suppressed except the pectorals and a well-marked dorsal (fig. 615). By means of the rapid movement of the latter from side to side the fish is able to swim with the long axis of its body in a vertical position, *i.e.* at right angles to its direction in an ordinary fish during progression. The contrast is as great as that between a dog and a human being when walking or running, the long axis of the body in these cases being respectively horizontal and vertical.

The remarkable peculiarities of the Sea-Horse are simply adaptations to an unusual mode of life. Its remote ancestors probably resembled sticklebacks in appearance.

The last fishes to be mentioned in this connection are the remarkable *Skates* and *Rays*, which belong to the same order as

Fig. 616.—Eagle-Rays (*Myliobatis aquila*) swimming (much reduced)

Sharks and Dog-Fishes (*Elasmobranchii*). The body is in this case flattened from above downwards (at right angles to the direction of compression in flat-fishes), and is of quadrangular form, the sides being constituted by the enormous pectoral fins. It is these fins which, by their upward and downward movement, enable the fish to flap its way through the water (fig. 616).

CHAPTER XLIV

MUSCULAR LOCOMOTION. AMPHIBIANS, REPTILES BIRDS, AND MAMMALS AS SWIMMERS

AMPHIBIANS (Amphibia) AS SWIMMERS

Although recent Amphibians are clearly marked off from recent Fishes, they are undoubtedly descended from fish-like ancestors, and both in structure and habits constitute a sort of half-way house between completely aquatic and thorough-going terrestrial Vertebrates. In almost all cases an Amphibian begins life as an aquatic tadpole larva (fig. 617), which is to all intents and purposes a fish, and swims by means of a long muscular tail, flattened from side to side and bordered by a membranous fin, which, however, is not supported by hard fin-rays, as is the case in a fish.

Fig. 617.—Tadpoles and young Frogs

There are three groups of Amphibia represented among living animals, *i.e.* Tailed Amphibians (*Urodela*), Tailless Amphibians (*Anura*), and Limbless Amphibians

(*Gymnophiona*). The last of these includes the blind, worm-like Cæcilians, which have a wide distribution in tropical and sub-tropical regions. After passing through the aquatic larval stage these creatures take to a burrowing life, and therefore do not concern us in the present chapter. As, however, the members of the other two groups are more or less expert swimmers when adult, it will be necessary to say a little about them.

Tailed Amphibians (*Urodela*).—The Newts and Salamanders which constitute this group are for the most part of thorough aquatic habit, and even those of them which are most adapted to a terrestrial life are found in damp places, and have by no means lost the power of progression in water. Average cases are presented by the Newts or Efts, of which three species are native to Britain, *i.e.* the Great Crested Newt (*Molge cristatus*), the Common Newt (*M. vulgaris*), and the Palmated Newt (*M. palmatus*). These animals and their immediate allies are terrestrial except during the egg-laying season, at which time they take to the water. The chief swimming organ is the strong flattened tail, which is moved from side to side like that of a tadpole. Its efficiency is increased by the presence of a membranous fin, and it is remarkable that this becomes larger when its owner temporarily abandons the land for the water. At the same time the males develop a crest along the upper side of the body, and this may also assist in swimming. It is particularly large in the Great Crested Newt, and its edge is saw-like (fig. 618). The limbs, no doubt, assist in swimming, and in the male of the Palmated Newt the hind-feet become webbed at the time when the crest is developed. Some species of Newt, however, have been seen swimming rapidly by undulating the body and tail in an eel-like manner, the limbs being at the same time folded back against the body. From this it would appear to follow that in such animals the limbs are at most of secondary importance in progression through the water.

The well-known Spotted Salamander (*Salamandra maculosa*) of Europe, Africa, and South-western Asia, though belonging to the same family as our native Newts (*Salamandridæ*), contrasts markedly with them as regards its habits. Though dependent on moisture for its well-being, it only enters the water voluntarily during the egg-laying season, and even then only immerses the hinder part of its body. Gadow (in *The Cambridge Natural*

History), after describing the difficulty of finding this animal in dry weather, even in places most affected by it, says:—"The same place after a thunder-storm will be literally swarming with sleek, lively salamanders in search of earthworms and all kinds of insects, especially at dusk or during the night. They disappear in the autumn, in October, to hibernate in the ground, out of the reach of frost, and they reappear again in April. Later on they

Fig. 618.—Great Crested Newt (*Molge cristatus*) above, and Spotted Salamander (*Salamandra maculosa*) below

congregate at little springs, always at running water, to reach which they have often to make long migrations. This is the only time when these thoroughly terrestrial creatures approach water, in which they easily get drowned." It would appear, however, that if thrown into water the Spotted Salamander is able to swim vigorously by powerful side-strokes of its strong flattened tail, though this is not so well suited for the purpose as that of a Newt (see fig. 618).

While the tailed Amphibians, so far mentioned, are either, like Newts, semi-terrestrial when adult, or, like the Spotted Salamander, entirely terrestrial, the remaining members of the group live mostly or entirely in the water during the whole of their lives. This is the case, for instance, with the Fish-Salamanders (*Amphiumidæ*), which include the Giant Salamander (*Megalobatrachus maximus*) of China and Japan, and the Mississippi Salamander or Hell-bender (*Cryptobranchus lateralis*). Both of these are tail-swimmers. Another interesting North American species of the same family, the Three-toed Salamander (*Amphiuma means*), has specialized along much the same lines as eels among bony fishes (see p. 43), and swims by undulations

Fig. 619.—Mud-Eel (*Siren lacertina*), reduced

of its elongated body. The limbs are much reduced in size, and are provided with only two or three digits.

The same kind of modification is carried even farther in the best-known member of another family (*Proteidæ*), *i.e.* the Olm (*Proteus anguineus*). This creature, which is blind and of white or pinkish colour, is a native of South-west Austria, where it lives in underground streams. The small fore- and hind-limbs are respectively provided with three and two digits (see vol. i, p. 249).

The most specialized family of tailed Amphibians, however, is that of the Siren Salamanders (*Sirenidæ*), including two species from the south-east of the United States. In both of these the hind-limbs have entirely disappeared, and the fore-limbs are folded back against the body during swimming. The more familiar of the two species (fig. 619) is locally known as the Mud-Eel (*Siren lacertina*), and possesses four digits to the fore-limb, while there are only three digits in the other species (*Pseudobranchus striatus*), which is native to Georgia.

TAILLESS AMPHIBIANS (*Anura*).—This subdivision of the Amphibia includes all the forms familiarly known as Frogs and

Fig. 620.—Surinam Water-Toad (*Pipa Americana*) swimming (reduced)

Toads, among which is exemplified an even greater variety of habit than is displayed by the tailed Amphibians. Many species are thoroughly aquatic, others are terrestrial, and some of the latter live in trees. In most cases these creatures seek the water during the egg-laying season, and many of them are expert swimmers. The organs of propulsion are the relatively long and powerful hind-limbs, the efficiency of which is often increased by the presence of well-developed webs between the toes.

Examination of a Frog in the act of swimming shows that the legs are simultaneously pushed back and widely separated from one another, being then drawn up again and at the same time brought together, so as to react upon the wedge-shaped mass of water between them. Meanwhile the arms are folded upon the breast. As far as this leg-action is concerned, a comparison may be made with a man swimming by means of his legs only. But the broad, flat, webbed feet of the Frog confer a great additional advantage, and render the comparison an imperfect one.

Among entirely aquatic species may be mentioned some of the Tongueless Toads (*Aglossa*), of which two notable examples are the African Clawed Toad (*Xenopus lævis*) and the Surinam Water-Toad (*Pipa Americana*), native to Guiana and some other parts of South America. In both these forms the feet are broad paddles of relatively large size (fig. 620).

Other thoroughly aquatic species are the "Water Frogs", of which the Bull-Frog (*Rana Catesbiana*) of North America, and the Edible Frog (*R. esculenta*), the kind eaten on the Continent, may be taken as typical examples. Although both the Common or Grass Frog (*R. temporaria*) and the Toad (*Bufo vulgaris*) are of terrestrial habit, they are both good swimmers, and are found in ponds, &c., during the egg-laying season.

REPTILES (Reptilia) AS SWIMMERS

Swimmers are represented in all the five orders of living Reptiles, *i.e.* Crocodiles and Alligators (*Crocodilia*), Lizards (*Lacertilia*), Snakes (*Ophidia*), Turtles and Tortoises (*Chelonia*), and Tuataras (*Rhynchocephala*).

Crocodiles and Alligators (*Crocodilia*).—The members of this order are eminently aquatic, and possess a powerful swimming tail, flattened from side to side, and provided with a saw-edged crest on its upper surface. There is a good deal of variation in the structure of the fore- and hind-feet. The former may be partly webbed, and the latter are always more or less so. Taking the Nile Crocodile (*Crocodilus Niloticus*) as a type (fig. 621), we find that the fore-feet are webbed at the base, while a well-developed membrane connects together the outer toes of each hind-foot. The spindle-shaped body may be regarded as an adaptation to rapid locomotion through the water, which is chiefly effected by powerful side-strokes of the tail. The fore-limbs do not appear to be of much use in this respect, for they are laid back against the body, much as is the case in a Frog during swimming. The hind-limbs, on the other hand,

THE WATER-MONITOR (*Varanus salvator*)

This Lizard, which may be as much as 6 or 7 feet in length, ranges from India to Australia, and is a representative of a widely distributed family (*Varanidæ*), the members of which exhibit a number of structural adaptations to different modes of life. In this case the most noticeable feature is the long powerful swimming-tail, which is rendered more efficient by being greatly flattened from side to side, much as in a Crocodile.

The Water-Monitor is particularly fond of birds' eggs, which it eats in a rather curious manner. Seizing one of these in its jaws, it raises its head, breaks the shell, and swallows the contents. The empty shell is then ejected.

are used as subsidiary propulsive organs, and there is a cut-water edge on the outer side of each which easily cleaves the water when the legs are drawn forward in preparation for their backward stroke. It may also be noted that the smooth surface of the horny plates which cover the body reduces friction with the surrounding water. The curious adaptations which the breathing organs exhibit in adaptation to the mode of life have been noticed elsewhere (vol. ii, p. 424).

LIZARDS (*Lacertilia*).—The members of this very large group exhibit a series of adaptations to almost every sort of condition,

Fig. 621.—Nile Crocodiles (*Crocodilus Niloticus*) swimming

and some of those which spend more or less of their time in the water are expert swimmers.

The Sea Lizard (*Amblyrhynchus cristatus*) of the Galapagos Islands is remarkable on account of its marine habits (see vol. ii, p. 192). The body and tail are flattened from side to side, especially the latter, and, as might be anticipated, the animal is a tail-swimmer (fig. 622). The large Lizards known as Monitors (*Varanus*), which range from Africa through South Asia to Australia, mostly live near water and swim with more or less facility, the swimming organ being the tail. It is very interesting to notice that this organ is flattened to a varying extent in the different species, the aquatic habit and power of swimming being most marked in cases where the flattening is greatest. A typical instance of considerable adaptation in this direction is afforded by the Water Monitor (*Varanus Salvator*), a species which ranges from India to North Australia, and concerning which Annandale says:—"*Varanus Salvator* is common in Lower Siam, where it is equally at home on land, in water, and among the branches of trees. . . . When in the water the lizard swims

Fig. 622.—Galapagos Sea-Lizard (*Amblyrhynchus cristatus*), reduced

beneath the surface, the legs being closely applied to the sides, and the tail functioning both as oar and rudder."

The large American Lizards known as Iguanas, which belong to the same family (*Iguanidæ*) as the Sea Lizard, possess a long powerful tail, which is strongly flattened from side to side, and by means of which they swim in much the same way as the Water Monitor. The Common Iguana (*Iguana tuberculata*) of tropical America and the West Indies lives for the most part on trees close to the water, into which it dives when alarmed. The Ring-tailed Iguana (*Cyclura carinata*) of the West Indies is also a good swimmer (see fig. 433, vol. ii, p. 193). Quite a different method of progression through the water is exemplified by the American Basilisk (*Basilicus Americanus*), which is another member of the Iguana family. The habits of these creatures are described by Gadow (in *The Cambridge Natural History*) as follows:—"These creatures are very common amidst the luxuriant vegetation on the banks of the rivers of the Tierra Caliente of Mexico and in Guatemala. They lie upon the branches of trees, preferring those which overhang the water, into which they plunge at the slightest alarm. The high crests, being restricted to the male sex, are not essential to their swimming; they propel themselves by rapid strokes of the fore-limbs, letting the long rudder-like tail drag behind."

The numerous Lizards which constitute the family *Agamidæ* play the same part in the Old World that Iguanas and their allies do in the New. They range from Australia through South Asia and the African continent, and include some few forms which are tail-swimmers. The Water-'guana of Queensland (*Physignathus Lesueuri*) will serve as an example. It is about 18 inches long, with laterally-flattened body and tail, which are provided with a narrow saw-edged crest on the upper side. Semon (in *The Australian Bush*) states that these creatures "are expert swimmers, and like to perch in the branches of the tea-trees, and on the tree-stumps of the river-side, whence they let themselves drop into the water with a big splash if anyone is approaching . . ."

SNAKES (*Ophidia*).—Some few Snakes are semi-aquatic in habit, and progress in the water by undulating movements, commonly keeping the head raised more or less above the surface. Examples are found in the gigantic Anaconda (*Euneces murinus*) of tropical South America, the common Grass Snake (*Tropidonotus natrix*) of Britain, the Wart-Snake (*Acrochordus Javanicus*) of the Malay Peninsula, Java, and New Guinea, and the Water Viper (*Ancistrodon piscivorus*) of the United States.

Marine Snakes.—A number of Snakes, belonging to several different families, inhabit the sea, and it may be the adjacent estuaries. The large majority of these are included in a special family (*Hydrophinæ*), of which all the members are extremely poisonous, and have their head-quarters in the Indian Ocean and the western part of the South Pacific, though some of them range as far as the west coast of Mexico and Central America. The most interesting feature about these Reptiles is the way in which they are adapted to their mode of life, for the tail is laterally flattened and serves as a propeller, while in some cases the trunk is also specialized in the same way. The former character is well seen in the species figured (*Hydrus bicolor*, fig. 623), which is one of those most widely distributed, as it ranges from the Cape of Good Hope to the west coast of America. Sea-Snakes are social in habit, and usually swim with

Fig. 623.—A Sea-Snake (*Hydrus bicolor*) swimming (reduced)

the head projecting above the surface. They dive when disturbed, and while under water their valvular nostrils are closed.

TURTLES AND TORTOISES (*Chelonia*).—These Reptiles present a very interesting series of gradations between limbs suited for progression on land and those much specialized for swimming purposes. Such a typically terrestrial form, for example, as the Grecian Tortoise (*Testudo Græca*) possesses stumpy legs, of which the short toes are provided with claws, and quite devoid of webs. Its carapace is strongly arched. The European Pond-Tortoise (*Emys orbicularis*) is flatter, but has limbs of much the same general character, though the extremities are broadened, and extensive webs spread between the somewhat longer toes.

Much greater specialization is exhibited by the Soft Tortoises (*Trionychoidea*), which live in some of the rivers of Asia, Africa, and North America, ranging also into estuaries and even into the sea, being thus intermediate in habit between purely fresh-water and purely marine forms. The body is here a good deal flattened, while the broadened limbs end in extensively-webbed paddles, of which only the three inner toes bear claws (fig. 624). The limbs are worked horizontally, and under ordinary circumstances those on one side alternate with those of the other side. On occasion, however, the two front paddles can be used together, in which case the swimming is more rapid. From this case we pass on to the purely marine Turtles (*Chelonidæ*), in which the limbs are converted into flippers, the fore ones being much larger than the others. The digits are much elongated for the support of these swimming organs, which are used diagonally, each fore-

Fig. 624.—Nilotic Soft Tortoise (*Triomyx triunguis*) swimming (reduced)

flipper moving forwards and backwards at the same time as the hind-flipper of the opposite side. In the Hawkbill Turtle (*Chelone imbricata*) only the two inner digits bear claws, and this is the case with young individuals of the Loggerhead Turtle (*Thalassochelys caretta*), but in the adults of this species there is only one clawed digit, *i.e.* the first or innermost. The same digit is, as a rule, the only claw-bearing one in the Edible Turtle (*Chelone mydas*). The largest and most specialized of recent Chelonians is the Leathery Turtle (*Dermatochelys coriacea*), which is the only living representative of its family (*Sphargidæ*). Its flippers are entirely devoid of claws (fig. 625).

TUATARAS (*Rhynchocephala*).—The only existing member of this order is the little New Zealand Tuatara (*Hatteria punctata*, see vol. i, p. 236). Its tail resembles that of a crocodile, and can be used on occasion as a swimming organ.

Fig. 625.—Leathery Turtle (*Dermatochelys coriacea*) swimming (much reduced)

BIRDS (AVES) AS SWIMMERS

A great many Birds are either semi-aquatic or aquatic in habit, and exhibit a series of adaptations to life in the water which are even more interesting than those presented by the Tortoises and Turtles among Reptiles. We have elsewhere seen (vol. ii, p. 426) that the breathing arrangements of Birds are extremely perfect, in relation to the unusually high temperature of the blood (from 103°–104° F.), and there are several devices by which aquatic birds are prevented from being unduly chilled by partial or complete immersion in water. For one thing, the plumage is very thick and extremely oily, so that the current saying about water falling off a duck's back is founded on fact. It is indeed characteristic of such forms that the oil-gland which opens on the upper side of the tail-region should be extremely large, and the greasy matter secreted by it is used for lubricating the feathers. These consequently do not get wet, and the water is unable to displace the air which they entangle, so that the actual surface of the skin is kept dry and warm. We find, too, in water-birds a considerable accumulation of fat below the skin, forming a non-conducting layer which goes far to prevent loss of heat from the outside of the body.

For the purpose of the present section it is convenient to draw a distinction between birds which swim entirely or mostly at the surface, and those which are more or less expert at swimming under water and diving. But it must, of course, be understood that the division is purely an artificial one, as all gradations may be traced between the two habits.

SURFACE-SWIMMING BIRDS

The small specific gravity of a Bird's body, due to the presence of extensive air-sacs connected with the lungs (see vol. ii, p. 426), is clearly an advantage in surface-swimming. We should expect, on the same principle, to find the bones of surface-swimmers richly provided with air-cavities, as is the case with a great many land-birds. But in many instances, *e.g.* Gulls, the bones are filled with marrow, as in amphibians, reptiles, mammals, diving birds, and many land birds. Lightness is clearly not the only thing to be considered, but our knowledge is at present too imperfect to explain all the facts in this particular case.

Fig. 626.—Herring Gull (*Larus argentatus*)

Typical Gulls (*Larus*) (fig. 626) may be taken as good

average examples of surface-swimmers, using their legs as paddles, of which the efficiency is greatly increased by the presence of webs between the three forwardly-directed toes. The inner or great toe (*hallux*) can be of little use for swimming, for it is small, backwardly directed, and shifted up a little, so as not to touch the ground when the bird is standing. The feet are used alternately during swimming, and, as in all limbs so modified, they present a minimum surface when being drawn forwards, but are spread out to their full extent during the powerful backward stroke.

Ordinary Surface Ducks, as they may be called to distinguish them from their diving cousins, include a number of well-

Fig. 627.—Sheld-Drakes (*Tadorna cornuta*)

known species, such as the Wild Duck (*Anas boschas*), Sheld-Drake (*Tadorna cornuta*) (fig. 627), Teal (*Querquedula crecca*), and Widgeon (*Mareca penelope*). These are more specialized in some respects than Gulls, as a result of still further adaptation to the aquatic habit. The plumage is particularly dense and oily, and the shape of the body is almost boat-like. Although the legs and feet (fig. 628) are much like those of gulls, they are a good deal shorter, and set on much farther back. Though this is no doubt conducive to rapid swimming, it is at the expense of walking power, and is the cause of the ungraceful "waddle" which distinguishes ducks on land. During swimming the two legs are pushed back almost but not quite at the same time. The remarks just made about ordinary surface ducks applies with equal force to the closely related Swans.

Fig. 628.—Foot of a Duck (*Anas boschas*)

BIRDS WHICH SWIM UNDER WATER AND DIVE

We have now to consider birds which are more perfectly adapted to an aquatic life than the surface swimmers, and which spend more or less of their time actually submerged in water. In such cases the plumage is markedly dense and oily, the general shape of the body is comparable to a rounded wedge suited for cleaving the water, and the legs are more specialized as paddles than those of ordinary Ducks and Swans, while at the same time they are set on even further back, till in the most extreme cases walking on land is effected in a very clumsy way. It becomes a matter of importance that the specific gravity of the body should be reduced as far as possible, for though lightness is an obvious advantage for purposes of flight, it clearly handicaps a diving animal. It is not, therefore, surprising to find that in diving birds all or most of the bones are solid, *i.e.* free from the air-spaces that are in so many other cases highly characteristic.

Although we can speak in general terms of birds less adapted or more adapted to diving and swimming under water, it is not possible to include them all in a single series, for different groups have specialized in somewhat different ways and along various lines. It will therefore be convenient to consider these groups separately.

Closely related to Surface Ducks and Swans are to be found a number of forms which may be termed collectively DIVING DUCKS, sometimes also called Sea Ducks, because the large majority of them are essentially marine. As in Surface Ducks, the feet are the swimming organs, but are here somewhat more specialized, for the great toe is bordered by a well-marked flap of skin, and thus increases the surface presented to the water. It may also be noted that the legs are set on further back than in surface forms, while the body is somewhat narrower from side to side. There is, in fact, as regards general shape, the same sort of difference between a surface-swimming bird and a diving bird as that between a life-boat and a submarine. Common examples of the present group are the Eider Duck (*Somateria mollissima*) (fig. 629), the Pochard (*Fuligula ferina*), the Canvas-back (*F. Vallisneria*) of North America, and the Logger-head or Steamer Duck (*Tachyeres cinereus*) of Chili. All these forms progress clumsily on land, and their heads are somewhat wedge-shaped. Even when swimming at the surface the body is more

Fig. 629.—Eider Duck (*Somateria mollissima*)

deeply sunk than in ordinary ducks, a peculiarity that is probably associated with the power of expelling some of the air in the air-sacs, thus reducing the specific gravity of the body. Increased

Fig. 630.—1, Red-breasted Merganser (*Mergus serrator*) and 2, Black-throated Diver (*Colymbus arcticus*)

diving power is commonly associated with reduced powers of flying as well as of walking. In these particular birds the wings are short, and flight, though it may be powerful, is more or less slow and heavy. In the Steamer Ducks it is said that the adults are unable to fly at all.

MERGANSERS (fig. 630) are closely related to the Diving

Ducks, but their bills are much longer and narrower. The two commonest British species are the Red-breasted Merganser (*Mergus serrator*) and the Goosander (*M. merganser*). These birds are very expert divers and swimmers, and it would seem that they are able to regulate the amount of air in the air-sacs, for they can either float high on the water, swim with only the head and neck projecting above the surface, or propel themselves at a great rate when completely submerged. In reference to a flock of Red-breasted Mergansers Macgillivray remarks (in *A History of British Birds*):—"The birds seemed to move

Fig. 631.—The Coot (*Fulica atra*), and its lobed foot drawn to a larger scale

under the water with almost as much velocity as in the air, and often rose to breathe at a distance of 200 yards from the spot at which they had dived".

Some of the RAILS (*Grallæ*) are of thoroughly aquatic habit, and of these may be mentioned among British forms the Moor-Hen or Water-Hen (*Gallinula chloropus*) and the Coot (*Fulica atra*) (fig. 631). The former bird possesses long toes that are not webbed, but are fringed with a narrow membrane, which increases their purchase upon the water. It is interesting that in an allied form, native to the southern parts of Australia, Mortier's Water-Hen (*Tribonyx Mortieri*), the toes are devoid of even this amount of extension, and, as might be expected, the powers of swimming and diving are feebler. The Coot, on the other hand, swims and dives with greater facility than the Water-Hen, and this is related to the fact that the three front toes are provided with broad folds of skin at the sides, so that they present a large surface to the water. It is also stated that these lobate toes are of use in enabling the bird to move rapidly over water-lilies and other floating plants.

CORMORANTS, &c. (*Steganopodes*).—The members of this group, though powerful swimmers, and often expert swimmers, have not sacrificed to any great degree their powers of flight, and some of them are pre-eminent in this respect. As in most other aquatic birds, however, their legs are set on rather far back, which renders the gait on land somewhat clumsy, though it is undoubtedly a great aid to swimming. The feet are more specialized than in any of the cases so far considered, for they are fully webbed, *i.e.* membranous expansions stretch between all four toes, the great toe included (fig. 633). These organs are therefore paddles of unusual power, and are used simultaneously, like the legs of a frog.

Probably the worst swimmers of this order are to be found in the Frigate Birds (*Fregatus*) and Tropic Birds (*Phaëthon*), both of which are thoroughly oceanic, being found in the open sea at great distances from land. As flying birds they are pre-eminent, and it is interesting to notice that the feet of the Frigate Birds differ from those of other members of the order in being less fully webbed. In fact the toes are united together for only about half their length. Pelicans both swim and dive, keeping for the most part to estuaries, rivers, and lakes. The diving powers, however, are not very great, except in the American White Pelican (*Pelecanus trachyrhynchus*). Here, as in all the members of the order except Tropic Birds, the nostrils are almost covered over by a membrane, an arrangement which is clearly advantageous when the head is frequently under water.

Gannets are well-known oceanic birds, of which the Common Gannet or Solan Goose (*Sula Bassana*) (fig. 632) breeds on the Bass Rock, on Ailsa Craig, and in a few other British localities. It is remarkable for the habit of diving from a great height in order to secure its prey. In this case a "flying start" is especially necessary, for the bones are hollow to an unusual extent, and air-sacs are found even under the skin. It has been suggested that these last act like an air-cushion to break the force of impact with the water. The birds known to sailors as "boobies" are of the Gannet kind.

The cosmopolitan Cormorants are the best swimmers and divers of their order, and it is not therefore surprising to find that their wings are shorter and their legs set further back than

Fig. 632.—Gannets (*Sula Bassana*)

in the other related forms. We have two native species, the Black Cormorant (*Phalacrocorax carbo*) (fig. 633) and the smaller Green Cormorant or Shag (*P. graculus*), both of which are essentially coast forms, though some foreign kinds frequent rivers and lakes. These birds can dive quite well from the floating position, and the shape of their bodies is admirably suited for cleaving the water, besides which they are known to be able to expel a large amount of air from their air-sacs, thus rendering themselves more weighty. Regarding the Green Cormorant Headley remarks (in *The Structure and Life of Birds*):—"Among the diving birds at the Zoological Gardens there is frequently a Shag, and as he chases the fish in the tank, he holds his wings motionless, just slightly lifted from the body. . . . Some birds dive to great depths. The Shag begins by jumping up in the water and taking a header, then he strikes hard up-

Fig. 633.—Black Cormorant (*Phalacrocorax carbo*)

ward. One was caught once in a crab-pot 20 fathoms below the surface."

The Darters or Snake-Birds (*Plotus*) (see vol. ii, p. 49) are river cormorants, which both fly and swim in much the same way as the forms just described. They often swim with only the head and long sinuous neck above the surface, presenting the appearance which has probably earned for them the name of "snake" birds.

GREBES, DIVERS and AUKS (*Pygopodes*) make up a group of birds distinguished by their great powers of swimming and diving. All of them exhibit in a greater or lesser degree the graceful curved outline associated with easy progression under water.

The short legs are set on exceedingly far back, and the feet are either much like those of a duck, or the three front toes are lobate, as in the Coot (p. 62). The wings are relatively short, and many of the species rely chiefly on diving when they are pursued.

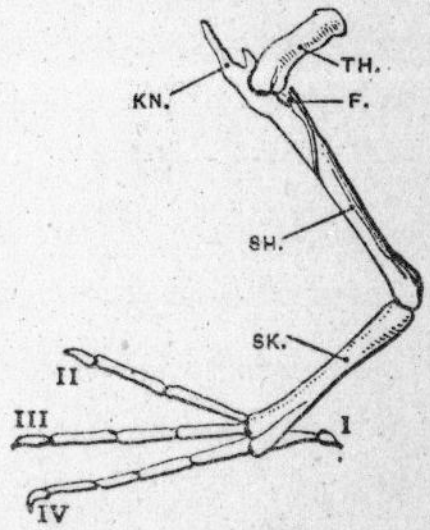

Fig. 634.—Bones of a Diver's Leg (reduced)

TH., Thigh-bone; KN., knee-cap; SH., shin-bone; F., fibula; SK., shank-bone; I–IV, toes.

Grebes and Divers agree in the possession of one or two interesting anatomical features related to their habits. A small great toe is present, and is fringed by membrane, while the shank is extremely flat, presenting a broad surface to the water during the effective backward stroke, but a narrow cut-water edge while being drawn forward again. The knee-cap and upper end of the shin-bone are drawn out into a sort of spike, which affords considerable purchase to some of the swimming muscles which are attached to it (fig. 634). In Grebes the long front toes are broadly lobed, presenting a considerable surface to the water

Fig. 635.—Little Grebe (*Podicipes fluviatilis*), and its broadly-lobed foot drawn to a larger scale

when fully expanded as they are thrust back, but folding up to small compass when moved in the other direction. The tail is exceedingly short. These are freshwater forms, of which we have one well-known species in Britain, the Little Grebe or

Dabchick (*Podicipes fluviatilis*) (fig. 635). Divers differ from Grebes in several respects, among which may be mentioned the presence of complete webs between the three front toes, somewhat longer wings, and a rather better developed tail. They are essentially marine in habit, but resort to inland waters during the nesting season. Our commonest native species is the Red-throated Diver (*Colymbus septentrionalis*). The Black-throated Diver (*C. arcticus*) (fig. 630) is much more rarely seen.

AUKS are here associated with Divers and Grebes in accordance with the common practice, but they are now often assigned

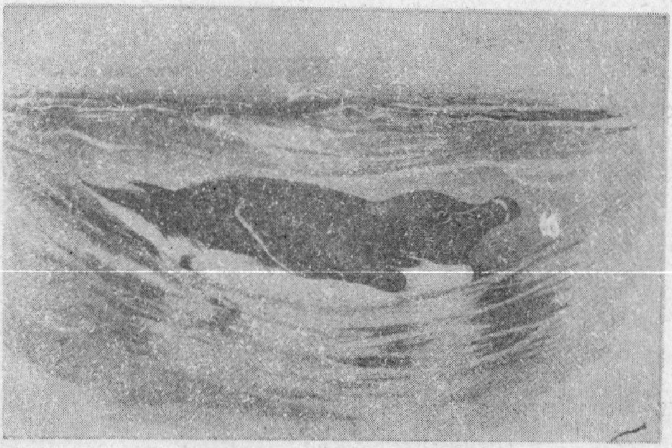

Fig. 636.—Razor-Bill (*Alca torda*)

to a distinct order, supposed to be most nearly related to Gulls. Their feet are pretty much like those of Divers, except that the great toe is either absent or extremely small. The shank and shin-bone do not exhibit the peculiarities described above for Divers and Grebes. Although the wings are short, the power of flight has not been lost in existing species, though the extinct Great Auk or Gare-Fowl (*Alca impennis*) was flightless (see vol. i, p. 183). Our commonest British species are the Razor-Bill (*Alca torda*) (fig. 636), the Guillemot (*Uria troile*), and the Puffin (*Fratercula arctica*). The most interesting point about the Auks is that they swim under water chiefly by means of their wings, while the webbed feet are used as rudders. In this sort of submarine flight the Great Auk appears to have excelled the forms now living.

PENGUINS (*Impennes*).—Although these extraordinary birds,

which have entirely lost the power of flight, are not unlike the Great Auk in appearance (indeed this bird was popularly called a "penguin"), this does not imply close relationship, but is the outcome of adaptation along similar lines to thoroughly aquatic habits. These birds are indeed more closely related to the Divers and Grebes, agreeing with the former in the structure of the feet and the flatness of the shank. The wings have been modified into stiff paddles or flippers, which are the chief propulsive organs, as the feet would appear to be mainly used for steering purposes. They are covered with short, almost scale-like feathers, and are, so to speak, twisted round, so as to give a very effective backward stroke, whereas in the wing of an ordinary flying-bird the downward movement is naturally the best marked. Penguins are characteristic of the southern hemisphere, the largest species being the Emperor Penguin (*Aptenodytes Forsteri*), native to Victoria Land and the neighbouring ocean area, and reaching the length of 3 feet. The smallest member of the order is the Blue Penguin (*Spheniscus minor*), which attains a length of 19 inches, and is found in the New Zealand and South Australian areas (fig. 637).

Fig. 637.—Blue Penguins (*Spheniscus minor*)

MAMMALS (MAMMALIA) AS SWIMMERS

Unlike Man, the great majority of Mammals are able to swim without difficulty for a greater or less distance when for the first time they enter or fall into the water. The facts are thus very clearly put by Pettigrew (in *Animal Locomotion*):—"Man, in order to swim, must learn the art of swimming. He must serve a longer or shorter apprenticeship to a new form of locomotion, and acquire a new order of movements. It is otherwise with the majority of animals. Almost all quadrupeds can swim the first time they are immersed, as may readily be ascertained by throwing a newly-born kitten or puppy into the water. The same may be said of the greater number of birds. This is accounted for by the fact that quadrupeds and birds are lighter, bulk for bulk, than water, but more especially, because in walking and running the movements made by their extremities are precisely those made in swimming. They have nothing to learn, as it were. They are buoyant naturally, and if they move their limbs at all, which they do instinctively, they swim of necessity. It is different with man. The movements made by him in walking and running are not those made by him in swimming; neither is the position resorted to in swimming that which characterizes him on land." All this is illustrated by a man who "swims like a dog", to use a well-known technicality, for he then imitates a quadruped and walks on all-fours through the water.

ADAPTATIONS TO SWIMMING EXHIBITED BY MAMMALS

It will be clear from what has been said that ordinary land Mammals are able to swim on occasion without being specialized for the purpose, and with these we have here no further concern. There are, however, many species which are more or less aquatic in habit, and such forms present, at least in most cases, obvious peculiarities which are clearly to be regarded as adaptations to the mode of life, and many of which are necessarily of the same nature as those already described in other classes of backboned animals.

We find, in the first place, that as regards shape the body of an aquatic mammal is more or less suitable for moving through the water with a small amount of friction, and the same end is furthered by the compact nature of the fur, or it may be by the reduction or even complete suppression of the hairy covering of the body. The external ear-flaps are commonly reduced in size, or perhaps absent altogether, while auditory apertures and nostrils are frequently valvular, so as to prevent free entry of water. Should the tail be used for swimming or even for steering, it will be found well developed and flattened either from side to

Fig. 638.—Duck-Mole (*Ornithorhynchus paradoxus*)

side, or from above downwards. And the limbs are typically modified in shape and sometimes position for propulsive purposes, very much on the same lines as in some aquatic reptiles (see p. 55). In extreme cases the hind limbs are absent altogether, a character which is correlated with the presence of a swimming-tail of exceptional efficiency. As in Birds, the same ends may be attained in somewhat different ways in different orders, and it is therefore best to consider such groups separately, ending with those where specialization is at a maximum.

EGG-LAYING MAMMALS (*Monotremata*).—One member of this primitive Australian group, the Duck-Mole (*Ornithorhynchus*) (fig. 638), is eminently aquatic in habit, presenting in this respect a strong contrast to its cousin, the Spiny Ant-Eater (*Echidna*). The body is flattened from above downwards, as also is the tail, and the fur is dense and closely set. Behind the small eyes no trace of ear-flaps is to be seen, and the auditory apertures are valvular. Both fore- and hind-limbs are short and webbed, the webs of the former being particularly well developed, and, when in use, extending beyond the claws. Swimming is chiefly effected by these paddle-like limbs, especially the front ones, but in diving the flat tail is used for both propelling and steering. Duck-Moles haunt the quiet reaches of streams in South Australia and Tasmania, living in long burrows, the openings of which are under the surface of the water. The feeding habits are correlated with the aquatic mode of life, and resemble those of ducks. There is indeed a striking resemblance between the snout of a Duck-Mole and the bill of a Duck, which is the outcome of specialization along similar lines.

Fig. 639.—Water Opossum (*Cheironectes variegatus*)

Pouched Mammals (*Marsupials*).—The only species belonging to this multifarious group requiring notice here is the Water Opossum (*Cheironectes variegatus*) of South America, which lives on the banks of rivers, upon the fishes of which it preys. Although an expert swimmer, it is not modified to nearly the same extent as the Duck-Mole in relation to the aquatic habit. But the fur is dense and short, and the hind-feet webbed, while the long scaly tail is not unlike that of an Otter (fig. 639).

INSECT-EATING MAMMALS (*Insectivora*).—Several animals included in this widely-distributed and somewhat lowly order are more or less specialized to fit them for an aquatic or semi-aquatic life.

Shrews.—The least-modified swimming Insectivore is one of our native forms, the Water-Shrew (*Crossopus fodiens*), which is a good deal larger than its non-aquatic relatives. Its fur is dense and not easily wetted, the long tail is somewhat flattened from side to side, and though the feet are not webbed, they are provided on their outer sides with stiff bristles which give an increased surface for application to the water. The movements of this species are thus described by Bell (in *British Quadrupeds*):—"Its swimming is principally effected by the alternate action of the hinder feet, which produces an unequal or wriggling motion. It makes its way, however, with great velocity, and as it swims rather superficially, with the belly flattened, the sides, as it were, spread out, and the tail extended backwards as a rudder, it forms a very beautiful and pleasing object, moving on the calm surface of a quiet brook, or diving in an instant after its food, its black velvety coat becoming beautifully silvered with the innumerable bubbles of air that cover it when submerged; and on rising again the fur is observed to be perfectly dry, repelling the water as completely as the feathers of the water-fowl. When submerged the ear is nearly closed by means of three little valves."

The Himalayan Swimming-Shrew (*Chimarrogale Himalayica*), and an allied Japanese species, closely resemble the Water-Shrew in structure and habits. But it is very interesting to note that an Insectivore native to Thibet, the Web-footed Shrew (*Nectogale elegans*), is more completely adapted to an aquatic life. In this case ear-flaps are entirely absent, and the feet are webbed.

The *Desmans* or *Divers* are aquatic Insectivores allied to Moles, which they somewhat resemble in the texture of their fur and in general appearance, though their tails are very much longer, and the feet quite different in structure. They are often termed Musk-Shrews (a name more properly applied to a group of land-shrews), but "Water-Moles" would be a better descriptive term. Of the two existing species the larger is the Wuychuchol or Russian Desman (*Myogale moschata*), and this is seen at a glance to be adapted to an aquatic life (fig. 640). The feet are not only fringed with strong bristles, as in a Water-Shrew, but are also fully webbed, and the powerful tail, laterally flattened and margined with stiff hairs, is evidently a swimming organ. The long bare narrow snout bears the nostrils at its tip, and is not only used for finding and seizing food, but is also of use in enabling the animal to breathe when under water, for its tip can readily be protruded above the surface. The smaller Spanish Desman (*Myogale Pyrenaica*), native to the streams of northern Spain, is not so highly specialized as its Russian cousin, for its tail is cylindrical instead of being flattened.

Fig. 640.—Russian Desman (*Myogale moschata*)

The largest known Insectivore is a remarkable otter-like creature (*Potamogale velox*), which lives in the rivers of West Africa. It is the type of a distinct family. The feet are not webbed, but the powerful flattened tail is a very efficient swimming organ, and passes gradually into the body instead of being sharply marked off. The animal is about 22 inches long, of which half is taken up by the tail.

Gnawing Animals (*Rodentia*).—A number of adaptations to an aquatic mode of life are exemplified by various species of this cosmopolitan order. All the swimming forms possess collar-bones, and the largest Rodents, like the largest Insectivores, inhabit the water. Some possess swimming feet, others swimming tails, and this furnishes a further parallel character of the two orders.

Voles.—The familiar water-"rat" of Britain, or, to speak more accurately, Water-Vole (*Microtus amphibius*), is an admirable swimmer and diver, though but little modified for the purpose, for its feet are not webbed, and its tail is not flattened, though, unlike that of an ordinary rat, it is hairy instead of scaly, thus presenting a fairly large surface to the water. The ears are short and rounded, but this can hardly be looked upon as

Fig. 641.—Musk-Rat (*Fiber zibethicus*).

a special aquatic character, as it is also found in land-voles, which very likely acquired it as an adaptation to burrowing. The Musk-Rat or Musquash (*Fiber zibethicus*) of Canada may be regarded as a large vole exhibiting marked aquatic specialization (fig. 641). Both fore- and hind-feet are furnished with hairy webs, while the tail is markedly flattened from side to side, and its edges are fringed with stiff hairs, as in so many other similar cases.

Beavers.—The Beaver (*Castor fiber*) is among the largest of its order, for the weight may be 60 pounds or more, and the length over 3 feet, of which nearly one-third is taken up by the tail. Of eminently aquatic habit, this creature presents numerous characters correlated to this particular mode of life. Not only is the general shape of the body well suited for cleaving the water, but the fur is unusually dense, the hind-feet are webbed, and the strong scaly tail is remarkably broad, being flattened from above downwards. During the act of diving eyes, ear-passages, and nose-cavities are all carefully guarded. For the eyes are small and provided with third eyelids (nictitating membranes), which can be pulled over them curtain-wise, yet without unduly obstructing vision; the valvular nostrils can readily be closed; and the small ear-flaps can be folded over the passages they adjoin, so as to effectively keep out water. The absence of webs between the toes of the fore-feet is readily understood, for these extremities are used in many delicate carpentry operations, during which it is clearly advantageous for the toes to be quite free. Although the webbed hind-feet are of great importance in swimming, the tail is the chief agent of propulsion in the water, and at first sight it seems curious that it should be flattened at right angles to the more usual direction of compression. But it appears that this organ can not only be moved up and down in a way which must be effective for diving purposes, but can also be twisted round so as to deliver side-strokes with its broad upper and lower surfaces. It acts, in fact, like a screw-propeller, but is not specially remarkable in this respect, since the same thing is true for most swimming and flying organs.

Coypus and Capybaras.—The last two examples of swimming Rodents will be taken from among the forms which inhabit South America, the head-quarters of the order. The Coypu (*Myopotamus coypu*) is particularly common in the Plate River and its tributaries, and from its appearance is often known as the "Plate Beaver". It is, however, much less specialized than its namesake, for though the hind-feet are webbed, the long hairy tail is not flattened. Though an excellent swimmer, it is asserted that the Coypu is a bad diver. It is at home in salt water as well as in fresh, an example of this being afforded by the numerous individuals which live on the shores of the Chonos Islands, in the south of Chili.

The Capybara or Carpincho (*Hydrochærus capybara*) is characteristic of South American rivers from Guiana to the Argentine Republic, and may be regarded as a huge guinea-pig, resembling its small relative in general appearance, practical absence of a tail, and the presence of little hoofs on its digits (fig. 642). It can both swim and dive with great facility, by means of its short strong limbs. Webs stretch between the toes, of which the fore-feet possess four and the hind-feet only three. Although mainly a freshwater animal, the Capybara is also found in the estuary of the Plate River. It is the largest existing Rodent, comparable in size to a yearling pig, and attaining a length of 4 feet and a weight of about 1 cwt.

FLESH-EATING MAMMALS (*Carnivora*).—These are divided into the two great groups of Land Carnivores (*Fissipedia*) and Aquatic

Fig. 642.—Capybara (*Hydrochærus capybara*)

Carnivores (*Pinnipedia*). Among the former Otters are specialized swimmers, and some few other forms are more or less modified for the purpose. Pinnipedes, including Sea-Lions, Walruses, and Seals, are altogether adapted to an aquatic life.

AQUATIC FISSIPEDES

Some of the terrestrial beasts of prey seek their food in the water, without exhibiting any noticeable features specially related to swimming or diving. Among these may be mentioned the Fishing Cat (*Felis viverrina*) of India and the Polar Bear (*Ursus maritimus*). The habits of the former are imperfectly known though it undoubtedly feeds on fish, and almost certainly pursues them in the water, as domesticated cats have been occasionally known to do. Polar Bears can swim and dive with great facility, and it is not impossible that the great breadth of their paws may in part be an adaptation to this habit, though primarily related to walking in plantigrade fashion, *i.e.* on the palms of the hands and soles of the feet. At any rate this great breadth must be of considerable assistance in swimming.

Visons, Otters, and Sea-Otters.—The Visons, or Minks, well known as fur-yielding forms, are native to the arctic and north temperate regions, where they spend a large part of their time in the pursuit of fishes, frogs, &c., in rivers and lakes. Three ill-defined species are known, the European Vison (*Mustela lutreola*), the Siberian Vison (*M. Sibirica*), and the American Vison (*M. vison*), inhabiting respectively the continents indicated by their names. These creatures are in effect water-polecats, and as regards both structure and habits are intermediate in character between creatures of the Weasel kind and Otters. Their feet are partly webbed, and are the chief swimming organs, but the large bushy tail probably serves as a rudder.

Otters.—The Common Otter (*Lutra vulgaris*) will serve as a type of this thoroughly aquatic group of Carnivores, which are not unlike Visons, but are more highly specialized (see vol. ii, p. 22). The cylindrical body presents a continuous curved outline, from the rounded head to the long tail, which is somewhat flattened from above downwards. As in some of the other types already described, the nostrils are valvular, the eyes small, and the ear-flaps much reduced, while the apertures of the ears can be closed at will. Both fore- and hind-limbs are remarkably short and strong, while the toes are fully webbed. The broadened extremities are the chief propulsive organs, the tail mainly serving as a rudder. Otters sometimes swim at the surface, but more commonly entirely submerged, and can make good headway against strong currents. The fur is extremely dense and smooth, serving the double purpose of preventing chill and reducing friction during swimming. Haacke (in *Das Thierleben der Erde*) says that the coat "takes up but little moisture, even if the animal remains for hours in the water, a characteristic which at once disappears in a dead or severely wounded otter. This results from the extraordinary quantity of electricity which is stored up in the coat of uninjured living individuals, but not in that of a dead or wounded one."

The Sea Otter (*Latax lutris*) of the North Pacific is more profoundly modified in relation to an aquatic life than its fresh-water cousins, and presents some features which are still further emphasized in Sea-Lions. The head is much rounder than that

Fig. 643.—Sea-Otter (*Latax lutris*)

of an Otter, the flattened tail much shorter, and the hind-limbs set on much further back (fig. 643). The hind-feet are very much larger than those in front, and constitute powerful flippers which do most of the work in swimming.

PINNIPEDE CARNIVORES

These are all highly-specialized aquatic forms, of which there are three groups, Eared Seals, Walruses, and Seals. In all cases the openings of the nose and ears are valvular, and there is a thick layer of fat below the skin. The limbs are modified into flippers.

Eared Seals (*Otaridæ*) include those forms popularly known as Fur-Seals, Sea-Lions, and Sea-Bears, which possess a very small ear-flap, an appendage entirely absent in the other Pinnipedes (fig. 644). The body is spindle-shaped, but the neck region is fairly distinct, while the ail is a mere stump. Both fore- and hind-limbs are converted into flippers, and the latter, though set on very far back, can be turned forwards under the body to assist in progression on land. Strong webs are developed between the digits, and project beyond the tips of these,

Fig. 644.—Pinnipedes. 1, Eared Seals (*Otaria*). 2, Common Seal (*Phoca*)

ending in a sort of scalloped edge with a lobe opposite the end of each of them. The claws are reduced in size, and those of the external digits in the hind-limb are absent altogether. Swimming is effected chiefly by means of the front flippers, which are almost comparable in shape to the wings of a penguin, this being largely due to the fact that the first or inner digit is the longest, while the others exhibit a gradual diminution in size (see fig. 645). The hind-flippers mainly serve for steering, and the inner and outer digits (first and fifth) are larger than the other three. Regarding the nature of the swimming movements of the Behring Sea Fur-Seal or Sea-Bear (*Otaria ursina*), Elliott writes as follows (in *An Arctic Province*):—"They all swim rapidly, with the exception of the pups, and may be said to dart under the water with the velocity of a bird on the wing. As they swim they are invariably submerged, running along horizontally about two or three feet below the surface, guiding their course with the hind-flippers as by an oar, and propelling themselves solely

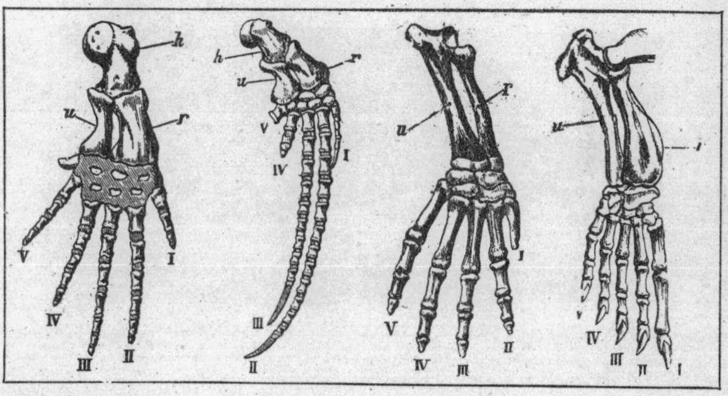

Fig. 645.—Skeleton of the Fore-limb or Flipper of the Whalebone Whale. Same of the Caaing Whale. Same of the Dugong. Same of the Seal

r, Radius; *u*, Ulna; *h*, Humerus; I–V, Digits.

by the fore-feet, rising to breathe at intervals which are either very frequent or else so wide apart that it is impossible to see the speeding animal when he rises a second time. . . . In all their swimming which I have had a chance to study, as they passed under the water, mirrored to my eyes from the bluff above by the whitish-coloured rocks below the rookery waters at Great Eastern Rookery, I have not been able to satisfy myself how they used their long, flexible hind-feet, other than as steering media. If these posterior members have any perceptible motion, it is so rapid that my eye is not quick enough to catch it; but the fore-flippers, however, can be most distinctly seen as they work in feathering forward and sweeping flatly back, opposed to the water, with great rapidity and energy."

Walruses (*Trichechidæ*).—The Walrus (*Trichechus rosmarus*) is bulkier and clumsier than any of the Eared Seals, and differs from them in many particulars (fig. 646). Leaving the teeth out of consideration (see vol. ii, p. 25), attention may be directed to the length of the head, the smallness of the eyes, and the complete absence of ear-flaps, while the neck is less well marked, and the hairy covering of the body not so well developed. In old individuals the skin is more or less bare, but its extreme thickness compensates for this. The limbs correspond pretty closely to those of a sea-lion, but are more enclosed, as it were, in the skin of the trunk, and blunt claws are present on all the digits.

Fig. 646.—Walrus (*Trichechus rosmarus*)

The front-flippers are used during swimming as in Sea-Lions, &c., but propulsion is also aided by the hind-flippers, which are actively moved from side to side, something like the tail of a fish. In spite of this, however, the Walrus swims neither so rapidly nor so gracefully as its eared relatives, for the shape of its body is not so well adapted to progression in the water, though its powers in this direction are of no mean order.

Seals Proper, or Earless Seals (*Phocidæ*) (fig. 644).—Of all Pinnipedes these are best adapted to the conditions of a thoroughly aquatic life, and it is not therefore surprising to find that they are more fish-shaped than either Eared Seals or Walruses, the head passing gradually into the trunk, owing to the absence of a clearly-marked neck. The front-flippers (fig. 644) are smaller than the hind ones, which are directed backwards, and so enclosed in the skin of the hinder part of the body that they cannot be turned forwards, as in a Sea-Lion or Walrus, to aid progression on land or ice. The webs do not extend beyond the tips of the digits, all of which are armed with claws. We have seen that the hind-flippers of a Walrus act to some extent like the tail of a fish, and this is true to a much greater extent of the corresponding organs in a Seal. Pettigrew (in *Animal Locomotion*) speaks as follows of the mode of swimming:—"It would appear that the swimming appliances of the seals (where the feet open and close as in swimming-birds) are to those of the sea-mammals generally what the feathers of the bird's wing (these also open and close in flight) are to the continuous membrane forming the wing of the insect and bat. The anterior extremities or flippers of the seal are not engaged in swimming, but only in balancing and in changing position. When so employed the fore-feet open and close, though not to the same extent as the hind ones; the resistance and non-resistance necessary being secured by a partial rotation and tilting of the flippers. By this twisting and untwisting the narrow edges and broader portions of the flippers are applied to the water alternately. The rotating and tilting of the anterior and posterior extremities, and the opening and closing of the hands and feet in the balancing and swimming of the seal, form a series of strictly progressive and very graceful movements. They are, however, performed so rapidly, and glide into each other so perfectly, as to render an analysis of them exceedingly difficult."

There can be no doubt that Pinnipedes are the specialized descendants of land carnivores, and we know that the group is a very ancient one. Unfortunately the geological evidence is too scanty to enable us to trace its evolution, though there is some ground for thinking that the adaptations to an aquatic life were first acquired in lakes, migration to the sea afterwards taking place.

SEA-COWS (*Sirenia*).—This small group of animals, which at the present time only includes Manatees and Dugongs, is not improbably an offshoot from the order of Hoofed Mammals (*Ungulata*), although there is an unfortunate lack of evidence on the subject. These creatures live in shallow coastal waters, estuaries, and certain large rivers (see vol. i, p. 101). The somewhat spindle-shaped body is flattened from above downwards, and there is a distinct neck. As in Seals, a deposit of fat underlies the thick skin, which, however, is but sparsely covered with hair. The fore-limbs are flippers, capable of movement both at the shoulder and elbow, but claws are either absent altogether (Dugong) or reduced to a few vestiges (Manatee). Hind-limbs are absent altogether, though traces are to be found by dissection, and the work done by these members in a Seal is here effected by a broad swimming-tail, rounded in the Manatee (fig. 647), and shaped like that of a bony fish in the Dugong (see vol. ii, p. 174). But the tail of a fish is flattened from side to side, that of a Sea-Cow from above downwards, a condition found in some of the swimming mammals already described, as *e.g.* in the Beaver (see p. 74). Though the main direction of movement for this organ appears to be up and

Fig. 647.—American Manatee (*Manatus Americanus*)

down, it can doubtless be twisted to some extent so as to act sideways upon the surrounding water, in the manner already described for the Beaver (see p. 74). Swimming is furthered by the comparative flexibility of the hinder part of the body as compared with a mammal where hind-limbs are present. For in such cases these limbs are united to a region of the backbone (*sacrum*) in which some of the constituent bones have fused together. In Sea-Cows the disappearance of the hind-limbs has involved the doing away with this fusion as no longer necessary. Hence a proportionate gain in flexibility. But neither the Manatee nor the Dugong can compare in swimming powers with Sea-Lions, Walruses, or ordinary Seals. The fact that vestiges of hind-limbs are still present, though they do not project externally, is enough in itself to prove that these members were present in remote ancestral forms, and it is particularly interesting to find that in a long since extinct fossil form (*Halitherium*) the remains of such limbs were rather better developed, though still insignificant and entirely sunk within the body.

WHALES, PORPOISES, &c. (*Cetacea*).—Of all aquatic mammals these are the most profoundly modified to fit them for life in water, and they have evolved on much the same lines as Sea-Cows, though to a very much greater extent. The general outline of the spindle-shaped body is so like that of a fish (fig. 648), that many uneducated persons imagine Whales to be simply huge

Fig. 648.—White Whale (*Delphinapterus leucas*)

fishes of peculiar kind, and this error is perpetuated by the term whale-"fisheries", which we still employ together with, may be noted, the expression seal-"fishery", for which there is even less excuse. The body of any one of these animals is somewhat flattened from side to side, just the opposite to what is found in Sea-Cows, and presents a continuous curve from side to side. As in the case of the best endowed swimmers among fishes (see p. 43), the curve is precisely that which expert marine engineers tell us is most suitable for cleaving water with the least amount of friction. Such a shape could not be attained without a practical absence of neck, and of this we accordingly find no trace visible externally. This region can, however, be identified in the skeleton, though it has undergone remarkable compression, not being more than a foot long even in the largest Whales. Nevertheless seven bones (*vertebræ*) enter into its composition, the typical number for Mammals (see vol. i, p. 66), though these bones are partly or entirely fused together. It is certainly a remarkable instance of adherence to a common plan of structure that the short-necked Whale and the long-necked Giraffe should have precisely the same number of bones supporting that region. The exceptions to this rule are so few that it may be of interest to note in passing that there are only *six* bones in the neck of a Dugong.

The hinder end of a Cetacean's body is terminated by a horizontally-flattened tail, comparable to that of a Dugong, for it is deeply notched and prolonged on either side into a triangular lobe or "fluke". In many cases, too, there is a triangular "fin" on the back, but fin and flukes alike are of fibrous texture, and are not supported by the firm rods or "fin-rays" characteristic of fishes (vol. i, p. 261). The fore-limbs are entirely converted into paddles which serve for steering and balancing, and though they usually possess five digits, these are not to be distinguished externally, and there is an entire absence of nails or claws. In ordinary mammals the digits never possess more than three supporting bones (*phalanges*), but the second and third fingers of a Whale may have a considerable number of such elements (fig. 645), and this increases the flexibility of the flippers. Hind-limbs are practically absent, as in Sea-Cows, but are represented by small internal vestiges. The thick smooth skin is devoid of fur or hair, though in very young specimens there may be a few bristles in the neighbourhood of the mouth. What is commercially known as "blubber" is a thick layer of fat under the skin, which, as in other similar cases, reduces the specific gravity of the body, and also keeps its owner warm.

Swimming is effected by the horizontal tail, which may be compared to a screw-propeller in its mode of action, for though no doubt there is a good deal of direct up-and-down movement, the hinder part of the body is sufficiently flexible to allow of more or less lateral strokes. This flexibility is partly due to the fact that, as in a Sea-Cow (see p. 82), the loss of hind-limbs has also obviated the necessity for a fused region in the backbone (*sacrum*) for the support of such extremities.

Cetaceans are so thoroughly adapted to an aquatic life that they soon die if stranded on the shore. They are able to traverse immense tracts of sea in a short time, and are incomparable swimmers and divers. Regarding the rapid movements of the

Killer-Whale (*Orca gladiator*), one of the toothed forms, Vogt (in *Mammalia*) says:—"The killer-whales swim in a line, one behind the other, with a speed that really makes one dizzy to look at them. I have often seen them on the coasts of Norway; they came only in heavy storms to sport round our ship." The same author makes the following remarks on the Rorqual or Fin-back Whale (*Balænoptera boöps*), a species in which teeth are replaced by whalebone:—"It is the longest, most slender, and most agile of all whalebone whales. . . . In the course of our voyage along the Norwegian coast we were accompanied for several days in the great Altenfjord by a rorqual of about the length of a two-master, which approached so near us that we could fire a bullet into its back, which appeared scarcely to tickle it. Without any apparent exertion this monstrous animal could traverse the waters with a rapidity which rendered it difficult for the gulls that swarmed around to follow it. On one occasion, when in the latitude of the Lofot Isles, we repeatedly heard thundering noises at a distance, as if proceeding from heavy artillery. When we approached we saw a large rorqual, which jumped out of the water, then plunged its head underneath the waves, turned itself vertically downwards, made two or three rapid vibrations with its enormous tail, which we guessed to be at least 20 feet in breadth, and then brought it down with a mighty stroke on the surface, producing a noise which resounded far and wide. It continued this exercise for hours together."

We know that the Cetacea are a very ancient group, but it is impossible to say much about their affinities with land mammals, for the oldest fossil remains with which we are so far acquainted are essentially whale-like, and furnish no certain clue as to their descent. By some the Hoofed Mammals (*Ungulata*) are regarded as their nearest allies, while others think their closest relatives are to be found in the Flesh-eating Mammals (*Carnivora*). But they have no close affinities with either Seals or Sea-Cows, and it is at least quite certain that they have not descended from the large marine reptiles which largely ruled the seas before the rise of the Mammalia.

Whether these creatures were first evolved as marine or as freshwater forms is another moot point. The late Professor Flower was inclined to take the latter view, on the ground that the freshwater dolphins of the Ganges and Amazons depart less than other Cetaceans from the plan of structure found among land mammals. The other view is, however, more generally held, these freshwater species being looked upon as types which have abandoned a marine life as the result of competition with better equipped forms, and it is certainly true that rivers and lakes have served in the past as havens of refuge for hard-pressed animals belonging to quite a number of different groups. Like many other problems, this can only be settled by geological evidence, which may perhaps be forthcoming when our knowledge of extinct types is greater than it is at present.

CHAPTER XLV

MUSCULAR LOCOMOTION—CREEPING ANIMALS

CREEPING

Having now dealt with the various ways in which swimming is effected in different animals, we pass to the means by which progression on a firm surface is brought about; in other words, to those forms of locomotion which are popularly termed Creeping, Walking, Running, Climbing, and so forth. It is by no means easy to distinguish clearly between creeping and some of the other kinds of movement, and as it is impossible to draw sharp boundary lines between them, it is perhaps best to be content with distinctions of somewhat artificial kind. Creeping, then, will be taken to mean progression along a firm surface in a continuous sort of way, in the absence of well-marked jointed limbs, such as are to be found in a lobster or insect, or in ordinary backboned animals which live on land. We shall therefore be mainly concerned here with the lower groups of animals, and it will be convenient to use the word "creeping" whether the surface along which movement takes place be horizontal or inclined. But it may be as well to state that a good deal of this kind of movement might just as well be called "climbing", if by this we mean a sort of pulling of the body along as opposed to pushing it forward, the front end of the animal being first fixed by some means or another, and the rest of the body afterwards drawn up to it. But the ordinary idea of climbing also means movement along an *inclined* surface, and this involves us in a further difficulty, as may be realized by considering the case of a leech (fig. 659). This has a sucker at either end of the body, to which we may apply the names of front-sucker and hind-sucker. With the aid of these the creature can move along a firm surface, the means adopted being precisely the same whether that surface be horizontal or inclined. Supposing the hind-sucker fixed, the body is stretched out in the desired direction, the front-sucker is then attached and the hind one loosened, after which the body is drawn forwards, and the same process is repeated indefinitely. Now, so far as the kind of movement is concerned, this certainly answers to the usual idea of climbing, but it is not usual to speak of climbing along a horizontal surface. To avoid continual hair-splitting, and mention of the same animal under two or more headings, the kind of movement described will here be called creeping, whether the surface be inclined or not, in the case of animals devoid of jointed limbs.

CREEPING ANIMALCULES (PROTOZOA)

Amœboid and ciliary movement as means of creeping have already been discussed (pp. 2 and 5), but certain other animalcules, which move about in a different fashion, deserve a brief

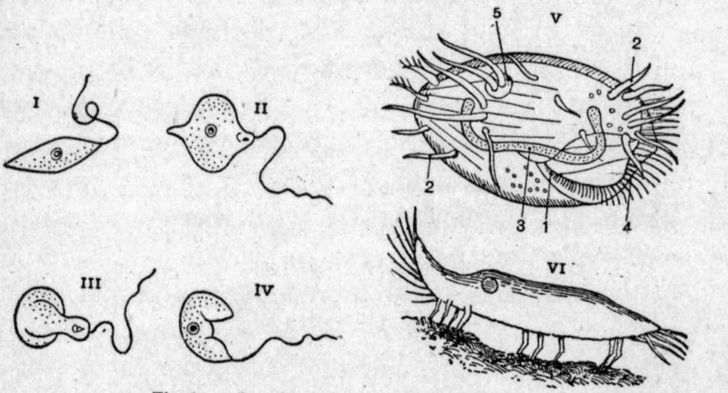

Fig. 649.—Creeping Animalcules (greatly enlarged)

I–IV, Stages in creeping movement of Euglena; V, Euplotes (under side); 1, mouth; 2, locomotor bristles; 3, nucleus; 4, cilia of mouth-groove; 5, pulsating vacuole; VI, Oxytricha creeping, as seen from the side.

notice here, though they are not, strictly speaking, illustrations of "muscular" locomotion.

One of these forms is the little worm-like creature Euglena (see vol. i, p. 494), which can wriggle along by altering the shape of its body in a fashion (fig. 649) which is so characteristic that it is technically known as "euglenoid" movement. The motive power is here afforded by the outer part of the animalcule's body, which is somewhat denser than the interior, and is specially contractile, *i.e.* is capable of shortening in one direction with corresponding broadening in other directions. As all parts of this layer do not necessarily contract at the same time, or even in the same direction, alterations of shape of the most varied kind can be brought about. And though there is a membrane covering over the contractile layer, it is extremely elastic, and therefore permits of such alterations.

Another kind of creeping is exemplified by the members of one subdivision of those Infusorians in which the body is more or less clothed as it were with cilia (Ciliata). The creatures in question (fig. 649) are of flattened shape, showing a well-marked distinction between upper and lower surfaces, this being a peculiarity related to the creeping habit. The upper side is altogether devoid of ordinary cilia, while the under surface is provided not only with these, but also with a number of bristle-like structures which can almost be called "legs", for they act as such. They have probably arisen by the fusion of groups of cilia, somewhat in the same way that rowing-plates have been formed in the Comb-Jellies (see p. 20). They are connected with a specially contractile external layer of the body, something like that of Euglena, but in this case partly made up of thread-shaped structures which are comparable in mode of action to muscle-fibres (see p. 8). It is some of these fibres which move the "legs" in such a way as to bring about creeping, and, as we shall see later, an interesting comparison may be made with certain sea-urchins, which move about by means of the spines on their under surface, thus progressing as it were on stilts.

CREEPING JELLY-FISHES OR MEDUSÆ (HYDROZOA)

An ordinary Jelly-Fish or Medusa is shaped in accordance with its swimming habit, as already described (see p. 18), but some such forms are also able to creep in a curious and characteristic manner. It may be well to recall the comparison, as to shape, elsewhere made between a jelly-fish and an umbrella with a straight handle. The expanded part of the former serves as a swimming organ, and the mouth is placed at the end of the "handle". Round the edge of the expansion are a number of tentacles, varying in kind and number according to species, and these we may liken to the fringe round the edge of an ornamental parasol. In such a creeping form as the one represented in fig. 650 (*Pectanthis asteroides*), many of these tentacles end in adhesive discs that can attach themselves to the underlying surface, thus enabling creeping movements to be executed. For some of the tentacles are stretched out in the direction of movement, and attached by their suckers, this being followed by a shortening or contraction which must clearly pull or drag the

Fig. 650.—Creeping Jelly-Fishes (*Pectanthis asteroides*)

animal forwards. And it appears to be a matter of indifference whether the handle-side is below or above. In the latter case, of course, the umbrella is partly turned inside out, a process to which its flabby nature offers no particular obstacle (see individual on left in foreground of fig. 650).

CREEPING HEDGEHOG-SKINNED ANIMALS (ECHINODERMATA)

Ordinary Star-Fishes (Asteroids), Sea-Urchins (Echinoids), and Sea-Cucumbers (Holothurians), when adult, are essentially creeping forms, though their movements are not all effected in precisely the same way.

STAR-FISHES (*Asteroidea*).—Ordinary Star-Fishes, as contrasted with Brittle-Stars, creep by means of very numerous *tube-feet*, lodged in five grooves which radiate from the mouth, on the under side of the body. In most cases these end in suckers, as for instance in the Common Star-Fish (*Uraster rubens*), and are used much in the same way as the tentacles of the creeping jelly-fishes already described. This will be obvious on examination of fig. 651, which shows one of these animals creeping up the glass side of an aquarium. Some of the tube-feet have stretched up and fixed their tips to the glass, and in the next stage the body will be dragged up a little by their shortening. These creeping organs form part of the *water-vascular system*, which is highly characteristic of Echinoderms generally, though it is not always used in creeping, as in this case (see vol. ii, p. 414). The nature and arrangements of its parts is briefly as follows (fig. 652):—On the upper side of the body, in the interval between two of the arms, a small round plate (madreporite) can be easily seen, the surface of which is marked by winding ridges. In the grooves between these there are a large number of small holes, through which sea-water enters by ciliary action into a tube (the stone canal) that runs down and opens into a hollow ring surrounding the gullet. From this ring a long tube (radial vessel) runs along each arm, lodged in the groove on its under side, and branching into a double series of tube-feet. At the base of each foot is a little swelling or bladder (ampulla) situated within the skeleton

Fig. 651.—Common Star-Fish (*Uraster rubens*) creeping up the glass side of an aquarium

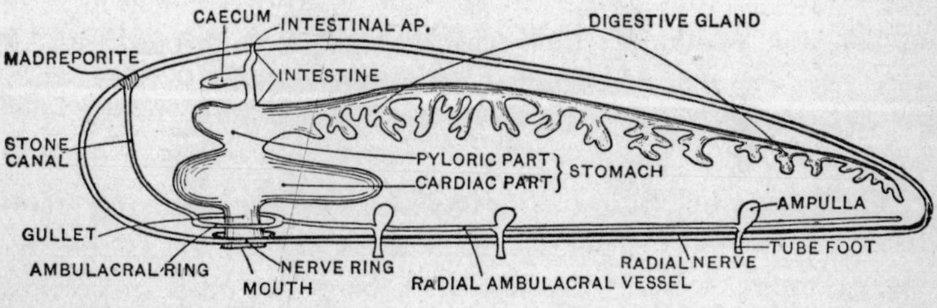

Fig. 652.—Vertical Section through disc and one arm of Common Star-Fish (*Uraster rubens*), diagrammatic

of the arm. By cutting open an arm from the upper side, and clearing away the branches of the stomach therein contained, these ampullæ will be easily seen. Their use is obvious, for muscle-fibres are contained in their walls, by the contraction of which water is squeezed into the corresponding tube-feet, just as a heart squeezes blood into arteries, the result being that these structures are lengthened and protruded. Valves are present which prevent the water from passing into the radial vessels instead of into the feet. The opposite process of shortening of the tube-feet is effected by contraction of muscle-fibres which run in their walls in the direction of their length, the ampullæ at the same time relaxing and receiving a fresh supply of water from the radial vessel. In many Star-Fishes, though not in the common sort here described, also in Sea-Urchins and Sea-Cucumbers, a number of stalked sacs (Polian vesicles) are attached to the water-vascular ring, and apparently serve as reservoirs of fluid, which by their contraction is forced into the radial vessels. It seems at first sight somewhat mysterious that the water-vascular system should permanently communicate with the exterior, from which water appears to constantly if slowly enter it. Regarding this point Shipley and MacBride (in *An Elementary Text-book of Zoology*) speak as follows, where they describe the valves already mentioned:—"These valves swing open into the tube-foot when the pressure in the radial tube is greater than the pressure in the tube-foot, but when the pressure in the latter is the higher, they close, so that under no circumstances can water escape from the tube-foot into the radial canal. So it appears that there is an arrangement which allows fluid to pass into the tube-foot but prevents its return, and this implies that under ordinary circumstances there must be a loss of fluid. We must, in fact, suppose that when the tube-foot is driven out by the contraction of the ampulla, the contained fluid slowly transudes through its thin walls, and the loss is supplied from the radial canal." Hence the constant inflow of water from the exterior to make good this waste.

There are some Star-Fishes in which the tube-feet have pointed ends, quite devoid of suckers, and this, of course, alters the character of their creeping movements. Romanes says of them (in *Jelly-Fish, Star-Fish, and Sea-Urchins*):—"These star-fish, therefore, assist themselves in locomotion by the muscular movement of their rays, while they use their suckerless feet to run along the ground somewhat after the manner of centipedes".

SEA-URCHINS (*Echinoidea*).—In a regular spheroidal form, such as the Edible Urchin (*Echinus esculentus*), the water-vascular system is constructed on much the same type as in a star-fish, except that the radial vessels run within the firm, continuous test through which the tube-feet protrude (see vol. i, p. 456). Speaking of the urchin as if it were a globe, we may say that the tube-feet are arranged in five meridional bands, equivalent to the five grooves on the under side of a star-fish; and if a broken test be held up to the light, a series of pairs of little holes will be seen on either side of each such band, every pair corresponding to a tube-foot. A Sea-Urchin is also covered with numerous spines, which are attached by ball-and-socket joints to knobs on the test. These spines can be moved in different directions by muscle-fibres which are attached to their bases. Creeping is effected much as in a star-fish, by the agency of the tube-feet, which have suckers at their ends. Some of them are protruded in the direction of movement, hold on with their suckers, and then shorten so as to drag the body onwards. But a compact creature like an urchin is more difficult to pull along than a flattened animal like a star-fish, and creeping is aided by the spines, as shown diagrammatically in fig. 653. The tips of certain spines are pressed against the underlying surface, constituting a series of firm points over which the body is swung as it were when the pulling tube-feet shorten. In this process the utility of the ball-and-socket joints is obvious. The arrangement is so effective that by its means even vertical surfaces can be ascended, though by no means so readily as in the case of star-fishes.

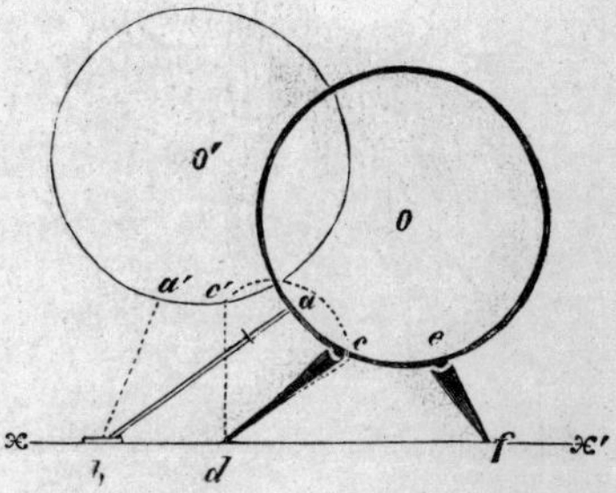

Fig. 653.—Diagram of Creeping Sea-Urchin. Only one tube-foot and two spines are represented

The tube-foot, *ab*, is extended, fixed to underlying surface *xx′*, and shortened, bringing it to position *a′b*. The body, *o*, is thus pulled forwards to *o′*, the tip of the spine, *cd*, serving as a fixed point, and its base travelling to *c′*; *ef*, a second spine supporting the body.

The oldest known extinct Sea-Urchins are spheroidal, as in the least specialized existing forms, and some of them are even melon-shaped. This is clearly an obstacle to rapid creeping, and it is not therefore surprising to find that the most specialized urchins have acquired a more or less flattened shape, which has no doubt been acquired in relation to the creeping mode of life. Such species have also become "irregular", *i.e.* they have acquired a marked two-sided or bilateral symmetry as opposed to the radial symmetry of the ordinary spheroidal type. In such cases only the tube-feet on the flattened under side are used for creeping, while those on the upper surface serve as breathing organs (see vol. ii,

p. 415). The bilateral symmetry has no doubt been evolved in relation to creeping with the same region of the body constantly kept in front. Indeed, it is only among the simpler forms of life that radial symmetry is to be found, especially among fixed forms such as corals and the like, where the influences to which the animal is exposed are similar in all directions, except above and below. For reasons chiefly connected with feeding, the

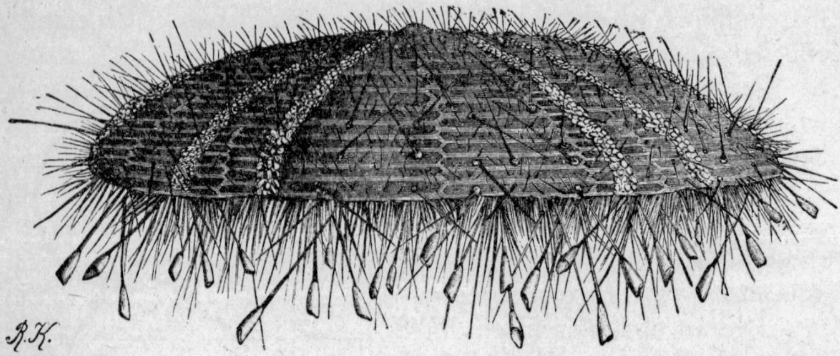

Fig. 654.—A Stilt Urchin (*Phormosoma luculenta*)

radial symmetry is by no means perfect in all these simple kinds of animal (see vol. ii, p. 417), and it is probable that the immediate ancestors of Star-Fishes, Sea-Urchins, and the like were bilaterally symmetrical (see vol. i, p. 450), so that in this group the radial symmetry exhibited is *secondary*, *i.e.* has been acquired during the history of the group and is not an inheritance from earlier types.

Speaking broadly, however, there can be no doubt that radial symmetry is a very primitive sort of regularity, and we are justified in thinking that bilateral symmetry as exemplified by Worms, Centipedes, Insects, Vertebrates, &c., was originally evolved in adaptation to locomotion with the same part of the body always leading, instead of any part, on the same principle, in short, as that employed to explain in the last paragraph the two-sidedness of an irregular urchin. The matter has previously been dealt with to some extent in vol. i, p. 21.

We have seen that the spines of a Sea-Urchin play an important part in creeping, and it now remains to be stated that there are certain flattened deep-sea forms, which creep by means of spines only. Such a "Stilt Urchin" (*Phormosoma luculenta*) is represented in fig. 654, from which it will be seen that the under surface bears a number of long spines with broadened ends. Tube-feet ending in suckers are most useful in cases where there are rocks or other firm bodies for them to lay hold of, but not so well adapted for crawling on the surface of the soft muds and oozes which cover the sea-floor where the water is very deep. And it is obvious that broad-ended spines here answer the purpose much better, for rigidity is desirable, and ordinary spines would be less effective, as their sharp tips would penetrate too deeply into the yielding underlying surface. It is also interesting to notice that the plates making up the test of Phormosoma, and some of the other urchins found in the deep sea, are so united together as to confer a certain amount of flexibility, while the tests of other forms are perfectly rigid.

SEA-CUCUMBERS (*Holothurians*).—The members of this group which live in shallow water are cylindrical in shape, with the tentacle-surrounded mouth at one end, and the opening of the intestine at the other (see vol. i, p. 462). In comparing such a creature with a regular spheroidal sea-urchin, we must suppose the latter drawn out into a cylinder in the direction of the vertical axis which passes from the upper pole of the body to the lower. In most respects the water-vascular system is constructed on the plan already described for a star-fish, there being a ring round the gullet from which five longitudinal radial vessels pass backwards, bearing tube-feet, which project externally, and are the chief agents in creeping. Variously-shaped calcareous plates are scattered through the skin, but these are not connected together into a firm test as in a sea-urchin, so that the body is perfectly flexible. Layers of muscle in the body-wall of a practically rigid sea-urchin would be of no use for locomotion, but here the case is different, and we accordingly find them well developed. Under the leathery skin is a continuous coat of muscle-fibres which run transversely, and inside this are five double bands of longitudinal fibres. Such an arrangement is common in worm-like lower forms, and is obviously able to help in creeping, for the body can be stretched out and narrowed by contraction of the circular layer, while the longitudinal bands when they contract of course make the body shorter and broader.

There is a remarkable peculiarity about the stone-canal of these ordinary kinds of Sea-Cucumber, for the madreporite in which it ends does not project at the exterior, but hangs down into the large cavity of the body in which the digestive and other organs are contained. And, as a result, the fluid lost by the water-vascular system by diffusion to the exterior through the tube-feet must be made good from the liquid contents of the body-cavity, and there must therefore be some means of renewing these contents in their turn. This means is supplied by the branching hollow structures (respiratory trees) which open into the last part of the intestine, and are constantly taking up sea-water from the exterior and expelling it again in the performance of their duties as breathing organs (see vol. ii, p. 414). It appears that the walls of these trees are pierced by innumerable minute holes through which fluid can pass into the surrounding body-cavity, a constant supply of liquid in which is thus kept up.

Fig. 655.—A Sea-Cucumber (*Psychropotes*) from the deep sea
The front end is placed to the right, and the back end bears a large tail-like projection on its upper side.

The members of one remarkable family of Sea-Cucumbers (*Elasipoda*) are peculiar to the deep sea, where they creep about on the mud or ooze, and swallow this for the sake of its nutritive contents. These forms vary greatly as to their shape, which is often extraordinary (fig. 655), but they nearly all agree in being markedly two-sided, and in the fact that one side of the body is modified into a flattened creeping sole, along which run three of the five longitudinal bands of tube-feet. The other two bands, which are not on the under side of the body, have lost their locomotor function and have become modified in shape, reminding us of the specializations which take place in the flattened forms of Sea-Urchin (p. 93). It is usual for the stone-canal of these deep-sea species to open directly to the exterior, so that the water-vascular system can renew its fluid as in a star-fish or sea-urchin. And in connection with this it is rather interesting to find that respiratory trees are either absent altogether or of very small size. One reason for this may perhaps be that as the stone-canal opens directly to the exterior it does not draw upon the fluid in the body-cavity, so that replenishment of this through the pores of such trees is not necessary as in the ordinary Sea-Cucumbers.

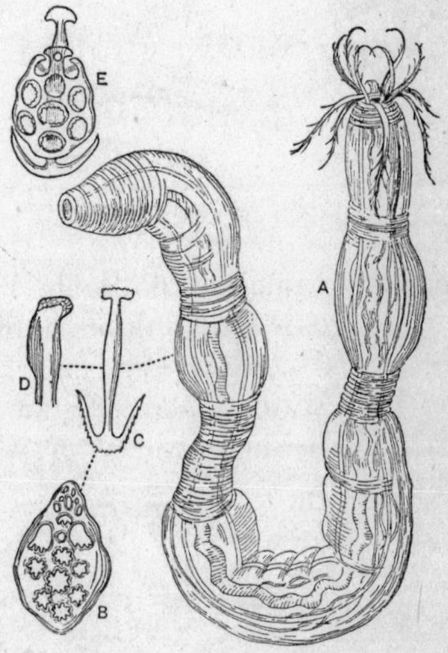

Fig. 656.—A, A Footless Sea-Cucumber (*Synapta*), reduced. B–E, Calcareous plates from skin of a Synapta, enlarged

Another very interesting case is that of the Footless Sea-Cucumbers (*Synapta*, &c., fig. 656), worm-shaped creatures in which radial canals and tube-feet are entirely absent. Creeping is effected by the tentacles, and by the muscular layers of the body-wall. And in this case too respiratory trees are entirely absent. They are certainly not required to keep up the supply of fluid in the water-vascular system. The calcareous plates in the skins of these footless forms are of characteristic shape, resembling wheels, anchors (fig. 656), &c., and they will be found in most general collections of microscopic slides, in which they are included on account of their attractive appearance. The anchors project externally, and are of use in crawling and burrowing. For supposing the front end of the body stretched out by contraction of the layer of circular muscle, these hooked plates afford a hold on the surrounding mud, which prevents backward slipping while the body is being dragged forwards by the active shortening of the longitudinal muscle-bands.

CREEPING ANNELIDS (ANNELIDA)

We are nere concerned with Bristle-Worms (*Chætopoda*) and Leeches (*Discophora*), the members of which groups crawl by somewhat different methods.

BRISTLE-WORMS (*Chætopoda*).—Examination of one of the wandering or errant Annelids, such as the Sea-Centipede (*Nereis*, fig. 657), will show that its much-elongated body is made up of a large number of successive rings or segments, each of which bears a pair of blunt foot-stumps (parapods) in which a considerable number of stiff bristles are imbedded. The animal can crawl with considerable rapidity, its body undulating from side to side, and a sort of wave-like movement passing from one end of the body to the other, with successive movement of the foot-stumps. The appearance presented strongly suggests a centipede, and the popular name has no doubt been given on this account.

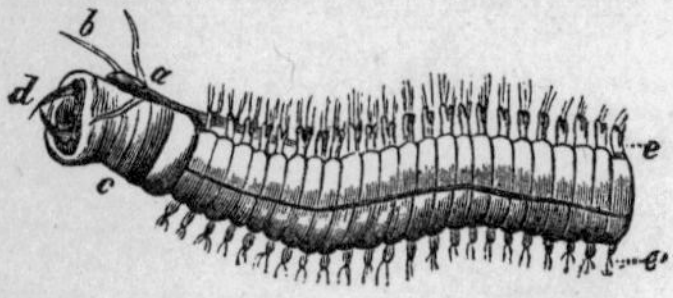

Fig. 657.—Front End of a Sea-Centipede (*Nereis*), seen from below. *a*, Head, with feelers, *b*; *c*, protruded pharynx, with jaws, *d*; *e e'*, bristle-bearing foot-stumps (parapods)

A cross-section through the body (fig. 658) shows that the body-wall contains muscular layers arranged on the same plan as in a sea-cucumber, *i.e.* an external circular coat, and within this longitudinal bands, of which in this case there are four, two above and two below. A foot-stump will be seen to be made up of an upper and a lower projection, each containing a long central bristle, of which only the tip projects, and which acts as a sort of stiffening, and numerous slender ones with curved ends.

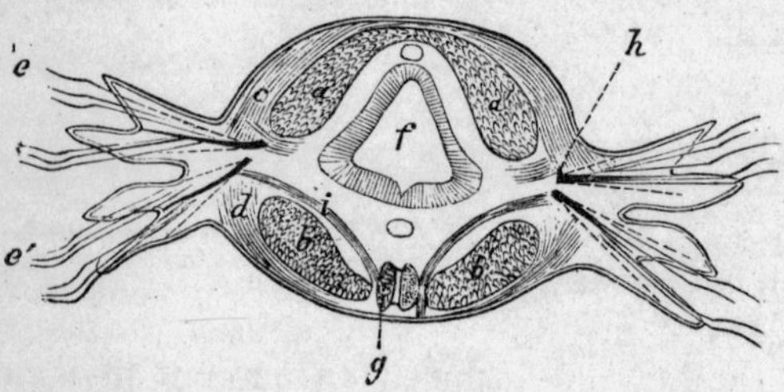

Fig. 658.—Enlarged cross-section through a Sea-Centipede (*Nereis*)

f, Intestine, above and below which are oval marks representing blood-vessels, *g*, nerve-cord; *a a'*, *b b'*, longitudinal muscle-bands, and outside this is circular muscle-layer, of which parts, *c d*, help to move foot-stumps; *i*, oblique muscle-bands connected with foot-stumps; *e e'*, small bristles; *h*, central bristle, special muscle strands connected with which are indicated by dotted lines.

Two effective ways of creeping are here practicable. The first is much after the fashion of that practised by a footless Sea-Cucumber (see p. 97). By contraction of the circular coat of muscle in the body-wall the front part of the animal can be stretched forwards, fixed by the agency of the bristles, and then the hinder part dragged up by shortening of the longitudinal muscle-bands. But the foot-stumps can also be employed as legs, for they can be moved in various directions by the little muscle-bands that are attached to them, so as to push back on the underlying surface, and give the body a forward shove. Though this kind of locomotion is here described under the head of crawling, it might with equal or even greater propriety be considered as a primitive sort of walking, and it is, in fact, the precise method of progression from which has been derived the walking of jointed-legged animals (Arthropods), such as Centipedes, Spiders, Insects, Lobsters, and similar forms of life.

It may be here remarked that there are a few very simple segmented Worms (Archiannelids, see vol. i, p. 431), which are entirely devoid of foot-stumps and bristles. One of these (*Polygordius*) is a much-elongated very slender creature, which creeps by means of the muscle-layers in the body-wall, in the manner already more than once described.

LEECHES (*Discophora*).—These Annelids never possess foot-stumps, and are almost always quite devoid of bristles. There is a sucker at either end of the body, by the alternate attachment

Fig. 659.—Stages in the Creeping of a Leech (diagrammatic). Direction of movement indicated by arrows

of which the animal is able to creep by "looping" itself along in the manner already described (p. 87). It only remains to add here that the stretching forward of the front part of the body, and the dragging up to the fixed front sucker, are both results of contraction in the muscular layers of the body-wall.

CREEPING MOSS-POLYPES (POLYZOA)

We have already seen that some colonial animals, *e.g.* the Compound Jelly-Fishes, are able to swim; the group now under consideration presents certain cases of creeping colonies, though this is the exception, and not the rule. In an ordinary Moss-polype the body is invested by a firm horny layer, which serves as a protection, and is well suited to a fixed habit of life. But in the creeping forms so far observed, all of which, by the way, inhabit fresh water, the individual members of the colony are imbedded in the upper surface of a gelatinous mass, into which they can be withdrawn by special muscular bands (retractor muscles), or from which they can protrude while feeding and breathing. The under side of the colony constitutes a creeping surface. Two such species are native to Britain. One is the beautiful little translucent Lophopus,. figured in vol. i, p. 437. The other is Cristatella (fig. 660), a flattened oval form, with a very definite sole-like creeping surface. The exact nature of the movement is not definitely known, but the observations so far made render it likely that muscle-cells belonging to the "sole" play some part in locomotion, which is probably also aided by the muscle-bands that retract the individual polypes, for these bands are attached below to the under side of the colony. Harmer (in *The Cambridge Natural History*) gives details concerning observations on the rate of movement of both Lophopus and Cristatella. A small colony of the former was observed to move from ¼ to ⅓ inch per day, *i.e.* its own length or a little more. A specimen of Cristatella rather more than ¼ inch long moved at an average rate of about ½ inch per day during the three days over which the observations extended. One very large creeping Moss-Polype (*Pectinatella*) has been found in Germany, Japan, and America. A Japanese species (*P. gelatinosa*) may attain the length of 6 feet, with a thickness of from 4 to 8 inches.

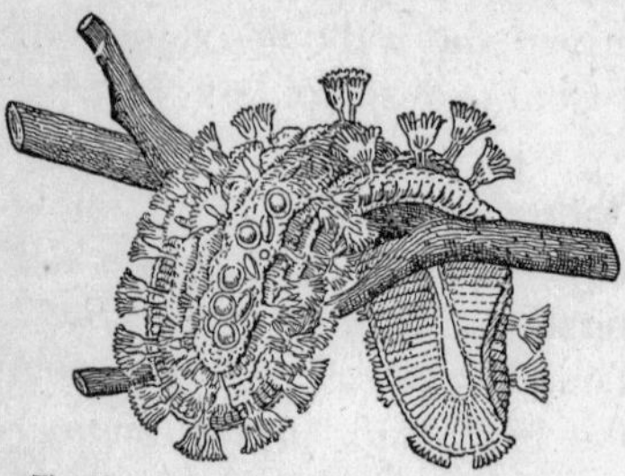

Fig. 660.—A Creeping Moss-Polype (*Cristatella*)

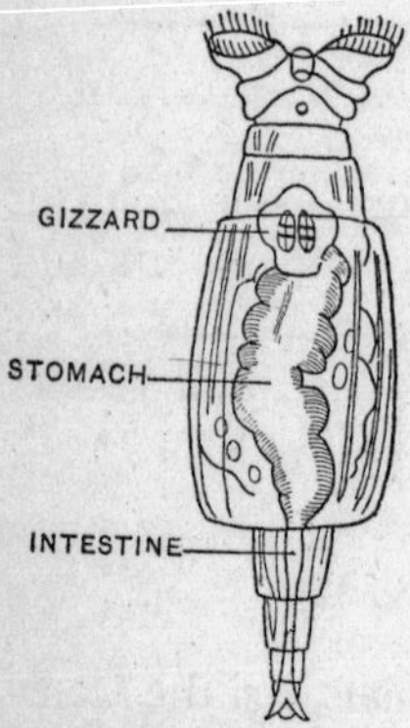

Fig. 661.—Rose-coloured Rotifer (*Philodina roseola*), enlarged

Below is seen the "foot", ending in pincers.

CREEPING WHEEL-ANIMALCULES
(ROTIFERA)

Some of these minute creatures, as, for instance, the Rose-coloured Rotifer (*Philodina roseola*, fig. 661), are able to creep by looping themselves along after the fashion of a leech. The hinder end of the body tapers into a sort of jointed tail (the "foot") provided with a pair of pincers, and capable of executing telescopic movements by the agency of muscle-fibres in the body-wall, some of these running longitudinally and others transversely. During creeping the wheel-organ is pulled in, and the front end of the body is employed after the same fashion as the anterior sucker of a Leech (see p. 87), while the pincer-bearing tail answers the same purpose as a posterior sucker.

CREEPING JOINTED-LIMBED ANIMALS (ARTHROPODA)

The two most interesting cases here meriting notice are afforded by the primitive form Peripatus, and the "Looper" Caterpillars, which are the larval stages in the life-history of certain moths.

PERIPATUS (see vol. i, p. 398) is a caterpillar-like creature native to many of the warmer parts of both Old and New Worlds, and presents so many peculiarities of structure that it is placed in a class of its own (Prototracheata). Although it is an undoubted Arthropod, resembling Millipedes and Centipedes in many respects, it differs from these and agrees with the Bristle-Worms in several particulars, especially as regards the organs by which locomotion is effected. As in such a worm the body-wall underneath the skin is made up of muscle, of which there is an external circular and an internal longitudinal layer (compare fig. 658). When examined under the microscope the fibres making up these layers are found to be unstriated, and this is a further point of agreement with a bristle-worm, and difference from an ordinary Arthropod, in which the fibres are well-striated (see p. 12), a feature which is always associated with vigorous powers of contraction. The limbs of such typical Arthropods as Millipedes, Insects, and Scorpions are solid, and sharply divided into a number of joints capable of being more or less bent upon one another. It is, indeed, this feature which has earned for the group both its popular ("jointed-limbed" animals) and scientific names (Arthropoda, from Gr. *arthros*, a joint; *pous podos*, a foot). Peripatus is possessed of many pairs of legs, all much alike, and the exact number varying according to the particular species. Each such limb is a conical hollow structure bearing a pair of sharp claws at its tip, and exhibiting only in an imperfect and incipient manner the characteristic jointing of the Arthropod group. Indeed, it strikingly resembles the hollow foot-stump of a Bristle-Worm (see p. 98), except that it is not divided into upper and lower portions, and we are almost tempted to compare its claws with the bristles of a foot-stump. In both a Peripatus leg and a Bristle-Worm foot-stump movement is brought about by muscle-bands which are connected with the wall of the body.

By successive movement of its legs Peripatus is able to crawl slowly along under the bark of decaying tree-stumps, or in the other dark places where it is found. Regarding this Sedgwick remarks (in *The Cambridge Natural History*):—"They avoid light, and are therefore rarely seen. They move with great deliberation, picking their course by means of their antennæ and eyes. It is by the former that they acquire a knowledge of the ground over which they are travelling, and by the latter that they avoid the light. The antennæ are extraordinarily sensitive, and so delicate, indeed, that they seem to be able to perceive the nature of objects without actual contact."

LOOPER CATERPILLARS.—The larvæ of a large and cosmopolitan family of Moths (*Geometridæ*), of which some 270 species are native to Britain, are the very interesting "Stick" Caterpillars, elsewhere described in regard to protective devices (see vol. ii, p. 297). They are also known as Loopers or Geometers, on account of their curious mode of progression, which is effected on much the same principle already described for leeches (p. 87). Near the front end of the long slender body are the three pairs of small jointed legs which correspond to those of the adult moth, and near the posterior end are two pair of unjointed sucker-tipped pro-legs. The entire absence of limbs from the rest of the body necessitates a looping kind of locomotion, which has suggested the popular names given to these caterpillars. By means of the pro-legs a firm hold is obtained on the underlying surface, the body is then stretched forwards and the three pairs of jointed legs fixed to some convenient point. The pro-legs are now detached, and the hinder part of the body drawn up to the front and thrown into a loop (fig. 662). By a repetition of

Fig. 662.—Looper or Stick Caterpillars of Brimstone Moth (*Rumia cratægata*), in characteristic attitudes

this procedure the caterpillar is able to creep with fair speed.

An ordinary caterpillar possesses a much larger number of pro-legs, by means of which and the ordinary jointed legs it is able to creep after the fashion of Peripatus. A case like this illustrates in a curious way the difficulty of drawing sharp boundary-lines between different modes of locomotion. It will be remembered that, for the sake of convenience, we have limited the use of the word "creeping" to animals devoid of jointed limbs, reserving for such forms the terms "walking" and "running". But it will not do to apply these terms too strictly in this particular case, as it would necessitate describing the locomotion of an ordinary caterpillar as partly creeping, partly walking: creeping in so far as brought about by the unjointed pro-legs, and walking as to the part of it effected by the three pairs of jointed legs. Similar anomalies would result in all probability if such words as "creeping" and "walking" were otherwise defined, and the matter may serve as an illustration of the difficulty of constructing definitions beyond cavil when dealing with the structure and actions of animals.

The caterpillars of some of the Owlet Moths (*Noctuidæ*) are intermediate in character between the Loopers and ordinary moth larvæ, as to the pro-legs, of which they possess a larger number than the former and a smaller number than the latter. As a result of this they "loop" to some extent while creeping, and on this account are known as Half-Loopers.

CREEPING MOLLUSCS (MOLLUSCA)

The characteristic locomotor organ of Molluscs is a muscular outgrowth from the under side of the body. This is known as the *foot*, and it varies greatly in shape and structure according to the uses to which it is put. It is sometimes a swimming organ (see p. 35), or it may be adapted to creeping, leaping, or burrowing. The sucker-bearing tentacles which surround the mouth of a Cuttle-Fish or Octopus (see p. 31) are believed by most zoologists to represent the front part of the foot, that has surrounded and fused with the head to constitute an arrangement for capturing prey, which can, however, also be used for creeping. And, as we have seen, this capture apparatus has in some instances become modified into a swimming-bell (see p. 33). In one of the most primitive of existing Molluscs, the Mail-Shell (*Chiton*, vol. i, p. 340), the foot is a broad sole-like expansion by which creeping is effected, and it is probable that this organ was either evolved in the first instance as a means of creeping, or else very soon acquired that function.

The Mail-Shells belong to the most simply organized subdivision of the Mollusca (class *Amphineura*), but creeping as a means of progression is also exemplified by animals which belong to three other classes, *i.e.* Snails and Slugs (*Gastropoda*), Cuttle-Fishes, &c. (*Cephalopoda*), and Bivalves (*Lamellibranchia*).

It will save repetition to remark here that the foot of a Mollusc is capable of being more or less altered as to shape and size in the same individual under different circumstances. This is partly due to contractions of the muscle so abundantly present, but is also dependent upon the amount of blood contained for the time being. In fact, blood can be pumped into the foot so as to make it larger, or withdrawn so as to make it smaller.

CREEPING SNAILS AND SLUGS (*Gastropoda*).—It is convenient to begin with this class, because most of its members creep, either under water or on the land. Many species, such as those which live between tide-marks, move about in this way with equal ease both when submerged and when left high and dry.

The creeping mode of progression can be easily observed in a Garden-Snail (*Helix aspersa*) placed upon a piece of glass so that the under surface of the foot can be seen through it, and equally favourable objects of investigation are a Limpet (*Patella vulgata*) moving along the glass front of a salt-water aquarium, or a Pond-Snail (*Limnæa stagnalis*) progressing in similar fashion on the surface of a bell-jar filled with fresh water. In any one of these or similar cases the movement may be described as a sort of slow gliding, friction being reduced by a kind of slime which exudes from special glands as well as from the skin of the foot. Probably everyone has noticed the gleaming track which marks the progress of a garden-snail over the surface of a wall or cabbage-leaf. Closer examination will show that a series of undulations indicated by dark transverse bands pass along the foot from back to front, and are clearly related to the creeping, for they cease when the animal comes to a stand-still. These waves are undoubtedly the expression of muscular contractions, but they do not, as might be at first sight supposed, prove the presence of a series of temporary wrinkles. The foot is closely applied all the time to the underlying surface, and the wave-like appearances are due to changes which take place within its substance.

The exact way in which a snail slides along in its own slime is by no means certain, but perhaps the most plausible explanation is one given by Simroth, though it is by no means free from objection. This observer finds that the foot of the snail is made up of a complicated network of muscle-fibres running in various directions, and he considers that creeping is mainly effected by the longitudinal fibres, which, according to him, do not shorten and thicken when they contract, as happens in ordinary muscle-fibres (see p. 10), but become longer and larger. Suppose this to take place in the front end of the foot, the result will be a slight forward advance of that region. And when the same fibres cease to contract they become shorter, and exert a pulling action that tends to drag up the foot to the front edge, which has gained ground. A succession of such contractions and relaxations, travelling along the longitudinal muscles of the foot, as indicated by the wave-like appearances, are supposed to bring about a gradual onward movement. However produced, the rate of progress is not very impressive, for it has been calculated that a garden-snail of average size and activity requires sixteen days fourteen hours to creep a mile. If we take two inches as a liberal estimate of the length of the extended foot, this calculation, otherwise expressed, means that a snail travels about 160 inches per hour, that is to say, eighty times its own length. A horse at the walk goes four miles in an hour, and its length may be taken at eight feet. It thus traverses 2640 times its own length per hour. We may say, therefore, that the horse, at its slowest pace, is thirty-three times as swift as a garden-snail. Nor can the latter adopt any swifter mode of progression, for as Scharff says: "Although this mode of locomotion may seem very pleasant, being at any rate quite unique among animals, the snail's lot is not a happy one. When the locomotor muscles are once set a-going . . . the snail can neither increase nor slacken its pace, nor can it go backwards. In that respect it is like a watch which may be wound up and which we can stop at will, but we cannot force the wheels to change their rate of velocity. Hence when the snail is pursued by an enemy, it is unable to run away, or rather slide away. The only possible manner to evade the enemy is to stop the motion of the foot and wind up another series of muscles by means of which the snail is enabled to retire within its shell."

It might at first sight be thought that the lubricating slime which a snail pours out would cause it to slip back, but it appears that in reality it enables the animal to adhere very closely to the underlying surface, for it can easily drag along relatively heavy weights, which further indicates that great expenditure of muscular power is necessary to produce a very tedious mode of locomotion. The relatively great size of the foot points to the same conclusion. Cooke (in *The Cambridge Natural History*) gives the following details as to experiments on the pulling powers of garden-snails carried out by Sandford:—"He found [a specimen weighing 1/4 oz.] could drag vertically a weight of 2 1/4 ozs., or nine times its own weight. Another snail, weighing 1/3 oz., was able to drag in a horizontal direction along a smooth table twelve reels of cotton, a pair of scissors, a screw-driver, a key, and a knife, weighing in all no less than 17 ozs., or more than fifty times its own weight. This latter experiment was much the same as asking a man of 12 stone to pull a load of over 3 3/4 tons."

Although the creeping movements of a snail or slug are slow, and involve a relatively large expenditure of energy, there are certain advantages in this mode of progression, especially in the case of aquatic forms. The sensitive and mobile foot is able to adapt itself to very irregular surfaces, and can clasp a narrow object. A Pond-Snail, for example, can creep with ease along the stem of a water-plant, round which its foot is wrapped, and though not able to move backwards can easily change the direction of its course.

Specialized ways of Creeping among Gastropods.—In addition to the ordinary method of locomotion as already described, there are interesting species of snail-like animals which creep in a somewhat different manner. A very remarkable specialization of the kind is exemplified by one of the Land-Snails (*Cyclostoma elegans*), and by the marine Pheasant-Shells (*Phasianella*). In these creatures the foot is divided by a longitudinal furrow into right and left halves, which are advanced alternately. And it is particularly interesting to note that these are in turn lifted from the underlying surface during the forward movement, so that there is a great reduction of friction.

FRESHWATER LUNG-SNAILS (*Pulmonata*)

These Molluscs creep in a characteristic manner by means of a fleshy expansion of the under side of the body, which is known as the foot. This possesses a sole-like surface that is closely applied to a stone or water-plant, as shown in the figure. The movement is of a gliding character, but exactly how it is effected is not clearly understood. The forms here represented are: 1, Fountain-Snail (*Physa*); 2, Amber-Snail (*Succinea*); 3, 4, 5, Pond-Snails (species of *Limnæus*); 3b, spawn of Pond-Snail (*Limnæus*); 6 and 7, Trumpet-Snails (species of *Planorbis*); 6a, spawn of Trumpet-Snail (*Planorbis*); 8a and 8b, male and female River-Snails (*Paludina vivipara*). A small freshwater bivalve (*Cyclas*), with extended siphons and foot, is also shown (9).

FRESHWATER LUNG-SNAILS (PULMONATA)

There are also a number of cases where the creeping is reminiscent of the looping mode of progression observed in a Leech (see p. 87), and here the foot appears to act as a whole, alternately lengthening and shortening. There is no longer the close adhesion to an underlying surface which is so characteristic of the gliding movement of average forms, and no longer therefore a large amount of retarding friction. Such special methods of creeping are associated with the presence of structures which play the same part as the suckers of a leech, and which are more particularly necessary when these animals are traversing steeply inclined and even vertical surfaces, or it may be crawling along the under side of a rock or piece of sea-weed. Some of these arrangements are outlined in fig. 663, only the head (top of figure) and foot being represented. In all these cases the mouth-region can be used as a sucker (indicated by the dark line in the figure), which may assist in the progress of the ordinary gliding forms (A). In Notarchus (B), a relative of the Sea-Hare (see p. 35) but with a very minute shell, there is a sucker on the front of the foot. In the lung-snail Pedipes (C), which lives just above high-water mark on rocks kept damp by the sea-spray, the front part of the foot (fore-foot) is clearly marked off by a transverse groove, and is of suctorial character. When the animal crawls, this region is extended forwards and holds on to the underlying surface, after which the body is drawn onwards, much as in a leech. There is a still further specialization in the marine Wing-Snails (*Strombus*, D), which possess a narrow pointed fore-foot, ending in a sucker (*a*), and also a well-marked hind-foot, upon the upper side of which is borne a toothed horny plate (*b*), the operculum, that serves as a kind of door when the animal withdraws into its shell. The fore-foot is used as in Pedipes, while the hind-foot can be bent round and used as a lever to shove its owner forwards.

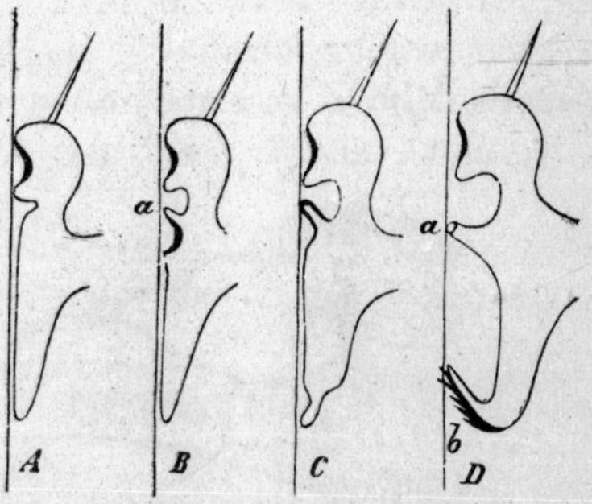

Fig. 663.—Diagram of Sea-Snails creeping up a vertical surface (only head and foot are shown)

A, Ordinary gliding type; B, Notarchus, with sucker, *a*, on front of foot; C, Pedipes, in which fore-foot (darkly outlined) is suctorial; D, Wing-Snail (*Strombus*), with sucker, *a*, and toothed operculum, *b*.

The preceding series of cases mean more or less reduction

of the area of the foot applied to the underlying surface, but arrangements of exactly opposite character are known in certain sea-snails which crawl on the surface of wet sand, into which there is a tendency to sink. In Bullia, for instance, a relative of the Dog-Whelk, the foot when in use is stretched out in all directions to a quite remarkable extent, assuming the form of a relatively thin plate.

Creeping Bivalve Molluscs (*Lamellibranchia*).—The foot of an average bivalve is specialized into a burrowing organ, as we shall have occasion to note in a subsequent section. There are, however, a few cases (*Nucula*, *Solenomya*, &c.) where this organ is possessed of a creeping sole-like under surface, which is used in much the same way as in an ordinary snail (fig. 664). In some instances an intermediate condition is found. There is good reason for believing that the remote ancestors of bivalves were creeping forms, and that in them the foot had a corresponding form. In view of this it is particularly interesting to note that most of those bivalves which at the present day are typical creepers may in other respects be regarded as the most primitive members of their class. They have probably therefore retained what must be regarded as the old method of locomotion. A limited number of more specialized bivalves, however, are able to creep. It is one of these which is depicted in fig. 664.

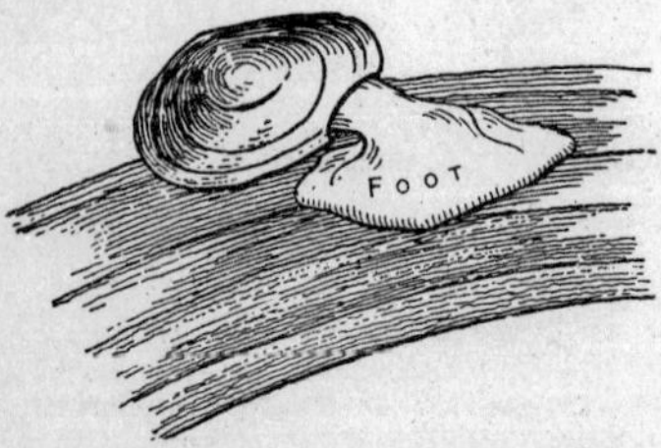

Fig. 664.—A Creeping Bivalve (*Erycina*)

Creeping Head-Footed Molluscs (*Cephalopoda*).—It has several times been pointed out in preceding sections that in this group of Molluscs the front part of the foot has grown round and intimately fused with the head, and that the development of suckers or other adhesive structures upon its surface have converted it into a very efficient organ for capturing prey. But these same structures also enable the greatly specialized fore-foot to act as a creeping organ. In the Pearly Nautilus (*Nautilus pompilius*), the most primitive member of its class, this foot consists of a number of lobes or lappets in the neighbourhood of the mouth, and these bear numerous tentacles of extremely adhesive nature, and capable of being drawn back into little sheaths. Dr.

Willey has shown by observations upon living specimens that the Nautilus is able to creep by successive attachment of these tentacles (fig. 665), almost after the manner of a Star-Fish (see p. 90), though the apparatus employed in the two cases is of widely different nature.

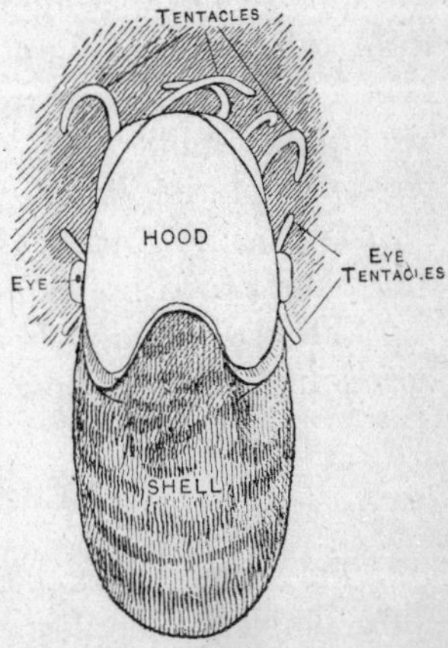

Fig. 665.—Pearly Nautilus (*Nautilus pompilius*) adhering to a smooth surface (reduced)

Animals of the cuttle-fish kind owe most of their peculiarities to specializations which they have undergone in relation to swimming (see p. 30), though there can be no doubt that the remote ancestors common to them and the other classes of molluscs were typical creeping forms. And living forms, such as Octopus and many of its allies, have found it advantageous to re-acquire the power of creeping, though still remaining good swimmers. One of these creatures is shown in the background of fig. 666 progressing in this way. The mouth being kept downwards, some of

Fig. 666.—Common Octopus (*Octopus vulgaris*)

the sucker-bearing tentacles are extended in the desired direction, hold fast to the underlying surface, and then shorten so that the body is dragged forwards. The comparison with a Star-Fish suggested for Nautilus is here much more appropriate, though the tube-feet of that animal are not only quite different in structure from the suckers of an Octopus, but are worked in a different way. And the comparatively rigid arms of the former animal are quite unlike the eminently flexible and highly muscular tentacles of the latter, which at one moment can be extended till they are no thicker than whip-cord, and at the next contracted into blunt broad projections.

The two individuals in the foreground of fig. 666 show characteristic resting positions.

CREEPING VERTEBRATES

The most remarkable creeping Vertebrates are SNAKES and other limbless Reptiles. Selecting the former for more detailed treatment, we find that the fore-limbs have disappeared altogether, and that at most the hind-limbs are represented by a pair of small projections, each of which may end in a little claw. More commonly, however, these extremities have completely vanished. The long cylindrical body is extremely muscular, and the ribs are extraordinarily numerous (fig. 667). The backbone is made up of a very large number of vertebræ, which are complex in nature, and united together in such a way as to permit of a large amount of movement, and yet at the same time to limit this to the extent necessary for the protection of the delicate spinal cord, any undue bending or stretching of which would result in partial or complete paralysis.

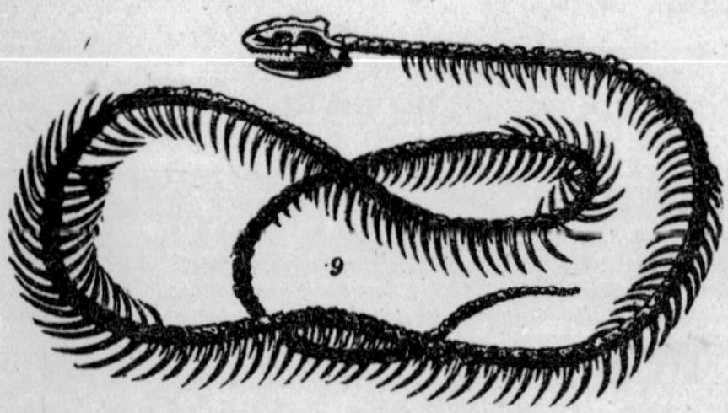

Fig. 667.—Skeleton of a Snake

Running along the under side of the body is a double series of large scales, the ventral shields, to which the ends of a corresponding pair of ribs are attached. The ribs are so hinged to the backbone that by means of appropriate muscles they can execute movements of considerable range. Whenever a rib is moved this way or that, the shield to which it is attached must at the same time be brought into action, and this provides a mechanism for creeping. The result is a sort of undulation passing from one end to the other, and throwing the body into a series of horizontal curves. Putting it in a popular way, we may say that a snake walks on the tips of its ribs, or, more correctly, by means of the large scales to which these are fixed. A comparison may well be made with the mode of creeping previously

Fig. 668.—The Blind-Worm (*Anguis fragilis*)

described for Bristle-Worms (see p. 98), and while in these creatures a firm hold of the underlying surface with prevention of slipping is attained by means of bristles imbedded in the foot-stumps, the same advantages are secured in Snakes by the sharp hinder edges of the ventral shields.

Some of the LIZARDS have been modified in much the same way as Snakes, for which they are often mistaken, though careful examination shows that there is not quite so much specialization. Of such forms the harmless little Blind-Worm (*Anguis fragilis*, fig. 668), which is one of our few native reptiles, may be taken as a good example. It has elsewhere been pointed out (see vol. i, p. 225) that various existing lizards exemplify successive stages in this remarkable kind of specialization.

CHAPTER XLVI

MUSCULAR LOCOMOTION OF ANIMALS—WALKING, RUNNING, &c.

As a matter of practical convenience, Walking, Running, and closely-related ways of progression upon a firm surface, as distinguished from Creeping, are here considered as forms of locomotion limited to those animals that possess jointed limbs or appendages, which are attached to the body they support so as to allow of well-marked movement at the place of union. Examples of such limbs are presented by the legs of a quadruped, lobster, or insect, and the five slender "arms" which radiate from the body of a brittle-star, these being very different from the five arms of an ordinary star-fish. These appendages may be looked upon as so many compound levers, and in most cases the locomotion they effect is chiefly brought about by a backward push against the underlying surface, a sort of action of which the nature is readily understood by fixing our attention on what happens when we ourselves walk. Progression of this kind may take place either upon a horizontal or upon an inclined surface, but in the latter case there is a degree of steepness beyond which ascent is a matter of climbing, in which an essential part of the process consists in pulling the body forwards from in front, rather than in pushing it onwards from behind, though the latter commonly plays a part as well. Almost everyone knows from experience that slopes are often encountered in mountaineering which can only be negotiated by using arms as well as legs. In other words, walking gives place to climbing.

The word "walking" can further be only properly applied to modes of progression in which the moving animal is never completely "off the ground" or other underlying surface. Contact between the two is always maintained, though of course the points of contact are continually being shifted, old ones being replaced by new. In running, on the contrary, which is a swifter mode of progression, the body leaves the ground for a fraction of time at every step. Jumping is effected in most cases by the sudden and vigorous straightening of well-developed hind-limbs, which push back against the ground with such force that the body is projected into the air.

Where typical walking and running are concerned the limbs employed are made up of several parts, which can be moved upon one another, and this greatly facilitates locomotion. In such modes of progression successive bending (flexion) and straightening (extension) of the limbs takes place, as a result of which much more effective pushes against the underlying surface can be given than would be possible if the extremities were stilt-like levers only movable at the place where they joined on to the body. Jumping, as briefly defined above, furnishes a very typical example of this. By carefully noticing what happens when we ourselves walk, run, and jump, the essential nature of the differences between these three methods of progression will be realized in a rough-and-ready fashion. In order, however, to gain detailed and accurate knowledge of what really happens during animal locomotion prolonged scientific investigations have been found necessary, in the course of which many ingenious kinds of special apparatus have been devised. The great improvement in photography which has taken place of late years has had much to do with the extension of our knowledge in this direction. A long strip of very sensitive film is moved at the rate desired through a camera by means of clockwork, and a series of photographs of a moving animal are taken upon it, thus enabling the exact nature of the movement to be determined. The eye alone is much too slow to detect all the details. By passing such a series through an optical lantern at a suitable speed, and projecting them upon a screen, the successive images fuse together and faithfully reproduce the movements as they appear to the eye. This is the principle of the well-known and much-appreciated cinematograph. Small portions of some such fims are depicted on pp. 126, 136, 145, and 146.

WALKING

We will now first consider the not very typical walking, &c., of Brittle-Stars (*Ophiuroidea*) and certain Fishes (*Pisces*), afterwards dealing with the more ordinary cases presented by Amphibians

(*Amphibia*), Reptiles (*Reptilia*), Birds (*Aves*), Mammals (*Mammalia*), and Jointed-limbed Invertebrates (*Arthropoda*). Arthropods are left to the last because the numerous legs which they possess renders their movements difficult to understand, and also because they have not been investigated to the same extent as the backboned forms.

LOCOMOTION OF BRITTLE-STARS (OPHIUROIDEA)

In an ordinary Star-Fish the arms, usually five in number, which are present, cannot be regarded as limbs or appendages, but rather as prolongations of the body. As we have elsewhere seen (p. 90), their typical mode of locomotion is slow creeping, effected by innumerable tube-feet. The case is quite different in an ordinary Brittle-Star (fig. 669), for here we find a distinction between "body" and limbs or appendages. The former is disc-shaped, while the latter are five slender and very flexible arms, encased in four longitudinal rows of scale-like plates, one above, one below, and one each side. There is no longer, as in ordinary star-fishes, a groove on the under side of the arm, from which numerous tube-feet protrude. What corresponds to this groove is covered over by the series of plates which invests the under side of the arm (ventral plates). There are, however, little pointed structures which protrude on either side between the ventral plates and the adjoining lateral plates, but these can only by courtesy be styled tube-"feet", for they take no part in locomotion. The name "brittle"-star expresses the ease with which the arms can be detached from the body, an indication of their separate nature. And the scientific name of the group, Ophiuroidea (Gk. *ophis*, a snake; *oura*, a tail; *eidŏs*, form), expresses their resemblance to the tail of a serpent as to shape and also with reference to the writhing movements they can execute. Running along the centre of each arm is a series of calcareous pieces, which suggest the joints of a backbone both in form and the way in which they are united together. These have therefore been called vertebral

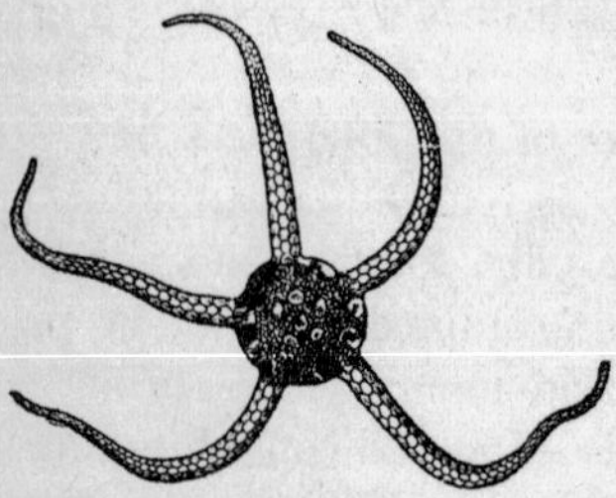

Fig. 669.—A Brittle-Star

ossicles. The resemblance is remote, for they are simply squarish blocks, and not nearly so complex as vertebræ. The presence and nature of these ossicles make the arms extremely flexible, and powerful muscle-bands attached to them bring about either simple bendings and straightenings, or curvings of complex character.

Romanes (in *Jelly-Fish, Star-Fish, and Sea-Urchins*) thus describes the locomotion of these creatures:—"The rays of the Brittle-Stars are very long, flexible, and muscular, and by their combined action the animal is able to shuffle along horizontal surfaces. When it desires to move rapidly, it uses two of its opposite arms upon the horizontal floor with a motion like swimming; at each stroke the animal advances with a leap or bound about the distance of two inches, and as the strokes follow one another rapidly, the Star-Fish is able to travel at the rate of six feet per minute. A common Star-Fish, on the other hand, with its slow crawling method of progression, can only go two inches per minute." In the more rapid kind of movement as thus described, one arm is kept pointing to the front.

LOCOMOTION OF CERTAIN FISHES (PISCES) UPON FIRM SURFACES

The above heading is purposely made rather indefinite, because the kind of locomotion to be dealt with is difficult to define.

The paired fins of an ordinary bony fish are flexible unjointed expansions, supported by firm rods (fin-rays), and chiefly useful in relation to swimming (see p. 41). In some few cases, however, they may be adapted to a kind of walking on the floor of the sea. In the Angler-Fish, for example (*Lophius piscatorius*, see vol. ii, p. 85), both pectoral and pelvic fins, equivalent to the fore- and hind-limbs of quadrupeds, are provided with powerful muscles, and can be employed for this purpose. A more remarkable instance is presented by Gurnards (*Trigla*), for part of each pectoral fin is modified into three finger-like projections, which can be turned forwards and used for walking. They have a curiously hand-like appearance.

The shore-haunting forms known as Mud-Skippers (*Periophthalmus*) (see vol. ii, p. 87) walk and spring with great facility, largely aided by their muscular pectoral fins, from the margins of which the hard tips of the fin-rays project, so as to give a firm grip on the underlying surface. Their extraordinary activity is well described by Day, who speaks as follows:—"These fishes, from the muscular development of the base of the pectoral fins, are able to use them for progression on mud or for climbing. It is a most curious sight to see *Periophthalmus Schlosseri* along the side of the Burmese rivers; at a distance the fishes appear like large tadpoles, stationary, contemplating all passing objects, or else snapping at flies or other insects; suddenly, startled by something, away they go with a hop, skip, and a jump, either inland among the trees or on to the water like a flat stone or a piece of slate sent skimming by a schoolboy. They climb on to trees and large pieces of grass, leaves, and sticks, holding on by their pectoral fins exactly as if these were arms. Now and then they plant these firmly as organs of support, the same as one places one's elbows on a table, then they raise their heads and take a deliberate survey of surrounding objects."

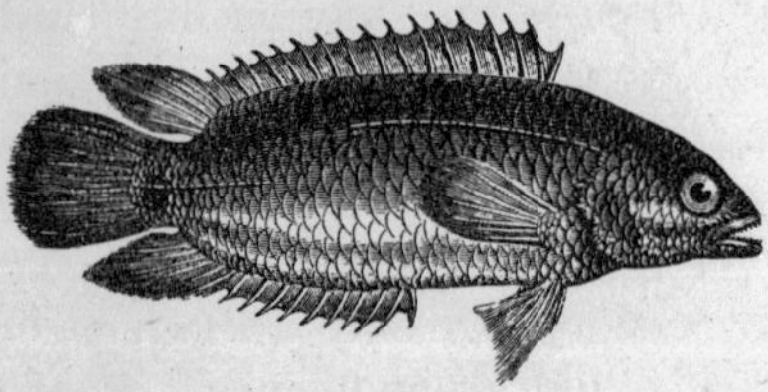

Fig. 670.—Climbing Perch (*Anabas scandens*)

As another example we may take the Climbing Perch (*Anabas scandens*) (fig. 670), which makes excursions on the land, forcing its way through vegetation. The strong pectoral fins appear to play an important part in this sort of progression, by hooking themselves round grass stems and the like, and pulling the fish forwards.

AMPHIBIANS (Amphibia) AS WALKERS

Backboned animals (Vertebrata), with the exception of Fishes and still lower forms, are for the most part inhabitants of the land, and have become adapted to a terrestrial life by a series of evolutionary modifications that have gone on for an immense period of time. The original ancestral stock was undoubtedly aquatic, suited in all respects for life in water, and in the course of evolution many structures and organs originally adapted to an existence of this kind have of necessity undergone profound modification, to fit them for playing useful parts in fresh and widely different surroundings. Some of the problems which have been solved as regards organs of circulation and breathing have already been dealt with (see vol. i, p. 244, and vol. ii, p. 421), and we have now to consider the evolution of structures related to the terrestrial locomotion of backboned animals.

In all questions connected with the evolution of land-vertebrates, the Amphibians are of singular interest. Not only do many of their characters clearly point to an aquatic ancestry, but also almost every member of the class in the course of its life-history presents us with an imperfect summary of the changes by which terrestrial vertebrates have sprung from aquatic forms, and we further know that this group is much older than those which include the other backboned animals that live on the land. Largely owing to this great antiquity, coupled with the fact that the skeletons of Amphibians are not well adapted for preservation in a fossil state, while of course the soft parts are not preserved at all, our knowledge of the origin of the group leaves much to be desired, and as Gadow says (in *The Cambridge Natural History*):—"The great gap within the Vertebrata lies between Fishes and Amphibia, between absolutely aquatic creatures with internal gills and 'fins', and terrestrial tetrapodous [*i.e.* four-legged] creatures, with lungs, and fingers, and toes".

LIMBS OF BACKBONED LAND-ANIMALS.—From what has already been said regarding the way in which a garden-snail creeps (p. 105) it will be realized that extensive contact with the underlying surface greatly retards progress, owing to the large amount of friction. And we have had occasion to note that certain snail-like animals have partly got over this difficulty by means of a sort of specialized creeping, during which the body is more or less lifted off the underlying surface. The evolution of walking-limbs has partly resulted from the necessity for raising the body so as to reduce the area of contact with the ground, which has also brought it to pass that such limbs have gradually become the chief agents of progression, and have consequently acquired a more or less complicated structure.

There can be no doubt that the fore- and hind-limbs of such a creature as a Newt or Salamander are strictly equivalent to the paired fins of a fish, *i.e.* the pectoral and pelvic fins, but it is not yet possible to speak with certainty as to the exact relation between the two. To put it another way—we feel assured that the remote ancestors of Newts and Salamanders were aquatic creatures possessed of paired fins much like those of a fish, and that these fins gradually evolved into the fore- and hind-limbs as we now see them, but we are ignorant as to the intermediate stages between the two sorts of limb. It is usual to adopt some such view as the one embodied in fig. 671, which is copied from Wiedersheim, and which tentatively compares the pectoral fin of a shark with the fore-limb of a newt-like animal. In either case there is a strong shoulder-girdle (indicated by dotted lines) imbedded within the body, and to which the free part of the limb is attached. In the shark this is a firm but flexible three-sided paddle, the part of which next the body is supported by three pieces of gristle, and to these are attached a number of jointed rods or fin-rays, of which those near the under edge are particularly large and prominent. All these parts are shaded black in the figure. Turning now to the fore-limb of the land-animal we find that it is comparatively narrow, and evolution from the fish-fin may have brought about this narrowing by suppressing two of the large pieces of gristle and most of the fin-rays. The bone of the upper arm, *i.e.* the humerus, may be the equivalent of the remaining gristly plate of the fish, while the two bones of the fore-arm (radius and ulna), and the supporting structures of wrist and hand, may be the outcome of modification in the large fin-rays near the under edge of the shark's fin (see diagram), and of some of the smaller fin-rays in connection with these. A similar comparison can be instituted between a pelvic fin and a hind-limb. Although what has been said is probably true in a general sort of way, it is impossible to feel sure about any of the details. For one thing, the pectoral fin of a shark, though undoubtedly a fairly simple structure of its kind, may be very different from the pectoral fin actually possessed by the fish-like amphibian ancestors. It might be supposed that the Law of Recapitulation, according to which an animal or an organ in the course of its individual development passes through ancestral stages, would clear up the matter, and that by investigating the growth of a Newt's limb from the time of its first appearance onwards we could get an idea of all the

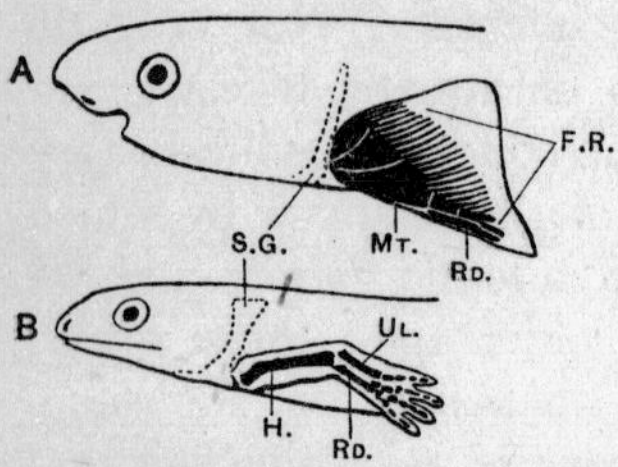

Fig. 671.—Comparison between Fore-limbs of Fish (A) and Land Vertebrate (B)

S.G. Shoulder-girdle; MT. gristly plate at base of fin; RD. large fin-ray; F.R. fin-rays; H, humerus; RD. radius in B, large fin-ray in A; UL. ulna.

transitional stages between fin and limb. But this is by no means the case, for though the law in question affords valuable clues as to many matters, it is not of much use here, so far as at present known. It may be broadly true that the development of an individual animal is an epitome of the ancestral history of the group to which that animal belongs, but that is all we have a right to expect. For if an animal repeated in detail all the ancestral stages of its group before it became an adult, its development would take an inordinate time. It has to be fitted as quickly as may be for the stern realities of existence: hence a condensation, a skipping, and even a transposition of chapters in the family history, especially in cases where recapitulation might prove a danger during the early stages of life. This is the Law of Hastening of Events, and in the particular instance under discussion it comes into operation. The limb of a Newt does not begin as a fin-like structure which undergoes gradual modification, but is first a mere knob, which soon lengthens and quickly acquires the shape, proportions, and structure of the adult extremity.

The narrowness of a typical land-limb as compared with a fin is easily intelligible, for a paddle-like shape would not be suitable for the work which the former has to perform. The evolution of digits by the free projection of fin-rays presents no particular difficulty, for even some of the fishes, *e.g.* Gurnards (see p. 115), have converted some of their pectoral fin-rays into fingers.

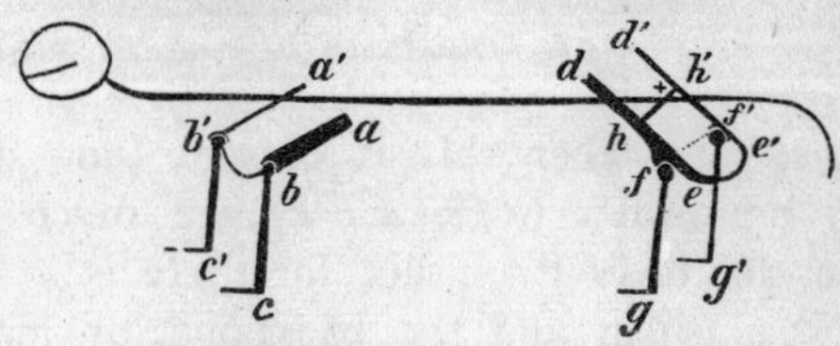

Fig. 672.—Diagram of Skeleton of Land Vertebrate

a b, *a' b'*, Shoulder-girdles united below: *b c*, *b' c'*, arms and hands; *d h e*, *d' h' e'*, hip-girdles united below, and with sacrum (*k*+*k'*) making up pelvis; *f g*, *f' g'*, legs and feet.

Another point is illustrated by fig. 672. A fish-fin is a simple lever, only movable where it is attached to the body; but the limb of a land-animal is a multiple lever, divided by transverse joints into a number of regions—upper arm, fore-arm, wrist, and hand in the fore-limb, corresponding to thigh, shin (or lower leg), ankle, and foot in the hind-limb. The importance of this has already been briefly indicated (see p. 113).

It is clear that walking- or running-limbs would not be able to support and move the body with efficiency unless they were firmly united to it. For this reason that part of the limb-skeleton which is imbedded in the body is of great importance. In the case of the fore-limb this is called the shoulder-girdle, while in the case of the hind-limb it is known as the hip-girdle. The general character of these arrangements is represented diagrammatically in fig. 672. The two shoulder-girdles (*ab*, *a′b′*) are firmly united by muscle and fibrous tissue to the body, and are often united together in the middle line below (*b b′*), or connected with the

Fig. 673.—Crested Newts (*Molge cristatus*). Male above, female below

breast-bone when this is present (not shown in figure). The two hip-girdles (*d f e*, *d′f′e′*) are much more intimately united with the body than this, for there is a more or less firm union between them and the backbone, by means of side projections from one or a larger number of vertebræ (*h* + *h′*) which constitute the sacrum. The two hip-girdles together with the sacrum are known as the pelvis. These two girdles are commonly united with one another below (*e e′*).

Amphibian Limbs.—Taking a Newt (fig. 673) as an example, we notice that the sacrum is of very primitive nature, for it consists of but one vertebra. The fore- and hind-limbs do not lift the body well off the ground, which is slung as it were between those of the two sides, and both elbow and knee are outwardly directed. Hence as a limb is used it pushes against the ground, straightens, and gives a sort of shove, the force of which partly impels the body onwards, but partly also moves it to one side. A Newt or similar creature consequently "wobbles" from one side to the other as it walks, and the result is to give the appearance of horizontal undulations. To put it popularly, the movement is rather "snaky". As in most cases of walking, the limbs are used *diagonally*, *i.e.* the two extremities of the same side do not move together nor in immediate succession, but the advance of a fore-limb is followed by the advance of the hind-limb diagonally opposite. We thus get this sequence—right fore-limb, left hind-limb, left fore-limb, right hind-limb, &c.

Though reduction of the area in contact with the ground is an important matter in the evolution of effective walking-limbs, such reduction can only reach a maximum where the underlying surface is hard and resistant. Amphibians live for the most part in marshy places, where the ground is soft and yielding, and the evolution of the walking-limbs of the group has taken place in relation to this condition. The extremities must therefore possess a sufficiently large walking-surface to prevent undue sinking into mud and the like, and, as might be expected, a Newt walks on the palms of its hands and soles of its feet, *i.e.* is *plantigrade*. Besides which, the fingers and toes spread out when they are pressed against the ground, thus giving an increased purchase. The typical number of digits in the limb of a land-vertebrate is five, as in the feet of most Amphibians; the hands of these creatures are four-fingered, though the vestige of a thumb is often found on dissection.

REPTILES (REPTILIA) AS WALKERS

What has been said about the walking of Amphibians is true in the main for Reptiles, but many of the latter are able to progress much more rapidly. There are some points of interest concerning Tortoises, Lizards, and Crocodiles which will now be considered.

TORTOISES (*Chelonia*).—In the section on Swimming we have had occasion to notice the interesting series of gradation which connect the walking-legs of the Land-Tortoises on the one hand with the flippers of Turtles on the other (see p. 54). It is with the former that we are here more specially concerned. The stumpy limbs of an ordinary Tortoise project from within the shell, which partly encloses them. Owing to this, and to the fact that they have to support a considerable weight, they are brought more under the body than in Amphibians or average Reptiles, but this does not mean speed of progression, for the deliberate walk of a Tortoise is proverbial. The limbs are used diagonally as in Newts, &c. (see p. 121). Fore- and hind-limbs alike possess five digits, indicated by a corresponding number of blunt claws. The European Pond Tortoise (*Emys orbicularis*, fig. 674) will serve as an example of an early stage in the series of changes which lead on from these typical land-limbs to the paddles of Turtles. The digits are much more distinct externally than in Land-Tortoises, their claws are sharper, and webs extend between them. This is a double advantage, for it not only increases the surface used in swimming, but also prevents the animal from sinking into the mud when it walks under water, or on the margin of its native pond or stream.

Fig. 674.—European Pond Tortoise (*Emys orbicularis*)

LIZARDS (*Lacertilia*).—The limbs of an average form, such as our native Sand-Lizard (*Lacerta agilis*, fig. 675), are not unlike those of a Newt so far as the general proportions and relation to the body are concerned, but there are five claw-bearing digits on each hand and foot, instead of four on the former and five on the latter, all unprovided with claws. The Sand-Lizard, however, like most of its kind, is able to cover the ground with great rapidity, and in this particular animal the specific name "agilis" is well chosen, for the little reptile is by no means easy to catch, and makes its way through grass or heather with astonishing celerity. So far as mere speed is concerned, it may be said to run, but as the body never entirely leaves the ground the word is not strictly applicable.

Fig. 675.—Sand-Lizard (*Lacerta agilis*)

Some few Lizards are able to walk upon their hind-legs, of which the most remarkable example is the Frilled Lizard (*Chla-*

Fig. 676.—Frilled Lizard (*Chlamydosaurus Kingi*)

mydosaurus Kingi, fig. 676) of Australia, a powerful form which attains a length of about three feet. Should danger threaten, it scuttles off on its hind-limbs with considerable speed for as far as 30 or 40 feet, in a half-crouching attitude, with the fore-limbs hanging down and the remarkable frill folded up. To this and certain other similar cases special interest attaches, for we know that many members of a long extinct order of Reptiles (*Dinosauria*) progressed habitually in this way, in accordance with which their hind-limbs were disproportionately long.

Crocodiles (*Crocodilia*).—In these creatures the relative proportions of limbs and body are much as in Lizards, and they progress on land in a similar manner. The way in

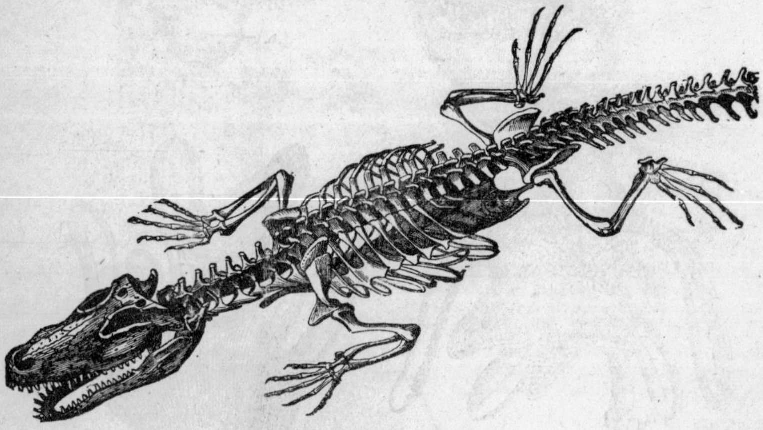

Fig. 677.—Skeleton of Crocodile

which elbows and knees stand out at the side, and the structure of the hands and feet, will be gathered from fig. 677. Cyrus W. Butler (in *The Big Game of North America*) speaks as follows regarding the mode of progression of the Alligator (*Alligator Mississippiensis*):—"In their common walk the central surface just clears the ground, and the end of the tail drags so as to leave a sharp cut in the mud between the footprints. But, when necessary, the Alligator can arch his back, straighten his legs so as to raise his body some distance from the ground, and shuffle off at a surprising gait. As a rule he seldom goes far from water, and when he does, it is in travelling from one body of water to another."

BIRDS (AVES) AS WALKERS AND RUNNERS

Since the fore-limbs of Birds are modified into wings, it of course follows that these animals must progress on land in a two-legged or bipedal fashion, as do we ourselves. But the walking of a typical bird differs in several respects from the walking of a man, the anatomical relations between trunk and hind-limbs being very dissimilar in the two cases. For in human beings the long axis of the body is vertical, and its weight is supported on a strong basin-shaped pelvis, formed by union of the two hip-girdles with a broadened part of the backbone known

Fig. 678.—Grey Wagtail (*Motacilla melanope*)

as the sacrum (see vol. i, p. 27). In Birds the attachments of the legs are, so to speak, shifted forwards, and the body is balanced between them, its long axis being oblique (fig. 678). The two hip-girdles are of extraordinary length, extending far in front of the hip-joints as well as a long way behind them, an arrangement which gives a very extended surface for attachment to the backbone. The corresponding region of the latter (sacrum) is formed by the fusion of a larger number of vertebræ than in any other class of vertebrates. Great firmness is thus secured, which is all the more necessary as the two hip-girdles do not, as a rule, unite with one another below, as is the case in Amphibians, Reptiles, and Mammals. If these girdles were not, therefore, very firmly fixed to a long piece of the backbone, a bird would walk or run in a very unsteady way, giving it a poor chance of escaping from enemies without having recourse to flight. There is also a remarkable peculiarity in the construction of a bird's leg, for the ankle-joint is not situated, as in a human being, between the shin-bone and the ankle-bones, but in the middle of the region which the latter support. A bird walks on its toes, of which never more than four are present, one (the great toe) being usually turned backwards, and the others forwards. It is therefore "digitigrade", like a cat or lion, and the instep region is upwardly directed, the ankle-joint being therefore lifted off the ground. The presence of a number of little ankle-bones would clearly tell against firmness under these circumstances, and so would the existence of several separate instep-bones. It is, therefore, not surprising to find that a good deal of fusion has taken place (fig. 679). The upper part of the ankle-skeleton (tarsus) has united with the lower end of the shin-bone (tibia) to form what is technically called the "tibio-tarsus", while the lower part of the ankle-skeleton and three instep-bones (metatarsus) have all united together into the "tarso-metatarsus", or shank-bone. Although these two words are long and clumsy, they are extremely lucid, and quite easy to understand if we remember that tibia, tarsus, and metatarsus are the scientific words for shin-bone, ankle-bones, and instep-bones. From what has been said it will be clear that the body of an ordinary land-bird is raised much further from the ground than is the case with a newt or lizard, and the limbs are more under the body, which successively rises and falls during progression.

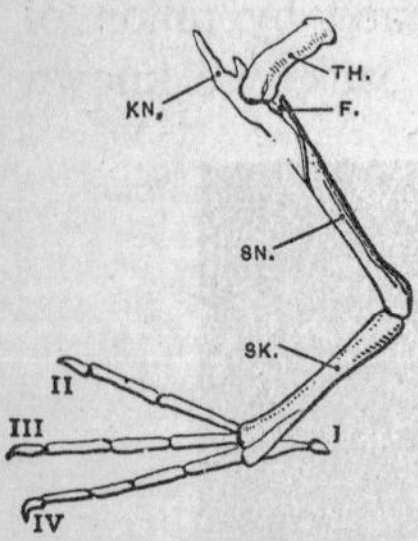

Fig. 679.—Bones of a Bird's Leg
TH., Thigh-bone; F., fibula; KN., knee-cap; SN., shin-bone; SK., shank-bone; I–IV, toes.

Fig. 680.—Series of instantaneous photographs of a Hen walking. Read from top to bottom.

In spite of the great difference as to structure, the legs of a bird are used in walking much in the same way as those of a human being. They are alternately swung to the front, and the body falls on to each of them in turn, so to speak. This is very well illustrated by fig. 680, which represents part of a series of photographs taken of a hen in the act of walking.

Birds which wade, or walk about in marshy places, often have long, stilt-like legs, which enable very long steps to be taken, and are of advantage in other ways, *e.g.* they confer on their owner a power of extended observation. The White Stork (*Ciconia alba*) (fig. 681) is a good instance of this. The toes of such birds are long and spreading, so as to prevent sinking into the soft under-

Fig. 681.—White Stork (*Ciconia alba*)

lying surface, and in many cases the same end is furthered by the presence of webs between the toes, or of membranous expansions which answer the same purpose. This is illustrated by fig. 682, which represents the feet of several members of the Plover group which frequent places where the ground is soft. On the left is seen the foot (*a*) of a Common Snipe (*Scolopax gallinago*), with strong spreading toes. This bird lives in marshy spots, and the legs are not very long. The Common Sandpiper (*Totanus hypoleucus*) haunts shores and inland waters, and its toes are webbed at the base (*b*). The digits of the Grey Phalarope (*Phalaropus fulicarius*), a shore form, are lobed (*c*). Those of the long-legged Avocet (*Recurvirostra avocetta*) are fully webbed (*d*), and this gives a sure footing while the bird is wading in shallow water or tide-pools, searching for food. This chiefly consists of small crustaceans, &c., which are scooped up from the sand by the long, slender beak, the end of which is bent sharply upwards. Phalaropes and Avocets are expert swimmers, and the structure of their feet is related to this as well as to use on a soft underlying surface.

The extremities of some few birds are well adapted to scrambling over the floating leaves of water-lilies or other aquatic

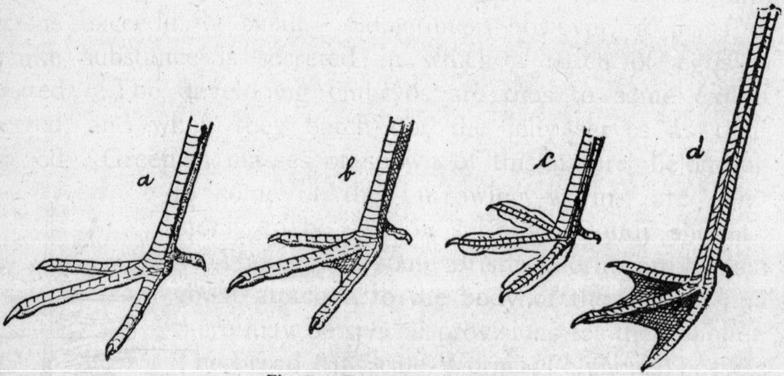

Fig. 682.—Feet of Plover-like Birds

a, Snipe (*Scolopax gallinago*); *b*, Sandpiper (*Totanus hypoleucus*); *c*, Grey Phalarope (*Phalaropus fulicarius*); *d*, Avocet (*Recurvirostra avocetta*).

plants, and this is said to be one of the uses of the lobed toes of the Coot (see p. 61). But the most remarkable arrangement of the kind is found in the Jaçanas, which inhabit parts of South America, Africa, South Asia, Australia, and New Guinea. The long and slender legs are supported by four toes of quite extraordinary length. A well-known species is the Water-Pheasant or Jaçana (*Parra jacana*) (fig. 683), which ranges from Guiana to Argentina.

Running Birds.—Existing Birds are divided into two groups, the Runners (*Ratitæ*) and Flyers (*Carinatæ*), of which the latter include the vast majority of species. These names are only appropriate in a general sort of way, for though none of the Runners can fly, many of the Flyers can run, while some of them have lost the power of flight, *e.g.* Penguins.

It is, however, undoubtedly true that the Ostriches, Emeus, &c., which together constitute the Ratite group, are the most expert runners in the class of Birds, and this is intelligible when we remember that their wings are so small and reduced as to be useless for flying purposes, and they therefore have to rely on legs alone.

The swiftest runners among both Birds and Mammals have several characters in common, resulting from their adaptation to easy and rapid locomotion upon a firm or fairly firm surface.

Fig. 683.—Jaçana (*Parra jaçana*)

Both in an Ostrich and a Horse the legs are extremely powerful and of great length, while at the same time they are placed well under the body, which prevents "wobbling" from side to side, as this would wastefully expend more or less of the muscular force exerted. Effective length of limb is partly gained in both cases by the body being raised as it were on tiptoe. It is further obvious that, given a firm surface, the successive pushes against the ground which bring about walking or running can be most effectively given when the pushing parts are of comparatively small size in comparison to the weight of the body. This end has been gained both in Ostrich and Horse by a reduction in the number of toes. The latter presents an extreme case of the kind, for all the digits have disappeared except the 3rd or middle one. Of all Ratite Birds the African Ostrich (*Struthio camelus*) is undoubtedly the swiftest, and when at full speed is said to take strides of 25 feet in length, and to easily outdistance a galloping horse. But in hunting it down, advantage is taken of the curious fact that it does not travel in a straight line, but in a curve. In correspondence with this great speed we find that the Ostrich has fewer toes than any other bird, only two being present (fig. 684). It is usual to number the digits 1, 2, 3, 4, 5, of which the first or great toe is the inner one. In an ordinary 4-toed bird the 5th has disappeared, but in the Ostrich two more have gone, the 1st and 2nd, leaving only the 3rd and 4th, of which the former is much the larger. Reduction in number of a series of organs commonly means an increase in size of those remaining, and this is the case here. Both toes are very stout, and their under sides are provided with thick pads, so as to prevent them from sinking into the sand.

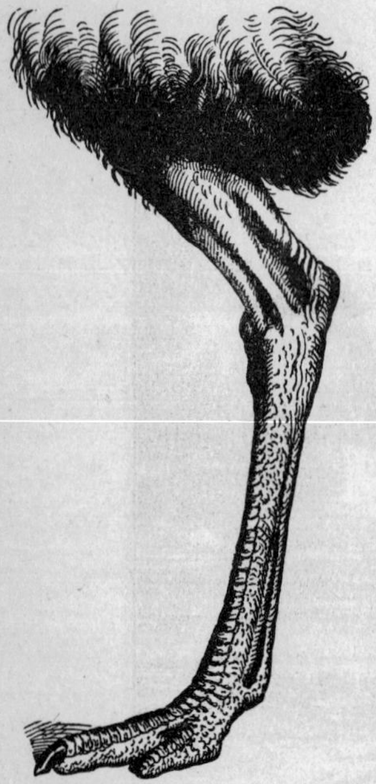

Fig. 684.—Left Leg of African Ostrich (*Struthio camelus*), seen from outer side

There are but two toes, 3rd and 4th, of which the former is the larger.

The feet of American Ostriches (*Rhea*) are similar in structure, but reduction has not gone so far, for three toes are present, *i.e.* the 2nd, 3rd, and 4th. These birds are also very swift runners. The Emeus (*Dromæus*) and Cassowaries (*Casuarius*, fig. 685) of the Australian region are also three-toed, but the little Kiwis (*Apteryx*) of New Zealand possess the usual four digits, though the 1st or great toe is small, and, being raised from the ground, does not assist in locomotion.

The wings of Running Birds, though too much reduced to

be of use for purposes of flight, would appear to help rapid progress on the ground. On this point Pettigrew speaks as follows (in *Animal Locomotion*):—"The wings of the Ostrich, although useless as flying organs, form important auxiliaries in running. When the Ostrich careers along the plain, he spreads out his wings in such a manner that they act as balancers, and so enable him to maintain his equilibrium. The wings, because of the angle

Fig. 685.—Cassowary (*Casuarius*). Three toes are present, 2nd, 3rd, and 4th

of inclination which their under surfaces make with the horizon and the great speed at which the Ostrich travels, act like kites, and so elevate and carry forward by a mechanical adaptation a certain proportion of the mass of the bird already in motion. The elevating and propelling power of even diminutive inclined planes is very considerable when carried along at a high speed in a horizontal direction. The wings, in addition to their elevating and propelling power, contribute by their short, rapid, swinging movements to continuity of motion in the legs. No bird with large wings can run well. . . . What, therefore, appears a defect in the Ostrich is a positive advantage when its habits and mode of locomotion are taken into account."

In African and American Ostriches the two hip-girdles are not only firmly united with the backbone, but also to some extent with one another, and the pelvis is thus firmer than in other birds. It may further be noted that in all Ratite forms, except Kiwis, many of the bones contain large air-spaces, giving a combination of strength with lightness which probably has relation to the great powers of locomotion.

MAMMALS (MAMMALIA) AS WALKERS AND RUNNERS

Although Land Mammals differ very much among themselves as regards powers of progression, they are on the average the best endowed quadrupeds in this respect, being far superior to Amphibians and Reptiles. This is largely due to the greater activity associated with relatively efficient circulatory and breathing organs. All parts of the body are provided with well oxygenated blood of constant and comparatively high temperature (about 98° F.), in which respect the cold-blooded Amphibians and Reptiles are not nearly so well off.

The well-nourished muscles which constitute the primary agents of locomotion are highly specialized, and the skeleton to which these are attached presents a number of mechanical arrangements which are directly related to efficient walking and running. Some of these will be gathered by reference to fig. 686, which represents the skeleton of a Dog.

As might be expected, the limbs are very firmly united to the trunk. The shoulder-girdle chiefly consists of the triangular shoulder-blade (scapula), which is firmly bound to the body by powerful muscles. In many Mammals, *e.g.* Man, each shoulder-girdle also includes a collar-bone (clavicle), stretching from scapula to breast-bone (sternum), and thus a transverse connection is established between the two girdles below. But in Dogs, Horses, and other forms able to run very rapidly, the collar-bones are either entirely absent (horse) or reduced to unimportant vestiges (dog). Why they have undergone such reduction is easily understood. Their presence would seriously hamper the forward and backward movements which have much to do with speed, and they would also be liable to fracture, as a result of the sudden strains brought to bear upon them during running, at the moment when the body suddenly alights upon a fore-limb.

In the skeleton of the hind-limb we notice that the two hip-girdles are closely united to part of the backbone (sacrum), in which several vertebræ immediately behind the region of the loins have fused together. This union is not so extensive as in Birds (see p. 125), which have to walk or run on two legs only, but on the other hand added stability is gained in the Mammal by fusion of the two hip-girdles together below. It must be admitted that this extremely firm connection of hind-limbs with body reduces to some extent the range of forward and backward movement in the legs, but this is more than counterbalanced by the gain in steadiness, and there is not the same liability to sudden shocks as is the case with the shoulder-girdles. For when a running animal, after a moment's suspension in the air, comes down on a fore-limb, it is obvious that the forward nature of the movement imposes a greater stress than when a hind-limb comes down first. No doubt, even in this case, a very considerable shock is experienced, but the pelvis (*i.e.* hip-girdles plus sacrum) is exceedingly strong, and built on the principle of the arch.

Turning to the parts of the limbs below shoulder- and hip-joints (see fig. 686), we see that these, especially the hinder ones, are relatively long, and lift the body well off the ground. During progression the limbs move practically from front to back, comparatively little force being wasted in side-pushes, as is the case in Amphibians and Reptiles (see p. 121), where the body is slung between the limbs, with both elbows and knees directed outwards. The mammalian arrangement is clearly better adapted to effective walking or running, during which the body moves up and down in a wavy vertical curve, and does not present the horizontal undulations so characteristic of quadrupeds lower in the scale.

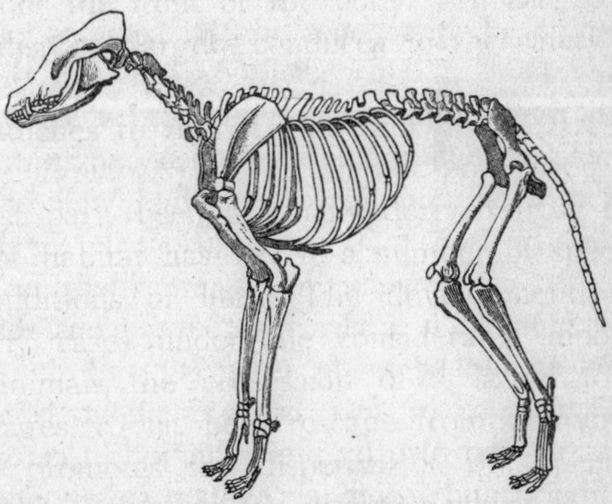

Fig. 686.—Skeleton of Dog. Described in text

In the Dog, and other Mammals possessed of great speed, there are well-marked angles between the several sections of the limbs, *e.g.* the elbow is directed well backwards and the knee well forwards. A double purpose is served by this arrangement, for the limbs are thereby converted into shock-reducing springs, while at the same time their sudden straightening enables powerful and effective backward pushes against the ground. This is particularly true for the hind-limbs, since these do much more work in a running animal than the fore-limbs, as necessarily follows from the fact that this kind of locomotion depends upon vigorous pushes against the ground, which are of course made with greatest effect from behind. This is one reason why the hind-limbs are so firmly united to the trunk, and the liability to shock which results from this is largely discounted by the conversion of these limbs into springs.

The amount of swing which the limbs can execute must not be judged from their length as seen in the skeleton, for in swift runners the upper arm and thigh are more or less imbedded in the trunk, and surrounded by the skin which bounds that region. This is to some extent the case in the Dog, but is still more marked in such creatures as the Horse. Union of limbs with trunk is thus rendered very intimate. But in these particular animals the shortening entailed by this is made up for by the length of the bones in the sections of the limbs below elbow and knee, and especially by the fact that the body is supported on the digits, *i.e.* the position is *digitigrade*. The palm-bones (metacarpus) and instep-bones (metatarsus) are almost vertical, so that wrist and ankle are lifted well off the ground. We have already seen that this is also true for Birds (see p. 126).

In cases where limbs are chiefly or mainly used for walking or running, it is clearly advantageous that their supporting skeleton should be made as strong and simple as possible. This has been more or less brought about by the firm union, or even fusion, and also by the reduction of certain bony elements. Both forearm and lower leg contain two bones—radius and ulna in the former, tibia and fibula in the latter. In running Mammals there is a marked tendency for radius and tibia, *i.e.* the two which have the larger surface of union with hand and foot, to increase in size, while the ulna and fibula dwindle to a corresponding extent. This is also true for the leg of a bird, in which (see fig. 126) the fibula is very small. In the case of the Dog this process has not affected the fore-limb, which is used for many purposes besides progression, but in the hind-limb the tibia is distinctly larger than the fibula, which is firmly united, but not fused with it. In this animal, too, the reduction of digits already noted in running birds (see p. 130) is beginning to take place, for the thumb is relatively small and does not reach the ground, while the great toe is usually only represented by a vestige. A comparatively primitive Mammal such as a Hedgehog has five fingers and five toes, *i.e.* is *pentadactyle,* while a dog has but four of each for locomotor purposes, *i.e.* is practically *tetradactyle.*

It is out of the question to attempt here any description of the immensely complicated muscular mechanism by which walking and running are effected, but we may well agree with the words of Graber, where (in *Die Werkzeuge der Wirbeltiere*) he compares the muscles of the body with the complicated ropes of a sailing-ship or the power-bands of a factory:—". . . the rigging of a sailing-ship, or the moving, power-transmitting bands of a large factory provided with numerous motors, appear to the lay mind as a bewildering arrangement. But if we look at all the muscles which cover and surround the backbone and limbs of vertebrates, we cannot but realize that the mechanical devices mentioned appear as children's toys when compared with the muscular machinery of backboned animals."

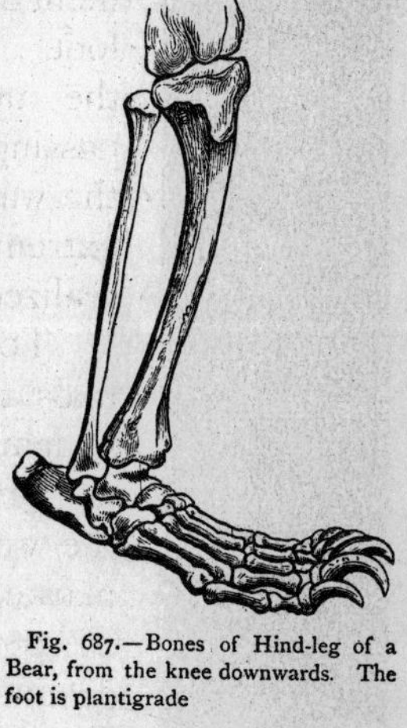

Fig. 687.—Bones of Hind-leg of a Bear, from the knee downwards. The foot is plantigrade

Many Mammals which are not so specialized as Dogs or Horses in regard to rapid progression, walk on the palms of the hands and soles of the feet, *i.e.* are *plantigrade.* It is inferred, from what is known of living and extinct forms, that this was the case in the earliest evolved members of the class. The more efficient digitigrade attitude is a later development, gradually acquired by forms to which considerable speed was a necessity, either for pursuit of prey, as in many of the Flesh-eating Mammals (Carnivora), or as a means of escape from enemies, as in the majority of Hoofed Mammals (Ungulata). Bears are typically plantigrade forms, and the bones of the lower part of the hind-limb are represented in fig. 687 to illustrate this. Compare also the drawing of Brown Bears given on p. 155.

Fig. 688.—Series of instantaneous photographs of Dog walking. Read from top to bottom

Having considered at some length the structure of the skeleton of the Dog (*Canis familiaris*) taken as a type, it will be convenient to consider the order in which the limbs of this animal are moved during walking. The same method is exemplified here as the one already described for Amphibians and Reptiles (p. 121), *i.e.* the limbs diagonally opposite succeed one another in their forward movement. Beginning, say, with the right fore-foot, the sequence is—right fore-foot, left hind-foot, left fore-foot, right hind-foot. Part of a series of photographs of a walking dog is given in fig. 688 to illustrate the movement of the right fore-foot. Beginning at the upper end and passing downwards, the way in which this extremity is brought to the front will readiiy be realized.

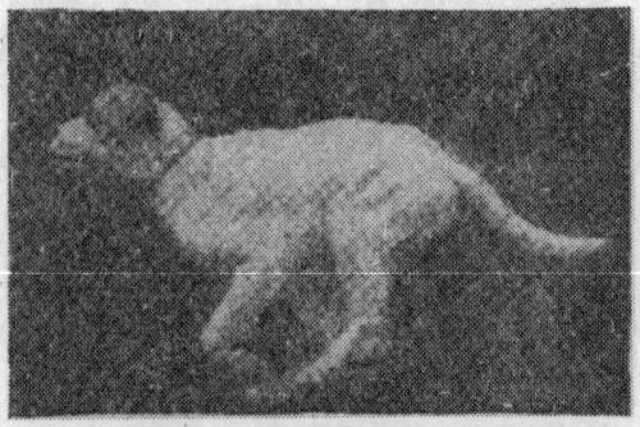

Fig. 689.—Instantaneous photograph of Dog running

To illustrate the nature of running in Mammals the Horse will be considered further on, as so many observations have been made upon it that no better example could well be selected. As to the way in which a dog runs, it need only be remarked here that, as in all other cases of this sort of progression, the body is completely off the ground for a very short time at regular intervals. Fig. 689 is an instantaneous photograph of one of the positions assumed, and shows the body resting on the hind-feet, while the fore-feet are preparing to move forwards, and it is clear from their positions that they reach the ground at different times.

That the hind-limbs have a considerable forward swing is obvious from the fact that they overlap the fore-limbs. Although the body rests on both hind-feet for the time being, the photograph shows that they do not work exactly together, or the right hind-limb would not be seen at all. Parts of it, however, are visible, owing to the fact that the left hind-limb is strongly bent. Its sudden straightening will give the body a vigorous forward push. The various joints can also be made out in the figure. In the fore-limb the elbow is directed backwards and the wrist forwards. Exactly the reverse is true for knee and ankle in the hind-limb. The position of the tail suggests its use as a balancing organ.

The more interesting cases of walking and running of members of some of the orders of Mammals will now briefly be reviewed.

HOOFED MAMMALS (*Ungulata*).—It will be convenient first to consider the Odd-toed Ungulates (Perissodactyla), so called in reference to the number of digits on the *hind*-foot, afterwards passing on to the Even-toed Ungulates (Artiodactyla). Most living species of these groups are characterized by the fact that they are entirely supported on the firm, horny hoofs which cover the end-joints of the digits, and this may be regarded as the most extreme case of digitigrade progression. The term *unguligrade* (*i.e.* hoof-walking) is employed to express it. Reference to fig. 693 will show exactly what is meant. Some few forms, however, cannot be so described, as will be seen in the sequel.

Odd-toed Ungulates (Perissodactyla).—The three groups of forms which these embrace—Tapirs, Rhinoceroses, and Horses—constitute a series of increasing specialization as regards locomotor organs.

Tapirs (fig. 690) are comparatively short-legged and rather clumsy animals, native to south-east Asia, South America, and Central America. Most of them live in dense, marshy forests, where there is not the same necessity for speed as in more open country. The wrist- and ankle-joints are lifted well off the ground, and the latter are well seen in fig. 690 at the back of the hind-limbs. For animals which constantly walk over yielding ground it is clearly necessary that the area of the surfaces of contact should not be too small (see p. 121). In Tapirs, although a reduction of these has resulted from the raising up of the palm and instep regions, this is to some extent made up for by the spreading nature of the toes, of which all the hoofs touch the ground. The full complement of digits (five), however, is not present, for there are but four in front and three behind.

It is the rule for Mammals that when such reduction takes place the 1st or innermost digit (thumb or great toe) first disappears, and then the 5th or outermost one (little finger or little toe). This is the case in Tapirs, which have lost thumb, great toe, and little toe. It is further to be noticed that the loss of certain digits is associated with increased size of those which remain, and in most Odd-toed Ungulates the central finger or toe (3rd) gradually becomes very large and dominant,

Fig. 690.—Malayan Tapir (*Tapirus Indicus*)

being also symmetrical in itself, a feature presented by none of the Even-toed Ungulates. This is, indeed, a much more distinctive character of the two groups than the mere number, odd or even, as the case may be, of the toes on the hind-foot.

Rhinoceroses (fig. 691) are such powerful and well-protected animals that they have but few serious enemies, and adequate support of the massive body is a more pressing necessity than speed in progression, especially as some of them inhabit marshy forests or grassy jungles, where the ground is yielding. The last remark is more particularly true of the Asiatic species, but the African forms live in more open country. Of these the White Rhinoceros (*Rhinoceros simus*) inhabits grass-covered steppes, while of the Common or Black Rhinoceros (*R. bicornis*) Sir Samuel Baker states (in *Wild Beasts and their Ways*):—"I have never found the African Rhinoceros in the neighbourhood of swamps, but, on the contrary, I have generally met them in dry and elevated places, at the base of rocky hills, or in woods, at some distance from a river". But at regular intervals these creatures also are obliged to step on yielding surfaces, at the times when they go to drink at streams or ponds.

The limbs of a Rhinoceros are comparatively short, while in shape they are stout and pillar-like. Reduction of digits has gone further than in Tapirs, for little finger as well as thumb

Fig. 691.—Indian Rhinoceros (*Rhinoceros unicornis*). Note the three-toed feet

has been lost by the hand, so that both fore- and hind-feet are three-toed (*tridactyle*). It may appear a little inconsequent to speak of the hand as a fore-"foot", and especially to use both terms in the same sentence. But in comparison of fore- and hind-limbs as regards digits it is more correct to use the words "hand", "fingers", "foot", "toes", and obviates clumsy expressions such as "fore-little-toe" and "hind-little-toe", while, on the other hand, it is obviously convenient when dealing with walking and running extremities to give the words "legs", "feet", and "toes" a wider meaning, and apply them indifferently to both pairs of limbs.

The third or central digits of a Rhinoceros are not markedly larger than the others, perhaps because in the case of such a heavy animal a uniform distribution of pressure is necessary. Nor is this creature a true hoof-walker, for the weight of the body is largely borne by large hard pads placed on the under sides of the palm- and instep-regions.

It must not be concluded from what has been said that Rhinoceroses are distinguished by great slowness of gait, for although the limbs are so constructed as to give a remarkably firm support, they are at the same time capable of vigorous and rapid movement, and the twelve hoofs present can accommodate themselves to irregular surfaces better than the four hoofs of a horse, which are better suited for swift progression on even ground. Speaking of the Black Rhinoceros (*R. bicornis*) Sir Samuel Baker gives a vivid picture (in *Wild Beasts and their Ways*) of the possibilities in this direction:—"When the vast bulk of a Rhinoceros is considered, it is astonishing to see the speed that this heavy animal can attain, and continue for a great distance. I have hunted them in company with the Arabs, and for at least two miles our horses have been going their best, keeping a position within five or six yards of the hind-quarters, but nevertheless unable to overtake them before they reached an impenetrable jungle. It is the peculiar formation of the hind-legs which enables the rhinoceros to attain this speed; the length from the thigh to the hock [*i.e.* ankle-joint] is so great that it affords immense springing capacity, and the animal bounds along the surface like a horse in full gallop, without the slightest appearance of weight or clumsiness. Upon a level plain, free from bushes or stones, a good horse would quickly overtake the Black Rhinoceros, but the animal is seldom found upon such favourable ground, and its strength and three-hoofed feet give it a peculiar advantage for travelling at a high speed over a rough surface that would test the endurance of the best horse."

Horses and their immediate allies are by far the most specialized of the Odd-toed Ungulates, and their powers of locomotion would appear to have been evolved with reference to rapid progression on even and tolerably firm tracts of country. The general proportions of the body, and the relation of the long limbs to the trunk, are clearly seen in fig. 692, and it will be observed that upper arm and thigh are largely merged in the latter. As a result of this the elbow and knee are very high up, and the so-called "knee" of a horse is really the wrist, while the "hock" is the ankle. A little way above each foot is a projection known as the "fetlock", on which grows a tuft of hair to which the name is also sometimes applied. This marks the position of a knuckle-joint in the fore-foot, and its equivalent in a hind-foot. It therefore follows that the long sections of the fore- and hind-limbs, situated respectively between "knee" and fetlock and "hock" and fetlock, correspond to the palm-region of the hand and the instep-region of the foot in, say, a man. The hind-limbs are obviously longer and stronger than the fore-limbs, and even in a resting attitude

Fig. 692.—Horse (*Equus caballus*). Note the one-toed feet

(fig. 692) present well-marked bends. Reference to fig. 696 will show where all the joints come in both fore- and hind-limbs.

Turning now to the skeleton of the Horse's limbs, we find that the fore-arm and lower leg are mainly supported by one bone, radius or tibia as the case may be, while the other bone of the same region (ulna and fibula) are correspondingly reduced. Wrist and ankle include a number of small bones, an arrangement first evolved in the interest of flexibility. But in a case like this, where these regions are lifted off the ground, firmness is more necessary than flexibility, and this is provided for in more than one way. By means of firm, fibrous bands known as ligaments, the wrist- and ankle-bones are very firmly united together, and the members of the two tiers which are present alternate with one another (see fig. 701), like two successive rows of bricks in a wall. This "bonding" obviously makes wrist and ankle very much firmer than they would be if the bones of one tier were immediately over those of the other, just as a "bonded" wall is greatly superior in this respect to one consisting of vertical rows of bricks.

The sections of the limbs which are situated between wrist and fetlock and ankle and fetlock contain the so-called "cannon-bones", which are simply the palm-bones of the middle or third digits in the fore-limb, and the instep-bones of the same digits in the hind-limbs (fig. 693). The region below the fetlock is supported by three bones, of which the lowest is greatly broadened for the attachment of the hoof. These complete the skeleton of the third digits, which are the only ones fully developed. The Horse is, in fact, one-toed or *unidactyle*. Reduction has gone a stage further than in the Rhinoceros, which is three-toed, and has retained the 2nd, 3rd, and 4th digits on each foot. By loss of the 2nd and 4th, with retention of the 3rd, the condition presented by the Horse would be reached. At this point we naturally enquire whether any traces of the 2nd and 4th digits are present in the skeleton of a horse's foot. The answer is in the affirmative, for lying on either side of the cannon-bone a narrow "splint-bone" is to be seen (fig. 693). These splint-bones are no other than the dwindled remains or "vestiges" of these two lost digits, corresponding to their palm-bones in the hand, and their instep-bones in the feet. We therefore conclude that the Horse was once, like the Rhinoceros, three-toed, and this conclusion is borne out by the facts of development, and by the study of extinct fossil forms.

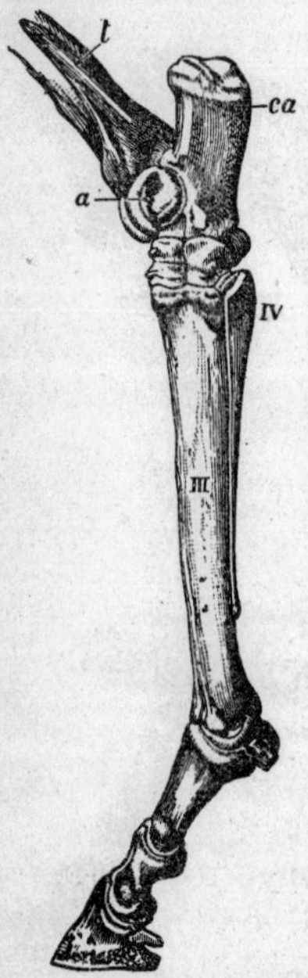

Fig. 693.—Bones of Left Hind-foot of Horse, seen from outer side

t, Shin-bone (tibia); *a*, pulley-bone (astragalus) of ankle; *ca*, heel-bone (calcaneum); III, instep-bone of large middle toe; IV, instep-bone ("splint-bone") of reduced 4th digit.

In the preceding parts of this book mention has several times been made of the Law of Recapitulation, according to which the development of an individual animal may broadly be taken as an epitome of the evolutionary history of the group to which it belongs. In this particular instance it has been shown by Cossar Ewart that each limb of a young unborn foal possesses a pair of little projections or "buttons" near its lower end, one on either side. There can be no doubt that these small knobs represent the tips of the 2nd and 4th digits.

Geological testimony is still more emphatic. A long series of fossil horses, or rather horse-like creatures, is now known, which proves conclusively that there has been a gradual reduction of digits, associated with other specializations, culminating in the forms which now exist. The hands and feet of some of these extinct creatures are shown in fig. 694, with the corresponding parts of a horse at the top for comparison. In the oldest form there represented (at the bottom) we see that there were four digits on the hand and three on the foot, *i.e.* the condition now found among Tapirs. The gradual dwindling of ulna and fibula is also indicated in the figure. Horse-like animals have been getting larger and larger during the progress of these various modifications. The oldest forms of the kind known to us were not much bigger than foxes. The facts just given form, however, but a very small part of our knowledge regarding the ancestry of Horses. It will be shown in a later section that there is good reason for believing that not only Horses, but all hoofed Mammals, together with Conies and Elephants, are descended from small swamp-inhabiting forms, which were plantigrade, and possessed the full complement of five digits on both fore- and hind-feet.

A few words are here necessary on the structure of the Horse's hoof, which is merely an exaggeration, so to speak, of

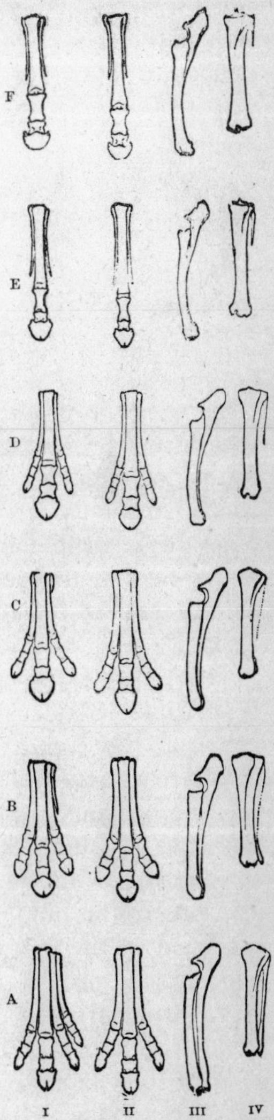

Fig. 694.—Evolution of Limbs of Horse

I, Fore-foot; II, hind-foot; III, fore-arm; IV, lower leg. A–E, Bones of extinct horse-like animals, Orohippus, Mesohippus, Miohippus (Anchitherium), Protohippus (Hipparion), Pliohippus. F, Bones of Horse (Equus). Read from below upwards (*i.e.* in order of geological age), and note gradual reduction in number of digits, and diminution of size of one forearm bone (ulna), and one lower leg bone (fibula).

what in ourselves we should call a finger-nail or a toe-nail. It constitutes a sort of horny box (fig. 695) supported by the expanded end-bone of the digit, and is composed of a complicated series of layers, so arranged as to combine great firmness with considerable elasticity. The latter property is of importance, as it mitigates the severe shocks to which the hoof is necessarily exposed. Although the locomotor organs of Horses were no doubt evolved with reference to swift progression on even and fairly firm ground, this was far more yielding in character than ordinary roads constructed by human agency. Hence arises the necessity for shoeing horses which constantly traverse these, as, if left unshod, the hoofs would wear away much too quickly. Really scientific farriery involves a thorough knowledge of the structure of the feet, and this important art, as practised in our own country, leaves much to be desired.

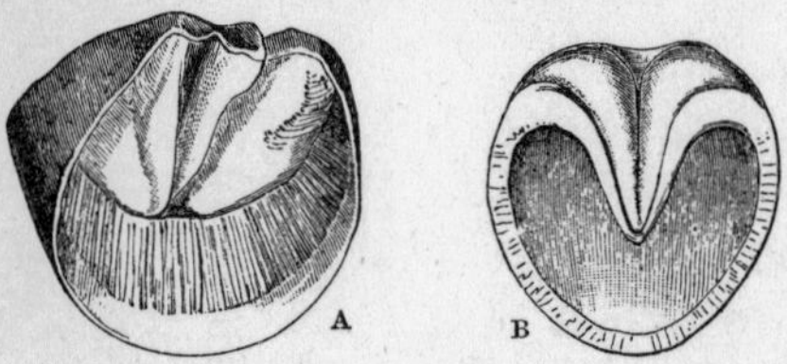

Fig. 695.—Horse's Hoof. A, Interior; B, under surface

Paces of the Horse.—The five chief kinds of pace which have been subjected to careful analysis are: the walk, the amble, the low trot, the ordinary trot, and the gallop. Of these the first three are varieties of walking, and the last two forms of running.

The ordinary *walk* of a Horse is effected in the same diagonal way already described for the Dog (see p. 136), the sequence, commencing with the right fore-foot, being—right fore, left hind, left fore, right hind. A regular series of equal sounds results, produced by the four successive hoof-falls. In both *amble* and *trot* two feet are placed on the ground simultaneously. The former is an artificial pace, which has to be taught to the animal. In it the two limbs of the same side move together, and two men walking one behind the other and keeping step would represent the succession, which would be—right fore and right hind together, left fore and left hind together. The sounds resulting would of course be a regular succession of double hoof-falls. What is known as the *low trot* agrees with this in so far that two feet are placed on the ground at the same time, but they are diagonally opposite one another, the sequence being—right fore and left hind together, left fore and right hind together.

In the *ordinary trot* the body entirely leaves the ground for a very short time between the successive impacts of the feet, and this kind of pace may therefore be considered a kind of running. The *gallop* is a more rapid run, and is distinguished from the trot by the irregularity of the sound produced, which is familiar to everyone, and is due to the fact that there is neither a regular succession of single hoof-falls, as in the walk, nor of double hoof-falls, as in the amble and trot, but a mixture of the two. Several kinds of gallop can be distinguished, which differ a good deal from one another. A simple variety is the one known as the gallop in three-time, because three successive sounds can be distinguished between one moment of suspension in the air and that next following. First comes a single hoof-fall, then a double one, and then a single one again. It appears that after suspension in the air the feet come down as follows—left hind, left fore and right hind together, right fore. Or it may be—right hind, right fore and left hind together, left fore. The first sequence applies to some horses, and the second to others. The instantaneous photographs represented in fig. 696 give two phases in such a gallop. Above is shown the horse resting on one fore-foot preparatory to leaving the ground altogether; below, the horse is seen actually suspended in the air. The times at which the hoofs reach and leave the ground are so related in one variety of this pace that the animal successively rests on the following number of legs: 1, 3, 2, 3, 1. In the first sequence given above these would be —left hind; left hind, right hind, left fore; right hind, left fore; right hind, left fore, right fore; right fore. In another variety of the three-time gallop the body alternately rests on one foot and on three feet.

Fig. 696.—Instantaneous Photographs of Horse Galloping. See text

What is known as the *full gallop*, the successive phases of which are given in fig. 697, is said to be in four-time, because four successive impacts are given by the hoofs, as follows (in

Fig. 697.—Series of Instantaneous Photographs of a Horse Galloping. Read from left to right beginning with uppermost row. See text

one of the two sequences)—left hind, right hind, left fore, right fore. It will be observed that the body is sometimes supported on one foot, at other times on two.

Mechanical devices have been invented, by which the hoofs can be made to register the exact times at which they reach and leave the ground. Diagrams of such automatic registration for walk, low trot, and one variety of three-time gallop, is given in fig. 698. Each foot is represented by a rectangle, the length of which is proportionate to the time the hoof rests on the ground. Perpendicular lines drawn across the diagrams show the number of feet (if any) resting on the ground in different phases of the movement.

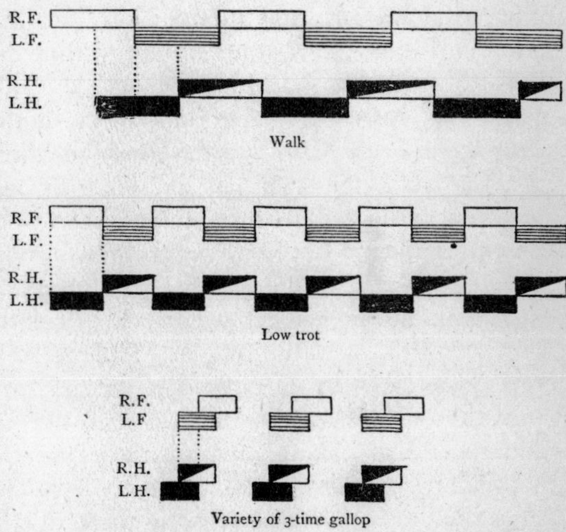

Fig. 698.—Paces of Horse Mechanically Registered

R.F., Right fore-foot; L.F., left fore-foot; R.H., right hind-foot; L.H., left hind-foot. See text.

Even-toed Ungulates (Artiodactyla).—As among the Odd-toed Ungulates, so also in this group, it is easy to pick out a series of forms which illustrate increasing specialization, resulting from adaptation to swift progression on firm surfaces. But the same end is here attained in a somewhat different manner, for *two* digits, the 3rd and 4th, become dominant, the axis of symmetry of the limb running between them, while in Odd-toed Ungulates only *one* digit, the 3rd, continues to increase in importance, and the axis of symmetry runs through it. The difference between the two types is clearly brought out in fig. 701.

These Even-toed or "cloven-footed" Ungulates include non-ruminating forms (Hippopotami and Swine), which are comparatively simple in structure, and far more numerous ruminants or "cud-chewers" (Cattle, Deer, &c.), some of which are as specialized as Horses, which they rival or even excel in speed.

The Hippopotamus is a creature of such vast bulk, and the ground upon which it walks when it comes out of the water is so soft, that we should naturally expect the feet to present a large surface of support, to be of spreading character, and to exhibit but little, if any, reduction in the number of digits. The structure of this animal fully justifies such expectations. The limbs are short and strong, with wrists and ankles raised but little from the ground, for palm- and instep-regions are both short. It is true that the innermost digits (thumbs and great toes) have been lost, but the four remaining in each foot are of about the same size, and terminate in pointed hoofs on which the body rests. The reason for absence of much reduction in the extremities is put very graphically by Oscar Schmidt (in *The Mammalia*), where, speaking of the primitive ancestors of hoofed Mammals, he says that these ". . . had to dwell principally in waters and on marshy ground. Their descendants adapted themselves gradually to life on dry ground, and this is connected with the advantageous reduction of the toes. The Hippopotamus . . . has taken an opposite course; from being an animal that liked the marshy soil of the primeval forests, it has become almost an aquatic creature, and accordingly has preserved the completeness of hand and foot, the four toes almost fully developed. . . . A one-toed hippopotamus in the natural course of development is an impossibility. The gradual reduction of the toes, as already said, can be connected only with the drying up of marshy lands. And if, by some extravagant flight of the imagination, we could conceive the existence of a one-toed leviathan, the very fact of its possessing a one-toed foot would be the cause of its speedy extinction."

It appears that the Hippopotamus can make its way very quickly along the bed of its native river, the body being buoyed up by the water to a convenient extent, and it can also climb with facility up mud-banks and on to shoals, the pointed hoofs of the spreading feet giving a sufficiently good hold for the purpose.

Swine and their immediate allies are comparatively short-limbed, and though possessed of considerable powers of speed, are in most cases essentially marsh-loving animals, so that feet capable of a certain amount of spreading are a necessary endowment. And we find accordingly that the extremities represent a sort of compromise between adaptations necessary for speed and arrangements suitable for progression on yielding surfaces. The bones of the forearm (radius and ulna) and lower leg (tibia and fibula) are both complete, palm-region and instep-region are of moderate length, and one digit (thumb or great toe) has been lost in each foot. Of the four digits which remain, two (third and

Fig. 699.—Collared Peccary (*Dicotyles torquatus*)

fourth) are large, and their ends are encased in hoofs upon which the animal walks, while the other two (second and fifth) are small, and possess little hoofs which do not touch the ground when this is firm enough to fully sustain the animal's weight. But when a pig traverses marshy ground, the two large toes separate to some extent and give an increased surface; while if, even in spite of this, the feet sink in to some extent, the two small toes act as "stops", which more or less check further sinking.

It is very interesting to note that the little, slender-legged Peccaries (fig. 699) of South America, animals which are included in the Pig family, are more specialized as regards the structure of the feet, for the two central palm-bones of the fore-limb are fused together into a "cannon-bone", which is also the case with the two central instep-bones of the hind-limb. [The structure so called in a horse is only *one* large bone (see p. 142).] And besides this, the hind-feet of a Peccary have lost the outermost (fifth) toes. The extremities, in short, are better suited for progression on firm surfaces than is the case in ordinary pigs, and, as we might expect, Peccaries are not such distinctively marsh-loving creatures. Nor is it surprising to find that they can run more quickly than pigs.

Ruminants (fig. 700) present a series of cases in which the kind of specialization seen in swine is carried to an increasingly greater extent. The two chief toes (third and fourth) become more and more dominant, and the two palm-bones or instep-bones which belong to them fuse together into a "cannon-bone", as in the Peccaries. At the same time the two side-toes (second and fifth) dwindle and ultimately disappear. As Vogt says (in *The Mammalia*): "There is thus a series of developments by which the two lateral digits get more and more reduced, and this series is the continuation of that which was presented by the preceding group (*i.e.* Hippopotami and Swine). At the same time the limbs become more slender and longer as the fleetness of the animal increases. Among the Ruminants we meet with runners which surpass all other known Mammals in point of speed." This acquisition of great powers of locomotion is undoubtedly in direct relation to the habit of ruminating or cud-chewing (see vol. ii, p. 169). For animals of this kind are able to hurriedly fill their paunches with food, after which they can rapidly seek places of safety on higher ground. This commonly necessitates a good deal of clambering, for which a spreading two-toed foot is much better suited than a one-toed foot like that of a horse (compare p. 140).

By far the least specialized Ruminants are the little Chevrotains (*Tragulidæ*) of South-east Asia and West Africa, which give us a good idea of the structure and habits of the remote ancestors from which all the even-toed Ungulates are descended. This is particularly true of the Water Chevrotain (*Dorcatherium*) from the latter region. The feet (fig. 701) are much like those of a pig, except that the two side-toes are relatively smaller. The two large palm-bones of the fore-foot have not fused into a cannon-bone (fig. 701), but the two large instep-bones of the hind-foot have, on the contrary, more or less united together. The Asiatic Chevrotain or Kanchil (*Tragulus*) is rather more

DORCAS GAZELLES (*Gazella Dorcas*)

Few animals are better able to escape from enemies by sheer speed than Antelopes, and among these the slender little Gazelles are particularly well endowed as regards running powers. The plate represents a herd of Dorcas Gazelles in rapid movement, and it will be noted that the attitudes assumed can scarcely be termed graceful. This particular species is common in the desert regions of North Africa and South-west Asia, and elegantly curved horns are present in both sexes, although those of the female are relatively slender. Gazelles frequently leap high into the air whilst running. As in desert animals generally, the colour closely matches the surroundings, thus promoting inconspicuousness. In the present instance this may be interpreted as a case of protective coloration.

Fig. 700.—Ruminants.—1, Giraffe (*Giraffa camelopardalis*); 2, Arabian Camel (*Camelus dromedarius*); 3, Fallow-Deer (*Cervus dama*); 4, Prongbuck (*Antilocapra Americana*); 5, Alpine Ibex (*Capra ibex*); 6, Musk-Deer (*Moschus moschiferus*).

specialized, for cannon-bones are present in both pairs of lin In Chevrotains, as in all other Ruminants, the ulna and fib are reduced, but the latter is complete though slender. In remaining cud-chewers it is only represented by a little noc (malleolar bone) just above the ankle-bones.

Deer (*Cervidæ*) are much larger and swifter animals tha Chevrotains, and, like the rest of the Ruminants, live on firme ground, to which their speed is an adaptation. The outer toes are reduced to insignificant vestiges, which project, however, at the exterior.

A very interesting case of adaptation to progression on a yielding surface is presented by the Reindeer (*Rangifer tarandus*), which may be said to possess "snow-feet", that can be so spread out as to give an increased walking surface, much as is the case with the marsh-feet of a pig or chevrotain. The hoofs of the two large toes are of considerable size and strongly curved, with concave sides facing one another, and convex outer edges. When pressed down on the snow they separate widely, so that the fairly large hoofs of the outer toes touch the ground and help to support the weight of the body, which is very considerable. A less-marked arrangement of similar kind is found in the Elk or Moose (*Alces machlis*), which is also a northern form, though it does not range into treeless wastes as does the reindeer.

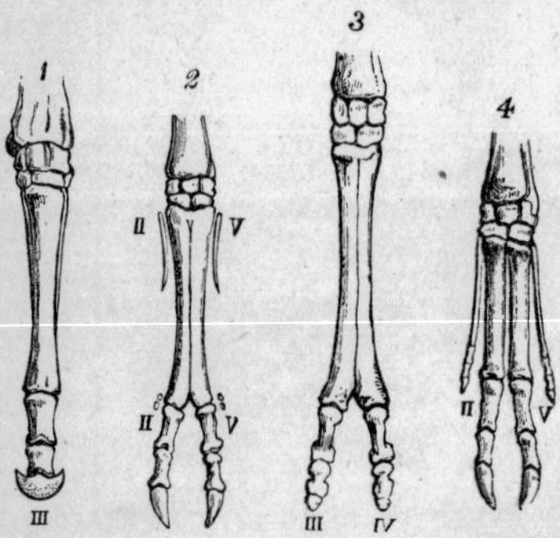

Fig. 701.—Bones of Fore-feet of Hoofed Animals
1, Horse; 2, Sheep; 3, Camel; 4, Water-Chevrotain (*Dorcatherium*). II–V, 2nd to 5th digits.

The Hollow-horned Ruminants (*Cavicornia*), including Antelopes, Cattle, Sheep, and Goats, present a further stage in the reduction of the side-toes, which are represented by traces of their supporting bones (fig. 701), and commonly also by little external projections bearing small accessory hoofs.

The Camel Family (*Tylopoda*), which includes the Camels of the Old World and the Llamas of the New, is characterized by the entire loss of the two small outer digits (second and fifth), which persist more or less in the Even-toed Ungulates so far considered. The two bones which have united together to form the cannon-bone in the Camel diverge below (fig. 701), an arrangement which gives a large surface of attachment for a firm pad on the under side of the foot. This is in relation to the yielding nature of the sand upon which the animal walks, for these pads greatly increase the surface of contact with the sand, and thus help to prevent the feet from sinking into it, at the same time preventing them from becoming unduly heated. The adaptation is remarkably like that found in the African Ostrich (see p. 130), where, however, one of the two toes present is very much larger than the other, and the foot is well cleft, while that of the Camel is only slightly so.

It is further interesting to note that the Camel is one of the very few animals of which the natural walk is an amble (see p. 144), other cases being the Giraffe and the Elephant. All three are more or less heavy creatures which habitually traverse yielding surfaces, and very probably their ambling may be explained by reference to these facts. For in this particular pace two feet are brought forward and set down together, thus doubling the surface of contact and halving the weight of the body between them, thus greatly reducing the tendency to sink into the ground.

Two wild species of camel-like animals, the Guanaco (*Lama guanacus*) and Vicunia (*L. vicunia*), are native to South America. Their structure is essentially like that of camels, but the body is smaller, the limbs more slender. Each toe of the more deeply-cleft foot bears a pad. Both animals are active mountain-climbers, especially the Vicunia, and the differences between their feet and those of camels are adaptations to this different way of life. The larger Guanaco, however, is also found in the plains, where it is associated with the South American Ostriches (*Rhea*), just as the Camel and African Ostrich (*Struthio*) are found together under similar conditions in the Old World.

Of all existing Even-toed Ungulates the Giraffes (*Giraffidæ*) are the most specialized (fig. 700). There is not the same disproportion between the length of fore- and hind-limbs as in other Ungulates, and the region between wrist or ankle and hand or foot is remarkably elongated. Both outer digits (second and fifth) have been lost entirely, and the two which still remain (third and fourth) possess very large hoofs. As already stated, the walking pace is an amble.

Until quite recently the Giraffe held a very isolated position among existing Ungulates, but the gap has partly been filled up by the discovery of what may be called a short-necked giraffe in Central Africa. This animal, the Okapi (*Okapia Johnstoni*), resembles its larger congener in many respects, but little is so far known regarding its habits.

FLESH-EATING MAMMALS (*Carnivora*) AS WALKERS AND RUNNERS.—Sufficient is known about extinct fossil Mammals to make it certain that the remote ancestors of the dogs, bears, lions, &c., of to-day were small marsh-inhabiting creatures, which had the full number of digits and walked upon the palms of their hands and soles of their feet. From animals of this sort Carnivores and Ungulates have both sprung (see p. 143). As we go back in time the characters of the two orders are less and less well marked, till we ultimately make the acquaintance of forms which cannot well be placed in either order, but give us a good idea of what the common ancestors of the two groups were like.

Existing Carnivores present us with a long series of stages in the evolution of efficient organs of locomotion, though even the most specialized do not parallel such animals as horses and giraffes in the matter of reduction of digits and lengthening of palm and instep regions. This is intelligible when we consider the habits of typical beasts of prey. Those of the dog kind excepted, there are but few of them which rely upon sheer speed to secure their prey, and the members of the highly-modified Cat family adopt more stealthy tactics, in the final stage of which a sudden and powerful spring is the most important matter. Besides this, the limbs have other work to do besides locomotion, and the necessity for lateral movement has checked specialization on ungulate lines. Effective seizing of prey, for example, is incompatible with great reduction in the number and mobility of digits.

The Dog has already been described at some length as an illustration of some of the main features of Mammalian locomotion, and the correlated characters presented by the bodily structure (see p. 132). It is typically digitigrade, *i.e.* walks upon its digits, and the wrists and ankles are well lifted off the ground (fig. 686, p. 133); but these regions are not elongated to the same extent as in many of the Hoofed Mammals, nor is there any fusion of the palm- or instep-bones. It is further to be remarked, that in the Dog and other digitigrade Carnivores the weight of the body is not borne upon the extreme

Fig. 702.—Brown Bears (*Ursus arctos*)

tips of the toes, as in, say, a horse, but upon elastic pads borne upon the under sides of the paws (fig. 707). The three joints of each digit are bent in a peculiar way, one result of which is to keep the claws off the ground, and in members of the Cat family these are even drawn back into special sheaths when not actually in use.

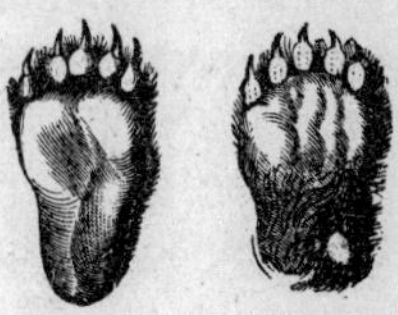

Fig. 703.—Under Surfaces of a Bear's Paws

The *Large Bears* (Ursidæ) (fig. 702) are not modified like dogs, &c., in relation to rapid progression, for they are typically plantigrade, walking on palms and soles. Both fore- and hind-feet possess the full number of five digits. It is a familiar fact that Bears are able to progress for some distance upon their hind-limbs only, especially when attacked by human beings. The broad soles of the hind-feet (fig. 703) render such a mode of progression comparatively easy to them.

The paws of the Polar Bear (*Ursus maritimus*) are of very great size, and their under surfaces are hair-clad. These features are not improbably related to the necessity for constantly traversing snow and the slippery surface of ice.

The *Weasel and Badger Family* (Mustelidæ) is one of great antiquity, and all five digits are present in fore- and hind-feet. There are considerable differences between the various members of the family as regards the way in which the feet are placed on the ground. A Common Badger (*Meles taxus*), for instance, is plantigrade, while the smaller creatures known as Martens, Weasels, &c., raise the wrists and ankles more or less off the

Fig. 704.—Sable (*Mustela zibellina*)

ground, and are therefore to some extent digitigrade. But as some part of the palm and instep regions touch the ground as well as the digits themselves, we have a sort of intermediate stage between plantigrade and digitigrade conditions. This *semi-plantigrade* arrangement, as it is usually called, is well seen in the Sable (*Mustela zibellina*, fig. 704), and is particularly interesting because it indicates the way in which a more specialized way of walking has been gradually evolved from a less specialized, constituting in this respect a sort of half-way house between what is found in a bear or badger on the one hand, and a lion or cat on the other.

The small Carnivores known as *Viverrines* (Viverridæ), including Mangoustis and Civets, constitute a group which is in many ways more primitive than the one last mentioned. Mangoustis, of which the best-known types are the Ichneumons, are semi-plantigrade, while the Civets have gone a stage further in specialization, for palm and instep regions are well lifted off the ground, so that the term digitigrade is here applicable. This is very well seen in the African Civet-Cat (*Viverra civetta*, fig. 705). As regards the mode of progression, Civets are therefore more highly modified than Mangoustis; but in spite of this the full number of five digits are present both on

Fig. 705.—African Civet-Cat (*Viverra civetta*)

fore- and hind-feet, while in Mangoustis and their immediate allies the first digits (thumbs and great toes) are reduced in size, or in some cases even absent altogether.

The members of the *Cat* family (Felidæ) are the most highly specialized of all Flesh-eating Mammals, and are completely digitigrade, as may be seen in the Common Cat (*Felis domesticus*, fig. 706). The weight of the body rests upon elastic pads on the under sides of the paws (fig. 707). Five digits are present on the fore-paw, but the first one (great toe) has been lost in the hind-paw.

Probably the fleetest of all existing Carnivores, at least for short distances, are the Hunting Leopards, of which the Indian Cheetah (*Cynailurus jubatus*, see vol. ii, p. 11) is a well-known example. In these forms the legs are unusually long and slender, and the claws cannot be drawn back into special sheaths, as in the other members of the Cat family.

MONKEYS AND MEN (*Primates*).—It would appear that the evolution of the members of this order has been related in the

Fig. 706.—Common Cat (*Felis domesticus*)

first instance to the climbing habit, and to the use of the limbs for various other purposes involving complex movements. In accordance with this we find the collar-bones well developed, as in all cases where the arms are capable of a large amount of lateral action. Both bones of the forearm (radius and ulna) and lower leg (tibia and fibula) are well developed, and so arranged in the former as to permit of twisting on the long axis, the radius, which carries the hand, rolling over the ulna as it were (see vol. i, p. 30). And in all cases the full number of digits is present, though it occasionally happens that the thumb is reduced in size.

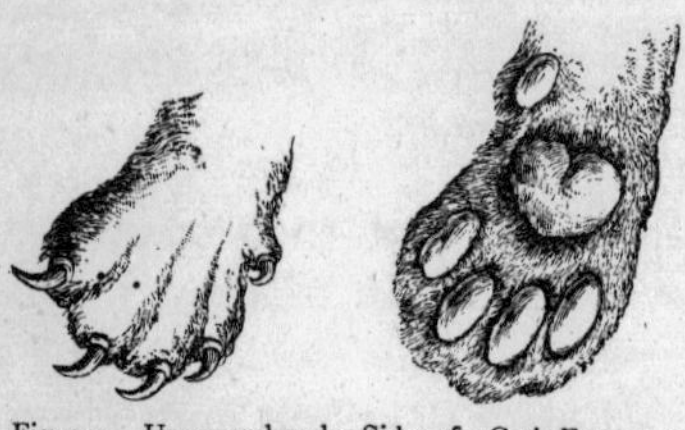

Fig. 707.—Upper and under Sides of a Cat's Fore-paw
The claws are protruded in the former and the "pads" are seen in the latter.

When an ordinary Monkey has occasion to walk on the ground, it does so on all-fours, in plantigrade fashion; and this is also the case in Baboons, which are in the main ground animals (fig. 708).

The higher or Anthropoid Apes, though all expert climbers,

present a series of adaptations to walking on the hinder limbs only, which lead up to the very perfect structural arrangements by which Man is eminently fitted for progression of this kind.

Bipedal locomotion in Primates is entirely different from what has already been described for Birds (see p. 125). In the latter the legs are set on far forwards, the body being as it were slung

Fig. 708.—Black Baboon of Celebes (*Cynopithecus niger*)

between them, with its long axis oblique. Birds are also digitigrade in a marked degree. In the higher Apes and Man, on the contrary, there is an increasing tendency for the pelvis to form a strong bony basin, built on the principle of the arch, and adapted to support the weight of the trunk, of which the long axis becomes vertical in the last stage of the evolutionary series. At the same time the tail has been reduced to an insignificant vestige. It must further be noted that the legs become relatively longer as the power of walking on them alone is gradually improved, and the feet more suited to bear the weight of the body. At the same time the arms become relatively shorter.

Higher Apes (Anthropomorpha, fig. 709).—The Gibbons of Asia are comparatively small creatures of eminently arboreal habit. Their arms are of extraordinary length, more than sufficient to enable them to touch the ground when the erect position

Fig. 709.—Higher or Anthropoid Apes
1, Gorilla (*Gorilla Savagei*); 2, Chimpanzee (*Anthropopithecus niger*); 3, Silver Gibbon (*Hylobates leuciscus*); 4, Orang-utan (*Simia satyrus*).

is assumed. Regarding their mode of walking, Vogt (in *The Mammalia*) speaks as follows:—"They [*i.e.* the arms] are so long that the Gibbons but seldom make use of them in walking on the ground, which indeed they touch only on exceptional occasions when living in freedom. They then waddle along upright, with their great toes widely spread out, with uplifted arms spread out sidewards as a balancing-rod, the long hands hanging down like goose wing-dusters, the head hanging a little forwards, and the back bent like a fiddle-bow." It is asserted by some authorities that Gibbons walk better on hind-limbs alone than the other higher apes.

The Orang-utan, Chimpanzee, and Gorilla mostly walk on all-fours, and usually bend their fingers so that the backs of these touch the ground. But on occasion all three are able to progress as bipeds. The Orang-Utan (*Simia satyrus*) is a thoroughly arboreal form, and its arms are only a little shorter than those of the Gibbons. In the erect posture the knuckles can be placed on the ground, and thus the animal is able to steady itself when walking on the hind-legs, as it sometimes does. The Chimpanzee (*Anthropopithecus niger*) and Gorilla (*Gorilla Savagei*), though good climbers, live on the ground to a much larger extent than their Asiatic cousins. Both are able to walk on the hind-legs with a rather tottering gait, and under these circumstances the fore-limbs give no help, for they are considerably shorter than in the Orang. But even in the Gorilla, which approaches most nearly to Man in its proportions, the legs are comparatively short, while the arms hang down below the knees.

WALKING AND RUNNING OF MAN.—The structure of the human skeleton, as adapted to the erect attitude, has already

Fig. 710.—Series of photographs of a Man walking. Read from right to left

been considered at some length (see vol. i, pp. 25–32). But the adaptation is by no means perfect, for after all, human beings are but highly-specialized quadrupeds, and the habitually upright position of the body is related to a number of complaints, chiefly as the result of undue pressure upon such internal organs as are situated in the lower part of the trunk.

Some of the successive stages of human walking are represented in fig. 710, taken from a series of photographs. By examining this from right to left a number of points will be observed. It is clear that the forward impulse, resulting from the backward push of each leg in turn against the ground, largely depends upon alternate bending and straightening of the limbs. Some little assistance is also given by the swinging of the arms, which move one after the other at the same time as the opposite leg. The purely plantigrade nature of this typical "heel-and-toe" work is also apparent, and it will be seen that the heel reaches the ground first. It will further be noted that the body moves in a wave-like curve, a fact which is best realized by following the successive positions of the head.

When a Man runs in the most advantageous way he lifts his heels from the ground and becomes a digitigrade animal for the time being. The legs now in turn bend and straighten with such vigour that the backward pushes they give project the body entirely off the ground at each stride. And as a matter of course the rate of progression is proportionate to the force with which the bending and straightening of the legs are effected.

WALKING OF JOINTED-LIMBED INVERTEBRATES (ARTHROPODA)

The problems presented by the locomotion of backboned animals are by no means easy to solve, but the study of Jointed-Limbed Invertebrates (*Arthropoda*) presents even greater difficulties. This is due to the great complexity of their structure, the number of their limbs, and the fact that each limb is made up of more numerous sections than is the case with the corresponding organs of Amphibians, Reptiles, and Mammals. And the comparatively small size of Arthropods of course renders investigation more difficult. A good deal of attention has been paid to the subject of late years, but it is beyond the scope of a work like this to do more than give some of the more elementary facts which have been determined.

The mechanical arrangements by which walking is effected in Arthropods are very different from those characteristic of Vertebrates. The bodies of the latter are supported by a complex internal skeleton, of which the parts are so jointed together as to permit of the necessary movements. The equally or perhaps more complex muscular system largely consists of fleshy bands (muscles) attached to the bones which make up the skeleton. But in an Arthropod, such as a lobster or insect, the skeleton is external, consisting of a hard layer covering the skin. Where movement is required, thin flexible places are found in this firm covering, and at such spots the thicker parts of the skeleton are provided with projections and sockets which so fit into one another as to constitute efficient joints of various kind, and comparable to the ball-and-socket joints, hinge-joints, &c., possessed by the internal skeleton of backboned animals. The numerous muscles which effect movement are of necessity attached to the inner surface of the hard covering of the body, as will be understood by reference to fig. 711, which represents diagrammatically the leg of an insect.

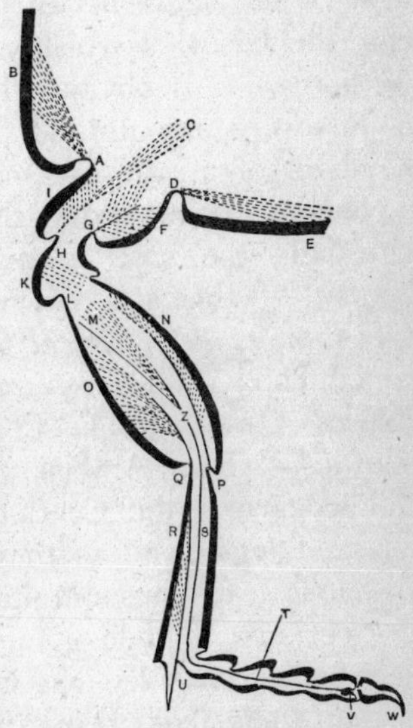

Fig. 711.—Diagram of an Insect's Leg in longitudinal section

The black outline represents the hard skeleton: the muscles are dotted and their tendons are drawn as thin unbroken lines. B E, Body; IF, hip (coxa); K, trochanter; ON, thigh (femur); R, shin (tibia); U V W, foot (tarsus) with end-claw. B A, C, E D, Muscles which move leg on body; K L, muscle which draws thigh inwards; F G, N P, muscles which straighten out the leg; I H, O Q, R U, M Z (with long tendon ZSTV), muscles which bend the parts of the leg upon one another.

There can be little doubt that Arthropods are descended from creatures resembling Bristle-Worms in many respects. We have seen (p. 98) that a typical worm of this kind is made up of a considerable number of rings or segments, each possessing a pair of hollow, unjointed foot-stumps, by the successive action of which creeping is effected in an undulating manner. As already mentioned (p. 101), the primitive air-breathing form Peripatus resembles a bristle-worm in certain particulars, as, for example, the structure of its many legs, which are much like modified foot-stumps, and are used in the same manner. It will now be convenient to consider the methods of walking practised by Centipedes and Millipedes (*Myriapoda*); Insects (*Insecta*); Scorpions, Spiders, &c. (*Arachnida*); and Crustaceans (*Crustacea*).

Centipedes and Millipedes (*Myriapoda*) as Walkers.—The creatures of this class present an advance upon Peripatus in the structure of their numerous legs, which are solid and distinctly jointed, as in all the other Arthropods to be considered. Myriapods walk on the claws with which their limbs are furnished, thus reminding us of the hoof-walkers among Mammals (see p. 137).

The vegetarian *Millipedes* are comparatively sluggish, and most of the segments of the body each bear two pairs of feeble legs, the bases of which are close together on the under side of the body. It is obvious that weak and numerous limbs attached in this way are not adapted for rapid locomotion. The two members of a pair are moved together, and a sort of wave of movement passes along the numerous legs during walking, as is usually the case in many-limbed animals. A very graphic account of this sort of movement is quoted by Heathcote (in *The Cambridge Natural History*) from an old and curiously-named book (*An Essay towards a Natural History of Serpents.* Charles Owen, D.D., London, 1742). The passage runs as follows:—"The Ambua, so the natives of Brazil call the Millipedes and the Centipedes, are serpents. These reptiles of thousand legs bend as they crawl along, and are reckoned very poisonous. In these Multipedes the mechanism of the body is very curious; in their going it is observable that on each side of their bodies each leg has its motion, one regularly after another, so that their legs, being numerous, form a kind of undulation, and thereby communicate to the body a swifter progression than one could imagine where so many short feet are to take so many short steps, that follow one another rolling on like the waves of the sea." The name Millipede, *i.e.* thousand-legs, is not very fortunate, for in average cases 100 pairs may be considered a liberal estimate, and in some short-bodied forms the number may sink as low as 13 pairs.

The carnivorous *Centipedes* are much more active than their vegetarian cousins, in accordance with which their legs are longer and stouter, and their bases farther apart. Most of the segments bear one pair each, and the two limbs of a pair move alternately and not together, an arrangement which would seem to favour speed. The body, being flattened from above downwards, is better suited for rapid progression than the almost cylindrical body of a Millipede. Here again the popular name Centipede, meaning hundred-legs, is not very appropriate, for some species are much elongated and may possess as many as 173 pairs of legs, while one form, common in our gardens (*Lithobius*, see vol. ii, p. 132), is quite short and has but 15 pairs. It is a curious fact that the number of pairs is always odd.

Typical Centipedes can move backwards as well as forwards, and the short forms progress more rapidly than the long ones, as might be expected. The Shield-bearing Centipede (*Scutigera*, vol. ii, p. 436), which differs so much from other forms as to be considered the type of a distinct order, is quite remarkable for its speed, and its legs, of which only 9 pairs are present, are remarkably long and stilt-like (fig. 712).

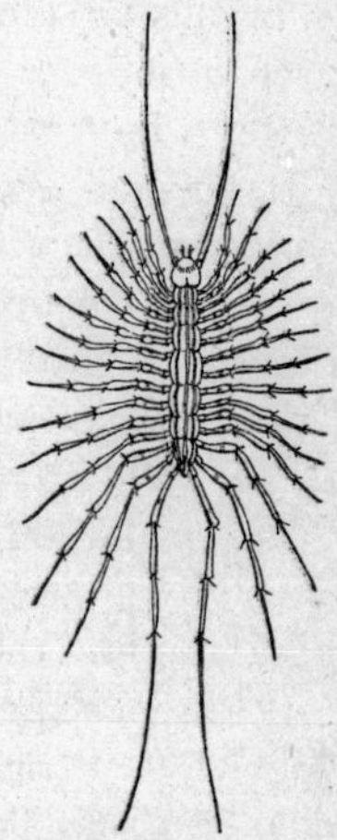

Fig. 712.—Shield-bearing Centipede (*Scutigera*)

INSECTS (*Insecta*) AS WALKERS.—Average insects possess but three pairs of legs, which are well developed, and attached to the central part or thorax of the comparatively short body. We find, however, that during development a number of abdominal legs begin to make their appearance, and may sometimes be retained as little stumps on the under side of the body in the adults of primitive wingless forms, though as a rule they disappear completely. From these and many other facts the conclusion has been reached that the remote ancestors of insects possessed more than three pairs of legs, and were probably not unlike short centipedes. And there can be no doubt that insects have gradually become compacter in form, while at the same time the number of legs has undergone reduction, in the interests of effective walking and climbing, among other things.

Elaborate investigations have been made upon the walk of Insects, a subject which is as interesting as it is complicated, though the simpler results are quite easy to understand. The elasticity of the legs appears to be a work-saving contrivance, for after a movement has been made this helps to bring them back to the position naturally assumed in a state of rest, when they are ready for a second effort. Just as if, say, a human limb, after having been bent by muscular action, could again straighten itself by elastic recoil without the use of muscles. On this point Packard, when summarizing (in his *Text-Book of Entomology*) the work of Graber, the most eminent authority on this particular subject, says: "Considering the respective positions of the individual levers of the leg and the nature of the materials of which they are made, the legs of insects may be likened, as Graber states, to elastic bows, which, when pressed down together from above, their own indwelling elasticity is able to raise them again and thus keep the body upright. This is very plainly shown in certain stilt-legged bark-beetles, in which, as in a rubber doll, as soon as the body is pressed down on the ground, the organs of motion extend again without the intervention of muscles; indeed, this experiment succeeds even with dead, but not yet wholly stiff, insects."

It further appears that most adult insects are *plantigrade*, walking on the whole of the surfaces of the feet or tarsi in which the limbs terminate, though, of course, these regions are not strictly comparable to the feet of backboned animals. The tips of the legs are provided with hooks which hold firmly to the underlying surface, unless this is very smooth. Hence the ease with which insects walk up inclined planes or upon narrow twigs. In the latter case the large feelers (antennæ) which certain forms possess appear to be used as balancers, playing the same part in this respect as the tail of the cat and many other Mammals.

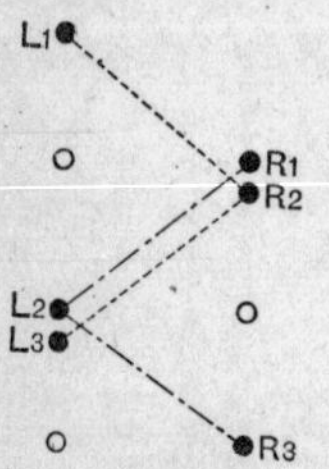

Fig. 713.—Diagram Plan of a Phase in an Insect's Walk

L1, L2, L3, First, second, and third legs of left side; R1, R2, R3, first, second, and third legs of right side. The legs which work together are connected by dotted lines. L1, R2, and L3 have just stepped forwards together (from positions indicated by unshaded circles).

As might be expected, the legs of an insect are moved diagonally, presenting a modification of the principle we have found to be usually applicable to quadrupeds (see p. 121). In considering their action it will be convenient to speak of the fore-, mid-, and hind-legs. These members work in two sets of three, on which account insects have sometimes been called "double-three-legged animals". One set includes left fore-, right mid-, and left hind-legs; the other, of course, right fore-, left mid-, and right hind-legs. These sets are advanced alternately (fig. 713), and there is a division of labour between the three legs of each set. The fore-leg pulls the body forwards, the hind-leg pushes it forwards, and the mid-leg is in the main a support, though it also does some pushing work. There must clearly be a certain amount of lateral movement, especially as the body is, so to speak, slung between the legs, as in an Amphibian (see p. 121), and as a result of this the gait is sinuous, the insect "wobbling" more or less from side to side. These creatures are also experts in varying degree in the art of walking backwards, during which reversal of the usual state of things the fore- and hind-legs exchange their rôles, the former pushing the body back, while the latter pull it back.

At this point the question naturally arises, "Why should an Insect have six legs, while Amphibians, Reptiles, and Mammals have only four?" It has been suggested that the answer to the first part of this question is to be found in the use of the legs of Insects for climbing, six being the smallest number which gives complete stability, and reduces to a minimum the risk of falling. The four-legged condition of ordinary back-boned land animals is, on the other hand, an inheritance from fish-like aquatic ancestors (see p. 117), of which the fore- and hind-fins have furnished the raw material for the evolution of legs. And it would seem that these ancestors acquired four fins rather than any other number because such fore-and-aft projections were best suited for balancing and steering purposes.

Returning to the walk of Insects, it appears that though the three members of each set are placed on the ground together they are not lifted at the same time. Cockroaches, house-flies, and certain beetles raise the hind-leg last, while blow-flies raise it first. We know that in human walking the arms move diagonally, each with the leg of the opposite side. And it is curious to notice that in cockroaches and earwigs the antennæ, and also the sensitive feelers of the second jaws, move diagonally with the legs. The successive limbs of these and other Insects are: *antennæ,* first jaws (mandibles), *second jaws* (first maxillæ). third jaws (second maxillæ), *fore-legs,* mid-legs, *hind-legs.* The first and third jaws do not possess parts which can swing with the legs. In diagonal movements alternate appendages on the same side must move together, and this is the case, for either side, with the appendages of which the names have been placed in italics, and which alternate.

Some Insects have become quadrupeds so far as walking is concerned, as the result of modifications which have affected the fore-legs. In a Praying Mantis, for example, these limbs are adapted for seizing prey (see vol. ii, p. 117), while in a number of Butterflies the same limbs are of small size and are not used in locomotion.

Spiders, Scorpions, &c. (*Arachnida*) as Walkers.—The walking of creatures of this kind is usually more complicated than that of Insects, for there are four pairs of walking-legs instead of three. All of them progress on the tips of the limbs.

In *Spiders* (Araneidæ) the legs are moved on the same diagonal principle as in Insects, but there are here, of course, two sets of *four*, *i.e.* right 1st, right 3rd, left 2nd, left 4th, and left 1st, left 3rd, right 2nd, right 4th. The four legs of a set do not all move at precisely the same time, but successively, either from before backwards, as in a Tarantula, or from behind forwards, as in a House-Spider. After all the legs of one set have executed their movements there is a pause before the legs of the other set begin to move (fig. 714).

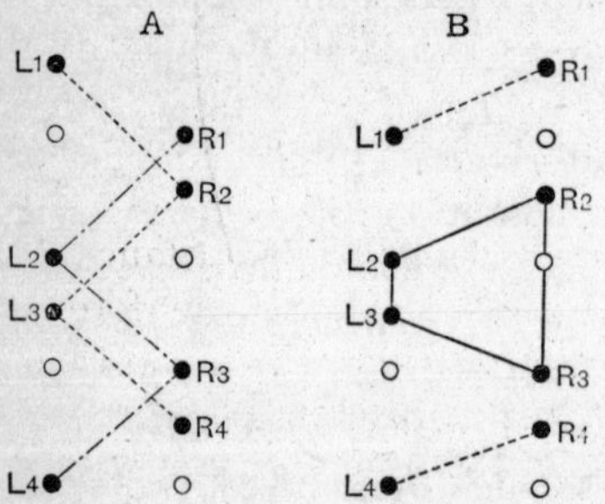

Fig. 714.—Diagram Plans of Phases in Walk of a Spider (A) and a Scorpion (B)

L1, L2, L3, L4, First, second, third, and fourth legs of left side; R1, R2, R3, R4, first, second, third, and fourth legs of right side. In A the legs which work together are connected by dotted lines; L1, R2, L3, and R4 have successively stepped forwards from positions indicated by unshaded circles. In B the legs which keep step are connected by dotted lines; R1 and R4 have just moved forwards from positions indicated by unshaded circles. The legs forming central supporting tripod are connected by an unbroken line; of these R2 and L3 have just stepped forwards from positions indicated by unshaded circles.

Peculiarities in gait are exhibited by some of those Spiders which hunt down their prey instead of constructing webs. The little Crab-Spiders (*Thomisidæ*), for instance, resemble their namesakes not only in shape but in walk, for they move obliquely forwards instead of directly to the front. In this curious kind of progression the legs of the side which goes first appear to pull the body, while those of the other side push it forwards.

Some of the Jumping Spiders (*Attidæ*) live in the company of ants, which they somewhat resemble in appearance. It is said that they make this resemblance more striking by holding up their first pair of legs to represent the feelers of their associates, walking on the remaining six legs, which are presumably moved in much the same way as those of Insects. This extraordinary sort of mimicry is not supposed, of course, to be the result of conscious intelligence.

Scorpions (Scorpionidæ) move in a somewhat differen fashion, which can best be understood by supposing four men walking behind one another in the following way:—The first and last men keep step, while the second and third keep step neither with one another nor with the first and last, but walk in such a way that their right and left feet are alternately close together. And further, the paces of these two men come between the left and right paces of the others. Supposing a halt to be called when all the men have completed a pace, then if the 1st and 4th men have their left feet advanced, the right feet of the 2nd and 3rd men will be close together, and their left feet far apart. But if, at the moment of halting, the right feet of the 1st and 4th men are advanced, the left feet of the 2nd and 3rd men will be close together and their right feet far apart (fig. 714). Applying this to a Scorpion, and considering for a moment only the 1st and 4th pairs of legs, these keep step, as in the amble of a horse (see p. 144). And it is really these limbs that are of most importance in walking, for the 1st pair pull and the 4th pair push, as do the fore- and hind-legs of an Insect. We have seen that the mid-legs of an Insect act as supports mainly (see p. 166), and this is also the case with the 2nd and 3rd legs of a Scorpion, which act like a progressing tripod, of which the apex (formed by two feet) is alternately right and left.

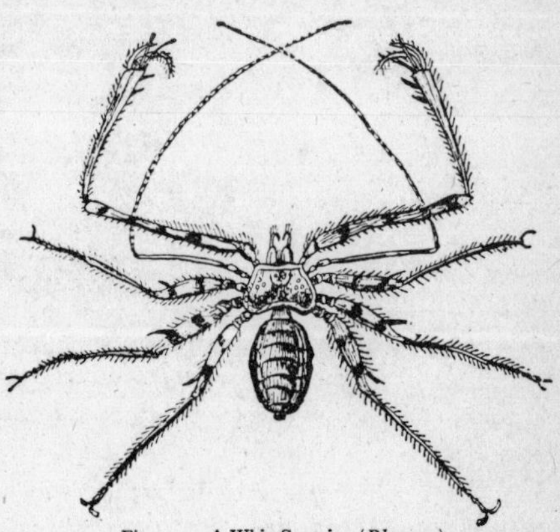

Fig. 715.—A Whip-Scorpion (*Phrynus*)
The first pair of legs are modified into slender feelers, which take no part in walking.

The Whip-Scorpions (Pedipalpi) and *False Spiders* (Solpugidæ), though possessing the usual eight legs characteristic of their class, agree with the insects in the manner of their walking, which is effected by the last three pairs only of these members, for the first pair are employed as feelers, and may be modified in shape for the purpose (fig. 715).

Crustaceans (*Crustacea*) as Walkers.—It appears that a Lobster (*Homarus vulgaris*) walks in the same way as a Scorpion, while a Common Prawn (*Palæmon serratus*) commonly uses only six legs for the purpose, and moves them like an Insect. These and the other Crustaceans walk on the tips of the legs, like Scorpions.

Since among the Higher Crustaceans it is the Crabs which have given themselves up most thoroughly to walking as opposed to swimming, and which have also been most successful in converting themselves in some cases into land-animals, we naturally turn to this group for instances of expert progression on firm

Fig. 716.—Cocoa-Nut Crab (*Birgus latro*)

The last pair of legs are small and take no part in walking.

surfaces. Average Crabs, however, would appear to be distinguished rather by the peculiar nature of their walking than by speed, though some of the ordinary shore forms are able to get along at a good rate. The peculiarity consists in the obliquely forward nature of the gait, and, as in the Crab-Spiders (see p. 168), the legs turned towards the direction of movement for the time being would appear to exert a pulling action, while the others shove the body along. The double tracks produced by this kind of walk constitute one of the most curious objects of interest to be seen on the sea-shore.

As might be expected, the Land-Crabs (*Gecarcinidæ*) are able to progress very rapidly, and the members of a closely-allied family (*Ocypodidæ*) are in most cases so noted for fleetness that they are commonly known as the Swift-Footed Sand-Crabs. Stebbing (in *A History of Crustacea*) speaks of them as follows:—"As the name *swift-of-foot* implies, these Crustacea are especially noted for their rapidity of movement. They are just the opposite of some of the strong-armed, thick-shelled, slow-moving Cancridæ [of which the common Edible Crab, *Cancer pagurus*, is a type]. On wind-swept stretches of sandy beach, and coloured like the sand, they sometimes seem rather to be borne on the wings of the wind than to run. . . .

Fig. 717.—Demon-Faced Crab (*Dorippe Japonicus*), much reduced
Note the small size of the last two pairs of legs

Krauss observed in South Africa the species *Ocypode ceratophthalmus* and others, and he says that while they are busy hunting, every now and then they look carefully round, raising their stalked-eyes upright, and standing on tiptoe. At the slightest movement towards them they run with uncommon rapidity to the nearest hole, or, if the danger is too close, press themselves flat on the sand, till an attempt is made to seize them, and then off they dart. In running, they carry their bodies high, doubling and dodging with such speed and cunning, that it is a difficult matter to lay hold of them."

Some of the Crabs and Hermit-Crabs exhibit a reduction in the number of effective walking-legs. In the Cocoa-Nut Crab (*Birgus latro*, fig. 716) of the Cocos-Keeling Islands, for example, we find that the last pair of these members are so small and feeble that the animal has to walk insect-fashion. But reduction may go even further than this, as strikingly exemplified by the Buffoon Crab (*Dorippe facchino*) of Hong-Kong and the Mediterranean coast, and its ally the Demon-Faced Crab (*D. Japonicus*, fig. 717), rapidly-moving forms which appear to have practically become quadrupeds in the interests of effective locomotion. For in them the two first pairs of legs are very long and strong, while the others are not only small, but attached to the body so high up that they are useless for walking purposes.

CHAPTER XLVII

MUSCULAR LOCOMOTION OF ANIMALS—LEAPING AND HOPPING

We have seen that in the different varieties of Walking the body is never entirely off the ground, while in the various modes of Running it is projected into the air for a short time at regular intervals. From this we naturally pass to Leaping or Jumping, where such projection is much more marked, and a curve drawn to represent the successive positions of any part of the body, say the head, would present a series of sharp convexities and concavities, the crests of the former corresponding to the maximum heights reached above the ground, and the lowest part of the concavities corresponding to the moments when the body actually rests upon the ground. Such a curve for an animal like a kangaroo would differ very greatly from the gentle undulation expressing the vertical movements which take place during walking (see p. 162), while a running curve would be of intermediate character.

It will be convenient to consider here not only that kind of Leaping which is employed for regular onward progression, but also springing movements of more irregular and occasional kind, some of which may be directed to a special object, such as the clearing of an obstacle in the case of a horse, or the seizing of prey by a lion, while other leaps again may be of somewhat aimless character, such as those often performed by the little crustaceans known as sand-hoppers.

But whatever purpose leaping may serve in a particular instance, or however different it may appear to be in diverse animals, the principle of the movement is always the same. Before a leap is taken, the part by which it is effected is bent, and then by a sudden straightening a push of such vigorous nature is given against the underlying surface that the animal is hurled, as it were, into the air, or it may be water. This alternate bending and straightening may take place in the body itself, in some of the limbs, or in structures of special kind, for some animals devoid of limbs in the ordinary sense may nevertheless possess springing organs. We will first consider typical cases of Backboneless Animals (*Invertebrata*) endowed with leaping powers, and then discuss some of the Backboned animals (*Vertebrata*) which best illustrate the same kind of movement.

BACKBONELESS ANIMALS (INVERTEBRATA) AS LEAPERS

We are here chiefly concerned with some of the Jointed-Limbed Invertebrates (*Arthropoda*) and a small number of Molluscs (*Mollusca*).

JOINTED-LIMBED INVERTEBRATES (*Arthropoda*) AS LEAPERS. Springing powers being related to a firm underlying surface, it is naturally among thoroughly terrestrial groups that we should expect to find them best developed. Insects constitute such a group, and some members of the class can leap higher and further in proportion to their size than any other animals. But there are also a few shore-dwelling Crustaceans and certain spiders which are more or less expert in this sort of movement, and these it will be convenient to consider first.

CRUSTACEANS (*Crustacea*) AS LEAPERS.—Springing powers of no mean order are possessed by some of the Amphipods, a division of Sessile-eyed Crustaceans (Arthrostraca), which includes *Sand-Hoppers* and their allies. Taking as an example the Common Sand-Hopper (*Talitrus locusta*, fig. 718), which literally swarms between tide-marks on many parts of our coast, the body will be seen to have a somewhat shrimp-like appearance, but to be greatly flattened from side to side. The numerous distinct rings of which it is composed give an extreme flexibility, and the hinder region can be bent sharply round so that the tail is brought into contact with the under surface. If now the animal suddenly and vigorously straightens itself it will be hurled into the air to a considerable height. On warm summer days the writer has often seen

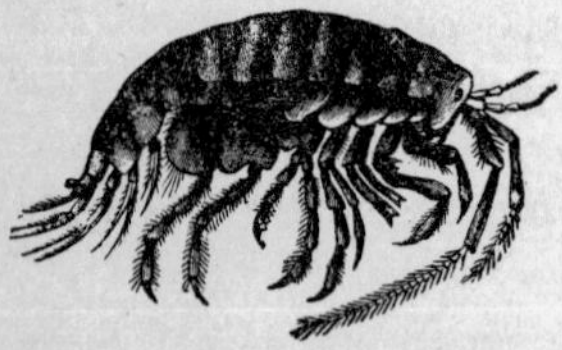

Fig. 718.—Common Sand-Hopper (*Talitrus locusta*), enlarged

a sort of haze quivering above the surface of sandy shores, an appearance caused by tens of thousands of these little creatures leaping about in all directions. To say that a Sand-Hopper half an inch long can spring to the height of 6 inches, *i.e.* twelve times the length of its body, is but to give a moderate estimate of the facts. We should consider it somewhat astonishing if a man 6 feet high could spring 72 feet into the air as an every-day proceeding.

Some of the *Crabs* are able to spring with facility, by means of first bending and then suddenly straightening their legs. Hickson (in *A Naturalist in Celebes*) thus describes a case of the sort:—"The rocks which lie below high-water mark are covered with a fine layer of acorn-shells. Upon them may be seen a number of brilliant little green-and-yellow crabs and jumping fishes. The crabs are called by naturalists *Grapsus varius*. They are curiously marked with dark olive-green stripes alternating with bright-yellow stripes and spots, and they are capable of making the most extraordinary leaps and bounds I have ever seen in crab-life. They would spring from rock to rock with the greatest skill and precision, and when a broad expanse of bare rock allowed it they would scamper along at such a rate that I found it impossible to catch them. Not being endowed with the wisdom of the crab, I wondered why, to escape from such an enemy as they evidently took me for, they did not immediately plunge into the water and hide beneath the rocks. Perhaps they have found that it is safer to trust to their powers of flight from rock to rock, which were, it is true, good enough for such an enemy as I was, than, by plunging in the waters, to run the risk of falling victims to larger crabs and other foes that lurk in the rocky pools."

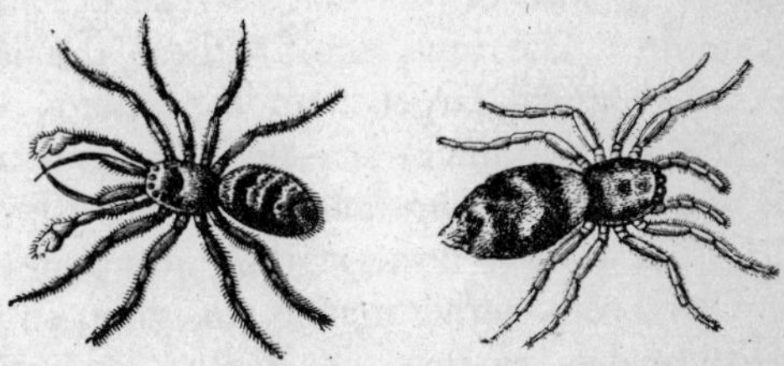

Fig. 719.—Jumping Spiders (*Salticus scenicus*), enlarged

SPIDERS (*Arachnida*) AS LEAPERS (fig. 719).—The Jumping-Spiders (*Attidæ*) are small forms which, instead of snaring prey by constructing webs, patiently stalk their quarry, terminating the proceeding by a sudden spring which usually attains the desired end. No doubt this leap is effected in the characteristic manner, by bending the legs first and then suddenly straightening them, but exact details have yet to be learned.

INSECTS (*Insecta*) AS LEAPERS.—A considerable number of springing Insects are known, belonging to various groups. The most primitive of these are undoubtedly the little wingless creatures known as *Spring-Tails* (Collembola, fig. 720), which are found in holes and corners in almost all parts of the world. They possess a curious springing organ, shaped like a two-pronged fork, which is attached to the tip of the tail, and when not in use is folded up under the body, there being in some cases a sort of "catch" for holding the prongs close to the body, by which a premature leap is prevented. When, mainly as the result of elasticity, the spring straightens out, the Insect is somewhat violently thrown into the air, an act which appears to be more of the nature of a protective measure than a regular means of progression. A well-known species, abundant on the ice in Alpine regions, is popularly known as the Glacier-"Flea" (*Desoria glacialis*) on account of its springing propensities.

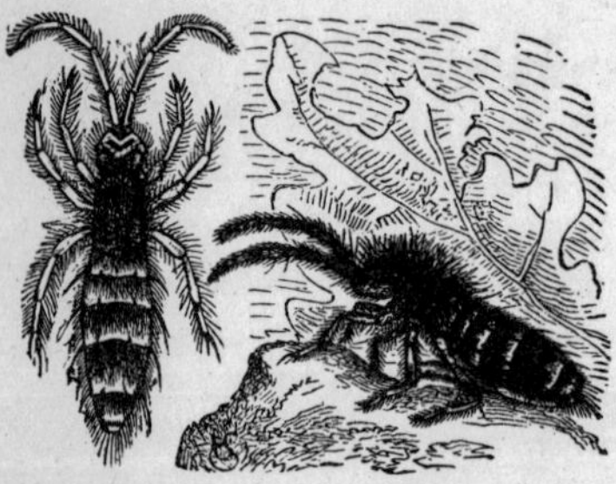

Fig. 720.—Spring-Tails (*Podura villosa*), enlarged

Among the *Straight-winged Insects* (*Orthoptera*) considerable leaping powers are possessed by Locusts, Grasshoppers, Crickets, and their allies. The Green Grasshopper (*Locusta viridissima*, fig. 721), one of our native insects, may be taken as a good example. The hind-legs are here the leaping organs, and they are very much larger than the others, while the region known as the thigh (femur) is especially stout and muscular. We have seen that in running animals the hind-limbs are better developed than the others, because their position enables them by sudden and vigorous straightening to give sufficiently powerful backward pushes against the ground to project the animal into the air (see p. 146). For effective leaping there has been an exaggeration of the same kind of action, and it is therefore but natural that the hind-limbs of so accomplished a leaper as a Grasshopper should have attained extraordinary size and strength. It is difficult to catch creatures of this sort by straightforward chasing, and it is very easy to lose sight of them among the vegetation they inhabit, with which they closely harmonize as to colour.

Beetles (*Coleoptera*) furnish a number of instances of leaping or springing forms. This is the case with the little *Click-Beetles*,

Fig. 721.—Green Grasshoppers (*Locusta viridissima*)

or *Skip-Jacks* (*Elateridæ*, fig. 722), of which many kinds are found in cultivated fields, their larvæ being the notorious "wire-worms". Most of these beetles possess a curious springing apparatus, by which they are able to right themselves if they happen to fall upon their backs. The leg-bearing region of the body (thorax) consists, as in Insects generally, of three rings or segments, upon the under side of which the springing organ is situated. It consists of a spine projecting back from the first segment and fitting into a groove in the second segment. If now the Click-Beetle finds itself upon its back, it draws in the legs and folds the antennæ against the sides, next arching the body so as to pull the spine as far out of the groove as possible (fig. 723). By a vigorous effort the spine is then driven forcibly into the groove, so that the insect's back comes into sudden and violent

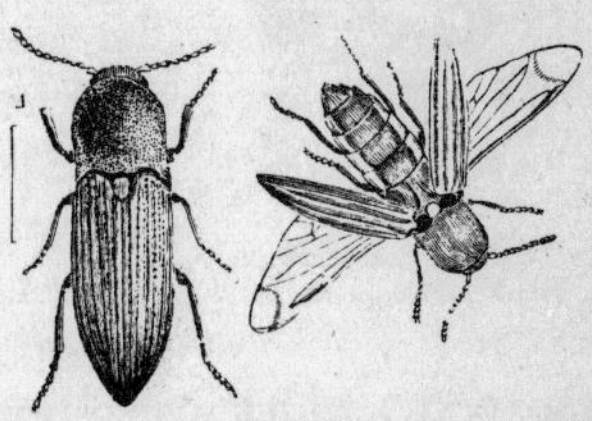

Fig. 722.—Click-Beetles or Skip-Jacks. Actual size indicated by the vertical line on the left.

contact with the underlying surface. The result is a sort of spring which hurls the beetle into the air, when, after describing one or more summersaults, it alights safely on its feet.

Fig. 723.—Click-Beetle lying on its back and about to spring. *a*, Head; *b c d*, rings of thorax; *e*, abdomen. The leaping-spine is shown at *b*. (Enlarged.)

The *Flea-Beetles* (*Halticidæ*) are also agricultural pests, the leaping powers of which are indicated by their name. A common species is the Turnip Flea-Beetle (*Haltica nemorum*, fig. 724), and we find here, but in lesser degree, the same kind of arrangement as in a Grasshopper. That is to say, the hind-legs are the best developed, but they are characterized by strength rather than length.

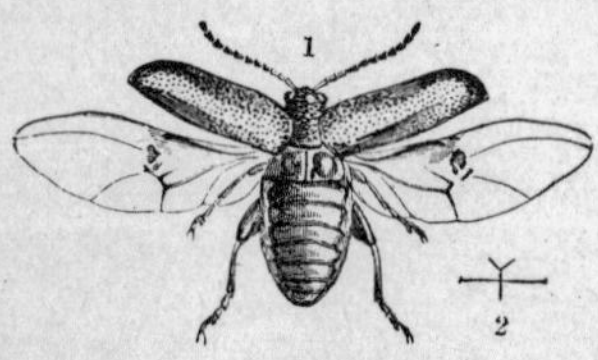

Fig. 724.—1, Turnip Flea-Beetle (*Haltica nemorum*), enlarged; 2, actual size of the same.

The *Fleas* (*Pulicidæ*), which are commonly regarded as aberrant wingless members of the order of Two-winged Flies (*Diptera*), are, of course, notable leapers. It has indeed been asserted that for a man to jump right over St. Paul's Cathedral would be a performance about equivalent to the saltatory feats of the Common Flea (*Pulex irritans*), taking into account the relative size of the two gymnasts. The hind-legs of a Flea are well-developed in relation to the characteristic mode of progression (fig. 725).

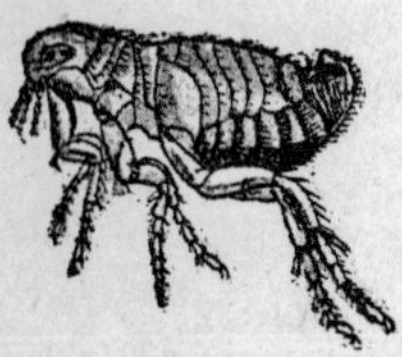

Fig. 725.—Common Flea (*Pulex irritans*), enlarged

Before leaving the two-winged flies it may be noted that the limbless maggots, which represent their early stages of life, are often able to spring with facility, of which a well-known example is afforded by the larvæ of the Cheese-Fly (*Piophilus casei*). The movement is brought about by sudden straightening of the body, which has previously been bent into a sharp curve.

Of insects belonging to the order of *Bugs* (*Hemiptera*), those included in the *Froghopper Family* (*Cercopidæ*) are noted for their leaping powers, in accordance with which the hind-legs are large and muscular. The frothy masses familiarly known as "cuckoo-spits" are the abodes of the larvæ of certain common species of these small insects.

Annandale has recently discovered a very remarkable leaping-mechanism in some of the widely-distributed tree-bugs known as Lantern-Flies, of which the Chinese Lantern-Fly (*Hotinus candelabrius*) (fig. 726) is a common species. In these insects the front of the head is drawn out into a "nose" of portentous length, which was formerly supposed to be luminous. Hence the popular name, which may perhaps turn out to be justifiable for some species. The nose is hollow and very elastic, and there is a transverse joint running across the middle of it, permitting its end half to be bent up. Supposing a Lantern-Fly which has

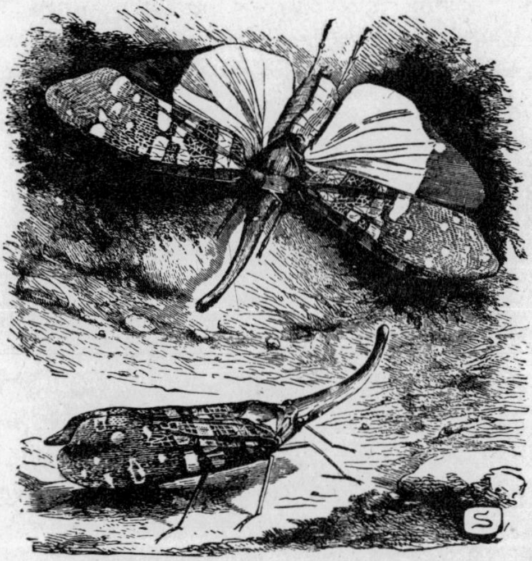

Fig. 726.—Chinese Lantern-Fly (*Hotinus candelabrius*).

settled on a branch suddenly wishes to leave its perch, the following appears to be the method adopted. The head is rapidly pressed down against the branch so as to bend up the nose. This organ then straightens itself again by elasticity, which results in a vigorous push against the underlying surface. As the legs give a "shove off" at the same time, the insect is launched into the air with considerable force. Annandale thus describes this peculiar kind of leaping as observed in a Malay species of Lantern-Fly:—". . . I noticed a specimen of *Hotinus spinolæ* seated on the trunk of a Durian tree in the village, and incautiously attempted to catch it in my hand. The insect remained almost still, merely drawing in its legs towards its body and pressing the claws firmly against the bark, until I had almost touched it. Then it lowered its head with very great rapidity, flew up into the air without spreading its wings, and alighted upon the roof of a house about six feet beyond the tree and considerably higher than the position on the trunk whence it had started." It is pretty clear that we have here a device for furthering escape from enemies.

MOLLUSCS (MOLLUSCA) AS LEAPERS.—Springing powers are possessed by some of the Bivalves and also by certain kinds of Snail, though such forms are in a small minority, as most Molluscs either swim, or creep, or burrow.

Bivalve Molluscs (*Lamellibranchia*) *as Leapers.*—Perhaps the most typical springing bivalves are the members of the *Cockle Family* (*Cardiidæ*), such as the Common Cockle (*Cardium edule*) and its allies. In these creatures the muscular foot is long,

Fig. 727.—Cockle (*Cardium*). The long bent foot is protruded

narrow, and sharply bent in a knee-like fashion (fig. 727). It is this foot which constitutes the springing organ, and it acts on the principle of which so many examples have already been given. That is to say, it is suddenly and vigorously straightened, pushing back with such force against the underlying sand that the body is thereby projected obliquely upwards and forwards.

Snails (*Gastropoda*) *as Leapers.*—In the *Wing-Shells* (*Strombidæ*, fig. 728) the hinder part of the foot is narrow and bent, enabling this region of the body to be used for springing purposes, after the fashion of Cockles.

Some of the *Land Snails* are also able to spring on occasion, the object being escape from enemies (see vol. ii, p. 373). Our little native Glass Snail (*Vitrina pellucida*), for instance, if alarmed when crawling exposed to view on a stone or the like, is able to suddenly bring down the hinder part of its foot on the underlying surface with such force as to jerk the animal on to the ground, where it has a chance of falling into some corner or crevice hiding it from view. A much more remarkable case has been described by Semper (in *Animal Life*) of certain small Philippine land-snails (species of *Helicarion*), which, when attacked or frightened, actually throw off this "tail" after it has served the purpose of jerking them on to the ground. This

Fig. 728.—Wing-Shell (*Strombus*)
a, Proboscis; *b*, notch in mouth of shell; *cc*, tentacles with eyes; *d*, front part of foot; *e*, sharply bent hind part of foot bearing a shelly plate (operculum).

is Semper's account:—"The numerous species . . . live on trees in damp woods, often in great multitudes; they are very active, and creep about with considerable rapidity upon the twigs and leaves of the trees. Every species that I personally examined possessed the singular property, which many lizards have—particularly the Geckoes,—of shedding their tail when they are seized somewhat roughly, at a little way behind the shell. This they do by whisking the tail up and down with extraordinary rapidity, almost convulsively, till it drops off; if the creature is held by the tail, it immediately falls to the ground, where it easily hides among the leaves. If it is laid flat on the hand, the rapid wagging movement is strong enough to raise the body with a spring into the air, so that it falls over on the ground. These snails at first constantly escaped me and my collectors in this way, and not unfrequently we had nothing but the tail left in our hand."

BACKBONED ANIMALS (VERTEBRATA) AS LEAPERS

Under this heading we shall have to successively consider various kinds of Leaping, Springing, and Hopping, as found among Fishes, Amphibians, Reptiles, Birds, and Mammals.

FISHES (PISCES) AS LEAPERS OR SPRINGERS.—It is a matter of familiar observation that many Fishes are able to leap or "rise" out of the water to a greater or less height, one of the most notable instances being that of the Salmon (*Salmo salar*). As everyone knows, this fish annually ascends some river or other for the purpose of spawning, and during this progress is able to spring right over weirs or falls which may be as much as 10 feet high. The leap is mainly effected by the powerful tail, which is brought down on the water with a tremendous smack that sends the salmon flying into the air. During this act the strongly-curved body is straightened out, and this, no doubt, increases the power of the leap.

The shore-haunting Mud-Skippers (see vol. ii, p. 87) of the Indian Ocean are able to get along with considerable rapidity by means of a succession of short leaps, partly effected, it would seem, by the alternate bending and straightening of the body, but chiefly by means of the pectoral fins, which are unusually muscular and well-developed. The leaps are sufficiently powerful to hurl the body several inches into the air.

Fig. 729.—Grass-Frog (*Rana temporaria*)

AMPHIBIANS (AMPHIBIA) AS LEAPERS.—The Tailless Amphibians (Anura), *i.e.* Frogs, Toads, and their allies, are pre-eminent as leapers, and their structure is greatly specialized in adaptation to this habit. Taking as a common example the Grass-Frog (*Rana temporaria*, fig. 729), we notice that the short, compact body is entirely devoid of tail, while the hind-limbs are of relatively enormous length and very muscular. It is these limbs which are the agents of leaping. When the animal is resting in a natural posture, as shown in the figure, their successive parts are folded upon each other, the knee being directed outwards and forwards, while the ankle points to the back. It is clear that a sudden straightening out must propel the small, compact body forwards with great force, and, since the backward push is given obliquely downwards, the animal rises to a considerable height into the air. Examination of the skeleton (fig. 730) shows how well it is adapted to leaping. The two long hip-girdles are united together at the back, thus bringing the hip-joints close together, so that when the hind limbs are straightened at the same time there is no waste of force in side-pushes. The tips of the girdles are attached fairly far forwards, to the last distinct vertebra (sacrum) of the backbone, at points where the forward pushes will have most effect. In the framework of the free parts of the limbs we see that in the interest of firmness the two bones of the lower leg (tibia and fibula) have completely fused together, while the foot is of great relative length. The presence of a lot of little bones or cartilages in the ankle-region (as in a Newt) would greatly militate against firmness, and to obviate this most of these elements have been either greatly reduced or suppressed altogether, except two, and these are long and strong, besides which they are firmly united together at both ends.

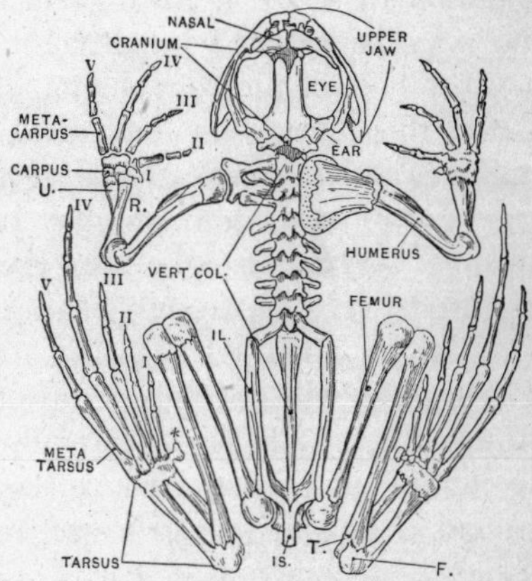

Fig. 730.—Skeleton of Frog

I–V, Digits; * extra digit (calcar) of foot; R, radius; U, Ulna; IL and IS, parts of hip-girdles; T, tibia; F, fibula; VERT.COL., vertebral column (backbone).

The Frog's leaping powers are useful not merely as a means of progression and for escape from enemies, but also in the capture of prey. Gadow (in *The Cambridge Natural History*) gives the following very interesting account of the habits of this animal, the extracts being selected with reference to the uses of its leaping powers:—"The Grass-Frog, when pursued, rarely takes to the water for safety. It trusts to flight, first by a few long and fast jumps, and then to concealment by squatting down between grass, under leaves; it rarely creeps into a hole, even if there be one near. The jumps soon become shorter and shorter after a few dozen repetitions. . . . The food, which consists chiefly of insects, snails, and worms, must be moving to excite interest; then the Frog, whose favourite position is half-squatting, half-supported by the arms, erects itself, and, facing the insect, turns round upon its haunches, adjusts its position anew by a shifting of the legs, and betrays its mental agitation by a few rapid movements of the throat. All this time the prey is watched intently till it moves; then there follows a jump, a flap of the tongue, and the insect is seen no more. As a rule these frogs do not crawl, they jump or hop even whilst stalking, and this takes place at any time of the day; in fact they are very diurnal, although they become more active towards the evening. When caught they are at first very wild, and, like all true frogs, very impetuous, committing acts of astonishing stupidity, without any apparent sense or appreciation of distance or height. The captive will not only jump off the table—whilst a toad stops at the edge and looks carefully down,—but without hesitation he jumps out of the window, regardless of the height above the ground. This is due to sheer fright; he loses his head. When at large in his native surroundings, nothing will induce him, although hotly pursued, to commit suicide by jumping down a precipice. But all this wildness calms down wonderfully soon. The captive no longer dashes his head against the glass; he does not struggle or twist when taken up; on the contrary, he makes himself at home, watches your coming with intense expectation, and without hesitation accepts the proffered meal-worm, maggot, butterfly, or earthworm; in short, he shows what a jolly and intelligent fellow he really is."

Reptiles (Reptilia) as Leapers.—Among existing forms there are no very interesting arrangements for effecting leaping, if we except the curious springs that some of the poisonous Snakes (*Ophidia*) appear to be able to make when seizing prey or defending themselves at close quarters. Under such circumstances the body can be coiled up and then suddenly extended, so that the snake is projected into the air.

Many Lizards (*Lacertilia*) are also able to leap with considerable facility, the hind-limbs being used for the purpose in the usual way, and the tail giving also some assistance by way of steadying the body, if it does not actually help in propulsion.

Birds (Aves) as Leapers.—There is no doubt that Birds have sprung from a reptilian stock, though we unfortunately know too little to feel sure of the stages by which the evolution has taken place. It is, however, not improbable that the immediate reptilian ancestors were springing or hopping forms, in which the hind-limbs were well-developed, and served as the chief means of progression. If this be so, the springing or hopping gait which is characteristic of many birds must be regarded as the primitive method of locomotion for members of the class, while walking was a later acquisition. A view of this kind harmonizes with the very specialized nature of the legs of Birds.

Fig. 731.—Two Hopping Birds
1, Chiffchaff (*Phylloscopus rufus*); 2, Wheatear (*Saxicola œnanthe*).

The word "hopping", as applied to human beings, means progression by a series of leaps on one foot, but in the case of Birds it signifies locomotion by means of a succession of relatively short jumps taken from both feet together. Hopping in this sense is practised by a large number of familiar forms, among which are included Thrushes, Blackbirds, Wheatears (fig. 731), Hedge-Accentors (Hedge-"Sparrows"), Robin Redbreasts, and Wrens. By measuring snow-tracks, R. Kearton estimated that the average hop of a Blackbird was 9 inches, as compared with 6½ inches for the average stride of a Rook. Although this kind of movement is very common among small birds that hunt for food upon the ground, many of them do not hop, but run, as is the case with Wagtails. Indeed walking and running are characteristic of those forms which have become best adapted to life on the ground, and fly comparatively little or not at all. Rails and Ostriches will serve as examples of this. Some birds, *e.g.* Rooks, both hop and walk.

For progress over very uneven surfaces hopping is particularly well suited, and the small Crested Penguins (species of *Eudyptes*), which when on land constantly have to make their way over rough boulders, are called "Rock-Hoppers" on account of their expertness in this direction.

It may further be observed that when birds take to wing from the ground they give a preliminary jump, which launches them fairly into the air. So important is this leaping start that the feeble-legged Swifts are often believed to be unable to rise from the ground at all. Competent observers deny the truth of this, though birds with short legs and very long wings must be at some disadvantage in the matter. Aflalo (in *Natural History of the British Isles*), speaking of our native Swift (*Cypselus apus*), says:—"It is not often seen to alight, though I have caught a few, a very few, in the act of dusting themselves in Kentish lanes, from which, in spite of the length of their wings, they can rise without quite so much difficulty as some chroniclers would have us imagine".

Mammals (Mammalia) as Leapers.—We have had occasion to note that the best runners in this class are distinguished by marked development of the hind-limbs as compared with the fore- (see p. 141), the reason being that the former do most of the work. Since leaping involves an even more vigorous use of the hind-limbs, we should expect to find the fleeter Mammals also well off as regards powers of leaping. This is usually the case, and some of the best examples are furnished by rock-dwelling members of the family of Hoofed Mammals (*Ungulata*), such as wild Sheep and Goats, Chamois, Ibexes, and the like. Creatures of this kind are able to spring from crag to crag in a very astonishing way, as hunters have reason to know. Brehm (in *From North Pole to Equator*) thus describes the movements of the large Archar Sheep (*Ovis Argali*, fig. 732) of Central Asia:—"Among the rocks they move, whether going upwards or downwards, with surprising ease, agility, and confidence. Without any apparent strain, without any trace of hurry, they clamber up and down almost vertical paths, leap wide chasms, and pass from the heights to the valley almost as if they were birds and could fly." The Rocky Mountain Sheep, or Bighorn (*Ovis montana*), is also capable of making extraordinary leaps, and will spring over a sheer precipice 10 to 15 feet deep without hesitation, always provided there is suitable foothold at the bottom, and for this a very little serves.

Many of the Hoofed Mammals specialized for swift running on level surfaces are also expert leapers, none more so than the Antelopes. The Springbok (*Gazella euchore*) is quite remarkable

Fig. 732.—Archar Sheep (*Ovis Argali*)

for its leaping powers, to which the popular name is an allusion. When suddenly alarmed it springs high in the air, assuming attitudes which are far from graceful, possibly as the result of intense muscular action. But indeed it may be said generally that many of the positions of swift animals in movement, as revealed by the camera, are not nearly so pleasing as the conventional postures by which they are rendered in some pictures, some of which render with sufficient accuracy the impression made upon the eye. The remark about the Springbok has reference to the general effect as thus given. Millais, who has studied this animal in its native wilds, thus describes its movements (in *A Breath from the Veldt*):—"I camped out on the

Karroo for a fortnight for this express purpose [*i.e.* study of the movements], where, with the aid of a powerful telescope, I could observe them from my tent door at all hours of the day. The peculiarity which struck me most was the stiff manner in which the legs are held in all cases of extreme movement. It is only when the buck is walking very slowly, and feeding as he goes along, that the joints seem to be relaxed, all his quicker and more energetic motions being performed from the shoulders and thighs in a constrained and 'collected' manner. I would especially call the attention of naturalists to this peculiarity on the part of the Springbuck and nearly all the South African antelopes I have observed. I do not consider that antelopes under *movement* have ever been correctly treated by any artist. Antelopes on the move are generally given the graceful movements of deer, whereas, with few exceptions, all their paces are performed with a certain stiffness and contraction of the limbs that are the reverse of graceful."

Of smaller animals which are fleet of foot, and at the same time endowed with considerable springing powers, the Hare (*Lepus timidus*) and its kind deserve mention among Gnawing Mammals (*Rodentia*). Here again we find that the hind-limbs are of disproportionate length and strength.

So far we have considered leaping as exhibited by Mammals whose powers of locomotion are mainly used in retreat from enemies, but among the cat-like species of Flesh-eating Mammals (*Carnivora*) springing is an important factor in securing prey (see p. 10). Such an animal first assumes a crouching attitude, in which the sections of the hind-limbs are strongly bent upon one another. By a sudden and powerful muscular effort these limbs are then extended, pushing back with such force against the ground that the animal is propelled forward like an arrow from a bow. Further details are here unnecessary.

We now have to deal with certain Pouched Mammals (*Marsupialia*) in which leaping constitutes the regular mode of progression, and which are greatly modified in structure in correspondence with this. Among such forms the Kangaroo presents a very typical case. This animal is practically a biped as regards progression, but the long, muscular tail is of great importance by way of balancing and steadying the body. It also helps to support its owner when in a resting attitude, supplementing the

Fig. 733.—Red Kangaroo (*Macropus rufus*) in resting attitude. From an instantaneous photograph

under surfaces of the long feet, which are provided with horny thickenings of corresponding length. This attitude is shown in fig. 733, which is taken from an instantaneous photograph of the Red Kangaroo (*Macropus rufus*). The striking disproportion between fore- and hind-limbs is also well seen in the same figure. The thigh, which is not particularly long, is largely enclosed within the boundaries of the trunk, as in other cases elsewhere described (see p. 134), but the lower leg is of quite extraordinary length, and the foot is also considerably elongated. As will be gathered from fig. 734, in which the skeleton is represented, a reduction of digits has taken place, in the interests of firmness. The great toe has gone altogether, while the second and third digits are extremely slender, bound up in a common fold of skin, and of no use in locomotion. On the other hand, the fourth and fifth digits, especially the former, are very large, and their instep-bones very long. There are only three bones belonging to the ankle (tarsus) which are of any size, and these are large and firm, and so connected as to prevent any "giving" in this region.

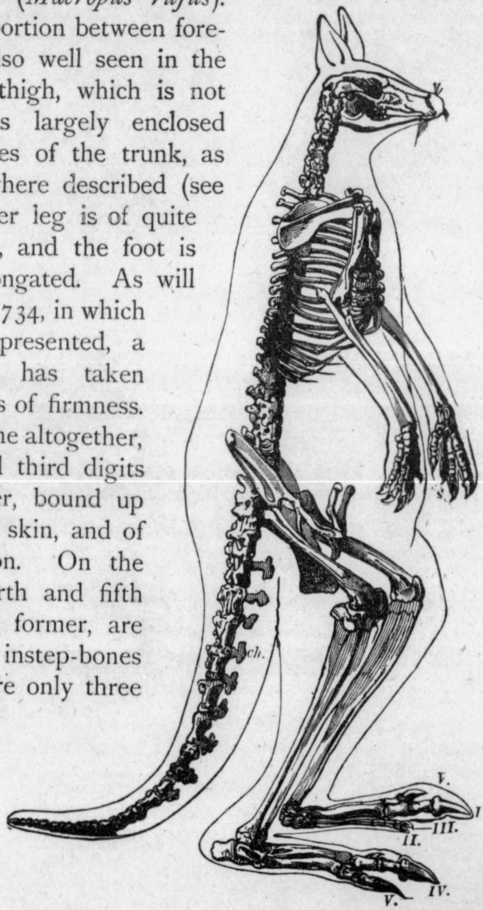

Fig. 734.—Skeleton of Kangaroo. II–V, Digits of foot

Though both bones of the lower leg (tibia and fibula) are present, they are united with sufficient firmness to prevent this being a source of weakness.

The relatively short fore-limbs of the Kangaroo possess the full complement of five digits, and they are capable of considerable lateral movement, as, for example, when employed for purposes of defence. And, as usually where side-action is marked, there is a strong collar-bone stretching from breast-bone to shoulder-blade, and serving as a firm prop on the inner side. The chief use of the fore-limbs, however, is to support the front part of the body when the animal is grazing, the attitude then assumed being extremely ungraceful. We have elsewhere seen (vol. ii, p. 182) that the kangaroo-like animals present a series of cases in which the disproportionate size of the hind-limbs becomes more and more apparent, leading up to the extreme case just described. Just as, in a lesser degree, the Okapi is intermediate between the Giraffe and other ruminants with shorter necks and limbs (see vol. ii, p. 170). The position of a Kangaroo which has just sprung from the ground is shown in fig. 735.

Fig. 735.—Kangaroo at beginning of leap

Kangaroos are not the only Pouched Mammals which are specialized in relation to leaping. The little Australian Bandicoots (*Peramelidæ*) also present us with similar adaptations related to the same habit, though the tail is comparatively short and weak, notwithstanding which it serves the same supporting function as in a Kangaroo. In the majority of these small creatures (species of *Perameles*) the hind-limbs are of similar construction to those of their larger cousins, but the fore-limbs are also much modified, for both thumb and little finger are of insignificant size, while the other three digits are long, and provided with powerful claws. This is related to the habit of digging holes as places of refuge. The Pig-footed Bandicoot (*Chœropus castanotus*, fig. 736) is of special interest, for it is more specialized than its immediate relatives as regards both pairs of extremities. In the hind-limb only one digit (the fourth) is well developed, being long, strong, and provided with an unusually powerful claw. The second and third digits are relatively even smaller than in a Kangaroo, while the fifth or little toe, which is large in that animal, is here greatly reduced. For practical purposes the Pig-footed Bandicoot may be considered a one-toed animal, like a horse, as regards the hind-foot; but it is here the fourth digit which has been retained and enlarged, while in a horse it is the third (see p. 142). The fore-foot is also more specialized than in an ordinary Bandicoot, and is practically only two-toed, for the first and fifth digits have gone altogether, and the fourth is a mere vestige. The presence of two large digits has earned for this animal the nickname "pig-footed", but the two large fingers of a pig are the third and fourth, while here they are the second and third; and a pig also possesses fairly well developed second and fifth fingers. (see p. 149). When leaping, the Bandicoots keep their fore-limbs pressed well against the body.

Fig. 736.—Pig-footed Bandicoot (*Chœropus castanotus*)

One more springing marsupial requires mention here. This is the Pouched-Jerboa (*Antechinomys laniger*) of Queensland and New South Wales. It is mouse-like in appearance, but with long hind-limbs and well-developed tail. Specialization with reference to leaping has not gone nea y so far as in Kangaroos, for reduction of digits has only affected the great toe, which has entirely disappeared.

Gnawing Mammals (*Rodentia*) *as Leapers.*—Some members of the North American family of Pouched Rats (*Geomyidæ*) are leapers, while the springing habit is eminently characteristic of most of the species included in the family of Jumping Mice or Jerboas (*Dipodidæ*), nearly all of which inhabit Asia or Africa, though the group is also represented in South Europe and North America.

As to the Pouched Rats (*Geomyidæ*) it may not be unnecessary to remind the reader that the first part of their name has reference to the possession of a "cheek-pouch" for the storage of food, and this has, of course, nothing to do with the pouch of the Pouched Mammals *par excellence* (*Marsupialia*), which is placed far back on the under surface of the body, and is used as a nursery for the immature young. The Common Kangaroo-Rat or Pocket-Mouse (*Dipodomys Phillipsi*, fig. 737) is a small, somewhat mouse-like animal which lives in the desert regions

Fig. 737.—Common Pocket-Mouse (*Dipodomys Phillipsi*)

to the east of the Rocky Mountain Highland, and it possesses the long tail and disproportionately-developed hind-limbs which we have already seen to be characteristic of Kangaroos and the like. But, being a gnawing Mammal, it is but very distantly related to these latter forms, the similarity in general build being the result of adaptation to the same kind of life. Or, to put it technically, we have a case of "convergence" of character in members of totally distinct groups. Just as thoroughly aquatic animals have acquired the same general shape of body, *i.e.* the shape best adapted to rapid progression through water. The

Kangaroo-Rat is not nearly so specialized as regards its hind-limbs as its Australian namesakes. Only one digit has suffered reduction, the first or great toe.

Jerboas (*Dipodidæ*) and their allies present us with a series of increasing modifications in adaptation to expert leaping. In all members of this series the tail and hind-limbs are relatively well developed, while the fore-limbs usually possess the full number of five digits, and since they are not only used to support the body during feeding, but also for burrowing and carrying food to the mouth, it is not surprising to find that fully-formed collar-bones are present (see p. 158). In the hind-limbs it is to be noticed that one bone of the lower leg, the fibula, is more or less reduced, as in some of the swift-running Mammals (see p. 141), on the principle that one large bone furnishes a better support than two smaller ones, while there is a large projection at the back of the heel-bone (calcaneum), which serves for the attachment of important muscles that straighten the leg in the act of springing. Kangaroos always progress by leaping, but these animals are also able to walk, in much the same way as a human being, except that the completely erect attitude is not assumed.

Perhaps the least specialized form as regards structure is the North American Jumping-Mouse (*Zapus Hudsonianus*), which ranges from the frozen north to Mexico. Five distinct toes are present on the hind-foot, but in the fore-foot the thumb is greatly reduced. Lydekker (in *The Royal Natural History*) quotes the following account of the habits of this animal, as observed by R. Slade:—"The Long-tailed Jumping-Mouse inhabits high land or low land, forest or pasture, cultivated field or swamp, and appears to be equally at home in either, and not numerous in any situation. It possesses a momentary agility second to no other rodent, and a muscular strength of enormous power for so small a creature. When suddenly disturbed it often moves away in a direct line, the first three or four leaps being 8 or 10 feet in length, but these distances rapidly decline to about 4 feet. This is not always the case, however, for it frequently takes an irregular course, and jumps at divers angles for several successive leaps, keeping the same general direction, or changing at will. It can double, and quickly too, if pursued, and by its manœuvres and instantaneous squattings can elude a hawk or an owl, and its spontaneous irregularities enable it to escape being brained by a weasel, or swallowed whole by the common black snake." Since the head and body are only a little over 3 inches in length, it will be seen that the leaps are of very great relative extent.

The Cape Jumping-Hare (*Pedetes Caffer*) is the largest member of its family, being about the size of an ordinary hare, which it somewhat resembles in appearance, except as regards

Fig. 738.—Cape Jumping-Hare (*Pedetes Caffer*)

limbs and tail (fig. 738). The hind-foot has lost the great toe, and the remaining digits, of which the third is best developed, bear thick, blunt nails. The ordinary leaps vary from about 6 to 9 feet, but it is stated that they can be increased on occasion to from 20 to 30 feet.

The remaining members of the family now being considered are generally known as Jerboas, and are particularly characteristic of the steppe and desert regions of Africa and Asia. The less specialized forms of the kind are called Five-toed Jerboas, because the hind-foot possesses the full number of digits, though only the three central ones reach the ground. The instep-bones (metatarsals) of these three toes are closely united, while the corresponding bones of the first and fifth toes have undergone reduction. A typical species is the Siberian Jerboa (*Alactaga decumana*), a creature about the size of a squirrel, which ranges from Siberia into the steppe-region of European Russia (see vol. i, p. 131).

The Three-toed Jerboas are smaller and more specialized animals, which have altogether lost the first and fifth digits of the hind-limb, while the instep-bones of the three central toes are

Fig. 739.—Egyptian Jerboa (*Dipus Mauritanicus*)

fused together into a "cannon-bone", reminding us of the fusion of corresponding elements which takes place in a bird (see p. 126). Cannon-bones formed by fusion of two bones are possessed by ruminants (see p. 149), and in all these various cases greatly increased firmness is gained by the arrangement. The best-known species is the Egyptian Jerboa (*Dipus Mauritanicus*, fig. 739), an essentially desert animal which ranges from Algeria to Persia. Of these little creatures Vogt (in *Mammalia*) thus speaks:—"The Jerboas run like long-legged birds, make enormous leaps, and in doing so draw their fore-feet towards their breast or lay them on their cheeks. . . . The three toes of the hind-feet are protected against the heat of the sand by small bunches of hair. The fine thick fur has the colour of the desert sand. The animal is especially fond of the alfa-covered steppes, lives socially, and digs holes of no great depth, which communicate with one another."

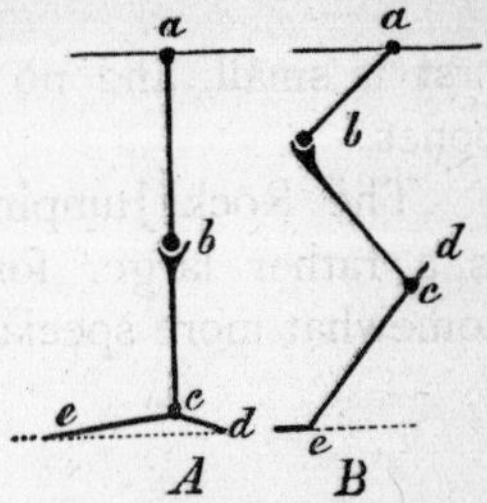

Fig. 740.—Diagram to illustrate relative length and position of regions in hind-limbs of Man (A) and Jerboa (B). *ab*, Thigh; *bc*, lower leg; *ecd*, foot. The knee-joint is at *b* and the ankle-joint at *c*; *d*, heel.

Some of the differences between the leg of a human being and the leg of a Jerboa, as to proportion of parts, and the positions assumed by them in a state of rest, are represented diagrammatically in fig. 740.

Insect-Eating Mammals (Insectivora) as Leapers.—One family of this widely-distributed and primitive order includes specialized leaping forms. These are the Jumping-Shrews (*Macroscelididæ*), native to the plains and deserts of Africa. A well-known South African species is the Cape Jumping-Shrew (*Macroscelides typicus*, fig. 741), often called the "Elephant" Shrew on account of its long, flexible snout. This feature at once distinguishes it from a Jerboa, which it otherwise resembles in general proportions. The long hind-limbs possess the full number of toes, although the

Fig. 741.—Cape Jumping-Shrew (*Macroscelides typicus*)

first is small, and no fusion has taken place between the instep-bones.

The Rock Jumping-Shrew (*M. tetradactylus*) of East Africa is a rather larger form which lives in rocky places, and it is somewhat more specialized, having completely lost the great toe.

CHAPTER XLVIII

MUSCULAR LOCOMOTION OF ANIMALS—BURROWING

Having now considered at some length a variety of forms which live on the surface of the sea-floor or on the ground, and progress by creeping, walking, running, or leaping, we naturally turn to those animals which live in the ground, or in marine and freshwater deposits of sand, mud, &c. Where the material is sufficiently firm these burrowing forms may construct more or less permanent underground "roads", which are from time to time extended; while in other cases burrowing is carried on continuously, and the passages excavated fall in as soon as they are made. In this chapter we are only concerned with creatures that live always or largely underground, or within the deposits that accumulate under water. Temporary or permanent excavations that serve as homes or retreats will be dealt with further on under Animal Dwellings.

Burrowing animals of thorough-going kind are found both among the Backboned Animals (Vertebrata) and Backboneless Animals (Invertebrata), and, as in other cases. these will be considered under separate headings.

BACKBONED ANIMALS (VERTEBRATA) AS BURROWERS

Typical underground species are found among Mammals (Mammalia), Reptiles (Reptilia), Amphibians (Amphibia), and Fishes (Pisces), as also among Primitive Vertebrates (Protochordata).

MAMMALS (MAMMALIA) AS BURROWERS.—Burrowing would seem to be a very ancient habit among land vertebrates, and has been attended with two advantages—rendering fresh food supplies available, and at the same time warding off the attacks of enemies. So far as the food existing underground consists of lower animals, some of these no doubt led the way to this kind of life, partly as a protective measure, the value of which has since been largely reduced by the fact of their example having been followed by some of their enemies. We find, for example, that insect larvæ often live underground, the habit having no doubt been acquired with reference to the food there to be found, and the immunity from attack enjoyed at the same time. But the adoption of the subterranean habit in creatures of this sort added greatly to the richness of the underground larder, and was no doubt one of the factors in the evolu-

Fig. 742.—Common Mole (*Talpa Europæa*). (From an instantaneous photograph)

tion of Moles and other forms adapted to make the most of the gastronomic advantages offered. A similar case has already been discussed (see vol. ii, p. 327) in speaking of the flight of insects, for by the acquisition of flying powers these animals were at first protected in a much higher degree than they have been since the evolution of Birds and Bats.

That the element of safety in an underground life had much to do with the evolution of burrowing Mammals appears very probable when we remember that the most thorough-going subterranean members of the class belong to the weaker and more primitive orders, and have therefore been specially subject to persecution by predaceous forms. The most highly-specialized burrowing Mammals, indeed, are to be found among insectivores, rodents, and marsupials.

Insect-eating Mammals (Insectivora) as Burrowers.—It would be difficult to select a better example of an animal thoroughly adapted to an underground life than the Common Mole (*Talpa Europæa*, fig. 742), a form with which almost everybody is acquainted. The nearly cylindrical body and the conical head, between which there is a scarcely appreciable neck, are well suited by their shape for easy passage through the surrounding earth. The same end is also furthered by the dense velvety fur, of which the short hairs grow out vertically, so as to yield equally in all directions (fig. 743). The powerful fore-limbs are largely included in the outline of the general body, and terminate in bare, hand-like extremities, provided with strong, curved claws (fig. 744). The palms are directed outwards and backwards, and we may say that in all respects these limbs are admirably efficient digging organs, by which the earth is excavated and thrown backwards. A life almost entirely underground is here, as usually, associated with very small eyes, and these organs are so hidden in the fur that they are only to be found with some difficulty. Large eyes would not only be useless, but would also be very liable to injury. It is equally difficult to detect the small ear-openings, these being similarly hidden. They are entirely devoid of external ear-flaps, which are just as unsuitable for a burrowing life as for an aquatic one (see p. 69). The tail is short and the hind-limbs are comparatively feeble. We have, in fact, as to this point, exactly the opposite state of things to that which is found among the most highly-specialized leapers (see p. 186).

Fig. 743.—Diagram Sections through Skin of a Mole (above) and a Non-burrowing animal (below).

Fig. 744.—Upper and Under Sides of a Mole's Hand

The skeleton exhibits a number of features associated with the burrowing habit, while those parts of the muscular system which are of special use in this connection are extremely well developed. The head has been compared, in shape and mode of action, to a drill or borer, and can be moved forwards and backwards by means of powerful muscles, in relation to which the neck-vertebræ are exceedingly strong, and the long shoulder-blade (scapula) is unusually stout. The tip of the snout ends in a little fibrous shield, covered with horny skin and supported by a piece of gristle, being thus well-fitted for boring purposes. On a small scale it is not unlike the snout of a pig, which, when used for "rooting" up the ground, plays much the same part. Well-developed collar-bones (clavicles), acting as firm props to the fore-limbs from the inner side, are always associated with marked powers of lateral movement, and to this rule the mole is no exception, for in it these bones are of great relative size and strength. The bones of the fore-limb are short and strong, and the breadth of the supporting framework of the hand gains additional breadth by the presence of a large curved "ploughshare"-bone (fig. 745). Some of the important digging movements of these limbs are effected by powerful muscles which take origin in the breast-bone (sternum), and this is provided with a well-marked ridge or keel that increases the surface for muscular attachment. The same thing is to be observed in the breast-bones of bats and flying birds, where also the breast-muscles are unusually well developed.

Fig. 745.—Skeleton of Hand of Mole (*Talpa Europœa*; I–V, digits; *Se*, "ploughshare" bone

The Common Mole and the other species included in the same genus (*Talpa*) are characteristic of the temperate parts of the Old World. Closely related to, and presenting a general agreement with them both in structure and habits, is the Star-nosed Mole (*Condylura cristata*) of eastern North America. In this creature the end of the snout is provided with a conspicuous shield, in the centre of which the nostrils open, and the edge of which is frayed out so as to suggest the popular name (see vol. iii, p. 37).

Much more specialized than the forms just described are the little Golden Moles of South Africa, which constitute a distinct family (*Chrysochloridæ*). The most striking peculiarity is found in the hand, which only possesses the three central digits. As will be seen from the accompanying figure of a common species (*Chrysochloris Capensis*, fig. 746), these are provided with claws of relatively enormous size and strength. These creatures owe their name to the peculiar metallic sheen which their fur presents.

Gnawing Mammals (Rodentia) as Burrowers.—Many of the members of this large and widely-distributed order are more or less distinguished by their burrowing powers, the usual end served being the excavation of dwellings, as in the case of the Rabbit. Some of the most typical burrowers are included in the remarkable family of Mole-Rats (*Spalacidæ*), of which the included species range widely through Africa and various parts of Asia, while some are native to South-east Europe. Most of them are larger than Moles, to which they present a superficial resemblance, as an outcome of closely similar habits. A typical form is the Common Mole-Rat (*Spalax typhlus*, fig. 747), which inhabits South-east Europe, South-west Asia, and Lower Egypt. Reference to the figure will at once show that the creature is a rodent

Fig. 746.--Cape Golden Mole (*Chrysochloris Capensis*)

and not an insectivore, for the exposed chisel-shaped front teeth characteristic of the order are here clearly visible. The head is rounded, and does not end in a tapering snout like that of a mole, while the tail is more reduced. The thumb is small, but the other four digits of the strong fore-limb bear powerful digging-claws. As in a mole, the velvety fur has no particular "set", and therefore presents no hindrance to either forward or backward movements, in both of which the animal is almost equally expert. The ear-flaps, though not entirely absent as in moles, are extremely small, and the minute eyes are not merely hidden in the fur, but covered over by skin. A review of these characters shows that this animal is in some respects less specialized than a mole, and in other respects more specialized.

The allied Bamboo-Rats (species of *Rhizomys*) of Central and South Asia, and also native to Abyssinia, are of interest in this connection because they are not quite so much modified in relation to the burrowing habit as the animal last described. In them the eyes, though extremely small, are not covered by skin, while tail and ear-flaps are decidedly less reduced.

The little Sand-Rats (species of *Heterocephalus*) of the North-east African deserts are no larger than mice, entirely devoid of

Fig. 747.—Common Mole-Rat (*Spalax typhlus*).

ear-flaps, but with minute, practically useless eyes. In the burrowing Mammals so far mentioned reduction of friction between the body and the surrounding earth is largely due to the velvety nature of the fur. In this case the same end is attained by the almost complete suppression of the hairy covering. We are here naturally reminded of the sharp contrast between the sleek coat of a seal and the naked skin of a porpoise, arrangements which are both related to diminution of friction with the surrounding medium (see p. 68).

The North American rodents include the family of Pouched-Rats (*Geomyidæ*), of which some members are thorough-going burrowers. Of these perhaps the best known is the Common Gopher (*Geomys bursarius*, fig. 748), a creature resembling a large rat in some respects, but presenting many of the features which we have seen to be characteristic of burrowers. The short limbs possess the full number of digits, all of which bear strong claws, though these are much better developed on the fore-feet. The fur is velvety and the tail fairly long. Although the ear-flaps are much reduced, the eyes are a good deal larger than is usual

Fig. 748.—Common Gopher (*Geomys bursarius*)

among animals that dwell underground, which suggests that these creatures live to some extent outside their burrows. That closely related animals may differ greatly in appearance, owing to the fact that they have become adapted to widely different habits, is well exemplified by comparing a Gopher with a Kangaroo-Rat, both being members of the same family. The latter form is distinguished by its well-marked leaping powers, and has already been briefly described (see p. 193).

Pouched Mammals (Marsupialia) as Burrowers.—We have

already had occasion to note that in Australia, to which most of the members of this order are confined, the absence during long ages of serious competition has led to a somewhat remarkable state of things. For Marsupials have specialized along the most diverse lines, and come to occupy many places in the economy of nature which are elsewhere filled by animals belonging to other groups.

In part of the desert region of South Australia the rôle of ordinary moles is played by a little creature known as the Pouched-Mole (*Notoryctes typhlops*, fig. 749), which has undergone modification along the lines of which so many instances

Fig. 749.—Pouched-Mole (*Notoryctes typhlops*)

have now been given. The head is rounded in front, and bears a firm protective shield of squarish shape. Both pairs of limbs are short and stout, and possess powerful digging claws. Those borne by the third and fourth digits of the hand are of relatively enormous size, and quite throw into the shade all structures of the kind which have so far been described in burrowing forms, the closest parallel being presented by the Golden Moles, where, however, three of the digging claws are especially large (see p. 202). It is characteristic of Marsupials that they should possess a pouch for the reception of the young, which are born in a very immature condition. That the Pouched-Mole is so provided is one of many features which prove that it belongs to this order of Mammals. The pouch is situated in the usual place, far back on the under side of the body, but its opening is posterior, instead of to the front as is usually the case. The short, stumpy tail is covered with very tough skin. There are no ear-flaps, and the small opening of the ear is buried in the surrounding hair; while the eyes have been reduced much more than in an ordinary mole, being represented by minute black dots imbedded in the skin. The coat is for the most part yellowish-brown in colour, but here and there patches of a golden hue are to be seen. Though soft, it is not distinguished, as in a true Mole, by a dense velvety texture, for the hairs are comparatively long. This is probably explained by the looseness of the sand in which the animal burrows. This is quite unsuitable for the excavation of permanent "runs"; indeed, it falls in immediately, so that there is no necessity for reducing friction during backward movements. Pouched-Moles burrow very near the surface, displaying remarkable energy in the matter.

Fig. 750.—Common Skink (*Scincus officinalis*)

Reptiles (Reptilia) as Burrowers.—Many animals of this class are able to burrow more or less, but our special concern here is with animals which live largely or entirely underground. This is the case with some of the Lizards (*Lacertilia*), and also with certain Snakes (*Ophidia*).

Lizards (Lacertilia) as Burrowers.—The family of Skinks (*Scincidæ*) includes a number of forms which burrow with facility, and of which the Common Skink (*Scincus officinalis*, fig. 750) of the desert regions of North Africa may be taken as a type. Although this lizard spends a good deal of its time above-ground, it is greatly specialized in relation to burrowing, its progression through sand being described as so rapid and easy as to suggest a comparison with swimming. The contours of the wedge-shaped snout, flattened from above downwards, pass gradually into those of the head and cylindrical body, and thence on into the short, gradually narrowing tail. The resulting outline is not unlike that of a fish, which is not unnatural, as the shapes of both types have been evolved with reference to easy passage through a resistant medium. And the resemblance does not cease here, for the Skink is clothed in closely-fitting armour of overlapping scales, the surface of which is highly polished, and which suggests the scaly investment of such a fish as the Mackerel (see p. 43), except that in the latter the surface is slimy. The last character is in adaptation to the surrounding water, but would not be effective in a desert animal, especially as it would involve too great an expenditure of moisture. That sand may be prevented from getting into the nostrils these are very small, and directed upwards rather than forwards, besides which each opens between two little protective shields. Since a Skink is by no means entirely subterranean in habit, its eyes, though small, are well developed. Injury by sand is prevented by the presence of well-marked eyelids, the lower one having a transparent area or window in its centre, enabling the animal to see pretty well without opening its eyes. The short, stout limbs are provided with strong digging claws, especially in the case of those in front.

For progress through dense vegetation, or for the purpose of burrowing, an elongated, snake-like body offers such advantages that it has been independently evolved in various groups of animals, presenting us with a case of the principle of "convergence" spoken of elsewhere (see p. 193). In plain English this means that close affinity is not necessarily indicated by mere shape and proportions, as these may have resulted from adaptation to the same or similar conditions in members of widely different groups. Internal characters are much more reliable in settling the actual relationship, although these also may be more or less modified as the result of alterations of the outward form.

But assumption of a snake-like form is associated with gradually increasing powers of locomotion by wave-like contractions of the muscular body-wall, in other words by "wriggling". As in the course of evolution along these lines certain animal forms became longer and narrower, they relied more and more on wriggling, and less on progression by limbs. Four legs are only efficient where the body is fairly short. At a certain point in the kind of evolution here considered they become a positive hindrance, increasing friction and tending to "catch" inconveniently in the surroundings, which were of such a sort as to hamper free progression. We therefore find that the limbs gradually dwindled and ultimately disappeared in the evolutionary series which culminated in snake-shaped forms. A very good case in point is afforded by one peculiar family of thoroughly subterranean lizards which may perhaps be called the Reversible Snake-Lizards (*Amphisbænidæ*), because they progress backwards or forwards with equal or almost equal facility, as their scientific name indicates (Gk. *amphis*, both ways; *bainō*, I move). The majority of these creatures are natives of Africa, the West Indies, and the hotter parts of America, but some of them are native to parts of South Europe and South-west Asia. The skin is much softer than in lizards generally, owing to the absence of scales, except on the head, where they are represented by horny plates.

Fig. 751.—Reversible Snake-Lizard (*Amphisbæna fuliginosa*)

Since this region acts as a borer, such a firm investment is clearly necessary, and in connection with this it may be noted that the skull is unusually firm and compact. The eyes are reduced to minute vestiges. Behind the head the soft skin is marked off into a large number of rings. In nearly all cases the limbs are entirely absent, scarcely any trace being left even of the shoulder- and hip-girdles. No less than half the species belong to the type genus Amphisbæna, of which one of the best-known species (*A. fuliginosa*, fig. 751) is a black-and-white creature abundant in South America and the West Indies. It is somewhat less than 2 feet in length.

One much smaller species of these curious worm-like lizards (*Chirotes canaliculatus*) differs from all its allies in the fact that it possesses small fore-limbs, each bearing four clawed digits. It is about 8 inches long, and is a native of California and Mexico.

The Reversible Snake-Lizards wriggle in a worm-like manner,

but the undulations into which the body is thrown are vertical, not horizontal, as is usually the case among elongated animals, *e.g.* Snakes. Bates (in *The Naturalist on the Amazons*) thus speaks of the habits of a South American species of Amphisbæna:—"Those brought to me were generally not much more than a foot in length. They are of cylindrical shape, having, properly speaking, no neck, and the blunt tail, which is only about an inch in length, is of the same shape as the head. This peculiar form, added to their habit of wriggling backwards as well as forwards, has given rise to the fable that they have two heads, one at each extremity. They are extremely sluggish in their motions. . . . The eye is so small as to be scarcely perceptible. They live habitually in the subterranean chambers of the Saüba ant, only coming out of their abodes occasionally in the night-time. The natives call the Amphisbæna the Mother of the Saübas, and believe it to be poisonous, although it is perfectly harmless. It is one of the many curious animals which have become the subject of mythical stories with the natives."

Snakes (*Ophidia*) *as Burrowers.*—There are several snake families of which the members spend the whole or a large part of their time in burrowing. None of these are poisonous, and the small mouth is not capable of being widely opened as in ordinary Snakes, a peculiarity which is in adaptation to their diet of earthworms, insects, and other small creatures, as compared with the relatively large prey which is swallowed by average members of the order. The small head passes without the intervention of a neck into the cylindrical body, which ends in a very short tail. And, as might be anticipated, the scales are very smooth. In an ordinary snake, as we have had occasion to notice (see p. 110), there is a double series of very large scales (ventral shields) on the under side of the body. To these the ribs are firmly attached, and they play a very important part in locomotion. But since the burrowing snakes move in a somewhat worm-like way, instead of being "rib-walkers", there is no need for special ventral shields, and as a matter of fact the scales on the under side of the body are no larger than the others in the forms which are entirely subterranean, and even in those which partly live on the surface of the ground are but little larger. In the latter, useful, though very small, eyes are present, but in the former they have been reduced to useless vestiges.

One of the less-modified families is that of the Cylinder-Snakes (*Ilysiidæ*), which includes but very few species, native to South America, Ceylon, and South-east Asia. One very interesting species, the Coral Cylinder-Snake (*Ilysia scytale*) of tropical South America, is beautifully marked with red and black rings, closely resembling what has elsewhere been described for the poisonous Coral Snakes from the same region (see vol. ii, p. 303.) It is generally considered to be a case of mimicry, the

Fig. 752.—Shield-tailed Snake (*Uropeltis grandis*)

harmless form enjoying comparative immunity from attack owing to its resemblance to its venomous relatives. Cylinder-Snakes have not entirely lost their hind-limbs, for these are represented by a pair of small projections, on each of which there is a claw.

The Shield-tailed Snakes (*Uropeltidæ*) of Ceylon and South India, though seen above-ground during the rainy season, are more thorough-going burrowers than the members of the last family, and consequently exhibit a greater degree of speciali-zation. No traces of the hind-limbs are present, and the ill-developed tail usually looks as if it had been cut off short. Its broad flat end is covered by a firm shield. The short cylindrical body is somewhat stiff, and the skull is unusually solid. In suggesting a use for the tail-shield, Gadow (in *The Cambridge Natural History*) says:—"The use of the characteristic tail-shield is not clear; perhaps it assists these rather rigid creatures in digging, by being pressed against the ground". A typical Ceylon species (*Uropeltis grandis*, fig. 752) is of black-and-yellow colour.

The little Blind Snakes (Typhlopidæ) are almost cosmopolitan so far as the warmer parts of the globe are concerned, and live

Fig. 753.—Blind Snake (*Typhlops vermiculatus*). The small drawing represents the head in side view, and shows the vestigial eye as seen by transparency through the shield which covers it

entirely underground. They are more thoroughly adapted to a burrowing life than the members of the two families just described. The front part of the small head is armoured with firm, horny shields, and the vestiges of the eyes are covered by similar shields. The mouth is placed on the under side of the head, and is extremely small. Teeth are present in the upper jaw only. The body is uniformly covered by small round scales, and the tail is very short. One outlying species (*Typhlops vermiculatus*, fig. 753) is native to South-east Europe and South-west Asia. Its tail is tipped with a horny spine.

AMPHIBIANS (AMPHIBIA) AS BURROWERS.—Some of the *Tailed*

Amphibians (*Urodela*) have become eel-like in shape, with accompanying reduction in the limbs, as an adaptation to burrowing in the mud of the ponds which they inhabit. The most notable case is afforded by the Sirens (Sirenidæ), which are found in the

Fig. 754.—Mud-Eel (*Siren lacertina*)

south-east of the United States, and of which the so-called Mud-"Eel" (*Siren lacertina*, fig. 754) is a well-known type. This creature possess no hind-limbs, while the fore-limbs are short and four-fingered. Although a large part of its time is spent in burrowing, it also swims about more or less, and occasionally leaves the water.

The *Limbless Amphibians* or *Cæcilians* (*Gymnophiona*) are snake-like burrowing forms which are more specialized than the Sirens, for they have entirely lost all traces of both pairs of limbs (fig. 755). They are not unlike the Reversible Snake-Lizards in appearance, giving us another case of the phenomenon of "convergence" as the result of adaptation to a particular mode of life. Cæcilians are widely distributed through the hotter parts of the globe.

Fig. 755.—A Cæcilian (*Siphonops annulatus*)

The body of one of these creatures presents a series of ring-like markings, and the eyes are mere vestiges, which are either imbedded in the skin or may even be covered by bones belonging to the upper jaw. As in several burrowing animals which have been already described, the skull is very compact and strong, a character which is no doubt related to the use of the head as a boring organ. As in Amphibians generally the skin is soft and slimy, but in most species a large number of little circular calcified scales are imbedded in it. With few exceptions the skin of members of other recent Amphibian groups is devoid of hard parts, although in remote geological ages an order (*Stegocephali*) flourished, of which one important character was the possession of well-developed external plate armour. Despite the peculiarities associated with the burrowing habit, Cæcilians are in many respects a primitive group, and undoubtedly of great antiquity, for it must have taken an immense time for them to get distributed all over the warmer regions of the world. It is therefore not at all improbable that the scales which many of them possess may be inherited from ancestors armoured like the extinct forms just mentioned.

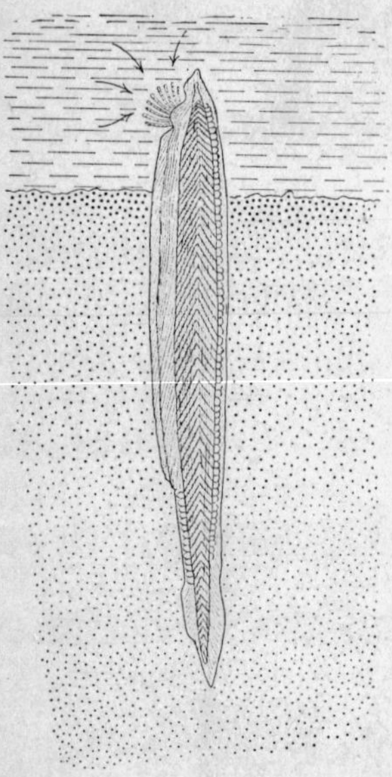

Fig. 756.—Lancelet (*Amphioxus*) Feeding

FISHES (PISCES) AS BURROWERS.—In the light of our knowledge concerning burrowing Lizards and Amphibians, we naturally turn to eel-shaped fishes for examples of the burrowing habit. The Common Eel (*Anguilla vulgaris*) is a good illustrative case, though only part of its time is occupied in wriggling through the mud, from which it comes out at night to feed. The narrow pointed head is well suited for burrowing, and the external openings of the gill-chambers are narrowed, no doubt for the protection of the gills (see vol. ii, p. 448).

PRIMITIVE VERTEBRATES (PROTOCHORDATA) AS BURROWERS.—The Lancelet (*Amphioxus*, fig. 756), with its pointed head and laterally flattened body, is well adapted for making its way through sand with facility. Willey (in *Amphioxus and the Descent of the Vertebrata*) thus speaks of its behaviour in this respect:—"Amphioxus possesses an extraordinary capacity for burrowing in the sand of the sea-shore or sea-bottom. If an individual be dropped from the hand on to a mound of wet sand which has just been dredged out of the water, it will burrow its way to the lowest depths of the sand-hillock in the twinkling of an eye." The delicate breathing organs are so situated that there is no danger of their sustaining injury from this procedure (see vol. i, p. 295), which is all the more necessary as during feeding the animal lies buried in the sand with only the head end projecting (fig. 756). The pointed front end of the body is supported by the forward extension of an elastic rod (the notochord) which underlies the nerve-chord, and has been aptly described as "the forerunner of a backbone". If the development of any backboned animal is followed, this rod will always be found, though usually partly or entirely squeezed out of existence later on by the appearance of a more serviceable backbone or its equivalent, but except in the Lancelet it never extends further forward than about the middle of the under side of the brain, where it tapers to a point. It is therefore regarded as probable that this structure has grown forwards to the extreme front end of the body in this animal, so as to make it sufficiently firm for burrowing purposes.

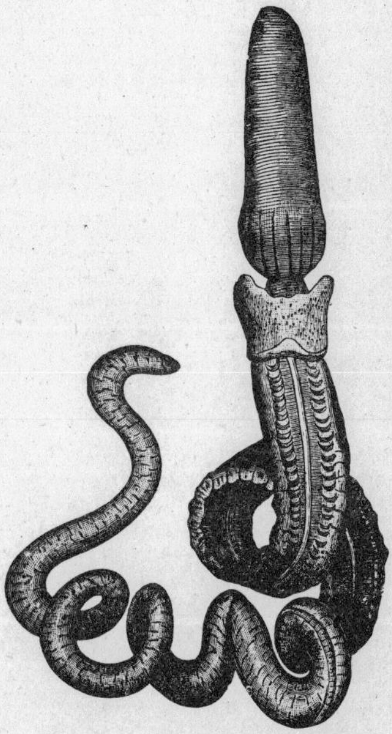

Fig. 757.—Acorn-headed Worm (*Balanoglossus*)

The Acorn-headed Worm (*Balanoglossus*) (fig. 757) is also a burrower, and its almost cylindrical worm-like body is well-suited to its habits. But here the chief agent would appear to be the curious acorn-shaped projection, usually called the "proboscis", which is attached by a comparatively narrow stalk to its front end. Blood can be squeezed into this organ so as greatly to lengthen it. By muscular contraction it is then made shorter, and the body is thus dragged up to it. No doubt assistance is also given by the layer of longitudinal muscle-fibres in the body-wall, by contraction of which the body can be shortened. The narrow stalk of the proboscis would be a source of weakness were it not that a support is afforded by a short elastic rod, which is developed as a forward growth from the digestive tube, and is usually regarded as representing the elastic notochord of the Lancelet, though it extends neither far forwards nor far backwards.

CHAPTER XLIX

MUSCULAR LOCOMOTION—BACKBONELESS ANIMALS (INVERTEBRATA) AS BURROWERS

Typical burrowers are found among the Molluscs (Mollusca), Jointed-Legged Animals (Arthropoda), Bristle-Worms (Chæto-poda), Siphon-Worms (Gephyrea), and Hedgehog-skinned Animals (Echinodermata). There are also parasitic animals belonging to various groups, which burrow within the bodies of other organisms, but these are best dealt with later on when Parasitism is being considered.

MOLLUSCS (MOLLUSCA) AS BURROWERS.—Animals of this kind are found among Snails and Slugs (Gastropoda) and Primitive Molluscs (Protomollusca), while the burrowing habit is eminently characteristic of Bivalve Molluscs (Lamellibranchia) and Tusk-Shells (Scaphopoda).

Fig. 758.—Burrowing Sea-Snail (*Natica Josephina*); *a*, boring organ

Snails and Slugs (Gastropoda) as Burrowers.—Some marine Snails burrow in sand or mud in pursuit of food, and are specialized in structure so as to fit them for this mode of life. This is clearly necessary, for the shape of an ordinary crawling form is in several ways unsuited for progression through sand and the like, as will at once be realized by recalling the configuration of an ordinary snail. Not only is the front end of the body quite different from what is required for such a purpose, but the head with its delicate sense organs would be liable to injury. Besides which the prominent rounded shell with its contents would be a great hindrance to progression. Reference to fig. 758 will show how these various difficulties have been got over in one typical burrowing Sea-Snail (*Natica Josephina*). The shell is not nearly so prominent as in an ordinary crawling form, and its surface is exceedingly smooth, so as to reduce friction with the surrounding sand. By modification of the front part of the foot (fore-foot) the head is protected, and at the same time a sort of burrowing wedge is produced in the following way:—The fore-foot is very large, and marked off transversely behind. Part of it is in the form of a muscular flap which can be folded back against the head, thus affording adequate protection, and at the same time giving a wedge-like outline. The manner in which this animal feeds has elsewhere been described (see vol. ii, p. 98).

Fig. 759.—Olive-Shell (*Oliva*)

The same sort of modification as that of which an account has just been given is found among the Olive-Shells (Olividæ, fig. 759). As will be seen by reference to the figure, the fore-foot is clearly marked off, and is crescent-shaped. It can be folded back against the head in the same way and for the same purpose as in a Natica.

A good many of the relatives of the Sea-Hares burrow in the sand, but here the necessary adaptation is of quite a different nature. In Actæon, for example (fig. 760), only the under side of the burrowing organ is made up of the front part of the foot, as it is mainly constituted by a modification of the head in front, to which the name of head-shield is applied. In a Sea-Hare (*Aplysia*, see p. 35) the head bears two pairs of feelers or tentacles. The eyes are placed at the bases of the front ones. It is thought that the head-shield has been formed by enlargement and fusion of the anterior tentacles, a view which is supported by the fact that a pair of vestigial eyes are to be seen on the front of the shield. The reduction of the organs of sight to mere useless vestiges is a phenomenon

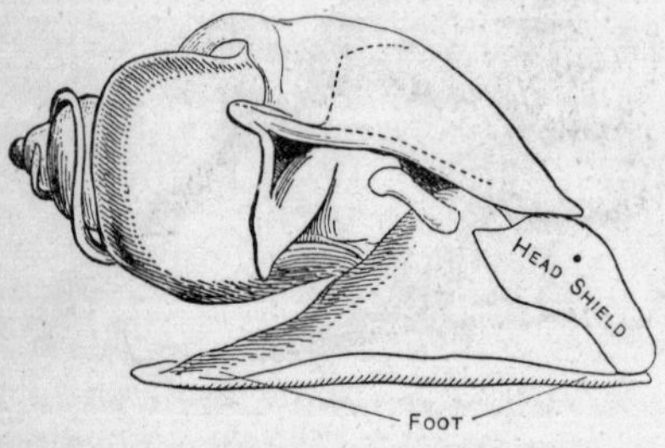

Fig. 760.—Actæon, showing head-shield, the black dot on which represents the vestigial eye

of which we have already found a number of illustrations among backboned animals which burrow.

Bivalve Molluscs (Lamellibranchia) as Burrowers.—The large majority of bivalves live in sand or mud, through which they make their way by means of their foot, which is modified accordingly. We have seen that the foot of a Snail is a fleshy projection on the under side of the body, possessing a flat, sole-like surface on which the animal creeps (see p. 104). The same thing is more or less true for a small number of primitive bivalves, and for still fewer of those which are much specialized as to the structure of their gills and in other ways. But in a fairly average form (fig. 761) the foot is placed rather to the front, flattened from

Fig. 761.—Burrowing Bivalve (*Scrobicularia*). Protruded foot on right, and extended siphons on left

side to side, and shaped like a ploughshare or axe-head. At the back in typical burrowers are to be seen a pair of tubes or siphons (see figure), not infrequently united together, but in either case playing an important part in feeding, breathing, and removal of waste (see vol. ii, p. 249). Without any previous knowledge of the way in which the foot is used we should probably imagine that it pushed against the mud or sand in front, thus causing the animal to progress backwards. This, however, is not the case. It is extended forwards between the two valves of the shell, being at the same time considerably enlarged by the pumping of blood into it. It is then shortened by contraction of the muscle of which it is mostly made up, and the blood is driven back into the body. The result is, that the animal is drawn forwards, and by continued repetition of the process is able to get along with a speed which varies greatly in different cases.

We have noticed that in some of the greatly specialized burrowers among Lizards and Amphibians the body has become long and narrow, thus facilitating progress through earth and the like.

Evolution along somewhat similar lines has taken place among those bivalves which are most notable for their burrowing powers. A step in this direction has been taken, for instance, in the Sand-Gaper (*Mya arenaria*, fig. 762), and a still further modification in the same direction in the Razor-Shell (*Solen*, fig. 763). It is also clear that as the foot is the burrowing organ, its most effective position is far forwards, and the way in which it has gradually been shifted to the front is well seen in the same two figures. The foot of a Razor-Shell is of remarkable length when extended, and its end then forms a sort of swollen knob, which holds firmly to the sides of the burrow during the shortening process by which the animal is drawn onwards. So rapidly can these creatures retreat, when alarmed, that their capture is a matter of considerable difficulty, but is rendered somewhat easier by the fact that they burrow obliquely when adult. It is only the small immature individuals which descend into the sand vertically, or nearly so, and this greatly increases their chances of escape from enemies, so that more of them become full grown than would otherwise be the case.

Fig. 762.—Sand-Gaper (*Mya arenaria*), showing foot and siphons

Fig. 763.—Razor-Shell (*Solen*), showing foot on left and siphons on right

In these burrowing forms, when the foot is very large, the two valves of the shell cannot be brought together in front, *i.e.* they "gape". And when the siphons are well-developed the shell gapes behind as well. An obvious advantage is thereby gained, for the animal can move, feed, and breathe without separating the two valves from one another, an operation which would not only take time, but also lead to unwelcome sand or mud getting in between them But this is also prevented by another kind of modification. In, say, a Freshwater Mussel, which has no siphons, and is not a rapid burrower, the two mantle-flaps, that invest the body right and left like the flaps of a coat, are almost entirely free from one another, so that they can easily be turned back, without cutting anything, when the shell is removed. But in many forms which burrow in sand they are not only fused together and drawn out into siphons at the back, but are also more or less united together below, except at the place where the foot is protruded (fig. 764).

Some bivalves can burrow in rock or wood, as, for example, the Piddock (*Pholas dactylus*) (vol. i, p. 336), which tunnels in

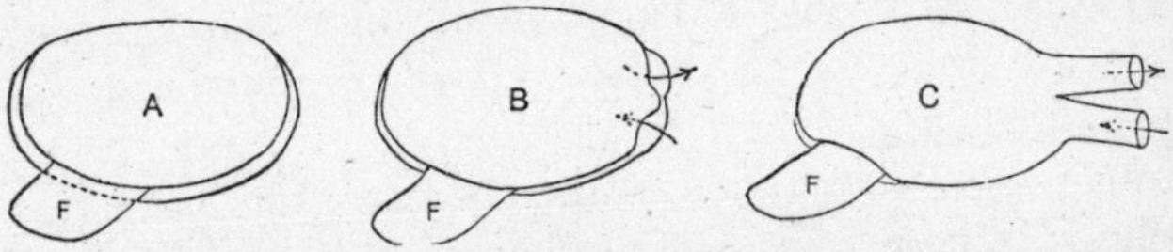

Fig. 764.—Bivalves in Side-view to show stages in Fusion of Mantle-lobes

F, foot; arrows represent water-currents entering and leaving mantle-cavity. In A there is no fusion, in B a small amount of union at back, with incipient siphons. C shows a large amount of fusion both at back, where well-developed siphons are present, and also below.

limestone, or even in siliceous matter. The shell gapes at both ends, in relation to the presence of a strong rounded foot and well-developed siphons. The front part of it is covered with transverse rows of short, strong spines, and the animal is able to twist itself round so as to use these after the fashion of a rasp. It is sometimes erroneously stated that the cylindrical foot is the chief excavating agent.

Since Piddocks and certain other bivalves bore in hard substances for the sake of securing sheltered homes, their operations in this direction are more naturally treated with relation to the subject of Animal Dwellings, and further details will be given when this is dealt with in a later section.

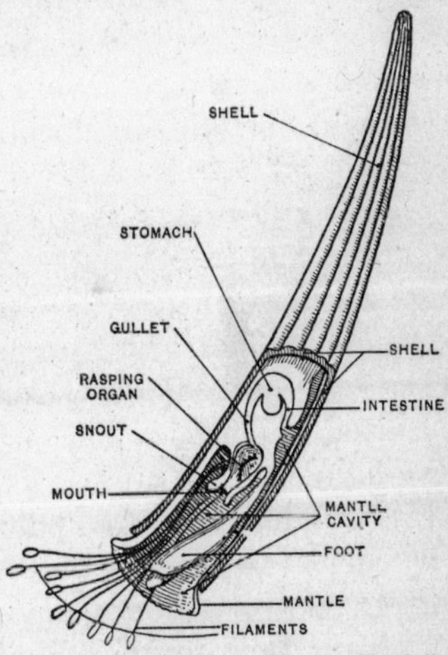

Fig. 765.—Tusk-Shell (*Dentalium*). The shell is partly removed

Tusk-Shells (Scaphopoda) as Burrowers.—These are widely-distributed marine animals of typically burrowing habit. The elongated, gradually-tapering, conical body (fig. 765) is well-adapted for progression through sand, and the smooth shell of corresponding shape by which it is invested greatly reduces friction. The burrowing organ is the three-lobed foot, which can be protruded from the broad end of the shell, and is used like the corresponding part of a bivalve. There are neither eyes nor tentacles.

Primitive Molluscs (Protomollusca) as Burrowers.—Most of the members of this small group are only known to professional zoologists, and very few facts have been determined as to their habits. Some of them are of cylindrical form, as, for instance, *Chætoderma* (fig. 766), a small, worm-like animal, which has probably acquired its shape as a result of burrowing in mud. In this particular case there is absolutely no trace of the muscular foot, which, as we have seen, is the characteristic locomotor organ of molluscs, but a sufficient number of the other structures by which the members of that group are distinguished are here present to make us feel pretty certain we are actually dealing with a specialized mollusc. Chætoderma presumably wriggles through mud, worm-fashion, by means of the muscular body-wall, and the numerous spicules with which the skin is studded must prevent it from slipping back.

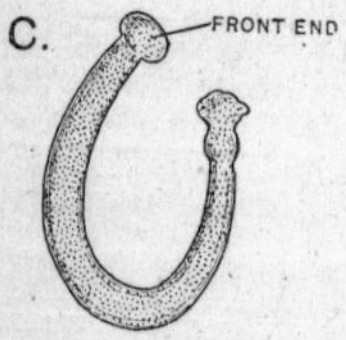

Fig. 766.—Chætoderma

JOINTED-LIMBED ANIMALS (ARTHROPODA) AS BURROWERS.—Typical burrowing animals are found in the following classes:—Insects (*Insecta*), Centipedes and Millipedes (*Myriapoda*), and Crustaceans (*Crustacea*).

Insects (Insecta) as Burrowers.—One of the most thoroughly subterranean insects is the Mole-Cricket (*Gryllotalpa vulgaris*) (fig. 767), which tunnels extensively in the ground. The front legs are the burrowing organs, and are remarkably specialized. They are exceedingly strong and broad, and their end-parts, the feet or tarsi, which in average insects are quite slender, several-jointed structures, look almost like the hands of a mole. This, coupled with the habits, accounts for the popular name. The digging part of the foot is mainly formed by the great enlargement of the uppermost joint, which comes next the shin or tibia. It is provided with four strong pointed projections. A Mole-Cricket in the course of its excavating work must frequently encounter roots, which cannot simply be burrowed through in the same way as the earth. To meet this exigency some of the end joints of the foot are provided with cutting projections, placed outside of the toothed spade, as will be seen by reference to the figure. The foot can be bent back against the shin, so as to work these against other sharp projections borne upon that region as well, and a pair of shears or scissors is thus constituted by which the roots are easily cut through.

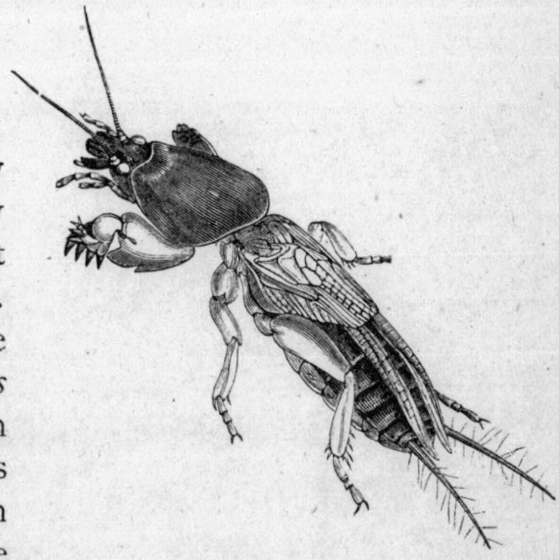

Fig. 767.—Mole-Cricket (*Gryllotalpa vulgaris*)

Some of the White Ants or Termites live in hollow trees, and bite out galleries by means of their powerful first pair of jaws, or mandibles. The curious little Book-Louse or Book-"Worm" (*Atropos divinatoria*, fig. 768), which belongs to a related family, is notorious for the way in which it drives tunnels through the leaves of books. Soft and weak as to its body, the hard-tipped mandibles of this creature are nevertheless strong enough to bite through paper, and each of the second pair of jaws (first maxillæ) bears a narrow pointed projection or "pick", which appears to help in this destructive operation. This insect and one of its equally small allies are sometimes known as the "lesser death-watches", because to one or both of them are possibly due some, at least, of the persistent tickings which rouse apprehensions in the minds of the superstitious.

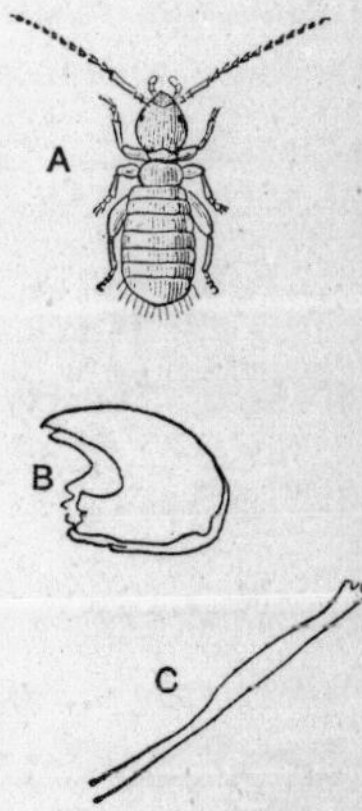

Fig. 768.—Book-Louse or Lesser Death-Watch (*Atropos divinatoria*)

A, much enlarged; B, mandible; and C, "pick" of second jaw, still further enlarged.

A large number of insects spend the early part of their existence burrowing in the ground, boring in wood, mining in leaves, or excavating articles of food, while others begin life as wriggling mud-dwellers.

The exigencies of space only permit mention of a few of the more interesting of these. Many instances of the sort are to be found among Beetles. Wood, for example, becomes "worm-eaten" owing to the ravages of the grubs of the "greater death-watches" (*Anobium striatum* and *A. tessellatum*), and the adult beetles are undoubtedly responsible for some of the ticking noises which have often been supposed to portend disaster. So far from this, however, the sound is really a love-call, which the insect produces by striking its hard head against the wood. It is said that apparently-worm-eaten, spuriously-antique furniture is manufactured by the simple device of firing small shot at the objects to which a deceptive appearance of age is to be given. So-called "weevilly" biscuit, which has stirred the discontent of many generations of sailors, owes its unpleasant condition to the grubs of a beetle related to the death-watches (*Anobium paniceum*).

Fig. 769.—Galleries of a boring Beetle-Grub (*Bostrichus typographus*)

The greater part of the life of the Common Cockchafer (*Melolontha vulgaris*) is spent underground, where its grubs burrow in the earth and feed on the roots of plants. This subterranean life lasts from three to five years. The grubs of the little Click-Beetles or Skip-jacks (*Elateridæ*) are the notorious "wire-worms", which gnaw the roots of crops. The Weevils (*Curculionidæ*) include some 20,000 species, of which the legless grubs bore in a great variety of plants, the kind and parts attacked varying in different sorts of these small insects. The wood of many trees is infested by the grubs of different beetles, and the borings are often very elaborate, and arranged in a way characteristic of the species. The galleries made by one of them (*Bostrichus typographus*) are shown in fig. 769.

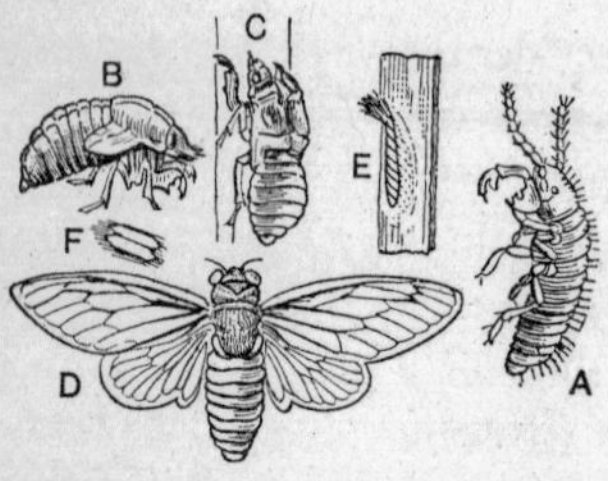

Fig. 770.—Seventeen-year Cicada (*Cicada septendecim*). Reduced to ½, except F, which is slightly magnified

A, larva; B, nymph; C, skin of nymph from which perfect insect D has emerged; E, batch of eggs; F, two eggs enlarged.

The larvæ of some of the Plant-Bugs are notable burrowers,

among which perhaps the most remarkable is the Seventeen-year Cicada (fig. 770), which during its subterranean life feeds upon roots. Regarding it, Sharp (in *The Cambridge Natural History*) speaks as follows:—"The North American *Cicada septendecim* is a most notorious insect owing to its life-cycle of seventeen years. It is considered that the individual, after nearly seventeen years of underground existence, comes to the surface and leads for a brief period the life of a noisy Insect. This is the only insect at present known having so considerable longevity. This fact, and several other peculiarities, have attracted much attention. . . . It is very difficult to obtain information as to their strange, prolonged, subterranean life; it is said that the insects sometimes penetrate to a great depth—10 feet, even 20 feet, are mentioned—and as great changes may take place on the surface during their long lives, these insect Rip Van Winkles sometimes emerge in very strange conditions, and may appear even in deep cellars."

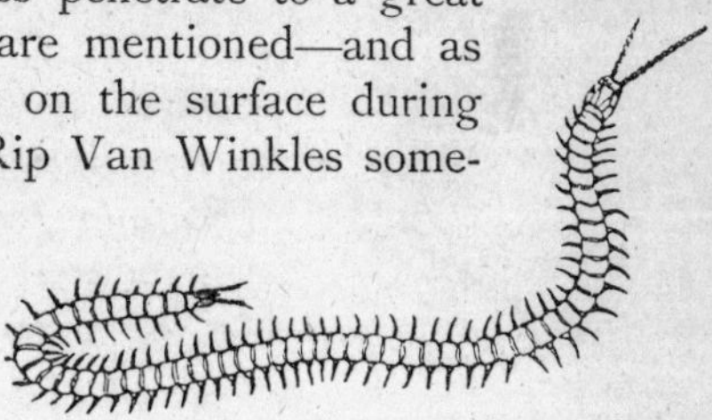

Fig. 771.—Earth-Centipede (*Geophilus*)

Centipedes and Millipedes (Myriapoda) as Burrowers.—The Earth-Centipedes (*Geophilidæ*, fig. 771) are widely-distributed, slender creatures, devoid of eyes, no doubt as an adaptation to their subterranean habits. They feed on earth-worms for the most part, and burrow in the ground in pursuit of their prey, a procedure which is no doubt facilitated by the narrow tunnels which the worms themselves make.

The little creatures known as Snake-Millipedes (species of *Julus*), the slender form of which is indicated by their name, are commonly found in soil, and are believed to injure the roots of crops. They are often called "false wire-worms".

Crustaceans (Crustacea) as Burrowers.—Many of the members of this class are able to excavate temporary or permanent burrows as homes or refuges, and a small number of them tunnel the submerged parts of wooden piles and the like. One such form (*Chelura terebrans*) is related to the Sand-Hoppers, but its body, instead of being flattened from side to side, is cylindrical, which is a more suitable shape for burrowing purposes. Associated with this is often found the Gribble (*Limnoria lignorum*), a relative of the Slaters and Wood-Lice. The burrows are bitten out in both instances, and the wood used as food.

BRISTLE-WORMS (CHÆTOPODA) AS BURROWERS.—Many of the marine members of this group burrow in sand or mud, by wriggling movements due to the contraction of the layers of muscle in the wall of the body. The hollow, conical foot-stumps (see p. 98) with the bristles imbedded in them are also of use for the same purpose, provided the sand or mud is of fairly loose texture. Such projections, however, if well-developed, greatly increase the friction, and we must regard them as organs which have been primarily evolved in the interests of crawling upon firm surfaces. In some of the best burrowers, such as the Lug-Worm (*Arenicola piscatorum*, fig. 772), they have been reduced to insignificant dimensions, so that the bristles are practically borne upon the main body-wall, and at the same time such burrowing forms have become cylindrical, the advantage of which is obvious. A great many of these animals swallow mud or sand for the sake of the nutritious matter therein contained, and they may therefore be said to eat their way through the deposits in which they are found, as well as to wriggle through them. The twisted heaps of material which are often seen on mud or sand are "castings" which have passed through the bodies of such creatures, and it is thought that the variously coloured muds which make up extensive deposits near the edge of the land in many places have, to a very large extent, been subjected to the swallowing process by marine worms and other creatures of similar habit. It may also be noted that the head region of the Lug-Worm is pointed, and devoid of the eyes and feelers which are characteristic features of free-living forms such as the Sea-Centipede (*Nereis*). The boring shape and reduction of sense organs liable to injury are strongly reminiscent of similar

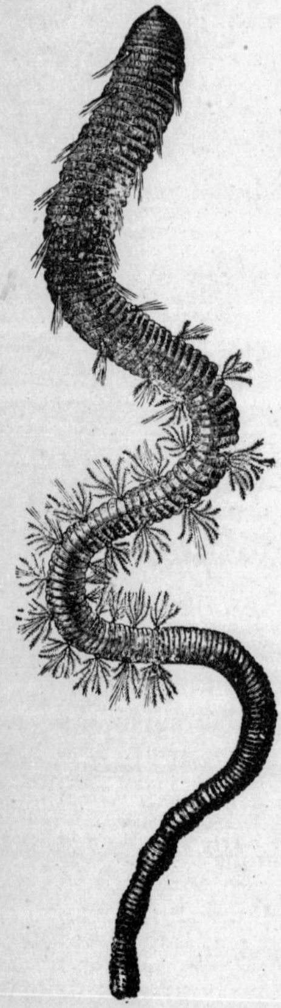

Fig. 772.—Lug-Worm (*Arenicola piscatorum*)

adaptations presented by moles and other burrowing Vertebrates.

The marine Bristle-Worms, in average cases, are distinguished by the possession of well-developed foot-stumps, in which many bristles are embedded, on which account they have been termed Many-Bristled Worms (*Polychæta*). We have seen, however, that the foot-stumps may be greatly reduced to facilitate burrowing, and it may be added that in these cases the bristles are also less numerous, and may be comparatively short. Such reductions enable us to understand the condition of freshwater and terrestrial forms, in which the foot-stumps have altogether gone, while the bristles are comparatively few in number. Hence these forms

Fig. 773.—Earth-Worms

are grouped together as Few-bristled Worms (*Oligochæta*). The head-region is pointed and devoid of tentacles, in most cases also of eyes as well. The freshwater forms are of delicate texture, and their bristles are more numerous and often longer and more complex in form than those of the earth-worms. This is easy to understand when we reflect that some of them do not burrow at all, while those that do only have to wriggle through soft mud which presents but little hindrance to their passage.

Earth-Worms (fig. 773) are the most specialized burrowers of all Bristle-Worms, and are able to make their way with ease through stiff soil as well as through that of looser texture. The body is pretty nearly cylindrical for most of its length, though in some species the hinder end is flattened from above downwards. It is clearly divided by transverse grooves into a large number of rings or segments. Nearly every one of these has bristles imbedded in it, there being in some earth-worms (*Perichæta*) a considerable number of them projecting at regular intervals all the way round the segment. But in the ordinary kinds of worm (species of *Lumbricus* and *Allolobophora*) to be obtained by digging in this country there are only eight bristles per segment. Except in very large specimens these can hardly be seen without the aid of a lens, as they are very short, and only their tips project to the exterior. But they are easily felt by passing the worm backwards between finger and thumb. The arrangement of the bristles is characteristic. Two double lines of them can be made out on either side of the body, placed rather nearer the under than the upper surface. A foot-stump of an ordinary marine worm is divided into an upper and

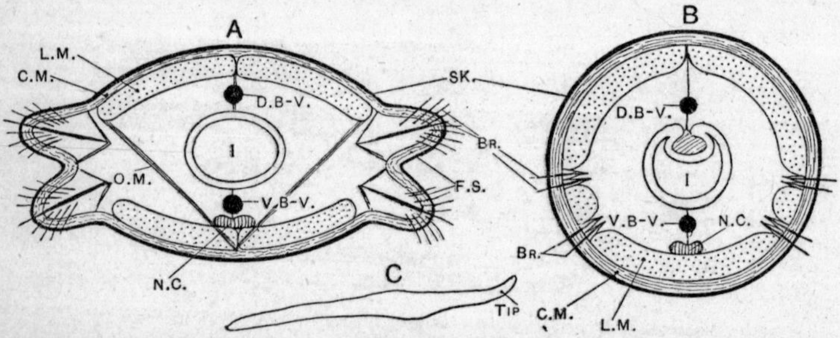

Fig. 774.—Diagrammatic Cross-sections through Marine Bristle-Worm (A) and Earth-Worm (B)

SK, skin; C.M., circular muscle; L.M., longitudinal muscle; O.M., oblique muscle; F.S., foot-stump; BR, bristles; I, intestine; D.B-V., dorsal blood-vessel; V.B-V., ventral blood-vessel; N.C., nerve-cord. C, bristle of Earth-Worm, greatly enlarged.

lower part, each bearing numerous bristles. If we suppose these to get smaller and smaller, and at the same time the number of bristles to be greatly reduced, the arrangement as seen in the earth-worm would ultimately be reached (fig. 774).

An earth-worm bores into the soil by means of the layers of muscles in the body-wall, in much the same way as it crawls. Under the skin is a circular layer, in which the fibres run transversely, and inside this is a longitudinal layer, of which the fibres are parallel to the long axis of the body. It is clear that the shortening or contraction of the fibres of the circular coat will make the body longer and at the same time narrower, while the contraction of the longitudinal fibres will have the opposite effect. The bristles serve as "hold-fasts", preventing the animal from slipping back, and their $\int$-shaped form gives them a very firm hold on the soil, while under ordinary circumstances their points are directed backwards, hence the rough feel of a worm passed the wrong way between the fingers. Suppose, now, that the front part of a worm is elongated, and forced forwards into the soil by contraction of the layer of circular muscle, a sufficient number of the bristles at the head end then grip the earth firmly, and the rest of the worm is dragged forwards by contraction of the longitudinal muscles. A little ground is thus gained, and by continuing the process gradual onward progression is brought about. Earth-Worms are only to be found where the soil contains a certain amount of moisture, for they breathe by the general surface of the body, a process which is dependent upon the skin being kept damp (see vol. ii, p. 444). This moisture also reduces friction, thus facilitating burrowing, and the same end is attained by the slimy nature of the skin.

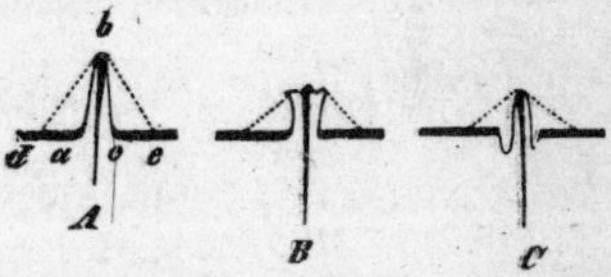

Fig. 775.—Diagram to explain Movement of Earth-Worm Bristles

A, bristle contained in pouch *a b c*; *d b*, *e b*, muscle-fibres. B and C, bristles protruded to varying extents.

These worms are able to move backwards as well as forwards in their burrows, which would scarcely be possible if the bristles were always projecting back. This, however, is by no means the case. Each bristle is provided with a special series of muscle-fibres, which take origin in the body-wall and converge to its imbedded end. The bristle is, so to speak, placed within a hollow cone, of which the side is composed of a series of such fibres. The arrangement is shown diagrammatically in section in fig. 775, and of course only two of the fibres can be indicated. If the one on the right shortens, the tip of the bristle will obviously move to the left, or to the right if shortening takes place in the fibre on the left. And if all the fibres making up the wall of the cone were to successively shorten, each relaxing immediately afterwards, the tip of the bristle would be moved round in a small circle. In fact there are appropriate muscle-fibres for moving the bristle in any required direction. If all the fibres contract together the bristle is protruded as shown in the figure,

As earth-worms continually swallow earth for the sake of the nutriment which it contains, they may also be said to eat their way through the ground, as some of the marine worms similarly facilitate their progress through sand or mud. These creatures continually bring up earth from below and deposit it on the surface in the form of "castings", and Darwin's observations on the subject led him to the conclusion that a large proportion of the soil of this country must have passed again and again through the bodies of worms.

Siphon-Worms (Gephyrea) as Burrowers.—A great many of these burrow in the sand and mud of the sea-floor, continually swallowing these substances in much the same way and for the same reason that earth-worms swallow earth. The most typical cases are afforded by the common Siphon-Worms (species of *Sipunculus*, fig. 776), which at first sight might almost be mistaken for earth-worms, though closer examination shows that their bodies are not divided into segments, and bristles are altogether absent. The muscular body-wall effects onward progression much in the same way as in worms which burrow in the soil.

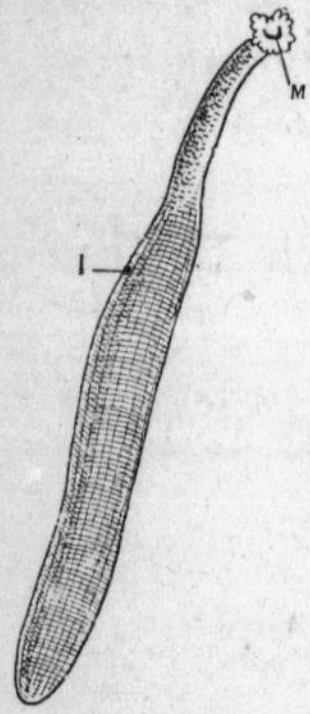

Fig. 776.—Common Siphon-Worm (*Sipunculus*); M, mouth; I, intestinal aperture

Hedgehog-skinned Animals (Echinodermata) as Burrowers.—The Sea-Cucumbers (*Holothuroidea*) swallow sand and mud, in which some of them are able to burrow like worms. As might be anticipated, those of them which are most markedly cylindrical are best adapted to this mode of life. One such form (*Synapta*) has already been described in relation to creeping, and the arrangements by which this is brought about are equally suitable for effecting progression through mud, &c. (see p. 97). Indeed this particular Sea-Cucumber is more notable as a burrower than as a creeper.

CHAPTER L

MUSCULAR LOCOMOTION OF ANIMALS—CLIMBING

We have elsewhere seen (p. 87) how difficult it is to sharply distinguish between Creeping and Climbing. The latter kind of progression involves fixing the front part of the body to some firm object or surface, the animal being then drawn forwards to the place thus affording a hold. In ordinary language climbing also means progression in a more or less upward direction by means of this pulling process. But as the lower animals devoid of jointed limbs pull themselves along in this way irrespective of the inclination of the surface traversed, we have found it convenient in their case to use the word "creeping" throughout. The sections on Walking, Running, &c., have been somewhat arbitrarily concerned with those forms only in which jointed limbs are present, *e.g.* Insects, Spiders, Crustaceans, and Land Vertebrates. And the present section on Climbing will be similarly restricted to the consideration of one particular variety of locomotion in the same set of forms.

Fig. 777.—Amœba climbing up a Stem, *a*; *b*, projection of body enclosing a mass of food, *c*

It may be well, however, to briefly describe a few cases of creeping up inclined surfaces by lower animals, as many naturalists would unhesitatingly use the word "climbing" in describing such movements.

Although the little Proteus Animalcule (*Amœba*) is a mere speck of protoplasm, quite devoid of any parts which can be called muscular, it has sometimes been observed creeping up the stems of water-plants in a way which strongly suggests climbing. This is very well shown in fig 777, taken from a drawing by Professor Mœbius. Four pairs of blunt lobes (pseudopods) of the body have been protruded, to be successively used as the means of pulling the animal up a vertical stem.

In fig. 778 are represented in a diagrammatic way the manœuvres of a Star-Fish which has been placed on its back at the bottom of a small glass aquarium. The tube-feet are successively extended, fixed to the vertical glass side, and shortened, so that in the end the animal is brought into a vertical position. By loosening the uppermost feet, stretching them up, attaching them to the glass, and then shortening them, the feet next below following suit, and so on, the animal is able to progress vertically upwards.

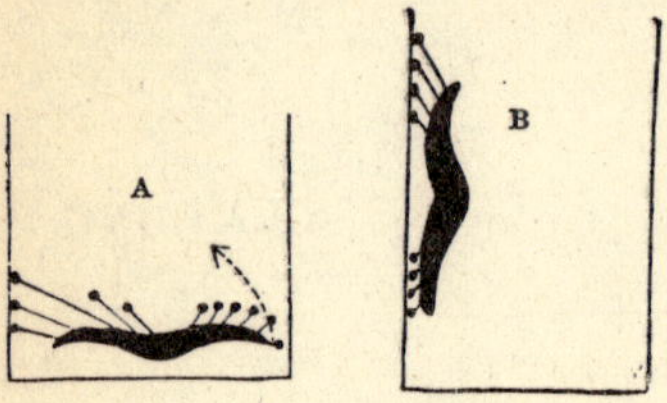

Fig. 778.—Diagram of Star-Fish Movements; in A the animal is beginning to right itself, and in B is climbing up vertical surface. See text

Another example is afforded by a small freshwater bivalve (*Cyclas*) which is able to make its way up the vertical side of an aquarium. The means employed are indicated in fig. 779. The first outline (A) shows the muscular foot stretched upwards to its fullest extent and holding firmly to the glass by its tip (*a*). This organ is then shortened, so that the animal is dragged up a little way (B), when it fixes itself by the hind part of the foot (*b*), used sucker-fashion. The foot is then stretched up again (*c*) and once more attached, and so on. Graber has calculated that in warm weather, which is favourable to activity, it will take a large individual about twenty minutes to creep up the side of a tumbler of water in which it has been placed.

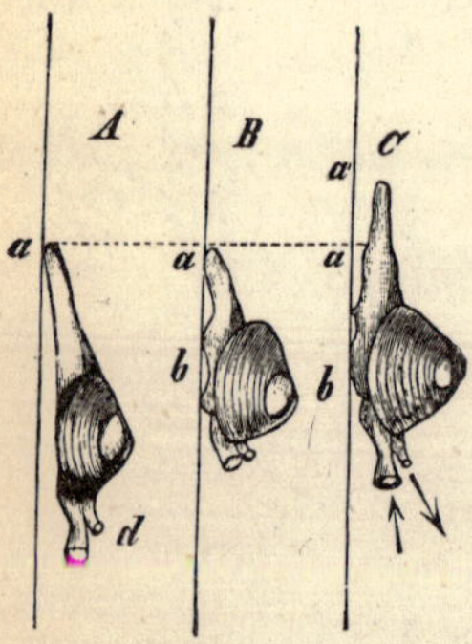

Fig. 779.—Bivalve (*Cyclas*) Climbing
Described in text

We now pass on to the consideration of Climbing in the narrower sense, as exhibited by animals which possess jointed limbs, beginning with Backboned Animals (Vertebrates), and then considering a selection of Backboneless Animals (Invertebrates).

BACKBONED ANIMALS (VERTEBRATA) AS CLIMBERS

Typical climbing animals are found among Mammals (Mammalia), Birds (Aves), Reptiles (Reptilia), Amphibians (Amphibia), and Fishes (Pisces).

MAMMALS (MAMMALIA) AS CLIMBERS.—We have here a large choice of examples, and it will only be possible to review a few of the most instructive cases, beginning with the highest order, most members of which are distinguished by their climbing powers.

Man and Monkeys (Primates) as Climbers.—The great majority of Apes and Monkeys are essentially forest animals, and many points of their structure are the result of adaptation to climbing among trees. Some of the chief principles involved in this sort of progression will be understood by reference to fig. 780, which may be taken to represent a Man or a Monkey climbing a pole. The upper limbs in A have been extended to grasp the pole above the head, while the strongly-bent lower limbs also grip it firmly. The next step is indicated in B, where the upper limbs have been bent so as to *pull* the body up, and the lower limbs straightened for the purpose of *pushing* it up. The dotted lines in A represent very diagrammatically the muscles which, by their contraction, bend the former and straighten the latter.

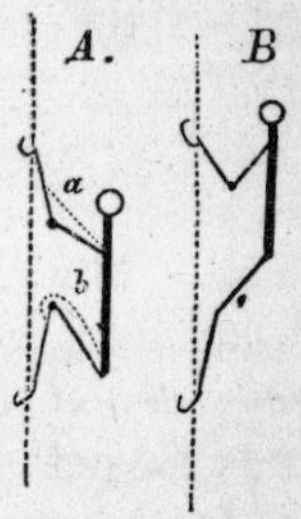

Fig. 780.—Diagram of a Man climbing a Pole, showing successive stages A and B; *a* and *b*, muscles which bend arm and straighten leg

In order that this kind of progression may take place rapidly and safely, it is clearly necessary that the limbs should terminate in efficient grasping organs. Monkeys are very well off in this respect, and were formerly termed the "Four-handed" Mammals (Quadrumana) in reference to the fact, for in ordinary language a "hand" means an extremity with well-marked clasping powers, and in this sense the feet of a Monkey may almost have the word applied to them. In an average Old World Monkey the hand is adapted for holding on to small branches and the like by a modification of the thumb-joint of precisely the same kind as that existing in a human being (see vol. i, p. 31). Examine your own hand and you will see that the projecting part of this digit is supported by two bones, while there are three such in each finger. The palm of the hand possesses five bones, the bases of which are jointed on to the wrist, but the joint between the palm-bone of the thumb and the wrist is of different character from the rest, for the surfaces of contact are saddle-shaped, an arrangement which permits of great freedom of movement. By means of a special muscle the thumb can be moved at this joint so as to be brought across the palm opposite to the fingers, and anything between it and them can thus be firmly gripped. In other words, the thumb is opposable. Examination of an Old World Monkey's foot shows that a similar modification exists there as well, for the great toe is opposable, and we also note that the toes are comparatively long, while the soles of the feet are inclined inwards. The human foot possesses entirely different proportions, since it has been greatly modified for the firm support of the body during walking (see vol. i, p. 32). All the toes are relatively short, and the great toe is not opposable. A Monkey therefore is able to hold on to trees by means of its feet alone in a way that would be quite impossible for a human being. This is very admirably shown in fig. 781, taken from an instantaneous photograph of a Pig-tailed Monkey (*Macacus nemestrinus*), native to South-east Asia.

It is perhaps only fair to remark that the contrast between the foot of a typical Monkey and that of an adult European is considerably emphasized owing to the unnatural cramping the latter has commonly undergone in badly-fitting foot-gear. The feet of savages are much more mobile, and are often used for purposes that would be quite out of the question with our own half-crippled extremities. And the feet of very young babies will well repay a careful examination. The toes here show remarkable freedom of movement, the soles are inclined inwards like those of a Monkey, and a number of creases are present which closely resemble those to be found in the inferior Mammal. We further note that the legs are not of disproportionate length as in the adult, while the strength of the hand-grip is extraordinary. Romanes (in *Darwin and after Darwin*) writes as follows regarding the last character:—"Dr. Louis Robinson has recently observed that the grasping power of the whole human hand is so surprisingly great at birth, and during the first few weeks of infancy, as to be far in excess of present requirements on the

Fig. 781.—Pig-tailed Monkey (*Macacus nemestrinus*), showing grasping feet

part of a young child. Hence he concludes that it refers us to our quadrumanous ancestry—the young of anthropoid apes being endowed with similar powers of grasping in order to hold on to the hair of the mother when she is using her arms for the purposes of locomotion. This inference appears to me justifiable, inasmuch as no other explanation can be given of the comparatively inordinate muscular force of an infant's grip. For experiments showed that very young babies are able to support their own weight by holding on to a horizontal bar for a period varying from one-half to more than two minutes." Enthusiasts are recommended to discreetly conceal their real motives when endeavouring to verify the foregoing facts by examination of very young specimens of the human species.

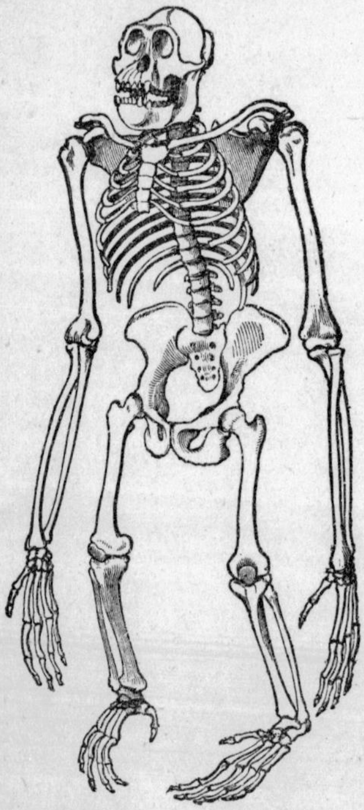

Fig. 782.—Skeleton of a Gorilla

It is difficult to resist the conclusion that our remote ancestors were expert climbers of arboreal habit. The fact that drowning persons invariably throw their arms out of the water has by some been referred to an instinctive attempt to attain safety by an endeavour to grasp as it were at the branches of the original tree dwelling. But this is extremely doubtful. Most readers will remember that Bret Harte has immortalized the grasping power of the infant hand in *The Luck of Roaring Camp*, and Robert Louis Stevenson has happily touched off the subject of our arboreal ancestry in the following passage (from *Memories and Portraits*):—"There is a certain critic, not indeed of execution but of matter, whom I dare be known to set before the best: a certain low-browed, hairy gentleman, at first a percher in the fork of trees, next (as they relate) a dweller in caves, and whom I think I see squatting in cave-mouths, of a pleasant afternoon, to munch his berries—his wife, that accomplished lady, squatting by his side: his name I never heard, but he is often described as Probably Arboreal, which may serve for recognition. Each has his own tree of ancestors, but at the top of all sits Probably Arboreal; in all our veins there run some minims of his old, wild tree-top blood; our civilized nerves still tingle with his rude terrors and pleasures; and to that which would have moved our common ancestors, all must obediently thrill."

The leading features of the skeleton in Monkeys and Apes having reference to climbing may be seen in fig. 782, which represents the skeleton of a Gorilla. Besides some of the points which have already been considered, we note in the fore-limb that the collar-bones are well-developed, propping up the shoulder-joints from the inner side, and facilitating lateral movement. The ball-and-socket joint at the shoulder permits, as in a human being, of extensive circular motion. The two bones of the fore-arm (radius and ulna) are both well developed, and the one on the thumb side (radius), which bears the hand, can be turned over the other one, carrying the hand with it, and bringing the back of this uppermost. This *prone* position is shown in the left arm of the figure, and it will be seen that radius and ulna cross one another. The right arm has been placed in the *supine* position, with palm uppermost, when these two bones are parallel. You can note both positions and verify the above facts in your own forearm by rotating it at the elbow. Both of the bones in the lower leg (tibia and fibula) are large, and a certain amount of inward twisting from the knee downwards can be effected, the movement being similar in kind to that taking place in the forearm, though its extent is much more limited. In a Man's leg only one of these two bones is large, *i.e.* the one on the great toe side (tibia), and very little inward twisting is possible.

The hands of the African Thumbless Monkeys (species of *Colobus*) are grasping organs of different character from those so far described. For, as their popular name implies, they have lost their thumbs, or, at most, these digits are represented by small vestiges. But the fingers are long and slender, and the hand can be bent round so as to form an efficient grasping hook. The great toe is well developed and opposable. A species of these Monkeys, the Guereza (*Colobus guereza*), native to North-east Africa is represented in fig. 783.

In Gibbons, the smallest of the man-like apes, and perhaps the most expert climbers of all the Old World Primates, the arms are exceedingly long, and the thumb very much shorter than the greatly elongated fingers. Indeed these animals use their hands for grasping boughs more as in the Thumbless Monkeys than as in the average Old World forms.

Fig. 783.—Guereza (*Colobus guereza*). Note reduced thumb on right hand

In the American Monkeys we find that the foot is used as a grasping organ much as in the Old World Monkeys, but the hand is employed more after the fashion already described for Thumbless Monkeys and Gibbons (fig. 709). It is true that a thumb is often present, and capable of considerable movement, but it cannot be called opposable. Many of these New World

WEEPER SAPAJOU OR CAPUCHIN MONKEYS
(*Cebus Capucinus*)

The extensive forests of South America are tenanted by a great many animal forms more or less specialized in relation to the climbing habit, and among these none are more characteristic than certain monkeys possessing prehensile tails. The Weeper Capuchin represented in the plate is a common and widely distributed Brazilian species, which is so well adapted to an arboreal life that it but rarely leaves the trees, except for the purpose of drinking. The wrinkled flesh-coloured forehead is very characteristic, and so is the dark patch of fur on the top of the head, which looks like a skull-cap, or close-fitting cowl, and has suggested the name "Capuchin" Monkey. The plate, representing a friendly scrimmage between two individuals, is designed to show the use of the tail. This organ is entirely covered with fur, and is not so much specialized as in the Spider Monkeys, South American forms in which its under side is bare near the tip, in the interests of touch.

WEEPER SAPAJOU OR CAPUCHIN MONKEYS (CEBUS CAPUCINUS)

forms have developed a new climbing organ, for the long tail is frequently prehensile, *i.e.* its tip can be coiled round a branch so as to give a very firm hold. Charles Waterton, the well-known naturalist-traveller, gives (in *Wanderings in South America*) the following graphic account of the way in which this organ is used by a Spider-Monkey:—"This prehensile tail is a most curious thing. It has been denominated, very appropriately, a fifth hand. It is of manifest advantage to the animal either when sitting

Fig. 784.—End of Tail of a Spider-Monkey

in repose on the branch of a tree, or when in its journey onwards in the gloomy recesses of the wilderness. You may see this monkey catching hold of the branches with its hands, and at the same moment twisting its tail round one of them, as if in want of additional support; and this prehensile tail is sufficiently strong to hold the animal in its place, even when all its four limbs are detached from the tree, so that it can swing to and fro and amuse itself solely through the instrumentality of its prehensile tail, which, by the way, would be of no manner of use to it did accident or misfortune force the monkey to take up a temporary abode on the ground. For several inches from the extremity, by nature and by constant use, this tail has assumed somewhat

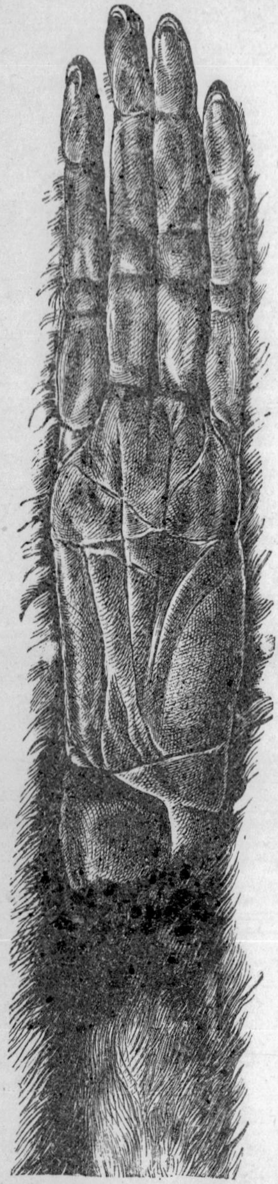

Fig. 785.—Thumbless Hand of a Spider-Monkey

the appearance of the inside of a man's finger, being entirely denuded of hair or fur beneath, but not so on the upper part."

Spider-Monkeys (fig. 799), to one of which the preceding extract applies, are slender, long-armed creatures which may be looked upon as the most notable climbers among the New World Monkeys. The under side of the prehensile tail, near its tip (fig. 784), has had its covering of hair suppressed in the interests of greater efficiency, for it is clear that a grasping organ cannot perform its work to best advantage unless it is very sensitive to contact, and the presence of dense fur would no doubt interfere with the sense of touch. And if we are justified in calling the Spider-Monkey's tail a fifth hand, we may also say that its end constitutes an extra finger-tip, which enables the animal to discover branches, &c., which will serve as a tail-hold.

The thumb of a Spider-Monkey is entirely absent, while the fingers and palm are of extraordinary length (fig. 785), and the hand is used hook-fashion, much as in the Thumbless Monkeys of the Old World. Even when a New World Monkey is provided with a thumb it employs its hands in a similar fashion, as will be seen from fig. 786, which represents the hand of a Black Saki (*Pithecia satanas*) grasping a branch. The Sakis have large bushy tails which are not prehensile.

Lemurs (Lemuroidea) as Climbers.—These curious Mammals are native to the warmer parts of Africa and Asia, while they are particularly abundant in Madagascar. Being specialized climbers of eminently arboreal habit, some of them superficially resemble monkeys, with which they are often confounded, but their structure proves them to be decidedly lower in the

Fig. 786.—Hand of Black Saki (*Pithecia satanas*)

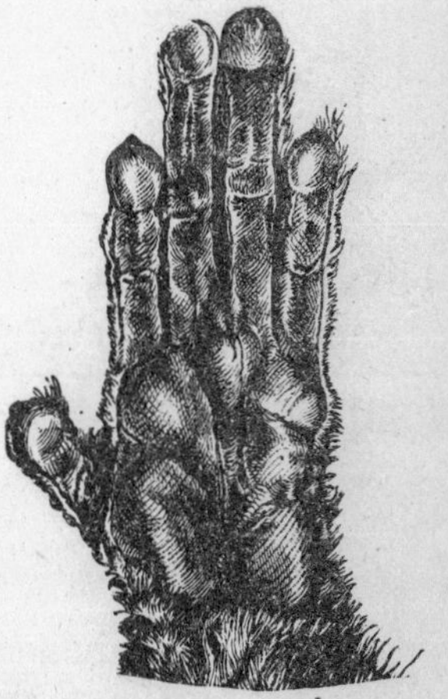

Fig. 787.—Hand of a Brown Lemur (*Lemur brunneus*), showing short but well-developed thumb

scale. Both thumb and great toe are markedly opposable, and the tail is often well developed, but is never converted into a grasping organ. In average Lemurs all the fingers and toes

Fig. 788.—1, Common Loris (*Nycticebus tardigradus*); 2, Slender Loris (*Loris gracilis*)

are well developed, and fig. 787 shows the formation of the hand in such a form. In some Lemurs there is a tuft of stiff hairs on the inner side of the forearm, ministering, no doubt, to the sense of touch, and playing much the same part as the sensitive tip of a Spider-Monkey's tail. A similar arrangement has been described in the Cat, Leopard, Squirrel, and several Pouched Mammals.

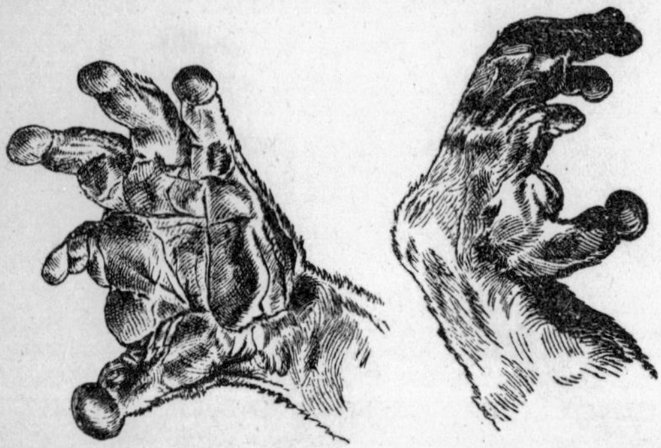

Fig. 789.—Hand of Common Loris (*Nycticebus tardigradus*), showing large thumb and reduced fore-finger

In the curious little Slow Lemurs of Africa and Asia, so named on account of the deliberate way in which they move about, the forefinger and its equivalent in the foot have undergone a large amount of reduction. The Asiatic members of the group are known as Loris (fig. 788), and of the two species represented, one, the Common Loris (*Nycticebus tardigradus*), is a clumsy-looking animal, comparable in size to an ordinary cat, while the other is the Slender Loris (*Loris gracilis*), a much smaller animal, with disproportionately small body. The structure of the extremities is much the same in the two cases, and may be illustrated by reference to the former species. We notice that in the hand (fig. 789) the fore-finger is much reduced, while the large thumb is opposed to the remaining fingers so as to constitute a grasping organ of unusual holding-power. Much the same is true of the foot (fig. 790), but the reduced second toe is provided with a claw. Both of these Lemurs are practically tailless.

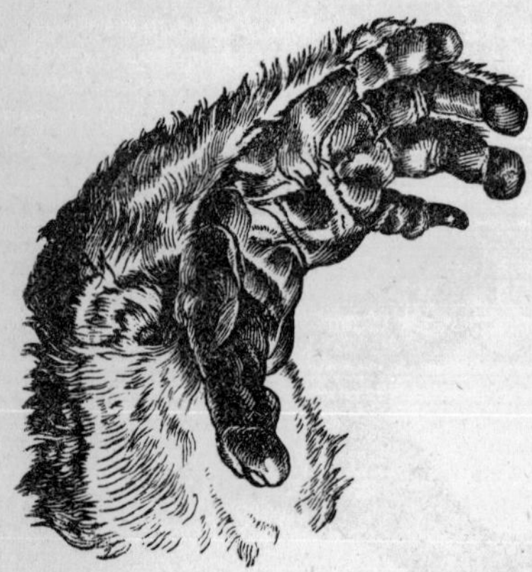

Fig. 790.—Foot of Common Loris (*Nycticebus tardigradus*), showing large first or great toe, and clawed second toe

The Slow Lemurs of Africa (fig. 791) are almost as remarkable in appearance as their Asiatic cousins, and are modified in a similar way so as to enable them to grip firmly to the branches. The two species represented are the only ones known to science, and both are natives of West Africa. The commoner of the two, which is distinguished by the possession of a short tail, is Bosman's Potto (*Perodicticus potto*), and the other is the Bear-Lemur (*Arctocebus Calabarensis*). The hands and feet of these creatures are constructed on much the same plan as those of the Loris, but the bases of the digits, with the exception of the great toe, are united together by folds of skin, which would appear to give additional firmness to the grip. Haacke (in *Der Schöpfung*

Fig. 791.—1, Bosman's Potto (*Perodicticus potto*); 2, Bear-Lemur (*Arctocebus Calabarensis*)

der Tierwelt) makes the following interesting remarks regarding adaptation of structure to habit in Slow Lemurs:—"To this group belong the Common Loris, the Slender Loris, the Potto, and the Bear-Lemur. In these four species, each of which belongs to a distinct genus, the arms and legs are of approximately equal length. In harmony with this is the reduction of the tail, which is almost absent in the Loris, very short in the Potto, and a mere stump in the Bear-Lemur. The build of the body in these creatures harmonizes with the character of their movements, for none of them are active leapers, like most Lemurs, but when night falls steal noiselessly through the foliage with slow but certain steps, with the object of catching insects, picking fruits, and surprising sleeping birds. Hence the necessity for a firm hold, for when the animal is seizing its booty it has to support itself steadily on three limbs. We consequently find that the hands and feet of these stealthy nocturnal animals are modified into tong-like grasping organs."

It has further been suggested that the unusual grasping powers of the Slow Lemurs are related to holding on to the same spot for a prolonged time. The Potto, at any rate, is able to sleep with comfort and safety, head sunk on breast, while holding on to a vertical branch or the bars of a cage by means of its hands and feet.

Specializations of quite another kind are found in the little Spectre Tarsier (*Tarsius spectrum*, fig. 792), an animal of the size of a small rat, native to the East Indies and Philippines, and remarkable among Lemurs for its bizarre appearance. That it is possessed of considerable powers of leaping might be at once inferred from the disproportionate length of the hind-limbs, especially as to the ankle-region, and the great length of the tail, both characters being strongly reminiscent of the proportions in a Jerboa (see p. 196). And this is, in fact, the case, for it leaps with great activity among the branches of trees in pursuit of insects and small reptiles. Its nocturnal habits are evidenced by the extraordinary size of the eyes. Its most remarkable peculiarity, however, is found in the broad adhesive discs in which the fingers and toes end, and the purpose of which is no doubt to obtain a firm hold upon the bark.

Fig. 792.—Spectre Tarsier (*Tarsius spectrum*)

Bats (Chiroptera) as Climbers.—When Bats are not flying about they usually settle on trees or masonry, a safer procedure than coming down to the ground, and under these circumstances they are able to climb about with greater facility than might be expected in creatures with such specialized fore-limbs. This is rendered possible by the existence of strong hooked claws on the toes, and a particularly strong claw of similar kind on the projecting thumb, in addition to which the large Fruit-Bats have a weaker claw on the forefinger. Many visitors to the Zoo must have noticed with interest the ease with which these particular bats clamber about the bars of their cage. Tickell (in *The Calcutta Journal of Natural History*) thus describes the movements of this sort which he observed in the Fruit-Bat or Kalong (*Pteropus edulis*) in its native haunts when settling down for the day among trees:—" From the arrival of the first comer until the sun is high above the horizon, a scene of incessant wrangling and contention is enacted among them, as each endeavours to secure a higher or better place, or to eject a neighbour from too close vicinage. In these struggles the bats hook themselves along the branches, scrambling about hand-over-hand with some speed, biting each other severely, striking out with the long claw of the thumb, shrieking and cackling without intermission. Each new arrival is compelled to fly several times round the tree, being threatened from all points, and when he

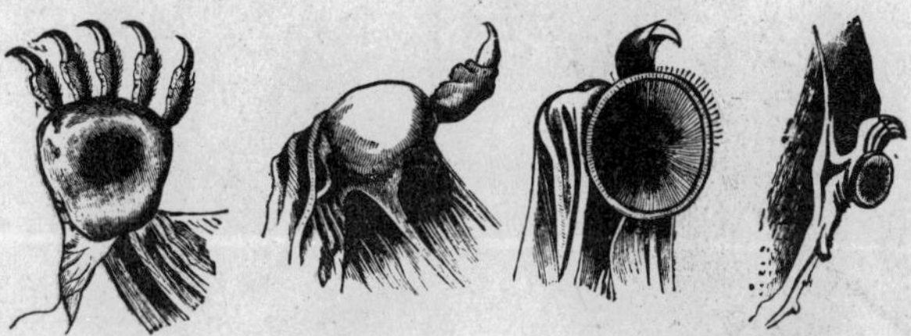

1. 2. 3. 4.

Fig. 793.—1 and 2, Incomplete Suckers on Foot and Hand of a Bat (*Vesperugo pachypus*). 3 and 4, Well-formed Suckers on Hand and Foot of another Bat (*Thyroptera tricolor*)

eventually hooks on he has to go through a series of combats, and be probably ejected two or three times, before he makes good his tenure." The hook-like claws also enable bats to hang themselves up during sleep or hibernation, usually head downwards. Some Bats possess more or less well-developed suckers on the hands and feet, augmenting their clinging powers (fig. 793).

Insect-eating Mammals (Insectivora) as Climbers.—This widely distributed order of rather primitive animals includes members adapted to almost every kind of life, and many of these we have already had occasion to conside in various connections. There are typical ground forms, such as Hedgehogs, aquatic Desmans, leaping Elephant-Shrews, and burrowing Moles. But this does not exhaust the possibilities, for the Banxrings or Tree-Shrews (*Tupaiidæ*) are typical arboreal Mammals, native to South and and South-east Asia, and much resembling squirrels in appear-

Fig. 794.—Bornean Tree-Shrew (*Tupaia tana*)

ance and movements. The largest species is the Bornean Tree-Shrew (*Tupaia tana*, fig. 794), and it will be seen from the illustration that, in spite of the bushy tail, this animal is decidedly unsquirrel-like as to the snout, which is long and pointed, after the manner of its kind. And examination of the front teeth would at once show the absence of the chisel-shaped incisors so characteristic of squirrels and other gnawing Mammals. The resemblance between these two sorts of climbing Mammal is generally supposed to be a case of "mimicry", the comparatively slow Tree-Shrew benefiting by the resemblance to the more nimble squirrels. But, curiously enough, there is at least one Squirrel (*Sciurus laticaudatus*) in this region of the world which has acquired a long snout and thus has come to resemble a Tree-Shrew, though the advantage to be derived from this is far from clear.

The adaptations to climbing present in a Banxring chiefly consist in sharp, curved claws, a large tail useful in balancing, and a relatively rather greater development of the hind-limbs, though the last feature has more to do with leaping about among branches than actual climbing.

Flesh-eating Mammals (Carnivora) as Climbers.—With the exception of the Lion most of the members of the Cat Family (*Felidæ*) are more or less expert climbers, *e.g.* Leopard, Puma, and Jaguar. Even Tigers have been known to climb low trees. The facility with which an ordinary cat ascends walls and trees is a matter of common observation. The large amount of lateral movement which is possible in these cases, largely as a result of adaptation to the seizing of prey, is obviously favourable to climbing, and the sharp curved claws are able to render valuable service as grappling-hooks, though this does not appear to have been the primary object of their evolution.

Many other Carnivores are climbers, as, *e.g.*, Bears, Civet-Cats, Martens, and Skunks, but it would hardly repay us to consider them in detail in this connection. The family of the Small Bears (*Sub-Ursidæ*), including Raccoons, Coatis, &c., is much more interesting. With one exception they are natives of the New World, and are particularly abundant in Central and South America. The toes are furnished with sharp, curved claws, which are partially retractile, and the large, often bushy, tail, present as a balancing organ in so many arboreal forms is noteworthy. The Common Raccoon (*Procyon lotor*) (see vol. i, p. 95) of North America is distinguished by the mobility of its fingers, which fits the hands for climbing as well as for various other purposes. But in many ways the most specialized and most interesting member of the family is the Kinkajou or Honey-Bear (*Cercoleptes caudivolvulus*, fig. 799), which ranges from Central Mexico to the River Amazon, and is a notable climber. The feature of greatest interest in this animal is the long prehensile tail, though this is not so specialized as the corresponding organ of a Spider-Monkey, as it is devoid of the bare patch of skin which in the latter is of importance in connection with the sense of touch (see p. 239). But the fur is "parted" in a curious way so as to expose the surface of the skin to some extent.

Hoofed Mammals (Ungulata) as Climbers.—We have so far been concerned with Mammals which are distinguished by the power of climbing trees, a habit which we should scarcely expect to find exemplified by the members of the present order, although a case has elsewhere been described of an Antelope that is able to ascend branches of some height for the purpose of feeding (see vol. ii, p. 169). But there are numerous Ungulates which climb steep slopes and rocky crags with extraordinary ease. Many of the cloven-footed forms are remarkable in this respect, especially wild Sheep and Goats, some Antelopes, and the Vicunias of South America, which are related to the Camels of the Old World. It is obvious that the split feet of these creatures, and the pointed shape of the hoofs, are well suited for giving a firm hold, and probably this type of extremity has been evolved in relation to clambering up precipitous places that furnished a secure refuge from carnivorous forms. A typical example of these rock-dwelling forms is the Grecian Ibex or Bezoar Goat (*Capra ægagrus*, fig. 795), which ranges from Crete to North-west India, and is probably the "goat" mentioned in Homer. Special interest of another kind attaches to this species, for it is probably the chief stock from which domesticated goats have descended. A wild Sheep, of which the habits are similar to those of the Grecian Ibex, is the Argali (*Ovis argali*), of which mention has been made in another place (see p. 186). The well-known Chamois (*Rupicapra tragus*) (see vol. ii, p. 365) may be taken as an example of a mountain Antelope.

The cloven feet of those even-toed Ungulates which do not chew the cud can on occasion be used for climbing up steep or slippery places, and this is particularly true of the Hippopotamus, which is thus able to ascend river-banks or clamber on to mud-banks without difficulty, in spite of its great bulk (see p. 148).

Conies or Rock-Badgers (Hyracoidea) as Climbers.—These curious little rabbit-like creatures present so many points of resemblance to the Hoofed Mammals that they are often classified with them. All the species are pretty much alike, which makes it at first sight rather surprising that though most of them live in rocky places, others make their homes in trees. It appears, however, that their spreading feet are well suited for climbing in both kinds of habitat. Vogt (in *The Mammalia*) thus describes the structure and mode of action of the feet of rock-dwelling Conies:—" The weak and short feet have four toes in front and three behind, and these toes are united down to their extremities by skin, and are covered with small, slightly-arched hoofs,

Fig. 795.—Grecian Ibex (*Capra ægagrus*)

with the exception of the inner toe of the hind-foot, which carries a small claw. The sole of the foot is covered with a firm, rough, naked skin, divided into several lobes by means of deep furrows. The Hyracoidea can make use of these little cushions and furrows for the production of vacua which act as suckers. In this manner they cling to the smooth surfaces of the rocks, in the clefts of which they have their retreats. They climb just as easily as geckos, and attach themselves like tree-frogs to smooth surfaces." The arrangement described is equally suitable for tree-climbing.

The species figured is a Tree-Cony or Tree-Hyrax (*Procavia* or *Dendrohyrax arborea*, fig. 796), native to East and South-east Africa. One of the rock-dwelling forms, the Abyssinian Cony or Hyrax (*Procavia* or *Hyrax Abyssinica*), has been figured in an earlier section of this work (vol. i, p. 104).

Gnawing Mammals (Rodentia) as Climbers.—It has been well remarked that the present order and that of the Insectivores

Fig. 796.—Tree-Hyrax (*Procavia arborea*)

resemble one another in the fact that they include members which are severally adapted to almost every kind of life. Nor is this surprising, for both orders are ancient and primitive, and there has been abundant time for them to evolve types able to exploit the supplies of food obtainable in the water, on the ground, under the ground, and above the ground. But whereas the Insectivores mainly subsist on animal food, the Rodents affect a vegetable diet, and the members of the two orders have not therefore competed keenly with one another in the struggle for existence, but have evolved side by side on the same lines. Some mention has already been made of aquatic Rodents, and of those which run or leap upon the ground, as well as of others which burrow in the soil, and we are here concerned with the climbing members of the order.

Pre-eminent among these are the Squirrels (Sciuridæ), in which the extremities are furnished with sharp curved claws, by

Fig. 797.—Dormice (*Muscardinus avellanarius*)

means of which these animals are able to take advantage of the smallest inequalities of the bark of trees, while the fore-paws can be used pretty much like hands for all sorts of purposes, of which climbing is one. The bushy tail is an important organ for the maintenance of equilibrium under circumstances where acrobatic feats become necessary, and possibly serves other purposes as well (see vol. ii, p. 367).

What is true of Squirrels is also true in the main of the pretty little Dormice (Myoxidæ), although in them the tail is not so well developed. The accompanying illustration of the Common Dormouse (*Muscardinus avellanarius*, fig. 797) shows very clearly how suitable the extremities are for climbing purposes, and in particular the hand-like character of the fore-paws. It will further be noted that, as in Squirrels (see vol. ii, p. 368), the hind-limbs are relatively long, which is indeed the case with very many arboreal forms, and this is related to the habit of leaping from branch to branch in the search for food, or in retreat from enemies.

In cases where the hind-limbs are the chief agents of progression, it commonly happens that the fore-limbs, being freed

Fig. 798.—Inner side, under surface, and outer side of Left Hand of Cape Jumping-Hare (*Pedetes Caffer*). In left and middle sketches the nearest claw, and in right sketch the furthest claw, is that of the "false thumb'

from the work of supporting the body, are used for other purposes, and become more or less hand-like. Such limbs are frequently of service in climbing, an instance of this being afforded by the Cape Jumping-Hare (*Pedetes Caffer*, see p. 195). This is a specialized leaping form, but with the aid of its hands is able to climb about among rocks with considerable facility. The thumb has been reduced, but the fingers bear strong curved claws, well suited for getting a grip on irregular surfaces. And, curiously enough, a sort of claw-bearing projection has been developed upon the wrist, which may almost be called a "false thumb" (fig. 798).

The Porcupines of the Old World are ground animals, but those of the New World are typically arboreal, the species inhabiting Central and South America reminding us of many of the monkeys of the same region in the fact that they are possessed of prehensile tails. The Brazilian Tree-Porcupine (*Cercolabes prehensilis*, fig. 799) may be taken as an illustration. As in a Spider-Monkey, the end of the tail presents a bare patch, but this is on the *upper* instead of the under side (see p. 239), in accordance with which the Porcupine coils its tail round a branch in exactly the opposite way to what is the case in the monkey. Thumb and great toe are reduced, while the remaining digits are provided with strong curved claws. The hind-foot possesses an arrangement which reminds one of that found in the fore-foot of the Cape Jumping-Hare, for there is a projection on its inner side which makes up for the absence of the missing toe. This "false great toe" is capable of a certain amount of bending, enabling it to serve as a grasping organ, and its value is enhanced by the fact that the hind-foot is set on obliquely. Both palms and soles are bare and rough on their under sides, this being an adaptation to holding on to the surface of bark. The Brazilian Porcupine and its allies move with great deliberation, suggesting a comparison with sloths. Being plant-eaters, there is no necessity for speed in the search for food, and they rely upon their sharp barbed spines for purposes of defence.

The Canadian Tree-Porcupine or "Urson" (*Erethizon dorsatus*), which is also native to the States, is a larger and clumsier animal, in which the strong tail is non-prehensile, its chief use being as a weapon. In this case, although the thumb has been reduced the great toe is retained. Hart Merriam states that if one of these porcupines "has selected and settled himself in a tree to his liking, he may not leave it, day or night, until he has denuded it of the whole of its foliage. I have seen many hemlocks thus completely stripped, not a green twig remaining even on the smallest bough. It seems incredible that so large and clumsy an animal should be able to climb out far enough on the branches of trees to reach the terminal leaves; but he distributes his weight by bringing several branches together, and then, with his powerful paws, bends back their ends and passes them through his mouth. When high in the tree-tops he is often passed unnoticed, mistaken, if seen at all, for the nest of a crow or hawk."

Mammals Poor in Teeth (Edentata) as Climbers.—The forest-regions of South America are tenanted by a great variety of animal which have become more or less specialized in relation to climbing (fig. 799), and among these the Sloths are perhaps the most remarkable. The fore-limbs are longer than the hind ones, and remarkably strong curved claws are borne by the digits, of which there are three in the hand and two or three in the foot. A set of climbing hooks is thus constituted, of equal service for suspending the animal from a branch, on the under side of which it is slung without effort, indeed it is said to be able to hang itself up quite comfortably by any one of the four limbs. The upside-down position is habitual, and it is in this position that a Sloth either climbs or walks, according as the particular branch traversed has a considerable or a slight inclination. The movements are deliberate, for the food consists of leaves, and the general appearance and colour harmonize well with the surroundings (see vol. ii, p. 295), so that the eyes of possible enemies are very liable to be deceived. Not only the external characters of a Sloth but also its structure are well adapted to its habits. The backbone possesses an unusual number of vertebræ and is very mobile, which is not only a help in reaching the food, but also enables awkward attitudes to be easily maintained, if they happen for the time being to be convenient. The fore-limbs play a particularly active part in locomotion, and are capable of very free movement: the fore-arm especially being capable of even a larger twisting movement from the elbow than in a human being or a monkey. The digits of the hand (and the same is true of the foot) are not capable of independent movement, being closely bound together by skin. The hind-limbs are constructed on a plan which gives firmness rather than mobility. The hip-bones, for example, are closely united with a considerable length of backbone, and the soles of the feet are kept turned inwards much as in a monkey (see p. 234), but here there is a special arrangement to maintain that position. The two bones of the ankle next the lower leg are, as elsewhere, the heel-bone, and the bone which is remarkable for its pulley-shaped surface in average Mammals, *i.e.* the astragalus. It is the latter which is often called the "knuckle-bone" in the case of a sheep, and furnishes the means of playing a well-known children's game that very likely originated in prehistoric times. In a Sloth the astragalus presents a well-marked smooth surface of peculiar form, for jointing on to

Fig. 799.—South American Mammals with Prehensile Tails

1, A Spider-Monkey (*Ateles Bartletti*). 2, Opossum (*Didelphys marsupialis*). 3, Brazilian Tree-Porcupine (*Cercolabes prehensilis*). 4, Lesser Ant-eater (*Tamandua tetradactyla*). 5, Kinkajou (*Cercoleptes caudivolvulus*).

the shin-bone, which is on the inner side of the leg (fig. 800). But there is also a sort of pit on the outer surface of this ankle-bone, into which a conical projection at the lower end of the other leg-bone (fibula) loosely fits. By this peg-and-socket arrangement the movement of the foot is limited to some extent, and great firmness is given. It may further be noted that in the Three-toed Sloth (*Bradypus*) a great many of the ankle and foot bones are fused together, which obviously contributes to firmness.

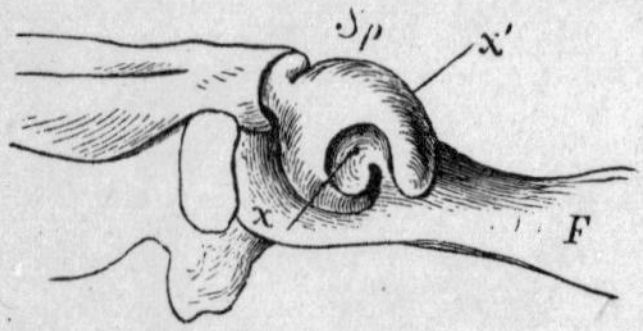

Fig. 800.—Ankle-bones of a Sloth

F, Heel-bone (calcaneum); *Sp*, pulley-bone (astragalus), showing pit for projection of fibula; *xx'*, axis of movement. Base of digits to left.

Sloths are probably to be regarded as the dwarfed descendants of the large extinct animals known as Ground-Sloths, which formerly existed in South America, and some of which were of huge size, and strong to pull down branches and even fairly large trees for the sake of their leaves.

The Ground-Sloths also appear to be ancestral to the South American Ant-eaters, which have lost their teeth and become adapted to an insect diet. Of these the largest is the Great Ant-eater (*Myrmecophaga jubata*), a ground form which has elsewhere been described (see vol. ii, p. 41). The fore-paws of this creature are provided with strong curved digging claws, for scratching open ant-hills, &c. But since trees furnish a happy hunting-ground for insect-eating animals, it is not surprising to find that some of the Ant-eaters have taken to an arboreal life, their strong claws serving admirably as climbing-hooks. One of these is the Lesser Ant-eater, or Tamandua (*Tamandua tetradactyla*, fig. 799), which is not unlike its larger relative in appearance, except that it possesses a prehensile tail that is constantly used during climbing.

A far more specialized arboreal species is the Two-toed Ant-eater (*Cyclothurus didactylus*, fig. 801), a creature about the size of a rat, native to the hotter parts of America. Were it not for the presence of a long, markedly prehensile tail, it might be taken for a diminutive sloth, for its general appearance and mode of progression are very similar. The snout is rounded instead of being slender as in the Tamandua, while hands and feet bare long hooked claws, to the number of two and four respectively.

Some of the Pangolins among the Old World Edentates (see vol. i, p. 138) climb by means of their sharp claws; and the overlapping scales, of which the pointed ends project backwardly, also appear to help as scaling-irons. This is only true, of course, of the lateral ones, especially those on the side of the

Fig. 801.—Two-toed Ant-eater (*Cyclothurus didactylus*)

tail, and a Pangolin is said to be able to hold on quite easily to the bark of a vertical tree-trunk by means of this organ and the hind-paws, and even to be able under such circumstances to allow the front part of its body to bend outwards at a considerable angle. It is then liable to be mistaken for a short rugged branch abruptly broken off.

Pouched Mammals (Marsupialia) as Climbers.—Tree-Kangaroos, Phalangers, and Opossums, all typical climbing forms, represent the arboreal members of this primitive and multifarious order. The Tree-Kangaroos (species of *Dendrolagus*) inhabit forest-regions in New Guinea and North Queensland. Just as Sloths and the smaller Ant-eaters of South America are the descendants of ground-forms, so are these creatures an offshoot from the main kangaroo group, of which the typical members are leapers of grazing habit. And in most respects they conform pretty closely to the appearance and structure of their immediate relatives, except that the hind-limbs are not of the same disproportionate length. We have seen, when dealing with the Spectre Tarsier (see p. 244), that leaping powers may be possessed by arboreal forms, and Tree-Kangaroos furnish an illustration of this, as might be expected. Of the movements of the Queensland species (*Dendrolagus Lumholtzii*) Semon speaks as follows (in *In the Australian Bush*):—"It seems very singular that a creature, the structure of which marks it out as a leaping animal adapted to life in the plains, should have accommodated itself relatively well to an arboreal life among trees and leaves, without really changing its character. It must be admitted that its movements among the trees differ somewhat from those of other tree-animals. It jumps upon a low tree at one leap, and thence ascends higher up, always moving by hops and leaps. But it can also climb the higher trees quite deftly by catching hold of the branches with the sharp claws of its fore-feet and applying its hind-feet tightly to the trunk. Arrived in the crown of the tree, it moves about in the same hopping manner; and I was told that it presents a very queer sight jumping about in the foliage of the native woods."

Phalangers constitute another group of climbing pouched Mammals, the members of which usually possess a long prehensile tail, the end of which is more or less destitute of hair, by which the sensitiveness is increased, as in a Spider-Monkey (see p. 239). There are five clawed digits on the hand, and the same number of toes on the foot, all of these being claw-bearing, except the great toe. There are one or two points in the structure of the hind-limb which are specially interesting. The two bones of the lower leg, tibia and fibula, are complete, and the former can be twisted round to some extent, carrying the foot with it, and thus enabling the sole to be turned inwards, a great accommodation in climbing. A similar arrangement has already been described for monkeys (see p. 237). The great toe is very large, devoid of claw, and opposable to the other toes, an admirable grasping organ being thus constituted as in monkeys. The second and third digits are relatively small, and bound together by a fold of skin, precisely as in a Kangaroo (fig. 802). A typical species, the Common Phalanger (*Trichosurus vulpeculus*) is represented in fig. 802. It is native to both Australia and Tasmania. The smallest and most elegant

Fig. 802.—Common Phalanger (*Trichosurus vulpeculus*)

member of the group, the Long-snouted Phalanger (*Tarsipes rostratus*), has already been spoken of in another connection (vol. ii, p. 181). The Koala or Pouched-Bear (*Phascolarctos cinereus*), on the other hand, is the clumsiest-looking Phalanger, and differs considerably from its congeners (see vol. ii, p. 180). The tail is reduced to a mere vestige, but the absence of this aid to climbing is fully made up for by the unique structure of the fore-foot. For the thumb and first finger together can be opposed to the other three fingers, and thus the hand is converted into a gripping organ fully as efficient as the clasping foot.

The Opossums of America, almost without exception, are expert climbers, and the general character of average species will be realized by reference to fig. 803, which represents the Common Opossum (*Didelphys Virginiana*). It is about the size of a cat, and much larger than any other member of the same family. The geographical range is considerable, for it is common

Fig. 803.—Virginian Opossum (*Didelphys Virginiana*)

throughout temperate North America, and its area of distribution stretches southwards into tropical South America. No other pouched Mammal is found in the northern half of the New World. The long, scaly, prehensile tail is one of the most striking features of its organization, and the foot is constructed on the same plan as that of a Phalanger, except that the second and third toes are neither reduced in size nor bound together by skin.

Some other pouched Mammals are arboreal, but the most interesting climbing adaptations in the order have now been described.

Birds (Aves) as Climbers.—So much space has been devoted to Climbing Mammals that it will be impossible to attempt anything like a detailed account of Birds adapted to the same habit. Besides, the purpose here kept in view will be sufficiently served by indicating the chief directions along which climbing specializations have been evolved. To these very great interest attaches, for it is reasonable to suppose that the remote ancestors of Birds first forsook life on the ground to dwell among trees, before conquering the realms of air, their proudest achievement.

Many Birds which obtain part or most of their food among trees, either in the form of buds, fruits, and seeds, or as insects and other small animals, have no need to be specialized for climbing. Their power of flight enables them to flit from branch to branch and levy toll on the abundant food-supplies that are thus to be easily reached. Many such forms also roost among the branches at night. It is therefore necessary that the feet should be constructed in such a way as to have a certain amount of grasping power, more especially as it is upon small branches and twigs that most food is to be found, and which also afford the securest sleeping-places. But these small branches at the same time furnish the scantiest foothold, and therefore require to be firmly gripped. As illustrating adaptation to this end the feet of ordinary Perching Birds (Passeres) merit special consideration. Some of the chief facts are easily verified by noticing the way in which tame Canaries, and most of the other small singing-birds kept in captivity, hold on to their perches. As in all Birds, the outer or little toe has been lost, and of the four which remain, the thumb, or inner toe, is backwardly directed. By means of flexor muscles all the digits can be bent, and the opposition of the thumb to the other three toes gives a very perfect grasping organ. The amount of bending is proportionate to the size of the twig upon which the bird has settled. The way in which the feet clasp small twigs is illustrated by fig. 804, in which two Titmice are drawn in different positions. There is an interesting arrangement enabling a bird which perches or roosts upon a small branch to hold on quite firmly without having to use muscular force at all. Two of the muscles which bend the toes are attached to the toe-bones by fibrous cords or tendons, of which one runs to the great toe, and the other divides into three branches for the three other toes. The weight of the body bends the leg at the ankle, and this pulls upon the tendons, as a result of which the toes are bent. It

Fig. 84.—Long-tailed Titmice (*Acredula caudata*)

is obvious that this "perching mechanism" greatly simplifies the task of grasping a twig firmly during resting or feeding, and it is so perfect that the bird can sleep in safety without any fear of falling. Everyone has noticed tame birds sleeping profoundly upon apparently perilous perches, and no doubt the question "How is it done?" has arisen in the minds of some. The answer has just been given, of course without going into minute anatomical detail. An equivalent mechanism is said to exist in some of the specialized climbing Mammals, such as squirrels.

Since the fore-limbs of birds have been transformed into wings, it is obvious that the feet must serve as the chief climbing organs, although these are often supplemented by beak and tail. And we are now prepared to understand the structure of "climbing" (*zygodactylous*) feet. Much importance was formerly attached to this in classification, and the pre-eminent climbers among birds possessing a particular type of such feet were

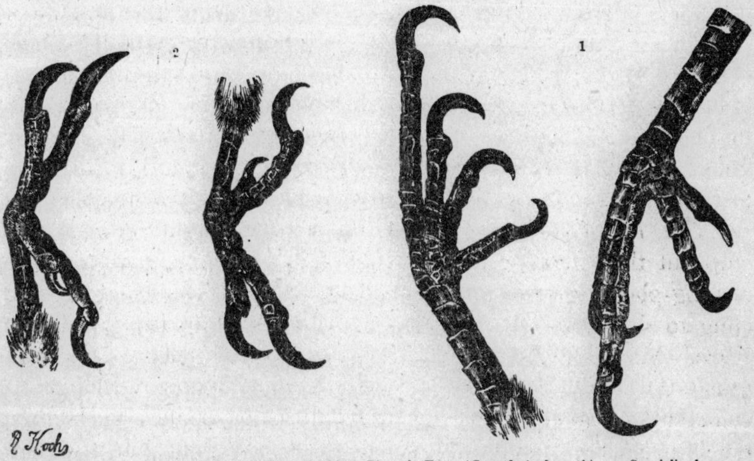

Fig. 805.—1, Imperfect Climbing Foot of African Plantain-Eater (*Corythaix leucotis*). 2, Specialized Climbing Foot of a Green Woodpecker (*Gecinus*).

lumped together into the group of CLIMBING BIRDS or SCANSORES, including Woodpeckers, Cuckoos, Parrots, &c. The peculiarity of the foot in question consists in the fact that not only the first toe is backwardly directed, but also the fourth or outer one (fig. 805). The sharp curved claws are another characteristic feature. The foot of an African Plantain-Eater (*Corythaix leucotis*) is also represented in the same figure, to illustrate a stage in the evolution of the climbing foot. In this case the outer toe can be turned back when required, but is not permanently fixed in that position. The ordinary perching foot is such a very perfect grasping organ that the climbing foot can scarcely have been evolved in relation to life among small branches and twigs, as under such conditions it would hardly be necessary. But these parts of a tree do not constitute the entire arboreal larder. The trunk, and branches too large to be encircled by a bird's foot, offer an abundant food supply, for numerous insects and other small creatures are to be found on their surface, and in the numerous small crannies and chinks which are present. And there are many insect larvæ which burrow in bark and wood, from which some birds are able to dig them out. It is clear that the climbing foot is better suited for clinging firmly to a tree-trunk than the ordinary perching foot; for the weight of the body has to be supported, and is mainly borne by the hinder part of the foot, so that two toes turned back are better than one. The ordinary perching foot can, however, be used for climbing up tree-trunks and walls, and clinging to these while food is being collected. A good example is that of the Common Creeper (*Certhia familiaris*), and here the stiff tail is of the greatest use in helping to support the body, thus aiding the great toe (see vol. ii. p. 59). The Nut-Hatch (*Sitta cæsia*) is a closely-related form which is able to cling to the smallest surface irregularities.

The *Woodpeckers* (Picidæ), which with their powerful bills chip out their food from bark and wood, and also excavate deep nesting-places in tree-trunks, possess powerful climbing feet, which cling so closely to the bark that Bowdler Sharpe remarks (in *The Royal Natural History*):—"The tenacity with which the claws grasp the bark of a tree is often illustrated even in death, for sometimes a woodpecker, when fatally wounded by shot, automatically grips the trunk with such vigour as to remain suspended". In most cases the short, stiffened tail also helps to support the body, as in a Creeper, the hard tips of the quill-axes being almost spiny in character. There are, however, some small Woodpeckers known as Piculets, native to both Old and New Worlds, in which the tail is quite short.

After what has been said about the advantages of the four-toed climbing foot, it seems rather curious to find that *Three*-toed Woodpeckers are known which have lost the great toe, but are notwithstanding as expert climbers as the ordinary species. But a plausible explanation of this seems possible. For of the two toes of the climbing foot which are turned back, the great toe is decidedly less useful, since it is not so firmly attached to the shank-bone as the fourth toe. And examination of the foot of an ordinary Woodpecker (fig. 805) will show that the great toe is a good deal smaller that the one which shares its work. From this we may gather that the great toe, with its comparatively loose attachment to the shank-bone, did not in the first instance prove a strong enough support. This led to its reinforcement by the fourth or outer toe, which became backwardly directed. The said toe, being well developed and having a firm attach-

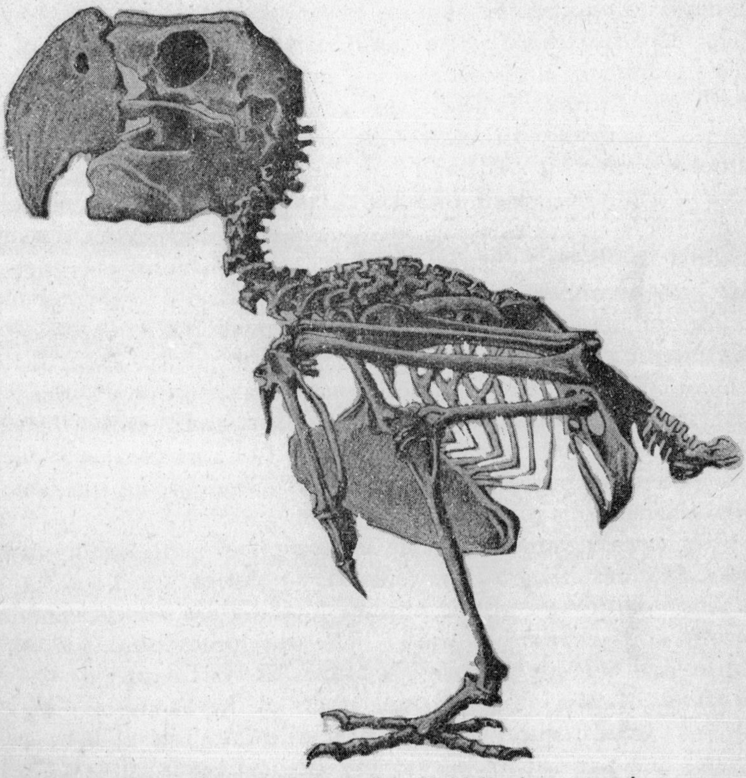

Fig. 806.—Skeleton of a Parrot. The limbs of the left side only are represented

ment to the shank, would seem to have become able to do all the supporting work required. Hence the gradual reduction of the less useful great toe, and ultimately, in Three-toed Woodpeckers, its entire suppression.

Parrots (Psittaci) constitute a large order of which the members are for the most part typical climbers. The legs are comparatively short, especially in the shank-region, and terminate in typical climbing feet (fig. 806 which constitute highly perfect grasping organs. So much is this the case that a Parrot often feeds when standing on one foot, the other being used to hold the food, as most of us have observed in captive specimens. No other birds use their feet for this purpose. The beautiful little Hanging Parrots of South-east Asia find another use for these mobile structures, for they habitually sleep suspended from a branch, to which they hold on by one foot.

In those species where the tail is short and broad, it no doubt helps in climbing, the most striking case being that afforded by the Pigmy Parrots of New Guinea, some of which are not so large as sparrows. In these little creatures the shafts of the tail-quills project at the end, very much as in a Creeper (see p. 264). But the powerful hooked beak of a Parrot is a much more valuable aid to climbing, its usefulness in this respect being enhanced by the fact that its upper half is capable of comparatively free movement.

The gorgeously-coloured *Trogons* (Trogonidæ) of Africa, Asia, and America possess grasping feet which look at first sight like those of Woodpeckers. But the two toes which are turned back are here first and *second* instead of first and *fourth*. This type of foot is termed *heterodactylous*, and the arrangement is to some extent comparable to that which is found in the hand of a Koala (see p. 259).

Still another variation of the climbing foot is found in the little *Colies* or *Mouse-Birds* (Coliidæ) of Africa, for here the first and fourth toes of the slender foot can be turned either forwards or backwards at will. The latter procedure converts the feet into efficient grasping organs. A. H. Evans (in *The Cambridge Natural History*) thus speaks of the habits of these birds:—"Colies frequent forest-districts, especially where the bush is thick; they are active, yet not very shy, and are usually found, except during the breeding season, in flocks of some six to eight individuals. The flight is laboured, with many a quick beat of the wings; but it is direct and fairly rapid, though seldom sustained beyond some neighbouring tree, where the bird may be seen stealing through the foliage, and aiding its creeping movements with its bill. The most peculiar habit, however, is that of climbing with the whole metatarsus [*i.e.* the shank-region next the foot] applied to the branch, a fact which adds greatly to the mouse-like appearance. When roosting, Colies are said to pack themselves together in masses, and to hang by the feet; rarely are they seen perching or hopping, though they often cling to the boughs with the head downwards." The Long-tailed Coly (*Colius macrurus*) is represented in fig. 807.

Fig. 807.—Long-tailed Coly (*Colius macrurus*)

REPTILES (REPTILIA) AS CLIMBERS.—We need only consider under this heading some of the Lizards (Lacertilia) and certain Snakes (Ophidia).

Lizards (Lacertilia) as Climbers.—Many Lizards, such as the American Iguanas, are arboreal in habit, and the Wall Lizard (*Lacerta muralis*) of the Mediterranean countries climbs about among masonry, &c. But as in these and most other cases of the sort climbing is simply effected by means of the sharp claws, there is nothing of special interest to detain us.

It is quite otherwise, however, with the little Geckos, which are widely distributed through the warmer parts of the world.

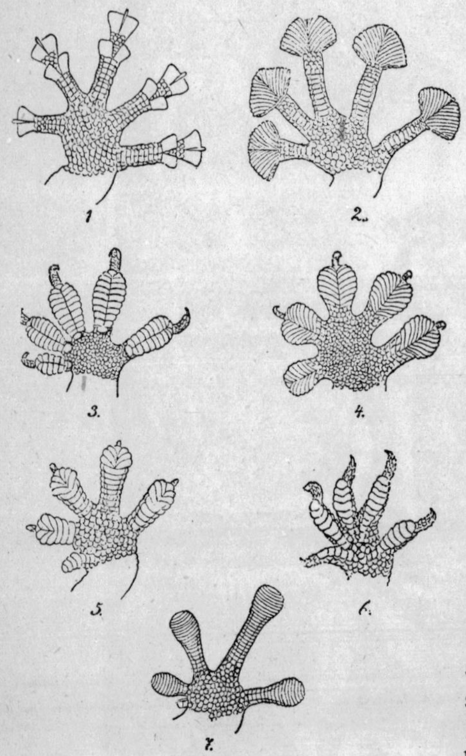

Fig. 808.—Under Sides of Feet of various Geckos

1, Calodactylus aureus; 2, Ptyodactylus homolepis; 3, Hemidactylus coctæi; 4, Gehyra mutilata; 5, Lepidodactylus aurantiacus; 6, Hoplodactylus Anamallensis; 7, Phelsuma Andamanense.

For here the fingers and toes are specialized into climbing organs of very peculiar nature, quite unlike anything with which we have so far met. In most species the under sides of the digits are broadened out, and provided with a variously arranged series of transverse overlapping folds (fig. 808). The projecting parts of these are thickly studded with curved climbing bristles, each with its tip swollen into a little knob. These are capable of fitting into the smallest inequalities, and no doubt help considerably in the ascent of even slightly rough surfaces. But when it is remembered that a Gecko can climb with facility up the face of a sheet of glass, it is clear that some sort of adhesive action must come into play, very probably of the "sucker" order, in which a vacuum is created by the pulling out of the central part of a smooth piece of skin applied to an equally smooth surface. Gadow (in *The Cambridge Natural History*) gives the following explanation:—"Many, perhaps the majority of Geckos, have adhesive digits, by means of which some kinds are enabled to climb absolutely smooth and vertical surfaces, for instance, a window-pane; or, what is more startling, they run along the smooth whitewashed ceiling, back downwards. The apparatus is complicated in its minute detail, but is very simple in principle. The adhesion is effected by small and numerous vacua. The under surface of each digit is furnished with many trans-

Fig. 809.—Common Chameleon (*Chameleo vulgaris*)

An outer view of the left fore-foot is given above and a similar view of the left hind-foot below.

verse lamellæ. The pressing down of the foot upon a smooth surface causes the lamellæ to spread asunder and drive out the air; partial retraction lets them return to their original position by virtue of their elasticity; and little vacua are produced. Each lamella is further beset with tiny hair-like excrescences, which secure adpression to even the slightest irregularity of surface, and at the same time enhance the elasticity of the pads."

Some of the Lizards possess grasping feet constructed more

or less on a plan of which so many examples have now been given for Mammals and Birds. There is, for instance, a good-sized species (*Lyriocephalus scutatus*) inhabiting Ceylon, in which thumb and great toe are opposable, somewhat as in an Old World Monkey. And this leads up to the much more remarkable case of Chameleons, where by union of the digits into two groups both hands and feet are converted into most efficient grasping organs (fig. 809). The united digits are grouped differently in the two extremities. The thumb is bound up with the two adjoining fingers, and the two other fingers (fourth and fifth) are similarly connected. But the great toe is united only with its neighbour, while the three outer toes (third, fourth, and fifth) are also joined together. The latter arrangement is reminiscent of the hand of a Koala (see p. 259). And as if such climbing hands and feet were not sufficient, the long curly tail is very prehensile.

Snakes (Ophidia) as Climbers.—Many Snakes climb most admirably by writhing round the trunks and branches of trees, a procedure which is rendered possible by the extreme flexibility of their bodies, and the great development of the lateral muscles. The backwardly projecting edges of the ventral shields prevent slipping back, just as in ordinary locomotion on the ground (see p. 110). Pythons and Boas, the largest of existing snakes, climb after this fashion, and their short prehensile tails enable them to hang from a branch on the look-out for prey. Among smaller forms which climb trees more or less in pursuit of food may be mentioned our common Grass Snake (*Tropidonotus natrix*), the Æsculapian Snake (*Coluber longissimus*) of Europe, and the American Black Snake (*Zamenis constrictor*). The Wood-Snakes of the West Indies and the hotter parts of Central and South America are thoroughly arboreal forms, and their dull green colour makes them inconspicuous among the foliage of their native forests. A well-known species is the Brazilian Wood-Snake (*Herpetodryas carinatus*, fig. 810), which may be as much as 7 feet long. Some very interesting Tree-Snakes (species of *Dendrophis* and *Dendrelaphis*) belonging to the Eastern Hemisphere, are distinguished by the conversion of the ventral shields into climbing structures. Each of these scales has a well-marked longitudinal ridge near either side, and the freely projecting back edge possesses a couple of notches corresponding to these. Gadow (in *The Cambridge Natural History*) speaks of these scales as—"arrangements which are of great assistance in climbing, these snakes being able to slide up the

Fig. 810.—Brazilian Wood-Snake (*Herpetodryas carinatus*). The head is drawn on a larger scale above

branches of trees in almost straight lines, instead of having to twist and undulate their way up".

All the preceding forms are non-poisonous. Most of the venomous serpents are ground forms, though to this there are exceptions, and some species which generally live on the ground can climb on occasion. Among typical arboreal forms may be mentioned the slender Whip-Snakes (species of *Dryophis*), native to India and South-east Asia, and the climbing Tree-Vipers (species of *Trimeresurus*) of India and Burmah. The tails of the latter are prehensile.

Amphibians (Amphibia) as Climbers.—The only forms of special interest in this connection are the little Tree-Frogs (*Hylidæ*), which have a wide distribution in both Old and New Worlds. One of the most familiar species is the common little Green Tree-Frog (*Hyla arborea*) of Europe and North Africa, which also ranges eastward to Japan. A novel kind of climbing apparatus is here present, in the form of little adhesive cushions on the under side of the tips of the digits. These appear to act by means of "adhesion", *i.e.* the mutual attraction of two surfaces which are brought into intimate contact. It is probably in the same way that a Limpet (*Patella vulgata*) adheres to its scar (see vol. ii, p. 197). The pad is supported by a gristly disc, and contains muscle-fibres which, by their contraction, help to adjust it to the surface of a twig or leaf. There are also small glands in the skin of the pad, and the slimy secretion poured out by these promotes adhesion by helping in the expulsion of air from between the two surfaces in contact.

Fishes (Pisces) as Climbers.—There is nothing of very special interest to engage our attention here. Of course such fishes as Eels, which from time to time leave the water, have to do a certain amount of climbing work. The shore-haunting Mud-Skippers (*Periophthalmus*), which have already been spoken of several times, are able to climb boulders and mangrove roots by means of their powerful pectoral fins, which are hooked over projections. It has also been stated that the Climbing Perch (*Anabas scandens*) is able to ascend the trunks of trees by means of the same fins but the statement requires confirmation.

BACKBONELESS ANIMALS (Invertebrata) AS CLIMBERS

We may here instructively consider how climbing is effected by some of the Jointed-Legged Animals (Arthropoda) and Hedgehog-Skinned Animals (Echinodermata).

Jointed-limbed Animals (Arthropoda) as Climbers.—Experts in this sort of locomotion are to be found among Insects (Insecta), Spider-legged Animals (Arachnida), and Crustaceans (Crustacea), and it will be well to remember in both cases that

THE EUROPEAN TREE-FROG (*Hyla arborea*)

This pretty little Tree-Frog has a wide distribution in Europe, from which it ranges east to Japan, and south into North Africa. It is extremely active, and possesses little rounded pads on the tips of its fingers and toes, which are able to adhere firmly even to perfectly smooth surfaces. The upper side of the body is green, shading off into a whitish tint on the under side. A considerable amount of colour-change is possible, enabling the animal to harmonize with different surroundings. By this "variable protective coloration" it often escapes the observation of its enemies; but the arrangement is also an "aggressive" one, helping to conceal the animal from its prey, which consists largely of insects. The male possesses a very large "croaking pouch" on the under side of its throat. This serves as a resonator, and when fully expanded looks something like a football.

THE EUROPEAN TREE-FROG (HYLA ARBOREA)

the limbs employed are quite different in structure from those of Backboned Animals (see p. 163).

Insects (Insecta) as Climbers.—The structure of the limbs in climbing insects depends upon the nature of the surfaces on which progression takes place. These may be either rough or smooth, necessitating two distinct kinds of adaptation, similar to those already exemplified among the backboned forms.

Fig. 811.—Long-horned Oak-Beetle (*Cerambyx heros*)

Undoubtedly the remote ancestors of Insects had numerous pairs of legs, as Peripatus, Centipedes, and Millipedes still have. The reduction to six pairs was very probably an adaptation to climbing (see p. 167), while at the same time the body became shorter and more compact.

Among insects capable of climbing upon a rough surface, such as that presented by bark, are many Tree-Beetles, especially those which are known as "longicorns", on account of the length of their feelers. An insect of this kind is shown in fig. 811, which represents the Long-horned Oak-Beetle (*Cerambyx heros*). The climbing mechanism will be understood by reference to the accompanying outline of a leg of the Cockroach (*Periplaneta orientalis*, fig. 812), an insect which is able to scale walls with undesirable facility. The parts of the leg are, beginning at the top,—hip (coxa), trochanter, thigh (femur), shin (tibia), and foot (tarsus). The last, with which only we are here concerned, is made up of five little joints, and bears a pair of curved claws at its tip. It is these which constitute the holdfasts by which climbing on a rough surface is rendered possible, and in this respect they are comparable to the claws of a cat or tree-lizard. Similar claws are present on the feet of a great many other insects, such as the beetles above mentioned, cockchafers, tree-grasshoppers, and tree-bugs. From the stand-point of evolution these structures are of very great interest. They are almost certainly to be regarded as an inheritance from the segmented worms, which were the ancestors of Arthropods. These worms, like the recent Bristle-Worms (see p. 98), no doubt had numerous pairs of unjointed foot-stumps, in which bristles were imbedded. There fortunately exists a recent form (*Peripatus*, fig. 813), which, though an undoubted Arthropod, resembles bristle-worms in many respects. Its numerous legs are very like foot-stumps, and each of them bears two sharp claws, which may be looked upon as specialized bristles. And if insects have descended from bristle-bearing worms through ancestors resembling Peripatus, their claws are probably to be explained in the same way.

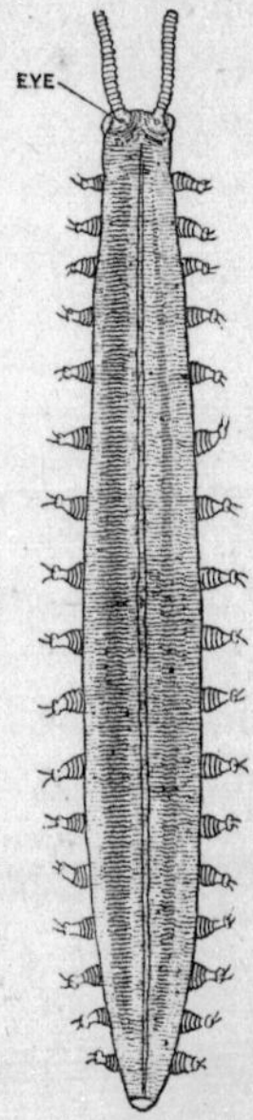

Fig. 813. Cape Peripatus (*Peripatus Capensis*)

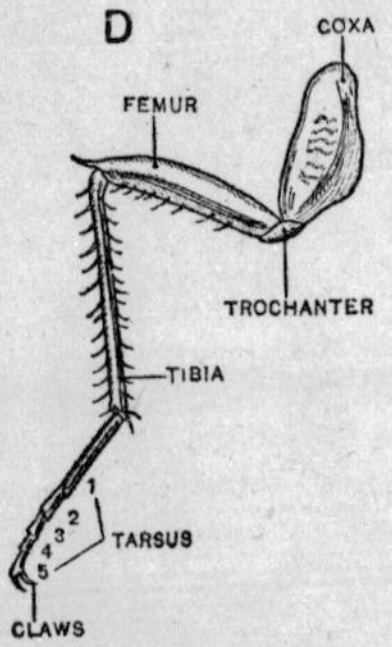

Fig. 812.—Leg of a Cockroach (*Periplaneta orientalis*)

Bees are able to climb both rough and smooth surfaces, and their feet are marvels of adaptation to this double power. Not only are two claws present for use as already described, but also an end-flap or *pulvillus*, which comes into action when the insect desires to ascend a smooth surface or to walk upside down in the fashion familiar to us all. The following quotation and the accompanying figures (figs. 814, 815) are taken from Cheshire, who has made a very thorough study of the Honey-Bee in this and other connections. On a rough surface "the points of the claws catch (as at E), and the pulvillus is saved from any contact, but if the surface be smooth, so that the claws get no grip, they slide back and are drawn beneath the foot (as at C), which change of position applies the pulvillus, so that it immediately clings. It is the character of the surface, then, and not the will of the bee, that determines whether claw or pulvillus shall be used in sustaining it. But another contrivance, equally beautiful, remains to be noticed. The pulvillus is carried folded in the middle (as at E), but opens out when applied to a surface; for it has at its upper part an elastic and curved rod (CR), which straightens as the pulvillus is pressed down; C and D (fig. 815) making this clear. The flattened out pulvillus thus holds strongly while pulled, by the weight of the bee, along the surface to which it adheres, but comes up at once if lifted and rolled off from its opposite sides, just as we should pull a wet postage-stamp from an envelope. The bee, then, is held securely till it attemps to lift the leg, when it is freed at once; and by this exquisite yet simple plan it can fix and release each foot at least twenty times per second." The pulvillus would appear to act by adhesion, much in the same way as the pads on the toes of a Tree-Frog (see p. 272). Nor does the resemblance cease here, for in the frog there are glands in the skin, which pour out a secretion that enables the air to be expelled from between pad and underlying surface, while in the insect the under side of the pulvillus is studded with holding-bristles from which a similar fluid exudes that answers the same purpose. We further notice the presence of a number of touch-bristles (H) on the end of the foot, and these probably help the insect in the selection of foot-holds. They are reminiscent of the stiff hairs on the wrist of some Lemurs, by which a similar purpose is served (see p. 241).

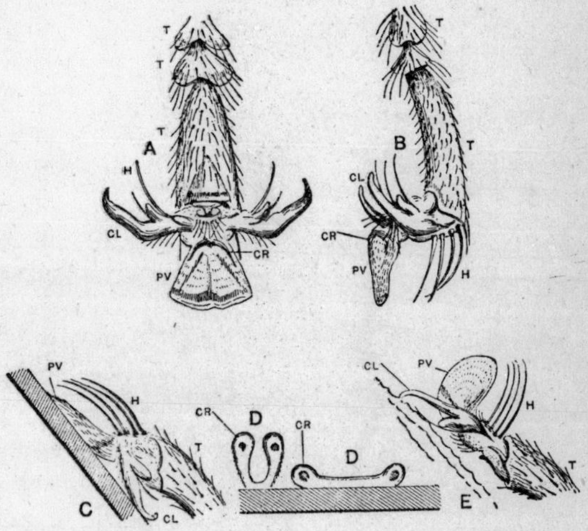

Figs. 814, 815.—Structure and Action of Foot of Honey-Bee (*Apis mellifica*)

A and B, Under surface and side of foot. C, Foot as used for climbing on smooth surface. D, Cross-sections of pulvillus in partly folded and fully unfolded conditions. E, Foot as used for climbing on rough surface. CL, Claws; CR, elastic rod of pulvillus; H, tactile hairs; PV, pulvillus; T, joints of tarsus.

A favourite microscopic object is the foot of the House-Fly (*Musca domestica*, fig. 816), which is constructed on a similar plan to that just described for the Bee, and possesses claws and two end-flaps. It is the adhesive power of the latter which enables the insect to walk along a ceiling.

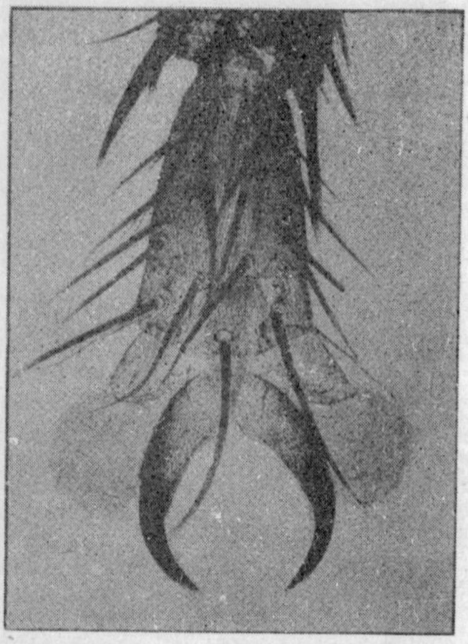

Fig. 816.—Under Surface of Foot of House-Fly (*Musca domestica*), greatly enlarged, showing claws and pulvilli.

It may be as well to state that the explanation of the adhesive power of the insect-foot, as just given, is not the only one possible, nor is it accepted by all zoologists. But it appears to the present writer to be the most plausible so far advanced, at any rate for the special insects named.

Spider-like Animals (Arachnida) as Climbers.—For our present purpose it will be enough to consider the case of web-spiders. The foot, for example, of a Garden Spider (*Epeira diadema*, fig. 817) terminates in three claws. Two of these (*a*), constituting a pair, are the comb-like weaving-claws which have to do with web-construction, and are helped in their work by some saw-edged bristles (*c*) on the under side of the foot. The unpaired third claw (*b*) is strongly hooked, and employed for climbing about the web, or on objects outside it. No doubt the specialized weaving-claws also help the spider to hold on to its snare.

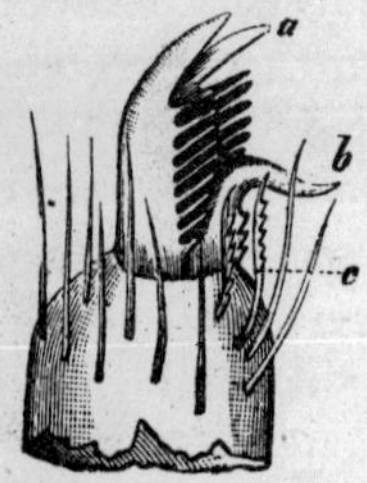

Fig. 817.—Side View of Foot of Spider, greatly enlarged *a*, Weaving-claws; *b*, climbing-claw; *c*, saw-edged weaving-bristles.

Among Spiders which construct no webs it is usual to find only a pair of claws, which play the same part as those on the tip of an insect's foot, and are equivalent to the weaving-claws of the web-spinners. In some species, such as the Harlequin Spider (*Salticus scenicus*), a well-known hunting form, there is a tuft of climbing-bristles on the under side of the foot. Their presence is associated with the power of scaling vertical surfaces and progressing upside down fly-fashion. We are reminded here of the similar structures on the feet of Geckos (see p. 268).

Crustaceans (Crustacea) as Climbers.—Two kinds of grasping organs, useful in climbing, are to be found in certain members of this class. One of these is exemplified by the little Skeleton Shrimp (*Caprella*, fig. 818), which climbs like a monkey on sea-weeds and zoophytes. The first pair of legs, immediately behind the head, have sharp end-joints which can be turned back so as to work against the part of the limb to which they are attached. The arrangement is comparable to a hand with one finger capable of being bent round against the palm. The hinder part of the body bears three pairs of legs with curved claws, which materially aid in the climbing movements.

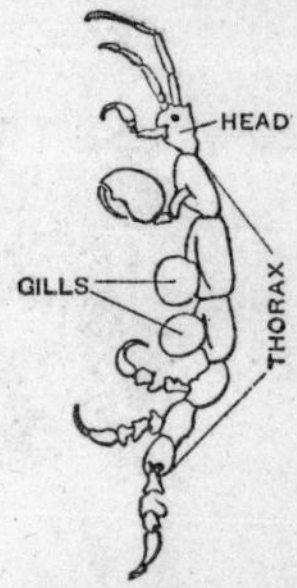

Fig. 818.—Skeleton Shrimp (*Caprella*), enlarged.

The great pincers of a Crab, Crayfish, or Lobster (fig. 819) are grasping organs of more complex nature, which serve many

Fig. 819.—Lobster (*Homarus vulgaris*)

purposes besides climbing. Here we find the smaller jaw of the pincers is the freely movable end-joint. This works against the large preceding joint, which is drawn out into a long toothed projection, constituting the other jaw of the pincers. The large size of this grasping organ is due to the presence of powerful muscles by which the jaws are opened and closed. In a Lobster or Crayfish the first two pairs of walking-legs terminate in nippers of similar nature, but of comparatively small size.

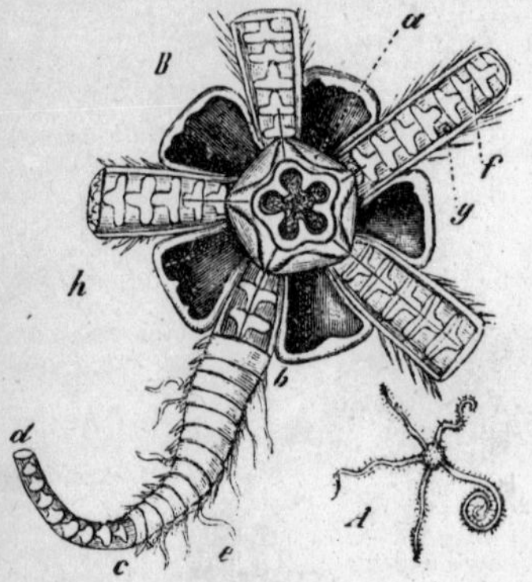

Fig. 820.—Brittle-Star

The flexibility of the arms is illustrated by the small figure A. B is partly dissected from below to show structure: *a*, mouth-plates; *becd*, an arm from which some of the under-plates have not been removed; the other arms have been cut off very short to show central plates (*f*) and their muscles (*g*); *h*, a breathing-pouch cut open.

HEDGEHOG-SKINNED ANIMALS (ECHINODERMATA) AS CLIMBERS.—The *Brittle-Stars* (*Ophiuroidea*) have aptly been called "Echinoderm Monkeys", as many of them are expert climbers. The five arms of an ordinary Star-Fish are merely prolongations of the body in which the digestive organs are partly lodged. But in Brittle-Stars (fig. 820) a sharp distinction can be drawn between a disc-shaped central body and five flexible, jointed arms, which may be looked upon as true limbs or appendages. Each arm is covered by overlapping limy plates, and its interior is mostly filled up by a series of hard pieces jointed together in such a way that all sorts of complicated curving movements can be executed by the agency of appropriate muscles. So

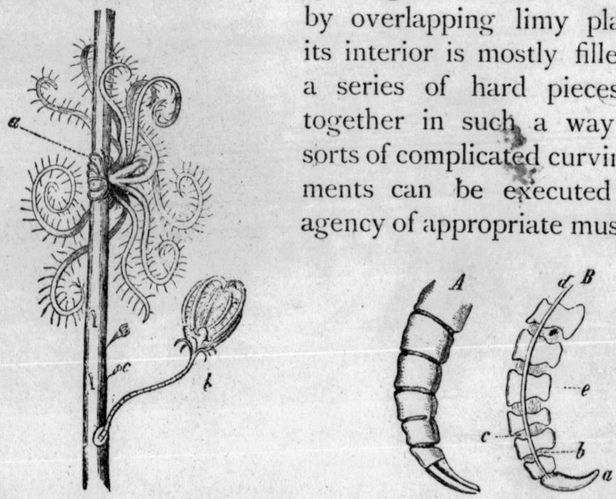

Figs. 821, 822.—A Feather-Star holding on by its Grasping-threads (*a*), and its larvæ (*bc*) attached by stalks. A and B (section) represent terminal part of a grasping-thread; *a*, end claw; *bc*, muscle; *d*, elastic band; *e*, limy joint.

much is this the case, that a parallel has often been drawn between the arm of a Brittle-Star and the sinuous body of a Snake.

The *Feather-Stars*, belonging to another group (*Crinoidea*), of which most members are fixed by long stalks, possess another sort of climbing apparatus (fig. 821). The very young animal is stalked, but soon becomes free, and close to the spot where the stalk was attached a circlet of slender grasping threads is developed. Each of these is made up of a series of limy joints, of which one end serves as a curved claw. The thread can be sharply bent by means of bundles of muscle-fibres which connect the successive joints, and straightened again by the elasticity of a fibrous band that runs through the centre of the thread. A grasping organ is thus constituted, which is almost like the foot of a bird, and may be used simply for fixing the animal to some firm body, or for climbing purposes.

The active Feather-Stars present a marked contrast to their sluggish stalked relatives the Sea-Lilies. But it is easy to understand how the difference between the two types has come about. We know that Sea-Lilies were once a dominant group, and flourished exceedingly in geological epochs very remote from our own times. It would seem that the competition for food among marine animals was much less keen than it is now, and fixed animals like the Sea-Lilies were at no great disadvantage. But as time went on the struggle for existence became more severe, and active rapacious forms such as higher Crustaceans and Fishes made it increasingly difficult for fixed species to maintain themselves. Sea-Lilies gradually diminished in numbers and importance, and the few forms which now exist are comparatively rare, and inhabit the deep sea, which has served as a refuge to them and other hard-pressed forms. But some creatures of the sort evolved along lines which have resulted in the Feather-Stars. These are simply to be regarded as Sea-Lilies which have given up their stalks and taken to an active life, though the larvæ are still stalked, as a sort of memento of the former state of things. That this step has proved successful is sufficiently shown by the great abundance and wide distribution of Feather-Stars at the present day. In very remote times, geologically speaking, Sea-Lilies were not the only stalked Echinoderms, there being two other groups of the kind, both of which have long been entirely extinct. Under present conditions a fixed life is decidedly unfavourable to Echinoderms, though it appears to answer well enough in certain other groups, *e.g.* Sponges and many Ascidians. Fixed animals are of necessity comparatively helpless, and when this kind of existence is a success there always appear to be effective protective arrangements. Rapid changes in the surroundings are usually unfavourable to highly specialized forms, which are not sufficiently plastic as it were to accommodate themselves with sufficient quickness to new conditions. This is probably why the Sea-Lilies are a declining group, of which, however, the Feather-Stars represent a vigorous branch that is probably able to hold its own for an indefinite time.

NUTHATCHES (*Sitta cæsia*) FEEDING YOUNG

The dominance of Birds in the vertebrate fauna of the world is largely due to their strongly developed parental instincts, by which the safety of eggs and young are secured. Such care is essential in cases where the nestlings are helpless, as in Perching Birds (*Passeres*), of which the Nuthatch is here taken as an illustration. This species is essentially a tree-form, and feeds upon insects during the greater part of the year, but when nuts, beech-mast, &c., are ripe, these constitute the chief article of diet. A nut is opened by being placed in a suitable crevice, and then cleft by the strong pointed beak. For nesting purposes a cavity in a trunk or branch is selected, and the opening plastered up with clay, leaving only a small round hole by way of door. The eggs are laid upon a heap of leaves or bark-scales within this cavity, and the parental duties of the old birds terminate soon after the young are fledged.

NUTHATCHES (SITTA CAESIA) FEEDING YOUNG

CONTENTS

ANIMAL MOVEMENT (*Continued*)

CHAPTER LI.—ANIMAL LOCOMOTION—PARACHUTING AND KITE-FLYING

PARACHUTING

KITE-FLYING

CHAPTER LII.—MUSCULAR LOCOMOTION—FLYING MAMMALS (MAMMALIA), BIRDS (AVES), AND REPTILES (REPTILIA)

ANIMAL DEVELOPMENT

CHAPTER LIII.—ANIMAL DEVELOPMENT—GENERAL PRINCIPLES—VEGETATIVE REPRODUCTION

CHAPTER LVI.—LIFE-HISTORIES, CARE OF EGGS AND YOUNG, AND DWELLINGS, IN BACKBONED ANIMALS (VERTEBRATA)

LIST OF ILLUSTRATIONS

PLATES

ILLUSTRATIONS

CHAPTER LI

ANIMAL LOCOMOTION—PARACHUTING AND KITE-FLYING

The present chapter is not headed "muscular" locomotion, as are those which precede it, because it deals with two kinds of progression which are of a passive nature, or mainly so.

PARACHUTING

The word "parachute" is applied by aeronauts to an umbrella-like arrangement by means of which perilous descents are made from balloons, &c. The opening out of the parachute offers so large a surface of resistance to the air that the fall is thereby broken.

In what may be called PARACHUTE ANIMALS we find expansions of the body which answer a similar purpose. As might be anticipated, it is among arboreal forms that we must chiefly look for examples of this kind of adaptation. Its practical use is obvious, for descent from one tree-branch to another, or even to the ground, is thus rendered comparatively safe and easy. And parachuting is of great evolutionary interest, for it probably constituted a prelude to flight. Unfortunately, however, our geological knowledge is as yet too incomplete to enable us to form any clear idea of the way in which wings were evolved from parachutes.

MAMMALS (MAMMALIA) AS PARACHUTISTS.—Striking instances of this adaptation are to be found in certain members of the following orders:—Insect-Eating Mammals (Insectivora), Gnawing Mammals (Rodentia), and Pouched Mammals (Marsupialia).

Insect-Eating Mammals (Insectivora) as Parachutists.—Only one species here included can claim to be a thorough-going parachutist. This is the Colugo or Flying "Lemur" (*Galeopithecus*) of South-east Asia, a much larger animal than its congeners, being about the size of a cat. In structure it is so peculiar that there is some doubt as to its classifactory position. But the Colugo is generally held to be an aberrant Insectivore, though, as a mark of its isolated position, it is placed in a distinct sub-order (*Dermaptera*). All the ordinary Insectivores (such as Shrews, Hedgehogs, Moles, &c.) are grouped in a second sub-order as True Insectivora (*Insectivora vera*).

The parachute consists of folds of hairy skin which run from neck to arm, connect the sides of the body with both pairs of limbs, and bind together hind-limbs and tail. Both feet and hands are webbed, but of course this simply means further extension of surface for parachuting, and has nothing to do with swimming. Comparatively little is known about the habits of this remarkable creature, but Wallace (in *The Malay Archipelago*) gives the following account of one which he observed in Sumatra:—"Once, in a bright twilight, I saw one of these animals run up a trunk in a rather open place, and then glide obliquely through the air to another tree, on which it alighted near its base, and immediately began to ascend. I paced the distance from the one tree to the other, and found it to be seventy yards; and the amount of descent I estimated at not more than thirty-five or forty feet, or less than one in five. This, I think, proves that the animal must have some power of guiding itself through the air, otherwise in so long a distance it would have little chance of alighting exactly upon the trunk."

Gnawing Mammals (Rodentia) as Parachutists.—So-called "Flying"-Squirrels inhabit the Northern Hemisphere and Africa. Of these the largest and best-known (species of *Pteromys*) are native to South and South-east Asia. A typical form is the Brown Flying-Squirrel (*Pteromys petaurista*), which may be as much as 18 inches in length, exclusive of the large bushy tail. In general appearance this creature is not unlike a common squirrel, were it not for the presence of parachute folds, resembling those of the Colugo. But only the base of the tail is in this case united with the hind-limbs, and the edge of the fold at the side of the body is supported in front by a bar of gristle stretching back from the wrist. The nature of the parachuting movement appears to be similar to those already described for the Colugo, and not far short of eighty yards is said to be the maximum length of the downward "flights" that are made through

PARACHUTING ANIMALS

In a number of arboreal backboned animals folds of skin are present that serve as parachuting arrangements, which facilitate progress from one branch or tree to another, and are useful in the search for food as well as in retreat from enemies. Three Parachuting Mammals are represented in the plate: 1, the Malayan Flying-Squirrel (*Pteromys petaurista*), native to south-east Asia; 2, the Colugo or Flying-"Lemur" (*Galeopithecus volans*), which is also from the Malay region; and 3, the little Sugar-"Squirrel" or Flying Phalanger (*Petaurus sciureus*) of eastern Australia. All these have a certain amount of steering power.

At 4 is depicted a Parachuting Reptile, the beautiful little Flying-Dragon (*Draco volans*) of the Malay region, in which there is a movable fold on either side of the body, supported by the ribs.

In the Common Flying-Fish (*Exocœtus volitans*) the pectoral fins are immensely large, and serve both as parachutes and kites. The peculiar shape of the tail gives an upward bias to the body in the water, greatly helping the fish to slide up, as it were, into the air.

PARACHUTING ANIMALS

the air. These squirrels are also credited with a certain amount of steering power as they descend in graceful curves from branch to branch or tree to tree.

The smaller Flying-Squirrels (species of *Sciuropterus*), represented in Asia, North-east Europe, and North America, are extremely graceful and pretty animals, which in most respects resemble their larger relatives. But the eyes are much larger, and even the base of the large tail is perfectly free. Being flattened from above downwards, this organ adds considerably to the area of the surface presented to the air. Audubon and Bachman thus describe the movements of the American Flying-Squirrel (*Sciuropterus volucella*), a community of which came under their observation:—"At times one would be seen darting from the topmost branches of a tall oak, and with wide extended membranes and outspread tail gliding diagonally through the air, till it reached the foot of a tree about fifty yards off, when, at the moment we expected to see it strike the earth, it suddenly turned upwards and alighted in the body of the tree. It would then run to the top, and once more precipitate itself from the upper branches and sail back again to the tree it had just left. Crowds of these little creatures joined in these sportive gambols; there could not have been less than two hundred. Scores of them would leave each tree at the same moment, seeming to have no other object in view than to indulge a playful propensity." This account certainly seems to furnish some evidence of steering power.

The African Flying-Squirrels (species of *Anomalurus* and *Idiurus*) are of somewhat smaller size than the Brown Flying-Squirrel and the species related to it. Notwithstanding an agreement with these both in general build, and especially as regards the nature and arrangement of the parachute folds, there are differences of sufficient importance to justify the inclusion of the African forms in a special family (*Anomaluridæ*). One of these is the absence of a piece of gristle stretching from the wrist along the front edge of the lateral fold. But the place of this is taken by a rod of similar character that runs from the elbow to the side of the fold. The other characteristic feature is the presence of a series of overlapping scales on the under side of the tail at its base. These would appear to be used as a help to climbing. In fig. 823 a drawing is given of a Gold Coast species (*Anomalurus peli*) to illustrate these features.

It may be interesting to notice that one member of the present family (*Aëthurus glirinus*), native to French Congo, is altogether devoid of parachute folds, although it possesses the distinctive climbing scales.

African Flying-Squirrels differ sufficiently from their Asiatic and American cousins to make it certain that the parachute folds

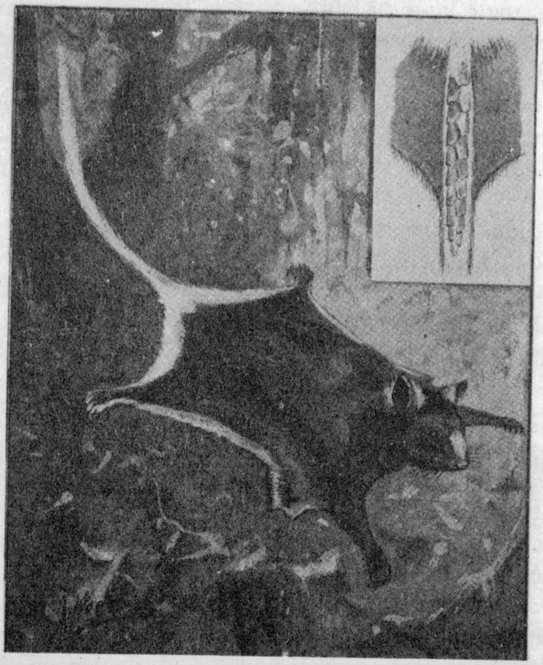

Fig. 823.—African Flying-Squirrel (*Anomalurus peli*). The small drawing shows the climbing-scales at the root of the tail

have been independently evolved in the two cases. And, on this view, the variation in detail already described is only what might be expected.

Pouched Mammals (Marsupialia) as Parachutists.—Different members of this order have adapted themselves to almost every conceivable mode of life, and it is not surprising to find that some of them are expert parachutists. These are the Flying Phalangers of the Australian region. One of the best-known species is the Squirrel Flying Phalanger or Sugar Squirrel (*Petaurus sciureus*) of East Australia, in which there is a well-developed fold stretching from hand to foot, while the tail is large and bushy. The length of the head and body is about 9 inches. The movements of this animal through the air, as indeed of flying phalangers generally, are much like those already described for other parachute mammals. Semon (in *In the Australian Bush*) gives the following account of the matter for this and an allied but smaller species (*P. breviceps*, variety

Fig. 824.—Australian Flying-Mouse (*Acrobates pygmæus*)

typicus):—"With the greatest agility they climb up the trunk of the eucalyptus-trees to the very tops. Then they spread out a fold of skin, which connects their limbs and tail and serves as a parachute, and noiselessly, in gentle flight, float downward towards the foot of a distant tree, to the top of which they immediately ascend. Thus I sometimes saw them float through distances of fifty yards, never failing their goal, and even managing to change their direction in the midst of their downward sweep, and to settle on another tree than that they had first chosen." We have here clear evidence proving considerable steering power.

The Taguan (*Petauroides volans*) of Queensland and Victoria is rather more than twice the size of the Sugar Squirrel, and the tip of its tail is devoid of hair. Besides this, the lateral parachute fold is very small in the region of the forearm and lower leg.

Fig. 825.—Instantaneous Photographs of a Pigeon descending to the Ground. Read from right to left

The smallest and most elegant of the Flying Phalangers is the diminutive Flying-Mouse (*Acrobates pygmæus*, fig. 824) of East Australia. The parachute fold extends only from ankle to knee, but its small extent is partly made up for by the long flat tail, the hair on which is so arranged as to give it the appearance of a feather.

Speaking of these three genera of parachute Marsupials (i.e. *Petaurus*, *Petauroides*, and *Acrobates*), Beddard remarks (in *The Cambridge Natural History*):—"As to these Flying Phalangers, it is exceedingly instructive to observe that the same method of 'flight' has been apparently evolved three times; for the three genera are each of them specially related to a separate type of non-flying Phalanger".

Birds (Aves) as Parachutists.—The wings of flying birds have passive as well as active uses. They are employed, for example, after the fashion of a parachute during descent from the air. This is illustrated in fig. 825 by a series of instantaneous photographs of a Pigeon taken during its downward course to the ground.

Reptiles (Reptilia) as Parachutists.—One of the Lizards native to the Malay region is a parachuting Gecko (*Ptychozoon homalocephalum*, fig. 826). Its fingers and toes are specialized for climbing, as in the better known members of its family (see p. 268). But it differs from these in possessing parachute folds on the sides of head, trunk, tail, and limbs, while a further increase of surface is afforded by webs which stretch between the digits.

Still more remarkable inhabitants of the same part of the world are the curious little lizards known as Flying-Dragons (species of *Draco*). But they are by no means so formidable as the name suggests, for the head and body are only some 5 inches in length, to which must be added a slender tail of about the same degree of elongation. These parachute organs consist of a pair of large wing-like folds at the sides of the flattened body, and these are supported by five or six pairs of the hinder ribs, which are of extraordinary length. The "wings" can be either expanded or folded up at will. These little dragons are very attractively coloured. In one well-known species (*Draco volans*), for example, the upper side is brown, with dark bands and flecks, and gleams like metal, while the parachute folds are black and orange. The little pouch (gular sac) under the throat affords an addition to the colour-scheme, for it is blue in the female and orange in the male. As to the habits of these lizards, Gadow (in *The Cambridge Natural History*) makes the following remarks:—"The 'Flying-Dragons use their wings as parachutes, but their sailing powers are said to be very moderate. Certainly they do not fly by moving the wings, but when at rest upon a branch amidst the luxurious vegetation, and in the immediate neighbourhood of gorgeously-coloured flowers, which partly conceal them by their likeness, they greatly resemble butterflies, especially since they have the habit of opening and folding their pretty wings."

Fig. 826.—Fringed Gecko (*Ptychozoon homalocephalum*)

Amphibians (Amphibia) as Parachutists.—A few species of tree-frog native to the East Indies are sufficiently specialized in connection (?) with the parachuting habit as to have earned the name of Flying-Frogs. The first known creature of this sort (*Rhacophorus nigropalmatus*) was seen in Borneo by Wallace, who makes the following remarks about it (in *The Malay Archipelago*):—"One of the most curious and interesting amphibians which I met with in Borneo was a large tree-frog, which was brought me by one of the Chinese workmen. He assured me that he had seen it come down in a slanting direction from a high tree, as if it flew. On examining it, I found the toes very long and fully webbed to their very extremity. The fore-legs were also bordered by a membrane, and the body was capable of considerable inflation. The back and limbs were of a very deep shining green colour, the under surface and the inner toes yellow, while the webs were black, rayed with yellow. . . As the extremities of the toes have dilated discs for adhesion, showing the creature to be a true tree-frog, it is difficult to imagine that this immense membrane of the toes can be for the purpose of swimming only, and the account of the Chinaman that it flew down from the tree becomes more credible. This is, I believe, the first instance known of a 'flying frog', and it is very interesting to Darwinians, as showing that the variability of the toes, which have been already modified for purposes of swimming and adhesive climbing, has been taken advantage of to enable an allied species to pass through the air like the flying lizard." Grave doubt has recently been thrown on the Chinaman's statement, and for the present the matter must remain undecided. This species also inhabits Sumatra and the Malay Peninsula, and an allied form (*R. Reinwardti*) is found in Java and Sumatra.

FISHES (PISCES) AS PARACHUTISTS.—In the cases so far described the parachuting organs facilitate descent from a height, but in Flying-Fishes (species of *Exocœtus*) the object attained is somewhat different. The so-called "wings" are constituted by the enormously enlarged pectoral fins, which, when one of these creatures vigorously projects itself out of the water, act kite-fashion, assisting the body to glide as it were up an inclined plane of air. At the same time the large resisting surface which they present hinders a too rapid return to the water. There is no evidence to show that these fins can be employed as wings, so that it is not a true case of flight. Under favourable circumstances a considerable speed (over 10 miles an hour) is attained, and a distance of some two or three hundred yards traversed; The "flight" is usually longest when directed *against* the wind. The tail of a Flying-Fish is of unusual form, being unsymmetrical, with the lower part better developed than the upper, and this is an adaptation to the habit of frequently leaving the water. For this particular shape of tail gives the body a bias upwards, and unless this is corrected by means of the pectoral fins the fish rises obliquely to the surface, thence passing into the air when the swimming movements are vigorous. As we have seen (p. 41), the tail of a Shark is also unsymmetrical, with the upper lobe better developed, thus facilitating progress downwards, while the symmetrical tail of an ordinary bony fish, such as a Herring, favours swimming directly forwards.

SPIDERS (ARANEIDÆ) AS PARACHUTISTS.—The Australian Flying-Spider (*Attus volans*, fig. 827), a hunting form, possesses para-

Fig. 827.—Australian Flying-Spider (*Attus volans*), showing the triangular parachute-flap on either side of the abdomen

chute organs having a similar use to the enlarged pectoral fins of a Flying-Fish. Either side of the abdominal region is provided with a flap, and when the spider launches itself into the air these flaps are spread out, presumably increasing the length of the leap, and diminishing shock when the ground is once more reached.

KITE-FLYING

We have seen that the wings of flying birds may be passively used as parachutes (p. 286), and they also serve as kites by which their owners are borne aloft without effort, under certain conditions to be spoken of more fully in the section Flight. Much the same thing is true of Flying-Insects, Flying-Fishes, and the Australian Flying-Spider.

A more remarkable case is presented by the larva of a two-winged fly, which, though unprovided with any special expansions of the body, is carried passively along by the wind, being reminiscent in this respect of certain small marine animals that drift along in the surface currents of the sea. The fly in question (*Hirmoneura obscura*) deposits her eggs in the tunnels which have been excavated in logs by wood-boring insects. When the maggots hatch out they make their way to the outside of the log, and sit up on their tails till they are blown away by the wind. When next met with they are found preying upon certain beetle-grubs which live in turf, but whether they attain their goal by pure chance is not known.

Many Spiders and some few Insects spin threads which present a sufficient surface to the wind to enable them to act as kites, bearing their constructors through the air, or at any rate rendering aerial progress more easy.

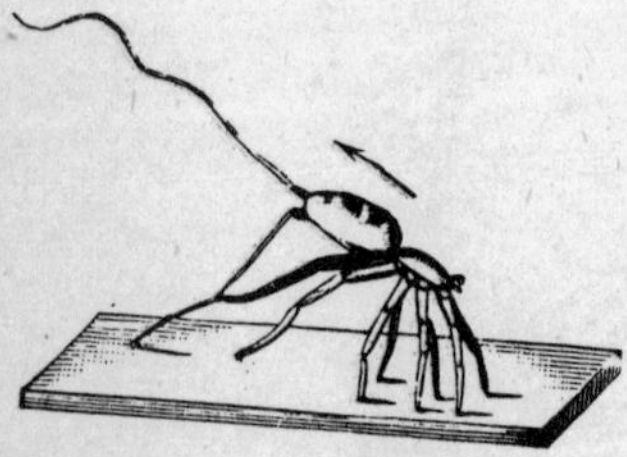

Fig. 828.—Young Spider spinning a "Gossamer" Thread. The arrow shows the direction of the wind

Spiders (Araneidæ) as Kite-Flyers. — The floating spider-threads familiar to all as "gossamer" were once believed to be produced by one particular kind of spider, but it is now known that they are spun by young individuals of many species. They are particularly abundant in early autumn, at the time associated with the slaughter of Michaelmas geese, and as the word is supposed to be a corruption of "goose-summer", it was possibly originally given on this account. A young spider desirous of floating through the air by this means stands firmly on its first three pairs of legs (fig. 828), and begins the work of spinning, using the last pair of legs for manipulating the threads. One of these is an anchor-line, and is severed when the gossamer thread is sufficiently long to serve its purpose. Krieghoff gives the following account of the matter (in *Das Tierreich*):—"Webs not only enable spiders to secure their prey, but also serve as a means of locomotion. In autumn young spiders begin to disperse themselves, casting out in any desired direction threads of such wondrous fineness as only to be visible in sunlight. By clinging to these with legs drawn in, these daring aeronauts are able to traverse considerable distances. The object of this procedure is probably to reach suitable winter quarters, as their weakness unfits them for the struggle for existence with older and stronger relatives in the original home. And by this instinct they unconsciously increase the area of distribution of their species, and contribute to its preservation. On fine autumn days we may see thousands upon thousands of these wind-borne gossamer threads, often compacted into thick web-like masses, some sweeping through the air, some hanging from flowers or other objects, others again spread out over meadows and stubble-fields, where, shining and sparkling in the sun like silver and diamonds, they produce what is known as 'wives' summer' or 'old wives' summer'. As soon as spiders emerge from their winter quarters in spring-time the same appearance repeats itself, though in much less degree, and is then known as 'maidens' summer'. These shimmering meteors in the air, woven of dew and silver, are described by folk-lore as the cunning handiwork of elves, taught by Freya and Holda, the renowned spinners of Asgaard."

TWO-WINGED FLIES (DIPTERA) AS KITE-FLYERS.—One family of this order includes a large number of predaceous forms called by the Germans Dancing-Flies (*Empidæ*), in reference to the complex aerial evolutions which many of them execute. In some of these (species of *Hilara*) small silken nets are carried about by the male, attached to his hind-legs, and probably serving as kites which facilitate the movements in the air. Another use of these singular constructions would appear to be the capture and storage of smaller flies to be used as food. It is suggested that the particular purpose served varies with the species.

CHAPTER LII

MUSCULAR LOCOMOTION—FLYING MAMMALS, BIRDS, AND REPTILES

The Bats (Chiroptera) among Mammals are expert flyers, and so, of course, are the vast majority of Birds, while probably all of them which do not now possess this power are descended from forms which did. One long since extinct order of Reptiles (Pterosauria) included a great variety of species capable of flight.

THE FLIGHT OF BATS (CHIROPTERA)

The Bats are probably an offshoot from the stock in which the Insect-Eating Mammals (Insectivora) took origin, though our knowledge of their past history is far too imperfect to throw any light upon the stages in the evolution of their organs of flight. But the order is one of very considerable antiquity, and such evidence as has been obtained proves that the oldest species so far known were fully equipped with flying membranes.

On examining a typical Bat, such as the Pipistrelle (*Vesperugo pipistrellus*, fig. 829), we find a thin flying-membrane (patagium) in the form of a fold of skin, extending between fore and hind limb on either side. There is also a fold between the neck and the front edge of the fore-limb, and a steering membrane which unites the hind-limbs with one another and the tail. In some bats the latter is partly free. As to their extent, the various folds are very like the parachuting folds of a Colugo (see p. 282), but are much thinner than in that animal. There is a remarkable difference between the two cases as regards structure. For the Bat's forearm is remarkable long, and bent sharply forwards on the upper-arm, and though the hook-bearing thumb is relatively short, the fingers are enormously drawn out, serving as supports to the main part of the flying membrane, and comparable to the ribs of an umbrella. And it may be added that both bat's wing and umbrella fold up in a similar way. The steering membrane is supported on either side by a gristly spur which projects from the ankle.

Examination of a Bat's skeleton (fig. 830) brings out some of he peculiarities more clearly. It will be seen that the fingers, in pite of their length, only possess three supporting bones apiece,

Fig. 829.—Pipistrelles (*Vesperugo pipistrellus*)

the usual number among Mammals. As in all cases where the fore-limbs have free lateral movements, there are well-developed collar-bones, propping up the shoulders from the inner side. There is a prominent ridge or keel running along the sternum, and correlated with the existence of large pectoral or breast-muscles, the principal agents in moving the wings. The hind-limbs are turned backwards in a remarkable manner, and the size of the flying-membrane is therefore greater in that direction than would otherwise be the case.

The parachuting arrangements in a Colugo (see p. 282) afford a hint as to the way in which the flying-membranes of bats have been evolved. For in this creature we find that though the fingers are not elongated they are webbed, and the steering power which is undoubtedly possessed may be associated with up-and-down movement of the arms. Here we probably have the first beginnings of the power of flight, which essentially depends upon movements of the kind. The webbed hands, being the parts brought down upon the air with greatest vigour, would have a very special value even at an early stage. Hence we are able to picture a gradual elongation of digits, with corresponding increase of the webs between them, the lateral parachuting membrane being at the same time gradually merged in the enlarging hand. We may, in fact, regard (see fig. 830) that part of the Bat's wing external to the little finger (*V*) as being the greatly-developed webbed hand, while the part between this and the body is the old lateral parachuting fold.

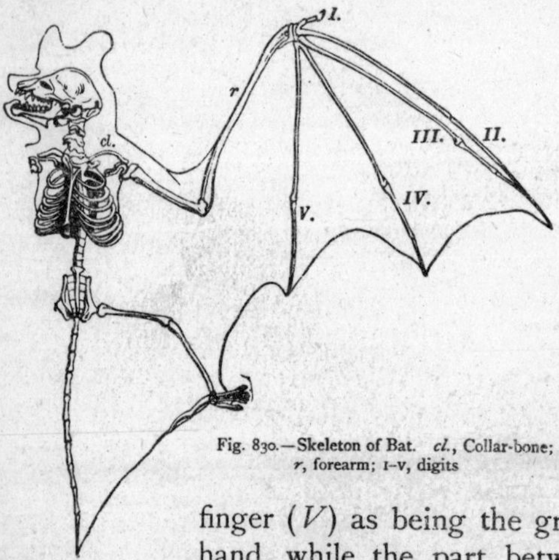

Fig. 830.—Skeleton of Bat. *cl.*, Collar-bone; *r*, forearm; I–V, digits

Considering the very considerable powers of flight which Bats possess, it is not surprising to find that they have a very wide geographical distribution. Speaking of the small forms which make up the largest family (*Vespertilionidæ*) of the order, Wallace says (in *The Geographical Distribution of Animals*):—"They range over almost the whole globe, being apparently only limited by the necessity of procuring insect food. In America they are found as far north as Hudson's Bay and the Columbia river; and in Europe they approach, if they do not pass, the Arctic circle. Such remote islands as the Azores, Bermudas, Fiji Islands, Sandwich Islands, and New Zealand, all possess species of this group of bats, some of which probably inhabit every island in warm or temperate parts of the globe." As to powers of flight, the same author remarks that Bats are capable of traversing considerable spaces of sea, since two North American species either regularly or occasionally visit the Bermudas, a distance of 600 miles from the mainland.

THE FLIGHT OF BIRDS (Aves)

In spite of the many elaborate investigations which have been made on this subject, there are numerous points in regard to which we are comparatively ignorant, and the whole subject is so exceedingly complicated that the space here available will only serve for a brief survey of the more salient facts.

It will be convenient to deal in the first place with the structure of Birds in relation to flight, and afterwards to consider the flying mechanism in action.

Structure of Birds in Relation to Flight.—The entire organism of Flying Birds has undergone very great specialization as a result of very perfect adaptation to aerial locomotion. The compact boat-shaped body and pointed head are well-suited to cleave the air with a minimum resistance, strongly reminding us of the "lines" of Fishes and Whales, which fit them to pass with ease through the water (see pp. 41 and 83).

The fore-limbs have undergone remarkable modification by which they have been converted into the chief agents of flight, but in spite of this they are merely one more variation on the common plan of structure that can be made out in the long series of land Vertebrates, from Amphibians to Mammals. If we look at the right-hand side of a Bird the partly-extended wing may be diagrammatically represented by a capital Z, the lower horizontal line corresponding to the upper-arm, the slanting stroke to the forearm, and the upper horizontal line to the hand. The digits have been reduced to three, which are usually considered to be the thumb, first finger, and second finger. The thumb may bear a claw, and this is occasionally the case with the first finger as well. Although a Bird's wing differs in many ways from that of a Bat, *e.g.* in the fact that the digits are not elongated, there are nevertheless certain resemblances between the two. For stretching between upper-arm and forearm there is a fold which may be called the front wing-membrane, while a much smaller hind wing-membrane extends between upper-arm and body (see fig. 834). The former is quite comparable to the front parachuting fold of a Bat, and the latter to that part of the "wing" of that animal which occupies the region of the arm-pit. As we shall see later, these folds have a purpose to serve in flight.

The direct evidence so far at our disposal as to the evolution of Birds' wings is unfortunately exceedingly scanty. For in the oldest known extinct member of this class (*Archæopteryx*, fig. 831) the fore-limb was a well-developed wing, though somewhat less specialized than in living forms. For example, claws were present on all three digits. Although an undoubted bird, with wings and feathers, this ancient type approximated to reptiles in several respects, notably in the presence of well-developed teeth and a long tail. There are good reasons for thinking that Birds are descended from reptilian ancestors, though none of the known groups of Reptiles can be worked into their pedigree. But it is permissible to picture those ancestors as hopping forms (see p. 185), which first took to climbing and then to parachuting. And it is quite conceivable that the two wing-membranes of a Bird are the last remains of parachuting arrangements, of which the hinder one has long since been superseded by feathers, the evolution of which was associated with the development of flying powers. This view, however, must only be regarded as a speculation.

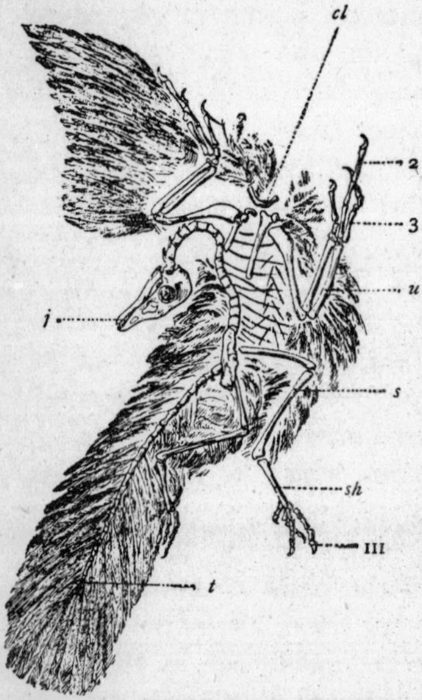

Fig. 831.—Extinct Toothed Bird (*Archæopteryx*)

j, Toothed jaws; *cl*, collar-bone; *u*, ulna; 2 and 3, second and third fingers; *s*, shin-bone; *sh*, shank-bone; III, third toe; *t*, axis of tail.

Feathers.—The possession of feathers is so eminently characteristic of Birds, that to define these as "Feathered Animals" would suffice to mark them off from all other creatures, living or extinct, of which we have at present any knowledge. As regards flight, the most important of these structures are the "quills" attached to wing and tail. The former are known as "rowing feathers" (remiges) and the latter as "steering feathers" (rectrices). Wing-quills and tail-quills are respectively covered to some extent by wing-coverts and tail-coverts.

The structure of feathers has already been dealt with (see vol. i, p. 142), and it need only be repeated here that they combine lightness with strength in a remarkable way, and that the little branches which make up the thin expansion on either side of the central shaft are hooked together in an elaborate manner. We have no direct evidence regarding the evolution of feathers, but they may be supposed to have originated by the fraying out of the scales no doubt possessed by ancestral forms. And it is interesting to note that the legs of birds are still partly clothed by overlapping scales.

The body of a Bird is light in proportion to its bulk, for although the bones have a dense external layer, they are otherwise of spongy texture, and commonly more or less traversed by air-spaces, especially in forms which fly well. The lungs communicate with large air-sacs, which take up a good deal of space within the body, and communicate with some of the air-sacs in the bones. Not only is an increase of lightness gained in this manner, but also a larger external surface for the attachment of muscles than would otherwise be the case. Too much stress must not be laid upon the lightness of the body, and it would be entirely erroneous to compare a bird with a balloon. It would be much more correct to draw a parallel between it and a flying-machine, for active flight is a matter of sheer muscular effort. Even here, however, the principles of the kite and parachute are involved, and this is still more the case in those varieties of movement through the air known as passive flight. The heavier parts of the body are placed towards the under surface, and stability is thus secured.

The immense amount of energy displayed by flying birds is associated with great activity of the circulatory and breathing organs, as to which they stand pre-eminent among backboned animals (see vol. ii, p. 426). The chief significance of air-sacs and air-spaces is probably to be found in the fact that they increase the efficiency of the lungs. This activity is of course associated with a rapid wasting of the substance of the body, which has to be made good by a correspondingly large amount of food. And it is therefore not surprising to find that birds are possessed of large appetites and great digestive powers.

The Skeletons of Birds in relation to Flight. —As in the case of the feathers, unusual lightness and great firmness are here combined. The joints of the backbone in the regions of the chest and loins are closely fused together so as to constitute a firm central support, to the front part of which the large breastbone is hung by means of the ribs. And the last few joints of the tail-region are fused into a ploughshare bone, from which the steering feathers radiate like a fan. This is a marked specialization as compared with the extinct toothed bird (*Archæopteryx*) already mentioned (see p. 296) as the oldest known member of its class. For this creature possessed a long tail like that of a lizard, with a series of quill-feathers along either side. Possibly this remarkable organ was used parachute fashion. It would, at any rate, be a hindrance rather than a help to active flight, and by gradual shortening became converted long ages since into the stumpy form with which we are familiar in recent birds.

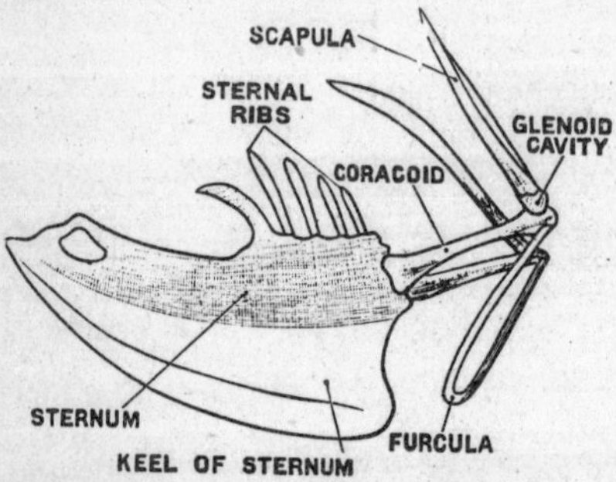

Fig. 832.—Shoulder-girdles and Breastbone of Pigeon

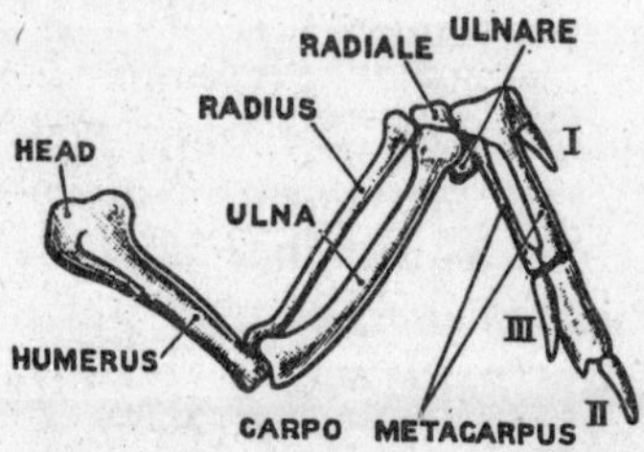

Fig. 833.—Wing-bones of Pigeon. I–III, digits

The skeleton of the wing naturally exhibits many modifications in relation to flight. The shoulder-girdle (fig. 832) consists of three bones. One is the sabre-shaped shoulder-blade (scapula), which is firmly bound by muscles to the skeleton of the trunk. From it a stout bone (the coracoid) runs down to the breastbone (sternum), with which it is closely united, thus acting as a prop. The third element of the girdle is the collar-bone (clavicle), which unites with its fellow to make up the "merry-thought" (furcula). This helps to keep the two shoulder-girdles apart, but, being elastic, also permits a certain amount of play. Passing now to the bones of the free part of the wing (fig. 833), we find that the head of the upper-arm bone (humerus) fits into a cup (glenoid cavity) where shoulder-blade and coracoid meet, and at this joint a good deal of rotatory movement is possible, a matter of great importance in adjusting the wing to advantageous positions for flight. The two usual bones (radius and ulna) are found in the forearm, but no twisting movement is possible at the elbow, as in ourselves. In this case it would detract from firmness and therefore be a disadvantage. A certain amount of fusion has taken place in the hand; here again, no doubt, in the interests of firmness. For though two of the little wrist-bones (radiale and ulnare) are separate, the remainder have united with the elements making up the palm-region (metacarpus). This bears the three digits, of which the middle one is the largest and most important.

The breastbone (sternum) of a flying bird is exceedingly large, and a vertical plate or keel projects from its under surface, giving additional surface for the attachment of the great muscles of flight which make up the flesh of the breast.

Chief Muscles of Flight (fig. 834).—So far we have been concerned with the supporting framework, and, as in other cases, the actual movements are brought about by the shortening or contraction of muscles. Of these the largest and most important are situated entirely or partly in the trunk, and are attached to the bones they move by means of inelastic cords or tendons. There are, however, a large number of smaller muscles situated entirely in the wing itself. And besides tendons there are other fibrous bands known as ligaments, which connect bones, &c., together. The advantageous situation of the large muscles is commented on very graphically in the following passage taken from Headley (*Structure and Life of Birds*):—"It is a strange thing that in these days when it is boasted that machines can be made to do most things that a man can do, that sailors should still have to run up the rigging, be the weather foul or fair, and straddle across the yards, in order to furl or set the sails. It would not seem to be beyond human ingenuity to devise machinery by the aid of which this work should be managed from the deck. Some progress towards this has, I believe, been made. In the bird we find such machinery brought to great perfection. Instead of men we have muscles, and by the machinery of tendons and ligaments these muscles, situated on or near the body, are able to spead the wings and regulate their utmost extremities. It is all-important that it should be so. All the weighty organs must be accumulated in the body. To speak metaphorically, the wings must be made up of very little besides masts, sails, and cordage."

The two largest muscles concerned with flight are those which make up the great fleshy mass of the breast, and of which the use is to lower and raise the wings (see fig. 834). By far the bigger of the two is the great breast muscle (*pectoralis major*), which is attached to the lower side of the humerus not far from the shoulder-joint, and by its contraction pulls down the wing.

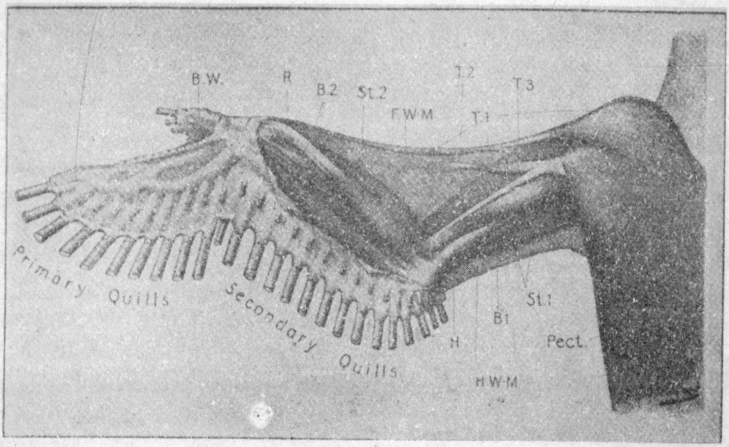

Fig. 834.—Structure of Pheasant's Wing

H, Humerus; R, radius; B.W., bastard-wing; F.W-M. and H.W-M., front and hind wing-membranes; St. 1 and St. 2, straightening muscles; B. 1 and B. 2, bending muscles; T. 1, T. 2, and T. 3, tensor muscles; Pect., part of great breast-muscle (*pectoralis major*).

It covers the smaller elevator muscle (*subclavius*), of which the work is to raise the wing. But being below this, its tendon has to take a rather curious course. It runs through a hole situated where the three bones of the shoulder meet, and then bends down to be attached to the upper side of the humerus not far from the shoulder-joint. We may compare it to a rope that passes over a pulley. Some other important muscles are shown in fig. 834. Among them may be mentioned:—(1) Muscles which straighten out the forearm on the upper-arm (St. 1), and the hand on the forearm (St. 2); (2) Muscles which bend the forearm on the upper-arm (B.1.), and the hand on the forearm (B.2.); (3) Tensor muscles (T.1, T.2, T.3), which keep the front wing-membrane stretched taut. There is another tendon (not shown in the figure) which performs the same office for the hind wing-membrane. Besides these muscles there are many others which adjust the parts of the wing in various ways. The thumb, for example, is well off in this respect.

One or two other points in the structure of the wing deserve notice here. The long tendon of one of the tensor muscles (T. 1) runs along the edge of the front wing-membrane to be attached to the hand. Unlike tendons in general it is elastic, and is stretched to three times its normal length when the wing is extended. This helps to keep the membrane taut, and the hand in line with the forearm. And when the bird folds up its wing the elasticity of this tendon comes into play and gives considerable assistance.

The large rowing-feathers are divided into two sets—primary quills attached to the hand, and secondary quills borne by the forearm. There is also a tuft of feathers on the thumb, making up the bastard-wing. When the wing is extended the quills spread out to give an expanded surface without muscular effort. This is effected by the agency of an elastic band or ligament which stretches from hand to arm-pit, and is pierced by the bases of all the secondary and some of the primary quills. Its work is aided by a second similar band which runs under the quills nearer their attachment to the wing. A still more beautiful mechanical arrangement affects the secondary quills only, bringing it about that during the down-stroke of the wing they are pressed firmly together so that no air can pass between them, while during the up-stroke they are slightly separated so as to allow of such passage, thereby diminishing the amount of work. Dissection reveals the cause of this. From the back edge of the muscle (B. 2) which bends the hand on the forearm a minute tendon passes to each secondary quill. When the wing is extended these tendons pull the overlapping quills together so that an unbroken surface is constituted. But when the up-stroke is made the hand is bent to some extent upon the forearm, the little tendons relax, and the quills being loosened, permit air to pass between them.

The stumpy tail with its radiating steering-feathers is well provided with muscles, by which it can be raised, lowered, and otherwise adjusted so that it may be able to perform its work in directing the course of flight. It also possesses elastic ligaments.

Active Flight.—For a bird, in the absence of wind, to rise from the ground involves very considerable muscular effort. If the legs are fairly long the start is greatly helped by a standing or running jump, but in any case the wings have to be moved rapidly up and down until the bird is fairly under weigh. As will be explained later, the support afforded by the air is dependent upon the speed attained. Let us now suppose that the bird is flying along, its wings having acquired sufficient "purchase" upon the air for propulsive purposes. It will be seen from fig. 835 that each wing may now be considered a lever of the third order, with the motive power acting between the fulcrum and the weight. The fulcrum here is not a firm fixed point, as in a crowbar used to raise a block of stone, but is constituted by the resistance of the air, and may be conveniently considered as located near the end of the wing. A similar yielding fulcrum is presented by the water to the blade of an oar used to propel a boat. The weight to be moved is that of the bird, and the power is supplied by the great pectoral muscle. That this is attached very near to the shoulder means great expenditure of force, with corresponding gain in speed, a matter which is of the greatest importance in this case. The most effective part of the wing is clearly that which is furthest from the body, for this moves most rapidly, and therefore gets the best grip upon the air. The near section, though less useful in this respect, is of greater value as a parachute to retard descent between the down-strokes, and the wing-membranes are of considerable use in this respect. It must also be remembered that the wing is not flat, but concave below and convex above, which gives a better hold on the air during the down-stroke and makes the upstroke more easy. The same ends are furthered by the arrangements for adjusting the quills, of which an account has already been given (p. 301).

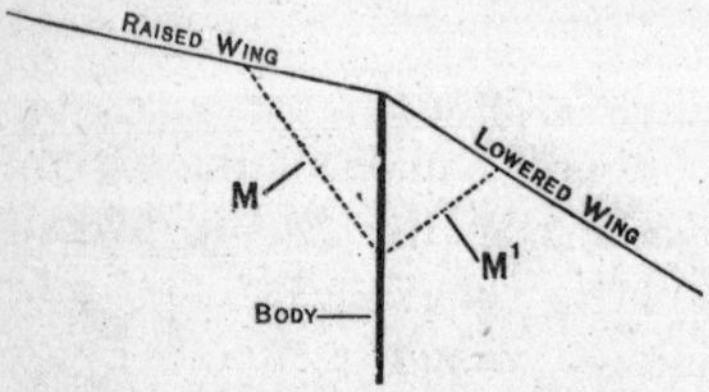

Fig. 835.—Diagram of Wing-Action (end view)

M and M[1], Great pectoral muscle relaxed and contracted respectively.

The action of the wings has so far been treated as if they

SWALLOWS AND MARTINS CHASING INSECTS

The plate represents our three native species of the Swallow Family (*Hirundinidæ*), *i.e.*, (1) the Common Swallow (*Hirundo rustica*); (2) the House-Martin (*Chelidon urbica*); and (3) the Sand-Martin (*Cotile riparia*). These summer visitors are remarkable for great powers of flight, associated with long pointed wings, a forked tail, and short, weak legs. They are untiring in the pursuit of insects, their short broad beaks and wide gape being adaptations for catching these on the wing. As weather-prophets they are justly esteemed, flying high when the air is dry, and low when it is charged with moisture, in accordance with the habits of their prey. The Swallow is the largest of the three species, and its mud-nests, resembling half a saucer in shape, are built by preference under the eaves of houses. Those of the House-Martin are to be seen in similar situations, and differ in being roofed over. The Sand-Martin, as the name indicates, nests in sand-banks, digging out a long burrow for the purpose. Swallows and Martins alike return to the same nest year after year.

SWALLOWS AND MARTINS CHASING INSECTS

simply raised the body in the air, and this would be the case if they merely moved up and down as though there were hinge-joints at the shoulders. But the joints in question allow of a certain amount of rotation, which actually takes place during onward flight. When the down-stroke is made the wing is brought forwards as well as downwards, its under side being inclined so as to face both downwards and backwards. And as a result of this the push of the wing, instead of being entirely expended in raising the bird and preventing it from falling, is only partly employed for this purpose, the rest of it acting backward, and therefore propelling the body onwards. And the angle of the wings can be so adjusted that the part of the push acting directly downwards is only just sufficient to maintain the height above the ground already attained, in which case the bird progresses in a horizontal direction, and does not continue to rise. Under these circumstances the hinder part of the body is raised by appropriate muscles when the down-stroke is given, which furthers the end in view.

During the up-stroke, which is the more rapid of the two, the wing is partly bent, and moved upwards and backwards, the under surface being now directed downwards and forwards. Some of the details of wing-movement may be gathered by reference to fig. 836, taken from serial photographs of flying birds.

A bird, such as a Lark, rises steeply into the air, not by adjusting the wing horizontally, as might be expected, but by inclining its body strongly, which increases the resistance to horizontal movement, and therefore favours upward progress.

The fact that the wings are not held horizontally but inclined during ordinary flight of course diminishes their efficiency when regarded as organs for preventing the body from falling. If the bird remained in one place this would be a serious matter, but it is in reality of little practical consequence, for it has been shown experimentally that the support given by the air increases very rapidly as speed is got up. Besides which, air-currents may help both in supporting the body and in furthering onward movement.

Steering and Stopping.—This is undoubtedly effected in various ways. The tail is an adjustable rudder, the body can be placed at various angles, and the wings are not of necessity moved together in precisely the same manner.

Some birds are able to stop quite suddenly, and turn with great rapidity. When a Pigeon does this its body assumes a vertical position, and the tail is fully spread out. In this way a maximum resistance to further onward progress is brought into play. It is possible that the bastard-wing may give some help in stopping and turning movements, but further investigation is needed before we can feel certain as to the part it plays in flight.

Powerful and rapid flight is commonly correlated with great

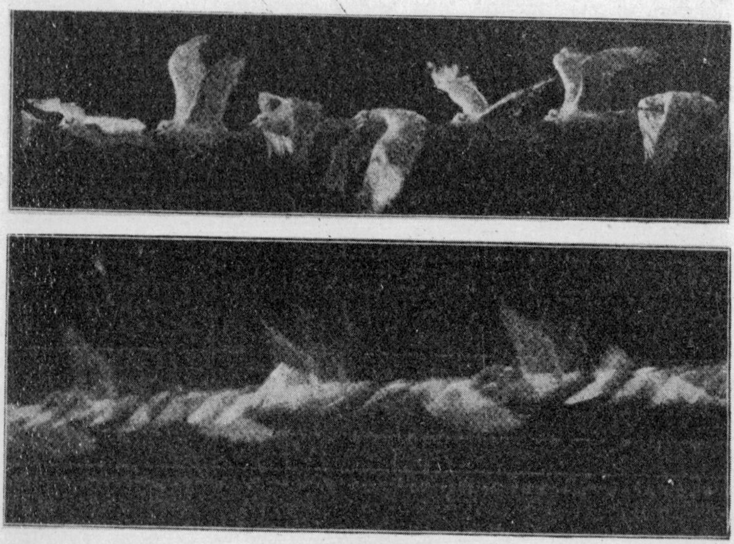

Fig. 836.—Instantaneous Photographs of Phases in Flight. The upper figure gives deliberate flight of a Gull (read from right to left), and the lower shows the rapid flight of a Pigeon (read from left to right). The photographs were taken at very short intervals in the latter case, and therefore overlap.

expanse of wing, but the flying possibilities of any particular bird depend upon many other things besides this. For instance, the shape of the wings is of importance. In expert flyers they are usually long and pointed, as may be seen to perfection in Swallows and Swifts. But short wings moved with great rapidity may also be very effective. And it is sufficiently obvious that long-distance flying and rapid flight for a short time are likely to be associated with arrangements of somewhat different kind.

There appears to be a dearth of accurate observations regarding the speed of various birds, especially the average that can be maintained for long distances. But it appears that 60 miles an hour is no extraordinary pace for Swallows and Swifts, while 36 miles an hour is a favourable average for Pigeons. Much higher speeds have, however, been recorded, *e.g.* 71 miles per hour (for a distance of 82 miles) in the case of a Pigeon, and 106 miles per hour (for 160 miles) in the case of a Swallow. The achievements of many migrant birds, extended as they often are over enormous distances, are remarkable as illustrating both speed and endurance. The American Golden Plover (*Charadrius Virginicus*), for example, during its autumnal migration to the South, is credited with being continuously on the wing for a distance of some 1700 miles, as it passes oversea from Nova Scotia to South America *viâ* the West Indies. In such a case the speed must be very considerable, as birds cannot remain without food for an indefinite time. Of course it must not be imagined that during a prolonged stay in the air the wings are in constant movement. For having once got up speed a bird is able to glide along for a considerable time without effort, especially by taking advantage of air-currents.

PASSIVE FLIGHT.— Birds may be often observed moving through the air with motionless outspread wings and expanded tail. Two chief kinds of this passive flight may be recognized, known respectively as Gliding and Soaring.

Gliding Flight.—This takes place when a bird simply moves onwards and does not describe the upward spirals that are characteristic of soaring. It is exemplified by many forms possessing considerable spread of wing, among the most familiar being Gulls and Pigeons. The simplest case is seen when one of the latter birds slides down obliquely from a roof to the ground, and this may be described as a parachute movement (see p. 286). Such a descent may also be made by a bird which is actually flying, as when a Falcon swoops steeply down upon its prey (fig. 837).

Gliding may also take place in an upward direction, and here again the Falcon will serve as an illustration. For in the middle of its swoop it can, if necessary, so adjust its wings and body as to utilize the momentum gained for an upward slide. Supposing that a bird which is flying horizontally forwards with considerable speed suddenly ceases to move its wings, but allows them to remain extended. It will then glide on for a considerable distance. And it has been proved experimentally that under such circumstances the upward pressure of the air is greatest on the front of the wings, tending to tilt up the fore part of the bird, and thus giving an upward bias. Unless this is corrected by some alteration of position an upward glide will result. A comparison may be made with a kite which a boy is sending up by the familiar process of running rapidly in front of it, a friend having previously "let go" at the psychological moment. At first the kite is dragged through the air at a slight inclination

Fig. 837.—A Falcon Swooping

with the ground, but as the pull of the string gradually gives it horizontal velocity an upward bias is developed, the string is paid out, and it glides up obliquely into the air. Birds which take wing from the ground, or from the water, always face the wind, and the assistance which this gives them is partly to be explained on the kite principle, the horizontal velocity required for a start being given by a preliminary leap aided by vigorous wing-flapping. The analogy is only an imperfect one, but the details are too complicated to give here.

It remains to be noticed that a bird which ceases active flight and commences gliding can easily adjust itself so as to correct the upward bias described above. The commonest methods employed appear to be slight folding of the wings and spreading out of the tail. Horizontal gliding is often the result. If the wings are folded more than necessary to correct the upward bias the bird will at once begin to glide downwards.

Soaring.—A bird is said to sail or soar when with outspread wings it circles up into the sky, describing a course that may broadly be termed spiral. It is only possible in cases where there is a large surface of wing compared to the weight of the body, and is characteristic of many of the Birds of Prey, the larger members of the Crow Family, Pelicans, and Storks. Roy (in *Newton's Dictionary of Birds*) thus summarizes the chief features of this kind of flight as described by competent observers:—"A certain amount of wind appears to be essential, soaring flight not being observed in a dead calm. Observers seem also to agree in this, that the soaring bird, with motionless outstretched wings (having raised itself some distance from the ground or sea by active wing-strokes), describes in its flight curves or circles which lead it to alternately sail up the wind and down the wind. It describes wide curves, and loses in vertical position while it is directed down the wind, while in going up into the wind it rises higher in the air. The bird may, in describing these curves or circles, rise as high or higher than the point from which it started, and may be as far or farther to windward, and this without any very evident expenditure of mechanical work on the part of the bird."

But it is easier to describe these evolutions than to explain how they are performed, and no entirely satisfactory explanation has so far been advanced. Some authorities have attributed them to the action of upward currents of air, and others have tried to explain it by the fact that an air current moves more rapidly in proportion to its height above the ground. But we know too little about the distribution and force of air-currents in the higher regions of the air, to feel sure that either explanation can account for the fact that Adjutants are able to soar up to an altitude of some two miles from the ground.

The following view on the subject is advanced by Headley (in *The Structure and Life of Birds*): "I believe myself that the irregularity of the wind may supply the explanation of soaring. The wind is a 'chartered libertine', and, even when steadiest, blows, as Professor Langley has shown, with great fitfulness. A bird, when soaring, if this explanation be sound, will face a strengthening breeze: when it begins to slacken, will turn round and go with it until conscious it is strengthening again, when once more he will sweep round and face it, his aim being always to feel the wind blowing in his face—sure evidence that he has momentum that will lift him. To do this, he would have to be perpetually feeling the pulse of the wind, and, moreover, soaring would be a much less regular progress upward than it is supposed to be. Some turns of the helix would be failures. There would be a loss instead of a gain of elevation, or nothing more than a maintenance of level would be achieved. But when we watch a bird circling at a great height, what can we tell of his progress during a particular minute? We only know that his general tendency is upward. Gulls make only partially successful turns when they soar, and it is possible that similar failures in a nobler performer like the Adjutant may remain undetected."

THE FLIGHT OF REPTILES (Reptilia)

Very few living Reptiles make any attempts at aerial locomotion, and those which do are merely parachutists (see p. 286). But in the remote epoch known to geologists as the Mesozoic or Secondary, when Mammals were but a feeble folk, not only the land and sea, but also the air were dominated by Reptiles, the majority of which belonged to groups now long extinct. The Flying Reptiles, or Pterosaurs, of this epoch are of great interest biologically, for they solved the problem of flight on quite different lines from those exemplified by Bats and Birds, approximating, however, more nearly to the former in this respect. As will be gathered by reference to fig. 838, which represents a restoration of the Paddle-Tailed Pterosaur (*Rhamporhynchus*), flying membranes connected fore- and hind-limbs, and (in some species) the latter with the tail, which in this particular form, however, was elongated, free, and broadened out at its end. There was also a

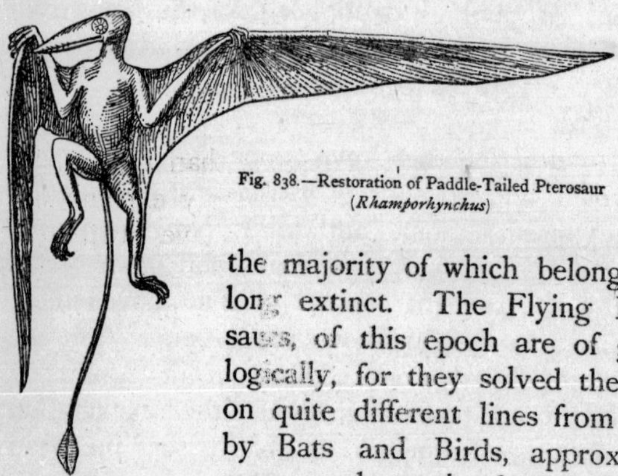

Fig. 838.—Restoration of Paddle-Tailed Pterosaur (*Rhamporhynchus*)

fold of membrane in front of the arm. We have seen that the wing of a Bat largely consists of a greatly developed webbed hand, of which all the digits, except the thumb, are much elongated. But the wing of a Pterosaur appears to have been entirely evolved from a lateral parachuting fold, the front end of this being supported by the arm, and also by the little finger, which was of extraordinary length. The species figured possessed very large eyes, and was no doubt nocturnal or dusk-loving.

The skeleton of Pterosaurs was specialized in relation to flight. There were, for example, extensive air-cavities in the bones, and the sternum possessed a strong keel, correlated with well-developed breast-muscles. In many species the tail was very short, and sometimes the jaws were toothless, being in that case no doubt covered by horny sheaths, as in the beak of a bird. The smallest of these creatures were no larger than sparrows, but some of the latest evolved forms, the toothless Pterosaurs (species of *Pteranodon*), which flourished during the Chalk period, attained gigantic dimensions, their spread of wing being sometimes as much as 25 feet.

The Flying Reptiles probably became extinct as a result of competition with the more highly organized Birds and Bats. Their organs of flight were perhaps less efficient than in those groups, but it is not likely that this was the only or even the chief cause of their failure in the struggle for existence. This must probably be sought in less perfect circulatory and breathing organs, but it is impossible to verify this conjecture, as our knowledge of the group is almost entirely limited to what can be deduced from the structure of the skeleton.

THE FLIGHT OF INSECTS (INSECTA)

Insects alone among Backboneless animals have evolved organs of flight, and to this must probably be ascribed their extraordinary abundance, both as regards number of species and number of individuals. In both respects they far surpass all other kinds of land animal taken together.

Structure of Insects in Relation to Flight.—The body of an insect is divided into three regions, *i.e.* head, thorax, and abdomen. The thorax consists of three successive rings, each of which bears a pair of legs, while in typical cases there are two pairs of wings, attached to the second and third ring respectively. These structures are developed as outgrowing folds of the body-wall, and are quite independent of the limbs, thus differing from the flying organs of backboned animals.

When fully developed, the wing may be regarded as an elastic membrane, horny in texture, and strengthened by a more or less elaborate system of thickened "veins" or "nervures", which have a constant arrangement in the same kind of insect, and are a great aid to classification. They prevent tearing, and the strongest of them run along the front part of the wing, which is thus rendered specially resistant, and plays the same part with reference to the more flexible region behind it as does the bone-supported front edge of a bird's wing with regard to the quill-feathers. A very young wing can be separated into upper and lower layers, between which run various structures. Each nervure, for example, is traversed by an air-tube, accompanied by a blood-channel. The wing is jointed on to the thorax in a complex manner, and its base projects into the body as a sort of fold, to which important muscles are attached.

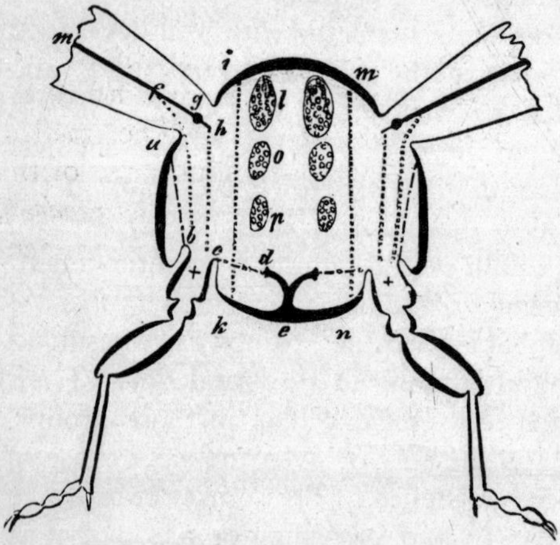

Fig. 839.—Diagrammatic Cross-section of a Butterfly

+ +, Thighs; *bu* and *cd*, muscles which pull the legs outwards and inwards. Muscles of flight described in text. The wings have been cut short

The diagrammatic cross-section through a butterfly represented in fig. 839 indicates the position of the chief muscles of flight. The thickened part of the wing to which some of these are attached may be regarded as a lever (*m h*), of which the fulcrum (*g*) is situated in the wing-joint. To the short arm of the lever internal to this a muscle is attached (*c h*), by which the wing is raised. The effective downward stroke is effected by a more powerful muscle (*b f*), which is attached to the wing a little way outside the fulcrum. Other muscles, which are not attached directly to the wings, but alter the shape of the thorax, help to bring about the upward and downward movements. This region of the body is flattened by vertical muscles (*i k*, *m n*), during the contraction of which the wings rise. There are also longitudinal muscles (*l*, *o*, *p*), by the action of which the thorax is shortened and the wings lowered. In Dragon-Flies, insects possessing quite extraordinary flying powers, and in which the two pairs of wings are capable of independent action as well as able to work together, the muscular arrangements are very complicated. In addition to elevator and depressor muscles there are others by which the wings can be rotated and otherwise adjusted.

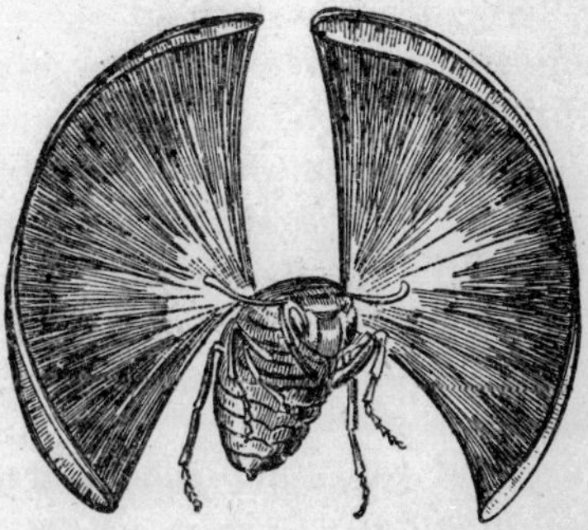

Fig. 840.—Wasp flying in the Sun, showing curves described by wings. To the tip of each a fragment of gold-leaf had previously been attached

Flight of Insects. — Marey and others have made elaborate experiments on the flight of insects, but the small size of these creatures and the great rapidity of their movements make such investigations exceedingly difficult. By allowing the wing-tips of captive insects to just brush against strips of blackened paper stretched upon revolving cylinders, Marey obtained curves which enabled him to calculate the rate of movement, some of his results being as follows:—

	Wing-beats per Second.
Common Fly	330
Drone-Fly	240
Bee	190
Wasp	110
Humming-Bird Moth	72
Dragon-Fly	28
White Butterfly	9

The rate is clearly greatest in insects of small size, and no doubt in these captive specimens it was diminished by friction against the blackened paper.

By attaching a fragment of gold-leaf to the tip of the front-wing in a Wasp, the same observer demonstrated the complexity of the actual movement (fig. 840). And by this and other means it has been shown that the wing-tip describes a figure-of-8 curve. Photography is here difficult of application, but it has at least shown that the plane of the wing is inclined during the upward and downward movements, and hence the body is propelled onwards as well as upwards, on the same principle as in Birds (see p. 303). The comparative rigidity of the front part of the wing conduces to obliquity. There appear to be several ways by which the direction of flight is regulated, and turning, stopping, and even reversing (in some cases) brought about. For example, the wings of opposite sides are capable of independent action, and the abdomen can be moved so as to throw the weight of the body to this or that side.

It is interesting to note that, as in Birds, air-sacs are present within the body, and these are especially large in swiftly-flying forms, such as bees, dragon-flies, moths, and flies (see vol. ii, p. 439). This undoubtedly reduces the weight of the body in proportion to its bulk, but, according to the most recent view, mere lightness is not the chief advantage thus gained. The large air-sacs are now thought to be important mainly because they render vigorous breathing possible, and this is a matter of great moment when muscular exertion is severe and prolonged.

Modification of the Wings in Different Insects (fig. 841).—In Dragon-Flies and some other forms the four wings are of equal or nearly equal size, and capable of acting independently. But in such insects as Bees and Moths there is an arrangement which to a great extent deprives the hind-wings of their independence, and makes them of secondary importance. The arrangement in question consists of an interlocking device, the nature of which varies in insects of different kind, whereby the hind-wings are attached during flight to the fore-wings. In a Moth, for instance, there are usually one or more bristles (*frenulum*) projecting from the front edge of the hind-wing, near its attachment, and capable of being made to catch in a small flap or tuft of scales (*retinaculum*) situated on the under surface of the fore-wing. A more elaborate arrangement fulfils the same purpose in Bees and similar insects, consisting of a series of hooks on the front of the hind-wing, which can be slipped over a ridge on the hinder edge of the fore-wing. The hooks are arranged "in a slightly-twisted or spiral direction along the margin of the wing, so as to resemble a screw, and when the wings are expanded attach themselves to a little fold on the posterior margin of the anterior wing, along which they play very freely when the wings are in motion, slipping to and fro like the rings on the rod of a window-curtain" (Newport).

The subordination of the hind-wings to the fore-wings has led in many cases, *e.g.* Bees, to a diminution in size of the former. And in ordinary Two-winged Flies (Diptera) this reduction has gone so far that the hind-wings have dwindled to a pair of club-shaped "balancers" (*halteres*) which appear to be chiefly useful as sense organs, though they also play a subordinate part in flight.

But, on the other hand, there are many insects in which the hind-wings are the chief agents

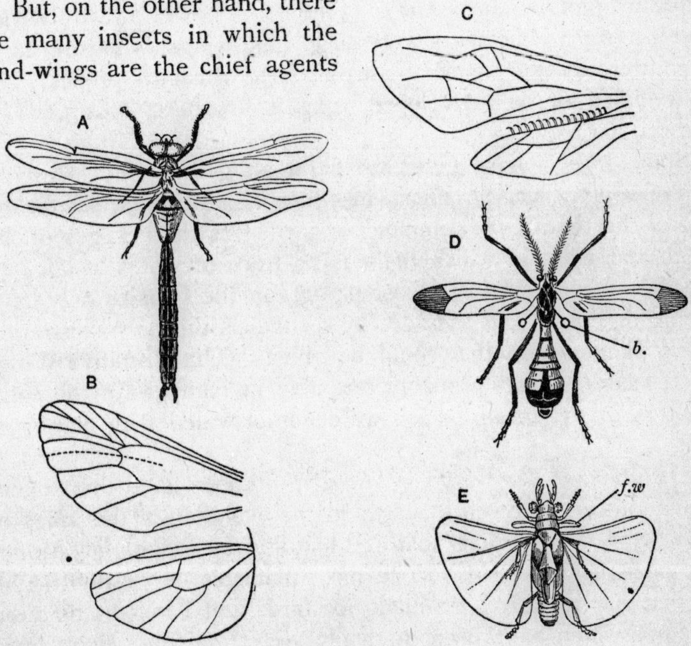

Fig. 841.—Wings of Insects

A, A Dragon-Fly. B, Left fore- and hind-wings of a Moth; note frenulum projecting from base of latter. C, left fore- and hind-wings of a Bee, showing row of hooks on latter. D, Two-Winged Fly; *b*, one of reduced hind-wings. E, Male Stylops; *f.w.*, reduced fore-wing. The figures have been drawn to various scales.

in flight, the fore-wings having become more or less hard and thick to constitute protective wing-covers. The most familiar case of the kind is afforded by the Beetles (Coleoptera), although it is supposed that in these insects the firm wing-covers (*elytra*) play a passive part in flight by acting as "wind-catchers", or kites. The membranous hind-wings of a Beetle, when not in use, are neatly folded up under the wing-covers, and are so long that they do not merely shut up like fans, but also have to be bent up along a transverse crease. In some Beetles which possess a long slender abdomen the tip of this is turned over the back to assist in stowing the membranous wings under their covers.

There are some curious little forms (species of *Stylops*, &c.), usually regarded either as aberrant beetles or as the representatives of a distinct order (Strepsiptera), which give us the exact opposite of the arrangement described for two-winged flies. They are parasitic in bees and some other insects, and the females are like minute maggots in appearance. The males, however, can fly with great activity by means of very large hind-wings, while the fore-wings are only represented by little scales, which are probably the last remains of well-developed wing-covers once possessed by ancestral forms.

Some insects have given up flight altogether, and lost both pairs of wings; such as Fleas, in which some little scales on the sides of the thorax are commonly regarded as the vestiges of the wings, and Lice, in which there is no trace of wings at all. In the forms mentioned in the last paragraph the females only have become flightless, and they are by no means the only illustration of this phenomenon that could be given. The Primitive Wingless Insects (Aptera) probably resemble in many ways the early ancestors of the group, which were not provided with organs of flight.

Evolution of the Wings of Insects.—There have been many speculations as to the early stages in the evolution of the wings of insects, and it is obvious that at their first inception they cannot have been flying organs. The most plausible suggestion is the one that has already been made for birds and bats, *i.e.* that the structures which have been gradually specialized into wings arose in the first instance as parachute-folds, in this case by outgrowth from the sides of the thorax. Possibly such folds were first developed as an aid to leaping, in which case comparison may be made with the Australian Flying-Spider (see p. 289). But, on the whole, it is more likely that the development of parachute-folds was a sequel to climbing, and this view becomes more probable when we recollect that the number of legs which insects possess, *i.e.* six, is best explained by reference to the climbing habit. The establishment of joints between the folds and the thorax would be of service in guiding even parachute movements, and from this stage on it is not difficult to imagine the gradual modification of the folds into wings.

Another possibility, however, must be borne in mind. The wings of an insect are traversed by air-tubes, with which blood-spaces are always associated in early stages of development. And there is reason to think that even in some adult insects the blood circulates in the wings to some extent. It is therefore quite possible that the original folds had reference to breathing as well as to parachuting. And this has led some authorities to surmise that wings have been evolved from tracheal gills possessed by primeval aquatic forms (see vol. ii, p. 463). But the evidence in support of this view is of the scantiest description, and it is in the highest degree improbable that the members of the original insect stock were of aquatic habit.

ANIMAL DEVELOPMENT

CHAPTER LIII

ANIMAL DEVELOPMENT—GENERAL PRINCIPLES—VEGETATIVE PROPAGATION

The preceding sections of this work have been devoted to Classification, and to those functions that maintain the life of the individual. We may now instructively consider the various means by which the continuance of the species is provided for. The Development of the individual, of course, includes a consideration of all the stages through which it has to pass before becoming adult, and might with propriety be considered under the heading of Life-Histories. But there are reasons which make it desirable to treat Development and Life-Histories as distinct sections. Under Development will be considered certain general principles as well as facts that can only be studied in the laboratory by means of the microscope, and technical methods associated with its use. The succeeding section on Life-Histories will broadly treat of facts which can be to a large extent made out by field naturalists, though many details can only be fully elucidated by work in the laboratory. And in that section it will also be convenient to deal with such topics as Protection of Eggs and Young, and Animal Dwellings, for these, of course, have an important bearing upon life-histories.

GENERAL PRINCIPLES OF DEVELOPMENT

All the different ways by means of which fresh individuals come into existence can be regarded as varieties of what may broadly be termed *overgrowth*. Every animal in the course of its existence builds up food into living body-substance, and this in its turn manufactures those components of the body which are not living, *e.g.* firm supporting structures and pigment granules. In early stages more food is taken in and utilized than is necessary to counterbalance the processes of waste that are constantly going on, and the result is *growth.* But when a certain size, varying with the species, is attained, the individual becomes adult, after which the chief use of food is to maintain the weight of the body by preventing the animal from gradually wasting away owing to the constant formation of various products of waste. In other words, the income and expenditure balance one another, in so far as the individual itself is concerned. But in all cases more food than is necessary for this particular purpose is taken into the body, and this is employed to build up living substance that becomes detached from the parent form and develops into new individuals. We have, in fact, a kind of overgrowth. A hen, for example, after it becomes adult, lays eggs, which may be regarded as detached parts of its body, and which, by developing into chickens, prevent the fowl species from becoming extinct.

It will be convenient to consider under separate headings Vegetative Propagation and Development from Eggs.

VEGETATIVE PROPAGATION

We have elsewhere (vol. i, p. 490) had occasion to note that the simple animals known as Animalcules (Protozoa) differ, as a rule, from all higher forms (Metazoa) in one very important particular. For any one of the latter is built up of more or less numerous units of structure technically known as *cells*, each of which is a fragment of living substance or protoplasm, part of this being specialized into a particle known as the *nucleus.* An Animalcule, on the contrary, consists of but one cell, though the parts of this may be very highly specialized. These facts are embodied in the technical statement that Protozoa are one-celled, while the Metazoa are many-celled. Any member of the latter group, *e.g.* a Worm, a Snail, or a Fish, may therefore be regarded as a cell-community, and the physiological work of the body is more or less divided among the members of this community, there being, in other words, a division of physiological labour. It invariably happens that some of the units or cells of the community are especially concerned with propagation, and either produce the eggs which develop into fresh individuals or else enable this development to take place. But many of the lower Metazoa do not entirely rely upon eggs for the perpetuation of their kind, but also give rise to other individuals by means of what is termed *vegetative propagation*, with which the egg-producing cells have nothing to do. There are, for example, some marine worms (fig. 842) in which the body becomes transversely divided into a number of sections, each of which ultimately breaks off and becomes a fresh worm. This phenomenon is much on a par with what is seen in many Flowering Plants. Here the production of seeds is related to egg-propagation, but this is frequently supplemented by one or more vegetative methods of multiplication. In Begonias, for example, buds sometimes grow out at the edges of the leaves, which, after developing into little plants, fall off and take root in the ground.

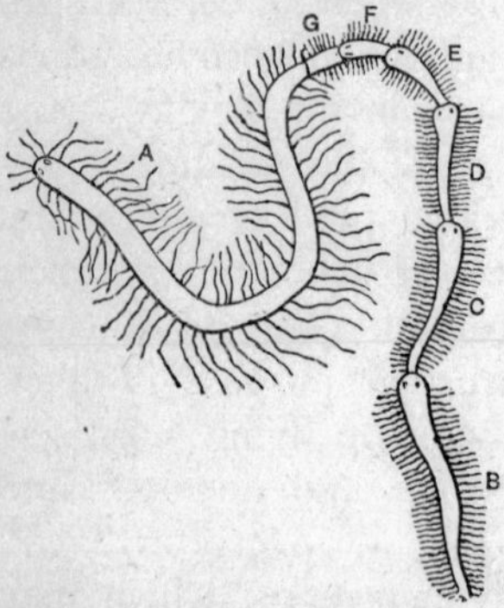

Fig. 842.—A Marine Worm (*Myrianida*) giving rise to a chain of individuals by transverse division. A, The parent worm; B–G, the new individuals, of which B is the oldest and G the youngest

VEGETATIVE PROPAGATION IN ANIMALCULES (PROTOZOA).—With rare exceptions the body of an Animalcule consists of but one cell, and there is therefore no question of egg-production, propagation being effected vegetatively. Three kinds of this are recognized: Splitting (Fission), Budding (Gemmation), and Spore-Formation. All are cases of cell-division.

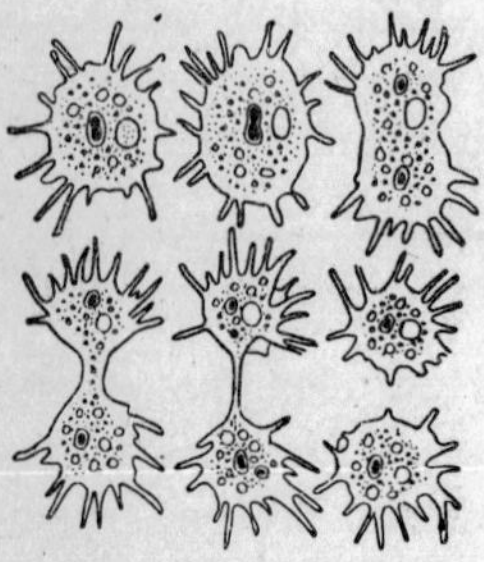

Fig. 843.—Stages in the Fission of a Proteus Animalcule (*Amœba*), much enlarged. Read from left to right, beginning at the top. The nucleus is represented black with a clear margin

Splitting (*Fission*).—A simple case of this is afforded by the Proteus Animalcule (*Amœba*, fig. 843). Division of the body is initiated in the nucleus, which becomes elongated and dumb-bell-shaped, after which the surrounding protoplasm gradually constricts into two, and ultimately there is complete separation, with the result that two Animalcules take the place of the original one. The parent Amœba is thus merged in its offspring, or at any rate has ceased to exist as a single individual. According to

Weismann, the products of this division later on divide in their turn, and so on indefinitely. And it is upon this belief that the distinguished zoologist in question founds his doctrine of the "immortality of the Protozoa", which involves the statement that death by "natural causes", as a coroner would put it, is unknown among Animalcules. But at present we do not know definitely whether or no division can go on for an indefinite number of generations, as Weismann's doctrine postulates.

We may take as further illustrations of fission (fig. 844) the Trumpet-Animalcule (*Stentor*) and the Bell-Animalcule (*Vorticella*), both of which are much more highly organized than Amœba, and belong to the group of Ciliata, in which the body is provided with cilia, *i.e.* short threads of protoplasm capable of movement. The Trumpet-Animalcule is elongated in form, with a narrow attached end, and a much broader free end, provided with a short spiral of cilia, by which food-bearing currents are set up in the surrounding water. The nucleus is elongated, and shaped something like a string of beads. Fission is here transverse, and though each half takes its share of the nucleus, one of the new individuals is constituted by the broad end and the other by the narrow end of the original body. This is of no great moment, as each of them develops the parts which it lacks before separation is completed.

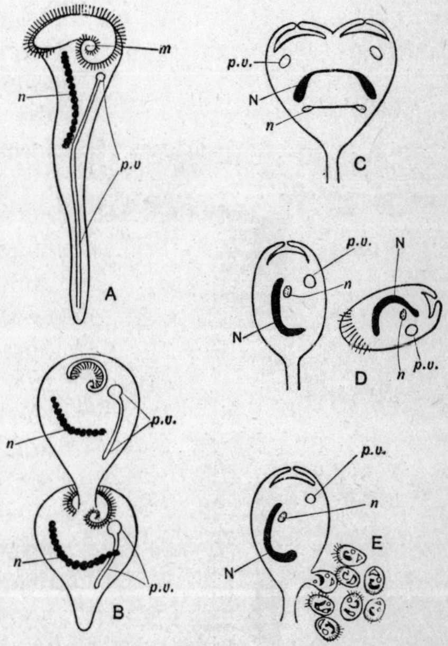

Fig. 844.—Fission of Ciliated Animalcules, enlarged

A and B, Stages in transverse division of Trumpet-Animalcule (*Stentor*); *m*, mouth; *n*, nucleus; *p.v.*, pulsating vacuole. C, D, Stages in equal longitudinal fission of Bell-Animalcule (*Vorticella*), and E, repeated unequal longitudinal fission of same. N, Large nucleus; *n*, small nucleus; *p.v.*, pulsating vacuole.

In the Bell-Animalcule fission is longitudinal, so that there is a fairer division of the parent Animalcule between the halves. One, however, keeps the stalk, which does not split, while the other has to swim away, attach itself to some firm body, and grow a new stalk. In some relatives of the Bell-Animalcule, and certain other Protozoa, colonies are formed by continuous fission, the products remaining united.

Budding (*Gemmation*).—This differs markedly from fission, because the parent Animalcule does not lose its individuality. One or more projections grow out from its body and receive a part of the original nucleus. These buds then become narrower and narrower at their attached ends, until at last they drop off, after which they gradually acquire the size and shape of the parent form from which they sprang. Comparatively simple illustrations of budding are afforded by the members of a curious group of Animalcules (Suctoria), which are devoid of mouth, but possess a number of slender outgrowths from the body that serve as a means of catching such prey as other Animalcules, and sucking the juices of these when secured.

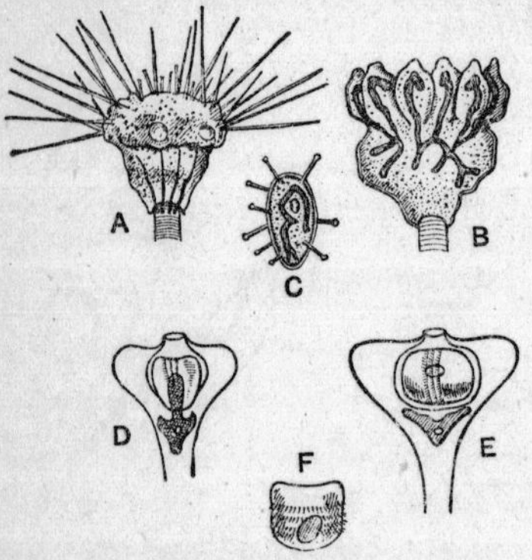

Fig. 845.—Budding Animalcules, enlarged

A–C, External budding of Ephelota: A, body of an adult (the stalk is cut short); B, an individual producing buds, each containing an outgrowth from the branching nucleus; C, a detached bud. D–F, Internal budding of Tokophrya, diagrammatic; D, young bud into which a branch from the nucleus is growing; E, mature bud lying in the brood-cavity; F, free-swimming bud.

A stalked member of this group (*Ephelota gemmipara*) is depicted in fig. 845, which shows a group of buds growing out from the body, and receiving twigs from the much-branched nucleus of the parent. A detached bud at a later stage is also represented, and it will be seen that this has begun to develop the curious suctorial projections that are characteristic of the group.

In some cases there may be an internal cavity (brood-cavity), within which a bud is formed. This is exemplified by a stalked Animalcule (*Tokophrya quadripartata*, fig. 845), belonging to the same group as the form last mentioned. Here the bud is provided with a broad ciliated girdle, and, when mature, squeezes out to the exterior through an opening present in the brood-cavity. After swimming about for some time by means of its cilia, the bud settles down, attaches itself to some firm body, loses its cilia, and develops the stalk and suctorial structures which are characteristic of the adult. This comparatively simple life-history appears to be a good illustration of the Law of Recapitulation, of which mention has already been made in this work. Otherwise expressed, the development of the individual epitomizes in a more or less perfect way the evolutionary history of the group to which the individual belongs, recapitulating ancestral stages. It is generally held that these suctorial Animalcules are an off-

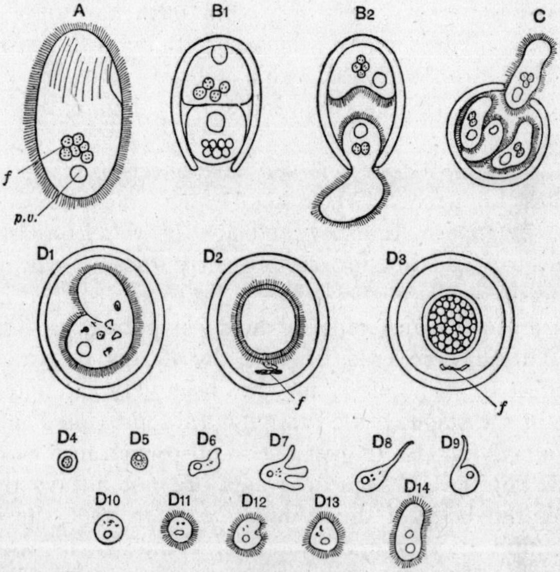

Fig. 846.—A Spore-forming Animalcule (*Colpoda*), greatly enlarged

A, Free-swimming individual. B and C, Encystment followed by division into two and four respectively. D 1–D 3, Encystment and Spore-formation; D 4–D 14, development of a spore. *f*, Food, *p.v.*, pulsating vacuole.

shoot from the ciliated group in which such forms as the Slipper- and Bell-Animalcules are included. And the existence of a ciliated stage in the life-history is not improbably reminiscent of ancestors in which cilia were present throughout life.

Spore-formation.—In the examples selected to give some idea of the nature of fission we saw that the body of the parent divided into two parts only. But many cases are also known of *multiple* fission, where several rapid divisions take place in succession, as a result of which several new individuals are brought into existence. In the Bell-Animalcule and its allies, for example, it often happens that a large fixed individual undergoes rapid unequal division to produce a number of relatively small free-swimming bells, which are simpler in structure than the parent Animalcule (fig. 844). The fate of these will be described in a later paragraph. Spore-formation is, so to speak, an exaggeration of this process, for where it takes place the body of the original form breaks up into a large number of minute parts, each of which is known as a *spore*. Such spores present a great variety of characters in different cases, and often form part of a remarkably complex life-history, of which something will be said elsewhere. They are developed within a firm capsule or *cyst*, with which the parent form surrounds its body before beginning to divide.

The formation of spores is very characteristic of the parasitic Animalcules known as Gregarines, which constitute the group Sporozoa (*i.e.* Spore-Animals), and also of the Fungus-Animalcules (Mycetozoa). But for our present purpose it will be better to take the simpler case afforded by a little bean-shaped organism (*Colpoda cucullus*) which often abounds in putrefying fluids. Its body is uniformly covered by cilia, by means of which swimming is effected. The life-history has been very carefully studied, and some of the stages passed through are represented in fig. 846. Before the body divides to give rise to offspring a firm case or cyst is formed, but the subsequent events are not always the same. Sometimes the body of the Animalcule, after losing its covering of cilia, simply divides into two (B) new individuals, which once more acquire cilia, and squeeze their way to the exterior through a hole in the cyst. In other cases there is a division into four (C). And lastly there may be spore-formation (D), which is a much more complicated process. After formation of a cyst devoid of any opening, the body of the Animalcule shrinks and becomes spherical, any food present within the body being expelled. The cilia then disappear, and a second firm membrane is formed outside the body, of which the substance now breaks up into a large number of minute rounded spores enclosed in firm coats. By rupture of the enclosing membranes the spores ultimately escape, and the firm coat of each of these splits open to liberate the tiny mass of living substance within. This at first resembles a minute Amœba, feeding and crawling in similar fashion. One end then grows out into a motile thread or flagellum, by which its owner is able for a time to swim about. Later on, the body assumes

GUENONS (*Cercopithecus sabæus*) RETREATING FROM A MAIZE-FIELD

The Guenons, of which one species is represented in the plate, are typical long-tailed African monkeys, native to the tropical parts of that continent. They are eminently arboreal, and live in troops, which make organized raids upon the crops of the natives. They are depicted here as retreating from threatened danger, of which the vigilant sentinel on the fence at the back has given warning. Maternal affection is well developed in monkeys, and in the background is shown the characteristic way in which the mother carries her helpless young one about. In the centre will be noticed another mother helping her partly-grown child over a difficult place. The intelligent individual in the foreground is retreating with a decent share of the plunder.

GUENONS (CERCOPITHECUS SABAEUS) RETREATING FROM A MAIZE-FIELD a rounded shape, cilia appear on its surface, and the size and shape of the adult are gradually attained.

Conjugation of Animalcules.—The vegetative propagation of Animalcules is commonly promoted by, and often dependent upon, a remarkable process to which the name of *conjugation* has been applied. This has been very carefully studied in some of the ciliated forms, as, *e.g.*, in the Slipper-Animalcule (*Paramœcium*) and Bell-Animalcule (*Vorticella*), which will serve as our illus-

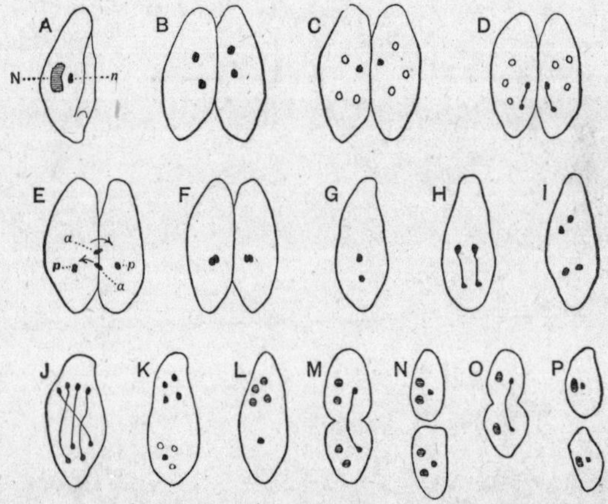

Fig. 847.—Temporary Conjugation of a Slipper-Animalcule (*Paramœcium caudatum*), diagrammatic and enlarged

A, A free individual; N, macronucleus; *n*, micronucleus. B–F, Stages in conjugation, showing successive divisions of micronuclei (macronuclei omitted), the fragments which disappear represented by clear circles—in E the active nucleus (*a*) of each individual is migrating towards the passive nucleus (*p*) of the other individual—in F each individual contains a compound nucleus. G–N, Changes in a conjugated individual leading to transverse fission, followed by (O, P) a further division in each half.

trations, though minute details will not be given, as the process is very complicated.

Within the body of one kind of Slipper-Animalcule (*Paramœcium caudatum*, fig. 847) two specialized particles of protoplasm can be seen, placed close to each other. The larger is the *macronucleus*, but it is with the smaller, or *micronucleus*, that we are here principally concerned. During conjugation two individuals apply themselves closely together, and remarkable changes take place in the nuclear structures. The macronucleus gradually disintegrates and disappears, but the micronucleus, by two successive divisions, is converted into four fragments, of which three break down and disappear. But the fourth fragment divides once more, and the fates of its halves differ. We may term them the active half and passive half. The active half, in each individual, migrates into the other Animalcule, and fuses with the passive half there present. After this interchange of nuclear material, which constitues the essential part of the process, the two conjugating individuals separate, each of them containing what may

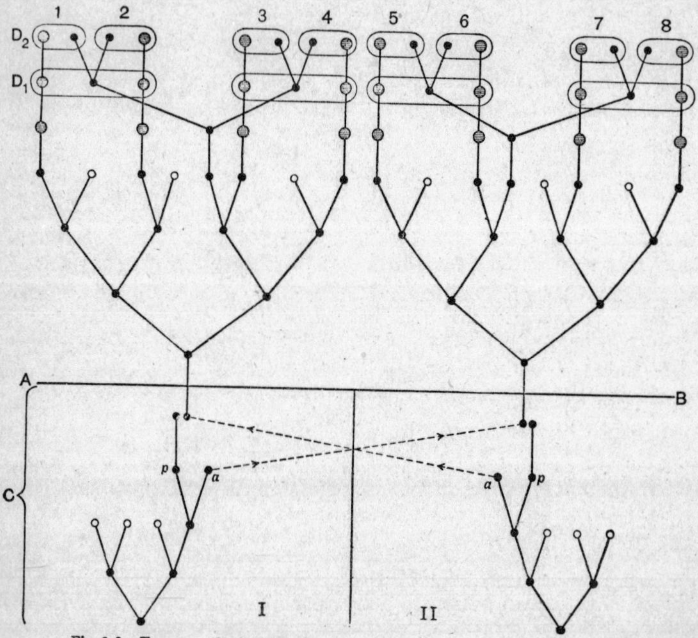

Fig. 848.—Temporary Conjugation of a Slipper-Animalcule (*Paramœcium caudatum*)

Diagram to show successive divisions, &c., of micronuclei. Fragments which disappear represented by clear circles, and fragments (of the compound nuclei) which become macronuclei shown as horizontally shaded circles. Read from below upwards. The changes during conjugation (c) of the two animalcules (I and II) are shown below AB: *a* and *p*, active and passive nuclei, the migration of the former indicated by dotted lines. The changes after conjugation shown above AB: at D_1, each conjugated animalcule has divided into two, and each of these (at D_2) has again divided, so that there are now eight new animalcules (1–8).

be called a *compound* or *fertilization nucleus.* The fusion of two nuclear masses, derived from different individuals, *i.e. fertilization*, is followed by increased activity in the vital processes. By it the living substance with which life is associated is, so to speak, stimulated and freshened, or, to use a more technical expression, *rejuvenesced.* Why this should be the case is still unknown. In the Slipper-Animalcule conjugation is followed by fission, a mark of increased activity. And it has been shown that without occasional conjugation between individuals not too nearly related the stock would degenerate and ultimately die out altogether. In this particular instance each of the two Animalcules which have conjugated divides into two, and each half at once divides again, so that multiplication is fourfold. By successive divisions of the fertilized nucleus eight fragments are produced, which become the macronuclei and micronuclei of the four new individuals. There are other fragments which come to nothing. The stages in conjugation and subsequent fission will best be followed by reference to figs. 847 and 848.

In a Bell-Animalcule (*Vorticella*) conjugation, instead of being *temporary*, as in the form just described, where two individuals exchange nuclear fragments and then separate, is *permanent*; *i.e.* two individuals completely fuse together to give a compound cell, which afterwards undergoes active fission. And the process differs in another important respect, for the individuals which fuse are of different size and nature. One is a large fixed bell, the other a small free-swimming individual (fig. 849), the latter being a product of multiple fission (see p. 321). Both conjugation and subsequent division are attended by complicated nuclear changes differing only in detail from those already described for the Slipper-Animalcule.

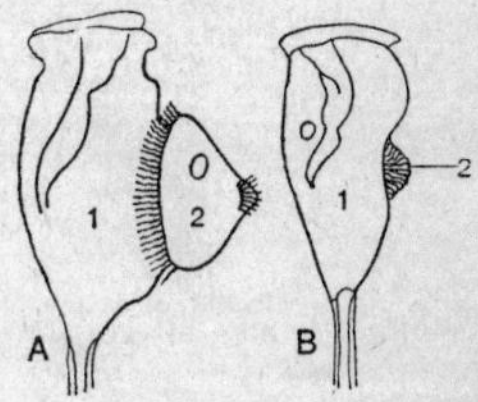

Fig. 849.—Permanent Conjugation of Bell-Animalcule (*Vorticella*), enlarged and diagrammatic

A and B are successive stages in the fusion of a large fixed bell (1) and a small free-swimming one (2).

VEGETATIVE PROPAGATION IN MANY-CELLED ANIMALS (METAZOA).—Some of the lower many-celled animals (Metazoa) regularly propagate by fission or budding, and are also able to regenerate lost parts with ease. The latter phenomenon is also exemplified by animals higher in the scale, and even the most specialized backboned forms are able to repair injuries to some extent.

Vegetative Propagation and Regeneration in Sponges (Porifera).—A simple Sponge is commonly in the form of a cup or vase, the walls of which are perforated by numerous small holes. Sea-water streams through these into the central cavity, and thence to the exterior through the larger opening (*osculum*) at the end of the body. Most Sponges, however, are far more complicated than this, and take all sorts of shapes. Some are compact masses, others flat incrustations attached to stones, &c.; others, again, branch like plants. Such forms as these are usually to be regarded as *colonies*, produced by budding or fission from a primary individual. A simple case of the kind is represented in fig. 862, 10, but it often happens that the boundaries between the members of the colony are extremely vague, though possibly each larger aperture (*osculum*) present corresponds to an individual.

Fig. 850.—A simple Cup-Sponge (*Polylophus*) producing External Buds. The curving bands below are bundles of siliceous spicules, bunches of which are also seen projecting from the buds.

In some kinds of Sponge external buds grow out (fig. 850), fall off, and develop into adults. A much more interesting phenomenon is presented by the formation of internal buds in certain species. The greenish Freshwater Sponge (*Spongilla*), common in this country, is a particularly instructive example, for it shows one way by which the unfavourable winter season can be tided over. The internal buds are here little packets of cells enclosed in protective coverings made up of peculiar spicules (fig. 851). They are developed on the approach of winter, the cold being fatal to the adult Sponge, which dies and decomposes. The buds (*gemmules*) then fall into the mud, and there remain dormant till the following spring, when the little mass of cells present in each of them creeps out of the protective investment through a hole present in one place, and grows into an adult Sponge.

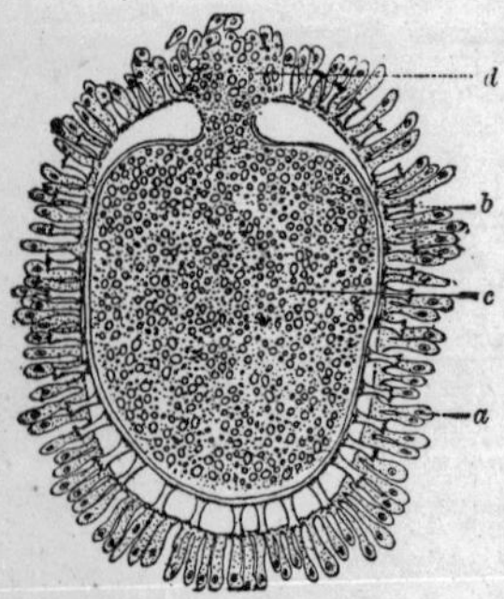

Fig. 851.—Section through Gemmule of Freshwater Sponge (*Spongilla*), enlarged. *a*, Cells which secrete the protective spicules (*b*); *c*, enclosed mass of cells; *d*, place where protective covering is incomplete.

If by accident a living Sponge gets cut or broken into pieces, each of these is able to repair its injuries, and continue growth on its own account. Advantage has been taken of this possibility in the case of the Bath Sponge (*Euspongia*), which can be propagated by means of cuttings almost as if it were a plant.

Vegetative Propagation and Regeneration in Zoophytes (*Cœlenterata*).—A simple case of budding is presented by the little Freshwater Polype (*Hydra*) during the summer months (fig. 852). A bud is formed by the outgrowth of a little projection from the wall of the body, which later on develops a mouth and tentacles, ultimately being pinched off from its parent as a new individual. And by vigorous budding a small temporary colony may be produced. The members of the group of Hydroid Zoophytes (*Hydromedusæ*), of which Hydra is a degenerate representative, are typically colonial, each colony resulting from the budding of a primary individual developed from an egg. And many kinds of Jelly-Fish are stages in the life-histories of such Zoophytes, from which they bud off.

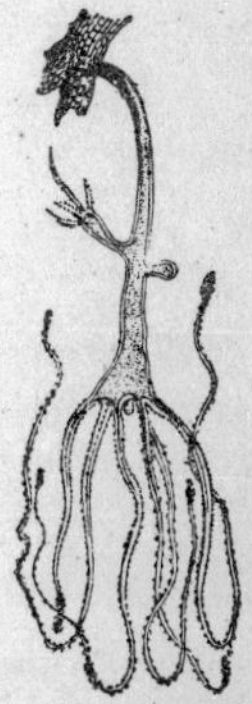

Fig. 852.—Budding Freshwater Polype (*Hydra*), enlarged. Two buds are shown.

The free-swimming colonies to which the name Compound Jelly-Fish (*Siphonophora*) is given are also the products of budding (see vol. i, p. 481), while other kinds of Jelly-Fish come into existence as the result of transverse splitting or fission of fixed individuals (see p. 352).

Vegetative propagation is eminently characteristic of the marine forms known as Sea-Flowers (*Anthozoa*), among which Sea-Anemones and most Corals are included. The former are familiar

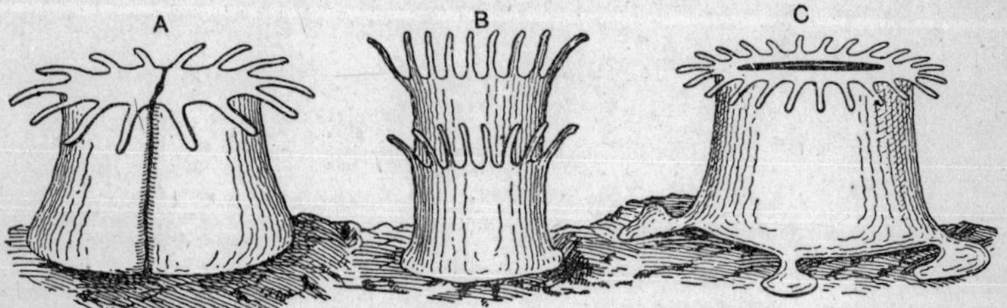

Fig. 853.—Vegetative Propagation of Sea-Anemones, diagrammatic

A, Longitudinal fission. B, Transverse fission. C. Laceration.

objects at the sea-side, and do not form colonies. Budding is known to take place in some species, but fission is a much commoner method of multiplication (fig. 853). When it takes place a groove makes its appearance, which gradually extends right across the Anemone, gets deeper and deeper, and ultimately splits the animal into two. Or the groove may be transverse, so that the upper and lower halves of the body are converted into separate individuals. In other cases the attached base of the Anemone grows out into little projections, which are pinched off, and grow into adults. This "laceration", as it has been called, is as much budding as fission.

Among Corals and allied forms some species are solitary, and these "cup Corals" chiefly differ from Anemones in the possession of a firm calcareous skeleton by which their basal half is supported. Such forms may propagate by budding or fission. But very many kinds of Coral are colonial, and, as in Hydroid Zoophytes, each colony has arisen by vegetative propagation of a primary individual. Budding and fission are both exemplified, and there is great variety in the shape of the colonies thus produced. Flat, massive, and branching forms abound in coral-reefs, and may be seen in any museum.

The regenerative powers of such creatures as Hydroid Zoophytes and Sea-Flowers are very considerable, so that "accidental death" is scarcely to be reckoned as one of the dangers to which they are exposed in the course of their existence. The best-known example is afforded by the Freshwater Polype (*Hydra*), a creature which can be artificially propagated by the simple device of cutting it into pieces.

Vegetative Propagation and Regeneration in Hedgehog-skinned Animals (*Echinodermata*).—The regenerative powers of members of this group are very considerable. Some of the Sea-Cucumbers when seized eject their digestive organs, which are afterwards re-developed. Sea-Lilies and Feather-Stars can also survive the loss of their soft parts, quickly replacing them by a new set. Star-Fishes and Brittle-Stars are quite notorious for the rapidity with which they renew lost arms. This is the origin of "comet" forms, in which some of the arms are of small size, being, in fact, new members which have yet to reach their full size.

Fission is definitely known to take place in some of the Star-Fishes and Brittle-Stars, the body being divided into two approximately equal parts. But the most remarkable illustration of vegetative propagation is met with in one family (*Linckiidæ*) of the former group. In Star-Fishes of this kind one or more arms can be deliberately thrown off. Not only is the original individual able to grow these again, but each detached arm can develop a disc and other arms, ultimately becoming a symmetrical adult (fig. 854).

Vegetative Propagation and Regeneration in Flat-Worms (*Platyhelmia*).—The members of this group are commonly able to repair injuries and re-grow lost parts with facility. As we shall see in a subsequent section, vegetative propagation plays an important part in the life-histories of such parasites as Flukes and Tape-Worms, and it will perhaps suffice for our present purpose to mention the transverse fission which regularly takes place in certain Planarian Worms (*Turbellaria*). A typical case is presented by a freshwater form (*Microstomum lineare*) depicted in fig. 855, and in which a temporary chain of individuals results from successive divisions.

Fig. 854.—Vegetative Propagation, &c., in Star-Fishes, reduced

A, A Star-Fish (*Ophidiaster diplax*), in which two arms (1, 2) are about to be pinched off, and three others (3, 4, 5) re-grown. B, A "Comet" Star-Fish (*Linckia multiflora*), in which a new disc and four arms are sprouting from a detached arm. C, A Star-Fish (*L. multiflora*) in which a new individual is growing from a wounded arm.

Fig. 855.—Fission-Chain of Planarian Worms (*Microstomum*), reduced

1, Original individual. 2, 3, 3, New individuals, numbered according to age.

Vegetative Propagation and Regeneration in Bristle-Worms (*Chætopoda*).—The body of a worm of this kind is made up of a varying number of rings or segments which, broadly speaking, resemble one another in structure. And supposing some of these rings to be accidentally cut off, or to fall a prey to some predaceous animal, the life of the worm is not thereby brought to an abrupt conclusion, for the injuries are speedily repaired. It has been suggested, with some show of probability, that segmentation of the body has been evolved as a protective measure (see vol. ii, p. 375), but this is rather doubtful, for unsegmented worms, such as Planarians, are also distinguished by great powers of regeneration.

It is not surprising to find ability to replace lost parts associated in some cases with vegetative propagation. This is the case in one of the marine Bristle-Worms already mentioned (p. 318), and the process essentially consists in the rapid growth or budding-out of the region immediately in front of the posterior end of the body. A transverse division is next effected, renewed growth takes place in front of this, a second division follows, and so on. In the temporary chain of individuals thus formed the youngest is therefore the one immediately behind the original animal. In other species a more complex arrangement may be found.

A more remarkable case is that of a Bristle-Worm (*Syllis ramosa*, fig. 856), in which lateral budding takes place, so that a temporary branching colony is brought into existence. This creature lives within the body of a sort of sponge.

Vegetative Propagation and Regeneration in Moss-Polypes (*Polyzoa*).—The vast majority of Moss-Polypes are colonial organisms and, as in Hydroid Zoophytes, the colonies result from a process of budding, and differ largely in shape according to the way in which this takes place.

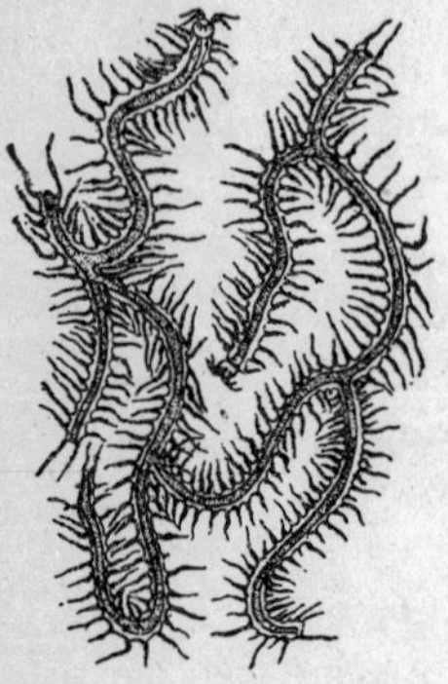

Fig. 856.—Part of Branching Colony of an Annelid (*Syllis ramosa*)

Our native freshwater species die down in autumn, but before this takes place *winter-buds* are produced (fig. 857), which remain dormant till the following spring, when they develop into new colonies. This affords another example of the method of tiding over an unfavourable season, which has already been described in the case of the Freshwater Sponge (see p. 326).

The winter-buds of Moss-Polypes are sometimes produced externally, but more commonly they arise internally, being known in that case as *statoblasts*. It is usual for these structures to be surrounded by a ring of air-containing cells, and in one case (*Cristatella*) there is also a circlet of grappling-hooks, which are likely to catch in water-plants or other objects. Harmer (in *The Cambridge Natural History*) makes the following interesting remarks regarding the buoyancy of these winter-buds:—"The production of *floating* statoblasts may seem a strange adaptation to the conditions of freshwater life, since it might be assumed, *a priori*, that these structures would be specially liable to be frozen during the winter. The following experiments made by Braem show, however, that the germinating power of the statoblasts is improved by a certain amount of frost. A number of statoblasts were taken; half of these were placed in water, which was then frozen; and these were found to germinate readily when afterwards exposed to suitable conditions. The other half were not subjected to the action of frost; and these could not be made to germinate, even though the water had been cooled to a point slightly above the freezing-point. It thus appears that the buoyancy, so far from being a risk, is a means of exposing the stato-

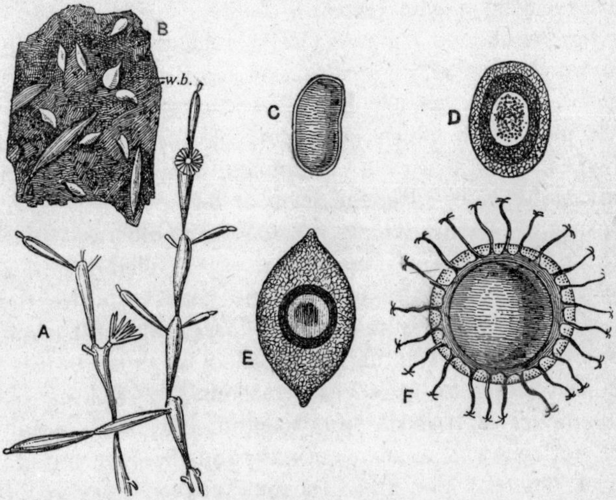

Fig. 857.—Winter-Buds of Moss-Polypes, enlarged to various scales

A, Small part of colony of *Paludicella*, with individuals expanded. B, Remains of part of colony of same, attached to stone and showing external winter-buds (*w.b.*). C, Simple statoblast of *Fredericella*. D, E, F, Floating statoblasts of *Plumatella*, *Lophopus*, and *Cristatella*.

blast to the conditions which are most favourable to its later development."

Moss-Polypes easily replace lost parts, and in most cases a large part of the body degenerates at regular intervals, and is as constantly re-grown from the part which remains. It has been suggested that this may be a radical sort of way of getting rid of waste products.

Vegetative Propagation and Regeneration in the Higher Groups of Many-celled Animals (*Metazoa*).—With increasing complexity of structure the possibilities in these directions become more and more limited. In Molluscs (Mollusca) and Jointed-limbed Invertebrates (Arthropoda) multiplication by means of budding or fission is no longer possible, though there is often considerable power of re-developing parts of the body which have been lost. The limbs of Crustaceans are a particularly good illustration of this. It is no infrequent thing to see a Crab or Lobster in which one pair of pincers is of insignificant size, the fact being that it is a new growth replacing an accidental loss. A creature of this kind which is getting the worst of a combat thinks nothing of abandoning a few limbs, leaving them in possession of the enemy, and thus securing a safe retreat.

Among Backboned Animals (Vertebrata) there are some lower types in which vegetative propagation regularly takes place. Of this the best examples are the Sea-Squirts (*Urochorda*), many of which produce colonies by means of budding. But in the higher types, from Fishes to Mammals, development from eggs is the invariable rule. Regeneration of lost parts may, however, take place to a varying extent. Among Amphibians (Amphibia), for instance, the limbs of Newts and other tailed forms, as also those of very young individuals of the tailless species (such as Frogs), can be completely re-grown if lost. The best example in the class of Reptiles (Reptilia) is afforded by those lizards which sacrifice their tails for protective reasons (see vol. ii, p. 371). These members afterwards sprout again, but the internal structures are not renewed in their entirety, and the covering of scales may be of different pattern. In the hot-blooded Birds (Aves) and Mammals (Mammalia) the regenerative processes are practically limited to the healing of wounds and the renewal of patches of skin which have been destroyed. It is obvious that the lives of many individuals would be sacrificed but for the possibilities in this direction. And it is a matter of common knowledge that remarkable results have been attained in modern surgery by "grafting" little bits of living healthy skin into the surface of extensive burns and the like.

CHAPTER LIV

ANIMAL DEVELOPMENT
PROPAGATION BY MEANS OF EGGS

DEVELOPMENT FROM EGGS IN ANIMALCULES (PROTOZOA)

The great majority of Animalcules are one-celled, a general rule which is but little upset by the fact that a number of forms are colonial, as the result of vegetative propagation. For in most such cases there is no division of labour between the members of the colony, all being precisely alike, and each of them having to discharge the various vital functions on its own account. For this reason a colony of this sort is said to be *physiologically* one-celled.

There can be no reasonable doubt that the remote ancestors of Many-celled Animals were one-celled forms, resembling Animalcules in essential respects, though many existing species of these have become greatly specialized on lines of their own, as the result of division of labour within the unit masses of living substance of which they are composed. And if this postulate be admitted, the Metazoa may be imagined to have arisen from colonial Protozoa in which the products of fission or budding remained united together. The operation of the principle of division of physiological work between the members of such a colony would ultimately result in the evolution of different *tissues*, *i.e.* groups of cells specialized in accordance with their particular duties, and the colony would then be in effect a simple kind of many-celled animal or Metazoon. Even the highest and most complex Metazoa are after all cell-communities in which division of labour is carried out into minute detail. An industrial illustration may serve to make this clearer. Supposing we take all the numerous processes involved in making boots to represent the sum-total of vital functions. Then a boot-maker who carries out all these processes with his own hands will correspond to a Protozoon. A number of boot-makers working together in the same house, each making boots on his own account, will correspond to the more usual type of Protozoan colony. But the workmen in a boot-factory, divided into sets, each set doing a different part of the work, and all therefore interdependent, will correspond to a Metazoon. Supposing the division of work to be carried out imperfectly a lower Metazoon will be typified, but if carried out into detail the nature of a higher Metazoon will be illustrated.

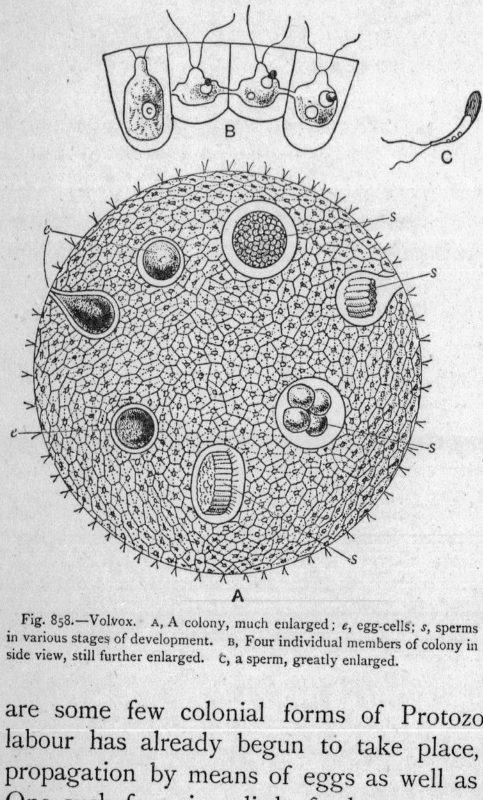

Fig. 858.—Volvox. A, A colony, much enlarged; *e*, egg-cells; *s*, sperms in various stages of development. B, Four individual members of colony in side view, still further enlarged. C, a sperm, greatly enlarged.

Between the numerous cells which make up the body of any Metazoon there is always a sharp division into (*a*) cells concerned with development from eggs, and (*b*) ordinary somatic cells which do the rest of the work. We may feel pretty sure that this distinction made its appearance very early in the history of the primitive Metazoa. It is therefore very interesting to know that there are some few colonial forms of Protozoa in which division of labour has already begun to take place, and in which there is propagation by means of eggs as well as by vegetative methods. One such form is a little freshwater organism (*Volvox*, fig. 858), which is about the size of a small pin's head, and of green colour. The colony is a hollow sphere with a gelatinous wall, in which are imbedded a large number of pear-shaped individuals the bodies of which are connected together by threads of living substance, while from each of them two filaments (*flagella*) of similar nature project to the exterior. The flagella execute lashing movements, by means of which the colony swims, at the same time constantly rotating. Vegetative propagation is effected by budding, some of the individuals dividing repeatedly to constitute daughter-colonies that are set free into the central cavity of the parent colony, which ultimately breaks up and liberates them. But development can also be effected in quite a different manner, *i.e.* by the formation of eggs. Some of the members of the colony increase in size and assume a spherical shape. These are the eggs, or, to speak more accurately, *egg-cells* or *ova*. Other members of the colony exhibit a similar increase, after which they divide into a multitude of small orange-coloured cells, which are set free into the surrounding water, and swim about actively by means of the flagella with which they are provided. They are known as *sperms*. Each ovum is fertilized by the permanent fusion with it of a single sperm, a process which is curiously like what happens during the conjugation of the Bell-Animalcule (p. 325), where a small free-swimming bell is completely incorporated with a large fixed one. And here also the fusion imparts increased vigour, which is manifested by active fission. But in the Bell-Animalcule the products of division separate from one another and become solitary adults, while in Volvox the corresponding products remain united together, and collectively make up a new colony.

DEVELOPMENT OF EGGS IN MANY-CELLED ANIMALS (METAZOA)

If vegetative propagation be left out of consideration, we may say that every many-celled animal, from a Sponge to a Vertebrate, begins its life-history as an egg-cell or ovum, which is fertilized, in the vast majority of cases, by fusion with it of a sperm, derived, as a rule, from another individual. The fertilized ovum then actively divides to form a little mass of cells, which, by further divisions and specializations, gradually shape themselves into the tissues and organs of the adult. There is, in fact, a gradual evolution of the individual (*ontogeny*), from a simple unit-mass of living substance, and that this should be so is broadly interpreted by the Law of Recapitulation as the result of inheritance, whereby is repeated the evolutionary history (*phylogeny*) of the particular group of animals to which the developing individual belongs. And if this interpretation be correct, the first stage in the life-history, *i.e.* the egg-cell, stands for the original one-celled ancestors of the many-celled animals. This gradual building up of the complex body of an animal is one of the most astonishing facts with which zoology has to deal, and can only be explained on an evolutionary basis. The early students of development held views which were totally at variance with the facts as we now know them. They believed, for instance, that the youngest discernible stage in the growth of the chicken within the egg differed from the adult bird only as regards size. This was the doctrine of Preformation, according to which development merely consisted in the enlargement of parts already present, by a process of "unfolding" or "evolution". The last expression was used, it will be noticed, in quite a different sense from the modern one. The rival doctrine of Epigenesis, according to which the body is gradually built up in the way already indicated, owes its first inception to the gifted investigator, Caspar Friedrich Wolff, who flourished in the latter part of the eighteenth century. In the realm of botany the errors of the Preformation theory linger even yet. The present writer has had the doubtful privilege of hearing eloquent discourses embellished by such statements as: "The tiny acorn contains in miniature every root, twig, and leaf of the mighty oak, of which it is the parent".

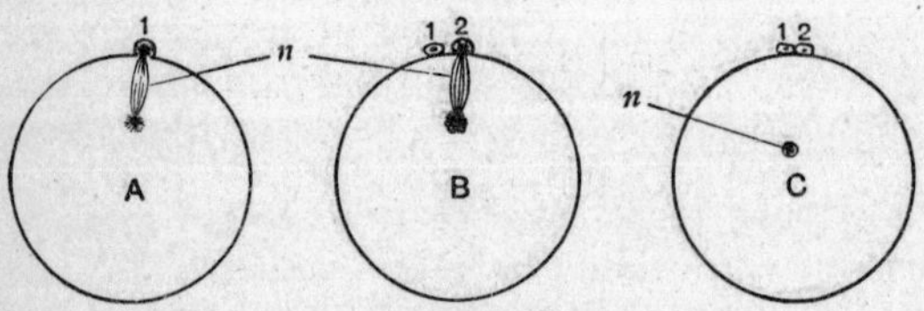

Fig. 859.—Formation of Polar Bodies, diagrammatic

In A and B is shown successive formation of first and second polar bodies (1 and 2). C, Egg-cell ready for fertilization; 1 and 2, first and second polar bodies; *n*, nucleus.

Polar Bodies (fig. 859).—Before an egg-cell is mature and ready to be fertilized it twice undergoes unequal division, of which the smaller products are known as "polar-bodies". They take no part in the development, but sooner or later disintegrate. As a result of their extrusion the egg-cell gets rid of three-quarters of its nuclear substance. The maturation of sperms is associated with a similar process. Why polar bodies should be formed at all is by no means clear, though they have been the object of a large amount of investigation and speculation. It is quite likely that, for one thing, the egg-cell is, so to speak, weakened, and thereby prevented from developing into an adult animal without fertilization, which is undoubtedly a process resulting in increased vigour. Presumably individuals developed from unfertilized egg-cells would be less fitted to struggle for existence than those arising in the usual way. The facts ascertained regarding the conjugation of Protozoa throw some light on this (see p. 323). Rare cases are known in which unfertilized ova do develop, and those which are thus distinguished do not as a rule give rise to more than one polar body. It may here be further noted that these bodies very probably have some bearing on the question of heredity, a point which will be dealt with further on.

Law of Recapitulation.—We have seen that certain colonial Animalcules, such as Volvox, help to bridge over the gap between one-celled animals (Protozoa) and many-celled animals (Metazoa), and that in the life-history of one of the latter the egg-cell which constitutes the starting-point is reminiscent of the original one-celled ancestors. But it would be a great mistake to suppose that the Law of Recapitulation enables us to work out in detail the evolutionary history of groups from the stages through which the members of those groups pass in the course of their development. For although, as Milnes Marshall picturesquely put it, an animal may be broadly said to "climb up its own genealogical tree" in the course of its life-history, yet the Law of Recapitulation is by no means the never-failing guide in matters evolutionary that many enthusiastic naturalists once supposed. The expression "*once* supposed" is used advisedly, for at the present time there is a tendency to discount the law in question to an extent which is hardly warranted by the facts. Balfour, the most gifted embryologist of last century, thus expressed the matter (in his *Comparative Embryology*) in his usual clear and vigorous way: "Were it indeed the case that each organism contained in its development a full record of its origin, the problem of phylogeny [*i.e.* evolution of animal groups] would be in a fair way towards solution. As it is, however, the law [of recapitulation] above enunciated is, like all physical laws, the statement of what would occur without interfering conditions. Such a state of things is not found in nature, but development as it actually occurs is the resultant of a series of influences of which heredity is only one. As a consequence of this, the embryological record, as it is usually presented to us, is both imperfect and misleading. It may be compared to an ancient manuscript with many of the sheets lost, others displaced, and with spurious passages interpolated by a later hand. The embryological record is almost always abbreviated in accordance with the tendency of nature (to be explained on the principle of the survival of the fittest) to attain her ends by the easiest means. The time and sequence of the development of parts is often modified, and finally, secondary structural features make their appearance to fit the embryo or larva for special conditions of existence. When the life-history of a form is fully known, the most difficult part of his task is still before the scientific embryologist. Like the scholar with his manuscript, the embryologist has by a process of careful and critical examination to determine where the gaps are present, to detect the later insertions, and to place in order what has been misplaced."

The difficulties mentioned above at once beset us when we attempt to explain on an evolutionary basis the processes through which the egg-cell goes immediately after fertilization. These consist of a series of divisions, technically known as *cleavage* or *segmentation* (not to be confounded with segmentation of the adult body), by which a little mass of cells, *i.e.* a *blastula*, is brought into existence. Nothing could be easier than to assert that this stage corresponds to the colonies of Protozoa which evolved into the earliest Metazoa, and such an assertion would no doubt be true in a general way. But it is rather disappointing to find that the blastula differs greatly in animals of different kind. Sometimes it is spherical and solid (*morula*), sometimes spherical and hollow (*blastosphere*), or it may be a two-layered plate of cells (*placula*). And occasionally it is not composed of cells at all, but is a mass of protoplasm containing numerous nuclei, which serve as centres round which cells are later on marked out. To decide which of these forms is *primary*, *i.e.* really represents an early ancestral stage, and which are *secondary*, *i.e.* modifications due to the exigencies of development, would puzzle Solomon himself, supposing that worthy to be posted in the facts and methods of modern science. And, as often happens, the triumph of one view over the rest might conceivably be not so much a contribution to fact as a tribute to the ability or ingenuity of some forceful authority. As the late Professor Huxley was wont to remark, in his characteristic way: "Theories which at first blush appear to be the most complete and beautiful are commonly those which are most easily upset". Without attempting to support the claims of any one kind of blastula to ancestral honours, the present writer would point out that all of them can be more or less completely matched by members of the group of Protozoa, though the placula comes off worst in this respect. And the possibility is by no means excluded that different groups of many-celled animals have arisen independently from colonial Protozoa which did not all conform to the same type.

A brief sketch of the chief stages in the development of a few typical animals will form a fitting conclusion to the present section.

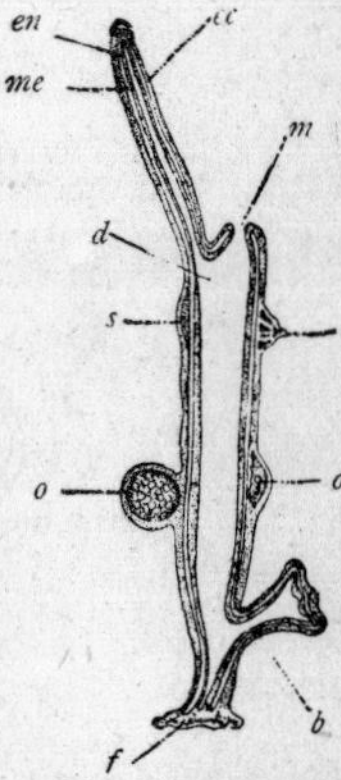

Fig. 860. — Diagrammatic Longitudinal Section of Freshwater Polype (*Hydra*), enlarged

m, Mouth; *f*, foot; *d*, digestive cavity; *ec*, ectoderm; *en*, endoderm; *me*, mesoglœa; *b*, bud; *oo*, ovaries; *ss*, spermaries.

Development of the Freshwater Polype (*Hydra*). — With the possible exception of Sponges (Porifera), the great group of the animal kingdom (Cœlenterata) of which Hydra is a member may be regarded as the lowest division of many-celled forms (Metazoa). Digestive arrangements are of such great importance to the well-being of animals that we might expect them to be evolved very early in the history of the Metazoa. And it has been remarked with truth that Cœlenterates may be epigrammatically defined as "living stomachs". This is certainly the case in Hydra, the body of which is a hollow cylinder, with a mouth at one end, surrounded by a circlet of tentacles that catch food, which is taken into the large central cavity and there digested. The numerous cells making up the body are disposed in two layers, and this may be taken to represent commencing division of physiological labour. The inner layer (*endoderm*), lining the central cavity, is concerned with digestion, and the outer layer (*ectoderm*) is not only protective, but also performs the duties which are carried out in higher forms by the nervous system and sense organs. In Hydra there is a thin structureless supporting membrane (*mesoglœa*) between the two cell-layers, and in many Cœlenterates, such as jelly-fishes, this may be extremely well developed, and contain various cells which have wandered into it from ectoderm and endoderm. But it is not a continuous sheet of closely-connected cells, as are the two latter, and therefore all Cœlenterates are regarded as being *two-layered* animals, as contrasted with still higher forms which, as we shall see, are essentially *three-layered.*

During the summer months Hydra propagates by means of budding, but as the autumn approaches, one or more rounded thickenings of the ectoderm appear near the attached end, and several pointed thickenings of the same layer near the mouth end (fig. 860). Each of the former is an *ovary*, and each of the latter a *spermary*. Within the ovary there are at first a number of little cells, one of which becomes bigger than its fellows, and uses these as food after the fashion of an Amœba. It has now become

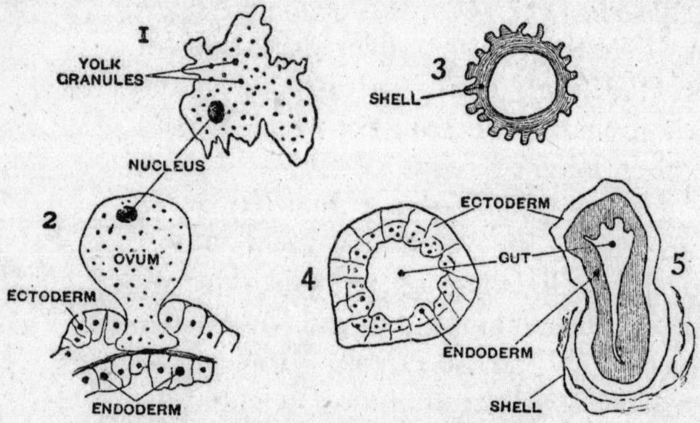

Fig. 861.—Development of Freshwater Polype (*Hydra*), enlarged

1, Ovum in amœboid stage. 2, Ripe ovum projecting from body-wall of adult. 3, Section through egg-shell. 4, Section through embryo in two-layered stage (shell omitted). 5, Section through ripe embryo escaping from shell (cells of ectoderm and endoderm not shown).

an egg-cell or ovum, within which are to be seen a number of granules of nutritious substance (yolk) which serve as food to the developing embryo. After a time the covering of the ovary is ruptured, and the egg-cell projects externally. Each spermary also contains a little mass of cells that divide repeatedly to form a large number of minute tadpole-shaped bodies, the sperms, which are ultimately set free into the surrounding water, where they swim about. Precisely as in Volvox (p. 335) the egg-cell is fertilized by fusion with it of a single sperm, derived from the same or another Hydra. The fertilized egg-cell next surrounds itself with a firm protective coating, and undergoes cleavage to form a mass of small cells (*morula*), which may be called an embryo (fig. 861). This now becomes detached from the body of the parent, and falls into the mud, where it remains in a dormant state during the winter. Since all or most of the adult animals die, these dormant embryos enable the species to tide over an unfavourable season, answering the same purpose as the winter buds of freshwater moss-polypes (p. 330) or the seeds of annual plants. During the following spring development is renewed, the changes which take place converting the solid Blastula (*morula*) into a two-layered *Gastrula*, possessing a central digestive cavity. The protective coat is ruptured, the embryo elongates, a mouth and tentacles are developed, and we have now a young Hydra, which feeds actively and grows into an adult.

The two-layered stage in development, *i.e.* the Gastrula, is of great interest, and in one form or other represents a stage in the life-history of the members of a great many groups of animals. In its most typical form a mouth is present from the first, and often is used as such, food passing through it into the central digestive cavity (*archenteron*, *i.e.* primitive gut). Some specialists, indeed, would not apply the term Gastrula to a two-layered embryo devoid of mouth. We have seen how difficult it is to decide which of the various kinds of Blastula are to be looked upon as representing an early ancestral stage. The Gastrula, however, probably repeats a somewhat later phase in the evolutionary history of Metazoa with some approach to accuracy. The Cœlenterates remain throughout life permanent and specialized Gastrulæ. And according to the Gastræa theory of Hæckel all the higher groups of animals are entitled to place some variety or other of the Gastrula in their picture-gallery of ancestors. Other authorities, however, are by no means unanimous on this point, though there seems to be a good deal of truth in Hæckel's view, the weak point in which lies in the assumption that the stage preceding the Gastrula was a hollow sphere, which attained the double-layered stage by in-pushing, much as an air-containing india-rubber ball, when collapsed, becomes a double-walled cup. Such a process certainly does not take place in the development of Hydra, but is true for a number of other animals, as we shall presently see.

Development of a Simple Calcareous Sponge.—The Sponges (Porifera) constitute a very problematic group of animals, of which the relationship to other forms is obscure. They are sometimes regarded as a branch of Cœlenterates, but it is more likely that they are a distinct group or phylum which has taken independent origin from Protozoan-like ancestors. It does not fall within the province of this work to discuss so difficult a technical problem, but the following sketch of the development of a simple typical sponge may not be without interest (fig. 862). The fertilized egg-cell divides repeatedly to give rise to a solid Blastula (*morŭla*), the cells of which next arrange themselves into two concentric layers (*ectoderm* and *endoderm*), while a central digestive cavity also makes its appearance, very much as in Hydra. The outer cells develop a covering of cilia, by means of which the embryo, or rather larva, which is now of oval form, swims about for a time. The term *larva* has elsewhere been explained, but it may not be superfluous to repeat here that it is applied to an embryo which leads an independent existence, and differs more or less markedly from the adult. This particular sort of larva is known as a Planula, and is also a stage in the life-histories of many Cœlenterates. It is at first mouthless, but a mouth is soon developed, and a typical gastrula stage is thus attained. The larva now fixes itself by the mouth end, and loses its covering of cilia. A new opening makes its appearance at the free extremity, and becomes the osculum of the adult. Further important changes consist in the appearance of a large number of small holes in the body-wall, and the development of a layer (*mesoglœa*) between ectoderm and endoderm. Cells pass into this, and some of them give rise to three-rayed spicules of calcareous nature, each ray taking origin from a separate cell; others become egg-cells. By subsequent budding a colony may be formed.

Early Stages in the Development of the Lancelet (*Amphioxus*).—While Cœlenterates and Sponges essentially consist of only two continuous sheets of cells (*ectoderm* and *endoderm*), although a third jelly-like layer (*mesoglœa*) afterwards makes its appearance between these, and usually contains cells of various kind, a further stage is reached in higher groups of animals. For in any one of these the embryo, after passing through a two-layered or gastrula stage, develops a third sheet of cells (*mesoderm*) between ectoderm and endoderm. Many difficult problems centre in the mesoderm, but with these we are not here concerned.

The three-layered animals, of which the Lancelet is selected as a type, illustrate the principle of division of physiological labour in a much higher degree than do the two-layered forms, and are consequently of more complex structure. This has already been abundantly illustrated in preceding sections, and will become still more obvious when we have to consider the Nervous System and

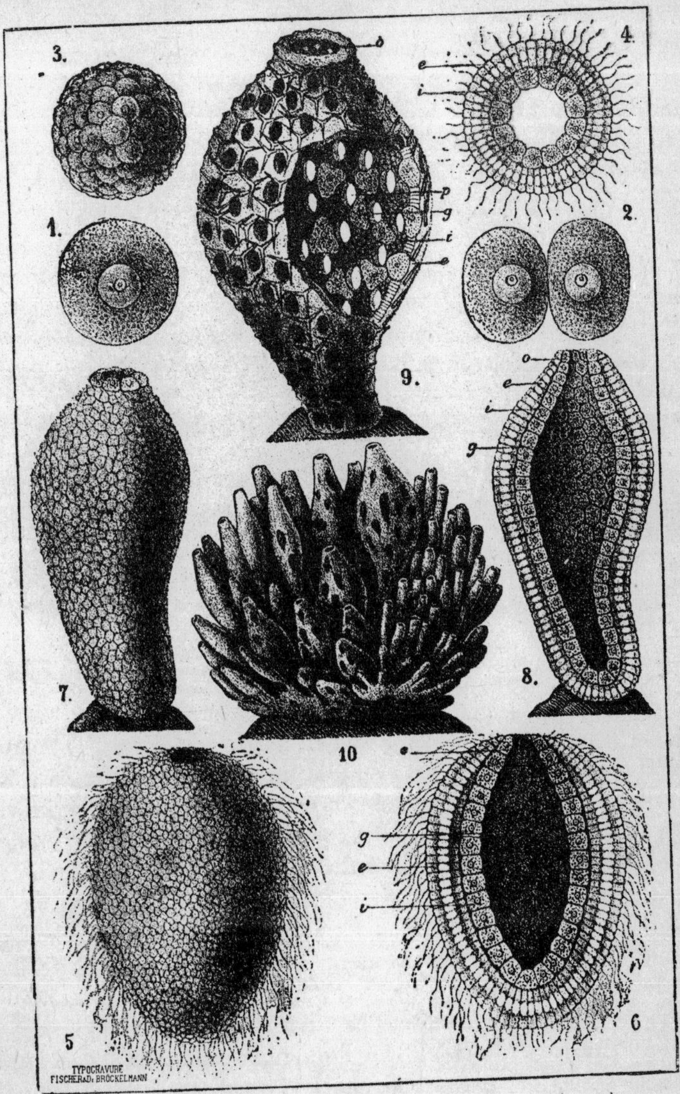

Fig. 862.—Stages in Development of a Sponge, enlarged (except 10) to various scales

e, Ectoderm; *i*, endoderm; *g*, digestive cavity; *o*, main opening (osculum) of digestive cavity; *p*, pore in body-wall. 1, Ovum. 2, First division of ovum. 3, Morula. 4, Two-layered embryo (in section). 5, Ciliated Planula, drawn at 6 in section. 7, Later fixed stage (in section at 8). 9, Adult stage (side-wall partly removed) showing numerous pores and three-rayed spicules. 10, Colony formed by budding.

Sense Organs, by means of which the activities of animals are regulated and directed.

The small egg-cell of the Lancelet passes out of the body, and is fertilized in the surrounding sea-water, after which it undergoes cleavage to become a Blastula, which in this case is a hollow sphere (*blastosphere*), the wall of which is formed by a single layer of cells (fig. 863). These are rather larger on one side of the sphere. The two-layered stage or Gastrula is then reached by a sort of in-pushing of the larger cells to constitute the lining of a large central digestive cavity (*archenteron*), that communicates with the exterior by a mouth, technically known as the *blastopore*. This internal layer of cells is the *endoderm*, while the smaller

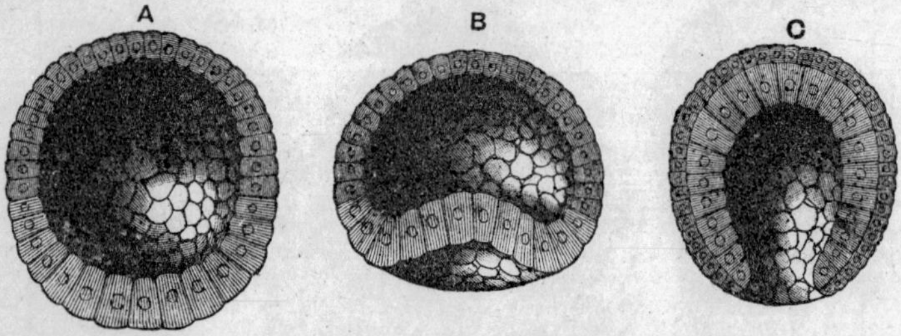

Fig. 863.—Young Embryos of Lancelet (*Amphioxus*), enlarged, and bisected to show interior. A, Blastosphere. B, Commencing gastrula. C, Gastrula. See text.

external cells are collectively known as the *ectoderm*. The two-layered Gastrula next gives rise to a three-layered stage, in a way which may be gathered by reference to fig. 864, which represents cross-sections through four embryos of different age, the youngest being on the left. The wall of the central digestive cavity bulges out at the upper corners, as indicated by dark shading in the figures, and the pouches thus formed gradually get pinched off, coming to lie between the ectoderm and endoderm. They subsequently grow right round the body and constitute the *mesoderm*, or middle embryonic layer. The cavities of the pouches become the body-cavity of the adult, *i.e.* the lymph-containing space, or in this case series of spaces between body-wall and the wall of the digestive tube.

It will be worth while to consider to what parts the three layers of the embryo respectively give rise. 1. The innermost layer (*endoderm*) becomes the thin cellular membrane (*epithelium*) which lines most of the digestive tube and also its outgrowths, such as the liver, which in the Lancelet is a simple pouch. And the endoderm also gives rise to the elastic rod or notochord, which represents the backbone in this particular animal, and is replaced partly or entirely by the backbone in higher Vertebrates. The origin of this rod is indicated in fig. 864. The wall of the upper part of the digestive cavity is seen to be grooved in B, just between the two mesodermic pouches. In C the groove is better marked, and in D a strip of the wall of the digestive cavity has been pinched off to form a rod, of which the section appears oval. 2. The outermost layer (*ectoderm*) naturally gives rise to the *epidermis*, or external part of the skin. From it the nervous system and the essential parts of the sense organs also take origin. The development of

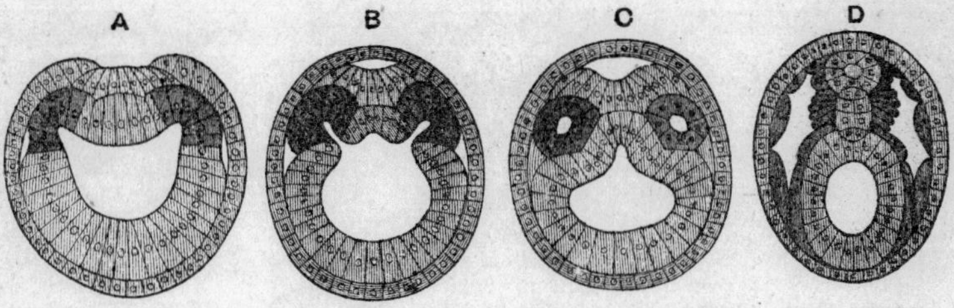

Fig. 864.—Cross-sections through older Embryos of Lancelet (*Amphioxus*), enlarged. Mesoderm darkly shaded. The central space is the digestive cavity. See text.

the hollow dorsal tube which constitutes the central part of the nervous system is seen in fig. 864. A central strip of ectoderm on the upper side of the body is thickened into a sort of plate, which sinks into the body and then folds up into a tube. Examination of the upper parts of A, B, C, and D will make this clear, remembering, of course, that only thin cross-sections of this strip are shown. 3. The middle layer (*mesoderm*) is the parent of all the remaining organs, as, for example, those concerned with circulation and development of eggs. The muscular system and the muscle in the wall of the digestive tube are also products of this layer, as are the deeper part of the skin (*dermis*) and all the supporting fibrous tissue found throughout the body.

The fate of the three embryonic layers, as just summarized, is practically the same in all three-layered animals, from backboned forms down to Worms and Echinoderms.

Influence of Food-Yolk on Development (fig. 865).—The egg-cells of different animals vary greatly in size, according to the amount of nutritive matter, or food-yolk, which is stored up in them, to be employed in building up the body of the embryo. The quantity and distribution of this material have much to do with the nature of the cleavage which succeeds fertilization. Unless a great deal of it is present the cleavage is *total*, the whole of the egg-cell taking part in the divisions which produce the blastula. But it happens in many cases that the yolk is not uniformly distributed, being concentrated towards one end (or "pole"), and the

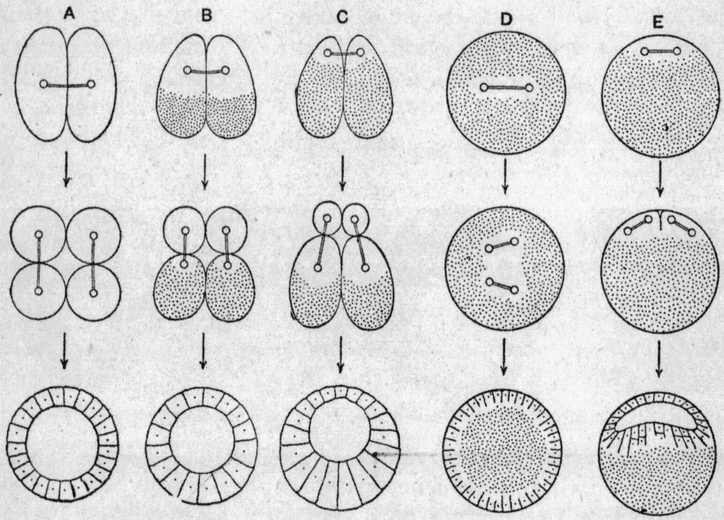

Fig. 865.—Influence of Food-yolk on Development. Diagrammatic sections

Read each column from above downwards. The food-yolk represented by dots. The two upper lines show early stages in division of the ovum, and the bottom line the blastula stage. A, Total equal cleavage (no yolk). B and C, Total unequal cleavage (yolk at one pole). D, Partial cleavage (central yolk). E, Partial cleavage (yolk at one pole). For convenience' sake all the figures are made of the same size, but the size of an ovum is proportionate to the amount of food-yolk it contains, *e.g.* A would be very small and E very large.

cleavage-cells are larger in this region. From this we pass to egg-cells which are so crammed with yolk that cleavage is *partial*, *i.e.* only that part of the cell which is not thus encumbered divides. This may be a patch at one pole, as in the eggs of Dog-Fishes and Birds, or it may be a surface layer, as in Arthropods, where the yolk is massed in the centre.

In egg-laying or *oviparous* animals, as opposed to *viviparous* forms, in which the young animal is brought into the world more or less ready to commence independent existence, the time of hatching depends upon the amount of yolk, or of this and other nutritive matters which may be enclosed in a protective covering with the developing embryo for its use. If these stores of food material are abundant, the changes which go on within the *egg*, as we may term the egg-cell together with accessory structures, may take a considerable time, and the young animal may hatch out in a form not very unlike that of the adult. A familiar example is afforded by the life-history of a Fowl. The egg is of large size, and made up of the developing egg-cell with the nutritive matter stored up in it (the "yolk"), of the extra food-supply known as the *albumen* (the "white"), and of two protective coverings, *i.e.* the double *shell-membrane* and the porous calcareous *shell* (fig. 866). As everyone knows, the chick which emerges from the egg after

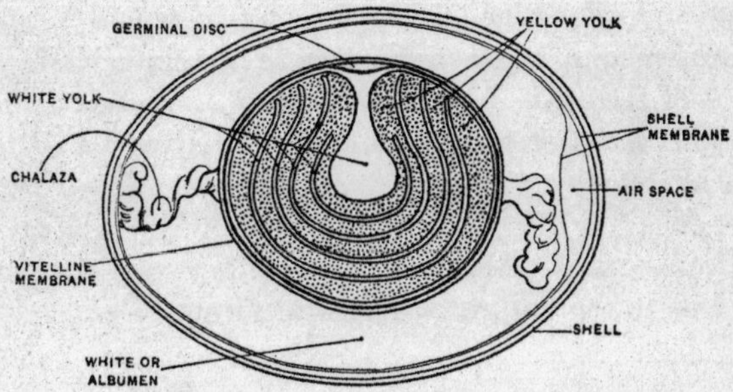

Fig. 866.—Diagrammatic Longitudinal Section through a Hen's Egg

three weeks' incubation is at once able to run about, and soon begins to pick up food.

On the other hand, hatching-out is a comparatively rapid process in the case of eggs which contain a small amount of nutritive matter, and the young animal is consequently in a very immature condition when it is thus prematurely forced to get its own living. It may often be described as a larva, which is very unlike the adult stage to which it ultimately attains. We have seen, for example, that a typical sponge is hatched out as a little ciliated oval Planula, and it may be added that the young Lancelet does not at first resemble the parent form. These, however, are somewhat extreme cases. Larval forms may result from the hatching of eggs containing a fairly large amount of yolk, as in the Frog. And it does not follow that the presence of large stores of nutritive material in the egg is correlated with such perfectly-formed young as those characteristic of Fowls. The nestlings of a Sparrow, for instance, are particularly helpless, and superficially unlike their parents. But this is largely due to their featherless condition, and they are obviously of bird nature, so not entitled to be called larvæ.

In applying the law of recapitulation to animals possessing a larval stage in their life-history, there is special need to exert care in making deductions as to the characters possessed by ancestral forms. There is great likelihood of organs developing out of their proper order, for those which are absolutely necessary to the life of the larva when it begins an independent existence take precedence of others which are not of such vital importance in the struggle for existence. This is particularly true for organs of locomotion and digestion, while few larvæ would survive if the nervous system and sense organs were not in an efficient state. Such parts of the body have to hurry up, as it were, or in other words there is a "hastening of events". Larvæ are also very apt to possess *secondary* characters, *i.e.* features specially related to the exigencies of larval life, which frequently differs in a marked way from adult existence. And it is obvious that such characters often afford no clue to the nature of ancestral forms.

ANIMAL LIFE-HISTORIES—PROTECTION OF EGGS AND YOUNG—ANIMAL DWELLINGS

CHAPTER LV

LIFE-HISTORIES, &c., OF BACKBONELESS ANIMALS (INVERTEBRATA)

To do full justice to the important question of Life-Histories, and related topics, a complete volume of this work would not afford too much scope. But, as full treatment of the kind would lead to undue limitation of the space to be devoted to equally interesting subjects, it is proposed to deal with only a small number of cases, selected with reference to general principles. Protection of Eggs and Young will include *passive protection* by mechanical devices, and also *active protection* on the part of parents. And it may be remarked that Animal Dwellings commonly owe their importance to the fact that they are employed as nurseries, and some of them are constructed solely for this purpose. Certain life-histories have already been dealt with more or less fully in earlier sections, and others will receive treatment in the later parts of this work, under such headings as Instinct and Intelligence, Parasitism, &c.

LIFE-HISTORIES, &c., OF ZOOPHYTES (CŒLENTERATA)

A great many of the familiar forms known as Jelly-Fishes are simply stages in the life-history of fixed colonial animals that have been produced by the budding of a single individual. A typical case is represented in fig. 867. We have here a simple illustration of the phenomenon known as *alternation of generations*. In other words the life-cycle does not consist of the continuous gradual growth of an individual from a bud, fission-product, or egg, but comprises at least two stages or generations, one propagating by vegetative means, and the other by eggs. In this case the former is the fixed branching colony (*hydroid zoophyte*), which not only buds to increase its size, but also produces special buds which are liberated as jelly-fishes or medusæ. These produce eggs, which develop into oval ciliated free-swimming larvæ (*planulæ*), something like those already described for Sponges (see p. 342). After a time each larva fixes itself to some firm body, and becomes an individual essentially resembling a Freshwater Polype (*Hydra*). By means of budding, a fixed colony (*hydroid zoophyte*) arises from this; later on, special buds grow into medusæ, and so on. If the hydroid zoophyte or *vegetative stage* be represented by V, and the medusa or *egg-producing stage* by E, the formula V–E–V–E–V–E, &c. will represent the succession of stages, V–E being a single cycle or life-history. But we cannot say that this is the life-history of an individual, since both V and E are individuals. And the singularity of the matter consists in this, that any given member of the series closely resembles its grandparents and grandchildren, but differs greatly from its parents and children.

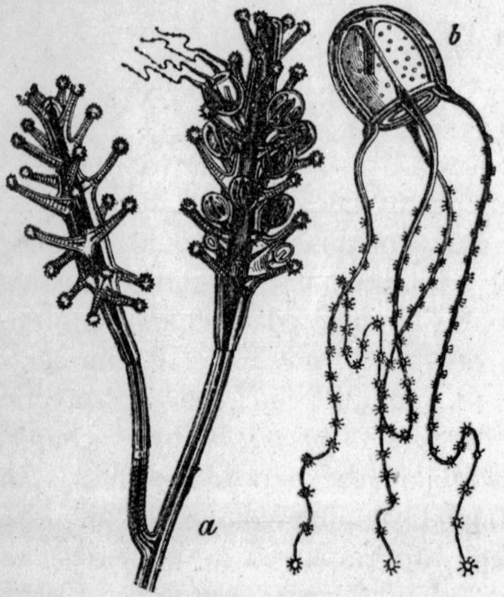

Fig. 867.—Life-history of Syncoryne

a, Two individuals from the fixed colonial stage (*hydroid zoophyte*) each studded with knobbed tentacles, between which (in one individual) are buds which become liberated as medusæ; *b*, a medusa.

In some of the Hydroid Zoophytes there are special arrangements for protecting the medusa-buds while they are being developed. Instead of projecting freely into the surrounding sea-water, a group of them is sheltered in a little horny case (*gonangium*, fig. 868).

It must not be supposed that all of the numerous species of Hydroid Zoophytes give rise to free-swimming jelly-fishes, for the egg-cells and sperms are often produced in special buds (*gonophores*) which are never liberated. These buds may be precisely like jelly-fishes in structure, obscurely like, or quite unlike (fig. 869). In the last case they are rounded projections known as *sporosacs*, a rather unfortunate name, for spores are certainly not produced in them. The ovaries and spermaries of Hydra (see p. 340) may be regarded as sporosacs of the simplest possible kind. The series of egg-producing buds just outlined, from the free-swimming medusa condition down to Hydra, appear to represent a set of evolutionary stages by which the jelly-fish stage as such has been practically superseded. A fixed colony, such as that represented by a Hydroid Zoophyte, is in some respects at a disadvantage, for if markedly unfavourable changes

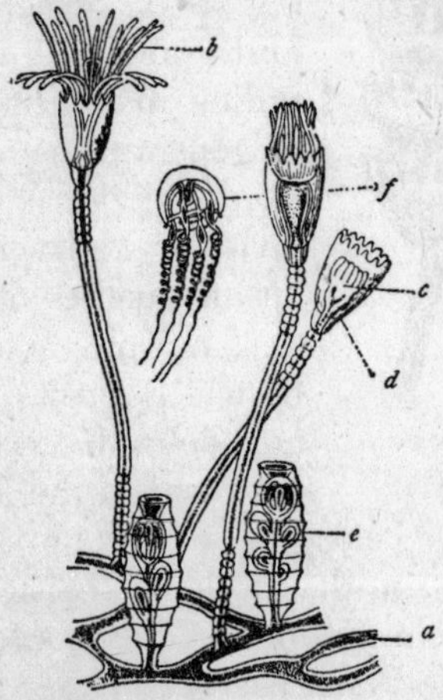

Fig. 868.—Life-history of Campanularia

a, Branching base of fixed colony; *b*, expanded individual; *c*, individual retracted into its cup (*d*); *e*, case within which medusa buds are developing; *f*, a free-swimming medusa.

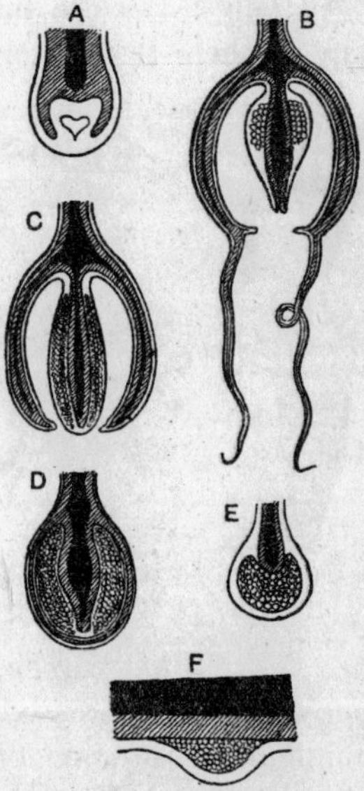

Fig. 869.—Gonophores of various Zoophytes in section —diagrammatic

Digestive cavity black, ectoderm white, endoderm shaded, egg- or sperm-producing cells as small circles. A, Developing gonophore. B–F, Stages in degeneration of gonophores (F is sporosac of Hydra).

take place in the surroundings it is not able to move away in search of a more desirable locality, and if the area occupied by the species were small, such changes might conceivably lead to its complete extinction, if there were no compensating arrangement. Probably the jelly-fish stage was originally evolved as an arrangement of the kind, whereby eggs could be carried to considerable distances, so that a reasonable percentage of the embryos produced from them would have a fair chance of reaching suitable spots for settling down and budding into fixed colonies of Hydroid Zoophytes. But if this view approximates to the truth, it is rather difficult to understand why some of the Hydroid Zoophytes have given up the jelly-fish stage, which presumably increased their chances in the struggle for existence. It can only be conjectured that since the production of eggs from which free-swimming *larvæ* hatch out takes less time and involves less expenditure of energy than the production of jelly-fishes that serve the same purpose, some Zoophytes have abandoned the latter plan altogether, while others are giving it up.

All jelly-fishes are not developed as buds on a fixed colony. Many of them result from the transverse fission of attached individuals, as, *e.g.*, the common form Aurelia (fig. 870), which affords another illustration of alternation of generations. The fixed individual here divides transversely into a number of little flat Ephyræ, each of which grows into an adult Medusa.

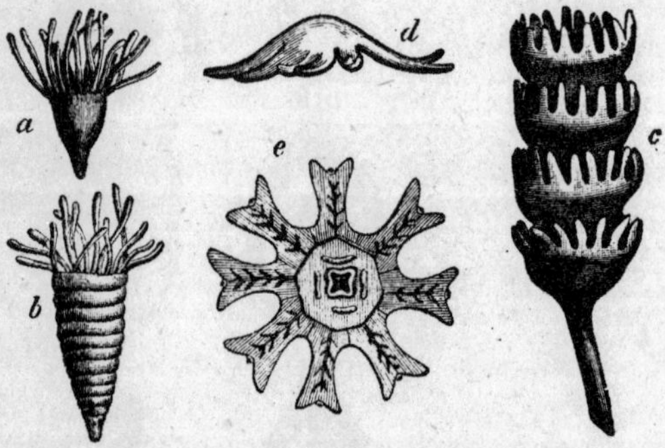

Fig. 870.—Life-history of Aurelia, enlarged. *a*, *b*, *c*, Stages in transverse division of fixed individual; *d e*, an Ephyra.

Some of the jelly-fishes related to Aurelia, and others belonging to certain other groups, have suppressed one stage in the cycle of existence, reminding us of some of the Hydroid Zoophytes. But in this case it is the fixed or vegetative stage which has been eliminated, while the egg-producing Medusa stage has been retained. In these species, which include some of the large forms of jelly-fish common in British seas, there is consequently a succession of Medusæ, instead of an alternation of these with fixed forms.

In some of the groups already mentioned there are interesting arrangements for securing the well-being of egg-cells, or, it may be, embryos. In Hydra, for example, as we have seen (p. 340), the single egg-cell in the ovary is the surviving member of a small mass of similar cells, with which it has had literally to struggle for existence. And it has not merely supplanted its sister-cells, but actually eaten them, affording us an illustration of cannibalism the precocity of which it would be hard to beat.

In fig. 871 a jelly-fish is represented in which the egg-cells resemble Amœbæ, and creep about in search of food on the outer surface of the mouth-bearing tube which hangs down from the umbrella of the parent.

In Aurelia there are four plaited projections from the corners of the mouth, in the folds of which part of the development takes place.

The life-histories of Sea-Flowers (Anthozoa), such as Sea-Anemones and Corals, are less sensational in character than

Fig. 871.—A Jelly-Fish (*Amalthœa amœbigera*), showing the eggs creeping on the large mouth-tube; enlarged

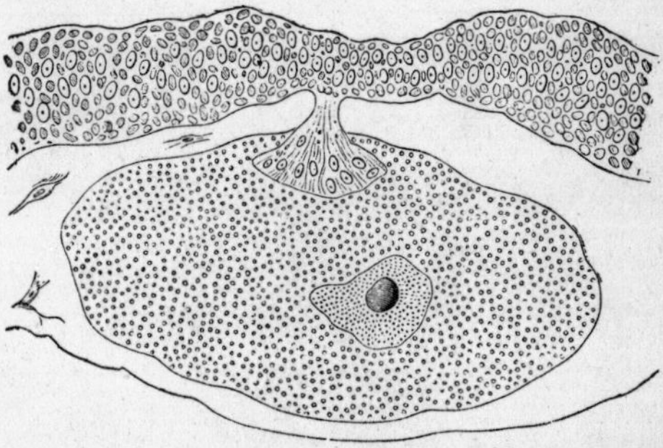

Fig. 872.—Egg-cell of a coral (*Corallimorphus rigidus*), with cells of the nutritive layer (above) projecting into it. Within the egg-cell are seen the large nucleus and numerous yolk-granules. Much enlarged.

those of the Cœlenterates already dealt with under this heading. But they are not lacking in interesting features. In fig. 872 is represented, on a greatly enlarged scale, the egg-cell of a sort of coral, which develops in the proximity of the nutritive layer, from which it is, in fact, derived. A little group of these cells project into its substance, and serve as a means of supplying it with food.

In both Sea-Anemones and ordinary Corals it usually happens that the early stages of development take place within the body of the parent, as far as the free-swimming ciliated larval stage (*planula*). These larvæ are then ejected through the mouth, later on become fixed, and grow into adults. Their locomotor powers prevent the fixed habit of the mature forms from becoming too great a disadvantage to the species.

LIFE-HISTORIES, &c., OF HEDGEHOG-SKINNED ANIMALS (ECHINODERMATA)

In most members of this group the eggs hatch out into larvæ, which are often of remarkable shape and extremely unlike the parent forms, the characters of which they ultimately acquire by passing through a complicated series of changes constituting a

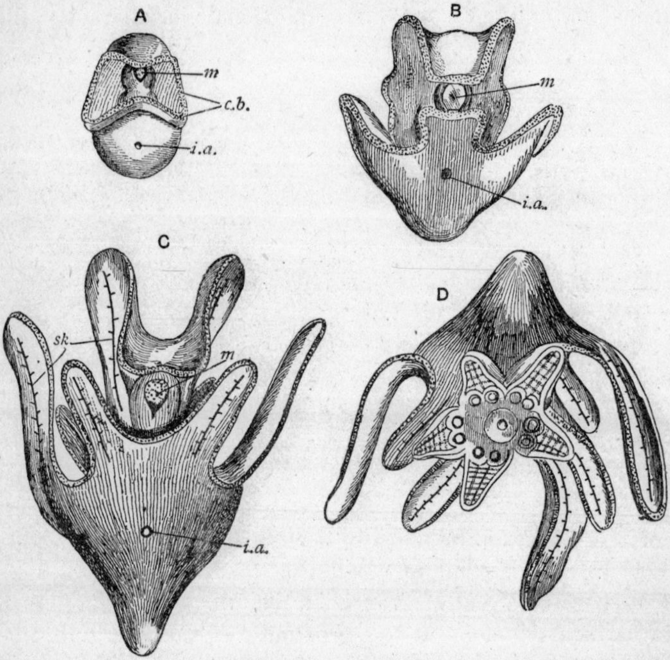

Fig. 873.—Life-history of a Brittle-Star

m, Mouth; *i.a.*, intestinal aperture; *c.b.*, ciliated band; *sk*, calcareous skeleton. A–C, Stages in development of Pluteus. D, Young Brittle-Star developing on the Pluteus. Enlarged.

metamorphosis. Each subdivision of the Echinoderms is characterized by a particular kind of larva, and we may take the Brittle-Stars (*Ophiuroidea*) as one of the most interesting illustrations.

The just-hatched young is oval in shape and bilaterally symmetrical, there being a well-marked distinction between front and back ends, and also between dorsal and ventral surfaces. Both mouth and intestinal aperture are on the ventral surface, and there is a ciliated band by means of which swimming is effected, and which is arranged as shown in fig. 873. Later on, the body grows out into a number of narrow "arms", on to which the ciliated band is continued. These are directed forwards, and supported by an internal skeleton of calcareous rods, which are united together in the hinder part of the body. The larva is known as a Pluteus. After a time the body of the adult star-fish begins to appear as a thickening in the body-wall of the larva, and as this increases in size the ciliated arms, with their supporting skeleton, are gradually absorbed. The internal organs of the Pluteus become the corresponding parts of the adult Brittle-Star. In some creatures of this kind there is not a free-swimming larva, but the fertilized eggs gradually assume the adult form, being sheltered in the meantime in pouches situated between the bases of the arms, and already spoken of in regard to breathing (see vol. ii, p. 414). This kind of life-history is, however, exceptional among Brittle-Stars, and has resulted from abandoning the method of *indirect development*, *i.e.* through a larval form, for *direct development*, by which the adult stage is gradually attained without any startling transformations. The use of free-swimming larvæ is doubtless to help in spreading the species, but the mortality of such immature forms is exceedingly large. The more sheltered direct type of development presents such advantages in this direction that we can understand why, in some species, it has superseded the larval type altogether, as, for example, in our commonest shore form (*Amphiura squamata*). If the eggs of this particular species developed into Plutei the chances of one of these becoming adult and reaching a suitable spot in which to live would be very remote. Direct development is here distinctly more favourable to survival, and as this species may also be said to possess a dwelling, since it is commonly found under stones near low-water mark, the chance of a given egg becoming an adult is still further increased.

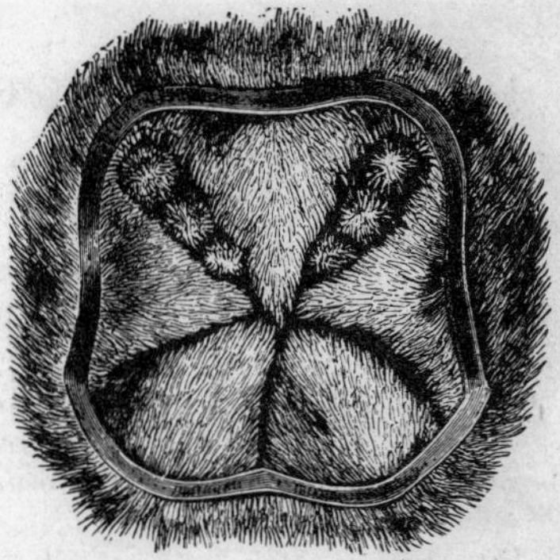

Fig. 874.—Young Sea-Urchins (*Hemiaster cavernosus*) sheltered in Grooves between the Spines of their Mother

Sea-Urchins (*Echinoidea*) usually have much the same sort of life-history as Brittle-Stars, being hatched out as Pluteus larvæ, though these differ in some respects from the kind already described. And in this case the mouth and gullet of the larva do not become those of the adult, which has to develop a second edition of these parts. Some Sea-Urchins resemble the exceptional Brittle-Stars already mentioned in having given up the larval type of development. And here also brood-pouches are present, in which the eggs are sheltered, as in the species represented in fig. 874, where parts of the areas from which the tube-feet project have become deep grooves which serve this purpose. Some Sea-Urchins hollow out dwellings for themselves in limestone rocks by means of their spines (fig. 875), and others attain the same end by burrowing in the sand (fig. 876). But as in both cases the eggs hatch into free-swimming larvæ, it cannot be said that these dwellings serve as nurseries.

Fig. 875.—Sea-Urchins burrowing in Limestone

Ordinary Star-Fishes (*Asteroidea*) as a rule present another type of indirect development, in which the larval forms (Bipinnaria and Brachiolaria) are in many respects unlike the Pluteus. Here again we find cases of direct development associated with arrangements for care of eggs or young. A remarkable instance is afforded by the members of one family (*Pterasteridæ*), for in these the upper side of the body forms the floor of a kind of pouch in which the young pass through their development, while the roof of this space is constituted by a special membrane supported on spines, and pierced by numerous small holes and a large central one. These apertures no doubt enable a free circulation of sea-water through the star-fish nursery to take place, a matter of considerable importance, since developing embryos require a plentiful supply of oxygen for breathing purposes. A simpler case is that of a Star-Fish (*Leptoptychaster*, fig. 877) in which the young are developed in grooves on the upper surface of their mother, on whose back they creep about after hatching out.

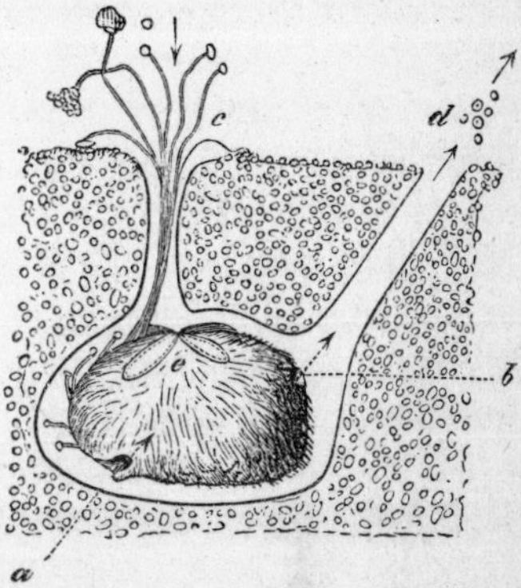

Fig. 876.—Heart-Urchin (*Amphidotus cordatus*) in its Burrow

As indicated by the arrows, food is entering by passage on left (through which some tube-feet, *c*, are protruding) to mouth (*a*), and waste matters (*d*) are being discharged through passage on right from intestinal aperture (*b*): *e*, rosette of respiratory tube-feet.

In most *Sea-Cucumbers* (*Holothuroidea*) the eggs hatch out into a simple kind of free-swimming larva (Auricularia, fig. 878), but in a few species there is direct development. In such cases the young are either simply attached to the skin of the parent without any special protective arrangement, or the upper side of the body may bear (as in *Psolus ephippifer*) a number of plate-like spines with narrow stalks.

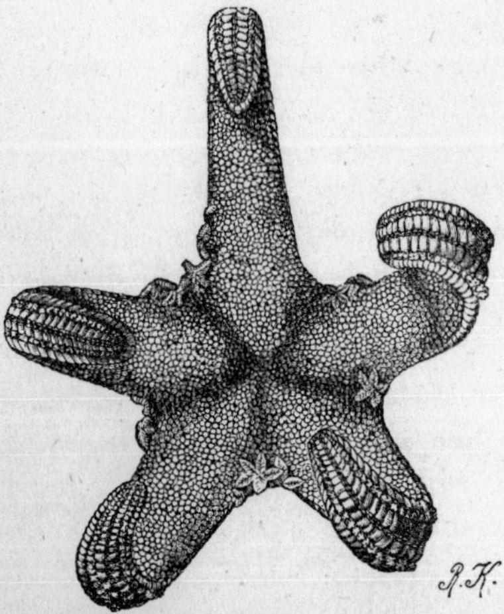

Fig. 877.—Young Star-fishes (*Leptoptychaster Kerguelensis*) creeping on the Body of their Mother

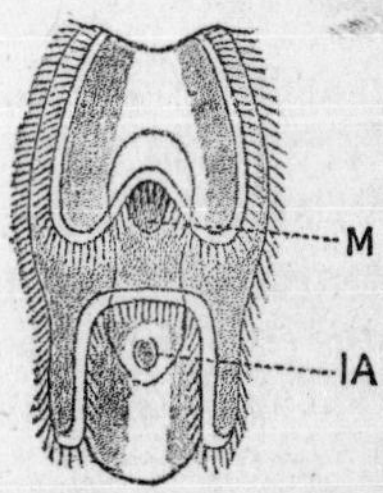

Fig. 878.—Auricularia, enlarged: M, mouth; IA, intestinal aperture.

The broad tops of these overlap, to roof in a space that serves as a brood-pouch.

LIFE-HISTORIES, &c., OF SEGMENTED WORMS (ANNELIDA)

Special arrangements for protection of eggs or young do not exist in the majority of the marine species of *Bristle-Worms* (*Chætopoda*), since in these, as a rule, the eggs are simply passed into the surrounding water, where their chance of developing into adults is exceedingly small. Sometimes, however, a mass of jelly-like substance is secreted in which a batch of eggs is deposited. The developing embryos are thus to some extent protected, and when they hatch out the jelly serves as their first food. Greenish masses of spawn of this nature, belonging to some of the burrowing worms, are commonly to be seen in spring on sandy shores.

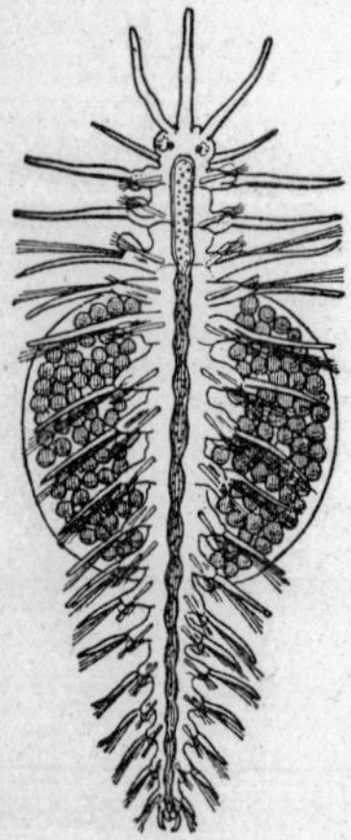

Fig. 879.—A Female Bristle-Worm (*Autolytus prolifer*) carrying Eggs in Pouch

The eggs of some Bristle-Worms are carried about attached to the body of the mother, and there may be special provisions for their shelter. The broad flat Scale-Worms (Polynoids) possess a double series of overlapping breathing-scales on the upper side of the body, and in some species the space underneath these structures is used as a brood-pouch. In one marine worm (*Autolytus prolifer*, fig. 879) the female carries her eggs about in a sort of bag attached to the under side of the body. The wall of this receptacle results from the hardening of a fluid which is secreted at the time the eggs are laid. In this particular case development is direct, and little worms hatch out from the eggs within the pouch, which resemble the adult, except in the fact that they are very much shorter.

A large number of marine Bristle-Worms may be said to possess dwellings, since they live in tubes of their own manufacture (see vol. ii, p. 339), which vary greatly in shape in different species, and are made up of the most diverse materials. To these tubes the eggs may be attached, either to their external surface, or to their inner surface, which is naturally a safer place. There is an interesting specialization in one worm (*Spirorbis*) (fig. 880) which lives in a flat spiral calcareous tube, for the head of this creature bears a kind of stopper (*operculum*), which is not only used to close the mouth of its dwelling, but is also hollowed out to serve as a brood-pouch.

Most marine Bristle-Worms hatch out in the larval form known as a Trochosphere, and this is also the case with Polygordius, a much elongated and very slender pink form, which is the largest representative of the closely-allied group of Simple Segmented Worms (Archiannelida). Being a typical case, it may well be taken to illustrate the kind of life-history which is usually found among marine Annelids.

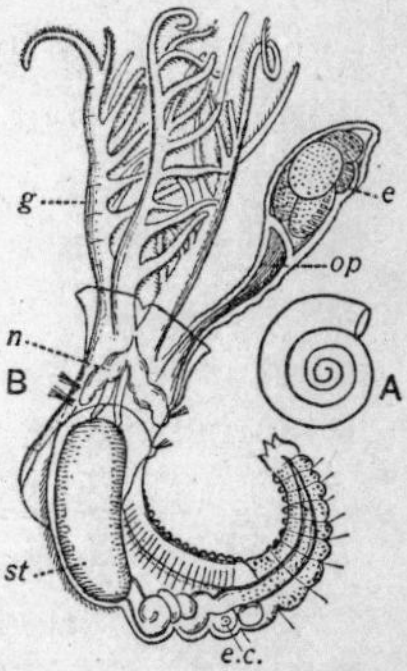

Fig. 880.—Spirorbis. A, Shell. B, Animal, enlarged: *e.c.*, egg-cells within body; *g*, gills; *n*, kidney tubes (*nephridia*); *op*, hollow operculum with eggs (*e*); *st*, stomach.

The form of a Polygordius larva (fig. 881) has been compared to that which would be presented by two blunt cones placed base to base. The broader and more rounded of these is the head-lobe (*prostomium*), which is kept uppermost during swimming, although at the front end of the body. At its base is a double row of long cilia, by which locomotion is effected. The lower and smaller cone narrows somewhat abruptly to a blunt point, which we may consider to be the tail end of the larva. On one side of the body a mouth is present which marks the under or ventral surface. It leads into a short gullet that is succeeded by a dilated stomach, and this again passes into a short intestine opening at the tail end. The ectoderm at the top of the head-lobe is thickened into a plate, which serves as a brain, and two eye-spots are embedded in it. A circlet of comparatively small cilia surrounds the body a little way below the mouth. With the internal changes that take place in the larva we are not here concerned, but it gradually becomes transformed into the adult by elongation of the tail end, and division of this region into rings or segments. It soon becomes apparent that

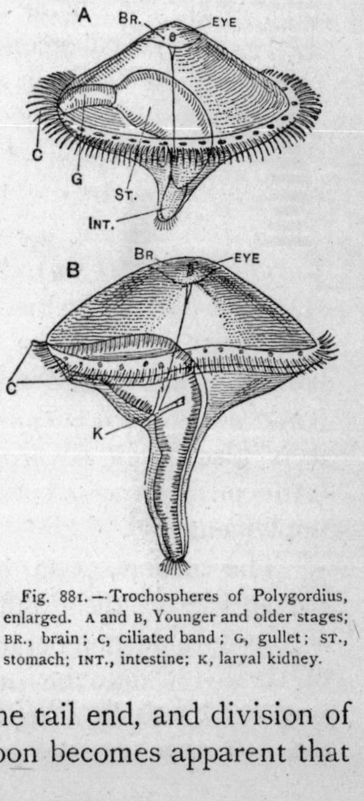

Fig. 881.—Trochospheres of Polygordius, enlarged. A and B, Younger and older stages; BR., brain; C, ciliated band; G, gullet; ST., stomach; INT., intestine; K, larval kidney.

this segmented region is destined to form the trunk of the worm, while the head-lobe and broad region immediately below it will together form the head. The latter is at first large out of all proportion, but as it grows more slowly than the trunk this ultimately ceases to be the case. For a long time the segments increase in number, the youngest being always the one adjoining the tip of the tail, while the oldest is next to the head. Among other events which take place before the free-swimming larva is converted into the adult worm may be mentioned: the sprouting of a pair of tentacles or feelers from the head-lobe, loss of the swimming bands of cilia, and degeneration of the eye-spots.

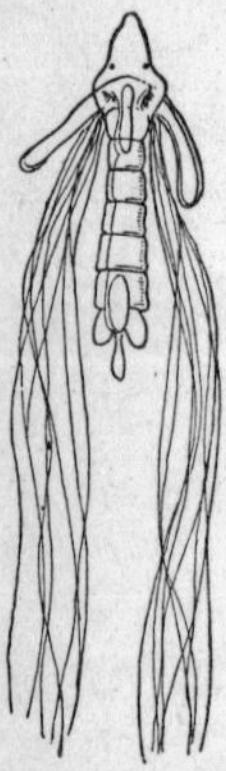

Fig. 882.—Larva of a Bristle-Worm, with bundles of slender Bristles. Enlarged

There are considerable differences between the trochospheres of different Annelids, especially in regard to the number of ciliated bands present, but of these the most constant is the one at the base of the head-lobe described above. In some cases the developing larvæ possess bundles of bristles, which differ greatly as to arrangement and length (fig. 882), but in all cases appear to serve the double purpose of balancing the body during swimming, and affording a certain amount of protection from enemies. They are secondary larval structures, and not retained by the adult.

In the Few-Bristled Annelids (*Oligochæta*), which include earth-worms and freshwater forms, as also in Leeches (*Discophora*), development is direct, there being no larval stage in the life-history. The members of the former group lay their eggs in a case of horny consistency (cocoon) formed by the hardening of a fluid that exudes from a glandular band of skin (*clitellum*), which is conspicuous in an ordinary earth-worm, where it is placed not far from the front end of the body, and often erroneously regarded as the result of injury by a spade or other implement.

The cocoons of earth-worms (fig. 883) are deposited either on the surface of the ground, or else buried in the soil. Although a considerable number of eggs are laid in each of them, but few of these—it may be only one—develop into adult worms, the successful members (or member) of any particular brood using the rest as food. As the eggs are very small, and do not contain much food-yolk (see p. 345), some such arrangement is necessary. It is true that a nutritive albuminous fluid is enclosed in the cocoon, but this is unfortunately not abundant enough to prevent the more vigorous embryos from becoming cannibals.

The small cocoons of freshwater worms are commonly attached to aquatic plants, in many cases near the edge of the native pond or stream. It sometimes happens that a considerable number of young worms emerge from each capsule, but this is exceptional.

The eggs of *Leeches* (*Discophora*) are usually enclosed in cocoons, which are generally deposited in damp places near the water, but not actually in it. Some species, however, do not form cocoons at all, but lay their eggs in gelatinous clumps attached to various objects under water, and the cocoons of other leeches are to be found in similar situations, *e.g.* those of the marine form Potobdella. We should scarcely expect to find "nursing" of young among Leeches, but this actually does take place in certain instances (species of *Glossiphonia*). Speaking of this sort of leech Beddard says (in *The Cambridge Natural History*) that it "carries its eggs upon the ventral face of the body, where the young remain for some time after they are hatched, attached by the posterior sucker to their parent's body, and from which situation of safety they make short excursions".

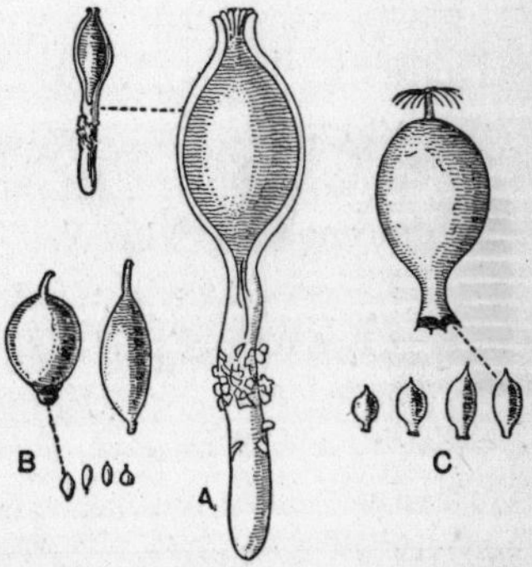

Fig. 883.—Cocoons of Earth-Worms, naturalsize and enlarged. A, Lumbricus rubellus. B, Allurus. C, Allolobophora fœtida.

The life-histories of animals belonging to the huge group of Jointed-Limbed Invertebrates (Arthropoda) include so many interesting and varied types that it may be well to consider separately the different subdivisions, *i.e.* Crustaceans (Crustacea), King-Crabs (Xiphosura), Primitive Tracheates (Prototracheata), Centipedes and Millipedes (Myriapoda), Spider-like Arthropods (Arachnida), and Insects (Insecta).

Up to this point the present section has dealt with the life-histories of Lower Invertebrates, in which the comparatively simple adult stage is reached after a correspondingly simple development. And though, as we have seen, there are many ways by which the early stages of life are protected, extreme fecundity is the most important safeguard against the extinction of species. With Arthropods we commence the study of Higher Invertebrates, which possess an extremely complex structure, and afterwards pass on to Vertebrates, the organization of which is even more elaborate. It naturally follows that in all these higher groups the development is more or less protracted, and there is therefore a greater necessity for elaborate arrangements by which eggs and young are protected. Such arrangements have reached a high degree of perfection in many cases, though marked fecundity is also characteristic of some higher animals. If the eggs or young are well protected, so that they have a good chance of becoming adult, they are produced in comparatively small numbers. But where the survival of the species depends chiefly on fecundity, an enormous number of eggs or young may be brought into existence.

LIFE-HISTORIES, &c., OF CRUSTACEANS (CRUSTACEA)

LOWER CRUSTACEANS (ENTOMOSTRACA).—The eggs and sometimes the newly-hatched young are here for a time protected by a variety of arrangements, which give them a better start in life than would otherwise be the case. Some of the *Leaf-Footed Crustaceans* (*Phyllopoda*) illustrate this point very well. In Apus, for example, one pair of limbs are modified into brood-pouches (fig. 884) comparable in appearance to a couple of watch-glasses applied together. These shelter the eggs from the time of laying until the larvæ are hatched out. The little Water-Flea (*Daphnia pulex*, fig. 885), so common in fresh water, uses the space between the upper side of the body and the enclosing shield as a brood-pouch. In this case the development is direct, there being no free-swimming larva, and the comparatively large eggs contain a good deal of yolk, which serves to nourish the embryos. The brood-pouch also contains a nutritive fluid employed for the same purpose. A lucky chance sometimes enables us to see the young Water-Fleas hatched out under the microscope, that is if

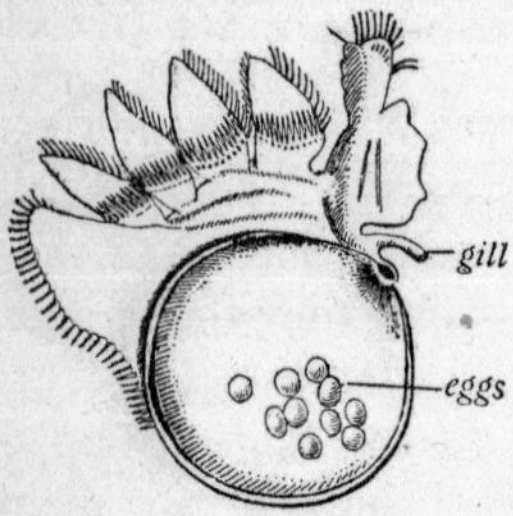

Fig. 884.—Brood-pouch of Apus, enlarged

our observations are made in the summer. Though much smaller than their mother they resemble her in appearance, and may be seen to play around her for some time. The qualification about the time of observation is made because these little creatures produce both summer-eggs and winter-eggs, the fate of which is somewhat different. The former are thin-shelled and develop without fertilization, hatching out during the season from which they get their name. The winter-eggs are fertilized, and, being destined to tide the species over the cold part of the year, are enclosed in firm, resistant shells. By thickening of a part of the parent shell a sort of case, known as a "saddle" (*ephippium*) is formed, which is cast adrift with a couple of eggs inside it, and floats about on the surface of the water. The young Water-Fleas hatch out the following spring. The number of winter-eggs enclosed in each case depends upon the species, varying from one to several.

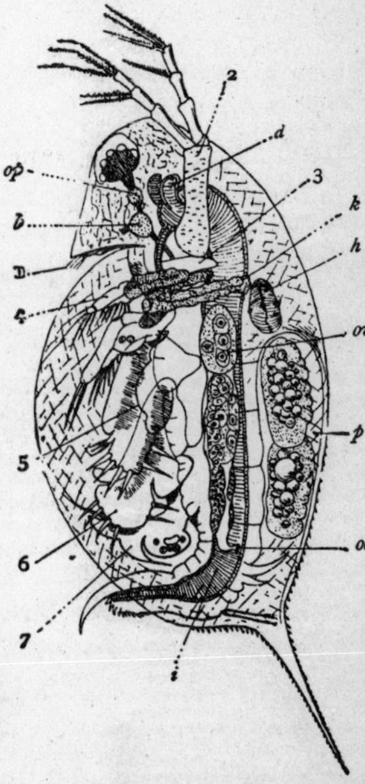

Fig. 885.—Water-Flea (*Daphnia*), with Eggs in Brood-pouch; enlarged

1-7, Appendages; *d*, digestive gland; *i*, intestine; *h*, heart; *k*, kidney; *b*, brain with larval eye (the black spot); *op*, optic ganglion and compound eye; *ov*, ovary; *od*, opening of oviduct; *p*, brood-pouch containing two developing eggs.

In *Fork-Footed Crustaceans* (*Copepoda*) the eggs, when laid, usually pass into curious little egg-bags, the material for making which is furnished by special cement-glands. A typical and easily-obtained example is furnished by Cyclops (fig. 886) which often abounds in ponds. The two ovoid egg-bags are carried about by the mother till the time of hatching. Some Copepods possess but one egg-bag, and these structures are differently shaped according to the species. The eggs of a few members of this group are sheltered in a dorsal brood-pouch, resembling that of a Water-Flea.

The most familiar examples of the group of *Barnacles* (*Cirripedia*) are the stalked Ship Barnacle (*Lepas*) and the stalkless Acorn Barnacle (*Balanus*), which is found in great numbers attached to rocks between tide-marks. In both these cases there is a protective armour of shelly plates, between which and the body is a considerable space that is made use of as a brood-pouch. The numerous eggs are glued, as it were, into relatively large masses, which are attached to a pair of triangular flaps.

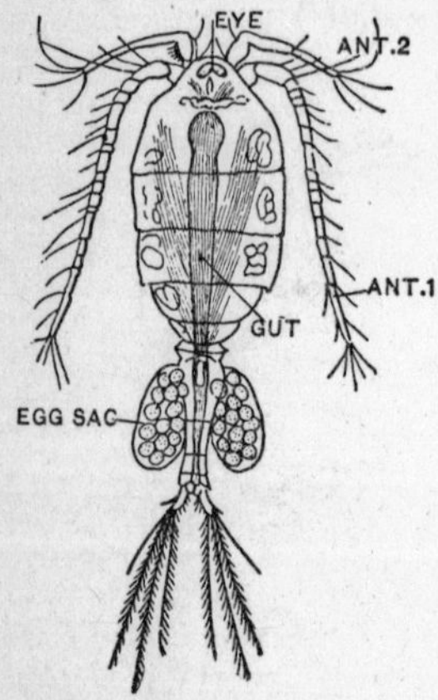

Fig. 886.—Female Cyclops with egg-bags, enlarged. ANT. 1 and ANT. 2, Antennules and antennæ.

Among the little *Mussel-Shrimps* (*Ostracoda*) it appears that the eggs may either be attached singly to water-plants, as in the commonest freshwater member (*Cypris*) of the group, or else, as in many marine forms (*Cypridina*, &c.), sheltered within the bivalve shield of the mother until such time as they hatch out.

In all the above groups of Lower Crustaceans, Mussel-Shrimps and most Water-Fleas excepted, development is indirect, the young animals hatching out in the form of a Nauplius larva (fig. 887) with oval unsegmented body and large unpaired eye in the middle of the fore-head. The swimming organs are three pairs of appendages, which afterwards become the small feelers (*antennules*), large feelers (*antennæ*), and first jaws (*mandibles*) of the adult. Many authorities at one time thought that the Nauplius repeats in its main features the characters of the simple ancestral forms from which all Crustaceans may be imagined to have taken origin, but this view is now practically abandoned. There can be little doubt that Crustaceans are the specialized descendants of animals resembling the recent Bristle-Worms, and an instructive comparison may be made between the Nauplius and the typical Trochosphere larva (p. 359) which is commonly an early stage in the life-history of such worms. If a Trochosphere were to lose its cilia and grow three pairs of appendages it would closely resemble a Nauplius, and evolutionary changes of the kind are quite conceivable, for such appendages would prove more efficient locomotor organs than the cilia which they superseded, and we are justified in making the general assertion that evolution always tends towards greater efficiency, *i.e.* to an increasingly perfect

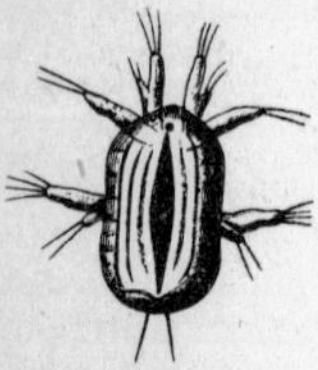
Fig. 887.—Nauplius Larva, enlarged

adaptation between animals and their surroundings. In this particular instance it is very interesting to find that the trunk of a crustacean develops in relation to the Nauplius in much the same way that the trunk of a worm develops with reference to the Trochosphere (see p. 359). For the hinder end of the Nauplius is a region of rapid growth and elongation, and while this is going on segment after segment comes into existence till the full number are formed. And, as in the worm, the oldest segment is next the head and the youngest next the tail.

HIGHER CRUSTACEANS (MALACOSTRACA).—In Nebalia and other *Mud-Shrimps* (*Leptostraca*), which are in some respects intermediate between Higher and Lower Crustaceans, the large shield which grows back from the head to partly cover the trunk affords a shelter to the eggs until the time of hatching. The development is direct, the young mud-shrimps closely resembling the adult form, except in size.

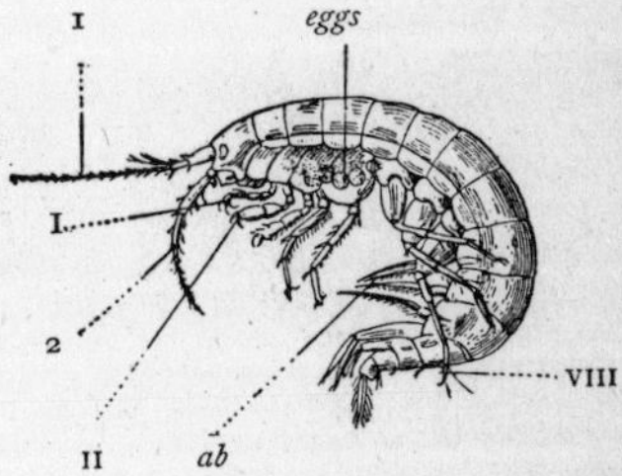

Fig. 888.—Female Sand-Hopper (*Gammarus neglectus*) carrying Eggs in Brood-pouch, slightly enlarged. 1 and 2, Antennules and antennæ; I, II, and VIII, first, second, and eighth thoracic limbs; *ab*, first abdominal limbs.

The *Sessile-Eyed Crustaceans* (*Arthrostraca*), including Sand-Hoppers and Slaters, usually incubate their eggs in a brood-pouch on the under side of the thorax, the floor of the pouch being formed by the growth of plates from the inner sides of the legs (fig. 888). There is no free-swimming larva, development being direct.

Stalk-Eyed Crustaceans (*Thoracostraca*) illustrate a number of ways by which the eggs or young are protected. The little Opossum Shrimp (*Mysis*), of which the development is direct, possesses a brood-pouch, as its name indicates. This is of similar character to the one found in Sand-Hoppers and their kindred. In Lobsters, Crayfishes, Crabs, Prawns, Shrimps, and the like, the eggs when laid are cemented to the numerous bristles with which the abdominal appendages of the mother are thickly studded. The material for this egg-glue is furnished by glands which open on the under surface of the thorax. Everyone must have noticed some creature of the kind "in berry", *i.e.* with numerous eggs firmly fixed to the lower side of the tail, in which safe position the early part of the development is gone through.

It will have been gathered from what has already been said, that development is direct in some of the Higher Crustaceans, but the stalk-eyed forms usually hatch out as larvæ. This early free-swimming stage in the life-history is, however, but very rarely

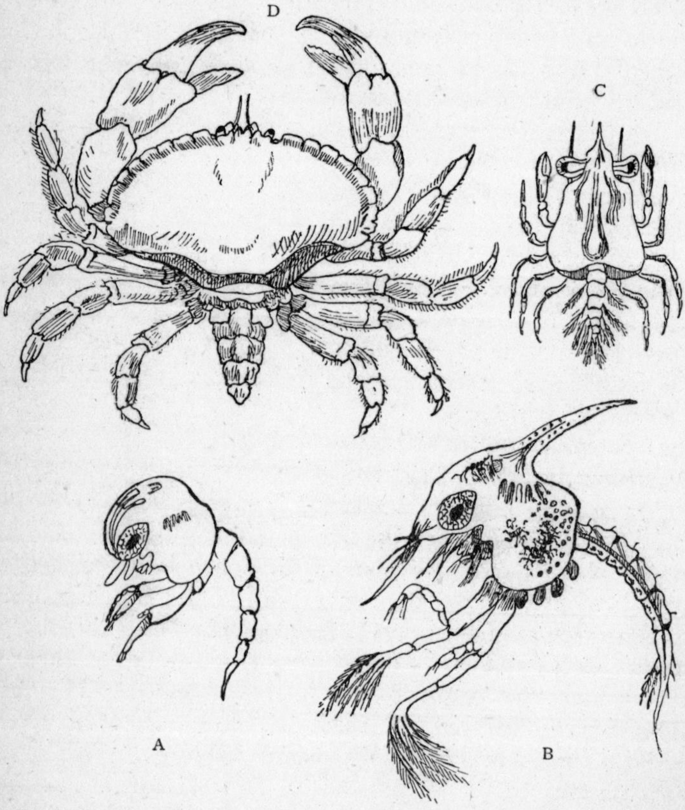

Fig. 889.—Life-history of Edible Crab (*Cancer pagurus*), enlarged. A, Young Zoæa. B, Fully formed Zoæa. C, Megalopa. D, Young Crab (during life the tail is bent up under body).

a Nauplius, the most characteristic variety of larva being the Zoæa, which is partially segmented, and otherwise of more complex nature. In the life-history of the Edible Crab (*Cancer pagurus*, fig. 889), for instance, the just-hatched Zoæa is a rather ungainly-looking little creature, with large rounded cephalothorax (*i.e.* head and thorax fused together) and slender limbless tail (A). The large appendages shown in the drawing are foot-jaws, which here serve for swimming-organs, and in front of these will be seen the sprouting jaws and feelers. At a somewhat later stage (B) the feelers and jaws have become much larger, the locomotor foot-jaws have attained a relatively enormous size, and behind them stump-like outgrowths have made their appearance which are destined to become pincers and legs. Long spines, that serve to balance the body, are now present on the strong shield which covers the front part of the body. There can be no doubt that Crabs, the most specialized of all Crustaceans, with their broad cephalothorax and absurdly small tail, have been derived from lobster-like forms, in which there was not the same disproportion between these two regions of the body. And the Zoæa, by completion of its set of appendages, loss of its balancing spines, and comparatively slow further growth of the precociously-developed foot-jaws, passes into the Megalopa stage (C), which would certainly seem to be reminiscent of such ancestors. Swimming is now effected lobster fashion, by strokes of the tail, but this mode of progression is soon abandoned in favour of walking. The tail now develops but slowly, while the front part of the body grows vigorously, especially in breadth, and thus the proportions of the adult are at last attained (D). The little tail is represented in the figure as projecting backwards, but is in reality folded up under the front of the body. In the adult female this method of disposal largely conduces to the safety of the eggs.

Particular interest attaches to the development of the Freshwater Crayfish (*Astacus fluviatilis*). The animal population of rivers has, for the most part, been originally derived from the sea, and this change of habitat has led to a number of special adaptations to new conditions of life. The development, for one thing, has in many cases undergone considerable modification. For marine animals the possession of a larval form presents certain advantages, *e.g.* it helps escape from unfavourable surroundings and promotes the dispersal of the species. But it would be positively dangerous for creatures which live in rivers to hatch out as larvæ, since these being small and weak would be liable to be swept away by the current, and would certainly perish if they reached the sea, for life in which their species have gradually become entirely unsuited. It is therefore not surprising to find that the freshwater representatives of marine groups that usually develop indirectly have either suppressed the larval stage in their life-histories, or else made special provision for its safety. The former is what has taken place in the Crayfish, in which the large eggs hatch out into little creatures that resemble their parents in all essential particulars (fig. 890). Nor do they at once leave the mother, but for a time attach themselves to the hardened egg-glue which covers her abdominal appendages, a safe means of attachment being afforded by their pincers, the ends of which are sharply hooked, one of the few points of difference from the adult. And it is said that even when the young begin to swim about on their own account, they at first make but short excursions, from which they return to the shelter of their mother's tail.

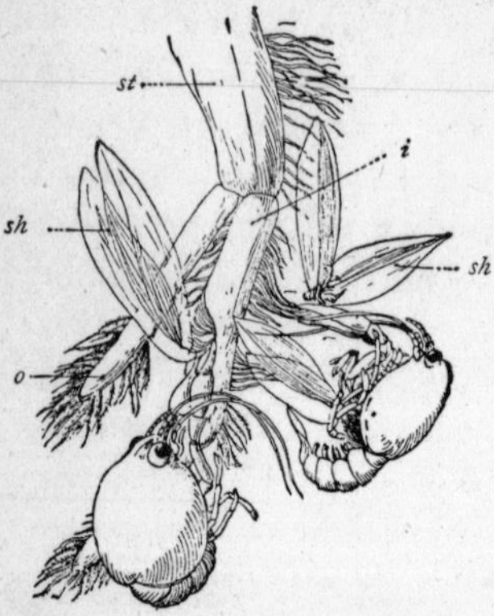

Fig. 890.—Two just-hatched Crayfishes clinging to Abdominal Appendage of their Mother, enlarged. *st*, *i*, and *o*—stalk, outer branch, and inner branch of appendage; *sh*, empty egg-shells.

Crustacean Dwellings.—Omitting the cases of those forms which obtain shelter by association with other animals, as these will be dealt with elsewhere, there is little that need be said here. Many Crustaceans live more or less in rock crevices, at the openings of which they lie in wait for prey. This is the case with many Crabs, and the Rock-Lobster (*Palinurus*) is distinguished by the same habit. By turning over stones at low tide one is pretty sure to find, in this country a curious little Crab (*Porcellana platycheles*) with hairy pincers, and also species of the Sand-Hopper group. Sea-Slaters shelter in rock crevices, and their terrestrial brethren, the Wood-Lice, are commonly to be found in the crannies of masonry and also under stones.

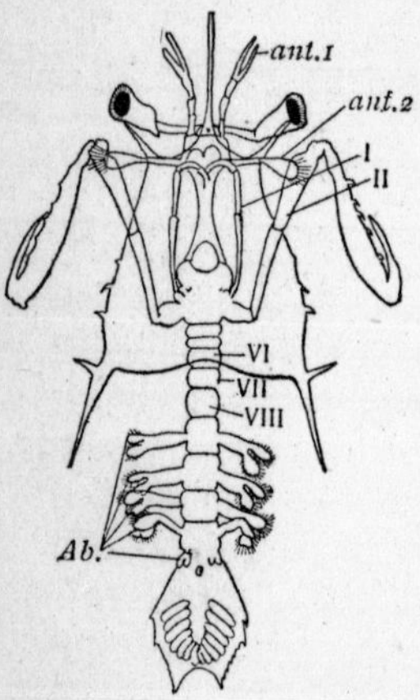

Fig. 891. — Alima Larva, enlarged. *ant.* 1 and *ant.* 2, antennules and antennæ; I and II, first and second pair of foot-jaws; VI–VIII, last three thoracic segments; *ab.*, abdominal appendages.

Some forms which burrow have already been mentioned

(p. 225), and the Mantis Shrimp (*Squilla mantis*) tunnels in banks covered with marine vegetation (Zostera). This creature is of special interest in the present connection, because it lays its eggs in these burrows, instead of carrying them about. The attenuated larva is known as an Alima (fig. 891).

Among Crustaceans of the Sand-Hopper kind (Amphipoda) the Caddis Shrimps (*Corophiidæ*) construct tubular or ovoid nests from fragments of sea-weed or other materials. The bodies of these creatures are cylindrical, in correspondence with the shape of their dwellings, and not flattened from side to side as in ordinary Sand-Hoppers.

LIFE-HISTORY, &c., OF KING-CRABS (XIPHOSURA)

The King-Crab or Horse-shoe Crab (*Limulus*), which is the only living representative of this ancient group, lives in

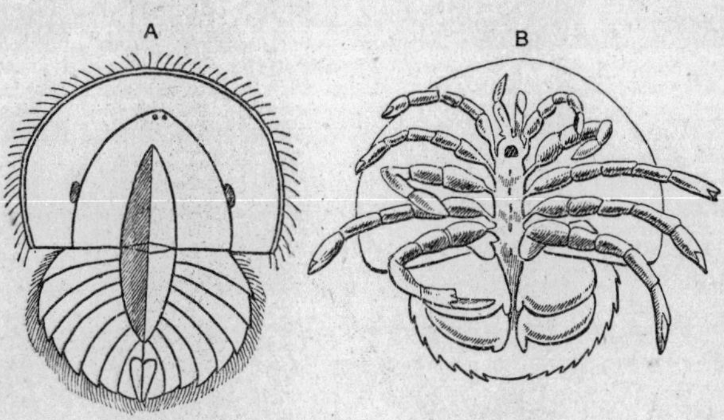

Fig. 892.—Trilobite Larva of King-Crab (*Limulus polyphemus*), enlarged

A, Upper side. B, Under side.

shallow water, and comes as near the coast as possible during spring-tides for spawning purposes. The female digs a hole for the reception of her eggs, which are afterwards covered over with mud by the movement of the water. One reason for choosing a spot near land for this purpose appears to be that incubation may be hastened by the warmth of the sun, at the times when the sea goes down. The eggs hatch out into little Trilobite larvæ (fig. 892), so called because they have a certain resemblance to the extinct animals of that name.

LIFE-HISTORIES, &c., OF PRIMITIVE TRACHEATES (PROTOTRACHEATA)

We are here only concerned with the archaic and widely-distributed form *Peripatus*, which has already been spoken of in several connections, especially as being a sort of link between Annelids and Arthropods. It is a light-shunning creature, and though in all the numerous species the young are born alive, there is a great deal of variation in respect to the amount of food-yolk contained in the egg. This is large in amount in species which live in the Australian region, much less in those inhabiting South Africa, and practically absent in the American forms. The newly-born young have been observed crawling over the body of their mother, and as she is not entirely devoid of means of defence (see vol. ii, p. 360) this association may be regarded as a protective measure.

LIFE-HISTORIES, &c., OF CENTIPEDES AND MILLIPEDES (MYRIAPODA)

The love of the beautiful is so marked a human characteristic that it has had a considerable influence upon the course of scientific research, though it has not swayed the professional zoologist to the same extent as the amateur naturalist. But it cannot be denied that the groups which include the more attractive-looking animals have received an undue share of attention. This is the case, for example, with Insects and Birds, while among the former Butterflies have been studied much more exhaustively than Flies or Bugs. Any investigator who desires to find a field of activity likely to quickly yield a rich harvest of results cannot do better than select a group of which the members are superficially unattractive, or, still better, downright repulsive, regarded from the lay stand-point. No animals are "common or unclean" in the light of science, and that any of them should be so regarded is one of the undesirable items of the legacy we have inherited from our prehistoric ancestors, whose stand-point was purely utilitarian. These worthy but uncultured gentlemen early discovered by painful experience that certain creatures could bite, sting, or otherwise cause annoyance, and in this we may discover the beginnings of a tendency to

FAMILY OF COMMON SQUIRRELS (*Sciurus vulgaris*)

As in Birds, parental affection has much to do with the success of Mammals in the struggle for existence. The chances of individual survival in the latter class are also furthered by development being internal (except in the egg-laying Duck-bills and Spiny Anteaters), and by the presence of milk-glands for the benefit of the young. In the large and widely-distributed order of Gnawing Mammals (*Rodentia*), fecundity plays a very important part in preventing extinction. The young may be born in a well-developed state, but the contrary is the case when they are brought up in some sort of dwelling or nest, as in the Common Squirrel. The "drey" of this animal is a snug habitation, built in a hole or tree-fork. Dry twigs are woven together into a rounded structure, with a hole on one side. Leaves, moss, lichen, and similar material are used for lining purposes. From three to four blind and naked young are born within this cosy dwelling, usually in June, and remain with their parents till the following spring, when they in their turn undertake family duties.

FAMILY OF COMMON SQUIRRELS (SCIURUS VULGARIS)

regard as "vermin" all and sundry forms even remotely resembling those actually known to be objectionable.

Centipedes and Millipedes have fallen under this ban, and as a result our knowledge of them is comparatively scanty, and mainly due to a few enterprising investigators. The structure of these creatures is of very great interest, throwing light as it does upon the origin of Insects, and that the habits deserve investigation may be judged from the following accounts which Sinclair gives (in *The Cambridge Natural History*) of two well-known British species, the Thirty-Foot (*Lithobius forficatus*), one of our commonest Centipedes (see vol. i, p. 394), and the Earth Snake-Millipede (*Julus terrestris*), which is even more abundant.

Sinclair speaks as follows of the Thirty-Foot:—"The female *Lithobius* is furnished with two small movable hooks at the end of the under surface of the body close to the opening of the oviduct. These small hooks have been observed by many naturalists, but their use has, so far as I know, never been described before. They play an important part in the proceedings following the laying of the egg. The time of breeding in *Lithobius* . . . . begins about June and continues till August. There are first of all some convulsive movements of the last segments of the body, and then in about ten minutes the egg appears at the entrance of the oviduct. The egg is a small sphere (about the size of a number-five shot) rather larger than that of *Julus*, and is covered with a sticky slime secreted by the large glands inside the body, usually called the accessory glands. When the egg falls out it is received by the little hooks, and is firmly clasped by them. This is the critical moment in the existence of the *Lithobius* into which the egg is destined to develop. If a male *Lithobius* sees the egg he makes a rush at the female, seizes the egg, and at once devours it. All the subsequent proceedings of the female seem to be directed to the frustration of this act of cannibalism. As soon as the egg is firmly clasped in the little hooks she rushes off to a convenient place away from the male, and uses her hooks to roll the egg round and round until it is completely covered by earth, which sticks to it owing to the viscous material with which it is coated; she also employs her hind-legs, which have glands on the thighs, to effect her purpose. When the operation is complete the egg resembles a small round ball of mud, and is indistinguishable from the surrounding soil. It is thus safe from the voracious appetite of the male, and she leaves it to its fate. The number of eggs is small when compared with the number laid by *Julus*."

The comparatively large size of these eggs, and their relatively small number, are correlated with direct development; for here, as in Centipedes generally, the just-hatched young closely resemble their parents except in size.

Sinclair's observations on the Earth Snake-Millipede are thus set forth:—"*Julus terrestris* is one of the most common of the English Millipedes, and can be easily obtained. I kept them in large, shallow glass vessels with a layer of earth at the bottom, and thus was able easily to watch the whole process. They breed in the months of May, June, and July. The female *Julus* when about to lay her eggs sets to work to form a kind of nest or receptacle for her eggs. She burrows down into the earth, and at some distance below the surface begins the work. She moistens small bits of earth with the sticky fluid secreted by her salivary glands, which become extraordinarily active in the spring. She works up these bits of earth with her jaws and front-legs till they are of a convenient size and shape, and places them together. When complete the nest is shaped like a hollow sphere, the inside being smooth and even, while the outside is rough and shows the shape of the small knobs of earth of which it is composed. She leaves a small opening in the top. The size of the whole nest is about that of a small nut. When she is ready to lay her eggs she passes them through the hole in the top, and usually lays about 60 to 100 eggs at a time. The eggs, which are very small, are coated with a glutinous fluid which causes them to adhere together. When they are all laid she closes up the aperture with a piece of earth moistened with her saliva; and having thus hermetically sealed the nest, she leaves the whole to its fate. The eggs hatch in about twelve days."

Numerous small eggs are associated in this and other Millipedes with indirect development. The young hatch out as short six-legged larvæ, which undergo a series of moults, increasing in length and number of legs each time, until the adult characters are fully acquired. It is stated that in one common

Continental species of Millipede (*Polyzonium Germanicum*) the female, after laying her eggs, coils her body round them and remains on guard till they hatch.

Sinclair's fascinating observations have been quoted in full in order that amateur naturalists may see the kind of result to which patient investigation may be expected to lead. And if any such are moved to turn their attention to this rather neglected group of animals, they will very likely be able, with a little patience, to make interesting additions to our present somewhat meagre knowledge as regards the habits of creatures of the kind.

LIFE-HISTORIES, &c., OF SPIDER-LIKE ANIMALS (ARACHNIDA)

Most of the animals belonging to this class are oviparous, and there is no metamorphosis, the just-hatched young differing from the adult mainly in respect of size.

Scorpions (*Scorpionidæ*) are distinguished from other Arachnids by being viviparous. The larger species commonly dig large holes in the ground to serve as habitations, while others lurk under stones, beneath the bark of trees, or in any convenient cranny.

The *Spiders* (*Araneidæ*) are of much greater interest in the present connection, and it has been suggested that their spinning powers were originally evolved in reference to the construction of investments for the eggs. However that may be, the eggs are laid in a little web, and a sort of bag is then spun round them. In those species where there is no fixed habitation the female often carries the egg-bag about with her, and defends it if attacked. This is the case, for example, in the *Wolf-Spiders* (*Lycosidæ*), in which the egg-bags are attached to the spinnerets on the under side of the body. Staveley (in *British Spiders*) thus speaks of these forms:—"The *Lycosæ*, or Wolf-Spiders, lead an entirely vagabond life, constructing no snares, and carrying their eggs, and afterwards their young, about their bodies. . . . The female *Lycosæ* will fight boldly for the protection of her cocoon, and it is said that if deprived of it she will conceal herself and die. She hatches two broods in the year, in spring and autumn, and has been known to hatch three. The eggs are not adherent to each other in the cocoon, which is constructed in a remarkable manner. The two halves of the silken case are strong and compact in texture, and at their suture is a band of much slighter substance. This gives way sufficiently to allow of the growth of the young after their escape from the egg and before they are disengaged each from its membranous envelope, and, in due time, it is at this weakest part that the young escape. Amongst snare-making spiders, the young commence weaving immediately after leaving the egg; but the young *Lycosæ*, requiring no snares, and being incapable of protecting themselves, remain for about a fortnight with the mother, giving rise formerly to a belief that they derived their nourishment from her body."

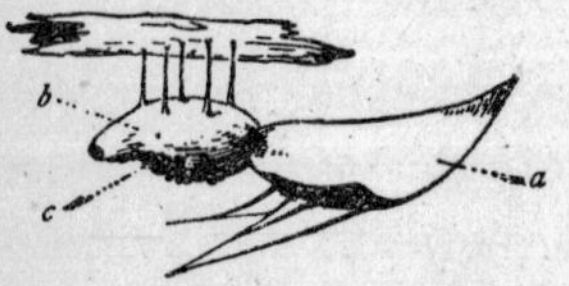

Fig. 893.—Nest of House-Spider (*Tegenaria domestica*). *a*, Part of web; *b*, nest with front-door to right and back-door to left; *c*, sand-grains which keep the nest steady.

The webs which snare-making Spiders construct are, as it were, an extension of a kind of tubular dwelling placed in their immediate neighbourhood. This may be seen in the cobwebs made by the *House-Spiders* (species of *Tegenaria*, fig. 893), where this home is placed in a sheltered corner, and has both a front-door opening on the web, and also a back-door which serves as a kind of emergency exit. The dense white horizontal webs of the *Hedge-Spiders* (species of *Agalena*) are associated with a similar provision. At the back a vertical tube hangs down, through which the spider retreats when alarmed. Connected with this tube are one or more dwelling-chambers, and in these the egg-bags, one or two in number, are deposited during August.

The domestic arrangements of one pretty little native species (*Theridium nervosum*) are described by Staveley (in *British Spiders*) as follows:—"This beautiful little spider, and her as beautiful snare and nest, are to be easily found in almost any kind of bush or shrub in June or July. The snare is . . . a very light mass of threads crossing each other in every direction, and altogether forming a pyramidal figure, or rather that of a long cottage roof. The nest is a perfect little tent, which is sometimes suspended by itself in the middle of the snare, and sometimes is sheltered under a growing leaf, which has been fastened by silken cords into a dome-like form to serve as roof. The tent is lined with white silk, and is covered with small dead leaves or flowers, or the stamens of larger flowers, or with anything which has presented itself, and is decorated with the wings and other parts of insects, as the wigwam of an Indian with scalps and other war-trophies. It is remarkable how often, where the insect is not uncommon, the beautiful wing-cases of the green nut-weevil are found among these ornaments. Within this tent is the little round green silk cocoon containing the eggs, and the mother is almost always to be found in an inverted position embracing this

Fig. 894.—Water-Spiders (*Argyroneta aquatica*) and Nests

treasure, and hiding it with her body, which it about equals in size. When the young are hatched, they live with their mother in this tent until they are able to make their own living."

The remarkable Water-Spider (*Argyroneta aquatica*, fig. 894) constructs below the surface a neat nest shaped like a diving-bell, and skilfully moored to some aquatic plant. Within this the cocoon is deposited. In such a spider the air used for breathing purposes is entangled in the downy covering of the abdomen, and, under water, shines like quicksilver. But this has nothing to do with the air-supply of the nest, which is provided for in a somewhat singular manner. We should naturally expect the walls of this elegant structure to be first woven, and air to be afterwards introduced, but this does not appear to be the case. The spider commences operations by protruding the tip of her tail out of the water, spreading her spinnerets, and entangling a small air-bubble between them. Diving down, she carries the bubble to the stem selected as the site of the dwelling, and leaves it clinging there. By successive additions the mass of air becomes large enough for her purpose, and a web is then spun over it to constitute the lining of the nest. Over this

Fig. 895 — Trap-door Spiders (*Cteniza cæmentaria*) and Nests

liquid silk is smeared, which soon hardens into an impervious membrane. Mooring lines complete the structure. The spider is, of course, able to introduce fresh air when necessary.

The *Trap-door Spiders* (*Ctenizidæ*, fig. 895) construct homes in many cases by digging a cylindrical hole in the ground, smoothing its interior, and adding a silken lining. A neat lid is then constructed of a mixture of earth and silk. It is smooth on its under side, but rough externally, so as to exactly match its surroundings, and is provided with a silken hinge. In some cases a refuge chamber branches out of the nest, from which it is separated by another neatly-made door, and it may also have a direct communication with the exterior of similar kind.

LIFE-HISTORIES, &c., OF INSECTS (INSECTA)

Many well-known insects, *e.g.* Bees, Butterflies, and Beetles, are striking illustrations of *indirect* development. They hatch out from the eggs as *larvæ*, which are exceedingly unlike the adult form, and pass later on into a quiescent *pupa* stage, from which the perfect insect or *imago* finally emerges. In such cases we may speak of a *complete metamorphosis*. There are also numerous instances where, as in Earwigs and Cockroaches, the just-hatched young differ far less from their parents, the character of which they gradually assume without, as a rule, passing through a quiescent stage. It is then convenient to speak of *nymphs*, not of larvæ, and the metamorphosis is said to be *partial*. And there are also some insects which begin life in a form which differs so little from the adult that the use of the term metamorphosis is hardly justifiable.

The time which elapses before an insect's egg hatches out varies greatly in different cases, and so does that consumed in the life-history taken as a whole. Hatching may take place on the day of laying, as in some Flies, or eggs deposited in late summer may remain dormant until the following spring, as in some Moths. The most remarkable case of a protracted life-history is afforded by the Seventeen-year Cicada (*Cicada septendecim*), which exists as a larva for the period indicated by its name (see vol. ii, p. 217).

A.—INSECTS WITH PARTIAL METAMORPHOSIS

PRIMITIVE WINGLESS INSECTS (APTERA).—Little is known as to the life-history of the Tassel-tails and Spring-tails which constitute this order, but many of them, though not all, closely resemble the adult stage at the time of hatching. More observations are badly needed, and might easily be made, for these little creatures are abundant almost everywhere.

STRAIGHT-WINGED INSECTS (ORTHOPTERA).—The appearance of the different stages in the life-history of the Common Earwig

(*Forficula auricularia*) will be gathered from fig. 896. The just-hatched nymph differs from the adult in the absence of wings, and in other particulars. But it quickly increases in size, and develops the parts which are lacking, these changes being associated, as in insects generally, with a series of moults or castings of the skin.

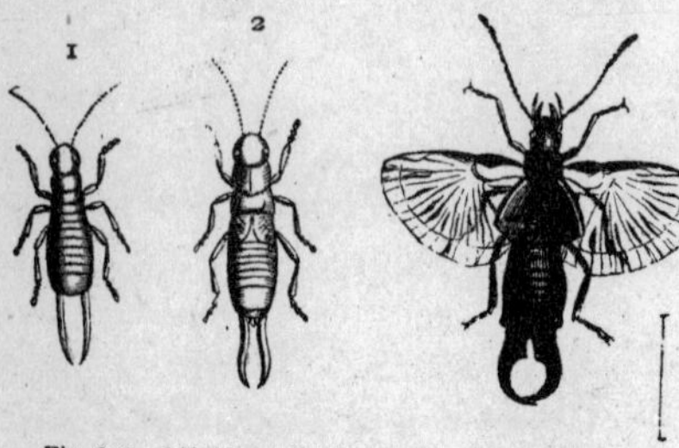

Fig. 896.—Life-history of Earwig (*Forficula auricularia*)
1 and 2, Nymphs. 3, Adult.

It is said that the female Earwig, after laying her eggs, collects them into a heap, over which she broods till the time of hatching. Beyond this maternal affection does not appear to go.

The eggs of the too familiar Cockroach (*Periplaneta orientalis*) are enclosed in a protective horny capsule, which the mother carries about with her for some time, ultimately leaving it in some safe corner. It is stated that she sometimes helps the young nymphs to make their way out of their tough investment. At this time there is about the same difference between them and the adult as in the case of Earwigs. They are, of course, much smaller.

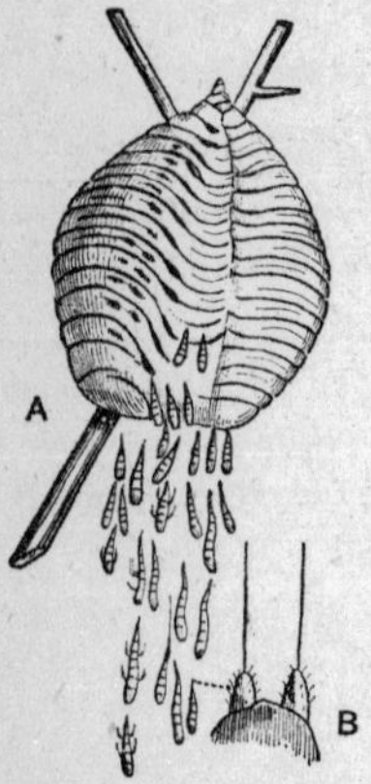

Fig. 897.—Praying Mantis. A, Young escaping from egg-capsule. B, Posterior end of a just-hatched Mantis, to show the two suspensory threads.

The *Soothsayers* or *Praying Insects* (*Mantidæ*) construct curious chambered egg-capsules, which are attached to plants or stones. In one species at least, the young, after making their way to the exterior, remain hanging to the capsule for some days by means of threads attached to their tails (fig. 897). They then undergo a moult, and lead an active existence for the rest of their lives.

Extraordinary circumstances attend the egg-laying of the curious *Stick-* and *Leaf-Insects* (*Phasmidæ*), which resemble in shape the objects after which they are named. Each egg is enclosed in a strong sculptured case, which makes it look very much like a seed, and this perhaps increases its chance of escaping the notice of certain predaceous Ichneumon-Flies which lay their own eggs within those of other insects. But it is known that this ingenious device is not always successful. Sharp (in *The Cambridge Natural History*) makes the following remark about one species:—"These eggs are not deposited in any careful way, but are discharged at random, simply dropping from the female; the noise caused by the dropping of the eggs of *Diapheromera femorata* from the trees on which the insects are feeding to the ground is said to resemble the pattering of rain-drops. The eggs of this species often remain till the second year before they hatch."

The eggs of *Locusts* and *Grasshoppers* (*Acridiidæ*) are usually deposited in the ground, a hole being excavated for the purpose. The tip of the abdomen in the female is provided with some hard-tipped rods which serve as spades for doing this work. A number of eggs are laid in the hole (fig. 898), and with them is discharged a sort of fluid, which subsequently hardens to form a protective case. All these devices are very necessary, as the eggs furnish much-appreciated articles of diet to a number of predaceous insects and other animals.

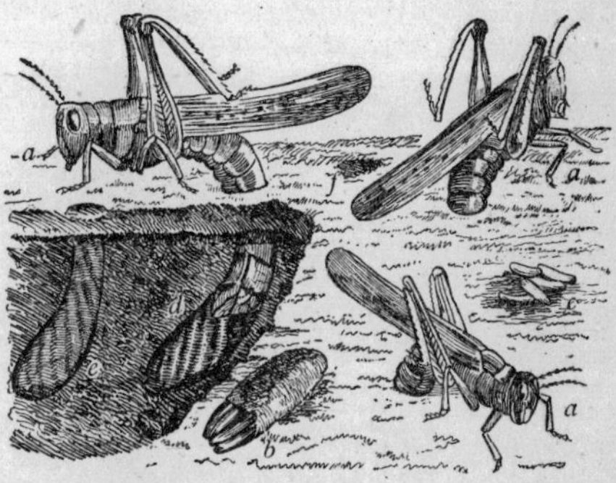

Fig. 898.—Red-legged Locust (*Melanoplus femur-rubrum*)

a, a, a, Females laying their eggs; *b,* egg-case opened; *c,* eggs; *d,* hole in the ground being filled with eggs; *e,* hole filled with eggs and closed above.

In *Green Grasshoppers* (*Locustidæ*), which are distinguished from the members of the preceding family by the great length of their feelers, the female possesses a long protrusible egg-laying tube or ovipositor, which is used for digging a shelter for the eggs, and afterwards directing them into it. The ground is usually selected for this purpose (fig. 899), but in some cases small twigs are chosen.

The *Crickets* (*Gryllidæ*) usually possess ovipositors, which are used for the same purpose as those of the Green Grasshoppers. The burrowing Mole-Cricket (*Gryllotalpa campestris*) is an exception to the rule, for in it all the digging is done by means of the specialized fore-legs (see vol. iii, p. 222). The excavations made in the interests of the young include an incubating chamber, and also a "nursery", in which the newly-hatched progeny can disport themselves (fig. 900). Our knowledge of these domestic details begins with old Gilbert White, who says (in *the Natural History of Selborne*):—". . . . A gardener at a house where I was on a visit, happening to be mowing, on the 6th of May, by the side of a canal, his scythe struck too deep, pared off a large piece of turf, and laid open to view a curious scene of domestic economy. There were many caverns and

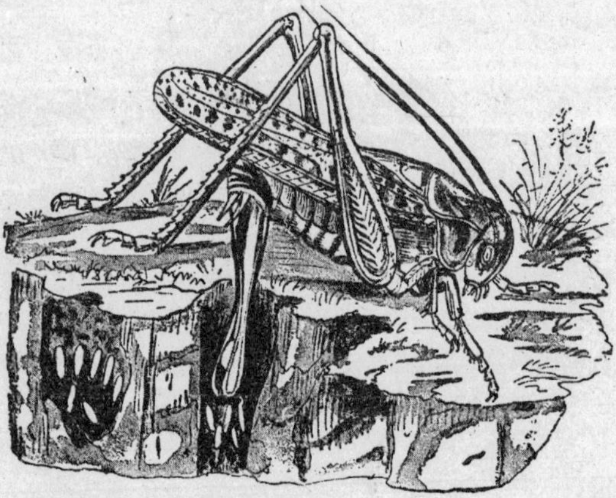

Fig. 899.—A Green Grasshopper (*Decticus verrucivorus*) laying her Eggs. Note the large ovipositor

winding passages leading to a kind of chamber, neatly smoothed and rounded, and about the size of a moderate snuff-box. Within this secret nursery were deposited near a hundred eggs of a dirty yellow colour, but too lately excluded to contain any rudiments of young, being full of a viscous substance. The eggs lay but shallow, and within the influence of the sun, just under a little heap of fresh-moved mould like that which is raised by ants."

Bugs (Hemiptera).—The members of this order emerge from the egg in a form which is usually not very dissimilar from the adult, though there is a good deal of variation in this matter. In *Tree-Bugs* (*Cicadidæ*), for instance, there is a considerable difference. Some account has already been given of the life-history of one of the most remarkable members of the family, the Seventeen-year Cicada (*Cicada septendecim*), which remains in the immature condition for an extraordinary length of time (see p. 225). These insects possess a strong ovipositor, and in this case it is used to bore a hole in a twig within which the eggs are laid.

Fig. 900.—Home of Mole-Cricket (*Gryllotalpa campestris*), in vertical section. *a*, Eggs in incubating chamber; *b*, young Cricket in "nursery"; *c*, adult.

In most of the *Scale-Insects* (*Coccidæ*) the wingless females are covered by a sort of shield (fig. 901), formed by the hardening of a fluid which exudes from the body, and in the construction of which the cast skins of the insect are also worked up. The shape and texture of these "scales" varies greatly according to the species. In most cases the female remains in the same spot, with her sharp beak driven into the plant on which she lives, for the purpose of sucking its juices. She lays numerous eggs, often dying and shrivelling up immediately afterwards, and these hatch out under the shelter of her body. The nymphs which emerge lead an active life for a time, but ultimately fix themselves by means of their beaks. Those which become females assume the adult shape by a series of gradual changes, but the males pass through a quiescent pupal stage, ultimately becoming, at least in some cases, active insects in which the fore-wings are present, while the hind-wings are reduced to vestiges, and the mouth-parts entirely absent.

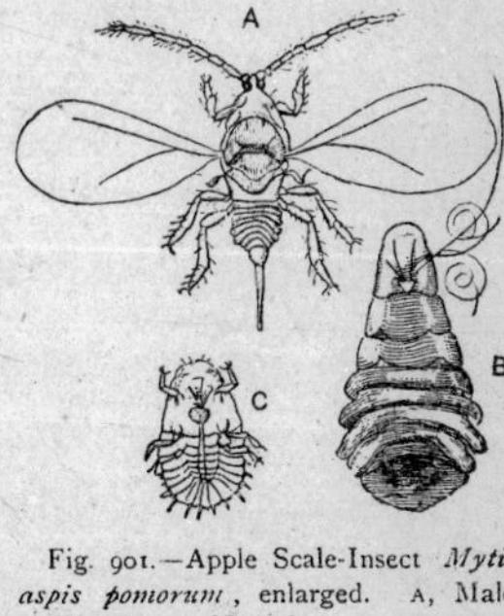

Fig. 901.—Apple Scale-Insect *Mytilaspis pomorum*, enlarged. A, Male. B, Female. C, Nymph.

Aphides or *Plant-Lice* (*Aphidæ*, fig. 902), often known as "green fly", are minute insects of astonishing fertility, in which the life-history is complex. During the warm part of the year, when food is abundant, there is a continuous succession of generations of females, some wingless, others possessing wings, which bring forth their young alive, *i.e.* are viviparous. These are all produced from unfertilized eggs. But on the approach of winter egg-laying or oviparous females come into existence, and also a certain proportion of males: in either sex wings may be present or absent. Fertilized eggs are now laid, which hatch out into viviparous females the following spring. We have here another example of the phenomenon of "alternation of generations", already illustrated by some of the Cœlenterates (see p. 349). But there is a great difference between the two cases. For in Cœlenterates vegetative propagation and egg-production alternate in the life-cycle (*metagenesis*), while in Aphides there is alternation between two kinds of egg, *i.e.* unfertilized eggs which develop internally, and fertilized eggs which develop externally. A life-cycle of this kind is technically described as a case of ***heterogeny***. If we denote the stage producing unfertilized eggs by E1, and that producing fertilized eggs by E2, the formula E1 E1 E1 E1, &c. &c., E2 will represent the life-history, a large number of viviparous generations (E1) succeeding one another before the single oviparous generation (E2) is reached.

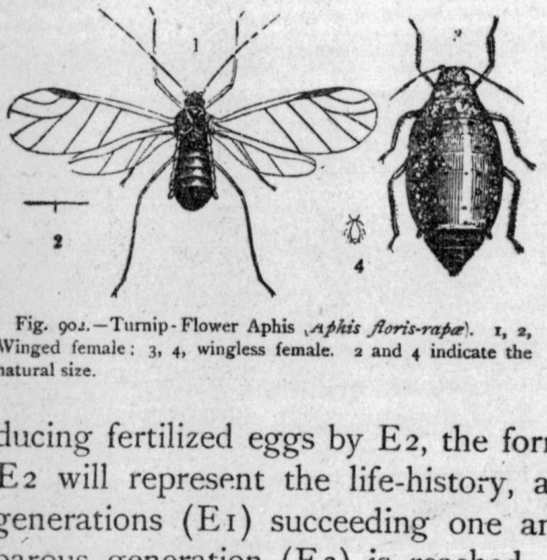

Fig. 902.—Turnip-Flower Aphis (*Aphis floris-rapæ*). 1, 2, Winged female: 3, 4, wingless female. 2 and 4 indicate the natural size.

Some of the aquatic bugs carry about their eggs with them until the time of hatching. This has been observed for one of the very few marine forms (*Halobates*), and has also been described for certain freshwater species (*e.g. Diplonychus*). In the latter case the eggs are sometimes, if not always, cemented to the back of the male.

Particular interest attaches to the eggs laid by the members of one family of freshwater Bugs (*Nepidæ*, fig. 903). In a Water-Scorpion (*Nepa*) the egg is provided with a tuft of threads at one end, and is deposited in the stem of a water-plant, the threads alone projecting. It has been suggested that they are of use in conducting air to the developing embryo, for they are of spongy nature, and continuous with a layer of the same character situated just within the egg-shell. But this requires confirmation.

The eggs of some of the slender water-bugs (species of *Ranatra*) are of elongated shape, with a couple of sharply-bent threads at one end. The female insect stands on a floating leaf

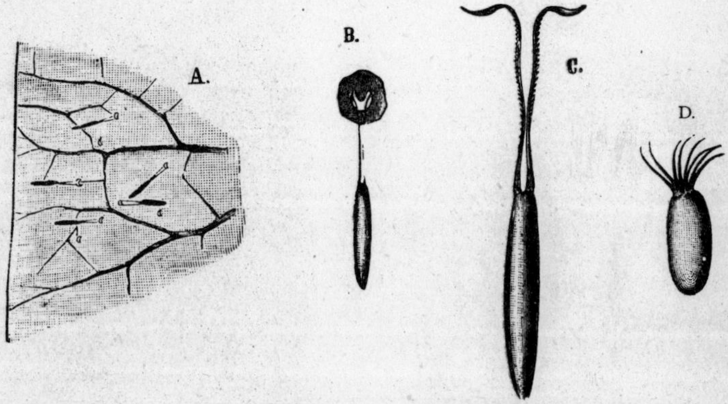

Fig. 903.—Eggs of Water-Bugs

A, Under side of bit of floating leaf, with attached eggs of Ranatra. B, Single egg of same with small piece of leaf, × 4. C, Isolated egg of same, × 8. D, Egg of Nepa cinerea, × 7.

and makes a small hole through which the egg is passed, when the threads catch at the side of the hole, acting as a suspensory arrangement. The leaf is thus converted into a nursery, and large numbers of these eggs may sometimes be found hanging down from its under side.

B. INSECTS WITH COMPLETE METAMORPHOSIS

NET-WINGED INSECTS (NEUROPTERA).—Of the purely terrestrial forms belonging to this order, the *Termites* or *White Ants* (*Termitidæ*), which live together in complex communities, are undoubtedly the most interesting, but these will be dealt with further on, under the heading ASSOCIATION OF ANIMALS.

Many Net-Winged Insects spend the early part of their existence in ponds or streams, and some of their adaptations to an aquatic life have already received attention (see vol. ii, p. 463). We may take the *Dragon-Flies* (*Odonata*, fig. 904) as a typical example. The eggs are laid either in water or upon aquatic plants, a number of them being usually imbedded in a jelly-like

Fig. 904.—Life-history of a Dragon-Fly (*Libellula depressa*). A, Perfect insect. B, Young Dragon-Fly emerging from nymph. C, C, Young nymphs. D, Full-grown nymph about to leave the water.

mass. They hatch out into flattened unattractive-looking nymphs, which lead a predaceous aquatic existence for some time, gradually increasing in size, and developing some of the adult characteristics. The fully-formed nymph ultimately creeps up the stem of some plant till it is out of the water, and then remains motionless. The

Fig. 905.—Caddis-Moth (*Phryganea striata*) and its Larva

skin of the back now splits, and the perfect insect makes its way out of the enclosing skin, its wings being at first flabby and shrivelled. They soon expand and assume their proper form, and the dragon-fly then takes wing, commencing a life in the air which is quite as predaceous as the life which its nymph led in the water. The amount of metamorphosis is not nearly so considerable as in some of the other insects to be described, and, as a matter of fact, the order of Net-winged Insects includes so many different kinds of life-history, that it really comes under the last heading as well as under this. But it is thought best to keep them together, so as to prevent confusion.

Caddis-Flies (*Phryganeidæ*) are net-winged insects which pass through a complete metamorphosis, hatching out as larvæ, which construct cases for themselves (see vol. ii, p. 337), and as "caddis-worms" are well-known inhabitants of fresh water. After a time the larva passes into a motionless pupa

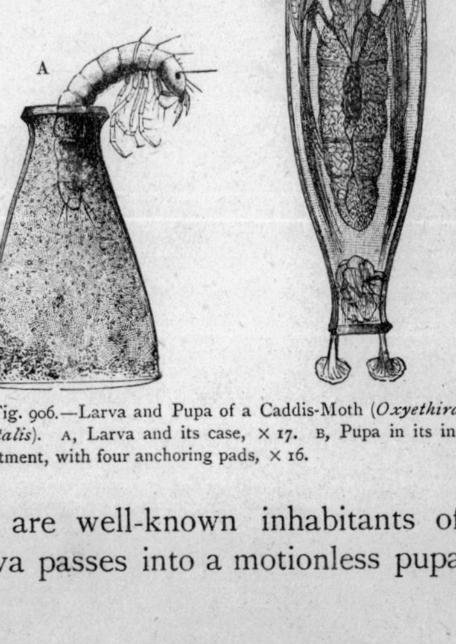

Fig. 906.—Larva and Pupa of a Caddis-Moth (*Oxyethira costalis*). A, Larva and its case, × 17. B, Pupa in its investment, with four anchoring pads, × 16.

stage, from which the moth-like perfect insect or imago ultimately emerges. The larva and imago of a species of Caddis-Fly are represented in fig. 905, the former having been removed from the water and placed on the bank. It is obvious that it would not do for the imago to come out of the pupa under water, and there is an interesting adaptation to meet this exigency. The larva, before passing into the motionless stage, closes its case by spinning silken screens, which do not prevent the passage of water, or it may employ bits of stick or stone for the purpose. In some species (fig. 906, B) the case is previously anchored to a floating leaf. It then becomes a pupa, which in general shape is much like the adult, and possesses a relatively enormous pair of jaws (mandibles). When fully formed it becomes active, bites its way out of the case, and swims on its back till some body is encountered up which it can climb out of the water. This transit to the outer air effected, the skin splits and the imago wriggles out, much as in the case of dragon-flies.

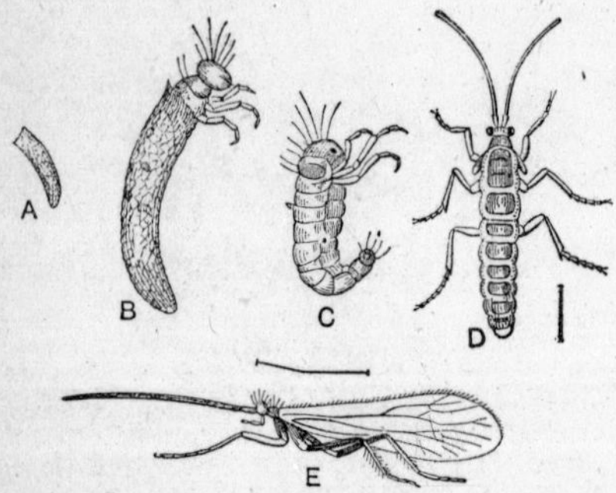

Fig. 907.—Land-Caddis (*Enoicyla pusilla*). A, Case of larva. B and C, Larva in its case, and removed from same, enlarged. D, Adult female. E, Adult male. The actual size of D and E is indicated by lines.

In rare instances the caddis-worms do not live in the water at all. The larvæ and adults of one such species (*Enoicyla pusilla*), in which the early part of life is spent in damp moss or among rotting leaves, is represented in fig. 907.

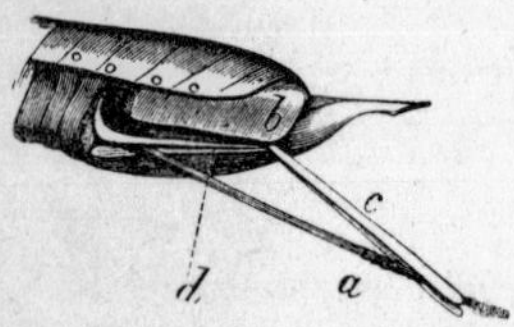

Fig. 908.—Hinder Part of Body of Female Wood-Wasp (*Sirex gigas*), enlarged. *a*, Ovipositor; *c*, *d*, its sheath, with a joint at *b*.

MEMBRANE-WINGED INSECTS (HYMENOPTERA). — Complete metamorphosis is characteristic of this order, as familiarly exemplified by the social Ants, Bees, and Wasps, whose complex communal life will receive our attention in a later section. A few simpler cases will suffice to illustrate the nature of the life-history.

The female of the Large Wood-Borer or Wood-Wasp (*Sirex gigas*, fig. 908) possesses a strong ovipositor, by means of which she bores holes in the trunks of sickly fir-trees, and lays her eggs therein. The structure of this organ is complex, but may be understood by reference to figs. 908 and 909. It consists of two protective pieces, which can be brought together so as to ensheathe the part by which the boring is effected. This is made up of three rods, one of which is relatively broad, and provided below with a pair of ridges, on which two boring spines can slide up and down. Each of these is studded with saw-like teeth near its tip. The larva is a pale grub-like creature practically devoid of limbs, though three pairs of little projections near the front end of the body correspond to the legs of the adult. It feeds on the wood of the tree, biting out long galleries, and is said to remain in the larval state for as much as two years. When full grown it travels towards the surface of the trunk or branch, and becomes a pupa, as which it may remain for a long time. The imago, after emerging from the pupal skin, gnaws its way to the exterior. Fabre states that in an allied species (*Sirex augur*) the galleries of the larva are longitudinal, and that it becomes a pupa in one of these, making no attempt to come near the surface before doing so. When the imago makes its appearance it does not try to get to the open air by travelling along the gallery in which it finds itself, but bores a transverse passage that takes it direct to the exterior. This is only one of many instances in which animals possess a sense of direction far more highly developed than our own somewhat imperfectly developed locality sense. There are possibly special sense organs related to this important faculty, which is here of vital importance, as without it many of the adult insects would never get out of the tree at all.

Fig. 909.—Cross-section through Ovipositor and Sheath of Wood-Wasp (*Sirex gigas*), greatly enlarged. *a b* and *a′ b′*, sheath; *e* and *e′*, boring spines, which slide on the ridges of a directing piece (*c d*).

The Corn Saw-Fly (*Cephus pygmæus*, fig. 910) passes through a life-history presenting similar stages to those described for the Wood-Wasp. Among cultivated plants wheat and rye are the special objects of its attentions. In such plants the stem or haulm is marked by a series of swollen solid nodes or "knots", from which the leaves grow out, and between which are long hollow internodes. The female Saw-Fly lays about a dozen eggs, depositing each of them in the lowest internode of a distinct plant. This takes place in early summer, and the larva spends the rest of this season in gradually working its way up the stem, biting through the knots as they are encountered. It then travels down again, and is fully grown by the time it gets near the ground. Now follows the most remarkable event, for the larva partly bites through the stem all the way round, about an inch from its base, the object unconsciously obtained being that later on it may be easily broken off by the wind, thus leaving a free means of exit for the fully-formed insect. This accomplished, the larva descends to the neighbourhood of the root and weaves a transparent silken cocoon, in which it remains dormant till the following May, when it becomes a pupa, the perfect insect making its appearance soon afterwards.

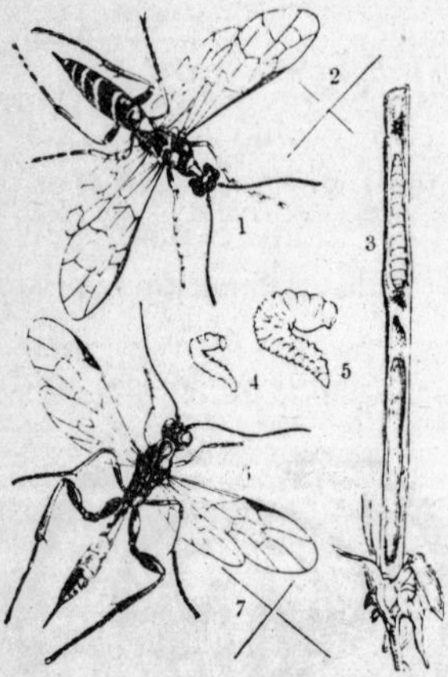

Fig. 910.—Corn Saw-Fly (*Cephus pygmæus*)

1, Adult female (2 indicates actual size); 3, larva within a haulm of rye; 4 and 5, the same, natural size and enlarged; 6, an Ichneumon-Fly which lays its eggs within the Saw-Fly larvæ (7 indicates actual size).

The numerous species belonging to the Saw-Flies Proper (*Tenthredinidæ*) are familiar pests, in which the female possesses an ovipositor constructed on much the same principle as that of the Wood-Wasp (see p. 387), but the two saws are elaborate curved plates, with teeth on their edges and sharp ridges on the outer side (fig. 911), the latter having a rasping function. When in use they are used alternately, sliding on their supporting pieces. Sharp remarks on these insects as follows (in *The Cambridge Natural History*):—"In the case of some species the Common Saw-Fly (*Hylotoma rosæ*) of our rose-bushes, for instance, there is no difficulty in observing the operation; indeed, old Réaumur, when speaking of the placid disposition of the Saw-Flies, suggests that it was given them so that we may easily observe their charming operations. We cannot but regret that in these days we are unable to take so complacent a view of the arrangements of nature.

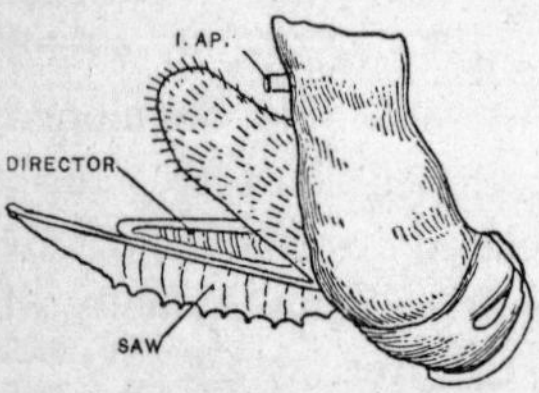

Fig. 911.—Side-view of Ovipositor of Rose Saw-Fly (*Hylotoma rosæ*), much enlarged. I. AP., intestinal aperture.

There is much variety in the details of the structure of these saws, so much, indeed, that it is possible to identify most of the species by means of the saw alone." The course of the life-history of a typical species, the Turnip Saw-Fly (*Athalia spinarum*, fig. 912), is as follows. The females lay their eggs during May in the edges of turnip leaves, or those of allied plants, cutting little slits for their reception. From 200 to 300 are deposited by a single turnip-fly. The egg increases in size after being laid, and the larva which hatches out in a few days closely resembles the caterpillar of a butterfly or moth, in the possession of three pairs of jointed legs in front, corresponding to the legs of the perfect insect, and sucker-bearing pro-legs behind these. But the head is rounder and the pro-legs more numerous than in a true caterpillar. The young larva is pale in colour, but with increasing size becomes first green and later on blackish. The full-grown larva creeps down to the ground and enters the earth, where it spins a silken cocoon, to which particles of soil adhere externally. Within this shelter it passes into the pupa stage, and the imago comes out about the end of July. Under favourable conditions a second brood makes its appearance the same year, and in this case the larva remains as such within its cocoon during the winter, completing the stages in its life-history the following May.

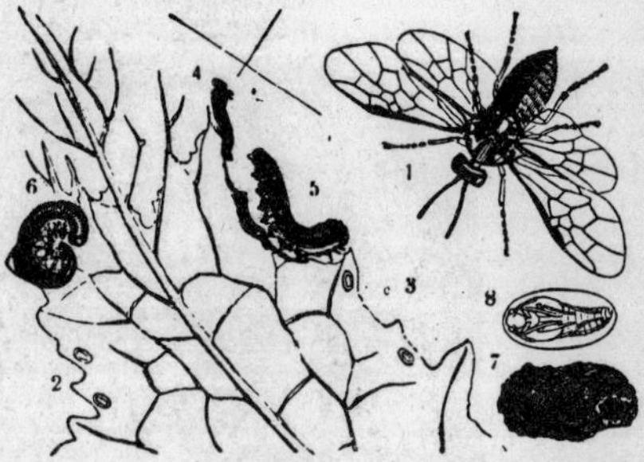

Fig. 912.—Turnip Saw-Fly (*Athalia spinarum*). 1, Adult female, enlarged (natural size indicated to left of it); 2, 3, eggs, enlarged and natural size; 4, 5, 6, larvæ; 7, cocoon; 8, pupa in cocoon.

Sharp (in *The Cambridge Natural History*) gives the following intensely interesting account of another kind of Saw-Fly:— "Although many kinds of Insects display the greatest solicitude and ingenuity in providing proper receptacles for their eggs, and in storing food for the young that will be produced, there are extremely few that display any further interest in their descendants; probably, indeed, the majority of Insects die before the eggs are hatched, one generation never seeing the individuals of another. It is therefore interesting to find that a fairly well authenticated case of maternal attachment, such as we have previously alluded to as occurring in Earwigs, has been recorded in *Perga lewisii*, an Australian Saw-Fly. . . . The mother, having deposited about eight eggs on the leaf of a eucalyptus, remains with them until they hatch, after which she sits over her brood with outstretched legs, and with admirable perseverance protects them, so far as she is able, from the attacks of parasites and other enemies; she quite refuses to be driven away from her charges.

Fig. 913.—Carpenter Bee (*Xylocopa violacea*) and Nest

Mr. Lewis, to whom we are indebted for this account, states that the Saw-Fly does not recognize her own special brood, but will give equal attention to another brood if she be transferred thereto; and he adds that many of the batches of larvæ were destitute of any maternal guardian."

The large purplish insect known as the Carpenter Bee (*Xylocopa violacea*, fig. 913), a European species which does not range into Britain, gnaws into dead wood, and excavates three or four parallel passages, which may be as much as a foot in length.

These are divided into a series of cells by partitions consisting of saw-dust stuck together with saliva, and each cell contains an egg, together with a supply of honey and pollen. The larva, as in bees generally, is a limbless grub, and after using up the food-supply allotted to it, becomes a pupa. The adult insect, after coming out of the pupa, bites through the saw-dust partitions which confine it, and makes its way to the exterior.

The Leaf-cutting Bees (species of *Megachile*) are widely distributed forms, which either excavate holes for their nests, or else use existing hollows for the purpose. These are then lined with pieces of leaf, bitten out for the purpose, and stuck together by a special secretion. Each cell is covered by a circular lid, composed of a number of pieces skilfully cemented together. Several cells are placed end to end, each containing an egg with a supply of food, much as in the Carpenter Bee. The Poppy Bee (*Osmia* or *Anthocopa papaveris*), a rare native form, lines its cells with the scarlet petals of the common poppy. Regarding the habits of this species, Shuckard (in *British Bees*) makes the following remarks:—"The habits of these bees . . . are to excavate vertical cylinders in hard down-trodden pathways and roads, by the sides of fields where corn is grown, and where consequently the common red poppy is abundant. From the petals of the flowers of this plant they cut out semicircular pieces, precisely as is done by *Megachile* with the more rigid leaves of shrubs and trees, and convey them home and line their nests with them, just as is practised by that genus with those leaves—with this difference merely, that a sufficient portion of the upper edge of the pieces of the petals used is left projecting, for the purpose of forming a covercle to the nidus, and which, when filled with provender and the egg deposited, is refolded over it and covered in, and it is closed up with earth. They then proceed to make another excavation, which is treated in the same manner, for they deposit only one larva in a tube. I would urge our collecting entomologists, especially those who have the opportunity of hunting up the west of England, to use due diligence and strive to confirm the native existence of this bee, and add specimens to the cabinets of their fellow-entomologists."

We now come to a number of Solitary Wasps and Wasp-like Insects which provide for their young by placing in the nest a store of caterpillars or other creatures, which they have previously disabled or killed by stinging. Of *Solitary Wasps* (*Eumenidæ*) we possess reliable information gained by the observations of Fabre. In one species (*Odynerus reniformis*, fig. 914) the nest is a little burrow at the end of which the egg is hung up by a thread. The female wasp next hunts for a small kind of caterpillar which rolls itself up when attacked, and, selecting an individual of suitable dimensions, packs it in the burrow near the egg, probably stinging it first to produce paralysis. A series of twenty or more caterpillars is thus packed away, the members of which are destined to be eaten in regular succession. The just-hatched larva remains hanging by its thread to devour the first (and weakest) caterpillar, and then descends into the little space at the end of the burrow, after which it polishes off the remaining victims, one after the other. It is suggested that in this and other instances the members of the living larder do not suffer any pain, being stupefied by the stinging process, but this is by no means certain.

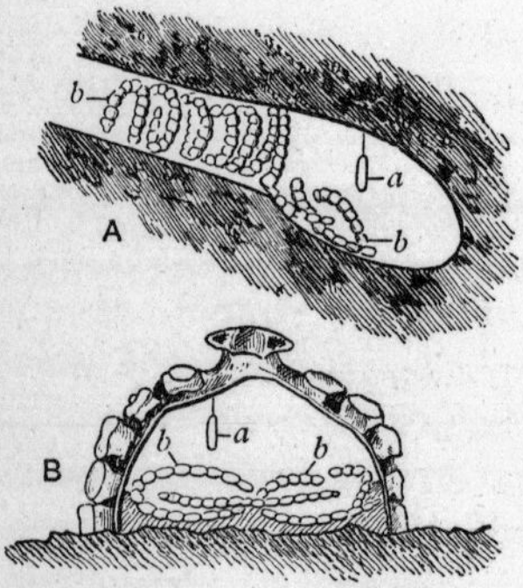

Fig. 914.—Nests of Solitary Wasps, in section

a, Suspended egg of Wasp; *b*, caterpillars stored as food for the larvæ. A, Subterranean nest of *Odynerus reniformis*. B, Dome-shaped nest of *Eumenes arbustorum*.

Fabre describes Solitary Wasps (species of *Eumenes*, fig. 914) of even greater interest, in which the female makes a little dome-shaped nest of mud and tiny stones, from the roof of which the egg is suspended as before, while a wriggling mass of stupefied caterpillars occupies the lower part. The minute larva is at first able to feed without quitting the egg-shell, and later on this splits into a spiral strip which, by augmenting the length of the thread, enables the occupant of the cell to get at the diminishing store of victims, so that it can make a further series of meals without running the risk of being squeezed or bitten to death. Ultimately the larva grows sufficiently big and strong to descend among its victims with safety, and this happens just at the time when it can no longer reach the diminishing heap of food from its thread.

The exceedingly numerous and widely distributed insects known as Solitary Digging-Wasps (*Fossores*), and which strictly speaking are not wasps at all, provide for the well-being of their young in a similar manner to that described for the last two cases.

Their nesting habits vary largely according to the species, from cases where no nest at all is formed, to others where burrows, or borings, or earthen cells are made for the purpose. There is an equal amount of variation in the nature of the victims selected. These not only include caterpillars, but also cockroaches, beetles, beetle-grubs, ants, flies, aphides, and spiders. The habits of these interesting forms will be reserved for treatment under the heading of Instinct and Intelligence, but the following general remarks of Sharp (in *The Cambridge Natural History*) are well worth quoting here:—"The habits are carnivorous; the structures formed are not for the benefit of the makers, but are constructed and stored with food for the next generation. Their remarkable habits attracted some attention even 2000 years or more ago, and were to some extent observed by Aristotle. The great variety in the habits of the species, the extreme industry, skill, and self-denial they display in carrying out their voluntary labours, renders them one of the most instructive groups of the animal kingdom. There are no social or gregarious forms, they are true individualists, and their lives and instinct offer many subjects for reflection. Unlike the social Insects they can learn nothing whatever from either example or precept. The skill of each individual is prompted by no imitation. The life is short, the later stages of the individual life are totally different from the earlier; the individuals of one generation only in rare cases see even the commencement of the life of the next; the progeny, for the benefit of which they labour with unsurpassable skill and industry, being unknown to them. Were such a solicitude displayed by ourselves we should connect it with a high sense of duty, and poets and moralists would vie in its laudation. But having dubbed ourselves the higher animals, we ascribe the eagerness of the Solitary Wasp to impulse or instinct, and we exterminate their numerous species from the face of the earth for ever, without even seeking to make a prior acquaintance with them. Meanwhile our economists and moralists devote their volumes to admiration of the progress of the civilization that effects this destruction and tolerates this negligence."

Beetles (Coleoptera).—Although this is the most dominant order of insects, and represented by the largest number of species, our knowledge of the habits of these is comparatively scanty, though at the same time sufficiently numerous observations have been made to render selection of illustrative cases difficult.

The stages in the life-history may be illustrated by reference to the Long-horned Oak-Beetle (*Cerambyx heros*, fig. 915), an insect of considerable size. The larva is a yellowish grub, which is practically limbless, though it possesses three pairs of little stumps corresponding to the legs of the adult. It lives in the wood of an old oak, which it tunnels in all directions, and passes into the pupa stage after three or four years. As in most beetles, the pupa is soft, and the outgrowths which are to form the append-

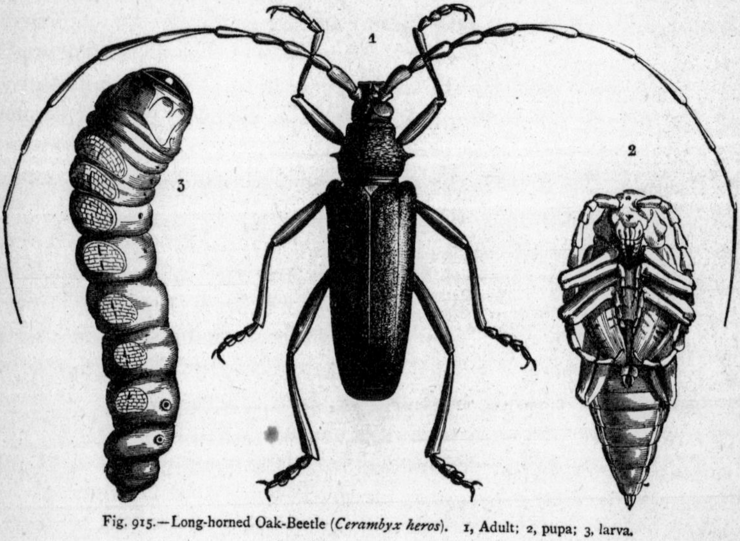

Fig. 915.—Long-horned Oak-Beetle (*Cerambyx heros*). 1, Adult; 2, pupa; 3, larva.

ages of the adult project freely at the exterior. After a short period of rest the skin splits and the imago comes out.

As a rule Beetles do not provide for the welfare of their eggs to anything like the extent which distinguishes the Net-winged Insects, but some of them display considerable solicitude in this direction. An illustration has already been given in the case of the Sacred Scarab (see vol. ii, p. 210). The little leaf-rolling Birch-Weevil (*Rhynchites betulæ*) constructs a receptacle for its eggs in a most ingenious manner (fig. 916), displaying an enormous amount of energy. Sharp (in *The Cambridge Natural History*) gives the following account of the operation:—"If young birches, or birch bushes from 5 to 10 feet in height, be looked at in the summer, one may often notice that some of the leaves are rolled so as to form, each one, a little funnel. . . . An inspection of one of these funnels will show that it is very carefully constructed. The whole of a leaf is not used in the formation of a funnel, cuts being made across the leaf in suitable directions. The beetle, standing on a leaf, as shown in the figure, proceeds to cut with its mandibles an incision shaped like an erect S, commencing at a certain part of the circumference, and ending at the midrib of the leaf; the beetle then goes to the other side of the midrib, and continues its incision so as to form another S-like curve considerably different from the first, being prostrate and less abrupt.

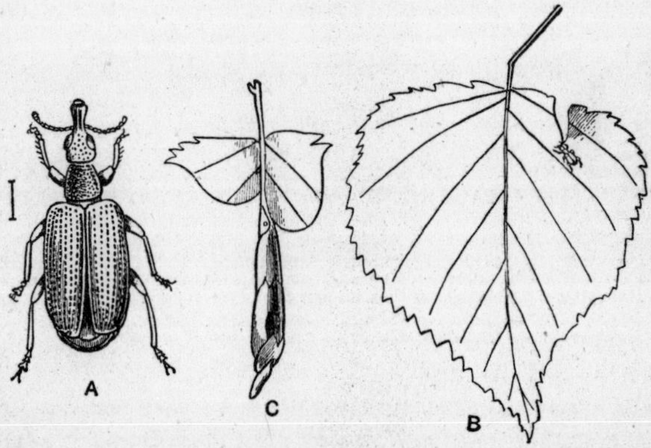

Fig. 916.—Birch-Weevil (*Rhynchites betulæ*). A, Adult Weevil (actual size indicated by line to left). B, Weevil constructing egg-case. C, Completed egg-case.

Thus the blade of the leaf is divided into two halves by certain curved incisions, the midrib remaining intact. The little funnel-twister now commences to roll up the leaf to form the funnel; and this part of the work is greatly facilitated by the shape of the incisions. Going back to the spot where it commenced work, by the aid of its legs it rolls one side of the leaf round an ideal axis, somewhat on the same plan as that adopted by a grocer in forming a paper-funnel for sugar. The incisions are found to be just of the right shape to make the overlaps in the rolling, and to retain them rolled up with the least tendency to spring back. After some other operations destined to facilitate subsequent parts of its task, the beetle enters the rolled-up part of the leaf and brings it more perfectly together; it again comes out, and, pursuing a different system, holds on with the legs of one side of the body to the roll, and with the other legs drags to it the portion of the leaf on the other side of the midrib, so as to wrap this part (*i.e.* the result of its second incision) round the part of the funnel already constructed. This being done, the insect again enters the funnel, bites three or four small cavities on the inside of the leafy wall, and deposits an egg in each. Afterwards it emerges and fits the overlaps together in a more perfect manner, so as to somewhat contract the funnel and make it firmer; then, proceeding to the tip, this is operated on by another series of engineering processes and made to close the orifice; this part of the operation being analogous to the closing by the grocer of his paper-funnel after the sugar has been put in. The operation of the beetle is, however, much more complex, for it actually makes a sort of second small funnel of the tip of the leaf, bends this in, and retains it by tucking in some little projections. The work, which has probably lasted about an hour, being now completed, the creature takes a longer or shorter rest before commencing another funnel. We have given only a sketch of the chief points of the work, omitting reference to smaller artifices of the craft-master; but we may remark that the curved incisions made by the beetle have been examined by mathematicians and dully extolled as being conducted on highly satisfactory mathematical principles." Perhaps the most extraordinary part of the whole thing is that we do not know the purpose of this elaborate arrangement, and closely related species get on quite well by simply laying their eggs in various parts of plants. Here is a good instance of a fascinating problem lying at our very doors, and probably to be solved by ordinary intelligence coupled with unlimited patience.

The grubs of *Burying-* or *Sexton-Beetle* (species of *Necrophorus*, fig. 917) feed on carrion, and the adults bury the corpses of small animals for the delectation of their progeny. The following amusing account of the obsequies of a bird as conducted by these creatures is given by Edward Newman (in *Introduction to the History of Insects*):—"The Sexton-Beetles hunt in couples, male and female; and where six or eight are found in a large animal, they are almost sure to be males and females in equal numbers; they hunt by scent only, the chase being mostly performed when no other sense would be very available, viz. in the night. When they have found a bird, great comfort is expressed by the male, who wheels round and round above it, like a vulture over the putrefying carcass of some giant of the forest—the female settles on it at once, without this testimonial of satisfaction; the male at last settles also, and a savoury and ample meal is made before the great work is begun. After the beetles have appeased the calls of hunger, the bird is abandoned for a while; they both leave it to explore the earth in the neighbourhood, and ascertain whether there is a place suitable for interment; if on a ploughed field there is no difficulty, but if on grass, or among stones, much labour

Fig. 917.—Sexton-Beetles (*Necrophorus*) burying a small Animal.

is required to draw it to a more suitable place. The operation of burying is performed almost entirely by the male beetle, the female mostly hiding herself in the body of the bird about to be buried, or sitting quietly upon it and allowing herself to be buried with it. The male begins by digging a furrow all round the bird at the distance of about half an inch, turning the earth outside. His head is the only tool used in this operation; it is held sloping outwards, and is exceedingly powerful. After the first furrow is completed another is made within it, and the earth is thrown into the first furrow; then a third furrow is made, and this is completely under the bird, so that the beetle, whilst working at it, is out of sight. Now the operation can only be traced by the heaving of the earth, which soon forms a little rampart round the bird. As the earth is moved from beneath, and the surrounding rampart increases in height, the bird sinks. After incessant labour for about three hours the beetle emerges, crawls upon the bird, and takes a survey of his work. If the female is on the bird she is driven away by the male, who does not choose to be intruded on during the important business. The male beetle then remains for about an hour perfectly still, and does not stir hand or foot; he then dismounts, dives again into the grave, and pulls the bird down by the feathers for half an hour: its own weight appears to sink it but very little. At last, after two or three hours' more labour, the beetle comes up, again gets on the bird, and again takes a survey, and then drops down as though dead, or fallen suddenly fast asleep. When sufficiently rested he rouses himself, treads the bird firmly into its grave, pulls it by the feathers this way and that way, and, having settled it to his mind, begins to shovel in the earth. This is done in a very short time by means of his broad head. He goes behind a rampart of earth and pushes it into the grave with amazing strength and dexterity, the head being bent directly downward at first, and then the nose elevated with a kind of jerk which sends the earth forwards. After the grave is thus filled up the earth is trodden in, and undergoes another keen scrutiny all round, the bird being completely hidden; the beetle then makes a hole in the loose earth, and having buried the bird and his own bride, next buries himself. The female having laid her eggs in the carcass of the bird, in number proportioned to its size, and the pair having eaten as much of the savoury viand as they please, they make their way out and fly away."

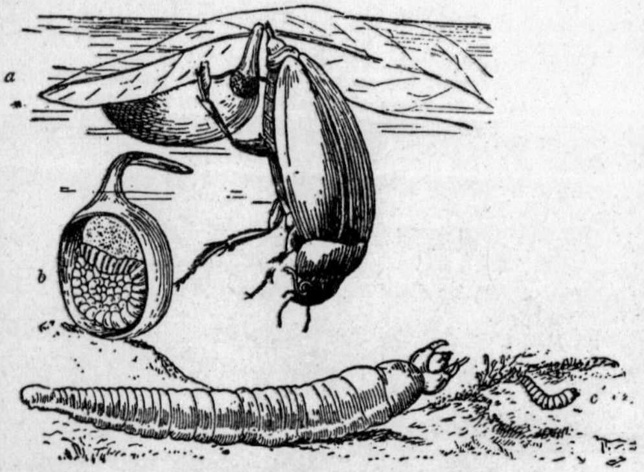

Fig. 918.—Great Black Water-Beetle (*Hydrophilus piceus*). *a*, Adult female, and cocoon attached to leaf; *b*, cocoon opened to show the eggs; *c*, young larva; *d*, full-grown larva.

Among freshwater forms the Great Black Water-Beetle (*Hydrophilus piceus*) is interesting in regard to its egg-laying arrangements. The hinder part of its body is provided with spinning glands, by the aid of which it constructs a pear-shaped silken case, within which the eggs are deposited, and which is attached to the leaf of a water-plant (fig. 918).

Scale-winged Insects (*Lepidoptera*).—The Butterflies and Moths which make up this order are often so attractive in appearance that there has never been a lack of naturalists willing to study them, and a vast amount of information has been collected regarding their structure and habits. The sequence of egg, caterpillar, pupa or chrysalis, and imago, is familiar to everybody.

Fig. 919.—Cabbage Butterfly (*Pieris brassicæ*). 1, Adult female; 2, eggs; 3, caterpillar; 4, chrysalis.

The large White or Cabbage Butterfly (*Pieris brassicæ*, fig. 919) furnishes a common and instructive illustration. The female lays clusters of bright yellow eggs on the under side of the leaves of cabbages, turnips, and allied plants. The external surface of the egg is sculptured in a characteristic manner. The caterpillars are gregarious, and when fully grown are bluish-green above and yellow below, with a yellow streak down the middle of the back, a series of large black spots along either side, and a sprinkling of black dots over the body. These colours make the larvæ conspicuous objects, especially as a number are associated together, and they are regarded as an illustration of warning coloration (see vol. ii, p. 301). After attaining its full size the caterpillar attaches itself by the tail to some firm object, spins a silken girdle for the front part of its body, casts its skin, and passes into the chrysalis stage. The observations and experiments of Poulton and others have shown that the colour harmonizes with the surroundings, varying from green to almost black, and this is interpreted as variable protective coloration (see vol. ii, p. 289). There may be several broods during the warmer part of the year, and the last set of chrysalides remain in a dormant state throughout the winter, the butterflies emerging the following spring.

The eggs of Lepidoptera vary greatly in shape, external markings, and colour, some of them being amongst the most beautiful objects commonly included in cabinets of microscopic slides. They are laid upon an appropriate food-plant, which is by no means the least astonishing fact in the natural history of insects, when we remember that the habits of larva and adult are totally different, the former feeding greedily on leaves or other vegetable matter by means of its powerful jaws, while the latter, if it feeds at all, is usually limited to the sipping of nectar through its suctorial proboscis. It sometimes happens that more elaborate provisions are made for the welfare of the eggs. In some of the *Eggers* or *Lappet-Moths* (*Lasiocampidæ*), for instance, the female covers them with fur taken from her own body.

When we come to consider caterpillars and chrysalides, we are at once encountered with a bewildering variety of adaptations to all sorts of conditions, to which it is impossible to do justice in small space. Among the most interesting are the protective devices found among Stick Caterpillars and others, which have been briefly dealt with in a preceding section (see vol. ii, pp. 287, 293, 297, 307, 313, 359, 374). The caterpillars of one family of small Moths (*Psychidæ*) are reminiscent of caddis-worms, for they construct protective cases of various shape, usually from earth or bits of plants. They are usually known as "basket-worms" on this account. In some instances the case is shaped exactly like a snail-shell, and made of closely-woven silk. The change into a pupa takes place inside the larval dwelling, and the female moth never quits it. Her eggs are laid and hatched out therein, and it is suspected that the young larvæ begin life by devouring their mother, but at present they are entitled to the benefit of the doubt.

In one great family of Butterflies (*Nymphalidæ*), including, among other forms, our native Fritillaries, Tortoiseshells, the Red Admiral, the Painted Lady, and the Peacock Butterfly, the chrysalis is hung up by the tip of its tail, which is provided with sharply curved hooks for that purpose. The caterpillars of a large number of species construct cocoons of various nature before they pass into the helpless chrysalis stage. The pupæ of the Silver-Y Moth (*Plusia gamma*, fig. 920), for instance, are to be found on the under sides of leaves, enclosed in a loose web of silk. The much denser cocoons of the Silkworm Moth (*Bombyx mori*) and other species are familiar as the source of commercial silk. Many caterpillars descend to the ground before they become chrysalides, an obviously protective habit. We may take as an example of this the Heart-and-Dart Moth (*Agrotis exclamationis*, fig. 921), a common agricultural pest in this country, in which the protective investment is supplemented by an earthen case. The caterpillar of another British species (*Brephos notha*) belonging to the same family of Owlet-Moths (*Noctuidæ*) adopts quite a different method. During its larval life it lives upon the aspen, the leaves of which it sticks together to form a shelter. When fully grown it bites out a snug receptacle in bark or wood wherein to become a chrysalis, previously spinning one or more partitions of silk across the entrance to its hiding-place. In this way prying enemies are to some extent kept off, while ventilation is at the same time not interfered with unduly.

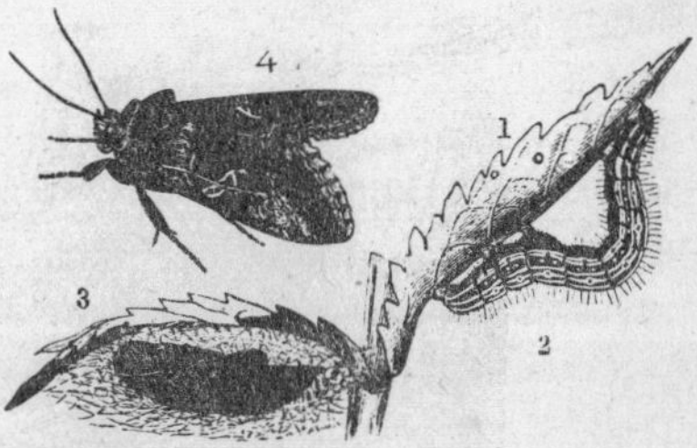

Fig. 920.—Silver-Y Moth (*Plusia gamma*)
1, Eggs; 2, caterpillar; 3, chrysalis in cocoon; 4, adult female.

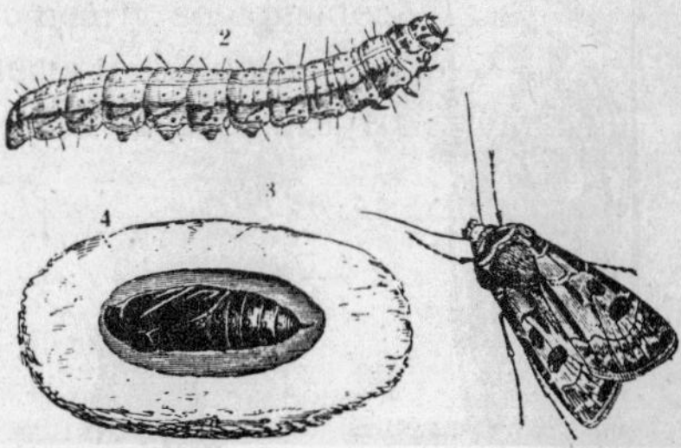

Fig. 921.—Heart-and-Dart Moth (*Agrotis exclamationis*). 1, Adult female; 2, caterpillar; 3, earthen case (cut open) enclosing chrysalis in cocoon (4).

The caterpillars of certain South American Moths (species of *Palustra*) inhabit fresh water, swimming about by alternately coiling and straightening their bodies. In most, but not all, species they construct their cocoons under water, and a number of these are found associated together. The larva of the Puss-Moth (*Cerura vinula*) makes a particularly firm cocoon, leaving, however, a thin place in front of its head, through which the imago later on forces its way. The exit is assisted by the ejection of a fluid containing caustic potash, which softens the barrier between the insect and liberty, and a piece of the chrysalis skin is used as a head-shield as a protection against the corrosive action of the liquid. In Burnet-Moths (*Zygænidæ*) the chrysalis is enclosed in a tapering, hammock-shaped cocoon, attached to a vertical stem. It is brownish in colour, with a shining surface. The chrysalis partly forces its way through the cocoon before the moth emerges. The caterpillar of an Indian Skipper Butterfly (*Badamia exclamationis*, fig. 922) makes very ingenious arrangements for the safety of the chrysalis, by fixing the edges of a leaf together, and constructing suspensory threads.

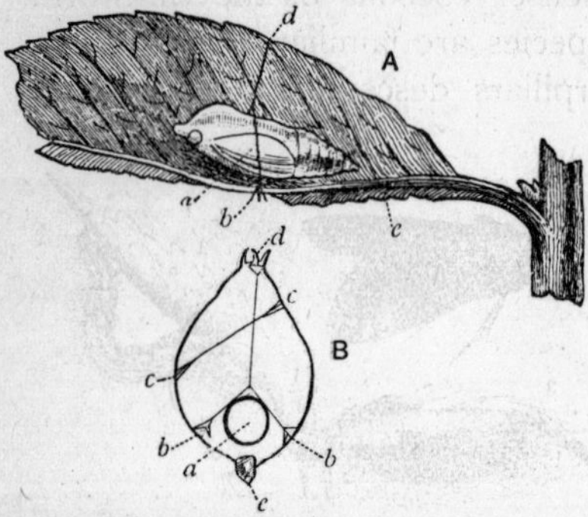

Fig. 922.—Indian Skipper Butterfly (*Badamia exclamationis*)

A, Chrysalis suspended in folded leaf, half of which has been removed. B, Diagrammatic section through same. *a*, Chrysalis; *b*, *b*, *d*, suspensory threads; *c c*, cross-thread holding leaf together; *e*, midrib of leaf.

Two-winged Flies (*Diptera*).—The Flies of this order undergo a more profound metamorphosis than any other insects, and as some of them lay their eggs in all sorts of animal food, most persons unwillingly acquire a certain amount of information on the subject of their life-history. The eggs of Diptera hatch out into limbless maggots, that later on become pupæ, which are either of firm texture, or else soft, and enclosed in a strong coat.

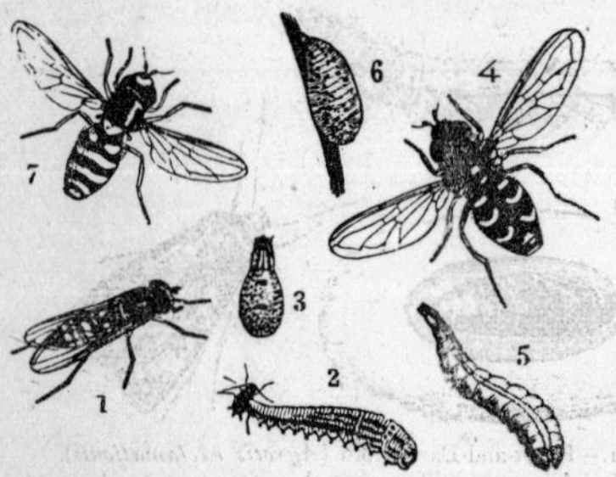

Fig. 923.—Hover-Flies. 1, 2, and 3, Female, larva (sucking an aphis), and pupa of *Syrphus balteata*; 4, 5, and 6, female, larva, and pupa of *S. Pyrastri*; 7, female of *S. ribesii*.

The *Hover-Flies* (species of *Syrphus*, fig. 923) commence independent existence as maggots which play havoc among aphides, sucking the soft contents of their bodies, and rejecting the shrivelled skins. The larvæ of a related insect, the Drone-Fly (*Eristalis tenax*), has been described elsewhere (vol. ii, p. 441) under the name of "rat-tailed maggot". This lives in liquid filth, but the larvæ of many flies are truly aquatic, *e.g.* those of

Gnats (*Culicidæ*). The life-history of one species (*Culex annulatus*) is represented in fig. 924. The female, when about to lay her eggs, holds firmly to some object by means of the first two pairs of legs, the last ones being stretched out at the back and crossed over one another (see figure). In the angle between their upper ends the elongated eggs are successively deposited, sticking together after leaving the body. As their number increases, the legs are gradually uncrossed and at last lie parallel to one another. The mass of eggs now floats away from between them in the form of a canoe-shaped raft. The wriggling larva makes its way

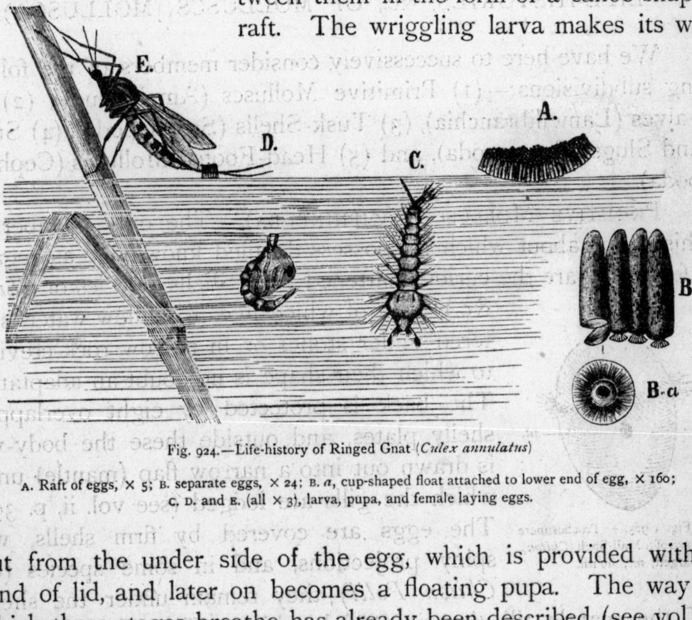

Fig. 924.—Life-history of Ringed Gnat (*Culex annulatus*)

A. Raft of eggs, × 5; B. separate eggs, × 24; B. *a*, cup-shaped float attached to lower end of egg, × 160; C. D. and E. (all × 3), larva, pupa, and female laying eggs.

out from the under side of the egg, which is provided with a kind of lid, and later on becomes a floating pupa. The way in which these stages breathe has already been described (see vol. ii, p. 442). The pupa is able to move when alarmed, on which point Hurst (in *The Pupal Stage of Culex*) makes the following remarks:—"The pupa is sensitive to light, and immediately darts backward when a shadow falls upon it suddenly. The movements, however, though very rapid, are devoid of anything like steering. The larva had to steer in its search for food, but the pupa has simply to get out of the way of danger, and the direction of its flight is of little importance, though, since the movement is always backward with reference to the pupa, it is chiefly downward with reference to the outer world. A sudden very loud noise, or a very gentle tap upon the vessel containing the pupæ, causes those at the surface to dart downwards, but as slight sounds of various kinds produce no effect upon them, I conclude that the tremor of the surface of the water, and not the sound itself, was recognized by them." The last stage in the life-history is reached when the adult gnat makes its way out of the floating pupa, which splits along its back, and the wings are very quickly ready for use: otherwise there would be considerable danger of drowning.

LIFE-HISTORIES, &c., OF MOLLUSCS (MOLLUSCA)

We have here to successively consider members of the following subdivisions:—(1) Primitive Molluscs (Amphineura), (2) Bivalves (Lamellibranchia), (3) Tusk-Shells (Scaphopoda), (4) Snails and Slugs (Gastropoda), and (5) Head-Footed Molluscs (Cephalopoda).

Primitive Molluscs (Amphineura).—The only members of this group about which we possess detailed knowledge as regards life-history are the curious flattened Mail-Shells (species of *Chiton*, &c.), most of which live in shallow water, sheltered under stones or in narrow rock-crevices, to which their shape is no doubt an adaptation. The back is protected by eight overlapping shelly plates, and outside these the body-wall is drawn out into a narrow flap (mantle) under which the gills are lodged (see vol. ii, p. 392). The eggs are covered by firm shells, with spiny projections, and in some species (e.g. *Chiton Polii*) they remain under the shelter of the mantle till the time of hatching. The development is indirect, and the just-hatched young is a ciliated Trochosphere (fig. 925), which resembles in many ways the larva of the same name characteristic of marine Bristle-Worms (see p. 359). Cuttle-fishes and the like excepted, most molluscs begin independent existence in the form of trochospheres, or else as larvæ which may be regarded as derived from these. This fact has been adduced by some zoologists in support of the view that the remote ancestors of Molluscs resembled marine Bristle-Worms in essential respects. If this "Annelid Theory" of molluscan descent be accepted, molluscs are profoundly different from their ancestors,

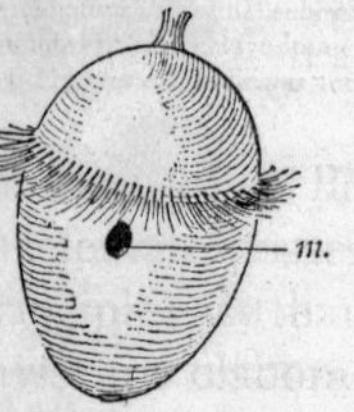

Fig. 925. – Trochosphere Larva of a Mail-Shell (*Chiton*), enlarged; *m.*, mouth.

for they are now unsegmented, and very unlike annelids in most respects. It is impossible to discuss so difficult and technical a problem here, but we should do well to look with suspicion upon the theory in so far as it is based upon the occurrence of a trochosphere larva in both annelids and molluscs. The peculiarities of this kind of larva have arisen as the result of adaptation to a free-swimming life, and they are of so simple a kind that they may quite conceivably have been evolved independently in half a dozen different distinct groups of animals, which have had the same life-problems to solve.

The Mail-Shell larva gradually undergoes a metamorphosis, ultimately losing its ciliated bands, developing shell-plates, foot, &c., and giving up swimming for creeping.

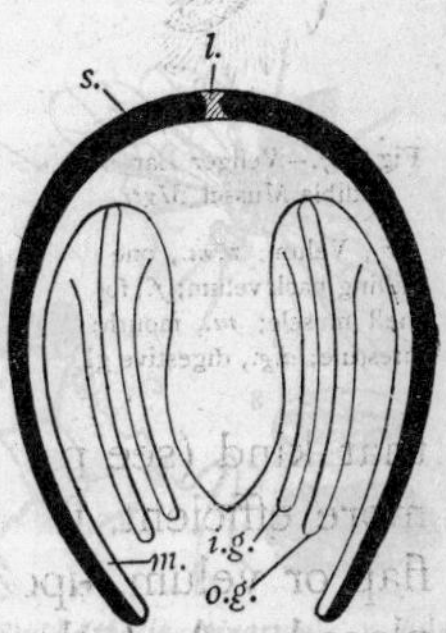

Fig. 926.—Diagrammatic Cross-Section through a Bivalve Mollusc. *l.*, Ligament; *s.*, shell; *m.*, mantle; *i.g.* and *o.g.*, inner and outer gill-plates.

Bivalve Molluscs (Lamellibranchia).—In most of the marine bivalves which have so far been studied the eggs are simply ejected into the surrounding water, and there pass through the stages of their development. This is the case, for example, in the American Oyster (*Ostrea Virginiana*) and the Edible Mussel (*Mytilus edulis*). But in some marine and most freshwater forms the eggs have a better chance of escaping destruction, for they hatch out between the protective shells of the parent. For such an arrangement the structure of a bivalve offers special advantages, as will be gathered from the diagrammatic cross-section represented in fig. 926. Hanging down on either side, and covering the body like the flap of a coat, is a mantle-lobe, the outer side of which bears a shell. The space between body and mantle-lobes is known as the mantle-cavity, and into this two gill-plates project on either side. Each plate consists of two layers, between which is a space divided into a series of tubes by vertical partitions. As a matter of fact, the gills of bivalves vary greatly in different species, and the statement just made applies to forms in which they are large and complex. Here, then, are a number of sheltered spaces within which eggs can be incubated, and a further advantage is secured by the fact that water is constantly streaming through the mantle-cavity and gills, in relation to the breathing and feeding of the adult form (see vol. ii, p. 398). The abundant supply of oxygen which developing eggs require is thus provided for. In the Common Oyster (*Ostrea edulis*) the eggs hatch out in the space between mantle-flaps and gills; in Freshwater Mussels (*Unio* and *Anodon*) the outer gill-plates serve as brood-pouches; while in some other fresh-water forms (*Cyrena* and *Cyclas*) the inner gill-plates discharge this office.

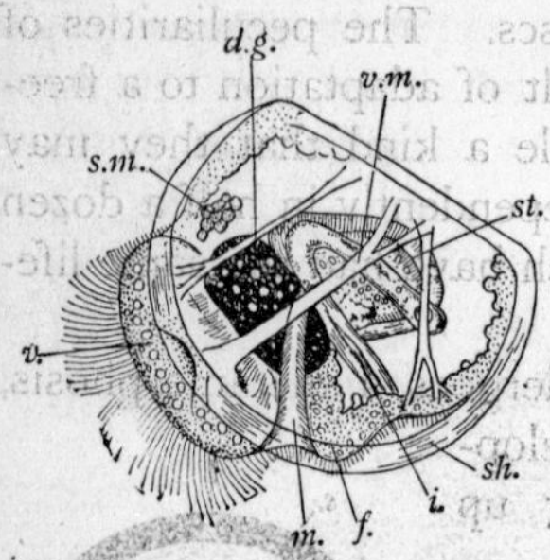

Fig. 927.—Veliger Larva (12 days old) of an Edible Mussel (*Mytilus edulis*), × 240

v., Velum; *v.m.*, one of the muscles for pulling back velum; *f.*, foot; *sh.*, shell; *s. m.*, shell muscle; *m.*, mouth; *st.*, stomach; *i.*, intestine; *d.g.*, digestive gland.

The egg of marine bivalves, and more rarely that of freshwater forms, hatches out into a free-swimming larva, which is usually a Veliger (fig. 927). This may be regarded as a modified Trochosphere, for it possesses the circlets of cilia, thickening of the skin to form a brain, and some of the other features which characterize a larva of that kind (see p. 359). But the swimming arrangements are here more efficient, for the base of the head lobe is drawn out into a flap or velum, upon the edge of which the front circlet of cilia is placed. And the velum can be drawn back by special muscle-bands so as to get a purchase upon the water, thus propelling the larva forwards. Slower movements are executed by means of the cilia alone. The fully developed Veliger is obviously a Mollusc, for it has grown a foot and secreted a shell.

Fig. 928.—Glochidium of Freshwater Mussel (*Anodonta*), enlarged. M, Shell-muscle; S, special sense-organs; Sh., shell; F, byssus thread (cut short).

An unusual and aberrant life-history characterizes most of the Freshwater Mussels (species of *Unio* and *Anodon*). The eggs hatch out in the outer gill-plates as an extraordinary larva known as a Glochidium (fig. 928), the name having been given at a time when it was thought to be an independent species. It possesses a pair of triangular shells with strongly hooked tips, a long trailing sticky thread (byssus), and several peculiar pointed projections believed to be special sense-organs. There is some difference of opinion as to what happens when the Glochidia are ejected from the gills of the parent. It is generally stated that they swim about actively by flapping their shells, but according to some highly competent observers masses of them remain passive on the surface of the mud with their long byssus threads waving about in the water. It will probably be found that their behaviour varies in different species. In any case the Glochidium's chance of further development entirely depends upon whether its sticky thread happens to touch the skin or gills of a fish. If this piece of good fortune should come about, it attaches itself firmly to the fish by means of the hooks on the shell. The irritation thus set up causes the skin or gill to grow out into a little capsule or cyst enclosing the Glochidium, and within this shelter development is continued. After a time, varying from a few weeks to several months, the form of the adult is fully acquired, and the little mussel falls out of the cyst into the mud. While attached to the fish it is provided not merely with shelter, but also with food, for it absorbs the juices of its unfortunate host. In Anodonta the hooks on the shell of the Glochidium are very well developed, and in this case the skin of the fish is attacked. But in Unio the hooks are much weaker, and fix themselves to the softer gills (fig. 929). The remarkable life-history just outlined is evidently an adaptation to freshwater conditions, for it prevents the delicate larvæ from being swept down to the sea, where they would perish, and is also important as regards distribution of the species. Some freshwater bivalves, such as Cyclas and Pisidium, gain the former end by suppressing the larval stage altogether, developing directly into the adult form by a series of gradual changes.

Fig. 929. — Glochidia of Freshwater Mussel (*Unio*), encysted on gills of Perch, enlarged

Dwellings of Bivalve Molluscs.—Most of these creatures live in mud or sand, through which they slowly plough their way; but some dwell in holes or crevices, others bore in various hard substances, and others again attach themselves to stones, &c., or construct a home from foreign bodies.

Attachment to firm objects is often effected by means of silky threads making up what is known as a *byssus*, springing from the back of the foot near its base. A well-known example is afforded by the Edible Mussel (*Mytilus edulis*, fig. 930), of which great numbers may often be seen adhering by their black threads to rocks or piles near low-water mark. But this animal is not necessarily doomed to spend the whole of its adult life glued to the same spot, for it is able to cast off the mooring-threads and creep away by means of its foot, which, however, is much smaller than in forms which lead a comparatively active life. Another well-known bivalve (*Tridacna*), which often attains a great size, also possesses a byssus and a small foot, and is common in the fissures of coral reefs with its under side facing upwards. The two openings, by means of which currents of water respectively enter and leave the mantle-cavity, are conveniently placed about the middle of the upturned margin, instead of being situated at the back end, as is usually the case. Some of the File-Shells (species of *Lima*) construct a sort of nest for themselves by fixing bits of stone and other foreign objects together with byssal threads. The curious Saddle-Oysters, of which one small species (*Anomia ephippium*) is common on our shores, settle down on their right sides when they leave the larval state, and become very unsymmetrical, as is usually the case when the two sides of the body are permanently exposed to conditions of different kind. The lower or right valve is here flat, and the upper or left one strongly curved. The flat valve is very closely applied to the underlying surface, to which it is firmly fixed by a hard conical plug that runs from the body of the mollusc through a hole in the shell, and is no other than the calcified byssus. As might be expected, the foot is very small, and its chief use is to act as a byssus-

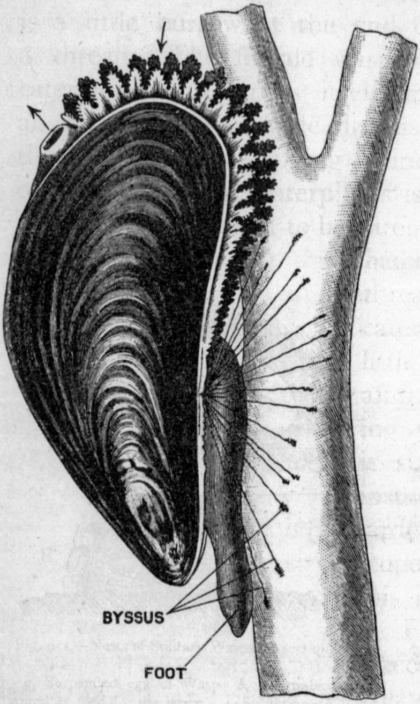

Fig. 930.—Edible Mussel (*Mytilus edulis*). The arrows indicate currents of water entering and leaving the mantle-cavity.

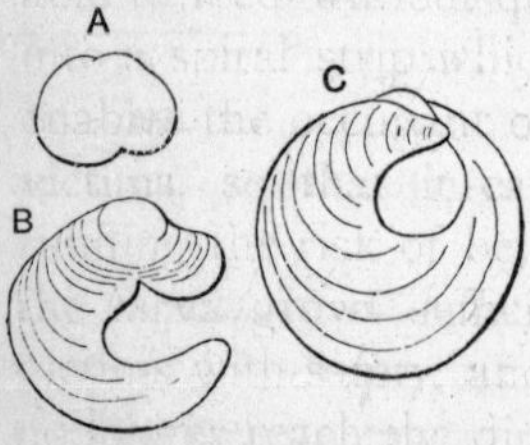

Fig. 931.—Shells of Saddle-Oyster (*Anomia*). A, B, and C, Successive stages of growth.

carrier. The perforation of the shell is at first a notch, as will be seen by reference to fig. 931.

The Scallops (species of *Pecten*) afford another example of bivalves with a very small foot, useless for locomotor purposes. Some of the species swim by opening and shutting their shells, while others are attached by means of a byssus, and rest on their right sides. As in Saddle-Oysters, there is well-marked asymmetry in such cases, but here, as usually, the valve which is kept below is strongly curved, while the other one is flat and forms a kind of lid as it were. This is an obviously advantageous arrangement, for the opening and closing of the shell are effected more easily than if the upwardly facing valve were convex and comparatively heavy, as, curiously enough, it is in the Saddle-Oysters. Another character which generally distinguishes bivalves that are permanently fixed on one side is the rounded or irregular shape of the shell, which loses the elongated form seen in so many active species.

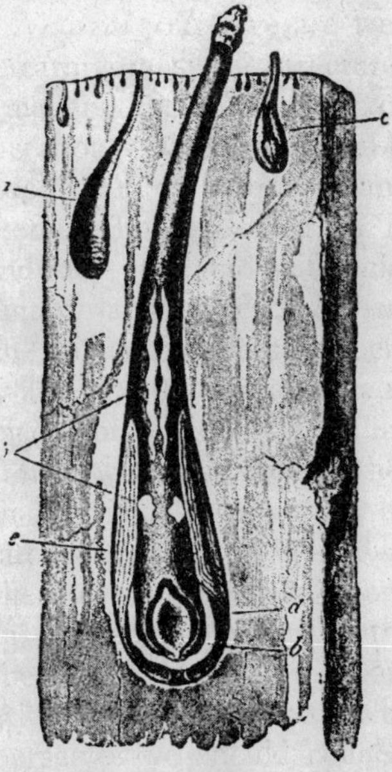

Fig. 932.—Piddocks (*Pholas*). *a*, Burrow of young individual; *b*, *b*, phosphorescent areas; *c*, young piddock; *d*, foot; *e*, shell.

The Thorny Oysters (*Spondylus*) are closely related to the Scallops, but all of them are fixed to firm objects by the substance of the right valve, which is relatively very large and thick. The foot is much reduced, and there is no byssus.

The Oysters (species of *Ostrea*) are the most familiar examples of fixed bivalves, and are attached by the substance of the *left* valve. Not only is there no byssus, but the useless foot has entirely disappeared, as an adaptation to the sedentary habit.

Those bivalves which bore into hard substances present a number of very interesting characters related to their mode of life. Some account has elsewhere been given (p. 221) of the habits of the Piddocks (*Pholas*, fig. 932) in this connection, but some interesting facts regarding them may be added or repeated here. There can be little doubt that burrowing is effected by means of the shell, the front part of which is raised into a system of intersecting ridges with sharp projections. These are brought into action by twisting movements on the long axis, during which the flat surface of the cylindrical foot holds on to the end of the burrow. Chemical action is excluded by the fact that piddocks are able to bore into hard siliceous rocks as well as into those of calcareous nature. In spite of its use for boring purposes the shell is quite thin, probably because it has not the same value for protective purposes as in non-burrowing forms. The later part of the life-history of a form (*Pholadidea*) closely related to the Piddock is of very great interest. To begin with, it bores into rock after the fashion of its relative, but when full grown loses its foot, closes up the front end of the shell, and remains stationary for the rest of its life. The hinder end of the shell is produced into a sort of hollow cylinder, directed towards the opening of the burrow, and enclosing the two tubes (siphons), through one of which currents bearing food and oxygen continually flow, while the other gives exit to return currents that carry off the various products of waste, and also enable the eggs to make their way to the exterior. Another form (*Jouannetia*), allied to the foregoing, bores into a block of coral, excavating a spherical cavity exactly corresponding to the shape of its body. When adult, the front of the shell is closed up, and the foot lost as in the form last mentioned. If the shell were perfectly round it is clear that there would be a danger of the animal slipping round so that the openings of the siphons were directed away from the exterior, the result of which would be fatal, as there would be no possibility of

Fig. 933.—Ship-Worms (*Teredo navalis*). A Bristle-Worm has appropriated an empty burrow on the left.

moving back to the proper position. Such slipping, however, is impossible, for there is a tongue-shaped projection from the back of the right valve which fits into the opening of the burrow and serves as a holdfast.

The notorious Ship-Worm (*Teredo navalis*, fig. 933), which in the days of entirely wooden vessels played such havoc with their timbers, belongs to a family which is closely related to that including the Piddocks and their allies. The body is not rounded like that of the last-mentioned bivalve, but resembles a long slender cylinder. The shell is of relatively very small size and placed at the front end of the body, while the two siphons project at the other. The burrow has a smooth calcareous lining, formed by the hardening of a fluid which is exuded from the skin. If in the course of its boring operations this mollusc reaches the outside of the wood it closes the opening with a shelly plate.

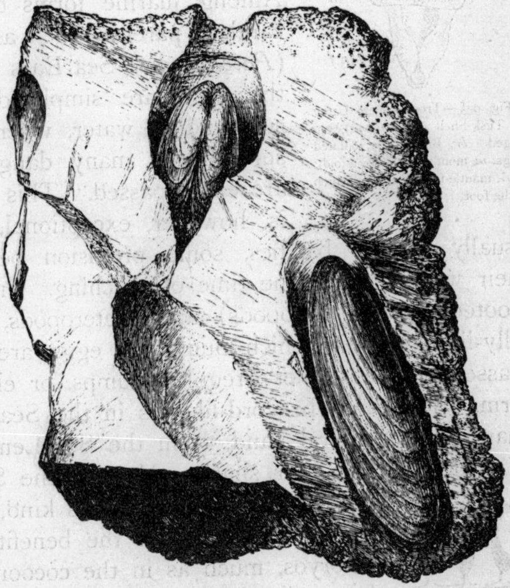

Fig. 934.—Date-Shells (*Lithodomus*)

The Date-Shells (*Lithodomus*, fig. 934) are relatives of the Edible Mussel that burrow only in limestone rocks. In this case the work is supposed to be chiefly done by an acid fluid, which acts as a solvent. The shell is covered by a tough horny layer, and is thus protected from the corrosive action to which its calcareous substance would otherwise be exposed.

Tusk-Shells (Scaphopoda).—These are burrowing forms with a curved conical shell open at both ends. As to their life-history, it need only be said that the eggs are discharged freely into the water, where they hatch out into trochospheres, which resemble the larvæ of marine annelids in some respects (fig. 935).

SNAILS AND SLUGS (GASTROPODA).—It will be convenient to consider in succession marine, freshwater, and terrestrial members of this group, afterwards adding some remarks on Gastropod Dwellings.

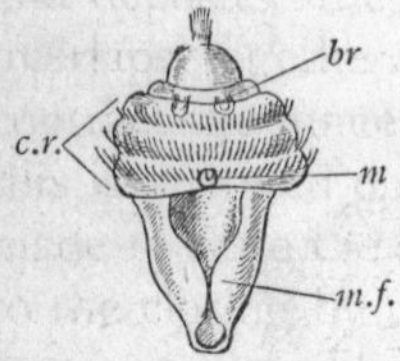

Fig. 935.—Trochosphere Larva of Tusk-Shell (*Dentalium*), enlarged. *br*, Brain; *c.r.*, ciliated rings; *m*, mouth (hidden by a fold); *m.f.*, mantle-folds, between which is the foot.

Egg-laying and Protection of Eggs.—Among marine forms there are some very careless parents, such as Common Limpets (*Patella*) and Sea-Ears (*Haliotis*), in which the eggs are simply discharged into the surrounding water, where but few of them survive the many dangers by which they are encompassed. This casual arrangement is, however, exceptional, and the eggs are usually laid in batches, some provision being also made for their welfare up to the time of hatching. In Sea-Slugs, Wing-Footed Snails (Pteropods), and Heteropods, the "spawn" is a jelly-like mass in which numerous eggs are imbedded. Such masses may be either irregular clumps, or else of more definite form. They may be cord-like, as in the Sea-Hare (*Aplysia*), or shaped like a spiral band, as in the Sea-Lemon (*Doris*), or else of some other regular shape. Most of the Sea-Snails lay their eggs in capsules of various kind, which also contain a nutritious fluid for the benefit of the developing embryos, much as in the cocoons of Earth-Worms (see p. 360). Among the common objects of our shores are the little stalked egg-capsules of the Purple-Shell (*Purpura lapillus*, fig. 936), of which a large number may be produced by the same individual. Each of them contains from 400 to 600 eggs, of which, however, only from 10 to 16 attain full development, while the rest are used as food by their successful brethren. More striking objects are the egg-capsules of the Common Whelk (*Buccinum undatum*, fig. 937), of which from 150 to 170 are aggregated together into a rounded mass. Each capsule contains from 5 to 30 eggs, of which only a small number hatch out. In certain other species, *e.g.* the Dog-Whelk (*Nassa*), all the eggs complete their development. Curious spirally-rolled bands, which are not infrequently cast up on the shore, are the

Fig. 936.—Egg-capsules of Purple-Shell (*Purpura lapillus*), × 2.

spawn of species of Natica (fig. 938), which are originally fixed by one edge, but have been torn from their attachment. They contain a very large number of eggs, imbedded in a hardened secretion, together with innumerable sand-grains, to which the brown colour is due.

The Violet-Snail (*Ianthina*), which swims freely through the

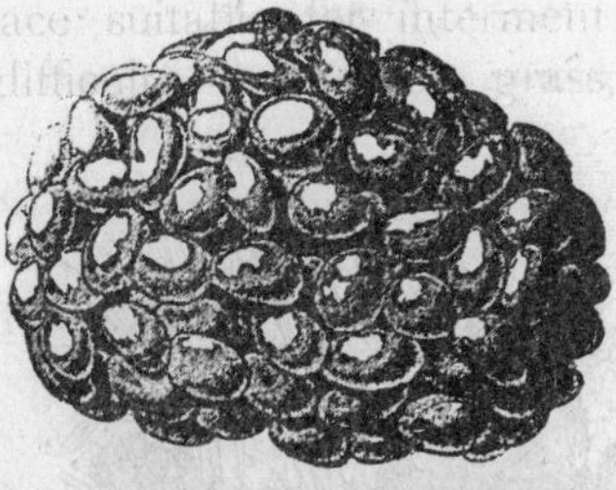

Fig. 937.—Spawn of Whelk (*Buccinum undatum*), × ½

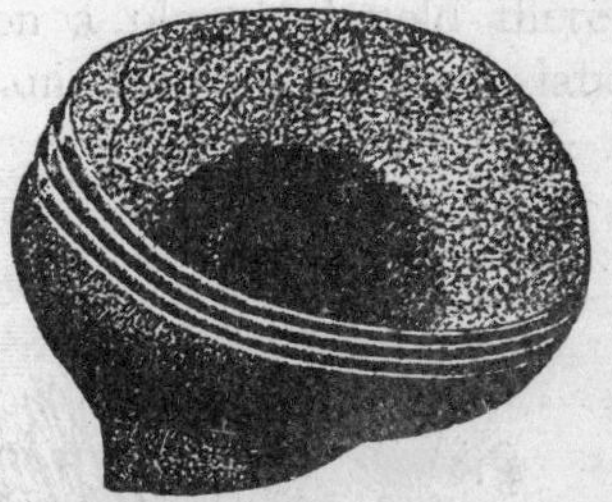

Fig. 938.—Spawn of Natica

water on its back, constructs a raft of hardened slime with enclosed air-bubbles (fig. 939), to the under side of which the egg-capsules are attached. The slime is derived from a gland imbedded in the foot, the front part of which during the construction of the raft is alternately raised above the surface and depressed below it, bringing down an air-bubble each time.

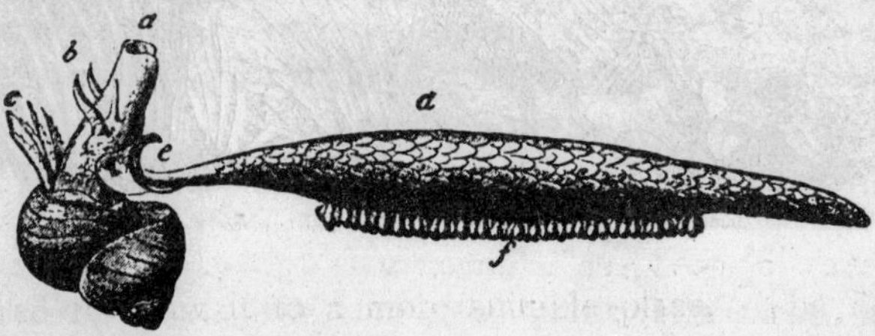

Fig. 939.—Violet-Snail (*Ianthina*) and Raft. *a*, Snout; *b*, tentacles; *c*, gills; *d*, raft; *e*, foot; *f*, eggs.

This snail drifts about for long distances, attached to its floating nursery.

Some of the Bonnet-Limpets (species of *Crepidula*), with a conical shell twisted into a little spiral at the top, appear to remain stationary, holding on to the underlying rock by means of the foot. The egg-capsules are deposited in the space sheltered by the edge of the shell, and possess very thin walls, in relation to their protected situation. In the Worm-Snails (*Vermetus*) the egg-capsules are deposited within the mouth of the shell, which is a loosely wound spiral tube with only the first few turns in contact.

Among air-breathing Freshwater Snails the spawn is usually gelatinous, common examples being afforded by the Pond-Snails (*Limnæa*), where the mass is elongated and sausage-shaped, and the Trumpet-Snails (*Planorbis*), in which it is oval. These collections of eggs are attached to water-plants, or, in captive specimens, are often fixed to the glass walls of the aquarium. A somewhat exceptional case is presented by our common River-Snail (*Paludina vivipara*), in which the eggs are not laid, but develop internally, and the young snails when they first enter the world resemble the adult except in size.

Of terrestrial forms many of the Land-Slugs (*e.g.* species of *Limax*) deposit gelatinous masses of spawn, in which numerous eggs are imbedded. Land-Snails lay a varying number of eggs, each enclosed in a more or less firm calcareous shell. The common Garden-Snail (*Helix aspersa*) digs a little hole in the earth, deposits from 40 to 100 eggs in this, and then covers them over with soil. Some of the large South American Land-Snails (species of *Bulimus*) lay very large eggs, which superficially resemble those of a pigeon, but have a widely different structure, for the included egg-cell is minute, most of the space within the shell being filled with a nutritive fluid. These eggs are deposited singly, and in the case of the arboreal species each of them is enclosed in a rolled-up leaf.

Gastropod Larvæ.—As in bivalves, the eggs of marine forms usually hatch out as free-swimming larvæ, which may be either trochospheres or veligers. These vary greatly in appearance, as may be gathered from fig. 940, in which a few typical forms are represented. Development is direct in freshwater and terrestrial species, there being no free-swimming larva, though a stage corresponding to it may be passed through before hatching takes place, proving that development was indirect in ancestral forms, and that the existing state of things is an adaptation to changed surroundings. In Onchidium, for example, a curious slug which lives on the upper part of the shore in various parts of the world, a typical veliger is developed within the egg (fig. 940), but this is gradually modified into the adult shape before the time of hatching.

Gastropod Dwellings.—Permanent homes constructed by the

animal itself are exceptional in this group, those forms with a large shell usually finding this a sufficient protection. Many of the creeping marine species shelter in rock-crevices, and others burrow (see p. 217). Some land-snails (species of *Helix*) excavate holes in limestone rocks, and the carnivorous slug *Testacella*, which pursues earth-worms underground, escapes many dangers by its mode of life. Many of the soft-bodied sea-slugs possess

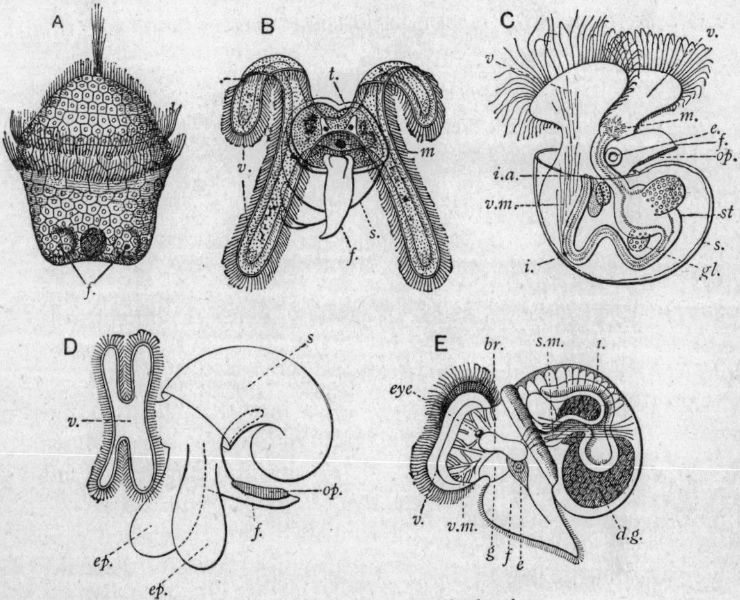

Fig. 940.—Gastropod Larvæ, much enlarged

A, Trochosphere of Limpet (*Patella*). B–E, Veligers of a Fore-gilled Snail, a Hind-gilled Snail, a Wing-footed Snail, and a Pulmonate (*Onchidium*). *br.*, Brain; *d.g.*, digestive gland; *e.*, ear (otocyst); *ep.*, epipodium; *f.*, foot; *g.*, gullet; *gl.*, gland; *i.*, intestine; *i.a.*, intestinal aperture; *m.*, mouth; *op.*, operculum; *s.*, shell; *s.m.*, shell-muscle; *st.*, stomach; *t.*, tentacle; *v.*, velum; *v.m.*, muscles of velum.

disagreeable properties, which are advertised by warning colours, and some marine gastropods resemble their surroundings so closely as to be inconspicuous (see vol. ii, pp. 306 and 285). These devices largely obviate the necessity for dwellings, while egg-capsules and the like play the part of nurseries.

The typical shape of a Gastropod shell is spiral, and it is commonly large enough to serve as an efficient refuge, the animal completely withdrawing into it, and often possessing a horny or limy plate (*operculum*) which serves as a door to close the weak place in the defences. But quite a number of sea-snails, and a few freshwater ones, have evolved a different type of shell, correlated with a creeping life on rocks, &c., in pursuit of vegetable food, and sometimes associated with a permanent home. This is the case with all those forms known as "limpets", in which the shell is cap-shaped or conical, sometimes with a small spiral at its tip. There can be no doubt that the ancestors of such species possessed the usual spiral shell, which may indeed be present in early life, recapitulating the former state of things.

Fig. 941.—Purple-Shell (*Purpura lapillus*)

The limpet-shaped shell is correlated with the presence of an unusually large oval foot, and when danger threatens this holds on to the underlying surface with great tenacity, and the shell is pulled down over the body. The two methods of defence just indicated may be seen side by side on 'tween-tide rocks. The Purple-Shell (*Purpura lapillus*, fig. 941) possesses an unusually thick shell and a strong operculum. When withdrawn into its dwelling it can defy most enemies, and stand a good deal of knocking about by the waves. The Common Limpet (*Patella vulgata*, fig. 942), on the other hand, unless it happens to be crawling over a very rough surface, is extremely difficult to detach unless taken unawares. The possession of a smooth place as a permanent residence is here so important that the animal returns to the same spot after every feeding excursion, and in course of time excavates an oval "scar" by means of the edge of the shell and the action of the foot. As these scars are formed in hard siliceous rocks as well as in calcareous ones, corrosion by an acid secretion plays no part in the matter, as has been suggested by some observers. The conical shape of the shell is calculated to resist the wash of the tide and waves, to which it offers but little purchase. It must not be supposed that all Gastropods with a limpet-shaped shell are of necessity

Fig. 942.—Limpet (*Patella vulgata*) leaving its Scar at Low Tide

closely related. The same arrangements would appear to have been independently evolved in several different groups, as the result of adaptation to similar conditions.

There is one brackish-water snail (*Potamides*) that lives in estuaries, and is reminiscent of those bivalves which attach themselves by means of a byssus (see p. 407). For it spins a number of strong threads, which serve to hold it firmly to the roots of mangrove-trees.

Head-Footed Molluscs (Cephalopoda).—The eggs are here comparatively large and contain a good deal of food-yolk. Those of Squids (*Loligo*, fig. 943) are enclosed in gelatinous tubes, of which a considerable number are associated, and radiate from a stone or other firm body to which they are attached. Each individual egg is surrounded by a firm investment. In the Common Cuttle-Fish (*Sepia*, fig. 944) each egg is enclosed in a firm spindle-shaped capsule about the size of a hazel-nut, and a number of these are fixed to sea-weeds or stones, looking something like a bunch of grapes.

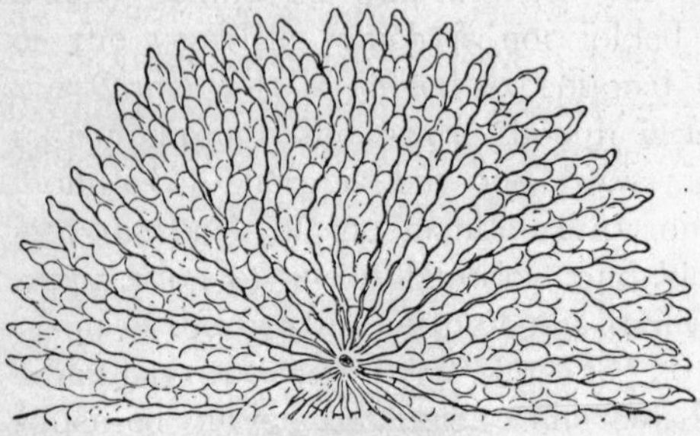

Fig. 943.—Spawn of Squid (*Loligo*), × ½

Among eight-armed forms (Octopods) a common British species (*Eledone moschata*) deposits small groups of egg-capsules, which are attached to various firm substances. The Poulpes (*Octopus*) lay their eggs in ovoid capsules, of which a large number are united by their stalks into a long necklace-like string. This is fixed to a rock, and the mother broods over it, hastening the development of the eggs by ejecting streams of water. The beautiful shell of the female Paper Nautilus (*Argonauta*) serves as a nursery, for to its inner side she attaches her grape-like mass of egg-capsules.

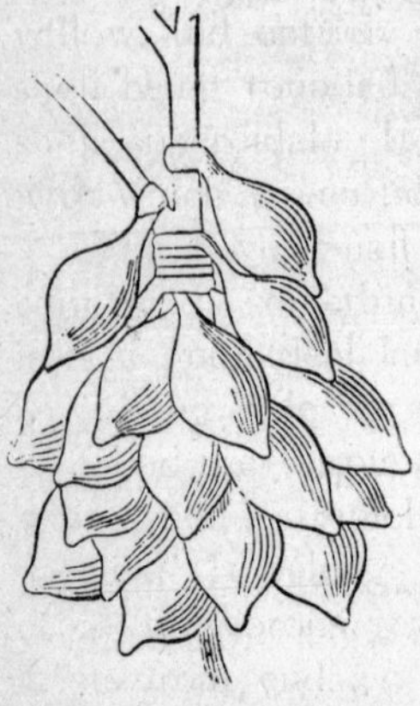

Fig. 944.—Egg-Capsules of Cuttle Fish (*Sepia*)

The eggs of one species of Pearly Nautilus (*Nautilus macromphalus*), according to the recent observations of Willey in the sea adjoining New Caledonia, are deposited singly during the night, being fixed by a spongy substance to some suitable surface. Each of them is enclosed in a double capsule, of gristly consistency. The inner layer of this forms a regular oval case, but the outer layer is very irregular.

So far as known development is always direct in Cephalopods, the egg containing sufficient yolk to obviate the necessity of premature hatching as a larval form.

Few members of the group can be said to possess dwellings, but creatures of the Octopus kind, which have to some extent given up swimming for creeping (see p. 109), lurk in caves and holes in the rock. Most readers will recollect the somewhat melodramatic account given by Victor Hugo (in *The Toilers of the Sea*) of an encounter with a gigantic animal of the sort.

LIFE-HISTORIES, &c., OF NEMERTINE WORMS (NEMERTEA)

The unsegmented ciliated worms included in this group are usually of rounded shape, and the vast majority of them are marine, though some few live in fresh water or on the land. Their structure has elsewhere been described (see vol. i, p. 305). Some Nemertines are quite small, but others may be many yards in length.

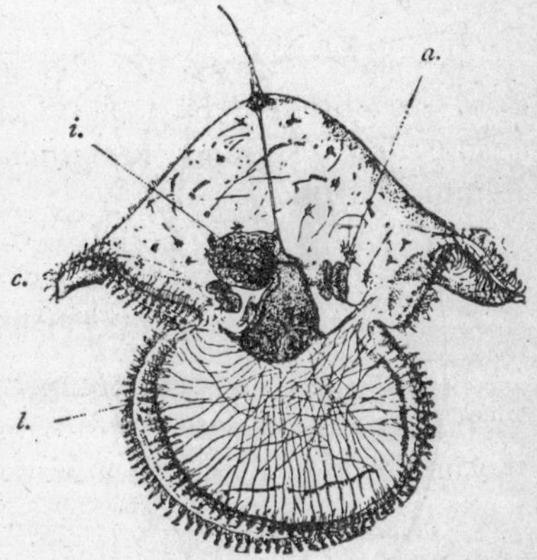

Fig. 945.—Pilidium Larva from the right side, enlarged. *c.*, Ciliated band; *d.*, two of the four disc-like ingrowths to form the young worm (the other two are seen to the left); *i.*, intestine; *l.*, side-lappet.

The marine forms are for the most part oviparous, and lay their eggs either singly or in clumps, surrounded by a gelatinous substance, much as in some of the molluscs. Development may be either direct or indirect, and in the latter case the larva which issues from the egg is often of the kind known as a Pilidium (fig. 945), which resembles an antique helmet in shape, and is like a trochosphere in some respects. The adult worm comes into existence by the ingrowth of four depressions of the skin, which surround the digestive tube. The remaining organs are gradually formed, and the metamorphosis is completed by the larval skin being thrown off. A few Nemertines are viviparous, the eggs developing internally, and in this case there is no larval stage.

The majority of marine forms live in shallow water among corals or sea-weeds, round which they twine their bodies. Many may be found under stones near low-water mark. A few species live in tubes, formed by the hardening of a fluid which exudes from the skin into a membranous or gelatinous substance. Others appropriate the empty shells of molluscs as dwellings, and some kinds excavate burrows for the same purpose.

CHAPTER LVI

LIFE-HISTORIES, CARE OF EGGS AND YOUNG, AND DWELLINGS, IN BACKBONED ANIMALS (VERTEBRATA)

We have here to consider in succession the classes of Primitive Vertebrates (Protochordata), Fishes (Pisces), Amphibians (Amphibia), Reptiles (Reptilia), Birds (Aves), and Mammals (Mammalia).

LIFE-HISTORIES, &c., OF PRIMITIVE VERTEBRATES (PROTOCHORDATA)

WORM-LIKE PROTOCHORDATES (HEMICHORDA).—The widely distributed species of Acorn-headed Worms (*Balanoglossus*) are marine forms which burrow in sand or mud. A viscid fluid exudes from the skin and glues the surrounding deposits into a sort of indefinite tube, which, however, is not of a permanent nature. Development is indirect, and two sorts of larva are known (fig. 946). The simpler of the two is somewhat egg-shaped, and covered with short cilia, there also being a circlet of longer ones near the hinder end. This larva gradually passes into the adult form without any striking metamorphosis. It first of all increases in length, and becomes divided by transverse furrows into three sections, which are destined to grow into the proboscis, collar, and trunk, of the mature form (see vol. i, p. 300). The gill-slits and other characteristic organs soon begin to make their appearance.

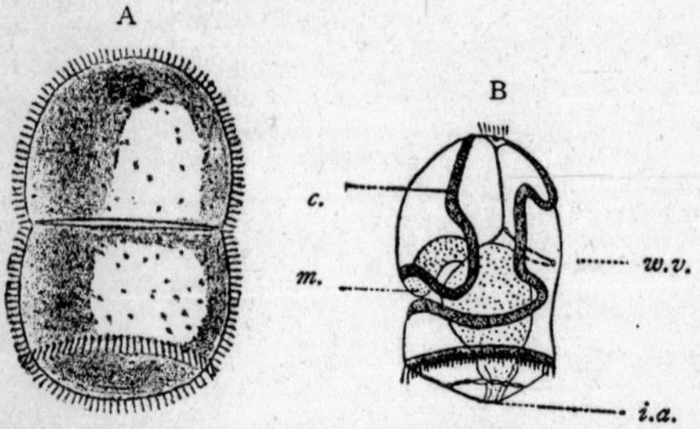

Fig. 946.—Larvæ of Acorn-headed Worms (*Balanoglossus*), enlarged. A, Simple form of larva. B, Tornaria; *c.*, anterior ciliated band; *m.*, mouth; *i.a.*, intestinal aperture; *w.v.*, water-vascular sac.

The second type of larva, characteristic of certain species, is known as a Tornaria (fig. 946). It resembles a trochosphere in some respects, while in others it approximates to the larvæ of star-fishes, and was originally believed to be a young Echinoderm. The uniform covering of short cilia and a posterior ciliary circlet, often found in the first-named type, are also present here, but there is in addition a complicated band of similar nature which passes round the mouth, and takes the course shown in the figure. It is comparable to the band of larval Echinoderms (pp. 355 and 357).

The large group of SEA-SQUIRTS, ASCIDIANS, or TUNICATES (UROCHORDA) presents a great variety of life-histories which are of special interest, because they illustrate quite a number of general principles. We may take as a first example a simple fixed Tunicate (*Ascidia*), of which the structure has already been briefly described (see vol. i, p. 297). The egg hatches out into a tadpole-shaped larva (fig. 947), which possesses the three characters which distinguish vertebrate animals from others. For it has (1) gill-slits, (2) a tubular central nervous system placed near the upper surface of the body, (3) an elastic rod, the notochord (the "forerunner of a backbone"), lying immediately below the nervous system, though in this particular instance limited to the tail-region. After leading a free-swimming life for some time the larva fixes itself by three sticky knobs on its head, and becomes an adult by a series of radical changes in its organization. The tail, with its notochord, shrivels up—the nervous system becomes reduced to a small solid mass or ganglion—and the gill-slits become so numerous as to convert the pharynx into a sort of ciliated basket, by which currents are set up which enable the animal to feed and breathe. A firm protective covering (test) is formed on the surface of the body, and the shape comes to resemble that of a skin flask with two openings, into one of which water streams, afterwards flowing out again through the other. The adult is therefore of lower grade than the larva, and only exemplifies one of the three crucial vertebrate characters, *i.e.* the

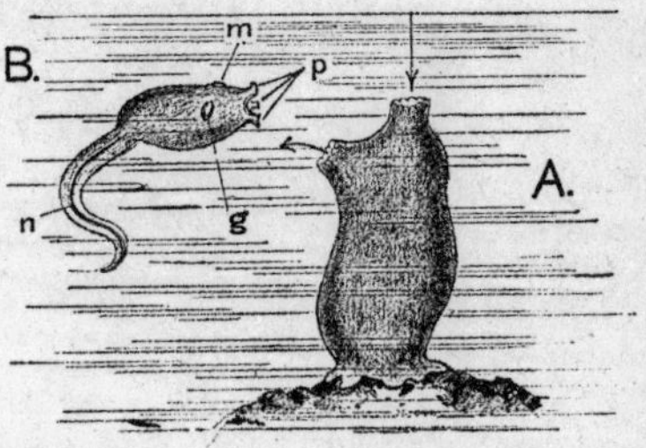

Fig. 947.—Adult (A.) and Tadpole Larva (B.) of Simple Ascidian (A. reduced and B. enlarged). g, Gill-slit; m, mouth; n, notochord; p, adhesive papillæ.

possession of gill-slits. This is a clear case of Degeneration, and is correlated with the fixed habit of life.

Many of the fixed Tunicates are colonial, as the result of a process of budding, though they also produce eggs from which individuals are developed that found fresh colonies. Vegetative propagation is unknown among vertebrates, except in this lowly group, and in certain relatives of the Acorn-headed Worms.

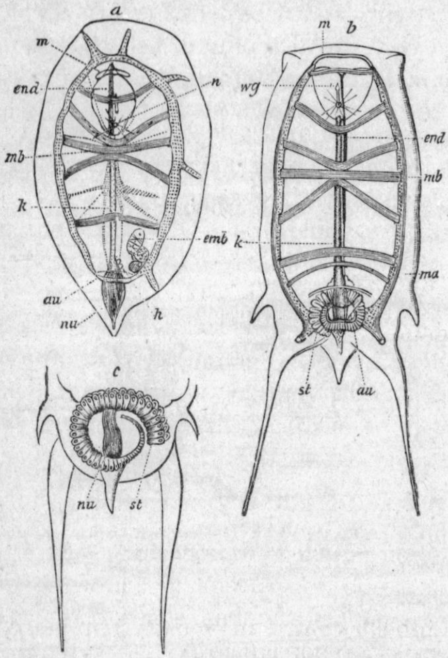

Fig. 948.—A Salp (upper side), enlarged

a, Egg-producing stage; *b*, budding stage; *c*, hinder end of *b* (further enlarged); *au*, atrial opening at hinder end out of which water streams; *end*, endostyle (a groove on floor of pharynx); *emb*, embryo of budding-stage; *h*, heart; *k*, gill; *m*, mouth; *ma*, protective covering; *mb*, muscle-band; *n*, central nervous system; *nu*, stomach and intestine; *st*, chain of egg-producing individuals (budding from *b*); *wg*, sense-organ.

The floating population of the sea includes a number of transparent Tunicates. Among these are the Salps, which illustrate the kind of alternation of generations (metagenesis) elsewhere described for the hydroid zoophytes (see p. 349). In these creatures there are two stages in the life-cycle—(1) an egg-producing stage, and (2) a budding stage (fig. 948). The latter is known as a Solitary Salp, from the hinder end of which a long string of egg-producing forms grows out, these being called Chain Salps, because they are at first united together. Later on the chains break up, and the eggs of each individual develop into the solitary stage.

LIFE-HISTORIES, &c., OF FISHES (PISCES)

Under this heading will be considered some of the more interesting facts regarding Round-Mouths (Cyclostomata), Sharks and Rays (Elasmobranchii), and Ordinary Bony Fishes (Teleostei).

Round-Mouths (Cyclostomata).—The only member of this group of which the life-histories and habits have been carefully studied are the Lampreys (species of *Petromyzon*), of which some are marine, others live in fresh water, while others again spend part of their adult existence in the sea and part in rivers. And even the marine forms enter fresh water for the purpose of spawning. We have three native species, the large Sea-Lamprey (*Petromyzon marinus*), the much smaller River-Lamprey or Lampern (*P. fluviatilis*), and the diminutive Small Lamprey (*P. Planeri*). In all of them the eggs are deposited in a sort of trench which is dug out for their reception, and hatch out in the form of a larva which differs so much from the adult that it was formerly believed to be a distinct species, and received the name of Ammocoetes (fig. 949), by which it is still known. The larva is blind and toothless, and is said to swallow mud for the sake of the contained organic matter. After several years of larval existence, during which it undergoes a gradual series of changes, it assumes the adult form, and the development of horny "teeth" enables it to adopt a carnivorous habit. The eyes, which are at first useless and covered by the skin, come to the surface, and other changes in the internal structure also take place.

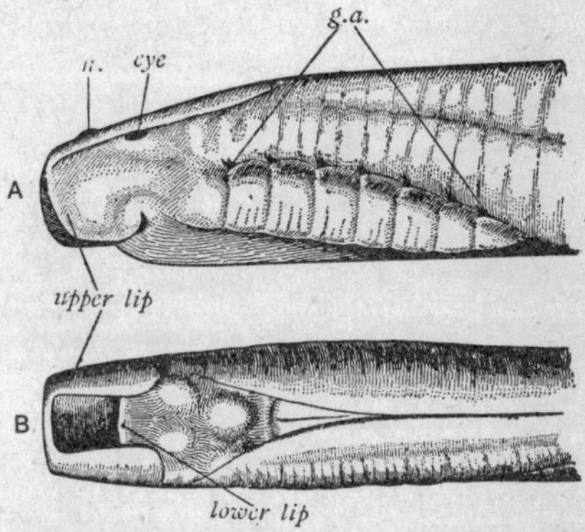

Fig. 949.—Front end of Ammocoetes from Left Side (A) and from below (B), enlarged. *n.*, nostril; *g.a.* (B), gill apertures.

In the case of the Sea-Lamprey and the Lampern, when larval life is over there is a migration to the sea, and there is no return to fresh water except for spawning purposes. It is said that the Lampern usually dies after laying its eggs. Regarding the habits of the Small Lamprey there is considerable divergence of opinion. Some observers believe that its entire life is spent in its native brook or river, while others assert that it migrates to the sea like the other two species. There can be little doubt that it dies after spawning, being thus reminiscent of what takes place in many Insects, where the greater part of life is spent in the larval state.

Sharks and Rays (Elasmobranchii).—Some few members of the order are viviparous, but, as a rule, the eggs are laid in horny cases (fig. 950), within the shelter of which development takes

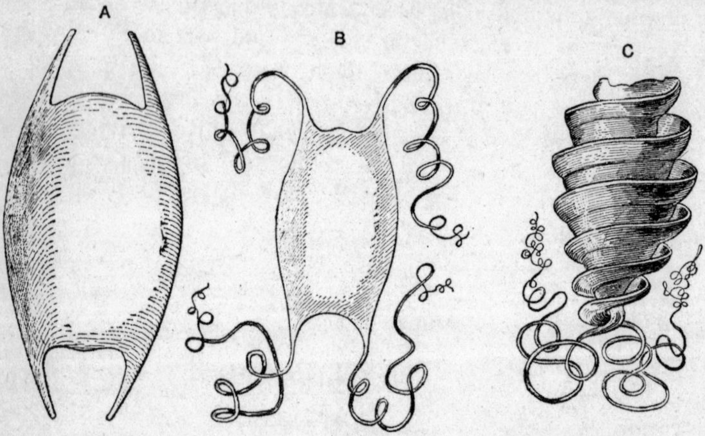

Fig. 950.—Egg-capsules of Skate (A), Spotted Dog-Fish (B), and Port Jackson Shark (C). C reduced.

place, and from which the young fishes ultimately emerge in a form closely resembling that of the adult. There is here no necessity for the early hatching of a larval form, since the egg is large, and contains abundant food-yolk. The egg-cases vary in shape in different species, and are popularly known as "mermaids' purses". Those of the Common Skate (*Raia batis*) are flat and squarish, with the corners drawn out into pointed processes, while in the Spotted Dogfish (*Scyllium canicula*) they are somewhat narrower and provided with four tendril-like threads, by means of which they are attached to sea-weeds. An external spiral fold and two tendrils are present in the case of the Port Jackson Shark (*Cestracion Philippi*).

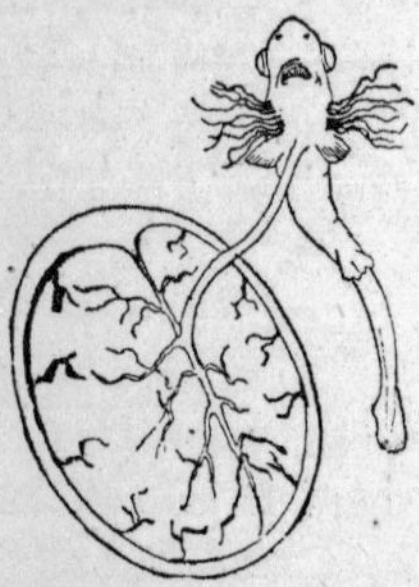

Fig. 951.—Advanced Embryo of Dog-Fish removed from the Egg-capsule. Note the large yolk-sac (with branching blood-vessels) to left. The embryo is provided with long external gills.

The abundant yolk makes up the greater part of the egg, and cleavage is consequently partial (see p. 346), the body of the embryo being developed from a small patch of living substance placed at one end. If the egg-case is cut open after development has gone on for some time the immature fish will be found within, and attached to its under surface will be seen a sort of bag (yolk sac) in which the yolk is contained, serving as a supply of food until hatching takes place (fig. 951).

Ordinary Bony Fishes (Teleostei).—A few members of this order are viviparous, but the large majority lay eggs, which are of much smaller size than those of Sharks and Rays, varying from $\frac{1}{25}$ to $\frac{2}{5}$ of an inch in diameter. They are produced in correspondingly large numbers, this fecundity being an important means of protecting the species, since but a very small percentage develop into adults. Günther says, in *The Study of Fishes*, "The small-sized roe in the Herring, Lump-fish, Halibut, and Cod-fish have been estimated at, respectively, 25,000, 155,000, 3,500,000, and 9,344,000". In individual Turbots, weighing 18, 21, and 23 lbs., the number of eggs respectively produced has been estimated at 5,612,000, 10,114,000, and 14,311,000. There is usually no special provision for the protection of the eggs, which in those forms which live in the open sea are usually found floating on the surface (fig. 952). Although so small, the eggs contain a large proportion of food-yolk, and cleavage is consequently partial (see p. 346), the body of the embryo developing from a small patch situated at one end.

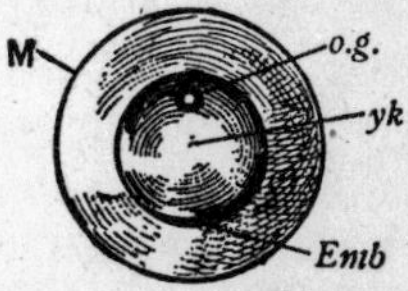

Fig. 952.—Floating Egg of Sea-Bass (*Serranus atrarius*), enlarged. M, Enclosing membrane; *Emb*, embryonic patch; *o.g.*, oil-globule imbedded in yolk (*yk*).

It is clearly advantageous that the patch which becomes the embryo should be below, and the egg naturally floats with this part downwards, the lighter yolk being on top, and in many cases containing an oil-drop which ensures the maintenance of this favourable position (fig. 952).

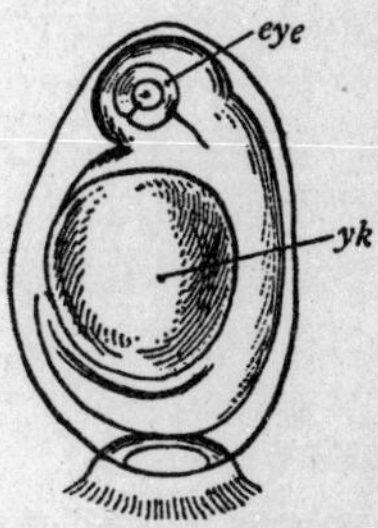

Fig. 953.—Embryo of a Blenny (*Blennius*) enclosed in its Capsule, much enlarged. *yk*, yolk.

In some marine fishes, notably in the Herring (*Clupeus harengus*), the eggs do not float, but are sticky, and adhere to stones and other substances on the sea-bottom. Some of the fishes known as Blennies (*Bleniidæ*), several species of which are common on our shores, lay their eggs in little horny capsules, which are attached to rocks (fig. 953). One of our native species, the Viviparous Blenny (*Zoarces viviparus*), is, as its name indicates, exceptional in the nature of its life-history. It is a comparatively large form, as it may be as much as 2 feet long, and development is entirely internal. A single brood consists of from 50 to 100 individuals, each about 1½ inch in length and resembling the adult in shape. The comparatively small size of the family is correlated with the protective nature of the development, which gives the young fishes a much better chance than usual of attaining maturity.

The fresh waters of the land are largely tenanted by forms which have been driven to take refuge there, as a result of the keen struggle for existence which is always going on in the sea. And some marine fishes increase the chance of survival of their species by using rivers as their nurseries. This has already been illustrated in the case of certain Lampreys (see p. 423), and the Salmon (*Salmo salar*) is a well-known instance of the same thing. These fishes periodically migrate into fresh water for the purpose of spawning, and they excavate by means of the tail a sort of trench in which the eggs are deposited, afterwards being covered by sand or gravel.

The parental duties of Fishes usually terminate when the eggs have been laid, but to this there are some interesting exceptions both among marine and freshwater species. One instance is afforded by the Butter-Fish or Gunnel (*Centronotus Gunnellus*), a slimy and rather eel-like Blenny, often to be found in the rock-pools of our coasts. Cunningham (in *Marketable Marine Fishes*) speaks as follows of it in this connection:—"At St. Andrews Mr. Holt saw the spawning of the Butter-Fish or Gunnel in the aquarium in February. The eggs were adhesive, and the parents were seen to roll the mass of eggs into a ball by coiling their bodies round them, not both parents together, but the male and female in turns. It has been observed by Professor M'Intosh and Mr. Anderson Smith, that in the natural condition the parents are found coiled round the balls of spawn, which are somewhat larger than walnuts and not attached to anything." Female Fishes are not remarkable for any great display of solicitude as regards their offspring, but some honourable exceptions, besides that of the Butter-Fish, have been recorded. In a form (*Aspredo*) native to Guiana, and belonging to the widely distributed freshwater family of Cat-Fishes (*Siluridæ*), the under side of the female's body becomes rough and spongy at the time of spawning. After the eggs are laid she presses against them, so that they adhere to this region, and are carried about till the time of hatching. Another instance is afforded by a curious little Pipe-Fish (*Solenostoma*) which inhabits the Indian Ocean, and, like other related forms, is distinguished by its tubular snout. The large pelvic fins of the female overlap each other, and also fuse with the adjacent skin so as to constitute a backwardly opening brood-pouch, within which the eggs develop. A large number of threads grow out from the inner side of this pouch, and among these the eggs are entangled.

Fishes often make very exemplary fathers, and among the most interesting instances of parental instinct are certain species allied to the two last mentioned. In some of the Cat-Fishes, for example, the male guards the hollows in which the eggs are laid, while in other members of the same family (e.g. *Arius*) he carries them about in his gill-chambers till the time of hatching, a situation which ensures not only protection but a constant supply of fresh oxygenated water. In the Greater Pipe-Fish (*Syngnathus acus*) and the little Sea-Horse (*Hippocampus*, fig. 954) the male possesses a brood-pouch on the under side of his body, rather far back. Within this the eggs hatch out. In the former case it is said that the young fishes make use of the pouch as a refuge for some time after they begin their free existence.

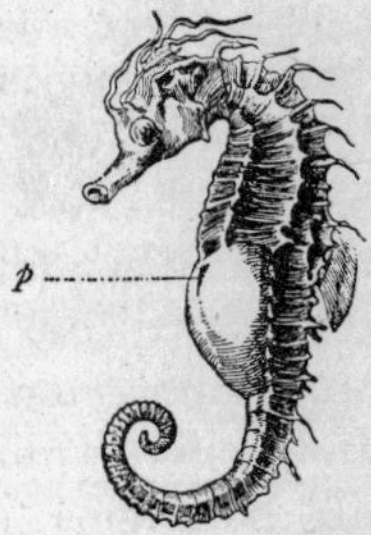

Fig. 954.—Male Sea-Horse (*Hippocampus*). *p*, opening of brood-pouch.

The male fish sometimes constructs regular nests for the reception of the eggs. This is the case, for example, in the beautiful little Paradise Fish (*Polyacanthus* or *Macropomus viridi-auratus*), distinguished by its bright colours and large forked tail. It has long been domesticated in China, from which country it was introduced into Europe, and probably differs a great deal from the wild parent species, of which nothing is yet known. At the time of spawning, the male constructs a floating nest of froth, bringing down air-bubbles and entangling these in slime to make a bowl-shaped construction. To this he conveys the eggs, and watches jealously over them till the time of hatching, and even afterwards, for it is said that if one of the tender fry escapes from the nursery he carefully takes it back again.

Male Sticklebacks (*Gasterosteidæ*) construct muff-shaped nests from bits of weed, glued together by sticky threads which their bodies provide, probably as the result of temporary kidney-disease (fig. 955). The matter is thus charmingly described by Fred Smith (in *The Boyhood of a Naturalist*), evidently as the result of first-hand observation, for the Common Three-Spined Stickleback (*Gasterosteus aculeatus*) of fresh water. After describing a combat in which a male stickleback, or "robin" (so

Fig. 955.—Ten-Spined Stickleback (*Gasterosteus pungitius*, upper figure), and Three-Spined Stickleback (*G. aculeatus*, lower figure). At the bottom is shown the nest of the latter.

named from his bright courtship colours), has engaged, the writer thus proceeds:—"But what is it all about, why is our friend so pugnacious? Well, I never! Fancy not knowing; even my brother knows that! Why, in that clump of weed the 'robin' has a home, as real a home as any human father has in this world. You may call it a nest if you like, but he considers it his home, so decidedly that no knight, even of King Arthur's Round Table, was ever more jealous of his castle than he is of that. And he has a wife there, perhaps two or more, but I think only one; and what is more, there is a group of as beautiful little eggs, almost ready to hatch, as anyone could wish to see. I could show them to you, but that would mean the destruction of the house, which I wouldn't have touched for the world. I haven't shown my brother where it is, for he might have a shy at it if I offended him. Now, look here, I must show you with a stick; and see how brave the gallant little 'robin' is—his spines are out, and he doesn't mean to leave his home undefended. See here a kind of green sponge about the size of a hen's egg; it is made up of gathered-up and broken . . . weed, the same as that which forms the clump. You certainly would not have noticed it; but now, if you can, look very closely. What do you see? If you have eyes at all you can see the tip, only the tip, of the tail fins; and if I gently put this weed aside with the stick, you can see the tip of a darling little nose. That is the lady keeping house and minding the prospective offspring. Now if I just apply my stick so, away goes the lady there, but not very far. And what happens? The instant my interfering stick is taken away, the 'robin' takes the lady's place in the nest; and now only the tip of *his* tail and the end of *his* nose is to be seen; and there he will remain till his spouse has the courage to come back, as he always does remain in possession when the lady goes out shopping—dear me! I mean foraging for food. Who told me it was a nest? . . . Why, nobody told me. I've seen them making a nest, *i.e.* working at it, even in this ditch; but I've seen them make one more than once from beginning to end in my own aquarium. There isn't much making about them, though, except with their mouths and their noses. When you see the sticklebacks, especially the 'robin', poking and picking away at bits of green rubbish, and when, every now and then, a whole mouthful of odd bits of anything is suddenly shot out before him, all of which he will catch like a conjurer without letting any fall to the ground, and then disappear, be sure a nest is being built. I think the swallowing, and tossing and turning of fragments of weed or decaying leaves, which I have repeatedly witnessed, is to give such items some property of hanging or attaching themselves together. In any case, a nucleus of the nest will soon be seen, which is added to in the way I describe; and so far as I can make out, nothing like structural arrangement is attempted. All that is apparently done is to make the ball of oddments sufficiently large—a process which has entailed many wild dartings about, and much poking and arranging with noses; and then one of them, generally again the male, makes a dart at the ball, or they do so in turns, and attempt to wriggle themselves through the middle of it. The object is to make a kind of tunnel right through, which is at last accomplished, and that is the nest. But there is a good deal of fussy procedure after that, or some mysterious arrangement is made inside, since, for a few days longer, material is often shot in or shot out; and sometimes, after it has been completed, it isn't thought sufficiently snug, and material is added on the outside. And they are clever little builders, for a house of theirs might be constructed under your very nose and you would probably not see it." This account may be supplemented by facts which other naturalists have ascertained. The nest has at first only one opening, and is made by the male, who is decidedly polygamous. When the nursery is ready he conducts his consorts to it one after the other, each laying from two to four eggs, after which they swim away and take no farther interest in domestic concerns. The second opening in the nest is made by the first female after laying her eggs, for instead of backing out she forces her way out through the further wall of the cavity. The existence of two apertures is favourable to development, for it promotes a constant flow of fresh water through the nest. When all the eggs have been laid the male stickleback, arrayed in brilliant war-paint, guards the nursery jealously till the young hatch out, which takes place in about ten days. Nor is his task a sinecure, for the time is spent in continual combat with other sticklebacks, especially females, who constantly try to reach the nest for the purpose of eating the developing eggs. After hatching has taken place the father protects the fry till they are large enough to look after themselves.

Sticklebacks have been treated at length, not only because their ways are particularly interesting, but also because anybody can easily stock a small freshwater aquarium for himself, and become an eye-witness of the curious domestic drama above described, which is enacted about mid-spring. Similar habits characterize our smaller native species, the Ten-spined Stickleback, or "Tinker" (*Gasterosteus pungitius*), in which the male becomes deep black during the spawning season; and also our Fifteen-spined Stickleback (*G. spinachia*), a rather larger form common on the coast, and perhaps also entering some of the rivers, as it does on the Continent.

The members of the present order usually hatch out as transparent larvæ, which are very unlike their parents, and have to go through a well-marked metamorphosis before they attain the adult condition. A particularly instructive case is afforded by the Flat-Fishes (*Pleuronectidæ*), of which we may take the Turbot (*Rhombus maximus*) as an example. No one but an expert would suspect that the larva (fig. 956) which hatches out

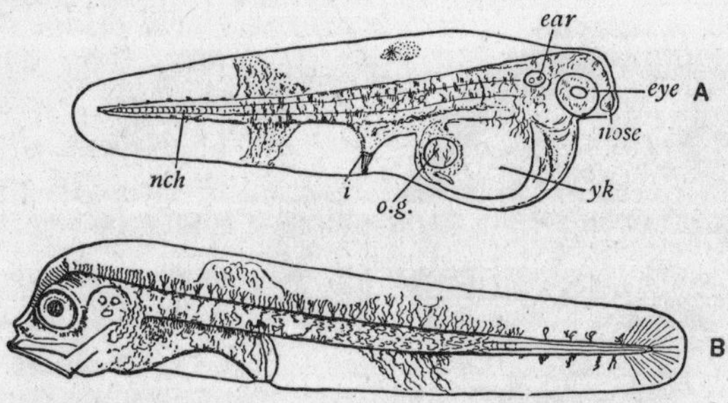

Fig. 956.—Turbot (*Rhombus maximus*). A, Just-hatched larva. B, Larva eight days old: *i*, intestine, *nch*, notochord; *o.g.*, oil-globule; *yk*, yolk. Enlarged.

from the floating egg of this form was destined to become a flat-fish. It is a transparent creature about $\frac{1}{12}$ of an inch long, and, since it possesses no mouth, is incapable of feeding. The food at this stage consists of the nutritive material contained in the bulging yolk-sac on the under side of the body. The second stage represented in the figure was taken from a larva eight days after hatching. Well-developed mouth and jaws were present, and the yolk was entirely used up. Somewhat later on the right eye begins to move up the side of the body, gradually passing over the top of the head to the left side. As this curious migration goes on the upright swimming position is gradually abandoned for an oblique, and finally for a horizontal one. A swim-bladder is present. Until a length of about an inch is attained the young Turbot lives at the surface, regarding which Cunningham (in *Marketable Marine Fishes*) thus speaks:—"The advantage of this power and habit of swimming at the surface is not difficult to discover. Even at these early stages the turbot and brill are rapacious, and feed on other fishes smaller than themselves. They might capture such prey when lying like the adult at the bottom, but in summer time the young of other kinds of fishes are much more plentiful in the open water and near the surface than at the bottom. In the aquarium at Plymouth the young turbot have been fed on pieces of dead fish, but both they and the brill much prefer living prey, and when kept with other young fish, such as flounders, speedily devour them or choke themselves in the attempt." Later on these little creatures settle down to a life on the sea-floor, and lose the swim-bladder, which is not required by a ground-fish. The left side of the body, which is kept uppermost (fig. 957), is strongly pigmented, while the other side is pale. Some of the points in this life-history are good instances of recapitulation, leading to the conclusion that the asymmetrical flat-fishes are descended from symmetrical forms in which a swim-bladder was present. While in Turbot and Brill both eyes are on the left side of the body, the right side being kept next the sea-bottom, the reverse is the case in most of our edible flat-fishes, such as Plaice, Flounder, Dab, Halibut, Sole, and Lemon Sole.

Fig. 957.—Turbot (*Rhombus maximus*)

Allusion has already been made to the spawning habits of the Salmon (*Salmo salar*). Shoals of these fishes ascend rivers in spring for the purpose of laying their eggs, which event takes place in the autumn. Development is a very slow process, for it is three or four months before the young hatch out. They are then only about $\frac{1}{25}$ of an inch long, and a large yolk-sac projects from the under side of the body (fig. 958). In the second year of life the young salmon, known in this stage as "parr", descend to the sea, apparently returning every year to their native river for the purpose of spawning. Several years elapse before the adult characteristics are fully acquired, and many different names, which vary with the locality, are given to the successive stages of life. Our knowledge of the habits of the Salmon still leaves much to be desired, especially as to its life in the sea.

The life-history of the Common Eel (*Anguilla vulgaris*) presents us with a curious reversal of events as compared with the Salmon. Until about twenty years ago no male eels had been discovered, but we now know that the so-called "broad-

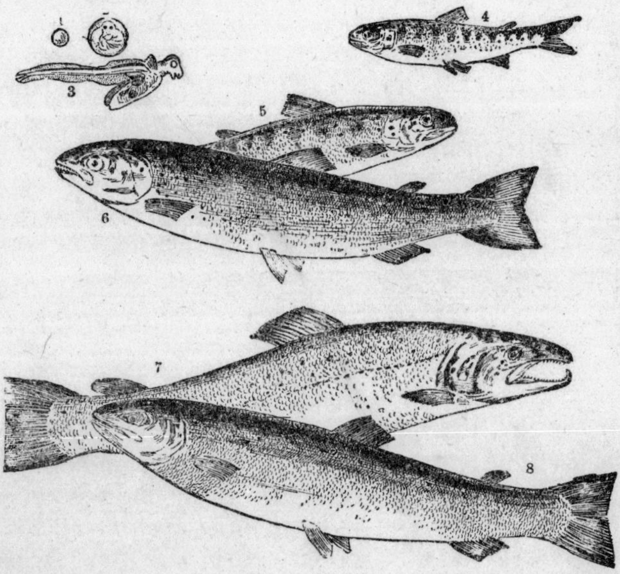

Fig. 958.—Salmon (*Salmo salar*). 1, Egg; 2, egg with embryo (enlarged); 3, young larva with yolk-sac (enlarged); 4, Parr; 5, Smolt; 6, Grilse; 7 and 8, adult male and female.

nosed eels" and "sharp-nosed eels", long believed to be distinct varieties, are respectively the males and females of this species. Thanks mainly to the painstaking observations of Grassi and Calandruccio, made on the Sicilian coast in 1891–92, the life-history has at last been elucidated as regards its main features. In October and November the adult eels migrate to the deep sea for spawning, after which they most probably die, since there is no reliable evidence of a return to fresh water. The eggs hatch out into larvæ of which the early stages are unknown, and we first meet them as transparent flattened creatures devoid of scales, which have long been familiar to naturalists under the name of Leptocephalus, and supposed to be either a distinct species, or else young fishes which have developed abnormally. The particular sort with which we are here concerned (*L. brevirostris*, fig. 959) is distinguished by the shortness of its snout, and the Italian naturalists named above have been able to show that it gradually assumes a cylindrical though still scaleless form, and undoubtedly grows into an eel. From February to May vast multitudes of these young eels, known as "elvers" or "eel-fare", ascend our rivers, those of them which survive reaching the adult state in fresh water, never returning to the sea again, except to spawn. It has also been proved that another kind of Leptocephalus (*L. Morrisii*) is the larval stage of the marine Conger Eel (*Conger vulgaris*). It is sometimes taken on our own coast, and has received the name of Morris.

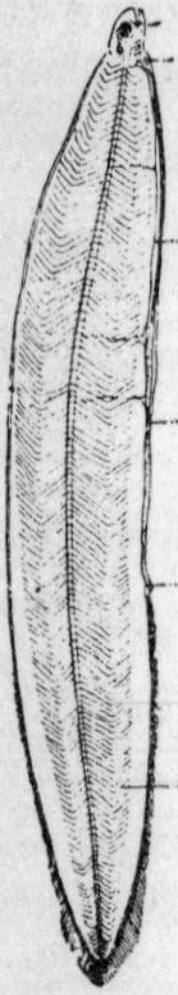

Fig. 959.—Larval Eel (*Leptocephalus brevirostris*); *h.*, heart; *b.*, body-cavity; *i.*, intestine; *i.a.*, intestinal aperture; *m.*, muscles.

LIFE-HISTORIES, &c., OF AMPHIBIANS (AMPHIBIA)

Some few members of this class are viviparous, but the vast majority lay eggs which usually hatch out into aquatic larvæ, familiarly known as "tadpoles" or "pollywogs". The life-history of the common Grass Frog (*Rana temporaria*) has been briefly described in an earlier section (see vol. i, p. 254). Amphibian eggs contain a considerable amount of food-yolk, and there are not infrequently special protective arrangements, in which case comparatively few are produced. We will consider in succession some of the more interesting facts relating to Tailed Amphibians (Urodela), Tailless Amphibians (Anura), and Limbless Amphibians (Gymnophiona).

TAILED AMPHIBIANS (URODELA).—This group is represented in our country by the familiar Efts or Newts, of which we have three native species (see p. 46). During the spawning season they enter the water for the purpose of laying their eggs, which, as in Amphibians generally, possess gelatinous investments. They are attached to stones or water-plants, and the little tadpoles, which hatch out in a fortnight or so, fix themselves for a time to water-plants by means of threads that project from the upper jaw.

Among other species of newt-like animals there may be more elaborate provision for the welfare of the eggs. These may be moored to stones by means of threads into which their investments are drawn out, as in one of the forms native to eastern North America (*Spelerpes bilineatus*); others again are deposited in little bags hung up on water-plants, as in a West Siberian species (*Salamandrella Keyserlingi*). Instances have also been described of maternal solicitude. The eel-like Three-toed Salamander (*Amphiuma means*) of the south-eastern United States, for example, coils her body round the string of eggs, which hatch out into tadpoles about three months later. In one little newt (*Desmognathus fuscus*, fig. 960), native to the east of North America, the stalked eggs are fixed to the body of the mother, who shelters in a hole during their development. Part of the tadpole-stage in the life-history is here passed through within the egg. This prepares us for what takes place in a form (*Autodax lugubris*) which lives in the western part of North America. The adult is entirely terrestrial, and the female retires to a hole underground for the purpose of laying her eggs, each of which is fixed to a bit of earth by means of a thread. They number about a score, and when all are deposited the mother coils herself round them until such time as they hatch out, a fortnight or three weeks later. The tadpole-stage is passed through entirely within the egg, and the young closely resemble their parents except in size and colour. This reminds us of the life-history of the slug Onchidium, where there is no free-living larva, although this is well represented before hatching (see p. 414). Such a life-history is intelligible when regarded as an adaptation to life on land, with entire abandonment of aquatic existence.

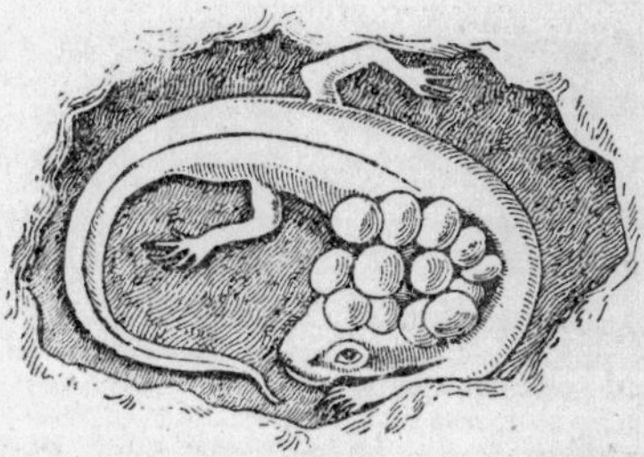

Fig. 960.—Female *Desmognathus fuscus* with her eggs

The famous case of the Axolotl, mentioned elsewhere (see vol. i, p. 249) is the exact reverse of what has just been described. For here the adult stage under certain conditions is entirely suppressed, and the animal remains a tadpole. It may therefore be regarded as a permanent larva, though one that has acquired the power of laying eggs. This peculiar state of things has come about in the absence of surroundings suitable for life on land. When such surroundings exist the Axolotl does become adult, and is then a kind of salamander.

A few Urodeles are viviparous, development taking place internally. This is the case, for example, in the Spotted Salamander (*Salamandra maculosa*), which does not lay eggs, but produces a brood of tadpoles. The Black Salamander (*S. atra*) of the Alpine region is also viviparous, and produces only a couple of young, which make their appearance in the world as minute facsimiles of their parents, though they pass through a tadpole stage before they are born. What has been said above about Autodax (p. 435) applies to this case also, except that development is internal instead of being external. The small number of young produced by the Black Salamander is clearly in relation to an improved chance of individual survival resulting from the sheltered nature of the development. It appears, however, that a great many eggs are actually formed, though the large majority of them disintegrate and serve as food for the two which are destined to perpetuate the species.

Tailless Amphibians (Anura). — The Frogs and Toads which make up this group are very specialized creatures, which differ remarkably among one another in respect of egg-laying and care of eggs.

In the majority of cases a very large number of comparatively small eggs are produced, from which typical tadpoles hatch out that are but ill adapted to cope successfully with the many dangers to which they are exposed. Relatively few of them become adult, and extreme fecundity alone prevents such species from becoming extinct. Comparison may be made with fishes in this respect (see p. 425). In average cases the eggs are laid in water, familiar instances being afforded by the Common Toad (*Bufo vulgaris*) and the Grass Frog (*Rana temporaria*), the jelly-like spawn of the former consisting of long cylindrical strings, while that of the latter is in the form of irregular clumps. Both kinds are to be seen floating in our ponds and ditches in early spring, quite uncared for by the parents, though not altogether unprotected. Examination of frog-spawn will show that each of the black shot-like eggs is inclosed in a sphere of jelly, which is

LIFE-HISTORY OF THE COMMON GRASS-FROG

(*Rana temporaria*)

This common Amphibian is an admirable illustration of evolutionary principles, for it begins its existence as a fish-like tadpole, which breathes by gills and feeds on vegetable matter, and later on is gradually transformed into a limb-bearing, lung-breathing, carnivorous frog, adapted to a life on land. Spawning takes place in spring, each egg being enclosed in a gelatinous sphere, which buoys it up, prevents overcrowding, and serves as a protection. The just-hatched tadpole is mouthless and tailless, and for a time holds on to a water-weed by means of adhesive discs on the under side of its head. It quickly grows a broad swimming-tail, and develops a mouth. Later on the limbs sprout out, and the bag-like lungs grow from the under side of the gullet. Ultimately the gills disappear, the gill-slits close, and the tail shrivels up. The life-history of the individual Frog gives us some idea of the evolutionary changes which have taken place in the past history of the groups of Reptiles, Birds, and Mammals, the remote ancestors of which were aquatic, fish-like creatures.

LIFE-HISTORY OF THE COMMON GRASS-FROG (RANA TEMPORARIA)

of importance in several ways. For it acts as a buoy, prevents overcrowding, and by concentrating heat upon the egg hastens development. It also serves as a protection against ducks and other birds, owing to its slippery nature and bitter taste.

A good many species lay their small eggs out of the water, this being the case, for example, with a little Brazilian frog (*Leptodactylus mystacinus*), which is purely terrestrial when adult. Spawning takes place before the advent of the rainy season, the mother scooping out a good-sized hole in the neighbourhood of water for the reception of her eggs, which are surrounded by a frothy mass that prevents them from drying up, and also appears to serve as food for the young tadpoles. They are afterwards washed out of their nest by the rain, and thus gain the adjacent pond, where they develop into adults. Should there be a drought the tadpoles live on in the nest till the following rainy season.

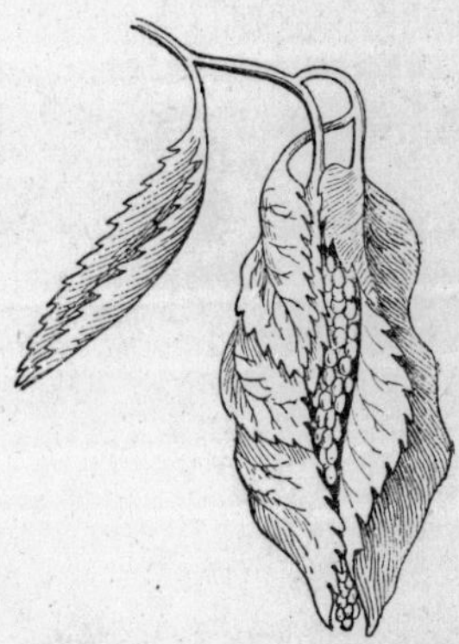

Fig. 961.—Egg-case of a Brazilian Tree-Frog (*Phyllomedusa Jheringi*)

Some of the Tree-Frogs deposit their eggs upon plants which overhang the water, one or more leaves being folded together into a sort of protective case. Such an arrangement has been described for a species (*Phyllomedusa Jheringi*, fig. 961) native to South Brazil, in which the eggs and the jelly by which they are surrounded are wrapped up in willow leaves. The tadpoles hatch out in this hanging nest and drop into the water below.

The two species last described display a certain amount of parental care, but are far surpassed in this respect by a Brazilian tree-frog (*Hyla faber*) known locally as the "Ferreiro", *i.e.* "Smith", on account of its curious voice, the sound of which has been compared to that produced by a copper plate beaten with a mallet. The female makes a circular nest in the shallow water at the edge of a pond (fig. 962) one or two nights being required for its construction. We are indebted to Goeldi for our knowledge of this interesting habit, of which he gives the following account, based on observations made in his own garden at Para: "We soon saw a mass of mud rising to the surface carried by a tree-frog, of which no more than the two hands emerged.

Diving again, after a moment's time, the frog brought up a second mass of mud near the first. This was repeated many times, the result being the gradual erection of a circular wall. From time to time the builder's head and front part of body appeared suddenly with a load of mud on some opposite point. But what astonished us in the highest degree was the manner in which it used its hands for smoothing the inside of the mud wall, as would a mason with his trowel. When the height of the wall reached about four

Fig. 962.—Nests of the Ferreiro (*Hyla faber*)

inches the frog was obliged to get out of the water. The parapet of the wall receives the same careful smoothing, but the outside is neglected. The levelling of the bottom is obtained by the action of the lower surface (belly and throat principally) together with that of the hands." (*Proceedings of the Zoological Society*, 1895.) The parents remain concealed near the nest till the time of hatching, which takes place in four or five days. Within their circular "nursery" the tadpoles live till the adult stage is attained.

When the eggs are small and numerous, as in ordinary Frogs and Toads, hatching takes place comparatively early, and the tadpoles are at first extremely helpless. They cannot even feed, for the mouth is not yet properly developed, and the absence of a tail in the earliest stage adds greatly to their disabilities. Some means of protection is obviously necessary, and this is found in the presence of one or a pair of modified sticky areas on the under side of the head, by means of which the larva adheres for some time to a water-plant.

We now pass to the consideration of certain tailless forms in which the eggs are less numerous and of larger size, containing indeed so much food-yolk that there is no necessity for early hatching, and the young animals begin their free existence either as advanced tadpoles which have already lost their gills, or else in the adult form. There is often some special provision for the care of such eggs during their development, and a comparison may well be made with those fishes which exert a certain amount of parental care (see p. 426). In the simplest case the eggs are simply deposited in damp places, as in a Japanese species (*Rhacophorus Schlegeli*) of tree-frog, where the female digs a hole near a pond or ditch and lays her eggs in it, also taking care to provide a supply of air by working up the jelly of the spawn into a sort of frothy mass by means of her hind-feet. Tadpoles hatch out from these eggs later on.

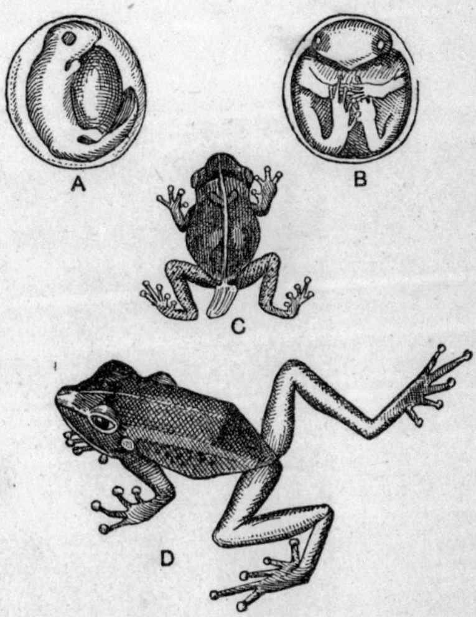

Fig. 963.—Development of a West Indian Tree-Frog (*Hylodes Martinicensis*). A and B, Eggs containing embryos seven and twelve days old; C, just-hatched Frog; D, adult male.

A pretty little West Indian tree-frog (*Hylodes Martinicensis*, fig. 963) lays about a score of large eggs upon a leaf, very often in the sheltered angle close to the stem. They are imbedded in a frothy mass of jelly. While development is going on it is said that the mother remains on guard not far off. Minute frogs of about one-fifth of an inch in length emerge from the eggs in about three weeks. The tadpole stage is thus passed through before hatching, and it is noteworthy that there is a certain amount of "hastening of events" in the development, since gills and gill-slits do not make their appearance, there being in fact no need for them.

In one species of toad (*Alytes obstetricans*, fig. 964) which ranges from Portugal to Central Germany, the eggs are taken care of by the male, reminding us of what happens in some fishes (see p. 427). They are laid in two long strings folded up into a gelatinous mass, through which he thrusts his legs and carries it about till the tadpoles are ready to hatch out, some three weeks later. During this critical time the father hides during the day in some hole or corner, digging a refuge for himself if necessary. At night he ventures out to feed, and prevents the eggs from drying up by moistening them with water or dew. When the

Fig. 964.—Male Alytes, carrying the eggs

time for hatching arrives he goes into the water, and the tadpoles wriggle out of their investments. They are well developed, for the eggs are fairly large, and contain a considerable amount of food-yolk, which enables the early part of the larval stage to be passed within the egg.

The male of a small species of toad (*Rhinoderma Darwini*) native to Chili tends the eggs in a still more curious way. He possesses a large croaking sac situated just within the skin on the ventral side of the body. The ordinary use of this, as in such creatures generally, is supposed to be that of a resonator by which the volume of the voice is increased. The pouch opens by a slit on either side of the tongue, and it serves as a receptacle for the eggs, though how they get into it is not known. The whole of the development takes place in this secure shelter, out of which the young ultimately escape as minute toads (fig. 965). No gills appear to be present in the tadpole stage. When not employed as a nursery the pouch is of modest dimensions, only stretching about half-way down the chest, but as the eggs develop it gradually extends along the whole under surface and round the sides.

In some tailless forms the eggs are carried about by the female, the arrangements made for their safety varying according

1 2

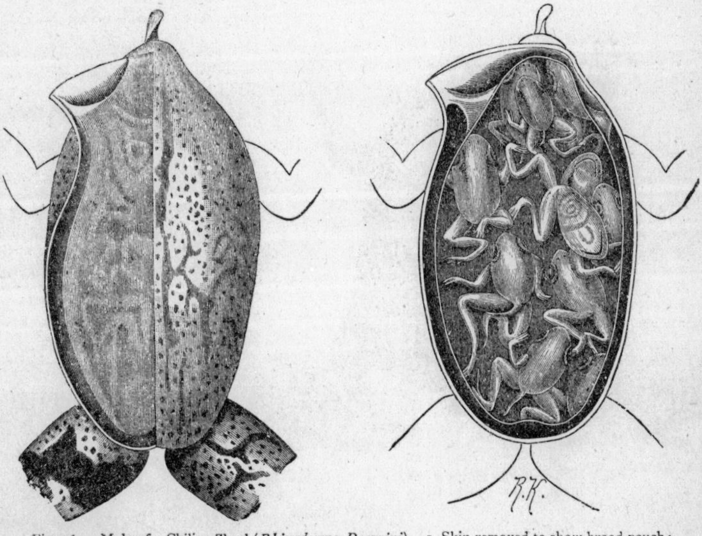

Fig. 965.—Male of a Chilian Toad (*Rhinoderma Darwini*). 1, Skin removed to show brood-pouch; 2, brood-pouch opened.

to the species. A well-known case is that of the Surinam Toad (*Pipa Americana*, fig. 966), in which the sticky eggs are spread by the male over the back of his mate. Where each of them is affixed a little pouch is formed in the skin, exactly how is unknown, and afterwards a lid comes into existence, possibly by hardening of the egg-investment. Within these sheltered recesses the whole of the development takes place, and when the young begin their free existence they have already attained the form of the adult.

In one of the Cingalese tree-frogs (*Rhacophorus reticulatus*) the female places her score or so of eggs on the under side of her body, where they sink into the skin, little pits being formed somewhat as in the form last described. Details are wanting, but the young are said to hatch out as tadpoles.

In some other cases there is a more or less well-developed pouch for the reception of the eggs on the upper surface of the mother's body. In a small Brazilian tree-frog (*Hyla Goeldii*), for example, the skin grows out into a narrow fold surrounding an oval area in which the eggs are placed, presenting an appearance suggestive of a shallow dish full of pale-coloured oranges. There is a large quantity of food-yolk, and the young have almost attained the form of the adult at the time they hatch out. In the pouched tree-frogs (*Nototrema*) of tropical South America the female possesses a permanent pouch on the upper side of her body, with an opening at the back. The young sometimes begin their free existence as advanced tadpoles, but in most of the species they have acquired the adult form before they make their way out of the pouch.

Fig. 966.—Female of Surinam Toad (*Pipa Americana*), carrying the developing young on her back

Limbless Amphibians (Gymnophiona).—The life-histories of these curious burrowing snake-like creatures have not been very exhaustively studied, but there are considerable differences between those species which have so far been the subject of investigation. One of the Cæcilians (*Ichthyophis glutinosa*, fig. 967) native to South and South-east Asia is one of the least aberrant species as regards development. The female excavates a hole in damp earth close to a stream, and lays some two dozen large eggs, round which she coils her body during their development. Shortly before hatching, the tadpole stage within the egg possesses three pair of long plume-like external gills of scarlet colour, and a pair of gill-clefts. There is also a small tail-fin. The gills are lost before the larva emerges, when it at once makes its way into the water, looking very much like a minute eel. After a somewhat prolonged aquatic existence the young Cæcilian loses its tail-fin, the gill-clefts close up, and other changes in structure take place. It then leaves the water, and spends the rest of its life as a burrowing terrestrial animal.

In certain Cæcilians which inhabit the Seychelles Islands (species of *Hypogeophis*) the free-living tadpole stage is eliminated from the life-history, as in some of the tailless Amphibians already described (see p. 440). As before, the female protects her eggs by coiling round them, and a tadpole stage is passed through

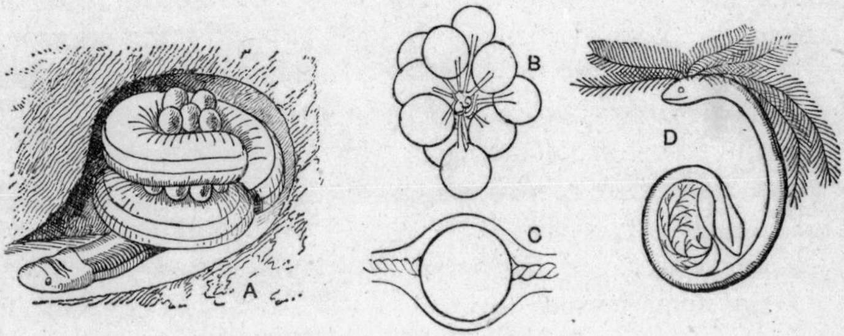

Fig. 967.—Development of a Cæcilian (*Ichthyophis glutinosa*)

A, Female coiled round her eggs, reduced; B, bunch of eggs; C, an egg, enlarged, showing investing membrane and supporting strings; D, an advanced embryo, with external gills and remains of yolk-sac, enlarged.

before hatching, in which external gills and four pairs of gill-clefts are present, but no tail-fin. When the young animal leaves the egg it resembles the adult in appearance, for the gills have disappeared and the gill-clefts closed up. It at once takes to the burrowing mode of life.

In a large Cæcilian (*Typhlonectes compressicaudata*) which inhabits the northern part of South America, development is entirely internal, and the young when born closely resemble their parents. A tadpole stage with reduced gills is passed through before birth, but, so far as we know, this species spends the whole of its life burrowing in the ground.

LIFE-HISTORIES, &c., OF REPTILES (Reptilia)

In the higher Vertebrates, including Reptiles, Birds, and Mammals, development is always direct, there being no larval form, though the young are sometimes in a rather embryonic state when they first make their appearance in the world.

Reptiles are for the most part oviparous, and their eggs contain a great deal of food-yolk. Protection is afforded by a tough or it may be calcareous shell. The group is not specially interesting in the present connection, but it will be worth while to briefly review the five orders in which all living species are included, *i.e.*—Tuataras (Rhynchocephala), Snakes (Ophidia), Lizards (Lacertilia), Turtles and Tortoises (Chelonia), and Crocodiles (Crocodiles).

Tuataras (Rhynchocephala).—The only living representative of this ancient and once extensive order is the Tuatara (*Hatteria punctata*) of New Zealand, which lives on some of the small islands in the Bay of Plenty. It digs a burrow in the ground, afterwards adding a lining of grass and other plants. This dwelling is not, however, used as a nest, a hole being scooped in the sand for the reception of the eggs, which thus have the benefit of the sun's heat. They are about ten in number, and closely resemble those of birds. The young hatch out some thirteen months afterwards, but the actual development only takes about half of this long period, the rest of the time being spent in a dormant condition.

Snakes (Ophidia).—The large majority of these creatures lay soft-shelled eggs, which are commonly deposited in earth or among decaying vegetable matter, where the heat generated by the processes of fermentation accelerates the development, which is also furthered by the sun's warmth. Manure-heaps are much favoured for this purpose by our native Grass Snake (*Tropidonotus natrix*), as may be illustrated by the following extract from Frank Buckland (*Log-Book of a Fisherman and Zoologist*):—"Just as I had put the lizard into a bag, I heard the squire's voice signalling me from the distance. He apologized for my want of sport in my snaking expedition, but at the same time he delighted me by promising to guide me at once to a dung-heap, where it was reported that some snakes had laid their eggs. This dung-heap was situated in the middle of a yard where the cows lived in the winter, and was just the very place snakes would choose to lay their eggs. The keeper got a dung-fork, and diligently turned over the straw at the top, while the squire and I worked away at the sides of the dung-heap. . . . I was dreadfully afraid we should draw the dung-hill blank, but at last I gave a view holloa, when, underneath a bit of the straw, I saw something of a milk-white colour.

'Avancez,' I said, 'go ahead; I'm certain that's a snake's nest.' Lifting up the straw most carefully, I was delighted to find first one, then two, then a dozen eggs. The squire and I then proceeded to dissect out the nest with our pocket-knives and a dung-fork most carefully. Snakes' eggs are not quite so large as a blackbird's; they are round at both ends like a sugar-plum. They have no hard shell like a hen's egg, but the shell is composed of a soft elastic substance, like thin wash-leather. Some eggs were lying quite separate. The greater part were, however, stuck firmly together, so tightly that it was almost impossible to tear them apart without breaking the skin. The eggs were not held by a ligature, but appeared pasted together by some strong adhesive gum, end on end. . . . The appearance of the eggs in this dung-heap, just as the parent snake or snakes had placed them, was so striking, that a gentleman, well-known for his artistic talent, took a sketch of the eggs and the nest. When the sketch was finished, I proceeded to examine the eggs more closely; there were sixty-four. I do not know from experience how many eggs the common snake lays, but I should say from twelve to twenty. It is, therefore, possible, even probable, that more than one snake had chosen the spot on the dung-hill to deposit their eggs. . . . The temperature of the spot where the eggs were deposited in the dung-heap was about 84 degrees in the sun, and the nest was buried about 18 inches deep on the southern aspect, as though the mother snake knew that that was the best place for the eggs." The unhatched snake is provided with a small "egg-tooth" on the tip of its snout, which helps it to make its way into the world.

Parental affection is rarely exhibited by snakes, but the female Python coils her body round her batch of eggs by way of protection. Some few species, such as Vipers, including our native Adder (*Pelias berus*), are viviparous. So also are marine snakes, which come to land for the purpose of producing their young.

LIZARDS (LACERTILIA).—Most of these are oviparous, and deposit their hard or soft-shelled eggs after the fashion of Snakes. Here too, the young animal possesses a sharp "egg-tooth" (fig. 968) on the tip of its upper jaw, and this is best developed in cases where the egg-shells are hard and calcareous. The Common Iguana (*Iguana tuberculata*) of tropical America digs out a deep burrow on a sloping bank for the reception of her eggs, the Eyed Lizard (*Lacerta ocellata*) commonly selects a hollow tree for the purpose, and the Spanish Sand-Lizard (*Psammodromus Hispanicus*) buries her eggs deeply in hot sand. Gadow (in *The Cambridge Natural History*) thus describes the nesting habits of the Common Chameleon (*Chamæleo vulgaris*):—"When the eggs are ripe, and this happens with the Common Chameleon about the end of October, the female refuses to take food, and becomes restless. One of my specimens searched about probing the ground for about a week before she dug a hole in some more solid soil. This took two days. In the evening I found her sitting in the hole to the middle of her body. On the following morning she was still there, but busy filling the hole with soil and covering it with dry leaves. A few eggs were lying about outside, two of which at least I saw her taking up by the hand and putting them on the nest, which was found to contain some thirty soft-shelled eggs closely packed upon each other. During the whole process she was very snappy, and hissed much when approached."

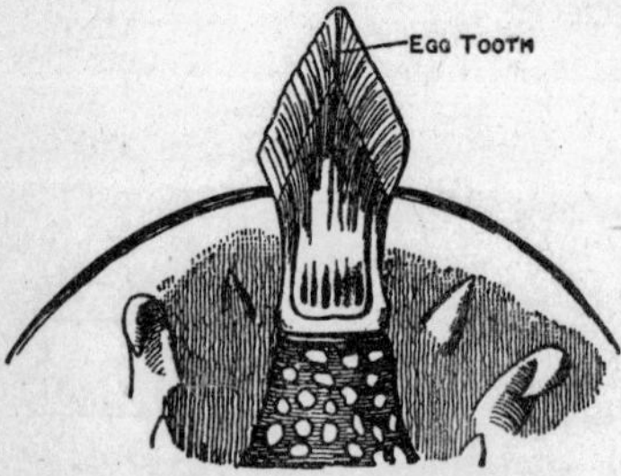

Fig. 968.—Tip of the upper jaw of embryo Lizard, showing Egg-tooth, enlarged

Some Lizards are viviparous to all intents and purposes, for the eggs hatch out immediately after they are laid. This is the case with two British species, the Viviparous Lizard (*Zoötoca vivipara*) and the Blind-Worm (*Anguis fragilis*).

TURTLES AND TORTOISES (CHELONIA).—All the members of this order are oviparous, and deposit their eggs in the ground. As in Lizards the shell may be either hard or simply tough, and there is a good deal of variation in shape. A typical instance is afforded by the European Pond Tortoise (*Emys orbicularis*), in which the female makes a hole in the ground, using first the tail and then the hind-limbs for the purpose. After depositing her eggs she replaces the earth, presses it down, and then scratches it with her claws, the object of this last procedure being to make the nest inconspicuous.

Even the thoroughly marine Turtles come to land for the purpose of egg-laying, regarding which habit in the Edible Turtle (*Chelone mydas*) Gadow makes the following remarks (in *The Cambridge Natural History*):—"The females come to their breeding-places from afar, reconnoitre the beach carefully, are extremely wary and shy, taking alarm at the slightest disturbance, and at last crawl on land. Well out of the reach of the tide the female scoops out a hole in the sand, deposits about one hundred or more of its round, rather parchment-shelled eggs, covers the nest carefully, obliterating all traces of the dug-out sand, and makes again for the sea by another route. At least they are said to make a sort of circuitous route so that nobody can tell the position of the nest, which may be anywhere beneath the broad trail left by the heavy creature on its way from and back to the sea."

Tortoises sometimes construct definite homes for themselves, as in the case of the Gopher Tortoise (*Testudo polyphemus*), a native of the south-eastern part of North America. Each pair live in a rather long burrow, which expands internally into a sort of dwelling-chamber. The eggs are not deposited in this underground retreat, but a hole is dug for their reception in the immediate neighbourhood. They are of large size, and only five in number.

CROCODILES (CROCODILES).—All the species of the order are oviparous, and the females lay a considerable number of white eggs, covered with firm calcareous shells. Crocodiles and their kind are much more affectionate than any other reptilian mothers.

The Nile Crocodile (*Crocodilus Niloticus*) constructs a nest for her eggs by digging a fairly deep hole in the sand, the floor being larger than the external opening, and somewhat raised in the middle, so that the eggs roll away to the margin. They are from twenty to thirty in number, and are laid in two batches, with a layer of sand between. After all have been deposited the mother fills up the hole, and uses the spot as a sleeping-place, an obviously protective measure. At the end of about three months the young crocodiles hatch out, and they possess a well-developed "egg-tooth" which enables them to break the shell. When ready to make their exit they make a peculiar sound, which has been compared to a hiccough, and it is said that the mother, on hearing this, digs them out of the nest, and leads them to the water.

This Crocodile also makes a sort of lair by excavating a long burrow in the bank of its native river, the entrance being under water. The roof is ventilated by air-holes, and at the inner end there is a fairly large space, to which the animal is supposed to retreat with its prey for the purpose of enjoying a quiet meal.

The somewhat similar habits of the American Alligator (*Alligator Mississippiensis*) are thus described by S. F. Clarke (in *The Journal of Morphology*, 1891):—"The nest of the alligator is very large, and is built by the female. A great quantity of dead leaves and twigs, together with much of the finely-divided humus underlying them, is scraped together into a low mound about 3 feet high; this varies considerably in its other dimensions, being in some instances 8 feet in diameter at the base. The nests are built on the bank of a stream or pool, and the female digs a cave under water in the bank close to the nest. Careful examination of the largest nest found showed a root of a neighbouring palmetto-tree, nearly an inch in diameter, running through it at about a foot above the ground; there were also roots of a grape vine growing near, which extended nearly through the nest. This furnishes strong support to the statement of many of the hunters, that the nests are used for more than one season. I could get no evidence whatever that the nests are used more than once a year. The eggs are laid near the top of the nest, within 8 inches of the surface, are four or five layers deep, and have no regular arrangement or uniform position of their axes in relation to the nest. The number of eggs to a nest varies from twenty to thirty, and averages twenty-eight; the maximum found was forty-seven."

LIFE-HISTORIES, &c., OF BIRDS (AVES)

All Birds, without exception, lay hard-shelled eggs, and at the time of hatching the young are either helpless (nidicolæ), as in the House-Sparrow, or else, as in Fowls, able almost at once to run about and feed themselves (nidifugæ). The eggs vary greatly in number, size, and appearance, and are commonly, though by no means always, laid in specially constructed nests, the nature of which is even more diverse than their contents. One parent, or each in turn, usually broods over the eggs, thus supplying the heat which is necessary for development. The skin on the under side of an incubating bird is plentifully supplied with blood and sometimes is more or less bare; increased warmth is the result. Sometimes, however, there is no such incubation, and the requisite warmth is otherwise supplied. Parental affection is commonly very strong, especially in those cases where there are helpless nestlings, which would speedily die if not carefully tended.

GANNETS OR SOLAN GEESE (*Sula Bassana*)

This plate reproduces photographs taken by Mr. R. A. L. Van Someren at the Bass Rock, a well-known breeding-haunt of this bird. A general view of part of the rock is given at 1, showing Gannets and nests. Two of the latter are represented on a larger scale in 2, each of them containing a large white egg, while a brooding bird is seen in 3. An unfledged nestling, with feathers beginning to sprout, is shown in 4, and the loose, untidy character of the insanitary nest will be noted. It is very roughly made of bits of sea-weed, pieces of turf, grass haulms, and other available materials. The young Gannets are hatched out as blind, featherless, unattractive-looking creatures, but soon become clothed with a thick covering of pure white down. Later on this is succeeded by speckled brown and white plumage, which, after passing through several other stages, gives place to the almost entirely white attire of the adult. Gannets are not fully mature until they have attained the age of four or five years.

GANNETS OR SOLAN GEESE (SULA BASSANA)

The Common Cuckoo is a familiar example of the shirking of such domestic duties. The unhatched bird generally has a little hard knob on the tip of its beak, which helps it to break the shell.

The habits of Birds have proved a never-failing attraction to a very large number of observers, and so much is known about them that choice of material for the present section is very difficult. There is, however, plenty of room for careful scientific investigation, since the work of many so-called ornithologists is extremely superficial, and only to be defined as periodical birds-nesting, undertaken for the purpose of adding rare eggs to a useless and often overstocked collection.

It will be convenient to consider separately the Running Birds (Ratitæ), and Flying Birds (Carinatæ).

Running Birds (Ratitæ).—In all living species the male bird does most if not all of the work of incubation, and also looks after the chicks when they are hatched. African and American Ostriches are polygamous, but Cassowaries, Emeus, and Kiwis are associated in pairs.

The African Ostrich (*Struthio camelus*) has often been unjustly regarded as a reprehensibly careless parent, an opinion commonly based on the following statement in the Book of Job (xxxix, 14–16):—"Which leaveth her eggs in the earth, and warmeth them in dust, and forgetteth that the foot may crush them, or that the wild beast may break them. She is hardened against her young ones, as though they were not her's: her labour is in vain without fear." In this species the hens of one establishment scratch out a hole in the sand, within which they lay eggs to the number of over thirty, afterwards covering them over. Other eggs are deposited outside the nest, possibly to serve as the first food of the newly-hatched chicks. Incubation lasts for six or seven weeks, and is undertaken by the cock, his duties in this direction being chiefly performed at night. During the day sufficient warmth is supplied by the sun, though it is said that at this time both sexes in turn brood over the eggs in the cooler parts of the area inhabited. Parents and young live together for some time, the father jealously guarding his offspring, and adopting various stratagems for the purpose of luring away inquisitive visitors whose designs appear to him questionable.

The habits of the American Ostriches (*Rhea*) are much the same as those of their African cousins.

Cassowaries (*Casuarius*) construct a careless nest of vegetation in a sheltered place, and the large eggs vary from three to six in number. They are of pale green colour, and usually rough from the presence of raised dark green spots. The plumage of the chicks is mottled.

The nest of the Emeu (*Dromæus Novæ-Hollandiæ*) is simply a shallow depression scraped out in the ground, and the roughened eggs are smaller and more numerous than those of Cassowaries. Their colour is usually blackish green. It is a common thing for young birds which are able to run about as soon as they are hatched to be protectively coloured, and this is well exemplified by Cassowary and Emeu chicks. Semon thus speaks of the latter (in *In the Australian Bush*):—"The young emeus are very different in colouring from the old birds. They are not of the modest grayish-brown of the latter, but bear a delicate design of a pretty dark gray with numerous stripes on their back and sides. A very similar design is to be seen in the young cassowaries. These stripes of the small birds fulfil a decidedly protective purpose. Young emeus are often pursued by the eagles and hawks so frequent in Australia. When (so my blacks told me) the young emeus see a bird of prey soaring above them they quickly lie down flat upon the ground. A body as big as theirs would surely be much more conspicuous, set off as it is by grass, if it were *evenly*, though ever so modestly coloured, than if its colouring be varied by stripes and spots. I myself have had occasion to notice how difficult it is to discover an emeu in the grass if it nestles to the ground. On an even level of sand its stripes would direct attention towards it, whereas here they render it inconspicuous." (Compare vol. ii, p. 285.)

The little Kiwis (*Apteryx*) of New Zealand have somewhat different nesting habits. The female digs a burrow which expands internally, and here places a thin layer of vegetation, on which she lays her remarkably large eggs. They are usually two in number, and of white or greenish colour.

FLYING BIRDS (CARINATÆ).—The order of Game Birds (Gallinæ) includes one family (*Megapodiidæ*) of which the members do not incubate their eggs, the requisite heat being furnished, as in the case of many reptiles, either by the sun or else by the fermentative processes which go on in decaying vegetation. Birds are undoubtedly of reptilian stock, and it may well be that we have here an exceedingly ancient habit. The family is very characteristic of the Australian region, but ranges north to the Philippines, and west to the Moluccas. The simplest method adopted is to lay the eggs among rotting leaves, as in a New Hebrides species (*Megapodius Layardi*), or to dig a hole in the sand for their reception, as in a form (*M. eremita*) native to the Solomon and other islands. From this we pass to the "mound-building" species, of which a typical example is afforded by the Scrub-Turkey (*Catheturus* or *Talegallus Lathami*), native to East Australia, of which the domestic arrangements are thus described by Semon (in *In the Australian Bush*):—"Within the scrubs one will look in vain for any bright colour, a sombre green reigning everywhere. The ground between the trees is almost bare of vegetation, strewed only with fallen trunks, dead branches, and fragments of plants. Here the 'scrub-turkey' . . . builds its nest by scraping together with its powerful claws great quantities of vegetable substance, mould, grass, leaves, branches, and mushrooms, out of which it builds an enormous mound of a flattish shape. The diameter of these mounds varies from 4 to 5 yards at their base, their height from 1½ to 2 yards, so that the material they represent would make up several cart-loads. It is undecided as yet whether one pair or a whole party of birds combine to construct these mighty nests. The circumstance of one's occasionally finding more than thirty eggs buried in one mound leads me to suppose the latter. The eggs are laid into these hills at a depth of one or of half a yard, and are incubated by the warmth arising from fermentation of the rotting vegetable substances. The parent birds do not abandon their brood entirely during this process, but appear once or several times during the day to air their eggs. They examine whether the places they occupy have an appropriate temperature, or whether this has grown either too hot or too cool, and they help the chickens ready to slip out from the depths of this hatching oven. In these scrubs I was able to note the interesting fact that the birds began to build their mounds already in August, while the laying of eggs takes place only about Christmas-time. . . . The facts that the hills are so extensive, and the decay of material in the lower parts of the nest is already so far advanced when the laying of the eggs commences, has led to the conclusion that the same mound is employed several years successively, being fitted up every time by the addition of new material. As to my own observations, the birds scrape together a new heap every year, as a rule, if not always. They, however, begin this work four or five months before laying the eggs, a provision which is very much to the purpose. For mighty erections of this sort, the material for which has to be carefully so gathered and chosen that the right temperature may develop in their interior, cannot be raised at a moment's bidding. Plausible as this appears to ourselves, we must admire the wonderful instinct prompting the animals to make such preparation for eggs to be laid more than three months later." In New Guinea and North-east Australia the place of the Scrub-Turkey is taken by another mound-builder (*Megapodius tumulus*, fig. 969), of smaller size, the mounds of which may be as much as ten feet high, with a correspondingly large diameter. The nest is largely made of sand, and Semon describes one he observed in Wednesday Island, which appeared to be constructed of this material only. He suggests that the greater heat of the sun in this warmer latitude renders the employment of vegetable matter unnecessary. The chicks of all these non-incubating birds emerge from the egg in a very perfect condition, and are soon able to fly.

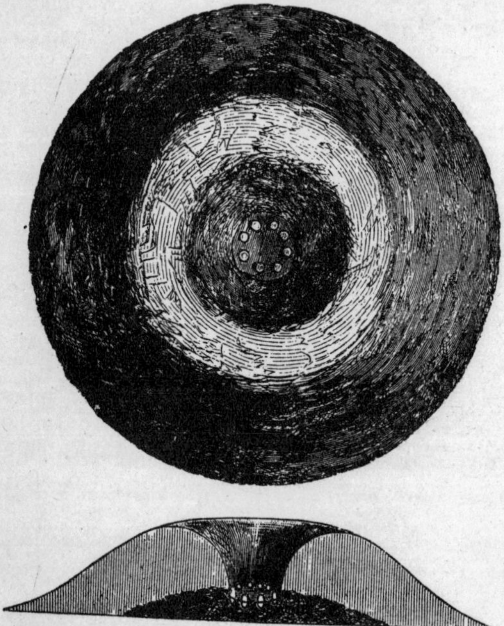

Fig. 969.—Mound of a Megapode (*Megapodius tumulus*), much reduced, as seen from above and in section

The vast majority of flying birds incubate their eggs, the old reptilian plan having been superseded. This is one of many results which have followed from the successful solution of the problem of separating the pure and impure blood in the circulation, a feat which reptiles have not yet accomplished. Hence the hot-bloodedness of birds, and the evolution of the incubatory habit.

Some birds make no nest at all, but simply lay their eggs in situations which are more or less exposed. The Common Guillemot (*Uria troile*), for example, lays her single egg on a ledge of rock or in a crevice, situated on a cliff or stack, the inaccessibility of which is a sufficient protection from most enemies, man excepted. The Common Tern (*Sterna fluviatilis*) lays two or three mottled eggs among shingle (fig. 970), and it will be seen from the illustration that it is scarcely possible to speak of a nest. The eggs are protectively coloured, as is usually the case when they are exposed to view, and by no means easy to detect. The Kentish Plover (*Ægialitis Cantiana*) affords another illustration of the same thing. Dixon (in *Among the Birds in Northern Shires*) says of the Nightjar or Goatsucker (*Caprimulgus Europæus*):—"It makes no nest, but the hen bird lays her two curiously oval eggs on the bare ground, sometimes beneath a spray of bracken or a furze bush, less frequently on the flat low branch of a convenient tree. These eggs are very beautiful, and he who finds them cannot confuse them with those of any other species that breeds in our islands. They are generally white and glossy, the surface mottled, blotched, streaked and veined with various shades of brown and gray."

Fig. 970.—Eggs of the Common Tern (*Sterna fluviatilis*)

Many birds make a burrow or hole in which to nest, or take advantage of an existing cavity, and the eggs are white, which is the general rule where they are not exposed to view. The Sand Martin (*Cotile riparia*) tunnels out a long (up to nine feet) and fairly horizontal gallery on the side of a steep bank often overlooking a stream. The inner end of this is enlarged, and the four to six eggs laid upon a layer of grass and neatly-arranged feathers. The Kingfisher (*Alcedo ispida*) digs out an upwardly slanting passage in an overhanging river-bank, and enlarges its end much after the fashion of a Sand-Martin. For a considerable time before laying this excavation is used for sleeping and feeding purposes, the result being an evil-smelling heap of fish-bones and other garbage upon which the six to eight pearly eggs are deposited. This has given rise to the erroneous idea that the bones are a special provision for the comfort(!) of the young. The beautiful Hoopoes are even more insanitary in their nesting-habits. The female lays her eggs in a hole in a tree or in rocks, and has sometimes been known to select a coffin or decomposing body for the purpose. A sort of lining is previously constructed of twigs, feathers, or hair, to which a liberal amount of filth is added. It is remarkable that the oil-gland of the nesting-female and also of the nestlings secretes an intolerably smelling fluid. This is perhaps a protective arrangement. The hen remains on this undesirable nest for practically the whole time of incubation, and is assiduously fed by her partner.

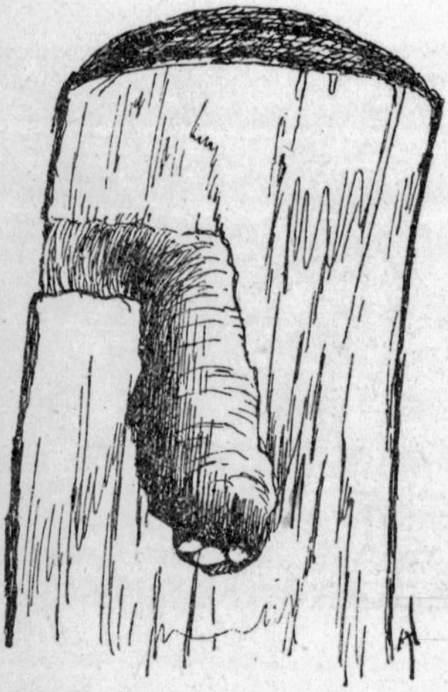

Fig. 971.—Nest of a Woodpecker, in section

Woodpeckers either nest in a ready-made hollow, or dig out a suitable cavity in the trunk of a tree, working at first horizontally and then vertically downwards (fig. 971). The white eggs are deposited on a layer of chips. The Nuthatch (*Sitta cæsia*) generally selects a hole in a decaying branch for its nesting-place, into which dead leaves or thin flakes of bark are taken to serve as a bed. The opening of the cavity is plastered up with clay, leaving only a round hole to serve for entry and exit.

We next have to consider nests of various degrees of complexity constructed from sticks, twigs, moss, and other plant material, to which feathers, wool, or hairs are frequently added. Many of the most familiar of these rest upon some firm support, and are circular in shape, with no roof except that which the surroundings may provide. Such nests may be of extremely primitive character, as in the Peewit or Lapwing (*Vanellus cristatus*), and the Golden

Plover (*Charadrius pluvialis*), where it is simply a slight hollow in the ground, with a scanty lining of dry herbage. Many sea-birds heap together such materials as are available into a somewhat rough nest, without any special attempt at concealment, as the inaccessible position gives a reasonable amount of security. Unfortunately the perverse ingenuity of man is difficult to baffle, and he is not the only egg-collector. Jackdaws, for example, are described by Dixon as making regular plundering expeditions around the Bass Rock, transfixing eggs with their beaks, and thus carrying them off to serve as food. The most prominent sea-bird in this famous spot is of course the Gannet or Solan Goose (*Sula Bassana*), and it is computed that not less than twelve thousand adult birds of this species find nesting-places there. The domestic arrangements are thus described by Dixon (in *Among the Birds in Northern Shires*):—"The nests are made almost anywhere—at the top of the cliffs amidst the broken rocks and crags, lower down the cliffs where any ordinary climber can reach them, and, most numerously of all, on the ledges far below which are only accessible with the aid of a rope. To say the least, the nest is not a very attractive one; it is often trodden out of all semblance to such a structure, and frequently covered with droppings and slime, whilst around it are dead and decaying fish, many of them disgorged when partly digested. The hot sun soon completes the work of decomposition, and generates a fearsome stench which it requires all the fortitude

Fig. 972.—Young Kittiwake (*Rissa tridactyla*) on Nest

Fig. 973.—Nest of Skylark (*Alauda arvensis*)

of an enthusiastic ornithologist to tolerate. The nests are made of sea-weed, turf, straws, and scraps of moss, the soil from the turf being trampled into a mortar-like mass and binding the whole together. In a shallow cavity at the top of this cone-like structure a single egg is laid, originally white and coated thickly with lime, but soon becoming stained into a rich brown from contact with the big webbed feet of the parent birds. Numbers of nests in some spots are crowded together, often so closely that the cliff is literally white with sitting birds." The nest of our smallest native gull, the Kittiwake (*Rissa tridactyla*) is a massive structure of similar kind (fig. 972). The illustration shows a young bird on the nest, as photographed by Mr. Van Someren at the Bass Rock.

Fig. 974.—Nest of Coot (*Fulica atra*)

Some birds build fairly well constructed nests in sheltered spots on or near the ground, as in the Sky-lark (*Alauda arvensis*, fig. 973), where dried grass, herbs, moss, and a little hair are used for the purpose. The Coot (*Fulica atra*, fig. 974) constructs a bulky nest of sedges, rushes, or flags, among the vegetation of its native stream. The illustration shows part of a sort of "road" trodden down by the birds in going to and from the nest. Sometimes this home is a floating one, as

Fig. 975.—White Swan (*Cygnus olor*) building a floating Nest

is regularly the case with the Little Grebe or Dabchick (*Podicipes fluviatilis*), which employs similar materials. The White Swan (*Cygnus olor*) frequently constructs a large floating nest of sticks and straw, though it often prefers an islet, when one is available. The former state of things is illustrated by fig. 975, taken at Duddingstone Loch, near Edinburgh, and showing building operations in progress.

Fig. 976.—Nest of Grey Wagtail (*Motacilla melanope*)

The cup-shaped nests of many common species built in various situations near the ground are more carefully finished than the domestic arrangements so far described. That of a Grey Wagtail (*Motacilla melanope*), shown in fig. 976, was built in a wall on the Pentlands. On this species Dixon (in *Among the Birds in Northern Shires*) makes the following remarks:—"Not every wanderer by the water-side is fortunate enough to get a peep at this bird's domestic arrangements. It has, fortunately perhaps, a happy way of concealing its nest under some large stone or overhanging rock, not necessarily in a secluded spot, but often close by the wayside, where the very audacity of the selection proves a source of safety. A scrappy little nest it is, dry grass and roots and such like litter thrown carelessly together, and lined with hair, or more rarely a few feathers; artless, yet possessing a rustic beauty if wanting that elaborate finish of more painstaking nest-builders. The five or six eggs are as unassuming as the nest that holds them, grayish-white freckled with brown, and perhaps with here and there a scratch of darker hue. . . . This pretty wagtail still further endears

Fig. 977.—Nest of Common Thrush (*Turdus musicus*)

itself to us by its attachment to a certain breeding-place, returning in many cases year by year to build its nest in one particular spot." A much neater nest is constructed in a hedge or bush by the Common Thrush (*Turdus musicus*, fig. 977), grass being the chief building material, while mud is used as a cement. An inner layer of finer material is added, and the whole is completed by a lining of cow-dung, decayed wood, or mud.

Fig. 978.—Nest of Wood-Pigeon (*Columba palumbus*)

We have next to consider nests made of sticks or fibres, and placed in trees or other precarious situations, often in such a way as to necessitate very considerable constructive skill. One of the least elaborate is the loose stick-nest of the Wood-Pigeon (*Columba palumbus*, fig. 978), through the crevices in which the two eggs can easily be seen from below. Contrary to the usual rule these are white in colour, and it has been suggested that they are thus rendered less conspicuous when seen from below against the bright sky.

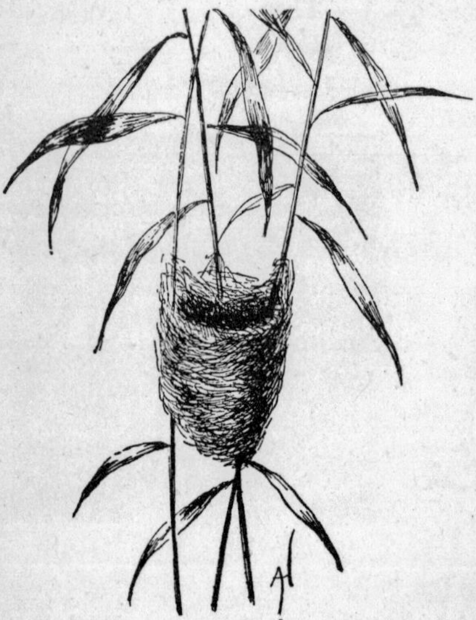

Fig. 979.—Nest of Great Reed Warbler (*Acrocephalus arundinaceus*)

Much more elegant are the deep woven nests of the Reed Warbler (*Acrocephalus streperus*) and Great Reed Warbler (*A. arundinaceus*, fig. 979), constructed of vegetable fibre, while moss, wool, feathers, and hair serve as materials for lining. It will be seen from the illustration how cleverly the stems of reeds are used as a support. Many woven nests are roofed over, and have an opening at the side, as in the case of the Long-tailed Tit (*Acredula caudata*), which has a more elaborate home than any other British bird. Compared to the owner it is of large dimensions, and ovoid in shape. Moss, wool, and cobwebs are the chief materials used, all carefully interwoven. The outside is studded with bits of lichen, while the inside is lined with hair and feathers. One observer had the curiosity to count the number of the latter embodied in a single nest and made a total of 2379, so that this item only must involve an enormous amount of patient labour. When the parents are "not at home" the aperture is said to be closed by a feather. Some of the glands of the mouth secrete a sticky fluid, which is of importance in softening and working up the material used in neat and elaborate nests like this one; cobwebs, too, prove useful as an adhesive. The Penduline Tit (*Ægithalus pendulinus*, fig. 980) of South Europe constructs an equally elaborate hanging nest, which is entered by a sort of passage, that has suggested comparison with a bottle, though a better simile would be afforded by a short-necked retort.

Fig. 980.—Penduline Tit (*Ægithalus pendulinus*) and Nest

The Indian Tailor-Bird (*Orthotomus sutorius*, fig. 981) constructs a hanging nest with extraordinary ingenuity, by sewing together a couple of long leaves into a sort of funnel, within which a soft bed of cotton is placed for the reception of the eggs. The sewing material is made of cotton, and sometimes, at least, is twisted by the bird itself, which is also credited with making a knot for the usual purpose. The Fan-tail Warbler (*Cisticola cursitans*) of South Europe builds a globular nest among grass, and makes a sort of awning by sewing together the leaves and stems above it. This bird too is said to make a knot at the end of its thread.

The nests of a good many birds are plastic structures made from earth or clay, with which bits of other material may be mixed.. That of the Common Flamingo (*Phœnicopterus roseus*, fig. 982) is built on the ground, and shaped like a broadly truncated cone, upon which the bird sits with its long legs folded up in an uncomfortable-looking position. Chapman and Buck (in *Wild Spain*) give the following interesting description:—"On reaching the spot we found a perfect mass of nests. The low, flat mud plateau was crowded with them as thickly as its space permitted. These nests had little or no height above the flat surface of the mud—some were raised an inch or two, a few might be five or six inches in height; but the majority were merely circular bulwarks of mud barely raised above the general level, and having the impression of the bird's legs distinctly marked upon them. The general aspect of the plateau was not unlike a large table covered with plates. In the centre was a deep hole full of muddy water, which, from the gouged appearance of its sides, appeared to be used as a reservoir for nest-making materials.

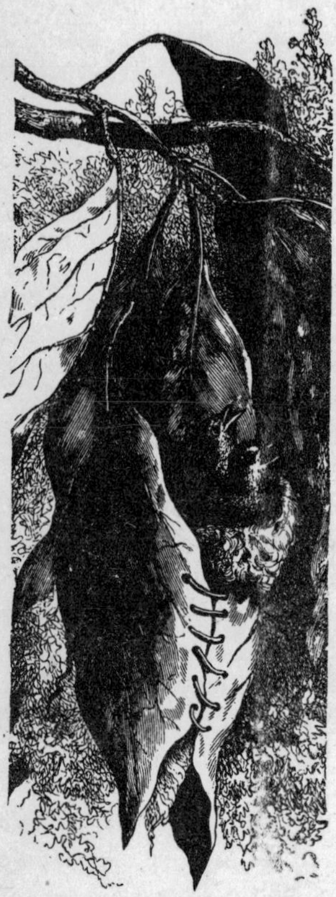

Fig. 981.—Nest and Young of Tailor-Bird (*Orthotomus sutorius*)

Scattered all round this main colony were numerous single nests, rising out of the water and evidently built up from the bottom. Here and there two or three of these were joined together—'semi-detached', so to speak: these separate nests stood six or eight inches above water-level, and as the depth was rather over a foot, the total height of the nests would be some two feet or thereabouts, and their width across the hollow top some fifteen inches."

Most persons are familiar with the little clay nests of the Common Swallow (*Hirundo rustica*), commonly built against a wall immediately under the eaves, and comparable in shape to half a saucer. Their construction involves much labour, for the material has to be brought in the bill in successive pellets. Consistency is given by bits of straw or stick, while in this and similar cases the sticky secretion of the mouth is probably of importance by way of cement. A lining of feathers is added. The nest of the House-Martin (*Chelidon urbica*) is made of similar materials, but roofed over.

Fig. 982.—Brooding Flamingo (*Phœnicopterus roseus*)

The Oven-Birds (species of *Furnarius*, fig. 983) of South America build on the branches of trees, their clay nests having

Fig. 983.—Nest of an Oven-Bird (*Furnarius*)

the shape which has suggested the popular name. A partition runs from back to front, dividing a cavity in which the eggs are contained from a sort of ante-chamber that communicates with the exterior.

The glands of the mouth, which are so often of importance in nest-building on account of their sticky secretion, are particularly well-developed in Swifts (*Cypselidæ*), birds which are often erroneously mistaken for Swallows. In our Common Swift (*Cypselus apus*) this secretion is used to glue straw, dry grass, and the like, into a flattish nest, which is built in some hole or cranny. A lining of feathers is added. A kind of Swift (*Panyptila Sancti Hieronymi*) native to Guatemala glues seeds together

Fig. 984.—Edible Nests of Collocalia

into a long hanging nest, shaped something like a knobbed walking-stick. The entrance is at the lower end, and the eggs are lodged in the "knob" at the top. Perhaps the most remarkable of all bird's nests, so far as the building material is concerned, are those which the Chinese prize as an article of diet. They are constructed by certain Swifts (species of *Collocalia*, fig. 984) which range from Madagascar eastwards to the Marquesas Islands. In form they resemble those of the Swallow, but are entirely composed of the sticky fluid secreted by the glands of the mouth, with an occasional admixture of other substances. They are mostly to be found in caves.

The majority of birds do not associate for nesting purposes, though a very large number are social in this respect, and several examples have already been described. Among British species Rooks, Herons, and Fieldfares may be added to the list. The most extraordinary instance of this kind is afforded by the Sociable Grosbeak (*Philhetærus socius*, fig. 985) of South Africa. By the combined efforts of a large number of these birds a huge structure resembling the top of a mushroom is built round a tree,

Fig. 985.—Nest of Sociable Grosbeak (*Philhetærus socius*)

grass being the material employed. It consists of from 100 to over 300 associated nests.

Related species not infrequently differ greatly as regards their nesting-habits, the most remarkable case being that of the South American Tree-Creepers or Picucules (*Dendrocolaptidæ*), which include the Oven-Birds already noticed. These Tree-Creepers differ remarkably among themselves in appearance and structure, as the result of adaptation to various modes of life. And that they provide for the welfare of their eggs in widely different ways will be obvious from the following account given by Hudson (in *The Naturalist in La Plata*):—"In the nesting habits the diversity is greatest. Some ground species excavate in the earth like kingfishers, only with greater skill, making cylindrical burrows often four to five feet deep, and terminating in a round chamber. Others build a massive oven-shaped structure of clay on a branch or other elevated site. Many of those that creep on trees nest in holes in the wood. The marsh-frequenting kinds attach spherical or oval domed nests to the reeds; and in some cases woven grass and clay are so ingeniously combined that the structure, while light as a basket, is perfectly impervious to the wet and practically indestructible. The most curious nests, however, are the large stick structures on trees and bushes, in the building and repairing of which the birds are in many cases employed more or less constantly all the year round. These stick nests vary greatly in form, size, and in other respects. Some have a spiral passage-way leading from the entrance to the nest cavity, and the cavity is in many cases only large enough to accommodate the bird; but in the gigantic structure of *Homoris gutturalis* it is so large that, if the upper half of the nest or dome were removed, a condor could comfortably hatch her eggs and rear her young in it. The nest is spherical. The allied *Homoris lophotis* builds a nest equally large, but with a small cavity for the eggs inside, and outwardly resembling a gigantic powder-flask, lying horizontally among the lower branches of a spreading tree. *Pracellodomus sibilatrix*, a bird in size like the English house-sparrow, also makes a huge nest, and places it on the twigs at the terminal end of a horizontal branch from twelve to fifteen feet above the ground; but when finished, the weight of the structure bears down the branch-end to within one or two feet of the surface. . . . *Synallaxis phryganophila* makes a stick nest about a foot in depth, and from the top a tubular passage, formed of slender twigs intertwined, runs down the entire length of the nest, like a rain-pipe on the wall of a house, and then becoming external, slopes upwards, ending at a distance of two to three feet from the nest." It must not be supposed that in this family the species of the same genus necessarily build in the same way. For example the Oven-Birds (*Furnarius*) are so named on account of the shape of the clay nests constructed by three species, but another species makes a stick nest, and still another lays its eggs in a burrow.

A nest having been constructed, both parents take part in the care of eggs and young. Probably in the majority of cases incubation is entirely or mostly performed by the mother, though the father may take his turn in brooding over the eggs, as in some Woodpeckers. More rarely, as in some of the Plover kind, the relations appear to be reversed, reminding us of what happens in the case of the Running Birds. Dixon thus speaks of the Dotterel (*Eudromias morinellus*, fig. 986) in this connection (in *Among the Birds in Northern Shires*):—"The Dotterel is one of the very few species in which the hen bird is larger and more brightly coloured than the cock, and the latter con-

Fig. 986.—Female Dotterel (*Eudromias morinellus*)

sequently incubates the eggs and takes the greater share in the task of rearing the young. The hen is even said to take the initiative in courtship, but we have yet to learn that the 'new woman' has quoted the fact in support of her advanced opinions! But then the Dotterel is widely known by the accompanying and preceding epithet of 'foolish', and its English name is said to be the diminutive of 'Dolt'; while its Latin name of *morinellus* is said by some to have been derived from *morus*, a fool—facts which those interested in so-called 'sex-problems' will also do well to bear in mind."

When the mother bird displays great devotion to the task of incubation, brooding on her eggs for long periods, she is diligently fed by her mate, as in the case of Hoopoes (see p. 454). The habits of some at least of the Hornbills (*Bucerotidæ*) are very remarkable in this respect. These birds range from Africa through South Asia into the East Indies. Evans thus summarizes what is known of the nesting habits (in *The Cambridge Natural History*):—"A hole in a tree or a cavity at the junction of two branches serves for the nest, wherein the hen is enclosed by a plaster of dung or like material; there, under penalty of death, she remains until she emerges, dirty, wasted, and enfeebled, when the brood is hatched. From one to four dingy white eggs with coarse pores are deposited upon the debris or a few feathers. Contrary to expectation, observations seem to show that the female walls herself in; but, however that may be, the cock feeds her through the small opening left, and is even said to knock with his bill to attract her attention as he clings to the bark. He shows great anxiety about his charge, and the hen screams and bites if molested."

The parental task of birds is by no means over when their eggs have hatched out, for the young are fed with anxious care, and jealously guarded from enemies. This is, of course, especially necessary when the nestlings are helpless. The devotion of birds to their offspring is well known, and they are often quite regardless of personal danger when the welfare of the brood is in question (fig. 987). Gilbert White (in *The Natural History of Selborne*) thus speaks in his own inimitable way of the solicitude which birds display for their young:—"This affection sublimes the passions, quickens the invention, and sharpens the sagacity of the brute creation. Thus a hen, just become a mother, is no longer that placid bird she used to be, but with feathers standing on end, wings hovering, and clocking note, she runs about like one possessed. Dams will throw themselves in the way of the greatest danger in order to avert it from their progeny. Thus a partridge will tumble along before a sportsman in order to draw away the dogs from her helpless covey. In the time of nidification the most feeble birds will assault the most rapacious. All the *Hirundines* [*i.e.* birds of the Swallow kind] of a village are up in arms at the sight of a hawk, whom they will persecute till he leaves that district. A very exact observer has often remarked that a pair of ravens nesting in the rock of Gibraltar would suffer no vulture or eagle to rest near their station, but would drive them from the hill with an amazing fury; even the blue thrush at the season of breeding would dart out from the clefts of the rocks to chase away the kestrel or the sparrow-hawk. If you stand near the nest of a bird that has young, she will not be induced to betray them by an inadvertent fondness, but will wait about at a distance with meat in her mouth for an hour together." The same naturalist describes as follows the way

Fig. 987.—Wild Duck defending her Brood against a Brown Rat

in which the House-Martin (*Chelidon urbica*) feeds its young in their later stages:—"As the young of small birds presently arrive at their . . . full growth, they soon become impatient of confinement, and sit all day with their heads out at the orifice, where the dams, by clinging to the nest, supply them with food from morning to night. For a time the young are fed on the wing by their parents; but the feat is done by so quick and almost imperceptible a flight that a person must have attended very exactly to their motions before he would be able to perceive it." White also observed young Swallows (*Hirundo rustica*) being fed on the wing, and says:—"In a day or two more they become *flyers*, but are still unable to take their own food; therefore they play about near the place where the dams are hawking for flies; and, when a mouthful is collected, at a certain signal given, the dam and the nestling advance, rising towards each other, and meeting at an angle, the young one all the while uttering such a little quick note of gratitude and complacency, that a person must have paid very little regard to the wonders of Nature that has not often remarked this feat." It must be added to these extracts that both in the Swallow and the House-Martin the father performs his full share of the arduous work of feeding the young.

Fig. 988.—Skylark (*Alauda arvensis*) at her Nest

R. and C. Kearton of recent years have made many remarkable photographs of bird-life, and by means of artificial rubbish-heaps and other ingenious devices have been able to hide themselves sufficiently near to the nests of a number of familiar forms to observe all the details of their domestic economy. The following passage (from *Wild Life at Home*) vividly describes the way in which a particular mother Skylark (*Alauda arvensis*) fed and tended her young (fig. 988):—"In a few minutes along came the lark, and hovering over her chicks for a few seconds, like a toy-bird suspended on the end of a bit of elastic, called to them in twittering notes, at which signal of her presence they all shot up their heads and opened their orange-coloured mouths ridiculously wide. She quickly alighted, and running up, gave each a small worm, which she appeared to fetch from the back of her throat. Generally, one of the worms which she brought was visible in her bill, but this was by no means always the case. When she had distributed her supply of food she waited for a moment, and then, thrusting her head into the depths of the nest, attended to its sanitary arrangements and flew away. . . . She heralded her return every time by a twittering call that was answered by her offspring, which she fed on an average once every quarter of an hour. . . . She did not appear to receive the slightest assistance from her mate, although I must say he sang very blithely over our heads on several occasions." All bird fathers, however, are not so careless as the Skylark, for in this same book we find the statement:—"A closer study of the domestic life of birds by means of our hiding appliances has resulted in the discovery that the males of many species share family cares to a far greater extent than I ever supposed. One day I erected our rubbish-heap close to a chaffinch's nest containing a brood of five half-grown young ones, and took up my station inside. The male bird fed the chicks four times for the female's once, and when he had distributed his harvest of caterpillars most impartially amongst his clamorous sons and daughters he attended to the sanitary requirements of his little establishment" (fig. 989). The frontispiece to the work from which the two last quotations are taken is a particularly charming picture of a male Bearded Tit feeding his young.

Fig. 989.—Cock Chaffinch (*Fringilla cœlebs*) at Nest

In many vegetarian birds the food of the adult is unsuitable for the young brood, and this is especially the case with some of the finch kind, which largely subsist on hard seeds and the like. There is more than one way of getting over this difficulty. The adult House-Sparrow (*Passer domesticus*, fig. 990), for example, lives chiefly on various plant parts, but feeds its young on worms, grubs, caterpillars, and other small creatures.

This is also true of the Tree-Sparrow (*P. montanus*). During the nesting season the Chaffinch (*Fringilla cœlebs*) abandons its diet of seeds and berries in favour of animal food, devoting

Fig. 990.—House-Sparrows (*Passer domesticus*) feeding their Young

special attention to the little caterpillars found in buds and flowers, which are also adapted to the tender digestions of the nestlings. Linnets (*Linaria cannabina*, fig. 991) are consistent vegetarians, but the seeds and other vegetable matters, with

Fig. 991.—A Nest of Linnets (*Linaria cannabina*)

which the young are fed, first undergo a softening process in the crops of the parents. A curious adaptation for the benefit of the young is found in Pigeons, which produce a special sort of "infants' food" popularly known as "pigeons' milk". This is not, however, a secretion, but consists of curd-like flakes derived from the lining of the crop, which undergoes rapid growth during the nesting season.

When the young bird is fed from the crop it sometimes makes the operation more easy by thrusting its head into the mouth of its parent, as in the case of the Black Cormorant (*Phalacrocorax carbo*, fig. 992).

The sanitation of the nest is sometimes entirely neglected, as in Gannets and Kingfishers, necessarily so in the case of Hornbills (see p. 466). But in probably the majority of birds it is attended to by the parents with scrupulous care, as will have been gathered from the accounts already given of the Skylark and Chaffinch. Sometimes, as in the House-Martin, the old birds teach the young ones how to avoid fouling the nest.

Fig. 992.—Black Cormorant (*Phalacrocorax carbo*) feeding its Young

Young birds which may almost be said to run from the egg are usually protectively coloured, and crouch when alarmed, as already described for the Emeu (see p. 450) and, in an earlier section, for some of the Plovers (see vol. ii, p. 285). Apparently the first case of the kind to attract observation was that of the Stone-Curlew (*Œdicnemus scolopax*), described, so long ago as 1768, by Gilbert White (in *The Natural History of Selborne*):—"The history of the stone-curlew . . . is as follows. It lays its eggs, usually two, never more than three, on the bare ground, without any nest, in the field; so that the countryman, in stirring his fallows, often destroys them. The young run immediately from the egg like partridges, &c., and are withdrawn to some flinty field by the dam, where they skulk among the stones, which are their best security; for their feathers are so exactly of the colour of our grey-spotted flints, that the most exact observer, unless he catches the eye of the young bird, may be deluded." Another familiar example is that of the Peewit or Lapwing (*Vanellus cristatus*, fig. 993), the chicks of which are exceedingly difficult to find, and when accidentally discovered are apt to disappear in the twinkling of an eye. The parent birds are adepts in the art of deceiving inquisitive strangers as to the exact whereabouts of their eggs or brood.

Remarkable arrangements exist for the safety of the young in a primitive South American bird, the Hoatzin (*Opisthocomus*),

Fig. 993.—Female Lapwing (*Vanellus cristatus*) and Young

which appears to be a distant relative of the Game-Birds (*Gallinæ*). Of these Headley gives the following interesting account (in *The Structure and Life of Birds*):—"Apparently about as large as a rather under-sized pheasant, the Hoatzin is really considerably smaller; his long tail, his large wings, and his crest suggest a larger bulk of body than he really possesses. . . . Among the trees and bushes that form a jungle-growth along the banks of the Berbice, and often overhang its waters, Hoatzins are plentiful. When a boat passes they will generally remain concealed among the leaves. . . . The nest is formed of a few sticks intertwisted. When the birds'-nester comes, cutting a way for his boat through the bushes, or wading thigh-deep through the mud, the old bird makes off upon the wing. The nestling, unless very recently hatched, crawls off on all-fours, making much use of not only his enormous feet, but of the great claws that grow at the ends of the two first digits of his hand (fig. 994). If you try to pull him from the nest by the legs, he holds fast by means of these wing-claws and his beak. Often a young bird may be found clawing his way onward some distance from the nest. If he tumbles into the water he proves to be a born swimmer and diver. . . . In the nestling Hoatzin the hand is longer than the forearm; gradually it grows shorter, while the other parts of the wing

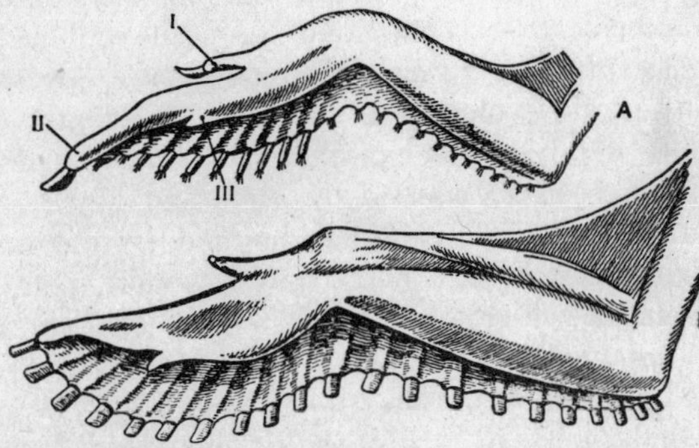

Fig. 994.—Wings of Young (A) and Adult (B) Hoatzin (*Opisthocomus*). The quills of the latter have been cut short. I, II, III, digits.

lengthen, till, in the fledged bird, the forearm surpasses it (fig. 994). The feathers, too, adapt themselves to changing circumstances; in the nestling the growth of the two outermost primaries is completely arrested, so that the use of the claws may not be impeded; when it is fledged and can fly, they begin again to grow and attain their full length. With maturity, too, the claw on digit No. 1 grows small, while that on No. 2 is lost altogether."

Before leaving Birds it may be well to remark that in the early history of the group precocious young were no doubt the rule, and it is interesting to note that they are characteristic of many species in which the organization is relatively low. The associated evolution of greater intelligence and increased parental affection is apparently responsible for the appearance of helpless nestlings. And we can only suppose that these have, on the whole, a better chance of surviving the struggle for existence than young birds which are soon able to take care of themselves, though this chance entirely depends upon the devotion of their progenitors. Such a conclusion is strengthened by a study of Mammals, the highest group of Vertebrates in many respects.

LIFE-HISTORIES, &c., OF MAMMALS (MAMMALIA)

Mammals agree with Birds in being of reptilian origin, and like them are hot-blooded, as a result of the perfect adaptation of their organs of circulation to air-breathing (see vol. ii, p. 426). The geological record shows us that Amphibians were the first backboned animals to become fitted for a life on land, where, in the absence of more specialized competitors, they were long dominant. But the evolution of Reptiles, still better suited to terrestrial life, deprived them of their supremacy, and these in their turn have been superseded by Birds and Mammals. Amphibians and Reptiles are still handicapped by the inheritance from fish-like ancestors of circulatory organs originally evolved in the interests of gill-breathing, and in none of them are these organs fully adapted to life on land. But Birds and Mammals, having finally overcome this initial difficulty, are thereby profoundly influenced in many ways. Increased energy and increased intelligence have resulted among other things, one manifestation of the latter being found in a remarkable solicitude for the welfare of their young, which is a factor of the first importance in the struggle for existence. Insects alone afford a parallel, and it is especially interesting to note that in them also the arrangements whereby the blood is purified are highly efficient, though very different in nature from those existing in land Vertebrates (see vol. ii, p. 437).

Birds, of course, are dominant in the realms of air, Bats alone among Mammals entering into competition with them. The fact that we ourselves belong to the Mammalia is enough to justify us in describing that class as the dominant one on land, though Birds flourish exceedingly, and there is still abundant foothold for both Reptiles and Amphibia. The prominent position which Mammals now occupy is largely bound up with two features in their life-history. One is the possession of milk-glands for the benefit of their young, and the other is the viviparous or internal development by which the vast majority of them are characterized. In both respects they contrast markedly with Birds, and have a decided advantage over them. For, given parents able to defend themselves, the sheltered nature of viviparous development increases the chance of survival, and feeding the young on milk is a simpler matter than collecting suitable nutriment for them, as so many birds have to do, with expenditure of an enormous amount of energy.

The three great groups of Mammals, beginning with the lowest, are: Egg-laying Mammals (Prototheria), Pouched Mammals (Metatheria), and Higher Mammals (Eutheria). By successively reviewing these we shall obtain some idea of what has taken place in the evolution of the class.

EGG-LAYING MAMMALS (PROTOTHERIA).—The one family (*Monotremata*) included in this group contains only the Duck-Bill or Duck-Billed Platypus (*Ornithorhynchus*) and the Spiny Ant-Eaters (*Echidna* and *Proëchidna*) of the Australian region. There can be no doubt that Australia was at one time continuous with the mainland mass of the Old World, but became isolated before any of the higher Mammals migrated into it, owing to which fortunate circumstance the lower members of the class have been able to maintain themselves there, in the absence of serious competition. Duck-Bills and Spiny Ant-Eaters alike are of comparatively lowly structure, and possess many reptilian characters, one of the most remarkable being that they lay large tough-shelled eggs containing a great deal of food-yolk, serving as a store of food for the developing embryo.

The domestic economy of the best-known species of Spiny Ant-Eater (*Echidna aculeata*) has of late years been the subject of careful study, and is of unusual interest. The milk-glands which distinguish Mammals from all other creatures almost always have teats, from which circumstance, indeed, the name of the class is derived (L. *mamma*, a teat). The Spiny Ant-Eater does not possess these, although it has two milk-glands, differing, however, in nature from those of other Mammals, the allied Duck-Bill excepted. It commonly happens that when "new" organs make their appearance they are in reality "old" structures which have undertaken new work, and been correspondingly modified (see vol. ii, p. 421). This appears to be the case with milk-glands. We find in the skins of various Mammals two important varieties of glandular structures, one

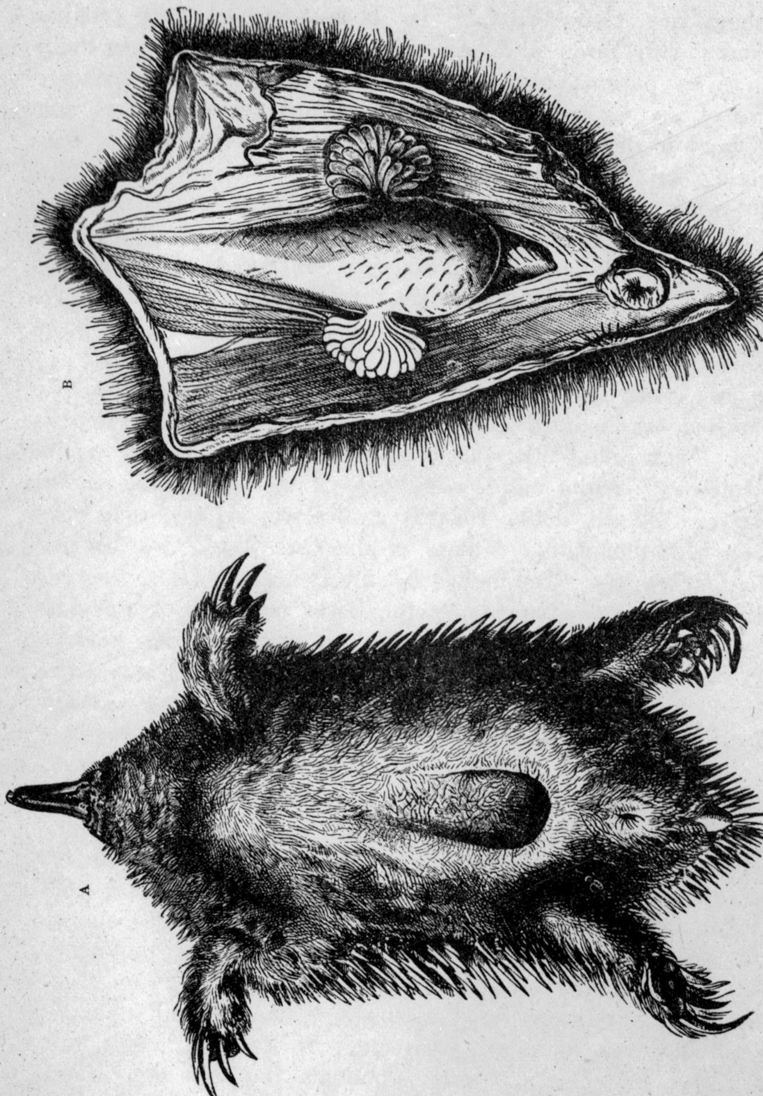

Fig. 995.—Female Spiny Ant-Eater (*Echidna*), reduced. A, under surface, showing pouch; B, dissection (from above), showing pouch, and two bunches of milk-glands opening into it.

for the secretion of sweat, the other for producing a greasy substance that acts as a sort of natural pomade. It appears that the milk-glands of Spiny Ant-eaters and Duck-Bills have been derived from the former (sweat-glands), those of other Mammals from the latter (sebaceous glands).

During the egg-laying season a sort of pouch develops on the under side of the Spiny Ant-eater, into which the milk-glands open (fig. 995). To this the single egg (about $\frac{3}{8}$ inch long) is transferred by the mother, by means of her snout. After a short incubation the young animal breaks through the egg shell with the aid of a little knob on its nose, something like that present in a young bird, and the mother is also said to give assistance. The little creature is entirely devoid of hair and not much like the adult (fig. 996). It is sheltered in the pouch till about three inches long, and feeds by licking up the milk which is secreted. The preceding facts are chiefly due to the investigations of Semon, who gives the following account of subsequent events (in *In the Australian Bush*):—"From the middle of October my blacks found several such older specimens outside the maternal pouch in little hollows of the ground. . . . The blacks all told me that the 'old woman' (as the natives call the mother animal) during the first weeks often returns to the young one to take it into her pouch and suckle it. On entering upon her nightly rambles, however, she deposits her weighty and inconvenient youngster, digging a little burrow for it, where she stows it away until her return from her roamings. I was able to substantiate this account. . . ." The very intimate relation between mother and offspring which suckling entails has probably played an important part in the evolution of the pronounced maternal affection for which Mammals are remarkable.

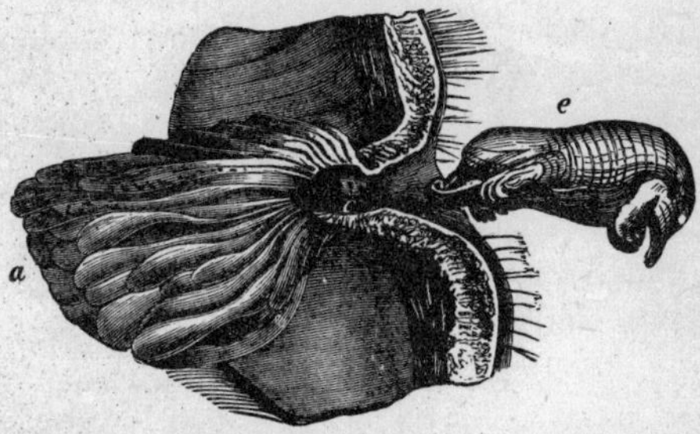

Fig. 996.—Pouch (*c*, in section), bunch of milk-glands (*a*), and Pouch-Embryo (*e*) of Spiny Ant-Eater (*Echidna*). The openings of the glands into the pouch are shown.

The aquatic Duck-Bill (*Ornithorhynchus*) digs out a burrow of from 20 to 50 feet in length, the inner end of which is enlarged, much as in the dwelling of a Kingfisher or Sand-Martin. The main opening is under water, but there is a second one above the surface, which appears to promote ventilation, though it may perhaps be used as an emergency exit as well. The milk-glands are comparable to those of the Spiny Ant-Eater, but there is no pouch, and the eggs are deposited in a rough sort of nest, lodged within the burrow, and made up of dry vegetation. Professor Gregg Wilson was the first naturalist to find this nest, and owed his success to the discovery that when the mother Duck-Bill goes out she throws up a little wall of soil between the nest and the rest of the burrow, an obviously protective arrangement. Anyone who dug out a burrow in ignorance of this fact would find that it appeared to end abruptly, whereas a little further excavation would reveal the nest.

POUCHED MAMMALS (METATHERIA).—Here again we are concerned with but one order (*Marsupialia*), the members of this also being limited to the Australian region, with the exception of Opossums (*Didelphyidæ*) and a small mouse-like creature (*Cœnolestes*), which are American. Here, as in all Mammals except the egg-laying forms, the ova are minute and develop internally, there being special arrangements compensating for the absence of food-yolk. Young Marsupials are born in an extremely immature condition, and in the majority of cases are at once placed by the mother in her large pouch, and attached to the long teats there present. In Kangaroos the opening of the pouch is in front (fig. 997), obviously the most convenient position for creatures so constantly assuming an upright posture. In other cases it is at the back. A number of forms, *e.g.* most of the Opossums, are entirely devoid of this structure.

The pouch of a Marsupial is supported by two "marsupial bones" (see fig. 734, p. 190) attached to the pelvis, and probably equivalent to similarly-placed "epipubic" elements, often present in Reptiles and Amphibia (see vol. i, p. 241, fig. 149). These bones are also present in the Duck-Mole and Spiny Ant-Eater. It would, however, be a mistake to suppose that the pouch of the last-named animal is equivalent to that of, say, a Kangaroo, for this is only one of many instances where organs of different nature perform the same function.

So helpless is a newly-born Marsupial that it is at first unable to suck properly, and the milk is squirted down its throat by the contraction of a layer of muscle covering the milk-

given locality the total number of rabbits may remain practically the same for long periods of time, but, as everyone knows, the introduction of this species into Australia has been followed by an extraordinary increase in numbers, chiefly owing to the absence of predaceous native forms. In respect of fertility the Rabbit is greatly surpassed by some other members of the same order, such as Mice and Voles. Certain species of the latter at times increase at such an alarming rate, both in this country and on the Continent, as to constitute a serious agricultural "plague", to successfully cope with which taxes all the resources of applied science.

Fig. 1000.—Harvest-Mice (*Mus minutus*) and Nest

Turning now to the Hare, we find that this animal does not burrow, its home being simply a sheltered spot known as a "form". The leverets are from two to five in number, their eyes are open from the first, and they are fur-covered when born. After being suckled for about three weeks they have to look after themselves.

The blind and naked young of the little Harvest-Mouse (*Mus minutus*, fig. 1000) are born in an elegant globular nest, usually found suspended from the stalks of corn or grass. Gilbert White (in *The Natural History of Selborne*), in his oft-quoted account of these mice, says that "they build their nests amidst the straws of the corn above the ground, and sometimes in thistles. They breed as many as eight at a litter, in a little round nest composed of the blades of grass or wheat. One of these nests I procured this autumn, most artificially plaited, and composed of the blades of wheat, perfectly round, and about the size of a cricket-ball; with the aperture so ingeniously closed, that there was no discovering to what part it belonged. It was so compact and well filled that it would roll across the table without being discomposed, though it contained eight little mice that were naked and blind."

The Common Squirrel (*Sciurus vulgaris*) is another nest-building rodent, and constructs its dwelling either in a hole in a tree or else in a convenient fork of the branches. The framework of this "drey", which is of rounded shape, consists of interwoven twigs, while moss, lichen, and leaves are used as packing and lining materials. The opening is on one side, and, unless a hole has been selected for a residence, its position may be altered from time to time in accordance with the exigencies of the weather. The blind and helpless young are born within this snug habitation, their number being usually three or four, though sometimes there is a much larger family.

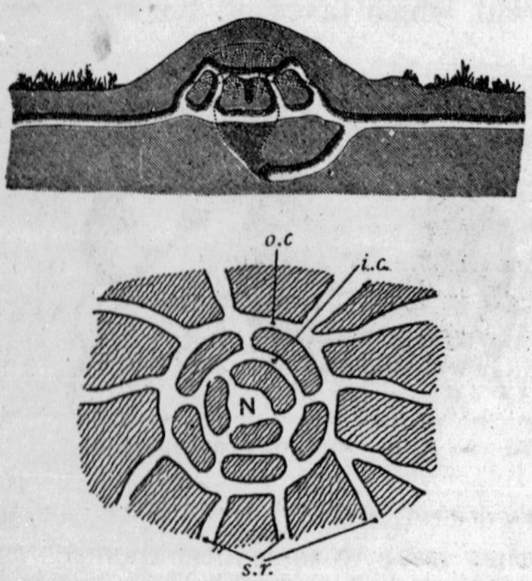

Fig. 1001.—Fortress of Mole (*Talpa Europæa*) in vertical section (above) and plan (below), reduced. N., nest; *i.c.*, inner circular passage; *o.c.*, outer circular passage; *s.r.*, side-roads.

Insect-eating Mammals (Insectivora).—The animals of this large order are usually small and defenceless. Like Rodents they are extremely prolific, and their young are born blind and naked. Several pairs of milk-glands are present. It will perhaps suffice to deal with two of our native forms, the Hedgehog (*Erinaceus Europæus*) and the Mole (*Talpa Europæa*).

The Hedgehog constructs a snug nest of dried leaves under a hedge or in some other sheltered situation, and here the young are born, to the number of five or six as a general rule. They are at first blind, practically bare, and devoid of the power of rolling themselves up. Growth is rapid, and these defects are soon remedied.

The Mole is remarkable for the ingenuity and skill it displays in the construction of a comfortable dwelling or "fortress", to which it is said to repair four times in the twenty-four hours, for the purpose of resting after its very considerable labours by way of tunnelling in search of food. This retreat is placed at a distance from the hunting-ground, in some inaccessible place, as under the roots of a tree, in the shelter of a thick hedge, or below a wall. As will be gathered from fig. 1001, it is of decidedly elaborate nature. What we may perhaps call the "home-road" leads into a rounded chamber, cosily lined with moss and dry grass. Surrounding this chamber at a little distance is a circular passage, and at a somewhat higher level a narrower gallery of the same shape. This last has some three direct communications with the central chamber, and about five with the larger circular passage, from which radiate a number of "side-roads", that ultimately bend round and open into the home-road. An enemy entering this labyrinth is likely to go wrong, and at the same time the owner of the dwelling has numerous ways of escape. The walls of all these various passages are compacted by pressure, so that they are permanent structures which do not readily fall in. But as in Rabbits (see p. 482), this convenient and well-appointed dwelling is not used as a nursery, for which purpose a sheltered spot not far from the fortress is selected, a suitable chamber being excavated and warmly lined. This is placed where three or more galleries meet, safety from weasels being the chief object attained. The family consists of five young ones in most cases, and these are born in a particularly helpless condition. They are fed and tended by their mother for at least five weeks, by which time they are about half-grown, and during this part of their existence are said to remain in the nest. The affections of the family are apparently distributed in a way that is somewhat reminiscent of the brief notes appended to the cast of a drama. The mother, as usual, is devoted to her young, and her affection is presumably reciprocated. The father is believed to be a noted instance of conjugal attachment, but his feelings towards his family are often expressed by attempts to devour them, and a probable guess might be made as to their feelings in regard to him.

The aberrant Insectivore known as the Colugo or Flying-"Lemur" (*Galeopithecus*), remarkable for its parachuting arrangements, is in some respects transitional to Bats. Instead of producing a numerous family, and possessing a proportionate number of milk-glands, it gives birth to only a single young one, so far as known. The milk-glands are two in number, and situated on the chest. Although the young Colugo comes into the world blind and hairless it is nevertheless able to hold firmly to the fur of its mother, and is carried about by her.

Bats (Chiroptera).—The milk-glands of Bats correspond to those of the Colugo in number and position; and the one or sometimes two young ones are born in much the same condition as the offspring of that animal. In the majority of cases the first act of a newly-born Bat is to crawl along the body of its mother till the source of nourishment is reached. The devoted parent carries her progeny about with her for a considerable time, but the power of holding on is so well developed that infant mortality is thereby obviated, so far as accidental death from falling is concerned.

Hudson (in *The Naturalist in La Plata*) gives the following interesting details regarding this habit of carrying about the young:—"While taking Bats one day in December, I captured a female of our common Buenos Ayrean species (*Molossus Bonariensis*), with her two young attached to her, so large that it seemed incredible she should be able to fly and take insects with such a weight to drag her down. The young were about a third less in size than the mother, so that she could carry a weight greatly exceeding that of her own body. They were fastened to her breast and belly, one on each side, as when first born; and possibly the young bat does not change its position, or move, like the young developed opossum, to other parts of the body, until mature enough to begin an independent life. On forcibly separating them from their parent, I found that they were not yet able to fly, but when set free fluttered feebly to the ground. This bat certainly appeared more burdened with its young than any animal I had ever observed. . . . The poor bat had to seek its living in the empty air, pursuing its prey with the swiftness of a swallow, and it seemed wonderful to me that she should have been able to carry about that great burden with her one pair of wings, and withal to be active enough to supply herself and her young with food." This mother-bat was released, and the young ones were found to be already expert climbers; their disposition was decidedly vicious. Maternal affection must have been strongly developed in this instance, and it is gratifying to read the following statement of what happened after the lapse of some hours:—"In the evening I placed myself close to the tree [from which the young were taken and to which they had been restored], and presently had the satisfaction of seeing the mother return, flying straight to the spot where I had taken her, and in a few moments she was away again, and over the trees with her twins".

HOOFED MAMMALS (UNGULATA).—We have seen that the

young of Rodents are either helpless or fairly well developed at birth, in correlation with the particular mode of life. For Insectivores and Bats the former is true, while the latter is the rule for the order now under consideration. The reason is not far to seek, and is thus tersely given by Flower:—"In the great order of Ungulates or Hoofed Mammals, where in the majority of cases defence from foes depends upon fleetness of foot, or upon huge corporeal bulk, the young are born in a very highly-

Fig. 1002.—Brazilian Tapirs (*Tapirus Americanus*) and striped Young

developed condition, and are able almost at once to run by the side of the parent". Swine, with the exception of the Peccaries, produce numerous offspring, but in all other Ungulates the number is limited to one, or at most two. In correlation with this the milk-glands are few in number. They are situated in the region of the groin, as familiarly illustrated by Sheep and other domesticated forms. Maternal affection is very strongly developed, nor, as a rule, is the father backward in defending his family. The majority of species are gregarious, and this greatly adds to the possibilities of defence. It will be convenient to consider Odd-toed and Even-toed Ungulates under separate headings.

Odd-toed Ungulates (*Perissodactyla*).—The three families of this sub-order include Tapirs, Rhinoceroses, and Horses respectively. The Tapirs are solitary animals, which produce a single young one at birth. While the adult is either uniformly coloured, as in the Brazilian Tapir (fig 1002), or dark with the hinder part whitish, the young are remarkable in being marked with yellowish streaks and spots. All these varieties in coloration would appear to be of protective nature, even that of the adult Malayan species, of which H. N. Ridley states (in *Natural Science*, 1895):—"When lying down during the day it exactly resembles a gray boulder, and as it often lives near the rocky streams of the hill jungles, it is really nearly as invisible then as it was when it was speckled". The peculiar markings of the young are precisely on a par with those so often exhibited by young birds (see p. 471). We learn from Ridley that in the Malayan species it is in the habit of taking its daily siesta under a bush, when "its coat is so exactly like a patch of ground flecked with sunlight that it is quite invisible". The same thing is no doubt true for the Brazilian form. The Rhinoceros produces a single young one, to which the strength of the mother is a sufficient protection. This animal is also of solitary habit.

Horses and their allies are gregarious, and as a rule only a single young one is brought forth at each birth. The chief point of interest in the present connection is afforded by the defensive tactics, which have elsewhere been noticed (see vol. ii, p. 350).

Even-toed Ungulates (*Artiodactyla*).—We have here to draw a distinction between the Non-Ruminating forms, including the Swine and Hippopotami, and the Ruminating or cud-chewing species, embracing Camels, Deer, Oxen, Sheep, Goats, Antelopes, and Giraffes.

Most wild Swine possess numerous pairs of milk-glands situated in the abdominal region, and their families are large. They live associated together in small droves. The young animals are striped, and this is no doubt a protective arrangement, as in the case of Tapirs. In the remarkable pig known as the Babirussa (*Porcus babirussa*), native to Celebes and certain adjacent islands, the young are more helpless than in other swine, and tax maternal affection considerably. This exceptional state of things is probably to be correlated with isolation on an island area which, in the absence of predaceous forms, minimizes the need for protective arrangements. In South America and the southern part of North America, the Swine of the Old World are replaced by the more specialized Peccaries. The smaller Collared Peccary (*Dicotyles torquatus*), which has the wider range, associates in small droves, while in the rather larger White-lipped Peccary (*D. labiatus*), a purely South American

Fig. 1003.—Hind and Fawn of Roe-Deer (*Capreolus caprea*)

form, a very large number of individuals herd together. Both are forest animals and lead a wandering life, and the young of both species are devoid of the stripes so characteristic of Old World Pigs. One, or at most two, young ones are born at a time, and the milk-glands are reduced to a single pair. Possibly the number of young may have undergone reduction as an adaptation to the exigencies of a roaming life.

The gregarious Hippopotamus (*Hippopotamus amphibius*) produces a single well-developed young one at a birth, which is tended by its mother with the most jealous care. It may frequently be seen riding upon her back, and under these circumstances she comes very frequently to the surface, seeming to be aware that her offspring requires to take a fresh breath more frequently than she does herself.

Ruminants (fig. 1003) usually give birth to a single young one, or more rarely to two. The power of chewing the cud is not at first possessed, since only the fourth or chemical division of the stomach (*abomasum*) is properly developed (see vol. ii, p. 169). This is quite able to deal with milk, to which diet the young animal is necessarily restricted till such time as the digestive organs are fully developed. The social habit, here very typical, is associated with interesting defensive tactics, such as setting sentinels to guard the feeding herd (see vol. ii, p. 365).

ELEPHANTS (PROBOSCIDEA).—As in the case of Ruminants, a single young one as a rule is produced at a birth in these gregarious animals, and from the first it is well able to accompany its mother in her rather extensive wanderings in search of food. It is scarcely necessary to remark that the young animal sucks with its mouth, and not with its trunk, though the contrary was long believed. There are but two milk-glands, placed on the chest.

SEA-COWS (SIRENIA).—Both in the Dugong (*Halicore*) and the Manatee (*Manatus*) there is but a single young one, born in a well-developed state, as might be expected in such thoroughly aquatic animals. There is a single pair of milk-glands, placed on the chest, and the mother has a curious habit of holding her offspring firmly by means of one flipper during the operation of sucking, swimming along at the same time with its head and her own above the surface.

WHALES, PORPOISES, &c. (CETACEA).—Of all Mammals these are by far the best adapted to an aquatic life. There is usually only a single young one, which, from the nature of the case, is born in a well-developed condition, and perfectly able to swim. Flower very justly remarks:—"This state of relative maturity at birth reaches its highest development in the Cetacea, where it is evidently associated with the peculiar conditions under which these animals pass their existence". The two milk-glands are placed far back on the under side of the body, the teat of each being lodged in a deep pit, an arrangement which is doubtless of a protective nature, besides which it may perhaps render suckling more easy. Maternal affection is very strongly manifested among Cetaceans, as whale-fishers have often found to their cost. At the approach of danger the Greenland Whale shelters her young one under her flippers. Most of the Cetaceans are markedly gregarious, being associated together in large "schools".

Fig. 1004.—Cubs of Brown Bear (*Ursus arctos*) at play

FLESH-EATING MAMMALS (CARNIVORA).—The helpless young which we have so far considered are safeguarded by being brought up in a sheltered dwelling, or it may be that the mother carries them about with her. The young of Carnivores are quite unable to look after themselves when born, as familiarly exemplified by kittens and puppies, but in this case their safety mostly depends upon the natural weapons with which their parents are liberally provided.

Among land Carnivores (Fissipedia) no general rule can be given as to the number of young, for this varies considerably within the limit of the group. A large family is usually typical of members of the Dog tribe (*Canidæ*), while three or four is the common limit in Lions, Tigers, and other large species of the Cat Family (*Felidæ*), and in the large Bears (*Ursidæ*) the number is usually restricted to one, two, or possibly three (fig. 1004). The safe up-bringing of the young is often furthered by the existence of some sort of dwelling or lair. It will suffice to instance the "earth" of the Fox and the "holt" of the Otter, the latter being simply a hole in the bank of a stream. That parental affection is strongly developed in Carnivores is a matter of common knowledge. All have had occasion to note this in the case of domesticated Dogs and Cats, and abundant examples are recorded in books on sport.

The Aquatic Carnivores (Pinnipedia) have much smaller families than the majority of their terrestrial cousins, the young being limited to one, or at most two. The Walruses, Seals, and Eared Seals which constitute the group all visit land at certain seasons, and remain there until their young are sufficiently advanced to share the aquatic life for which these forms are so eminently adapted. The crowded "rookeries" established at this time by the Northern Fur-Seal (*Otaria ursina*) on the Pribyloff Islands, in Behring Sea, have been described in detail by Elliott and other observers. The first comers are the mature males, of which vast numbers have arrived by about the first of June, the far more numerous females making their appearance about three weeks or a month later. As, too, many of the younger and weaker males are "bachelors", from compulsion and not from choice, polygamy naturally results. The males who have contracted family ties take once more to the sea at the beginning of August, though a small minority return to the land in September; and the large majority of individuals have left the islands by November. The young seals are born soon after their mothers reach land, and their eyes are open at birth. After their fathers have resumed an aquatic life the cubs make their first attempts in swimming, and though said to be clumsy at first, are efficient in the art after about a month's practice. From observations made on captive Eared Seals in the zoological gardens at Cologne, Wunderlich believes that the current accounts representing the cubs as having to "learn" to swim are somewhat exaggerated, and he says that they are quite at home in the water shortly after birth. But it is certain that fairly prolonged sojourn on land is necessary before they are strong enough to undertake long-distance swimming, the adaptation to an aquatic life being much less complete than in the case of young Cetaceans (see p. 490). Parental affection is said to be far from strong in the Northern Fur-Seals.

LEMURS (LEMUROIDEA).—In these purely arboreal animals

there is a pair of milk-glands situated on the chest, but these may be supplemented by others placed in the abdominal region. In the majority of species the number of young is limited to one, or it may be two, and all Lemurs are born in a helpless condition. In many cases the mother carries her young one about with her, and it holds on firmly to the under side of her body, lying crosswise, in the position which is of least hindrance to climbing (fig. 1005). One species at least possesses a well-marked vestige of a marsupial pouch, which fact has suggested to Beddard the

Fig. 1005.—Lemur (*Lemur rufifrons*) carrying her Young

following interesting remark (in *The Cambridge Natural History*):—"One is tempted to wonder how far the habit which certain Lemurs have of carrying their young across the abdomen with the tail wrapped round the body of the mother is a reminiscence of a marsupial pouch". The little Mouse-Lemurs somewhat resemble Dormice in appearance and habits. Lydekker (in *The Royal Natural History*) makes the following remarks about the Dwarf Mouse-Lemur (*Microcebus pusillus*), one of the smallest of these:—"The dwarf mouse-lemur builds beautifully-constructed nests of twigs, lined with hair, in the tops of the lofty trees where it delights to dwell. These nests somewhat resemble those of a rook both in form and size, and are used not only as diurnal resting-places, but as cradles for the young."

Apes, Monkeys, and Men (Primates).—Even if the human species be left out of consideration we must regard this order as including the Highest Mammals, if a well-developed brain associated with great intelligence is to be taken as the criterion. The single pair of milk-glands is situated on the chest, and a single young one is the general rule, though an exception is afforded to this by the Marmozets, the lowest members of the order, for in these there is a family of two or three. Parental affection, especially on the part of the mother, is very strongly developed, and necessarily so, for the newly-born young are extremely helpless, and it is a considerable time before they are fully able to look after themselves. One of the most extraordinary features in the evolution of human civilization consists in the relatively late age at which maturity is attained, and the large amount of parental sacrifice which this involves. The altruistic attitude to which this has largely contributed is a factor of no small importance in social progress. And it may be added that the study of biology is, or should be, an indispensable preliminary for those who interest themselves in the as yet imperfect science of sociology.

Most Monkeys are arboreal and social in habit, and the immature young are commonly carried about by their mothers, pretty much as in some of the Lemurs. The extraordinary grasping-power of newly-born human infants has been explained as an inheritance from remote tree-living ancestors (see p. 234). Much sagacity is often shown, especially in Old World forms, in the precautions taken for the safety of the community, on similar lines to those adopted by some of the social Ungulates (see p. 365). This is true not only for the arboreal forms but also for the Baboons which are typical ground-dwellers (see vol. ii, p. 363).

The highest of the man-like Apes, Orang, Chimpanzee, and Gorilla, do not live in troops, but are associated in family parties. They appear to be in the habit of constructing rough shelters in trees, some 50 or 60 feet from the ground in the case of the Orang, according to Wallace.

2/4

The
Natural History
of Animals

The animal life of the world in its
various aspects and relations

IN FOUR VOLUMES

BY

J.R. AINSWORTH DAVIS

Volume IV

GIAN PUBLISHING HOUSE
New Delhi-110002

Gian Publishing House
4348, Madan Mohan Street
4C, Ansari Road, Darya Ganj.
New Delhi - 110002

First Indian Edition 1989
First Printed 1905

ISBN 81 - 212 - 0253 - 1 Set
ISBN 81 - 212 - 0259-3

Printed In India
at
Goyal Offset Printers, Delhi.

CONTENTS

NERVOUS SYSTEM AND SENSE-ORGANS

CHAPTER LVII.—GENERAL PRINCIPLES—NERVOUS SYSTEMS OF BACKBONELESS ANIMALS (INVERTEBRATA) AND BACKBONED ANIMALS (VERTEBRATA)

CHAPTER LVIII.—SENSE-ORGANS OF BACKBONELESS ANIMALS (INVERTEBRATA) AND BACKBONED ANIMALS (VERTEBRATA)

ANIMAL INSTINCT AND INTELLIGENCE

CHAPTER LIX.—GENERAL PRINCIPLES—INSTINCT AND INTELLIGENCE IN HIGHER BACKBONELESS ANIMALS (INVERTEBRATA) AND BACKBONED ANIMALS (VERTEBRATA)

INSTINCT AND INTELLIGENCE IN HIGHER INVERTEBRATES (INVERTEBRATA)

INSTINCT AND INTELLIGENCE IN VERTEBRATES (VERTEBRATA)

ASSOCIATION OF ORGANISMS—THE WEB OF LIFE

CHAPTER LX.—ASSOCIATION OF ORGANISMS—GENERAL PRINCIPLES—ANIMALS AND PLANTS

PLANTS AND ANIMALS

CHAPTER LXIV.—ASSOCIATION OF ORGANISMS—COURTSHIP AND MATING

CHAPTER LXV.—ASSOCIATION OF ORGANISMS—MESSMATES OR COMMENSALS (COMMENSALISM)

CHAPTER LXVI.—ASSOCIATION OF ORGANISMS—PARASITES

DOMESTICATION OF ANIMALS

LIST OF ILLUSTRATIONS

Vol. IV

PLATES

ILLUSTRATIONS

N.B.—Figs. 1123, 1124, 1125, 1129, 1130, and 1131 are from Alcock's *A Naturalist in Indian Seas*, by the courtesy of Mr. John Murray.

NATURAL HISTORY

NERVOUS SYSTEM AND SENSE-ORGANS

CHAPTER LVII

GENERAL PRINCIPLES—NERVOUS SYSTEMS OF INVERTEBRATES AND VERTEBRATES

GENERAL PRINCIPLES

Some of the properties of living matter or protoplasm have already been pretty fully considered, in sections which may be regarded as expansions of part of the brief sketch of Human Physiology given in vol. i, pp. 24–59. We have seen that protoplasm is a very complex and eminently unstable substance, which is continually breaking down into simpler compounds, with the result that stored or potential energy is transformed into actual or kinetic energy, without which movement and other life-manifestations would be impossible. The breaking-down process ultimately results in the formation of waste products, which being physiologically useless are cast out of the body. One such product is carbonic acid gas or carbon dioxide, and a primary object of Breathing or Respiration is to get rid of this. But Breathing also includes the taking in of free oxygen, without which the breaking down of the complex body-substance would not take place at the rate necessary for liberating the energy required. We have also seen that the gradual wasting of the body associated with the breaking-down process requires to be made good; hence the necessity for Food, which is built up into fresh protoplasm. In cases where Growth is taking place the food taken in must obviously be larger in amount than when it is merely a question of compensating for waste. By a process of over-growth with subsequent separation from the parent-body new individuals are developed, capable of leading independent existences, and ultimately giving rise to a further generation in their turn. Another very characteristic property of protoplasm is Contractility, *i.e.* spontaneous change of shape. Hence all the various kinds of Animal Movement, without which food could not be secured, enemies escaped, or unfavourable surroundings quitted.

The present section is an expansion of the last part of the brief sketch of Human Physiology already mentioned, *i.e.* the part headed Nervous System and Sense Organs. What these are, and why they should exist, cannot be understood without reference to another fundamental property of protoplasm, which we may broadly term Sensitiveness and Spontaneity, there being, unfortunately, no briefer way of putting it. The surroundings of an animal are constantly changing; all sorts of external agents are continually acting upon it to varying extents; and life wholly depends upon successful adjustment or adaptation to this perpetually altering Environment. Alternations of day and night, succession of seasons, tidal flow and ebb, variations of food-supply, the diminution or increase in number of enemies, may be taken as examples of changes which have much to do with the preservation or extinction of old species and the evolution of new ones. That protoplasm is *sensitive* means that it is not inert to its surroundings, but reacts, in ways which tend to the preservation of life, to the influences which are constantly affecting it. If, when you are not looking, someone touches your hand with a red-hot poker, the member thus treated is drawn back without the exercise of will-power, and immediately after a painful sensation is experienced. This practically illustrates the fact that human protoplasm is sensitive to one external agent, *i.e.* heat, and the usefulness of reaction is sufficiently obvious. If animals were not sensitive to heat many of them would very quickly perish in an untimely manner. And a little consideration will make it apparent that Sensitiveness to a great variety of external agents is absolutely necessary to existence. All actions, however, are not the direct results of external agents acting for the time being. Protoplasm is *spon-*

taneous, i.e. it performs actions which find their starting-point within the body itself, as in the case of many voluntary human actions.

Any change in the surroundings which brings the sensitiveness of an organism into play is technically known as a stimulus (L. *stimulus*, an ox-goad), and stimuli may broadly be classified as mechanical, chemical, thermal, photic, and electrical. The corresponding stimulating agents are pressure, change in chemical nature of the surroundings, heat, light, and electricity, which are scientifically defined as different forms of energy, or, to use the old expression, "force". Protoplasm, like every other kind of matter, may be regarded as made up of excessively minute particles or molecules, much too small to be seen with even the most powerful microscope, which are in a state of constant vibration, throbbing, or to-and-fro movement. The pendulum affords a simple example of vibratory movement. It may further be said that every sort of stimulus is of the nature of a vibration, *e.g.* in a sound-wave transmitted through air the particles of air move in a particular way and at a rate depending upon the pitch of the sound. All the changes that take place in living matter result from modifications in the movement of its molecules, but we are profoundly ignorant of what exactly takes place when, say, a muscle-fibre contracts or an impulse passes along a nerve. The adjustment to surroundings that is necessary for the maintenance of life results from these molecular changes in the body, which take place in response to the action of pressure, heat, light, &c., these themselves being of a vibratory nature, as has already been stated. So far as an animal is "sensitive" to its surroundings it is comparable to a complex musical instrument capable of playing all sorts of tunes with all kinds of variations, in response to external influences of different kind. The reaction of an animal to its environment at any given moment depends upon how external agents are acting upon it at that moment: it is they which "call the tune". If the supposed musical instrument could also play tunes of its own accord, independently of the *direct* action of the surroundings, such tunes might be taken to represent the "spontaneous" actions of an animal.

That Sensitiveness and Spontaneity, as above defined, are essential properties of living matter, may best be realized by studying a very simple organism, such as the Proteus Animalcule (*Amœba*), which is a particle of comparatively pure protoplasm (fig. 1006). That this creature is sensitive to mechanical stimuli is easily proved by tapping the glass slide on which one is crawling about under the microscope. The protruding lobes of the body (pseudopods) by which creeping is effected will be drawn in, and the animal will assume a spherical form (fig. 1006, A).

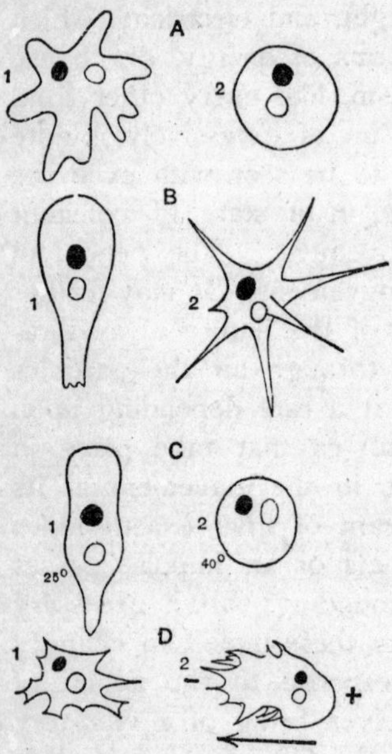

Fig. 1006. — Proteus Animalcules (*Amœba*), much enlarged, showing effect of various stimuli. 1 and 2, Appearance before and after application of stimulus. See text.

A good example of chemical stimulation is afforded by the addition of very weak caustic potash to the water in which the slug-shaped species of Amœba (*A. limax*) is moving along, the reaction consisting in this case of the protrusion of long pointed pseudopods (fig. 1006, B). The same kind of Amœba reacts in a marked way to changes of temperature (fig. 1006, C). At freezing point (0° C.) it is spherical and inert; as the temperature increases from 0° C. to 35° C. it moves about with ever-increasing activity; above this the activity gradually diminishes; and at about 40° C. the animal has assumed a spherical form, and dies in a condition of "heat-stiffening" or coagulation. This illustrates very well the fact that any particular stimulus has only a certain range of action, the range in this case being between 0° C. and 40° C., which are known as the *minimum* and *maximum* points of heat-stimulation for this particular animal. Between these two points is an *optimum* one (35° C. in this instance), at which the stimulus exerts its greatest effect by way of promoting activity. Light does not appear to affect the creeping movements of Amœba, but is said to check the taking in of food, which process goes on most actively at night. If a constant current of electricity is passed through the body of an Amœba which is protruding pseudopods in all directions it will begin to creep against the current, and all those pseudopods will be drawn in which are not at the front end for the time being (fig. 1006 D).

Since a hungry Amœba creeps actively about for a long time we are probably justified in concluding that some of its movements are spontaneous, and these are probably initiated by chemical changes which take place within its body, and may be called internal stimuli.

NERVOUS SYSTEMS OF INVERTEBRATES

The Amœba, like most other animalcules, is a single cell or structural unit, which has to discharge all the functions of life, and does not exhibit the principle of division of labour to the same extent as animals belonging to the higher groups, which are collectively termed Metazoa, as contrasted with the Animalcules or Protozoa. Every member of the former group is made up of more or less numerous cells, and may therefore be styled a *cell-community*. It is clear that in such a case advantageous adjustment to the surroundings is best secured on the principle of division of labour, by which the vital activities are shared among the members of the community. Evolution on these lines has resulted in the development of Digestive Organs, Respiratory Organs, Organs of Movement, &c., the complexity of which is very great in some of the higher groups of animals. Hence the need for some means of central control, some way of correlating the diverse parts of the body, and at the same time of adjusting the body to its environment. These duties are discharged by the Nervous System, with the aid of Sense Organs, which keep it in touch with external agents. The Sensitiveness and Spontaneity of a Metazoon, in fact, are more or less centred in the Nervous System and Sense Organs, and this is true to an increasing extent as we consider animals higher and higher in the scale. At the same time it must not be forgotten that every cell in the body is endowed with *all* the primary properties of protoplasm, though cells specialize as it were in different directions, according to the nature of the organs of which they form a part.

NERVOUS SYSTEMS OF ZOOPHYTES (CŒLENTERATA). — The members of this primitive group, comprising Freshwater Polypes (*Hydra*), Hydroid Zoophytes, Jelly-Fish, Sea-Anemones, and

Corals, correspond to a fairly early stage in the evolution of the Metazoa from simple colonies of Protozoa, and furnish us with some idea of the way in which nervous systems have arisen. Reduced to its simplest terms the body of such an animal is practically a living stomach, and is made up of two layers of cells—an inner one (endoderm) and an outer one (ectoderm). We are here more especially concerned with the outer layer. It would appear that the nervous system was first evolved in the interest of adjustment to the surroundings, and it is not therefore surprising to find that it has come into existence by modification of some of the cells making up the ectoderm, since this layer immediately adjoins the outer world. The same is also true for the essential parts of all the sense-organs. These specialized nervous elements are known as *nerve-cells* or *ganglion cells*, which constitute so many centres of correlation and control. A typical cell of the kind is star-shaped and possesses a large nucleus, but it may also be round or ovoid. In Vertebrates, of which our knowledge is considerable, it is usual for a nerve-cell to be prolonged into a number of branching prolongations, and one nerve-fibre, which may be of very great length (fig. 1007). It is convenient to speak of the cell with its extensions as a *neuron*, and investigation will probably show that the neurons of Invertebrates are broadly similar to those of Vertebrates, though in many instances our knowledge is here very incomplete. It is clear that the nerve-cells need to be in communication with the environment, the parts which they control or correlate, and other similar cells with which they co-operate. This is provided for by the slender extensions of the cell-body, which constitute lines of communication. There is reason to think that the branching extensions are paths of conduction *to* the cell, while the nerve fibre is a similar path *from* the cell. It was formerly believed that the neurons in a nervous system are united together by their processes into a complicated net-work or *plexus*, but it is now known that in Vertebrates at any rate this is not so, though the slender extensions of one neuron are closely adjacent to those of others. The same thing is probably usually true for Invertebrates.

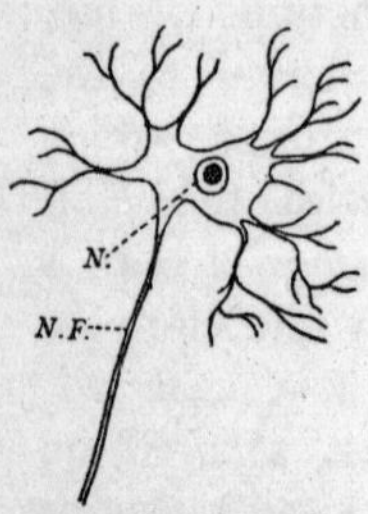

Fig. 1007. — A Typical Neuron, much enlarged. *N.*, Nucleus; *N.F.*, nerve-fibre (cut short).

Although neurons belong to the external cell-layer they do not remain at the surface of the body, but sink as it were more or less inwards to take up a more sheltered position, leaving to sense-cells the duty of reception of stimuli from external agents. In some Jelly-Fish we find cells of the external layer which are beginning to sink in to constitute neurons, while others have actually done so and acquired at the same time a more specialized shape (fig. 1008, A).

A nervous system of very primitive kind is found in a Sea-Anemone, which, leading as it does a sluggish life fixed to some firm object, does not require any very elaborate correlating mechanism. There is here a delicate continuous nerve-layer underlying the ectodermal cells that directly adjoin the exterior, and made up of innumerable neurons of which the extensions run in all directions (fig. 1008, B). Even in this case, however, there is a certain amount of centralization, for the nerve-layer is thicker in the upper side of the body where the mouth is placed, and in the tentacles which fringe this region.

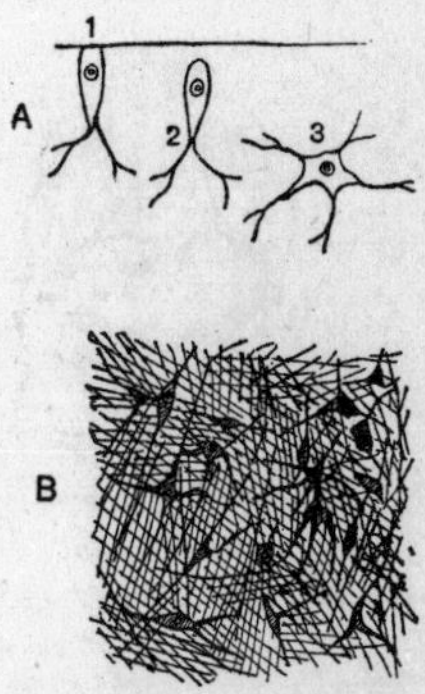

Fig. 1008.—A, Stages in the Evolution of the Neurons of a Jelly-Fish, enlarged. B, Part of the Nerve-Layer in a Sea-Anemone, showing Neurons, enlarged

The free-swimming Jelly-Fish, having more complex adjustments to effect with the environment than their fixed relatives, possess, as might be anticipated, a more centralized nervous system. It is true that there is here also a continuous nerve-layer in the deeper part of the ectoderm, but part of this is concentrated into what may be called a *central nervous system*. This may be either in the form of a double nerve-ring placed near the edge of the umbrella, or it may consist of small masses of neurons placed at regular intervals in the same region.

NERVOUS SYSTEMS OF SEGMENTED WORMS (ANNELIDA).—The members of this group are comparatively complex in structure, and possess a well-defined nervous system, that conforms to the two-sided or bilateral symmetry of the body. The primitive nerve-layer in the ectoderm is retained more or less, but it is largely superseded by the central nervous system, which consists of a nerve-ring surrounding the front end of the digestive tube, and a double nerve-cord running along near the under side of the body (fig. 1009). In the lower Annelids this system is closely connected with the ectoderm or outer layer of the skin, but in the more specialized members of the group it has sunk within the muscular layers of the body-wall, where it is much better protected. Connected with these central organs are a large number of slender nerves, that come into intimate relation with the various organs of the body, and are made up of excessively minute nerve-fibres which are prolongations of the nerve-cells. On the upper side of the nerve-ring are two little swellings, that may be regarded as an incipient brain or chief central organ, and are technically known as ganglia. A ganglion is a thickened part of a nerve-cord, where nerve-cells are concentrated as a result of evolution along centralizing lines. The ventral cord swells into a pair of ganglia in each segment of the trunk, for which they act as controlling organs. In such a form as the Earth-Worm the ganglia are not very distinct, and nerve-cells are scattered throughout the whole of the central nervous system, but in the free-living Bristle-Worms and Leeches concentration of nerve-cells has taken place to a much greater extent, and the ganglia are clearly marked. The relations of these active forms to their surroundings are comparatively complex; hence greater concentration of nerve-cells with increased efficiency of the nervous system. The complex nature of the neurons will be gathered from fig. 1010, which represents a few of them in part of the ventral cord of an Earth-Worm.

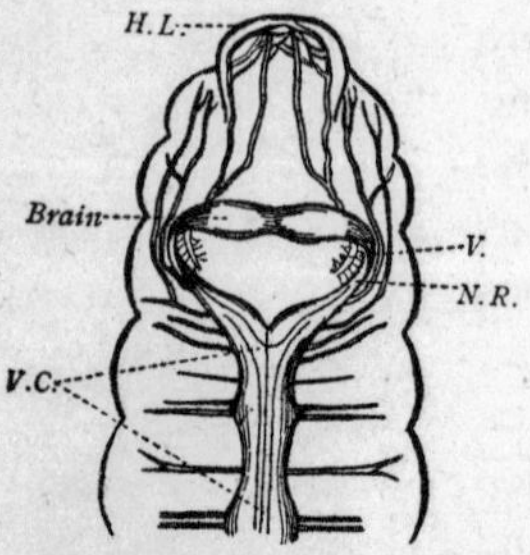

Fig. 1009.—Front Part of the Central Nervous System of an Earth-Worm, enlarged. *H.L.*, Head-lobe; *N.R.*, side of nerve-ring; *V.*, visceral or sympathetic nerves; *V.C.*, ventral cord, giving off nerves, and swollen into indistinct ganglia

The front end of a bilaterally symmetrical animal, such as a segmented worm, is more subject to the action of external agents than the rest of the body, and becomes specialized into a *head*, in which the most important part of the nervous system, *i.e.* the brain, and the chief organs of sense are located. Even in a segmented worm we are justified in considering the brain as the highest part of the nervous system, because it is the chief centre of correlation and administration. Voluntary action, consciousness or awareness of existence, sensation, and intelligence, so far as these exist in so lowly an animal, are dependent upon it. That this is so in the common earth-worm we know from the fact that the mole stores up these unfortunate creatures as a sort of living larder, having previously bitten off the front ends of their bodies, and consequently removed such brains as they possess. This does not destroy life, but prevents the victims from crawling away. The ventral nerve-cord is subordinate to the brain, but exerts a considerable amount of independent control, each pair of ganglia dominating the ring or segment to which it belongs. To these collections of nerve-cells are due what are technically known as *reflex actions*, which are quite independent of will. We may instructively consider one common sort of reflex action which manifests itself in muscular movement. If the skin of one of the segments is stimulated mechanically, chemically, or otherwise, some amount of contraction in the muscle of the body-wall immediately follows. For the performance of this or any other reflex action three nervous elements are requisite: (1) a nerve-centre consisting of one or more, usually of several, nerve-cells, which in the latter case co-operate with one another; (2) one or more nerve-fibres constituting an *afferent* tract carrying impulses *to* the nerve-centre from sensitive ectodermal cells which have been acted upon by the mechanical, chemical, or other stimulus; and (3) one or more nerve-fibres forming an *efferent* tract carrying impulses *from* the nerve-centre to the executive structures which perform the reflex action, these being muscle-fibres in the case supposed (fig. 1011). Even in ourselves many actions are of reflex nature, *e.g.* the involuntary withdrawal of the hand from a red-hot substance as described on an earlier page (p. 2).

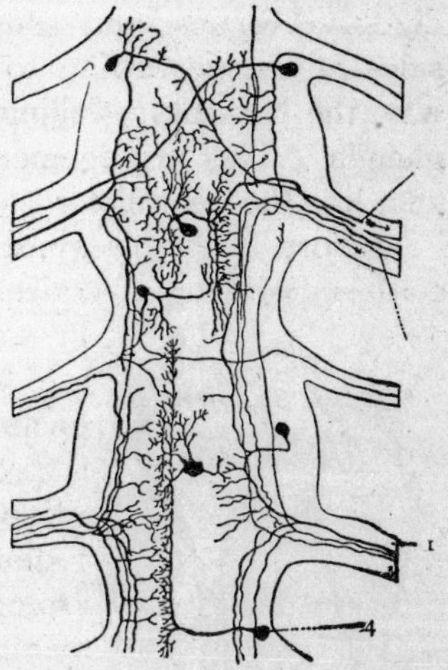

Fig. 1010.—Diagram of part of the Ventral Cord of an Earth-Worm, showing a few Neurons, enlarged. The two arrows (on the right) indicate the direction of nerve-impulses. 1, Nerve-roots; 2, afferent nerve-fibres; 3, efferent nerve-fibres; 4, a neuron, of which the branches extend through three segments

Fig. 1011.—Diagram of a Simple Reflex Action. *S.*, Stimulus; *S.O.*, sense-organ; *aff.n.*, afferent nerve; *N.C.*, nerve-centre; *eff.n.*, efferent nerve. Direction of nerve-impulses indicated by arrows.

It has already been stated that one of the duties of a nervous system is to correlate the organs of the body itself, and even in an earth-worm there is a special arrangement for controlling the digestive organs, and consisting of nerves which run from the sides of the nerve-ring to the gut, and branch out in a complex way, the branches swelling here and there into extremely minute ganglia. This arrangement is called the *visceral nervous system*, and, like the ventral cord, is subject to the control of the brain.

Before leaving segmented worms one feature in the nerve-cord is deserving of notice. It is distinctly of double nature, and in some cases its two longitudinal halves are widely separated (fig. 1012). In the evolution of this type of nervous system it is probable that each side of the body developed and was regulated by its own longitudinal nerve-cord, and this is actually the arrangement found in the curious unsegmented forms known as Nemertine Worms. Though these constitute a special group quite distinct from Annelids, they are descended from common ancestors, some of the primitive characters of which they have probably retained, one being the possession of a strong lateral nerve on either side, instead of a double ventral cord (fig. 1013). Such an arrangement is not a desirable one, for it means imperfect correlation between right and left sides of the body. The ventral cord of an Annelid has quite likely been derived from lateral cords of the kind, which have migrated downwards and come into more or less intimate relation with one another in the interests of centralization.

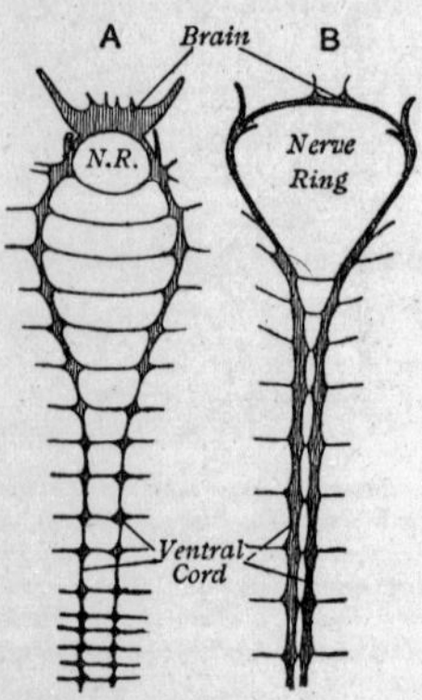

Fig. 1012.—Front Part of Central Nervous System in two Marine Annelids, enlarged. In A the two halves of the ventral cord are fairly far apart, while in B they are close together but not fused. *N.R.*, nerve-ring.

NERVOUS SYSTEMS OF JOINTED-LIMBED INVERTEBRATES (ARTHROPODA).—There can be little doubt that the members of this huge group have sprung from ancestors which resembled Annelids in many respects. But they have specialized in various ways, partly as the result of centralizing tendencies which have resulted in increased complexity of structure, associated with very perfect adjustment to surroundings. The body, instead of being greatly elongated and made up of a large number of rings or segments, is comparatively short, and composed of relatively few segments.

In the higher members of the group, *e.g.* lobsters and insects, the segments in front have fused into a well-developed head, followed by a thorax, to constitute which other segments have coalesced, while this is succeeded by an abdomen, where the amount of union of segments varies greatly in different cases. These three successive regions of the body differ greatly from one another as to size and shape, and may undergo further fusion. Thus, in a

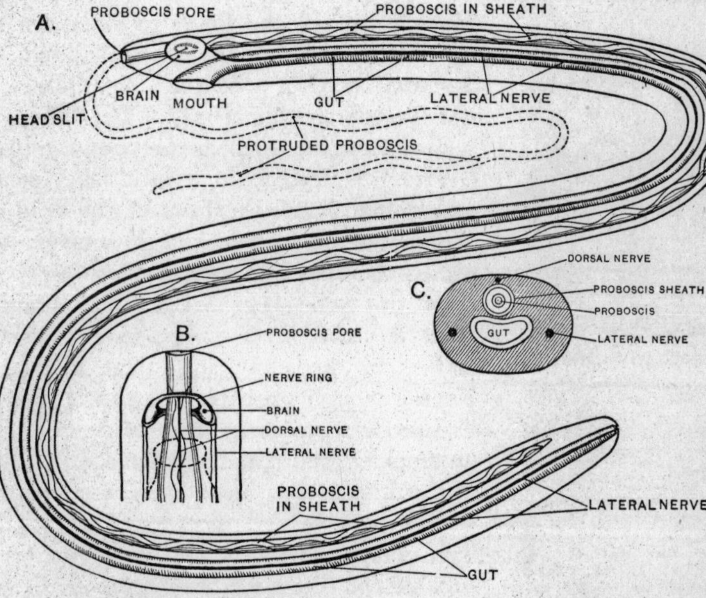

Fig. 1013.—Diagrams to illustrate Structure of a Nemertine Worm, represented as a transparent object

A., Side view; B., front end, seen from above; C., cross section.

Lobster, head and thorax are welded together, and in a Spider not only is this so, but the abdominal segments have closely united into a rounded mass.

The nervous system of an Arthropod, like that of an Annelid, consists of nerve-ring and double ventral nerve-cord, but the ganglia are better developed, and in the higher members of the group they are more or less fused together into larger nerve-masses, just as the segments to which they belong are similarly united. There is, in other words, an increasing amount of centralization in the nervous system as we pass from lower to higher forms in any subdivision of the Arthropods. And this is clearly advantageous in regard to correlation of the different parts of the body, and adaptation to the environment. It may also be noted that while in many lower Arthropods the two halves of the ventral cord are more or less separate, they are intimately united together in higher forms.

Nervous Systems of Crustaceans (*Crustacea*).—Successive stages of fusion in the nervous system may be illustrated by comparison of Apus, Crayfish, and Crab. In the first of these, which is one of the lower forms, there is a nerve-ring with clearly-marked brain, and a ventral cord of which the two halves are widely separate (fig. 1014). The brain of a typical Annelid, such as the Sea-Centipede (*Nereis*), is lodged in a head-lobe (prostomium) that forms the front of the head and overhangs the mouth, and it supplies with nerves the eyes and feelers which are borne upon this lobe (fig. 1014). The brain of Apus is placed in a corresponding position, and is in the main equivalent to that of Nereis, though probably not entirely so. A Crustacean possesses two pairs of feelers (antennules and antennæ) situated in front of the mouth, but most likely their original position was behind that aperture, and they have shifted forwards into a position more suitable for the work they have to perform, by way of exploring the surroundings. These two pairs of feelers belong to two segments of the head, each of which is provided with a corresponding pair of ganglia. In Apus those of the segment to which the antennæ belong are the first pair of the ventral cord (see figure), but the nerve for each front feeler or antennule arises from the side of the nerve-ring, and can be traced into the brain. This is intelligible if we suppose that organ to be equivalent to the brain of an Annelid, plus the ganglia supplying the antennules, which have shifted forwards along the sides of the nerve-ring. If this view be correct, a certain amount of fusion and centralization has taken place at the front end of the nervous system in Apus, as compared with an Annelid. But it is here necessary to state that

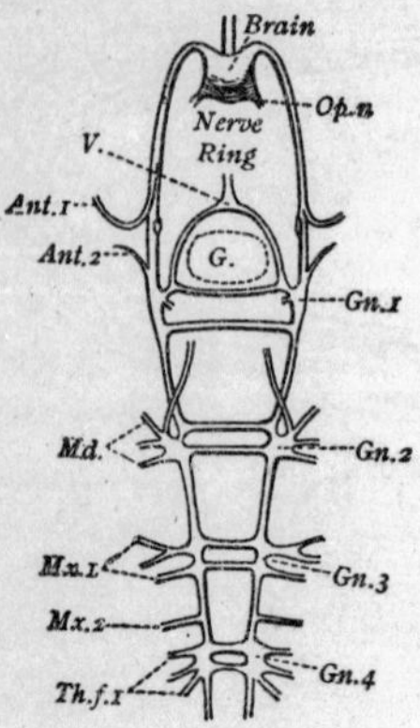

Fig. 1014.—Front Part of the Central Nervous System of Apus, enlarged

G., Place where gullet runs through nerve-ring; *Gn.1–Gn.4*, ganglia of one half of ventral cord; *Op.n*, *Ant.1*, *Ant.2*, *Md.*, *Mx.1*, *Mx.2*, *Th.f.1*, nerves to eyes, antennules, antennæ, mandibles, first and second maxillæ, and first thoracic feet; *V.*, visceral nervous system.

some authorities hold a different view as to the antennules, believing that these have always been situated in front of the mouth, and are in reality outgrowths from the head-lobe. If so they are comparable to the sensitive palps on the head of a Nereis, and the brain of Apus is strictly equivalent to the brain of an Annelid. We shall assume here the truth of the first view, as the balance of evidence is in its favour.

The body of Apus is made up of a comparatively large number of segments, while in Crayfish and Crab, as in all members of the highly-organized group (Decapoda) to which they belong, there are relatively few, *i.e.* twenty, so far as can be definitely made out. Five belong to the Head, eight to the Thorax, and seven to the Abdomen, each with a pair of ganglia and, except the last, provided with a pair of limbs. The nervous system of the Crayfish has undergone a certain amount of fusion and centralization (fig. 1015). The brain is larger and more complex than that of Apus, and it supplies not only the first but also the second feelers, the ganglia corresponding to which have shifted along the nerve-ring. Even greater fusion has taken place at the front end of the ventral cord, where there is a large ventral ganglion, which has resulted from the union of the last three pairs of head-ganglia (supplying the three pairs of jaws), and the three first pairs of thoracic ganglia (supplying the three pairs of foot-jaws). It is interesting to notice that the third thoracic ganglia are caught as it were in the act of uniting with those in front of them. The last five pairs of thoracic ganglia (supplying pincers and walking-legs) are clearly defined, although by reference to the figure it will be seen that the last two are beginning to unite, while just in front of this the doubleness of the cord is practically demonstrated by the fact that its two halves diverge, for the passage of an artery which runs vertically downwards from the heart to supply the ventral region of the body. The first five pairs of abdominal

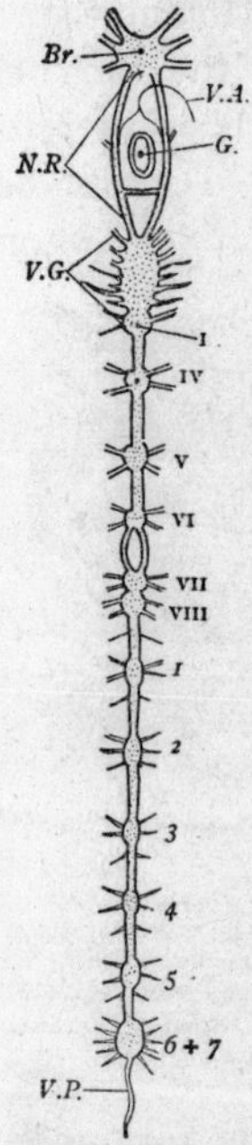

Fig. 1015.—Central Nervous System of Crayfish

G., Gullet (in cross section); *Br.*, brain; *N.R.*, side of nerve-ring; *V.G.*, ventral ganglion; III–VIII, ganglia of third to eighth thoracic segments; 1–7, ganglia of abdominal segments; *V.A.* and *V.P.*, anterior and posterior visceral nerves.

ganglia are quite distinct, and smaller than those of the thoracic region, in correspondence with the relatively small size of their segments. But the last two pairs have united into a somewhat larger nerve-mass, which supplies the last two segments of the body, that include the large tail-fin. It has been shown by experiment that the brain of the Crayfish is the dominating centre of the nervous system, while the remaining nerve-masses are centres of reflex action for the segments which they supply.

Turning now to the Crab, in which the head and thorax are relatively short and broad, and the abdomen insignificant, the brain is comparable to that of a Crayfish, but all the ganglia of the short ventral cord have fused together into a single mass, placed near the under side of the thorax, and perforated by the artery which runs down from the heart (fig. 1016).

Fig. 1016.—Central Nervous System of a Crab. The brain forms the thickened front end of the nerve-ring, while the large ventral ganglion is seen behind, with numerous radiating nerves.

In all the three Crustaceans described there is a visceral nervous system, the roots of which are indicated in the figures.

Nervous Systems of Air-breathing Arthropods (*Tracheata*).—Comparison of Peripatus, Myriapods, Arachnids, and Insects will show that the same lines are followed as in Crustaceans. In the less-specialized forms, where the body is elongated and there has been but little fusion between segments, the nervous system is very like that of an Annelid. But in cases where the body is comparatively short and much fusion has taken place, the nervous system is concentrated to a corresponding degree.

We have already had occasion to see that Peripatus is the most primitive of all living air-breathing Arthropods, and has the closest affinity to Annelids. This view is fully borne out by examination of the nervous system. The upper side of the nerve-ring is swollen into a relatively large brain, and the two halves of the ventral cord are widely separate, though united by numerous transverse bands of nerve-fibres. The outer part of each cord, through its entire extent, contains numerous nerve-cells, and these are not aggregated into well-marked ganglia (fig. 1017).

Myriapods, such as ordinary Centipedes and Millipedes, are rather more specialized than Peripatus, and possess a well-marked head, although there is no distinction between thorax and abdomen. The central nervous system consists of the usual nerve-ring and double ventral cord, and well-developed ganglia are present, between which the two halves of the cord commonly remain distinct (fig. 1018). In Centipedes there is a certain amount of fusion between the ganglia at the front end of the cord, the region from which spring the nerves of the three pairs of jaws, and also those of the poison-claws.

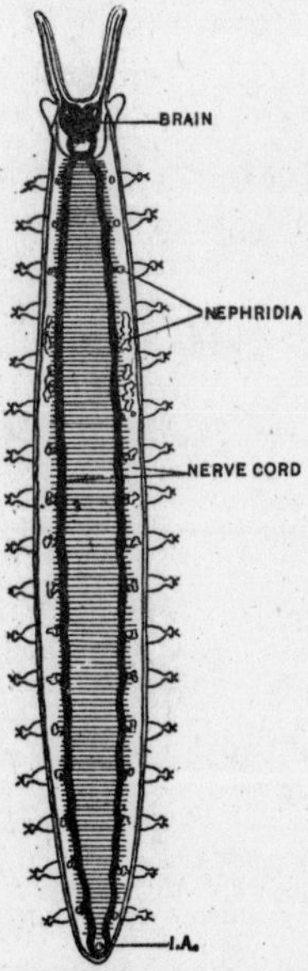

Fig. 1017.—Dissection of Peripatus from the upper side, to show Central Nervous System. I.A., Intestinal aperture.

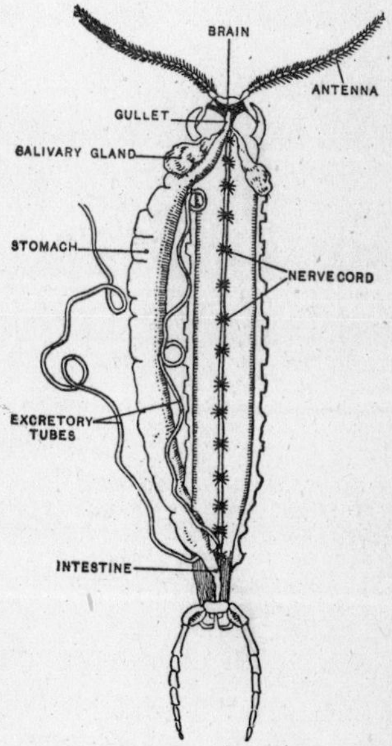

Fig. 1018.—Dissection of a Centipede (*Lithobius*) from above, enlarged

In regard to Arachnids, it will be sufficient for our present purpose to remark that the relation between the nervous system of an elongated form, such as a Scorpion, with that of a shortened form, such as a Spider or Mite, is much like that existing between a Crayfish and a Crab (p. 14). For in a Scorpion many of the pairs of ganglia of the ventral cord remain distinct, though there is a good deal of fusion between those at its front end, while in a Spider or Mite all the ganglia of the cord have consolidated into a single nerve-mass.

Among the Insects, again, we find the same principles exemplified. Some of the simpler forms possess a nervous system very much like that of a short Centipede, and from this condition all degrees of fusion and concentration are found, the maximum being reached where all the ganglia of the ventral cord have united into a single nerve-mass, precisely as in Crabs and Spiders. Three such stages, as exemplified by a Termite, a Water-Beetle, and a Fly, are represented in fig. 1019. In those insects which begin life as larvæ, it commonly happens that in this early stage of life the nervous system is simpler than in the adult, exhibiting less fusion and concentration. This is exemplified by comparison of a caterpillar with the butterfly or moth which it becomes, or a bee-grub with an adult bee. Cases are known, however, where the nervous system is condensed both in larva and adult, *e.g.* the House-Fly and its allies (*Muscidæ*). A curious reversal of the ordinary state of things is found in the Ant-Lion (*Myrmeleo*), for here the nervous system of the relatively short and squat larva is more concentrated than that of the elongated adult. That this should be so is probably not merely due to difference in shape, for the complex habits of the rapacious larva involve elaborate adjustments to the surroundings, which need an efficient and centralized nervous system for their proper performance (see vol. ii, p. 111). So far as we know, the life of the adult is relatively simple.

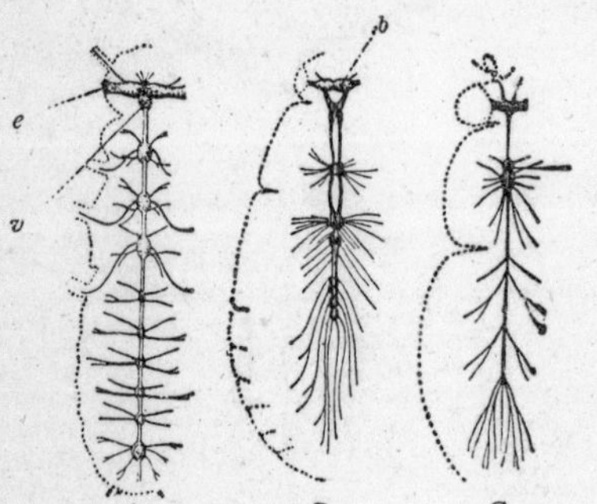

Fig. 1019.—Central Nervous Systems of a Termite (*Termes*, A), a Water-Beetle (*Dytiscus*, B), and a Blow-Fly (*Musca*, C), to illustrate stages in concentration. *b*, brain; *e*, eye; *v*, ventral ganglion.

It remains to be added that all the air-breathing Arthropods possess a visceral nervous system, which may attain considerable complexity, and takes origin from the nerve-ring.

Nervous Systems of Molluscs (Mollusca).—The least concentrated type of nervous system is found, as might be expected, among some of the Primitive Molluscs (Amphineura). The central nervous system of a Mail-Shell (*Chiton*), for instance, consists of a nerve-ring from which four thick nerves run back (fig. 1020). Two of these are *pedal cords*, that traverse the substance of the muscular foot, while the others are *lateral cords* placed at a higher level, and uniting with one another behind above the intestine. The nerve-cells are distributed pretty uniformly throughout both ring and cords, in the course of which are no distinct ganglia. The pharynx with its rasping organ receives branches from the nerve-ring, which *do* swell into small ganglia, and this is also the case with a pair of nerves running from the lateral cords to the under side of the stomach (see figure). In this sluggish animal digestion is the dominant function, and that is possibly why the only distinct ganglia in the nervous system are related to the digestive organs. The visceral nervous system consists in this case of (1) the nerves which run from the nerve-ring to the pharynx, (2) the lateral cords and their branches.

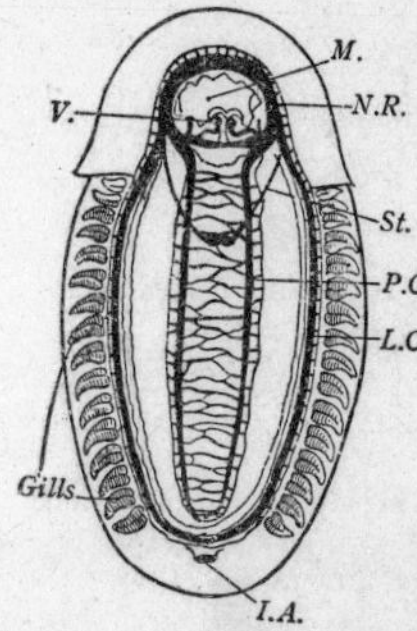

Fig. 1020.—A Mail-Shell (*Chiton*) dissected from above, to show Central Nervous System

M., Mouth; *I.A.*, intestinal aperture; *N.R.*, nerve-ring; *P.C.*, pedal cord; *L.C.*, lateral cord; *St.*, stomach nerve passing back to pair of gastric ganglia; *V.*, part of Visceral nervous system.

Passing from a simple form like the Mail-Shell to those which are more specialized, we shall find that as we ascend the scale to higher and higher types the nervous system becomes more and more centralized, in the same sort of way as in Arthropods. The nerve-cells are no longer scattered throughout the central nervous system, but are collected into definite ganglia, of which the most important are thickenings of the nerve-ring. This is very well seen in Snails and Slugs (Gastropoda), a vast number of which present a similar arrangement to that represented in fig. 1021 for the River-Snail (*Paludina*). In the middle of the figure is seen the nerve-ring, which is thickened into three distinct pairs of ganglia —(1) brain-ganglia above, (2) side-ganglia laterally (dotted in the figure), and (3) foot-ganglia below. The brain-ganglia, as shown at the top of the figure, give origin to a cord that supplies the pharynx, and swells into a pair of small ganglia from which nerves run to the pharynx. This is part of the visceral nervous system, the rest of it consisting of a nerve-loop by means of which the

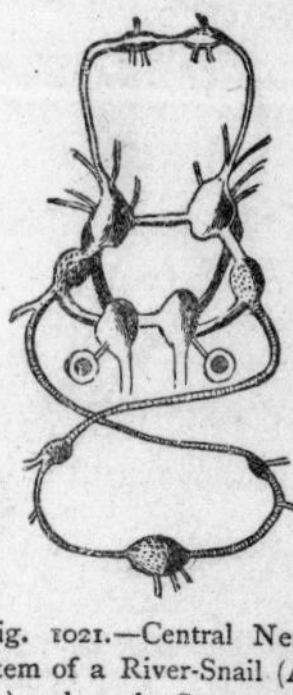

Fig. 1021.—Central Nervous System of a River-Snail (*Paludina*), enlarged. See text. The circles shaded in the centre and connected with the pedal ganglia are the so-called "ears" (*Otocysts*)

two side-ganglia are connected together, and in the course of which are three ganglia supplying many of the organs of the body. As in all Gastropods, the upper part of the body of the River-Snail has been subjected to a sort of twisting process, as the spiral shell suggests, and this has affected the nerve-loop, making it 8-shaped, as shown in the figure. This well-specialized central nervous system is associated with the presence of a clearly defined head, while just the contrary is the case in a Mail-Shell. Centralization has taken place to a still greater extent in some of the Gastropods, *e.g.* in the Pond-Snail (*Limnæus*) and Garden-Snail (*Helix aspersa*, fig. 1022), where the nerve-loop, which here has not been inflenced by the twisting of the body, is so short that its three ganglia are closely approximated to one another, and also to the foot-ganglia and side-ganglia of the nerve-ring.

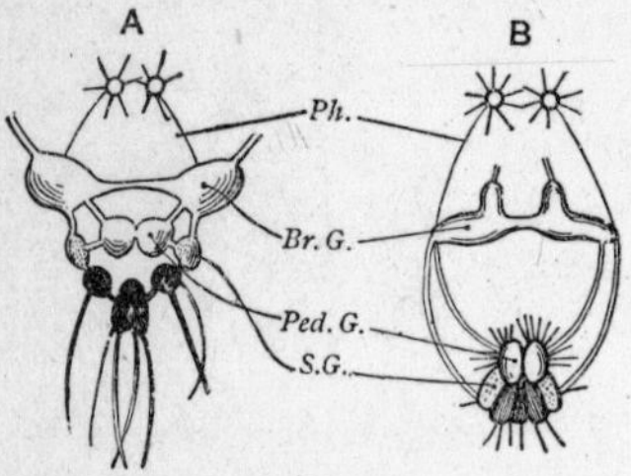

Fig. 1022.—Central Nervous Systems of Pond-Snail (*Limnæus*, A) and Garden-Snail (*Helix*, B), diagrammatic and enlarged

Br.G., Brain ganglia; *Ped.G.*, pedal ganglia: *S.G.*, side ganglia (dotted). Above are seen the small buccal ganglia connected by pharyngeal nerves (*Ph.*) with the brain ganglia, while below, the short nerve-loop with its ganglia is represented (darkly shaded).

Both in Bivalve Molluscs (Lamellibranchia) and Tusk-Shells (Scaphopoda) the nervous system follows the type described for Gastropods, but is less concentrated, and the brain-ganglia are relatively small, which may be correlated with the absence of any definite head in the former group, and its imperfect development in the latter.

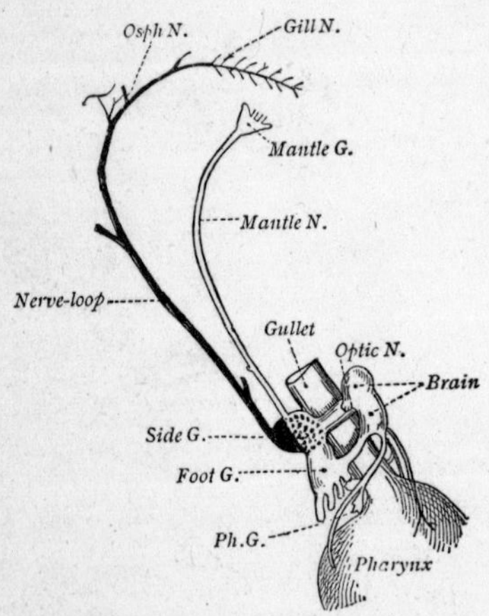

Fig. 1023.—Central Nervous System of Cuttle-Fish (*Sepia*), seen from the right side

G., Ganglia; *N.*, nerve; *Ph.G.*, pharyngeal or buccal ganglia; *Osph.N.*, osphradial nerve of water-testing organ (*Osphradium*).

Among the Head-Footed Molluscs (Cephalopoda) various degrees of concentration are found, there being the least amount of this in the Pearly Nautilus, which is a primitive and isolated type, while in the active Cuttle-Fishes, Squids, and Octopi centralization is at a maximum. The Common Cuttle-Fish (*Sepia officinalis*, fig. 1023) possesses a nerve-ring of which the ganglia are exceedingly large and closely connected. In one respect the nerve-ring is less complex than that of the Garden-Snail, for it here includes two only of the three ganglia of the nerve-loop, which is long, distinct, and, like the body, not twisted. The nerve-ring of Cephalopods is more or less enclosed in a gristly case, serving as a sort of skull.

NERVOUS SYSTEMS OF BACKBONED ANIMALS (VERTEBRATA)

The nervous system attains its maximum complexity in backboned animals, especially in the highest Mammals. The chief part of the central organs consists of a tube, which is placed near the upper side of the body, and in all but the lowest members of the group is sheltered within a skull and backbone. The front end of this nerve-tube is usually swollen into a brain, which is the chief organ of correlation and adjustment, while the rest of it is known as the spinal cord or spinal marrow. The central structures also include a visceral, or, as it is here usually called, a sympathetic nervous system, which where best developed consists of a couple of cords running longitudinally near the under side of the backbone, and swelling at intervals into sympathetic ganglia. Besides these there are outlying ganglia of similar nature in close connection with some of the internal organs, and connected with the cords just mentioned.

The body of a Vertebrate is undoubtedly made up of rings or segments, and although this is not at first sight apparent, the serial arrangement of certain structures shows it to be the case. We find, for example, that a regular succession of spinal nerves is given off from the spinal cord, one pair to each segment. From the brain arise from 10 to 12 pairs of cranial nerves, the number of which, however, does not tell us how many segments are fused to form the head. The number would be a guide if cranial nerves were precisely equivalent to spinal nerves, but this does not appear to be the case. While on the one hand some of them are complex, and equivalent to more than one pair of spinal nerves, others are only comparable to bits of such nerves, so to speak. The sympathetic system is closely connected with the brain and spinal cord, to which it is subordinate, and its nerves branch out in the organs of digestion, circulation, &c. A few further details have already been given with regard to the nervous system of Man (see vol. i, p. 49).

It was stated at the commencement of this section that the essential elements of the nervous system, *i.e.* the neurons, are derived from the ectoderm or outer cell-layer. Considering that brain and spinal cord are far removed from the surface, while the body is traversed in all directions by nerves, it seems very difficult to believe such a statement, but the study of development shows that there is no doubt at all about the matter.

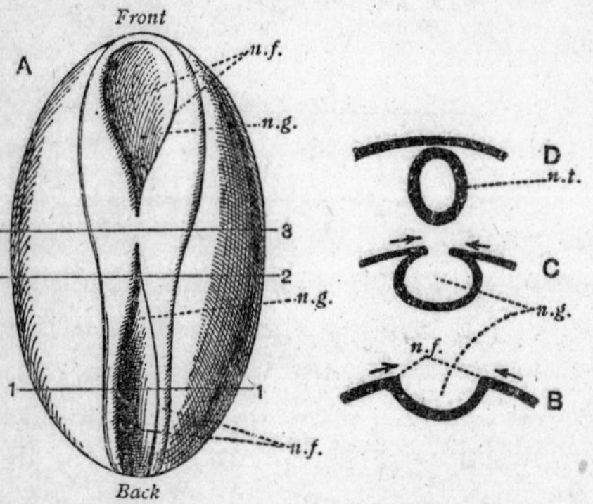

Fig. 1024.—Development of Central Nervous System in a Vertebrate Embryo, diagrammatic

A, Upper side of embryo, showing folding-up of the nerve-plate; B, C, and D, stages in folding-up of nerve-plate, as seen in cross-sections through upper part of A, taken at levels 1–1, 2–2, and 3–3; *n.g.*, nerve-groove; *n.f.*, nerve-folds; *n.t.*, nerve-tube.

At a comparatively early stage in the development of an embryo part of the ectoderm covering the upper surface thickens into a nerve-plate, which sinks below the surface, and at the same time folds up to constitute the nerve-tube. The details for the Lancelet have already been given (vol. iii, p. 345), but in that animal the nerve-plate sinks below the surface before it is completely folded into a tube, while in average cases the two processes go on simultaneously, as will be gathered from fig. 1024.

The walls of the nerve-tube thicken, and by a process of unequal growth the spinal cord and the various regions of the brain come into existence. The rest of the nervous system grows out from the nerve-tube, *e.g.* the spinal nerves grow out from the spinal cord to the parts of the body which they supply. It therefore follows that these and the other nerves, as well as the sympathetic system, are really *ingrowths* from the ectoderm or outer cell-layer, although in the adult they are far removed from the surface.

The Brain of Vertebrates.—At first sight the brains of Fishes,

Amphibians, Reptiles, Birds, and Mammals look so extremely unlike that comparison seems hopeless, but such an idea is soon dispelled by a study of development, which is the key to the whole matter. What takes place is broadly as follows (fig. 1025). The front end of the nerve-tube grows rapidly, and divides into three successive swellings, which we may term the Fore-, Mid-, and Hind-Brains. These three original swellings are converted into the central part or axis of the adult brain, the front part of which is called the 'Twixt-Brain, and the hind part the Medulla Oblongata or Spinal Bulb (continuous behind with the Spinal Cord), while the roof of the middle section is thickened

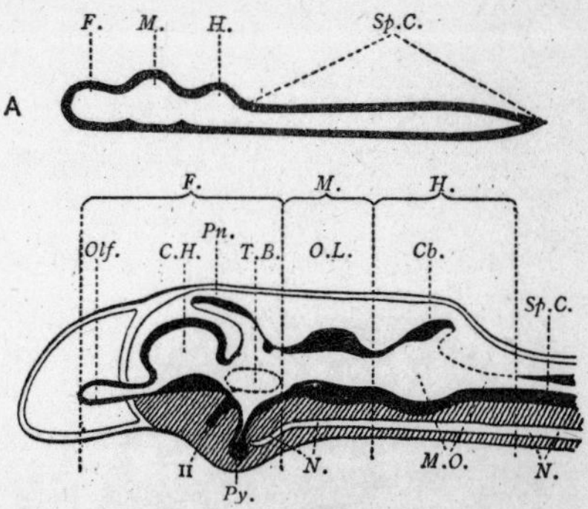

Fig. 1025.—Development of Vertebrate Brain, as seen in longitudinal section. diagrammatic

A, Brain and spinal cord at early stage; B, brain at later stage enclosed in brain-case, the floor of which is shaded with oblique lines; *F.*, *M.*, *H.*, *Sp.C.*, fore-, mid-, and hind-brains, and spinal cord; *T.B.*, 'twixt-brain; *C.H.*, cerebral hemispheres; *Olf.*, olfactory lobe projecting into nasal capsule; *Pn.* and *Py.*, pineal and pituitary bodies; *O.L.*, optic lobes; *M.O.*, medulla oblongata; *Cb.*, cerebellum; *N. N.*, notochord; II, optic nerve.

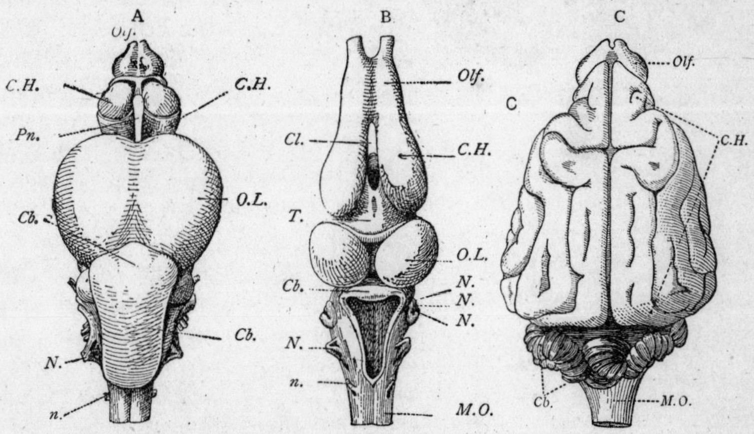

Fig. 1026.—Brains of Trout (A), Frog (B), and Dog (C), seen from above, and drawn same length

Olf., Olfactory lobes; *C.H.*, cerebral hemispheres (*Cl.* is a cleft between them in B); *T.*, 'twixt-brain; *Pn.*, pineal body; *O.L.*, optic lobes; *Cb.*, cerebellum; *M.O.*, medulla oblongata; *N.*, *N.*, *N.*, cranial nerves; *n.*, *n.*, spinal nerves.

into a pair of swellings known as Optic Lobes, each of which, in Mammals only, is divided into two smaller projections by a transverse groove. The differences between various classes of Vertebrates mainly depend upon the relative size and structure of certain outgrowths from the axis, the position of which will be realized by reference to fig. 1026. From the 'twixt-brain two lobes grow out, which become the Cerebral Hemispheres (represented in some Fishes by a single lobe), from the front end of which spring Olfactory Lobes, related to the organs of smell. An unpaired outgrowth, the Cerebellum, arises from the upper side of the hind-brain. In Birds and Mammals the Cerebral Hemispheres and Cerebellum are of such great relative size that they largely overlap and conceal the central axis. That the brain should be made up of so many parts is a result of the division of physiological labour, these different parts sharing between them the work that has to be done. The most responsible duties are vested in the Cerebral Hemispheres, to which all the other regions are subordinate. The other regions of the brain, the spinal cord, and the sympathetic system, all have important shares in the work of the nervous system, but all are subsidiary to the cerebral hemispheres, which exercise supreme control over the body at large, and are the chief centres of correlation and adjustment. And besides this, consciousness, sensation, will, and intelligence are dependent upon them. As we ascend the scale among the Vertebrates we shall find the hemispheres getting relatively larger and more complex, as the expression of a centralizing tendency (fig. 1026). There is also a great deal of division of labour between the parts of the hemispheres themselves, and their highest duties appear to be discharged by what is known as the cerebral *cortex*, an external layer of nerve-cells. In all the higher Mammals the extent of this cortex is more or less increased by the presence of winding furrows, resulting from a process

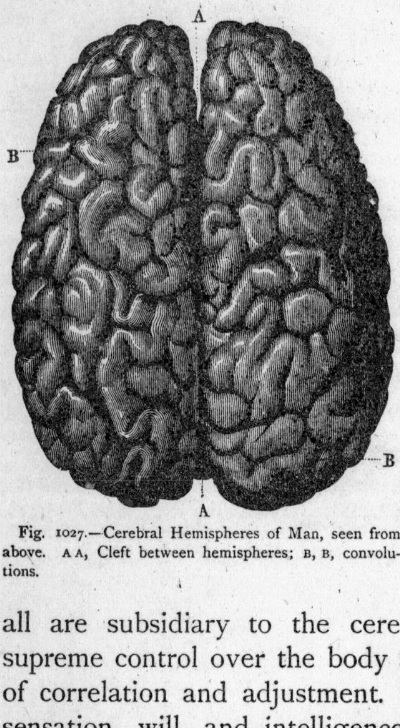

Fig. 1027.—Cerebral Hemispheres of Man, seen from above. A A, Cleft between hemispheres; B, B, convolutions.

of folding or convolution. These attain their maximum complication in the human subject, where also the hemispheres are of relatively enormous size (fig. 1027). The amount of convolution is related to the intelligence of the particular species, but hasty deductions must be avoided, since they are also proportionate to the bulk of the body. Some of the most brilliant advances in modern surgery are due to the discovery that the cerebral cortex is divided into nerve-centres, some of which are concerned with sight, hearing, and other special sensations, while others again control definite sections of the muscular system. But so far it has not been found possible to locate the higher mental functions, such, for example, as memory. The Cerebellum also possesses a very complicated cortex. As might be expected, the minute structure of the brain in a higher Mammal is most remarkably complex. Details would be out of place here, but fig. 1028, which represents one of the most specialized neurons from the cortex, will suggest the elaboration which exists, bearing in mind that the number of neurons in the brain is enormous. And it is particularly interesting to know that, as recent investigations have proved, these ultimate elements of the nervous system maintain themselves during the entire life of the animal. There are not successive crops of nerve-cells as once supposed. Were this the case, indeed, such things as memory would be almost unintelligible.

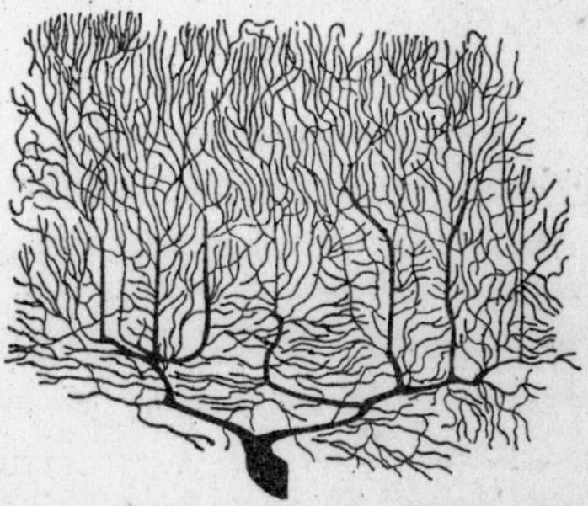

Fig. 1028.—Complex Neuron from Cortex of Human Brain, greatly enlarged

CHAPTER LVIII

SENSE-ORGANS OF INVERTEBRATES AND VERTEBRATES

Sense-organs are the intermediaries between the nervous system and the environment, and essentially consist of ectoderm cells (end-organs) capable of being influenced by external agents or stimuli. The stimulation of a sense-organ may be immediately followed by a reflex action, or it may lead to a voluntary action, and it is commonly associated, in higher animals at least, with what is technically termed a *sensation*, *i.e.* an awareness of something in the surroundings. Supposing that in ourselves a light is suddenly flashed in the eyes when it is night. The eye is first affected, then the optic nerve, and then some of the nerve-cells in the brain. It is not till these last are brought into operation that we "see a light", and by comparison with past experiences are put into possession of a piece of information about our surroundings. It must be added, that besides special sensations, such as those of hearing, sight, &c., there are others of obscurer nature, which tell us something about the state of the body itself, and are known as *organic sensations.* Such are feelings of hunger, discomfort, &c., which, though of great importance for the well-being of the body, since they often guide to actions, *e.g.* feeding, which conduce to its welfare, will not be considered here, since they are not related to special sense-organs. Nor will reference be made to the "muscular sense", by which muscular efforts are gauged.

It will be convenient to place the subject-matter ot the present chapter under the time-honoured headings of Touch, Taste, Smell, Hearing, and Sight, for it is by means of sensations which can be broadly classified in this way that we derive most of our knowledge of surroundings. But many of the lower animals possess sense-organs of which we can only conjecture the use, and the stimulation of which must result in sensations of which we can form little if any idea. And even when with reasonable certainty we can correlate sense-organs possessed by such animals with some of our own, it by no means follows that the *range* of a given sensation is the same for one of them as for ourselves. As regards hearing, for example, there is reason to think that some animals can hear sounds which are pitched much higher than any by which we are affected; nor is this very surprising when we reflect that the range of hearing is not the same in all human beings. Many persons, for example, cannot hear the high and piercing sounds made by Bats. These remarks are made as a warning against applying the results of human physiology to lower animals with too great assurance.

TOUCH

Undoubtedly the most primitive of all the senses is that of Touch, and we may broadly state that the skin is the Tactile Organ, remembering that its outer layer, commonly known as the epidermis, is no other than the ectoderm or outer cell-layer of the embryo. We must also include here the cellular lining of the mouth-cavity and, when such exist, the nasal cavities,

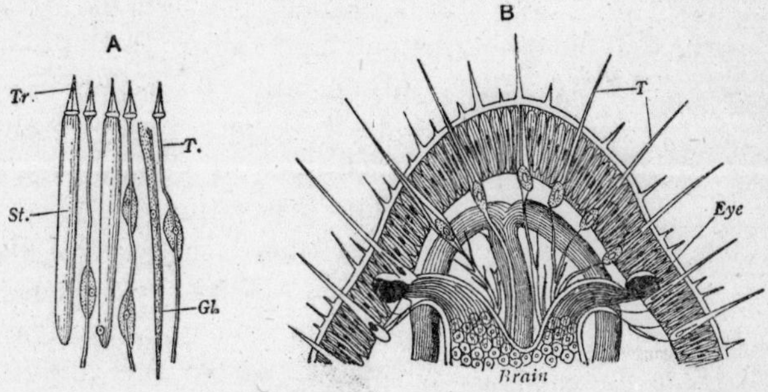

Fig. 1029.—Tactile Organs. A, Cells from the ectoderm of a Sea-Anemone (*Actinia*); *T.*, a touch-cell, with outer end produced into a stiff process; *St.*, stinging cell, with sensitive trigger-hair (*Tr.*); *Gl.*, glandular cell. B, Head of a Freshwater Annelid (*Bohemilla comata*), seen from above, and showing epidermis in optical section, enlarged; *T.*, tactile processes of some of the epidermic cells, which are continuous internally with nerve-fibres.

since these have been developed as in-pushings of the ectoderm. The external agents of stimuli which by their action upon the skin evoke sensations of touch are of two sorts. There are, in the first place, mechanical agents, such as contact or pressure, and, in the second place, heat-rays. The sensations which result are respectively known as *haptic* and *thermal*.

Single epidermal cells or groups of such cells are specialized for the reception of stimuli leading to sensations of touch, but in such forms as Cœlenterates and Annelids many scattered cells of the kind probably minister to other senses besides that of touch. And it must be remembered that even the special sense-cells of hearing and sight are derived from the skin, which is in fact the primitive sense-organ. Cells which are regarded as tactile, from some of the lowest animals, are represented in fig. 1029.

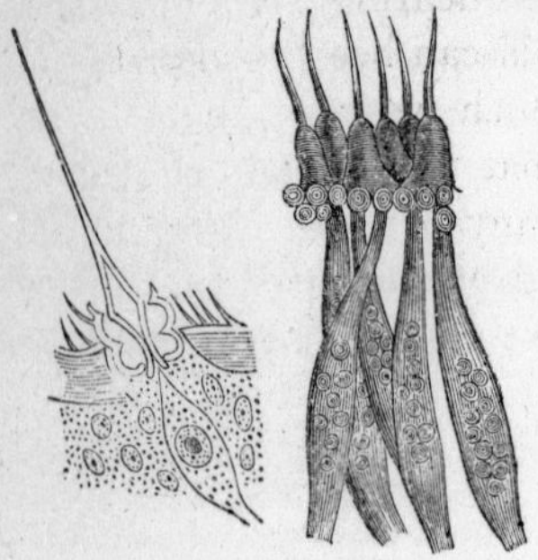

Fig. 1030. — Tactile Organs of Insects, greatly enlarged. On the right is a group of such structures, and on the left a single one, in section.

The firm external covering with which the bodies of Arthropods are clothed is naturally a hindrance to the reception of stimuli by the underlying epidermis. The difficulty is got over by the existence of little pores in the hard investment. Under each pore is an enlarged sense-cell, placed at the base of a stiff tactile bristle, with which external bodies come into contact (fig. 1030).

In aquatic Vertebrates the sense-cells of the skin are in direct contact with the surrounding medium, although they are not infrequently protected by being lodged in pits, grooves, or canals which open at intervals to the exterior. But in terrestrial Vertebrates there are special end-organs of touch which have sunk below the epidermis, though they remain sufficiently near to the surface to be stimulated when the body comes into contact with surrounding objects. Such are the groups of touch-corpuscles which are to be found in the skin of the Frog, and around the edge of the Duck's bill (fig. 1031). The latter animal feeds upon small worms, &c., which live in the mud that is strained through its bill, and such special arrangements are clearly necessary to aid in the discrimination between what is edible and what is not. Another example is afforded by the

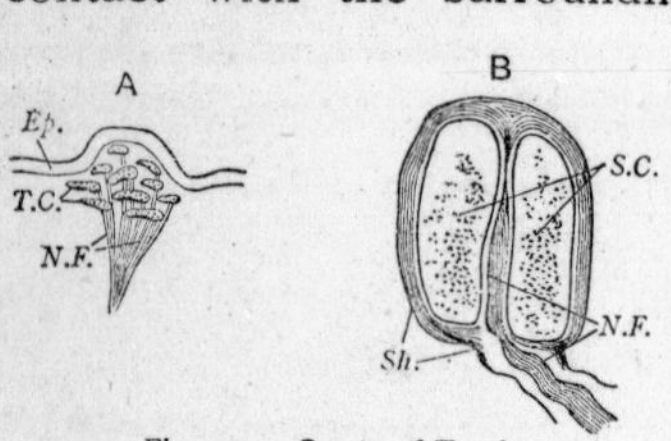

Fig. 1031.—Organs of Touch

A, Small piece of the skin of a Frog, in vertical section, enlarged; *Ep.*, epidermis; *T.C.*, touch-corpuscles; *N.F.*, nerve-fibres. B, Touch-corpuscle from the bill of a Duck, much enlarged; *S.C.*, sense-cells; *N.F.*, nerve-fibre; *Sh.*, fibrous sheath.

numerous touch-corpuscles which underlie the little ridges seen on the tips of our fingers and thumbs (fig. 1032). In Reptiles, Birds, and Mammals there are also curious structures known as Pacinian bodies (fig. 1033), in which the ending of a nerve is surrounded by a series of layers arranged almost like the coats of an onion. There is reason to think that these are very sensitive to slight pressures. They abound, for instance, in the wing-membranes of Bats, and it is well known that these creatures can easily steer their way in the dark through a veritable maze of obstacles, such as that afforded by a series of strings running in various directions. Pacinian bodies are also found connected with tendons, ligaments, and various internal organs. The use of these is probably to apprise the central nervous system of variations in pressure and tension which take place as between the different parts of the body itself.

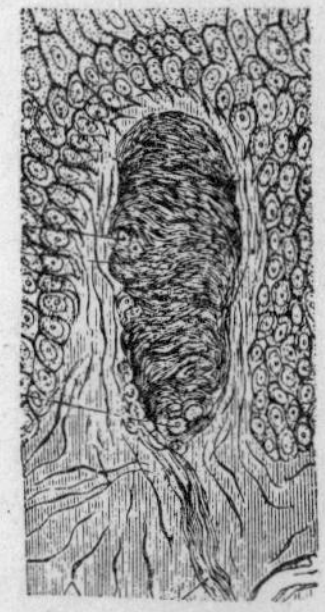

Fig. 1032. — Touch-Corpuscle from Finger Tip of Man, in section, greatly enlarged

We are still very much in the dark as to how far there do or do not exist special end-organs which are affected by variations in temperature. It is known that definite spots in the human skin are sensitive to such variations, but there do not appear to be any special sense-organs in these spots. Some of the sensory nerve-fibres terminate in the skin by dividing into a number of little branches which do not become continuous with modified epidermal cells, and it has been suggested that these "free nerve endings" are related to the temperature sense.

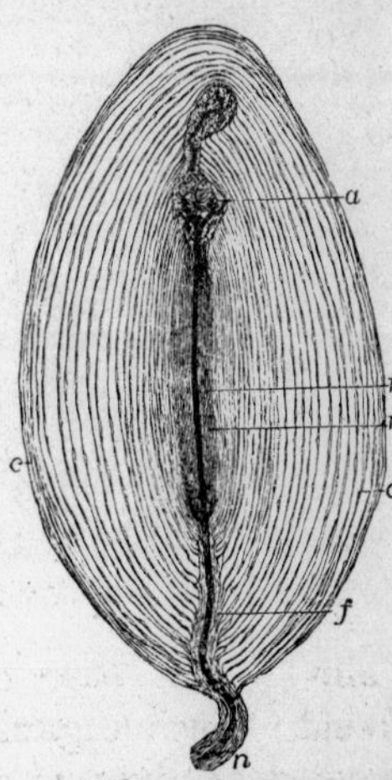

Fig. 1033.—A Pacinian Corpuscle in Longitudinal Section, enlarged. A nerve-fibre (*n n′*), surrounded by a sheath (*f*), enters the base of the corpuscle, loses its sheath, traverses a central core (*m*), and ends in an irregular expansion (*a*). The corpuscle is mostly made up of numerous concentric fibrous layers (*c*, *d*).

While the entire external surface of the body is sensitive to contact, pressure, and changes in temperature, this is in many cases insufficient to enable the requisite adjustments to the environment to be brought about. And we accordingly find that in many animals organs of active touch have been evolved, which explore the surroundings, and help to detect the presence of food, or to give warning of danger. Such are the tentacles of Jelly-Fish and Sea-Anemones, the slender outgrowths on the head of a Sea-Centipede, the two pairs of antennæ on the head of a Crayfish, the single pair on the head of an Insect, and the tentacles on the heads of Snails and Slugs. The "whiskers" of a Cat or Rabbit belong to the same class of structures. They are stiff

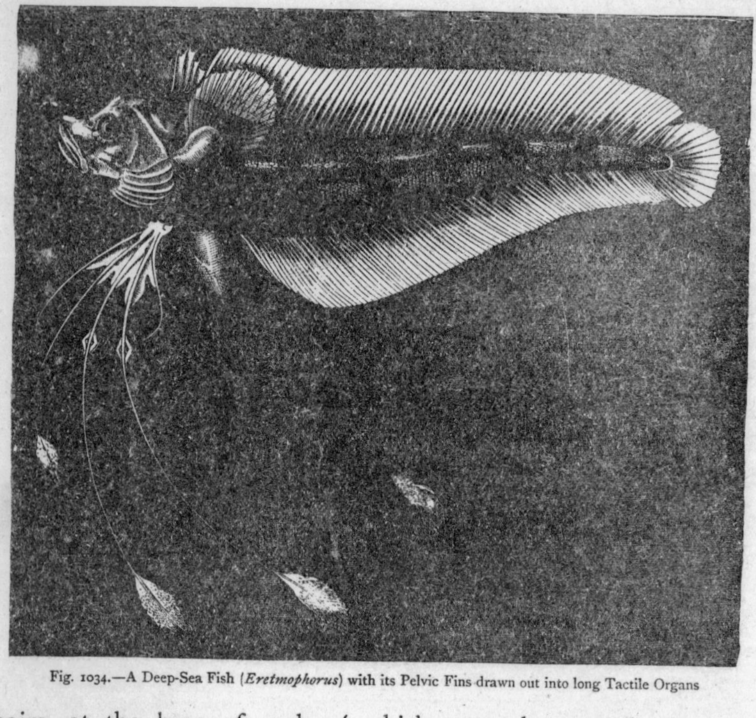

Fig. 1034.—A Deep-Sea Fish (*Eretmophorus*) with its Pelvic Fins drawn out into long Tactile Organs

hairs, at the base of each of which a touch-corpuscle is to be found. Such organs of active touch may either from the first have done duty as sensory organs, or may have originally been evolved in the interests of some other function. The former is probably true for the feelers of a Sea-Centipede or Insect, but the large feelers of a Crayfish (and very likely the small ones too) were probably jaws at an earlier stage, having later on been shifted in front of the mouth, and modified in shape and structure to do duty as sense-organs. There can be no doubt that the paired fins of Fishes were originally evolved in relation to swimming, but it sometimes happens that they have been transformed into tactile organs, as in the deep-sea form (*Eretmophorus*) represented in fig. 1034. Snakes employ their tongues as tactile organs, as also do Woodpeckers and Ant-eaters. This, however, is probably only an extension of the original duties, for the primary use of the tongue seems to be that of a tactile organ in relation to the mouth-cavity.

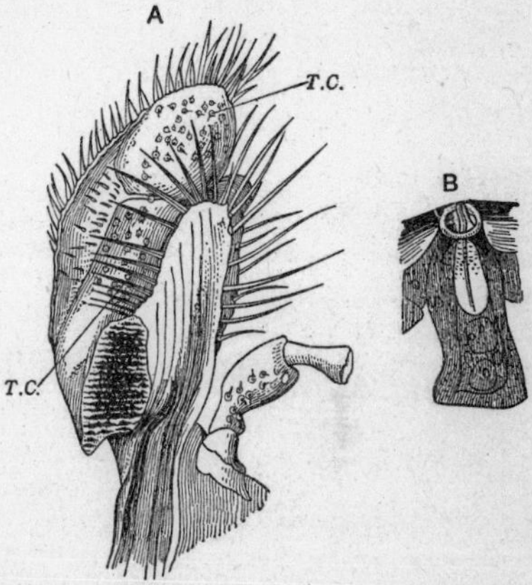

Fig. 1035.—Taste-Organs of a Wasp. A, Under side of left maxilla, enlarged, showing group of taste-cups (*T.C.*). B, A single taste-cup, greatly enlarged.

TASTE

Sensations of Taste are primarily important because they assist in the selection of suitable food. The stimulus is a chemical one, and consists of substances in solution. We know but little about the gustatory organs of lower forms, but as these show a preference for certain kinds of food it is probably correct to assume that such organs are present. In the Earth-Worm, for example, groups of modified epidermal cells in the neighbourhood of the mouth are very likely related to taste.

Fig. 1036.—Taste-Bud from the Tongue of a Rabbit, in longitudinal section, greatly enlarged. The bud contains slender taste-cells, the external ends of which project into a little pit continuous with the mouth-cavity.

Certain regions of the mouth-parts of some Insects are studded with minute pits, beneath each of which is a sense-cell, drawn out externally into a short bristle, and continuous with a nerve-fibre internally. They are present, for example, in Bees and Wasps, and are almost certainly of a gustatory nature (fig. 1035).

Cuttle-Fishes and many Snails possess a sense-organ on the floor of the pharynx, below the front end of the rasping-ribbon. It probably has to do with taste.

In Lung-Fishes, Amphibians, Reptiles, Birds, and Mammals the organs of taste consist of groups of sense-cells in the lining of the mouth-cavity, and since this cavity is developed as an in-pushing from the exterior the cells in question are of ectodermic nature. The largest amount of specialization takes place in Mammals, where the "taste-buds", as the group of cells are called, are associated with small projections or papillæ of the surface of the tongue (fig. 1036).

SMELL

Many of the lower animals can undoubtedly smell as well as taste, though to definitely associate this sense with special cells or groups of cells is not at present possible. Our knowledge is more complete in the case of Arthropods, Molluscs, and Vertebrates, where experiments lead to results of more de-

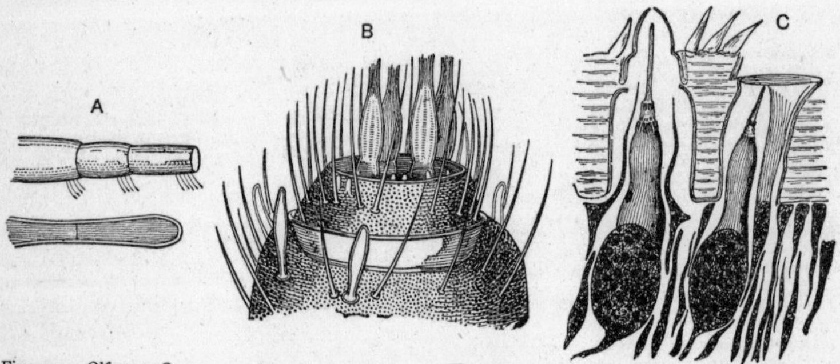

Fig. 1037.—Olfactory Organs. A, A small part of the outer branch of antennule of a Crayfish is shown at *a*, with groups of olfactory setæ on its under side, enlarged; *b*, an olfactory seta, further enlarged. B, Tip of feeler of a Millipede, greatly enlarged, showing olfactory cylinders among the ordinary tactile bristles. C, Two olfactory cones from feeler of a Wasp, in section, greatly enlarged.

finite kind. In all cases the stimulus is of a gaseous nature, and in aquatic animals the gases that are smelt are dissolved in the surrounding water. The sense of smell is obviously of great importance as regards adjustment to the environment. By its means food is in many cases detected, while it often enables animals to recognize friends or foes, even when these are at a considerable distance. This is, of course, due to the nature of the stimulus. Since Smell, Hearing, Sight, and the Temperature Sense are able to give information about objects which are more or less far away, they may be grouped together as Distance-Senses (telæsthetic senses), and are in marked contrast to Touch (so far as haptic sensations are concerned), which only conveys knowledge regarding things that actually come into contact with the skin.

There is naturally a tendency for olfactory organs to be developed at the front end of the body, where they can be most usefully employed, and they are commonly to be found on the feelers of Arthropods. In the Crayfish, for example, the small first feelers (antennules) bear groups of flattened bristles which undoubtedly have to do with smell, and similar structures are present on the antennæ of Millipedes and Insects (fig. 1037).

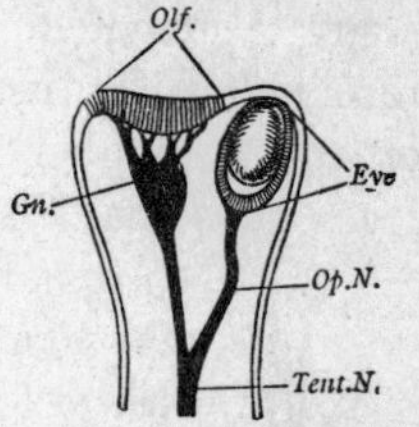

Fig. 1038.—Tip of Optic Tentacle of Garden-Snail, in diagrammatic longitudinal section, enlarged. The tentacular nerve (*Tent. N.*) gives off an optic nerve (*Op.N.*) to the eye, and then expands into a ganglion (*Gn.*) which sends fibres to an olfactory patch (*Olf.*) of cells on the tip of the tentacle.

Land-Snails and Slugs, among the Molluscs, are known to be endowed with a keen sense of smell. In the common Garden-Snail (*Helix aspersa*) some of the epidermic cells at the tips of the long eye-bearing tentacles are believed to minister to this function (fig. 1038), though experiments have been made which appear to show that olfactory cells are elsewhere present.

Among aquatic Molluscs what is known as a water-testing organ (osphradium) is usually present in the neighbourhood of the breathing organs (fig. 1039). This is generally considered to be of olfactory nature.

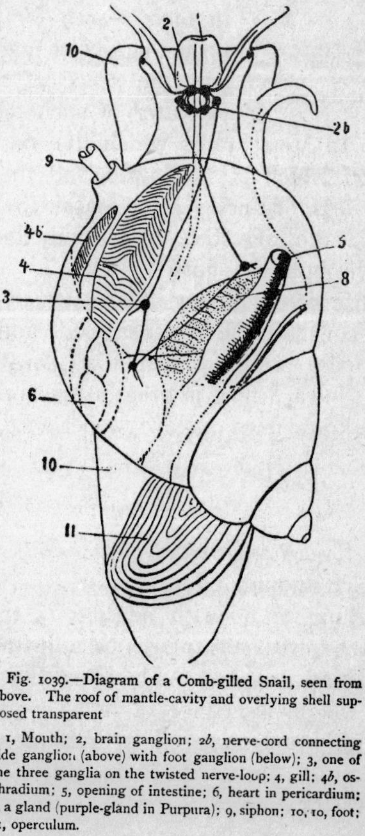

Fig. 1039.—Diagram of a Comb-gilled Snail, seen from above. The roof of mantle-cavity and overlying shell supposed transparent

1, Mouth; 2, brain ganglion; 2*b*, nerve-cord connecting side ganglion (above) with foot ganglion (below); 3, one of the three ganglia on the twisted nerve-loop; 4, gill; 4*b*, osphradium; 5, opening of intestine; 6, heart in pericardium; 8, a gland (purple-gland in Purpura); 9, siphon; 10, 10, foot; 11, operculum.

In Vertebrates the sense-cells related to smell form part of the lining of the cavities of the nose, and since these are developed as pits in the external surface, such cells must necessarily be of ectodermic character. When the sense of smell is keen the nasal cavities are large and complex, and folds project into them which increase the surface over which olfactory cells are distributed. These cells are frequently of the shape represented in fig. 1040, from which it will be seen that from the outer end a number of slender processes project into the nasal cavity. In some Fishes, such as the ordinary bony forms, the originally single nostril of each half of the nose is divided into two apertures, which respectively serve for the entry and exit of water, that appears to flow continuously through the nasal cavity. There can be no doubt that many fishes possess a very keen sense of smell, and the experiments of Bateson have proved that some of them (*e.g.* Dog-Fish, Conger-Eel, and Sole) are mainly guided by this in their search for food. This being so, the nocturnal habits of many species is readily intelligible, and the sense of smell must also be very useful in water of such depth that the light is dim.

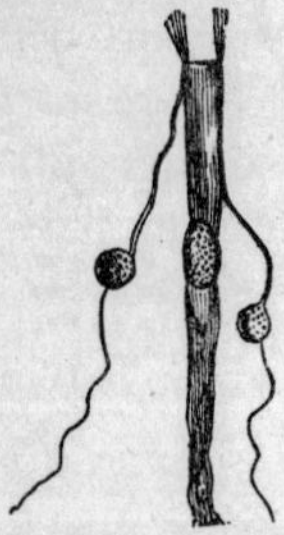

Fig. 1040.—Two Olfactory Cells from an Amphibian (*Proteus*), greatly enlarged

In Vertebrates which live on land the courses taken by the food which is swallowed and the air that is breathed are more or less distinct. Each nasal cavity, in fact, opens at the back into the digestive tube, and the natural way of breathing is "through the nose". This is clearly to the advantage of the sense of smell, for the air which passes over the olfactory cells is constantly being renewed, and the incoming current is continually bringing with it gaseous matter capable of being smelt. An inward flow is greatly promoted by the act of "sniffing", as we know from our own experience.

BALANCE AND HEARING

There are certain sensory structures among the Invertebrates which though often classified as Auditory Organs have probably nothing to do with hearing in the ordinary sense, but are concerned with advantageous adjustment of the body as regards its position in space. This is of the greatest importance in reference to the maintenance of balance and the direction of movement. They are stimulated by vibrations in the surrounding medium, water or air as the case may be, and there can be little doubt that they have furnished the material from which undoubted organs of hearing have been evolved. Indeed the auditory organs still retain, in ourselves for instance, the old function side by side with the new.

BALANCING ORGANS OF JELLY-FISH (HYDROZOA).—Jelly-Fish are often provided with balancing organs placed at regular intervals round the edge of the umbrella. In the simplest case these are little pits lined by specialized sense-cells, from each of which a bristle projects. Within the pit one or more calcareous particles (otoliths) are found, and these also have been derived from the ectoderm. In many species the mouths of these pits close up, converting them into little sacs (otocysts) which lie close to the surface. Other kinds, again, possess short balancing-tentacles (tentaculocysts), evolved no doubt from some of the ordinary sort (fig. 1041). In such instances the otoliths are derived from the entoderm cells which make up the inner part of the tentacle. Though these different organs may be constructed in various ways they are affected by the same sort of stimulus. Their sensory cells are jolted by movements in the surrounding water and by the swimming movements of the animals themselves, and the otoliths appear to intensify the action, as it were. The sense-cells are closely connected with the nervous system, and this again with muscle-fibres. We have present, in fact, the necessary machinery for muscular reflex actions (see p. 9), under which may be included the checking or stopping of swimming movements actually in progress.

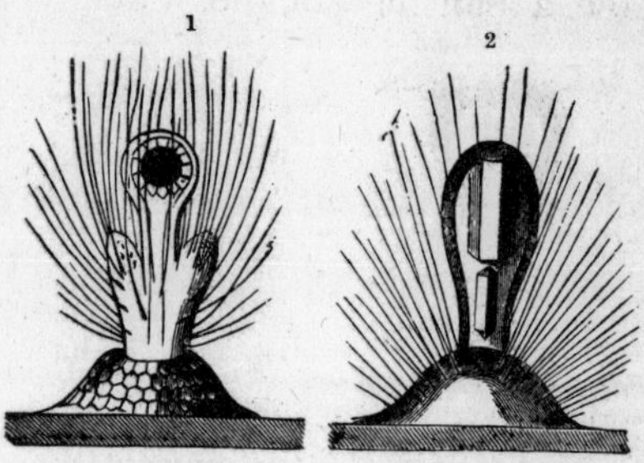

Fig. 1041.—Tentaculocysts of Jelly-Fish, enlarged
1, Of *Solmaris coronantha*; 2, of *Polyxenia cyanostylis*.

One of the most obvious uses of the sense-organs described appears to be that of enabling their possessors to keep well below the surface of the water during rough weather, for creatures of such flabby and delicate structure are quite unfitted to withstand the buffets of the waves. Supposing that on a stormy day a jelly-fish is swimming obliquely upwards. When it comes sufficiently near the surface for the balancing organs to be stimulated with a certain degree of vigour by the swing of the water, reflex modification of the swimming movements will take place, and the upward course will be altered into a downward one.

BALANCING ORGANS IN SEGMENTED WORMS (ANNELIDA).—Members of this group commonly react very quickly to jolting or agitation of the surrounding medium, and this may lead to movements promoting escape from danger. Earth-Worms, for example, when partly protruding from their burrows, will often draw back with extreme rapidity on the approach of a heavy footstep. The skin is no doubt the sense-organ in this case, but we are ignorant as to details. A few Annelids, however, have a pair of otocysts in the front part of the body, as, *e.g.*, the Common Lob-Worm (*Arenicola piscatorum*), where they are closely connected with the brain (fig. 1042). They have undoubtedly been evolved from pits in the ectoderm like the similar sacs found in some of the jelly-fish, and three stages in this evolution are permanently retained in three kinds of Lob-Worm. In one of these (*A. Claparedii*) there is simply a pair of depressions on the head, in another (*A. piscatorum*) otocysts which are still in communication with the exterior, and in a third (*A. Grubii*) closed otocysts. The otoliths of the second species are minute sand grains taken in from the exterior, while those of the third are calcareous particles secreted by the ectoderm.

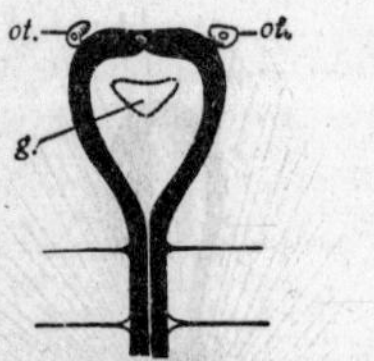

Fig. 1042.—Front Part of Central Nervous System of Lob-Worm (*Arenicola piscatorum*), enlarged. *g.*, Gullet (in cross section) traversing nerve-ring; *ot.*, otocysts in close connection with the brain (canals to exterior not shown).

BALANCING ORGANS IN MOLLUSCS (MOLLUSCA).—Most Molluscs possess a pair of otocysts, developed as pits in the ectoderm, which become closed and travel inwards to the neighbourhood of the foot. They are attached to the foot-ganglia, although their nerve-supply is derived from the brain (see fig. 1021, p. 17). It occasionally happens in Bivalves that the communication with the exterior is retained. The lining of these organs partly consists of sense-cells provided with stiff processes, and one or more calcareous otoliths are present.

The otocysts of Cuttle-Fishes and their allies are lodged in the gristly case which surrounds the thickened nerve-ring, pretty much as in backboned animals the corresponding organs are sheltered in gristly or bony capsules that form part of the wall of the brain-case. And it is definitely known that in Molluscs of this kind maintenance of equilibrium and adjustment of the swimming movements are seriously interfered with if the otocysts are injured, which leaves little doubt as to the use of these organs.

The otocysts of some of the free-swimming Sea-Snails (Heteropods) are particularly large and well-developed (fig. 1043), and are undoubtedly related to balance and steering. The majority of Snails and Slugs, however, are adapted to a creeping mode of life, the organ of locomotion being the muscular flat-soled foot, which is also concerned with maintaining the balance of the body. Since the otocysts are presumably related to both these uses, it is not surprising to find them placed close to the upper surface of the foot, by the slightest movement of which they must therefore be affected, and H. J. Fleure has described an interesting arrangement in the Limpet and Sea-Ear which probably conduces to this. In the two forms mentioned each otocyst is connected with the foot by a fibrous band, and there is a similar bond between the two otocysts (fig. 1044). These organs are thus kept "in touch" with the foot and with one another, and, being also moored by their nerves to the foot-ganglia, are kept steady, which seems desirable when their functions are considered.

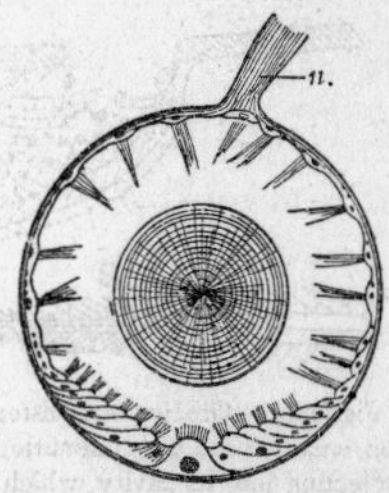

Fig. 1043.—Otocyst of a Heteropod (*Pterotrachea*), in section, enlarged. The large otolith is seen in the centre of the vesicle, which is lined below by sensory cells, provided with bunches of short, stiff projections; the rest of the vesicle is lined by cells bearing long cilia; *n.*, nerve.

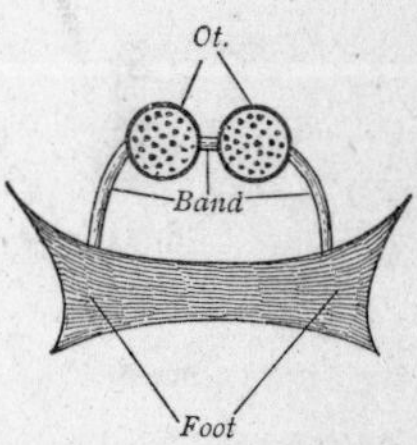

Fig. 1044. — Diagrammatic Cross Section through Otocysts (*Ot.*) and Foot of a Limpet, enlarged

Organs of Balance and Hearing in Crustaceans (Crustacea). — Such higher forms as Lobsters, Prawns, Shrimps, and Crabs are provided with otocysts lodged in the bases of the small feelers or antennules. These organs arise, as in cases already described, as pits in the ectoderm, and they usually, though not always, remain open through life. In a Lobster, for example, they are lined by a thin horny membrane continuous with the hard covering of the body, and studded with delicate bristles, at the bases of which are sense-cells (fig. 1045). The otoliths are sand grains which have been taken in from the exterior.

That the otocysts are concerned with equilibrium and adjustment of movement has been definitely proved by experiments upon the Prawn (*Palæmon*). When this creature moults it sheds not only the defensive armour of the body but also the lining of the otocysts, getting rid at the same time of the sand grains which serve as otoliths. Under ordinary circumstances these would be replaced by a fresh supply of the same material, but the specimens experimented upon were only provided with iron filings, some of which in due course were introduced into the otocysts. It was then found possible by means of a magnet to move the particles in various ways, and as a result of this the Prawns could be induced to assume all sorts of positions, under the impression, so to speak, that they were falling over in this or that direction, which they would have been if the shifting of the otoliths had been produced by ordinary causes.

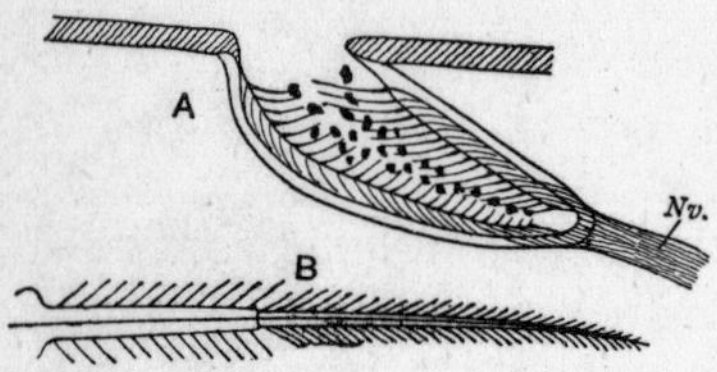

Fig. 1045.—Otocyst of Lobster (A) in longitudinal section, enlarged and diagrammatic; sensory bristles are seen projecting into its cavity, which contains numerous otoliths; *Nv.*, nerve. B, A sensory bristle, further enlarged

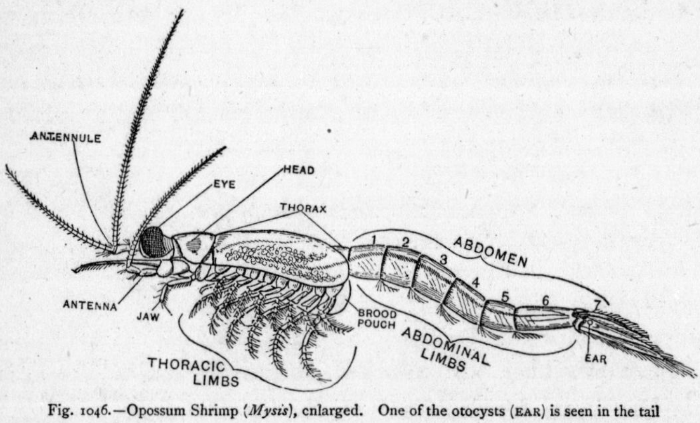

Fig. 1046.—Opossum Shrimp (*Mysis*), enlarged. One of the otocysts (EAR) is seen in the tail

In one Crustacean, the Opossum Shrimp (*Mysis*), the otocysts, in this case closed, are lodged in the flaps of the tail-fin, but why they should have this position is not known (fig. 1046).

It is generally assumed that animals which are endowed with a voice or its equivalent also possess powers of hearing, at least if the voice is used for the benefit of one another. Since some of the higher Crustaceans are able to emit sounds, it is quite possible that their otocysts are beginning to acquire a new use, *i.e.* that of serving as auditory organs. The Rock-Lobster (*Palinurus*), for example, makes a creaking noise by moving the basal joints of the large feelers, which then rub against their sockets. An unpleasant sound of similar nature can be produced by twisting a glass stopper in the neck of its bottle. A more specialized case is that of the Musical Strand-Crab (*Ocypoda macrocera*), which has been described by Alcock (in *A Naturalist in Indian Seas*). In this animal the inner side of the large nippers is provided with a ridge or scraper placed near the base of the limb, and a rasp-like ridge or key-board on the fixed joint of the claw. By drawing the scraper over the key-board a sort of chirping sound is produced, not unlike the one with which our native grasshoppers have made us familiar. The same zoologist speaks of the Squeaker Crab (*Psopheticus stridulans*) of the Andaman Sea as making a dismal noise by rubbing a spine which projects from the base of its nippers against a rough knob near the eye-socket.

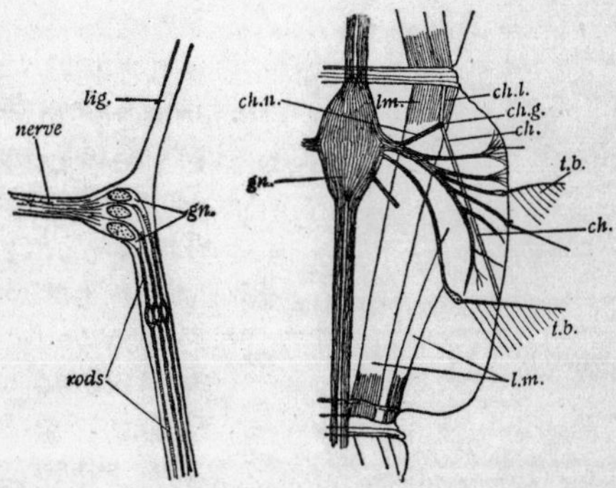

Fig. 1047.—Chordotonal Organs. On the right is shown part of an abdominal segment of the larva of a Gnat (*Corethra plumicornis*), seen as a transparent object, enlarged. In the centre is the nerve-cord (darkly shaded) with the ganglion (*gn.*) of the segment; *l.m.*, longitudinal muscles; *ch.n.*, *ch.g.*, *ch.l.*, and *ch.*, chordotonal nerve, ganglion, ligament, and organ; *t.b.*, branched tactile bristles. On the left is seen part of the chordotonal organ with its rods, ganglion (*gn.*), nerve, and ligament (*lig.*) still further enlarged.

Organs of Balance and Hearing in Insects (Insecta).—A variety of organs situated in different parts of the body are probably connected with balance or hearing, or both. Among those which are most likely concerned with equilibrium and movement are certain peculiar structures (chordotonal organs) that are especially characteristic of aquatic larvæ, though not limited to these. Gnat larvæ, for example, possess such organs, one of which is represented in fig. 1047. It consists essentially of a group of rod-shaped cells contained in a tube that opens to the exterior.

Many insects make sounds which are doubtless heard by

their fellows, a well-known instance being afforded by Grasshoppers and Crickets. A Grasshopper possesses a chirping arrangement something like that of the Musical Strand-Crab (p. 37). The wing-cover is provided with a sharp edge or scraper which is rubbed along a key-board placed on the inner edge of the thigh of the hind-leg (fig. 1048). The chirping sounds audible to our own ears are produced by the male insect, but the females of some species are also provided with these "stridulating" organs, which no doubt make sounds that can be heard and appreciated by the opposite sex. These sound-producing insects also possess what we may feel justified in calling "ears". On either side of the first ring of the abdomen there is a membrane comparable to a drum-head (fig. 1048) stretched over an air-space, and closely connected with sensory arrangements somewhat like those already described for a gnat-larva. The ears of Green Grasshoppers and Crickets are situated in the shins of the fore-legs, just below the knee.

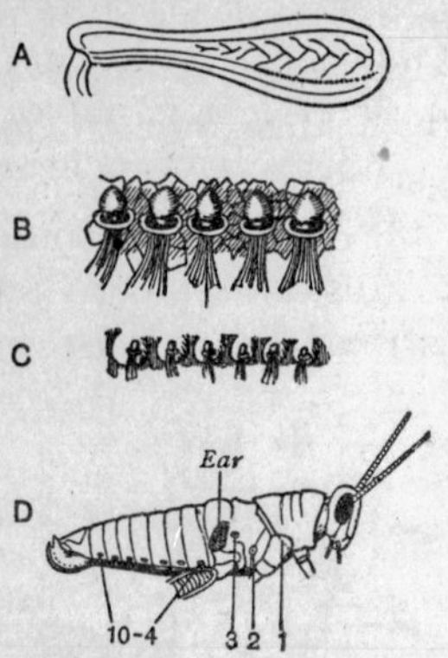

Fig. 1048.—Stridulating Organs and Ears of Grasshoppers. A, Hind-thigh of a male Grasshopper (*Stenobothrus*), showing beaded key-board (dotted line on right), enlarged; B, five beads of same, further enlarged; C, six of the much smaller beads of key-board of a female (same scale as B); D, side view of a Grasshopper (*Acridium*), to show ear; wings and legs cut short; 1–3, thoracic stigmata; 4–10, abdominal stigmata.

Organs of Balance and Hearing in Backboned Animals (Vertebrata).—The tadpole larvæ of Sea-Squirts possess remarkable sense-organs formed by specialization of part of the wall of the brain, and projecting into its cavity. One of these is of the nature of an otocyst, and is probably a balancing organ (fig. 1049).

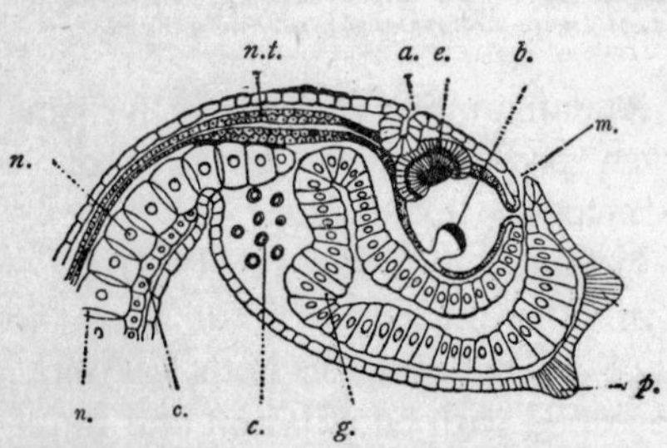

Fig. 1049.—Body of an Ascidian Tadpole, in longitudinal section, enlarged. The tail is cut short; the dorsal nerve-tube (*n.t.*) swells into a brain, into which project a balancing organ (*b.*) and an eye (*e.*); *a.*, atrial cavity; *c.*, groups of embryonic cells; *g.*, gut; *m.*, mouth; *n.*, notochord; *p.*, adhesive papillæ.

From Fishes onwards we find undoubted ears, similar, broadly speaking, to the essential parts of our own organs of hearing, and there can be no doubt that these also have to do with equilibrium and movement. If we trace the development of the ear we shall find that it begins as a pit in the skin, and by closure of the mouth of this a vesicle is produced, which if it underwent no further modification would be called an otocyst. As it is, however, a very complex shape is assumed, the final result being known as the membranous labyrinth, or internal ear (fig. 1050). This sometimes, as in a Skate or Dog-Fish, remains in communication with the exterior throughout life. It is significant that in Fishes the auditory pit arises in close connection with the "lateral line", which is a groove or tube containing groups of sense-cells belonging to the skin. And this suggests that the ear is no more than a bit of this line which has sunk beneath the surface and become specialized as regards structure and function. It is extremely probable that the lateral line of Fishes and Amphibian larvæ has to do with maintenance of balance and direction of movements, and if so, the fact that the ear has to do with these functions is quite intelligible. We know so little about the division of physiological labour between the different parts of the complex labyrinth that a discussion of details would be out of place here. But experiments have shown that the semicircular canals have some connection with movement and equilibrium, and it is interesting to note that they lie in three planes which are mutually at right angles. It is also certain that the labyrinth is the sense-organ of hearing proper. In land-vertebrates there are more or less perfect arrangements for conducting air-waves from the exterior to the deeply-seated and well-protected internal ear. This has already been sufficiently illustrated by the brief account of the auditory organs of Man given elsewhere (see vol. i, p. 56).

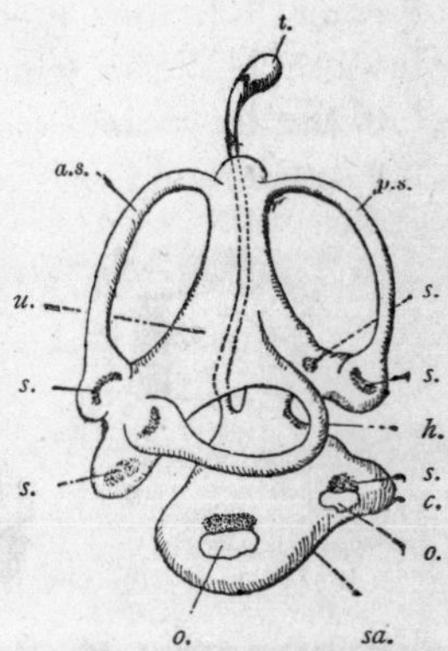

Fig. 1050.—Diagram of the Left Membranous Labyrinth of a Lower Vertebrate, seen from the outer side. *t.*, A tube representing the outer part of the original ingrowth; *a.s.*, *p.s.*, and *h.*, anterior vertical, posterior vertical, and horizontal semicircular canals; *u*, utricle; *sa.*, saccule; *c.*, cochlea; *o.*, *o.*, otoliths; *s.*, *s.*, *s.*, *s.*, *s.* (and other dotted patches), groups of sense-cells.

SIGHT

Skin-Seeing.—The simplest kind of sight is literally that of "seeing without eyes", and it amounts to no more than the power of distinguishing between light and darkness, or detecting sudden variations in the amount of illumination. But even this limited sort of vision may be of the greatest importance to its possessor, since it often gives valuable information about the surroundings. In such skin-seeing (*dermatoptic vision*) it is usual to find colouring-matter or pigment in or below the epidermis, which localizes the action of light-rays upon sensitive cells in this layer. This is the case, for instance, in Earth-Worms, the safety of which must often depend upon their avoidance of light. A further and more interesting illustration is afforded by many of the bivalve Molluscs which live in sand or mud, and which feed and breathe by means of two tubes, the siphons, which project from the hinder end of the body (vol. ii, p. 249). Such animals are often found hidden in their burrows with only the extreme tips of the siphons projecting. But even though thus concealed they would more frequently fall victims than they do to octopi and fishes, or, in the case of those which live between tide-marks, to strand-haunting birds, were they not provided with some means of detecting the proximity of such enemies. Warning is often given by the siphons themselves, which are commonly pigmented and sensitive to changes in light-intensity. And experiments on specimens kept in aquaria have shown that the fully-extended siphons are rapidly drawn in if a shadow is suddenly cast upon them, an event that would happen under natural conditions on the approach of a voracious fish or too inquisitive bird.

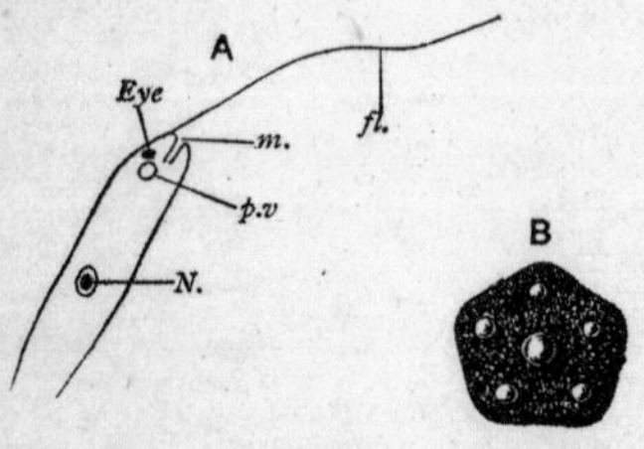

Fig. 1051.—A, *Euglena viridis*, enlarged; *fl.*, flagellum; *m.*, mouth; *N.*, nucleus; *p.v.*, pulsating vacuole. B, Eye-spot, greatly enlarged, showing six rounded lenses resting on a mass of pigment.

EYES.—Localization and improvement of the powers of sight have led to the evolution of definite visual organs or eyes, though many of the lower Invertebrates have more or less retained the old faculty of diffuse skin-seeing. The simplest organs of the kind are known as *eye-spots*, and their presence is marked by dense pigment. These are possessed even by some Animalcules, *e.g.* by a little green creature (*Euglena viridis*) which often swarms in stagnant water (fig. 1051). The eye-spot in this case is marked by the presence of a tiny patch of red colouring-matter on which rest several little lenses that serve to concentrate the light.

In some of the Jelly-Fish the margin of the umbrella bears

a number of compound sense-organs (rhopalia) derived from tentacles, and having to do with balance and adjustment of movements, sight, and possibly smell. Their visual part consists of a group of pigmented ectoderm cells, upon which a lens may rest (fig. 1052).

Examination of a Common Star-Fish (*Uraster rubens*) will

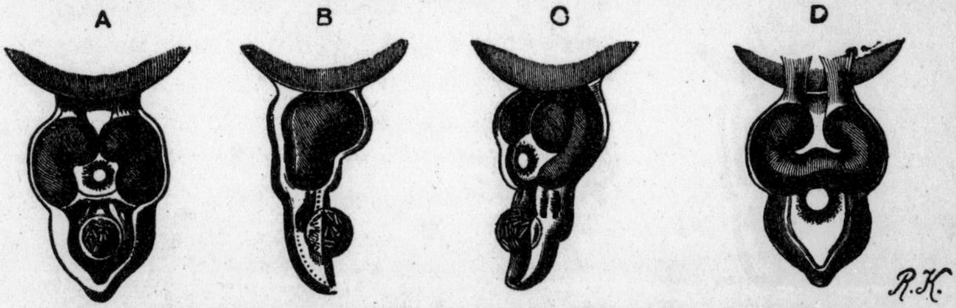

Fig. 1052.—Rhopalia of *Pericolpa quadrigata*, seen from various points of view, enlarged. The otocyst, containing numerous otoliths, is seen in the lower part of A, B, and C; the rounded pigmented eye, with clear, central, refracting portion, is indicated in A, C, and D.

reveal the presence of a bright-red spot at the tip of each arm, borne upon an unpaired tube-foot. This is undoubtedly an eye, and microscopic examination shows that it is made up of a multitude of little cups, each of which is lined with elongated cells, some of which are sensory, while others contain pigment (fig. 1053). Sea Urchins possess a circlet of somewhat similar eyes placed near the upper pole of the body. In some of these animals each of the minute cups may be provided with refracting structures, which presumably concentrate the light.

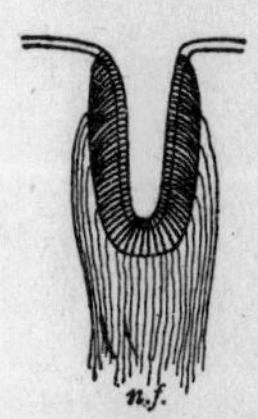

Fig. 1053.—An Eye-Cup of a Star-Fish, greatly enlarged, in section. The retina is supplied with numerous nerve-fibres (*n.f.*).

Jelly-Fish, Star-Fish, and Sea-Urchins are radially symmetrical animals, and their eyes are correspondingly disposed. But in "Worms", Arthropods, Molluscs, and Vertebrates, where the body is bilaterally symmetrical, and there is a more or less well-developed head, the eyes are usually situated upon this, as being the most useful position. But eyes may be present elsewhere, especially in some of the Planarian Worms, and certain Bivalve Molluscs.

The visual organs so far described may be called DIRECTION-EYES, as they can do no more than detect the direction from which the light-rays which influence them are coming. Eyes of the sort are present in many Worms and Molluscs, and some of them are less complex than those of a Jelly-Fish or Star-Fish. Nothing, for example, could be much simpler than the eye-spots on the head of the common freshwater worm Naïs. Each of these is simply an enlarged epidermal cell, along one side of which are several much smaller cells containing pigment (fig. 1054). We may take as examples of greater complication the eyes of a Leech, a Limpet, and an Arrow-Worm, the nature of which is sufficiently indicated in fig. 1055. They essentially consist of a group of visual or retinal cells, associated with pigment and refracting structures. Those of the Leech are particularly interesting, because they closely resemble in structure certain organs of touch which are present in the skin of the same animal, differing from these, however, in being larger, surrounded with pigment, and limited to the front end of the body. It is, in fact, a case of tactile organs which are acquiring a new function. The simple

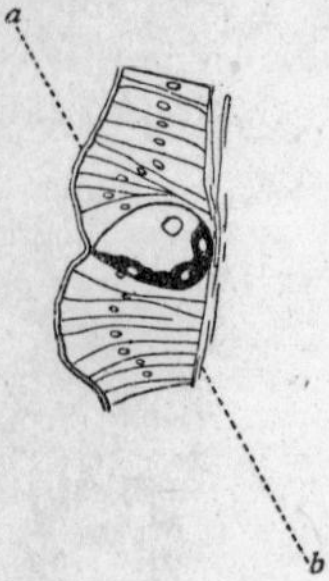

Fig. 1054.—Section through an Eye-Spot of a Freshwater Annelid (*Naïs*), with adjacent epidermic cells, enlarged. *a b*, optic axis

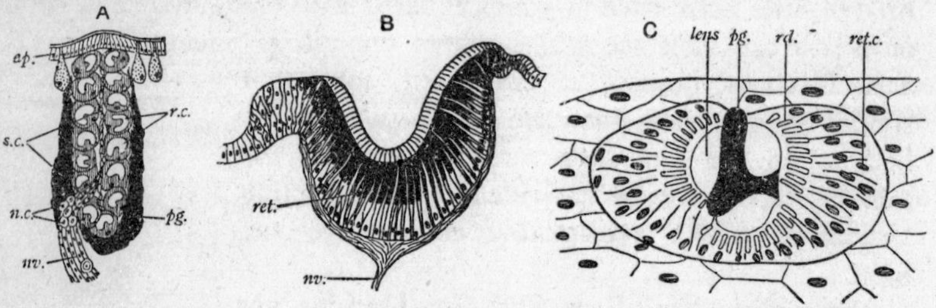

Fig. 1055.—Direction-Eyes of a Leech (*Hirudo*, A), a Limpet (*Patella*, B), and an Arrow-Worm (*Sagitta*, C), in section, and enlarged to various scales

In A the elongated eye is placed below a transparent patch of the epidermis (*ep.*); it is enclosed in a pigmented sheath (*pg.*), and consists of an external layer of large refracting cells (*r.c.*), surrounding a core of slender sense-cells (*s.c.*), which are continuous with nerve-cells (*n.c.*), and these again with nerve-fibres (*nv.*). B is an open cup, lined by a thickened retina (*ret.*) with clear refracting part externally, and dark pigment between its cells; *nv.*, nerve. In C there are three lenses imbedded in pigment (*pg.*), external to which are retinal cells (*ret.c.*), that contain refracting rodlets (*rd.*) in their inner ends.

eye-cups, of which one is to be found at the base of each tentacle in a Limpet, are interesting for quite a different reason. For they are almost certainly to be regarded as degenerate structures, which have been greatly simplified as a result of adaptation to the mode of life characteristic of their possessor. The activity of a Limpet is practically limited to feeding excursions in the vicinity of its home, and the eyes are under the shadow of the large conical shell. Under such circumstances complex visual organs are unnecessary.

Picture-Eyes.—The development of refracting structures in direction-eyes has led to the possibility of further specialization in vision, and has resulted in what we may call Picture-Eyes, capable of giving more or less definite information about the form and colour of external objects. Two kinds of these may be distinguished, *i.e.* Compound Eyes and Camera Eyes.

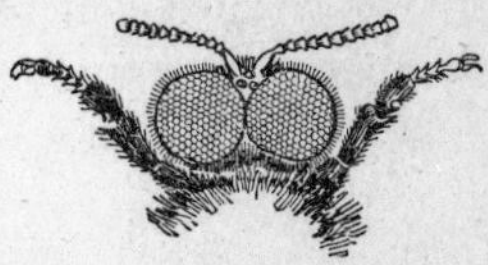

Fig. 1056.—Head of Male Honey-Bee (*Apis mellifica*) and Beginning of Thorax with First Pair of Legs, enlarged. The antennæ are seen in front, and three small simple eyes near their bases, but the most conspicuous structures are the enormous compound eyes, with their minute hexagonal facets.

Compound Eyes are characteristic of a great many Arthropods, such as Lobsters and Crabs, where they are placed at the end of stalks, and Insects, where they are in the form of two large projections on the head (fig. 1056). Examination with a lens shows that such an eye is covered by a transparent patch of the hard covering of the body, which is divided into a multitude of minute square or polygonal areas, commonly known as facets. These may be exceedingly numerous, as will be seen from the following calculations made by Leeuwenhoek more than a century ago:—house-fly, 4000; gadfly, 7000; goat-moth, 11,000; death's-head moth, 12,000; swallow-tail butterfly, 17,000; dragon-fly, 20,000; a small beetle (Mordella), 25,000. It was originally believed that these elaborate structures were aggregates of simple eyes, acting independently; and they were therefore called "compound" eyes, a rather misleading term. Sections through such eyes (fig. 1057) have demonstrated that each facet is the outer end or base of a very slender visual pyramid (ommatidium), the external part of which consists of various refracting structures, while internally is a group of sensitive visual cells connected with nerve-fibres. Adjacent pyramids are optically separated from one another by means of pigment. Comparison of various compound eyes shows that there are

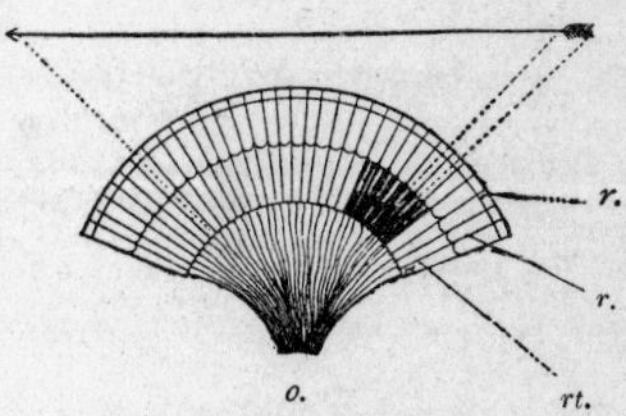

Fig. 1057.—Diagram of a Compound Eye, in section, enlarged, to illustrate theory of "mosaic vision". Numerous radiating visual pyramids are indicated, each consisting of external refracting structures (*r.*, *r.*) and internal groups of retinal cells (*rt.*). On the right side part of the pigment of several pyramids is inserted. The course of light-rays from an external object is indicated for three pyramids; *o.*, optic nerve.

great differences in detail, and much has yet to be learnt regarding the exact structure and use of the numerous parts which are present. The most plausible explanation which has yet been given of the mode of action of this sort of eye is that of "mosaic vision". According to this a visual pyramid is only stimulated by light-rays which exactly correspond in direction with its long axis, and numerous pyramids co-operate so as to enable the shape and colour of surrounding objects to be perceived (fig. 1057).

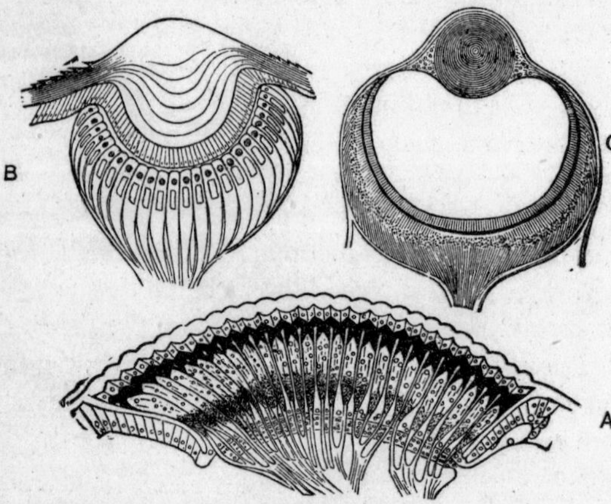

Fig. 1058.—Sections through the Compound Eye of an Earwig (*Forficula*, A), and the Camera Eyes of a Spider (*Epeira diadema*, B), and a Marine Annelid (*Alciope*, C), enlarged

In A numerous radiating visual pyramids are seen, ending externally in the facets of the thickened cuticle, and connected internally with nerve-branches; one of the pigmented zones is indicated. In B the cuticle is thickened into a rounded lens, and behind this is a transparent layer, upon which abut the retinal cells, continuous with nerve-fibres; each retinal cell contains a refracting rodlet. C is a vesicle, of which the external part is thickened into a spheroidal lens, while the rest constitutes a retina, consisting of an internal refracting layer, separated by pigment from the external sensitive part, into which nerve-fibres are seen running.

Camera Eyes are found in Annelids, Arthropods, Molluscs, and Vertebrates. Just as in a photographer's camera a picture of external objects is imaged on a sensitive plate by means of a lens, so also in a camera eye do we find refracting structures which focus light-rays on a retina, or layer of sensitive visual cells. Scattering of light is prevented in the former case by a blackened lining, in the latter by a layer of pigment.

One of the two exceptionally large eyes present on the head of a marine Bristle-Worm (*Alciope*) is represented in fig. 1058. A Sea-Centipede (*Nereis*) possesses four smaller and less complex eyes of similar kind on the upper side of its head-lobe, and in some of the tube-inhabiting Bristle-Worms (*e.g. Branchiomma* and

Dasychone) there are eyes of elaborate nature on the gill-filaments of the head.

Spiders, among Arthropods, have a group of simple eyes (ocelli) on the top of the head. These are constructed on the camera principle, though they differ in detail from those of Alciope (fig. 1058). The spherical shape of the lens and its closeness to the retina suggest that only near objects can be seen with any degree of distinctness. A great many Insects possess ocelli in addition to the two large compound eyes. In Bees, for instance, there are three of these arranged in a triangle on the top of the head. In this and similar cases it is extremely probable that the compound

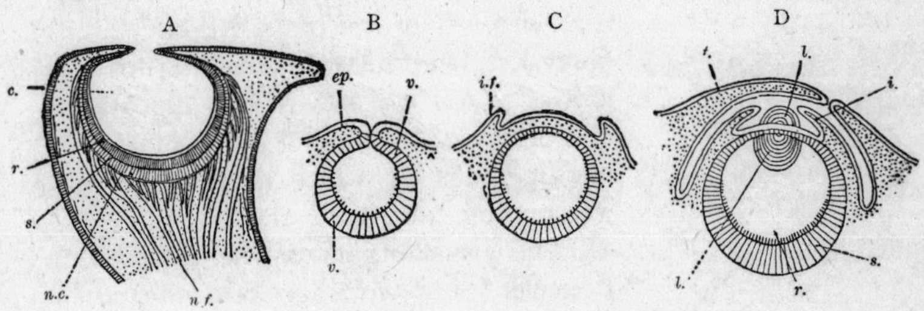

Fig. 1059.—Diagrammatic Sections through Camera Eyes of Cephalopods

A, Eye of Nautilus; *c.*, internal cavity; *r.* and *s.*, refracting and sensitive layers of retina; *n.c.*, layer of nerve-cells; *n.f.*, nerve-fibres. B–D, Stages in development of eye of Cuttle-Fish (*Sepia*); in B the epidermis (*ep.*) has folded in to produce a vesicle (*v.*, *v.*); in C a fold (*i.f.*) is growing out to form the iris; D is the adult eye; *f.*, protective external fold; *i.*, iris; *l.*, *l.*, outer and inner parts of lens; *r.* and *s.*, refracting and sensitive layers of retina.

eyes are used for seeing things at a distance, while the ocelli are used at close range. As focussing arrangements are entirely absent this would certainly be a great convenience.

The most familiar example of camera eyes among Molluscs is afforded by the Garden-Snail (*Helix aspersa*, fig. 1038), where they are placed near the tips of the long front tentacles. It is extremely short-sighted, as we might expect, in view of the fact that the lens is practically spherical and very close to the retina. The Pearly Nautilus possesses eyes which are constructed on the "pinhole camera" principle. There is no lens, and sea-water is admitted by a minute hole into the large internal cavity (fig. 1059). Large and complex eyes are found in the rapacious Squids and Cuttle-Fishes, and some idea of their structure and mode of development will be gathered from fig. 1059. A few of the Bivalve Molluscs possess numerous complex camera eyes situated on the edges of the mantle-flaps, as in the Scallops (*Pecten*), where they are bright-red in colour. Their presence is possibly in relation to the fact that some species are active swimmers.

Before speaking of the camera eyes of Vertebrates, it may be well to mention certain simpler visual structures which are found in some of the most primitive members of that group. In the tadpole larva of a Sea-Squirt there is a simple cup-like direction-eye formed by thickening of the wall of the brain, and projecting into that organ (see fig. 1049, p. 38). Since the larva is transparent light-rays are able to reach it. The adult condition results from a remarkable series of modifications (see vol. iii, p. 421), which include simplification of the nervous system with loss of the brain-eye and brain-otocyst. The only compensation for this loss of vision consists in the appearance of a circlet of pigmented eye-spots round the openings by which currents of sea-water enter and leave the body.

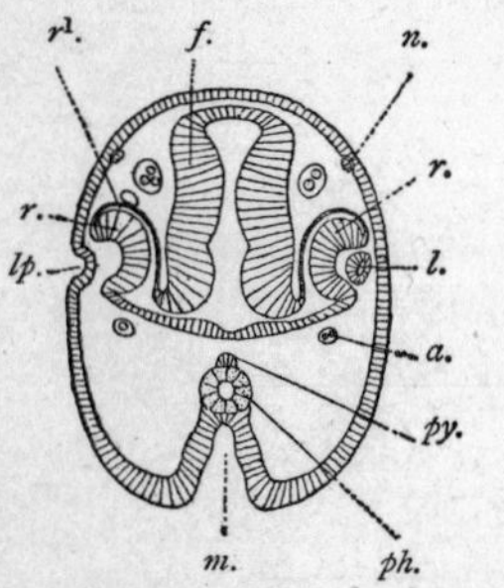

Fig. 1060.—Diagrammatic Cross Section through the Head of a Tadpole, to Illustrate the Development of the Eyes, enlarged. *f.*, Fore-brain; *r.* and *r*¹., retina and its external pigment-layer; *lp.*, lens-pit; *l.*, lens; *a.*, an artery; *m.*, mouth cavity; *n.*, a nerve; *ph.*, pharynx; *py.*, pituitary body.

The visual organs of the transparent Lancelet (*Amphioxus*) are of even simpler kind. The so-called "eye" is merely a deeply-pigmented spot in the extreme front end of the nerve-tube, and there is in addition a series of similar but smaller spots in the floor of the nerve-tube behind the head-region.

The facts just mentioned prepare us for the statement that the ordinary camera eyes of Fishes and still higher Vertebrates are partly derived from the brain, and in this they differ from the camera eyes of Invertebrates, which are of epidermic nature. Two stages in the development of the Vertebrate eye are represented in fig. 1060. From either side of the fore-brain of the embryo an *optic vesicle* grows out towards the ectoderm, in which a corresponding pit makes its appearance. The end of the vesicle becomes as it were pushed in to form a double-walled *optic cup*, of which the inner and thicker layer is destined to produce the greater part of the retina, or sensitive eye-screen, while the outermost pigmented layer of this is derived from the outer part of the cup. The external ectodermic pit closes, and is pinched off as a vesicle, which lies in the optic cup (see right-hand side of figure), and ultimately thickens into the lens. The stalk of the optic cup becomes the optic nerve. Since the brain itself is of ectodermic origin (see p. 20), it is clear that the parts of the eye so far mentioned are all derived from ectoderm. The rest of the eyeball, including its two outer coats and refracting contents (see vol. i, p. 57), are formed from the middle embryonic layer (mesoderm). This curious kind of development clearly suggests that in the remote ancestors of Vertebrates the eyes were internal projections from the brain, and received their light through the transparent tissues external to them, as is still the case in the single eye of the tadpole of a Sea-Squirt. The free ends of the visual cells (rods and cones) were directed towards the cavity of the brain. As in the course of evolution the brain became more and more complex, an opaque skull was developed for its protection, and the brain-eyes, having their supply of light thus cut off, were obliged, so to speak, to grow outwards. Subsequently they were improved into camera eyes by the development of a lens. Further improvements consisted in the evolution of eye-muscles, eyelids, and complex focussing arrangements. The visual cells (rods and cones) of the Vertebrate eye present the remarkable peculiarity of pointing *away* from the light, one result of the manner in which the retina is developed.

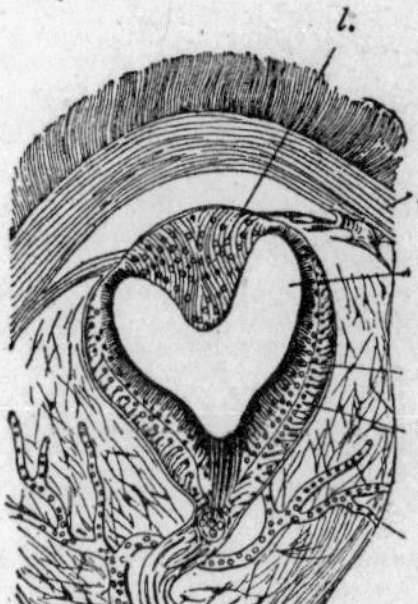

Fig. 1061. — Section through the Pineal Eye of a Tuatara (*Hatteria*), enlarged. *f.*, Fibrous covering; *l.*, lens; *r.*, *r.*, retina; *b.*, blood-vessel; *o.n.*, optic nerve.

In Vertebrates, such as Fishes, which have to see under water, the lens of the eye is spheroidal, and one mark of the aquatic ancestry of the Amphibia is the possession of a lens of similar shape. But thoroughgoing land Vertebrates have lost this primitive character, for in them the lens is more or less flattened and biconvex, as an adaptation to seeing in air.

An extremely interesting and remarkable arrangement is found in certain bony fishes known as Double-Eyes (*Anableps*), native to the coasts and estuaries of tropical America. The name has been given because either eye, as seen from the exterior, is marked off into upper and lower halves by a dark transverse band. Dissection shows that the upper half of the lens is biconvex, and the lower half spheroidal. And since these fishes habitually swim at the surface, with only the lower part of the eye immersed, we can only conclude that this half can see clearly in water, while the upper half has been so modified that distinct vision in air has also become possible.

Some of the Reptiles possess a more or less degenerate third or *pineal eye* on the top of the head (fig. 1061). It is connected with the roof of the 'twixt-brain. There seems good reason to believe that the ancestral Vertebrates had at least one visual organ in this position, probably serving as a means of detecting enemies attacking from above, a contingency to which aquatic forms are peculiarly liable. We may perhaps compare it with the internal brain-eye of the Ascidian tadpole, which also is unpaired and dorsal.

ANIMAL INSTINCT AND INTELLIGENCE

CHAPTER LIX

GENERAL PRINCIPLES—INSTINCT AND INTELLIGENCE IN HIGHER INVERTEBRATES AND VERTEBRATES

GENERAL PRINCIPLES

Having briefly surveyed the salient facts regarding the Nervous System and Sense-Organs we naturally pass on to the consideration of those higher manifestations of life known as Instinct and Intelligence, which play a very important part in the adjustment of animals to their surroundings. To do anything like full justice to the subject at least half a volume would be required, and it is only possible here to attempt a brief summary of general principles, adding to this a few typical illustrations. Many other examples, however, will be found in other parts of this book. As regards the present section, the writer wishes to acknowledge his great indebtedness to the works of Principal Lloyd Morgan, *i.e. Habit and Instinct*, *Animal Life and Intelligence*, and *Animal Behaviour*, to which are referred those readers who wish further information on this branch of zoology.

Something has already been said about Reflex Actions (see p. 9), which are comparatively simple responses to external stimuli. In very lowly animals, such as Animalcules (Protozoa), these, together with equally simple spontaneous actions, are sufficient to meet all the contingencies of existence. So apparently purposeful, however, are many of these actions, that some observers are inclined to ascribe mental powers to such forms. Either to prove or to disprove such a view is impossible, for we have no direct knowledge of the mind of any animal save Man, and can only make more or less probable guesses about other forms. We may feel pretty sure, however, that the evolution of the nervous system through increasingly complex stages has been associated with a corresponding evolution of mind, and there is considerable justification for doubting whether animals devoid of a nervous system, or possessed of a very imperfect one, are endowed with more than a dim consciousness or awareness of existence, or are capable of manifesting either Instinct or Intelligence.

An animal which inherits the power of performing more or less complex actions helping to adjust it to its surroundings, independently of experience or instruction, is said to display Instinct, and such actions may be termed instinctive. They differ from Reflex Actions in being more elaborate, and many of them are partly or entirely spontaneous. But our knowledge is at present too incomplete to enable us to draw the line between actions which are of reflex character and those which are instinctive. It is only when dealing with the higher Invertebrates and the Vertebrates that we can use the latter term with any degree of certainty. The Birch-Weevil (see vol. iii, p. 394), for instance, certainly displays instinct when she constructs an elaborate leaf-funnel for the reception of her eggs. This very complicated piece of work is performed, so far as we know, with unerring certainty and without previous experience. Nor can the weevil have more than a hazy knowledge of the purpose of her work, which is probably done quite mechanically.

An animal is said to show Intelligence when it profits by experience, accommodating its actions to the exigencies of changed or changing surrounding. There is an inherited basis to such actions; it is the controlling power which makes them intelligent. The difference between Instinct and Intelligence is explained with admirable lucidity in the following passage from Lloyd Morgan (in *Animal Behaviour*):—"Such an animal as a newly-hatched bird or an insect just set free from the chrysalis is a going concern, a living creature. It is the bearer of wonderfully complex automatic machinery, capable, under the initiating influence of stimuli, of performing instinctive acts. But if this were all, we should have no more than a cunningly-wrought and self-developing automatic machine. What the creature does instinctively at first it would do always, perhaps a little more smoothly as the organic mechanism settled down to its work—just as a steam-engine goes more smoothly when it has been running for a while; but otherwise the action would continue unchanged. Instinctive behaviour would remain unmodified throughout life. The chick, however, or the imago insect, is something more than this. It affords evidence of the accommodation of behaviour to varying circumstances. It so acts as to lead us to infer that there are centres of intelligent control through the action of which the automatic behaviour can be modified in accordance with the results of experience. When, for example, a young chick walks towards and pecks at a lady-bird, the like of which he has never before seen, the behaviour may be purely instinctive; and so, too, when he similarly seizes a wasp-larva. . . . But when, after a few trials, the chick leaves lady-birds unmolested while he seizes wasp-larvæ with increased energy, he affords evidence of selection based on individual experience. And such selection implies intelligence in almost its simplest expression. We may say, therefore, that, whereas instinctive behaviour is prior to individual experience, intelligent behaviour is the outcome and product of such experience. This distinction is presumably clear enough; and it is one that is based on the facts of observation. But we must not fail to notice that, though the logical distinction is quite clear, the acquired modifications of behaviour, which we speak of as intelligence, presuppose congenital [*i.e.* inherited] modes of response which are guided to finer issues. We may say then, that where these congenital modes of response take the form of instinctive behaviour, there is supplied a general plan of action which intelligence particularizes in such a manner as to produce accommodation to the conditions of existence." The quotation just given implies, what is no doubt true, that in the course of mental evolution Instinct does not *become* Intelligence, but is gradually *replaced* by it, *i.e.* inherited specialized behaviour is replaced more or less by self-specialized behaviour. The larger the amount of such replacement the greater the intelligence. And this enables us to understand the peculiar helplessness of the young of higher Mammals, especially those of our own species. The complex instincts of lower forms have been lost, and it takes a long time to learn how to act intelligently. The remark does not apply to all helpless young, for in some of these, *e.g.* in nestling birds, such instincts are only deferred. The influence of strongly-developed parental affection is noticeable in both cases.

To interpret the action of animals with any likelihood of accuracy it is necessary to avoid two extreme views of opposite kind. One of these ascribes almost human attributes to even the lowest animals; it is a case of interpreting the observed in terms of the observer. The other and older view regards Man as the only intelligent animal, all the others being simply living machines worked by Instinct and Reflex Action. There has been in the past a great dearth of patient unbiassed observation on living animals, but the number of competent investigators is now fortunately increasing, and the results already obtained clearly point to the conclusion that extreme opinions in either direction are inadmissible.

The difference between Instinct and Intelligence may also be realized by taking some metaphorical illustration. Let us then compare the successful adjustments of an animal to its environment to the effective shots of a rifleman aiming at a series of targets. And let us also suppose that a certain minimum score is necessary for the maintenance of a bare existence, while marriage is only permitted as the reward of a good score. The shooting of such a rifleman would be comparable to the actions of an animal actuated by pure Instinct, if he were provided with a series of loaded rifles previously sighted and adjusted in such a way that he would merely have to press the triggers to mechanically secure a large number of points—a sort of "you-press-the-button-and-we-do-the-rest" arrangement. If the targets remained fixed the privileges attached to success would be easily secured. But the actions of life have to bring about adjustments to surroundings which are constantly altering, and this may be represented in the illustration by substituting moving targets for stationary ones. The purely "instinctive rifleman" would do pretty well if his targets moved but slightly, though bull's-eyes would be infrequent, and his total would be smaller. But with increasing movement the percentage of hits would dwindle till first of all the prize of matrimony would be denied him, and finally the score would be so small that even bare existence would not be permitted.

Our illustration can easily be modified to represent the gradual replacement of Instinct by Intelligence. By endowing our imaginary rifleman with increasing capacity to adjust his rifles, so as to secure a reasonable score with shifting targets, we make his shooting more and more intelligent, less and less instinctive. And were he simply given the loaded rifles, and left to learn the art of marksmanship for himself, success would require a high degree of intelligence. The loaded rifles would represent the gift of inheri-

YOUNG ORANG-UTANS (*Simia satyrus*

The Orang-utan, a man-like ape native to Sumatra and Borneo, is characterized by the great relative length of its arms, a peculiarity associated with purely arboreal habits. The long hair is of a reddish colour. Orangs are undoubtedly very intelligent, and the rounded intellectual-looking forehead gives a very human appearance. The mental powers of the Gorilla and Chimpanzee, however, are more considerable, though the powerful brow-ridges which these forms possess greatly detract from their personal appearance.

The Orang builds a kind of stick-nest in the fork of a tree as a temporary shelter, from which it does not sally forth to feed until the day is well advanced. Small family parties are commonly found associated together, though the male appears to lead a solitary life during a large part of the year. The young are as helpless as those of the human species, and those which have been brought up in captivity present many similar traits. Their wants are expressed by loud lamentations, and they protest loudly if their food is not to their taste. They also greatly appreciate being nursed and "cuddled". Unlike human infants, however, they are eager to be washed and combed.

YOUNG ORANG-UTANS (SIMIA SATYRUS)

tance; but were there no profiting by experience most of the shots would go wide. Parental care might be here symbolized by supposing the raw beginner protected and instructed by an expert shot until the necessary experience had been acquired.

We do not know how far down in the scale of animal life some sort of consciousness exists, but the dawn of intelligence is marked by the appearance of what Lloyd Morgan calls "effective consciousness", *i.e.* a realization of existence which enables more or less successful adjustments to a changing environment.

In ourselves we find Intelligence reinforced by Reason, the "ideational stage" in mental evolution, where actions depend upon motive, instead of being due to mere impulse dictating certain sorts of behaviour "on the spur of the moment". It involves appreciation of abstract ideas with powers of reflection and deliberation, leading us to trace the relations between cause and effect, and to construct ideals of existence by which our conduct is more or less regulated. The dim beginnings of Reason are probably to be found among the higher animals, but the body of facts with which we are at present acquainted is far too small to justify positive statements or wide-sweeping generalizations.

INSTINCT AND INTELLIGENCE IN HIGHER INVERTEBRATES (INVERTEBRATA)

The most instructive cases so far investigated are to be found among Insects (Insecta) and Molluscs (Mollusca), and it will be enough for our present purpose to briefly describe a few of these.

INSTINCT AND INTELLIGENCE IN INSECTS (INSECTA).—A good example of the stereotyped nature of complex instincts is given by Fabre (in *Souvenirs entomologiques*) in his account of one of the Mason-Bees (*Chalicodoma muraria*) native to South Europe. The female makes a nest consisting of nine or ten cells placed one on top of the other, using cement made of a mixture of earth and saliva, to which little stones are added. After each cell is built it is stored with honey and pollen, after which an egg is laid in it, and a roof is added. The entire series is then thickly covered with cement till the nest assumes a hemispherical form. The three operations of building, storing, and egg-laying which take place in regard to each cell follow one another with automatic regularity, and there is no harking back to an earlier stage. For conditions artificially imposed with a view to altering the order do not succeed in this, as they would do if the actions were of very intelligent kind. For example, a nest with fully-constructed top-cell partly stored was substituted for the original nest in which the uppermost cell had only been commenced. The bee did not apparently detect the imposture, and proceeded to raise the walls of the substituted cell till it was one-third greater than the normal height. In another experiment a bee had completed the construction of a cell, and was preparing to store it, when another nest with an incomplete top-chamber was substituted. On her return with honey and pollen she appeared greatly puzzled at the change, and finally deposited her load in the nest of a neighbour. The result of another similar experiment was somewhat different, for the bee removed the roof of the last complete cell and stored this a second time, afterwards laying a second egg in it. The last two experiments seem to prove the existence of a certain infusion of intelligence, as shown by the attempts to meet the altered circumstances, though these attempts were not of very satisfactory kind. It is somewhat remarkable that this bee is apparently unable to recognize its own nest, though we must not forget that its visual powers are of different kind from our own, but it has a well-marked memory for localities, returning to the spot selected for building-purposes from considerable distances. Fabre also showed that individuals removed as far as four kilometres from their nests, into what was probably unknown country to them, were able to find their way home. Quite a number of animals are endowed with a strong "homing faculty" of this kind, but how far this may be due to a "locality sense" which cannot be explained by applying the known principles of human physiology, it is as yet impossible to say. In this particular instance, even if we were to assume that the bees had some previous acquaintance with the distant place to which they were taken, we should still be quite unable to explain exactly *how* they got home. Locality-memory, however, would seem to imply some amount of intelligence. Readers desiring further details of the fascinating observations and experiments by Fabre on Mason-Bees and many other insects are referred to the original work, or the translation of the same which has recently appeared.

Suggestions have more than once been made in the course of this book as to the kind of investigation which amateur naturalists might profitably attempt. The habits of Insects and other higher Invertebrates offer an inexhaustible and intensely-interesting field to multitudes of such workers. Accurate observations recorded with scrupulous exactness are here badly needed, and those who enlarge our knowledge in this direction are contributing to the advance of two branches of knowledge, zoology and the science of mind (psychology), not to mention sociology and education, both of which are intimately connected with the latter.

It is indispensable that observations on instinct and intelligence should be made with a perfectly open mind, and not with the object of collecting material for the support of this or that view. And it is peculiarly necessary to remember that the mental standard of human beings can only be applied with many reservations in explanation of the actions of animals, especially when dealing with creatures like Insects which, though of highly complex structure, have specialized on lines of their own. A series of observations made in this spirit, and which are not only of the utmost value but of absorbing interest, have been recorded by Dr. and Mrs. Peckham (*On the Habits and Instincts of the Solitary Wasps*). These insects have attracted much attention on account of their habit of storing up caterpillars, flies, spiders, &c., for the benefit of their progeny, the victims having previously been stung (see vol. iii, p. 391). Instincts of very complex nature are here involved, but the zoologists just mentioned have shown that these instincts are not so stereotyped as commonly supposed, there being a certain amount of adaptability to circumstances, which is strong presumptive proof of some degree of intelligence. Pure instinct is manifested by the fact that any particular species of these wasps is always found to select the same kind of prey, and, for a given species, there is so much uniformity in the mode of nest-construction, the way of disabling the victims, the manner of taking them into the nest, &c., that instinct is undoubtedly the dominant factor. But, except in regard to the kind of prey, there is a sufficient amount of adjustment to varying circumstances to warrant the conclusion that intelligence also plays some part in the complex series of operations. It appears, for example, that the prey is not uniformly stung in the nerve-cord, as once believed, and it may be killed instead of paralysed by its injuries, proving in either case suitable food for the larvæ. This certainly discounts the view that this part of the series of actions is stereotyped by instinct.

And a convincing proof of the power of profiting by experience which constitutes intelligence is given in a letter of Dr. Peckham's, quoted by Lloyd Morgan (in *Animal Behaviour*), in reference to a species (*Sphex ichneumonea*) which preys upon grasshoppers, and after leaving them a short time while she makes an excursion into the nest, returns and drags them in by their feelers. One individual, being several times thwarted in her storing work by removal of the victim to a short distance when she was in the nest, soon learnt the inadvisability of losing sight of her booty, and either at once dragged it into the hole or, straddling over it, substituted pushing for pulling.

One of the most remarkable points about the nesting-instinct in so many solitary insects is the elaborate provision made for the welfare of offspring which will never be seen, and which commonly require food of quite different nature from that taken by the adult. The parent would seem to be urged on by irresistible impulses, and can hardly be supposed to realize the meaning of its work, except perhaps in a very dim sort of way. Butterflies and Moths illustrate the food-question very clearly. It is true that they do not construct and store nests, like the solitary wasps just mentioned, but they instinctively lay their eggs on special sorts of plant, upon the leaves of which their voracious offspring are destined to feed. A Peacock Butterfly (*Vanessa Io*), for example, selects a nettle for the purpose, but her own food consists of nectar drawn from the recesses of flowers by means of suctorial mouth-parts, differing greatly from the powerful biting jaws of the leaf-eating caterpillar. It is almost impossible to believe that remembrance of her own larval days guides to the choice of a suitable place for egg-laying, for the caterpillar is converted into the adult by a series of revolutionary changes which amount to reconstruction.

INSTINCT AND INTELLIGENCE IN MOLLUSCS (MOLLUSCA).—Comparatively few observations have been made upon the members of this group, some of which are very highly organized. Several good illustrations of both instinct and intelligence have, however, been recorded.

The Octopus is one of the highest Molluscs, and appears to be a very intelligent creature. Schneider saw a young one seize a hermit-crab and then let it go, being stung by the zoophytes covering its shell. For some time at least this individual was observed to avoid hermit-crabs, having learnt to associate them with painful sensations. Other Octopi manifested still greater intelligence, for they pulled hermits out of their shells, taking care not to touch the zoophytes, realizing apparently that these were the stinging element. More remarkable than this is an observation made by Madame Jeannette Power. This lady on one occasion saw an Octopus, that held a stone by one of its arms, watching a large bivalve (*Pinna*) of which the shell was beginning to open. When this operation was complete the Octopus quickly inserted

Fig. 1062.—A Limpet (*Patella vulgata*) leaving its Scar at Ebb-tide

the stone between the valves so as to prevent them from coming together again, and then proceeded to make a meal of the helpless bivalve.

Some of the Gastropods possess a well-marked "homing instinct", a particularly good example of this being afforded by the Common Limpet (*Patella vulgata*, fig. 1062). As elsewhere described (see vol. ii, p. 197) this creature lives on a particular spot, which in course of time becomes a more or less well-marked "scar", to which it can hold so firmly as to defy waves and tide. From this home it wanders out to feed when uncovered by the water, and also when well covered. From such excursions, which may extend to a distance of several feet, it later on returns to settle down again on the scar, the surface traversed being often very irregular and covered with acorn-barnacles. When the animal gets back to the scar it of course arrives wrong way on, so to speak, and it quickly shuffles round so as to get into the proper position. A memory of locality certainly exists, and this would seem to imply intelligence. In the course of time a Limpet acquires a very accurate knowledge of the topography of a fair-sized area around its home, and if picked up when on the crawl and placed within this area is able to get home, though the time taken varies considerably. Exactly *how* it gets home we do not know. The simple cup-like eyes cannot render assistance, nor can we very well suppose that the otocysts help to guide it. Experiments appear to demonstrate that the animal does not smell its way back, and we are therefore reduced to touch, or to a "locality sense", or to both. The most obvious organs of touch are the two large tentacles on the head, with which the Limpet constantly touches the rock as it crawls, and it is no doubt by means of these that a good deal of the topographical knowledge is acquired. But as it can get home without the aid of these organs there must be some other organs of guidance. The edge of the mantle-flap is provided with a very large number of small tentacles which can be stretched out and actively moved, as they are sometimes, if not always, when the animal is adjusting itself on its scar. These perhaps have something to do with the matter, and so may still other sense-organs, but further investigation is required. The problem here to be solved, like most of those connected with locality-knowledge, is of a particularly baffling kind, though not to be regarded as insoluble. The Garden-Snail (*Helix aspersa*) is another Mollusc possessed of a "homing instinct"

INSTINCT AND INTELLIGENCE IN VERTEBRATES (VERTEBRATA)

There is here an almost unlimited amount of material which might be discussed, but a few examples must suffice.

WARNING COLORATION.—A large number of animals possessed of noxious properties advertise their objectionable nature by means of bright though somewhat crude colours, and simple but striking patterns, the net result of which is to render them extremely conspicuous (see vol. ii, p. 301). Such are the striped "blazer" of the Wasp, and the spotted jacket of the Lady-Bird. Unless very hard pressed by hunger it appears that the foes of animals so coloured and marked give them a wide berth. But without careful observation and experiment it would remain an open question whether this resulted from Instinct or Intelligence, or a mixture of the two. The cases which have so far been properly investigated appear to prove that Intelligence here comes into play, and that a young animal has to learn from experience that some things are good to eat and others not. The thorough and long-continued researches of Lloyd Morgan upon artificially-hatched chicks definitely prove that they at least have to acquire such useful knowledge for themselves. He thus describes (in *Animal Behaviour*) how some of his chicks learnt that alternate bands of black and orange, as possessed by the caterpillars of the Cinnabar Moth, are associated with disagreeable sensations:—"The following experiment was made with young chicks. Stripes of orange and black paper were pasted beneath glass slips, and on them meal moistened with quinine was placed. On other plain slips meal moistened with water was provided. The young birds soon learnt to avoid the bitter meal, and then would not touch plain meal if it was offered on the banded slip. And these birds, save in two instances, refused to touch cinnabar caterpillars, which were new to their experience. They did not, like other birds, have to learn by particular trials that these caterpillars are unpleasant. Their experience had already been gained through the banded glass slips; or so it seemed. I have also found that young birds who had learnt to avoid cinnabar caterpillars left wasps untouched."

NEST-BUILDING IN BIRDS.—There can be no reasonable doubt that in its main features the nest-building of birds is a matter of instinct. One of the best proofs of this is afforded by cases where individuals kept in captivity from the time of hatching, under conditions which excluded the possibility of instruction or imitation, have nevertheless constructed nests of the kind proper to their species. Further experiments, however, are much to be desired, especially on birds which indulge in architecture of such characteristic kind as to be quite unmistakable. It would, of course, be necessary to make the nesting conditions in such cases as natural as possible. Other instincts, tending to the benefit of the eggs or young, are often associated with that for nest-building. Of this the Eider-Duck (*Somateria mollissima*, fig. 1063) may be taken as an example. Egg-laying and building are here not consecutive acts, but the former takes place at intervals during the latter, in a somewhat variable fashion. Three successive stages are shown in the illustration, which is taken from photographs by Mr. R. A. L. Van Someren. The first represents four eggs resting in the incomplete nest, and the second (on a larger scale) the complete down-lined nest with its full complement of eggs. The third figure shows the same nest during the temporary absence of the mother-bird, and illustrates an interesting associated instinct. Before leaving her duties she had pulled the down over the eggs, so as to cover them completely, an act distinctly conducive to their welfare. For, snugly tucked up under their "eider-down quilt", they were not only kept warm, but also, as the figure clearly proves, effectively screened from observation.

Fig. 1063.—Nest of the Eider-Duck (*Somateria mollissima*). See Text.

But although nest-building is almost certainly instinctive in the main, it is subject to modification in individual cases in ways which vouch for the intelligence of the builders. And such modification may affect the style, materials, and place of construction. Often-quoted illustrations are those of the House-Swallow and House-Martin, which have taken advantage of the evolution of human civilization so far as concerned with domestic architecture.

This change of habit, of course, took place in the remote past, but the following very interesting modern example of precisely similar kind is given by Headley (in *The Structure and Life of Birds*):—"The Palm Swift in Jamaica till 1854 always built in palms. But in Spanish Town, when two cocoa-nut palms were blown down, they drove out the Swallows from the Piazza of the House of Assembly and built between the angles formed by the beams and joists." Of other such cases Newton thus writes (in *A Dictionary of Birds*):—"But though in a general way the dictates of hereditary instinct are rigidly observed by Birds, in many species a remarkable degree of elasticity is exhibited or the rule of habit is rudely broken. Thus, the noble Falcon, whose ordinary eyry is on the beetling cliff, will for the convenience of procuring prey condescend to lay its eggs on the ground in a marsh, or appropriate the nest of some other bird in a tree. The Golden Eagle, too, remarkably adapts itself to circumstances, now rearing its young on a precipitous ledge, now on the arm of an ancient monarch of the forest, and again on a treeless plain, making a humble home amid grass and herbage. Herons also show the same versatility, and will breed according to circumstances in an open fen, on sea-banks, or (as is most usual) on lofty trees. Such changes are easy to understand. The instinct of finding food for the family is predominant, and where most food is, there will the feeders be gathered together. This explains, in all likelihood, the associated bands of Ospreys or Fish-Hawks, which in North America breed (or used to breed) in large companies where sustenance is plentiful, though in the Old World the same species brooks not the society of aught but its mate."

Migration of Birds.—Nothing can be more familiar than the fact that innumerable species of birds undertake periodic journeys, often of extreme length, from one region to another, and at the same time nothing in the entire realm of natural history is more mysterious. Broadly speaking, the same migrant species has its own line of travel between its two places of residence. The Golden Plovers, for example, of the northern part of North America, fly south to the north of South America *via* the Bermudas and Antilles. The paths of a number of species are more or less coincident, in many cases, to form what is known as a "migration route", and some of these routes have been determined with some approach to accuracy. A vast number of facts concerning migration have already been collected, and these receive large additions every year, so that in the course of time we may expect to have a fairly complete knowledge of the movements of many migratory birds. To discover *how* they find their way is a much more difficult problem, especially in cases where there can have been no previous experience. Many of them, *e.g.* the Common White Stork (*Ciconia alba*), "assemble" before migration, as if to practise their powers of flight, and the writer once saw the roof-ridges in the street of a midland town "lined" with hundreds of swallows at 6 a.m. one morning, less than two hours after which all had disappeared. It has been suggested that the old birds impart geographical knowledge to the young, and also that the migrant flocks are "personally conducted" by experienced leaders. But many well-ascertained facts militate strongly against such views, at any rate for certain species. Some young birds go off by themselves, even the first time they migrate, and this may take place under conditions which preclude the possibility of their having previously acquired information from their elders. The Common Cuckoo (*Cuculus canorus*), for example, winters in Africa, and, as everyone knows, its offspring are reared by other birds. The old Cuckoos have all left this country by the end of August, and the young ones take their departure later. In such a case we cannot doubt the existence of a "migratory instinct", but how far this is modified by intelligence has yet to be determined. We are equally ignorant as to the sense-organs which are the agents of the instinct, and its possible modifications by intelligence, even more than we are in the cases of insects and molluscs which possess a keen sense of locality. We ourselves are not entirely devoid of a faculty of the kind, and it appears to be comparatively well developed in savage races. It is to be hoped that extended observation and experiment will some day throw more light upon the subject, till when it will be wise to suspend our judgment, and remain in a critical attitude, rather than indulge in premature generalization. It is scarcely necessary to add that there is room for a host of unprejudiced observers in this field of work.

WHITE STORKS (*Ciconia alba*) ASSEMBLING FOR MIGRATION

The seasonal Migration of many birds is a phenomenon familiar to all, and one which, in spite of much research, is still but little understood. Food-supply has no doubt much to do with it, but the reasons for migration are the least mysterious part of the matter. *How* birds are able to find their way over vast stretches of land and sea to regions suitable for their purposes is at present quite beyond our comprehension. In most cases it appears that the young birds are the first to depart on what must be for them an unknown journey, which greatly adds to the difficulty of the problem to be solved. One of the best-known migratory birds is the White Stork, the rough stick-nests of which are such common objects on roofs and chimneys in Holland, Denmark, and North Germany. The locality-sense is strongly developed, for year after year a nest is tenanted by the same pair of birds. They arrive in spring, leaving again in late summer, by which time the young are well grown. Before their departure they "assemble" in large numbers on the meadows, and fly away in troops, some of which have been estimated to include as many as five thousand individuals. They winter in Africa, some of them getting as far south as Cape Colony.

WHITE STORKS (CICONIA ALBA) ASSEMBLING FOR MIGRATION

ASSOCIATION OF ORGANISMS—THE WEB OF LIFE

CHAPTER LX

ASSOCIATION OF ORGANISMS—GENERAL PRINCIPLES—ANIMALS AND PLANTS

GENERAL PRINCIPLES

The study of natural science during the last half-century has advanced so rapidly that it is no longer possible for one man to grapple seriously even with a single subject, and there is an ever-increasing tendency towards specialization. No doubt the sum of our knowledge is thereby constantly being increased at a rate which would otherwise be impossible, but there is another side to the question. For extreme specialization is somewhat apt to lead to a neglect of general principles, and to a more or less complete loss of the sense of proportion. To be unable to see the wood on account of the trees is bad enough, but to have one's vision restricted to a single tree, or perhaps a single branch, is very much worse. In no department of knowledge is the cramping tendency of specialization more apparent than in natural history. There seemed at one time a chance of establishing a science of Biology, designed to deal with both plants and animals, but this has now been merged into botany on the one hand and zoology on the other, and many of the important relations that exist between plants and animals are not given the prominence which they undoubtedly deserve. This cannot altogether be helped, but even under existing circumstances it is both desirable and possible that work of specialist kind should be preceded by studies of a wider and more general nature. This is one of the aims of the new subject of Nature-Study, so far as biology and geology are concerned, another object being to foster that intelligent interest in and accurate observation of natural objects upon which much of the future happiness of our embryo citizens will depend. If properly taught as a connected whole, and not as a string of isolated facts (to be "learnt"), this subject ought to fare better than physiography and general elementary science, which, though designed with the laudable intention of giving a broad foundation in non-biological science, are now somewhat discredited.

The relations which bind together the innumerable plants and animals now living on the globe are so numerous, and often so complex, that from this point of view the world has been compared to a spider's-web of elaborate texture, in which all the threads are directly or indirectly connected, so that when one is touched the entire structure is thrown into vibration.

It is not within the scope of this work to deal with the complex relations which link together the members of the vegetable kingdom, and students who desire information of this kind are referred to the English edition of Schimper's *Plant Geography*, to Kerner von Marilaun's altogether admirable book *The Natural History of Plants*, and also to Scott Elliot's *Nature Studies*, which gives an excellent account of the leading facts and principles in small compass. But it may be well to attempt here a brief description of the salient features which mark the relations existing between plants and animals. This is much more fully dealt with by the authors just mentioned.

PLANTS AND ANIMALS

It may not be superfluous to remark here that the vegetable world is divided into the following great groups, beginning with the highest:—1. SEED PLANTS (Spermaphyta), including most of the large and obvious forms, such as ordinary forest-trees and the inhabitants of our flower-gardens. 2. FERN-LIKE PLANTS (Pteridophyta), comprising not only ferns, but also horse-tails, club-mosses, &c. 3. MOSSES AND LIVERWORTS (Bryophyta). 4. LOWER PLANTS (Thallophyta), in which the body is not divided into stem, root, and leaf, or such a division is only incipient. Multitudes of Thallophytes are minute or microscopic, and in any case they may broadly be assigned to one of three sub-groups: (*a*) *Algæ*, embracing brown, green, and red sea-weeds (with a smaller number of freshwater weeds), with a host of smaller forms living not only in water but in most damp places; (*b*) *Fungi*, including toad-stools, moulds, mildews, the microscopic yeast-plants, and the still smaller bacteria; and (*c*) *Lichens*, which are intimately connected communities of algæ and fungi.

All these plants, except fungi (and a few seed-plants), contain leaf-green or chlorophyll, a substance of great biological importance, as elsewhere explained. It is convenient to distinguish forms which possess it as "green plants", though the chlorophyll

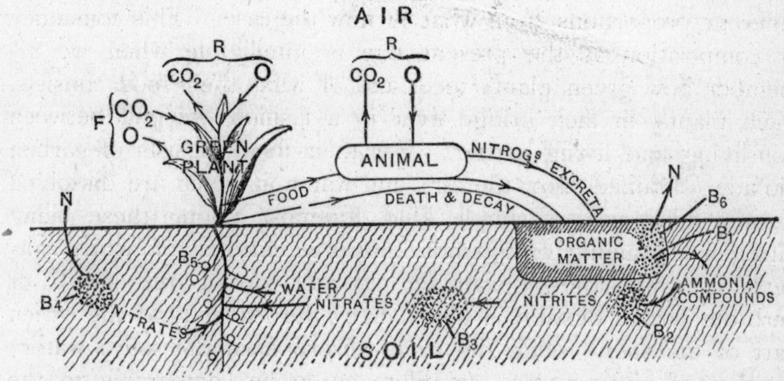

Fig. 1064.—Relations between Animals and Plants: arrows indicate the taking in or giving out of various substances

Both green plant and animal take in oxygen (O) and give out carbon dioxide (CO_2) in the course of respiration (R). The animal feeds on plants, and by nitrogenous excretion and ultimate death adds to the store of organic matter in the soil. The green plant in the course of feeding (F) takes in carbon dioxide (CO_2) from the air, returning oxygen (O), and also takes up water with dissolved salts from the soil; its dead parts contribute to the store of organic matter in the soil. The groups of bacteria B_1–B_3, respectively produce ammonia compounds, convert these into nitrites, and these again into nitrates. The bacteria B_4, and the tubercle-fungi B_5, fix the free nitrogen (N) of the air, with production of nitrates. The bacteria B_6, in the absence of oxygen, decompose organic matter with liberation of free nitrogen (N).

may be obscured by the presence of other pigments, as, for example, in brown and red sea-weeds.

Relations between Organisms and the Constituents of the Atmosphere (fig. 1064).—In considering this question it must not be forgotten that the gases which are mixed together in air are also found dissolved in both fresh and salt water, and the relations between these dissolved gases and aquatic organisms are pretty much the same as those subsisting between ordinary air and land organisms. The most important of these gases are carbon dioxide (carbonic acid gas, CO_2), oxygen, and nitrogen. It has already been explained in the section on Breathing (vol. ii, p. 379) that plants and animals respire in the same way, taking in oxygen to facilitate the breaking-down processes which continually go on in the body, and giving out carbon dioxide as a product of waste. It is quite a mistake to suppose that plants "breathe in carbon dioxide and breathe out oxygen", as often supposed. If there were not some compensating arrangement, it is clear that the amount of oxygen in air would rapidly diminish and the quantity of carbon dioxide rapidly increase. But it appears that this is not so, for the composition of air remains practically the same, at least for very long periods of time, though probably in earlier periods of the earth's history its constituent gases were in different proportions from what is now the case. This constancy of composition at the present day is intelligible when we remember how green plants feed, and of what their food consists. Such plants, in fact, bridge over in a fashion the gulf between non-living and living matter. For their food consists of carbon dioxide (obtained from the air), and water in which are dissolved certain substances of simple kind, foremost among these being nitrogen-containing compounds known as nitrates, of which saltpetre is a well-known example. In any sort of tree, shrub, or herb the carbon dioxide is taken in by the leaves (and the green part of the stem), while the roots absorb from the soil a watery solution of nitrates, &c., so dilute as to be comparable to the ordinary drinking water of most districts. These simple constituents of the food are converted step by step into the living substance of the plant by the agency of that substance itself. The first step in this series of up-building processes takes place in the leaves (and the green parts of the stem), and consists in a reaction between carbon dioxide and water, giving rise to a substance which is more complex in nature than either of them. This can only go on in daylight and in the presence of chlorophyll, which in some way not clearly understood enables the living substance associated with it to press the energy of sunlight into its service for the purpose of building up a comparatively complex substance from simple ones. And this first step in the manufacture of living matter is accompanied by the liberation of free oxygen into the surrounding air as a by-product. For the carbon dioxide and water, which are the raw materials in this work, contain more oxygen than is required for the purpose, and the surplus passes away to the exterior. It therefore follows that green plants in the course of their feeding (1) take carbon dioxide *from* the air, and (2) give out free oxygen *to* the air. And these gases are respectively taken in and given out in such proportions that the amount of carbon dioxide in the air does not rapidly grow larger, and the amount of free oxygen rapidly get smaller, as would undoubtedly be the case if the results of breathing were not compensated.

The action and reaction between organisms and the air also involve chemical processes which have to do with nitrogen, and in which a leading part is played by various bacteria which live in the soil. Green plants get the nitrogen which they require for feeding purposes in the form of dissolved nitrates, which are derived from more than one source. It is a familiar fact that ordinary earth or soil, such as is to be found in a garden, is more or less dark in colour, largely as the result of the presence of organic matter. This partly consists of the remains of organisms which have died and decayed, and partly of substances derived from the nitrogen-containing excreta of animals. The rotting, decomposition, or breaking down of such materials is the result of chemical changes brought about by certain bacteria in the presence of oxygen, with production of ammonia compounds. Another set of bacteria convert these compounds into salts known as nitrites, from which nitrates are then produced by the action of still another group of bacteria. The nitrates serve as food to green plants, which in their turn are devoured by animals. We thus see that by the death and decay of organisms material is produced which helps to build up the bodies of new generations. This, however, is not the only source of nitrates in the soil, for what are known as *nitrifying* bacteria are there present, which possess the remarkable power of abstracting free nitrogen from the air, and causing it to enter into combination. There is another arrangement by which, in leguminous and a few other plants, the same end is attained. If, say, a pea- or bean-plant is dug up, and the earth washed away from its roots, these will be found to bear a number of rounded thickenings. Within each such "root-tubercle" live a number of microscopic fungi (possibly bacteria) that appropriate the free nitrogen of the air which circulates in the soil, employing it to build up nitrates. We have here a striking example of Mutualism (symbiosis), *i.e.* the intimate association of two organisms for their common benefit. The leguminous plant has a supply of nitrates ready to hand, while the tubercle-fungus is sheltered, and no doubt nourished.

It is clear that by the action of nitrifying bacteria and tubercle-fungi the nitrogen of the air is steadily diminished, but here again we find a means of compensation. For there are certain *denitrifying* bacteria, which, in the absence of oxygen, act upon decaying organic matter in such a way that free nitrogen is liberated.

Relations between the Nutrition of Plants and Animals.—A little reflection will show that animals are entirely dependent upon plants in the matter of food. This is obviously so as regards purely vegetarian animals, while carnivorous forms are indirectly dependent upon the vegetable world. Many flesh-eaters feed entirely upon vegetarians, but if they prey upon other flesh-eaters, and these again upon still other carnivorous creatures, and so on, we get to plants in the end.

Plants, considered as food for animals, have been concerned in the evolution of burrowing, climbing, parachuting, and flying forms, especially the last three. (For details, see vol. iii, pp. 231, 281, 292.)

On the other hand, animals contribute to the store of plant food. For, as we have already seen (pp. 65–67), they breathe out carbon dioxide, which green plants take up, while their nitrogenous excreta and dead bodies are partly converted into nitrates, which the same plants are able to use for the purposes of nutrition.

There are also a number of Carnivorous Plants, which do not altogether rely upon simple substances as food, but are provided with "traps" for the capture and digestion of insects or other small creatures. One of Darwin's most interesting books (*Insectivorous Plants*) is devoted to these forms, some of which are native to our own country, while several others may be seen in botanic gardens. One of the simplest kinds of arrangement is seen in the Butterwort (*Pinguicula*), that is often to be found growing in damp places among our mountains. The pale-green slippery leaves are arranged in a rosette, from the centre of which violet flowers grow up. Small flies alighting on the leaves are held fast by a sticky fluid, secreted by a multitude of little knobbed hairs which project from the surface. The edges of the leaves then curl over the prey, and there is an increased exudation of the fluid in question, which acts very much like gastric juice, converting the flesh of the booty into a soluble form that is then absorbed as food. The widely distributed members of the Sundew family (*Droseraceæ*) exhibit greater specialization in relation to the catching of insects than the Butterworts, though the means employed are essentially the same. Our native forms, the Sundews (species of *Drosera*), are fairly common in marshy places, and are often found growing side by side with the Butterwort. Here, again, the leaves are arranged in a rosette, from the centre of which rises a stem bearing a number of small flowers. The end of each leaf is thickly studded with long reddish "tentacles", shaped something like pins, upon the heads of which are little drops of sticky fluid that glisten like dew (fig. 1065). Should an unfortunate insect alight on one or more of these tentacles it sticks fast, other

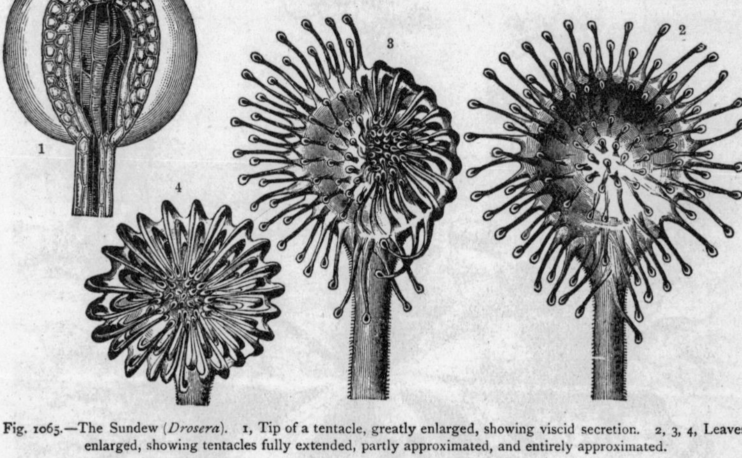

Fig. 1065.—The Sundew (*Drosera*). 1, Tip of a tentacle, greatly enlarged, showing viscid secretion. 2, 3, 4, Leaves, enlarged, showing tentacles fully extended, partly approximated, and entirely approximated.

tentacles bend towards it, there is an increased flow of the digestive juice, and the final result is the same as in a Butterwort.

Venus' Fly-Trap (*Dionæa muscipula*), growing on marshy ground in the east of the United States, is a near relative of our Sundews, but its "traps" are much more elaborate (fig. 1066). The end of each leaf is divided into halves which can move towards each other almost as on a hinge, while their edges are fringed with bristles. The upper side of each half is studded with small violet hairs, which secrete a digestive fluid, and three large sensitive hairs project from its centre. If an insect happens to visit one of these leaves, and touches one or more of the six sensitive hairs, the result is somewhat dramatic. For the halves of the leaf close rapidly together, the bristles on their edges interlocking, so that a very perfect trap is constituted, in which there is plenty of room for an average victim, since as the two halves move together they become concave towards each other. As in the other cases, digestion and absorption complete the tragedy.

Among the most notorious of carnivorous forms are the widely-distributed Pitcher Plants, in which the leaves are hollowed into structures which may be described as a combination of lure, pit-

Fig. 1066.—Venus' Fly-Trap (*Dionæa muscipula*)

fall, and stomach. Such are the species of *Nepenthes*, which range from Madagascar through South Asia and the East Indies to the Philippines. In this case the lidded pitchers look something like hot-water jugs, and are attractively coloured. The way in which they serve their purpose is thus described by Kerner (in *The Natural History of Plants*):—"The bright pitchers of *Nepenthes*, visible from afar, are sought, just as flowers are, by insects, and probably by other winged creatures as well; and this occurs all the more because there is a copious secretion of honey by the epidermal cells upon the under surface of the lid, and on the rim round the mouth of each pitcher. The swollen and often delicately-fluted rim, in particular, drips and glitters with the sugary juice, and it would be permissible in this connection to speak of a honeyed mouth and sweet lips in the most literal sense of the words. Animals which suck honey from the lips of *Nepenthes* pitchers wander, as they do so, only too readily upon the interior surface of the orifice. But the inner face is smooth and precipitous, and rendered so slippery by a bluish coating of wax that not a few of the alighted guests slip down to the bottom of the pitcher and fall into the liquid there collected. Many of them perish in a short time; others try to save themselves by climbing up the internal face of the pitcher, but they always slip again on the polished, wax-coated zone, and tumble back once more to the bottom." In some species the inwardly bent rim of the pitcher is fringed with sharp teeth which curve downwards and facilitate entry but forbid exit.

Another very interesting Pitcher-Plant (*Sarracenia variolaris*), native to the marshes of Alabama, Carolina, and Florida, presents arrangements of somewhat different kind. It possesses a rosette of elongated hollow leaves, of which the ends bend sharply over like hoods. The narrow opening of a pitcher is just under the hood, from which a little flap hangs down. Allurement by colour is not wanting, for though most of each pitcher is green, its hooded top is veined with red, and there are purple blotches here and there. In this region, too, there are numerous translucent patches between the veins, which from inside the pitcher must look like openings or "windows". As in *Nepenthes*, honey is provided on the inner surface of the hood and round the margin of the aperture, from which a sugary ridge runs right down to the ground, serving as an attractive but fatal pathway to many wingless insects, especially ants. The pitcher is a pitfall of the deadliest kind, for its interior is clothed with slippery overlapping scales, of which the narrow pointed ends are directed downwards, so that insects, once imprisoned, are quite unable to climb out again. And if a winged insect tries to fly out it naturally makes for the apparent windows in the hood, for the actual opening faces downwards and is veiled in darkness, and in most cases falls back exhausted into the putrid fluid which fills the lower part of its prison. The unfortunate victims are not digested, as in *Nepenthes*, but either drown or starve, after which their bodies decompose to form a sort of liquid manure, parts of which are no doubt absorbed as food. Yet, strange to say, a few flies, and a small moth, regularly lay their eggs in the decomposing mass contained in these pitchers, and possess climbing-irons, so to speak, which enable them to get out again with the greatest ease. One such form is a species of Blow-Fly (*Sarcophaga Sarraceniæ*), own cousin to the speckled nuisance (*S. carnaria*) that lays her eggs in our meat, and to which we give the same name. Each foot of this fly is possessed of a long and sharp claw, which can be pushed between the scales of the pitcher, and firmly fixed into the underlying tissue. The maggots which hatch out of her eggs feed on the putrefying substances surrounding them until they are full grown, when they easily get out of the pitcher, not by climbing, which would be impossible in their case, but by the simple device of eating a hole in the wall. Once outside, they enter the ground, and there pass into the motionless pupa stage, from which the adult fly later on emerges. The small moth (*Xanthoptera semicrocea*) for which the Sarracenia pitchers have no terrors is adapted for climbing in much the same way as the Blow-Fly. For each of the second legs possesses a pair of long sharp spines at the end of its shin (tibia), while two pairs of such spines are similarly situated on each of the hind-legs. The caterpillars do not, like the fly-maggots, eat their way out of the pitcher, but climb out, though in quite a different way from their mother. Their solution of the problem is equally effective, for they spin a web of silken threads over the slippery scales, and thus secure the necessary foothold.

All the carnivorous forms so far mentioned, though they live in marshy places, are land plants, more or less perfectly adapted for the capture of insects and other small terrestrial animals. Some of them, however, have aquatic relatives, which are to be found floating in ditches and ponds, where they prey chiefly upon small crustaceans, such as water-fleas, mussel-shrimps, and copepods, though the larvæ of gnats and other insects are also among their victims, besides which they catch large numbers of the minute motile plants known as Diatoms. The floating habit conduces to success in this matter, for small crustaceans, &c., are

PITCHER-PLANTS (*Nepenthes*)

The plate represents a typical species (*Nepenthes destillatoria*) of a group of pitcher-plants which ranges from Madagascar through south and south-east Asia to the East Indies, Philippines, and tropical Australia. They live in damp forest-regions, at the side of pools, in the shallow water of which their seeds germinate. The leaves are modified in a remarkable manner for the purpose of catching and digesting flying-insects. The attached end of the leaf-stalk is broadened into a green expansion, followed by a tendril-like section, while the end of the stalk swells into a pitcher, which is overhung by a lid representing the blade of the leaf. Insects are attracted by the bright colours of the pitchers, and the nectar which is abundantly secreted around their openings and on the under side of their lids. But the inner side of the pitcher is as slippery a glass, and any insect that steps upon it quickly slides down into the contained fluid, which partly consists of a powerful digestive juice that reduces to solution the nutritious parts of the victim. The "peptonized insect-extract" thus prepared is absorbed by the lining of the pitcher, and constitutes a highly nutritious and stimulating food.

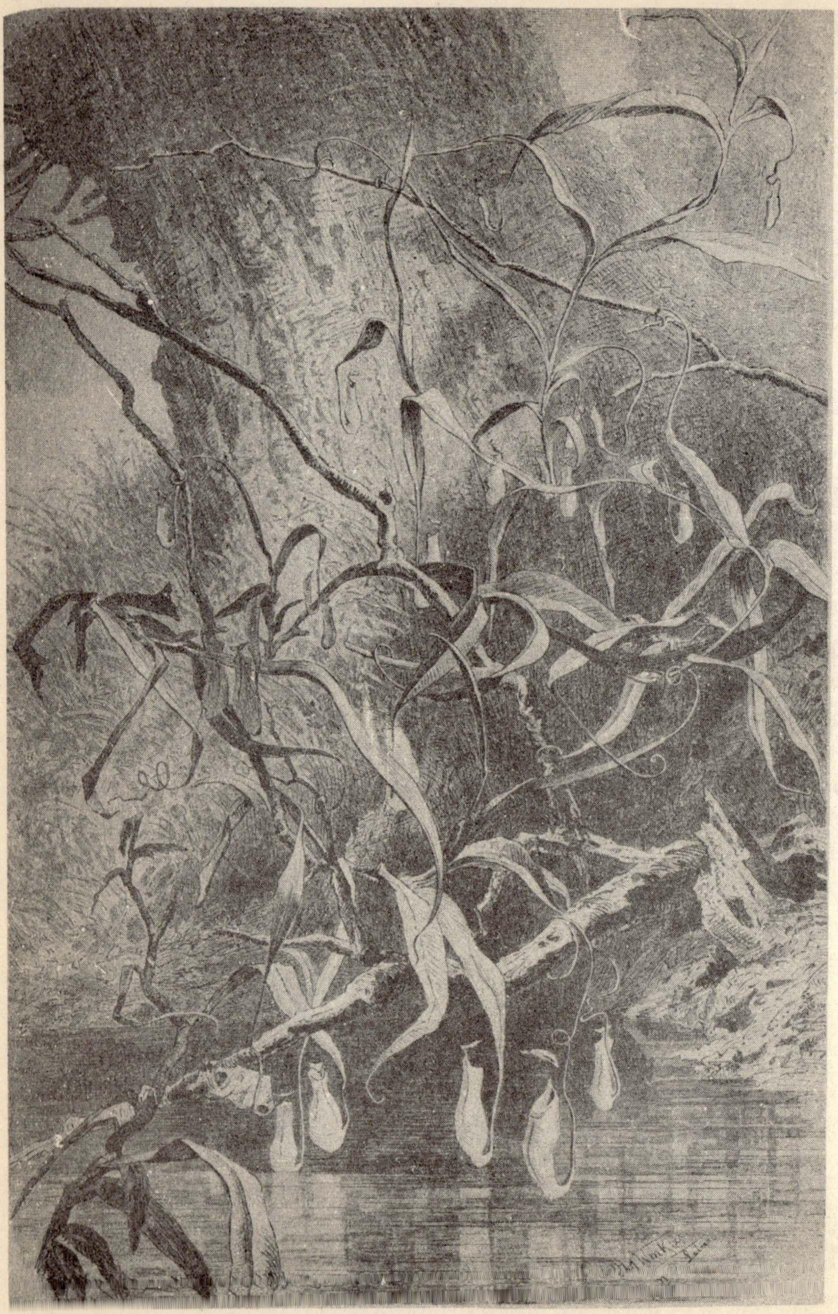

PITCHER-PLANTS (NEPENTHES DESTILLATORIA) AT THE EDGE OF A TROPICAL POOL most abundant at or near the surface. Among these aquatic carnivores are certain small cousins (species of *Aldrovandia*) of Venus' Fly-Trap, which are specialized in much the same way. They are native to South and Central Europe, India, and Australia.

The Bladderworts (species of *Utricularia*, fig. 1067) are widely-distributed ditch-plants, closely related to the Butterworts, and

Fig. 1067.—Bladderworts (*Utricularia*)

represented in the British flora. They feed in part upon small aquatic organisms, and catch their prey in little bladder-like traps formed by modification of parts of the feathery leaves (fig. 1068). Each of these snares is not unlike a large water-flea in shape, and the resemblance is greatly increased by the presence of two branching bristles at the free end. Here, too, is placed the small opening into the bladder, guarded by a little transparent flap serving as a door, which opens inwards with the greatest ease, but prevents exit. Why little creatures should be attracted to these traps is by no means clear, but minute crustaceans, &c., are fond of prying into holes and corners in search of food, while some of them may make use of the two branching bristles as a place of refuge from their enemies. And as the two bristles act as guides to the mouth of the trap the result is often tragic. Slimy hairs grow in this dangerous neighbourhood, which possibly have attractions to offer, while the little transparent door

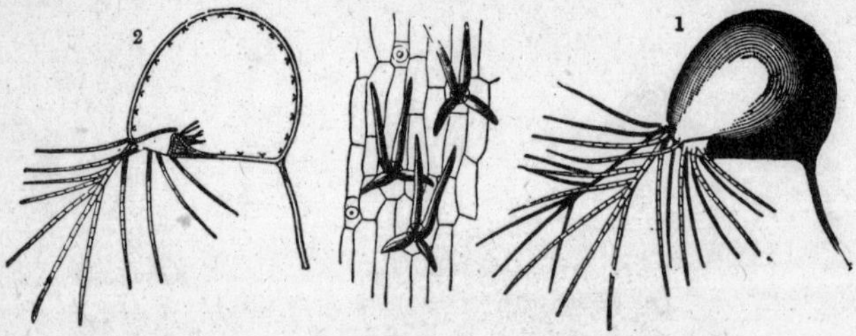

Fig. 1068.—Traps of Bladderwort (*Utricularia*), enlarged. 1, External view. 2, Longitudinal section. 3, Three absorptive branched hairs from interior. 1 and 2, × 4; 3, × 250.

must look like a spot of light, and perhaps acts as a lure. It is at any rate certain that victims are numerous, and their decomposed remains are absorbed by curious branched hairs which line the trap. The prey is apparently not digested as in Sundews and Butterworts.

The remaining topics dealt with in this chapter also more or less involve questions of nutrition, but are placed under separate headings for the sake of clearness.

ASSOCIATION OF PLANTS AND ANIMALS AS MESSMATES, MUTUALISTS, AND PARASITES

COMMENSALISM.—Two associated organisms are known as Messmates or Commensals when they live together to the benefit of one or both; the union, however, not being of so intimate a nature as to be essential to the life of either. The term commensalism was coined to express such relations as existing between different animals, but there appears to be no reason why its meaning should not be extended to cover cases where two plants, or a plant and an animal, are similarly related. As an instance of the former we may take those tropical Orchids which regularly live upon trees, and are on that account said to be Epiphytes (Gk.

epi, upon; *phyton*, a plant). The advantage to the Orchids is obvious, though they do not absorb the sap of the plants upon which they live. These last, however, apparently derive no benefit from this one-sided arrangement.

There are numerous cases of commensalism between plants and animals in which the latter alone are benefited. In one of the Liverworts (*Frullania dilatata*, fig. 1069) which grow on tree-trunks there are little cup-like outgrowths on the under sides of the leaves, serving as the abodes of a species of Wheel-Animalcule (*Callidina symbiotica*). Marine plants often bear animals as messmates, which do them no harm. On a kind of brown sea-weed (*Fucus serratus*), for example, are frequently to be seen the little spiral tubes of a sort of Annelid (*Spirorbis*), which no doubt secures an increased supply of nutriment and dissolved oxygen by being moved about in the water when the tide is up. The Australian Sea-Horse (*Phyllopteryx eques*) also benefits by its association with the sea-weeds to which it bears a resemblance (see vol. ii, p. 296).

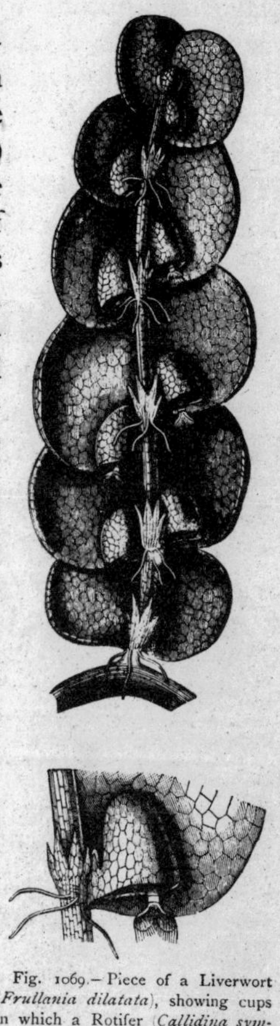

Fig. 1069.—Piece of a Liverwort (*Frullania dilatata*), showing cups in which a Rotifer (*Callidina symbiotica*) lives: enlarged. The small drawing is of one cup with its Rotifer (further enlarged).

Some instances are known of commensalism between a plant and an animal, in which both derive advantage from the association. Ant-plants illustrate such an arrangement (see p. 81), and so do the Sloths of South America, in which minute algæ live in the grooves of the fluted hairs. For these algæ are provided with a sheltered home, and at the same time give a greenish tint to the hairs, the Sloths being thereby rendered less conspicuous to their enemies.

Mutualism (Symbiosis).—Organisms living together as Mutualists are very intimately associated for mutual benefit. Mutualism between two plants is well illustrated by leguminous forms and the minute fungi which live in the tubercles on their roots. And every Lichen may be regarded as a joint-stock community, consisting as it does of an alga and a fungus closely interwoven (fig. 1070).

Animals and plants may also be associated in an intimate way. It appears, for example, that the process of digestion in many animals is aided by certain bacteria which always live in their internal organs, as, *e.g.*, *Sarcina ventriculi* in the human stomach (fig. 1073). Bacteria of the sort are provided with a sheltered home and abundant food. Among the Animalcules (Protozoa) a well-known example is afforded by some of the Radiolaria, which always contain so-called "yellow cells", that are regarded as a kind of alga (fig. 1071). These cells are not only sheltered, but also absorb carbon dioxide, water, and salts from the fluids of the Radiolarian, which in its turn is provided with abundant free oxygen for breathing purposes, and possibly benefits in other ways. A somewhat similar association between some Sea-Anemones and minute algæ has been described. It is, however, possible that "yellow cells" and "algæ" are not plants at all, but specialized parts of the Ray-Animalcules and Sea-Anemones themselves.

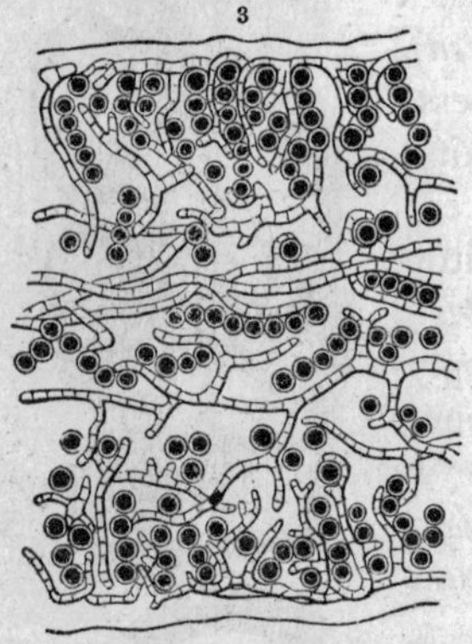

Fig. 1070.—Cross-section through a Lichen (*Collema*), showing the colourless threads of the Fungus, and the dark necklace-like filaments of the Alga. ×450.

PARASITISM.—An organism is known as a *parasite* when it feeds upon the substance of another organism, to the serious or fatal detriment of this unwilling "host". An *ectoparasite* lives on the outside of its host; an *endoparasite* within it.

Many plants prey upon other plants in one way or the other. Clover-Dodder (*Cuscuta*), for example, is ectoparasitic upon Clover, while various fungi live as endoparasites within higher plants, *e.g.* Potato-Fungus (*Phytophthora infestans*) within the tissues of the Potato plant.

A large number of plants are known which are endoparasitic with regard to animals. In autumn many dead flies will be seen adhering to various objects by a sort of fluffy halo which surrounds them. These have been killed by the Fly-Mould (*Empusa muscæ*, fig. 1072), the delicate threads of which branch in all directions through their tissues. Other fungi attack various caterpillars, *e.g.* the silk-worm disease known as "muscardine" is due to the Silk-worm Mould (a species of *Cordiceps*). A number

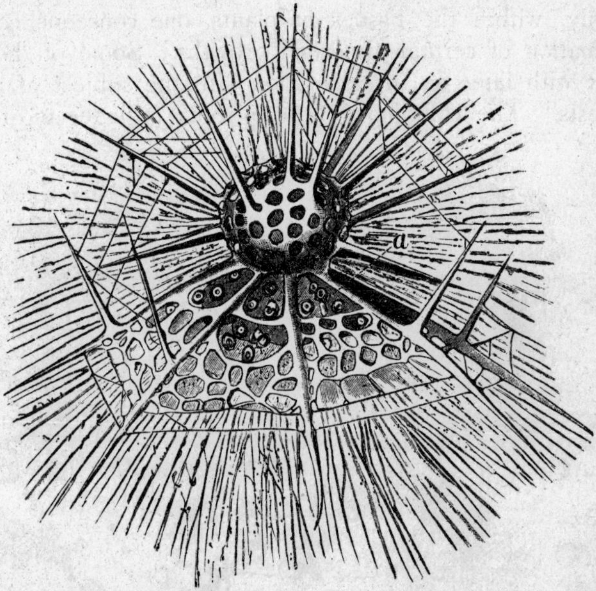

Fig. 1071.—A Ray-Animalcule (*Arachnocorys circumtexta*) with yellow cells (*a*), much enlarged

of skin-diseases, such as ringworm and "barbers' rash" are caused by parasitic plants of somewhat similar nature.

But the most notable, and at the same time the smallest, of the endoparasitic plants which attack animals are certain kinds of bacteria, which may literally swarm within the body, and give rise to a host of diseases, such as relapsing fever, typhoid, leprosy, Asiatic cholera, tuberculosis, diphtheria, anthrax, lock-jaw, and bubonic plague. Some idea of the small size of bacteria will be gathered from fig. 1073, or from statements that make some appeal to the imagination. It is said, for example, that 250,000,000 individuals of the species associated with bubonic plague could be crowded into the small space of a square inch. A number more than six times as great as the population of the United Kingdom at the last census.

Fig. 1072.—A House-Fly (*Musca domestica*) killed by Fly-Mould (*Empusa muscæ*), enlarged

In dealing with those animals that feed upon plants it is impossible to draw any clear line between vegetarians and parasites. We shall, however, be justified in applying the latter name to a number of small forms which live, generally for part of their lives only, within the tissues of plants, one consequence being the formation of certain abnormal growths. Some of these will be dealt with later on in connection with the subject of agricultural pests. The clubbing of turnip-roots ("finger-and-toe" or

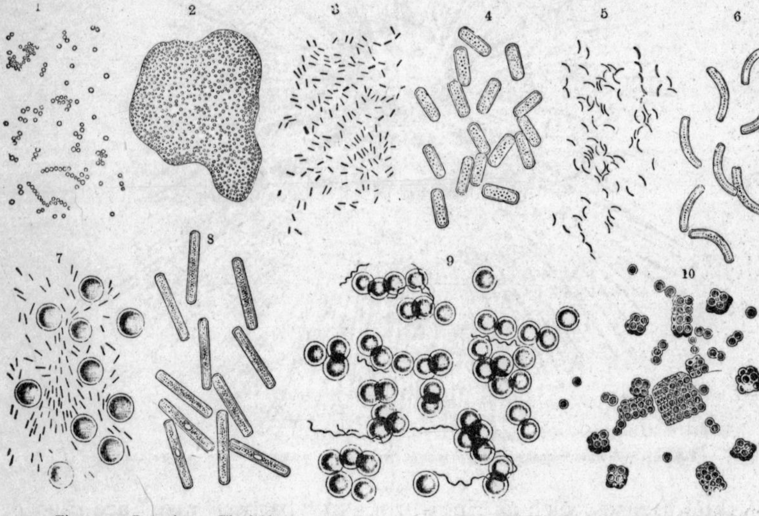

Fig. 1073.—Bacteria. 1, The "blood portent" (*Micrococcus prodigiosus*); 2, gelatinous stage of the same. 3, Bacteria which produce acetic acid (*Bacterium aceti*); 4, the same on larger scale. 5, Bacteria of Asiatic cholera (*Spirochæte choleræ asiaticæ*); 6, the same on larger scale. 7, Anthrax bacilli (*Bacillus anthracis*) with red blood-corpuscles; 8, the same on larger scale. 9, Bacteria of relapsing fever (*Spirochæte Obermeieri*) and red blood-corpuscles. 10, Symbiotic bacteria (*Sarcina ventriculi*) from human stomach. 1, 2, 3, 5, 7, and 9, × 300. 10, × 800. 4, 6, and 8, × 2000.

"anbury"), for example, is caused by one of the Fungus-Animals (*Plasmodiophora brassicæ*), which interferes with the nutrition of the plant, causing it to grow in an unusual way. And it not infrequently happens that cereals and some other cultivated forms are attacked by small Eel-Worms, the presence of which has a stunting or distorting effect.

Most persons have noticed the curious local outgrowths known as "galls" that are common upon some plants, and tempt comparison with the tumours and cancers of animals. They are due to the attacks of Gall-Flies, small forms belonging to the order of Membrane-winged Insects (*Hymenoptera*). The female gall-fly punctures a bud, or leaf, or stem, by means of her sharp ovipositor, and lays an egg in the incision. The injury is trifling, but sets up irritation, probably caused by some secretion, and the result is an abnormal growth. Some of the different galls to be seen on oak-leaves are represented in fig. 1074. Other examples are furnished by the familiar "oak-apples", and the "bedeguars" of rose-bushes. A particular species of gall-fly always selects the same sort of plant, and attacks the same region, the resulting gall being of definite size, shape, and colour. A remarkable case is cited below (see p. 81), where the gall benefits the plant on which it is found.

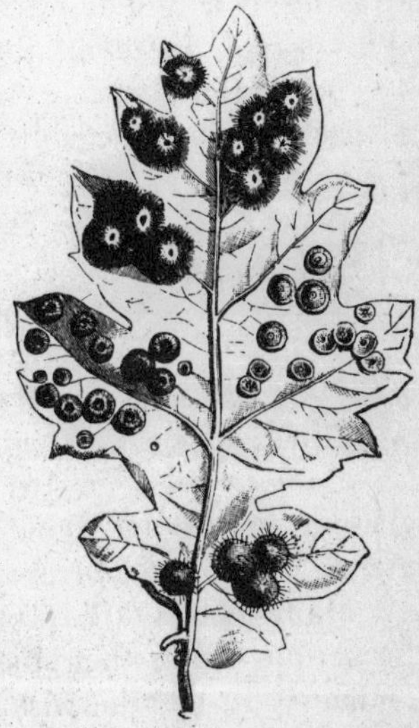

Fig. 1074.—Various Insect-Galls on Leaf of Oak (*Quercus*)

Defences of Plants and Animals against One Another.—A good deal of space has already been devoted (vol. ii, p. 275) to the innumerable devices by which various animals are more or less protected in reference to carnivorous forms; but animals are also liable to be attacked by plants, especially by microscopic but deadly bacteria that induce many sorts of disease, particularly those of infectious or contagious nature. One important function of the white or colourless corpuscles which live in lymph or blood appears to be to repel the attacks of dangerous "germs" of the sort (see vol. iii, p. 4). The principle involved in vaccination or inoculation is related to the fact that animals which have been purposely subjected to the influence of a disease-germ that has been weakened by artificial methods (or to the action of a related but less dangerous kind of germ), are thereby rendered able to resist more or less successfully the onslaughts of the same sort of germ in its more virulent form. Another important application of preventive (and curative) medicine has resulted from the discovery that some animals are protected from particular disease-germs by means of complex substances (defensive proteids or anti-toxins) contained in their blood. The best-known example is afforded by diphtheria, which can be warded off, or combated if contracted, by means of an anti-toxin extracted from the blood of the horse.

Turning to the other side of the question, we find that numerous plants are protected by various means against vegetarian animals. Many species, for example, more or less successfully ward off the attacks of browsing forms by mechanical devices. Of this nature are the thorns, spines, prickles, and stinging hairs with which painful experience has made most of us more or less familiar. Good illustrative cases are such common forms as gorse, blackthorn, holly, thistle, and stinging-nettle. This is not, however, the only use of sharp-pointed outgrowths, for not a few forms, *e.g.* the bramble, are "hook-climbers". It is particularly noticeable that ripening fruits are often mechanically guarded, the prickly husks of horse-chestnut being a case in point.

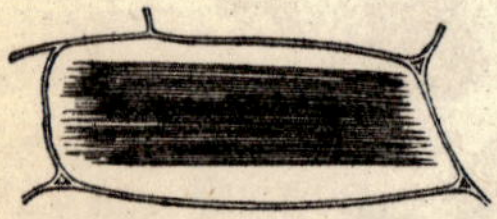

Fig. 1075.—Cell from Leaf of Virginia Creeper (*Ampelopsis*), containing a bundle of needle-crystals (raphides) of oxalate of lime; highly magnified

Quite a number of herbaceous plants contain in their soft tissues bundles of exceedingly sharp needle-like crystals (raphides, fig. 1075) which protect them against the ravages of slugs and snails, as experiment has shown. Many such crystals are to be found, for example, in the leaf-stalks of the Arum-"Lily" (*Richardia Æthiopica*).

Many plants are protected by chemical means, *i.e.* by the formation within their tissues of substances which are poisonous or nauseous, or otherwise detrimental to the well-being of would-be consumers. Forms such as Foxglove, Aconite, Monkshood, Hemlock, and Yew no doubt ward off to a great extent the attacks of browsing animals in this way. Fruits and seeds are often thus protected, and may be either simply nauseous (especially when unripe) or else contain active poisons, as in the case of the seeds of Laburnum and *Strychnos nux-vomica*. The attacks of both large and small animals are checked in many cases by means of a sticky fluid known as *latex*, which flows from an injured part, and when fresh has a milky appearance. Common examples among British plants are the Spurges (*Euphorbia*), Poppy, Greater Celandine, and Dandelion. This secretion hardens when dry, and forms a protective coat over the wound. Some tropical trees produce a kind of latex which, in the solidified condition, is known to us as india-rubber. It is almost certainly to be regarded as a means of defence against wood-boring insects, especially beetles. The many varieties of resin and gum are also of protective nature.

We have already had occasion to note (vol. ii, p. 301) that quite a number of animals advertise their disagreeable properties by conspicuous colours or by other means. Such warning coloration also appears to be present in certain plants, as, for instance, in some of the poisonous toad-stools, which are of glaring and repulsive appearance. And here also it would seem that, as among animals, cases of Mimicry are to be found, for some harmless toad-stools closely resemble their poisonous brethren, and thus gain some amount of protection. The highly desirable *Boletus edulis*, for example, is very liable to be mistaken for its virulently poisonous cousin (*B. Satanas*).

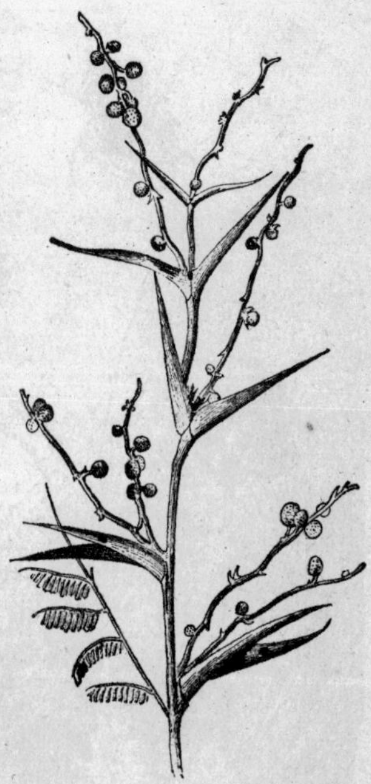

Fig. 1076.—Acacia (*A. sphærocephala*), possessing hollow thorns in which ants finds shelter, and pear-shaped food-bodies on tips of leaflets.

Another set of plants contain aromatic or fragrant essential oils which, though pleasant enough to our own sense of smell, act as deterrents to many animals. Such are sage, mint, lavender, and many spice-producing forms.

There is still another means of defence, and one which is more interesting from the zoological standpoint than those so far described. Certain forms are known which may appropriately be termed ant-loving (*myrmecophilous*), because they maintain a "police-force" of ants, by which they are protected from leaf-cutting insects and other unwelcome visitors. The services of these hirelings are secured by means of material benefits of substantial character. A well-known case is that of a sort of Acacia (*Acacia sphærocephala*, fig. 1076), which bears little pear-shaped "food-bodies" to appease the appetites of its retainers, and also hollow thorns which furnish them with shelter. Another curious instance is afforded by a kind of Oak (*Quercus pubescens*) in which a gall-fly (*Cynips argentea*) lays her eggs. The abnormal growths or "galls" which result from this process secrete nectar that serves to attract ants, and thus a body-guard is secured by which the attacks of caterpillars and snails are repelled. The following account is given by Kerner (in *The Natural History of Plants*) of the way in which ants protect the flower-heads (capitula) of certain Composites:—"A similar state of affairs is met with on

Fig. 1077.—A Saw-Wort (*Serratula lycopifolia*) defended by Ants (*Formica exsecta*) against the attacks of a Beetle (*Oxythyrea funesta*)

the capitula of several Composites indigenous to South-eastern Europe, *e.g. Centaurea alpina* and *Ruthenica*, *Jurinea mollis*, and *Serratula lycopifolia*, the last of which is here figured [fig. 1077]. The young heads of these Composites are particularly liable to the attacks of voracious beetles, especially of *Oxythyrea funesta*, which bites big holes in them, destroying crowded flower-buds and involucral scales [*i.e.* the overlapping scales which surround the head] without the least difficulty. To meet this danger a garrison of warlike ants is employed. Honey is secreted from big stomata [*i.e.* pores in the epidermis] on the overlapping scales of the still-closed heads in such quantities that one can see a drop of it on every scale in the early morning, whilst later in the day, as the water evaporates, little masses, or even crystals, of sugar are to be found. This sugar, either in its liquid or solid form, is very palatable to the ants, which habitually resort to these heads during the period of its secretion. And to preserve it for themselves they resent any invasion from outside. If one of the aforementioned beetles appears they assume a menacing attitude. They hold on to the involucral scales with their last pair of legs and present their fore-legs, abdomen, and powerful jaws to the enemy, as shown in the figure. Thus they remain till the beetle withdraws, if necessary hastening its retreat by squirting formic acid in its direction. Then they quietly begin to feed on the honey again."

Much has yet to be learnt about the relations between British plants and insects in the present connection, and no undoubted case of ant-guards has so far been described. Some of our native trees, however, harbour mites that appear to discharge defensive duties. Scott Elliot (in *Nature Studies*) thus speaks of them:—"Almost any common tree, such as the Lime, Ash, Elm, or Horse-Chestnut, will show on the lower side of the leaves little hairy patches which occupy the forks of the veins. If these are examined in summer with a strong magnifying glass, and stirred up with a pin, very small active . . . mites will be found. They run about quickly, and once seen, can be observed with ease, whenever looked for. The hairy grottoes which they inhabit are often rather neatly formed; but they are difficult to describe. As a rule the colour of the mite is that of the hairs amongst which it lives. These mites come forth at night, and appear to live upon bacteria and upon the spores of fungi, lichens, or algæ. But here again it is not possible to give as exact details as would be desirable." The arrangement described is of special interest, as it appears to be a case of animals defending a plant against other plants lower in the scale.

THE POLLINATION OF FLOWERS BY ANIMALS.—Of all the numerous kinds of relation between plants and animals none has attracted more attention than the one now to be briefly described. So much is this the case that, though of absorbing interest, it is almost in danger of becoming hackneyed. But its study has done much towards revolutionizing the old cut-and-dried method of studying botany, and has caused so many persons to pay some attention to the world of life, that no excuse is made for presenting here a few facts which will be familiar to most readers, especially as the scheme of this work would be incomplete without them.

To understand the meaning of the word "pollination" it is first of all necessary to say something about the structure of flowers. These are concerned with the production of seeds, in each of which is to be found an embryo or plantlet in a dormant state, capable, under favourable conditions, of growing into a new plant. We have elsewhere seen (see vol. iii, p. 335) that in animals the first stage in propagation by means of eggs consists in the fertilization of an egg-cell or ovum by fusion with it of a smaller cell or sperm, the fertilized egg-cell afterwards developing into an embryo. The embryo in a seed has also arisen from an egg-cell, which has been fertilized by material formed in the same flower (self-fertilization) or in some other flower (cross-fertilization). The result in the latter case is better than in the former, since cross-fertilized egg-cells develop into more vigorous embryos, and many floral arrangements are to be explained as means by which cross-fertilization is brought about.

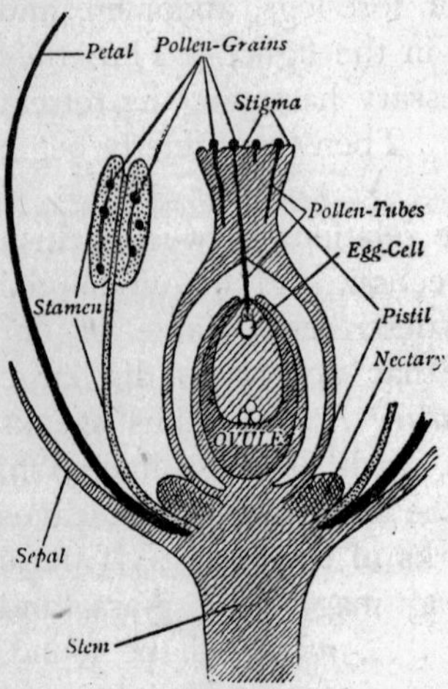

Fig. 1078.—Diagrammatic Section through a Simple Flower

Examination of a typical flower (fig. 1078) shows that it is made up of four sets of structures, all of which are specialized leaves. Beginning at the outside they are as follows:—(1) *Calyx*, consisting of a circlet of *sepals*, which may be green (as in a Buttercup), or brightly coloured (as in a Tulip); (2) *Corolla*, made up of *petals*, which are commonly conspicuous; (3) Thread-like *Stamens*, within the thickened ends (*anthers*) of which is formed the powdery substance, *pollen*, from which the fertilizing living substance is derived; (4) *Pistil*, consisting of one or more *Carpels*, which in the latter case may be either separate or fused together (a single carpel is shown in the figure). The carpels contain a varying number of small bodies known as *Ovules*, destined to become seeds, and the most important part of an ovule is a minute *egg-cell* or *ovum*. On the top of the pistil is a rough and sticky surface, the *Stigma*.

Pollination is a necessary preliminary to fertilization, and consists of the transfer of ripe pollen-grains to the stigma. Supposing this to have been effected, a thread-like *pollen-tube* grows from each grain into the cavity of the carpel until it reaches that part of the ovule where the egg-cell is located. A nucleus-containing fragment of protoplasm (equivalent to a sperm) from the tip of the tube is then transferred to this cell, with which it fuses. The egg-cell, thus fertilized, develops into an embryo, and the rest of the ovule undergoes certain modifications, the total product being a seed.

A stigma may be pollinated by grains developed in the stamens of its own flower (self-pollination), or by grains derived from other flowers (cross-pollination). The latter, since it is followed by cross-fertilization, is the more desirable event, and the actual transfer of pollen from flower to flower is effected by water, wind, or animals, according to the nature of the arrangements which have been evolved. We are here only concerned with animal-pollinated (zoophilous) flowers, and in the large majority of these the agents are insects. Many of the characters of insect-pollinated (entomophilous) flowers have been evolved with reference to the attraction and reception of suitable guests. It was at one time the general belief that the varied odours and hues of flowers came into existence simply and solely for the delectation of mankind; as a matter of fact their significance is utilitarian, and has reference to the needs of plants themselves. For scent and colour are the means employed to attract insects (and sometimes other animals) capable of doing the work of cross-pollination. It is fortunate that the odours generally commend themselves to us, but this is not always so, for certain flowers (*e.g.* some Arums) smell like carrion, the object being to attract those flies which revel in putridity. As to colour there is of course a great variety, and some tints appeal to special visitors. Typical "bee flowers", for example, are commonly reddish-purple, purple, or blue. Other forms depend upon dusk-loving insects, especially moths, for their cross-pollination, and these are white or pale in hue, which gives them the best chance of being seen (fig. 1079).

Such flowers open in the evening, and are then most fragrant. Conspicuousness is often increased by numerous flowers being associated together.

For the entertainment of their insect-guests flowers may provide sweet sap, or produce a great excess of pollen, a highly nutritious substance, or secrete nectar. In highly-specialized forms at least the last sort of food is generally the most important, and is usually produced deep down in the recesses of the flower, often in long spur-like tubes, where it is only accessible to long-tongued insects, such as bees and butterflies.

Fig. 1079.—The Nottingham Catch-Fly (*Silene nutans*) by Night, a flower being visited by a moth (*Dianthœcia albimacula*); the remains of dead creeping insects are seen adhering to the viscid stem

Flowers not only attract guests and provide refreshment, but their whole structure is often modified, it may be in a very complex way, to secure the benefits of cross-pollination, *i.e.* to ensure that pollen which is brought is deposited on the stigma by arriving guests, and make certain that departing guests take with them a fresh supply of the same material.

In many cases the adaptations existing between flower and insect are so perfect as to leave no room for doubt that each has influenced the evolution of the other. Some of the adjustments that have come into existence will best be understood by reference to concrete examples, the first two of which will be taken from the remarkable Orchis Family, the members of this being notable for the great variety of arrangements which they display in relation to insect-pollination. In one large and handsome species (*Phalænopsis Schilleriana*, fig. 1080) the attraction of colour is provided by five spreading leaves, equivalent to sepals and petals, of which the most remarkable (the *labellum*) is one which hangs down from the centre of the flower. It begins in a narrow stalk, but soon broadens into three lobes, of which one curves up on each side, while the third takes a downward course and divides at its end into a couple of curved projections. Just at the place where the stalk expands into lobes a small double projection arises from its upper side, and this serves as a footstool for flies, which are here

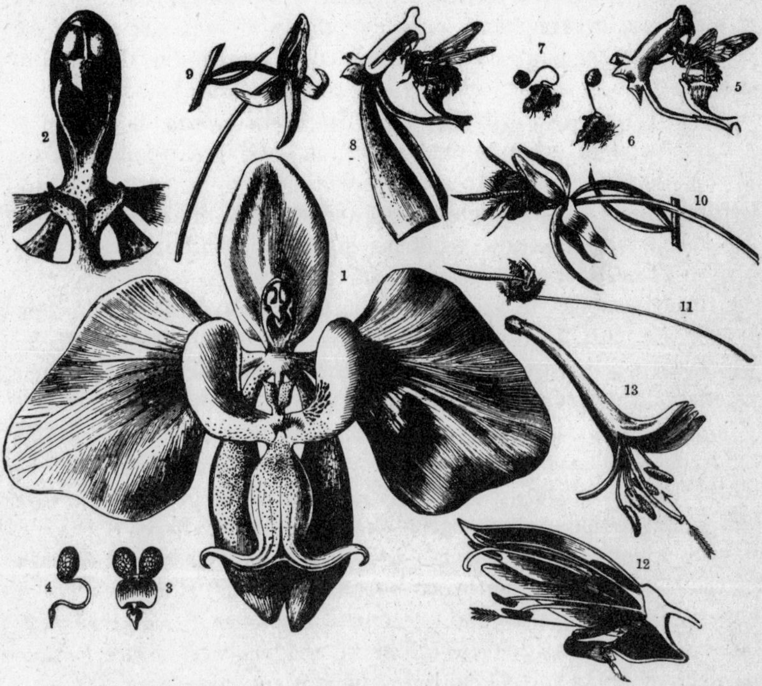

Fig. 1080.—Cross-Pollinated Flowers. 1, Front view of a fly pollinated orchid (*Phalænopsis Schilleriana*); 2, column of same, showing bilobed footstool; 3, pollen-masses of same attached to sticky heart-shaped gland; 4, side view of pollen-masses; 5, side view showing a fly on the footstool; 6, head of the fly with attached pollen-masses; 7, the same after the pollen-masses have bent forwards; 8 (in vertical section), shows a fly introducing pollen-masses to another flower. 9, Flower of the moth-pollinated Lesser Butterfly Orchis (*Habenaria bifolia*); 10, the same, with head of a moth (*Sphinx pinastri*) probing the long spur with its proboscis; 11, head and extended proboscis of the moth. 12, Side view of a bird-pollinated flower (*Melianthus major*) with outer part removed, four stamens and the long curved style are seen; the arrow indicates the way to the honey-containing spur. 13, Flower of a moth-pollinated honeysuckle (*Lonicera Etrusca*) with long honey-containing tube; the arrow shows how to reach this the rounded stigma and stamens must be successively touched. 2, 3, 4, 6, and 7, slightly enlarged; the other figures natural size.

the invited guests. In the middle of the flower, just behind the footstool, may be seen a short projecting "column", the rounded top of which is constituted by a short stamen, immediately beneath this being a deep hollow, the stigma. The pollen is aggregated into two masses (*pollinia*), attached to a little curved plate, which passes below into a heart-shaped sticky knob (*rostellum*) that projects into the cavity of the stigma. If now a fly alights on the footstool and begins to lick up the nectar from the stigma, its head will come into contact with the rostellum, and on leaving the flower it will carry away the pollinia, which very quickly bend forwards. When the fly visits another flower and thrusts its head into the stigma, the sticky surface of this will catch and retain the pollinia, another pair of which will become attached to the head of the insect, to be carried on in their turn to another blossom.

The Lesser Butterfly Orchis (*Habenaria bifolia*, fig. 1080) is a much smaller form native to Britain, and cross-pollinated by Hawk-Moths. A number of whitish very fragrant flowers are borne upon a long upright stalk, and there is here no platform for the arriving guests, as these sip nectar without having to alight. The nectar is contained in a slender spur, the length of which corresponds to that of the unrolled proboscis of the moth. As before, the departing guest carries away the two pollinia, which then bend downwards, and converge together into the exact position necessary to ensure their striking the stigma of the next flower visited. In regard to these movements, and the somewhat different ones made by the pollinia of other species, Darwin remarks (in *Fertilization of Orchids*):—"A poet might imagine that whilst the pollinia were borne through the air from flower to flower, adhering to an insect's body, they voluntarily and eagerly placed themselves in that exact position, in which alone they could hope to gain their wish and perpetuate their race". To this same book of Darwin's are referred those readers who desire further particulars regarding Orchids in the present connection.

The different species of Honeysuckle (*Lonicera*, fig. 1080) are also "moth-flowers", and exhibit three of the leading features just detailed for the Butterfly Orchis, *i.e.* absence of an alighting platform, pale colour, and marked fragrance. But, as in most flowers except Orchids, the pollen is dust-like, and not aggregated into pollinia.

Insects are not the only animals by which cross-pollination is brought about, for in some instances this work appears to be discharged by Snails and Slugs, Birds, or Mammals. In our two native species of Golden Saxifrage (*Chrysosplenium*), snails and slugs are said to be the agents. These plants live in damp places, and possess groups of small greenish-yellow flowers, over which the slimy visitors crawl, transferring the pollen from one blossom to another.

The Humming-Birds of America, and the little Sun-Birds of Africa, which resemble them in appearance, suck nectar while on the wing from certain flowers. Regarding bird-pollinated forms, Scott-Elliot, who made a special study of the subject in South Africa, speaks as follows (in *Nature Studies*):—"Many tropical flowers, such as the Banana, or the beautiful *Lobelia cardinalis*, are visited by the Sun-Birds and Humming-Birds. A great proportion of these flowers have a scarlet colour, and a curved tube which exactly fits the head and beak of the bird. Others, which are visited by these beautiful and lively creatures, have the flowers massed together in large cup-shaped heads, such as the *Proteas*, or Sugarbush of South Africa. The bird stands on the edge of this cup and plunges its beak into the mass of honey flowers which fills it. There are no bird flowers in the British Flora, at least so far as the writer's knowledge goes; but sparrows can be seen to dip their beaks into the heads of the Ragwort, after insects, and it is very likely that the flower-haunting habits of the Sun-Birds began in this way." One of the bird-pollinated African forms (*Melianthus major*) is represented in fig. 1080.

Few observations have been made upon cross-pollination by mammals, but some tropical Bats are supposed to further the transference of pollen, and Kerner suggests that the same kind office is discharged by Kangaroos for Dryandra bushes. The flowers in the latter case are at a suitable height above the ground, and are arranged round the edge of a sort of cup, into which a fluid resembling sour milk trickles down from them. It is not improbable that the little Long-Snouted Phalanger (*Tarsipes rostratus*, see vol. ii, p. 181) transports the pollen of the flowers which it constantly visits.

Prevention of Self-Pollination.—The various arrangements related to cross-pollination have been so evolved that they also, at least for some time, prevent self-pollination. It may be that a particular flower contains stamens only or a pistil only, and these distinct staminate and pistillate flowers may either be on the same plant (*e.g.* Spurges,—*Euphorbia*) or on different plants (*e.g.* Willows,—*Salix*). And even where stamens and pistil are present in the same flower the pollen is commonly produced before the stigma is mature, or, more rarely, the stigma is first ready. Of other kinds of arrangement we may take the common wild Monkey-Musk (*Mimulus luteus*, fig. 1081) as an interesting example. An insect visiting this flower first touches the bilobed stigma, which receives any pollen that the visitor may bring. But the stigma is very sensitive to contact, and immediately closes, almost like a book, remaining in this state for some time. Hence it does not receive from its own flower any of the pollen with which the departing guest has been loaded.

It ought, however, to be stated that some flowers are regularly self-pollinated, while others exemplify a number of most ingenious devices for effecting this as a last resort. The whole structure of

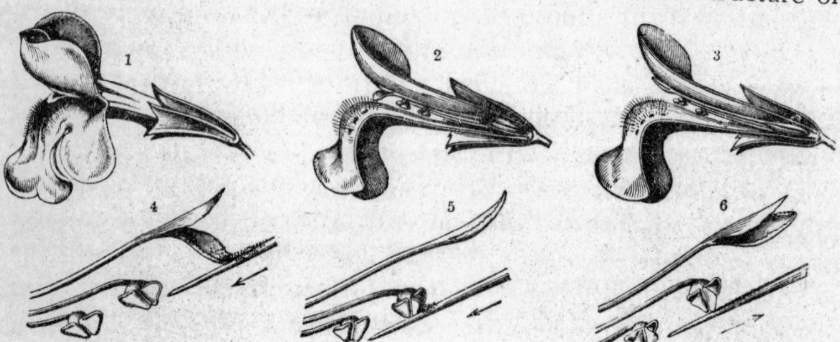

Fig. 1081.—Pollination of Monkey Musk (*Mimulus luteus*). 1, External view of flower; 2, same in longitudinal section, with open stigma; 3, ditto with closed stigma. 4, Pollen is deposited on the lower lip of the stigma by a proboscis passing in the direction of the arrow; 5, the stigma has closed, and the proboscis passing on opens the closed anthers and becomes covered with pollen; 6, proboscis being withdrawn in direction of arrow, but does not deposit pollen on the stigma as this is closed. 1, 2, and 3, natural size; 4, 5, and 6, somewhat enlarged.

a Foxglove flower, for example, is wonderfully adapted to cross-pollination by humble-bees, but after a time the purple corolla falls off, and in so doing drags the stamens attached to it over the stigma, so that this is self-pollinated, and if it has not already received foreign pollen, the egg-cells will be self-fertilized. Full details of this sort of arrangement will be found in Kerner and other botanical works, but would be out of place here. It is perhaps desirable to add that some authorities believe the importance of cross-pollination to have been somewhat exaggerated.

Defences of Flowers against Unbidden Guests.—The animals which are most serviceable as agents of cross-pollination are those capable of carrying pollen from one plant to another, though interchange between flowers on the same plant is beneficial to a lesser degree, and is often the chief kind of crossing which takes place in cases where a considerable number of small flowers are crowded together. The most specialized plants lay themselves out, so to speak, to attract insects with well-marked powers of flight, or in some cases birds, and it may be mammals. These are the "bidden guests". But there are also "unbidden guests" with a liking for nectar, especially wingless insects, such as ants. In many cases these undesirable visitors simply rob the flowers without conferring any benefit. There are also numerous snails and slugs which eat up flowers altogether if they get the chance. It is for all reasons desirable that these useless and dangerous visitors should be kept away. Ogle, in the preface to his translation of a work by Kerner (*Unbidden Guests*), thus presents the matter:—"Now Nature, who at first sight often appears a prodigal, is always found, on closer examination, to be the most rigid of economists. If no insects are to be allured, she gives . . . no nectar; she cuts off the bright petals and suppresses the attractive odours. Nor even when a bait is wanted will she give it one minute sooner than is necessary. The brilliancy, the scent, and the nectar are only furnished when the flower is ready for its guests and requires their presence; just as a thrifty housewife lights her candles when the first guest is at the door. The mature bud is furnished with no such attractions. Still more, even when the flower is mature, when its pollen is ready for transference or its stigma for pollination, when all the allurements are consequently displayed and insects invited to the feast, she still shows her economy. Guests might come who were not of sufficient importance, and the banquet be wasted on them; for it is only when insects have a certain shape, size, or weight that she requires their visits, and can use them profitably for her purposes. She requires, moreover, that they should make their entrance by the main portal, which she has specially adapted to suit their and her requirements. All insignificant and unremunerative visitors, all such, moreover, as would creep in by the back entrance, must be kept out. . . ."

It will be convenient to first describe the chief ways by which wingless insects are kept away from the flowers. One rather curious device is found in some of the Balsams, *e.g.* in a species native to the Himalayan region (*Impatiens tricornis*) which has been carefully studied. Here, as in many other plants, there are little expansions (stipules) at the bases of the leaves, where they join the stem. Of each pair of stipules one is transformed into a nectar-secreting gland (nectary) in the form of a thick curved plate, so situated that insects creeping up the stem are sure to find it. As soon as the Balsam begins to open its flowers nectar is abundantly secreted by these nectaries, and being both abundant and more accessible than that in the flowers, unwelcome guests are diverted from these. Regarding this sweet fluid and its use Kerner makes the following remarks:—"The honey-loving ants lick it up eagerly, and are content not to stray farther upwards. Actual observation shows that the flowers of *Impatiens tricornis* are free from ants, whilst these stipular nectaries are much frequented by them. Their presence in the flowers is very undesirable, since they could readily get at the honey there without touching the pollen or stigma. And more than this, they would not only pilfer the honey, but they would also drive away those winged insects for which the honey is prepared—the welcome guests that pollinate the flowers. We are justified on the facts in regarding this diversion of the unbidden guests as an indirect protection of the floral honey."

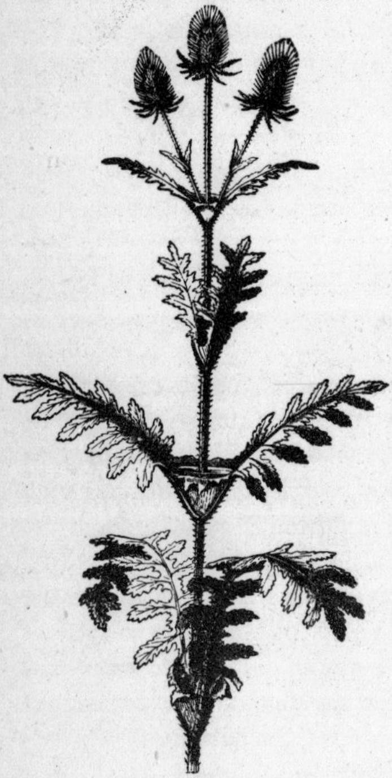

Fig. 1082.—A Teasel (*Dipsacus laciniatus*), showing water-cups formed by fusion of bases of leaves

Insects are not infrequently prevented from reaching the flowers by means of a watery barrier. This is obviously so in the case of water-lilies and other aquatic plants, and may also be observed in some land forms. In Teasels, for example, the leaves are arranged in pairs, the bases of each pair being united together to form a sort of cup, in which water collects, so as completely to surround the stem (fig. 1082).

Slippery surfaces are often present, on which creeping insects can find no foothold. There is sometimes a smooth coating of wax, as in certain Willows, where the catkin-bearing twigs are thus protected. Another interesting case is that of the Snowdrop

(*Galanthus nivalis*, fig. 1083). Here the smooth flower-stalk is bent over, so that the flower hangs down, and a creeping insect trying to reach it is almost certain to fall when it reaches the sharp bend. The nectar secreted in the green grooves of the petals is intended for flying insects. If one of these approaches from below it will first touch the stigma, effecting pollination if it has previously visited another snowdrop. And in getting the nectar it is sure to jolt the stamens, causing a shower of pollen to fall on its back, ready for transfer to other blossoms.

Fig. 1083.—Flower of Snowdrop (*Galanthus nivalis*)

A more drastic method of dealing with creeping insects is found in many plants which exude a sticky fluid, especially in the neighbourhood of the flowers, or actually upon them. Sometimes this is of the nature of latex, as in the Lettuce (*Lactuca sativa*), where the flower-heads are surrounded by overlapping scales from which the milky secretion readily escapes, quickly coagulating into a sticky mass that catches and smothers ants and the like. The flower-stalks of Catch-Flies (see p. 86) and various other forms are covered by a glutinous layer, to which the bodies of trespassers are often found adhering. But more commonly the secretion is poured out by variously-situated glandular hairs. In Plumbago, for instance (fig. 1084), they are borne on the calyx. It would appear that in some instances the captured insects are used as food, after the fashion of the carnivorous plants already described (see p. 68).

Fig. 1084.—Flower of *Plumbago Europæa* (enlarged), showing glandular hairs on the calyx

So far we have dealt with the exclusion of wingless insects, but in the case of large flowers evolved in relation to bees, wasps, butterflies, &c., small-winged insects are equally undesirable visitors, since they steal nectar without effecting cross-pollination. Such forms are altogether excluded, or else made effective by arrangements in the flowers, which Kerner thus describes in general terms (in *The Natural History of Plants*):—"Peculiar folds and cushions, walls and gratings, brushes and thickets of hairs are present, guarding the entrance and rendering access difficult, whilst still allowing it. Large and powerful animals find these obstacles no hindrance, and readily brush them aside; small ones, however, cannot do this, but have to climb over or circumvent the obstacles. And in many cases this enforced divergence by small insects from the direct path brings about the desired result. For, in circumventing these folds and barricades and hairs, they are unconsciously led past the anthers and stigmas, contact with which is unavoidable. Thus, what would otherwise be useless visitants become welcome guests. They are conducted indirectly to the honey by these curious structures, which may, in a sense, be termed 'path-finders'." Cursory examination of such flowers as Foxglove or Pansy will show the presence of barricades of the kind mentioned (see also fig. 1085). Path-finders for the guidance of invited guests are often present in the form of conspicuous colour-streaks, which converge towards the source of nectar. Pansy, Azalea, and Pelargonium are particularly good examples of this.

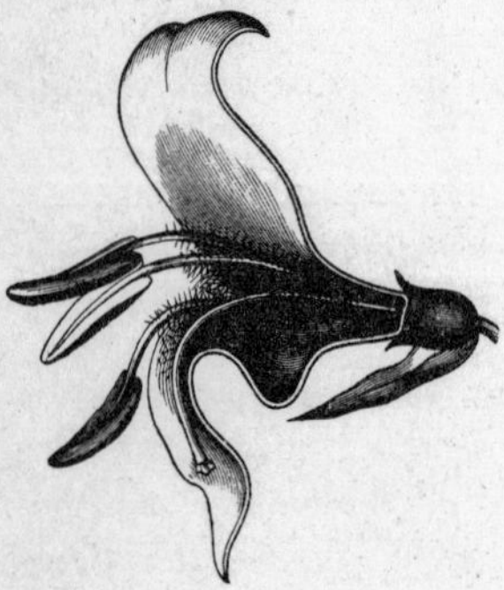

Fig. 1085.—Section through Flower of a Honeysuckle (*Lonicera alpigena*), showing protective tufts of hair; enlarged

The defences and other arrangements which have been evolved in various connections by plants and animals are never completely successful, and with changed surroundings are apt to fail. This applies not only to "mice and men", but also to flowers. Kerner states, for example, that the flowers of some 300 European plants are systematically robbed by humble-bees, which take a short cut to the nectar by biting through the calyx or corolla. The result may be disastrous, for in some of these plants but few seeds are produced, so that they are becoming rare, and in course of time will probably die out altogether. Certain Alpine Catch-Flies (*Silene Pumilio* and *S. Elizabethæ*) are in this evil case. Kerner suggests that such plants date back to a time when there were no, or but few, humble-bees in the region where they now grow, and that they have since failed to evolve means of defence against the new kind of attack.

Wingless enemies of soft-bodied character, especially snails and slugs, are not kept off by smooth surfaces or sticky secretions. But such creatures are easily baffled by prickles, bristles, thorns, and other sharp structures, and these are often found in the neighbourhood of the flowers.

Dispersal of Plants by Animals.—Since the large majority of plants are fixed, means of dispersal are clearly a necessity, as otherwise they would have to struggle for existence with their own offspring. And it is only when numerous individuals of a species are placed in favourable surroundings that the species has any chance of escaping extinction. It is not therefore surprising to find that there are almost innumerable ways by which dispersal is effected. Sometimes the plant itself is the agent, sending out creeping stems above or below ground, or ejecting its fruits, seeds, or spores to a distance by explosive or elastic mechanisms. Currents of air and water are also of great importance in this connection. But we are here only concerned with the chief ways in which animals are pressed into the service of plants for this purpose, or it may be render assistance of more casual kind.

Many of the small plants which float in ponds, such as Duckweeds (*Lemna*) and various algæ, must often cling to the legs of water-birds, and get carried bodily from place to place. And it is noticeable that the buds of somewhat larger aquatic plants, such as Frog-bit and Bladderwort (*Hydrocharis* and *Utricularia*), possess a slimy covering by means of which they readily adhere to the plumage of such birds. Among marine plants a curious means of transit is exemplified by various sea-weeds which certain crabs plant on their backs to make themselves inconspicuous (see vol. ii, p. 287). On the decease of such a crab his little "garden" goes on growing, unless perchance he has been swallowed whole by some predaceous form.

A good many land-plants propagate by means of "offshoots", *i.e.* specialized branches, &c., which grow into new individuals, and cases have been noted where animals assist in the dispersal of such offshoots. Some of the rounded Mexican Cacti (species of *Mammillaria*), for example, produce little spherical shoots studded with barbed bristles, and which are very readily detached from the parent plant. They readily cling to the coats of various mammals and may thus be carried for a considerable distance.

Dispersal of Seeds and Fruits by Animals.—As already explained (p. 85), a seed may be regarded as a matured ovule, in which is contained a dormant plantlet, that has resulted from the fertilization of an egg-cell. The fertilizing process stimulates the growth of various parts external to the ovules, leading to the production of what may broadly be called a "fruit", which for our present purpose may be considered as a seed-carrier. A cherry or plum, for example, is a fruit, within which is a single seed—the "stone". A long account of the different kinds of fruit would be out of place here, but it may be well to add that many are hard and dry, *e.g.* hazel-nuts (of which the "kernels" are the seeds), poppy-"heads", and the so-called "seeds" of Sunflower or Carrot.

The dispersal of seeds in many plants results from the fact that a considerable number of animals are fruit-eaters. And in such cases the seeds being protected by hard coats often escape digestion. It would appear that the attractive colours and palatable qualities of numerous fruits have been evolved with direct reference to this. While still unripe such fruits are inconspicuous and more or less nauseous, but become extremely conspicuous by the time they are ready for consumption, thus advertising their desirable properties as articles of diet. Though monkeys and other fruit-eating mammals no doubt largely assist in plant dispersal, birds seem to play a more important part in the matter. Kerner made a large number of experiments which tend to prove this. He found, for example, that the hard-coated seeds of stone-fruits and berries passed quite uninjured through the bodies of ravens and jackdaws; also that the blackbird, song-thrush, rock-thrush, and robin, which eagerly devour fleshy fruits, throw up the seeds if these are large, as in Barberry and Privet. The fate of small seeds swallowed by the last four birds is thus described by him (in *The Natural History of Plants*):—"Of the fruits and seeds which passed through the intestine of one or other of these birds, 75 per cent germinated in the case of the blackbird, 85 per cent in the case of the thrush, 88 per cent in the case of the rock-thrush, and 80 per cent in the case of the robin. . . . From these experiments it is evident that the dispersal of edible fruits through the agency of thrushes and blackbirds is not, as was formerly supposed, an exceptional phenomenon obtaining in the mistletoe only, but one that may take place in the case of many other plants, and other observations prove that, as a matter of fact, it does take place."

Some animals store up seeds and fruit for future use, and as for various reasons many of these escape being eaten, the storing habit undoubtedly promotes dispersal. Squirrels, jays, and many ants may be cited in illustration. The case of ants is peculiarly interesting. According to Kerner's observations the seeds which prove attractive to these little creatures are those which, although smooth, possess a little rough outgrowth technically known as a "caruncle", as in Violet, Greater Celandine, Snowdrop, Periwinkle, and some Spurges. It is only this caruncle which is eaten, the rest of the seed being left untouched, and capable of germination.

Besides the seeds and fruits which specially appeal to the appetites of animals, there are many others which become attached to their bodies, and are thus effectively dispersed. This may take place without any special adaptations to clinging, as in the case of the floating seeds of many aquatic plants, which adhere to the plumage of birds, or where moist earth containing seeds sticks to the feet of birds or other animals.

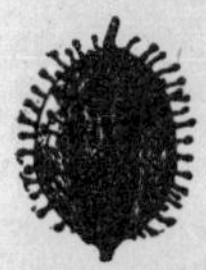

Fig. 1086.—Fruit of *Linnæa borealis* (×5) studded with glandular hairs

There are, however, a large number of fruits and seeds which are either sticky or else studded with hooks, their chances of transport by animals being thus greatly increased. Stickiness results in many cases from exposure to moisture, as in the seeds of Meadow Saffron (*Colchicum*) which have often been observed adhering to the feet of sheep, cattle, and horses. A somewhat more specialized case is afforded by fruits which owe their viscidity to the presence of glandular outgrowths, *e.g. Linnæa borealis* (fig. 1086).

A firmer means of attachment is found in seeds and fruits provided with hooks, and its efficiency would seem to be proved by the fact that about ten per cent of Flowering Plants are provided with such arrangements. They have apparently been evolved, at least in many cases, in relation to the hairy coats of Mammals, for they are particularly characteristic of plants of low stature, with which such animals are likely to come into contact. Many examples are found among the members of our native flora, as everyone who knows the country must have observed. The little globular fruits of the Goosegrass or Cleavers (*Galium aparine*, fig. 1087) are studded with little recurved bristles which prove very effective holdfasts, and the "burrs" of Burdock (*Arctium majus*, fig. 1088) cling with great tenacity to sheep and other animals. Each burr consists of a number of fruits enclosed by a great many narrow scales, each one of which is bent into a hook at its tip. A different but equally effective arrangement is present in Avens (*Geum urbanum*, fig. 1088). The group of fruits is not surrounded by clinging scales, but each is provided with a long hook. In some foreign fruits the holdfasts are of formidable character, and cause much pain to the unfortunate animals which unwillingly promote dispersal. A well-known instance is that of the Harpoon-Plant (*Harpagophytum*) of South Africa, the large fruits of which are covered with stout radiating projections provided with powerful hooks. They are the source of much inconvenience to such animals as antelopes and lions, being said to sometimes cause the death of the latter.

Fig. 1087.—Fruits of Goose-Grass (*Galium aparine*) covered with Hooks; a few of the hooks, magnified, are shown below

Dispersal of Spores by Animals.—Fleshy fungi are eaten by various insects that swallow vast numbers of the minute spores by which such plants propagate, these passing uninjured through their bodies. In some cases flies are attracted by a sweet fluid (as in Ergot, *Claviceps purpurea*), or by evil-smelling moisture that exudes on the spore-producing surface (as in the Stinkhorn, *Phallus impudicus*). Earth-Worms and other burrowing forms no doubt help to disperse the spores of underground fungi, such as truffles. The last-named plants are also eagerly sought and devoured by pigs, with similar results. The dissemination by animals of disease-producing bacteria is too notorious to require emphasizing.

Fig. 1088.—Group of Hooked Fruits of Avens (*Geum urbanum*) is shown to left, with a single fruit on larger scale. On the right is shown a group of the Fruits of Burdock (*Arctium majus*) surrounded by hooked scales.

CHAPTER LXI

ASSOCIATION OF ANIMALS—COLONIES

Having considered the chief sorts of relation which exist between animals and plants, we have now to deal with the association of individual animals, whether of the same or different species. In the sections on Food and Defences (volume ii) one kind of connection has been treated at considerable length, *i.e.* that which links carnivorous (and to some extent omnivorous) forms with their prey, and we have seen that the bodily structure of both attackers and attacked have been more or less perfectly adapted to the exigencies of attack and defence. Another chapter of the same story will engage our attention rather later on, when Animal Parasites receive consideration, but it will be convenient in the meantime to enter into some particulars regarding other kinds of relation.

Animals of the same species may be associated together in three chief ways, conveniently described under the headings of Colonial Animals, Social Animals, and Courtship and Mating of Animals.

COLONIAL ANIMALS

Colonial Animalcules (Protozoa).—The minute and lowly creatures known as Animalcules are distinguished from animals higher in the scale by the fact that they are single cells or units of structure, *i.e.* they are unicellular. They propagate, as a rule, by splitting (fission) or budding (gemmation), and in a number of species the new individuals which thus come into existence remain connected together, forming a *colony* (fig. 1089). The members of such a colony are usually all alike, each of them performing all the duties of life for itself, and species for which this is true have therefore been described as "physiologically unicellular". Most of them are fixed, as, for instance, in Epistylis (fig. 1089), which is closely allied to the common Bell-Animalcule (*Vorticella*), a non-colonial form. And another colonial form (*Codosiga*), represented in the same figure, also has solitary relatives. In cases where a number of units are associated together it is clearly advantageous that there should be a "division of labour", on similar principles to those which have increased

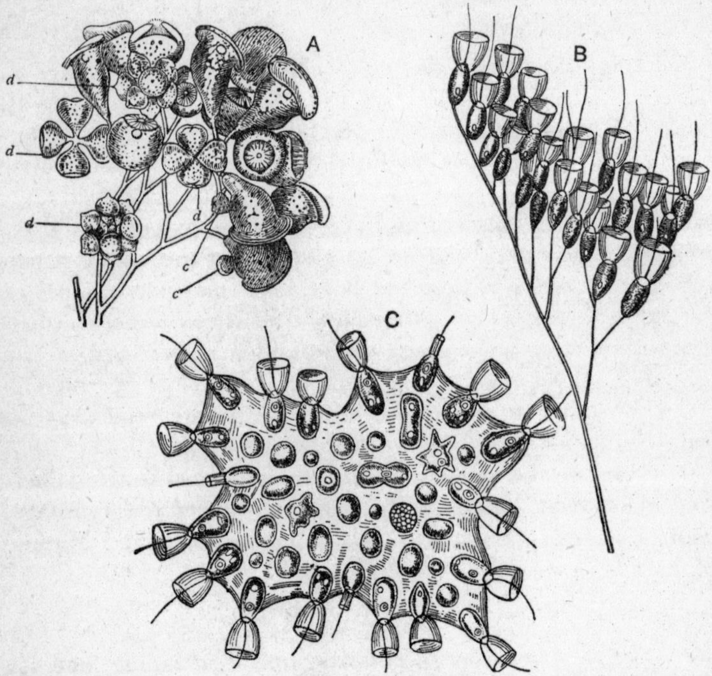

Fig. 1089.—Colonial Animalcules, enlarged to various scales. A, *Epistylis*; *c*, *c*, small individuals conjugating with large ones; *d*, *d*, *d*, *d*, individuals undergoing fission. B, *Codosiga*. C, *Proterospongia*.

the output and improved the quality of manufactured articles. There are certain colonial Animalcules which exhibit an early stage in division of "physiological" labour. Of this an excellent example has already been given (see vol. iii, p. 333) in Volvox, where some members of the colony become specialized in connection with propagation by means of eggs. As another instance we may take Proterospongia (fig. 1089), which consists of numerous individuals imbedded in a gelatinous substance. Some of these are charged with the duty of securing food for the colony, and the projecting end of each such individual is surrounded by a "collar" from the centre of which springs a thread (flagellum) which executes lashing movements. Within the jelly are other amœba-like individuals, which divide actively, some of the products of division serving to increase the size of the colony, while others are probably liberated to found fresh communities. Proterospongia is of special interest, as it suggests the way in which Sponges have possibly been evolved from simpler animals, for it is characteristic of Sponges that the spaces within their bodies should be more or less lined with "collar cells" that strikingly resemble the collar-provided individuals of the colonial Animalcule just described.

All forms higher in the scale than the Protozoa are collectively known as Many-celled Animals or Metazoa. In any one of these, *e.g.* a Zoophyte, a Worm, or a Mollusc, the body is a more or less complex community of cells, exemplifying in various degree the principle of division of physiological labour, with accompanying specialization. And there can be little doubt that these cell-communities have been gradually evolved from colonial Protozoa. This view has been discussed to some extent in an earlier section (see vol. iii, p. 333).

Colonial Sponges (Porifera).—In this group of animals the colonial condition is the rule, a colony being produced by the budding or incomplete fission of an original individual. Sometimes the members of a community are fairly distinct (see vol. iii, p. 343), but in other cases it is difficult or even impossible to say where one ends and others begin. The absence of sharp boundary-lines between adjacent individuals is well exemplified by a very common British species, the Crumb-of-bread Sponge (*Halichondria panicea*), which may be seen as an encrustation of light-brown colour on rocks near low-tide mark.

Colonial Zoophytes (Cœlenterata).—Vegetative propagation by means of budding or fission is very characteristic of members of this large group, and the buds or fission-products commonly remain united together to form colonies, of which the members are usually clearly marked off from one another. They are united together by what may be termed a "common flesh" (cœnosarc), and their digestive cavities all communicate with a more or less complex system of canals by which this is traversed. It therefore follows that food taken in and digested by one individual may benefit other members of the same community, a fact which has had much to do with the course of evolution in certain species. Reference should be made to vol. i, pp. 474–481, where some of the Colonial Zoophytes are figured and described, and also to vol. iii, pp. 327–328, for a brief account of the life-histories of such colonies. We are here only concerned with the characteristic features of colonial life, and it will be convenient to consider separately the two sub-groups of Sea-Flowers (*Anthozoa*) and Hydroids (*Hydrozoa*).

Colonial Sea-Flowers (*Anthozoa or Actinozoa*).—To students of the British fauna the most familiar Sea-Flowers are the solitary forms known as Sea-Anemones, which abound on our shores. But in warmer parts of the globe Corals are equally abundant, and these may be either solitary or colonial. The former, or cup-corals, may be compared to anemones, but the lower part of the body is supported by a limy skeleton, while the latter may be regarded as colonies of cup-corals, and present wide variations in shape, according to the mode of growth. In the majority of cases the members of the colony are all alike (fig. 1090), but this is not invariably the case. For in some of the Eight-rayed Sea-Flowers (*Octactinia*), *e.g.* the Sea-Pen (*Pennatula*), some of them are devoid of tentacles, and participate neither in active feeding nor in the production of egg-cells. Their special duty appears to be that of promoting breathing by setting up currents of sea-water which circulate through the fleshy substance of the colony. Ciliary action is the agency employed.

Fig. 1090.—Small Colony of a Coral (*Astroides calycularis*)

Hydroids (*Hydrozoa*).—The branching or encrusting colonies known as Hydroid Zoophytes exemplify division of labour more or less. As we have elsewhere seen, some of the individuals are specially concerned with egg-propagation, and these may be liberated as little free-swimming jelly-fish or medusæ (see vol. iii,

p. 350). This, however, is not the only possibility, as will be seen by reference to fig. 1091, which represents a small part of a species of hydroid (*Aglaophenia*). In addition to the ordinary members of the colony, each provided with mouth and tentacles, there are two kinds of small mouthless individuals. One of these is in the form of a slender thread, which can be stretched out to some little distance, and is possessed of a thickened sticky tip. It acts as a food-catcher, ensnaring small animals to be swallowed and digested by its larger fellows for the benefit of the community. The other kind of mouthless individual is somewhat stouter, and richly provided at its free end with "batteries" of stinging-cells, capable of dealing effectively with larger prey, or warding off the attacks of enemies. When these fighting individuals are called into action, the other members of the colony can be withdrawn into the little cups that surround their bases, being thus out of harm's way.

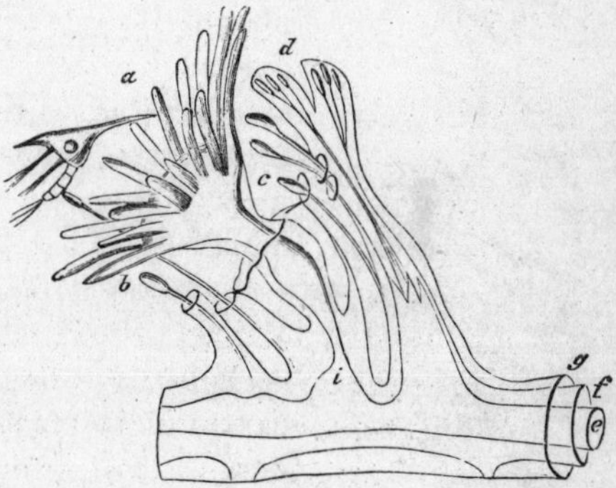

Fig. 1001.—Small part of a Colony of *Aglaophenia*, enlarged

a, Ordinary individual: *b*, *c*, food-catchers, between them another is seen capturing a crustacean larva; *d*, fighting individual; *e*, digestive cavity of colony; *f*, outer layer of body; *g*, horny investment.

An extreme case of division of labour is presented by the free-swimming colonies of Hydroids known as Compound Jelly-Fish (Siphonophora), which have probably been evolved from simple medusæ by a process of budding (see vol. i, p. 481). The shape of the colony depends upon the way in which this process has been effected. Sometimes the buds have arisen from the "umbrella" of the original medusa, or they may have grown from the walls of the mouth-bearing "handle". The chief kinds of individual that have been thus produced are represented diagrammatically in fig. 1092. The umbrella of the original medusa loses its function as a swimming organ and becomes a float, while (in the case represented) the handle, of which part only is shown, carries a variety of members which contribute in various ways to the common weal of the community. Some are swimming-bells which, by alternately opening and closing, effect propulsion through the water. Others are transformed into fishing-lines that catch food, and at the same time are so well provided with stinging-cells as to effectively keep off enemies. There are also digestive individuals, which devour and digest the animals caught by the fishing-lines. Some members are reduced to tentacles, ministering to the sense of touch (and possibly smell); others again are in the form of protective plates, covering and sheltering adjacent individuals. And there are also egg-producing members of the colony which may be liberated as little medusæ, thus promoting dispersal. In different species there are considerable variations in detail, and the actual arrangements in one case (*Stephalia corona*) are shown in fig. 1093.

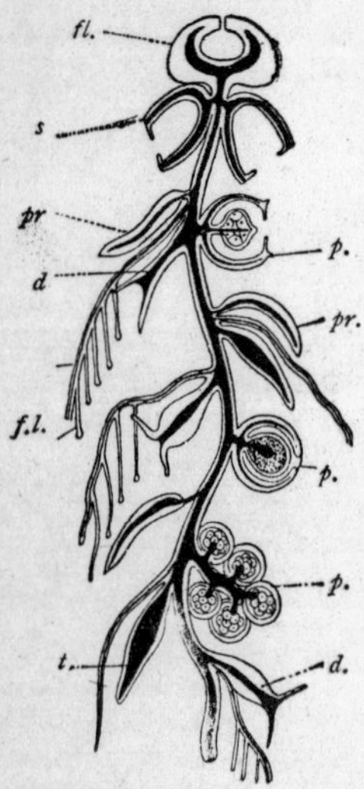

Fig. 1092.—Diagram of various individuals in a colony of Compound Jelly-Fish (*Siphonophora*), central cavity of colony indicated in black. *fl*, Float; *s*, swimming-bell; *d*, *d*, digestive individuals; *f.l.*, branched fishing-line; *pr*, protective individual; *p*, *p*, *p*, various forms of propagative individual; *t*, tentacle.

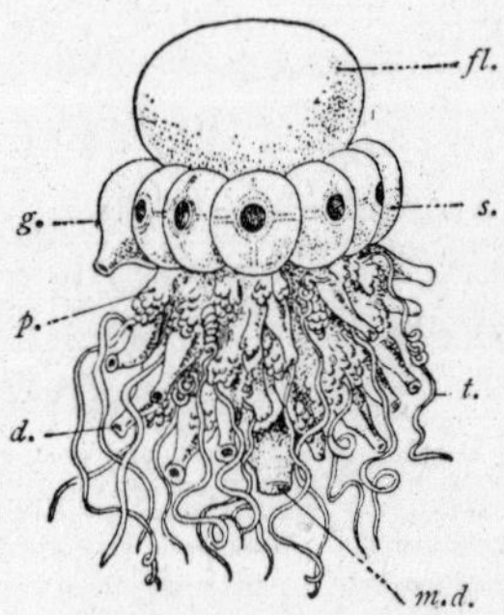

Fig. 1093.—A Compound Jelly-Fish (*Stephalia corona*), reduced. *fl*, Float; *s*, swimming-bell; *g*, gas-conducting individual; *d*, small digestive individual; *m.d.*, large central digestive individual; *t*, tentacle; *p*, group of small propagative individuals.

Colonial Moss-Polypes (Polyzoa).—With a single exception the members of this group produce colonies by budding, after the fashion of Hydroid Zoophytes, for which they are sometimes mistaken, though in reality much higher in the scale. Some of the members of such a colony may be greatly specialized for various purposes (fig. 1094), *e.g.* they may be modified into rounded receptacles (ovicells) in which the eggs develop till the time of hatching. In certain species there are bird's-head individuals, which execute vigorous snapping movements, the object of which is extremely doubtful. Cleanliness is possibly promoted, or perhaps the attacks of small parasitic forms may thus be warded off. It has also been noticed that the powerful jaws often succeed in catching little worms, crustaceans, &c., apparently holding them tenaciously till they die and decompose. The suggestion has been made that the decayed fragments of these victims are carried by ciliary action into the mouths of the unmodified members of the colony, thus serving as food. But there is no definite proof that such is the case. Individual Moss-Polypes may also undergo still greater modification into whip-like threads that actively lash about in all directions. Cleanliness and defence have here again been suggested as the ends to be served, and cases have been observed where the action is so vigorous as to move the entire colony about. That the surrounding water should be thoroughly stirred up is probably advantageous with reference both to feeding and breathing. The only thing, however, that we definitely know about these curious structures is, that they have been evolved from bird's-head individuals by suppression of the "head", and prolongation of the "lower jaw" into a slender filament.

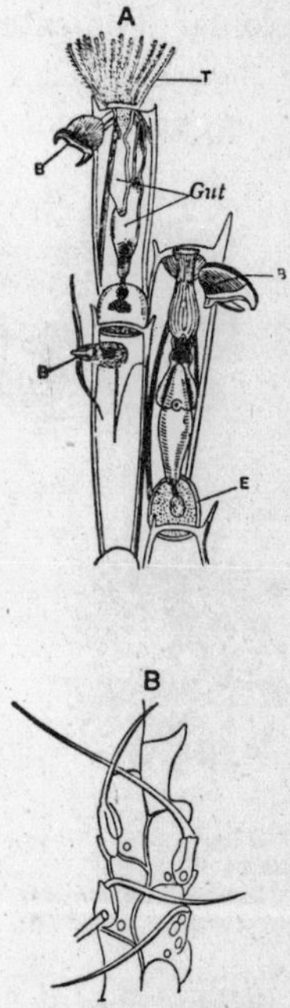

Fig. 1094.—Parts of Colonies of Moss-Polypes, enlarged. A, *Bugula*; B, B, B, bird's-head individuals (one holding a small worm); E, ovicell; T, tentacles of an ordinary individual. B, *Scrupocellaria*, showing three whip-shaped individuals.

Colonial Tunicates (Urochorda).—The formation of colonies is clearly related to powers of increase by means of budding or fission, and consequently all the members of certain animal groups devoid of such powers, *e.g.* Arthropods and Molluscs, are non-colonial. This is also true for the vast majority of Backboned Animals, the most notable exception being afforded by many species of the lowly and degenerate forms known as Sea-Squirts, Tunicates, or Ascidians. Most of these are fixed to some firm object when adult, and their sedentary life has no doubt had much to do with the degeneration they have undergone (see vol. iii, p. 421). A good many Tunicates are non-colonial or "solitary", but others bud to produce colonies of various shape. In such species the individual members may be borne on a creeping stem and clearly marked off from one another, much as in a hydroid zoophyte, or the association may be much more intimate. In the latter case the individuals are sunk within a sort of common body (like the cœnosarc of colonial corals), and there is a continuous protective investment or common test. A good instance is afforded by Botryllus (fig. 1095), to be found at low tide on our coasts as a sort of bluish encrustation on sea-weeds and stones. It presents at regular intervals a number of flower-like markings, each of which is made up of a circlet of individuals, with their mouths near the tips of the "petals". A small hole in the centre of the flower leads out of a cavity ("common cloaca") into which are discharged the waste products of the members of the group. The surface population of the sea is also partly made up of colonial Tunicates. The Salps, for instance, present two stages in their life-history, one of which propagates by budding, the other by eggs (see vol. iii, p. 422). A large number of the latter stage are connected together when young into "chains", which may be regarded as temporary colonies. These ultimately break up into their constituent members. A notable example of a permanent free-swimming Tunicate colony is afforded by the Fire-Cylinder (*Pyrosoma*, fig. 1095), abundant in the Mediterranean and elsewhere, and giving off a bright phosphorescent light, possibly as a means of protection. The colony is shaped like a hollow cylinder which, in one large species (*Pyrosoma gigantea*), may be as much as 5 feet long, and possesses a contracted aperture at one end, the other being closed. The external surface is covered with pointed projections of the firm test. The small but very numerous individuals are imbedded transversely in the wall of the cylinder, their mouths being external. The large central cavity receives all the products of waste, and is comparable to the common cloaca of a Botryllus circlet. The size of the colony is augmented by budding, and eggs are also produced, which develop into minute colonies that are liberated into the surrounding water, there to grow to their full size.

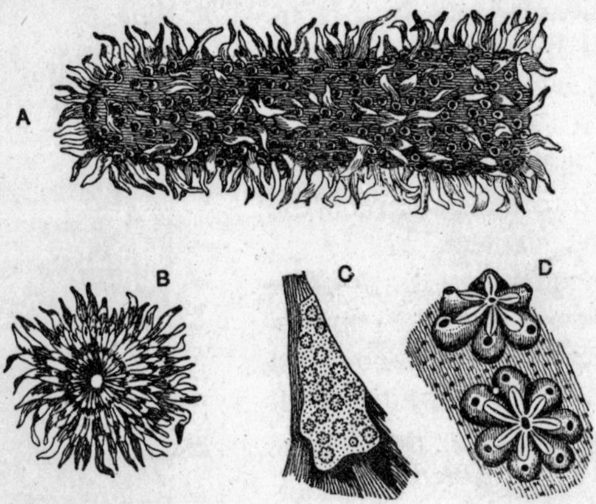

Fig. 1095.—A, Fire-Cylinder (*Pyrosoma*) in side view, the small rounded areas are the mouths of members of the colony. B, Open end of same. C, Small colony of *Botryllus*, showing circlets of individuals. D, Two circlets, enlarged.

CHAPTER LXII

ASSOCIATION OF ORGANISMS—SOCIAL BACKBONELESS ANIMALS (INVERTEBRATA).

Many animals are social or gregarious, and in such cases division of labour between the members of a community is more or less perfectly exemplified. The mere fact that many individuals of the same species live together in the same place does not entitle them to be termed social, in the sense here intended, unless there is some sort of co-operation which benefits the animals living together. It would hardly be justifiable, for example, to describe oysters, cockles, or star-fishes, as colonial animals. But even here the species may be benefited, *e.g.* weakly individuals are weeded out in the keen struggle for existence, so that the stock becomes increasingly healthy and strong. And from such casual kinds of association communities of very complex kind have gradually been evolved, the benefits to be derived from division of labour between individuals giving various species a greatly improved chance of survival in the competition with other species. But here a qualification must be made. For in the world of organisms, by the irony of fate, an extreme penalty attaches to elaborate specialization resulting from adjustment to the exigencies of a certain set of conditions. The surroundings of animals (and plants) are constantly changing, and if these alter suddenly, as they are liable to do, a well adapted species may be unable to adjust itself with sufficient rapidity to the new order of things, and hence be doomed to extinction, while simpler but more plastic forms may survive. Many lowly organisms have endured through countless ages, while others of more complex kind have quickly succumbed to rapid alterations of their environment at a time when their continued dominance seemed most certain. Innumerable instances of this far-reaching principle are to be drawn from the geological record, which preserves for us the past history of the globe.

The most interesting cases of the social habit are to be found among Insects and Backboned Animals, which it will be well to consider separately.

SOCIAL INSECTS (INSECTA)

Some of the most remarkable facts in natural history have been made known by those who have studied the complex communities existing among various species of Membrane-Winged Insects (Hymenoptera) and Net-winged Insects (Neuroptera). The extent to which division of labour is carried varies greatly in different cases, so that we are able to get some notion of the successive stages which have marked the evolution of the social habit.

SOCIAL MEMBRANE-WINGED INSECTS (HYMENOPTERA).—The most salient point distinguishing highly organized communities of Bees, Wasps, and Ants is the presence of a varying number of "castes" or kinds of individual. In the Honey-Bee (*Apis mellifica*), for instance, a hive contains not only males (drones) and an egg-producing female (queen), but also numerous "workers", which are a second kind of female, having nothing to do with the production of eggs, but, as their name indicates, labouring for the benefit of the republic. And in other cases there may be more than three castes, as we shall see in the sequel. Worker honey-bees differ markedly in size and structure from the queen, as the result of a long course of evolution, and it will be desirable to begin with simpler communities, where such sharp distinctions do not exist.

BEES.—Some account has already been given of Carpenter-Bees, Mason-Bees, and Leaf-cutting Bees, solitary forms in which the female not only lays eggs but also makes and stores a nest (see vol. iii, p. 390). These and many other non-colonial insects exhibit very elaborate adaptations to their surroundings, and it would be a mistake to consider them as necessarily lower in the scale than colonial forms, which have evolved on entirely different lines. Here, as in all other cases, success in the struggle for existence may be attained in widely different ways.

From the purely solitary life led by the bees above-mentioned, we pass to a curious case described by Fabre (from his observations in South France), where a certain amount of co-operation is associated with a large amount of independence. The case is that of certain rather small "short-tongued" bees (species of *Halictus*), which are represented in the British fauna. There are here no workers, but by the united labours of a number of females a branching underground passage is dug out at night, there being a single opening to the exterior, and close to this an enlargement or "hall" for the greater convenience of individuals wishing to pass one another. Within this underground home each female makes her own particular nest, consisting of ovoid waterproof cells, and attends to her domestic duties after the fashion of solitary species. A sentinel is said to be posted at the common opening of the burrow, so that some understanding would seem to be arrived at in the matter of mounting and relieving guard. But, apart from this, the individuals living together have no more social organization than the different families occupying a dwelling made up of a set of "flats", who use a common stair and the same street door. If the said families had constructed these by their joint efforts the analogy would be more complete.

The last example is a sort of side-branch in social evolution; for a comparatively simple case in the direct series of adaptations we may turn to the large insects familiarly known as Humble-Bees (species of *Bombus*), which are well represented in our own country, and live above or under the ground in communities which endure for a single year only. They exemplify the beginning of the caste-system, for in addition to males there are three varieties of the opposite sex, *i.e.* queens, small females, and workers, which in appearance and structure resemble one another pretty closely. We do not find the same marked differences that exist between the queen and worker in honey-bees, while the power of egg-laying is not restricted to the queen, though she is the mother of most of the members of the community. The habits of several species have been closely observed, and the succession of events is somewhat as follows. A queen which has survived the winter begins her work as foundress of a society when the spring is well advanced, and food in the form of nectar and pollen is abundant. Selecting a sheltered spot, on the surface or below the ground according to the species, she successively constructs two or three large waxen cells, the material for which is derived (as in social bees generally) from a number of small glands that open on the under side of her abdomen: a proportion of pollen being added. When a cell is of full size it is lined with a mixture of pollen and honey, several eggs are laid in it, and a roof is put on. After several days' rest the next cell is made, and stocked in the same way. About the time that the second cell is completed duties of another kind are added to the tale of work. For, meanwhile, the eggs first laid have hatched out, and the bee-grubs, having exhausted their scanty store of provisions, require feeding. To do this their mother bites a hole in the enclosing cell, and supplies honey from her mouth as required. Here, and in other cases, the "honey" is not the same thing as the "nectar" found in flowers. A bee swallows the latter, taking it into a crop or "honey-bag", into which the gullet dilates. Within this receptacle it undergoes a kind of fermentation by which it is converted into honey. So far the life-history is much like that of a solitary form, all the work being done by the mother. But in the next stage division of labour begins to play an important part. The full-fed grubs spin silken cocoons, and pass into the quiescent or pupa stage, from which they emerge as "workers". By gnawing away the wax the queen assists their escape from the enclosing cell. As workers become numerous they justify their name by undertaking the labours of building and storing, ultimately enabling the queen to devote herself entirely to egg-laying. For each egg a separate cell is constructed. As the community increases in size small females may be produced, and towards autumn larger "drone cells" are made, and still larger "queen cells". It is stated that these are not stored with food, the corresponding grubs being from the first assiduously nursed by the workers. By the time that drones and queens are mature the community has attained its full size, and may consist of from 300 to 400 individuals, under favourable circumstances. The pairing of the young queens in the course of a nuptial flight constitutes the climax of the year's drama, for as winter approaches the temporary community becomes disintegrated. All the workers and drones perish, together with many of the queens, but some of the latter live through the winter in a torpid state to found fresh societies the following spring. It should be added to this account that when the community is in full working order special unclosed cells are made, to be stored with honey or pollen for general use. These "honey tubs" and "pollen tubs" serve as a larder, which is constantly being replenished during fine weather, to be drawn upon when it is wet. Old brood-cells may be enlarged for the same purpose, but are never put to their original use a second time.

For one species of Humble-Bee (*Bombus ruderatus*) a remarkable arrangement has been described. It is said that in every nest one bee is told off as a "trumpeter". This individual sounds *reveillé* at from 3 to 4 a.m., rousing her fellows to the labours of the day, and if removed is replaced by another. The habit of storing food, existing to some extent in Humble-Bees, is carried much further in the Honey-Bee (*Apis mellifica*) and its numerous relatives, and has probably had much to do with the evolution of the complex social life which these exhibit. It enables a community to live on through the unfavourable season of the year, thus becoming permanent, and this continuity has rendered possible division of labour to a greater degree, being at the same time associated with well-marked differences between the castes, so far as queen and workers are concerned. The former is of comparatively large size, and her only duty is to produce eggs, while the varied labours of the hive fall to the lot of her smaller sisters. The community is only temporary as regards the drones, none of which survive the winter, but are replaced by a fresh set which hatch out the following year. A few further details regarding the Honey-Bee will be given in a later section.

The Social Wasps (*Vespidæ*) live in communities which, so far as at present known, exist for one season only, as in Humble-Bees, to which they present a further resemblance in the fact that the workers are not markedly unlike the queen, and are more or less capable of laying eggs. The building-material, however, is not wax but a sort of paper, made by chewing woody matter and mixing it with a fluid secreted by certain glands of the mouth-region. We may take to illustrate the annual cycle one of three British species (*Vespa Germanica*, fig. 1096) in which the nest is constructed underground. The foundress queen begins work in spring, making a small number of cells in the place which is to be the top of the nest, and depositing an egg in each. The cells are neither stored nor closed. Her next task consists in feeding the grubs as they hatch out, first with honey or fruit-juice, and later with the bodies of insects, especially flies. By means of her strong jaws she removes the hard parts of the prey, chewing up the rest into a kind of mince-meat adapted to the tender digestions of her offspring. When they have reached their full size the grubs spin cocoons and pass into the pupa stage, from which they emerge as worker wasps about four weeks after the date when the eggs were laid. Without loss of time these take over the work of building and nursing, and even feed their mother, who soon has nothing to do but lay eggs in the cells as they are constructed. The complete nest consists of a series of combs, connected by little pillars, and the building operations are carried on from above downwards. Each comb is made up of a large number of roughly hexagonal cells, the mouths of which are directed downwards. Towards the end of summer cells of larger size are made, in which queens and drones are reared, but many of the latter are brought up in the ordinary small cells. After mating has taken place the community is soon broken up; most of the insects die, but some of the queens survive the winter, and found the communities of the following year. Wasps appear to be extremely sensitive to cold, and it is perhaps partly for this reason that the nest is surrounded with a covering made up of layers of paper (see fig. 1096).

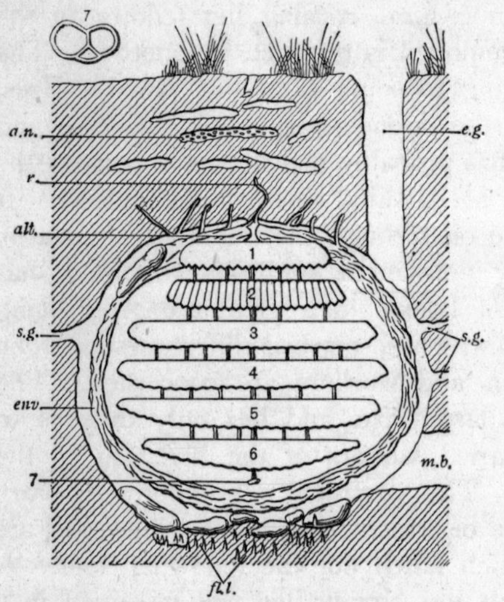

Fig. 1096.—Section through Nest of a Social Wasp (*Vespa Germanica*), rather less than ¼ natural size

e.g., Entrance gallery; *s.g.*, side galleries; 1–7, combs connected by pillars (7 above main figure shows arrangement of the three cells of the youngest comb); *env.*, papery envelope of nest; *r.*, root to which first foundation is attached (other roots with secondary attachments also shown); *a.n.*, part of an ant's nest; *fl.l.*, larvæ of a fly; *m.b.*, mole burrow.

The nests of many species of social Wasp are suspended from plants, while the Hornet (*Vespa crabro*) prefers to build in a hollow tree. There is a large amount of variation as to size, shape, and durability, while in some cases earth is added to the ordinary building material.

The social habits of Ants are even more complex than those of Bees and Wasps, and some account has already been given of the way in which the members of certain species procure and store food (see vol. ii, pp. 103 and 206). There is no more fascinating department in the whole realm of natural history than the study of ant life, for these little creatures live in a wonderland which is all their own. The elaboration of some of their communities is very considerable, and the welfare of the individual is rigorously subordinated to the interests of the species. Some of the more salient points are thus ably summarized by Sharp (in *The Cambridge Natural History*):—"Observation has revealed most remarkable phenomena in the lives of these insects. Indeed, we can scarcely avoid the conclusion that they have acquired in many respects the art of living together in societies more perfectly than our own species has, and that they have anticipated us in the acquisition of some of the industries and arts that greatly facilitate social life. The lives of individual ants extend over a considerable number of years—in the case of certain species at any rate,—so that the competence of the individual may be developed to a considerable extent by exercise; and one generation may communicate to a younger one by example the arts of living by which it has itself profited. The prolonged life of ants, their existence in the perfect state at all seasons, and the highly social life they lead are facts of the greatest biological importance, and are those that we should expect to be accompanied by greater and wider competence than is usually exhibited by Insects. There can indeed be little doubt that ants are really not only the 'highest' structurally or mechanically of all insects, but also the most efficient. There is an American saying that the ant is ruler of Brazil. We must add a word of qualification; the competence of the ant is not like that of man. It is devoted to the welfare of the species rather than to that of the individual, which is, as it were, sacrificed or specialized for the benefit of the community. The distinctions between the sexes in their powers or capacities are astonishing, and those between the various forms of one sex are also great. The difference between different species is extreme; we have, in fact, the most imperfect forms of social evolution coexisting, even locally, with the most evolute. These facts render it extremely difficult for us to appreciate the ant; the limitations of efficiency displayed by the individual being in some cases extreme, while observation seems to elicit contradictory facts. About two thousand species are already known, and it is pretty certain that the number will reach at least five thousand."

The caste-system is well-marked among Ants, and there are at least three sorts of individual, males, queens, and workers or modified females. The two former are commonly winged, and pairing usually takes place in the air. After this has been accomplished the males soon die, while the females cast, or it may be bite off, their wings, and enter upon their further duties. In some species the male alone possesses wings, while it more rarely happens that the contrary is true. Cases are also known where both kinds of male exist in the same species, the female being winged, or both kinds of female are associated with winged males. There may also be distinct castes of workers, one consisting of large individuals (workers major), and the other or others of small ones (workers minor). In many cases, too, there is a caste of "soldiers" distinguished by the great size of their mandibles. Like workers they are modified females. To all intents and purposes, indeed, the societies of Ants, like those of Bees and Wasps, are female republics. The "queen", it is true, has all her wants attended to by the workers, but does not actively direct the affairs of the community, having no special authority. The care bestowed upon her, indeed, would appear to be simply in recognition of the fact that she is necessary for the continuance of the society. In ant-societies there may be more than one queen. There appears to be no doubt that these insects are able to communicate certain kinds of information to one another. Indeed, without some power of communication there would be endless confusion in a large community. As it is, we find that foraging expeditions, warfare, and the complex economy of the nest are all carried out in an orderly fashion. In human societies even republics require some sort of government for the direction of individual efforts, but this often appears not to be the case here. The armies of our native species, for example, so far as we know, are entirely made up of rank and file, without officers and non-commissioned officers. Yet such an army often seems to conduct its campaigns strategically, and deals very effectively with tactical problems which arise after it has taken the field. How this is possible we are not yet able to say, for our own mental powers have been evolved on very different lines. There is certainly a basis of instinct, *i.e.* inherited capability of doing certain things on impulse when appropriate occasions present themselves; but since individual ants profit largely by experience, we may also say without hesitation that many of their actions are intelligent. There can be little doubt that young workers receive a practical education in their duties, learning by example if not by precept. If so, we have a very convincing proof of marked intelligence. Where, as in some tropical ants, there are numerous castes, the mental life of the community is probably more complex, but comparatively few observations have been made on this difficult subject.

The early stages in the formation of societies have been observed in some species, and are probably substantially the same in all. A foundress queen lays her first batch of eggs, and carefully tends the larvæ when they hatch out, until they pass into the pupa stage, from which they emerge as workers, who at once concern themselves with the industrial work of the young community. The queen is therefore soon able, as in the ordinary social wasps and bees, to restrict herself solely to the duty of egg-laying. One important point in the domestic economy of all ant-societies may here be mentioned. Special cells of paper or wax are not constructed for the reception of eggs, as in Bees and Wasps, but these are deposited in chambers, variously situated, according to the species. It is further to be noted that the larva may or may not spin a cocoon before passing into the pupa state. When a cocoon is made it is removed by the workers at the proper time, so as to facilitate the escape of the perfect insect.

There is a large amount of variation as to the number of individuals contained in an ant-society. This is very large in most of the kinds which have been carefully studied, and it is naturally so in cases where the social life is very complex. Simple instances are afforded by some of the Indian Ants (species of *Polyrhachis*), where a single queen and less than a dozen workers live together in a little one-chambered dwelling that looks almost like a miniature bird's-nest, and is constructed of a papery substance with a lining of silk. These small homes are found on leaves, and are commonly so placed or made as to be inconspicuous. Another sort of Asiatic Ant (*Œcophylla smaragdina*) lives in larger communities upon foliage, of which the leaves are converted into dwellings in a very remarkable manner. The workers roll them up and fix their edges together by means of a viscid fluid derived from the silk-glands opening near the mouths of the larvæ. A worker engaged in this task holds a larva firmly in her jaws, and holds it to the required spot, using it in fact as a living gum-bottle.

Some of the leading features in the communal life of a large society of the industrious insects under discussion may be learnt from the study of our largest native species, the reddish-coloured Wood-Ant or Horse-Ant (*Formica rufa*). It abounds in the fir-woods of our southern counties, where the large "ant-hills" which it constructs are conspicuous objects. The winged males and females are not far short of half an inch in length, and there are two kinds of worker, which are respectively about one-fourth, and from one-fifth to one-sixth of an inch long. The nest may be nearly three feet high and some eighteen feet round at its base, and is made up of fir-needles, together with all sorts of plant fragments. The vicinity of the nest is trodden down into a number of "ant-roads", which are the scene of much busy going and coming. The larger workers are principally concerned, when outside the nest, with collecting building materials, while an important duty of the smaller workers is to collect the "honey-dew" of aphides, insects which are often picturesquely described as "ant-cows". The substance in question is a sugary fluid that exudes in considerable amount from the intestines of these little creatures, and is eagerly swallowed by the workers, a great deal of it passing into their dilated crops. Having filled themselves up with this desirable food, the workers hurry back to the nest, and obligingly distribute some of their store for the benefit of the larvæ, and their adult friends who have meanwhile been engaged with the internal economy of the nest. There are no special receptacles corresponding to the honey-tubs of humble-bees or comb-cells of ordinary bees, for storage of what is not immediately needed. Indeed none of our native ants indulge in the luxury of a larder, and remain in a torpid condition during the winter. The food is by no means limited to honey-dew, but is of very mixed nature, for caterpillars, various adult insects, and miscellaneous vegetable matter all figure in the bill of fare. There is a constant return of foraging parties to the central home (fig. 1097).

The ant-hill is literally riddled with labyrinthine galleries expanding at intervals into rounded chambers, and for some depth the underlying ground is mined with passages continuous with those above. It is easier to destroy an ant-hill than to get any clear idea of its internal economy, but J. G. Wood (in *Insects at Home*) thus describes a very ingenious device by which he was enabled to gain some knowledge of the kind:—"I have, however, succeeded in obtaining an excellent view into the interior of a Wood-Ants' nest, though it was but a short one. Accompanied by my friend Mr. H. J. B. Hancock, I was visiting some remarkably fine Wood-Ants' nests near Bagshot. We took with us a large piece of plate-glass, placed it edgewise on the top of an ant-hill, and, standing one at each side, cut the nest completely in two,

Fig. 1097.—Horse Ants (*Formica rufa*) collecting Food and Building Materials

leaving the glass almost wholly buried in it. After the expiration of a few weeks, during which time the Ants could repair damages, we returned to the spot, and, with a spade, removed one side of the nest as far as the glass, which then served as a window through which we could look into the nest. It was really a wonderful sight. The ant-hill was honey-combed into passages and cells, in all of which the inhabitants were hurriedly running about, being alarmed at the unwonted admission of light into their dwellings. In some of the chambers the pupæ were treasured, and these chambers were continually entered by Ants, which picked up the helpless pupæ and carried them to other parts of the nest where the unwelcome light had not shown itself. Unfortunately, this view lasted only a short time."

The most important and arduous duty of the workers is to look after the eggs, larvæ, and pupæ, and these are distributed through the nest with due regard to variations of moisture and temperature, since both of these affect development. The queens are carefully tended, and their eggs are carried off to suitable chambers. From time to time these are carefully licked, and it is also said that they are smeared with nutritious fluid that is absorbed by the embryos. When the larvæ hatch out they are fed with great assiduity and their toilet requirements attended to. The full-grown larvæ spin cocoons, within which they become pupæ (the so-called "ants' eggs"), which also receive unremitting attention. The workers bite away the enclosing cocoons when the perfect insects are ready to come out. Some of them are workers, others winged males and females which fly about in swarms. After mating, the large majority of the swarming individuals perish, but some of the females survive to found fresh communities, or sometimes to be taken into existing nests.

The stings of Wood-Ants are not sufficiently well developed to be of use, but their poison-bags contain formic acid, which can be squirted to a considerable distance, and is an effective defence. This particular acid, as its name indicates (L. *formica*, an ant), was first known as a product of insect-life. The strong mandibles of the workers are also weapons of no despicable character. These ants co-operate for offence and defence, and Lord Avebury (in *Ants, Bees, and Wasps*) thus describes their tactics, and those of a related species:—"*Formica rufa*, the common Horse Ant, attacks in serried masses, seldom sending out detachments, while single ants scarcely ever make individual attacks. They rarely pursue a flying foe, but give no quarter, killing as many enemies as possible, and never hesitating, with this object, to sacrifice themselves for the common good. *Formica exsecta* is a delicate, but very active, species. They also advance in serried masses, but in close quarters they bite right and left, dancing about to avoid being bitten themselves. When fighting with larger species they spring on to their backs, and then seize them by the neck or by an antenna. They also have the instinct of acting together, three or four seizing an enemy at once, and then pulling different ways, so that she on her part cannot get at any one of her foes. One of them then jumps on her back and cuts, or rather saws, off her head. In battles between this ant and the much larger *F. pratensis*, many of the *F. exsectas* may be seen on the backs of the *F. pratensis*, sawing off their heads from behind." Such practices would be greatly deprecated in human warfare.

Some of the most remarkable features in ant-life have reference to the use they make of aphides (fig. 1098), and some species, instead of merely sallying forth to collect honey-dew, in the way described above for the Wood-Ant, have advanced to the pastoral stage of social life, and may be described as cattle-keepers. This is well illustrated by our native species of Lasius. The common little Black Garden-Ant (*Lasius niger*), which lives in elaborate underground dwellings, is particularly partial to aphides which live on twigs and leaves, moving them to convenient places for "milking" operations, and carrying their eggs into its sheltered home for the inclement winter season. The small Yellow Ant (*Lasius flavus*), another underground species, goes further than this, for Lord Avebury states that four or five distinct kinds of aphis are found in some numbers in its nest, belonging to root-feeding species. The same observer made some most interesting observations (on captive specimens) of the way in which (like *L. niger*) these ants tend another sort of aphis, which is not a root-feeder, and he gives the following summary of the facts (in *Ants, Bees, and Wasps*):—"Here are aphides, not living in the ants' nests, but outside, on the leaf-stalks of plants. The eggs are laid early in October on the food-plant of the insect. They are of no direct use to the ants, yet they are not left where they are laid, exposed to the severity of the weather and to innumerable dangers, but brought into the nests by the ants, and tended by them with the utmost care through the long winter months until the following March, when the young ones are brought out and again placed on the young shoots of the daisy. This seems to me a most remarkable case of prudence. Our ants may not perhaps lay up food for the winter; but they do more, for they keep during six months the eggs which will enable them to procure food during the following summer, a case of prudence unexampled in the animal kingdom." It should be added that after carrying the young aphides to the appropriate food-plant the ants wall them in with earth, and the enclosures thus made may be almost

Fig. 1098.—Ant (*Myrmica rubra*) "Milking" an Aphis (*Aphis sambuci*)

called "cattle-pens." Some remarks will be made in a subsequent chapter on ants as slave-owners, and on the beetles, &c., which live in their nests.

The caste-system is carried to an extreme in one of the common Foraging-Ants (*Eciton hamata*, see vol. ii, p. 104) of Tropical America, a carnivorous species which possesses a powerful sting. Besides winged males and wingless females there are "soldiers" with enormous jaws, large workers, and two sizes of small worker. These ants and those of allied species have no permanent abode, but wander about from place to place after the fashion of armies. After carrying on offensive operations for some time they construct temporary quarters, where they cultivate the domestic virtues and bring up their offspring. Belt gives the following account of ants of the sort in regard to this matter (in *A Naturalist in Nicaragua*):—"They make their temporary habitations in hollow trees and sometimes underneath large fallen trunks that offer suitable hollows. A nest that I came across in the latter situation was open at one side. The ants were clustered together in a dense mass, like a great swarm of bees, hanging from the roof, but reaching to the ground below. Their innumerable long legs looked like brown threads binding together the mass, which must have been at least a cubic yard in bulk, and contained hundreds of thousands of individuals, although many columns were outside, some bringing in the pupæ of ants, others the legs and dissected bodies of various insects. I was surprised to see in this living nest tubular passages leading down to the centre of the mass, kept open, just as if it had been formed of inorganic materials. Down these holes the ants who were bringing in booty passed with their prey. I thrust a long stick down to the centre of the cluster, and brought out clinging to it many ants holding larvæ and pupæ." Ants as agriculturalists and mushroom-growers have been dealt with in an earlier section (see vol. i, p. 207).

Social Net-Winged Insects (Neuroptera).—The interesting social insects known as Termites live in complex communities somewhat resembling those of Ants, with which, under the name of "White Ants", these forms are often confounded. The resemblance, however, is very superficial, while the differences are profound. Termites are not invested in strong plate-armour, their exo-skeleton being comparatively thin, nor do they possess poison-glands or stings. But the jaws of the individuals which do the work of the community are very powerful, as in Ants. Most species shun the light and are pale in colour (hence the name "White" Ants), and in such cases only the kings and queens possess eyes, the other castes being blind. There are, however, leaf-cutting Termites in South Africa which move about in open daylight. Eyes are here present in all castes. There is no marked metamorphosis, for the young do not hatch out of the egg as helpless grubs, but as active nymphs, which attain their full size after several moults. The number of castes varies greatly in the different species, and matters are complicated by the presence of nymphs in various stages of development. But in all cases which have been investigated the just-hatched nymphs are to all appearance alike, and it is probable that their subsequent fate depends upon the nature of the food, the matter being more or less regulated by the mature inhabitants of the nest. The same thing is, indeed, largely true for social Bees and Wasps. In the Honey-Bee, for example, the grubs destined to become queens are fed differently from their fellows.

Only the fully mature queens and kings (as the full-blown males are here usually termed) are provided with wings, both pairs being of equal size, the arrangement of veins being quite unlike that characteristic of Bees and Wasps, as might be anticipated from the fact that Termites belong to an entirely different order. Near the base of each wing there is a weak place, facilitating detachment after the first and only flight has taken place. Queens and kings swarm from the nest much as in Ants, and associate themselves in pairs. The vast majority fall a victim to insectivorous birds and other animals, but enough survive to secure the formation of fresh societies, at least in some cases. Nor do we find that speedy death is the necessary sequel to mating for a king termite, as in the case of drone bees, for a nest commonly contains, in some species at any rate, a royal couple, both of whom are carefully tended for the term of their natural lives. Of other kinds of individual, soldiers are always found and generally workers, some of both these castes being modified females and others modified males. A Termite society is not, like those of Bees and Wasps, a female republic.

The only two known species of European Termite have been carefully studied, in Sicily, by Grassi and Sandias, whose chief results will be briefly summarized. The societies of some of the African forms are still more complicated, but here our knowledge is in many respects very incomplete, though it may prove interesting to give a few details. Rather more than 100 species of Termite have been so far described, and these are probably only a tithe of those which actually exist. They abound in the tropical and warmer temperate regions of the world.

The Yellow-Necked Termite (*Calotermes flavicollis*) of the Mediterranean littoral is of peculiar interest, for its communities are small (under 1000 individuals), and the habits are comparatively simple. The home is a hollow within a dead or decaying tree, and the architectural operations are limited to increasing the size of the hollow as may be necessary, and making partitions or the like with waste matter ejected from the intestine, saliva being employed as a cement. Within this simple home are found a king and queen, together with a number of soldiers and nymphs. There are no workers. The soldiers are distinguished, as in Termites generally, by the possession of huge heads and formidable jaws. The habits as regards food are somewhat remarkable, and promote sanitation of the nest in an unusual degree. Wood is the staple diet, but it is a substance very difficult of digestion, and the pellets which are voided from the intestine are eaten again and again, until their nutritive properties are exhausted, when they are either employed as building materials, heaped up in remote parts of the nest, or dropped outside. Partly digested food may also be ejected from the crop, suggesting the arrangement found in other social insects as regards sweet substances. The salivary secretion is also highly nutritious, and not a mere digestive juice. All the cast skins are used as food, and burial rites are simple, the bodies of deceased friends augmenting the bill of fare. The young nymphs are fed at first on saliva, from which they are promoted to material ejected from the crop and intestinal pellets, wood pure and simple being eaten more or less at a still later stage. A grim sort of fate attends the soldiers, for their huge jaws would appear to cut them off from the most abundant items in the dietary, and they are driven to cannibalism. Not only do they devour the dead, but shorten the sufferings of the sick and dying by eating them alive. It is supposed that they are in a state of permanent hunger, and may be well excused for sometimes doing a little private slaughter among their healthy relatives, as they are said to be apt to do when excited. It is on the whole a good thing that human social life has evolved on rather different lines, in spite of the horrors of war and other matters which an intelligent Termite would deprecate.

Winged queens and kings swarm from the nest at certain seasons of the year, and any pair fortunate enough to escape the appetites of birds or other foes is capable of starting a fresh society

The Light-shunning Termite (*Termes lucifugus*) is the second and only other European species. A society consists of many thousands of individuals, and there are workers as well as soldiers. Winged queens and kings swarm from the nest as in other cases, but in Sicily these all perish, so far as yet known. It seems probable, however, that the existing societies there were founded in the first instance by royal pairs, though Grassi has never found these in any of the very numerous Sicilian nests he has examined. In France, however, the investigations of Perris and Perez show that in that country communities can be founded in the usual way. Since fresh individuals are constantly being produced in the Sicilian nests, we naturally enquire how this is possible in the absence of true queens and kings, *i.e.* termites which at one time possessed wings and were fully adult. The answer is found in the existence of remarkable castes which may be termed "substitution royalties". Here, as in other species with complex social life, the workers seem to be aware of the necessity for continued egg-production, and appear to feed some of the nymphs in such a way that they become capable of continuing their kind, though wings are not developed, and certain immature characters are retained. The substitution queens and kings are not all alike, as may be gathered to some extent from fig. 1099. Even this apology for a king is rarely found in a nest, a possible explana-

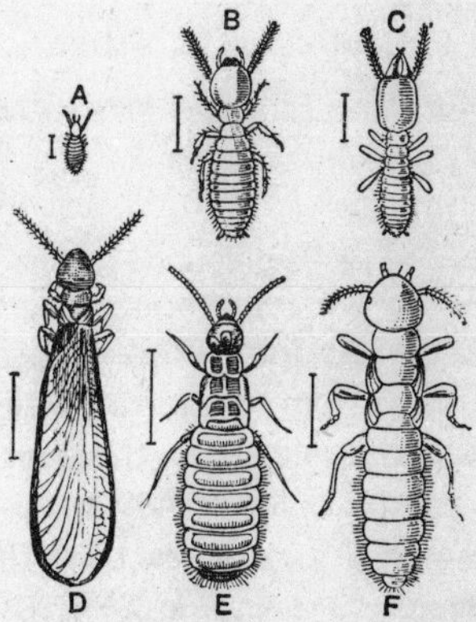

Fig. 1099.—Light-Shunning Termite (*Termes lucifugus*). A, Young larva; B, adult worker; C, soldier; D, winged adult; E and F, reserve or substitution queens. Actual sizes indicated by the vertical lines.

tion being that this particular species is given to regicide, though this would be contrary to the usual habit of Termites. The following table (modified from Grassi) will show the various kinds of individual that have been found in the dwellings of *Termes lucifugus*:—

- 1. Young, undifferentiated nymphs.
  - 2. Nymphs that are not to be concerned with egg-production.
    - 5. Soldier nymphs.
      - 7. Soldiers.
    - 6. Worker nymphs.
      - 8. Workers.
  - 3. Nymphs that will be concerned with egg-production.
  - 4. Reserves for royalties (present if 14, 15, and 11 are absent, or 14 and 15 not sufficiently numerous).
    - (from 3 and 4:)
    - 9. Nymphs of the first form.
      - 12. Winged insects.
        - 14. True royalties.
      - 13 Reserve royalties (?).
    - 10. Nymphs of the second form.
      - 15. Substitution royalties.
    - 11. Reserves for royalties (present if 14, 15, and 4 are wanting, or if 15 and 4 are not sufficiently numerous).

When we remember that the societies of this and other species may exist for a very long time, the reason for the production of substitution royalties becomes tolerably clear. We may suppose that a society is in the first instance founded by a fully-developed royal pair, after they have shed their wings. When a sufficient number of workers have been matured to do the ordinary work, the royal pair for the rest of their lives are carefully tended (though possibly in some species the king may be destroyed), being afterwards replaced by substitution royalties, devoid of wings, these being unnecessary under the circumstances. Provision would, of course, be made for a continuous succession of queens and kings of this kind, and the society would only die out when the environment became in some way very unfavourable.

The Light-shunning Termite lives in wood, like the Yellow-necked species, but its building operations are much more elaborate. Complex galleries and chambers are tunnelled out, and, as before, the exhausted intestinal pellets are employed in constructive work, the cement being saliva. The same sorts of food are used as in the other species.

The societies of certain Termites native to tropical Africa are the largest and most complex yet discovered, though our knowledge regarding them is unfortunately very incomplete. The most famous species is the Warrior Termite (*Termes bellicosus*), which was long ago investigated by Smeathman in West Africa. His description in the *Philosophical Transactions* for 1781 is astonishingly correct, considering the date at which it was written. Each of the vastly numerous communities constructs and lives in a wonderfully solid dwelling in the form of a mound that may be as much as 20 feet high, and is shaped something like a sugar-loaf. It is chiefly made of earth glued together with saliva, while a good deal of the interior work is carried out with the materials already mentioned for other species. A single

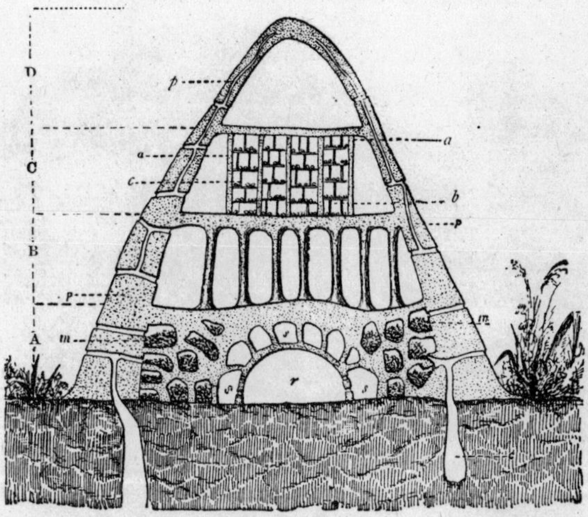

Fig. 1100.—Section through Mound of Warrior Termite (*Termes bellicosus*), greatly reduced. For description see text.

royal couple constitute the centre of social life, and there are both worker and soldier castes, the members of the former being much the larger. The name "soldier" is not altogether a happy one, for it appears that the workers fight much better, while the supposed military individuals are rather fond of looking on. Below the termite dwelling (fig. 1100) are excavations (*c*) from which earth for building is procured, while the dwelling itself is divided into four stories (A–D), surrounded by a common external wall (*p* on left), which is traversed by transverse and longitudinal galleries (*p* on right). The centre of the ground-floor (A) is occupied by the royal chamber (*r*), which is of considerable size, and enclosed by a curved wall in which there are numerous apertures, giving free access to the workers, and furthering ventilation. The king lives here of his own free-will, while the queen is obliged to be a prisoner, for her abdomen is so filled with eggs as to be of relatively enormous size. Attendant crowds of workers are constantly to be found within the royal chamber, attending to the various wants of the king and queen, and carrying away the eggs, which are sometimes laid at the rate of 60 per minute (fig. 1101). Numerous worker-dwellings (*s*) adjoin the abode of their titular sovereigns, and the outer part of the ground-floor is

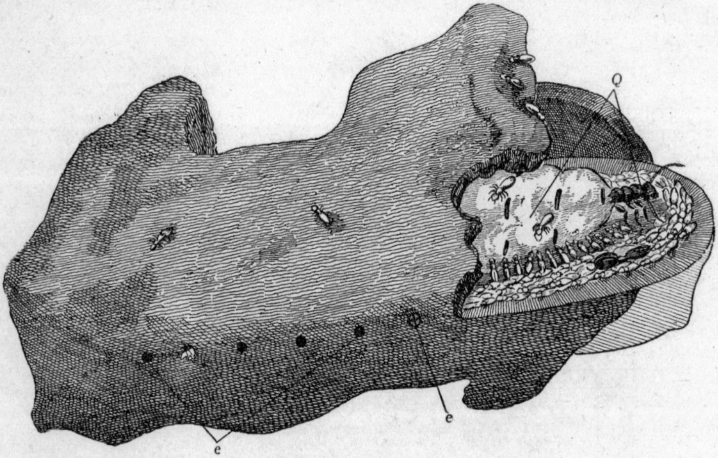

Fig. 1101.—Royal Cell of Warrior Termite (*Termes bellicosus*), broken open to show queen (Q) and her attendants *e* (on left), Openings into royal cell; *e* (on right), an opening that has been closed up; about ⅔ natural size.

occupied by numerous store-chambers (*m*) in which are heaped up gums and other dry vegetable products. The first floor (B) is a large pillared hall, which has no known use except that of serving as an air-space. The second floor (C) may be called the "nursery", for here the eggs are hatched out, and the young nymphs carefully tended. The space is subdivided by means of strong vertical partitions (*a*), and the central portion is marked off into a large number of small compartments (*b*), separated from one another by more delicate party-walls (*c*). The third story or attic is simply an air-space. It will be noted that the arrangements are such as to further the maintenance of equable conditions as regards temperature and moisture, to variations in which Termites appear to be particularly sensitive.

In concluding this chapter it may be noted that the larvæ of many insects are found feeding together in "companies", which have hatched out from batches of eggs laid at the same time and place. Probably the most remarkable case of associated larvæ is afforded by the maggots of certain of the little two-winged flies known as Fungus Gnats (*Mycetophilidæ*). One of these is familiar as the "Army Worm" (*Sciara militaris*) of Europe, and allied forms are native to the United States. The maggots live among rotting leaves, and are sometimes found moving from place to place, united together by sticky threads, and writhing along like a snake. The largest armies of this sort may include millions of individuals, and are stated to reach an extreme length of 100 feet, with a breadth of 6 inches, and a depth of 1 inch. The migrations are probably dependent on the question of food-supply.

CHAPTER LXIII

ASSOCIATION OF ORGANISMS—SOCIAL BACKBONED ANIMALS (VERTEBRATA)

That many backboned animals are of gregarious habit is too well known to require emphasis. Our vocabulary includes many words signifying communities of animals, *e.g.* we speak of a "shoal" of fishes, a "flock" of birds, a "pack" of wolves, a "herd" of antelopes, and so on. The societies of which the existence is implied by many such words exhibit a type of communal life differing greatly from that described for insects, and one that is in some respects less interesting, except in so far as it throws light on the problems of sociology, with which all intelligent persons are more or less concerned. The complex conditions resulting from numerous individuals living together have not here led to profound anatomical specialization, as they have in the case of such insects as ants.

SOCIAL FISHES (PISCES).—That so many Fishes should be associated together in shoals would seem to be dependent in many instances on the place and manner of spawning. In ordinary bony fishes (Teleostei) the eggs are nearly always fertilized externally, and it is obvious that this process is facilitated when numerous individuals seek the same locality for the purpose. The Herring (*Clupea harengus*), fig. 1102), for example, approaches our shores in order to deposit its eggs in shallow water, where they adhere to various objects; the Salmon (*Salmo salar*) ascends rivers for the same purpose; and the Common Eel (*Anguilla vulgaris*) migrates in vast numbers to the deep sea in order to spawn. How far the movements of migratory fish involve division of labour is not at present known. It is not impossible that some of the older individuals may act as "leaders", though this is little more than a conjecture.

The gregarious habit of many predaceous fishes, such as Sharks, Dog-fishes and Mackerel, may conduce to success in procuring prey, and certainly gives an opportunity for co-operation to the benefit of the community. On the other hand, living in shoals must tend very greatly to increase mortality among ill-defended species, which thus are bound to attract the notice of their foes. The well-being of the individual is here, as generally, subordinated to the interests of the species, the matter apparently being determined by the exigencies of spawning.

Though some of the AMPHIBIANS and REPTILES may be more or less gregarious, but little of interest is known about them in

Fig. 1102.—Part of a Shoal of Herrings (*Clupea harengus*)

the present connection, so that we may pass on to the more intelligent animals included in the two highest vertebrate classes, *i.e.* Birds and Mammals. A comparatively large and complex brain is here associated with sagacity that may make itself manifest in social developments.

SOCIAL BIRDS (AVES).—Many Birds are eminently social in their habits, and migrant forms may be associated in vast numbers when making their long journeys (see p. 61). But we have yet much to learn regarding the way in which the living together of numerous individuals results in division of labour, or in concerted action. Of two closely related birds the one may be solitary, and the other markedly gregarious, the Raven and the Rook affording a good instance of this. Each is adapted to its surroundings in a different way, and both adaptations are admirable of their kind, though possibly the social habit gives a better chance in the struggle for existence, and it certainly has a tendency to promote the development of comparatively high mental qualities. As elsewhere remarked (p. 107), the remarkable caste-system which distinguishes social insects has a serious penalty attached to it, for extreme specialization involves a loss of plasticity which, if surroundings change quickly, may mean extinction. But in social Birds and other Vertebrates improved mental powers may be expected to confer increased ability to cope with changing surroundings, and a community of the kind does not suggest a complicated machine easily thrown out of gear, as a nest, say, of Termites, irresistibly does.

As an example of a common social bird we may take the Rook (*Corvus frugilegus*), where there is abundant evidence to show that individuals may render services to the community, and that there may be co-operation to bring about certain common ends. We must, however, receive with caution some of the accounts that have been given of these crafty birds, and which would endow them with almost human attributes. It would appear that when raiding cultivated fields they commonly set sentinels on adjoining trees, and these worthies promptly give warning in raucous tones of the approach of danger in the shape of an agriculturalist. They certainly seem to have acquired knowledge, based on painful experience, of the lethal properties of firearms. Bernard observed Rooks co-operating to hunt field-voles, and his observations are thus summarized by Houssay (in *The Industries of Animals*):—"His curiosity was excited by the way in which numerous rooks stood about a field cawing loudly. In a few days this was explained: the field was covered with rooks; the original assemblage had been calling together a mouse-hunt, which could only be successfully carried out by a large number of birds acting in conjunction. By diligently probing the ground and blocking up the net-work of runs, the voles, one or more at a time, were gradually driven into a corner. The hunt was very successful, and no more voles were seen in that field during the winter." The social nesting-habits of Rooks are familiar to all, for the cheerful sights and sounds of the rookery lend to the country a

CRESTED PENGUINS OR ROCK-HOPPERS

(*Eudyptes chrysocome*)

Penguins are more thoroughly aquatic than any other existing birds, their wings having been converted into paddles of great efficiency, though entirely useless for purposes of flight. The group is characteristic of the Southern Hemisphere, and practically limited to the shores of the Antarctic Ocean. The species represented is the Crested Penguin or Rock-hopper (*Eudyptes chrysocome*), which ranges from the Falkland Islands to New Zealand. It is a handsome black-and-white bird, with an orange-coloured crest on either side of the head. Like so many sea-birds the Rock-hoppers are social in habit. Their favourite breeding-grounds are boulder-strewn slopes at some little distance from the sea, and near fresh water, in which they are fond of bathing. The nest is often a mere hollow scratched in the earth, though stems and leaves may be roughly drawn together to form it. The Rock-hopper, like Penguins generally, broods over its eggs in an erect or semi-erect position, bringing them into contact with a bare patch on the under side of the body, an arrangement which secures a maximum of heat.

CRESTED PENGUINS OR ROCK-HOPPERS (EUDYPTES CHRYSOCOME)
ON THE SHORES OF THE ANTARCTIC OCEAN

charm of their own (fig. 1103). The following vivid account given by Dixon (in *Among the Birds in Northern Shires*) will call up pleasant memories to the minds of many readers:—"And then their home in the cluster of elm-trees yonder is a place fraught with interest if full of noise. Towards the close of February, or, if the weather be still inclement, not until the

Fig. 1103.—A Rookery

beginning of March, and at least a fortnight or three weeks later than in Devonshire, the rooks begin to tidy up their big nests in the slender branches at the tree-tops. Others, less fortunate, commence to build entirely new nests. But this building is by no means universal for a week or more; the mania for collecting sticks and turf has not yet spread through the entire colony, and numbers of birds may be seen looking on with indifference at the efforts of more industrious neighbours. What a noisy animated scene the old rookery is for the next month, until the eggs are laid in the big massive nests; then there is comparative quietness until the young are hatched, when the noisy clamour begins again with greater volume until nestlings and parents get on to the adjoining fields. They return in many cases to the nest trees to roost, and then each evening the din is deafening as troop after troop of tired birds come straggling in from all directions and caw themselves hoarse before dropping off to sleep in the tall trees." The Social Grosbeak has been spoken of in an earlier section as a remarkable example of social nesting-habits (see vol. iii, p. 463).

The social habit is not infrequently conducive to successful defensive measures against enemies. Birds of the swallow kind will unite together to "mob" a hawk that ventures too near their nests, and other instances might easily be given.

Recognition Marks in Birds.—It is obviously advantageous for the members of a community of animals to be able to recognize one another with ease and certainty. They are safer, on the whole, when they keep together, for approaching danger is pretty sure to be perceived by some of them, and these individuals are able to communicate the fact to their fellows. Co-operation in the pursuit of food is also promoted, and, in migrant species, long journeys are more likely to be successfully made in fairly close order.

Wallace has given the name of "recognition marks" to certain colour-arrangements which appear to be of importance in the present connection, and he speaks as follows about the matter (in *Darwinism*).—"Among birds, these recognition marks are especially numerous and suggestive. Species which inhabit open districts are usually protectively coloured; but they generally possess some distinctive markings for the purpose of being easily recognized by their kind, both when at rest and during flight. Such are, the white bands or patches on the breast or belly of many birds, but more especially the head and neck markings in the form of white or black caps, collars, eye-marks, or frontal patches . . . (see fig. 1104). Recognition marks during flight are very important for all birds which congregate in flocks or which migrate together; and it is essential that, while being as conspicuous as possible, the marks shall not interfere with the general protective tints of the species when at rest. Hence they usually consist of well-contrasted markings on the wings and tail, which are concealed during repose, but become fully visible when the bird takes flight. Such markings are well seen in our four British species of shrikes, each having quite different white marks on the expanded wings and on the tail-feathers; and the same is the case with our three species of Saxicola—the stone-chat, whin-chat, and wheat-ear—which are thus easily recognizable on the wing, especially when seen from above, as they would be by stragglers looking out for their companions. . . . Those birds

Fig. 1104.—1, Lesser Tern (*Sterna minuta*), and 2, Ringed Plover (*Ægialitis hiaticola*)

which are inhabitants of tropical forests, and which need recognition marks that shall be at all times visible among the dense foliage, and not solely or chiefly during flight, have usually small but brilliant patches of colour on the head or neck, often not interfering with the generally protective character of their plumage. Such are the bright patches of blue, red, or yellow by which the usually green Eastern barbets are distinguished; and similar bright patches of colour characterize the separate species of small green fruit-doves. To this necessity for specialization in colour, by which each bird may easily recognize its kind, is probably due that marvellous variety in the peculiar beauties of some groups of birds." If we admit the truth of the view just set forth, it follows that, in many birds, comparatively slight differences in plumage will often prove a safe guide in the discrimination of species. Though trivial in themselves they may nevertheless be regarded as natural "labels", which indicate the presence of other specific differences that may be much more difficult to detect. The theory of recognition marks is strongly supported by the fact that animals which turn white in winter commonly do not do so completely, but retain small dark patches. The Ptarmigan (*Lagopus mutus*, fig. 1105), for example, retains black markings on the side of the tail, while the male in winter plumage is further distinguished by black streaks near the eye.

Social Mammals (Mammalia).—A large number of mammals affect the gregarious habit, and some examples of the benefits

Fig. 1105.—Male Ptarmigan (*Lagopus mutus*) in Winter Plumage

accruing have elsewhere been given. Wolves, for example, hunt in packs, and sometimes secure their prey by very ingenious devices (see vol. ii, p. 16). The herding together of various Hoofed Mammals is distinctly of advantage in defence, and many such forms post sentinels to warn them of approaching danger (see vol. ii, p. 365). Troops of Baboons and Monkeys make well-organized raids, while their tactics during retreat from foes are often decidedly skilful, and have reference to the well-being of the community (see vol. ii, p. 363). The cubs of the Fur-Seal benefit by the mode of life in their "rookery" (see vol. iii, p. 492). To consider in detail all the groups of mammals in regard to social habits would be an almost endless task, and the present purpose will perhaps be sufficiently served by taking one or two typical and interesting cases.

PRAIRIE DOGS (*Cynomys Ludovicianus*)

These animals have received their somewhat inappropriate name from the curious way in which they "bark" on the approach of danger, but in reality there is nothing dog-like about them, for they are social burrowing Rodents or Gnawing Mammals, not distantly allied to the Marmots of the Old World. They are among the most characteristic inhabitants of the great plains to the east of the Rocky Mountain Highland in North America. The earth thrown out from each burrow is heaped up into a mound that serves as a sort of watch-tower, on which a sentry may be posted.

The Rattlesnake or the Burrowing Owl may take possession of a burrow, but the old idea that snake, bird, and prairie-dog live together in the same quarters on amicable terms is quite untenable.

PRAIRIE DOGS (CYNOMYS LUDOVICIANUS) AT HOME

The Common Prairie-Marmot (*Cynomys Ludovicianus*), more familiarly known as the Prairie-"Dog", on account of the barking sound to which it gives utterance when alarmed, is a social burrowing rodent native to the dry open plains on the east of the Rocky Mountain highland. Several individuals live together in the same burrow, and a very large number of these homes may be associated together into a "city". The excavated earth is partly heaped up into a mound at the entrance to the burrow, and this may almost be called a watch-tower, since it is commonly occupied by a sentinel, who performs the usual duties of his office. On hearing his warning bark the neighbouring individuals scuttle down into their underground dwellings. The opening of each burrow is somewhat funnel-shaped, some of the earth dug out having been regularly arranged round it, and pressed together till firm: the use probably being to prevent flooding out during sudden showers. Owing to the fact that Burrowing Owls and Rattlesnakes are not infrequently found in the dwellings of this rodent, the conclusion has somewhat hastily been drawn that the three kinds of animal constitute a kind of "happy family", living together on the best of terms. This, however, is not the case, for the Owl simply takes possession of a deserted burrow, while the Rattlesnake appropriates one at random, ejecting the rightful owner if necessary, and thereafter visits his neighbours, levying a tax upon their offspring. The Common Prairie-Marmot is about a foot in length, exclusive of the short tail, but a larger and a smaller species are also indigenous to North America. The former is the Mexican Prairie-Marmot (*C. Mexicanus*), while the smaller sort is the Columbian Prairie-Marmot (*C. Columbianus*), which inhabits higher ground in the western part of North America. Their habits are much the same as those of the common form. It appears that there is a winter-sleep in the case of individuals which live pretty far north. The True Marmots (species of *Arctomys*) are somewhat larger animals allied to the preceding, and like them gregarious burrowers. They have a wide range through the northern parts of North America and Eurasia, living on plains except in the southern part of their distributional area, where they are typical mountain-animals. It is a familiar fact that they indulge in a long winter-sleep.

The Beaver (*Castor fiber*) is a very large social Rodent which formerly had a wide extension in Europe and North America, but has been hunted down to such a deplorable extent, chiefly for the sake of its fur, that it now exists in greatly diminished numbers, and in all probability will become extinct at no distant period, except in cases where it is strictly preserved. It was once a native of Great Britain, though its range never extended to Ireland. According to Geraldus Cambrensis it lived in the river Teifi (Cardiganshire) so late as 1188, and is thought to have survived in Scotland to a still later period. The American Beaver is probably a distinct species (*C. Canadensis*), and its habits have been more carefully studied than those of the European kind. The animal is an expert swimmer and diver, being modified in structure in connection with this habit, as elsewhere described (see vol. iii, p. 73). In all probability it was originally a bank-dweller, excavating an upwardly sloping burrow, with the top end expanded into a living chamber, and the entrance below the surface of the water. And where this unfortunate animal is subjected to much persecution its architectural efforts do not attain anything of more elaborate nature. Under normal circumstances, however, much more complex homes are made, which may be regarded as having been evolved by gradual stages from the primeval burrow. They involve the construction of "dams" and "lodges", a narrow stream being converted by the former into a series of ponds, of which the surface-level remains fairly steady, thus giving favourable conditions for building the lodges or houses. It is essential that the district should be well wooded, as the chief material used in making the dams consists of the trunks and branches of trees, some of which may be as much as 40 inches round at the base and 120 feet high. The tools employed are the powerful incisor teeth, and a tree is felled by being bitten round in a neat manner near the ground. As H. T. Martin says (in *Castorologia*):—"No better work could be accomplished by a most highly-finished steel cutting tool, wielded by a muscular human arm".

Trees growing near water usually slant towards it, and when sufficiently weakened by the gnawing process must, as a rule, fall that way. It was once supposed that the Beaver secured this end by biting more wood from the side facing the stream, but this appears to be incorrect. When the tree is felled its branches are gnawed off, and the timber is cut up into lengths of five or six feet, the bark being peeled off to serve as food. It is, indeed, quite possible that the habit of bark-feeding was the original one, and that the use of the wood for constructive purposes has been evolved subsequently. The process described provides for the framework of a dyke, and twigs, &c., are added, together with much earth. The nature of the work is adapted to the local conditions: in the case of brooks or large streams with ill-marked banks there is a "stick-dam", in which the earth is of comparatively small amount; where the water is deeper and the banks clearly defined there is a "solid-bank dam", with enough earth to cover up all the woody framework. In the former case no special channel is made through which the water may make its way, while in the latter case a suitable exit is scooped out on the top of the dyke. In order the better to resist water-pressure, the upper side of the barrier is sloping; its lower surface is approximately vertical. The foundation is from about 9 to 12 feet, the upper part about 2 feet in thickness. The dam is built straight across if the current is gentle, while the greater pressure existing in a rapid stream is compensated by making the work curved, with its convex side facing upwards. The following careful account of this preliminary engineering work is given by Lewis H. Morgan (in *The American Beaver and his Works*), and it will be noted that he does not favour the common view that several or a large number of families co-operate for the benefit of the "village":—"The dam is the principal structure of the beaver. It is also the most important of his erections as it is the most extensive, and because its production and preservation could only be accomplished by patient and long-continued labour. In point of time, also, it precedes the lodge, since the floor of the latter and the entrances to its chamber are constructed with reference to the level of the water in the pond. The object of the dam is the formation of an artificial pond, the principal use of which is the refuge it affords to them when assailed, and the water connection it gives to their lodges and to their burrows in the banks. Hence, as the level of the pond must, in all cases, rise from one to two feet above these entrances for the protection of the animal from pursuit and capture, the surface-level of the pond must, to a greater or less extent, be subject to their immediate control. As the dam is not an absolute necessity to the beaver for the maintenance of his life, his normal habitation being rather natural ponds and rivers, and burrows in their banks, it is, in itself considered, a remarkable fact that he should have voluntarily transferred himself, by means of dams and ponds of his own construction, from a natural to an artificial mode of life. Some of these dams are so extensive as to forbid the supposition that they were the exclusive work of a single pair, or of a single family of beavers; but it does not follow, as has very generally been supposed, that several families, or a colony, unite for the joint construction of a dam. After careful examination of some hundreds of these structures, and of the lodges and burrows attached to many of them, I am altogether satisfied that the larger dams were not the joint product of the labour of large numbers of beavers working together, and brought thus to immediate completion; but, on the contrary, that they arose from small beginnings, and were built upon year after year, until they finally reached that size which exhausted the capabilities of the location; after which they were maintained for centuries, at the ascertained standard, by constant repairs. So far as my observations have enabled me to form an opinion, I think they were usually, if not invariably, commenced by a single pair, or a single family, of beavers; and that when, in the course of time, by the gradual increase of the dam, the pond had become sufficiently enlarged to accommodate more families than one, other families took up their residence upon it, and afterwards contributed by their labour to its maintenance. There is no satisfactory evidence that the American beavers either live or work in colonies; and if some such cases have been observed, it will either be found to be an exception to the general rule, or in consequence of the sudden destruction of a work upon the maintenance of which a number of families were depending. The great age of the larger dams is shown by their size, by the large amount of solid materials they contain, and by the destruction of the primitive forest within the area of the ponds; and also by the extent of the beaver-meadows all along the margins of the streams where dams are maintained, and by the hummocks formed upon them by and through the annual growth and decay of vegetation in separate hills. These meadows were undoubtedly covered with trees adapted to a wet soil when the dams were constructed. It must have required long periods of time to destroy every vestige of the ancient forest by the increased saturation of the earth, accompanied with occasional overflows from the stream. The evidence from these and other sources tends to show that these dams have existed in the same places for hundreds and thousands of years, and that they have been maintained by a system of continued repairs.

"At the place selected for the construction of a dam the ground is usually firm and often stony, and when across the channel of a flowing stream, a hard rather than a soft bottom is preferred. Such places are necessarily unfavourable for the insertion of stakes in the ground, if such were, in fact, their practice in building dams. The theory upon which beaver-dams are constructed is perfectly simple, and involves no such necessity. Soft earth, intermixed with vegetable fibre, is used to form an embankment, with sticks, brush, and poles imbedded within these materials to bind them together, and to impart to them the requisite solidity to resist the effects both of pressure and of saturation. Small sticks and brush are used, in the first instance, with mud and earth and stones for down-weight. Consequently these dams are extremely rude at their first commencement, and they do not attain their remarkably artistic appearance until they have been raised to a considerable height, and have been maintained by a system of annual repairs for a number of years."

The beaver-house or "lodge" is a domed structure, constructed of clay and wood on the upper side of the dam. A lodge is from 6 to 8 feet high, and its base is 9 to 12 feet broad, or rather more. The living-room within, which also serves as a "nursery", is lined with grass, and its floor is at water-level. There are several entrances which open well below the surface, so that there is no danger of blockage by ice during the winter. The beaver does not hibernate, and its pond is deep enough to enable it to swim about under the surface of the ice in the most rigorous seasons. The lodge includes a store-chamber, in which large quantities of the succulent rhizomes of certain water-lilies are heaped up for winter use. Tree-branches are also accumulated in the deeper parts of the pond for the same purpose. Martin (in *Castorologia*) makes the following interesting remarks regarding the popular misconception as to the highly-finished character of the lodge, and also as to the way in which it has evolved from the simple burrow:—"The beaver-lodge is generally included in the list of marvels reserved for the investigation of those who visit beaver-districts, and yet no greater disappointment awaits the inquirer than the first inspection of one. Somehow the minds of all lovers of natural history become affected by the fabulous accounts concerning this structure, and it is a shock to stand for the first time before a pile of twigs, branches, and logs, heaped in disorder upon a small dome of mud, and to learn that this constitutes the famous lodge. Of course the superficial glance does not convey all that can be learnt in connection with this work, but it does most completely disillusionize the mind. On breaking through the upper walls, the interior is found to be similar to the general type of an animal's sleeping apartment, and has scarcely any distinguishing characteristic. . . . Starting with the simple burrow, the next step is the accumulation of logs and branches about its entrance, forming what is called a 'bank-lodge'. In places where the water is shallow towards the shore, a great advantage would be derived from extending this artificial covering of brushwood, so that in time a natural evolution of the lodge disconnected entirely from the shore would take place, and form an independent and very convenient refuge from landward enemies." It may be well to add that the large flattened tail of the beaver is a swimming organ, and is not employed as a trowel. Clay is manipulated entirely by means of the fore-paws.

Recognition Marks and Odours.—Many of the gregarious Mammals possess contrasted light and dark markings which possibly enable the individuals of the same species to recognize one another, as in the similar cases already described for birds (p. 132). The most familiar instance is the white patch on the under side of a Rabbit's tail, which, though it does not interfere with the general protective character of the coloration, makes the animal easily seen when it moves rapidly. On this account it has also been described as an illustration of "signalling coloration", by which, when retreating from danger, an unconscious warning is given by the animal to its fellows. Other instances cited by Wallace (in *Darwinism*) are antelopes (fig. 1106), zebras, monkeys, and lemurs. In regard to the first of these, he suggests that the great variety in the shape of the horns has to do with recognition.

Gregarious Mammals are commonly distinguished by the possession of a keen sense of smell, which has various relations to habits. In herbivorous forms, for instance, it is of great importance with reference to detecting the approach of carnivores. But it would also seem to play a part in facilitating mutual recognition between individuals of the same kind. At any rate we often find that social forms are provided, in various parts of the body, with peculiar glands, the secretions of which emit

Fig. 1106.—Hartebeest (*Bubalis caama*)

characteristic odours, often, to us, of disagreeable kind. The Rabbit (*Lepus cuniculus*) is a case in point, for its "rabbity smell" is due to the products of a pair of glands (perineal glands) in the hinder part of the body. The little Peccaries (*Dicotyles*) of South America possess a good-sized gland under the skin of the back, the secretion being here a stinking oily fluid, the emanations from which no doubt assist in keeping the members of a troop together.

There is good reason why they should, for, as Beddard says (in *The Cambridge Natural History*), "they owe, too, their safety from many foes to their sociable habits. Being nocturnal animals they are liable to the attacks of the jaguar, which will speedily overpower and devour a peccary that has strayed from its herd."

In Deer there is usually a scent-gland (the *crumen*) opening into a pit below the eye; so also in most Antelopes. The latter may also possess other scent-glands in the groin or between the toes. Bottle-shaped structures of the sort are found between the digits in Sheep (fig. 1107). It is interesting to note that a captive specimen of the Klipspringer Antelope (*Oreotragus saltator*) has been observed to deliberately deposit upon various objects the secretion that oozes out under its eyes. Such a habit if practised under natural conditions would no doubt help these animals to find one another. But the glands in the feet of Sheep, &c., are of special interest here, for drops of the strong-smelling secretion must constantly be squeezed out on to the ground, leaving a well-marked "trail".

Fig. 1107. —Foot of Sheep (*Ovis aries*) dissected to show scent-gland, the opening of which is indicated by an arrow

Many other examples of scent-glands might easily be given. The exact use no doubt varies in different cases, and may have nothing to do with the social habit proper. For example, an animal may thus be assisted in the search for a mate, and Beddard suggests that some scents are possibly of mimetic nature. The odour of the Musk-Deer is perhaps of this kind, for it may suggest to aggressors the musky smell of the Crocodile, an animal which they would think twice before attacking. Stink-glands as a direct defence have been spoken of elsewhere (see vol. ii, p. 301).

CHAPTER LXIV

ASSOCIATION OF ORGANISMS—COURTSHIP AND MATING

It is well known that among a number of savage tribes well-developed thews and sinews are an invaluable possession to a young man inclined towards matrimony; he has, in short, to fight for a wife. Among civilized human communities good looks play no unimportant part in the matter, though financial considerations are sometimes said to be paramount. We have, in fact, the Law of Battle and the Law of Beauty, both very clearly enunciated by Darwin in the case of animals, and illustrated by a wealth of fact. The former law is admitted by all to have great influence in many cases in deciding which individuals shall mate together, but Wallace, whose opinion in all zoological matters is entitled to the greatest respect, does not think that ornamental males are preferred as partners by those of the opposite sex. The part of his argument, so far as the human species is concerned, is thus expressed (in *Darwinism*):—"A young man, when courting, brushes or curls his hair, and has his moustache, beard, or whiskers in perfect order, and no doubt his sweetheart admires them; but this does not prove that she marries him on account of these ornaments, still less that hair, beard, whiskers, and moustache were developed by the continued preferences of the female sex. So, a girl likes to see her lover well and fashionably dressed, and he always dresses as well as he can when he visits her; but we cannot conclude from this that the whole series of male costumes, from the brilliantly-coloured, puffed, and slashed doublet and hose of the Elizabethan period, through the gorgeous coats, long waist-coats, and pigtails of the early Georgian era, down to the funereal dress-suit of the present day, are the direct result of female preference." One is inclined to believe, however, that an average girl does prefer a good-looking young man, and that female preference has had a directive influence on the evolution of male attire. And there are so many facts supporting the view that the females of many animals are influenced by the ornamental endowments of prospective partners, that the existence of the Law of Beauty will be here taken as provisionally proved. At the same time it must not be applied to explain facts in too sweeping a manner. Every case should be considered on its own merits, and our knowledge of animal habits is so very imperfect that it is easy to fall into error. It is also necessary to carefully avoid the pitfall of unconsciously assuming that the mental endowments of lower animals closely resemble our own. There is no reason to think, for example, that a hen-bird exerts a deliberate choice in the selection of a mate. She may be strongly attracted towards one of several possible partners, and beauty of plumage or voice may have to do with such attraction, but that is not the same thing as "deliberate choice" in the usual sense.

It is only among comparatively specialized animals that the Laws of Battle and Beauty are exemplified, and a few examples will fittingly illustrate the subject.

COURTSHIP AND MATING OF MAMMALS (MAMMALIA)

THE LAW OF BATTLE.—A complete list of species in which the males fight in order to secure mates would be a fairly complete catalogue of Mammals, for in this class the question of Beauty would appear to be subordinate. One would naturally expect combats to be most frequent in cases where the females were comparatively few in number, but as a matter of fact it is better marked among polygamous species, which are necessarily social, though it by no means follows that all gregarious animals are polygamous. Deer and various other Hoofed Mammals afford good illustrations, and as these lead a wandering life it is possible that the practice of polygamy has arisen from the desirability of keeping a herd together, an end to which it is more favourable than monogamy. In nearly all species of Deer the males alone possess antlers, and this is correlated with the fact that they fight furiously together in the struggle to secure mates. In the case of our native Red Deer (*Cervus elaphus*) the adult stags live by themselves except for about three weeks in the autumn, this being the mating-season. Fierce combats are then frequent, that result in the discomfiture of the weaker males, some of which may be killed outright. Every victor is able to secure a number of partners, but he has to be continually on the look-out to repel other stags wishing to interfere with his family life, and may have to yield his privileges to an intruder. Might as usual is the only right.

THE LAW OF BEAUTY.—Adult male Mammals are not infrequently distinguished from those of the other sex by the possession

Fig. 1108.—Male Mandrill (*Papio mormon*)

of various ornaments, among which may be mentioned the mane of the Lion and the beard of the Goat. An extreme case is presented by the West African Baboon known as the Mandrill (*Papio mormon*, fig. 1108), the name of which probably means "man-like baboon". If so, it is rather a libel upon the human species, for the appearance of the adult male is decidedly startling. Either side of the face presents a furrowed blue swelling, the grooves being purple, while between these ornaments is a strip of bright red, passing down to the end of the nose, which is of the same lively hue. A pointed beard of orange yellow completes a scheme of colour that is effective in its way. The large bare patches on the hinder part of the body are also of a vivid scarlet, with a tinge of blue. The teeth are of formidable nature, as in many apes and monkeys, the canines being particularly large, partly no doubt with reference to defence, but partly also in relation to combats with other males of the same species. The female Mandrill is faded-looking in comparison to her mate. The swellings on her face are comparatively small and pale, while there is never more than a faint display of red.

The attractions of male mammals often include a relatively well-developed voice, as in the Red Deer, where during the mating season the stag makes a characteristic roaring sound, known as "belling", though whether this serves any special purpose is doubtful. The last remark also applies, it would seem, to the American Howling Monkeys, regarding one of which Darwin thus speaks (in *The Descent of Man*):—"The vocal organs of the American *Mycetes caraya* are one-third larger in the male than in the female, and are wonderfully powerful. These monkeys in warm weather make the forests resound at morning and evening with their overwhelming voices. The males begin the dreadful concert, and often continue it during many hours, the females sometimes joining in with their less powerful voices. An excellent observer, Rengger, could not perceive that they were excited to begin by any special cause; he thinks that, like many birds, they delight in their own music, and try to excel each other." One is irresistibly reminded here of the "dreadful concerts" held nightly by the common Cat. The males appear to take the leading parts, and their unearthly cries seem to express defiance of one another, rather than to be a means of attracting the softer sex.

COURTSHIP AND MATING OF BIRDS (Aves)

The Law of Battle.—Most male birds are exceedingly pugnacious, fighting for the possession of mates in the most determined manner, the habit being perhaps best-marked in the polygamous species. They may be provided with special weapons, the spurs of cocks being a familiar example. The methods of fighting of some birds are described as follows by Brehm (in *From North Pole to Equator*):—"Rival ostriches fight with their strong legs, and, striking forwards, tear deep wounds with their sharp toe-nails in the breast, body, and legs of their opponent. Jealous bustards, after spending a long time challenging each other with throat inflated, wings and tail outspread, and much grumbling and hissing, make use of their bills with very considerable effect. Sand-pipers and other shore-birds, particularly the fighting ruffs, which fight about everything, about

Fig. 1109.—Cock Chaffinches Fighting

a mate or about a fly, about sun and light, or about their standing-ground, run against each other with bills like poised lances, and receive the thrusts among the breast feathers, which in the case of the ruffs are developed into what serves as a shield [much as in the Lion]. Coots rush at each other on an unsteady surface of water-plants, and strike each other with their legs. Swans, geese, and ducks chase each other till one of the combatants succeeds in seizing the other by the head and holding him under water, till he is in danger of suffocating, or at least until he is so much exhausted that he is unable to continue the struggle."

A battle-royal between two cock chaffinches is represented in fig. 1109.

THE LAW OF BEAUTY.—It is familiar to all that male birds very often differ markedly from the females in the possession of more ornamental characters, and a more powerful or more beautiful voice. And it is significant that their charms are in full perfection at the time of mating. The contrast between the sexes is obvious on looking round any poultry-yard. Among ordinary fowls the striking plumage of the cock, and his scarlet wattles and comb, make him a handsome bird by contrast with the rather dowdy hen. The drake is distinctly handsomer than the duck. But such examples are far excelled by some of the allies of domesticated fowls, for in many of these the plumage of the male is beautiful beyond mere verbal description. Such in particular are the Golden Pheasant (*Chrysolophus pictus*), Amherst's Pheasant (*C. Amherstiæ*), the Argus Pheasant (*Argusianus giganteus*), and the Peacock (*Pavo cristatus*). Gorgeously decorated male birds of the sort display their charms during courtship in a remarkable manner. We may take as an example the Scarlet Tragopan (*Tragopan satura*), of which the following description by Ogilvie Grant (in *The Royal Natural History*) will convey some idea of the brilliancy of the colour-scheme:—"The male has the top and sides of the head black, the neck, mantle, and under-parts orange-carmine, and the rest of the upper parts olive-brown, each feather being ornamented at the tip with a round white spot, partially or entirely margined with black; the outer wing-coverts being edged on each side with dark orange-carmine. The throat-wattle is salmon-colour with transverse blue bars, and the legs are pale flesh." Brehm, after describing the love-dances of various birds, thus speaks (in *From North Pole to Equator*) of this particular form:—"More remarkable than all the rest is the behaviour of the male tragopans or horned pheasants of Southern Asia, magnificently decorative birds, distinguished by two brightly-coloured horn-like tubes of skin on the sides of the head, and by brilliantly-coloured extensible wattles. After the cock has walked round the hen several times without appearing to pay any attention to her, he stands still at

COURTING OF THE TRAGOPAN (*Ceriornis satyrus*)

Among highly organized groups of animals the male is commonly more beautiful than his partner, and the matrimonial chances of the former are supposed to be often proportionate to his decorative endowments. According to this view the æsthetic taste of females has had an important influence in the evolution of male adornments. The Horned Pheasant (*Ceriornis satyrus*) or Tragopan of Northern India, which is one of a small group of extremely handsome species, affords a good illustration of the striking difference in appearance which often distinguishes the sexes. As will be gathered from the plate, the hen-bird (in the foreground) is comparatively dowdy, but the cock possesses adornments of no common order, which he is represented as fully displaying with a view of securing the favour of a desired partner. His ornaments include a couple of blue outgrowths on the head, which can be made to stick up like horns, and a pair of brilliantly coloured wattles capable of inflation to form a sort of horseshoe-shaped collar. Details of the colour-scheme and of the love-antics are given in the text.

THE HORNED PHEASANT (CERIORNIS SATYRUS) OR TRAGOPAN OF NORTHERN INDIA a particular spot, and begins to bow. More and more quickly the courtesies follow each other, the horns meantime swelling and tossing, the wattles dilating and collapsing again, till all are literally flying about the head of the love-crazed bird. Now he unfolds and spreads his wings, rounds and droops his tail, sinks down with bent feet, and, spitting and hissing, lets his wings sweep along the ground. Suddenly every movement ceases. Bent low, his plumage ruffled, his wings and tail pressed against the ground, his eyes closed, his breathing audible, he remains for a while in motionless ecstasy. His fully unfolded decorations gleam with dazzling brightness. Abruptly he rises again, spits and hisses, trembles, smooths his feathers, scratches, throws up his tail, flaps his wings, jerks himself up to his full height, rushes upon the female, and, suddenly checking his wild career, appears before her in olympic majesty, stands still for a moment, trembles, twitches, hisses, and all at once lets all his glory vanish, smooths his feathers, draws in his horns and wattles, and goes about his business as if nothing had happened."

The combination of "spitting and hissing" with "olympic majesty" in the tragopan strikes one as somewhat lacking in dramatic fitness, from the human stand-point, but it serves as a reminder that the most gorgeously decorated male birds are not remarkable for beautiful voices. The unpleasant scream of the Peacock is no doubt familiar to all. On the other hand, the most gifted songsters are often modestly attired, and it is further to be noted that birds of small size are particularly notable in the matter of vocal attainments. In some cases, at any rate, love-songs would appear to prove more attractive to the female than elaborate colour-displays or amorous antics. On this point Darwin makes the following remarks (in *The Descent of Man*):—"Naturalists are much divided with respect to the object of the singing of birds. Few more careful observers ever lived than Montagu, and he maintained that the 'males of song-birds and of many others do not in general search for the female, but, on the contrary, their business in the spring is to perch on some conspicuous spot, breathing out their full and amorous notes, which, by instinct, the female knows, and repairs to the spot to choose her mate'. Mr. Jenner Weir informs me that this is certainly the case with the nightingale. Bechstein, who kept birds during his whole life, asserts 'that the female canary always chooses the best singer, and that in a state of nature the female finch selects that male out of a hundred whose notes please her most'. There can be no doubt that birds closely attend to each other's song." It seems, however, to be certain that birds take a delight in their musical powers quite apart from the question of courtship, often singing from emulation or from sheer "joy of life".

Fig. 1110.—Male Australian Bustard (*Otis australis*), with Throat-pouch inflated

It is almost superfluous to remark that in appraising the attractions of male birds we must remember that what to us is merely comical, may nevertheless be well adapted to its purpose. In the Common Bustard (*Otis tarda*), for instance, the male indulges in strange antics and displays of plumage, and often possesses a large pouch that can be dilated to serve as a resonator, no doubt making the love-call more sonorous, though this is no more than the syllable "oak" often repeated. The Australian Bustard (*Otis australis*, fig. 1110) also has such a pouch, which in this case is simply a greatly dilatable part of the gullet.

Odorous attractions are sometimes possessed by the male, as in the Musk-Duck (*Cairina moschata*), a species which ranges from Mexico to the Argentine Republic, and is known in captivity by the erroneous name of "Muscovy"-Duck.

It must not be imagined that the courtship of any particular species necessarily exemplifies the Law of Battle or the Law of Beauty only, for in many cases strength and æsthetic qualities are both called into play.

COURTSHIP AND MATING OF REPTILES (REPTILIA).

THE LAW OF BATTLE.—Some male Reptiles engage in combats with one another during the mating season, a habit which has been observed in Alligators, some Tortoises, and certain

Fig. 1111.—Owen's Chameleon (*Chamæleo Oweni*). Female on left; male on right

Lizards. Among the latter the males may be provided with strong spines or horns on the head, especially so in some of the Chameleons (fig. 1111), and these weapons are no doubt used in their fights with one another. The jealous ferocity of the American Alligator (*Alligator Mississippiensis*) is thus graphically touched off by Cyrus W. Butler (in *Big Game of North America*): —"On the whole, he is a sluggish, very sluggish, animal, not even being an active hunter; but loafs around in hope that something may turn up—that probably a fish may unwittingly swim near enough to be snapped up by a quick motion of his long jaws. But lazy and sluggish as he is, and cold as is his blood, there are times when it must course swiftly through his veins; for on a little island of muck, in the centre of a pond, a female is heaping up a pile of saw-grass and dirt for a nest, while upon opposite sides of the pond, and just upon the edge of the saw-grass, eyeing her with warm glances of admiration, and each other with the sullen glare of hatred, lie two old males, whose scarred and bleeding bodies testify that even a 'gator's cold blood is thicker than water. The smaller one moves painfully, for his right fore-foot is missing — the larger one got his jaws upon it, a few rapid turns, and the foot was gone, probably soon buried in the stomach of the victor. The loss of a foot in fighting is quite common, for I have taken three thus maimed, and heard of others."

THE LAW OF BEAUTY.—The most striking examples among Reptiles of relatively ornamental males is afforded by some of

Fig. 1112.—Male Lizard (*Sitana*) with Throat-pouch

152-E

the Lizards. In certain Indian species of the genus Sitana (fig. 1112), for instance, the male is provided with a brilliantly-coloured throat-pouch, which can be either folded up or dilated, and is only fully displayed during the mating-season. It also appears that at this time the scent-glands of Crocodiles, Snakes, and Lizards are particularly active in the male.

COURTSHIP AND MATING OF AMPHIBIANS (AMPHIBIA)

THE LAW OF BATTLE.—Our information here is somewhat scanty, but male Frogs have been observed fighting together with great ferocity during the mating season, at which time also male Toads wrestle with one another in a determined manner, discomfited athletes being at a discount among the females.

THE LAW OF BEAUTY.—Here we may take as an example

the Great Crested Newt (*Molge cristatus*, fig. 1113), which is one of our few native forms. During the time of courtship the male possesses a special adornment in the form of a high saw-edged crest on the upper side of his body and tail, besides which his colours are brighter than those of the other sex.

The vocal attractions of male Frogs are often considerable. In the Edible Frog (*Rana esculenta*), for instance, the male possesses a pair of croaking sacs at the corners of the mouth, which can be dilated to serve as resonators, imparting a mellow tone to his voice. The "concerts" of this and other species

Fig. 1113.—Great Crested Newt (*Molge cristatus*). Male above; female below

are as striking in their way as the musical efforts of Howling Monkeys and some other Mammals. The following picturesque account of an evening performance of the kind is given by Thoreau (in *Walden*):—"In the meantime all the shore rang with the trump of bull-frogs, the sturdy spirits of ancient wine-bibbers and wassailers, still unrepentant, trying to sing a catch in their Stygian lake,—if the Walden nymphs will pardon the comparison, for though there are almost no weeds, there are frogs there,—who would fain keep up the hilarious rules of their old festal tables, though their voices have waxed hoarse and solemnly grave, mocking at mirth, and the wine has lost its flavour, and become only liquor to distend their paunches, and sweet intoxication never comes to drown the memory of the past, but mere saturation and water-loggedness and distention. The most aldermanic, with his chin upon a heart-leaf, which serves for a napkin to his drooling chaps, under this northern shore quaffs a deep draught of the once-scorned water, and passes round a cup with the ejaculation *tr-r-r-oonk, tr-r-r-oonk, tr-r-r-oonk!* and straightway comes over the water from some distant cove the same pass-word repeated, where the next in seniority and girth has gulped down to his mark; and when this observance has made the circuit of the shores, then ejaculates the master of ceremonies, with satisfaction, *tr-r-r-oonk*, and each in his turn repeats the same down to the least distended, leakiest, and flabbiest-paunched, that there be no mistake; and then the bowl goes round again and again, until the sun disperses the morning mist, and only the patriarch is not under the pond, but vainly bellowing *troonk* from time to time, and pausing for a reply."

COURTSHIP AND MATING OF FISHES (PISCES)

THE LAW OF BATTLE.—During the spawning-season a number of male fishes are very pugnacious, fighting one another on the least provocation. We may take as examples the Salmon (*Salmo salar*) and Three-Spined Stickleback (*Gasterosteus aculeatus*). At the time when Salmon make their annual ascent of rivers the lower jaw of the mature male grows out into a sort of hook (fig. 1114), which is supposed to serve as a protection against the furious charges of his rivals, while at the same time his teeth become long and sharp, being frequently over half an inch in length. Two males have been observed fighting together a whole day, and the mortality is often considerable.

The little Stickleback is no less savage during the days of courtship, at which time he becomes of a vivid red colour, that has earned him the local name of "robin". Fred Smith (in *The Boyhood of a Naturalist*) thus graphically describes a combat:—"Oh, we needn't be so cautious in approaching, at least not this ditch, for the stickleback is monarch of all he surveys here; and though just a bit scared when our shadows fall athwart the water, he immediately reappears in a defiant attitude which there is no mistaking. I speak of 'he', because the only stickleback at present visible, and which I knew

I should find at the spot, is an acquaintance of quite long standing, and is a 'robin', *i.e.* a gentleman stickleback, as beautiful as he is brave. Now see him turn over and show himself when I drop in this little red worm—there, what a gorgeous crimson breast, with sides of brightest silver, and back like the sheen of a sunset sky, and eyes like points of living light! All this, in his efforts to master the poor worm's wriggling, or to break it in two before attempting to swallow. And now that is accomplished, he takes his stand under that dense clump of weed [which contains his nest]. And here comes another stickleback,

Fig. 1114.—Head of Adult Male Salmon (*Salmo salar*), showing hooked lower jaw

innocently looking for something to eat, and approaches within a foot of that clump of weed. Like a lightning flash the 'robin' shoots himself at the intruder, and she, a lady stickleback, turns one or two somersaults, goes very pale and almost transparent, and beats a precipitate retreat. This looks cruel, but he only meant to frighten the brazen female who dared to venture so near to his domain. See him now. Another 'robin' has approached, perhaps the husband of the frightened lady. Now it is war; now he is ready to be cruel if he can. Before we can think, green and crimson and golden lights play madly before our eyes; and this brilliant display is all that can be made out till it is suddenly resolved into two gorgeous robins, more brilliant than ever in their rage, their eyes very balls of fire, their dorsal and lateral prickles erect, and red as though touched with fire. Only an instant are they quiet, when our older friend renews the attack with such ferocity that our later acquaintance deems discretion the better part of valour, and, not in too great a hurry, but with a certain dignity, follows his lady-love, to whom he no doubt describes the tremendous thrashing he has given to her ungallant molester." Lloyd Morgan (in *Animal Sketches*) gives the following very interesting account of a complete stickleback love-story, the scene being an aquarium:—"I began by putting into one of my glass tanks, in which there grew sufficient healthy weed to ensure the purity of the water, a male Thornie and three females. The male was just beginning to assume the bright colours (blue and crimson and creamy white) of courtship. But the largest and stoutest of the females bullied him so unmercifully — reversing the usual order of things *among sticklebacks*—that in two days he was utterly dejected and crestfallen, and had completely lost all sign of colour. I then put into the same tank another male. Him, too, the irascible old lady bullied unmercifully, pulling his fins and his tail in the most vulgar fashion, until he leapt out of the water in his agony. I felt that such conduct could not be allowed. It pained me to see my little friend treated worse than 'the Private Secretary', and that by a lady whom he would fain have made his wife. I therefore removed the offending party, and kept her in solitary confinement in a separate tank, introducing in her stead one quieter and less quarrelsome. This was at about ten o'clock in the morning. But I shortly found that there was a new element of difficulty in getting my finned family to dwell together in peace and harmony. After some slight angry skirmishing, the two little males began a regular downright battle, using freely the strong spines which form the outer rays of the ventral fins. Never were seen more infuriated little monsters. It was, however, soon evident which was master, for ere long the victor was chasing the vanquished round and round the tank, seizing him at times by the pectoral fin, holding on and shaking him like a young bull-dog, the three females timidly looking on the while. At about three o'clock the victor's angry passions began to subside to some extent. He still had a suspicious mien; but with well-feigned nonchalance he began to carry about somewhat aimlessly any little bits of stick or broken pieces of alga he could find, as though he thus intended to proclaim that, now he was master of that tank, he was going to settle down there and build his nest. He was, however, evidently too perturbed in his mind to do any serious work, for he continually left off to go and give the other fellow an additional bit of a drubbing; so that at five o'clock I took pity on the dejected little fish, and removed him to another tank. (A description of the way in which the victorious male built a nest here follows. See vol. iii, p. 428.) He was by this time in glorious colour, bright red all over the gills and along the ventral region, light creamy pink or blue on the back, his eye a very sapphire for brightness and purity of blue. Yet would not his mates be coaxed to the nest. Dress as he might, and air his finery as he would, they remained obdurate, insensate, and unmoved. Then would he show his not unnatural pique and annoyance by running at them from a distance and giving them most ungallant digs in the ribs. This is, however, it should be stated in extenuation of his conduct, a recognized part of the mysteries of stickleback courtship. I therefore removed the females, placing them in a tank close by, so that the little gentleman could show off his attire in one tank, while the ladies gazed at him admiringly from the other, without danger of being pestered by his too urgent attentions. After a time one of the females put on her wedding finery, her sides becoming marked with bands of deeper brown; and as she seemed anxious to join the merry little monarch of the other tank, I transferred her thither. He at once became much excited, and looked, if possible, rosier and bluer-eyed than ever. He soon dashed off to the nest to see that all was there in readiness, and passed through it, remaining inside half a minute or so. After having thus prepared his nest for her reception he returned to the female, and swam slowly round and round her, frequently passing in front of her. The gay rogue! He knew that she could not resist those rosy cheeks and that bright blue eye. Nevertheless he found it his duty to dig her several times in the ribs, and was clearly somewhat annoyed that she delayed so long to come to his nest. Unfortunately I was then called away from my room, so that I did not on this occasion see her pass through the nest and lay her eggs there." For further particulars regarding the home-life of this and other kinds of stickleback, the reader is referred to the delightful book from which the above extract is taken.

THE LAW OF BEAUTY.—We have just seen that a male fish

may assume courtship colours of brilliant kind, but in some species the attractions are of a more elaborate nature. A good instance among British marine fishes is afforded by the Gemmeous Dragonet or Golden Skulpin (*Callionymus lyra*, fig. 1115), where the female is of a dull brown, and was formerly, under the name of the Sordid Dragonet, considered to be a distinct species. The male, however, is yellow, with spots and stripes of blue, besides which his first dorsal fin is relatively large, and

Fig. 1115.—Gemmeous Dragonet (*Callionymus lyra*). Male above; female below

its first ray is drawn out into a long slender filament, which appears to be of the nature of an ornament. Holt has described the courtship of an allied species, the Spangled Dragonet (*C. lineatus*), and says regarding the male that—"its head and body are indescribable mingled harmony of many shades of brown and blue and green, set off with light-blue spots and pearl-coloured stripes; the anterior dorsal fin, which can be erected like a high sail, is golden yellow, studded with many white-edged blue ocelli; the tail fin is a blend of brown and yellow, set with turquoise spots; the belly fin is like dark-blue velvet sown with rows of turquoise; the pelvic fins are like golden-green satin, fringed with dark blue, and spangled with small turquoise spots; and the pectoral fins are of a delicate lavender-gray, with serried dark-brown spots. The female is but a dish-clout in respect of him." In still another species of Dragonet (*C. carebares*), however, it is the female which is beautiful, and she no doubt takes the lead in courtship. It is interesting to note that Alcock has described an Indian flat-fish (*Arnoglossus macrolophus*) in which the male possesses a long crest, owing to the excessive development of the rays at the front end of the dorsal fin, somewhat as in the Dragonets above described.

COURTSHIP AND MATING OF INSECTS (INSECTA)

THE LAW OF BATTLE.—The jaws of some male beetles are of enormous size (fig. 1116), and to these are sometimes added conspicuous horn-like outgrowths from the head or thorax. These features have suggested such names as "stag beetle",

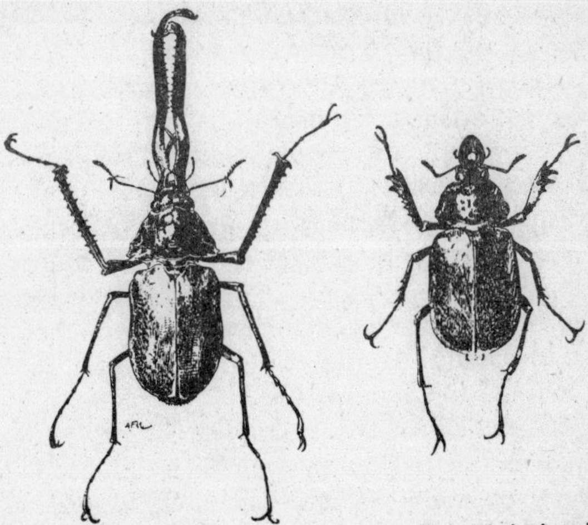

Fig. 1116.—A Tropical Beetle (*Chiasognathus Grantii*). Male on left; female on right

"rhinoceros beetle", &c. Such structures may possibly be used in fights for the possession of mates, but this has not so far been proved, and the matter must remain unsettled until our knowledge of habits is more complete.

Various male insects have, however, been observed fighting for partners, and Darwin (in *The Descent of Man*) gives apparently well-authenticated instances of this among digging wasp-like forms (*Cerceris*), Saw-Flies, Bees, and even Butterflies.

THE LAW OF BEAUTY.—Male insects, especially Butterflies, are often more beautiful and more conspicuous than individuals of the other sex, but it is necessary here to be cautious in drawing conclusions, for courtship is not the only business of life. That the female should often be in plain attire would often appear to be a protective measure, as it is more important for the welfare of the species that she should escape from enemies than her comparatively useless partner. The same explanation may be given where female butterflies are conspicuous as the result of protective mimicry (see vol. ii, p. 311). This line of argument, however, may easily be carried too far, and the usually brighter colours of the male in insects (and other animals) cannot be satisfactorily explained simply as one of the results of greater energy and activity. In many groups the eyes are complex and highly developed, and that they often minister to a "colour-sense" is generally admitted, the relations between insects and flowers, for example, affording much evidence in this direction (see p. 85). Admitting this, Wallace suggests that his theory of recognition marks (see pp. 132, 140) may account for many of the distinctive colours and markings of insects. In arguing against this view Poulton says (in *The Colours of Animals*)—"that the beauty of the colours and patterns displayed in courtship can never be explained by this principle. For the purposes of recognition, beauty is entirely superfluous and indeed undesirable; strongly-marked and conspicuous differences are alone necessary. But these, which are so well marked in Warning Colours, are not by any means characteristic of those displayed in courtship. If an artist, entirely ignorant of natural history, were asked to arrange all the brightly-coloured butterflies and moths in England in two divisions, the one containing all the beautiful patterns and combinations of colour, the other including the staring, strongly-contrasted colours, and crude patterns, we should find that the latter would contain, with hardly an exception, the species in which independent evidence has shown, or is likely to show, the existence of some unpleasant quality. The former division would contain the colours displayed in courtship and when the insect is on the alert, concealed at other times. The immense difference between the two divisions, the one most pleasing, the other highly repugnant to our æsthetic susceptibilities, seems to me to be entirely unexplained if we assume that the colours of both are intended for the purposes of recognition. But these great differences are to be expected if we accept Mr. Darwin's views; for the colours and patterns of the latter division appeal to a vertebrate enemy's sense of what is *conspicuous*, while those of the former appeal to an insect's sense of what is *beautiful*. It is, of course, highly remarkable that our own æsthetic sense should so closely correspond with that of an insect. I believe, however, that it is possible to account for this wonderful unanimity in taste. Our

Fig. 1117.—Orange-Tips (*Anthocharis cardamines*) in Centre (male left; female right). Cabbage-Whites (*Pieris brassicæ*) at Sides (male right; female left)

standards of beauty are largely derived from the contemplation of the numerous examples around us, which, strange as it may seem, have been created by the æsthetic preferences of the insect world."

Among our native species the Orange-Tip Butterfly (*Anthocharis cardamines*, fig. 1117) may probably be taken as a good example of courtship coloration. As in most other butterflies, these insects bring their wings together when they settle, and are then inconspicuous, as the under surfaces of these organs are protectively coloured, being white with greenish mottlings. This is more particularly true for the female Orange-Tip, which is often found sleeping among the blossoms of Wild Chervil (*Anthriscus sylvestris*), with the colour-scheme of which it harmonizes wonderfully. In both sexes the upper sides of the wings are whitish, while the front ones are tipped with black and have a spot in the centre. This can hardly be regarded as a protective arrangement, for it renders the insects conspicuous, though it is not a case of warning coloration; and in the male the effect is greatly heightened by the beautiful orange tips of the fore-wings, and since these present this peculiarity on their under as well as on their upper sides, the members of this sex are not sc inconspicuous when they settle as are their partners. We can only conclude that the magnificent orange patches are courtship adornments.

It is very interesting to find that there are certain Moths in which the females are degenerate, their eyes, among other parts, having undergone retrogressive changes. Attractive colours and patterns in the male would be here superfluous, and, as a matter of fact, the males of such species are commonly dull and plain in appearance.

In some insects the usual rule is reversed, and the female is more beautiful than the male, as in the Cabbage Butterfly (*Pieris brassicæ*, fig. 1117) and other Whites, where there are black markings on the fore-wings of the former sex. Careful observations have demonstrated that in these species the females are the active wooers, while the males are coy (compare vol. iii, p. 465).

A considerable number of male insects proclaim their feelings in an audible manner, as in Grasshoppers and Crickets (see p. 38). Many beetles too, and some other sorts of insects, such as the Cicadas, are possessed of variously situated and constructed sound-producing organs, of which one or the chief use appears to be the production of love-calls (see vol. i, p. 352 and vol. iii, p. 224). Some male insects are also known which emit a strong musky odour.

That some female insects show a preference for one particular admirer seems to be pretty clearly demonstrated in the case of certain Moths, where a large number of males "assemble" round a female that has just come out of the chrysalis (fig. 1118). The following first-hand evidence on this point is given by Poulton (in *The Colours of Animals*):—"In many species of moths the males 'assemble' round the freshly-emerged female, but no special advantage appears to attend an early arrival. The female sits apparently motionless while the little crowd of suitors buzz around her for several minutes. Suddenly, and, as far as one can see, without any sign from the female, one of the males pairs with her and all the others immediately disappear. In these cases the males do not fight or struggle in any way, and as one watches the ceremony the wonder arises as to how the moment is determined, and why the pairing did not take place before. All the males are evidently most eager to pair, and yet when pairing takes place no opposition is offered by the other males to the successful suitor. Proximity does not decide the point, for long beforehand

Fig. 1118.—"Assembling" of Oak Eggar Moths (*Lasiocampa quercus*). The female is the large pale moth, with simple antennæ, at the top of the cut.

the males often alight close to the female, and brush against her with fluttering wings. In watching this wonderful and complicated courtship one is driven to the conclusion that the female must signify her intention in some way unknown to us, and that it is a point of honour with the males to abide by her decision. I have watched the process exactly as I have described it in a common northern Noctua, the Antler Moth (*Charæas graminis*), and I have seen the same thing among beetles. The fact is well known to entomologists, and, as far as the evidence goes, it supports Darwin's theory."

THE FINDING OF MATES.—As implied in the preceding paragraphs, an insect may be guided to a suitable mate in several ways. One of the most remarkable is found in the possession of an exceedingly delicate sense of smell by male insects, especially in cases where sight would often be useless. The moths which "assemble" are no doubt a case in point. When an adult female makes her appearance in the world she is quickly attended by a large number of admirers, although immediately before none were to be seen in the immediate vicinity. This fact is well known to collectors, who by the simple device of putting a female that has just left the chrysalis into a little box, with gauze sides,

Fig. 1119.—The Emperor Moth (*Saturnia carpini*). Male left; female right

and carrying the same into a suitable locality, are often able to capture large numbers of the corresponding male. In such cases the antennæ of the latter are large and complicated (fig. 1119), no doubt ministering to an unusually acute sense of smell. The mouth-parts of an insect of the kind are often much reduced, his last meal having been taken when he was still a voracious larva. Courtship and mating fill up the brief span of his adult life, and unless a partner be quickly found he is doomed to speedy death in a celibate condition. Hence the extraordinary development of the olfactory organs, to aid him in his quest.

In other cases the visual organs are unusually large, apparently with the same purpose. An instance of the kind is thus described by Carpenter (in *Insects, their Structure and Life*):— "Some male Mayflies are provided with peculiar large frontal eyes, carried on columnar outgrowths of the head, in addition to normal lateral eyes like those of the females. The reduction of pigment and the presence of a thick layer of homogeneous fluid . . . has led to the conclusion that the special function of these eyes is to discern moving objects in the dusk, to enable the male to secure a mate in the airy twilight dance of the short-lived Mayflies" (fig. 1120).

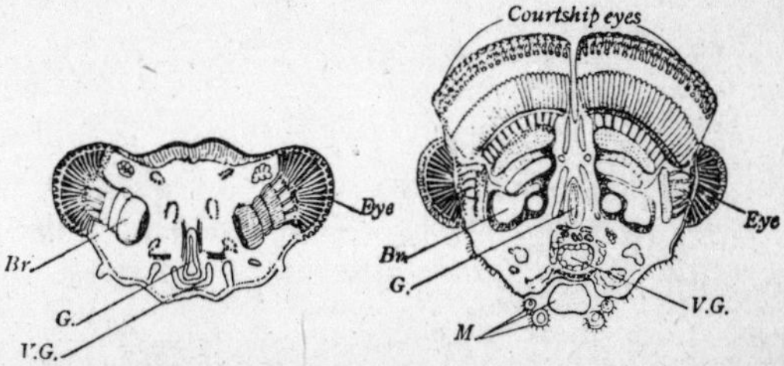

Fig. 1120.—Horizontal Sections through the Heads of a Male (right) and Female (left) Mayfly (*Cloë fuscata*), enlarged. *Br.*, Brain; *V.G.*, ventral ganglion; *G.*, Gullet; *M.*, mouth-parts.

In many of the nocturnal Beetles which are known as Glow-Worms the female is wingless and grub-like, as in our familiar native species (*Lampyris noctiluca*), and practically monopolizes the power of emitting a clear light from peculiar patches of skin along the sides of the body. As the eyes of the male in such cases are well developed, sometimes remarkably so, the object of the arrangement is tolerably clear. In some of the insects of this sort, native to South America, the difference in appearance between the male and female is particularly marked, the latter sex closely resembling the larva (fig. 1121). In Paraguay some of these grub-like females are known as "railway-beetles", being said to exhibit a "danger signal" at either end, and a row of "caution signals" along each side, or, to speak less metaphorically, possessing luminous organs in the positions indicated which respectively emit red and green light. A cynical remark might here be made, as to the appropriateness of such colours in the female sex.

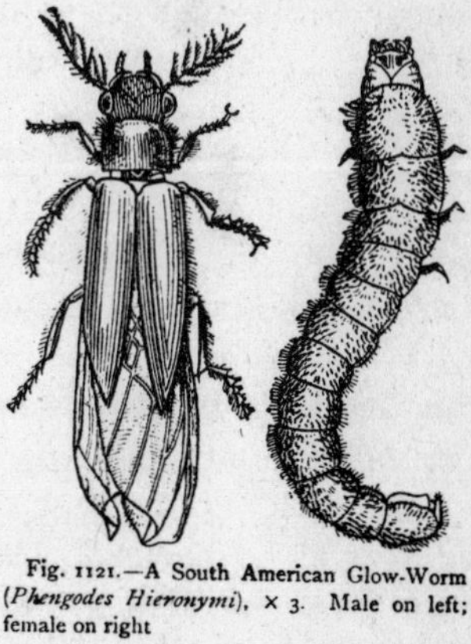

Fig. 1121.—A South American Glow-Worm (*Phengodes Hieronymi*). × 3. Male on left; female on right

There is still, however, much to be learnt as to the meaning of luminous organs in insects, for it appears that in species belonging to the same family as the Glow-Worms, *e.g.* the well-known Fire-Flies (*Luciola*) of South Europe, the light-giving power is more strongly developed in the males. Nor can it well be deemed as probable that they are here the sought and not the seekers, for we should then expect to find the eyes of the female better developed than those of the opposite sex, but this is not the case.

COURTSHIP AND MATING OF SPIDERS (ARANEIDÆ)

The lot of a male spider is not altogether desirable, for he is much smaller than his prospective partner, who sometimes makes a meal of him. It is scarcely worth while in this case to make separate headings of the Laws of Battle and Beauty, for both may find their application at the same time. Dr. and Mrs. Peckham have investigated this subject as regards species of the family of Hunting Spiders (*Attidæ*). Their observations, some of which are quoted below (from *Papers of the Natural History Society of Wisconsin*, 1889), are intensely interesting, and clearly prove that the females of various species do not mate at random with any swain that offers, often being exceedingly fastidious, and sometimes tragically cruel. The males generally possess special markings and ornaments, which they display in ways that often appear grotesque; they also perform complex evolutions, some of these being rather weird "dances" (fig. 1122), of which one (for *Saïtis pulex*) is thus described:—"He saw her as she stood perfectly still, 12 inches away; the glance seemed to excite him, and he moved toward her; when some 4 inches from her he stood still, and then began the most remarkable performances that an amorous male could offer to an admiring female. She eyed him eagerly, changing her position from time to time so that he might be always in view. He, raising his whole body on one side by straightening out the legs, and lowering it on the other by folding the first two pair of legs up and under, leans so far over as to be in danger of losing his balance, which he only maintained by sidling rapidly towards the lowered side. The palpus, too, on this side was turned back to correspond to the direction of the legs nearest it (see fig. 1122). He moved in a semicircle for about 2 inches, and then instantly reversed the position of the legs and circled in the opposite direction, gradually approaching nearer and nearer to the female. Now she dashes towards him, while he, raising his first pair of legs, extends them upward and forward to hold her off, but withal slowly retreats.

Again and again he circles from side to side, she gazing towards him in a softer mood, evidently admiring the grace of his antics. This is repeated until we have counted 111 circles made by the ardent little male. Now he approaches nearer and nearer, and when almost within reach, whirls madly around and around her, she joining and whirling with him in a giddy maze." One feels quite glad to hear that the suit of this particular male was successful. He was decidedly in luck, for we learn that the females

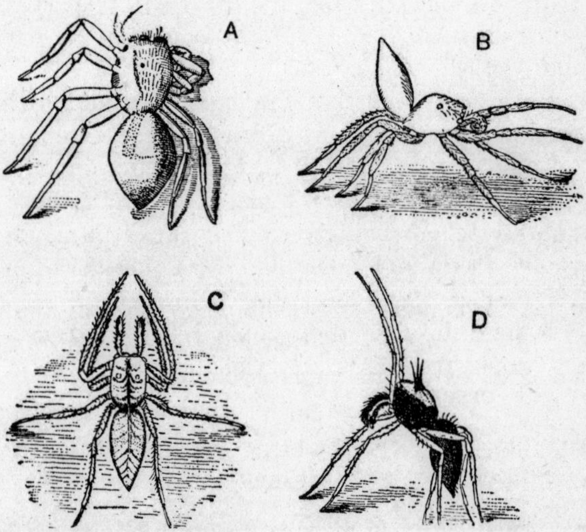

Fig. 1122.—Courtship Attitudes of Male Spiders, enlarged. A, *Saitis pulex*, dancing. B, *Habrocestum splendens* approaching female. C and D, Red and black varieties of *Astia vittata* in approaching attitudes.

of his species are very fastidious, and frequently turn admirers away.

A number of males often compete for the good graces of a single female in some of the species observed, in which case the latter takes some time to make up her mind. Competing wooers from time to time interrupt their antics to tussle with one another. Boldness or persistence sometimes wins the day. The male of one species (*Dendryphantes capitatus*) may frisk around for hours displaying his special beauties, until "at last the female, either won by his beauty or worn out by his persistence, accepts his addresses". And in another form (*Hasarius Hoyi*) a male was brave enough to walk up to an evidently displeased female, "when she seized him and seemed to hold him by the head for a minute, he struggling. At last he freed himself and ran away." Only to come back again, however, for we read that: "This same male after a time courted her successfully". Tragic courtships were also observed, as in the case of a particularly ruthless female (of *Phidippus morsitans*) who behaved thus:—"The two males that we provided for her had offered her only the merest civilities, when she leaped upon them and killed them".

In one remarkable species (*Astia vittata*) the female is red, and there are two kinds of male, red and black respectively, which court in different ways (fig. 1122). When they are rivals, black is invariably the winning colour.

It has been suggested that the small size and great activity of male spiders are adaptations which to some extent reduce the appalling dangers of courtship. In leaving this group the writer ventures to express a hope that many field naturalists may feel moved to observe the habits of common native forms on the lines so successfully followed by Dr. and Mrs. Peckham, in this and other fields (see p. 55). Anything approaching the skill and devotion of these investigators, applied to the study of almost any species, would most assuredly yield a rich harvest of valuable results.

COURTSHIP AND MATING OF CRUSTACEANS (CRUSTACEA)

Comparatively little is known about the love affairs of the higher members of this group, which deserves far more attention in this matter than has so far been bestowed upon it. It will perhaps suffice here to quote an exceedingly interesting account which is given by Alcock (in *A Naturalist in Indian Seas*) of a little Fiddler Crab (*Gelasimus annulipes*, fig. 1123), which is very abundant on the mud-flats at the mouths of the Godávari and Kistna. The pincers of the female are small, and only used in feeding, but in the male one of them is of great size and bright pink in colour, serving as an ornament and also as a weapon. Alcock thus describes the courtship of these little

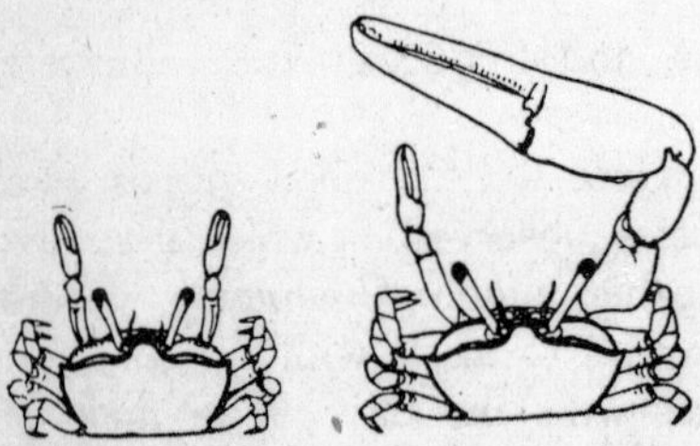

Fig. 1123.—Indian Fiddler Crab (*Gelasimus annulipes*). Female on left; male on right

animals:—" Landing one afternoon in March upon a cheerful mud-flat of the Godávari sea-face, I was bewildered by the sight of a multitude of small pink objects twinkling in the sun, and always, like will-of-the-wisps, disappearing as I came near to them, but flashing brightly on ahead as far as the eye could reach. It was not until I stayed perfectly quiet that I discovered that these twinkling gems were the brandished nippers of a host of males of *Gelasimus annulipes.* By long watching I found out that the little creatures were waving their nippers with a purpose—the purpose apparently being to attract the attention of an occasional infrequent female, who, uncertain, coy, and hard to please, might be seen unconsciously sifting the sand at the mouth of her burrow. If this demure little flirt happened to creep near the burrow of one of the males, then that favoured individual became frantic with excitement, dancing round his domain on tiptoe and waving his great cherry hand as if demented. Then, if another male, burning with jealousy, showed a desire to interfere, the two puny little suitors would make savage back-handed swipes at one another, wielding their cumbrous hands as if they had no weight at all.

Some of the Crustaceans possess the power of emitting sounds (see p. 37), possibly to serve as love-calls, and the courtship habits of such species would probably prove interesting.

CHAPTER LXV

ASSOCIATION OF ANIMALS—MESSMATES OR COMMENSALS (COMMENSALISM)

Messmates are organisms of different species which are more or less closely associated, to the benefit of at least one partner in the concern. Cases of this sort are grouped under the head of Commensalism Mutualism (*Symbiosis*) is a much more intimate kind of relation between two organisms, to the advantage of both, as already described. The best examples of such Mutualism or Symbiosis involve a partnership for certain cases where plants and animals are thus associated (see p. 75). It is doubtful whether any two kinds of animal live together in this intimate fashion. Parasites are animals which live on or in other animals, at their expense, and to their detriment. Parasitism also includes cases where one organism concerned is a plant (see p. 76).

In a broad sense all the animals which live and feed together in the same place may be regarded as messmates, and the relations between such species may be very complex. It will, however, be well to restrict the term to cases where the connection is of closer and more constant nature, involving the interests of definite species. But it must not be forgotten that this kind of association has no doubt gradually arisen from relations which were originally of more casual kind. So many instances of Commensalism are known that it will only be possible to describe a few of the more striking examples.

FISHES (PISCES) AS MESSMATES

Some extraordinary cases have been described where small bony fishes take up their quarters within the digestive organs of lower animals, sallying forth from these peculiar refuges as circumstances dictate. The most familiar instance of this is afforded by a slender form (*Fierasfer*) living in the gullet of a kind of Sea-Cucumber, which does not appear to gain anything by way of return for its hospitality. Some of the giant sea-anemones living on the Great Barrier Reef of Australia harbour gaily-coloured little fishes belonging to the Perch family, a given species of anemone being the home of a particular species of fish. The fish-guest (*Amphiprion percula*) of one such obliging zoophyte (*Discosoma Kenti*) is orange-red in colour, marked by three cross-bands of pearly white, these and the fins being edged with black. An allied anemone (*D. Haddoni*) entertains a little fish (*A. bicinctus*) which differs from its relative in possessing two bands only, while the black edging is absent.

Fig. 1124.—Indian Rock Perch (*Minous inermis*) with Commensal Polypes (*Stylactis minoi*)

The same anemone also extends its hospitality to a red-and-white Prawn (*Palæmon*). In these cases the fishes not only find a secure shelter, the stinging properties of which ward off attack, but also probably filch some of the food of their living homes. On the other hand, it is possible, as suggested by Saville Kent, who has described the associated animals, that the bright tints of the gue ts serve as "lure colours", enticing animals which serve as food for the anemones.

The relations just described are occasionally reversed, as when a fish serves as a moving home to zoophytes. Alcock describes a Rock Perch (*Minous inermis*, fig. 1124), native to the Indian Ocean, as being always more or less encrusted with small polypes (*Stylactis minoi*), which, being of course carried about from place to place, have a better chance of getting abundant food than if they were attached to a stone or sea-weed. The fish may perhaps derive some protection from the stinging properties of its guests.

MOLLUSCS (MOLLUSCA) AS MESSMATES

A marine snail (*Pleurotoma symbiotes*, fig. 1125), living in the deep water of the Indian Ocean, always has its shell more or less encrusted with colonial sea-anemones (*Epizoanthus*). Both animals are no doubt benefited, for the mollusc is protected, while the anemones are carried about.

A number of small Bivalve Molluscs are associated with burrowing Sea-Urchins or Crustaceans. One such bivalve (*Montacuta ferruginosa*), native to South Devon, lives in the dwelling which a Heart-Urchin (*Echinocardium cordatum*) excavates in muddy sand. The circulation of sea-water which takes place within the burrow (see vol. iii, p. 357) ensures a constant supply of food by which the mollusc benefits. In places where the sand is loose and wet the Heart-Urchin is in the habit of coming to the surface, along which it makes its way, but the lodger is not thereby left behind, for it spins byssus threads that attach it to its partner.

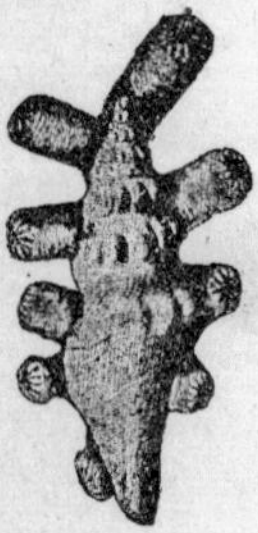

Fig. 1125.—An Indian Sea-Snail (*Pleurotoma symbiotes*) with Commensal Sea-Anemones (*Epizoanthus*)

A rare little British Bivalve (*Lepton squamosum*) inhabits the burrow of a prawn-like Crustacean (*Upogebia stellata*), and, having an exceedingly flat shell, does not interfere with the movements of its protector. A similar partnership exists on the coast of Florida between two species related to the preceding, while on the shores of Oregon and California a third association of the sort is more intimate, for here the Lepton attaches itself to the abdomen of the Upogebia. A burrowing Australian prawn (*Axius plectorhynchus*) harbours two species of a kind of bivalve (*Ephippodonta*), which is never found elsewhere. The flatness, so necessary to allow of the restless movements of the prawn, is here produced by the valves of the mollusc opening to their fullest extent. This particular prawn appears to be a specialist in the matter of providing lodgings, for four other bivalves (one species of *Kellia* and three of *Mylitta*) find a commodious home in its burrow, which also contains an orange-coloured sponge. The last possibly serves as a protection to the crustacean, but the arrangement would appear to be quite one-sided so far as the molluscs are concerned.

As with Fishes (see p. 171), Bivalve Molluscs are not always lodgers in the case of partnerships, but may afford shelter to weaker creatures. A well-known instance is that of the little rounded Lodger-Crabs (*Pinnotheridæ*), in which the eyes have undergone great reduction. Among bivalves which provide them with homes may be mentioned Horse-Mussels (*Modiola*), Oysters (*Ostrea*), Pinnas, and Tridacnas, while some crabs of the kind take up their quarters within ascidians or sea-cucumbers. Van Beneden thus speaks of these little lodgers (in *Animal Parasites and Messmates*):—"It is not a taste for voyaging which tempts them, but the desire of having always a secure retreat in every place. The pinnothere is a brigand who causes himself to be followed by the cavern which he inhabits, and which opens only at a well-known watchword. The association redounds to the advantage of both; the remains of food which the pinnothere abandons are seized upon by the mollusc [or, rather, some of its remains may be carried by ciliary action into the mouth of the mollusc]. It is the rich man who instals himself in the dwelling of the poor, and causes him to participate in all the advantages of the position. The pinnotheres are, in our opinion, true messmates. They take their food in the same waters as their fellow-lodger, and the crumbs of the rapacious crabs are doubtless not lost in the mouth of the peaceful mussel. There is no doubt that these little plunderers are good lodgers, and if the mussels furnish them with an excellent hiding-place and a safe lodging, they themselves profit largely by the leavings of the feast which fall from their pincers. Little as they are, these crabs are well furnished with tackle, and advantageously placed to carry on their fishery in every season. Concealed in the bottom of their living dwelling-place (a den which the mussel transports at will) they choose admirably the moment to rush out to the attack, and always fall on their enemy unawares. Some of these pinnotheres live in all seas, and inhabit a great number of bivalve molluscs." The habits of these curious little crabs attracted attention in remote times, and have been the subject of much curious speculation. Stebbing (in *A History of Crustacea*) makes the following remarks upon the ancient views, and discusses the origin of the commensal habit:—"The name *Pinnoteres* means one that watches or guards the *Pinna*, and there can be little doubt that it was the form used by Aristotle [and not *Pinnotheres*, meaning one that 'hunts the *Pinna*'], seeing that he also speaks of *Pinnophylax*, a word of precisely the same meaning. Not only Aristotle, but many succeeding writers of renown, such as Cicero, Pliny, and seemingly Linnæus himself, accepted the opinion that there was a compact between the mollusc and the crustacean for their mutual benefit. Whenever little fishes swam in between the expanded valves of the mollusc, it was supposed that its companion gave it a little friendly nip, upon which the valves snapped together, the prey was secured, and shared between the confederates. A similar policy was pursued to exclude the intrusion of a dangerous foe. The great antiquity of the belief is attested by the fact that the Egyptians in their hieroglyphics made use of the pinna and crab to symbolize the helplessness of a man without friends. That the belief was untenable was pointed out by many naturalists, from Gesner down to Cuvier, on the ground that molluscs do not feed on little fishes, and that the residence of the crabs within the valves was sufficiently explained by the prevailing softness of the carapace in this family. This indeed applies chiefly to the females, and it is the females that appear to be most frequently found thus domiciled. It is so much the nature of crustaceans to take refuge in any sort of cleft or cranny that the first entrance of the *Pinnotheres* into any sort of bivalve can be easily understood. When the residence proved to be peculiarly secure, the shell of the crab would by degrees lose a hardness that was no longer especially necessary. That the crab may at times be useful to the mollusc seems after all not so very improbable, for at the approach of an enemy so nervous a creature as a crab would no doubt begin to scuttle about, and in this way communicate its terror to its more apathetic companion, which would then naturally close its doors against the danger."

JOINTED-LIMBED ANIMALS (ARTHROPODA) AS MESSMATES

We are here especially concerned with Insects and Crabs, regarding which groups there is a great wealth of material from which to select, so that only a few examples can be here given, supplementing, for the latter animals, what has just been said about Pinnotheres.

INSECTS (INSECTA) AS MESSMATES.—It will be convenient to limit our attention to Bees and Ants, remembering that both belong to an order (Hymenoptera—Membrane-winged Insects) of which the members are distinguished by an extraordinary amount of specialization, associated with mental qualities of no mean order.

Bees as Messmates.—Many species are known of what may be called, for want of a better word, Lodger Bees (*Psithyrus*), each kind of which lives in the nest of some sort of Humble-Bee (*Bombus*). In nearly all such cases the guest closely resembles its entertainer in appearance, and the two dwell together in a perfectly friendly way. The arrangement is of a one-sided nature, for the lodger not only has free quarters, but also makes free use of the provisions stored up by the industrious humble-bee, which, however, is not directly harmed by the association. But as a result of the raids made upon the larder by its lazy lodger, it is not able to rear nearly so many young ones as would otherwise be the case. A nest of a species of Humble-Bee (*Bombus variabilis*), examined by Hoffer in early autumn, contained only a queen and fifteen workers, together with eighteen Lodger-Bees (*Psithyrus campestris*), of which eight were females. But for the strain on the commissariat there would, it was estimated, have been 200 humble-bees in the colony, or even more.

Ants as Messmates.—Occasion has already been taken to note the curious relations which exist between Ants and Aphides, the latter being fed and tended in return for their services as "cows" (see p. 119). Even more extraordinary are the habits of certain Slave-making Ants, which press other ants into their service, employing them in all the varied duties of the nest. The slavers conduct organized raids from time to time, in order to keep up the number of their dependants, and it must be said that these take very kindly to their enforced labours. A notable European example is afforded by the large Amazon Ant (*Polyergus rufescens*), which enslaves the small Brown Garden Ant (*Formica fusca*). The following graphic account of the matter is given by Newman (in *An Introduction to the History of Insects*), and some of the details are set forth in fig. 1126:—"The most remarkable fact connected with the history of ants is the propensity possessed by certain species to kidnap the workers of other species, and compel them to labour for the benefit of the community, thus using them completely as slaves; and, as far as we yet know, the kidnappers are red or pale-coloured ants, and the slaves, like the ill-treated natives of Africa, are of a jet black [or at any rate dark in hue]. The time for capturing slaves extends over a period of about ten weeks, and never commences till the male and female ants are about emerging from the pupa stage, and thus the ruthless marauders never interfere with the continuation of the species; this instinct seems specially provided, for were the slave ants created for no other end than to fill the

Fig. 1126.—Slave Raid of Amazon Ants (*Polyergus rufescens*)

station of slavery to which they appear to be doomed, still even that office must fail were the attacks to be made on their nests before the winged myriads have departed, or are departing, charged with the duty of continuing their kind. When the red ants are about to sally forth on a marauding expedition, they send scouts to ascertain the exact position in which a colony of negroes may be found; these scouts having discovered the object of their search, return to the nest and report their success. Shortly afterwards the army of red ants marches forth, headed by a vanguard, which is perpetually changing; the individuals which constitute it, when thev nave advanced a little before the main body, halting, falling into the rear, and being replaced by others; this vanguard consists of eight or ten ants only. When they have arrived near the negro colony, they disperse, wandering through the herbage and hunting about, as if aware of the propinquity of the object of their search, yet ignorant of its exact position. At last they discover the settlement, and the foremost of the invaders, rushing impetuously to the attack, are met, grappled with, and frequently killed by the negroes on guard; the alarm is quickly communicated to the interior of the nest; the negroes sally forth by thousands, and, the red ants rushing to the rescue, a desperate conflict ensues, which, however, always terminates in the defeat of the negroes, who retire to the innermost recesses of their habitation. Now follows the scene of pillage; the red ants with their powerful mandibles tear open the sides of the negro ant-hill, and rush into the heart of the citadel. In a few minutes each of the invaders emerges, carrying in its mouth the pupa of a worker negro, which it has obtained in spite of the vigilance and valour of its natural guardians. The red ants return in perfect order to their nest, bearing with them their living burdens. On reaching the nest the pupæ appear to be treated precisely as their own, and the workers, when they emerge, perform the various duties of the community with the greatest energy and apparent goodwill; they repair the nest, excavate passages, collect food, feed the larvæ, take the pupæ into the sunshine, and perform every office which the welfare of the colony seems to require; in fact, they conduct themselves entirely as if fulfilling their original destination." The Amazon Ants are practically incapable of feeding themselves, being thus almost entirely dependent upon the good offices of their slaves. They are, however, so fierce and warlike that their dominance in the mixed community is easily understood. Far more remarkable is the mode of life of a rare ant (*Anergates atratulus*), native to Central Europe, in which there is no worker caste, but only females and wingless males, both sexes being weak and helpless. Small numbers of them are found associated with numerous workers of a small species (*Tetramorium cæspitum*), by which they and their offspring are tended, and which are vastly their superiors in strength and energy. How the association comes about is unknown, but it has been suggested that a young fertile Anergates female makes her way into a Tetramorium nest, destroys the queen and young, and is accepted by the workers as their nominal sovereign. A more likely view is that such a female enters a Tetramorium nest containing only workers, and it appears that such nests do sometimes occur More observations are necessary in order to settle the question. Lord Avebury makes the following conjectures (in *Ants, Bees, and Wasps*) as to the past history of Anergates:—"We may safely conclude that in distant times their ancestors lived, as so many ants do now, partly by hunting, partly on honey; that by degrees they became bold marauders, and gradually took to keeping slaves; that for a time they maintained their strength and agility, though losing by degrees their real independence, their arts, and even many of their instincts; that gradually even their bodily force dwindled away under the enervating influence to which they had subjected themselves, until they sank to their present degraded condition—weak in body and mind, few in numbers, and apparently nearly extinct, the miserable representatives of far superior ancestors, maintaining a precarious existence as contemptible parasites of their former slaves."

Ants not only keep cattle and slaves, but are also known, in many cases, to entertain quite a number of insect guests, which they feed and otherwise look after, their attentions being probably often rewarded by some sort of sweet substance produced by their visitors, though this does not appear to be invariably the case. Beetles are especially common among such true guests, and many species (as also of other sorts of insect) are to be found nowhere else, being then known as ants'-nest insects (myrmecophilous insects). They often somewhat resemble their entertainers in appearance, and are fully versed in the ways of the nest. The latter point is well illustrated by the way in which they stroke ants that have returned from foraging, to induce them to disgorge some of the honey with which the crop is distended (fig. 1127, A). One very remarkable case has been described in which certain ants (*Lasius*) carry about mites on their bodies, feeding them from time to time, and otherwise treating them with great consideration, though apparently without deriving any corresponding benefit.

Besides the true guests just mentioned, there may be also various sorts of tolerated guest, which the ants treat with more or less indifference. A case in point is afforded by a small ant (*Formicoxenus nitidulus*), which is permitted to live unmolested in the hills of the large Horse-Ant (*Formica rufa*). A somewhat amusing instance is that of a species of Tassel-tail (*Grassiella polypoda*), which maintains itself in the nest of a kind of ant

(*Lasius mixtus*). In fig. 1127, B is represented a little drama which appears to be frequently enacted by the two kinds of insect. One ant is seen in the act of feeding another by squeezing a drop of sweet fluid out of its crop. A tassel-tail is just about to steal this drop, being also prepared to beat a hasty retreat after accomplishing the impudent theft.

Fig. 1127.—Scenes in Ant Life, enlarged. A, an Ants'-nest Beetle (*Atemeles*) asking to be fed. B. A Tassel-Tail (*Grassiella polypoda*) about to steal a drop of food which one ant is giving to another.

CRABS (BRACHYURA) AS MESSMATES.—Partnerships between Crabs and Sea-Anemones are of common occurrence, the former being benefited by the stinging properties of the Zoophytes, which in their turn are placed under favourable conditions as regards feeding. Such an association between a Buffoon-Crab (*Dorippe facchino*) and an Anemone (*Cancrisocia expansa*) is shown in fig. 1128. An arrangement, differing in detail, has been described in the case of two kinds of crab native to Mauritius, each of which has two anemones as messmates, one fixed to each of the large pincers.

Fig. 1128.—Buffoon-Crab (*Dorippe facchino*) with Commensal Sea-Anemone (*Cancrisocia expansa*), reduced

Hermit-Crabs are particularly notable for the partnerships which they contract with Zoophytes, probably because the shells in which they shelter their soft tails afford a convenient surface for attachment. Two British species, for example, *Eupagurus Bernhardus* and *E. Prideauxii*, have as their respective associates two different species of Cloak-Anemone (*Adamsia Rondeletii* and *A. palliata*). Regarding the latter hermit-crab Stebbing (in *A History of Crustacea*) speaks as follows:—"Surmises are sometimes made as to the advantages which the companions may hope to gain from the alliance. The anemone may obviously obtain a greatly increased range for supplies of food, by the superior locomotive powers of the hermit, and though the weight of both anemone and shell may seem an unnecessary encumbrance to the crustacean, that objection is gradually diminished by the circumstance that the anemone in course of time almost entirely absorbs the shell. On the other hand, the presence of the anemone may be a very valuable protection to the hermit, since numerous fishes are in the habit of swallowing these recluses, shell and all, merely spitting out the shell after they have digested its inmate. But it is most probable that to many fishes an *Adamsia palliata* would be by no means an agreeable morsel, even when flavoured with crab-sauce. It is also not unlikely that the anemone may contribute to the commissariat by throwing out its darts as some swift-gliding shrimp passes by, and thus reducing it to a condition in which it can be captured by the pagurid." In some of the hermit-crabs the shelly dwelling is coated by a hydroid zoophyte (*Hydractinia echinata*), which by its growth is able to enlarge the hermit's home, thus saving him the trouble of looking out for fresh quarters, as in other cases is done from time to time as the exigencies of growth may determine. It is said that when a hermit in partnership with an anemone changes his abode he carefully detaches his messmate from the old domicile and attaches it to the new one.

The messmate of an American hermit (*Eupagurus pubescens*) is a colonial sea-anemone (*Epizoanthus*), which gradually absorbs the protective shell, constituting thereafter an expansible covering, which obviates change of residence. Anderson's Blanket-Crab (*Chlænopagurus Andersoni*, fig. 1129), native to the Indian Ocean, is associated with a similar anemone, and is said never to use a cast-off shell as a refuge. Alcock (in *A Naturalist in Indian Seas*) thus summarizes in an interesting way the salient features of associations of the kind:—"Sea-anemones here [*i.e.* on the Orissa coast], for the most part, were found attached to the shells of hermit-crabs, &c., a case of Hobson's choice sometimes, no doubt, but also sometimes illustrating that happy bond of commensalism, or Platonic union, which is one of the most valuable object-lessons for man's edification that marine zoology affords. When two animals of different grades in the zoological scale live together in such a fashion that each one assists the other in some definite way, while doing it no manner of harm, they are termed commensals or messmates. For instance, when a hermit-crab and a sea-anemone live together, the hermit-crab, being by nature a very ill-clad and vulnerable animal, acquires by the partnership a thick and easily-adjustable greatcoat, while the sea-anemone, being by nature a hopeless lump of an animal, dependent on chance currents for its food and oxygen, acquires an engine and intelligent engine-driver all in one, which are always carrying it in the way of the necessaries of life; and yet with this mutual assistance there goes absolute independence in all other respects, such as mistresses and servants, who would both be none the worse for a little knowledge of the principles of zoology, never dreamt of."

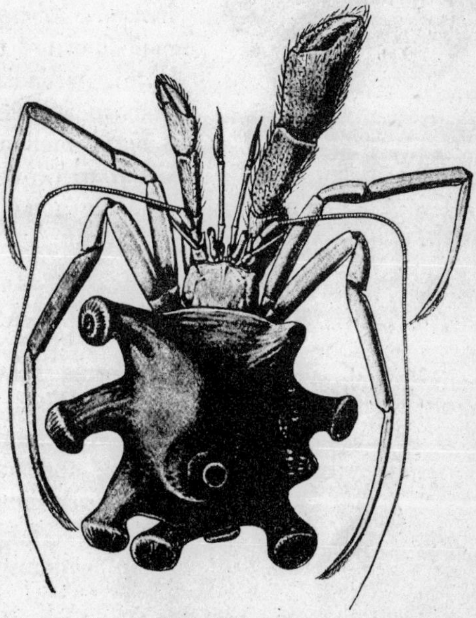

Fig. 1129.—Anderson's Blanket-Crab (*Chlænopagurus Andersoni*) with Commensal Sea-Anemones (*Epizoanthus*)

Certain crabs have sponges as messmates, the mutual advantages being much the same as before, it being remembered that sponges are usually avoided by predaceous creatures which appreciate the flavour of crustaceans. In the members of one family of crabs (*Dromidæ*) the last pair of legs are modified in relation to the commensal habit, being small, with more or less hook-like tips, and having shifted somewhat towards the upper side of the body. They are used to hold a sponge or some other passive messmate that serves as a sort of living cape, promoting concealment and protection. In the common Sponge-Crab (*Dromia vulgaris*), as the popular name indicates, this companion is a sponge. So also in a little species (*Cryptodromia pileifera*, fig. 1130) from the coral-reefs of the Andaman Islands, and in this case the messmate is cap-shaped, and fits very neatly to the back of its active partner.

Fig. 1130.—Under View of an Andaman Sponge - Crab (*Cryptodromia pileifera*) with Commensal Sponge

Hermit-Crabs are also in some instances associated with sponges, one of them (*Eupagurus Cuanensis*) being particularly notable in this respect, for the shell in which it lives is completely overgrown by an orange-coloured species (*Suberites domunculus*), leaving only a small aperture to serve as a front door. As this particular sponge is not only full of sharp spicules, but also disagreeable to both smell and taste, we might expect it to prove a very efficient protection, and Garstang has found by actual experiment that fishes find it extremely repulsive.

SIPHON-WORMS (GEPHYREA) AS MESSMATES

Some of these curious worms take up their quarters in empty shells, and in certain cases this has led to a curious kind of commensalism, to some extent teminiscent of what happens in hermit-crabs. For just as anemones attach themselves to the dwellings of hermits, so do certain simple corals affix themselves to the shells appropriated by siphon-worms, afterwards increasing in size so as to conceal these from view, so that in the end we find the base of the coral traversed by a kind of tunnel serving as the home of the worm (fig. 1131). Three different species of coral (*Heteropsammia Michelini*, *Heterocyathus æquicostatus*, and *Stephanoseris Rousseaui*) have been described from the Indian Ocean, each living with a distinct species of a kind of siphon-worm (*Aspidosiphon*). Shipley has carefully examined the species (*A. corallicola*) associated with the first-named coral, and makes the following interesting remarks about the partnership (in *Ceylon Pearl Fishery Report*):—"The whole question of such com-

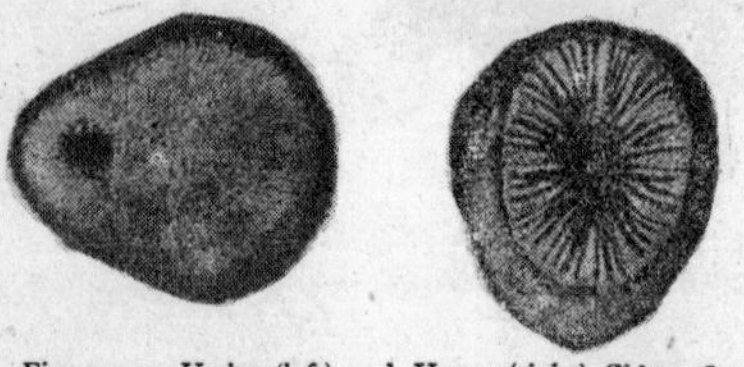

Fig. 1131.—Under (left) and Upper (right) Sides of a Cup-Coral (*Heteropsammia Michelini*), showing opening of the dwelling of its Commensal Siphon-Worm (*Aspidosiphon corallicola*)

mensalism as exists between the *Aspidosiphon* and the coral is an interesting one. Commensalism is usually looked upon as conferring some mutual advantage on the contracting parties, and one or the other of these usually seeks the other out. But in the case in question the mutual advantage is far to seek. It can hardly help the coral to have a large proportion of its base burrowed by a spacious canal, but the fact that the Gephyrean pulls the otherwise immovable coral about may be, and probably is, an advantage to the Cœlenterate. On the other hand, the Gephyrean gains protection and a home more spacious than the Gastropod shell affords. The *Aspidosiphon* can hardly find or attract the larval coral to come to rest on its borrowed shell, and it is unlikely that the larva is especially on the outlook for such shells as are inhabited by Gephyrea. It seems more probable that the *Aspidosiphon* may select for its home a Mollusc shell which already bears a young coral, but the whole matter seems to demand more careful study. It is certainly remarkable that three distinct genera of coral, each with but one species, should be inhabited by three distinct species of *Aspidosiphon*, and that neither commensal has hitherto been found apart from the other." In some cases, at least, there would appear to be a third partner in the concern, for numbers of a kind of minute bivalve mollusc were found closely attached to the outside of the siphon-worms. Regarding them Shipley remarks:—"These were so closely adpressed to the skin of the *Aspidosiphon* as to indent it, appearing as little pearls set in a matrix. The advantage they obtained by taking up such a position is not very evident, but there they were, and as far as one could judge they were, until Professor Herdman dropped them into his collecting-jar, flourishing."

CHAPTER LXVI

ASSOCIATION OF ANIMALS—PARASITES

Parasites live at the expense of larger animals, either using various parts of them as aliment, or robbing them of the food which they have digested. The less modified forms (ecto-parasites) attack their "hosts" from the outside, making either an occasional visit, as in the blood-sucking Leeches, or dwelling permanently upon the skin, a condition familiarly illustrated by many of the Fleas. Much greater modification is found among those parasitic animals (endoparasites) which live within their hosts, *e.g.* Flukes and Tape-Worms, and many of these pass through a complicated life-history, in the course of which two or more hosts may be utilized as homes. Many forms are parasites for a part of their lives only, being free-living when young or adult as the case may be, and not infrequently there is a difference between the sexes in this respect, one of them (especially the female) being a parasite and the other not.

The origin of parasitism is not far to seek. It may be regarded in many cases as an outcome of the carnivorous habit. Small animals attacked larger ones which they were unable to kill and devour in a straightforward fashion, so to speak, and the convenience of preying upon a highly nutritious living food-supply, at which it was possible to "cut and come again", naturally led to further evolution of the habit. And it is not difficult to imagine the stages by which external parasites gradually became internal parasites. Sometimes, too, no doubt, parasitism has resulted from the association of messmates (commensalism) in which the partnership was from the first one-sided, or ultimately became so. It would also seem that in many instances the habit possessed by many female animals of seeking out some secure refuge for egg-laying purposes has been the starting-point of parasitic relations. However originated, it is at least certain that the phenomenon of parasitism is very widely spread, and there is probably no animal which does not unwillingly entertain unwelcome guests that make no return for services rendered. As De Morgan sings (in *The Budget of Paradoxes*):—

"Great fleas have little fleas upon their backs to bite 'em,
And little fleas have lesser fleas, and so *ad infinitum*;
And the great fleas themselves, in turn, have greater fleas to go on,
Whilst these again have greater still, and greater still, and so on".

The general progress of evolution has been from the less to the more specialized as a result of adaptation to increasingly complex surroundings, but to this parasites constitute a striking exception. Free quarters and free rations having been provided for them, they have taken but little part in the active struggle for existence, and well illustrate the principle of Degeneration. They are on the down-grade, adapting themselves to comparatively simple conditions. Hence we find that complex organs of digestion, circulation, respiration, and locomotion, together with nervous system and sense-organs, have undergone more or less reduction in thoroughgoing parasites, though, on the other hand, they have frequently developed special piercing, sucking, and adhesive structures, enabling them to exploit their living food-supply, and to maintain their position. The great danger attending this particular mode of life is constituted by the smallness of the chance of transfer from one host to another. In the more helpless forms this difficulty is often met by the practice of living in two or more different hosts which eat or prey upon one another; the adult egg-producing stage, being the most important, is commonly associated with the strongest and most highly organized of these, the so-called "final host". The biological relations between the successive living refuges is always such as to maintain most surely "the vicious circle of parasitism". Even more important is the immense fecundity of parasites, a necessary provision, for the chances of survival are extremely small. Leuckart calculated, for example, that any one egg of a tape-worm has only one chance in some 83,000,000 of giving rise to an adult.

What is called Brood Parasitism, where an animal shirks the duty of bringing up its own young, will be considered in this section, although it is by no means the same thing as true parasitism.

BIRDS (AVES) AS BROOD-PARASITES

The Common Cuckoo (*Cuculus canorus*), as everyone knows, deposits her just-laid egg in the nest of some small bird, carrying it there in her bill. The proceedings of the young cuckoo, as observed by Mrs. Blackburn, are thus described by Lloyd Morgan (in *Animal Behaviour*):—"One of the most remarkable instincts of young birds is that of the cuckoo, which ejects eggs and nestlings from the home of its foster-parent. Mrs. Hugh Blackburn found a nest which contained two meadow-pipits' eggs, besides that of a cuckoo. On a later visit the pipits were found to be hatched, but not the cuckoo. At the next visit, which was after an interval of forty-eight hours, 'we found the young cuckoo alone in the nest, and both the young pipits lying down the bank, about ten inches from the margin of the nest, but quite lively after being warmed in the hand. They were replaced in the nest beside the cuckoo, which struggled about until it got its back under one of them, when it climbed backwards directly up the open side of the nest, and hitched the pipit from its back on to the edge. It then stood quite upright on its legs, which were straddled wide apart, with the claws firmly fixed half-way down the inside of the nest, among the interlacing fibres of which the nest was woven, and, stretching its wings apart and backwards, it elbowed the pipit fairly over the margin, so far that its struggles took it down the bank instead of back into the nest [fig. 1132]. As it was getting late, and the cuckoo did not immediately set to work on the other nestling, I replaced the ejected one and went home. On returning next day, both nestlings were found dead and cold, out of the nest' (*Birds from Moidart and Elsewhere*)." Similar habits have been described for the Cow-Birds (species of *Molobrus*) of America. One species of these (*M. rufaxillaris*) actually lays its eggs in the nest of a related species (*M. badius*), which is industrious enough to build one for itself. It may further be remarked in passing that some kinds of Cuckoo also construct nests, and bring up their young in the usual way.

Newton, after speaking of the social nesting-habits of certain birds, makes the following suggestions as to the origin of brood-parasitism (in *A Dictionary of Birds*):—"In the strongest contrast to these amiable qualities is the parasitic nature of the Cuckows of the Old World and the Cow-Birds of the New, but this peculiarity of theirs has already been dwelt upon. Enough to say here that the egg of the parasite is introduced into the nest of the dupe, and after the necessary incubation by the fond fool of a foster-mother the interloper successfully counterfeits the heirs, who perish miserably, victims of his superior strength. The whole process has been often watched, but the reflective naturalist will pause to ask how such a state of things came about, and there is not much to satisfy his enquiry. Certain it is that some birds, whether by mistake or stupidity, do not unfrequently lay their eggs in the nests of others. It is within the knowledge of many that Pheasants' eggs and Partridges' eggs are often laid in the same nest, and it is within the knowledge of the writer that Gulls' eggs have been found in the nests of Eider-Ducks, and *vice versâ*; that a Redstart and a Pied Fly-Catcher, or the latter and a Titmouse, will lay their eggs in the same convenient hole—the forest being rather deficient in such accommodation; that an Owl and a Golden-Eye will resort to the same nest-box, set up by a scheming woodsman for his own advantage; and that the Starling, which constantly dispossesses the Green Woodpecker, sometimes discovers that the rightful heir of the domicile has to be brought up by the intruding tenant. In all such cases it is not possible to say which species is so constituted as to obtain the mastery; but just as it is conceivable that in the course of ages that which was driven from its home might thrive through the fostering of its young by the invader, and thus the abandonment of domestic duties would become a direct gain to the evicted householder, so the bird which, through

Fig. 1132.—Young Cuckoo (*Cuculus canorus*) ejecting a Fledgling Meadow-Pipit from the Nest

inadvertence or any other cause, adopted the habit of casually dropping her eggs in a neighbour's nest, might thereby ensure a profitable inheritance for endless generations of her offspring. This much granted, all the rest will follow easily enough, but it must be confessed that this is only a presumption, though a presumption which seems plausible if not likely."

FISHES (PISCES) AS PARASITES

The Lampreys and Hags (*Cyclostomata*) are scaleless, eel-shaped creatures, devoid of jaws, and intermediate in habit between carnivorous forms and external parasites. On the under side of the head is a bell-shaped sucker, the lining of which is thickened into a varying number of sharp horny teeth. At the top of the bell is the true mouth-opening, provided with a projecting "tongue", also tooth-bearing (fig. 1133). By means of the sucker these creatures are able to attach themselves to other fishes, the flesh of which they rasp away, using the tongue for the purpose, this being moved by means of powerful muscles.

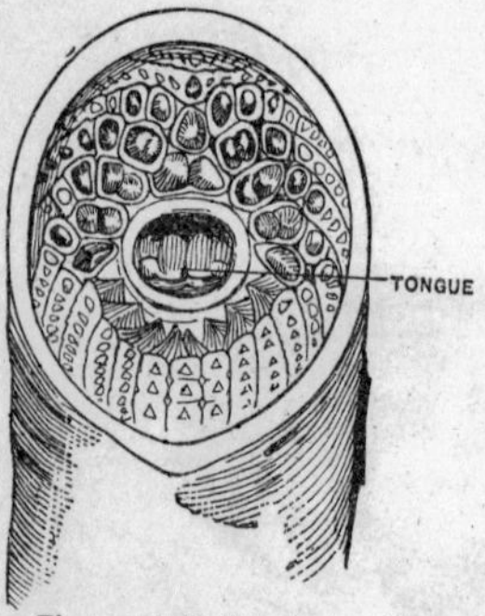

Fig. 1133.—Sucker of a Lamprey (*Petromyzon*)

MOLLUSCS (MOLLUSCA) AS PARASITES

Certain Sea-Snails afford the best illustrations of the parasitic habit as occurring among Molluscs. One of the Cap-Shells (*Thyca ectoconcha*, fig. 1134) is an external parasite upon a kind of Star-Fish (*Linckia multiforis*). It will be seen from the illustration that this form is still easily recognizable as a mollusc, though the influence of its particular mode of life is also obvious. The mouth has shifted backwards, and is on the end of a short proboscis, which penetrates into the body of the host, and is surrounded by an adhesive disc, formed by the fusion of parts of the foot with an outgrowth from the head. The characteristic rasping-organ (odontophore) has entirely disappeared, and the pharynx has been converted into a sort of suction-pump by which the juices of the star-fish are drawn in. The body of the same unfortunate star-fish may also present a number of rounded swellings in which are lodged parasitic snails of another species (*Stilaster Linckiæ*) that have undergone much further modification, being practically endoparasites in which the proboscis has become very long, while the rest of the body is much smaller in proportion, and the shell has disappeared. Communication with the exterior is still kept up, however, by means of a small hole, in the interests of breathing and the getting rid of waste products. From this case we pass on to degenerate worm-like snails, which are true internal parasites, and have lost most of the typical organs of the group to which they belong, though the study of their life-histories renders no doubt possible as to their classificatory position. Their bodies hang freely into the interiors of their hosts, one end being fixed to the inner side of the body-wall of the same. A degenerate of the kind (*Entocolax Ludwigii*) lives within a species of sea-cucumber (*Myriotrochus Rinkii*), and one still more strongly modified (*Entoconcha mirabilis*) within another creature of the same sort (*Syapta digitata*).

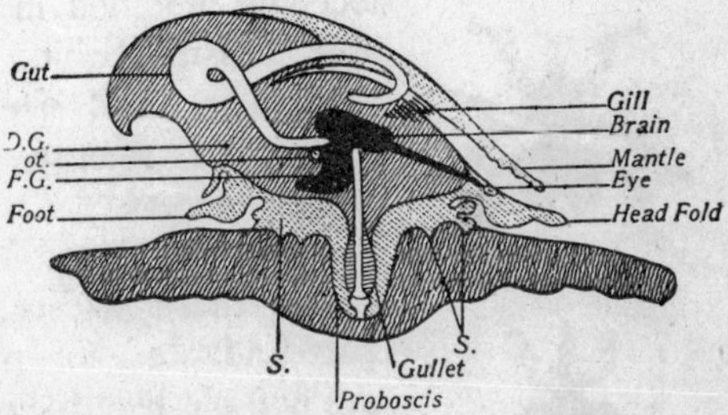

Fig. 1134.—Parasitic Cap-Shell (*Thyca ectoconcha*) attached to the Skin of a Star-Fish (*Linckia multiforis*); diagrammatic section. *D.G.*, Digestive gland; *F.G.*, foot-ganglion; *S.*, *S.*, suctorial disc; *ot.*, otocyst.

The parasitic habit of the larvæ of Freshwater Mussels has been dealt with elsewhere (see vol. iii, p. 406).

INSECTS (Insecta) AS PARASITES

Innumerable insects have adopted the parasitic habit, either for the whole of their lives or for some particular stage of existence. It will only be possible to give a limited number of examples in illustration of the more interesting kinds of adaptation.

Bugs (Hemiptera) as Parasites.—The fact that the insects of this order possess piercing and sucking mouth-parts naturally suggests that some of them attack other animals, which is indeed the case, though the majority would appear to devote themselves to plants. Where, as largely in Water-Bugs, small creatures are selected as victims, these are killed as a result of the feeding operations, and the true carnivorous habit is illustrated. But Bugs which feed on the blood of relatively large animals may be described as external parasites. The most notable example is the wingless Bed Bug (*Cimex lectularius*), which is fortunately a favourite prey of several other insects, including some belonging to the same order (*e.g.* species of Reduvius). The True Lice, which live entirely upon the blood of Mammals, are very possibly to be regarded as minute Bugs, which have lost their wings and become modified in other ways as a result of the parasitic habit. Considering the mode of life, their small size is clearly an advantage, and their remote ancestors were probably larger insects.

Fig. 1135. — Swallow - Fly (*Stenopteryx hirundinis*) above and Sheep-"Tick" (*Melophagus ovis*) below. The short lines to left show actual length.

FLIES (DIPTERA) AS PARASITES.—A number of these insects are endowed with mouth-parts adapted for piercing and sucking, and are notable blood-suckers, the habit being commonly restricted to the females. Gnats and Mosquitoes, Midges, Sand-Midges, Breeze-Flies, and Tsetse-Flies, may be cited in illustration. A very interesting series of modifications is found within the limits of one family (*Hippoboscidæ*), which illustrates the reduction of wings resulting from the parasitic mode of life. The feet are provided with strong claws for holding firmly to the animals attacked, and males as well as females are blood-suckers. One of the least modified species is the Forest-Fly (*Hippobosca equina*), which infests horses. Well-developed wings are present, but not much used, as these insects fly unwillingly. Another somewhat similar form (*Lipoptena cervi*) lives on the Red-Deer, and its wings are either shed or bitten off as soon as a host has been secured. The wings of the Swallow-Fly (*Stenopteryx hirundinis*) are small and narrow, while in the so-called Sheep-"Tick" (*Melophagus ovis*) they are altogether absent (fig. 1135). So also in the Bee-"Louse" (*Braula cæca*), a minute insect that infests bees, and some curious little parasites (species of *Nycteribia*) that have been found among the fur of bats.

Some of the insects of this order live within the bodies of

other animals during the early part of their existence, as, *e.g.*, the Bot-Flies (*Œstridæ*), which are only too well known to the owners of stock. The mouth of the adult is greatly reduced, so that there is no question of blood-sucking, while the larvæ do not devour the living substance of their hosts, but absorb the fluid which surrounds them, and is generally a morbid product resulting from the irritation due to their presence. The Horse-Bot (*Gastrophilus equi*, fig. 1136) lays her eggs upon those parts of the horse's body which are easily reached by the tongue, and the young larvæ, when they hatch out, are thus conveyed to the mouth, whence they make their way to the stomach. The head of the maggot is provided with hooks by which it bores into the lining of that organ. In later stages it becomes ovoid

Fig. 1136.—Horse-Bot (*Gastrophilus equi*). 1, Male; 2, female; 3, egg (much enlarged) attached to hair; 4, young larva (enlarged); 5, older larva; 6, empty pupa-case.

in shape, and is known as a "bot". Its powers of adhesion are considerably increased by the presence of circlets of short spines on the body. When a large number of these larvæ are present they set up inflammation, &c., sometimes with fatal results, and they have even been known to bore right through the wall of the stomach. After about nine or ten months the larva looses its hold, and is carried through the digestive organs of the horse to the exterior, where it passes into the motionless pupa stage, from which the adult fly later on emerges.

The eggs of the Sheep-Bot (*Œstrus ovis*) are developed internally, and the female fly deposits the just-born larvæ near the nostrils of the sheep. Thence they pass into the nose, and ultimately into spaces (frontal sinuses) in the bones of the head, where they become "bots". After some nine months' growth these make their way back into the nose, from which they appear to be sneezed out, and pass into the pupa stage. One or two more pests of the kind will be dealt with later, in the section on ANIMAL FOES.

Before leaving the order of Flies, it may be noted that the

wingless blood-sucking Fleas are here included. The modifications which they have undergone have no doubt been in relation to the parasitic habit.

BEETLES (COLEOPTERA) AS PARASITES AND BROOD-PARASITES.—To this order possibly belongs a family of small insects (*Stylopidæ*) parasitic upon Bees, Wasps, and, to some extent, upon certain Bugs. Many zoologists, however, place them in a distinct order (*Strepsiptera*). The adult female is little more than a shapeless bag, living in the abdomen of a bee or other host, with one end projecting externally (fig. 1137). The adult male, on the other hand, is a very active creature, possessing large hind-wings, but only vestiges of fore-wings. His free life is short, three days being the maximum on record, while in some species (of *Xenos*) fifteen to twenty minutes is the limit, though during this brief period extraordinary energy is shown. The numerous eggs are developed internally, hatching out into minute six-legged larvæ, which make their way into the bodies of bee-grubs or the like, though the way in which these hosts are found is in many cases but imperfectly understood. Their presence in the interior of the grubs does not cause death, for they feed upon the fatty substance (fat-body) between the various organs. Having once become parasitic they lose their legs and assume the appearance of minute maggots. Later on, when the bee-grub passes into the pupa stage, the parasitic larva pushes out one end to the exterior, and, if a male, also passes into the pupa stage, but if a female, undergoes comparatively slight modifications. When the adult bees come out of the pupæ the male parasites also emerge to lead their free existence, but the females remain fixed in their hosts. Individual bees harbour but one or a few of these curious parasites; in wasps they may be more numerous.

Fig. 1137.—A Bee-Parasite (*Stylops aterrimus*), enlarged. The male is shown above, the female (with two contained embryos) below to right, and the larva below to left.

The parasitic habits of some of the Oil-Beetles (*Meloidæ*) are both remarkable and highly interesting. Fabre has worked out the life-history of one species (*Sitaris humeralis*, fig. 1138), of which the larvæ feed on the eggs and honey of certain bees

(*Anthophora*) that make underground nests, storing each cell with honey, and then laying an egg therein. In early autumn the female beetle lays her numerous eggs (as many as 2000) near the openings of bees' nests, and these hatch out into minute six-legged larvæ, which hibernate till the following spring. After the winter-sleep is over these little creatures hold on to any hair-clad insects that pass sufficiently near, and are thus carried away. Only those which have by good fortune attached themselves to the right sort of bee have any chance of surviving, and a great many are undoubtedly transported by unsuitable insects, merely to die. Hence in all probability the reason for the production of so many eggs. Some of the successful larvæ unconsciously select female bees as carriers, but most appear to attach themselves to drones, whence they transfer themselves to individuals of the opposite sex. When one of these female bees lays an egg in a honey-filled cell, a predatory larva immediately transfers itself to the egg, and the bee roofs in the cell. To fall into the honey would be fatal to the larva, but it stands firmly on the floating egg, and thus avoids this danger. This scene in the drama lasts for eight days, the larva being busily employed eating up the nutritious contents of the egg. Moulting now takes place, and the once active robber is transformed into a plump grub with breathing-holes (stigmata) placed in the upper part of its body, so that it can float in the honey without fear of suffocation. The sweet food-supply is exhausted in about forty days, by which time it is mid-July, and the grub next becomes a motionless false-pupa, but without shedding its skin, which remains as a dry covering to the body. The further stages in the life-history may follow immediately, but are usually postponed till the following spring, after a long winter-sleep. In either case the false-pupa assumes once more the form of a grub, the skin, however, being retained as a second dry investment. In about two days the grub becomes a true pupa, from which the perfect insect emerges a month later.

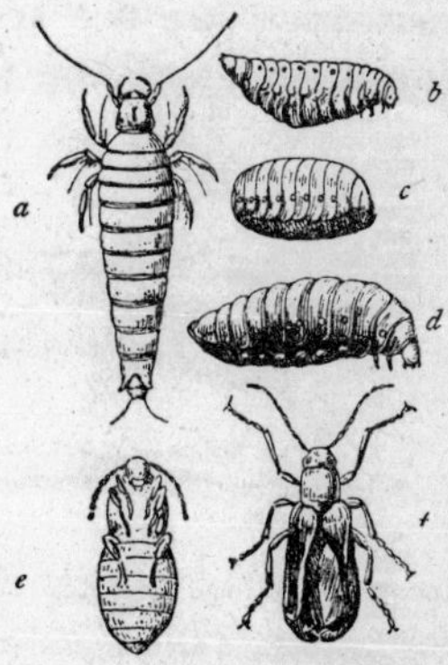

Fig. 1138.—Stages of *Sitaris humeralis*, enlarged. *a*, Six-legged larva; *b*, floating grub; *c*, false pupa; *d*, second grub-stage; *e*, true pupa; *f*, adult beetle.

Some other Oil-Beetles (species of *Meloë*) have much the same kind of life-history as the form last described, and are parasitic on bees of the same sort. The female beetle does not, however, lay her eggs near a suitable nest, but simply deposits them in the ground. The six-legged larvæ climb up various plants, and commonly lie in wait on or near their flowers, attaching themselves at random to any hairy insects that come near enough. The chances of a given larva reaching a suitable destination are exceedingly small, but as a set-off against this each female beetle lays some 10,000 eggs, which allows for considerable wastage.

MEMBRANE-WINGED INSECTS (HYMENOPTERA) AS PARASITES.—Among the most interesting members of this order in the present connection are the Ichneumon-Flies, and other forms of similar habits, in which the female is provided with a sharp ovipositor,

Fig. 1139.—The Yellow-Legged Ichneumon-Fly (*Microgaster glomeratus*). *a*, Adult; *b*, larva; *c*, dead caterpillar of Cabbage-Butterfly, surrounded by cocoons of the Ichneumon. Size of *a* and *b* indicated by the short lines.

by means of which she deposits her eggs within the bodies of the larvæ, pupæ, or even eggs of other insects. In some cases deposition takes place not in, but on or sufficiently near, suitable victims. The early stages of Butterflies and Moths are particularly liable to such attacks, and in this way the ravages of many of our familiar agricultural and garden pests are kept within bounds. Some of these parasites are in turn similarly attacked by insects not distantly related to them, a case of the biter bit. The common Cabbage-Butterfly (*Pieris brassicæ*) is subject to the attentions of a number of these forms. By one (*Polynema gracilis*) its eggs are pierced, two others (*Microgaster glomeratus*, fig. 1139, and *Pimpla instigator*) lay their eggs in its caterpillars, and still another two (*Pteromalus puparum* and *P. pontiæ*) attack its chrysalides.

Certain larvæ and pupæ, that live where one would expect them to be quite secure from these parasitic insects, are nevertheless sought out by them, and exposed to the murderous assaults of their brood. One kind of Ichneumon-Fly (*Agriotypus armatus*) boldly plunges into water, and lays her eggs in the larvæ of caddis-moths. Others (species of *Rhyssa* and *Thalessa*, fig. 1140) possess powerful ovipositors three or four inches long, with which they penetrate trees tunnelled by the larvæ of wood-wasps (*Siricidæ*). The grubs which hatch out from the eggs of such ichneumons attach themselves as external parasites to the wood-boring larvæ. Fabre has described the even more remarkable habits of another parasitic form (*Leucopsis gigas*), that seeks the nests of the Mason-Bee (*Chalicodoma muraria*), in which a number of cells, each containing a larva, are surrounded by little stones cemented together (see p. 53). The parasite thrusts her stout ovipositor through weak spots in this masonry, never failing to reach the contained cells, in each of which she deposits an egg. It is only when such a cell contains a full-grown bee-larva, on the point of becoming a pupa, that the operation attains the desired object. In this case the parasitic grub first wanders round the cell to destroy any other eggs that may have been there deposited, and then attaches itself to the bee-larva, the juices of which nourish it for two or three weeks. Next follows a quiescent period of ten or eleven months, after which the larva becomes a pupa, from which the perfect insect soon emerges.

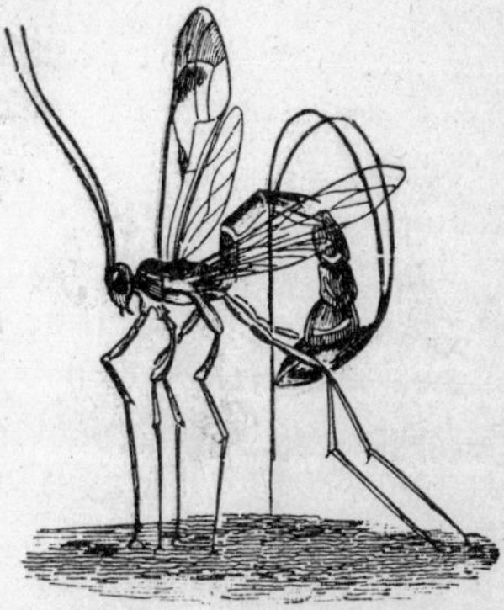

Fig. 1140.—A Female Ichneumon-Fly (*Thalessa*) using her Ovipositor

SPIDER-LIKE ANIMALS (ARACHNIDA) AS PARASITES

Many of the Ticks and Mites (Acarina) are parasitic upon other animals, and some of them have earned considerable notoriety on this account. Ticks are greedy blood-suckers which lurk on plants, and attach themselves to passing birds or mammals, human beings not excepted (fig. 1141). One of the best-known species is the Dog-Tick (*Ixodes ricinus*). A victim once secured, the tick buries its piercing mouth-parts in the skin, and takes in so much blood that it swells visibly. When satiated it drops off, and digests the meal at leisure.

Fig. 1141.—A Tick (*Ixodes*), enlarged

Mange- or Itch-Mites exhibit degrees in parasitism. Some of them (*Dermatophagus*) simply devour the loose scales which are constantly being detached from the epidermis, while others (*Dermatocoptes*) suck blood. But the most objectionable (*Sarcoptes*, fig. 1142), those responsible for the unpleasant disease known as "itch", actually burrow in the skin, within which the female lays her eggs, and may therefore be described as true internal parasites. They live on the blood and other juices of their hosts.

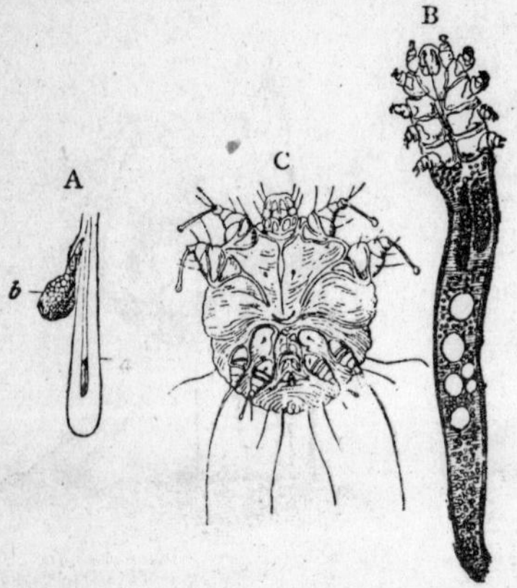

Fig. 1142.—A, Root of hair; (*a*) enlarged, showing a swollen sebaceous gland (*b*), containing a Hair-Mite (*Simonea folliculorum*). B, A Hair-Mite, greatly enlarged. C, An Itch-Mite *Sarcoptes scabei*), greatly enlarged.

A curious little elongated mite (*Simonea folliculorum*, fig. 1142) lives in the little bag-like glands attached to the roots of hair, in which a sort of fatty matter is secreted.

The degenerate Tongue-Worms (*Linguatulida*), which live in the noses of dogs and wolves, are doubtfully classed with the Arachnida (see vol. i, p. 393).

CRUSTACEANS (CRUSTACEA) AS PARASITES

A large number of the lower Crustaceans are parasitic, and some of them have become extremely degenerate as the result of their mode of life, especially in the case of the females. A few examples must suffice.

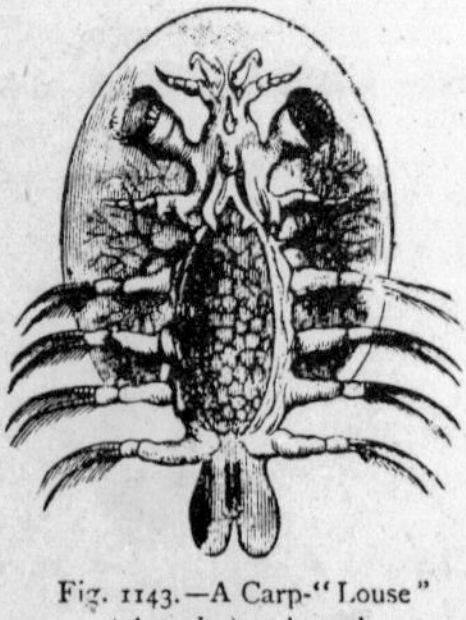
Fig. 1143.—A Carp-"Louse" (*Argulus*), enlarged

FORK-FOOTED CRUSTACEA (COPEPODA) AS PARASITES.—Many of the members of this group are found attached to fishes, usually by means of their suctorial mouths. They are popularly, though somewhat inappropriately, known as Fish-"Lice". Among the least modified kinds are those (*Argulus*, fig. 1143) found attached to the skins of carp and sticklebacks, holding on by a couple of suckers formed by the modification of parts of two limbs. The piercing jaws are enclosed in a sharp beak-like projection.

A larger amount of modification is found in the female parasite (*Achtheres*) depicted in fig. 1144, and which is not infrequently found attached to the gills or living in the throat of the perch. Creatures of the kind also infest a large number of marine fishes. One (*Lernæa*, fig. 1145) is sometimes found attached to the eye of the sprat, and, as it is phosphorescent, the little fishes which harbour these unwelcome guests are known to fishermen as "lantern sprats".

Fig. 1144.—A Perch-"Louse" (*Achtheres percarum*), enlarged

BARNACLES (CIRRIPEDIA) AS PARASITES.—Some of the members of this group have undergone an extraordinary amount of degeneration as a result of parasitism. This is carried to an extreme in a form (*Sacculina*, fig. 1146) that is sometimes found projecting from the under side of the tail of the Shore-Crab (*Carcinus mœnas*). Only a professed zoologist would suspect it to be a Crustacean, for in appearance it is simply a rounded bag, which dissection shows to be provided with numerous branching root-like threads that grow through the body of the unfortunate host, extending even to the tips of the limbs. A study of its weird life-history (fig. 1146) definitely proves that it is really a distant relative of its unfortunate host. From the egg hatches out a little larva, of the kind (nauplius) typical for lower Crustaceans (see vol. iii, p. 364). After undergoing several moults it assumes a form not unlike that of a mussel-shrimp, and continues to swim about for three days or more. At the end of this period it seeks a very young crab, and fixes itself by means of a feeler to the soft membrane at the base of one of the bristles on a limb or on the back of its victim. The hinder part of its body is then thrown off bodily, and the organs contained in the remainder fuse together into a soft mass. Around this a membrane is developed, part of which becomes converted into a tube that is pushed into the interior of the crab. Through this the soft substance of the parasite squeezes itself. Within the body of its host it migrates to the region of the intestine, in

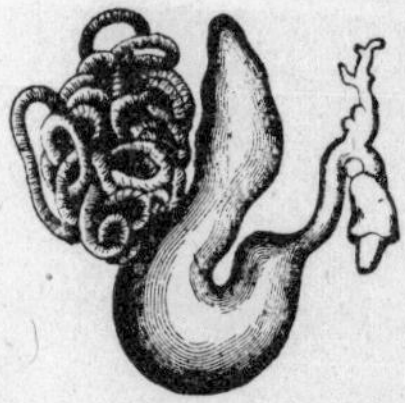

Fig. 1145.—Sprat-"Louse" (*Lernæa*), enlarged

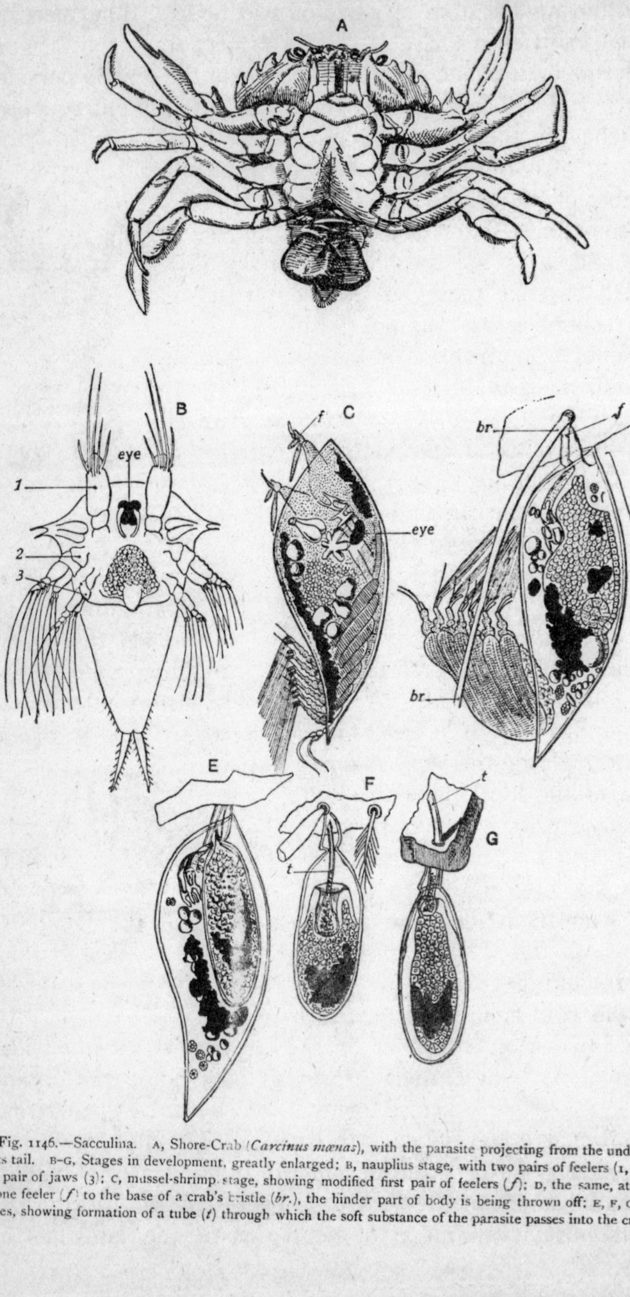

Fig. 1146.—Sacculina. A, Shore-Crab (*Carcinus mænas*), with the parasite projecting from the under side of its tail. B–G, Stages in development, greatly enlarged; B, nauplius stage, with two pairs of feelers (1, 2) and one pair of jaws (3); C, mussel-shrimp stage, showing modified first pair of feelers (*f*); D, the same, attached by one feeler (*f*) to the base of a crab's bristle (*br.*), the hinder part of body is being thrown off; E, F, G, later stages, showing formation of a tube (*t*) through which the soft substance of the parasite passes into the crab.

the neighbourhood of the tail, and root-like threads grow out from it in all directions. Fed by these it grows rapidly, and exerts so much pressure on the muscles and skin which are placed between it and the under side of the tail that they become thinner and thinner. Ultimately, as the final result of this process, the parasite projects to the exterior, its roots, however, remaining inside the crab.

Some of the higher Crustaceans belonging to the group of Slaters (Isopoda) are also parasitic, and have undergone profound modifications.

SEGMENTED WORMS (ANNELIDA) AS PARASITES

We are here concerned with various Bristle-Worms (Chætopoda) and Leeches (Discophora).

BRISTLE-WORMS (CHÆTOPODA) AS PARASITES.—A number of marine worms are external parasites upon hosts of widely different nature, including star-fishes, sea-urchins, sea-cucumbers, corals, and even other annelids. Cases have also been described where one species of marine worm lives parasitically within the body of another species. Much more interesting than these, however, are certain small flattened creatures (e.g. *Myzostoma*, fig. 1147), which live upon, or more rarely within, feather-stars and sea-lilies, sometimes causing gall-like growths that serve as habitations. Since these curious little parasites possess a small number of foot-stumps, each terminating in a pair of bristles, they are probably to be regarded as bristle-worms that have become modified in consequence of their mode of life. And this view is supported by the fact that they begin existence as larvæ which closely resemble those of typical worms of the kind.

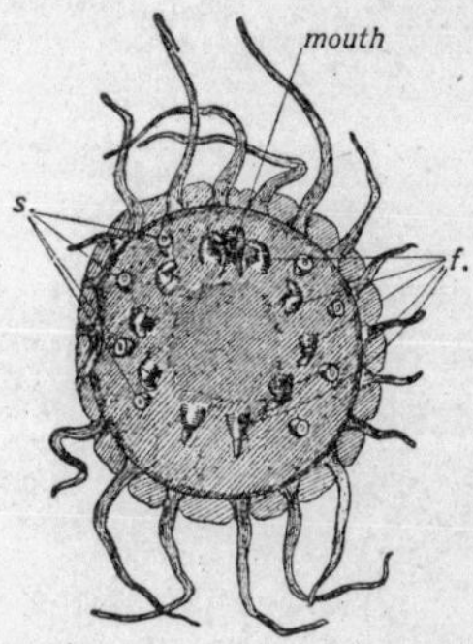

Fig. 1147.—Under Side of *Myzostoma*, enlarged. *s*, Suckers; *f*, foot-stumps.

One large group of Annelids (Few-bristled Worms, *Oligochæta*), of which earth-worms and certain freshwater forms are the typical representatives, includes a small number of species resembling leeches in appearance, as well as in the fact that bristles are entirely absent. They are ectoparasites upon crustaceans, the

Crayfish (*Astacus fluviatilis*), for example, being infested by several of them (species of *Branchiobdella*), which suck its blood and devour its eggs.

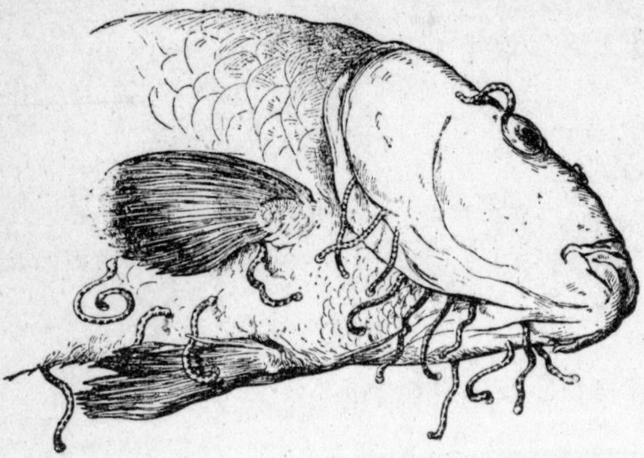

Fig. 1148.—Fish-Leeches (*Piscicola*) attached to the Head of a Carp

LEECHES (DISCOPHORA) AS PARASITES.—While some leeches prey upon animals smaller than themselves, others are true external parasites, and the habits of these have been sufficiently described elsewhere (see vol. ii, p. 147). Some of these creatures (e.g. *Piscicola*, fig. 1148) attach themselves to the exterior of fishes, their presence causing great annoyance or even proving fatal.

FLUKES (TREMATODA) AS PARASITES

The flattened unsegmented animals included in this group are, almost without exception, of parasitic habit. They are provided with organs of adhesion in the form of suckers, and the mouth leads into a muscular pharynx, which serves as a sort of suction-pump by which blood and other substances are taken into the body.

As ectoparasites, flukes are only found upon the bodies of aquatic animals, and in this case three or more suckers are present, since efficient means of holding on are clearly a matter of primary importance. The gills of fishes are particularly liable to such attacks, and it is only natural that this should be so, for their sheltered position, delicate texture, and abundant blood-supply are great advantages, from the parasitic point of view.

We may take as an example a form (*Octobothrium pollachii*, fig. 1149) which lives upon the gills of the pollack, adhering by means of eight stalked suckers. A related species (*O. merlangi*) lives on the whiting, and the herring is infested by a similar parasite, in which, however, the suckers are not stalked. A curious case, where the host is not a fish, is presented by a minute three-suckered fluke (*Udonella caligorum*), numbers of which attach themselves to the egg-bags of a degenerate crustacean (*Caligus*), living as a parasite upon the gills of the hake.

Aquatic Amphibians do not escape from the attacks of Flukes, a notable instance being afforded by one of these creatures (*Polystomum integerrimum*) which lives, when adult, in the urinary bladder of the frog, and illustrates the transition from external to internal parasitism. It adheres to the lining of the bladder by means of a rounded projection at its hinder end, on which are situated six suckers and many small hooks. The numerous eggs are laid in spring, and pass from the frog's body to the exterior, where they hatch out into minute ciliated larvæ, which actively swim about in search of tadpoles. To understand what happens next, it must be remembered that at a certain stage in development a fold grows back from the head of a tadpole, covering the gill-slits, and uniting with the adjacent skin so as to enclose a gill-chamber opening to the exterior by a small hole or spiracle on the left side. The continued existence of the fluke-larva depends upon its finding a tadpole within twenty-four hours, preferably one in the stage described. If successful in this quest it swims into the gill-chamber through the spiracle, and becomes parasitic upon the gills. After living for two months or so in these comfortable quarters a change of residence becomes necessary, for the tadpole is becoming a frog, the gills are disappearing, and the gill-slits are closing up. The larva now makes its way into the pharynx of its host, and passing through gullet, stomach, and intestines, reaches and enters the bladder, where it becomes adult in about three years.

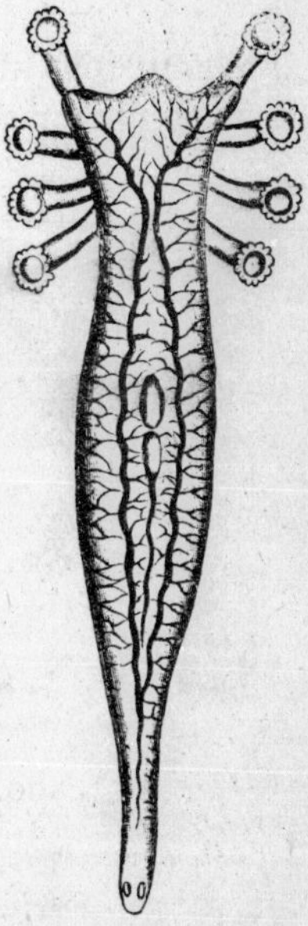

Fig. 1149.—Eight-suckered Pollack-Fluke (*Octobothrium pollachii*), enlarged

Mention must here be made of a singular species of many-suckered Fluke (*Diplozoön paradoxum*, fig. 1150) which lays its eggs upon the gills of the minnow. Minute ciliated larvæ hatch out, which perish in from five to six hours unless they find another host of the same kind. In that case, after further growth, they fuse together in pairs, and become X-shaped adults, capable of producing eggs. The adult is therefore a compound animal, for each stroke of the X was originally a distinct individual, and has a mouth at one end.

A great many Flukes live in the internal organs of various animals, and differ in several important respects from those already described. There is less occasion for adhesive organs, and the usual number of suckers is two, one surrounding the mouth at the front end of the body, and the other situated upon the under surface. In some cases the latter is absent. Two or three different kinds of host are infested in the course of the life-history, the reason probably being that unlimited increase in the same sort of host might ultimately lead to its exinction, when a similar fate would overtake the parasite. Although the relations existing between the two or three hosts are such as to favour transfer, the chances are greatly against the survival of a given larva, to meet which contingency immense numbers of small eggs are produced, fewer and correspondingly larger eggs being the rule for external parasites attacking but one kind of host. And, as might be anticipated, the life-history is very complicated.

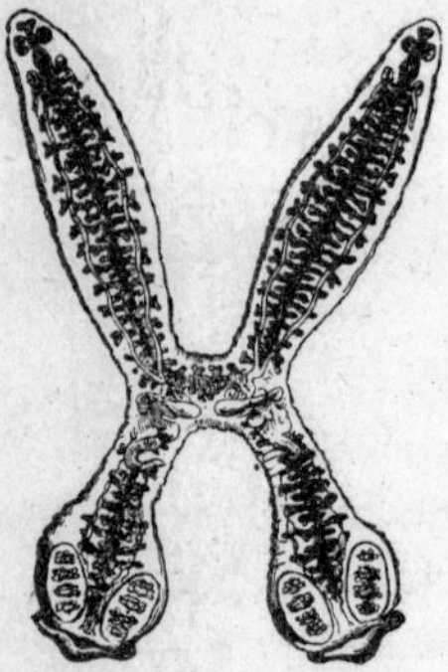

Fig. 1150.—Diplozoön paradoxum

The best-known form is the notorious Liver-Fluke (*Fasciola hepatica*, see vol. i, p. 443), which, when adult, infests the liver of the sheep, producing what is known as "liver rot". To this and other especially injurious species reference will be made later. It will suffice here to describe a form (*Distomum macrostomum*, fig. 1151) in which the life-history is rather simpler, but at the same time of greater interest. This little Fluke, when adult, lives in the intestine of various small birds, such as sparrows, warblers, and tits. Its eggs pass out to the exterior, and many of them get scattered over leaves. If one of them happens to be swallowed by a particular species of small Snail (*Succinea putris*) it hatches out into a minute larva, which bores through the wall of the digestive tube, and penetrates between the organs contained in the body of its host. Being now surrounded by nutritious and easily-absorbed fluid it grows rapidly, becoming converted into a shapeless sac (sporocyst), from which branches are given off in all directions. Those which lie near the surface of the head, and penetrate into the tentacles, assume a worm-like form, and are brightly coloured with rings of white and green, while the end of each of them is marked with a red spot. These tints are easily seen through the stretched and translucent skin of the snail. The resemblance of these structures to worms is increased by the fact that they expand and contract in a rhythmic way, and they were at one time actually supposed to be a kind of parasitic worm, and received a special name (*Leucochloridium paradoxum*). Attracted by the colours and movement, small birds nip off the tentacles of the snail, the bright-hued tubes of which contain numerous tiny flukes that have developed within them. The fate of these now trembles in the balance, for if they are swallowed by the adult bird itself they are simply digested, but if, on the other hand, they are fed to its nestlings, they are able to develop into adult flukes.

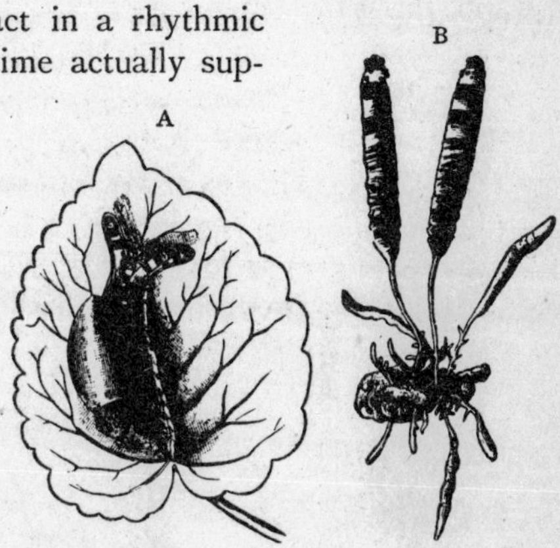

Fig. 1151.—*Distomum macrostomum*. A, A Land-Snail (*Succinea putris*) infested by sporocyst, some of the banded worm-like branches of which can be seen through skin of head and tentacles. B, A sporocyst, enlarged, and showing two worm-like branches.

TAPE-WORMS (CESTODA) AS PARASITES

Creatures resembling Planarian Worms (see vol. i, p. 445) were probably ancestral to Flukes, and they, in their turn, stand in a similar relation to the degenerate internal parasites known as Tape-Worms. In these the peculiar mode of life has had a still more far-reaching influence, for there are no digestive organs, and the nutriment consists either of the fluids or the already digested food of the animals which play the part of hosts. In either case it is absorbed by the general surface of the parasite.

The simplest kind of Tape-Worm known (*Archigetes Sieboldi*, fig. 1152) is a minute creature, less than one-eighth of an inch long, which lives within the body of the small Red River-Worm (*Tubifex*), and there attains the egg-producing stage, which elsewhere is only reached within the digestive tube of a backboned animal. It may possibly be a specialized larva, like the Axolotl (see vol. i, p. 249), but our knowledge is too incomplete to justify such a conclusion.

The best-known Tape-worms consist of a head, provided with organs of adhesion, and passing behind into a series of flat joints (proglottides), in which vast numbers of eggs are produced. The complex life-history of the Common Tape-Worm (*Tænia solium*) has been briefly described elsewhere (see vol. i, p. 441). In the adult condition it lives in the intestine of man, sometimes attaining the length of 9 feet, while in an earlier stage it is found encapsuled in the muscles of the pig, producing the disease known as "measles".

Fig. 1152.—A Simple Tape-Worm (*Archigetes Sieboldii*), greatly enlarged

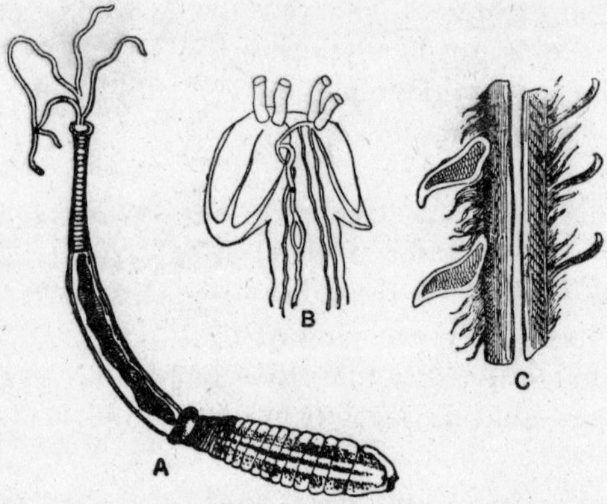

Fig. 1153.—A Fish Tape-Worm (*Tetrarhynchus*). A, Adult worm, enlarged, showing the four proboscides; B, head of same still further enlarged, showing double suckers, and proboscides slightly protruded; C, part of a proboscis, very highly magnified, to show the hooks.

In one small kind of Tape-Worm (*Tetrarhynchus*, fig. 1153) the adhesive apparatus on the head is somewhat complex, consisting of two double suckers, and four tubes studded with numerous hooks. When adult it lives in the intestines of fishes of the shark and ray kind (Elasmobranchii). The life-history of one species has been worked out by Herdman and Hornell, and is of particular interest. In this case the host of the adult worm is a large Ray (*Trygon*), which is common in Indian seas. The eggs pass from the body of the fish, and hatch out into minute active larvæ, which perish unless they succeed in entering the shells of the Pearl-Oyster (*Margaritifera vulgaris*), a well-known bivalve on account of the pearls which it yields. The Gulf of Manaar, in particular, has been the seat of an important pearl-fishery for between two and three thousand years. Successful larvæ bore into the bodies of the oysters, and undergo further development, attaining the size of a small pin's head. One of the mollusc's enemies is the Trigger-Fish (*Balistes*), and if this swallows an infested oyster the tape-worm embryos bore through the wall of the stomach, and become encapsuled in the body of the fish. The trigger-fish in its turn may be devoured by a sting-ray, in which case the young tape-worms become adult. The life-history of this parasite is therefore passed within the bodies of three distinct kinds of animal, the final host being the most powerful, as usual in such cases. It remains to add that many of the tape-worm embryos die while still within the oysters, and, proving a source of irritation, are covered by successive layers of calcareous matter. It is in this way that the best or "orient" pearls are formed.

THREAD-WORMS (NEMATHELMIA) AS PARASITES

The members of this large group are cylindrical unsegmented worms, most of which are internal parasites in the bodies of animals or plants. They are less degenerate than tape-worms, and the very numerous species differ greatly in respect of the complexity of their life-history, and the hosts infested. One or two of them have already been briefly described (see vol. i, p. 447), and something will be said about others in the section on ANIMAL FOES.

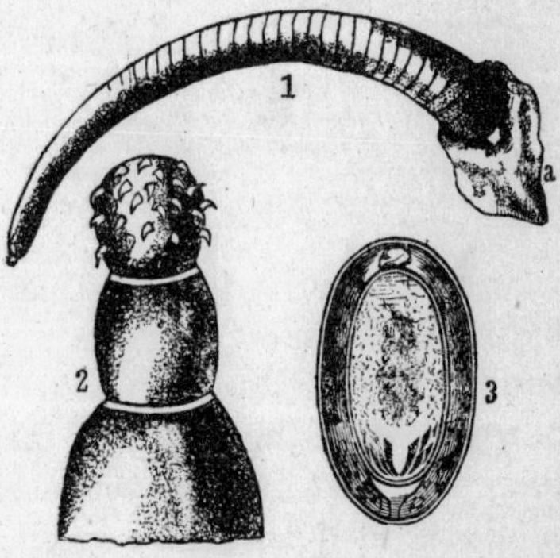

Fig. 1154.—Thorn-headed Worm (*Gigantorhynchus gigas*). 1, A worm attached to the lining (*a*) of a pig's intestine; (2), hooked proboscis of same, enlarged; 3, egg containing an embryo, greatly enlarged.

Some curious internal parasites, the Thorn-headed Worms (*Echinorhynchidæ*), are generally regarded as related to the Thread-Worms, and in them the digestive organs are entirely absent. We may take as an example a form (*Gigantorhynchus gigas*, fig. 1154), which, when adult, lives in the intestine of the pig, maintaining a firm hold by means of a formidable hollow "proboscis", thickly studded with hooks. The eggs pass out of the body of the pig, and some of them are swallowed by beetle-grubs, within which the development is carried on to a certain stage. If an infested grub happens to be eaten by a pig the life-history of the parasite is completed.

ANIMALCULES (PROTOZOA) AS PARASITES

The large group of Gregarines (Sporozoa) includes typical internal parasites, in which the body is surrounded by a firm elastic membrane, through which the body-fluids or digested food of the host are easily absorbed. A well-known form (*Clepsidrina blattarum*, fig. 1155) infests the intestines of the cockroach. The young parasite is worm-like in shape, and its body is divided into three regions, one of which bears hooks, and serves as a means of adhesion to the host. Later on this part is thrown off, and the gregarine lies freely in the intestine, where it absorbs food, and increases considerably in size. The life-history is somewhat peculiar. Two parasites adhere together, and become enclosed in a firm case or cyst, which is passed out of the body of the host. If the surroundings are sufficiently damp the outer part of the cyst swells up into a gelatinous layer, and complex changes go on in the interior. The bodies of the two contained parasites break up into a large number of minute spores, with firm coats, scattered through a kind of net-work. A number of tubes are also formed which turn inside out, and since they convey the spores out of the cyst are termed *sporoducts*. If these spores are swallowed by a young cockroach their firm coats

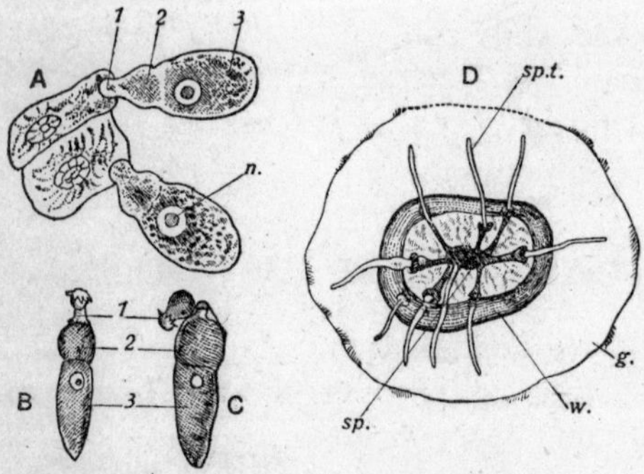

Fig. 1155.—Cockroach Gregarine (*Clepsidrina blattarum*), enlarged to various scales. A, Young gregarines attached to cells of intestine; B and C, later stages lying free within intestine; D, spore-cyst in section. 1, 2, 3, Three body-regions, of which 1 is thrown off by adult; *n.*, nucleus; *g.*, gelatinous covering of cyst; *sp.*, mass of spores in middle of cyst; *sp.t.*, spore-tubes; *w.*, firm wall of cyst.

are dissolved by the digestive fluids, and the soft protoplasmic contents make their way into the cells which line the intestine, there to develop into worm-like gregarines.

A great number of the Sporozoa are excessively minute parasites living within the bodies of hosts of various kinds, and often giving rise to disease. It has been proved, for example, that malarial fever is due to a blood parasite of the kind introduced by the agency of a Mosquito (*Anopheles*). The complex life-history of this form will be briefly given in the section on Animal Foes.

UTILITARIAN ZOOLOGY

CHAPTER LXVII

ANIMAL FRIENDS—ANIMALS AS A SOURCE OF FOOD—DOMESTICATION—DOMESTICATED MAMMALS

The view taken in this work as to the scope of Utilitarian Zoology has been sufficiently indicated in the Introduction (see vol. i, p. 18), and if by no means free from objection, it may serve to marshal important facts and principles in a fairly orderly manner.

Although the feeding habits of Man differ greatly according to the environment, he may fairly be described as omnivorous (see vol. ii, p. 225), but the proportion of animal food taken increases as we pass from tropical and sub-tropical regions into higher latitudes. The commissariat question has necessarily been a dominant factor in the evolution of human civilization, and this is abundantly evident if we recall the oft-told story of that evolution so far as Western Europe is concerned. In this area, as is generally known, there have been successive Ages of Stone, Bronze, and Iron, names indicating the materials employed in making the chief weapons and implements. During the first of these ages prehistoric man passed through the three most important stages marking the progress of civilization, *i.e.* those of (1) the Hunter and Fisherman, (2) the nomad Herdsman and Flock-Master (pastoral stage), and (3) the Tiller of the Soil (agricultural stage). The first two of these (and of course the third) still find parallels among existing races. In an interesting little book by Jenks (*A History of Politics*) the native Australians are taken as an illustration of the first stage:—"The material side of Australian existence may be best described in a series of negatives. The savages understand neither the cultivation of the land nor the rearing of sheep and cattle. Their only domestic animal (if 'domestic' it can be called) is the dog. . . . They have no food but the scanty game of the 'bush' or forest, such as the wallaby and the opossum, and the natural products of the earth. . . . It is the custom to speak of the Australians and other savages as living in 'tribes'. But the term is most misleading; for the word 'tribe' always suggests to us the notion of descent from a common ancestor, or at any rate, of close blood relationship. Now there is . . . a most important stage in human progress, in which descent from a common ancestor plays a vital part in social organization. But the Australian 'tribe' does not really play a very important part in savage life, at least on its social side. It appears to be mainly a group of people engaged in hunting together, a co-operative or communal society for the acquisition of food-supply. It would really be better to call it the 'pack'; for it far more resembles a hunting than a social organization. All its members are entitled to a share in the proceeds of the day's chase, and, quite naturally, they camp and live together." To make a complete list of wild animals that minister to the appetite of mankind would be an unnecessary task, but a brief summary is given in the sequel. Savages in particular are often far from fastidious in such matters. Lord Avebury (in *Prehistoric Times*) compiles from various authorities the following somewhat varied bill of fare of these same Australians:—"The food of the Australian savages differs much in different parts of the continent. Speaking generally, it may be said to consist of various roots, fruits, fungi, shell-fish, frogs, snakes, honey, grubs, moths, birds, birds'-eggs, fish, turtles, dogs, kangaroos, and sometimes of seal and whale. The kangeroo, however, forms only an occasional luxury, nor are the natives, so far as I am aware, able to kill whales for themselves, but when one is washed on shore it is a real godsend to them. Fires are immediately lit to give notice of the joyful event. Then they rub themselves all over with blubber, and anoint their favourite wives in the same way; after which they cut down through the blubber to the beef, which they sometimes eat raw, and sometimes broil on pointed sticks. As other natives arrive, they 'fairly eat their way into the whale, and you see them climbing in and about the stinking carcase, choosing titbits'. For days 'they remain by the carcase, rubbed from head to foot with stinking blubber, gorged to repletion with putrid meat —out of temper from indigestion, and therefore engaged in constant frays—suffering from a cutaneous disorder by high feeding—and altogether a disgusting spectacle. There is no sight in the world more revolting than to see a young and gracefully-formed native girl stepping out of the carcase of a putrid whale' (Gray's *Explorations in North-West and Western Australia*). The Australians also mash up bones and suck out the fat contained in them. Like other savages, they are excessively fond of fatty substances."

To illustrate a predominatingly animal diet we may take the following *menu* of an Esquimaux feast, given by comparatively civilized individuals:—"A factor being invited to a great entertainment with several topping Greenlanders counted the following dishes:—1. Dried herrings. 2. Dried seal's flesh. 3. Boiled ditto. 4. Half-raw and rotten ditto, called mikiak. 5. Boiled willocks [sea-birds]. 6. A piece of a half-rotten whale's tail (this was the dainty dish or haunch of venison to which the guests were properly invited). 7. Dried salmon. 8. Dried reindeer venison. 9. A dessert of crowberries mixed with the chyle out of the maw of a reindeer. 10. The same, enriched with train oil." (Crantz—*History of Greenland.*) It may be added that blood is a favourite Esquimaux drink.

Even among civilized nations fish and molluscs are important articles of food, and it is interesting to know that this was also the case during the Stone Age. Along the shores of Denmark and many other countries, including Britain, are to be found, more or less abundantly, shell-mounds or "kitchen-middens" (Danish *kjökkenmöddings*), the sites of many a prehistoric meal. In Danish mounds the shells of oysters, cockles, mussels, and periwinkles are by far the most abundant, and with them are associated the bones of fishes (herring, dab, eel, &c.), birds, (capercailzie, duck, swan, goose, &c.), and mammals (deer, wild boar, &c). Remains of domesticated animals are entirely absent, except of the dog, and many of the bones have been gnawed by this half-wild attendant at the feasts. Darwin's account (in *A Naturalist's Voyage*) of some of the inhabitants of Tierra del Fuego furnishes a modern parallel to the kind of life led by the prehistoric men of the shell-mounds, except that the latter were probably in better case. He says:—"The inhabitants, living chiefly upon shell-fish, are obliged constantly to change their place of residence; but they return at intervals to the same spots, as is evident from the piles of old shells, which must often amount to many tons in weight. . . . These poor wretches were stunted in their growth, their hideous faces daubed with white paint, their skins filthy and greasy, their hair entangled, their voices discordant, and their gestures violent. Viewing such men, one can hardly make one's self believe that they are fellow-creatures, and inhabitants of the same world. It is a common subject of conjecture what pleasure in life some of the lower animals can enjoy. How much more reasonably the same question may be asked with respect to these barbarians! At night, five or six human beings, naked, and scarcely protected from the wind and rain of this tempestuous climate, sleep on the wet ground, coiled up like animals. Whenever it is low water, winter or summer, night or day, they must rise to pick shell-fish from the rocks; and the women either dive to collect sea-eggs, or sit patiently in their canoes and, with a baited hair-line without any hook, jerk out little fish. If a seal is killed, or the floating carcase of a putrid whale discovered, it is a feast; and such miserable food is assisted by a few tasteless berries and fungi."

WILD ANIMALS AS A SOURCE OF FOOD

MAMMALS (MAMMALIA).—The large majority of the members of this class, from the Spiny Ant-Eater (*Echidna*) and the Duck-Bill (*Ornithorhynchus*) of Australia up to Man, are, or have been, used as food. As to the two first, it will be seen from the following remarks made by Semon (in *In the Australian Bush*) in regard to Queensland, that even uncivilized races have marked preferences in the matter of diet, when not under stress of famine:—"My blacks were hardly able to furnish me with any information as to the customs of this animal, *i.e.* the Duck-Bill, which they called 'Jungjumore', for they despise its flesh, and consequently never hunt it. In fact, it has an 'ancient and fish-like smell', even after it has been skinned. The blacks showed utter contempt for 'jungjumore', and could hardly be brought to help me in digging up their burrows or to trouble themselves in any way about this, to their minds, useless and inferior creature. The taste for Echidna is quite the reverse, since their regard for it amounts almost to adoration, and they consider its flesh a first-rate dainty, superior even to beef, which is the greatest compliment they can pay to any food. According to Bennett, the blacks near the Wollondilly and Yas rivers in New South Wales have a different taste, and are very partial to Ornithorhynchus." The *Pouched Mammals* (*Marsupialia*) of Australia have naturally been largely eaten by the natives, and the Kangaroo, at any rate, is decidedly palatable. Semon says of it, in the work just quoted:—"The muscular tail of the kangaroo furnishes a delicious soup, and its flesh is not to be despised".

Hoofed Mammals (*Ungulata*), especially Ruminants, are more important than any others as a source of food, and this is the primary reason why they have been so largely domesticated. Elephants (*Proboscidea*) have been in times past of great importance to the African larder. Sir Samuel Baker remarks (in *Wild Beasts and their Ways*):—"There is no animal that is more persistently pursued than the elephant, as it affords food in wholesale supply to the Africans, who consume its flesh, while the hide is valuable for shields; the fat when boiled is highly esteemed by the natives, and the ivory is of extreme value. No portion of the animal is wasted in Africa, although in Ceylon the elephant is considered worthless, and is allowed to rot uselessly upon the ground where it fell to die." Of *Gnawing Mammals* (*Rodentia*), Hares and Rabbits have always been most esteemed, while *Insect-eating Mammals* (*Insectivora*) are of no particular importance, though gipsies appear to relish the Hedgehog (*Erinaceus*). The related Bats (*Chiroptera*) are not in much favour, but Fruit-bats (*Pteropus*) are eaten by the Malays.

Flesh-eating Mammals (*Carnivora*) inhabiting the land are less useful as a source of food than most other Mammals, though the omnivorous Bears, and to some extent Dogs, must be excepted. It would appear, in some cases at least, to be a matter of prejudice. Wallace found Jaguar steaks good eating, and this suggested to him the following remarks:—"It appears evident to me that the common idea of the food of an animal determining the quality of its meat is quite erroneous. Domestic poultry and pigs are the most unclean animals in their food, yet their flesh is highly esteemed, while field-rats and squirrels, which eat only vegetable food, are in general disrepute." There can be no doubt that the Cat is good eating, and, under numerous aliases, it is said to figure in the dietary of various European nations. Simmonds (in *Animal Products*) thus speaks of the culinary value of the Lion:—"The flesh of the lion is eaten by the Hottentots; and a tribe of Arabs between Tunis and Algeria, according to Blumenbach, live almost entirely upon it when they can get it. When a lion has been killed and the skin removed, the flesh is divided, and the mothers take each a small piece of the animal's heart and give it their male children to eat in order to render them strong and courageous. They take away as much as possible of the mane, in order to make armlets of it, which are supposed to have the same effect. It would seem from the journal of the Marquess of Hastings, that this superstition as to eating lion's flesh is as strong in India. On the death of a lion it is stated: 'Anxious interest was made with our servants for a bit of the flesh, though it should be the size of a hazel-nut. Every native in the camp, male or female, who was fortunate enough to get a morsel, dressed it and ate it. They have a thorough conviction that the eating a piece of lion's flesh strengthens the constitution incalculably, and is a preservative against many particular distempers. This superstition does not apply to tiger's flesh, though the whiskers and claws of that animal are considered as very potent for bewitching people.' But the flesh of lions has also been eaten with gusto by Europeans, for Madame Bedichon in her work on Algeria states, that at Oran a lion was killed which three days before had eaten a man, and the prefect gave a grand dinner, the principal dish being the lion, which the French gentlemen assembled ate with the greatest relish. More recently still . . . a magnificent quarter of lion, shot in the neighbourhood of Philippeville, Algeria, by M. Constant Cheret, was sent to the Restaurant Magny, Paris, and served up to a party of nineteen guests, who enjoyed with gusto 'Estouffade de lion à la Méridionale' and 'Cœur de lion à la Castellane'." Among aquatic Carnivores the Seals are valuable as a source of food to Esquimaux and other tribes inhabiting cold latitudes.

Of other aquatic Mammals used as food may be mentioned the Manatees (*Manatus*) and Dugongs (*Halicore*), which constitute the order of *Sea-Cows* (*Sirenia*); while reference has already been made (p. 209) to Whales (*Cetacea*) in this connection.

BIRDS (AVES).—Birds are eaten even more indiscriminately than Mammals, though birds of prey and fish-eating forms are avoided. The eggs of some wild birds, *e.g.* Plovers, are esteemed a delicacy. Edible birds'-nests have been mentioned elsewhere (see vol. iii, p. 462).

REPTILES (REPTILIA).—The high reputation of the Green Turtle (*Chelone mydas*) is familiar, and other members of the same order (*Chelonia*) are also eaten in various parts of the world, besides which the eggs of such creatures may also figure as an article of diet.

Some of the larger *Lizards* (*Lacertilia*) are regularly used as articles of food, especially the Iguanas (*Iguanidæ*) of America and the Water-Lizards (*Varanidæ*) of South and South-East Asia.

To a less extent *Crocodiles* and *Alligators* (*Crocodilia*) and *Snakes* (*Ophidia*) serve as a source of food.

AMPHIBIANS (AMPHIBIA).—The only members of the group of importance in this connection are some of the Frogs, which are eaten in India and Europe. In the latter case it is the Edible Frog (*Rana esculenta*) that falls a victim.

FISHES (PISCES).—Fishes are, and always have been, of great importance as a source of food. A very large number are regularly eaten, and it will be most convenient to deal with these in a special chapter.

MOLLUSCS (MOLLUSCS).—Many kinds of shell-fish are used as food, and some of the more important, *e.g.* the Oyster, will be dealt with separately.

Cuttle-fishes, Squids, and Octopods (*Cephalopoda*) are eaten in various parts of the world, particularly by the Chinese and Japanese, while one species (*Eledone*) is a common article of diet in South Europe, nor is it the only one.

Of *Snails and Slugs* (*Gastropoda*) utilized as food by Europeans many examples might be given. The commonest marine form thus employed is probably the Periwinkle (*Littorina*), and after this come Whelk (*Buccinum*), Limpet (*Patella*), and the Ormer or Sea-Ear (*Haliotis*). But there are many more, and in other parts of the world the list is much larger. The marine slug known as the Sea-Hare (*Aplysia*) is eaten in the South Sea Islands.

Land Snails (species of *Helix*) are largely used on the Continent, and to some extent in Great Britain.

Bivalve Molluscs (*Lamellibranchia*) are more important as a source of food than shell-fish of other kinds. Besides Oysters, Cockles, and Mussels there are the esteemed "Clams" of North America (species of *Mya*, *Mactra*, and *Venus*), and Razor-Shells (*Solen*) are also appreciated. The last are known in Scotland as "Spout-Fish", on account of the jet of water they squirt out when disturbed. On the Ayrshire coast the "hunting of the Spout-Fish" is pursued with great zeal at certain times of the year, a pointed instrument being thrust between the valves. These molluscs burrow obliquely in the sand with great rapidity, and are easily alarmed by the approach of footsteps, so there is considerable room for skill in their capture. Other bivalves commonly used for food are Piddocks (*Pholas*), Date-Shells (*Lithodomus*), and Ark-Shells (*Arca*). But the list might be extended almost indefinitely.

Among *Primitive Molluscs* (*Amphineura*) Cooke (in *The Cambridge Natural History*) says of the Mail-Shells (*Chiton*):—"West Indian negroes eat the large chitons which are abundant on their rocky coasts, cutting off and swallowing raw the fleshy foot, which they call 'beef', and rejecting the viscera"

INSECTS (INSECTA).—Bees (*Apis*) as a source of honey are most prominent here, but they will be noticed in a later section. Next to these, Locusts are perhaps of greatest importance, but Ants and Termites are also eaten. The Malays appreciate Cicadas or Tree-Bugs, and by rhythmic hand-clappings are able to lure them down from among the branches. Some of the Scale-Insects (*Coccidæ*) secrete sweet or waxy substances, and regarding one such species Sharp says (in *The Cambridge Natural History*):—"The manna mentioned in the book of Exodus is pretty certainly the honey-dew secreted by *Coccus* (now *Gossyparia*) *mannifera*, which lives on *Tamarix* in many places of the Mediterranean basin. This substance is still called by the Arabs 'man', and is used as food; in its natural state it is a substance very like honey; it is doubtless excreted by the *Coccus*, and is not produced directly by the *Tamarix* as some have supposed." Livingstone mentions a peculiar "kungu cake" eaten by the natives on the shores of Lake Nyassa, and which is made by compressing the bodies of vast numbers of the aquatic larvæ of gnats and related insects.

CENTIPEDES AND MILLIPEDES (MYRIAPODA).—These are mentioned here merely as a matter of curious interest. Sinclair remarks as follows (in *The Cambridge Natural History*):—"It is hard to believe that any human being could under any circumstances eat Centipedes, which have been described by one naturalist as 'a disgusting tribe loving the darkness'. Nevertheless, Humboldt informs us that he has seen the Indian children drag out of the earth Centipedes eighteen inches long and more than half an inch wide and devour them. This, I believe, is the only account of human beings using the Myriapoda as food, if we except the accounts of the religious fanatics among the African Arabs, who are said to devour Centipedes alive; though this is not a case of eating for pleasure, for the Scolopendras are devoured in company with leaves of the prickly pear, broken glass, &c., as a test of the unpleasant things that may be eaten under the influence of religious excitement."

CRUSTACEANS (CRUSTACEA).—This group is of obvious importance as a source of food, as the mention of Crab, Lobster, Prawn, and Shrimp is enough to show. A few details will be given in a later section, and it is enough to say here that a very large number of species are eaten in one country or another. One would scarcely expect Barnacles to be used in this way (though they are often mentioned in old accounts of shipwrecks), but certain species are exposed for sale in Spain and South America.

BRISTLE-WORMS (CHÆTOPODA).—The only marine Annelid used to any great extent as human food is the Palolo Worm (*Palolo viridis*) in the Samoa and Fiji islands. The chief facts regarding it are thus summarized by Benham (in *The Cambridge Natural History*):—"The worm . . . . lives in fissures among corals on the reefs, at a depth of about two fathoms. At certain days in October and November they leave the reefs and swim to the shores of the above islands, probably to spawn; and this occurs on two days in each of the above months—the day on which the moon is in her last quarter, and the day before. The natives, who call the worm 'Mbalolo', give the name 'Mbalolo laili' (little) to October, and 'Mbalolo levu' (large) to November, thereby indicating the relative abundance of the worms in these two months. The natives eat them either alive or baked, tied up in leaves; and they are esteemed so great a delicacy that presents of them are sent by the chiefs who live on shore to those living inland." Another worm, of which the habits are much the same, abounds on the shores of Mota Island, in the New Hebrides, and is also eaten.

HEDGEHOG-SKINNED ANIMALS (ECHINODERMATA).—The "roe" of *Sea-Urchins* (*Echinoidea*) was prized as a luxury by the ancient Romans, and is still eaten on the shores of the Adriatic, as well as in other parts of the world. The "sea-eggs" mentioned in the quotation from Darwin's account of the Fuegians given at the beginning of this chapter (p. 211) are animals of the kind. The collection of sea-urchins (chiefly *Hipponoe esculenta*) for food is an important but decaying industry in Barbados, amounting in value to £4000 per annum.

The dried bodies of *Sea-Cucumbers* (*Holothuroidea*) constitute what is commonly known to commerce as *Bêche-de-Mer* or Trepang, an important article of food to the Chinese. The most extensive fishery is on the Great Barrier Reef of Australia, the annual return of which is worth some £23,000 to Queensland. These animals abound in the West Indies, of which the marine resources are not sufficiently developed. One desideratum is a properly-organized trepang fishery.

ZOOPHYTES (CŒLENTERATA).—This group of animals is unimportant as a source of food, but Sea-Anemones (*cul de mulet*) are eaten in France, Sicily, and along the shores of the Adriatic.

DOMESTICATION OF ANIMALS

The domestication of certain animals by man has been one of the most important factors in the evolution of civilization, enabling the prehistoric huntsmen and shore-dwellers to pass into the more civilized pastoral stage, from which gradual transition is easy to the still more civilized agricultural stage.

Although the Dog can claim to be the earliest domesticated animal, our greatest debt is obviously due to various Hoofed Mammals (Ungulata), which include all the larger inhabitants of our farmyards, the Camels of the Old World, and the Llamas of the New, while Elephants belong to an order which is not distantly related. The most important domesticated birds belong to two orders, (1) Ducks and Geese (Anseres), and (2) Game-Birds (Gallinæ), including, more particularly, Fowls (descended from an Indian stock) and Turkeys (natives of North America).

One Insect, too, the Honey-Bee (*Apis mellifica*), has played no mean part in the drama of human civilization, and to this may be added the Silk-Worm (*Bombyx mori*) and the Cochineal Insect (*Coccus cacti*)

The following remarks on the origin of Domestication and some of its results are quoted from Jenks (*A History of Politics*):—"The art of taming wild animals and making them serve the purposes of man, is one of the great discoveries of the world. . . . But as to the man or men who introduced it we have no knowledge, except through vague and obviously untrustworthy tradition. . . . In all probability the discovery was made independently by many different races, under combinations of favourable circumstances. But if we cannot speak with confidence of names and dates in the matter, we can make certain tolerably shrewd guesses as to the way in which domestication of animals came about. We start with the fact that the most valuable of the world's domestic animals—the sheep, horse, ox, goat, &c.—are known to exist, or to have existed, in a wild state. It is practically impossible to suppose that these wild animals are (except in rare cases) the result of the escape from captivity of tame animals. It follows, therefore, that the start which a pack of savages could obtain in the matter of domestication would depend upon the character of the wild animals in the neighbourhood. For it is fairly obvious by this time that many wild animals are not suitable for taming. Thus, it is hardly possible that the lion, tiger, or bear will ever really become domestic animals, in spite of the fact that their strength and endurance would prove valuable qualities if they could be used. And so some peoples may have remained utterly savage because of the fact that their country does not produce animals capable of domestication. Again, some races, like the Eskimos, appear to have had only the wild ancestors of the dog and the reindeer (fig. 1156), and thus to have been very limited in their opportunities. Other races have been able to tame the sheep, one of the most valuable aids to civilization; others, again, have had the still more valuable ox. But still the question remains—how was the process of domestication discovered? Here, again, we can only proceed by speculation; but a most valuable account of his experiences in Southern Africa (Damara Land), published by the late Sir Francis Galton in the middle of last century, affords us some suggestive hints

(*Narrative of an Explorer in Tropical South Africa*). . . . Two of the most striking features of the savage character are *recklessness* and *greed.* Being quite unable to make provision for the future, or even to realize the wants of the future, the savage consumes in disgusting orgies the produce of a successful hunt. A stroke of luck, such as the capture of a big herd of game, simply means an opportunity for gorging. But even the savage capacity for food has its limits; and, in exceptionally good

Fig. 1156.—Reindeer (*Rangifer tarandus*)

seasons, there is a superfluity of game. A civilized man would strain every nerve to store the surplus away against future wants. The savage simply wastes it; partly because he knows that meat will not keep, partly because he cannot realize the needs of the future. The 'pemmican' or sun-dried meat of the Red Indian, and his 'caches' or buried hoards, are the limits of the savage capacity for storing up against a rainy day. But if the savage is reckless and greedy, he is often affectionate and playful. If he has had as much food as he can eat, he will amuse himself by playing with his captives instead of killing them. At first, no doubt, there is a good deal of the cat and the mouse in the relationship; but in time the savage comes positively to love his captives, and even to resist the pangs of hunger rather than kill them. In other words, the earliest domestic animals were *pets*; preserved, not with a view to profit, but for sport or amusement. And it is most important to observe that animals so selected would naturally be the handsomest and finest of the catch, whose appearance would delight the eye. . . . But, of course, feelings of affection would be bound to give way in the long run to feelings of hunger, and then the tame animals would be slaughtered for food. And so it would ultimately dawn on the savage that the keeping of pets was really a profitable business, because it afforded some protection against famine. Gradually it would become more and more common. Finally, the savage would learn by experience that, even without destroying them, his pets could be put to valuable use. Thus the wool of sheep, the hair of goats, the milk of cows, would be to a savage like a gift from an unknown Power. . . . But, when he had got thus far, the savage would have ceased to be a savage; he would have become a *pastoralist*. . . . And then, as all the advantages of the rearing of animals come to be realized, the savage 'pack' gradually changes into a society of shepherds or herdsmen, in which the men are engaged in tending cattle, sheep, or goats, while to the women fall the subordinate offices of spinning the wool, milking the cows and goats, and making the butter and cheese. The men drive the flocks to pasture and water, regulate the breeding, guard the folds against enemies, decide which of the animals shall be killed for food, and break in the beasts of burden." The nomad tribes of the Asiatic steppes, Kirghiz, Kalmucks, &c., are still in the pastoral stage.

A brief account of some of the chief domesticated animals may now appropriately follow.

DOMESTICATED MAMMALS (MAMMALIA) AND THEIR USES

THE DOG (*Canis familiaris*).—It is not likely that the some 180 breeds of Dog which exist at the present day (figs. 1157 and 1158) have all descended from the same wild stock. Various kinds of Wolf, Jackal, and Wild Dog have more probably been domesticated at various times by different races, and the

Fig. 1157.—Greyhound

very wide distribution of the family (*Canidæ*) to which such creatures belong lends probability to this view. We have already

Fig. 1158.—Dachshund

seen (p. 217) that it was the first animal tamed by Man. At a much later period, the monuments of Assyria and Egypt afford evidence, as Darwin says that (in *Animals and Plants under Domestication*), "four or five thousand years ago, various breeds, viz. pariah dogs, greyhounds, common hounds, mastiffs, house-dogs, lap-dogs, and turnspits, existed, more or less closely resembling our present breeds. But there is not sufficient evidence that any of these ancient dogs belonged to the same identical sub-varieties with our present dogs" (fig. 1159). Although Australia is singularly lacking in higher Mammals, it nevertheless possesses a kind of dog, the Dingo (*Canis dingo*), probably introduced by human agency at a remote period. Friend and companion, guardian of flocks, and protector of the home, no animal has been so closely and so long associated with man as the Dog.

Fig. 1159.—Types of Ancient Egyptian Dogs. A, Turnspit; B, House Dog; C, Hunting Dog.

The Cat (*Felis domestica*).—Here again we have almost certainly to do with an animal of multiple origin, the Wild Cat (*Felis catus*) of Europe and North Asia being probably not the chief ancestor. On this point Beddard (in *The Cambridge Natural History*) speaks as follows:—"The domestic cat is, in fact, regarded as the descendant of the Eastern *F. caffra*, or (perhaps *and*) the closely allied *F. maniculata* (fig. 1160). It is highly probable, however, that after its introduction into this country as a domestic animal it has interbred with the Wild Cat. Many allied species of Cats will interbreed, even two so far apart as the Lion and the Tiger. There are interesting archæological and linguistic reasons for regarding the Domestic Cat as an importation. The legend of Dick Whittington's Cat points to it being a rare and valuable animal, which a tamed *F. catus* would not at that time have been. There was an enactment in Wales against him who should kill the king's Cat, again suggestive of its rarity and consequent value. The very name 'Puss' is a hint of a foreign origin. Some would derive it from Perse, and upon this is based the notion that the

Cat is from Persia. But it seems that Puss is the same as Pasht and Bubastis, showing so far an Egyptian origin for the animal. The ancestral Cats mentioned above are native of Egypt." So far as we know the ancient Egyptians were the first to discover the domestic virtues of this animal, and Herodotus tells us that they treated it with no little consideration (though it scarcely ranked so high as the dog):—"When a fire breaks out a wonderful thing happens to these animals; for the Egyptians, heedless of extinguishing the flames, stand in a line to take care

Fig. 1160.—Fallow Cat (*Felis maniculata*)

of the cats; but those creatures, slipping in between the men, or leaping over them, rush into the fire; and when that happens deep grief seizes the Egyptians. If in any house a cat dies naturally, all the inmates shave merely their eyebrows: those in whose house a dog happens to die, shave the whole of their bodies and heads. The dead cats are taken to some sacred buildings in Bubastis, where, when embalmed, they are buried. With respect to the dogs, they bury them in sacred repositories, each in his own town."

It is not proposed to refer to Kipling as a zoological authority, but those who have not done so (if such exist) should read the story of domestication in "The Cat that Walked by Himself", as a brilliant *tour de force* of imagination (in *Just So Stories*).

In the same place he neatly hits off the mental difference between Puss and the Dog Binkie:—

"Pussy will rub my knees with her head,
 Pretending she loves me hard;
But the very minute I go to my bed,
 Pussy runs out in the yard.
And there she stays till the morning-light,
 So I know it is only pretend;
But *Binkie*, he snores at my feet all night,
 And he is my Firstest Friend!"

OXEN (BOS) AND BUFFALOES (BUBALUS).—The domesticated cattle of various parts of the world are no doubt, like the dogs.

Fig. 1161.—Hungarian Oxen

descended from several wild stocks, and some of them would seem to represent a mixture of strains. The two most notable oxen that appear to have been domesticated in Europe during the Newer Stone Age (Neolithic period) were the great Urus (*Bos primigenius*), and a second much smaller species (*B. longifrons*). It is often considered that the wild White Cattle of Chillingham Park are the direct but dwarfed descendants of the former, while the small dark cattle of Wales and the Scottish Highlands can probably be traced back to the latter. And we have also to take into consideration the European Bison or Aurochs (*Bison Europæus*), a large and savage form now only surviving in parts of Russia, especially in the Lithuanian forest of Bielovege, where it is jealously preserved. This is not the place to consider in detail how far the various breeds of European Oxen (*Bos taurus*) take origin from one or more of the forms just mentioned, or from still others, for the subject is still in the controversial stage. It need only be stated that even in prehistoric times there were

Fig. 1162.—Dwarf Zebus of Ceylon

several domesticated breeds, while now there are a great many. The large pale Hungarian cattle with their formidable horns are amongst the most remarkable (fig. 1161).

Humped Cattle were domesticated by the ancient Egyptians, and we find them still both in Africa and South Asia, under the name of Zebus (*Bos Indicus*, fig. 1162). Their ancestry is doubtful, and it is also a moot point as to whether or no the race of them living in North-East Africa has contributed a strain to certain European breeds. The curious little grunting long-haired Yak (*Bos grunniens*), characteristic of Tibet, is probably quite distinct. Further India possesses another kind of humped ox, the Gayal (*Bos frontalis*).

Differing in many ways from oxen is the tame Buffalo (*Bubalus buffelus*), ranging from India and Ceylon to South Europe. It is a descendant of the wild Indian Buffalo (*Bubalus arni*).

It is scarcely necessary to remark that oxen, besides serving as an important source of food, are useful in many other ways. In South Africa, for instance, it would be difficult to exaggerate their value for purposes of transport, while in many countries they are used to draw the plough, as, *e.g.*, in Hungary (fig. 1161). Tallow, hoofs, horns, and hides are the most valuable products of the carcase, meat alone excepted. This may be illustrated by the fact that raw hides were imported into this country in 1902 to the value of £2,441,000. It may be added that in June, 1903, the total number of cattle in the United Kingdom amounted to 11 408,560, *i.e.* about 148 head per thousand acres.

The Sheep (Ovis aries).—Wild Sheep of various species are characteristic of the Northern Hemisphere, and different origins must be sought for the domesticated forms of different areas. Regarding the breeds with which we are familiar in this country there is much difference of opinion, but it is probable that some of them represent a mixture of several different strains. We know that during the Newer Stone Age (Neolithic period) the sheep existed in a tame condition, though it would appear to have been domesticated subsequent to the ox, and the bones that have been found, *e.g.* in connection with some of the Swiss lake-dwellings, indicate a slender and rather goat-like creature. But here, as in the case of our other familiar farm mammals, the question of origin is complicated by the consideration that the invading Neolithic tribes, who drove out the rude hunters and fishermen of the Older Stone Age (Palæolithic period), probably brought domesticated animals with them. If we knew with certainty whence these immigrants came, the problem would be rather less complex, but our knowledge on this point is unfortunately very incomplete. Grave doubt has been cast upon the picturesque view that Central Asia is the "cradle" of the Aryan race, and that the mixed populations of Europe mainly result from successive "waves" of immigration which have radiated from this centre. It is more likely that Neolithic man was of North African stock, and invaded Europe from the south. He certainly at one time inhabited Corsica, Sardinia, Sicily, and South Italy. In view of the possible correctness of the view indicated, it may be well to remember that a wild species of

WILD CATTLE OF CHILLINGHAM

The origin of our domestic breeds of cattle is a question regarding which many conjectures have been made, though the matter is still involved in considerable doubt. They are possibly in part descended from the gigantic prehistoric Wild Ox (*Bos primigenius*) of Western Europe, which survived into historic times and was probably the form known to the ancient Romans by the name of Urus. In Chillingham Park, Northumberland, and elsewhere, wild white cattle are still preserved, and it is considered by some authorities that these are to be regarded as the dwarfed descendants of the Urus. This view, however, cannot be regarded as definitely established.

BRITISH WILD CATTLE (BOS PRIMIGENIUS) IN CHILLINGHAM PARK

sheep, *i.e.* the Barbary Sheep (*Ovis tragelaphus*), is now peculiar to North Africa, and another, the Mouflon or Musimon (*O. musimon*, fig. 1163), is limited to Corsica and Sardinia, though it probably once had a wider distribution. One or both these species have possibly contributed a strain towards the formation of our ordinary tame varieties.

Fig. 1163.—The Mouflon (*Ovis musimon*)

As dwellers among mountains and rocky uplands, Sheep occupy a different place in nature from Oxen, and being close browsers are able to live comfortably on herbage quite unsuitable for horned stock, as may be seen in the barren "sheep-walks" of Central Wales. The practical importance of this is sufficiently obvious. In assessing the value of these animals from the economic stand-point, we have to reckon not only with meat and, to a less extent, milk, but also with wool, a material that has played an important part in the history of textile industries. In the colder parts of the globe clothing of some sort ranks as a necessity, which the prehistoric hunter supplied by roughly stitching together the skins of various animals, sinews being used as thread. This kind of clothing is still in vogue among many savage or half-civilized races. Lord Avebury thus speaks (in *Prehistoric Times*) of the Esquimaux in this connection:—"The clothes of the Esquimaux are made from the skins of reindeer, seals, and birds, sewn together with sinews. For needles they use bones either of birds or fishes; yet with these simple instruments they sew very strongly and well. The outer dress of the men resembles a short greatcoat, with a hood that can be pulled over the head if necessary, and which serves as a substitute for a hat or cap. Their under-garments or shirts are made of bird-skins with the feathers inwards; or of skins with the hair inside; sometimes, however, they wear in addition another shirt made of seal's entrails. Their breeches are either of seal-skin or reindeer-skin, and their stockings of skins from very young animals. The boots are of smooth black dressed seal's leather, and sometimes when at sea they wear a great overcoat of the same material. The dress of the women does not differ much from that of the men."

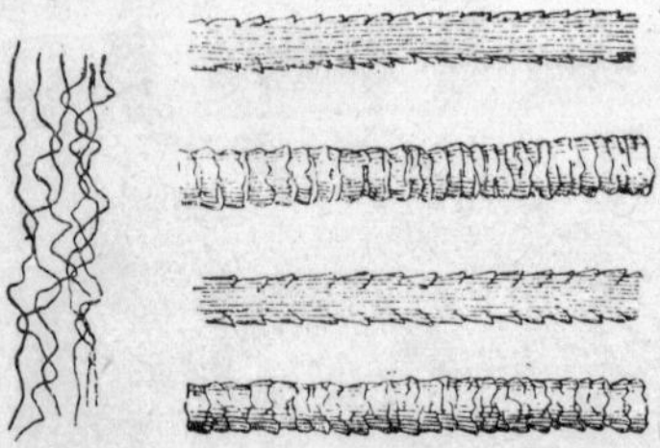

Fibres of Wool — Fibres of Wool as seen under Microscope

Fig. 1164

For temperate climates skins are far from being a convenient form of clothing, and among the prehistoric races of Europe were gradually replaced by woven fabrics. Coarse materials of the sort made from flax or straw fibres, have been discovered in connection with some of the Swiss lake-dwellings referred to the Stone Age, at a time when tame sheep were few in number. But when this animal became an important domesticated form the possibility of replacing flax, &c., by wool came to be realized. And among the remains of the Bronze Age in Jutland various woollen garments have been found.

The coat of a Mammal typically consists of outer hair, more or less harsh in texture, and soft under-fur, the two being present in different proportions in different cases. The "wool" of Sheep is a specialized kind of under-fur, the individual hairs of which are wavy or crimped, and covered with well-marked overlapping scales, that promote felting together (fig. 1164). Considerable variations exist as to length, fineness, &c., and the fleeces of certain existing breeds are noted for their valuable qualities. In South-west Asia there is a remarkable variety of the domestic form, known as the Flat-Tailed Sheep, in which the tail is enormously large and fat, weighing as much as 40 or 50 lbs. A miniature sledge or cart is often attached to animals of the kind, for the more convenient carriage of this monstrous appendage. The nomad races of the steppes of Asia possess vast flocks of a related variety, in which, however, the flat tail is very short, and the fat is concentrated on the sides of the rump. The colour of the breed is black, white, or a mixture of the two, and the familiar "Persian lamb" and "astrachan" of commerce are the product of young animals of this breed. The Merino Sheep, originally confined to Spain but now widely distributed, is noted for the length and fineness of its wool.

Fig. 1165.—Angora Goats

The economic importance of wool may be illustrated by the statement that in 1902 our import (worth £20,236,000) amounted to 678 million pounds, and the home production to 136 million pounds. Of these amounts 320 million pounds were exported, while the remainder, *i.e.* 494 million pounds, was worked up for home use.

THE GOAT (CAPRA HIRCUS).—Although this animal does not rank so high as the sheep from the economic stand-point, it possesses considerable value as a source of meat, dairy products, and clothing. We know that it was domesticated by the Swiss lake-dwellers during the Stone Age in rather greater numbers than the sheep. In the same remote period goats, as well as sheep and oxen, were among the tame animals possessed by prehistoric man in Britain.

The most important wild animal from which the domesticated Goat of Europe has taken origin is probably the Grecian Ibex or Bezoar Goat (*Capra ægagrus*), which at the present time ranges from Crete to North-west India. But there is very likely an admixture of one or more other strains.

So far as civilized nations are concerned, the most important products obtained from the Goat are kid-skin, for glove-making, and "mohair", which is the long silky over-hair of certain Asiatic breeds. The chief source of the latter is the well-known Angora Goat, native to Asia Minor, and distinguished by the beauty of its long white silky coat (fig. 1165). The Kashmir Goat, which also ranges into Tibet and the Asiatic steppes, possesses an undercoat of fine soft wool, and it is this which is made into the familiar Kashmir shawls. Large herds of the steppe variety are among the most valuable property of the nomad tribes, not only on account of their skins and wool, but also as a source of meat, milk, butter, and cheese.

THE CAMEL (CAMELUS).—Being eminently adapted to desert conditions the Camel has been a most valuable domestic animal in Asia and Africa from very remote times. There are two species, the one-humped Arabian Camel (*Camelus dromedarius*), which is the familiar kind introduced by the Arabs into Africa, and the two-humped Bactrian Camel (*C. Bactrianus*, fig. 1166) of Central Asia. It is doubtful whether either species exists in the wild condition. Both are represented on the Assyrian monuments. The most important use of Camels is to serve as beasts of burden, a large animal being able to carry 1000 pounds weight or more for a distance of 30 to 35 miles a day. Several breeds exist, and a distinction may be drawn between baggage-camels and racing-camels or dromedaries. The latter are capable of maintaining a pace of from 8 to 10 miles an hour for a considerable part of the day. There are also various crosses between Arabian and Bactrian camels.

Camels are most valuable as beasts of burden, both in peace and war, but they are also an important source of meat and milk, while the thick wool of the Bactrian species is greatly esteemed for textile purposes. The Arabian Camel is by no means limited to Africa and Arabia, for it ranges also from Syria to North-west India, and has been introduced into Italy, Spain, the Canary Islands, North America, and Australia. It is probably of Indian stock.

THE LLAMA (LAMA LAMA) AND ALPACA (L. PACOS).—We know from geological evidence that creatures of the camel kind first came into existence in North America. Thence some of them migrated into the Old World, passing over a land area that once existed in the North Atlantic (or *viâ* land uniting Alaska and

Fig. 1166.—Kirghiz with Bactrian Camels (*Camelus Bactrianus*)

Asia), while others made their way into South America. From the former Camels took origin, and from the latter the cameline forms of South America, with which we are now concerned. All animals of the sort having become extinct in the intervening area, and submergence of the connecting land having isolated the Old World from the New, the group has come to be distributed in a discontinuous manner.

The domesticated camelines of South America are the Llama

and Alpaca, both probably derived from the wild Guanaco (*Lama guanacus*), which now ranges from the mountain regions of Ecuador and Peru to Tierra del Fuego.

The Llama (*Lama lama*), an animal much smaller than the camel, has been an important beast of burden in Peru and Bolivia from ancient times, though now largely replaced by horses, mules, and oxen. Its flesh and wool are also of value. At the time of the Spanish Conquest it is said that some 300,000 llamas were employed in transporting silver from the famous mines of Potosi.

Fig. 1167.—Alpacas (*Lama pacos*)

The Alpaca (*L. pacos*, fig. 1167) is somewhat bigger than a large goat, and is bred for the sake of its flesh, and more especially on account of the fine qualities of its fleece, which is distinguished for its softness and elasticity. The fine straight hairs average from 7 to 9 inches in length, and are strong without being coarse, differing in this respect from wool of other kinds.

THE PIG (SUS SCROFA).—While oxen, sheep, and goats are well adapted to the needs of pastoral nomad races, it is quite otherwise with swine, which are notoriously difficult to drive from place to place. Their domestication is, in fact, one mark that their owners have abandoned a wandering life, and entered upon the agricultural stage of civilization, which is a distinct advance upon the pastoral one. We should expect therefore that the prehistoric

THE LLAMA (*Lama lama*)

This animal was domesticated in very remote times by the ancient Peruvians, and even now is an important beast of burden in the high Andes of Peru and Bolivia, though the original breed has been replaced to a great extent by domesticated forms introduced from the Old World. In former times it was used in great numbers for the transport of silver ore from the famous mines of Potosi in Bolivia, more than 13,000 feet above the sea.

The Llama may be described as an American cousin of the Camel, belonging, as it does, to the same group (*Tylopoda*) of Ruminants or Cud-chewers. The earliest known members of this group were, however, native to North America, from which area the stock spread on the one hand into South America, and on the other into the Old World, having since become extinct elsewhere.

LLAMAS (LAMA LAMA) CARRYING GOODS IN THE ANDES

races of the Old World would tame the ox, the sheep, and the goat before turning their attention to the pig, and the evidence of the lake-dwellings of Switzerland favours such a conclusion, for in that area at any rate swine were not domesticated till the Age of Stone had given way to the Age of Bronze. And positive evidence is also available to show that the Swiss lake-dwellers of the latter period cultivated several kinds of grain, and were, in fact, agriculturists of a primitive kind.

Ordinary European Swine are probably not an unmixed race, but the predominant strain in them is derived from the Wild Boar (*Sus scrofa*), which at the present time is widely distributed through Europe, North Africa, West Asia, and Central Asia. It inhabited Britain down to the end of the sixteenth century. The Wild Boar of India, Ceylon, and Further India is probably a variety of the same species. The domesticated pigs of China and Japan would appear to be of entirely different origin.

The uses of the Pig are manifold, and too well known to require detailed notice. As Simmonds says (in *Animal Products*): "It is the animal in which there is the least waste between the dead and living weight, nearly all the carcase being utilized. The blood, the skin, the head, and most of the entrails, which are useless in other animals, serving as food." Leather, bristles, and lard (employed for a great variety of purposes) are the most valuable of the remaining products. In 1902 this country imported about 328,600 tons of bacon and ham, the value of which was £17,285,867. And it was estimated that in June, 1903, the number of swine in the United Kingdom amounted to 4,085,764.

THE HORSE (EQUUS CABALLUS).—Wild Horses were among the animals hunted by prehistoric man in Europe during the Stone Age, as we know from contemporary drawings that have come down to us from the times (Newer Palæolithic period) which immediately preceded the final (or Neolithic) epoch of that age, when the implements and weapons of stone were either neatly chipped or carefully polished. It is remarkable that the men of the Newer Palæolithic period were possessed of considerable artistic power, as is now the case with the Esquimaux, their possible descendants, and they whiled away part of their leisure time by scratching spirited outlines of various wild animals on pieces of bone, ivory, or antler. One such drawing representing two hog-maned horses is depicted in fig. 1168. It would appear, however, that the Horse was not domesticated in Europe until the Bronze Age, or at least not to any large extent.

At the present time there do not appear to be any truly wild horses of the same species as our domesticated breeds, and the so-called "wild horses" of South America, for example, are simply feral, *i.e.* the descendants of tame animals which have escaped from captivity. There is, however, a small kind of horse (*Equus Przewalskii*, fig. 1169) native to the desert regions of Central Asia, which possibly approaches in some respects to the ancestral

Fig. 1168.—Prehistoric Hog-Maned Horses (from Isaac Taylor's *The Origin of the Aryans*, by the courtesy of Mr. Walter Scott)

Fig. 1169.—Przewalsky's Horse (*Equus Przewalskii*)

stock. The mane is not well developed, and the tail resembles that of a donkey. The greatly specialized limbs of horses and their allies have undoubtedly been evolved as an adaptation to swift progression on plains of desert or steppe nature (see vol. iii,

p. 140), and it is probable that in colour and markings the ancestral forms harmonized more or less with their surroundings. Darwin long ago suggested that the bars and stripes so often present on various parts of the bodies of domesticated horses may be a case of atavism, *i.e.* "reversion" or "throw back" to ancestral characters. Cossar Ewart has greatly elaborated and adduced fresh evidence in support of this view; in his opinion primeval horses were clothed in "striped khaki", with short forelock and hog-mane (as in

Fig. 1170.—Head of "Matopo", Prof. Cossar Ewart's Zebra (*Equus Burchelli*), and of a Norwegian Pony

the prehistoric drawings). Fig. 1170, which Professor Ewart has kindly permitted me to borrow from his book (*The Penycuik Experiments*), shows how the head-stripes possessed by a particular Norwegian pony compare with those on the head of a Zebra, an animal which might almost be described as a striped and hog-maned latter-day horse. The following quotation is taken from the book just mentioned:—"We can only guess as to the colour of the remote ancestor of the horse, but nearly all who have made a special study of the subject have come to the conclusion that the less remote ancestors were dun-coloured. But it is hardly sufficient to say the ancestors were dun-coloured, for in Norway four shades of dun are recognized, which include nearly every colour from white to black. There are (1) white duns (white and light creams) with white mane and tail; (2) yellow duns with black mane and tail, including creams and light bays; (3) elk duns, frequently approaching in hue bays, chestnuts, and browns; and (4) mouse duns, some of which are nearly black. After a full consideration

Fig. 1171.—Arabian Horse

of the subject, I am inclined to believe the body-colour of the striped ancestral horse of the temperate regions was mainly of a yellowish-brown colour. As the descendants extended their range the ground-colour would change, a sand colour probably prevailing in desert areas, a reddish dun in the vicinity of forests, a mouse dun in the far north, a light tint near the tropics, and in the uplands a gray or ash tint." There is a marked resemblance between Norwegian ponies and certain Indian breeds, in view of which it is interesting to notice that according to the traditions of Scandinavia the horse was introduced into that region from the East by the god Odin. But though the body of evidence is on the whole in favour of the view that Central Asia is the old home of the domesticated species of horse, it must not be forgotten that equines, like camelines, were originally evolved in North America.

The horse, like many other forms domesticated from ancient times, presents a great variety of breeds, produced by artificial selection, and suitable for widely different purposes. Arabians, Clydesdales, and Shetland ponies or "shelties", may be taken as examples (figs. 1171–1173).

Fig. 1172.—A Clydesdale

It is unnecessary to dwell upon the important services rendered by the horse to man, alike during peace and in times of war, as a draught animal and for riding purposes. And among our dumb intimates he ranks second only to the dog. The return of live stock of the United Kingdom for June, 1903, included 2,069,859 horses, a modest total compared to over 16½ millions possessed by the United States, and over 22 millions by Russia.

Horse-flesh is by no means unimportant as an article of food, and probably plays a more prominent part in the dietary of Europe than is commonly suspected. The hide is of considerable value, and horse-hair is put to various uses, though the once familiar hair-cloth, figuring as an eminently respectable if slippery covering for chairs and sofas, has been replaced by cheaper and more attractive materials.

THE ASS (EQUUS ASINUS).—Many of the purposes served by the horse are discharged with considerable efficiency by his

Fig. 1173.—A Shetland Pony

humbler cousin, a comparatively late-comer to Western and Central Europe, though domesticated from a very remote period by the Egyptians and other races (fig. 1174). It would be a mistake to base our judgment of the species upon the ill-fed and

Fig. 1174.—Egyptian Sculpture

too often cruelly treated donkeys seen in this country, for some of the breeds of South Europe and the East are handsome and even graceful. White asses have long been esteemed, as may be illustrated by an allusion in the Old Testament, "Speak, ye that ride on white asses, ye that sit in judgment, and walk by the way" (Judges v. 10). The undeserved obloquy from which the modern "moke" suffers is, however, the survival of a very ancient prejudice. Possibly the original source of derision is to be looked for in the shockingly inharmonious voice of this unfortunate creature. The views of the ancient Egyptians on the subject are thus summarized by Houghton (in *Natural History of the Ancients*):—"The ass was sacred to Typho, 'the Evil Being'. According to Plutarch, the Coptites had the custom of throwing an ass down a precipice; and the inhabitants of Busiris and Lycopolis carried their detestation of it so far as never to make use of trumpets, fancying that their sound is similar to the braying of an ass. Even the colour of the unfortunate ass—which, in Egypt, as in ancient Palestine, was of a redder tint than is usual with the domestic ass of England—was looked upon as indicative of the Evil Being, and any unhappy man who was of a ruddy complexion, or had decidedly red hair, was thought to be related to the Evil Being (Typho)."

Several species of wild donkey are native to Asia and Africa. One of the latter, the Nubian Ass (*Equus Africanus* or *tæniopus*), is probably ancestral to the domesticated form. The original stock most likely resembled in colour and markings that from which horses have sprung.

It may conveniently be noted here that the the striped Tiger-Horses or Zebras, of which Africa possesses three indigenous species, are not the wild and intractable creatures once supposed, but are susceptible to domestication. Nor do the zebras of the "fly" districts succumb to the bites of the tsetse-fly, an insect that makes considerable tracts in tropical Africa impossible for horses.

MULES AND ZEBRA-MULES.—It is a familiar fact that ordinary mules are crosses or hybrids between horse and ass. On account of their strength, endurance, and sure-footedness they are invaluable beasts of burden in mountainous countries, and play a more important part both in peace and war than is commonly realized in England, where there is considerable prejudice against them. Probably Spain has made more use of them than any other nation, especially in the New World. The importance of the mule in war so far as the British Empire is concerned has been abundantly demonstrated in our African and Indian campaigns, and its value in peace is also considerable.

Unfortunately mules are often vicious, stubborn, and difficult to manage, and probably on this account have not so far been used so much as might be desired in the development of the resources of the mountainous parts of the empire. A partial solution to the problem may perhaps be found in the employment of zebra-mules, *i.e.* crosses between horse and zebra (fig. 1175), which are much more docile than ordinary mules. This step has been advocated by Captain Lugard, Major von Wissmann, and Professor

Fig. 1175.—"Sir John", one of Prof. Cossar Ewart's Zebra Hybrids (sire "Matopo", see fig. 1170; dam "Tundra", an Iceland pony)

Cossar Ewart, the last of whom makes the following remarks on the subject (in *The Penycuik Experiments*):—"I have already referred to the views of Captain Lugard. He writes: 'Some years ago I advocated experiments on taming the zebra, and I especially suggested that an attempt should be made to obtain zebra-mules by horse or donkey mares. Such mules, I believe, would be found excessively hardy, and impervious to the 'fly' and to climatic diseases. . . . I would even go further, and say that their export might prove one of the sources of revenue and wealth in the future; for, as everyone knows, the paucity of mules both for mountain batteries and for transport purposes has long been one of the gravest difficulties in our otherwise almost perfect Indian Army Corps.' Since this was written much information has been gained as to the dreaded tsetse-fly, but apparently there is extremely little chance of horses being made immune, *i.e.* so treated by inoculation or otherwise that they will be able to survive if once infected by the peculiar minute organism so intimately associated with the all too fatal disease. Further, owing to the destruction of cattle by the rinderpest, the transport difficulties have been increased in Africa, while the frontier wars have increased the demand for mules in India. On the other hand, it has been proved that it is a comparatively simple matter to cross various breeds of mares with a Burchell zebra, and if experts are to be trusted, the hybrids (zebra-mules, as some call them) promise to be as useful and hardy as they are shapely and attractive. The preliminary difficulties having been overcome, it remains for those in authority to ascertain of what special use, if any, zebra hybrids may be in various parts of the Empire, but more especially in Africa and India." Prof. Ewart, in a recent letter (March, 1904), has kindly supplied me with further information.—"Some of the hybrids are constantly being driven in Hamburg. Eight of those I bred are going to the St. Louis Exposition. Apparently a hybrid withstands the tsetse poison better than a zebra which has not been reared in the 'fly' country. Some of the hybrids out of Iceland (inbred) ponies are extremely tractable, and can be used for carrying children."

The Elephant.—Although both African and Indian Elephants can be tamed, it is only the latter species that has been of very great service to man as a domesticated animal. Its considerable intelligence and enormous strength make it useful as a beast of burden and for lifting heavy weights (fig. 1176). For such purposes, and also in war, it has been employed in the East from very remote times. But its nervous temperament and uncertain temper constitute serious drawbacks, especially in the case of the males. Some of the characteristics of this animal are thus described by Sir Samuel Baker (in *Wild Beasts and their Ways*):—"Although I may be an exception in the non-admiration of the elephant's sagacity to the degree in which it is usually accepted, there is no one who more admires or is so foolishly fond of elephants. . . . There is, however, a peculiar contradiction in the character of elephants that tends to increase the interest in the animal. If they were all the same, there would be a monotony; but this is never the case, either among animals or human beings, although they may belong to one family. The elephant, on the other hand, stands so entirely apart from all other animals, and its performances appear so extraordinary owing to the enormous effect which its great strength produces instantaneously, that its peculiarities interest mankind more than any smaller animal. Yet, when we consider the actual aptitude for learning, or the natural habits of the creature, we are obliged to confess that in proportion to its size the elephant is a mere fool in comparison with the intelligence of many insects. . . . It actually does nothing remarkable, unless specially instructed; but it is this inertia that renders it so valuable to man. If the elephant were to be continually exerting its natural intelligence, and volunteering all manner of gigantic performances in the hope that they would be appreciated by its rider, it would be unbearable; the value of the animal consists in its capacity to learn, and in its passive demeanour until directed by the mahout's commands." The same writer advocates, in the following words, the domestication of the African species:—"It is much to be regretted that no system has been organized in Africa for capturing and training the wild elephants, instead of harrying them to destruction. In a country where beasts of burden are unknown, as in equatorial Africa, it seems incredible that the power and the intelligence of the elephant have been completely ignored. . . . When we consider the peculiar power that an elephant possesses for swimming long distances, and for supporting long marches under an enormous weight, we are tempted to condemn the apathy even of European settlers in Africa, who have hitherto ignored the capabilities of this useful creature. The chief difficulty of African commerce is the lack of transport. The elephant is admirably adapted by his natural habits for travelling through a wild country devoid of roads. He can wade through unbridged streams, or swim the deepest rivers (without a load), and he is equally at home either on land or water. His carrying power for continued service would be from 12 to 14 cwts.; thus a single elephant would convey about 1300 lbs. of ivory in addition to the weight of the pad. The value of one load would be about £500. At the present moment such an amount of ivory would employ twenty-six carriers; but as these are generally slaves which can be sold at the termination of the journey, they might be more profitable than the legitimate transport by an elephant." Sir Harry Johnston, while in favour of experiments in this matter, thus expresses his forebodings as to the result:—"The question of its domestication and usefulness to man is a very doubtful one. It is relatively easy to obtain young African elephants, and to tame them in a few days or a few weeks. It is also easy to train them to bear burdens on their backs or to perform other simple tasks, but it cannot be

Fig. 1176.—An Indian Elephant (*Elephas Indicus*) lifting Timber

said as they grow up that they evince the same docility that is characteristic of the Indian elephant, while after the males have reached maturity they are positively dangerous. Something might be done with the adult female African elephant." (*Nature*, 1904.)

THE RABBIT (LEPUS CUNICULUS) AND HARE (L. TIMIDUS).—The various breeds of Rabbit which are domesticated in Europe are all descended from the common wild form, which was originally restricted to the countries bordering the Western Mediterranean, and the islands of the same region. Some of the races, especially Chinchillas and Angoras, are valued on account of their fur, the flesh being also utilized (fig. 1177). In this country they are chiefly kept as pets, and for show purposes.

The Rabbit has long played a minor part in the civilization of various peoples, regarding which Darwin gives the following information (in *Animals and Plants under Domestication*):—"The tame rabbit has been domesticated from an ancient period. Confucius ranges rabbits among animals worthy to be sacrificed to the gods, and, as he prescribes their multiplication, they were probably at this early period domesticated in China. They are mentioned by several of the classical writers. In 1631 Gervaise Markham writes: 'You shall not, as in other cattell, looke to their shape, but to their richnesse, onely elect your buckes, the largest and goodliest conies you can get; and for the richnesse of the skin, that is accounted the richest which has the equallest mixture of blacke and white hair together, yet the blacke rather shadowing the white; the furre should be thicke, deepe, smooth, and shining; . . . they are of body much fatter and larger, and, when another skin is worth two or three pence, they are worth two shillings'. From this full description we see that silver-gray rabbits existed in England at this period; and, what is far more important, we see that the breeding or selection of rabbits was then carefully attended to."

Fig. 1177.—Angora Rabbit

Although the Hare cannot now be called a domesticated animal, it was so in ancient Rome, as it happened to be one of the numerous animals relished by the epicure, its shoulder in particular being esteemed a dainty. The animals were kept in a hare-preserve or leporarium, which was a large enclosed park. They were sufficiently tame to come and be fed in winter, a horn being blown as a signal to them. At first, it would seem, intended for hares only, the leporaria were at a later date tenanted by rabbits as well, these having been introduced from Spain.

The Fat Dormouse or Loir (Myoxus glis, fig. 1178).—This was another animal that appealed to the palate of the Roman epicure. Houghton gives the following account of the way in which it was treated (in *Natural History of the Ancients*):—"Dormice (*glires*) were very highly esteemed as food by the old Romans. Small yards were walled around, in which were planted oak-trees to supply the animals with acorns. These preserves were called *gliraria*; holes were dug in the inside of the yard for the dormice to breed in; a little water was supplied to them, but dry soil was necessary. They were fattened in large jars (*doliis*), and were plentifully supplied with acorns, chestnuts, and walnuts. In these dark places they soon got fat. . . . Dormice

Fig. 1178.—The Fat Dormouse or Loir (*Myoxus glis*)

were considered articles of such luxury that one of the consuls, M. Scaurus, prohibited them by a censor's edict, and, as Pliny says, 'they were banished from our tables'. Notwithstanding this edict, however, a *glirarium* appears to have been an ordinary adjunct of a Roman gentleman's villa. . . . I believe the fat dormouse is still eaten in some parts of Italy, but how far the flavour depended on the inherent good quality of the creature's flesh, or on the mode in which it was cooked, I am unable to say."

BIRD (AVES) AS DOMESTICATED ANIMALS

THE FOWL (GALLUS DOMESTICUS).—The very numerous breeds of domesticated fowls, some of which differ greatly from one another in appearance, are generally held to be all descendants of the Red Jungle Fowl (*Gallus bankiva* or *ferrugineus*), which at the present time ranges from North India through South-east Asia and part of the East Indies to the Philippines. Among the domesticated races Game-Fowls most nearly resemble the original type (fig. 1179).

Fowls are valuable not only because they and their eggs are important articles of diet, but also on account of their feathers, which are put to various uses. Poultry-farming is now rightly regarded as one of those minor agricultural industries upon which the prosperity of the small farmer and the peasant largely depends. A good instance is afforded by the Irish egg-industry. Not many years ago the product was notorious in England on account of the uncertain age of the eggs which were put upon the market; these being only in great demand for election purposes. And the industry, such as it was, benefited the Irish farmer but little, being exploited by persons having no stake in the development of the agriculture of the country. But now, thanks to the co-operative policy of Sir Horace Plunkett, which has been in every way of enormous benefit to Ireland, the Irish eggs, sorted, cleansed, and properly packed, can be sold in the London market within three days after being laid; and the very considerable profits directly benefit the farmers and peasantry. A similar story regarding Irish butter might have been told when the importance of horned stock was emphasized in an earlier paragraph.

Fowls do not appear to have formed part of the live stock of the prehistoric races of Europe, but that they have been tamed for a long period of time will be gathered from the following quotation (Newton—*A Dictionary of Birds*):—"Several circumstances seem to render it likely that Fowls were first domesticated in Burma or the countries adjacent thereto, and it is the tradition of the Chinese that they received their poultry from the West about the year 1400 B.C. By the Institutes of Manu, the date of which is variously assigned from 1200 to 800 B.C., the tame fowl is forbidden, though the wild is allowed to be eaten—showing that its domestication was accomplished [in India] when they were written. The bird is not mentioned in the Old Testament, nor by Homer, . . . nor is it figured on ancient Egyptian monuments. Pindar mentions it, and Aristophanes calls it the Persian bird, thus indicating it to have been introduced to Greece through Persia, and it is figured on Baby-

Fig. 1179.—Game-Fowls

lonian cylinders between the sixth and seventh centuries B.C. It is sculptured on the Lycian marbles in the British Museum (*circa* 600 B.C.), and Blyth remarks (*Ibis*, 1867) that it is there represented with the appearance of a true Jungle Fowl, for none of the wild *galli* have the upright bearing of the tame breeds, but carry their tail in a drooping position."

THE DUCK (ANAS BOSCHAS).—Ducks are of less importance than Fowls, but their uses are much the same. There is little if any doubt that the ordinary breeds of domesticated Duck are descended from the Mallard or Wild Duck (*Anas boschas*), which has a wide distribution in the Northern Hemisphere. This bird seems to have been tamed at a later date than the Fowl, but it was apparently kept in a state of semi-domestication by the Greeks so long ago as the time of Aristophanes (448(?)-388 B.C.). From them the Romans appear to have learnt its virtues, but we gather from Varro (116–27 B.C.) that in his time the taming process was not complete, for he states that duck-enclosures should be covered with nets, to prevent the escape of their inmates, as well as to exclude predaceous animals.

Fig. 1180.—Gray Lag Geese (*Anser cinereus*)

Other species of duck are also domesticated in Europe, especially the Musk or "Muscovy" Duck (*Cairina moschata*), native to South America.

THE GOOSE (ANSER DOMESTICUS).—Geese have been domesticated from very remote times, on which point Darwin remarks (in *Animals and Plants under Domestication*):—"That geese were anciently domesticated we know from certain verses in Homer; and from these birds having been kept (388 B.C.) in the capitol at Rome as sacred to Juno, which sacredness implies great antiquity". It is generally held that the tame European breeds are descended from the Gray Lag Goose (*Anser cinereus*, fig. 1180), native to Britain and most countries of the Continent, and ranging east to China. There are but few domesticated varieties, and these resemble one another and the parent stock more than might be expected; there having been far less variation than, *e.g.* in the case of Fowls. The most obvious difference between a tame and a wild bird consists in the lighter or even perfectly white plumage of the former.

The soft under-feathers of geese are largely used for stuffing pillows and beds, being of greater value in this connection than those of other domesticated birds. And before steel pens came into general use the large feathers from the wing were in great demand for the making of quill-pens, which even now have many admirers.

THE TURKEY (MELEAGRIS GALLOPAVO).—A native of the southern part of North America, this bird was first described in 1527, and is known to have been domesticated in Europe by 1530, having very likely been introduced early in the century. That it soon found favour in this country is evident from the following facts quoted by Newton (in *A Dictionary of Birds*):—

Fig. 1181.—Guinea-Fowls (*Numida meleagris*)

"The earliest documentary evidence of its existence in England is a 'constitution' set forth by Cranmer in 1541. . . . This names 'Turkeycocke' as one of 'the greater fowles' of which an ecclesiastic was to have 'but one in a dishe'. . . . Moreover, the comparatively low price of the two Turkeys and four Turkey-chicks served at a feast of the serjeants-at-law in 1555 (Dugdale, *Origines*) points to their having become by that time abundant, and, indeed, by 1573 Tusser bears witness to the part they had already begun to play in 'Christmas husbandlie fare'."

THE GUINEA-FOWL (NUMIDA MELEAGRIS, fig. 1181).—This form is native to West Africa, and appears to have been domesticated at two different periods, *i.e.* in the times of the ancient Romans, and during the sixteenth century.

Under the term "poultry" may be included fowls, ducks,

geese, turkeys, and guinea-fowl, and the importance of these (especially the first) to agriculture in this country may be seen from the following statistics:—The value of the poultry and eggs consumed in the United Kingdom during 1902 amounted to £16,408,994, including foreign produce worth £7,358,934, Irish produce worth £2,300,000, and produce of Great Britain worth £6,750,000.

THE PIGEON (COLUMBA LIVIA).—The wild Blue Rock-Pigeon (*Columba livia*), the races of which have at the present day a

Fig. 1182.—Ostriches (*Struthio camelus*) on a South African Farm

very wide range through Europe, Asia, and North Africa, is believed to be the original stock from which the very numerous domesticated breeds are descended. The ancient Egyptians would seem to have tamed it over 5000 years ago, and it was valued by them not only as a source of food, but also as a means of communication. Its military importance in the latter connections has been abundantly demonstrated in modern times, and it seems destined to play a leading part in the campaigns of the future.

As we shall see in the sequel the theoretical importance of pigeons is very great, for they throw considerable light upon the question of evolution. The various breeds were studied with the utmost thoroughness by Darwin, and more recent observations show that the subject is by no means exhausted, and that these birds are most desirable subjects for experiment when heredity problems have to be considered.

THE AFRICAN OSTRICH (STRUTHIO CAMELUS).—Although ostriches have been domesticated or semi-domesticated by some of the native tribes of Africa from remote times, the "ostrich farms" of the south are of comparatively recent date (fig. 1182). The inducement to this industry is of course found in the valuable plumage, the white wing-feathers being most esteemed, while those of the tail and also some of the back plumes are also marketable. Birds are in their prime when from three to four years old, and the feathers of the males are of better quality than those of the females. They are plucked or cut off about twice in three years, and are subjected to a number of processes before being fit for use. Ostrich-feathers constitute an important export from Cape Colony, yielding not far short of a million pounds sterling annually. The industry has been introduced with more or less success into several other parts of the world, notably Southern California and Australia.

DOMESTICATED INSECTS (INSECTA)

Under this heading may be placed the Honey-Bee (*Apis mellifica*), the Silk-Worm Moth (*Bombyx mori*, &c.), and the Cochineal Insect (*Coccus cacti*). The industries which these insects render possible are all of ancient date, and the two first of very considerable importance.

THE HONEY-BEE (APIS MELLIFICA).—A liking for sweet things is a wide-spread human weakness, and appears to be of very old standing. Wild bees of different kind are native to many parts of the world, and the honey which some of them store in abundance no doubt soon attracted the attention of primitive peoples, whose most important business in life consisted in the discovery of edibles (compare vol. ii, p. 63). Of a small Brazilian species Bates says (in *The Naturalist on the Amazons*):—"A hive of the Melipona fasciculata, which I saw opened, contained about two quarts of pleasantly-tasted honey. The bees . . . have no sting, but they bite furiously when their colonies are disturbed." Semon complains of the time wasted in the search for honey by the blacks he employed to hunt out the Spiny Ant-Eater (*Echidna*):—"About a dozen black families had gathered in my camp at that period, but only two or three of them performed any work worth mentioning. The control of their day's labour was very difficult, as we were not able to follow them on their rambles, and to make sure of their really pursuing the track of Echidna and not giving themselves up to sweet idleness or to the search of nests of the stingless Australian bee, of the honey of which they are excessively fond. . . . Many an hour destined for labour did they spend in the pursuit of these bees' nests. Still greater was the loss of time when they discovered a nest of our European honey-bee. Mr. Cole, the doctor in Gayndah, was an eager apiarian, and from his hives European bees, which soon became wild, had spread all over the Middle Burnet. . . . Whenever it happened that my blacks discovered a tree which the immigrated bees had chosen as a dwelling, and the hollow of which they had filled with their sweet stores (often to a height of eleven yards or so above the ground), all the mob would at once assemble to fell the mighty tree, often the work of a day." (*In The Australian Bush.*) Readers will doubtless be able to recall appreciative biblical allusions to the desirable properties of honey.

In the case of the Honey-Bee (*Apis mellifica*), with which we are here more especially concerned, the primitive appreciation of sweets led in very early times to the practice of apiculture. As in so many other things the ancient Egyptians would seem to have led the way, their example being zealously followed by both Greeks and Romans. The littoral of the Eastern Mediterranean was possibly the original home of the species, and, if we include varieties, it now has a wide range in the Old World, and has also been introduced into America, the West Indies, Australia, and New Zealand.

As elsewhere sufficiently indicated, the Honey-Bee represents the final term of specialized social life among its kind, though very possibly some features have been brought about by the influence of long-continued domestication. The leading facts about it are so well known that a brief outline may here suffice. A populous hive will contain a queen, several hundred drones or males, and from 30,000 to 50,000 "workers", *i.e.* imperfectly-developed females, specialized in various ways so as to be able to perform efficiently the varied duties necessary to the maintenance of the community (fig. 1183). The queen is comparatively large, with slender body, short wings, and a curved sting. Maternity is her sole function, and she is fed and tended with the greatest assiduity by the workers. Except for the nuptial flight, and when migrating with a "swarm" to fresh quarters, she does not leave the hive. Only a single queen is tolerated by workers in the same community, and if one should happen to emerge from a "royal cell" while the reigning queen is still in the hive a duel to the death ensues. If a queen should intrude from outside the result may be similar, or the workers may mob the interloper, though they will not sting her, and death by starvation or suffocation is commonly her fate. A queen is astonishingly fertile, and under favourable circumstances is capable of laying from two thousand to three thousand eggs in a day. Some of these are unfertilized, and develop into drones, but the majority are fertilized, and are usually destined to produce females, though it is not impossible that some of these also may give rise to drones. The life of a queen extends over four or five years.

Fig. 1183.—Honey-Bee (*Apis mellifica*), enlarged

A, Queen; B, worker; C, drone.

The stingless drones are smaller and stouter than the queen, and distinguished by the enormous size of their compound eyes. They do absolutely no work, but their presence is patiently submitted to until the end of the summer, because a minute percentage of them are destined to become the fathers of communities. At the approach of autumn, when food is becoming scarce, the drones are mercilessly expelled from the hive, or even, according to some authorities, ruthlessly slaughtered.

The workers are smaller than the drones, and distinguished

by many special characters. One of the most remarkable consists in the possession of a "pollen basket", consisting of a hollow covered by transverse rows of hairs on the inner side of the first joint of the hind-foot (fig. 1184). There are also wax-glands on the under side of the abdomen, by which scales of wax are secreted, this being the chief building material (fig. 1185). The sting is straight, and the mouth-parts better developed than in queen and drones, the proboscis in particular being longer, and well adapted to probe the recesses of flowers in the search for nectar (fig. 1186). These and other specializations are, of course, related to the fact that the workers discharge all the duties of the hive, egg-production alone excepted. A few of them may, however, be fertile under exceptional circumstances, but in that case their eggs invariably hatch out into drones. Workers born late in the season may survive till the following year, but the rest live only for six or eight weeks.

Fig. 1184.—Part of Hind-leg of a Worker Bee, greatly enlarged, to show Pollen-Basket, above which, on right side, may be seen a pincer-like arrangement used for various purposes.

Fig. 1185.—Under Side of a Worker Bee, enlarged, showing plates of wax

The waxen combs made by the workers for storage of food and reception of eggs are suspended vertically, and consist of six-sided cells, of which there is a set on either side of the comb, separated by a thin party-wall (fig. 1187). The long axes of these cells slope slightly outwards and upwards. The smallest of them are for storage and worker-brood, and there is a larger size in which the drones are reared. A comparatively small number of "royal cells" are constructed at the edges of the combs as circumstances may require. These are somewhat acorn-shaped, with downwardly-directed mouths, and a good deal larger than any of the hexagonal cells. In them the young queens are reared. The workers that produce the wax for comb-construction hang suspended in dense clusters for many hours, until eight little scales of wax have been secreted on the under side of each of them. They then successively visit the highest part of the hive, and work the scales into a lenticular mass. The hind-legs are used for detaching the scales, and the jaws for kneading them. Other workers excavate areas corresponding to the cells, building up the walls of these from the wax scooped out, and as the work proceeds the two sides of the comb are simultaneously operated on by two gangs of labourers. At the same time fresh wax is added as required to the edges of the growing comb.

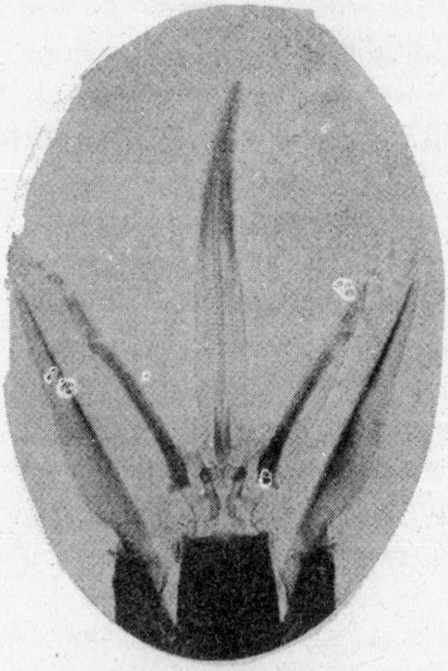

Fig. 1186.—Extended Mouth-parts of a Worker Bee, seen from above, with the different regions separated, enlarged. The long "tongue" is seen in the centre, and the second jaws (1st maxillæ) below.

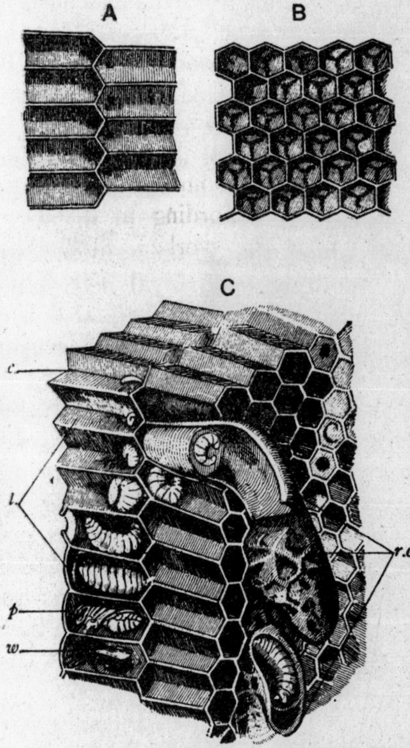

Fig. 1187.—Honey-Comb. A, Small cells in section. B, Ditto in surface view. C, Comb with brood, on left development of a worker; egg (*e*), larvæ (*l*), pupa (*p*), imago (*w*); on right are seen royal cells (*r.c.*), the middle one unopened.

For filling up the crevices of the hive bees employ "propolis", which consists of resin collected from the buds and bark of trees, especially horse-chestnuts and pines. It is carried to the hive in the same way as pollen.

The limbless grubs which hatch out from the eggs in three days' time are fed and tended by the younger workers, and at first receive a soft substance consisting of honey and pollen that have been swallowed and partly digested by their attendants, with which is mixed a fluid secreted by certain glands of the head. This mixture is commonly known as "royal jelly". Larvæ hatched from unfertilized eggs always become drones, but those emerging from fertilized eggs may become either workers or queens, according to the way in which they are fed. A larva which the workers intend shall become a queen is nourished entirely upon royal jelly, possibly differing in composition from that which the others at first receive. It would appear to be of stimulating nature, for queens develop more quickly than members of the other castes, requiring only 15 days (from the laying of the egg) as against 21 for a worker, and 24 for a drone. The larvæ destined to become workers or drones are quickly "weaned", honey, pollen, and water being substituted for jelly. After being fed for 5 days (or 6 in the case of drones) the larvæ attain their full size, when the workers seal the cells with a mixture of pollen and wax, that permits the diffusion of air. Within its cell the larva spins a silken cocoon, imperfect at the hinder-end in the case of queens, and passes into the motionless pupa stage, from which, later on, the perfect insect emerges, to bite its way out into the hive.

When a hive becomes overcrowded the surplus population, accompanied by the reigning queen, "swarms" out of the hive to seek fresh quarters. This never takes place unless one or more royal cells with inmates are present in the deserted home. When the first young queen emerges from these, her first act is to tear open the remaining royal cells and sting the inmates to death, an operation which is rendered possible by the imperfect nature of the cocoons in which these are enclosed. After a nuptial flight the young queen settles down as the new mother of the community. Sometimes the workers will prevent the first emerged young queen from destroying her sisters, and in that case there is a possibility of the first migration being succeeded by after-swarms or "casts". Domesticated bees are more given to swarming than wild ones.

Bee-Keeping or Apiculture.—The remarks already made about the importance of poultry-keeping (p. 246), as an adjunct to agriculture, apply here also, though to a less extent. To give a long account of the industry is unnecessary, and readers requiring details will do well to consult Cowan's *British Bee-Keeper's Guide Book.* This writer thus speaks of the paying nature of the industry, and the essentials to success:—"The culture of the honey-bee is now universally admitted to be one of the most profitable of rural pursuits. It has engaged the attention of intelligent persons of all ages; yet it is only comparatively recently—by the introduction of improved movable-comb hives, the honey-extractor, and comb-foundation—that this pursuit has been rendered no longer a matter of chance, but as certain and more remunerative with small outlay than any other rural occupation. Much has been written about the enormous profits to be derived from bee-keeping; and, stimulated by what they have read, persons have purchased a few stocks, and, after keeping them without any attention for some years, have given them up, having failed for want of a knowledge of the first principles of bee-culture. Although anyone may keep bees, it is not everyone who can become a proficient bee-master. Energy and perseverance, together with aptness for investigation, can only ensure real success. While some degree of talent is essential, in this as in every other pursuit, ordinary ability directed to the attainment of a specific end will be more likely to be rewarded by success, than the most extraordinary talent divided among half a dozen different pursuits. The man who is thoroughly conversant with his business, is familiar with its requirements, has mastered its every detail, and who is industrious and energetic, will be likely to succeed; and if, in addition to this, he possesses good executive abilities, his success will be very apt to be above the average."

A few words may be of interest on the three requisites to enlightened apiculture mentioned in the above extract, *i.e.* movable-comb hives, honey-extractors, and comb-foundation. The familiar bell-shaped straw hive or "skep" may be picturesque, but is eminently undesirable. It renders regulation of the bees' labours impossible, necessitates destruction of the combs, and too often means that the industrious insects are choked by the fumes of burning sulphur as a preliminary to taking their honey. All this is altered in the movable-comb or "frame" hives (fig. 1188). These are square wooden boxes, which open at the top, and contain a number of wooden frames for holding the combs, and easily taken out at pleasure for the purposes of the bee-keeper. They render it easy to regulate the bees, including the swarming, in almost any required way. The reigning queen, for example, can be deposed, and replaced by a more fertile successor, or one of more desirable race.

The honey-extractor is a simple device for rapidly rotating combs so that the honey flies out by centrifugal force, and this is a vast improvement on the old method of crushing and straining. As Cowan very justly remarks:—"When we bear in mind that bees consume about 20 pounds of honey in order to produce one pound of wax, we can realize the advantages of a machine which enables us to give them empty comb, and thus save them the labour of comb-building".

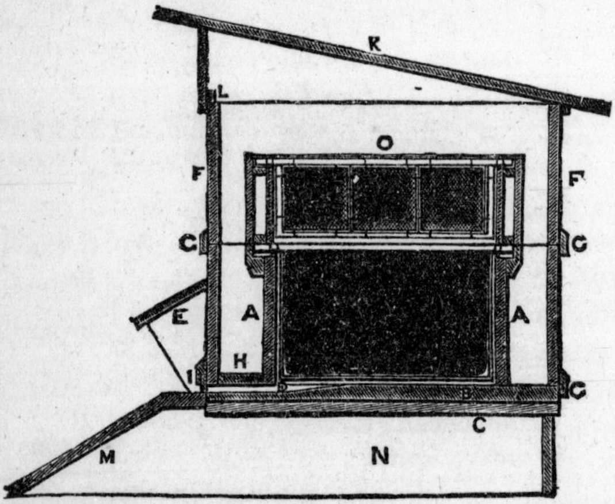

Fig. 1188.—Cowan Hive in Longitudinal Section. A, Body-box; B, floor-board; C, strengthening piece; D, entrance gallery; E, entrance porch; F, outer case; G, protective plinths; H, roof of entrance gallery; I, sliding door at entrance; K, roof; L, roof-catch; M, alighting board; N, stand; O, rack with three sections, below which is seen a frame of comb.

To supply comb-foundation is the next best thing to giving empty combs. This consists of thin plates of wax, which have been passed between suitably-embossed rollers, so that the "foundations" of the cells are laid, and there are also projecting ridges of wax, furnishing enough material for the completion of the cells, save that required to cover them. Foundation is made with either small cells suitable for worker-brood (or storage), or with larger cells adapted for drone-brood. It is possible, by supplying one or other kind as desired, to regulate within certain limits the number of workers and drones produced in the hive.

There unfortunately appear to be no means of ascertaining how far British apiculture is profitable. Honey to the value of £30,349 was imported into this country in 1903.

The Silk-Worm Moth (Bombyx mori, &c., fig. 1189).—The most important and best-known kind of Silk-Worm Moth is the one (*Bombyx mori*) of which the caterpillar or "silk-worm" feeds upon the leaves of the mulberry-tree. The life-history is sufficiently familiar. From the egg a minute larva hatches out which is full grown in about five weeks, during which time it casts its skin several times. At the end of this period the silk-worm spins a cocoon, which consists of two long threads, the hardened secretion of two large glands that open on the under-lip.

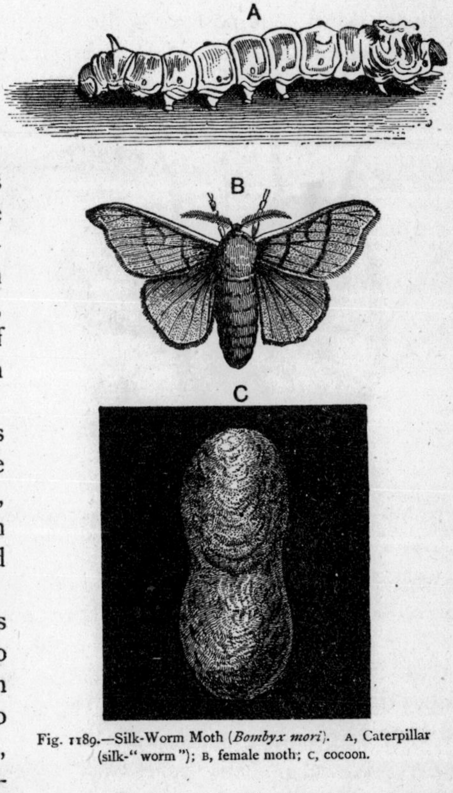

Fig. 1189.—Silk-Worm Moth (*Bombyx mori*). A, Caterpillar (silk-"worm"); B, female moth; C, cocoon.

The material known as "cat-gut" is made from the secretion of the silk-glands, which are removed from the caterpillar and subjected to suitable treatment.

The culture of silk-worms is generally supposed to have been first practised in China, the first allusion to it dating back to 2640 B.C., according to Chinese records. Thence the industry spread through Korea into Japan, and also into India, Persia, and Central Asia. Its introduction into Europe is ascribed to the Emperor Justinian, who is said to have induced a couple of Persian monks to undertake a journey to China with the view of surreptitiously obtaining eggs. These worthies are stated to have been successful in their mission, reaching Constantinople with a supply of eggs (concealed in bamboos) in the year 550 A.D. To this source the silk-industry of Southern Europe may be traced, and to France and Italy, in particular, it is now of great importance. In the former country about 137,500 cwts. of raw silk (worth £1,080,000) is produced annually, while the Italian yield in 1902 was 823,718 cwts. (worth £12,355,057).

Of late years the Chinese have engaged in the culture of the Oak Silk-Moth (*Saturnia Pernyi*), of which the larvæ feed on oak-leaves. The silk is coarser and less valuable than the ordinary kind, but possesses the merit of greater strength. An allied species (*S. yama-mai*) is cultivated in Japan.

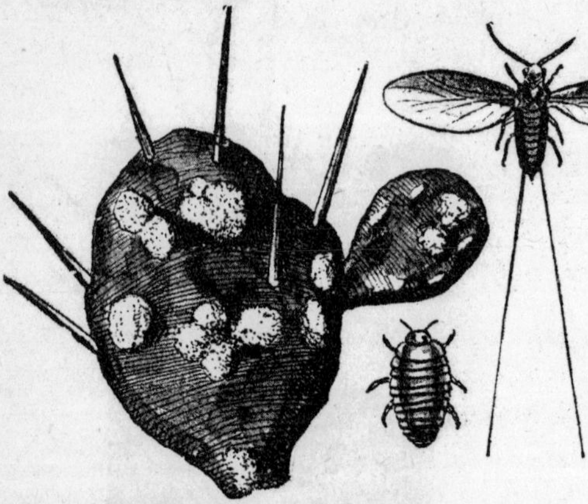

Fig. 1190.—Nopal (*Opuntia coccinellifera*) and Cochineal Insects (*Coccus cacti*), enlarged, female to left, male to right

How far silk is important to Britain may be gathered from the fact that in 1902 we imported 1,252,848 lbs. of raw silk worth £728,020, and silk goods to the value of £14,321,541.

The Cochineal Insect (Coccus cacti, fig. 1190).—The colouring-matter known as cochineal, as also (to some extent) the pigments known as carmine and lake, are derived from a species of bug native to Mexico, which feeds upon the Nopal (*Opuntia coccinellifera*), a plant of the cactus sort. The culture of this insect dates back to the times of the ancient Mexicans, and is now of some importance in Central America. The insect and its food-plant have also been successfully introduced into the Canary Islands, Algeria, Java, and Australia. The colouring-matter is obtained from the dried bodies of the female insects, which are ground and extracted. It requires about 70,000 of them to produce a pound of cochineal. The introduction of cheap aniline dyes has caused this industry to decline, while carmine and lake can now be manufactured chemically.

HUMMING-BIRDS (*Trochilidæ*)

These brilliantly-coloured little forms, of which between 400 and 500 species have been described, are perhaps the most attractive members of their class, and some of them are the smallest known birds. Excluding the tail, which is often long out of all proportion, they vary in length from 8½ to rather less than 2½ inches. They are wholly American (and West Indian), ranging from Tierra del Fuego to Canada, and from sea-level to a vertical height of 16,000 feet. The mountains and hills of the northern parts of South America are inhabited by the largest number of beautiful species. Unfortunately, like many other birds of attractive plumage, they are ruthlessly hunted down to minister to the vanity of womankind.

The species represented in the plate are: 1. *Lamprolæma rhami*, 2. *Thalurania furcata*, 3. *Lesbia sparganura*, 4. *Calypte Helenæ*, 5. *Diphlogæna hesperus*.

HUMMING-BIRDS (TROCHILIDAE) OF AMERICA

CONTENTS

UTILITARIAN ZOOLOGY (*Continued*)

CHAPTER LXVIII.—ANIMAL FRIENDS—FISHES, MOLLUSCS. AND CRUSTACEANS AS FOOD—FISHERIES

FISHES (PISCES) AS FOOD

SKINS AND DOWN OF WILD BIRDS (AVES)

WILD ANIMALS YIELDING LEATHER, HORN, FAT, &c.

MEDICINAL AND MISCELLANEOUS ANIMAL PRODUCTS

WILD ANIMALS BENEFICIAL TO MAN ON ACCOUNT OF THEIR HABITS

CHAPTER LXX.—ANIMAL FOES—THE PERSONAL ENEMIES OF MAN

CHAPTER LXXI.—ANIMAL FOES—FORMS INJURIOUS TO HUMAN INDUSTRIES

CHAPTER LXXII.—THE ZOOLOGY OF SPORT

MAMMALS (MAMMALIA) AS AIDS TO SPORT

BIRDS (AVES) AS AIDS TO SPORT

MAMMALS (MAMMALIA) HUNTED FOR SPORT

BIRDS (AVES) HUNTED FOR SPORT

REPTILES (REPTILIA) HUNTED IN SPORT

FISHES (PISCES) HUNTED IN SPORT

CHAPTER LXXIII.—UTILITARIAN ZOOLOGY—ANIMAL PETS

MAMMALS (MAMMALIA) AS PETS

ANIMAL ÆSTHETICS

DISTRIBUTION IN SPACE AND TIME

CHAPTER LXXV.—GEOGRAPHICAL DISTRIBUTION

SUPPLEMENTARY FACTORS OF EVOLUTION

VARIATION

HEREDITY

LIST OF ILLUSTRATIONS

HALF-VOLUME VIII

COLOURED PLATES

BLACK-AND-WHITE ILLUSTRATIONS

N.B.—The figs. followed by "from Alcock" are from Alcock's *A Naturalist in Indian Seas*, by the courtesy of Mr. John Murray.

CHAPTER LXVIII

ANIMAL FRIENDS—FISHES, MOLLUSCS, AND CRUSTACEANS AS FOOD—FISHERIES

To do anything like justice to the "harvest of the sea", not to mention the "freshwater harvest", would require a very considerable space, but the importance of the subject may be sufficiently illustrated for the purposes of this book by a few salient facts and figures. It will be convenient to successively consider Fishes, Molluscs, and Crustaceans, beginning in each case with a brief account of the more valuable species, and adding a few remarks on fisheries, culture-methods, &c. In the preparation of this chapter the writer has been greatly helped by Mr. J. T. Cunningham's *Marketable Marine Fishes*, as well as by papers and MS. notes by Professor J. Travis Jenkins.

Much kind assistance has also been given by the Secretaries to the French, German, Italian, Russian, and U.S. Embassies, the Legations of Holland and Scandinavia, the Italian Chamber of Commerce, the Imperial Russian Financial Agency, our own Department for Agriculture and Fisheries, and the Whitstable Oyster Fishery Company; also by the U.S.A. and Newfoundland Fisheries Departments, the High Commissioner for Canada, and the British Consuls-General in Christiania, Paris, and St. Petersburg.

FISHES (PISCES) AS FOOD

Without entering into minute technical details, it will be desirable in the first place to say a little about the three chief methods by which fishes are captured on a commercial scale, *i.e.* line-fishing, net-fishing, and trawling.

Line-Fishing.—Before the prehistoric races of Western Europe had learnt the use of metals there is evidence to show that large fishes, such as salmon, were secured by means of bone harpoons, and the earliest fish-hooks were made of bone or shell. The remains from the Age of Bronze include a number of fish-hooks of that metal, and of these our modern devices of the same nature are doubtless lineal descendants. The most extensive development of line-fishing in this country is exemplified on the Scottish coasts, where such fishes as cod, haddock, and ling are thus caught. A series of cod-lines may reach the great length of eight miles, and carry 4680 hooks on attached "snoods", the favourite bait being whelks. The somewhat shorter haddock-lines are mostly baited with mussels or lug-worms.

Net-Fishing.—This more wholesale method of capture has the advantage of obviating the trouble and expense of bait. *Drift-nets* afford the chief means of catching fishes which, like herrings, pilchards, and mackerel, swim in large shoals at or near the surface, and they are nearly always worked at night. Such a net is practically a curtain, of which the upper edge is floated by corks, while the lower edge is sunk by weights. If by skilful manœuvring a shoal can be induced to dash against the meshwork, their heads easily pass through (the size of mesh being adapted to the particular species), and the projecting gill-covers prevent withdrawal. For herrings a series or "train" of drift-nets may extend a distance of 1¼ mile, while for mackerel the length may be twice as great. *Seines*, which may be as much as 1200 feet in length, are hanging nets which are drawn round shoals of fishes so as to enclose and secure them as in a bag. After the catch is made it may be hauled on to fishing-boats or drawn to shore according to circumstances. Certain other smaller nets will be mentioned as occasion arises.

Trawling.—This is, of course, a variety of net-fishing, and specially adapted for the wholesale capture of fishes that live on or near the bottom. The "trawl" or "beam-trawl" (fig. 1191) is essentially a large, flat, tapering net, which is dragged over the sea-floor, and may be as much as 100 feet long, with a mouth 50 feet wide. The "beam" is a horizontal spar by which the mouth is kept open, and which does not scrape along the bottom as sometimes supposed. It would be out of place here to describe all the elaborate details of construction. For most purposes trawling, especially as practised by steam-vessels, is rapidly superseding some of the older methods of fishing. And as it not only means the capture of vast quantities of adult fishes, but also destruction of great numbers of immature individuals, trawling cannot but tend to deplete the natural supply. It is to be hoped that our knowledge will ultimately be sufficiently extensive and accurate to grapple with the question as to how best to regulate this kind of fishing, with a view to maintaining the more important species in sufficient numbers. At present our ignorance on many points is considerable, not to say profound, and there is no lack of exaggeration on a slender basis of fact.

THE HERRING FAMILY (CLUPEIDÆ).—The members of this family are widely distributed in the coastal waters of both tropical and temperate seas, but are not found in the deeper parts of the ocean. From the economic standpoint they are the most valuable of all food-fishes, which is partly due to the fact that they live in large surface-feeding shoals. The chief method of capture is by means of "drift-nets". The most important British fishes belonging to the family are Herring, Sprat, Pilchard, and Anchovy.

Fig. 1191.—Trawl-Net attached to Fishing-Boat

The Herring (*Clupea harengus*, fig. 1192).—Of all European marine fishes this contributes most largely to the human food-supply, especially when converted by curing methods into the familiar "red herring" "kipper", and "bloater". It was long supposed that herrings migrated periodically from northern waters to the south, on both sides of the North Atlantic, but their movements are now believed to be of much more local character. It may, in fact, be stated that the direction of these movements is alternately towards and from the land, the former being undertaken for the purpose of spawning in shallow water, where the heavy, sticky eggs sink to the bottom and adhere to various objects. In British seas a distinction may, somewhat doubtfully, be drawn between "summer" and "winter" herrings, which appear to be two distinct varieties or races that spawn respectively at the seasons indicated. Winter herrings favour estuaries, and it is they which are fished, for example, in the Firth of Forth, Firth of Clyde, and Plymouth Sound. Summer herrings, on the other hand, avoid estuaries, and their spawning-grounds may be at some distance from the coast. They are the

Fig. 1192.—Part of a Shoal of Herrings (*Clupeaharengus*)

more important race, and are caught in vast numbers on the north-east coasts of Scotland and the east coast of England.

The Sprat, Pilchard, and Anchovy, which next fall to be considered, lay floating eggs, like the large majority of marine fishes.

The Sprat (*C. sprattus*).—This small species ranges from the north of Europe to the Mediterranean, and is largely fished from the coast of Kent round our south-east and south shores to Devonshire.

It appears that what is popularly known as "whitebait" is not a distinct kind of fish, but is chiefly made up of very young herrings and sprats, both of which are fond of making their way into sheltered estuaries.

The Pilchard (*C. pilchardus*).—This fish is pretty much like a herring in appearance, but its body is of rounder shape, the scales are very large, and there are several other points of difference. It ranges from the south of Ireland and England to Madeira, and into the Mediterranean. As is well known, the pilchard fishery of Cornwall is one of the most important industries of that county.

Sardines are simply young pilchards, and not a distinct species as sometimes supposed. They are fished on a large scale on the west of France, and also off the coast of North-west Spain (Galicia). Sardines are caught by the French to the value of some £400,000 per annum. Our own import of preserved fish (largely sardines) from France in 1902 was worth £373,960.

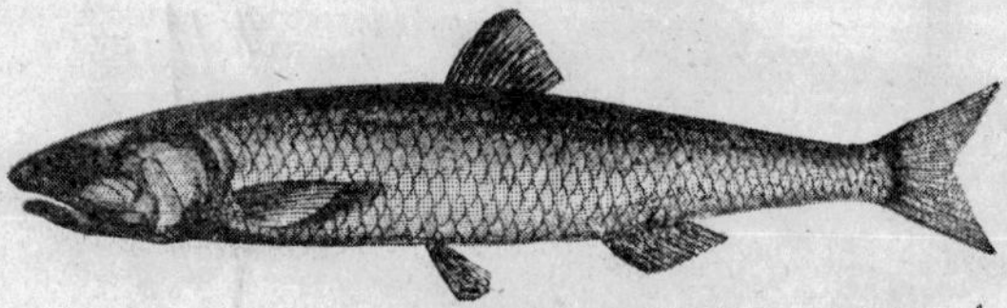

Fig. 1193.—Anchovy (*Engraulis encrasicholus*)

The Anchovy (*Engraulis encrasicholus*, fig. 1193).—This slender little fish, which is best known to us as the source of various flavourings, is easily distinguished from its congeners by the way in which its snout projects in front of the mouth, so that this opens on the under side of the head, much as in a shark. The anchovy ranges from the coast of Norway down the sea-board of Western Europe, and through the Mediterranean. Although native to our seas it is not the object of a British fishery, but the Dutch capture it in large numbers, in the Zuyder Zee and the estuary of the Scheldt, by means of small drift-nets fixed at either end, netted gaps between willow- and poplar-fences (near Bergen-op-Zoom), and by large sweep-nets. The importance of the anchovy-fishery to Holland will be realized from the fact that in 1902 the catch amounted to 100,000 ankers (an anker = about 88 lbs.). At Bergen-op-Zoom in that year 127 cwts. of these fishes were cured, over 77 cwts. of salt being used in the process. In the anchovy-fisheries along the Mediterranean littoral of Spain, France, and Italy drift-nets and seines are employed.

THE COD FAMILY (GADIDÆ).—From the economic stand-point

this family ranks second only to the one just considered. The fishes it includes are voracious ground-feeders characteristic of polar and temperate regions. With few exceptions they are marine, and their favourite habitat is in water under 200 fathoms in depth. Trawling and line-fishing are the chief methods by which they are captured. The most notable British species are Cod, Coal-Fish, Haddock, Whiting, Ling, and Hake. All of these lay floating eggs.

The Cod (*Gadus morrhua*, fig. 1194).—This large and important fish is the most valuable member of its family so far as its range extends, *i.e.* from Arctic seas to the Bay of Biscay on one side of the North Atlantic, and as far as

Fig. 1194.—Cod-Fish (*Gadus morrhua*)

New York on the other side. Günther thus summarizes some of the chief points regarding it (in *The Study of Fishes*):—"The Cod-Fish occurs between 50° and 75° lat. N. in great profusion, but is not found nearer the equator than 40° lat. Close to the coast it is met with singly all the year round, but towards the spawning-time it approaches the shore in numbers, which happens in January in England and not before May on the American coasts. The English resorted to the cod-fisheries of Iceland before the year 1415, but since the sixteenth century most vessels go to the banks of Newfoundland, and almost all the preserved cod consumed during Lent in the various Continental countries is imported from across the Atlantic. At one time the Newfoundland cod-fishery rivalled in importance the whale-fishery and the fur trade of North America." The Newfoundland catch for 1902 weighed about 140,000 tons.

The Coal-Fish (*Gadus virens*).—This fish, locally known as "green cod" and "saith", is somewhat smaller than the ordinary cod, and ranges from the Arctic Ocean into the Mediterranean. It is largely fished in northern British waters, and is cured to a considerable extent.

The Haddock (*Gadus æglefinus*, fig. 1195).—Though of superior quality in the fresh condition, this fish is perhaps more familiar in the cured state, under the names of "yellow fish", "Finnan haddie", and so forth. In British seas average specimens are decidedly smaller than cod, and are easily recognizable by the blackness of the lateral line, and by the presence of a black blotch above the pectoral fin, attributed by tradition to

Fig. 1195.—Haddock (*Gadus æglefinus*)

the finger and thumb of the apostle Peter, though the John Dory is another candidate for the honour of the association. The range of the haddock is much the same as that of the cod, but it is only of marked importance in regard to the northern half of the British fishery area.

The Whiting (*G. merlangus*).—This comparatively small species is noted for delicacy of flavour, but to fully appreciate this it must be eaten immediately after capture, for it rapidly deteriorates, and stands carriage badly. Though ranging from Norway to the Mediterranean, and found all round our coasts, it is of more importance to the fisheries of the English Channel than to those farther north.

The Ling (*Molva vulgaris*).—This is a large and rapacious fish, which is largely cured, but is decidedly inferior to the haddock. It ranges from the Arctic Ocean as far as Gibraltar on the east of the North Atlantic, but only to Newfoundland on the west. It is mostly fished in the northern parts of the North Sea, and around the shores of the Orkneys, Shetlands, and Faroe Islands.

The Hake (*Merluccius vulgaris*).—Like the last-named species this is a rapacious fish of large size. Its range is similar to that of the cod, except that it is found throughout the Mediterranean, and is most abundant on the southern shores of Britain. Like most large forms it is somewhat coarse and not greatly esteemed as food, though hake steaks are not to be despised.

THE FLAT-FISH FAMILY (PLEURONECTIDÆ).—These are carnivorous ground-fishes of great economic importance, especially in the north temperate region, and for delicacy of flavour some of the species are unrivalled. The valuable British forms which deserve notice are Turbot and Brill, with eyes on the left side; and Sole, Plaice, Flounder, Dab, and Lemon Dab, in which the eyes are on the right side. All these species lay buoyant eggs. Trawling is by far the most important method of capture, after which comes line-fishing.

The Turbot (*Rhombus maximus*).—This is the most esteemed of the larger flat-fishes, and may attain a weight of over 20 lbs. It is a shallow-water form, and ranges from the Black Sea, through the Mediterranean, up the eastern coast of the North Atlantic as far as Denmark and South Scotland. Bony tubercles are imbedded in the skin of the left side. In accordance with the fact that the turbot is highly predaceous, feeding upon other fishes, its mouth is larger than in most members of the family.

The Brill (*R. lævis*).—Except in its smaller size, and the absence of tubercles on the skin, this species resembles the turbot in appearance, mode of feeding, and distribution.

The other flat-fishes to be noticed here all have the eyes on the right side of the body and (except the Halibut) have small mouths, adapted to feeding on worms and other small creatures.

The Halibut (*Hippoglossus vulgaris*).—This is the largest of all flat-fishes, and is said to sometimes reach the length of 20 feet, while individuals of 6 or 7 feet long are often caught in British seas. A 7-foot halibut weighs somewhere about 300 pounds or rather more. It is a decidedly northern species, and appears to range right round the southern shores of the Arctic

Ocean. In the Atlantic its area of distribution extends as far south as the English Channel. The halibut feeds on fishes and crustaceans.

The Sole (*Solea vulgaris,* fig. 1196).—This valuable and delicately-flavoured food-fish, adult specimens of which average from 12 to 18 inches in length, is distinguished from many other forms by its shape, which is a narrow oval with continuous outline, free from sharp curves or projections. It ranges from the Mediterranean to the south of Scotland, and is captured for the most part in water under 30 fathoms deep.

Fig. 1196.—Soles (*Solea vulgaris*)

The Plaice (*Pleuronectes platessa*).—This common British species is of considerable economic importance, though its flesh is rather flavourless. Average specimens vary from 15 to 18 inches in length, but a larger size is often reached, especially in northern waters. The plaice may easily be recognized by the large orange - coloured or rust-red blotches on the dark side of the body. It ranges from the north coast of Europe as far south as the Bay of Biscay.

The Flounder (*P. flesus*).—This is a rather small species, the pigmented side of which is dark-brown or black. It ranges along the entire west coast of Europe, and is also found in the Baltic and Mediterranean. Flounders are estuarine fishes, and are able to live in fresh water.

The Dab (*P. limanda*).—This is about the same size as the flounder, but its pigmented side is of light-brown colour, with darker spots, and the skin is rough. It ranges from the north of Europe to the Bay of Biscay, and is found both in estuaries and the open sea.

The Lemon Dab (*P. microcephalus*).—This is often sold under the name of Lemon "Sole", but it is a poor substitute for the true Sole, which it resembles in shape though not in colour. The dark side of the body is of a yellowish-brown, marked with numerous spots. The range is practically the same as that of the Dab, but it is most abundant in fairly deep water.

THE MACKEREL FAMILY (SCOMBERIDÆ).—The members of this family are highly predaceous tropical and temperate fishes which swim in shoals in the open sea, but approach the land in pursuit of prey. Their form admirably adapts them to swift progression (see vol. iii, p. 41). It will be necessary here to consider two

Fig. 1197.—Mackerel (*Scomber vernalis*)

species, the Mackerel and Common Tunny, both of which lay floating eggs.

The Mackerel (*Scomber vernalis*, fig. 1197).—This is one of the most beautiful of our native marine fishes, and adults vary in length from about 1 foot to 17 inches. The range is from the Mediterranean to the Canaries, and north along the shores of Europe to the south of Norway. So far as British fisheries are concerned mackerel are of importance from the coast of Norfolk round the Straits of Dover to Devon and Cornwall. Drift-nets and seines are the chief means of capture, but lines are also employed, especially in the south-west of England.

The Common Tunny (*Orcynus thynnus*).—This can be described as a gigantic mackerel, which may reach a length of 10 feet, and a weight of about half a ton. Although sometimes taken in the North Sea and Baltic it is essentially a native of the Mediterranean, where it has been the object of an important fishery from very early times. Its flesh is eaten both when fresh and in the preserved condition. Pickled Tunny (*Saltamentum Sardicum*) was considered a delicacy by the ancient Romans. The Italian tunny-fishery, of which Sardinia and Sicily are the chief centres, is a considerable industry, which yielded over £111,000 in 1902. It commences in spring, when the fish approach the shore to spawn, and the shoals are either driven into shallow water and surrounded by a series of strong nets, or else chased into a sort of net-labyrinth, in the innermost compartment of which they are slaughtered with clubs, boat-hooks, and the like.

Fig. 1198.—Striped Red Mullet (*Mullus surmulletus*)

THE RED MULLET FAMILY (MULLIDÆ).—The members of this family are mostly tropical fishes, but one species, the Striped Red Mullet (*Mullus surmulletus*, fig. 1198), is common in the Mediterranean, from which it ranges to the Canaries and Norway. It is taken in some numbers off the south and south-west shores of England by means of small drift-nets known as trammels. Average specimens weigh about half a pound. It is a particularly handsome fish, of bright-red colour (except below), with several narrow yellow bands along its sides. There is also a Plain Red Mullet (*M. barbatus*), without the stripes, which is common in the Mediterranean, and is occasionally taken in British waters. Most probably it is a distinct species.

The Red Mullet is universally regarded as a delicacy, and its flavour has suggested the popular name of "sea woodcock". The epicures of ancient Rome were extravagantly fond of it. On this point Günther remarks (in *The Study of Fishes*): "The Romans prized it above any other fish; they sought for large specimens far and wide, and paid ruinous prices for them. . . . Then, as nowadays, it was considered essential for the enjoyment of this delicacy that the fish should exhibit the red colour of its integuments. The Romans brought it, for that purpose, living into the banqueting-room, and allowed it to die in the hands of the guests, the red colour appearing in all its brilliancy during the death struggle of the fish. The fishermen of our times attain the same object by scaling the fish immediately after its capture, thus causing a permanent contraction of the chromatophores containing the red pigment."

Fig. 1199.—John Dory (*Zeus faber*)

The John Dory Family (Cyttidæ).—The members of this family inhabit temperate seas, and, so far as known, lay floating eggs. The body is greatly flattened from side to side. Other fishes constitute the food. Only one species requires notice, *i.e.* the *John Dory* (*Zeus faber*, fig. 1199), which may be of considerable size (up to 18 lbs. in weight). Its narrow body is very deep, while the elongated first dorsal fin and large staring eye give it an extraordinary appearance. The colour is greenish-brown, banded with yellow, and on either side of the body there is a large round black patch with a yellow border. Günther says (in *The Study of Fishes*):—"The fishermen of Roman Catholic countries hold this fish in special respect, as they recognize in a black round spot on its side the mark left by the thumb of St. Peter when he took the piece of money from its mouth". (See also p. 267.) The John Dory ranges from the Mediterranean to Madeira and Norway. It is trawled in considerable numbers in the English and Bristol Channels.

The Gurnard Family (Cottidæ).—Here are included widely

distributed ground-fishes, living in shallow water. Among them are the little *Bull-Heads* (*Cottus*), some of which are common on our coasts, while one, the Miller's Thumb, is a familiar inhabitant of our brooks. They are of no economic importance, though the Germans make soup of the last-named form. The larger Gurnards, however, are valuable food-fishes, of which several are British. They lay floating eggs. The head is large and covered with strong plates, while some of the rays of the pectoral fins are free and serve as feelers. The commonest native species are the *Grey Gurnard* (*Trigla gurnardus*) and the *Red Gurnard*

Fig. 1200.—Thin-lipped Grey Mullet (*Mugil capito*)

(*T. cuculus*), both of which range from the Mediterranean to Norway. The latter is most abundant in the English Channel, and the former in the North Sea.

THE GREY MULLET FAMILY (MUGILIDÆ).—Grey Mullets are handsome forms common on temperate and tropical coasts. They frequent inlets and estuaries, where they feed on vegetable food. There appear to be two species, the *Thin-lipped* and *Thick-lipped Grey Mullets* (*Mugil capito*, fig. 1200, and *M. chelo*), which range from the Mediterranean into British seas. Both are silver-grey in colour with longitudinal black streaks, and distinguishable from each other by the nature of the lips as indicated in their names. They are taken in large numbers by seines and other nets on the south coast of England, but the thick-lipped species seems to be more common off the western part of this area.

So far we have considered marine food-fishes, and it will be now appropriate to make some reference to the members of the Eel and Salmon families, which, in a sense, link together the forms of sea and fresh water.

THE EEL FAMILY (MURÆNIDÆ).—Eels are more or less cylindrical fishes, which may either be scaleless or possess minute scales sunk in the skin. They are widely distributed through the fresh waters and seas of the tropical and temperate regions, some of the most specialized kinds inhabiting the abysmal parts of the ocean. They are captured either by hook and line or by means of wicker-work (or metal) traps, provided with funnel-shaped openings. Trident-shaped eel-spears, with numerous tines, are also used in some localities. Creatures of the kind have been esteemed as a savoury food from very remote times, the ancient Greeks and Romans, for example, being extremely partial to them. There are two British species, the Conger and the Common Eel.

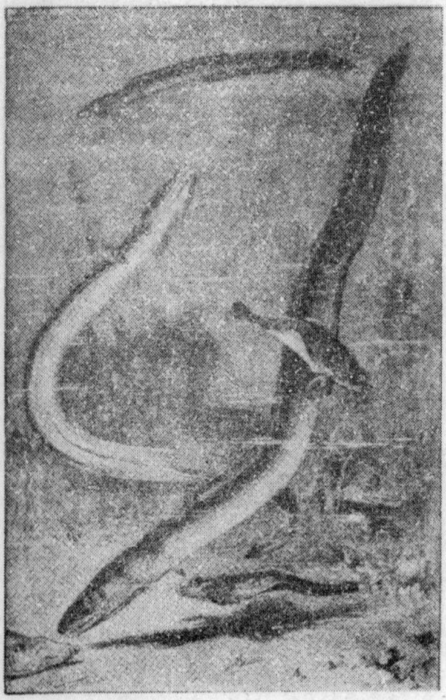

Fig. 1201.—Conger Eels (*Conger vulgaris*)

The Conger (*Conger vulgaris*, fig. 1201).—This is a large, scaleless marine eel, which not uncommonly attains the length of 6 or 7 feet and a weight of 60 lbs. It is a shallow-water form, and has a very wide distribution, occurring all round the shores of Europe, and also inhabiting the coastal waters of St. Helena, Japan, and Tasmania.

The Common Eel (*Anguilla vulgaris*).—This is a good deal smaller than the Conger, but full-grown specimens attain a length of 3 feet. When adult it inhabits fresh water, but repairs to the deep sea to spawn, the young eels or elvers making their way up rivers after undergoing a rather startling kind of transformation (see vol. iii, p. 433). This species has a wide distribution in the river-systems that discharge their waters into the North Atlantic (west as well as east coast) and Mediterranean.

THE SALMON FAMILY (SALMONIDÆ).—Salmonoid fishes are both commercially important and also of interest from the sporting point of view. About the middle of the back there is a dorsal fin of the usual character, and some distance behind this a small fatty or adipose second dorsal, unsupported by fin-rays. The nature of this second fin is a distinctive character. The family includes various species of Salmon, Trout, Charr, Grayling, and Smelt. All are natives to the non-tropical parts of the Northern Hemisphere, with the exception of a kind of Smelt (*Retropinna Richardsoni*) found in New Zealand and the Chatham Islands.

Fig. 1202.—River Trout (*Salmo fario*)

Some of the salmonoids are purely marine, others never leave fresh water, and others again may be described as marine forms which ascend rivers to spawn. The eggs are heavy and adhesive. Only a few important species require mention here.

The Salmon (*Salmo salar*).—This universally esteemed fish spawns in the rivers of temperate Europe as far south as 43° N. lat., and those of temperate North America down to 41° N. lat. In Britain it reaches commonly a weight of 20 to 40 lbs., and much larger specimens have been recorded. Salmon are eaten not only when fresh, but also, especially in North Europe, in the smoked condition. The chief method of capture is by netting at the time when the fish are ascending rivers, but large numbers are also taken with the rod.

The River Trout (*Salmo fario*, fig. 1202).—Average adult specimens of this well-known angler's fish attain the weight of about 1½ lb., but this may be greatly exceeded, especially in the case of local races. It is a purely freshwater species, and more delicate in flavour than is usual with such forms.

The Smelt or *Sparling* (*Osmerus eperlanus*, fig. 1203).—This rather small fish is generally considered a dainty. It abounds in the tidal parts of many of the rivers of Europe and North America, ascending these for some distance for the purpose of spawning. Günther says of it (in *The Study of Fishes*):—"In the sea it grows to a length of 8 inches, but, singularly, it frequently

Fig. 1203.—Smelt (*Osmerus eperlanus*)

migrates from the sea into rivers and lakes, where its growth is very much retarded. That this habit is one of very old date is evident from the fact that this small freshwater form occurs and is fully acclimatized in lakes which have now no open communication with the sea." Smelts are taken in large numbers by seines in some of the English estuaries which open into the southern part of the North Sea.

There are several other families of ordinary bony fishes (Teleostei) of which the freshwater species are used as food, such as the Carp Family, Pike Family, &c. As, in this country at any rate, they are of no particular economic importance, it is scarcely necessary to deal with them here. A few words, however, about a few of the families of lower fishes will not be out of place.

Those of most note include Sturgeons, Skates and Rays, and Lampreys.

THE STURGEON FAMILY (ACIPENSERIDÆ).—This belongs to an ancient group of Fishes (Ganoidei), closely related to the ordinary bony type. There are about twenty species of Sturgeon, all inhabiting the temperate part of the Northern Hemisphere. Like Salmon, they ascend rivers to spawn, and also in some cases for wintering, and some of them are altogether confined to the waters of the land. The Common Sturgeon (*Acipenser sturio*, fig. 1204) belongs to the British fauna, for it enters some of our rivers, as

Fig. 1204.—Common Sturgeon (*Acipenser sturio*)

the Severn and Thames, and, being the property of the Crown, is known as a "royal" fish. Though perhaps 6 feet may be taken as the length of an average adult, a much larger size—up to about 12 feet—may be attained. The species is found on both sides of the Atlantic, on the one side entering the rivers of the Eastern United States, and on the other those of West Europe and the Mediterranean. It is absent from the Black Sea. The much smaller but more esteemed Sterlet (*A. ruthenus*) is native to the rivers that debouch into the Black and Caspian Seas, and also inhabits the Siberian rivers. It does not, as a rule, descend into salt water. The Giant Sturgeon or Hausen (*A. huso*), on the other hand, is much larger than the common species, but somewhat coarse. It lives in the Black Sea, Sea of Azov, Caspian, and the corresponding river basins. Güldenstädt's Sturgeon (*A. Güldenstädti*) ascends the rivers of the Black Sea.

So far as Europe is concerned. the sturgeon-fishery is of most importance to Russia. The flesh of all the species is used as food, the hard roes (ovaries) are cleaned and salted to figure as caviare, to the extent of some 10,000 tons annually, and isinglass is prepared from the swim-bladders. For all these purposes the smaller sorts of Sturgeon, especially the Sterlet, are most esteemed. The Volga fishery is on the largest scale, and goes on at two seasons, autumn and winter. During the former, ground-lines with numerous hooks are used, and operations cease when the river begins to freeze. With increasing cold the fishes congregate at certain spots for hibernation, and such places are carefully marked by the fishermen. Later on, in January, when the cold is at its maximum, the winter-fishing is ushered in with great festivities. Good-sized holes are broken through the ice at the spots previously noted; the fishes, disturbed by the noise, come to the surface, and are promptly secured by means of harpoons and iron hooks.

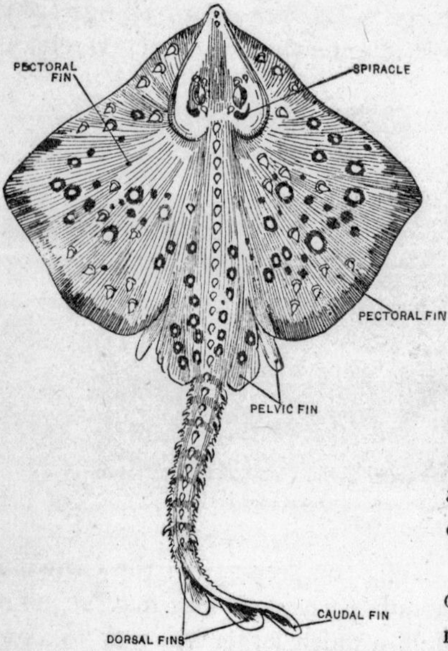

Fig. 1205.—Thornback (*Raia clavata*)

SKATES AND RAYS (BATOIDEI).—These flattened, narrow-tailed, rhomboidal forms constitute, with Sharks, Dogfishes, &c., the great group of cartilaginous fishes (Elasmobranchii). The two most important British species are the comparatively smooth-skinned Skate (*Raia batis*) and the Thornback (*R. clavata*, fig. 1205), of which latter the characters are sufficiently indicated by the name. The Skate may attain a length of 6 feet or more, and the Thornback about half as much. Both are common in British waters, where they are captured by trawling and by line-fishing. Though not among the choicer food-fishes, they are largely eaten, the enormous pectoral fins, cut into strips and rolled, constituting what is commonly known as "crimped skate".

ROUND MOUTHS (CYCLOSTCMATA).—The eel-shaped scaleless

Lampreys, which can be only called fishes by courtesy (see vol. i, p. 291), are considered great delicacies in some Continental countries, but are not abundant enough in Britain to be of economic importance. The best-known of our three native species are the Sea Lamprey (*Petromyzon marinus*), which may grow to the length of 3 feet, and the much smaller River Lamprey or Lampern (*P. fluviatilis*), less than half that size, both of which are marine forms that ascend some of our rivers to spawn, the Severn

Fig. 1206.—Herring-Boats leaving Aberdeen Harbour

being especially notable in this respect. In *Cassell's Dictionary of Cookery* the following remarks are made about the lamprey, apparently the large species:—"This not very wholesome, but rare and rich fish, was a great favourite in ancient times, and is well known to the student of English history, as it was an attack of indigestion, brought on by eating of it too freely, which caused the death of Henry I. . . . Probable cost uncertain, lampreys being seldom offered for sale."

FISHERIES

In practical fishery matters a distinction is drawn between "wet" fish, *i.e.* fishes proper, and "shell"-fish, among which both molluscs and crustaceans are included. We are here for the present concerned with the former only (except as regards some of the statistics). The importance of the matter to this country may be realized by giving a few figures.

In 1901 the number of fishing-boats registered in the United Kingdom (including the Isle of Man and Channel Islands) was as follows:—First class (15 tons or more), 7083; second class, 14,067; third class, 4647; total tonnage, 302,188. And to this must be added a large number of unregistered boats, chiefly of the third class. During the same year 68,878 persons were regularly employed in fishing, and 37,599 more found occasional employment.

The amount and value of the British catch for 1902 were as follows:—

Wet Fish.			Shell-Fish.		
	Quantity in Cwts.	Value.		Number.	Value.
		£			£
Soles	76,624	512,596	Crabs ...	8,680,645	79,968
Turbot ...	64,094	245,215	Lobsters	1,632,110	73,317
Other prime fish	33,184	81,550	Oysters ...	43,482,711	119,086
Cod	1,584,528	865,934	Other shell-fish	cwts. 613,436	138,544
Haddock ...	2,941,264	1,787,942			
Herrings ...	8,437,566	2,531,912			410,915
Ling	252,627	115,925			
Mackerel ...	599,983	390,321			
Sprats	76,066	16,636			
Whiting ...	403,247	161,392			
Other fish ...	3,432,862	2,586,675			
	17,902,045	9,296,098			

Total Value of British Catch for 1902,

£9,707,013.

We do not entirely rely upon the British fishing industry for supplies, for in 1902 our imports of fresh and cured fish amounted to 2,587,370 cwts., valued at £4,105,800. Of this amount, however, 439,773 cwts. (worth £809,322) were re-exported, while we exported a part of our own catch to the value of £3,706,002, which included 2,249,976 barrels of herrings, worth £2,933,864. Of the exported herrings no less than 1,364,613 barrels were cured in Scotland, and the greater part of these were for Russian consumption, some of them finding their way as far east as Vladivostock.

During the last few decades it has gradually been realized by maritime nations that the supply of fish is not inexhaustible, and

DEEP-SEA FISHES (drawn to various scales)

The fishes of the deep sea are highly carnivorous forms, often provided with formidable teeth. The eyes are either very large or else greatly reduced. Luminous organs are often present. Many of these fishes are of bizarre appearance, as may be gathered from the plate, which represents eight species, as follows:—

1. *Sternoptyx diaphana*: small and translucent, with rounded luminous organs on the sides of head, body, and tail.
2. *Cyema atrum*: a small deep-sea eel, with reduced eyes.
3. *Malacosteus Indicus*: very large eyes, two luminous organs on the side of the head, and enormous mouth.
4. *Idiacanthus ferox*: a greatly attenuated form, with numerous small rounded luminous organs on the side of the body.
5. *Nemichthys ingens*: a greatly elongated deep-sea eel, with large eyes, and jaws drawn out into a slender beak.
6. *Saccopharynx ampullaceus*: a large deep-sea conger-eel, which has succeeded in swallowing a fish much bigger than itself.
7. *Bathypterois longicauda*: a deep-sea fish with reduced eyes, and much elongated fin-rays serving as feelers.
8. *Macrurus crassiceps*: a species of a widely distributed deep-sea family related to that including the cod, &c. Eyes extremely large, and mouth on the under side of the head.

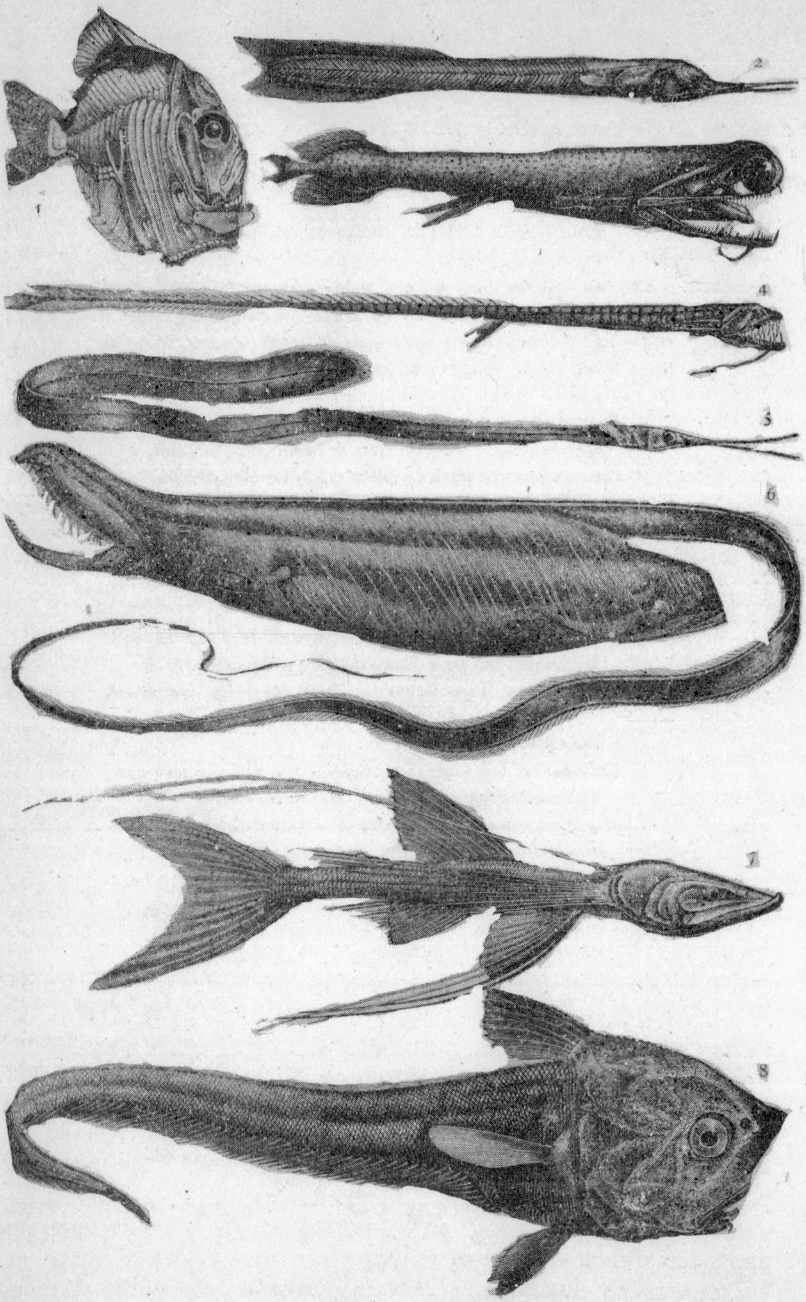

DEEP-SEA FISHES

DRAWN TO VARIOUS SCALES

this is partly due to the steady increase of steam-trawling, which means capture on a wholesale scale. Practical men are recognizing more and more that expert scientific advice must be requisitioned if the supply of fish is to be maintained, and still more so if it is to be increased. As Cunningham very justly remarks (in *Marketable Marine Fishes*):—"It can scarcely be expected that the fisherman or fish merchant will spend his short and hard-earned leisure moments in the study of the blue-books and technical memoirs in which the results of research are described; and when certain newly-established facts are brought before them in other ways it frequently happens that they either deny these facts, as contrary to their own experience, or turn a deaf ear, from the conviction that such matters are of no practical importance. With reference to the contradiction of the naturalist's conclusions, it may be urged that, although he may not be able to climb the rigging of a smack, and is generally sick while at sea, although also he may be as ignorant as a baby of the mysterious and complicated practice of the fish-trade, still he has two advantages over the professional fish-man in attempting to get at the truth concerning the life and habits of fish. Firstly, he has been trained to appreciate the value of scientific evidence, and is on his guard against jumping at conclusions; secondly, he can use instruments of precision, which are as essential to the investigation of some of the matters in question as the compass and the lead to the handling of a fishing-vessel With regard to the practical importance of the naturalist's researches and results to the fishing industry, it can only be said that there is no doubt about it. It is an undeniable fact that parliamentary legislation and local by-laws are at the present time constantly being demanded or proposed for the benefit of the fisheries, and the reasons by which these proposals and demands are supported consist largely of statements concerning the natural history of the fishes and other marine creatures concerned. It is necessary, therefore, that we should be able to test the correctness of these statements, and should be able to judge correctly of the most probable effect of the measures proposed on the productiveness of the fisheries."

A few epoch-making dates in fishery work may here be appended with advantage, and the reader may draw his own conclusions as to the relative enterprise displayed by the nations concerned. 1862, Professor Allman of Edinburgh investigated the spawning of herrings at the request of the Scottish Fishery Board. 1864, Professor Sars of Christiania commissioned by the Norwegian Government to investigate the natural history of the cod and the cod-fisheries of the Lofot Islands. 1870, the Prussian Minister of Agriculture instituted a Commission for the Investigation of the German Seas. 1871, institution of the United States Commission of Fish and Fisheries. 1882, establishment of the new Fishery Board for Scotland; this marked the first commencement, on a large scale, of the application of scientific methods to British fishery problems. 1884, inauguration of the Marine Biological Association of the United Kingdom (active work at the Plymouth Marine Station commenced in 1887) on the initiative of Professor Ray Lankester. The late Professor Huxley was the first president. In the same year the marine laboratories at St. Andrews and Granton (near Edinburgh) were completed. 1886, a Fishery Department of the Board of Trade was organized, but without power to make scientific investigations. 1899, an annual sum of £10,000 was devoted to Irish Sea-Fisheries. More recently the countries interested in the fisheries of the North Sea have agreed to jointly investigate that area with regard to fishery problems on scientific lines. In 1901 the Board of Trade appointed a Committee on Ichthyological Research, with the view of ascertaining the best methods of carrying out scientific investigations of problems affecting British fisheries. The committee presented their report in the following year, suggesting greatly increased expenditure, with a view to solving certain pressing problems, and recommending, among other things, the establishment of a Fishery Council for England.

Some varieties of fishery work which are of special importance may now be very briefly indicated.

Statistics.—Until we know with some approach to definiteness the amount of each kind of fish captured yearly, together with the time, place, and method of capture, it will be impossible to form a sound opinion as to whether the natural supply is actually diminishing generally or locally.

Habits and Life-Histories of Food-Fishes.—It is clear that full knowledge on these points is absolutely necessary from the practical stand-point, for upon such knowledge must ultimately depend the various means adopted for regulating the fishing industry. Full information of the sort regarding any particular form, joined to that derived from statistics, would enable us to determine with a reasonable approach to accuracy the best methods, times, and places for capturing such fish, securing on the one hand a profitable result, and on the other hand obviating wasteful depletion of the natural supply.

Food of Fishes.—Directly or indirectly the most important source of fish food is found in "plankton", *i.e.* the various floating organisms which are found in vast numbers at or near the surface of the sea (and of lakes). Minute plants, animalcules, small crustaceans (especially Copepods), various larvæ, and floating eggs (including those of fishes themselves) are among the more important constituents. Some valuable food-fishes, such as the herring, feed solely on plankton.

The amount of this food available bears a direct relation to the fish-supply, and Professor Hensen of Kiel has devised ingenious and elaborate methods of estimating it in a quantitative manner. Details cannot be given here, but the following extracts from a paper by J. Travis Jenkins (*The Methods and Results of German Plankton Investigations*) will serve to give some idea of the importance of the matter:—"The plankton estimation methods of the Germans, the credit for initiation of which is due to Hensen, differ from and mark an advance upon the methods hitherto employed in England, inasmuch as no attempt is made in the latter country to arrive at a quantitative as distinguished from a qualitative result. The questions that Hensen attempts to answer are—(1) What does the sea contain at a given time in the shape of living organisms in the plankton? and (2) How does this material vary from season to season and from year to year? It may be pointed out that the results obtained by the German investigators are largely due to the liberal attitude taken by their Government with regard to subsidizing scientific investigation of problems connected with the sea-fisheries. It is to be hoped that the Irish Sea may be subsequently investigated in like manner. A comparison with the results already obtained for the North and Baltic Seas could not fail to be of interest and to yield important results." Some of the most striking estimations were made on the number of Fork-footed Crustaceans (Copepoda) in plankton, since it is these which constitute the chief food of herrings, sprats, and their allies. The following results were yielded by the method:—"For a square mile of surface-water the annual consumption of Copepoda can be regarded as approximately 975 billion, or for the 16 square miles of the Eckenförde fishery district [in the West Baltic] a grand total of 15,600 billion. A billion Copepoda yield not less than 1500 kilograms of dry organic substance, so that the 15,600 billion weigh not less than 23,400,000 kilograms [*i.e.* more than 22,982 tons]. Taking the average weight of an adult West Baltic herring as being 60 grams, and allowing that every herring uses in fifty days its own weight of organic substance, we find that every herring consumes annually 438 grams. In the 16 square miles of the Eckenförde fishery district there exists food in the shape of Copepoda for 534,000,000 herring of an average body weight of 60 grams. This result may, of course, be largely problematical, but it is at any rate extremely interesting. The North Sea, in a similar manner to the Baltic, contains an abundant wealth of Copepoda. The open ocean, on the other hand, contains much less." The number of floating fish-eggs of a particular kind contained in plankton may be used as a basis for determining the number of fish of the sort present in a given area at a given time. Applying this method to the cod and plaice of the Eckenförde, Hensen estimates that "man captures for his own use every year about one-fourth of the total number of adult fish in this particular area of the West Baltic. This result is surprising to those who consider the resources of the sea as inexhaustible, and believe that the number of fish caught by man bears only a small proportion to the number actually present in the sea." It is also interesting to learn that the northern seas are richer in plankton than those in warmer latitudes. The possibilities of the Hensen methods are thus seen to be very considerable, but it is unsafe to generalize from a small number of determinations, for the distribution of plankton in a given area is by no means uniform. In this, and many other matters involving accurate scientific research, large government subsidies are urgently needed in this country. We are co-operating, it is true, with other nations in a scientific survey of the North Sea for the space of three years, but during that period the annual grant of £2000 per annum to the Scottish Fishery Board is suspended, thus seriously crippling an organization that has long been engaged in work of the most valuable kind.

Fish-Culture (Pisciculture).—The rearing of fishes in ponds is a very ancient art, which was practised by the Egyptians,

Greeks, and Romans, of antiquity. The young of various species were made to enter lagoons, prevented from again escaping, and kept till large enough for the table. Culture in freshwater ponds has been an important Chinese industry from time immemorial, and was well understood in England during the Middle Ages, especially by the monks, who did not care to rely on chance for the periodic fish repasts prescribed by the Church. Remains of old "fish-stews", in which carp, eels, &c., were reared, abound in this country.

A very interesting outcome of the fish-culture of the old Romans still exists in the lagoon of Comacchio, at the mouth of

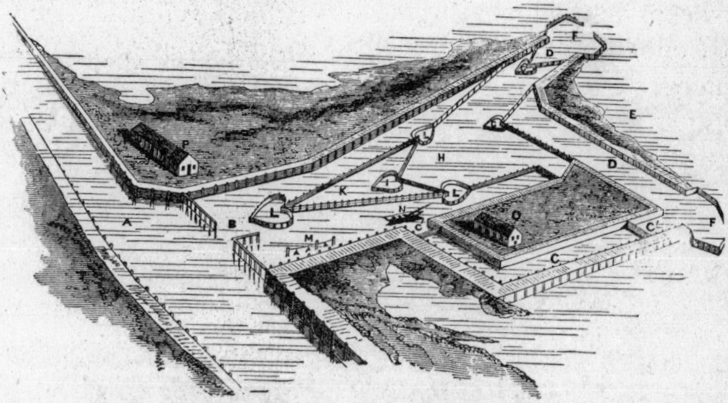

Fig. 1207.—A Division of Comacchio

A, Canal Palotta. B, Entrance from canal. C, Canal for boats. C', Sluices. D, First compartment of labyrinth. E, Outer basin. F, Antechamber of first compartment. G, Chamber of ditto. H, Second compartment. I, Chamber of ditto. K, Third compartment. L, L, L, Chambers of ditto. M, Wicker-work baskets for keeping fish alive. N, Boat and tackle. O, Dwelling-house. P, Storehouse.

the Po, where eels are grown on a large scale, and distributed throughout Italy both fresh and in a preserved condition. The definite records of the industry date from 1229, and so long ago as the end of the sixteenth century the annual revenue derived from the culture amounted to £16,000 annually, a sum which, of course, represented much more at that time than it does now. The eels sold in 1903 fetched over £28,000. The whole lagoon, which is bounded at the sides by the Reno and Volano mouth of the Po, is a perfect labyrinth of ponds and canals, of which a faint idea may be gained by examining fig. 1207. The conduct of this industry is a very elaborate matter. The ascending swarms of eivers have to be guided to their destination, the supply of fish-food maintained, full-grown eels captured (from August to December), and the catch prepared for the market.

The pond-culture of Carp is carried on in a very systematic manner in some parts of Germany, and it need only be said that the fish are transferred from one pond to another according to age.

The discovery of the possibility of artificial fecundation, by mixing eggs and milt together, constituted an epoch in fish-culture which opened up far-reaching possibilities the importance of which has only been fully realized of late years. It appears to have been first practised, for salmon and trout, by S. L. Jacobi of Hohenhausen, in Westphalia, so long ago as 1748, and was continued by him and his sons, with profitable results, till 1825. George III (of England) gave a pension to Jacobi in 1771.

Fig. 1208.—Staby's Californian Trough

A, Hatching tank, into the outer part of which (*b*) water flows from a tap (*a*); *c* and *d* are hatching trays with floors of fine wire-gauze; *e*, outflow. *B*, Tank to catch fry which escape from *A* when *d* is removed; they pass into the space *f*, but are prevented by the gauze partition *g* from getting washed away in the outflow to the right.

Scotland, as usual, was one of the first of other countries to profit by an improvement on old methods, for we find that in 1837 John Shaw, a gamekeeper at Drumlanrig of the Duke of Buccleuch, introduced Jacobi's system. But the beginning of fish-culture on a national scale only dates from 1850, when the French Government instituted a large fish-hatching establishment at Huningue, in Alsace. At the present time America has profited most by the pursuit of fish-culture, which is largely practised with reference to their rivers and lakes. One type of hatching apparatus suitable for trout and salmon is represented in fig. 1208 as constructed by Dr. Ludwig Staby, and named by him "the deep Californian trough".

The fact that most marine fishes lay floating eggs renders fish-culture in their case comparatively easy, for any quantity of fertilized eggs can be collected from the surface of spawning-ponds in which adult fishes are confined. In a hatchery for such fishes the eggs are placed in various receptacles, where they are kept aerated by suitable devices. MacDonald's hatching-bottle (fig. 1209) is largely employed in the United States for the small eggs of shad and other fishes, of which one bottle will accommodate about 70,000.

An important hatchery for cod has for some years been in operation at Flödevig, near Arendal, in Norway, under the superintendence of Captain Dannevig. In Scotland there is an important hatchery, chiefly used for plaice, connected with the marine station at Nigg, near Aberdeen, and there is also one at Piel, on the coast of Lancashire. There are, of course, important hatcheries for marine fishes in America.

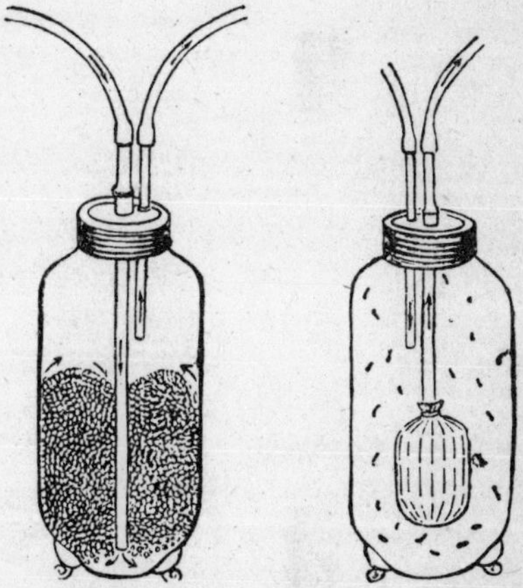

Fig. 1209.—MacDonald's Hatching Bottle. The one on the left is arranged for hatching purposes, and the other contains fry. Course of water indicated by arrows.

Regarding the value of hatcheries for freshwater forms, and fishes which, like the salmon, spawn in rivers, there can be no doubt. As to marine fish-hatcheries, which aim at maintaining or even increasing the supply by liberating great numbers of fry in the sea, the data are at present too incomplete to estimate their utility. It appears to be certain in some cases that good has been done by them, one instance of the sort being afforded by the Norwegian hatchery near Flödevig, but the expense involved is considerable, and for some species and some localities may well turn out to be so great as not to be justifiable. The large majority of the just-hatched fry which are now from time to time placed in the sea are destined to perish before growing to a marketable size, and it may in the end turn out to be necessary to carry the culture to a stage which will give a greatly increased chance of survival. But this is notoriously difficult, and a large amount of experiment is necessary before success is likely to be attained. And even in the event of the various obstacles being surmounted, the greatly increased expense of such a method may prevent its adoption.

There is a second possibility of exactly opposite kind, suggested by Cunningham, *i.e.* to give up hatching, and largely increase the extent of spawning-ponds, contenting ourselves with setting adrift vast numbers of fertilized eggs. Both the possibilities mentioned require testing on a large scale, and afford suitable objects for large Government expenditure. The money spent on a single battle-ship, or even on a cruiser, if devoted to this purpose, would quite conceivably settle the whole vexed question of British marine fish-hatcheries so far as some of the more important food-fishes are concerned. And unless scientific research, both pure and as applied to our important industries, fisheries of course included, is not far more largely endowed in future than it has been in the past, it may come about in the course of time that the country will be unable to afford a sufficient number of battle-ships, cruisers, and similar expensive necessaries.

MOLLUSCS (MOLLUSCA) AS FOOD

Brief mention has already been made (see p. 214) of various molluscs used for food in different parts of the world. A few of these are of such importance that they require somewhat more detailed treatment. They are Oysters, Mussels, Cockles, and Periwinkles.

The Oyster (*Ostrea*).—The most important European species is the "Flat" Oyster (*O. edulis*), to which our "natives" belong. There is also the large, somewhat triangular, Portuguese Oyster (*O. angulata*), which is of considerable economic importance, though of coarser kind. The American Oyster (*O. Virginiana*), commonly known in this country as "blue point", is the object of valuable and extensive fisheries on the Atlantic coast of the United States. In spite of typhoid scares it is probable that oysters will continue to be popular delicacies in this country, those from Whitstable and other fisheries in the Thames estuary being most esteemed.

Oyster Culture.—Some nations engage on a large scale in oyster culture as well as oyster fishing. Italy, Holland, France, and the United States may be particularly mentioned in this connection. This kind of culture mainly depends on the fact that the larvæ, fry, or "spat" readily attach themselves to various foreign objects, and can then be reared to "seed" oysters, which may be further grown where produced, or else despatched elsewhere. The practice varies largely in different countries, and perhaps the most interesting case is afforded by France. It may be remarked in passing that the Italian oyster-industry has existed continuously from the times of the ancient Romans, and that the oysters are commonly grown upon bundles of twigs (*fascines*). The Dutch largely employ earthenware tiles, and the numerous estuaries of Holland afford suitable localities.

The large development of oyster-culture in France during the last few decades is very remarkable, and is the outcome of some experiments made in 1853 by M. de Bon, commissaire of marine at St. Servan. At that time the natural oyster-beds of France had been so much depleted by over-dredging that not only was strict legislation regarding them necessary, but the question of future supply naturally demanded attention. The observer mentioned found that the oyster-fry readily attached themselves to pieces of stone or stick, and this was the first step in the evolution of "collectors" to serve this end. The earliest attempts to revive the industry by artificial culture were unfortunately not successful, but many natural obstacles were gradually overcome, the final result being a flourishing and highly-specialized trade, in which there is much division of labour. The total annual value of the industry considerably exceeds half a million pounds sterling. In 1902 the fresh oysters imported into this country from France were worth £30,000.

Public dredging of the natural oyster-banks of France is so stringently limited by Government that they are of little importance as regards the direct supply of the market. They are, in fact, regarded as a reserve of spawning individuals, by which vast quantities of spat are produced. One important branch of the industry is to catch the spat on collectors ingeniously adapted to the conditions of particular localities. Some of these devices are made of boards, fixed together in successive tiers; but most of them consist of curved earthenware tiles, arranged in wooden crates, wired together, or otherwise associated (fig. 1210). Whatever their precise nature, they are mostly to be found fixed in their appointed places near low tide-mark or in shallow water, by the beginning of July, *i.e.* at the time when the fry are liberated from between the shells of the parent oysters. The tiles (or boards) have previously been covered with a thin layer of a mixture of lime and sand (or mud), and it is the under surfaces which, under ordinary circumstances, serve for the attachment of the larval oysters when these give up a free-swimming existence for a sedentary life. It may be added that in some localities it has been found possible to construct large spawning-ponds instead of relying on the supply of spat from the oyster-banks off the shore.

Fig. 1210.—The Gabarét Collector (Ruche) in position (at Arcachon). Young oysters are seen attached to the tile which is being lifted, and to another that is up-ended on the right. The collectors are covered with sea-weed, so that when left by the tide they are kept moist, and protected from heat and light.

A "set" of spat having been secured on the collectors, the tender molluscs are left till about October, by which time they have grown to the size of a finger-nail, and are known as "seed-oysters". They are then flaked off the tiles (or boards), which the thin layer of lime renders possible with trifling loss, and carefully packed. This ends the stage of production (*production*), and the little oysters are now committed to the care of another set of specialists, who rear them to a marketable size. This process of *élevage* is much more difficult. The *éleveur* places the seed in rectangular rearing-cases, the upper and lower sides of which are chiefly made of wire-gauze. As growth proceeds, sorting from time to time becomes necessary, so as to give increased room. The cases are placed in oyster "parks", which are simply enclosed areas of shallow water, with boundaries of the most various character, from lines of waving saplings to solid masonry pierced by flood-gates (fig. 1211). When the oysters have attained a fair size they may be trans-

Fig. 1211.—A Norwegian Oyster-Park

ferred from the cases to the floor of the park, which sometimes has to be specially prepared for their reception.

There are still two more stages which some French oysters have to go through before they reach the market. One is the process of "greening", as at Marennes, the products of which are greatly esteemed. The oysters are here kept for a long time in small and muddy salt ponds (*claires*), where they gradually acquire a green colour owing to the nature of the food available, which consists of minute algæ. At the same time a peculiarly delicate flavour is imparted. Healthy British oysters from the estuaries of the Roach and Crouch, in Essex, may also be green, and for the same reason. Certain green oysters, however, should be looked upon with suspicion, as, for example, some of those from Cornwall, in which the colour is due to the presence of copper.

The last process to which some of the French oysters are subjected is that of education for transport. They are gradually accustomed to be out of water, and to close their valves closely, which clearly enables them to be sent in a good condition for long distances.

English Oyster-Industry.—That this industry is of considerable importance will already have been gathered from the statistics on page 280. We may take as an example the Whitstable Oyster Fishery Company, which is one of the most notable. As to its yield of oysters, the Secretary of the Company, Mr. W. H. Reeves, writes in a private letter: "With regard to statistics I can only say that our own sales of oysters average about 10 million to 12 million yearly, and of this number about two-thirds are English Natives and the rest imported from France, with a small percentage of East River oysters from America". As most persons are aware, Whitstable is on the north coast of Kent, east of the Isle of Sheppey, and has been an important seat of the oyster-trade from very remote times. The details here given are derived from a book by A. O. Collard (*The Oyster and Dredgers of Whitstable*), to which readers are referred for further information. The following quotation from this book will give an idea of the length of time for which "natives" have been popular:—"Among some valuable notes attached to the evidence taken on oath in the Committee of the House of Lords in 1866, on certain bills promoted by the Herne Bay Fishery Company, I find the following observations: 'The Whitstable Company are a most ancient body of 'free fishers

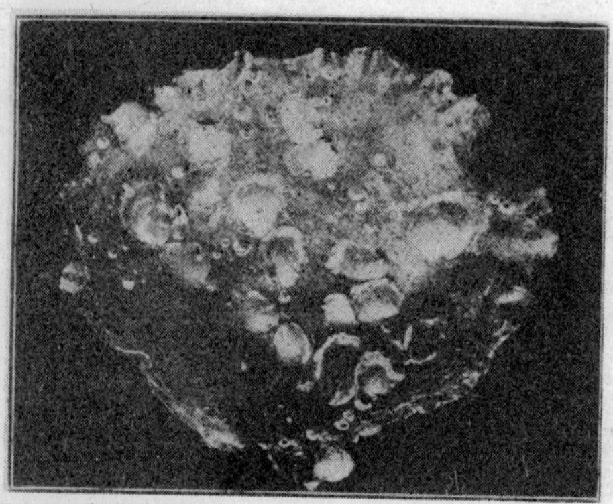

Fig. 1212.—Shell of a Whitstable Native, with young Oysters attached. Reduced.

and dredgers', who, from father to son, have carried on the business of an oyster fishery during, it is probable, a period of

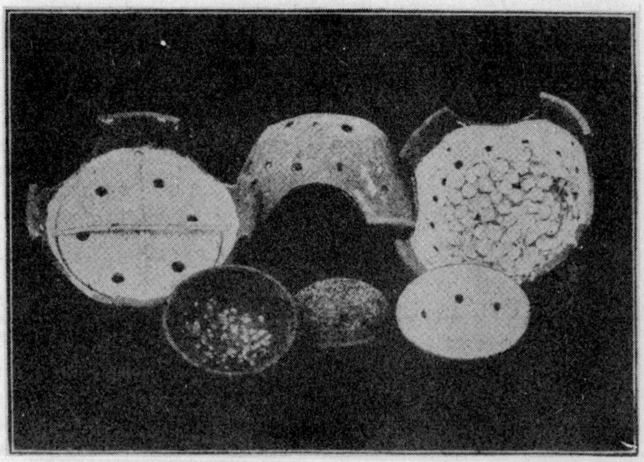

Fig. 1213.—Wheeler's Beehive Collector. Much reduced

at least two thousand years. It was about A.D. 80 that Julius Agricola first exported oysters from the neighbourhood of the

Fig. 1214.—Whitstable Oyster-Dredger at Work. Dredges on the rail.

Reculvers to Rome, and for the ancestors of the Whitstable free dredgers Rome was, during about three centuries, their

Billingsgate.' . . . When we remember what is known of the early state of Great Britain, we can scarcely be surprised that Sallust, who lived and wrote about fifty years before Christ, had a better opinion of our oysters than our ancestors, for he said, 'The poor Britons—there is some good in them after all—they produce an oyster'. Whitstable may certainly claim some share in creating that good impression."

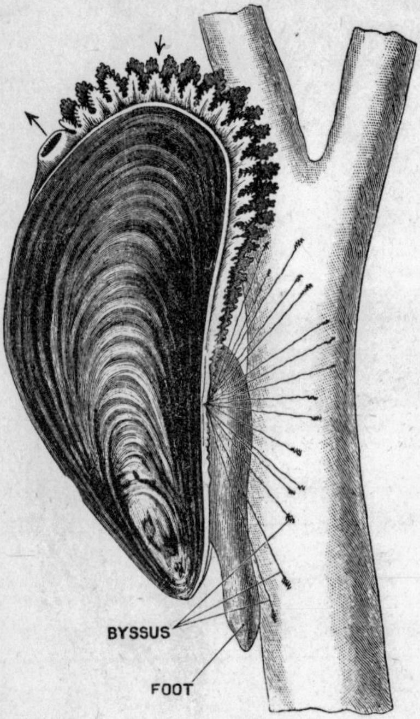

Fig. 1215.—Edible Mussel (*Mytilus edulis*)

The superior quality of the Whitstable Natives is mainly due to the character of the in-shore beds where the oysters live, for not only is the soil favourable, but there is the necessary admixture of fresh water of suitable nature from the land. Upon these beds are planted the seed oysters dredged further out in the estuary, while some of these are imported from France. The "cultch" to which the bivalves attach themselves is largely made up of empty oyster-shells (fig. 1212). One ingenious method that has been tried for catching the spat is by means of Wheeler's Beehive Collector (fig. 1213), made of perforated earthenware, and partly filled with empty shells. Space forbids reference to the way in which the mature natives are treated after they have been dredged (fig. 1214) and before they are finally packed in barrels for the market.

The Edible Mussel (*Mytilus edulis*, fig. 1215).—This mollusc is used to a considerable extent as human food, though there is rather a prejudice against it on account of the fact that occasional batches turn out to be poisonous, causing serious illness or even death. That mussels are nevertheless eaten largely in England may be deduced from the fact that in 1902 no less a quantity

INTERTIDAL AND SHALLOW WATER ANIMALS

The plate represents a tide-pool on the British coast, and introduces a number of familiar marine animals. Beginning with those lowest in the scale they are:

1. Sea-Anemones (*Actiniæ*).
2. Common Star-fish (*Uraster rubens*).
3. Acorn-Barnacles (*Balanus*).
4. Shore-Crab (*Carcinus mœnas*).
5. Cockles (*Cardium*). The one on the left belongs to the edible species (*C. edule*).
6. Sea-Mussels (*Mytilus edulis*).
7. Scallop (*Pecten*).
8. Periwinkles (*Littorina*). Those on the right are of the edible sort (*L. littorea*), while the small yellow ones on the left belong to another species (*L. obtusata*).
9. Purple-Shells (*Purpura lapillus*).
10. Gulls (*Larus*).

A TIDAL POOL WITH FAMILIAR MARINE ANIMALS

1. Sea-Anemones. 2. Star-fish. 3. Acorn-Barnacles. 4. Shore-Crab. 5. Cockles.
6. Sea-Mussels. 7. Scallop. 8. Periwinkles. 9. Purple-shells. 10. Gulls.

than 43 tons 10 cwts. of them was seized and condemned at and near Billingsgate Market. On the Continent the consumption is much greater than with us.

The mussel is greatly valued as a bait in British line-fishing, particularly on the coast of Scotland. The yield in that country for 1902 amounted to 95,663 cwts., valued at £5445, which contrasts strongly with the 247,186 cwts., worth £14,506, collected in 1892. The meaning of the steady diminution which has been going on for some years has reference to the displacement of line-fishing by trawling. The same thing has been happening with regard to "clams" (species of *Pecten* and various other bivalves), another valuable bait in Scottish line-fishing. The quantity of clams taken in 1892 was 20,769 cwts. (£2736), but in 1902 only 4320 cwts. (£586).

Mussel-Culture.—As in the case of the oyster, the eggs hatch out into free-swimming "fry", which after a time attach themselves to various objects, not, however, by the substance of one valve, but by silky byssus threads. Nor is the mussel obliged to spend the whole of its fixed life in one spot, for it can cast off the threads, and crawl away to some distance, if adverse circumstances render a change of residence desirable. Important musselries were established some years ago at Montrose, and previously barren ground was made very valuable. The principle involved essentially consists in reserving certain beds for the production of "seed", as in the case of the strictly-preserved natural oyster-banks on the French coast (see p. 289). From these beds the young mussels are collected and planted out on other areas.

On the Baltic coast of Germany tree-branches are thrust into the sea-floor in shallow water (fig. 1216), serving as collectors for the fry, which grow upon them to a marketable size. After from three to five years they are pulled up, weighed, and sold with their living crop still adhering.

At some points of the French sea-board, especially at Esnaudes on the west coast, elaborate mussel-farming is practised, on what is known as the "bouchot" system. Each bouchot is a **V**-shaped or **W**-shaped collection of stakes driven into the mud, with the opening directed seawards. Adjacent stakes are connected by interwoven branches, and the 500 bouchots of the Esnaude musselry have a collective length of not far short of

130 miles. During the first two months of the year the mussel-fry attach themselves to the bouchots next the sea, and by May have grown sufficiently large to be scraped off without difficulty. They are then placed in small bags made of old canvas and the like, which are fixed to stakes further from the sea. Ultimately the bags rot away, leaving the mussels hanging in bunches by their byssal threads. As time goes on they are transferred further and further landwards, till by the time the

Fig. 1216.—Part of a Baltic Musselry

innermost stakes are reached they are large enough to gather for sale. The annual yield of Esnaudes is valued at not less than £52,000.

The Cockle (*Cardium edule*).—As a cheap, if indigestible, substitute for the oyster this bivalve is largely eaten by the populace in this and other countries. It burrows in the sand or mud of bays and estuaries, and is captured by raking at low tide. Morecambe Bay, Caermarthen Bay, and the estuary of the Teign are notable localities. Statistics for this country are not available, for even in the Reports of the Scottish Fishery Board the cockle is an "unclassified" shell-fish. But most of us have seen small detachments of this mollusc displayed for sale on stalls, with vinegar and pepper as accompaniments, and have speculated as to what kind of customer might be expected. And we have the significant fact that, in 1902, 7 tons 18 cwts. 2 qrs. of cockles were seized and condemned at or near Billingsgate Market.

The Periwinkle (*Littorina littorea*).—The popular 'winkle is gathered between tide-marks on many parts of our coasts, the greater part of the London supply being derived from Scotland. The large quantity of 54 tons 5 cwts. was seized and condemned at or near Billingsgate Market in 1902.

CRUSTACEANS (CRUSTACEA) AS FOOD

We are here chiefly concerned with Lobsters, Prawns, Shrimps, and Crabs (fig. 1217), though these are far from being the only edible species.

The Lobster (*Homarus vulgaris*).—Of all large crustaceans this is the most esteemed in this country, and vast numbers are annually consumed. Along the rocky parts of the coast of the British Isles, Norway, Canada, and many other countries, lobster-fishing is a very important industry. A large part of the English supply is derived from Scotland, for which the yield in 1902 was 786,400, valued at £37,114. The home-supply is by no means equal to the demand, and our imports of lobsters, fresh and canned, are very considerable. Of the former we relied upon Norway for 38,538 (worth about £1850) in 1902, and upon France for many more. Lobster-canning is an important industry for Newfoundland, Canada, and the United States. It should be added that the American Lobster (*H. Americanus*) is not of the same species as our native form, though closely allied.

Lobsters are caught in "pots" or "creels", contrivances of the nature of traps, constructed of a wooden framework covered with netting (fig. 1218). Fish-entrails or other garbage is used as bait, the creel being sunk in a suitable spot by means of stones, a cord with a cork at the end serving to mark the spot.

Lobster-fishing has to be regulated with considerable stringency, as it is only too easy to deplete the supply. Hatching has been carried on to a considerable extent in several countries with a view to maintain or, if possible, increase the numbers available. The difficulties to be overcome are far less formidable than in the case of fishes, for the female or "hen" lobster carries about her

Fig. 1217.—1, Common Prawn (*Palæmon serratus*). 2, Common Shrimp (*Crangon vulgaris*). 3, The Edible Crab (*Cancer pagurus*). 4, The Lobster (*Homarus vulgaris*)

eggs attached to the under side of the tail, at which time she is said to be in "berry". So long ago as 1887 Captain Dannevig, at the Norwegian fish-hatchery near Arendal, found it possible to rear lobster-fry from the eggs, and such rearing is now resorted to by Scotland, Canada, and the United States, among other countries. The Aberdeen hatchery, for example, liberated some

3000 minute lobsters during 1902. The value of these hatcheries is doubtful.

The Edible Crab (*Cancer pagurus*).—This savoury crustacean is also of considerable economic importance (see p. 280). The chief method of capture is the same as for the lobster. Hatching methods are here also being made the subject of experiment. The Aberdeen hatchery cast adrift in the open sea no less than 4,500,000 of juvenile crabs in the year 1902.

Shrimps and Prawns.—A Common Shrimp (*Crangon vulgaris*) is distinguished from a Prawn (*Palæmon serratus*, &c.) not only

Fig. 1218.—Crab-Pots

by its smaller size, but also by several structural features, of which the most obvious is the absence of the sharp saw-edged spine which projects from the head of the latter. Prawns are often known as "red shrimps". The annual consumption in this country must be very large, judging from observation, and the fact that in 1902 shrimps (presumably including prawns as well) to the amount of over 54 tons were seized and condemned at or near Billingsgate Market. We also know that in the year mentioned over 900 fishing-boats (mostly second class) were engaged in capturing shrimps and prawns, chiefly by trawls, round the coasts of England and Wales. The catch of three small third-class Scottish trawlers working for that period in the Solway Firth was worth £3571, and if the earnings of the English boats were proportionate the total value of their catch must have been very considerable. And we have further to consider the great army of shrimpers working by means of various kinds of hand-net (fig. 1219), or dragging similar contrivances along by means of carts.

Fig. 1219.—Shrimper working a Push-Net

The Fresh-Water Crayfish (*Astacus fluviatilis*).—This inhabitant of many of our rivers and canals, which resembles a small lobster in appearance, is of no great economic importance to this country, although of decidedly delicate flavour. On the Continent, however, an allied but larger species (*A. nobilis*) is much eaten.

CHAPTER LXIX

ANIMAL FRIENDS—WILD ANIMALS CAPTURED FOR VARIOUS ECONOMIC PURPOSES—BENEFICIALS

The present section has mainly been concerned with the animal kingdom as a source of food, although in dealing with domesticated forms it has been found convenient to mention commodities of other kinds, such as wool.

We now have to deal with economic products other than food, for the sake of which wild animals of various kinds are captured. Prominent among these desiderata are furs, skins, fats, and oils, besides which there are a great number of less important articles of commerce, such as sponges and medicinal substances, that call for passing notice. Animal products employed entirely or mainly for decorative purposes will be reserved for treatment under Animal Æsthetics.

FUR-BEARING MAMMALS (MAMMALIA)

Although in temperate regions, as we have seen (p. 228), woven clothes have replaced for ordinary purposes the garments of skin and fur devised by prehistoric races, this by no means applies to the colder parts of the world, where ordinary clothing does not afford sufficient protection from the rigorous climate. The nomad tribes of the Russian steppes, for example, make large use of such garments, and the heathen Ostiaks of North Siberia do so to a still greater extent (fig. 1220). Of the latter Brehm says (in *North Pole to Equator*) that ". . . they use nothing but the skin of the reindeer for clothing, and only employ the furs of other animals for the occasional decoration of the reindeer, or, as the Russians call them, stag skins. Their dress consists of a close-fitting skin coat reaching to the knee; in the men it is slit down the breast, in the women it is open down the whole front, but held together with leather thongs; a hood of the same material is usually attached to or forms part of the dress; mittens also are sewn on; leather breeches reach below the knee; and leather stockings, which fasten over the knee, complete the attire. The fur garment worn by the women is edged down the sides of the

Fig. 1220.—Heathen Ostiaks

opening with a carefully-pieced border of variously-coloured little squares of short-haired fur, and always has a broad band of dog-skin round the foot; that worn by the men has at most a border of dog-skin round the foot; the leather stockings, if they are decorated at all, are composed of many prettily-combined, diversely-coloured stripes of skin from the leg of a reindeer, with a stout shoe partly sewn on, partly laced over the foot." The Esquimaux dress is spoken of elsewhere (see p. 227).

That we ourselves have not altogether abandoned the dress-materials of our remote prehistoric ancestors is sufficiently attested by the fact that in 1902 over 97,000,000 skins and furs, worth £5,578,452, were imported into this country, though of course only a part of these were destined for personal wear.

The list of fur-bearing Mammals is a very long one, but the most important orders in this connection are the Flesh-Eaters (Carnivora) and the Gnawers (Rodentia), and the purpose of the present section will be sufficiently attained by dealing with a few species belonging to these. It may be noted that we look to the colder parts of the world, especially Canada and Russia, for our chief supply, for the growth of a dense under-coat of fur is an adaptation to rigorous climatal conditions. And it is the pelts obtained in winter that are valuable. In 1902 Canada exported furs to the value of £98,000.

FUR-YIELDING FLESH-EATERS (CARNIVORA).—Some of the most important furs of commerce are derived from the members of the Weasel and Marten Family (Mustelidæ). Pre-eminent among these is the Russian Sable (*Mustela zibellina*), which formerly abounded throughout the forest regions of Siberia, but is now mostly to be found in the eastern part of that country, including Kamschatka, where the seaport of Petropavlosk is an important depôt for the pelts. A single skin may be worth as much as £30 in this country. The chief method of hunting is by means of dogs, which force the sables to take refuge in trees, from which they are shaken or knocked down into suitably disposed nets. The closely allied American Sable (*M. Americana*), largely trapped in Canada, is also of considerable importance.

The white skins (with black tails) known as "ermine", which custom leads us to associate with the "great ones of the earth", are no other than the winter coats of the Stoat (*Putorius erminea*), one of our native "vermin". It is widely distributed through the arctic and temperate regions of both Old and New Worlds, but only assumes full winter livery in the colder parts of its area of distribution.

The *Minks* or *Visons* are comparatively large aquatic animals of the weasel kind, with brown fur. The pelts of the American Mink (*Putorius vison*) are most esteemed, and are of importance in the Canadian fur-trade. Those of the Russian Mink (*P. lutreola*) are less valuable.

Passing over Bears, Foxes, Leopards, &c., mention must be made of Sea-Otters and Fur-Seals, of which the latter in particular are of great economic importance.

The *Sea-Otter* (*Latax lutris*), native to the coastal waters of the North Pacific, has been so persistently hunted down that its numbers have rapidly diminished during the last twenty years, and it is probably doomed to speedy extinction. Spearing, clubbing,

Fig. 1221.—Northern Fur-Seals (*Otaria ursina*) on the Pribyloffs

and netting are the chief modes of capture. The fur of the adult is very dense, and of a beautiful dark colour. Owing to their rarity skins are now of great value, a single one being worth at least £100, or, in exceptional cases, double that amount or even still more.

Certain species of *Sea-Lions* or *Eared Seals* (Otaridæ) are the "fur seals" of commerce, which furnish the valuable skins with which most of us are familiar. Some of them are native to the Southern seas, but the most notable kind is the *Northern Fur-Seal* (*Otaria ursina*, figs. 1221 and 1222), or Sea-Bear of the Pacific. The Pribyloff Islands of the Behring Sea have long been famous as one of the most important centres of the industry to which this

THE SABLE (*Mustela zibellina*)

This small carnivore, a near relative of our native Pine-Marten, is one of the most valuable of fur-yielding animals. It formerly ranged across the northern parts of Asia, from the Urals to the Behring Sea, but has been so persistently hunted down that it is now chiefly found in the forests of eastern Siberia and Kamschatka, Petropavlovsk on the coast of the latter being the chief depôt for sable-skins. It is only the thick winter-fur that is valuable, and a good pelt may be worth as much as £30.

Sables were formerly caught for the most part by trapping, and sometimes guns were resorted to, though with great risk of injury to the skins. At the present time they are usually hunted down with dogs, and forced to take refuge in trees, from which they are shaken or knocked down into suitably disposed nets.

THE RUSSIAN SABLE (MUSTELA ZIBELLINA), THE KING OF THE MARTENS species gives rise. As elsewhere briefly described (vol. iii, p. 492), large numbers of the fur-seals repair to these islands during the summer for the purpose of bringing up their young. It is the young "bachelor" males, or "holluschickie", that are not strong enough to secure establishments, which are slaughtered for the sake of their skins. These are carefully driven to inland "killing grounds", knocked on the head, and flayed as quickly as possible. Very full details of the industry are given by H. W. Elliot in his well-known book *An Arctic Province*, from which the following extract is taken:—"The common or popular notion in regard to seal-skins is, that they are worn by those animals just as they appear when offered for sale; that the fur-seal swims about, exposing the same soft coat with which our ladies of fashion so delight to cover their tender forms during inclement winter. This is a very great mistake; few skins are less attractive than a seal-skin is when it is taken from the creature. The fur is not visible; it is concealed entirely by a coat of stiff over-hair, dull, gray-brown, and grizzled. It takes three of them to make a lady's sack and boa; and in order that a reason for their costliness may be apparent, I take great pleasure in submitting a description of the tedious and skilful labour necessary to their dressing by the furriers ere they are fit for use. A leading manufacturer writing to me says: 'When the skins are received by us in the salt, we wash off the salt, placing them upon a beam somewhat like a tanner's beam, removing the fat from the flesh side with a beaming-knife, care being required that no cuts or uneven places are made in the pelt. The skins are next washed in water and placed upon the beam with the fur up, and the grease and water removed by the knife. The skins are then dried by moderate heat, being tacked out on frames to keep them smooth. After being fully dried, they are soaked in water and thoroughly cleansed with soap and water. In some cases they can be unhaired without this drying process and cleansed before drying. After the cleansing process they pass

Fig. 1222.—Northern Fur-Seals

to the picker, who dries the fur by stove-heat, the pelt being kept moist. When the fur is dry he places the skin on a beam, and while it is warm he removes the main coat of hair with a dull shoe-knife, grasping the hair with his thumb and knife, the thumb being protected by a rubber cob. The hair must be pulled out, not broken. After a portion is removed the skin must be again warmed at the stove, the pelt being kept moist. When the outer hairs have been mostly removed, he uses a beaming-knife to work out the fine hairs (which are shorter), and the remaining coarser hairs. It will be seen that great care must be used, as the skin is in that soft state that too much pressure of the knife would take the fur also; indeed, bare spots are made. Carelessly-cured skins are sometimes worthless on this account. The skins are next dried, afterwards dampened on the pelt side, and shaved to a fine, even surface. They are then stretched, worked, and dried, afterwards softened in a fulling-mill, or by treading them with the bare feet in a hogshead, one head being removed and the cask placed nearly upright, into which the workman gets with a few skins and some fine hardwood saw-dust, to absorb the grease while he dances upon them to break them into leather. If the skins have been shaved thin, as required when finished, any defective spots or holes must now be mended, the skin smoothed and pasted with paper on the pelt side, or two pasted together to protect the pelt in drying. The usual process in the United States is to leave the pelt sufficiently thick to protect them without pasting. In dyeing, the liquid dye is put on with a brush, carefully covering the points of the standing fur. After lying folded, with the points touching each other, for some time, the skins are hung up and dried. The dry dye is then removed, and so on, until the required shade is obtained. One or two of these coats of dye are put on much heavier and pressed down to the roots of the fur, making what is called the ground. From eight to twelve coats are required to produce a good colour. The skins are then washed clean, the fur dried, the pelt moist. They are shaved down to the required thickness, dried, working them some time while drying, then softened in a hogshead, and sometimes run in a revolving cylinder with fine saw-dust to clean them. The English process does not have the washing after dyeing.'"

Fur-Seals are also hunted in the open sea, at times when the herds are migrating. The United States endeavoured to put an end to this "pelagic" sealing in the Behring Sea on the part of other nations, but the matter being submitted to arbitration, it was decided that, subject to certain restrictions, the practice should be allowed to continue. The yield of the fur-seal industry of British Columbia in 1900 was 35,523 skins (value $562,845), and in 1901 24,422 skins (value $366,330).

FUR-YIELDING GNAWERS (RODENTIA).—Beaver, Chinchilla, Musquash, Squirrel, and Rabbit are here of greatest importance.

Fig. 1223.—Musquash (*Fiber zibethicus*)

The Beaver (*Castor*).—The American Beaver (*Castor Canadensis*) is largely trapped in Canada for the sake of its fur, which is greatly esteemed, though no longer used in the manufacture of top-hats, silk having proved both cheaper and better for the purpose. The animal has been slaughtered in so wholesale a manner that beaver-fur is becoming increasingly rare and expensive.

The European Beaver (*C. fiber*), once abundant, is now too scarce to be of economic value. Regarding the value attached to the skins of those which existed in Wales down to 1188, Beddard (in *The Cambridge Natural History*), after stating that the species was extinct in England before the historic period, remarks: " . . . they were rare in the Principality for a hundred years or so before the Norman Conquest. The king Hywel Dda, who died in 948 A.D., fixed the price of a Beaver skin at 120 pence, the skins of Stag, Wolf, and Fox being worth only 8 pence apiece."

The Musquash (*Fiber zibethicus*, fig. 1223).—This is a large North American vole, which is of considerable importance to the Canadian fur-trade, chiefly, it would seem, because it is made into imitation seal-skin.

The Chinchilla (*Chinchilla lanigera*).—The cold climate to which the soft gray fur of this pretty little rodent is an adaptation, is here a result not of latitude but of altitude. Chinchillas live in the high Andes of Peru and Bolivia, and are something like squirrels in appearance, except that the tail is far less bushy (see vol. i, p. 134).

The Common Squirrel (*Sciurus vulgaris*).—This species has a remarkably wide distribution, ranging from Ireland to Japan, and also being native to North Africa. It is the chief source of "squirrel" fur, which is of grey or drab colour, quite unlike the reddish-brown of our ordinary native specimens. The skins of commerce are, in fact, taken from individuals inhabiting the colder parts of Russia, the grey hue being, as in many other cases, an adaptation to the severe climate of winter.

The Rabbit (*Lepus cuniculus*).—Among the cheaper kinds of fur that of the rabbit is best known, and by means of dyeing and other processes it is worked up into passable imitations of more costly pelts.

SKINS AND DOWN OF WILD BIRDS (AVES)

Deferring for the present the question of the wild birds which are subjected to wholesale butchery on account of their beautiful plumage, mention may here be made of Grebes and Eider-Ducks.

Grebes (species of *Podicipes*).—These widely-distributed aquatic birds are distinguished by the density and beautiful silver-white colour of the plumage on the under side of the body. Muffs and other articles made of "grebe" are manufactured from the skin of this region, with the feathers attached as in nature.

Eider-Ducks (*Somateria*, fig. 1224).—Two species of these essentially Arctic birds are of commercial importance on account of the valuable down developed on the nest as a climatal adaptation. The Common Eider (*Somateria mollissima*), which has a wide range, and is included in the British avifauna, is carefully preserved in Iceland and Norway. In Labrador and Greenland it is replaced by an allied species (*S. Dresseri*).

The Scandinavian eider-industry is based on the fact that the female bird lines and covers her nest with down plucked from her own breast (see p. 60). The breeding-places are on low ground near the coast, or upon rocky islets, and each "eder-fold" (*i.e.* eider-fold) is worked for profit by a special proprietor. Both eggs and down are collected at regular intervals during the nesting-season, but the amount obtainable from a particular nest

Fig. 1224.—Eider-Drake (*Somateria mollissima*)

is, of course, limited, and care is taken to allow the despoiled mother-birds to hatch out some at least of the final batch of eggs. The last lot of down is collected when the nests have been deserted for the season. About three-quarters of the Danish supply is derived from Greenland. Newton (in *A Dictionary of Birds*) thus disposes of two popular errors regarding these birds:—"The story of the drakes furnishing down after the duck's supply is exhausted is a fiction. He never goes near the nest. . . . Equally fictitious is the often-repeated statement that eider-down is white. Mouse-colour would perhaps best describe its hue."

WILD ANIMALS YIELDING LEATHER, HORN, FAT, ETC.

It has been considered desirable in this book to deal with domesticated animals in a special section, but the plan (like any other) has certain disadvantages, especially when treating of economic products. Leather, horn, fat, &c. &c., are, of course, derived from both tame and wild animals, and this must be kept in mind here. The importance of leather and horn will be realized by reading the following extracts from Simmonds (in *Animal Products*):—"The leather manufacture is one of our most ancient and important industries. . . . The old adage that there is nothing like leather is certainly verified in the multifarious uses to which leather has been or is now put. We make coverings of it in articles of personal use, for a man may be clothed in leather garments from the head to the foot. In saddlery and harness its use is universal, and nothing can supplant it for durability. In articles for household or domestic use, we have leather hangings and coverings for furniture, buckets and bottles, cups and hose. . . . For travelling we have portmanteaus, valises, and hand-bags, pocket-books, purses, and cigar-cases. . . . We write on leather, and we cover our books with it, and it has even been used by photographers to take likenesses on. It is the packing and baling material in many countries from its cheapness and durability. Hammocks, boats, and even cannon have been made of it, whilst the leather apron is the most durable and serviceable protection for many an artisan. Leather shields were and are still in use in many countries. It serves for the grip-handle of swords, and for the sheaths of knives. We use leather in balls for cricket and football, and we cover musical instruments with it, as well as telescopes and many philosophical instruments, for protection. It is the most ancient, useful, and generally applied animal substance for an infinite variety of purposes. And, moreover, leather can be made of the skin or hide of almost every quadruped, and of many fishes, serpents, and reptiles. Human skin has even been tanned, but it is too thin for any serviceable use." In the following remarks about horn it will be remembered that the antlers of deer are of bony nature:—"The rights and privileges of the 'horn-workers' and 'horn-pressers' in former times occupied the prominent attention of the Legislature. But there is no fear in the present day 'of the trade being ruined, and the business lost to the nation', as was the cry when the statutes 6 Edward IV, c. 1, and 7 James I, c. 14 were passed, forbidding the sale of horns to foreigners, and prohibiting the export of our wrought horns. The invention of horn lanterns has been by some ascribed to King Alfred, who is said to have first used them to preserve his candle time-measurers from the wind. . . . A lantern [was formerly] an indispensable family article; there was no going into the yard or out of the door on dark nights without one. A piece of horn was sometimes placed over the title of mediæval MSS. to preserve the letters from injury, while the transparent material allowed them to be read. The child's horn-book of later times had its leaves of alphabet and spelling covered entirely with thin sheets of this material. Although the principal manufacturing applications of horn are for combs, umbrella-tops, and knife-handles, yet there are other uses as extensive and varied as the descriptions of horn which come into the market, or bristle on the head of the animals characterized by these frontal appendages. Ox, buffalo, and deer horns are those mostly worked up, but the horns of the rhinoceros, ram, goat, and some other animals are also employed to a limited extent for different purposes. . . . While many of the former uses of horns for glazing purposes, for drinking-cups, for horn-books, and for the bugle of the bold forester have passed away, other and more elegant and varied applications have been found for this plastic and durable substance. Extensive as is the present use of horns, we believe that many further manufacturing purposes may be found for them, and that they will become even still more important in a commercial point of view. They receive a great variety of applications at the present day, owing to their toughness and elasticity, as well as their remarkable property of softening under heat, of welding, and of being moulded into various forms under pressure." It may be added that for many purposes both leather and horn are now replaced by cheap substitutes.

As most of the horns used on a large scale for manufacturing purposes are those of oxen, it will suffice to devote the rest of this sub-section to the consideration of certain wild animals captured chiefly for the sake of the leather and fat which they yield.

THE WALRUS (TRICHECHUS ROSMARUS).—This huge aquatic carnivore, which may attain the weight of 3300 lbs., is a purely Arctic form, and once abounded in the Behring Sea, the Gulf of St. Lawrence, and on the coasts of Newfoundland and Labrador. Like so many other wild animals, however, it has been so much hunted down that the walrus industry is a declining one. Rifle, lance, and harpoon are all employed in its destruction. The economic products are skin, fat, and ivory. The skin is very thick and tough, but tanning reduces its value. It is employed for some of the coarser purposes to which leather is put, and in former times was largely used in North Europe for making ropes and cables, to which end strips of it were plaited together. The fat or blubber, though of good quality, is yielded in relatively small quantities. The ivory making up the large tusks is inferior to that of the elephant.

SEALS (PHOCIDÆ).—These are often confounded with the Fur-Seals (Otaridæ) and their allies, from which, however, they are distinguished by their more complete adaptation to an aquatic life, as seen more particularly in the complete absence of an external ear, and the backwardly-directed hind-flippers, which are bound together by a fold of skin (see vol. iii, p. 78).

Seals are hunted for the sake of their blubber, which makes excellent oil for lighting and lubricating purposes; and also on account of the value of their skins, which are dressed as one of the coarser furs; while they yield leather that, especially when enamelled, finds increasing favour. The animals are killed by clubs, harpoons, or rifles, according to circumstances. By far the most important species for the sealing industry is the Harp or Greenland Seal (*Phoca Grœnlandica*, fig. 1225), the former name of which has reference to the presence of a curved black mark on the back of the male. Next to this species in importance, and like it native to the Arctic Ocean, is the curious Hooded or Bladder-Nosed Seal (*Cystophora cristata*), so named from a dilatable swelling on the nose of the male. The most noted sealing centres are the coasts of, and the parts of the sea adjacent to West Greenland, Newfoundland, Jan Mayen Island, and North Russia (including the White Sea and the vicinity of Nova Zembla). From the British stand-point it is most interesting to notice that sealing is one of the chief industries of Newfoundland, its products in 1902 reaching the value of £166,747. The young are born on ice-floes, the "whelping ice", off the coast of Labrador, during January and February, and do not take to the water for about three months. The cold Labrador current, which sets southward along the American coast, brings the "whelping ice" to the latitude of Newfoundland by about mid-March, and the well-equipped steam-sealers of St. John's begin their annual sealing-trip at the commencement of that month, timing their journey to reach the floes before the "whelps" are old enough to leave the ice.

Lake Baikal and the Caspian Sea were once connected with the Arctic Ocean, one proof of which is found in the fact that each is inhabited by a special kind of seal (*Phoca Sibirica* and *P. Caspica*), both of which are largely captured by means of

Fig. 1225.—Harp or Greenland Seal (*Phoca Grœnlandica*)

strong wide-meshed nets, worked on the same principle as the "drift-nets" used for catching herring and mackerel. The Caspian sealers let down their nets from boats, those of Lake Baikal take advantage of the holes in the ice, to which the seals come up in order to breathe.

THE DUGONG (HALICORE DUGONG).—This member of the order of Sea-Cows (Sirenia), which ranges from Ceylon to East Australia, is, when adult, about the size of an ox, and is captured for the sake of its flesh, fat, and hide. Its pursuit is one of the Queensland industries, and harpooning is the method adopted. Semon (in *In the Australian Bush*) says of it:—

"The whites capture dugong principally for their fat, which is said to possess therapeutic qualities. It is considered an excellent remedy for consumption, but, happily for the dugongs, this seems to be a mere superstition. I have not tasted their meat myself, though some whites are very fond of it, and compare it to veal. Others, however, describe its taste as disagreeable and insipid. The aborigines of Torres Straits consider it a great delicacy." The hide is thick and tough, rendering it suitable for machine-straps.

WHALES, &c. (CETACEA).—Whales and their kind have been systematically hunted down from very remote times, chiefly for the sake of their fat or blubber, but some species also for their baleen or "whale-bone", and others on account of the value of their skins. As elsewhere stated (p. 209), the flesh of cetaceans is regarded as a great luxury by the Esquimaux and many other primitive peoples. A distinction is drawn between the Toothed Whales and the Toothless Whales, in which transverse plates of baleen, with fringed edges, hang down from the roof of the mouth (fig. 1226), serving as a sort of strainer by which water is removed from the plankton used as food.

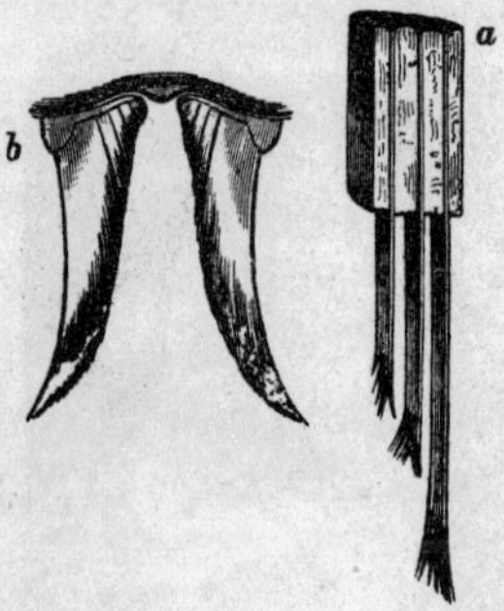

Fig. 1226.—Baleen. *a*, Three plates in section; *b*, a pair of plates. Greatly reduced.

Toothless Whales (*Mystacoceti*).—The most important member of this group is the Greenland or Northern "Right" Whale (*Balæna mysticetus*), a purely Arctic species. The British whaling industry, of which the chief ports engaged are Peterhead and Dundee, is chiefly concerned with the capture of this animal, but unfortunately has greatly declined of late years. To Newfoundland the pursuit of whales is a matter of much greater relative importance.

The old method of capture was from open boats, by means of harpoons thrown by hand, lances being afterwards used to despatch the wounded animals. The harpoon-gun afforded an improvement upon this, while a modern steam-whaler can dispense with the use of open boats, and discharge harpoons (sometimes loaded with explosives) from a platform in the bows.

Adult Greenland whales now attain a length of 50 or 60 feet, but much larger specimens were often captured in the palmy days of the whaling industry. The average product from a single animal is said to be about 15 tons of oil and 15 cwts. of whalebone. The former, like that of seals, is valuable as a lubricant and for other technical purposes, but the discovery of petroleum has greatly lessened the value of this and other animal fats as a source of artificial heat and light. Whalebone is becoming increasingly expensive in proportion to the diminishing supplies, and is still in great demand for a number of purposes, owing to its toughness, durability, and elasticity. It is now largely replaced by steel, as, *e.g.*, for umbrella-frames and corsets.

The Southern "Right" Whale (*B. australis*), which closely resembles the Greenland form, though its baleen is not of such good quality, has a very wide area of distribution, but is absent from the Arctic Ocean. The chief interest attaching to it is that at one time it was common in the Bay of Biscay, where it formed the object of an important industry, especially to the Basques of North Spain. Some points relating to this are thus summarized by Beddard (in *The Cambridge Natural History*):—"Among the small towns which fringe the bay it is very common to find the whale incorporated in the armorial bearings. 'Over the portal of the first old house in the steep street of Guetaria', writes Sir Clements Markham (*P. Z. S.*, 1881), 'there is a shield of arms consisting of whales amid waves of the sea. At Motrico the town arms consist of a whale in the sea harpooned, and with a boat with men holding the line.' Plenty of other such examples testify to the prevalence of the whaling industry on these adjoining coasts of Spain and France. It appears that though the fishery began much earlier—even in the ninth century—the first actual document relating to it dates from the year 1150. It is in the shape of privileges granted by Sancho the Wise to the city of San Sebastian. The trade was still very flourishing in the sixteenth century. Rondeletius the naturalist described Bayonne as the centre of the trade, and tells us that the flesh, especially of the tongue, was exposed for sale as food in the markets. M. Fischer (*Actes Linn. Soc. Bordeaux*, 1881), who, as well as Sir Clements Markham, has given an important account of the whaling industry on the Basque shores, quotes an account of the methods pursued in the sixteenth century. It was at Biarritz

—or as Ambroise Pare, from whom Fischer quotes, spelt it, Biaris—that the main fisheries were undertaken. . . . The inhabitants set upon a hill a tower from which they could see 'the balaines which pass, and perceiving them coming partly by the loud noise they make, and partly by the water which they throw out by a conduit which they possess in the middle of the forehead.' Several boats then set out in pursuit, some of which were reserved for men whose sole duty it was to pick out of the water their comrades who had overbalanced themselves in their excitement. The harpoons bore a mark by which their respective owners could recognize them, and the carcass of the animal was shared in accordance with the numbers and owners of the harpoons found sticking in the dead body of the whale. At this period the fishery was at its height, but it continued to be an occupation along those shores until the beginning of the eighteenth century, after which it gradually declined. The fishery of whales began to be carried farther afield than the shore, and for a long time the Basques furnished expert harpooners to whaling vessels proceeding to the Arctic seas."

Toothed Whales (*Odontoceti*).—The largest of these is the Cachalot or Sperm Whale (*Physeter macrocephalus*, fig. 1227), which has been credited with reaching a length of over 80 feet, though this is probably an exaggeration. It ranges throughout the warmer seas of the world. The great head possesses a squarish snout that projects in front of the mouth, which is consequently placed on the under side of the body, obliging the Cachalot, it is said, to turn over like a shark when it wishes to bite. Many stories are current regarding the fierceness of this animal, and no doubt many whale-boats have been crushed in its formidable jaws, but that whaling and other vessels have at times been reported "missing" as a result of the attacks of Cachalots, as has been suggested, would appear to be more problematical. Like other cetaceans, this whale has a thick coat of blubber under the skin, and the front part of the skull is modified into a curious basin-shaped receptacle, which is full of the liquid fat known as spermaceti. As much as forty-five barrels of this have been taken from a single individual. Mixed with a small percentage of bees'-wax it was formerly much used in manufacturing candles of the better sort.

The White Whale or Beluga (*Delphinapterus leucas*) is an

Arctic species related to the Dolphins and Porpoises. The average length of adults is about 10 feet, but this may be considerably exceeded. It is chiefly hunted on the north of Russia and north-east of Canada, and is one of those cetaceans which ascend rivers. The blubber is of good quality, and the skin is made into the "porpoise leather" of commerce, which is of considerable value for the manufacture of shooting-boots and some other articles.

Fig. 1227.—Cachalot or Sperm Whale (*Physeter macrocephalus*)

REPTILES (REPTILIA).—It need only be said here that ornamental leather is made from the skins of Crocodiles and various Lizards, while "tortoise-shell" is obtained from certain Turtles. Of the last something will be said in a succeeding section.

FISHES (PISCES).—The skins of various members of this group are of economic value. Those of certain sharks and dog-fishes, for instance, are the source of "shagreen", used to some extent as ornamental leather, but chiefly for polishing wood. Their value for the latter purpose depends upon the fact that they are full of little hard-pointed scales, covered with enamel. The skins of some of the ordinary bony fishes (Teleostei) are employed for clarifying beer, while in Eastern countries, such as India and China, they are converted into fish-glue, which is a very powerful adhesive.

Other fishes serve as a source of oil for technical purposes, as, *e.g.*, the Menhaden or Pogy (*Clupea menhaden*), a member of the herring family. This species is largely captured on the eastern coasts of the United States for this particular purpose. The livers of sharks and dog-fishes are also of considerable value as a source of oil.

INSECTS (INSECTA).—One would scarcely expect this group to be included under the present heading, but it appears that in Algeria locusts are utilized in the preparation of a kind of oil.

MEDICINAL AND MISCELLANEOUS ECONOMIC PRODUCTS

ANIMALS AND ANIMAL PRODUCTS AS MEDICINAL AGENTS.—In former days large use was made of animals in medicine, the prescriptions being usually fanciful and often revolting. To consider these ancient practices at length would be here superfluous, and the subject will be sufficiently illustrated by the following quotation from Hulme's *Natural History Lore and Legend*, a book in which much curious matter is brought together:—"Cogan in his *Haven of Health* declares 'thus much will I say as to the commendation of the hare, and of the defense of hunters' toyle, that no beast, be it never so great, is profitable to so many and so diverse uses in Physicke as the hare', and he then proceeds to give numerous prescriptions in which it is the principal feature. 'The knee-bone of an Hare taken out alive and worne abute the necke is excellent against Convulsion fitts', we are told, and perhaps it may be so, but the point that more especially strikes us, and it impresses one over and over again in these mediæval recipes, is the cold-blooded cruelty and indifference to animal suffering that is shown in so many of them. Fried mice were considered a specific in small-pox, but it was necessary that they should be fried alive; while for cataract a fox should be captured, his tongue cut out, and the animal released; the member thus barbarously procured was placed in a bag of red cloth and hung round the man's neck. For erysipelas a favourite old remedy was to cut off one-half of the ear of a cat and let the blood drop on the part affected, while for fits one popular recipe was to take a mole alive, cut the tip of his nose off, and let nine drops of the blood fall on to a drop of sugar: the swallowing of this was held to be a certain cure."

"The shrew-mouse, one of the most inoffensive of creatures, was by our ancestors held to be of terribly poisonous nature. Its bite was thought to be most venomous, and even contact with it in any way was accounted extremely dangerous. Cattle and horses seized with any malady that appeared to cause any numbness of the legs were at once reputed shrew-struck. 'It is a ravening beast,' quoth Topsell, 'feigning itself gentle and tame, but being touched it biteth deep and poysoneth deadly. It beareth a cruel minde, desiring to hunt anything, neither is there any creature that it loveth.' On whatever limb it crept was 'cruel anguish', often ending in paralysis. These calumnies have prevailed in many countries and for many ages, the Romans being as firmly convinced of the deadly nature of the shrew-mouse as any British rustic of a century ago. . . . Happily there was a certain antidote against the evil wrought by this malevolent beast. A large ash-tree being chosen, a deep hole was made in its trunk, and after certain incantations were made a shrew-mouse was thrust alive into the opening, and the hole securely plugged. 'A shrew-ash', says Gilbert White in his *Natural History of Selborne*, 'is an ash whose twigs or branches, when gently applied to the limbs of cattle, will immediately relieve the pain which a beast suffers from the running of a shrew-mouse over the part affected. Against this accident, to which they were continually liable, our provident forefathers always kept a shrew-ash at hand, which when once medicated would maintain its virtue for ever.' One of these shrew-ashes, now but a fragment of what was evidently once a massive stately tree, may still be seen (1895) near the Sheen Gate in Richmond Park, and there are those still living who can remember cattle and horses being brought to it for its healing virtues."

"To cure a stye our forefathers had great faith in rubbing it with hairs from a cat's tail, two essential points being that the cat should be a black one, and that the operation should take place on the first night of the new moon; but to cure warts the hairs must be taken from the tail of a tortoise-shell cat, and even then the remedy is only efficacious during the month of May."

"Toads were in great repute in sickness. 'In time of common contagion,' writes Sir Kenelm Digby in 1660, 'men used to carry about with them the powder of a toad, and sometimes a living toad or spider shut up in a box, which draws the contagious air which otherwise would infect the party'; and many other illustrations of their employment as preventive or remedies might be given. The spider and the toad seem to have been each regarded as most venomous creatures, and in many of the old remedies one or other of them at will are recommended, either alternative being regarded as equally efficacious; thus for whooping-cough, if one cannot find a toad to thrust up the chimney, two spiders in a walnut-shell will serve equally well."

The physicians of former times were particularly fond of administering all sorts of animal extracts, some of them noisome enough, and it is somewhat curious that of recent times large use has been made of certain such extracts with beneficial result, though it need hardly be said that our modern methods of preparation are not on the old lines. Pepsin, for instance, a well-known aid to gastric digestion, is prepared from the lining of the pig's stomach, while pancreatin, which facilitates intestinal digestion, is obtained from the pancreas of domestic animals. Disease of the thyroid "gland" in the throat leads to serious mal-nutrition, or even to cretinism, palliation if not cure of which can be effected either by grafting a healthy piece of thyroid from an animal into the patient, or by administering thyroid extract. Several other preparations of the kind are also in use. Certain specific germ-diseases can also be prevented or combated by animal preparations, the most familiar instance being that of vaccination as a safeguard against small-pox. Diphtheria is now often cured by an extract (antitoxin) derived from horse's blood. Different principles are involved in the uses of the extracts, &c., mentioned, but details would here be out of place.

Various kinds of animal fat are used in pharmacy in the preparation of ointments, &c. They include mutton suet, hogs' lard, spermaceti, and lanoline, the last being the natural grease of wool. Gelatine is employed for making "gelatine lozenges" and various jujubes, also as the adhesive medium for "court plaster". It is obtained from bones, hides, horns, and hoofs by steaming. Isinglass (see p. 278) is a superior kind of gelatine.

It should not be forgotten that the careful study of the anatomy and physiology of lower animals has played a leading

VARIETIES OF THE FIELD-SNAIL (*Helix hortensis*)

Variation is one of the fundamental phenomena upon which the Evolution Theory is based. No two individuals of the same species are ever precisely alike, a fact familiarly illustrated by the dissimilarity which often exists between children of the same parents. It appears that all parts of the body are liable to variation, which may be of very marked kind and is no doubt, at least in part, due to the action of surroundings. A typical case, selected for this plate because it appeals to the eye, is that of the Field-Snail (*Helix hortensis*), of which some 90 races or varieties have been described. In some of these the shell is "self-coloured", yellow or pinkish-brown being common tints. In other cases there are in addition dark bands, the number of which is distinctive of the race, while the ground colour has also to be considered. Enough varieties have been introduced into the plate to illustrate the principle.

VARIETIES OF THE FIELD-SNAIL (HELIX HORTENSIS)

part in the evolution of modern medicine. Without skilled researches on such animals it would never have been possible for operative surgery to reach its present high pitch of perfection. The prevention and cure of disease, other than by surgical methods, have also benefited greatly in the past by such investigations, and seem likely to benefit to a much larger extent in the immediate future.

Medicinal Value of Fish-Oil.—It need only be said here that the preparation of cod-liver oil, of which the Cod-Fish (*Gadus morrhua*) is the recognized source, is a by no means unimportant industry.

Medical Uses of Insects.—The Oil-Beetles (*Meloidæ* or *Cantharidæ*) are so called because they abound in an irritant sort of oil, which no doubt protects them to some extent from the attacks of insectivorous animals. Some of them are used to make preparations for blistering the skin, and of these "blister-beetles" the most notable are the "Spanish flies" (*Cantharides*), belonging to South and Central Europe. For commercial purposes a bright-green species (*Lytta vesicatoria*, fig. 1228), collected in Hungary, is most important. Various officinal extracts and plasters are prepared from the dried bodies of these insects.

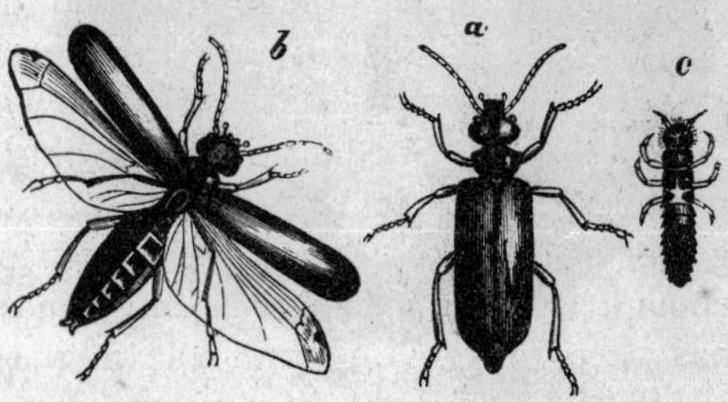

Fig. 1228.—Spanish Fly or Blister Beetle (*Lytta vesicatoria*) *a* and *b*, Adults; *c*, larva.

Although Cochineal, another insect product (see p. 260), appears to have no value as a drug, it is largely used to give liquid medicines an attractive appearance.

Medicinal Use of Leeches (*Discophora*).—Two kinds of Leech are used for blood-letting, the commoner being the Medicinal Leech (*Hirudo medicinalis*), which is mostly collected in Spain, France, and Italy. The Green Leech (*H. officinalis*) of Hungary answers the same purpose. In these days the extent to which these creatures are employed is comparatively small, but in the Middle Ages, when blood-letting was esteemed a sovereign cure for every ailment, the physician took his name from this favourite remedy, and was familiarly known as a "leech".

Miscellaneous Animal Products.—It will be convenient to consider here a few odds and ends, which are difficult to place under other headings.

Miscellaneous Products of Molluscs (*Mollusca*).—The internal shell of the Cuttle-fish (*Sepia officinalis*, fig. 1229), under the name of "cuttle-bone", is ground up to form an ingredient of various tooth-powders. Before the invention of blotting-paper it was largely used (as also was fine sand) to sprinkle upon wet writing. It was known as "pounce", and a "pounce-box", with a perforated top, was part of the regular equipment of an old-fashioned ink-stand or standish.

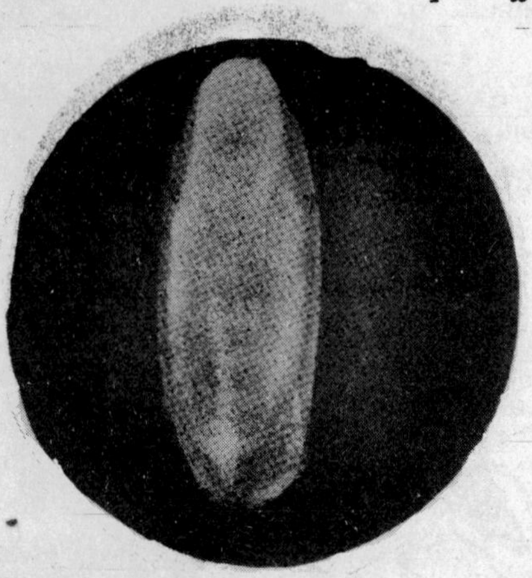

Fig. 1229.—A Cuttle-bone

Cooke (in *The Cambridge Natural History*) makes the following interesting remarks about the miscellaneous uses of shells:—"The employment of shells as a medium of exchange was exceedingly common amongst uncivilized tribes in all parts of the world, and has by no means yet become obsolete. One of the commonest species thus employed is the 'money cowry' (*Cypræa moneta*, L., fig. 1230), which stands almost alone in being used entire, while nearly all the other forms of shell money are made out of portions of shells, thus requiring a certain amount of labour in the process of formation. . . . In British India about 4000 are said to have passed for a shilling, but the value appears to differ according to their condition, poor specimens being comparatively worthless. According to Reeve a gentleman residing at Cuttack is said to have paid for the erection of his bungalow entirely in cowries. The building cost him 4000 Rs. sicca (about £400), and as 64 cowries = 1 pice, and 64 pice = 1 rupee sicca, he paid over

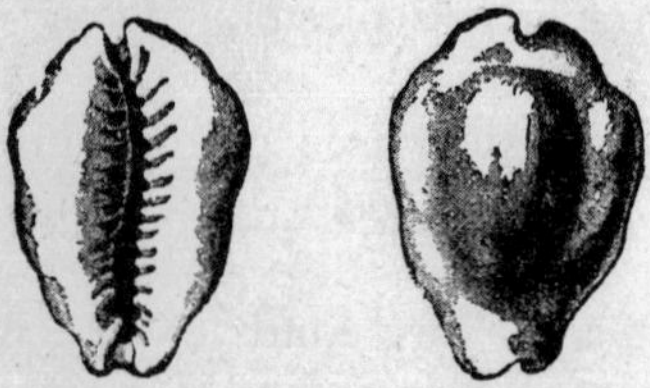

Fig. 1230.—Money Cowry (*Cypræa moneta*)

16,000,000 cowries in all. Cowries are imported to England from India and other places for the purpose of exportation to West Africa, to be exchanged for native products. The trade, however, appears to be greatly on the decrease. At the port of Lagos, in 1870, 50,000 cwts. of cowries were imported. A banded form of *Nerita polita* was used as money in certain parts of the South Pacific. The sandal-wood imported into the China market is largely obtained from the New Hebrides, being purchased of the natives in exchange for *Ovulum angulosum,* which they especially esteem as an ornament. Sometimes, as in the Duke of York group, the use of shell money is specially restricted to certain kinds of purchase, being employed there only in the buying of swine. Among the tribes of the north-west coasts of America, the common *Dentalium indianorum* [a tusk-shell] used to form the standard of value, until it was superseded, under the auspices of the Hudson's Bay Company, by blankets. A slave was valued at a fathom of from twenty-five to forty of these shells, strung lengthwise. Inferior or broken specimens were strung together in a similar way, but were less highly esteemed; they corresponded more to our silver and copper coins, while the strings of the best shells represented gold. The *wampum* (fig. 1231) of the eastern coast of North America differed from all these forms of shell money, in that it required a laborious process for its manufacture. Wampum consisted of strings of cylindrical beads, each about a quarter of an inch in length and half that breadth. The beads were of two colours, white and purple, the latter being the more valuable. Both were formed from the common clam (*Venus mercenaria*), the valves of which are often stained with purple at the lower margins, while the rest of the shell is white. Cut small, ground down, and pierced, these shells were converted into money, which appears to have been current along the whole seaboard of North America from Maine to Florida, and on the Gulf Coast as far as Central America, as well as among the

Fig. 1231.—Indian Wampum. Reduced.

inland tribes east of the Mississippi. Another kind of wampum was made from the shells of *Busycon carica* and *B. perversum*. By staining the wampum with various colours, and disposing these colours in belts in various forms of arrangement, the Indians were able to preserve records, send messages, and keep account of any kind of event, treaty, or transaction. Another common form of money in California was *Olivella biplicata*, strung together by rubbing down the apex. Button-shaped discs cut from *Saxidomus arata* and *Pachydesma crassatelloides*, as well as oblong pieces of *Haliotis*, were employed for the same purpose, when strung together in lengths of several yards."

Shells are put to various uses in the islands of the Pacific, as, *e.g.*, the making of fish-hooks, spoons, knives, and axe-heads. The ingenious Chinese convert the thin translucent shell of a flat bivalve (*Placuna placenta*) into window-panes, grind up cockle-shells for lime, or, by mixing the powder with oil, make a sort of putty.

Speaking of the West of Scotland, Anderson Smith (in *Benderloch*) thus describes an old-time practice:—"There is a curious old custom that used formerly to be in use in this locality, and no doubt was generally employed along the sea-board, as the most simple and ready means of arrangement of bargains by a non-writing population. That was, when a bargain was made, each party to the transaction got one half of a bivalve shell—such as a mussel, cockle, or oyster—and when the bargain was implemented, the half that fitted exactly was delivered up as a receipt. Thus a man who had a box full of unfitted shells might be either a creditor or a debtor; but the box filled with fitted shells represented receipted accounts. Those who know the difficulty of fitting the valves of some classes of bivalves will readily acknowledge the value of this arrangement."

Sponges (*Porifera*).—The horny skeletons of certain sponges have been used for toilet and other purposes since the times of the ancient Greeks. The best kind of Bath Sponge (*Euspongia officinalis*), known to commerce as "Turkey Sponge", comes from the Mediterranean and Red Sea, as well as the less esteemed Zimocca Sponge (*Euspongia zimocca*) and Horse Sponge (*Hippospongia equina*). Other kinds, both fine and coarse, are imported from the Bahamas, and sponges of commercial value are to be found off Australia and some of the South Sea Islands.

Three methods of sponge-fishing are practised in the Mediterranean, according to the depth of water. Where this is very shallow a five-pronged fork is employed, beyond the range of which (up to about 30 fathoms) diving is resorted to, while specimens growing in comparatively deep water (up to 200 fathoms) are dredged. The yield of the Italian sponge-fisheries for 1902 was worth £24,720.

WILD ANIMALS BENEFICIAL TO MAN ON ACCOUNT OF THEIR HABITS

From the economic stand-point many wild forms are of very considerable benefit to man, because they prey upon other creatures which are injurious to himself, his stock, and his crops. To some such animals we should extend the "protection" which they deserve at our hands, while for others equally beneficial (*e.g.* certain insects) we can do nothing in that direction. And it should be remembered that without very full knowledge it is very risky either to mercilessly persecute native forms, or to introduce species from other countries. The result of the ruthless slaughter of bats in a particular locality has been elsewhere mentioned (see vol. ii, p. 346), while the introduction of rabbits into Australia has led to unexpected and undesirable consequences.

Certain other wild species deserve the name of "beneficials" because they promote the health of mankind, or unconsciously assist in the work of agriculture, &c.

It will sufficiently serve the purposes of this work if the general nature of our indebtedness to certain groups of animals is indicated in a few paragraphs. For this and the other aspects of applied natural history readers who may be interested are specially recommended to consult Theobald's *First Report on Economic Zoology* (1902), one of the publications issued under the auspices of the British Museum (Natural History). This is rendered particularly valuable by the Introduction ("A Classification of Animals from the point of view of Economic Zoology") written by Ray Lankester. The word "beneficials" is applied by him in a somewhat narrower sense than it is here.

Beneficial Mammals (Mammalia).—The destructiveness of Foxes, Weasels, Stoats, and the like, is so obvious, that the idea of their being "beneficials" would be scouted by many, though they probably do more good than harm. The Fox, for instance, in spite of his ravages on poultry, destroys large numbers of field-voles and field-mice, together with noxious insects, such as cockchafers. And, of the Weasel (fig. 1232), Ritzema Bos says (in *Agricultural Zoology*):—"The weasel does some damage in fowl-houses and dove-cots, and is also destructive to game. This, however, does not outweigh its very great use, since it is above all an untiring vole-catcher. When in any region the field-voles have multiplied excessively, an immigration of weasels takes place from surrounding parts. In years when there is a plague of voles the usual breeding-time in spring is followed by another later on. A very large number of weasels may be found in a vole-infected district, and they thin out the mischievous rodents in a surprising manner. Nor are the weasels less useful in winter than in summer. They even follow under the snow the voles which winter in the country, and the slaughter effected at this period must exert a great influence on the following season, when these animals recommence their injurious work." The feelings of poultry-keepers and game-keepers are readily intelligible, but without full knowledge it is unwise to stigmatize as "vermin" apparently undesirable animals. Foxes only escape the libel for sporting reasons.

Fig. 1232.—Weasels (*Putorius vulgaris*)

The Insect-eating Mammals (Insectivora), such as Mole, Hedgehog, and Shrews, destroy enormous numbers of noxious insects and insect-larvæ, and are beneficials of the first rank. The mole is also of use in mixing and draining the soil. The vast majority of Bats (Chiroptera) feed on insects, and do much to keep down the numbers of the innumerable species which are injurious to stock and cultivated plants, as well as to forest-trees.

In the hotter parts of the globe some Mammals do useful work as scavengers, *e.g.* Hyænas (see vol. ii, p. 14). Rats and the like also act as sanitary agents.

Fig. 1233.—Barn Owl (*Strix flammea*) and Nest

BENEFICIAL BIRDS (AVES). — By destroying field-voles, &c., and small birds of injurious character, many of the smaller birds of prey, such as Kestrels, Buzzards, and Merlins, do much good, though it must be confessed that there is another side to the matter. Aflalo says of the Kestrel (in *Natural History of the British Isles*):—"Its food consists almost entirely of mice, so that its persecution is wanton folly". Even should it prove requisite to classify any of our native species, unfortunately now existing in greatly diminished numbers, as "vermin", they ought to be destroyed in a merciful way. Some of the steel traps used for slaughtering these and other wild animals (such as rabbits) are a disgrace to civilization, and only fit for the days of rack and thumb-screw.

Owls are more useful, but even more disliked than the diurnal birds of prey, partly as a result of the superstitions associated with them. Aflalo makes the following apposite remarks in this regard about the Barn Owl (*Strix flammea*, fig. 1233).—"Its disappearance from neighbourhoods where it once was plentiful is doubtless due to the short-sighted policy of persecution meted out to the unoffending bird by gamekeepers. As rats, shrews, and voles are among its favourite articles of food, a few of these voracious birds on an estate should be worth a ton of poison. . . . The way in which gardener, farmer, and game-preserver unite in persecuting this owl has been mentioned, and it is to be doubted whether they would achieve a far different result, were they actually to breed and turn down rats and voles, of which this bird must annually destroy hundreds of bushels."

A great many birds render us invaluable service by destroying vast numbers of injurious insects and insect-larvæ. The Cuckoo (*Cuculus canorus*), for example, is a great protector of fruit-culture and forestry, for it greedily devours certain hairy kinds of caterpillar, which most other birds refuse to touch. Among other benefactors may be particularly mentioned—Swifts, Swallows, Martins, and Tit-Mice. In Germany various useful species are provided with suitable nesting-boxes and wintering-boxes, the size of the opening being adjusted to the particular kind of bird.

The African Secretary Bird (*Serpentarius secretarius*) is a notable destroyer of poisonous snakes, and is domesticated by the farmers of South Africa for the sake of its services in this direction.

There are also scavenging birds, such as Vultures, which in hot countries discharge a most useful office.

Beneficial Reptiles (Reptilia).—Lizards are certainly to be regarded as beneficials, for they feed largely upon injurious insects and the like. Many Snakes are also useful, and some of them render conspicuous service by preying upon small rodents. Some species may even be domesticated on this account, as, *e.g.*, the Corn Snake (*Coluber guttatus*) in North America, and the Rat Snake (*Zamenis mucosus*) in India.

Beneficial Amphibians (Amphibia).—All the members of the class are beneficial, inasmuch as they live upon insects, snails, slugs, and other destructive creatures. Ritzema Bos states that . . . . "in the research garden attached to the Rouen entomological laboratory the snails were entirely exterminated in 1891, as a result of introducing a hundred toads and ninety frogs". The Toad in particular is one of the most useful animals that can be put into a garden, effectually protecting strawberries from the ravages of slugs and performing other valuable offices of like nature.

Beneficial Fishes (Pisces).—Much of the scavenging work in the sea and fresh water is efficiently discharged by members of this class. Among freshwater fishes Carp are particularly valuable in maintaining the purity of our drinking supply, keeping it free from insects, insect larvæ, and decaying matter. They are not infrequently kept in reservoirs on this account. And since the larvæ of such notorious pests as gnats, mosquitoes, and sand-midges are all aquatic, we are largely saved from annoyance and even from disease by the good offices of these and various other freshwater fishes.

Beneficial Insects (Insecta).—There are quite a large number of insects which either when adult or in the larval state, or it may be throughout life, are the natural enemies of many notorious insect pests. Sufficient examples have already been given in vol. ii, chap. ix, vol. iii, pp. 391–393, and in pp. 194, 195 of the present volume.

Carrion is also largely destroyed by insect-larvæ, such as the grubs of Burying-Beetles and the maggots of various Flies. Nor must we forget the large part which insects take in the fertilization of plants (see p. 83), including many which are of great importance to mankind.

Beneficial Spider-like Animals (Arachnida).—Of the members of this group it need only be said that Spiders, in particular, largely assist in keeping the numbers of insects within due limits.

Beneficial Myriapods (Myriapoda).—The numerous kinds of Centipede undoubtedly destroy large numbers of noxious ground-insects, and have therefore a claim to be included among beneficial animals.

Beneficial Crustaceans (Crustacea).—A large amount of scavenging work is carried on by the members of this class, and, so far as the sea is concerned, Crabs are particularly notable in this respect.

Beneficial Annelids (Annelida).—Earth-Worms render considerable service to agriculture (see vol. ii, p. 258) in more than one way. They reduce large quantities of soil to a finely-divided state, making it into a suitable seed-bed, bring earth to the surface as a sort of natural "top-dressing", and it may be added that their burrows in the ground help on the work of drainage and aeration. In short, the habits of these animals benefit the land in much the same way as the operations of ploughing, harrowing, and the like.

BENEFICIAL PARASITIC WORMS.—At first sight one is rather apt to imagine that the members of the several groups of these not altogether pleasing creatures do nothing but harm. This is not, however, strictly true, for many of them pay special attention to noxious animals, and assist considerably in keeping down their numbers.

CHAPTER LXX

ANIMAL FOES—THE PERSONAL ENEMIES OF MAN

Personal Enemies among Mammals (Mammalia).—We are not justified in calling the fiercer and larger Mammals or other animals our enemies, simply because they defend themselves when attacked, and in most cases man will probably be found to have been the first aggressor. And even when that is not the case, at least when carnivorous forms are in question, casualties are usually the outcome of the Law of Hunger, or it may be parental solicitude.

Partly owing to its comparatively straightforward habits, the Lion (*Felis leo*), when left alone, does not attack human beings to the extent that might be supposed, unless pressed by hunger. Speaking of North-East Africa, Sir Samuel Baker says (in *Wild Beasts and their Ways*):—"In the locality which I have mentioned, the lions, although numerous, were never regarded as dangerous unless attacked; there was an abundance of game, therefore the carnivora were plentfully supplied, and a large area of country being entirely uninhabited, the lions were unaccustomed to the sight of human beings, and held them in respect. During the night we took the precaution to light extensive bonfires within our camp, which was well protected by a circular fence of impenetrable thorns, but we were never threatened by wild animals except on one occasion."

Where the country is thickly populated it is only to be expected that individual animals may at times acquire bad habits, or, as Vogt puts it (in *Mammalia*):—"Old experienced lions who know how little danger they are exposed to in breaking in upon the villages of the badly-armed negroes will, it appears, hanker after human flesh".

The stealthy cat-like habits of the Tiger (*Felix tigris*, fig. 1234) render it a good deal more dangerous to man than its nobler cousin. But even the "man-eaters", which at one time undoubtedly accounted for a considerable number of the Indian natives, must have been but a small percentage of the tigers actually in existence. Of these once-dreaded marauders G. P. Sanderson gives the following graphic account (in *Thirteen Years among the Wild Beasts of India*):—"This truly terrible scourge to the timid and unarmed inhabitants of an Indian village is now happily becoming very rare; man-eaters of a bad type are seldom

Fig. 1234.—Tiger (*Felis tigris*)

heard of, or, if heard of, rarely survive long. Before there were so many European sportsmen as there now are in the country, a man-eater frequently caused the temporary abandonment of whole tracts; and the sites of small hamlets abandoned by the terrified inhabitants, and which have never been reoccupied, are not uncommonly met with by the sportsman in the jungles. The terror inspired by a man-eater throughout the district ranged by him is extreme. The helpless people are defenceless against his attacks. Their occupations of cattle-grazing or wood-cutting take them into the jungles, where they feel that they go with their lives in their hands. A rustling leaf, or a squirrel or bird moving in the undergrowth, sets their hearts beating with a dread sense of danger. The only security they feel is in numbers. Though the bloodthirsty monster is perhaps reposing with the remains of his last victim miles away, the terror he inspires is always present to every one throughout his domain. The rapidity and uncertainty of a man-eater's movements form the chief elements of the dread he causes. His name is in every one's mouth; his daring, ferocity, and appalling appearance are represented with true Eastern exaggeration; and until some European sportsman, perhaps after days or weeks of pursuit, lays him low, thousands live in fear day and night. Bold man-eaters have been known to enter a village and carry off a victim from the first open hut. Having lived in a tract so circumstanced until I shot the fiend that possessed it, and having myself felt something of the grim dread that had taken hold of the country-side, where ordinary rambling about the jungles, and even sitting outside the tent after dark except with a large fire, or moving from the encampment without an escort, were unsafe, I could realize the feelings of relief and thankfulness so earnestly expressed by the poor ryots when I shot the Jezebel that had held sway over them so long. The man-eater is often an old tiger (more frequently a tigress), or an animal that, through having been wounded or otherwise hurt, has been unable to procure its usual food, and takes to this means of subsistence." In a recent article (in *The Sports of the World*) Lieutenant-general Sir Montagu G. Gerard thus speaks on this subject:—"Man-eaters are very rare indeed, and . . . probably become so accidentally. The accepted belief that they are necessarily mangy is a myth; it may be the cause, not the effect. For whatever reason, they seem to acquire preternatural cunning, and natives believe that the soul of a man is imprisoned within them. I once spent a fortnight following one, who never during that time killed within ten miles of her last victim. . . . A former colonel of the C.I. Horse, the most celebrated tiger slayer of thirty years back, killed an exceptionally mischievous one, which in a year had accounted for eighty-seven known victims. . . . I have only killed four undoubted ones, whose victims ranged from thirty-three to about a dozen apiece; but I have known of several others, generally sulky males, who had killed cattle-herds or wood-cutters disturbing them."

Of other members of the Cat family (Felidæ) large enough to

be dangerous to man, it need only be said that, since they are expert climbers, trees afford no refuge to human beings if they chance to be attacked.

Bears (Ursidæ), from their great strength and powerful claws, are dangerous antagonists when roused, but they can scarcely be considered the natural enemies of mankind, for most of them leave human beings alone unless provoked, or impelled by hunger. It may be gathered from accounts of Arctic expeditions, for example, that a hungry Polar Bear (*Ursus maritimus*) will not hesitate to attack men, and similarly for the Brown Bear of Europe (*U. arctos*), and the North American variety of that species commonly known as the "Grizzly". It is rather curious that the Indian Sloth-Bear (*U. labiatus*), which chiefly lives on fruit, honey, and insects, is somewhat given to turning upon our species, though, obviously, not as the result of hunger. At least Sir Samuel Baker says (in *Wild Beasts and their Ways*):—"This species is very active, and although it refuses flesh, it is one of the most mischievous of its kind, as it will frequently attack man without the slightest reason, but from sheer pugnacity". And under these circumstances the long-curved claws are capable of inflicting "terrible wounds upon a human being".

Wolves, when pressed by hunger, are destructive to human life in several countries, their habit of hunting in large packs greatly aggravating the danger, as everyone is aware. The annual casualties due to wolves in parts of the Russian Empire are by no means inconsiderable.

Even without special provocation some of the larger wild Mammals of purely herbivorous habit may injure or kill human beings, as in the case of Hippopotami, Buffaloes, Rhinoceroses, and Elephants. All have heard, for example, of "rogue" Elephants, ill-natured males which have been expelled from their herds for general misbehaviour. But details are here unnecessary. Some of the smaller forms, such as Wild Boars, are also dangerous, and the Peccaries (*Dicotyles*), which range from South America to Mexico and Texas, are even more so. A. G. Requa recounts the following amusing adventure (in *The Big Game of North America*) with a herd of White-lipped Peccaries (*D. labiatus*), which sufficiently illustrates their ferocity:—"I had not sat there more than five minutes before I heard the sharp noise of the Peccaries. They came in sight not more than twenty yards below me. There were not more than a dozen that I could see, and there were plenty of small pines near by; so I thought that I would just kill the whole herd, provided they showed fight. As they came into the open ground they seemed to wind me, as they began to snuff and paw. I fired at one, and, just as I intended, only crippled him. He set up a great squealing, and, sure enough, here they came! I was just a little excited, and started for a tree, forgetting my coat and turkey. I had scarcely time to get up when they were around the tree, and instead of twelve, they kept coming till there were at least two hundred. I commenced shooting, and killed five with my rifle, that being the number of shells in my gun. It then occurred to me that my rifle-shells were in my coat; so, having no further use for my rifle, and realizing that it would become a burden to me if compelled to stay in the tree several hours, as seemed likely, I threw it down. Fortunately I had both revolvers, and a belt full of cartridges for them; so I went at them. They were chewing the tree, and climbing over each other trying to get at me. Each shot laid one out, and each shot seemed to make them more and more furious, as they would rush at the tree, and gnaw the bark and wood, while the white flakes of froth fell from their mouths. I tried to count them, and found that there were over two hundred left, and I had killed twenty-three. The position I had was not a comfortable one, but I had to stand it. Then for the first time I thought of the boys. Had they heard my shooting? if so, would they come? Then I remembered I had not fired the signal agreed on, and that I had followed the turkeys up the mountain and down again, and by this time the boys must be four miles up the cañon and on the opposite side. The Peccaries showed no signs of leaving. It was now noon, and very warm. They would root around, then come back to the tree, and grunt, and paw, and bite the tree; then they would cool down a little, would go a short distance away, root around awhile, then come back again. I was getting tired of being treed, but it was just what we had planned the night before, only we were not all together. If the boys could only hear my firing, and come over, how quick we would wipe them out! Such thoughts ran through my head; but still the pigs stayed. One o'clock came, then two; still they stayed. Then I thought I would fire a signal with my revolver—maybe the boys were hunting for me; so I made a noise, and back to the tree they came. I killed three of them in about a second; then I waited. Three o'clock came, then four, and no sign of the boys. Some of the pigs would feed while the others stood guard; then they would change off. I was so tired I could scarcely stay in the tree; so I took my belt off and buckled myself fast to the trunk, so that I would not fall out. Seven o'clock! I could see no change; they still camped near me, showing no signs of weakening. Then the sun went behind the mountain; darkness came on, and I was thirsty, hungry, and tired; but, worse than all, I was a prisoner. Twelve o'clock! The moon shone brightly, and I could see my sentinels scattered around. Two o'clock! Then came a signal from some of the outside ones; the rest snuffed the air, then away they all went. I could hear them far below, going down the mountain. . . . Hereafter, anyone who wants to hunt Peccaries can hunt them, and be blanked; but I prefer some kind of game that is not so fond of human flesh as they are." Without the friendly tree the adventure might have ended differently, for the same writer tells us of these animals that—"If one of their number is wounded so that it squeals, the whole herd becomes ferocious, will charge their enemy on sight, and speedily destroy him, unless he escapes by climbing a tree or by flight".

The blood-sucking Bats have been spoken about elsewhere (see vol. ii, p. 39).

PERSONAL ENEMIES AMONG REPTILES (REPTILIA).—The larger Crocodiles and Alligators are particularly destructive to human life, though their sphere of operations is obviously much limited by their aquatic habits. Speaking of Ega on the Upper Amazons, Bates says (in *The Naturalist on the Amazons*):—"Alligators were rather troublesome in the dry season. During these months there was almost always one or two lying in wait near the bathing-place for anything that might turn up at the edge of the water—dog, sheep, pig, child, or drunken Indian." With reference to Crocodiles in Madagascar, Sibree remarks (in *The Great African Island*): —"They are regarded with a superstitious dread by many of the Malagasy tribes, and are so dangerous in some parts of the island that at every village on the banks of the rivers a space is carefully fenced off with strong stakes, so that the women and girls can draw water without the risk of being seized by the jaws or swept off by the tail of these disgusting-looking creatures". Tales about the ferocity of Crocodiles are sufficiently numerous, many of them, of course, having reference to that notable species, the Nile Crocodile (*Crocodilus Niloticus*, fig. 1235). The following remarks by Sir Samuel Baker (in *Wild Beasts and Their Ways*) will sufficiently illustrate the point:—"The throat of a crocodile is not only large, but is capable of great expansion, and although the habits of the creature usually permit the body of a victim to rest in quiet until it is devoured in piecemeal, there are many exceptions to the rule; large crocodiles will swallow a small person without the slower operation of dismemberment. . . . When I was in

Fig. 1235.—Nile Crocodile (*Crocodilus Niloticus*)

command of the Khedive's expedition, our losses through crocodiles were very distressing, all of which were terrible examples of the ferocity, combined with cunning, which characterizes this useless scourge. On one occasion the vessels were sailing up the White Nile with a strong north wind, making at least 7 knots an hour; one of the cavasses was sitting upon the deck, with his legs dangling over the sides of the deeply-laden vessel, his feet being half a yard above the water. Suddenly a rush was made by a very large crocodile, and the man was seized and carried off in a shorter time than it would take to announce the fact. This was done in the presence of a hundred men on board the vessel, and nothing was ever heard of the unfortunate cavass."

Mention may here be made of the fact that two species of poisonous Lizards exist, both native to North America. One (*Heloderma horridum*, fig. 1236) is a Mexican form, while the other, commonly known as the "Gila Monster" (*H. suspectum*), inhabits New Mexico and Arizona. The sharp curved teeth of these creatures are grooved in front and behind for the purpose of conducting the poison, which is secreted by a series of small glands opening along the edge of the lower jaw. Of the Gila Monster,

Fig. 1236.—Mexican Poisonous Lizard (*Heloderma horridum*)

Gadow states (in *The Cambridge Natural History*):—"Frogs are probably paralysed or killed by the bite, which, although not so dangerous as that of poisonous snakes, is effective enough to produce severe symptoms even on man, and a few cases of death of people who had been bitten are on record".

Poisonous Snakes are among the most formidable personal enemies of man, and are justly dreaded in the countries they inhabit, which embrace all but the coldest parts of the globe. There is also reason to think that at least one of the larger non-poisonous snakes, *i.e.* the Anaconda or Water-Boa (*Euneces murinus*) of northern South America, may now and then crush and devour human beings. This species is said to attain the length of 33 feet, or possibly more.

The mechanism by which a venomous serpent bites its victim, so as to introduce poison into the wound, has been described already (see vol. ii, p. 80), so does not require mention here. In justice to such creatures it may be said that, as a rule, they only attack human beings when interfered with, as, *e.g.*, by being accidentally trodden upon. Among the most dreaded species are the Indian Cobra (*Naia tripudians*); the even more dangerous Krait (*Bungarus cœruleus*) of the same country; the Australian Death-Adder (*Acanthophis antarcticus*); the Coral-Snake (*Elaps corallinus*) of tropical South America; the Sea-Snakes (*Hydrophinæ*) of the Indian Ocean; the African Puff-Adder (*Vipera arietans*); Russell's Viper (*V. Russelli*), native to South Asia; and the American Rattle-Snakes (species of *Crotalus*). The following remarks by Semon (in *In The Australian Bush*) will prove of interest:—

Fig. 1237.—Indian Cobra (*Naia tripudians*)

"It is decidedly no exaggeration to say that 500 persons are yearly bitten on the Australian continent, although the majority of these cases do not prove fatal. The population of Australia is at present supposed to amount to 3,000,000 [in 1901 it was nearer 4,000,000]. About 20,000 deaths by snake-bite are yearly reported from the British provinces of India, containing 120,000,000 inhabitants [population of India in 1901 was 294,266,701]. This record may indeed be somewhat exaggerated, and may owe its enormity to conscious or unconscious deception of the magistrates by the native officials. Decidedly, however, the figures are not so much overrated as is frequently believed. In India, as well as in Australia, in the course of a year about one person in 6000 falls a victim to snake-bite."

PERSONAL ENEMIES AMONG FISHES (PISCES).—Some of the larger Sharks injure or devour bodily a good many human beings every year. The most notable is the Rondeletian Shark (*Carcharodon Rondeletii*), which ranges through the warmer parts of the ocean, and may attain the length of 40 feet.

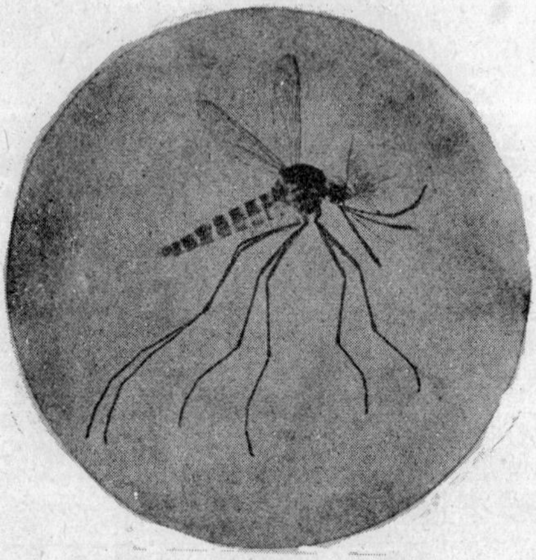

Fig. 1238.—A Gnat (*Culex*), enlarged

Those fishes also which possess poisonous spines (see vol. ii, p. 355) may cause serious injury, while some species are poisonous as food, such, *e.g.*, as Globe-Fishes (*Diodon* and *Tetrodon*) and Coffer-Fishes (*Ostracion*).

PERSONAL ENEMIES AMONG MOLLUSCS (MOLLUSCA).—Some of the giant Squids, and larger creatures of the Octopus kind, are certainly capable of injuring or destroying human beings. How far they do so, or have done so, it is impossible to say. And a few Sea-Snails, such as Cone-Shells (see vol. ii, p. 357), give poisonous bites.

PERSONAL ENEMIES AMONG INSECTS (INSECTA).—It is quite impossible here to pass in review the host of insects which bite or sting, and many of which make up by numbers what they lack in size. Bees, Wasps, Ants, Gnats (fig. 1238), Mosquitoes, Midges, Sand-Flies, Fleas, Bugs, and Lice are all more or less notable in their way, or perhaps notorious would be a better word. And many insects which do not bite or sting may nevertheless be a serious nuisance, *e.g.* House-Flies and Flesh-Flies.

But a fresh and unwelcome interest attaches to insects now that it is known that some of them are the means of conveying the germs of serious disease into the human body. The recent work of Major Ross in reference to malarial fever is the best illustration that can be given. It appears that a particular sort of Mosquito (*Anopheles*) is infested with certain stages in the life-history of a parasitic animalcule (*Hæmamœba*) which are introduced into the blood of persons bitten. Further development is there possible, serious disturbances of the system resulting. And when the mosquito bites a human being whose blood harbours these further stages it is in turn infected. In short the mosquito infects man, and man infects the mosquito. Some of the details are given in fig. 1239. Fortunately the researches of Ross enable preventive measures to be adopted. The early part of the life of the insect is passed in stagnant water (compare vol. iii, p. 403), from which the immature stages can be cleared out by the use of petroleum, if applied at a suitable time. The method has been exceedingly successful at Havannah, formerly a great breeding-ground for yellow fever and other disorders of malarial type. The subject suggests another homily on the necessity for properly endowing scientific research.

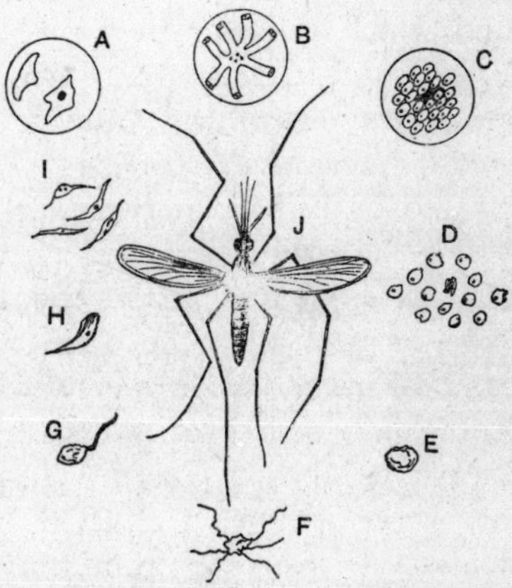

Fig. 1239.—Malaria Parasite (*Hæmamœba*)

A, Two parasites within a red blood-corpuscle of man; B, one of the same branching; C, division of same into minute spores; D, spores liberated by breaking up of the corpuscle; when taken up into the body of the mosquito with human blood some spores assume the form E, others the form F; G shows fusion of an E-spore with a thread from an F-spore; H, the fusion is complete, and at this stage the parasite pierces the wall of the mosquito's digestive tube; after complex changes the parasites reach the salivary glands of the insect, where the stage I is produced, which is introduced into the blood of a human being and attacks the red corpuscles; J, the mosquito (*Anopheles*). All but J greatly enlarged.

PERSONAL ENEMIES AMONG SPIDER-LIKE ANIMALS (ARACHNIDA).—It need only be noted that Scorpions possess poisonous stings, while some of the larger Spiders inflict poisonous bites. At one time an exaggerated virulence was ascribed in Italy to the latter. Violent exercise was the reputed cure, hence the origin of the rapid dance known as a "Tarantella" (*i.e.* the diminutive of "Tarantula", the name of the spider).

The unpleasant skin-disease known as "Itch" is caused by the attacks of a kind of Mite (*Sarcoptes scabei*, see p. 196).

PERSONAL ENEMIES AMONG MYRIAPODS (MYRIAPODA).—The

large Centipedes (Scolopendra) which abound in tropical countries are well known on account of their painful and poisonous bites.

PERSONAL ENEMIES AMONG ANNELIDS (ANNELIDA).—Some of the Leeches, especially the Land-Leeches of tropical countries, are peculiarly unpleasant to encounter (see vol. ii, p. 148).

PERSONAL ENEMIES AMONG FLAT-WORMS (PLATYHELMIA).—Among the Flukes (*Trematoda*) about eleven different species have been described as parasitic in human beings, including the kind which causes "liver-rot" in sheep, and which will be the subject of further notice. On one notorious scourge of the sort (*Bilharzia hæmatobia*) Gamble remarks as follows (in *The Cambridge Natural History*):—"This formidable parasite was discovered by Bilharz in 1853 in the veins of the bladder of patients at the Cairo Hospital, and is remarkable from its abundance on the east coast and inland countries of Africa from Egypt to the Cape, as well as in the districts bordering Lake Nyassa and the Zambesi river, while westwards it occurs on the Gold Coast. Mecca is a source of infection whence Mohammedans carry the disease to distant places. In Egypt about 30 per cent of the native population is affected by the serious disease known as hæmaturia, resulting from the attacks of *Bilharzia*, so that, of the many scourges from which in Africa man suffers, this one is perhaps the most severe."

A number of Tape-Worms (*Cestoda*) infest the human subject, and one example has been given in an earlier volume (vol. i, p. 441), *i.e.* the Common Tape-Worm (*Tænia solium*), which is a common consequence of eating "measly" pork in a partially cooked condition. Another not infrequent human parasite in Western Europe is the Beef Tape-Worm (*Tænia saginata*), derived from "measly" beef. The Broad Tape-Worm (*Bothriocephalus latus*), which is well known as a parasite of man in Russia, Switzerland, North America, and Japan, results from eating diseased fish, especially pike, which have not been sufficiently cooked. All these three forms attain their adult state in the human intestine, from which they can be expelled with comparative ease by suitable drugs. Another tape-worm (*Tænia echinococcus*) which when adult is found in the dog's intestine, is a much more dangerous parasite to man, in whom it may occur in its earlier bladder-worm form of existence as a swelling or cyst in the lungs or liver (*Echinococcus veterinorum*, fig. 1240), often with fatal consequences.

Pigs and ruminants are also liable to the disease. Gamble says of the bladder-worm stage (in *The Cambridge Natural History*):—"*Echinococcus* is most frequent in Iceland, where it affects 2 to 3 per cent of the population, and a still larger proportion of sheep; while in Copenhagen, Northern Germany, some districts of Switzerland, and Victoria it is not uncommon, but is frequently found during *post-mortem* examinations when no definite symptoms of its presence had been previously noticed."

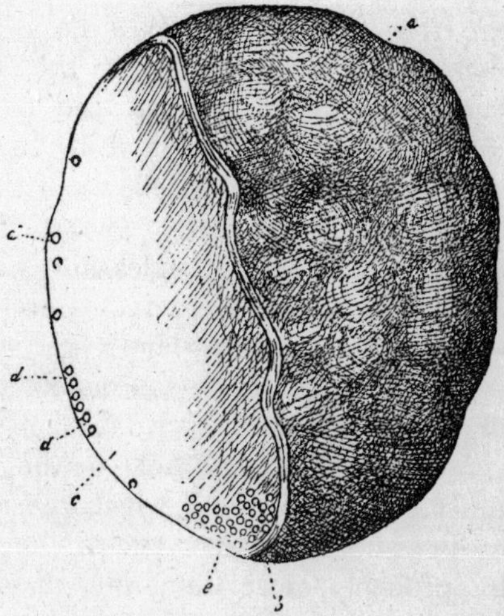

Fig. 1240.—Echinococcus Cyst from the Liver of a Cow

a, Outer covering of cyst, which has been cut away along *b* to show the cyst itself (*c*); *d*, *d*, *d*, secondary cysts each of which may produce several tape-worms. Reduced.

PERSONAL ENEMIES AMONG ROUND-WORMS (NEMATHELMIA).—A number of species of these objectionable forms are found as internal parasites within the bodies of human beings. The Round-Worm (*Ascaris lumbricoides*) and Thread-Worm (*Oxyuris vermicularis*) are two of the commonest sorts. Far more dangerous than these is one of the Palisade-Worms (*Dochmius duodenalis*), which possesses spines in the neighbourhood of the mouth, enabling it to burrow in the wall of the small intestine of its host. This worm is the cause of the fatal disease called "miners' anæmia".

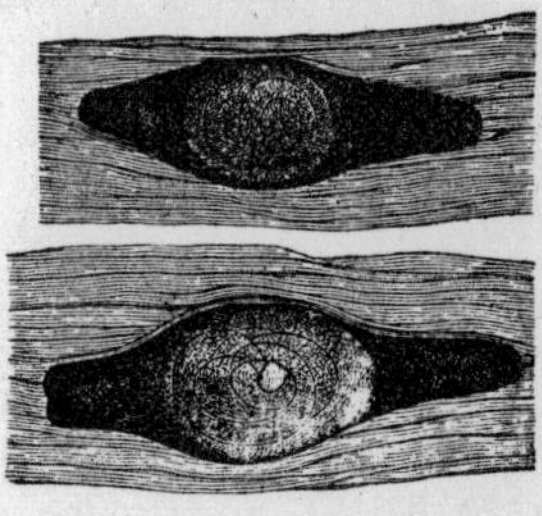

Fig. 1241.—Trichinæ encysted in Muscle. Much enlarged.

The Guinea-Worm (*Filaria medinensis*), only too well known in tropical countries, is the cause of serious tumours, especially in the legs. These are caused by the female, an elongated (usually 20 to 32 inches) slender creature which lives under the skin of the person affected.

Trichinosis is an extremely dangerous disorder contracted by eating diseased pork, containing the encapsuled stage of a minute thread-worm (*Trichina spiralis*, fig. 1241). On reaching the human stomach the capsules are dissolved, the minute worms become adult, and myriads of larvæ are produced, which bore into the walls of the intestine. They are then carried in the blood to different parts of the body, especially the muscles, where they come to rest, and pass into the encapsuled stage. Pigs contract the complaint by eating diseased rats, or the offal from their slaughtered fellows, if the latter are infected.

PERSONAL ENEMIES AMONG HEDGEHOG-SKINNED ANIMALS (ECHINODERMATA).—Unpleasant wounds may be given by the long sharp spines of some sea-urchins, especially when these are provided with poison-glands (see vol. ii, p. 361).

PERSONAL ENEMIES AMONG ZOOPHYTES (CŒLENTERATA).—The larger Jelly-Fishes, such as the Portuguese Man-of-war (*Physalia*), possess innumerable nettling capsules, by which they can inflict painful stings, of which the effects may long be felt.

PERSONAL ENEMIES AMONG ANIMALCULES (PROTOZOA).—These are probably more numerous than at one time suspected. The malaria-parasites introduced by means of Mosquitoes (see p. 341) are the most serious at present known.

CHAPTER LXXI

ANIMAL FOES—FORMS INJURIOUS TO HUMAN INDUSTRIES

A large volume would be required to give anything like an adequate account of the innumerable animal pests which more or less diminish the success of many human operations. Keepers of stock or poultry, crop-growers, gardeners, foresters, and the like, all have constant and painful experience of some such forms. Other animals damage buildings, food, clothes, and various manufactured articles. To cope successfully with many of these foes requires much knowledge of their habits and life-histories, and such knowledge can only be acquired by patient and long-continued scientific research, carried out by trained experts. Although an increasing amount of this kind of work is done in the United Kingdom, we are at present very far behind such countries as Germany and the United States, where the value of research is fully appreciated by the authorities. Our own government is comparatively apathetic in the matter, and our universities are too much occupied in turning out graduates by the score to undertake more than a small fraction of the original investigations upon which the prosperity of many of our industries ultimately depends.

It is only possible here to briefly review the animal kingdom with a view to pointing out some of the more injurious forms.

Injurious Mammals (Mammalia).—It goes without saying that the carnivores which attack man (see p. 331) are still more mischievous by way of raiding flocks and herds. Besides which, members of the same group which are not powerful enough to be considered our own personal enemies, may nevertheless be very destructive to domesticated animals. Foxes, Weasels, and Stoats may be mentioned in illustration. But at the same time it ought to be remembered that the damage inflicted is not infrequently balanced, or even outweighed, by benefits conferred in other ways (see p. 325).

Cultivated plants are often injured or destroyed by herbivorous or omnivorous Mammals—Deer and various gnawing mammals, such as Rats, Mice, Voles, Hares, and Rabbits. Such creatures may also be injurious in gardens, orchards, and woods, by injuring the bark of trees. In this respect Goats are particularly destructive. A remarkable instance of this is given in the following passage from Wallace (*Island Life*):—"When first discovered [over 400 years ago], St. Helena was densely covered with a luxuriant forest vegetation, the trees overhanging the seaward precipices and covering every part of the surface with an evergreen mantle. This indigenous vegetation has been almost wholly destroyed; and although an immense number of foreign plants have been introduced, and have more or less completely established themselves, yet the general aspect of the island is now so barren and forbidding, that some persons find it difficult to believe that it was once all green and fertile. The cause of the change is, however, very easily explained. The rich soil formed by decomposed volcanic rock and vegetable deposits could only be retained on the steep slopes so long as it was

Fig. 1242.—Common House-Mouse (*Mus musculus*)

protected by the vegetation to which it in great part owed its origin. When this was destroyed, the heavy tropical rains soon washed away the soil, and has left a vast expanse of bare rock or sterile clay. This irreparable destruction was caused in the first place by goats, which were introduced by the Portuguese in 1513, and increased so rapidly that in 1588 they existed in thousands. These animals are the greatest of all foes to trees, because they eat off the young seedlings, and thus prevent the natural restoration of the forest. They were, however, aided by the reckless waste of man."

Fig. 1243.—Tree "ringed" by a Woodpecker

Rats, Mice (fig. 1242), and other small rodents are destructive to stored grain and other commodities, and may become a thorough nuisance in dwellings, as most of us have found by experience. Such creatures may also be productive of serious harm by disseminating various diseases. Rats, for example, often cause trichinosis in swine (see p. 344), and hence indirectly in human beings, or may spread such virulent germs as those of bubonic plague.

Injurious Birds (Aves).—Large birds of prey, such as Eagles, may attack various domesticated animals, and even the Raven (*Corvus corax*) is known to injure lambs, among other forms. The Kea Parrot (*Nestor notabilis*) of New Zealand has acquired the reprehensible habit of killing sheep by biting deep holes in their backs, its object being said to be to reach the fat in the neighbourhood of the kidneys. The smaller Birds of Prey may raid poultry-yards or game-preserves, and some of them destroy useful insectivorous birds. Certain species, however, do more good than harm (see p. 327).

Among insectivorous birds the Woodpeckers damage trees in the course of their search for food (fig. 1243), and also sometimes by excavating nesting-holes in sound trunks. A great many plant-eating or omnivorous birds do much mischief in cultivated fields, gardens, and orchards, the exact nature of the depredations depending upon the species. Most, if not all, omnivorous birds also do a certain amount of good, sufficient, in some cases, entirely to outweigh their misdeeds. Crows, Rooks, and Sparrows are among the most hurtful forms in Western Europe. Some of the mainly beneficial species are: Thrushes, Starlings, and Chaffinches.

Injurious Reptiles (Reptilia).—It is only necessary to note that Crocodiles, Alligators, and poisonous Snakes destroy a number of domesticated animals.

Injurious Fishes (Pisces).—Some of the more voracious freshwater forms, especially the Pike (*Esox lucius*) destroy other species of greater value, or interfere with the work of fish-culture. Skate and Rays are destructive to oysters.

Injurious Molluscs (Mollusca).—Forms like the Octopus and its kind destroy oysters, as also do several species of boring sea-snail. Of the latter the "whelks" detrimental to British oyster-culture are chiefly the Common Whelk (*Buccinum undatum*), the Dog-Whelk (*Nassa reticosa*), and the Purple-Shell (*Purpura lapillus*). Various North American species which do harm in the same way are popularly known as "drills".

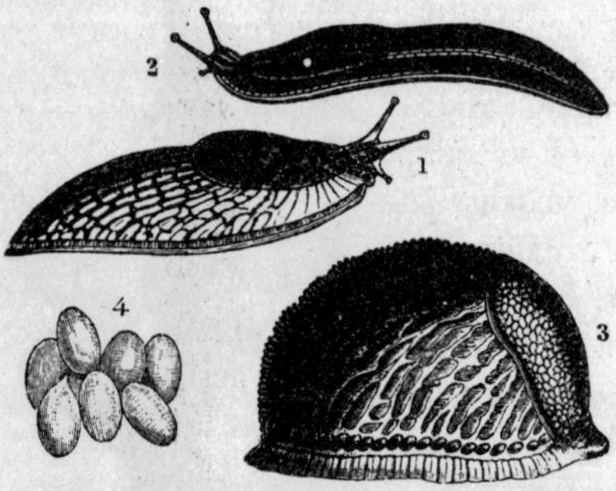

Fig. 1244.—1, Field-Slug (*Limax agrestis*); 2, Black Slug (*Arion ater*); and 3, a related species (*A. empiricorum*) with its eggs 4.

Cultivated plants of almost all kinds are liable to the attacks of various Land-Snails and Land-Slugs (fig. 1244), which are probably by far the most injurious of all molluscs from the human stand-point.

Among injurious bivalves the Ship-Worm (*Teredo navalis*) is notorious for the way in which it has damaged the timbers of ships and wooden piles. At one time it worked such devastation in the sea-dykes of Holland that serious disaster was threatened. The Edible Mussel (*Mytilus edulis*) is sometimes an enemy to oyster-culture, as it may cover up and smother beds of young oysters.

Injurious Insects (Insecta).—These are so excessively numerous, and at the same time so destructive, that they are the subject of a particularly extensive literature, and constantly engage the attention of many skilled naturalists, especially at the numerous experimental Entomological Stations of America.

Domesticated animals are attacked by a great variety of insects, of which only a few can be here mentioned. Something has elsewhere been said about Bot-Flies (see p. 191). Two such forms, the Ox-Warble Flies (*Hypoderma bovis* and *H. lineatus*, fig. 1245), lay their eggs on the legs of cattle, usually near the heels. It is probable (but not absolutely certain) that the maggots when hatched pierce the skin, under which they make their way to the back. At any rate they are found in that region later on, living in swellings ("warbles") which open to the exterior. Of the injuries inflicted Somerville says (in *Farm and Garden Insects*): — "The damage done by this insect is enormous, the Newcastle Hide Protection Society, for instance, reporting that the hides dealt with in that town alone in 1892 had been damaged by warbles to the extent of £14,000. Besides the injury to the leather *H. bovis* causes great damage by unsettling cattle and preventing them thriving properly. When cattle discover that the fly is hovering near they rush wildly about the field; and the constant irritation to which the larva subjects them when located in the skin is no less detrimental to the animals. The flesh in the neighbourhood of the warbles is also much reduced in value, being covered by a jelly-like substance known as 'licked beef'."

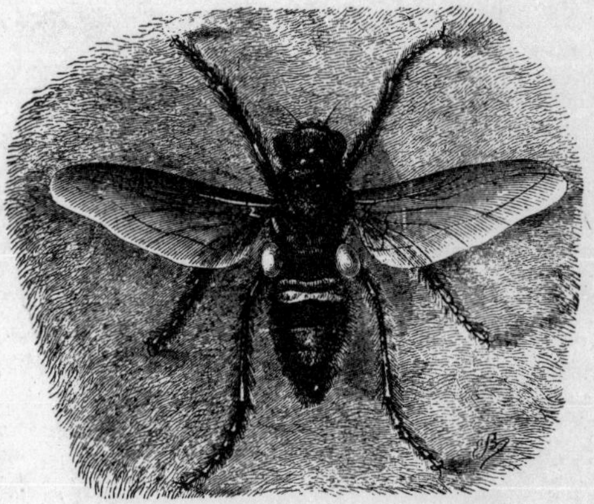

Fig. 1245.—Ox-Warble Fly (*Hypoderma*), enlarged

The bite of the much-dreaded Tsetse Fly (*Glossina morsitans*) of tropical Africa is fatal to horses, producing "nagana" or "fly-sickness" (see p. 241). This is because the bite introduces into the horse's blood certain stages in the life-history of a parasitic animalcule (*Trypanosoma*), which attacks the red corpuscles. Other biting flies may introduce fatal germs, as, *e.g.*, the bacilli which are the cause of anthrax (splenic fever, quarter evil).

The insect pests which damage stock are mostly Flies and

Fleas (*Diptera*), but forms extremely injurious to cultivated and other plants are to be found in several orders, as a brief summary will show. It will be convenient to mention at the same time some of the species which damage food, clothing, buildings, &c. &c.

Bugs (*Hemiptera*).—By means of their piercing and suctorial mouth-parts innumerable members of this order are able to feed upon the sap of plants, often with the most deplorable consequences. Aphides or Green-Flies (*Aphidæ*) and Scale-Insects or Mealy Bugs (*Coccidæ*) are among the most mischievous, for though of small size they are astoundingly pro-

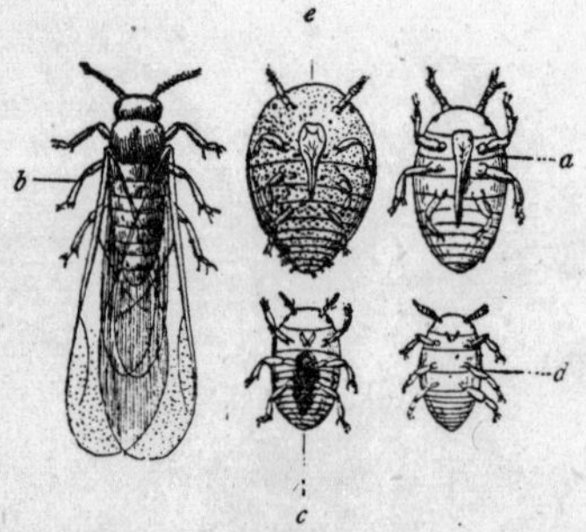

Fig. 1246.—Vine Aphis (*Phylloxera vastatrix*)

a, Wingless root-sucking female; *b*, winged overground female; *c*, wingless overground female; *d*, male; *e*, gall-producing female.

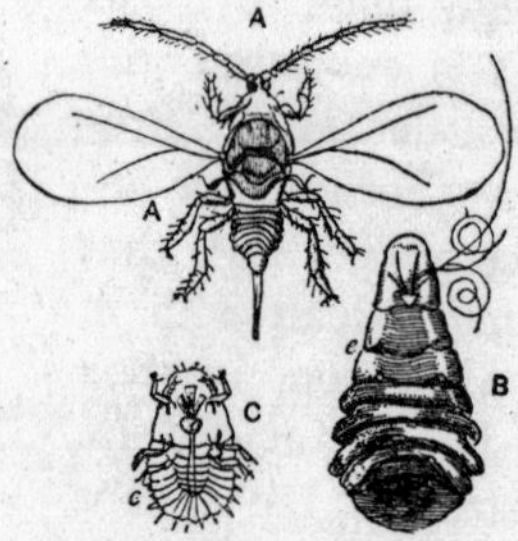

Fig. 1247.—Apple Scale-Insect (*Mytilaspis pomorum*), enlarged. A, Male. B, Female. C, Nymph.

lific. Aphides are often popularly known as "blight", and nearly 200 species of them are British, while some 800 have altogether been described. Many important cultivated plants are infested by particular kinds of Aphis, as will be gathered from the names of the following:—Corn Aphis (*Aphis cerealis*), Oat Aphis (*A. avenæ*), Bean Aphis (*A. fabæ*), Cabbage Aphis (*A. brassicæ*), Turnip Aphis (*A. rapæ*), Hop Aphis (*A. humuli*), Cherry Aphis (*A. cerasi*), Plum Aphis (*A. pruni*), &c. &c. Enormous damage is done in vineyards by the Vine Aphis (*Phylloxera devastatrix*, fig. 1246). During the spring and summer wingless females work havoc upon the roots, which swell up into small galls. They lay unfertilized eggs, which hatch out into forms like themselves, and there may be as many as eight generations of the kind produced during the season. But the last batch of these eggs produced in autumn gives rise to wingless males and winged females, that live above-ground and attack the leaves. The fertilized "winter-eggs" of this generation survive, lie dormant during the winter, and wingless females hatch out from them in the following spring.

Scale-Insects (*Coccidæ*), of which one kind has already been described (see vol. iii, p. 381), are particularly harmful in fruit-culture. Well known in Britain are—Apple Scale (*Mytilaspis pomorum*), white woolly Currant Scale (*Pulvinaria ribesiæ*), and Gooseberry and Currant Scale (*Lecanium ribis*).

Fringe-Winged Insects (*Thysanoptera*). See vol. i, p. 355.

Flies (*Diptera*).—The most familiar pests belonging to this group are the Crane-Flies or "Daddy-Long-Legs" (*Tipulidæ*), of which there are at least some thirty British species. The larvæ, known as "leather-jackets", are very destructive to the roots of grasses and cereals (fig. 1248). A species which has been responsible for great damage to cereal crops in America is the Hessian Fly (*Cecidomyia destructor*), so called because it is supposed to have been introduced into the New World in 1778 by means of straw brought by Hessian mercenaries. The female fly lays her eggs in pairs in the angles where the leaves of wheat, barley, or rye join the stem. The maggots feed upon the juices of the haulm, causing this to bend or break, and interfering greatly with the development of the grain. The Wheat-Midge (*Cecidomyia tritici*) is chiefly destructive to wheat and rye, the eggs in this case being laid in the flowers. The Frit-Fly (*Oscinis frit*) is injurious to cereals in much the same way as the Hessian Fly, but its eggs are here laid on the under sides of the leaves. Some flies lay their eggs on food, and cause great annoyance. The Blow-Fly or Blue-Bottle (*Musca vomitoria*) and the Cheese-Fly (*Piophila casei*) are well-known examples.

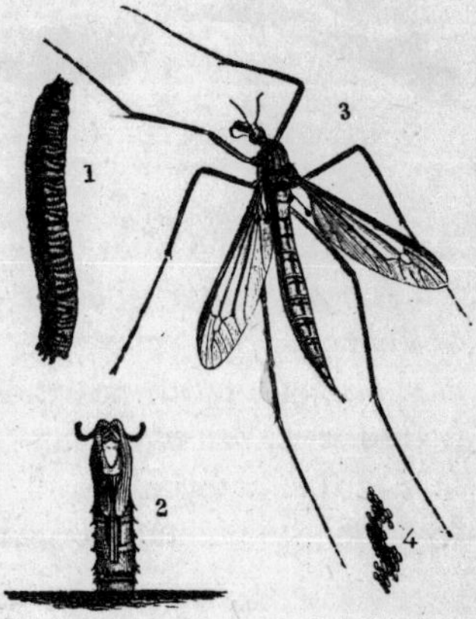

Fig. 1248.—Crane-Fly (*Tipula oleraceæ*). 1, Larva; 2, pupa; 3, adult; 4, eggs.

Moths and Butterflies (*Lepidoptera*).—Almost everyone has noticed the way in which the caterpillars of these insects voraciously devour plants of various kind, and a mere list of destructive species would occupy a considerable space. Among injurious

Butterflies the Whites (*Pieridæ*) are only too familiar. They include, for example, the Large Garden White or Cabbage Butterfly (*Pieris brassicæ*), the Small White (*P. rapæ*), and the Green-veined White (*P. napi*). The leaves of cabbages, cauliflowers, turnips, and other cruciferous plants are ravaged by the insatiable caterpillars.

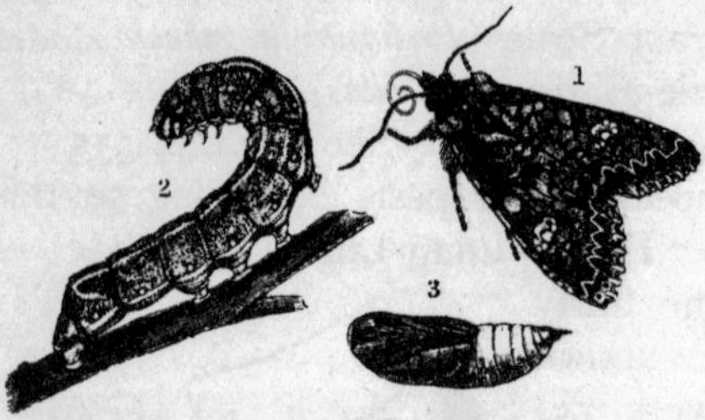

Fig. 1249.—Cabbage Moth (*Mamestra brassicæ*). 1, Adult female, 2, larva: 3, pupa.

The larvæ of many species of Owlet Moths (*Noctuidæ*), under the name of "surface caterpillars", are responsible for a large amount of damage to various cultivated plants. Notable forms are the Turnip Moth (*Agrotis segetum*), Heart-and-Dart Moth (*A. exclamationis*), and Great Yellow Underwing (*Triphæna pronuba*).

Among other species of which the larvæ are destructive to ordinary crops may be mentioned—Silver-Y Moth (*Plusia gamma*), inimical to most cultivated herbs; Cabbage Moth (*Mamestra brassicæ*, fig. 1249); Pea Moth (*Grapholitha nebritana*), the caterpillars of which penetrate the young pods and feed on the immature peas; Grass Moth (*Charæas graminis*), a pasture pest; and Diamond-back Moth (*Plutella cruciferarum*), destructive to various crucifers.

Fig. 1250.—Codlin Moth (*Carpocapsa pomonella*). Adult female on left, larva in centre, pupa to right (its actual size indicated by a line).

Various trees of economic importance are liable to be attacked by voracious caterpillars. What are known as "worm-eaten" apples, for instance, commonly owe their condition to the larvæ of the Codlin Moth (*Carpocapsa pomonella*, fig. 1250). The large caterpillars of the Goat Moth (*Cossus ligniperda*) bore great holes in forest-trees, while the larvæ of other species ravage their foliage. The Nun (*Psilura monacha*) is a very serious forest pest in Germany, for its caterpillars devour pine-needles and the leaves of hardwood trees in a wholesale manner. The Gipsy Moth (*Ocneria dispar*), introduced from Europe into the United States some thirty years ago, has within the last decade proved a veritable scourge to many trees. Fletcher Osgood makes the following observations about this particular pest (in *Harper's Magazine*, 1897):—"The careful reckoning of science has demonstrated that the unrestricted caterpillar increase of a single pair of gipsy moths would suffice in eight years to devour the entire vegetation of the United States. In the ordinary course of nature (let Heaven be thanked for it!) such increase is never left wholly unrestricted. . . . Since the work [of extermination] began [in Massachusetts], some forty-two millions of trees have been inspected, while the number of the buildings, walls, and fences thus looked over exceeds four hundred thousand. Besides myriads of the gipsy kind destroyed by burning and in other ways, and hosts escaping record in the first years of the outbreak, the force employed against the caterpillar has killed directly by hand, to date, about two billions and three millions of these dreadful creatures. The unrecorded destruction will doubtless bring the list of killed to at least some four billions. The results so far have more than justified the necessary outlay."

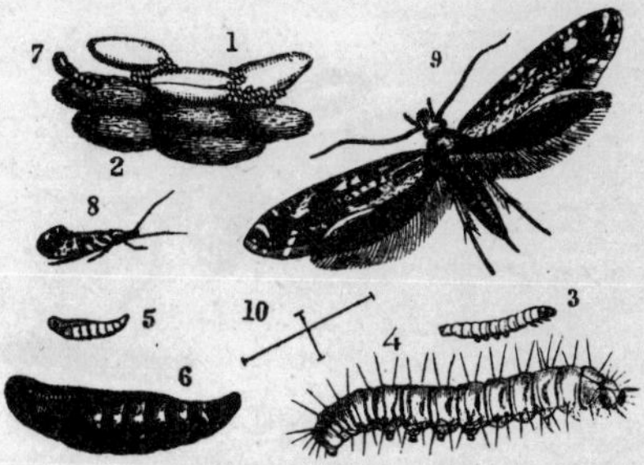

Fig. 1251.—Corn Moth (*Tinea granella*). 1, Infested grains held together by threads of silk; 2, cocoons; 3, larva; 4, the same enlarged; 5, chrysalis; 6, the same, enlarged; 7, empty chrysalis skin projecting from cocoon; 8, adult female; 9, the same, enlarged (actual size in same position indicated at 10).

The Corn Moth or Corn Wolf (*Tinea granella*, fig. 1251) is a small granary-pest that does much damage to stored grain. The Clothes-Moths, so destructive to garments of cloth and fur, are closely related.

The last species to be here mentioned is the Wax Moth (*Galleria mellonella*), one of the enemies of apiculturalists. The female tries to enter a bee-hive, and, if successful, lays her eggs there. When the caterpillars hatch out they burrow into the combs, and feed upon the wax.

Injurious Beetles (*Coleoptera*).—Many notorious malefactors belong to this order. Among the most injurious are "wire-worms", which do great damage to the underground parts of cereals, grasses, and root-crops, and are no other than the larvæ of the little Click-Beetles (*Elateridæ*). The still smaller Turnip Flea-Beetles (*Haltica nemorum*, fig. 1252, and *H. undulata*), popularly known as Turnip-"Flies", are very injurious to turnips and related plants, for the adults attack the leaves from the outside, while their larvæ burrow within them. Some of the "Chafers" are very injurious to trees, crops, and pastures. The Common Cockchafer (*Melolontha vulgaris*), when adult, ravages the foliage of trees, while its grubs live underground, and attack the roots of grasses, various crop-plants, and many trees. A form which created a "scare" in this country some years ago is the Colorado Beetle (*Chrysomela decemlineata*), a particularly prolific insect which, both in the larval state and when adult, devours potato leaves.

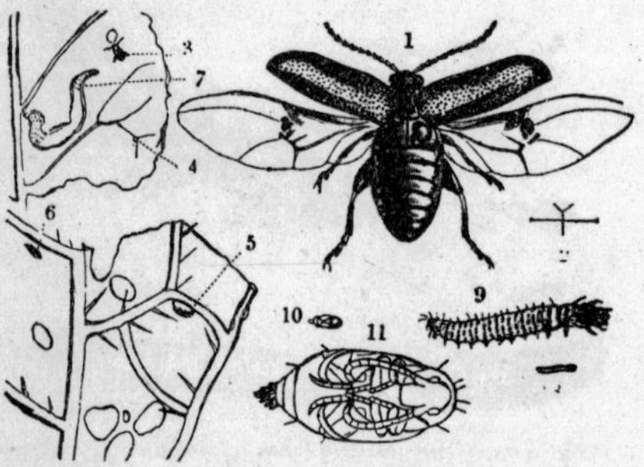

Fig. 1252.—Stages of Turnip Flea-Beetle (*Haltica nemorum*). 1, Adult (enlarged), showing wing-covers and wings spread out; 2, 3, natural size of same; 4, 5, eggs (5 enlarged); 6, 7, burrows of larvæ (7 enlarged); 8, 9, larva (natural size and enlarged); 10, 11, pupa (natural size and enlarged).

The larvæ of Beetles belonging to one family (*Bruchidæ*) burrow in seeds, and some of them infest plants of economic value, *e.g.* Pea-Beetles (*Bruchus pisi*) and Bean-Beetle (*B. fabæ*).

The little long-snouted Weevils (*Curculionidæ*), of which something like 20,000 species have already been described, include a large number of pests, of which both adults and larvæ feed on vegetable matter. The Pea-Weevil (*Sitones lineatus*), for example, devours the leaves of pea, bean, clover, &c., while its larvæ prey upon their roots. The Apple-blossom Weevil (*Anthonomus pomorum*) is very destructive in orchards to both apple and pear. The female insect deposits her eggs in the young flower-buds, one in each, and may carry on this injurious operation for two or three weeks. The Corn-Weevil (*Calandria granaria*, fig. 1253) bores holes in young grains of corn, and each of the some 150 eggs of a single female are deposited within separate grains. Some of the Weevils are among the pests of forestry, certain forms attacking conifers, *e.g.* species of *Hylobius* and *Pissodes.*

Some of the Beetles are indoor pests, their larvæ feeding on all sorts of substances. The members of one small family (*Dermestidæ*) devour animal substances, and are very destructive in museums. To one species at least (*Anthrenus fasciatus*) the horse-hair coverings of furniture prove palatable. The larvæ of the Bacon-Beetle (*Dermestes lardarius*) indulge in a more luxurious diet, as the name indicates. The larvæ and adults of certain species belonging to another family (*Ptinidæ*) are not often seen, though some of them are frequently heard, and their "works" are familiar. A kind of literary flavour attaches itself to the Biscuit-"Weevil" (*Anobium paniceum*), for its larva is most likely the "original bookworm" which finds its pabulum in libraries, though paper is not the only item in its bill of fare, for Sharp remarks (in *The Cambridge Natural History*) that ". . . it must possess extraordinary powers of digestion, as we have known it to pass several consecutive generations on a diet of opium; it has also been reported to thrive on tablets of dried compressed meat; in India it is said to disintegrate books; a more usual food of the insect is, however, hard biscuits; weevily biscuits are known to every sailor, and the so-called 'weevil' is usually the larva of *A. paniceum*". The "Greater Death-Watches" belong to allied species (*A. striatum* and *A. tessellatum*), and are the cause of "worm-eaten" wood and much superstition.

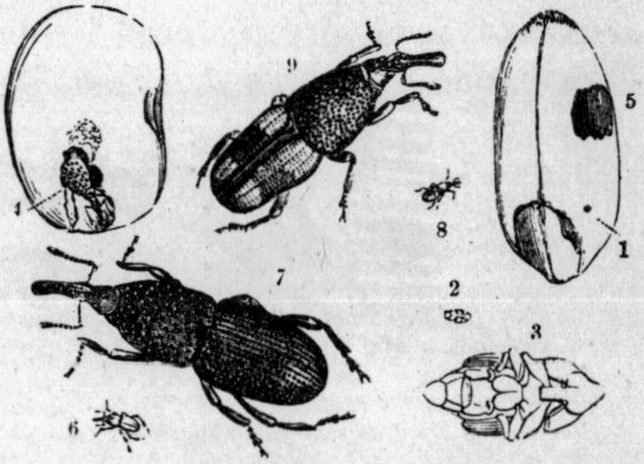

Fig. 1253.—Weevils. 1, Grain of wheat, showing the punctured hole; and 5, the exit of the perfect weevil. 2. Pupa (natural size); 3, magnified. 4, Grain of Indian corn, with weevil inside. 6, 7, Corn-Weevil (*Calandra granaria*), natural size and magnified; 8, 9, Rice-Weevil (*C. oryzæ*), natural size and magnified.

Injurious Membrane-Winged Insects (*Hymenoptera*).—To farmers and fruit-growers the Saw-Flies are here most deleterious, while Wood-Borers are among the pests of forestry. Their operations have been already sufficiently described (see vol. i, p. 371; vol. ii, p. 203; and vol. iii, p. 386). Prominent pests are the Corn Saw-Fly (*Cephus pygmæus*), Turnip Saw-Fly

(*Athalia spinarum*), Apple Saw-Fly (*Hoplocampa testudinea*), Gooseberry and Currant Saw-Fly (*Nematus ribesii*), Cherry and Pear Saw-Fly (*Eriocampa limacina*), Plum Saw-Fly (*Hoplocampa fulvicornis*), and Pine Saw-Fly (*Lophyrus pini*, fig. 1254).

Other net-winged insects may at times be injurious, *e.g.* Wasps sometimes damage large quantities of fruits, while Ants make raids on provisions (especially those containing sugar), and Carpenter-Bees (*Xylocopa*) destroy woodwork.

Injurious Net-winged Insects (*Neuroptera*).—The Biting-Lice (*Mallophaga*) live as ectoparasites on birds or mammals, and feed on their feathers or hairs, at the same time causing much irritation. Domestic fowls are pestered by no less than five species of these insects, one (*Menopon pallidum*) being particularly common. The

Fig 1254.—Pine Saw-Fly (*Lophyrus pini*). On the branch to the left are two larvæ, a cocoon, and an adult male on the right is an adult female, enlarged (actual size indicated by the line).

Biting Dog-Louse (*Trichodectes latus*) not only torments its host, but also harbours a stage in the life-history of a tape-worm which lives when adult in the dog's intestine.

In some of the hotter countries of the world Termites or "White Ants" are very harmful to furniture and woodwork, on account of their habit of excavating and feeding upon wood (see p. 120). An interesting example is giving by Sharp (in *The Cambridge Natural History*), who says:—"A Termite (*Termes tenuis*) was introduced—in what manner is not certainly known—to the island of St. Helena, and committed such extensive ravages there that Jamestown, the capital, was practically destroyed, and new buildings had to be erected".

Injurious Straight-winged Insects (*Orthoptera*).—Locusts have been one of the scourges of mankind from the earliest times, owing to their enormous fertility and the wholesale manner in which they devour all sorts of vegetation (see vol. i, p. 382, and vol. iii, p. 379). The species which migrate from place to place in vast swarms are those which do most mischief. The following quotation from Sharp (in *The Cambridge Natural History*) regarding such forms will give an idea of the possibilities:—"In countries that are liable to their visitations they have a great influence on the prosperity of the inhabitants, for they appear suddenly on a spot in huge swarms, which, in the space of a few hours, clear off all the vegetable food that can be eaten, leaving no green thing for beast or man. It is difficult for those who have not witnessed a serious invasion to realize the magnitude of the event. Large swarms consist of an almost incalculable number of individuals. A writer in *Nature* [Carruthers, 1889] states that a flight of locusts that passed over the Red Sea

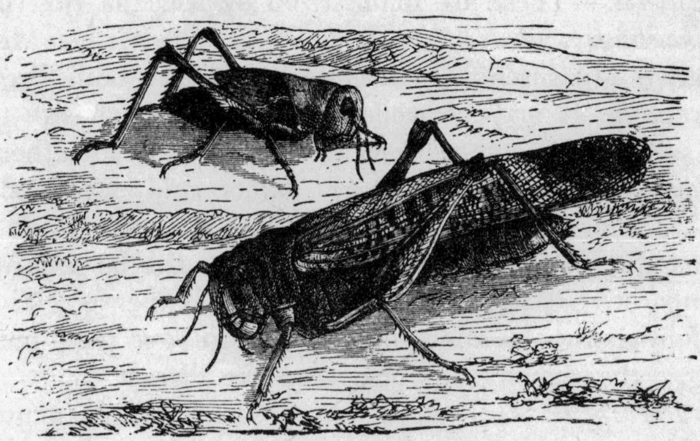

Fig. 1255.—Larva and Adult Female of the Migratory Locust (*Schistocerca peregrina*)

in 1889 was 2000 square miles in extent, and he estimated its weight at 42,850 millions of tons, each locust weighing $\frac{1}{16}$ of an ounce. A second similar, perhaps even larger, flight was seen passing in the same direction the next day. That such an estimate may be no exaggeration is rendered probable by other testimony. From official accounts of locusts in Cyprus we find that in 1881, up to the end of October, 1,600,000,000 egg-cases had been that season collected and destroyed, each case containing a considerable number of eggs. By the end of the season the weight of the eggs collected and made away with amounted to over 1300 tons, and, notwithstanding this, no less than 5,076,000,000 egg-cases were, it is believed, deposited in the island in 1883. When we realize the enormous number of individuals of which a large swarm of locusts may consist we can see that famine is only a too probable sequence, and that pestilence may follow—as it often has done—from the decomposition of the bodies of the dead insects. This latter result is said to have occurred on some occasions from locusts flying in a mass into the sea, and their dead bodies being afterwards washed ashore."

Of other well-known members of the present order which are to be regarded as pests may be mentioned: The Earwig (*Forficula auricularia*), which attacks flowers and fruits; Cockroaches (our common species is *Periplaneta orientalis*), that are troublesome in houses and on board ships; and the Mole-Cricket (*Gryllotalpa vulgaris*), which is injurious to pasture.

Principles regulating the Methods employed in Combating Injurious Insects.—These are summarized by Ritzema Bos (in *Tierische Schädlinge und Nützlinge*) under (1) Preventive Measures, (2) Curative Measures, (3) Measures which are both Preventive and Curative. It may be well once more to emphasize the fact that to successfully combat harmful insects (and all other pests) an intimate knowledge cf their habits and life-histories is essential. There is commonly, for example, some stage in the development of a particular animal which can be exterminated with comparative ease and at relatively small expense. This must be carefully borne in mind, or it may turn out that, financially speaking, "the remedy is worse than the disease".

(1.) *Preventive Measures.*—Sickly plants are in many cases more subject to infestation than healthy ones, and it therefore follows that all the means adopted by farmers, gardeners, and foresters to promote the vigour of the forms with which they are concerned assist in warding off the attacks of injurious insects, &c. It is also well known that seedlings are less able to resist their enemies than plants in a later stage of development, from which it follows that crops should be stimulated to rapid growth at the time when sprouting begins.

One of the benefits to be derived from rotation of crops is to check the ravages of various injurious insects, &c., which only feed upon one or a few kinds of plant. They are often, so to speak, starved out. Clean seed is another important preventive, for without precaution in this direction sowing may mean a distribution of pests as well as plants. And as during part of their existence some noxious forms are harboured in straw, another preventive measure is thereby suggested.

It is also sufficiently obvious that the natural enemies of pests should be protected and encouraged as far as possible. This particular preventive measure chiefly applies to insectivorous birds and mammals.

(2.) *Curative Measures.*—It is possible to collect and destroy many sorts of pest (see p. 353), although this is usually an expensive matter. The question as to which stage in the life-history of a particular form most readily lends itself to the method is clearly one of great economic importance.

Collection is sometimes facilitated by "luring" pests by means of something which serves to attract them. Slices of potato, for example, have been found to draw large numbers of wire-worms.

Fig. 1256.—Winter-Moth (*Cheimatobia brumata*); male (centre), female (right), and chrysalis (left). The vertical lines indicate actual sizes.

Many creatures can be destroyed in the places where they live by means of certain powders and sprays, distributed by various ingenious appliances. Soot, quick-lime, "Paris green" (an aceto-arsenite of copper), soap-suds, paraffin emulsion, &c. &c., all have their special uses.

(3.) *Measures which are both Preventive and Curative.*—These may be illustrated by "tar-rings", employed in combating the Winter-Moth (*Cheimatobia brumata*, fig. 1256), destructive to fruit-trees, and the Gipsy-Moth (*Ocneria dispar*), which is an enemy to all sorts of trees. In both these species the dormant chrysalis stage is passed through in the ground. As the wings of the female Winter-Moth are small and useless, while the female Gipsy-Moth cannot (or at any rate does not) fly, both of them have to creep up the tree-trunks in order to lay their eggs. This can be prevented by means of a tar-coated band of suitable material fixed round the trees a short distance above the ground. Collection and destruction of moths and eggs naturally follow.

Injurious Spider-like Animals (Arachnida).—The only forms of great importance here are the Mites (*Acarina*). Mange- and Itch-Mites, injurious to domesticated animals, have already been mentioned (see p. 196). Poultry are attacked as well as quadrupeds. Fowls are also liable to be infested by Red Fowl-Mites (*Dermanyssus gallinæ*), which suck their blood and set up an intolerable itching.

Domesticated animals are also often attacked by Ticks (*Ixodidæ*), which are able to draw large quantities of blood, and, what is more serious, may convey the germs of disease. Infection by means of one such Tick (*Ixodes reduvius*) is, for example, the cause of "louping ill" in sheep.

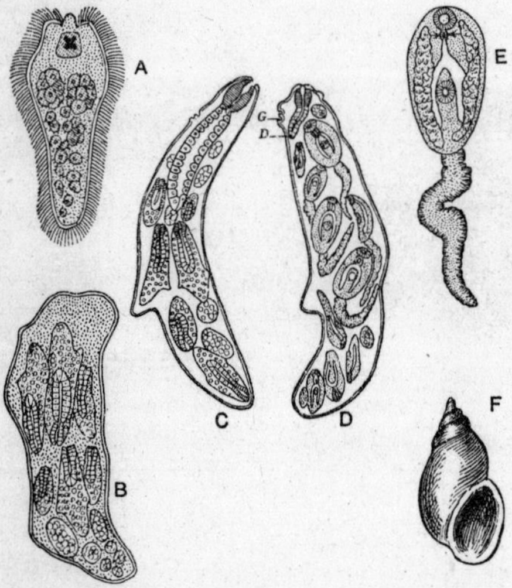

Fig. 1257.—Stages in Life-History of Liver-Fluke (*Fasciola hepatica*), enlarged. A, ciliated larva; B, sporocyst, within which rediæ are developing; C, redia, within which a new generation of rediæ is developing; D, redia, with contained cercariæ (*G*, opening by which these escape; *D*, intestine); E, cercaria. B to E are parasitic within the water-snail F (*Limnæa truncatula*), from which E escapes to encyst on the stem of a plant.

Cultivated plants also suffer from the attacks of Mites, among which the following may be mentioned:—Currant Gall-Mite (*Phytoptus ribis*), Red Hop-"Spider" (*Tetranychus telarius*), Red Plum-"Spider" (*T. rubescens*), and Harvest or Gooseberry-"Bug" (*T. autumnalis*).

Other kinds of Mite spoil furniture and attack food, especially meal, cheese, and sugar.

Injurious Myriapods (Myriapoda).—Some of the Millipedes ("false wire-worms") attack the underground parts of various plants, or may damage soft fruits.

Injurious Flat-Worms (Platyhelmia).—A large number of Flukes (Trematoda) and Tape-Worms (Cestoda) are parasitic within the bodies of domestic animals, as previously stated in dealing with the personal enemies of man (see p. 342). A few details may be appropriately added.

Flukes (*Trematoda*).—It is only necessary here to refer to the

Liver-Fluke (*Fasciola hepatica*, fig. 1257), a brief account of which has already been given (see vol. i, p. 443). The adult Fluke is parasitic in the liver of the sheep, causing the serious disease known as "liver-rot", while certain earlier stages of the life-history are passed within a small water-snail (*Limnæa truncatula*). The following extract from Gamble (in *The Cambridge Natural History*) will give some idea of the serious losses which may be caused by this destructive parasite:—"Over the whole of Europe, Northern Asia, Abyssinia, and North Africa, the Canaries, and the Faroes the fluke and the snail are known to occur, and recently the former has been found in Australia and the Sandwich Islands, where a snail, apparently a variety of *Limnæa truncatula*, is also found. Over these vast areas, however, the disease usually only occurs in certain marshy districts and at certain times of the year. Meadows of a clayey soil, liable to be flooded (as in certain parts of Oxfordshire), are the places where this *Limnæa* occurs most abundantly, and these are consequently the most dangerous feeding-grounds for sheep. The wet years 1816, 1817, 1830, 1853, and 1854—memorable for the occurrence of acute liver-rot in England, Germany, and France—showed that the weather also plays a considerable part in extending the suitable ground for *Limnæa* over wide areas which in dry years may be safe pastures. In 1830 England lost from this cause one and a half million sheep, representing some four millions of money, while in 1879–80 three millions died. In 1862 Ireland lost 60 per cent of the flocks, and in 1882 vast numbers of sheep perished in Buenos Ayres from this cause. In the United Kingdom the annual loss was formerly estimated at a million animals, but is now probably considerably less." This extract clearly shows the importance of scientific research to agriculture, as preventive measures clearly depend upon an accurate knowledge of the life-history of the fluke.

Tape-Worms (*Cestoda*).—The disease of sheep known as "staggers" or "sturdy" is due to the presence of large cysts that cause pressure on the brain, and are the bladder-worm stage (*Cœnurus cerebralis*) of a Tape-Worm (*Tænia cœnurus*) that lives when adult in the intestine of a sheep-dog (fig. 1258). A sheep contracts the disease by swallowing eggs of the parasite which have passed out of the body of a dog, while in its turn a dog becomes infected if it devours cysts from the brain of a sheep that has died of staggers.

Dog and Rabbit (or Hare) are the two hosts of another kind of Tape-Worm (*Tænia serrata*), of which the adult lives in the intestine of the former animal, while the bladder-worm stage (*Cysticercus pisiformis*) is harboured in the body of the latter.

INJURIOUS THREAD-WORMS (NEMATHELMIA).—Many of the worms belonging to this group are injurious to domesticated animals and cultivated plants. The large Horse-Worm (*Ascaris megalocephala*), for example, often infests in great numbers the intestine of the horse and its allies, while smaller species of round-worm live as parasites within dogs and cats. Much more dangerous is the minute Trichina (*Trichina spiralis*) that sets up trichinosis in pig and man (see p. 343).

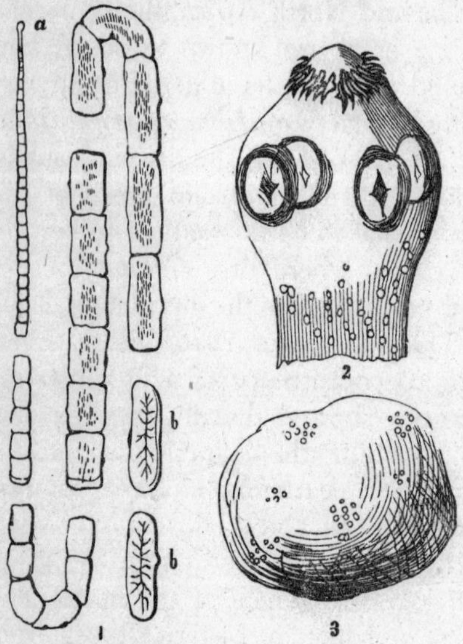

Fig. 1258.—The Tape-Worm (*Tænia cœnurus*), of which the cyst causes "staggers" in Sheep. 1, parts of the adult worm (*a*, head; *bb*, ripe joints); 2, head of same (× 30) showing hooks and suckers; 3, cyst from sheep's brain. Several groups of developing tape-worm heads are indicated.

Much harm is caused by the Palisade-Worms or Strongyles (*Strongylidæ*), related to the species which produces "miners' anæmia" in human beings (see p. 343). The Giant-Strongyle (*Eustrongylus gigas*), of which the female may be from a foot to over a yard long, lives in the kidneys of horse, ox, dog, and, it may be, man. Swellings in the arteries of the horse are caused by the presence of Armed Strongyles (*Strongylus armatus*), while other deadly parasites are the Stomach-Strongyle (*S. contortus*) of the sheep, and the Lung-Worm (*S. filaria*) of the lamb. The disease known as "gapes", to which young poultry and game-birds are liable, is caused by the presence of a related species, the Red- or Forked-Worm (*Syngamus trachealis*).

Some of the little Eel-Worms (*Anguillulidæ*) are serious agricultural pests. They possess a spine at the front end of the body, by which they bore into the tissues of plants. One species, the Wheat Eel-Worm (*Tylenchus scandens*), has been described in an earlier section (see vol. ii, p. 222). The Stem Eel-Worm (*T. devastatrix*) attacks the stems and leaves of rye, oats, buckwheat, clover, &c., leading to stunted growth, or even killing the plants outright. "Clover sickness" is set up by the presence of this parasite. The Beet Eel-Worm (*Heterodera Schachtii*, fig. 1259) infests the roots of its host-plant, and causes "beet sickness". The related Root-knot Eel-Worm (*H. radicicola*) produces galls on the roots of clover, lucerne, cucumber, tomato, and many other cultivated plants.

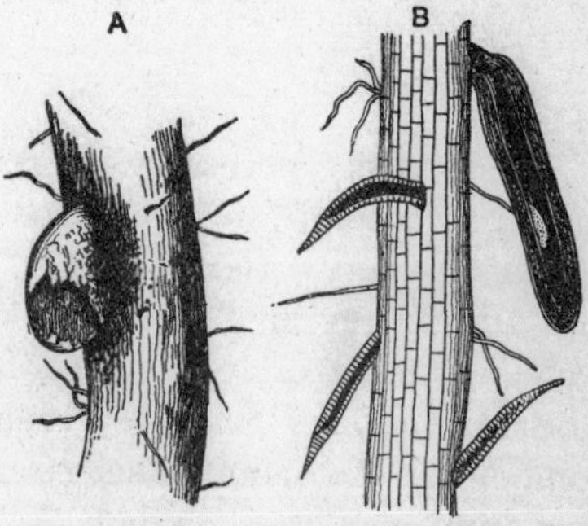

Fig. 1259.—Roots of Beet, infested by Beet Eel-Worm (*Heterodera Schachtii*), enlarged. A shows a swelling containing adult female; B, larvæ attacking a root.

INJURIOUS ANIMALCULES (PROTOZOA).—Nagana or "fly-sickness" (see p. 241) is the best example of disease resulting from the presence of parasitic animalcules in the bodies of domesticated animals.

Some ailments of cultivated plants are also the result of the attacks of certain Protozoa. One instance is afforded by "finger-and-toe" or "anbury", a turnip disease associated with curious deformation of the roots. It is due to the presence of one of the Fungus-Animals (Mycetozoa) within the tissues (i.e. *Plasmodiophora brassicæ*).

CHAPTER LXXII

THE ZOOLOGY OF SPORT

It is hardly necessary to remark that the literature of those forms of "sport" which depend upon the existence of wild animals is very extensive, and includes accounts of experiences and adventures in all parts of the world. Much of it is highly technical, most of it is anecdotal, and but a small part is the work of authors who represent the sportsman and naturalist combined. To name a selection of books for the benefit of expert huntsmen and anglers is of course quite superfluous, but general readers may profitably refer to the following works:—The volumes of *The Badminton Library*, *Fur and Feather Series*, and *The American Sportsman's Library*; Izaak Walton's *Compleat Angler*; Selous' *A Hunter's Wanderings in Africa*; Sir Samuel Baker's *Wild Beasts and their Ways* and *With Rifle and Hound in Ceylon*; *The Big Game of North America*, *English Sport*, *Sport in Europe*, and *The Sports of the World*, edited respectively by G. O. Shields, Alfred E. T. Watson, and (the two last) by F. G. Aflalo.

We have already had occasion to notice (p. 208) that the first stage in the evolution of civilization was represented by the primeval hunter and fisherman, a stage still in evidence to-day among various savage races. But our remote prehistoric ancestors, like modern savages, were "pot-hunters" rather than sportsmen, while the intimate knowledge they must have acquired of the habits of wild animals imparted a certain flavour of the field naturalist. Many primitive races have also had, and some still have, to defend themselves and (in the pastoral and agricultural stages) their domesticated animals from the attacks of predaceous forms. Even when hunting and fishing were necessary for existence, however, a good deal of pleasurable excitement must have attached to the pursuit of wild animals, rivalry and emulation playing no unimportant part in the matter. When the further evolution of civilization diminished the material importance of hunting and fishing, these arts continued to be pursued for pleasure as well as for profit; hence the origin of modern sport.

This is not the place to enter into a long disquisition regarding the ethics of field-sports, but such of them as deserve the name involve certain obvious fundamentals. There must be room for skill, the quarry must have a fair chance, and every precaution should be taken to prevent a miserable and lingering death on the part of maimed or wounded animals. The hunter of "big game" would no doubt add that "the greater the danger the greater the sport". Selous, for instance, remarks (in *The Sports of the World*):—"Lion-hunting by savages, armed only with spears or bows and arrows, must have been incomparably more dangerous, and therefore infinitely finer sport, than the pursuit of these animals by civilized man at the present day armed with modern rifles". On the other hand, it is quite possible for a recognized form of sport to become so highly artificial as to demand hardly more skill to make a "bag" than would be required to slaughter the inhabitants of the poultry-yard with a shot-gun. Under such circumstances "massacre" and not "sport" would be the proper word to employ.

Our pluck, vigour, and enterprise as a nation are undoubtedly due in no small degree to the influence of field-sports, and to entirely exclude these from our national life, as some would have us do, on the ground of cruelty to animals, would be as inexpedient as it is impossible. On the other hand, the view of the matter which suggests that it is rather a pleasure than otherwise to be hunted may be regarded as a little optimistic. Lady Augusta Fane, for example, makes the following remarks on fox-hunting (in *English Sport*):—"Worthy folks who fancy that they are more humane than their neighbours write about the cruelty of fox-hunting, drawing fancy pictures of a poor, timid, terrified little creature pursued by savage dogs, ruthless viragoes, and brutal men! As a matter of fact, foxes constantly live to a green old age, and defeat their pursuers season after season. They do not even pretend to be frightened. How often we have seen a fox break out of covert, look around, give himself a good shake, and, whisking his brush, trot off without the slightest sign of fear! He knows where he means to go, and all the safe refuges *en route*; and if he gets tired he is familiar with the woods, where he can find a friend to take his place."

The limited space here available must necessarily be devoted to briefly reviewing the animals which are of importance from the sporting stand-point, including those which assist man in the chase. Mammals, Birds, Reptiles, and Fishes are the only groups with which we are concerned, though the "naturalist" who hunts down insects or the like merely to add to his collection is more of a sportsman (in a very small way) than a man of science; often, however, he is neither!

MAMMALS (MAMMALIA) AS AIDS TO SPORT

It is a natural consequence of the slow rate of human locomotion that several Mammals have been pressed into the service of man in order to make up for this deficiency, or, it may be, reduce the element of danger. From time immemorial, in many sorts of sport, horse and elephant have saved him the work of using his own legs, while dog or falcon have pursued the quarry and tackled it at close quarters.

THE HORSE (EQUUS CABALLUS).—The combination of intelligence and speed by which the horse is characterized, and its susceptibility to thorough domestication, have naturally led to its large employment in the chase. The extraordinary way in which the long-continued influence of man has resulted in the production of widely different breeds of the same kind of animal is here very strikingly exemplified. A well-bred hunter combines to perfection the two desiderata of speed and endurance, and it is, to all intent and purposes, a product of human ingenuity, without which many forms of sport would be comparatively tame and featureless. It may also be remarked in passing, that without highly specialized breeds of horses certain forms of sport which do not depend upon the existence of a quarry, such as horse-racing and trotting, could never have attained their present high pitch of perfection. By the practice of what may almost be called a species of artificial evolution, man has been here able to further his own ends in a remarkable manner.

THE INDIAN ELEPHANT (ELEPHAS INDICUS).—The use of this animal in tiger-shooting is too well known to need description.

It is here not so much a question of speed as of size and strength, by which otherwise impracticable ground can be traversed, while the personal risk of the sportsman is reduced. On the other hand, an element of different kind is introduced by the nervousness and uncertain temper of the elephant, both of which are decidedly in favour of the quarry.

THE DOG (CANIS FAMILIARIS).—The Dog has been the companion of man in the chase from the remotest times, and to all appearance keenly shares in the exhilarating pleasures of pursuit.

Fig. 1260.—Pointer

He has proved singularly susceptible to the selective influence of man, practised for unnumbered centuries, the result of which has been the evolution of a very large number of breeds, many of which have been brought into existence for sporting purposes. We know that the ancient Egyptians possessed several breeds of dogs, one of which was a sort of white hound (see p. 222) used in hunting antelopes, for which sport a similar kind of dog is to this day employed in North Africa. They also used packs of mixed character, though the nature of the breeds is doubtful. Upon the Assyrian sculptures we find hunting-mastiffs and greyhounds figured, while inscriptions inform us that still other breeds existed, some of which appear to have been used in sport.

Sporting Dogs (*Canes venatici*) of various kinds were possessed by the ancient Romans, some hunting by scent (*nare sagaces*), while others, more fleet (*pedibus celeres*), were let slip when the game was in sight.

To enumerate all the existing breeds employed in sport would be both tiresome and unnecessary. The names of many, *e.g.* fox-hound, deer-hound, and otter-hound, to some extent serve as an indication of their character. The exaggeration of natural instincts in artificial directions would appear to have led to the evolution of "pointers" (fig. 1260) and "retrievers". Darwin suggests that the original act of "pointing" was simply the pause which a carnivorous animal often makes before springing upon its prey.

Fig. 1261.—Cheetah (*Cynailurus jubatus*) pursuing an Indian Antelope 368-d

It is further interesting to note, that when we employ a pack of hounds to hunt down an animal by scent we are simply making use of the natural methods used by similar forms, when wild, in the pursuit of prey.

THE CHEETAH, OR HUNTING LEOPARD (CYNAILURUS JUBATUS, fig. 1261).—This long-legged animal, which is enabled by its fleetness to capture prey in a more straightforward way than is usual among felines, is employed by the native dignitaries of India for coursing antelopes. In former times this variety of sport was practised very largely, and is of ancient origin, having been known to the Persians so far back as 865 B.C., while at a still earlier period it was familiar to the Assyrians.

THE FERRET.—The slender bodies of the bloodthirsty members of the weasel kind enable them to pursue their prey underground, and advantage is taken of this peculiarity when rabbits are driven from their burrows by means of Ferrets, which are a domesticated variety of the Pole-Cat (*Putorius fœtidus*).

BIRDS (AVES) AS AIDS TO SPORT

Certain Birds of Prey have been employed from very remote times in the pursuit of wild animals, mostly other birds, but the art of Falconry in Europe has steadily declined since firearms came into general use. Another contributing cause has been the gradual increase of the area under cultivation. Lord Granville Gordon (in *Sport in Europe*) thus speaks of the antiquity and wide popularity of this form of sport:—"Records of hawking and falconry are supplied in the writings of Pliny and Aristotle. In Japan, in India, Arabia, Persia, and Syria, we can find it has been practised, and in our own Middle Ages stringent laws were passed referring to it. Hawks and falcons were allotted to men according to their rank and station. An earl had a peregrine, a yeoman a goshawk, a priest a sparrow-hawk, and so on. The king of birds in falconry in our Middle Ages was, and even now is, the peregrine, and the noble game at which to fly this bold and splendid bird was the heron; but I do not think this form of sport is followed any longer in our island." Hawking for rooks or larks is still, however, to be included in the list of British sports.

What may be termed a magnified variety of falconry is practised by the Kirghiz of the Asiatic steppes, the "falcon" in this case being no less noble a bird than the Golden Eagle, while the quarry is often the fox or the wolf (fig. 1262).

MAMMALS (MAMMALIA) HUNTED FOR SPORT

FLESH-EATING MAMMALS (CARNIVORA).—The Lion (*Felis leo*, fig. 1263) is undoubtedly the noblest quarry that falls to the rifle of the sportsman, while the attendant danger and excitement appeal so strongly to those who engage in this form of sport that it will be popular so long as lions continue to exist. Regarding the antiquity and characteristics of the pursuit Selous makes the following remarks (in *The Sports of the World*):—" Lion hunting must undoubtedly be reckoned amongst the most ancient and

Fig. 1262.—Kirghiz hunting the Wolf with the Golden Eagle

time-honoured of all field-sports, for ages and ages before the days when Assyrian kings pursued the king of beasts for pleasure, and shot him with bow and arrow from their light two-wheeled chariots, the prehistoric races of man, inhabiting the whole of Africa, as well as large areas in Asia and Europe, must have hunted lions as a sporting necessity, in defence of their flocks and herds as well as of their own lives. . . . Speaking generally, it is a difficult matter to find and hunt lions in the daytime, and shooting them at night cannot be called hunting. Lion hunting on horseback, as it used to be commonly practised in South Africa, is the most exciting form of big game hunting I have had experience of, as lions almost always turn vicious when chased on horseback, and charge freely, and whether you

Fig. 1263.—Lion (*Felis leo*)

are galloping after a lion or a lion is close behind your horse's heels, your nerves are kept strung as long as the hunt lasts. It will be many a long day yet before the lion has ceased to haunt the wilds of Africa, but when that day comes, one of the grandest forms of wild sport will also have become a thing of the past."

The hunting of the Tiger (*Felis tigris*) appears at the present time to be an increasingly rare and expensive form of sport, when conducted in an orthodox way with numerous elephants, some for beating, and others with howdahs for the accommodation of the actual huntsmen. In some parts of India packs of dogs also help in the sport, and are more feared by the quarry than one would be apt to imagine. Advantage is also often taken of the fact that the tiger is not a climbing animal to shoot him from a secure station in a tree, a goat or buffalo-calf having been previously tied up within easy range to serve as a "bait". Although justifiable for the destruction of man-eaters, this can hardly be dignified by the name of "sport".

The different species of Bear (*Ursus*) are hunted, and also slaughtered in a variety of ways, but do not take a very high place in the estimation of most sportsmen. In parts of Russia,

Fig. 1264.—Fox (*Canis vulpes*)

for example, Brown Bears (*Ursus arctos*) are considered to be "vermin". The Lapps, however, do not hesitate to attack this animal in its den, a method sufficiently dangerous and exciting to satisfy the most exacting in such matters.

The European Wolf (*Canis lupus*) is the object of more than one form of popular Russian sport. A favourite variety involves the use of fox-hounds and wolf-hounds, the former being employed for drawing the coverts, and the latter for the actual work of coursing. As previously mentioned (p. 369), the Kirghiz practise a species of falconry, of which the wolf is a favourite quarry.

The Fox (*Canis vulpes*, fig. 1264) is familiar to all as the object of one of the most popular, sociable, and exhilarating forms of British sport, but Lord Granville Gordon tells us (in *Sport in Europe*) that "it is doubtful if fox-hunting can long continue in a congested country like England. Bad agricultural seasons and barbed wire point to its doom." Otter-hunting is undoubtedly a declining sport in Britain, on account of the increasing diminution in numbers of the quarry.

ELEPHANTS (PROBOSCIDEA).—Wild Elephants, whether African or Indian, naturally take high rank among "big game", chiefly because their enormous strength, and great ferocity when thoroughly aroused (especially if they are "rogues"), are liable to make them exceedingly dangerous antagonists. But the great perfection to which firearms have now attained render even these great beasts no match for the most destructive member of the Mammalia—Man.

HOOFED MAMMALS (UNGULATA). — Rhinoceroses, of course, reckon as "big game", and, as a rule, seem to be inoffensive enough, though sufficiently dangerous when wounded. Under such circumstances the two-horned White and Black Rhinoceroses of Africa (*Rhinoceros simus* and *Atelodus bicornis*) bring the long front horn into action, while the one-horned Indian species (*R. Indicus*) can bite with terrible effect.

The Hippopotamus (*Hippopotamus amphibius*) is sufficiently formidable when attacked from boats to give it a place among sporting mammals. But to kill it with a rifle from a place of security on the bank of its native river is simply a variety of target-shooting.

Among the many other Ungulates that are pursued for sport some are especially esteemed on account of their pluck and dangerous qualities, *e.g.* the African or Indian Buffaloes and the Wild Boar, while the great speed or agility in climbing of others furnish the requisite zest to the chase, as in the case of Deer, Antelopes, or Ibexes.

The joys and dangers of "pig-sticking", as pursued with reference to the Wild Boar (*Sus scrofa*) of Europe, his Indian cousin (*S. cristata*), and the African Wart-Hog (*Phacochœrus*), have been fully described by many authors, and need no mention here. Regarding the Peccaries (*Dicotyles*) of America, something has already been said (see p. 334).

To give here even a brief account of the numerous swift runners or active climbers which belong to the Ungulata, and provide many varieties of sport, is both impossible and unnecessary. Among them the Red Deer (*Cervus elaphus*, fig. 1265) may perhaps be given first place, at least from the English stand-point, and though the glories of stag-hunting have faded so far as Britain is concerned, innumerable trophies still attest the important place it once held in our national life. Deer-stalking in the "deer forests" of Scotland is excellent sport, but not comparable to hunting the wild animal in the old-time fashion, which, in this country, is now only possible on Exmoor. Regarding a third variety of the sport once popular in Britain Lord Granville Gordon makes the following very apposite remarks (in *Sport in Europe*):—"True we can still pursue him in what might be described as a pickled state, with horns shorn off, around the purlieus of Windsor, or in one or two other places, but, pleasant though the run may actually be, the 'sport' cannot stand close investigation, for sport consists in the strategy and skill of man in pursuing and capturing a wild animal. It loses all its charm and all its poetry when the game is first, as it were, tethered". Wild Red Deer are fortunately more numerous in other parts of Europe, *e.g.* in Hungary, than in Britain, but stalking and driving are in most cases the chief methods employed. The following remarks by Paul Caillard (in *The Sports of the World*) are of interest as showing that stag-hunting is to this day practised in France on a considerable scale:—"If hunting generally is known as the 'sport of kings', then surely is stag-hunting particularly associated with the memories of mediæval courts, and, although some might not perhaps expect it, modern France preserves above all other lands the tradition and even the outward forms of the ancient *chasse*. . . . In many of our French forests it would be as great a heresy to kill a deer otherwise than before the hounds as ever it would on Exmoor, and many visitors to our meets have expressed their pleasure at the survival of such picturesque sport."

Fig. 1265.—Red-Deer Trophy

GNAWING MAMMALS (RODENTIA).—Coursing the Hare with greyhounds is a very ancient form of amusement, which appears to have been indulged in by the Assyrians (fig. 1266). We next hear of it in Greece, and many details are given by Arrian (born

A.D. 90) in his work on coursing. The ancient Gauls were experts in this form of sport, which was probably introduced into Britain from their country. With us, however, it is now almost entirely replaced by hare-hunting with harriers, which supplies much of the interest of fox-hunting at considerably less expense. We know from Xenophon (B.C. 400) that the ancient Greeks in his time pursued the hare with two kinds of dog, the nature of which is doubtful, though they were certainly not greyhounds. It is hardly necessary to add that the sporting value of the Hare is found in its great speed, coupled with considerable ingenuity in "doubling", calculated to baffle even the swift greyhound.

The passion for sport, which is so thoroughly British, is

Fig. 1266.—Hares coursed by Greyhounds, as depicted on the edge of an Assyrian bronze dish.

gratified and kept alive among those with slender means by the possibilities which the inexpensive Rabbit (*Lepus cuniculus*) offers. The use of the Ferret has already been indicated (see p. 369). Nor even here do we reach the lowest plane, for the Brown Rat (*Mus decumanus*) undoubtedly seems to minister in no small degree to the sporting instincts of a considerable fraction of the community, though it would not be admitted into an orthodox work on Sport.

BIRDS (AVES) HUNTED FOR SPORT

In the palmy days of falconry the Grey Heron (*Ardea cinerea*) was, of course, the chief bird pursued for sport, but hawking (for Rooks, Larks, &c.) is now practised by the few (see p. 369), having fallen from its once high estate owing to the introduction of and constant improvement in firearms. Among the numerous species which now fall victims to the art of the gunner the GAME-BIRDS (GALLINÆ) take first place, and of these, in this country, three are pre-eminent, *i.e.* Pheasant (*Phasianus Colchicus*), Red

Grouse (*Lagopus Scoticus*), and Partridge (*Perdix cinerea*). Other well-known members of the group are: Capercailzie (*Tetrao urogallus*), Black Grouse (*Lyrurus tetrix*), Ptarmigan (*Lagopus mutus*), and Quail (*Coturnix communis*).

In many kinds of shooting one is rather inclined to think that things are made too easy for the gunners, not all of whom can be called good shots, and the size of the "bag" too often appears to be the object of overmuch attention. It is clear that both these tendencies greatly diminish the true "sporting" element. The following quotations show that some sportsmen are inclined to compare our own methods unfavourably with those of "the good old days". Nicholas Everitt (in *The Sports of the World*) thus speaks on the point:—"In England, in the old days, our forbears were wont to sally forth in the early morning, before the autumnal dews had left the grass and undergrowth, accompanied by their favourite pointers, setters, or spaniels, to double the hedgerows and to hunt the commons and likely places for pheasants, when, if they obtained as many single birds as some of the modern school of sportsmen now require hundreds, they would return home contented with their bag and lot". The Marquess of Granby (in *English Sport*) speaks still more strongly: —"But, nevertheless, it is open to question whether there is as much real keenness about working for their sport amongst the younger generation of gunners as there used to be twenty or thirty years ago, let alone a century. A wild, rough day's shooting does not nowadays apparently appeal to many. The large majority of gunners would not say 'thank you' for the offer of such a day's sport. It would look as if the deliberately competitive system of shooting, which now so largely prevails—by which I mean that very often the owner of one shooting-place seems to vie with the next-door one as to the amount of game he can kill off his property, and appears seriously annoyed if he hears that anyone round about him has had an exceptionally heavy day's sport, or one better, as regards numbers, than any he can produce—has to a great extent unfamiliarized the rising and just risen race of sportsmen with those days when hard walking, and consequently good condition, coupled with some knowledge of wood and field craft, were necessary if any satisfactory results were to be obtained."

The Red Grouse (*Lagopus Scoticus*) is a game-bird of par-

RED GROUSE (*Lagopus Scoticus*) GLIDING UP TO THE GUNS

The Red Grouse or Muirfowl is here selected for illustration not only on account of its importance as a game-bird, but also because it is the only member of its class peculiar to our islands. In Great Britain it ranges from the Orkneys to Shropshire and Glamorgan, and is also found in Ireland, though less abundantly. The Red Grouse is closely related to the Willow Grouse (*Lagopus albus*), which ranges right round the colder parts of the Northern Hemisphere, but it does not, like this species and the Ptarmigan (*L. mutus*), turn white in winter, though there are seasonal changes in the plumage. It is popularly supposed that the date at which grouse-shooting begins determines the rising of Parliament, and although the notion is erroneous its origin is not far to seek.

RED GROUSE (LAGOPUS SCOTICUS) GLIDING UP TO THE GUNS

ticular interest, as it happens to be peculiar to Britain. The old method of "walking" has now mostly given place in this country to "driving". The latter practice, curiously enough, is more favourable to the maintenance of sufficient numbers on a grouse-moor than the former. It is suggested that when the birds are driven the old ones are the first to glide up to the guns, so that the undue destruction of immature individuals is obviated. Besides which the old birds are said to be so quarrelsome as seriously to interfere with the domestic plans of their juniors.

Fig. 1267.—Flamingoes (*Phœnicopterus roseus*)

PERCHING BIRDS (PASSERES).— Hawking for Rooks (*Corvus frugilegus*) and Sky-Larks (*Alauda arvensis*) has already been mentioned (see p. 369).

PLOVERS (LIMICOLÆ). — Woodcock (*Scolopax rusticola*) and Snipe (*Gallinago cœlestis*) are familiar sporting birds.

BUSTARDS (ALECTORIDES).—The Great Bustard (*Otis tarda*), once a native of Britain, affords good sport in several European countries, including Hungary, Russia, Roumania, Spain, and Portugal. The Little Bustard (*O. tetrax*) is also the object of sporting attentions.

DUCKS, GEESE, SWANS, AND FLAMINGOES (ANSERES).—The art of wild-fowling is largely applied to the members of this group (also to Woodcock and Snipe) on inland waters, in swampy districts, and along low shores. Our own Norfolk Broads furnish an example. In sport of the kind punting plays a large part.

The Flamingo (*Phœnicopterus roseus*, fig. 1267) is one of the most interesting birds that falls to the gun of the fowler in the Peninsula. Chapman & Buck (in *Wild Spain*) thus describe the method pursued:—"Flamingoes are always shy and watchful birds, and their great height gives them a commanding view of threatening dangers; but there are degrees in intensity of wildness, and despite the unquestionable difficulty of flamingo-shooting, we would certainly not place these long-necked birds in the first rank among impracticable wild-fowl. Wild geese, for example, many of the duck-tribe, and nearly all the larger raptores far exceed them in incessant vigilance and downright astuteness. Flamingoes, however, will not, as a rule, permit of approach by the ordinary Spanish method of the stalking-horse, or *cabresto*: while the treacherous pony is still two gunshots away, the warning croak of the sentries is given, and at once the whole herd start to walk away, opening out their ranks as they move off. The method we found most effective to secure them was by partially surrounding a herd with a line of mounted men, who rode far out beyond them and then drove them over our two guns, each concealed behind his horse and crouching knee-deep in water. Of all the dirty work that wild-fowling in its many forms necessitates, this flamingo-driving takes the palm. It is mud-larking pure and simple, man, horse, and gun alike encased in a clinging argillaceous covering like the street-Arab amphibians below London Bridge. It is a fine sight to see a big flight of flamingoes, say five hundred, coming well in to the gun—*entrando bien á la escopeta*! The whole sky is streaked with columns of strange forms, and the still air resounds with the babel of discordant croaks and cries. How wondrously they marshal those long uniform files, bird behind bird, without break or confusion, and how precisely do those thousand black wing-points beat in rapid regular unison! Flamingoes are not 'hard' birds: their feathers being loose and open, and the extremely long neck a specially vulnerable part, they may be brought down from a considerable height even with small shot."

REPTILES (Reptilia) HUNTED IN SPORT

About the only Reptile that can be considered as furnishing anything in the nature of sport is the American Alligator

(*Alligator Mississippiensis*), native to the south-eastern part of the United States. The " 'Gator " is shot from the bank or from a boat, and is sometimes attracted by tying up a dog as a bait.

FISHES (PISCES) HUNTED IN SPORT

The "gentle craft" has always had, and always will have, a large number of supporters. It of course finds its highest expression in fly-fishing, as applied to species the capture of which

Fig. 1268.—Grayling (*Thymallus vulgaris*)

calls for the exercise of patience, skill, and other sportsmanlike qualities.

Salmon (*Salmo salar*) and Trout (*S. fario*, &c.) are generally regarded as taking first rank among game-fishes, and the Grayling (*Thymallus vulgaris*, fig. 1268) may also be given an honourable place. H. A. Rolt's appreciation of the last-named fish (in *The Sports of the World*) is well worth quoting, especially as the pleasures of angling for Grayling are much less familiar than the joys of the fisher for salmon or trout:—"It is remarkable what a peculiar fascination there is in connection with the capture of the grayling with the artificial fly. Some men who have killed hundreds of trout fall hopelessly in love with the sport the 'gray lady of the stream' affords from the very first moment they enter the lists against it, and infinitely prefer the autumn and winter pastime it provides to any other branch of angling.

The enthusiasm and all-absorbing interest it evokes in the angler are incomprehensible even to many disciples of the good and observant Walton himself, for to sally forth, fly-rod in hand, when the ground is hard with frost or the fields are white with snow, seems to them to savour somewhat of folly and madness. In the soft, bright spring-time it is delightful to wander by the rippling stream and stalk the spotted trout, to the accompaniment of the glorious melody of birds—to watch the budding foliage bursting into new life, and gaze upon the river shining like gold

Fig. 1269.—Pike (*Esox lucius*)

in the dancing sunlight. On quiet, restful summer evenings, too, the splash of the fish as they enjoy an abundant feast of Duns is the sweetest of music to the angler's ear, and he may perchance induce his quarry to look with favour upon the artifically-dressed copy of the fly he offers them, and grass a brace or two of lovely specimens ere darkness compels him, as a thorough sportsman, to leave the stream. But it is amid different and far less exhilarating surroundings that the grayling fisher's labours begin and are continued to the end. As autumn approaches, the rise of fly becomes sparse and erratic, and when September's days are out, the trout fisher finds his occupation gone. Thymallus steps in to fill what would otherwise be a great gap in his piscatorial life. But for the grayling, his rods would hang upon the wall during the long winter months, 'a mournful, half-accusing row', unused, and perhaps uncared for."

Some of the "coarse fish" also provide good sport, particularly the Pike (*Esox lucius*, fig. 1269), the Barbel (*Barbus vulgaris*), and the Perch (*Perca fluviatilis*).

Sea-fishing in many forms also has innumerable votaries. If size, strength, and game qualities are taken as the criteria, the great Tarpon (*Megalops thrissoides*), common off the coast of Florida, must be given a prominent position. It is to all intents and purposes a gigantic herring, which may be as much as five feet in length; and W. H. Grenfell says of it (in *The Sports of the World*) that ". . . until a new sporting fish is found I think the tarpon in the sea, as the salmon in fresh water, can still claim to be the most exciting quarry of the angler with the rod and line". Fishing for the Tunny (*Orcynus thynnus*) off the south coast of Spain would also seem to be a worthy occupation for the brethren of the rod, and specimens captured in this way have scaled as much as 50 pounds.

Among native marine fishes, the Grey Mullet (*Mugil capito*) and Bass (*Labrax lupus*) are perhaps the most esteemed, on account of their sporting qualities and the difficulties attending their capture. Both frequent estuaries, and the Bass is a near relative of the Perch.

CHAPTER LXXIII

UTILITARIAN ZOOLOGY—ANIMAL PETS

It is the merest commonplace to say that a considerable number of animals are either domesticated or kept in captivity as pets, and those which have perhaps the best right to the name simply afford gratification to human tastes, or, it may be, serve as objects of affection. In the latter case the pet-keepers may either have a genuine liking for animals, or else the over-fed lap-dog, the spoilt feline, or the loquacious parrot may be the recipient of caresses that under different circumstances might have been bestowed upon some specimen or other of that alleged highest Mammal—*Homo sapiens.*

MAMMALS (MAMMALIA) AS PETS

MONKEYS (PRIMATES).—On account of their intelligence many species of Monkey find favour as pets among both civilized and uncivilized races. But most of them are so terribly mischievous that only a sailor or the late Frank Buckland could put up with their pranks for any lengthened period. It is said that even Buckland found his two favourites, "Tiny" and "The Hag", trying at times, and a friend recommended him to build a cage for himself in the middle of his study. It is interesting to note that the keepers in Zoological Gardens often make great pets of their charges, especially when these happen to be intelligent apes, as, *e.g.*, Chimpanzees (fig 1270).

The Marmosets are attractive little creatures, so far as appearance goes, and are not infrequently kept as pets; but they are rather lacking in intelligence, and apt to impose a tax on the olfactory organs.

FLESH-EATING MAMMALS (CARNIVORA).—The fact that this order includes both Dog and Cat makes it of primary importance from the present stand-point.

The Dog (*Canis familiaris*), man's earliest friend among the animals, is undoubtedly the "king of pets", for even the commonest mongrel is full of intelligence, and overflows with affection for his owner, even when subjected to much ill treatment, as is but too often the case. Among the breeds which have been brought into existence simply to be petted may be mentioned—the Italian Greyhound, the Pug (a diminutive and

Fig. 1270.—Young Chimpanzee (*Anthropopithecus niger*)

particularly ugly relative of the mastiff, fig. 1271), the King Charles Spaniel, the Skye Terrier, the "Toy" Terrier, and the Poodle. The last is particularly clever in learning tricks, as may often be noted in exhibitions of performing dogs. The Dalmatian and the Hairless Dog of Japan are both curiosities in their way. No better example than these and other breeds of Dog could be given to show the effect of human interference upon the normal course of evolution. Modifications in shape, size, proportions, colour, hair, and even temperament have been brought about within a comparatively short space of time, in a way that suggests nothing so much as "clay in the hands of the potter". By taking advantage of variations that occur naturally it is possible to "make to order" almost any desired pattern of the canine race.

The Cat (*Felis domesticus*).—The differences between the various breeds of this animal are by no means so striking as those existing between the different sorts of dog, and chiefly relate to colour, character of the fur, and relative length of the tail. It has been suggested that the stripes of the "tabby" indicate a strain derived from the ordinary Wild Cat (*Felis catus*) of Europe. Among both wild and tame animals it is not uncommon to find individuals in which pigment is either present in excess, or else largely deficient. Illustrations of this are afforded by "nigger" rabbits and white blackbirds. Such "sports" are respectively described in technical language as examples of "melanism" and "albinism". The jet black cat once associated with magical practices, and the pure white pussy with blue eyes are thus classed. Why albino cats should be usually deaf, as appears to be the case, is as yet unexplained. The long and handsome coats of the Persian or Angora Cats (fig. 1272) renders them great favourites among those who admire felines, though they seem rather apt to be short-tempered, if one may be permitted to say so.

Fig. 1271.—Pug Dog

That the indigenous cats of the Isle of Man are devoid of tails is known to all; some of the Crimean cats are said to be similarly deficient, and the same peculiarity has been noticed in some Japanese individuals. Lydekker (in *The Royal Natural History*) thus speaks of some other peculiar varieties:—"In Siam there is a breed of cats reserved for royalty, characterized by their uniform, and often dark, fawn colour, their blue eyes, and the presence of two or more perfectly bald spots on the forehead. Siam, together with Burma, also possesses a breed known as the Malay cat, in which the tail is but of half the usual length, and is often, through deformity in its bones, tightly curled up into a knot."

The present writer is not a great lover of cats, but, desiring to be just, adds the following appreciation by Romanes (in *Animal Intelligence*) of this domestic carnivore:—"The cat is unquestionably a highly intelligent animal, though, when contrasted

Fig. 1272.—Persian Cat

with its great domestic rival the dog, its intelligence, from being cast in quite a different mould, is very frequently underrated. Comparatively unsocial in temperament, wanderingly predaceous in habits, and lacking in the affectionate docility of the canine nature, this animal has never in any considerable degree been subject to the psychological transforming influences whereby a prolonged and intimate association with man has so profoundly modified the psychology of the dog. Nevertheless, the cat is not only by nature an animal remarkable for intelligence, but, in spite of its naturally imposed disadvantage of temperament, has not altogether escaped those privileges of nurture which unnumbered centuries of domestication could scarcely fail to supply. Thus, as contrasted with most of the wild species of the genus when tamed from their youngest days, the domestic cat is conspicuously of less uncertain temper towards its masters

—the uncertainty of temper displayed by nearly all the wild members of the feline tribe when tamed being, of course, an expression of the interference of individual with hereditary experience. And, as contrasted with all the wild species of the genus when tamed, the domestic cat is conspicuous in alone manifesting any exalted development of affection towards the human kind; for in many individual cases such affection, under favouring circumstances, reaches a level fully comparable to that which it attains in the dog."

Passing notice may be given to the Mangoustis or Mungooses, also known as Ichneumons, of which one, the Egyptian Mungoose

Fig. 1273.—Indian Mungoose (*Herpestes griseus*)

(*Herpestes ichneumon*), has been domesticated in Egypt from time immemorial, while the common Indian Mungoose (*H. griseus*, fig. 1273) is commonly kept as a pet in its native country, and appears to be both intelligent and affectionate. The latter species is known to the readers of Kipling as "Rikki-tikki".

Gnawing Mammals (Rodentia).—Human influence has resulted in the production of a large number of varieties of Rabbits, Rats, and Mice, some of which have been alternately tended and neglected by almost every boy. Upon the Rabbit (*Lepus cuniculus*) one of the most remarkable results of domestication has been, in certain breeds, the great elongation of the ears, and the drooping position they have assumed. There has also been a large amount of variation in the colour and character of the fur.

The various domesticated breeds of Rat (*Mus rāttus*) and

Mouse (*M. musculus*) differ chiefly from one another in colour. The curious evolutions of "waltzing mice" appear to be due to defects in the structure of the internal ear.

Among other rodents serving as pets may be mentioned—the Alpine Marmot (*Arctomys marmotta*), the Dormouse (*Muscardinus avellanarius*), the Squirrel (*Sciurus vulgaris*), and the Guinea-Pig.

BIRDS (AVES) AS PETS

The number of species represented among pet-birds, including those which are better described as "captives", is very large indeed, and it will be unnecessary to mention more than a few of them.

PERCHING BIRDS (PASSERES).—Many of these are domesticated on account of their beauty or vocal powers, or both, and not a few of these have exchanged the sweets of liberty for a small and uncomfortable cage. To treat small birds in this fashion is scarcely less than criminal. Large aviaries, of course, are on a somewhat different footing. Fortunately the objection does not apply to the most popular of all pet birds, the Canary (*Serinus canarius*, fig. 1274), of which countless generations have been brought up in captivity, and of which the numerous strikingly different breeds may almost be regarded as artificial products. Newton makes the following remarks about this bird (in *A Dictionary of Birds*):—"It abounds not only in the islands whence it has its name, but in the neighbouring groups of the Madeiras and Azores. It seems to have been imported into Europe very early in the sixteenth century. Turner in 1544 speaks of the birds '*quas Anglia aues canarias uocat*', a statement confirmed by the poet Gascoigne, who died in 1577, and speaks . . . of 'Canara byrds'. Gesner had not seen one in 1555, but he gave an account of it . . . , communicated to him by Raphael Seiler of Augsburg under the name of *Suckeruögele*. The wild stock is of an olive-green, mottled with dark-brown above and greenish-yellow beneath. All the bright-hued examples we now see in captivity have been induced by carefully breeding from any chance varieties that have shown themselves; and not only the colour but the build and stature of the bird have in this manner been greatly modified. The change must have begun early, for Hernandez, who died in 1587, described the bird . . . as being wholly yellow (*tota lutea*), except the end of its wings. Of late the ingenuity of 'the fancy', which might seem to have exhausted itself in the production of top-knots, feathered feet, and so forth, has brought about a still further change from the original type. It has been found by a particular treatment, in which the mixing

Fig. 1274.—Canaries (*Serinus canarius*). 1, Wild form; 2, common yellow; 3, crested variety; 4, Scotch fancy.

of large quantities of cayenne-pepper with the food plays an important part, the ordinary 'canary yellow' may be intensified so as to verge upon a more or less brilliant flame colour. Birds which have successfully undergone this forcing process, and are hence called 'hot canaries', command a very high price, for a large proportion die under the discipline, though it is said that they soon become exceedingly fond of the exciting condiment." Space forbids any attempt to describe the methods by which the German fanciers of the Harz valleys teach canaries the notes of other birds, or even various tunes.

Another well-known and extremely pretty cage-bird is the Java Sparrow (*Munia oryzivora*), which has long been an object of domestication, and is distinguished by its extreme tameness.

On account of their intelligence, sprightliness, and imitative powers, the Raven, Jackdaw, Magpie, and Starling appeal to many persons more than Canaries and other small singing-birds. They are not, however, so frequently seen in captivity, partly on account of the thievish propensities of all but the last.

PARROTS (PSITTACI).—Among the many species of this group which are kept in captivity, the common Grey Parrot (*Psittacus erithacus*), native to tropical Africa, probably stands highest in public estimation. This is partly due to its extreme liveliness, but chiefly on account of the clever way in which it learns fragments of human speech, and imitates familiar sounds, such as the drawing of corks and the like. The often singularly malapropos nature of the remarks and sounds greatly increase their charm.

Parrots have been known and appreciated for more than two thousand years as clever imitative birds, often with brilliant plumage. Some of the Indian species appear to have been those first known to Europeans, while the resources of Africa were exploited later on. Regarding this, Newton (in *A Dictionary of Birds*) speaks as follows:—"That Africa had parrots does not seem to have been discovered by the ancients till long after, as Pliny tells us (vi, 29) that they were first met with by explorers employed by Nero beyond the limits of Upper Egypt. These birds, highly prized from the first, reprobated by the moralist, and celebrated by more than one classical poet, as time went on were brought in great numbers to Rome, and ministered in various ways to the luxury of the age. Not only were they lodged in cages of tortoise-shell and ivory, with silver wires, but they were professedly esteemed as delicacies for the table, and one emperor is said to have fed his lions upon them. . . . With the decline of the Roman Empire the demand for parrots in Europe lessened, and so the supply dwindled, yet all knowledge of them was not wholly lost, and they are occasionally mentioned by one writer or another until in the fifteenth century began that career of geographical discovery which has since proceeded uninterruptedly. This immediately brought with it the knowledge of many more forms of these birds than had ever before been seen, for whatever races of men were visited by European navigators—whether in the East Indies or the West, whether in Africa or the islands of the Pacific—it was almost invariably found that even the most savage tribes had tamed some kind

Fig. 1275.—Macaw (*Ara*)

of parrot; and, moreover, experience soon showed that no bird was more easily kept alive on board ship and brought home, while, if it had not the merit of 'speech', it was almost certain to be of beautiful plumage."

One of the prettiest pets among these birds is the Grass-Parakeet or Budgerigar (*Melopsittacus undulatus*) of Australia. Yellow, green, and black are the chief components of the colour scheme, but the two central tail-quills are blue, and there is a patch of the same hue on either side of the face.

The affectionate little Love-Birds are deservedly popular.

The name is properly applied to certain African species (of *Agapornis*), but it may also be taken to include the Parrotlets (*Psittacula*) of South America.

The sprightly crested Cockatoos (*Cacatuidæ*) of the Australian region do not lack their admirers, while for gaudy coloration few birds surpass the long-tailed Macaws (species of *Ara*, fig. 1275), which range from Mexico into South America.

REPTILES (REPTILIA) AS PETS

Reptiles make no appeal to the affections or fancies of most persons, though various species prove attractive to some. The ancient Egyptians, as everyone knows, regarded the Nile Crocodile (*Crocodilus Niloticus*) as sacred, and made a sort of pet divinity of the creature, but this hardly comes within the scope of the present section. Some persons have a fancy for certain Snakes, such as our common and innocuous Grass-Snake (*Tropidonotus natrix*), and the Indian snake-charmers tame the Cobra (*Naia tripudians*), actuated, however, by strictly business motives. Regarding the latter, Gadow (in *The Cambridge Natural History*) speaks as follows:—"This cobra is used by Indian conjurers. The 'dance' is the habit of these snakes of erecting themselves, when agitated, upon the hinder third or quarter of their length, whilst they spread out the hood and sway the head and neck to the right and left, always in an attitude ready for striking. They are docile, and by nature not vicious. Most of the performing cobras have their teeth drawn, and they then know well that they cannot bite. They only strike at the hand, just as uninjured specimens soon avoid biting into the iron rod with which they are lifted up in menageries. The drawing of the teeth is an operation which has to be repeated, since reserve-teeth soon take the place of the lost pair."

Various Lizards are or have been tamed, and some of them are very attractive, *e.g.* the beautiful Green Lizard (*Lacerta viridis*). The Common Gecko (*Tarentola Mauritanica*) of North Africa and South Spain and Portugal often lives in houses in a half-domesticated condition, running over the walls and ceilings in pursuit of flies. And such lizards are sometimes actually tamed.

The most familiar domesticated reptile in this country is the Grecian Tortoise (*Testudo Græca*), though it can scarcely be called an interesting pet. Gilbert White has immortalized one specimen, which was over forty years old when it came into his possession in 1780, and died fourteen years later. But, for longevity, it would be hard to beat some of the huge land-tortoises which were at one time common in the islands of the Indian Ocean. Regarding one species (*Testudo Sumeirei*) Gadow makes the following interesting remarks (in *The Cambridge Natural History*):—"This kind is supposed to have been the species peculiar to the Seychelles. In 1766 five large tortoises were brought from the Seychelles to Mauritius by Chevalier Marion de Tresne. Of these only three were alive in 1898, two in Mauritius and one in London; the latter specimen soon died in the Zoological Gardens. One of the two survivors, the last of their race, is famous. It was kept at Port Louis, and when Mauritius became a British possession in 1810 the tortoise was especially mentioned and taken over. It still [1900] lives there in the grounds of the barracks of the garrison. According to the proverbial oldest inhabitants, it had in 1810 already reached its present size, namely, a shell-length of about 40 inches, with a greatest circumference of . . . 8 feet 6 inches. When walking it stands about . . . 25.4 inches high, . . . and it can then carry with ease two full-grown men on its back. This old male is now nearly blind, but is otherwise of regular habits and in good health. Although it has been known for nearly 150 years, it had to wait for its scientific name until the year 1892."

AMPHIBIANS (AMPHIBIA) AS PETS

Ordinary Toads and Frogs have at times been subjected to domestication, and are by no means wanting in interest and intelligence. The pretty little Green Tree-Frogs of Europe (*Hyla arborea*) are less known as pets than they deserve to be. In North and Central America the Horned Toad (*Phrynosoma*) is subjected to a certain amount of domestication.

FISHES (PISCES) AS PETS

The greatest favourite in the aquarium is probably the Gold-Fish (*Carassius auratus*, fig. 1276), a kind of carp native to China and Japan. Domestication has eliminated dark pigment from its skin, leaving only the golden-yellow hue from which its name is derived. Various monstrosities have also been produced, especially the "Telescope Fish", with eyes on short projections, and a large abnormal tail-fin. It is stated that the Gold-Fish was originally introduced into this country in 1691.

Another aquarium favourite is the Paradise-Fish (*Polyacanthus viridi-auratus*, fig. 1276), domesticated in China from very remote

Fig. 1276.—Pet Fishes. 1, Gold Fish (*Carassius auratus*; 2, "Telescope" variety of same; 3, Paradise Fish (*Polyacanthus viridi-auratus*).

times, and only known in captivity. Its golden sides are cross-barred with red, and some of its fins are abnormally developed (see also vol. iii, p. 427).

The Siamese keep certain pugnacious fishes in captivity in order to enjoy the sight of their combats.

INSECTS (INSECTA) AS PETS

Some Insects are excitable, and can easily be induced to fight together. The ingenious Chinese keep various species in captivity in order to enjoy these mimic combats. Their list includes Mantids, Beetles, Grasshoppers, and Crickets. The same curious kind of amusement is practised to some extent in Italy. Nor must the evolutions of performing Fleas be forgotten.

CHAPTER LXXIV

UTILITARIAN ZOOLOGY—ANIMAL PRODUCTS USED FOR DECORATIVE PURPOSES—ANIMAL ÆSTHETICS

We have here first to consider the chief animal products employed for decorative purposes, and afterwards briefly to review the principles of Animal Æsthetics.

ANIMAL PRODUCTS USED FOR DECORATIVE PURPOSES

A number of animal products which were originally valued by mankind chiefly as ministering to the primary necessities of life, now derive their main worth from the ornamental or decorative possibilities they present, or they are, at any rate, in increased demand on that account. Furs, horns, silk, and the skins of some birds belong to this category (see pp. 303, 310, 259, and 308).

We are especially concerned in this chapter with products which from the first have been employed by way of ornament or decoration, sometimes also as a means of heightening the attractions of materials of other kind.

DECORATIVE PRODUCTS OF MAMMALS (MAMMALIA).—Some Mammals have been ruthlessly hunted down by man for the sake of the ivory furnished by their teeth. Prominent among these are the Elephants (*Elephas*), and, as will be gathered from fig. 1277, the tusks of the African species may attain very large dimensions. The extinct Mammoth (*E. primigenius*) has also long been known as a source of "fossil ivory". The tusks of Walrus (*Trichechus rosmarus*) furnish a further supply, as does the long spirally-grooved "horn" of the male Narwhal (*Monodon monoceros*), of which two are occasionally present in the same animal. While the tusks of the Walrus are canine teeth, those of the other animals mentioned are incisors.

Many of the trophies of sport are decidedly ornamental, such as the skins of beasts of prey, the antlers of deer, the heads of fox or wolf, the prepared feet of the elephant, &c. &c. Among primitive races such things as necklaces of tigers' or lions' claws are greatly esteemed.

DECORATIVE PRODUCTS OF BIRDS (AVES).—The beautiful plumage of many birds seems always to have appealed to the human colour-sense or appreciation of form, and much slaughter of certain members of the feathered race has resulted on the part of savage races, often to minister to the vanity of other races sometimes supposed to be fully civilized. The trade in ostrich-feathers (see p. 251) is a legitimate branch of the plume-industry, and nothing can be said against the use of the cast feathers of beautiful forms like the different species of Peacock. But, on the other hand, the wholesale massacre that takes place every year of many exquisitely lovely species, purely to satisfy the love of finery which has been inherited by civilized nations from barbarian ancestors, deserves the most unsparing censure. Birds of Paradise, Sun-Birds, Humming-Birds, and Egrets are prominent in the long list of victims.

Fig. 1277.—Tusks of African Elephant

DECORATIVE PRODUCTS OF REPTILES (REPTILIA).—The skins of Crocodiles and various lizards are used for ornamental purposes, but the most important reptilian product is tortoise-shell, which consists of the horny epidermic shields of the widely-distributed Hawksbill Turtle (*Chelone imbricata*, fig. 1278). When softened by heat these can be worked up into all sorts of artistic objects. Very undesirable practices are often resorted to in procuring the raw material, as will be seen from the following quotation from Tennent (in *The Natural History of Ceylon*).—"If taken from the animal after death and decomposition, the colour of the shell becomes clouded and milky, and hence the cruel expedient is resorted to of seizing the turtles as they repair to the shore to deposit their eggs, and suspending them over fires till heat

Fig. 1278.—Hawksbill Turtle (*Chelone imbricata*)

makes the plates on the dorsal shields start from the bone of the carapace, after which the creature is permitted to escape to the water. At Celebes, where the finest tortoise-shell is exported to China, the natives kill the turtles by blows on the head, and immerse the shell in boiling water to detach the shields. Dry heat is only resorted to by the unskilful, who frequently destroy the tortoise-shell in the operation."

DECORATIVE PRODUCTS OF FISHES (PISCES).—Ornamental leather is made from the skins of Dog-Fishes and Sharks (shagreen), while the scales of Dace (*Leuciscus vulgaris*) and

Bleak (*L. alburnus*) are employed in the manufacture of artificial pearls.

DECORATIVE PRODUCTS OF MOLLUSCS (MOLLUSCA). — The shells of the Pearly Nautilus, of many univalves, and numerous bivalves, are largely used for purposes of personal decoration by savage races, and to some extent by civilized ones. Some of them are worked up into ornamental knick-knacks even in British watering-places, while the Chinese are singularly skilful in the construction of the images of gods, human beings, animals, and plants, from a variety of small shells (fig. 1279).

Fig. 1279.—Chinese Shell-ornament

Sea-Snails (*Gastropoda*).

The thick shells of some Sea-Snails (species of *Cassis*, &c.) are made up of layers of different tints, which has rendered them a favourite material upon which to carve cameos (fig. 1280). Pink pearls are the pathological products of certain species, especially the large Conch-Shell (*Strombus gigas*) of the West Indies.

The most famous product of Sea-Snails was, however, the royal dye known as Tyrian Purple, prepared by the ancient Phœnicians from species of Purpura and Murex (fig. 1281). It is secreted by a gland in the gill-cavity, closely connected with the intestine.

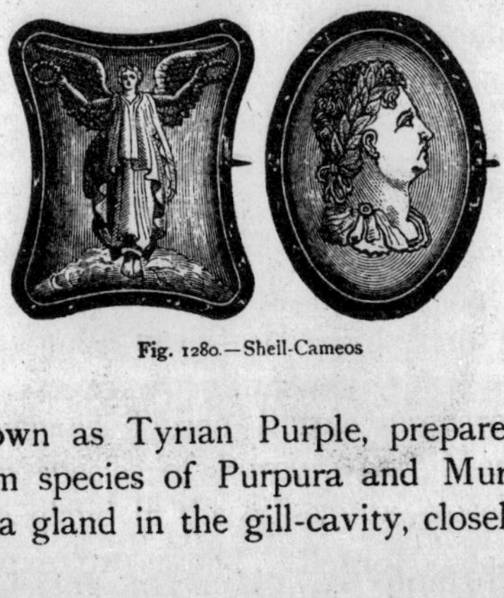

Fig. 1280.—Shell-Cameos

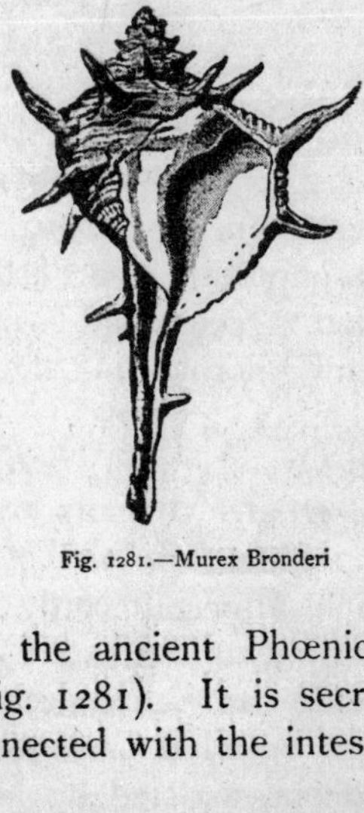

Fig. 1281.—Murex Bronderi

The explorations of the Phœnicians westward, which had no small influence upon the course of history, were partly conducted with the object of securing larger supplies of these molluscs.

Some of the travellers of the seventeenth and eighteenth centuries state that the natives of Ecuador and Costa Rica obtained a purple fluid from a species of Purpura, and used it to dye cotton. A kind of Sea-Slug (*Aplysia camelus*) is still used by the Portuguese for a similar purpose.

Bivalve Mollusca (*Lamellibranchia*).—Pearls and mother-of-pearl are chiefly derived from members of this group. Mother-of-pearl or nacre is the iridescent internal layer of the shell,

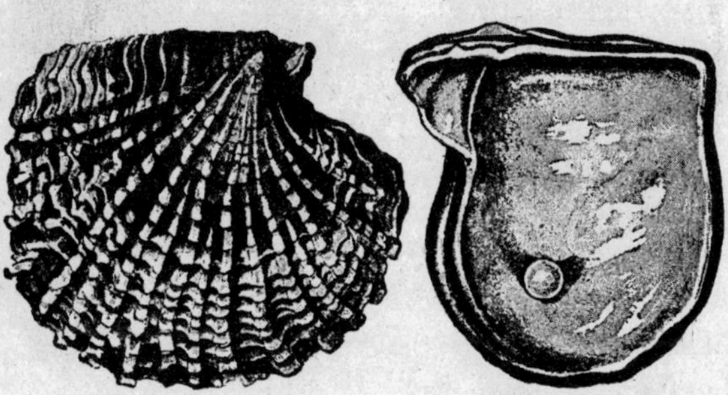

Fig. 1282.—Shells of Pearl-Oyster (*Margaritifera vulgaris*), and pearl of same.

while pearls consist of layers of similar material deposited round various foreign bodies which, in the most valuable kinds, are stages in the development of parasitic forms (see p. 204). The most important pearl-fisheries are those of the Red Sea, India, Ceylon, Queensland, some of the South Pacific archipelagoes, lower California, and the Pacific coast of Central America. The bivalve of greatest economic value in this connection is the Pearl-Oyster (*Margaritifera vulgaris*), which in reality is more of a mussel than an oyster, but belongs to a different family from either (*Aviculidæ*). The once important pearl-fisheries of Ceylon, after a record yield in 1891, benefiting the revenue of the island to the extent of hard on a million rupees, completely failed for an entire decade. As the outcome of this the pearl-oyster question has recently been investigated by Professor Herdman, assisted by Mr. James Hornell. These two experts have fully worked out the life-history of the tape-worm which leads to the formation of "orient pearls", and it is hoped that the knowledge acquired will form the basis of measures by which the industry may be resuscitated. The first part of Herdman's *Report on the Pearl-Oyster Fisheries of the Gulf of Manaar* includes a very interesting historical sketch from which the following extract is taken:—"The pearl-fisheries of Ceylon, India, and the Persian Gulf, yielding the highly prized 'Oriental' pearl, are of very great antiquity. They are probably the most ancient fisheries still in existence, and seem to be carried on at the present day under very much the same conditions as 2000 or perhaps even 3000 years ago. These fisheries are referred to by various classical writers, and Pliny, after saying how highly valued the pearls are at Rome, refers to Taprobane [Ceylon] as 'the most productive of pearls of all parts of the world'. . . . But the Singhalese records take us to still earlier times. According to the 'Mahawanso', pearls figure in the list of native products sent as a present from King Vijáya of Ceylon to his Indian father-in-law in about 540–550 B.C.; and again when, in B.C. 306, King Devanampiyatissa sent an embassy to India the presents are said to include eight kinds of Ceylon pearls. The King's Hall in the Brazen Palace at Anuradhapura (B.C. 161) is said to have been decorated with native pearls. The mortar in the ruins of Polonaruwa shows the remains of the pearl-oyster shells which were used in its manufacture—no doubt the refuse of an early fishery. Many other references could be given. In the eighth to eleventh centuries, trade in the East was in the hands of the Persians and Arabs, and we find Arab writers alluding to the pearls. We know also that they enriched the kings of Ceylon in the days of Marco Polo (1291). One record, given by Friar Jordanus, says that in 1330 about 8000 boats were engaged in the pearl-fisheries of the Gulf of Manaar."

From the remote times mentioned in the above extract down to the present day the pearl-oysters have been collected by native divers, but it is not improbable that dredging will ultimately be the chief method employed.

Pearls are formed within a number of bivalves besides the one mentioned, nor are all of these marine, for the once famous British pearls were obtained from Fresh water Mussels. Purple pearls are formed within some of the Ark-Shells (*Arca*).

DECORATIVE PRODUCTS OF INSECTS (INSECTA).—There is not much to mention with regard to this group of animals. The hard metallic-looking wing-covers or elytra of certain Beetles serve for various decorative purposes, and some of the more beautiful Butterflies are sometimes placed in glass cases and used as ornaments. Some of the Scale-Insects (*Coccidæ*) are the source of economic products of some importance in the present connection, *e.g.* the Cochineal Insect (*Coccus cacti*) furnishes red pigment (see p. 260). Objects known as "ground pearls" are found in the earth in various parts of the world, *e.g.* in the island of St. Vincent (West Indies), where they are made into necklaces, &c. They are in reality the encysted pupæ of Scale-Insects, covered by a hard substance looking like pearl or glass. The West Indian ones mentioned above belong to a species of Margarodes.

ANIMAL ÆSTHETICS

The course of human evolution has necessarily involved a gradually improving adaptation to surroundings, of which the outcome is seen in all the intricate details of modern civilization. Imaginative literature and the various branches of art are among the most remarkable results of this evolution, and the full discussion of their nature and origin is the province of that branch of philosophy known as Æsthetic. But as, after all, man is an animal, who has always lived among other animals that have profoundly influenced the course of his mental development, it naturally follows that the study of Æsthetic, as indeed of all other departments of philosophy, must look for its foundations among the principles of biology. The interdependence of natural science and philosophy is well brought out in the following quotation from Karl Groos (in *The Play of Animals*):—"Man's animal nature reveals itself in instinctive acts, and the latest investigators tell us that man has at least as many instincts as the brutes have, though most of them have become unrecognizable through the influence of education and tradition. Therefore an accurate knowledge of the animal world, where pure instinct is displayed, is indispensable in weighing the importance of inherited impulses in men. . . . The animal psychologist must harbour in his breast not only two souls, but more; he must unite with a thorough training in physiology, psychology, and biology the experience of a traveller, the practical knowledge of the director of a zoological garden, and the outdoor lore of a forester. And even then he could not round up his labours satisfactorily unless he were familiar with the trend of modern æsthetics." To briefly indicate some of the chief points of contact between Biology and Æsthetics is all that can be attempted here, and those who wish to pursue the subject fully are referred to the works of Herbert Spencer, Bain, Baldwin, Romanes, and Lloyd Morgan, as also to Grant Allen's *Physiological Æsthetics*, Knight's *Philosophy of the Beautiful*, Bosanquet's *History of Æsthetic*, and Groos's *Play of Animals*.

No human being or highly-organized animal would be able to live for any length of time, nor would the preservation of its species be possible, if constant adjustment to the surroundings was not brought about by the agency of the nervous system and sense-organs (see p. 2). This is seen, for example, in the utilitarian significance of pleasure and pain. Pleasure, broadly speaking, promotes actions which conduce to self-preservation and the maintenance of the species, while pain as constantly forbids other actions which would mean self-destruction. Unless pleasure were associated, for instance, with the act of eating, an animal would probably be content to starve, while if contact with burning substances caused no pain it would be very liable to self-cremation. Now there can be no doubt at all that the feelings to which Beauty and Ugliness give rise are simply to be regarded as finer manifestations of pleasure and pain, and since Æsthetics is concerned with such feelings it clearly rests upon a physiological basis.

THE SENSE OF SIGHT AND ITS BEARING ON ÆSTHETICS.—We have only to reflect for a moment on the deprivations suffered by a man blind from birth to realize that artistic enjoyment depends most upon the sense of sight. And our criteria of what is beautiful in colour, form, and movement have largely been evolved with reference to the animal world, including human beings. To mention examples is unnecessary, for the illustration scheme of this work provides them in abundance. But a few generalities are perhaps desirable.

No one will deny that the human colour-sense has been largely educated by the materials which flowers provide. But the exquisite tints and colour-schemes of the floral world are strictly utilitarian with reference to plants themselves, being simply devices for attracting beneficial insects (see p. 85). To insects, therefore, our æsthetic debt is very large.

The Courtship Colours of Insects, Birds, and some other animals (see p. 143) are also as a rule beautiful to us, and have played no small part in the evolution of our artistic sense. With reference to the animals which display them it is pretty certain that they are purely utilitarian.

Were we similarly to consider the materials upon which our ideas of the beautiful in form and movement are based, we should once more have to acknowledge that the evolution of the æsthetic sense has largely progressed on lines determined by the animal world.

Ugliness in the first instance appears to have been associated with what was harmful or dangerous. The repugnance which most of us feel towards snakes, scorpions, and centipedes is probably part of the legacy which has been handed down to us by our prehistoric ancestors (see vol. iii, p. 370). It is also generally admitted that "warning coloration", which marks undesirable properties in many animals, is crude and inartistic from the human stand-point.

THE SENSE OF HEARING AND ITS BEARING ON ÆSTHETICS.—Next to sight, hearing is the most important sense, from the æsthetic stand-point. The song of birds and the chirp of insects, which further the courtships of their owners (and hence are of utilitarian nature), must have had something to do with the evolution of our standards of what is beautiful in the realm of sound.

THE SENSE OF SMELL AND ITS BEARING ON ÆSTHETICS.—That certain odours are, to our thinking, of fragrant nature, is largely due to the direct or indirect influence which animals have had upon human development. Many species emit strong musky odours, serving for purposes of recognition, and also as courtship accessories. Civet-cats are an example of this, and at one time "civet", obtained from certain glands in these animals, was a favourite perfume, though it would now be considered rank. It has been replaced by musk, obtained from glands possessed by the Musk Deer (*Moschus moschiferus*), though even this perfume is too coarse for cultivated tastes, which show a preference for floral odours. But, as we have elsewhere seen (see p. 85), the delicate scents of flowers are of utilitarian meaning to the plants which possess them, being so many baits to attract useful insects.

One substance used as a sort of basis in the manufacture of perfume, *i.e.* ambergris, is on an entirely different footing from such things as musk or attar of roses, its properties being, so to speak, accidental. It consists of concretions, which are formed in the intestine of the Sperm-Whale as a result of disease.

THE SENSE OF TASTE AND ITS BEARING ON ÆSTHETICS.—The organs of taste were, in the first instance, undoubtedly evolved in relation to food-testing, a purely utilitarian matter. Adaptation to diets of particular kind would have been difficult, if not impossible, without this, and there would also have been a liability to take in poisonous substances. Pleasurable sensations would gradually come to be associated with the taste of desirable food, and sensations of opposite kind with that of unsuitable aliment, to say nothing of poisons.

Tastes pure and simple, such as that of sweetness, do not rank very high in the æsthetic scale, but it is otherwise with "flavours", which are combinations of tastes and odours. The triumphs of the art of cookery, so dear to the gourmand, are of necessity largely based on the properties of animals in the dead state. But this of course is a mere commonplace.

THE EVOLUTION OF ART AND CERTAIN FORMS OF LITERATURE.—In the evolution of Æsthetics, Groos considers that "play" has been a dominant factor. By Spencer (and Schiller before him) play was regarded as a manifestation of surplus energy, an expression of the "joy of life". But Groos interprets the play of animals as being an instinct whereby preparation is given for the stern realities of existence. A kitten, for example, by playing with various objects, including its own tail, acquires fitness for the pursuit of mice. According to this view an animal or young child does not play because it is young, but has a period of youth in order that it may play. Imitation is here of importance in helping the acquisition of powers that will later on be useful. Baldwin regards it as standing between instinct and intelligence, sometimes promoting the preservation of the former, and in other cases enabling it to be more or less discarded in favour of intelligent actions. Groos summarizes his ideas regarding the relation between play and art in the following table, which, though susceptible of criticism, will serve as the basis for a few remarks.

PLAY

Experimentation

(Joy in being able)

(Pretence: conscious self-deception)

Self-exhibition.	Imitation.	Decoration.
The Personal.	The True.	The Beautiful.
With animals { Courtship arts.	Imitative arts.	Building arts.
With man { Dance with excitement.	Imitative dance.	Ornamentation.
Music.	Pantomime.	Architecture.
Lyric poetry.	Sculpture.	
	Painting.	
	Epic Poetry.	
	Drama.	

Plenty of examples of each of the three primary groups above are to be found in the animal world. *Self-exhibition* as manifested in Courtship arts is sufficiently illustrated by Birds and Spiders, and some account of it has already been given (see pp. 148 and 166).

No better instance of *Imitation* could possibly be given than the concerted Dances of some birds, graphically described by Hudson (in *The Naturalist in La Plata*). The following is his account of the evolutions of the Spur-winged Lapwing (*Hoplopterus cayanus*, fig. 1283) of South America:—"The lapwing display, called by the natives its 'dance', or 'serious dance'—by which they mean square dance—requires three birds for its performance, and is, so far as I know, unique in this respect. The birds are so fond of it that they indulge in it all the year round, and at frequent intervals during the day, also on moonlight nights. If a person watches any two birds for some time—for they live in pairs—he will see another lapwing, one of a neighbouring couple, rise up and fly to them, leaving his own mate to guard their chosen ground; and instead of resenting this visit as an unwarranted intrusion on their domain, as they would certainly resent the approach of almost any other bird, they welcome it with notes and signs of pleasure. Advancing to the visitor, they place themselves behind it; then all three, keeping step, begin a rapid march, uttering resonant drumming notes in time with their movements; the notes of the pair behind being emitted in a stream, like a drum-roll, while the leader utters loud single notes at regular intervals. The march ceases; the leader elevates his wings and stands erect and motionless, still uttering loud notes; while the other two, with puffed-out plumage and standing exactly abreast, stoop forward and downward until the tips of their beaks touch the ground, and, sinking their rhythmical voices to a murmur, remain for some time in this posture. The performance is then over, and the visitor

Fig. 1283.—Dance of Spur-winged Lapwings (*Hoplopterus cayanus*)

goes back to his own ground and mate, to receive a visitor himself later on."

As to the third kind of artistic development, placed under the head of *Decoration*, we once more find among Birds the best illustrations. Their nests not only exemplify, in some cases, the art of building carried to a high pitch of perfection, but may also involve a certain amount of decorative skill. Both, however, are most strikingly seen in the curious "runs" made by the Bower-Birds, native to the Australian region. They appear to play some part in courtship, and their original discoverer, Gould, describes them as follows (in *Proceedings Zool. Society*, 1840):—"These constructions are perfectly anomalous in the architecture of birds, and consist in a collection of pieces of stick or grass, formed into a bower; or one of them (that of the *Chlamydera*) might be called an avenue, being about 3 feet in length, and 7 or 8 inches broad inside; a transverse section giving the figure of a horse-shoe, the round part downwards. They are used by the birds as a playing-house, or 'run' as it is termed, and are used by the males to attract the females. The 'run' of the Satin-Bird is much smaller, being less than 1 foot in length, and moreover differs from that just described in being decorated with the highly-coloured feathers of the parrot tribe; the *Chlamydera*, on the other hand, collects around its

Fig. 1284.—Gardener-Birds (*Amblyornis inornatus*), with hut and garden; male in foreground, female at back.

'run' a quantity of stones, shells, bleached bones, &c.; they are also strewed down the centre within."

Newton thus describes (in *A Dictionary of Birds*) some even more remarkable kinds of Bower-Bird, unknown to science at the time of Gould's observations:—"A bird of New Guinea, . . . *Amblyornis inornatus*, fig. 1284, has been found by Signor Beccari to present not only a modification of bower-building, but an appreciation of beauty perhaps unparalleled in the animal world. His interesting observations . . . show that this species, which he not inaptly calls the 'Gardener' (*Gjardiniere*), builds at the foot of a small tree a kind of hut or cabin (*capanna*) some 2 feet in height, roofed with orchid-stems that slope to the ground, regularly radiating from the central support, which is covered with a conical mass of moss, and sheltering a gallery round it. One side of this hut is left open, and in front of it is arranged a bed of verdant moss, bedecked with blossoms and berries of the brightest colours. As these ornaments wither they are removed to a heap behind the hut, and replaced by others that are fresh. The hut is circular and some 3 feet in diameter, and the mossy lawn in front of it nearly twice that expanse. Each hut and garden are, it is believed, though not known, the work of a single pair of birds, or perhaps of the male only; and it may be observed that this species, as its trivial name implies, is wholly inornate in plumage. Not less remarkable is the more recently described 'bower' of *Prionodura*, a genus of which the male . . . is conspicuous for his bright orange coloration. This structure is said by Mr. Devis . . . to be piled up almost horizontally round the base of a tree to the height of from 4 to 6 feet, and around it are a number of hut-like fabrics, having the look of a dwarfed native camp."

With the stages in the evolution of human art we are here not directly concerned, but enough has been said to show that a careful study of the habits of animals is likely to throw a good deal of light upon the subject.

ANIMALS AS MATERIAL FOR ART AND LITERATURE.—Animals form such an important part of the environment of man that they naturally figure largely in art and literature. If, in imagination, we entirely eliminate animal forms from galleries of sculpture or pictures we shall realize this very fully, and ideas derived from the animal world are also embodied to some extent in music. As we have elsewhere seen (p. 341), the Tarantella originated with reference to a kind of spider.

The art of decoration is also indebted to the animal world, some of the most beautiful designs being based upon animal forms. Mr. Talwin Morris' "peacock design" on the covers of this book is a particularly charming example.

In literature our debt to animals is no less great. The very letters of the alphabet, which, as everyone knows, are the descendants of Egyptian picture-symbols or hieroglyphs, were in some instances originally based on animal forms. V, for example, represents the last remains of a drawing of the Horned Viper (*Cerastes*) of Egypt (fig. 1285).

Animals make no inconsiderable figure in both prose and

poetry. In fables, from the time of Æsop downwards, they often supply the principal characters. Sterne has immortalized the Starling, Shakespeare and Shelley the Sky-Lark, Poe and Dickens the Raven, Aristophanes and Thoreau the Frog. Other examples are scattered broadcast through the literatures of the world, and to name them would be a work of supererogation. They often supply the *motif* for poetic efforts which express our

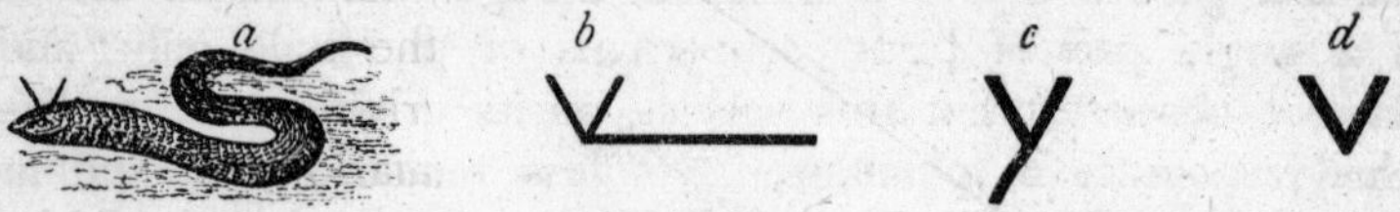

Fig 1285.—Evolution of V. *a*, Egyptian hieroglyphic; *b*, abbreviation of same; *c*, Phœnician form; *d*, final form.

sympathy with Nature, and appeal more particularly to those of us who are counted among the worshippers of "the great god Pan". The poem "Enchanted Tones", by J. S. Welhaven, may serve to illustrate this point, and it will be unknown to most readers, for its native language is Norwegian.

"A bird flew over the pine-clad hill
Of the old, old legends singing,
And carried me out of life's beaten way
Into dreamland's dim beginning.
I came to the moorland's secret spring
Where fairies their thirst were slaking,
But ever those magical notes I heard
'Midst the sighs that the breeze was making.

"I stood in the beech-trees' silver shade
As the sunset rays low slanted,
When glimmered the dew in the darkling glade
And on hill shone like gold enchanted:
Then rustled the branches, a sound drew nigh
As of wings that were rising and falling,
And ever from fell-top, and ever from tree
Those magical flute-notes were calling.

"Away in the woodland, far away,
Is the songster's leafy dwelling,
From under the pine-trees, ever and aye,
His melody's tide is swelling;
And though I never may reach his home,
The song there is no forgetting,
That sounded sweet when eve's dewy wings
Shut soft as the sun was setting."

DISTRIBUTION IN SPACE AND TIME

CHAPTER LXXV

GEOGRAPHICAL DISTRIBUTION

To consider, and so far as possible explain, the way in which animals are now spread over the surface of the globe is the province of Geographical Distribution, or, as it is sometimes called, Zoogeography. Alfred Russel Wallace, more than any other man, has been the means of placing this branch of Natural History on a really scientific footing, and his invaluable works *The Geographical Distribution of Animals* and *Island Life* will long remain standard sources of information on the subject. Smaller books by Heilprin and Beddard (*Geographical and Geological Distribution of Animals*, and *Zoogeography*) will also be found extremely useful by the student.

A good deal of information about the parts of the world to which a number of animals belong has already been given in the preceding sections of this work, but certain facts and principles require special mention here, though only elementary treatment is possible, or, it may be, desirable.

Before the theory of evolution became dominant it was commonly believed that any particular kind of animal found within a certain area was specially created there, and speculation was deemed out of place, though it was assumed that one sort of climate suited certain species, and another sort of climate other species. But we are not now contented with the statement "This is so", and always ask "*Why* is this so?" To which question we sometimes get a fairly satisfactory answer.

Areas of Distribution.—If we consider any kind or species of animal, or any one of the larger groups, such as a genus, a family, an order, or a class, we shall find that it may occupy a limited or an extensive area, or that it may be found in two or more widely distant parts of the world, and be entirely absent from the intervening regions. The last and perhaps the most interesting case is technically described by speaking of a "discontinuous area of distribution". Believing that existing species have been evolved in course of time from other species, it is pretty obvious that any sort of animal which occupies a restricted area must either have come into existence comparatively recently, or else be an ancient form which has gradually lost ground and is progressing towards extinction. A good example of the latter state of things is afforded by the Tuatara (*Hatteria punctata*), now only to be found on some islets in the Bay of Plenty, off the North Island of New Zealand, upon which larger land-mass we know that it formerly existed. The evidence of geology also proves that it is the last living representative of an order of Reptiles (*Rhychocephala*) which was once widely distributed and dominant, being very likely the parent reptilian group from which all the other orders took origin.

In dealing with questions of distribution it is important to remember that the outlines of land and sea have undergone many changes in the course of the world's history. At various periods, for example, the land-masses of the Old and New Worlds have been connected together in the North, while Australia and the East Indies are the surviving remnants of an extension of the mainland of Asia. Comparatively recent union between land-areas now distinct is often indicated by intervening shallow water, more ancient union by deeper water. From this and other facts we conclude that the British Isles were part of the continent of Europe in comparatively recent times, while many ages have elapsed since Madagascar was continuous with Africa, and the connection of Australia with Asia was still more remote. On the other hand, there are certain small islands isolated in mid-ocean, such as St. Helena and Ascension, which probably never formed part of any existing continent. Using this principle as a basis, Wallace classifies islands as "continental", *e.g.* the British Isles and Madagascar, which once were united with adjacent mainlands; and "oceanic", *e.g.* St. Helena, in which this has never been the case. That such a view explains many of the features of island faunas we shall presently see: the bearing of the former existence of "land-bridges", long since submerged, upon questions of discontinuous distribution is, for the moment, our immediate concern.

One of the best examples of discontinuous distribution is afforded by the order of Pouched Mammals (*Marsupialia*), now mainly limited to the Australian region, though also represented in America by the Opossums and one other form (*Cœnolestes*). Without the aid of the geological record the reason for this would ever remain a matter of the merest conjecture. We know, however, from the evidence this record affords, that in the remote past Pouched Mammals were common enough in Europe, and there are enough facts upon which to base the view that the earliest representatives of the order were evolved in the land-mass of Eurasia. From this area the Pouched Mammals gradually spread, entering what are now America and Australia over tracts of land since submerged beneath the sea. Elsewhere, owing to the competition of more highly specialized mammals, they have died out. But the Australian region having been cut off from the northern land-mass before the higher mammals had a chance of entering it, the pouched forms of that region had a field free from serious competition, in which have since been evolved numerous species adapted to many diverse modes of life. In America they had a harder struggle for existence, and at the present time are poorly represented there, chiefly by Opossums, the ancestors of which no doubt reached the New World by one or more formerly existing land-bridges in the north. There is also good reason for thinking that South America also received a population of pouched mammals from Australia, by means of a southern land-bridge, of which some existing islands appear to be remnants. This Australian stock has since died out almost entirely, being now only represented by two small species of Opossum-Rats (*Cœnolestes*), native to Colombia and Ecuador.

Discontinuous distribution explained on somewhat different lines is exhibited by the Lung-Fishes (*Dipnoi*), now represented only in the fresh waters of Africa, South America, and Queensland (see vol. i, p. 264). Once more a clue is afforded by the geological record, from which we know that the ancestors of the Lung-Fishes were at one time a dominant and widely distributed *marine* group. Hard pressed by fishes better adapted to life in the sea, some of them took refuge in estuaries, ultimately passing into the fresh waters of the land. It is only these which in widely distant parts of the world have left descendants, while all the marine types were doomed to extinction.

DISPERSAL OF ANIMALS.—A species which meets with any success in the struggle for existence increases largely in numbers and, led chiefly by the search for food, comes to occupy a tract of land or sea of continually increasing size (*i.e.* it widens its area of distribution) until prevented by natural causes from migrating farther. The means of locomotion possessed by such a species necessarily plays an important part in the matter. The power of flight, for example, often renders wide dispersal possible, as in the case of Bats. But there are usually certain physical barriers which put a stop to the migratory movements of most kinds of animal. Mammals other than Bats are unable to cross even narrow arms of the sea, while mountain chains and deserts often prove potent checks to further advance. And for every other group of land forms obstacles of varying kind present themselves. Even in the case of marine species limits are imposed by temperature, depth of water, supply of suitable food, competition with other species, and so on.

ZOOGEOGRAPHICAL REGIONS OF THE LAND.—It is generally considered that Mammals afford the best means of dividing the land into regions possessing characteristic faunas, and as the areas thus demarcated answer fairly well for Birds, the subdivisions made by W. L. Sclater on this basis, and afterwards adopted by Wallace, will here be given. A reference to the accompanying map (fig. 1286) will show that the boundaries between Sclater's six great regions are largely constituted by physical barriers. Each of these primary subdivisions is again divided into sub-regions. All that can be attempted here is a brief account of the leading features of the large distributional areas, especially with reference to Mammals and Birds. So many incorrect ideas are current, even among educated persons, about the distribution of well-known animals, that no attempt will be made to avoid details that will be commonplace to some readers. Most of the forms of life mentioned in this chapter will be found to have received notice in other connections. It may be well first of all to enumerate the regions and sub-regions.

I. PALÆARCTIC REGION.—Europe,—all but the south of Asia,—and Africa north of the Sahara. Sub-Regions:—1. European; 2. Mediterranean; 3. Siberian; 4. Manchurian.

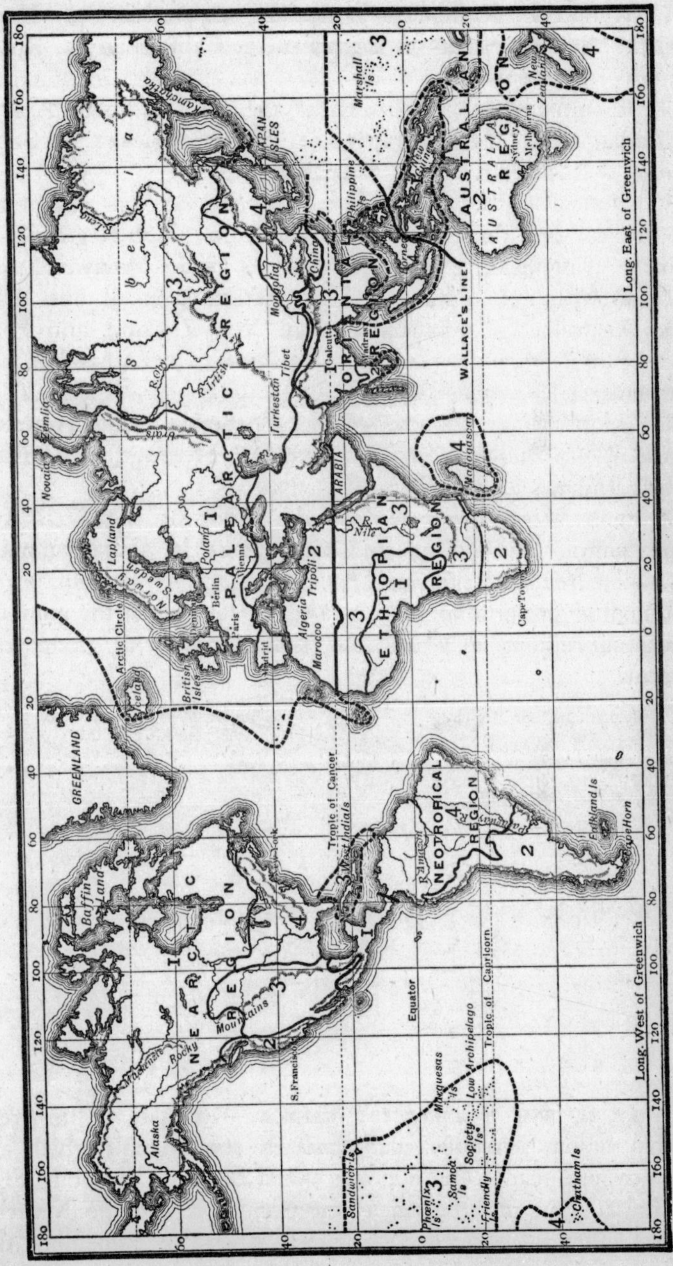

Fig. 1286.—Zoogeographical Regions of the Land. The figures indicate the sub-regions (see text).

II. Nearctic Region. — Practically equivalent to North America. Sub-Regions:—1. Canadian; 2. Californian; 3. Rocky Mountain; 4. Alleghany.

III. Ethiopian.—Africa south of the Sahara, south Arabia, and Madagascar. Sub-Regions:—1. West African; 2. South African; 3. East African; 4. Mascarene.

IV. Oriental Region.—South Asia, the western part of the East Indies, the Philippines, and Formosa. Sub-Regions:—1. Indian; 2. Cingalese; 3. Indo-Chinese; 4. Indo-Malayan.

V.—Australian Region.—The eastern part of the East Indies, Australia and adjacent islands, New Zealand, and Polynesia. Sub-Regions:—1. Austro-Malayan; 2. Australian; 3. Polynesian; 4. Novo-Zelanian.

VI. Neotropical Region.—Central America, South America, and the West Indies. Sub-Regions:—1. Mexican; 2. Chilian; 3. West Indian; 4. Brazilian.

Chalmers Mitchell has devised the following ingenious way of representing the regions and sub-regions in a diagrammatic form, which readily lends itself to expressing the distribution of any animal or group of animals, by simply leaving out the numbers of those sub-regions in which that particular form or group does not occur.

Regions and Sub-Regions.

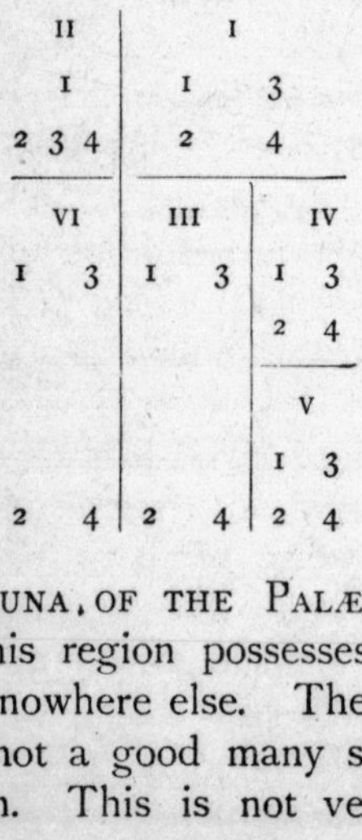

Distribution of Crocodiles and Alligators (Crocodilia).

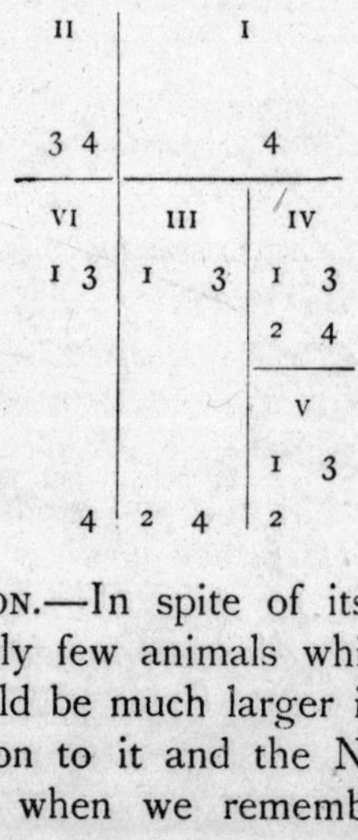

Fauna of the Palæarctic Region.—In spite of its great size this region possesses comparatively few animals which are found nowhere else. The number would be much larger if there were not a good many species common to it and the Nearctic Region. This is not very surprising when we remember the comparative narrowness of the Behring Straits, across which there was a land-bridge at no very remote period, geologically speaking. At one time, too, Europe and North America were connected by land occupying the North Atlantic, and the sea between Britain and Greenland is still comparatively shallow. It may be objected that even if such unions once existed the rigour of the northern climate would prevent land animals from migrating across them; but we know that there have been many changes in climate during the past history of the globe, and that for part of the time when these land-bridges existed a much higher temperature prevailed in the areas they occupied than is now the case. Besides which, the objection, even if valid, would not apply to Arctic forms; and, further, many animals which we now associate with the warmer parts of the earth are able to endure a larger amount of cold than is sometimes supposed. It may be added that the resemblances between the faunas of the Palæarctic Region and the northern part of North America are so striking that many writers associate these together under the name of the Holarctic Region. This fact is mentioned because in dealing with certain forms it will be convenient to speak of them as being "holarctic".

Palæarctic Mammals (*Mammalia*).—Among Insect-eating Mammals (*Insectivora*) our common Mole (*Talpa Europœa*) and related species of the same genus are confined to this region, as also are the Desmans (*Myogale*), while Hedgehogs (*Erinaceidæ*) are very characteristic, though not peculiar. Of the Flesh-Eaters (*Carnivora*) very few are entirely limited to the region, the most notable being the Raccoon-Dog (*Nyctereutes*, fig. 1287) of north-east Asia, and the Common Badger (*Meles taxus*) with some of its immediate allies. It should be stated, however, that a number of Carnivores are purely holarctic, *e.g.* the Polar Bear (*Ursus maritimus*), the Glutton (*Gulo luscus*), Lynxes, and Arctic Foxes; while some others are very characteristic, *e.g.* Wolves, Bears (other than the Polar species), Martens, and Weasels. Some aquatic Carnivores are entirely holarctic, such as the Sea Otter (*Latax lutris*), the Greenland Seal (*Phoca Grœnlandica*), the Walrus (*Trichechus rosmarus*), and the Greenland Whale (*Balæna mysticetus*).

The Palæarctic region is comparatively rich in Hoofed Mammals (*Ungulata*) native to no other part of the world. Among these are conspicuous typical Oxen (*Bos*), Goats (*Capra*), and Sheep (*Ovis*), which are hardly represented elsewhere; also a number of Deer (*Cervidæ*), such as the Fallow-Deer (*Dama vulgaris*), Roe-Deer (*Cervus capreola*), and Water-Deer (*Hydropotes*); while, besides these, certain Antelopes, such as the Chamois (*Rupicapra tragus*) and the Saiga Antelope (*Saiga Tartarica*), are peculiar. Nor must mention of the Camels

Fig. 1287.—Raccoon Dog (*Nyctereutes*)

(*Camelus*) be omitted. The Reindeer (*Rangifer tarandus*), Elk (*Alces machlis*), and Musk-Ox (*Ovibos moschatus*) may be mentioned as typically holarctic Ungulates.

Among Gnawing Mammals (*Rodentia*), Dormice (*Myoxus*) and Mole-Rats (*Spalax*) are Palæarctic, while Marmots (*Arctomys*) and Calling Hares or Pikas (*Lagomys*) are holarctic. Beavers (*Castor*), Voles (*Microtus*), Ground-Squirrels (*Tamias*), and most of the Hares and Rabbits (*Lepus*) are also holarctic.

Palæarctic Birds (*Aves*).—Among the genera which are limited to this region are some of those including a number of our familiar British forms, *e.g.* Grasshopper Warbler (*Locustella*), Robin Redbreast (*Erithacus*), "Bearded Tit" or Reedling (*Panurus*), Long-tailed Tit (*Acredula*), Buntings (*Emberiza*), Chaffinch (*Fringilla*), Bullfinch (*Pyrrhula*), Jay (*Garrulus*), Nutcracker (*Nucifraga*), and Partridge (*Perdix*). Ordinary Pheasants (*Phasianus*) and some of their more ornamental relatives are also very characteristic Palæarctic forms. Some other British birds belong to holarctic genera, *e.g.* Red Grouse and Ptarmigan (*Lagopus*), Capercailzie (*Tetrao*), Divers (*Colymbus*), Razor-Bills (*Alca*), Guillemots (*Uria*), and Puffins (*Fratercula*).

Palæarctic Reptiles (*Reptilia*).—A solitary species of Alligator (*Alligator Sinensis*) is native to South China. Our indigenous Blind-Worm represents a purely Palæarctic genus (*Anguis*) of limbless lizards, while that (*Lacerta*) which includes the Sand-Lizard, Green-Lizard, and Wall-Lizard is hardly represented outside the region.

Palæarctic Amphibians (*Amphibia*).—Peculiar to this region are the genera including the Fire-bellied Toads (*Bombinator*), that form (*Alytes*) in which the male carries about the egg-masses, and the Salamanders (*Salamandra*). It is also interesting to notice that the great majority of Tailed Amphibians (*Urodela*) are limited to the Northern Hemisphere.

Palæarctic Fishes (*Pisces*).—Among British freshwater fishes, Carp and Tench may be mentioned as representing genera (*Cyprinus* and *Tinca*) peculiar to the region, as also are the Gold-fishes, &c. (*Carassius*), of China and Japan. There are also some families of fishes which are very characteristic of the Northern Hemisphere, *e.g.* those containing Pikes (*Esocidæ*), Sticklebacks (*Gasterosteidæ*), and Salmon (*Salmonidæ*). Most of the curious archaic Ganoids (*Ganoidei*) also belong to the same hemisphere. These forms (see vol. i, p. 266) present a good example of a discontinuous area of distribution to be explained in the same way as that of the Lung-Fishes (see p. 266).

Palæarctic Insects (*Insecta*).—Perhaps the most striking feature of the region is the great abundance of predaceous Ground-Beetles (*Carabidæ*) which it possesses, regarding which Wallace says (in *Island Life*) that ". . . the large and handsome genus Carabus, with its allies Procerus and Procrustes, containing nearly 300 species, is almost wholly confined to this region, and would alone serve to distinguish it zoologically from all other parts of the globe".

FAUNA OF THE NEARCTIC REGION.—It will be remembered that the "holarctic" forms already mentioned are common to the Palæarctic region and northern part of the Nearctic region, and need not, therefore, be mentioned again, though it may be well to state that the Musk-Ox (*Ovibos*) is almost entirely Nearctic.

Fig. 1288.—Star-nosed Mole (*Condylura*)

Nearctic Mammals (*Mammalia*).—Among the Insect-Eaters (*Insectivora*) the Star-nosed Mole (*Condylura*, fig. 1288) is the most remarkable of the purely Nearctic forms. A number of the Flesh-Eaters (*Carnivora*) differ from those of the Old World, but as the most important of these are even more characteristic of the Neotropical region, mention of them will be postponed. Two of the Hoofed Mammals (*Ungulata*) are essentially Nearctic, *i.e.* the Pronghorn (*Antilocapra*) and the Rocky Mountain Goat (*Haploceros*). Two families of Gnawers (*Rodentia*) are confined to this region, the Pouched Rats (*Saccomyidæ*), including Gophers, Kangaroo-Rats, and Pocket-Mice, and the Sewellels (*Haplodontidæ*), including two species of small rodents allied to the squirrels but with the habits of marmots. Besides these, two very typical Nearctic genera belong to this order, *i.e.* those to which the Tree-Porcupine (*Erethizon*) and the Prairie-Dogs (*Cynomys*) belong. Opossums (*Didelphyidæ*) represent the Pouched Mammals (*Marsupialia*) in this region, but are more typical of the Neotropical.

Nearctic Birds (*Aves*).—Many of the familiar Palæarctic

species are replaced by members of characteristic American families. There are also a number of peculiar Nearctic genera, but to give a list of them would serve no useful purposes. Turkeys (*Meleagris*) are well represented, but also range south into Central America.

Nearctic Reptiles (*Reptilia*).—It need only be said that poisonous Lizards (*Heloderma*) are characteristic, as also are Rattlesnakes (*Crotalus*), though both range into the Neotropical region, while Crocodiles and Alligators are represented in the south of the United States.

Nearctic Amphibians (*Amphibia*).—The region is richer than any other part of the world in Tailed Amphibians (*Urodela*), and among the peculiar forms are the curious Mud-Eels (*Amphiuma*) and Sirens (*Siren*).

Nearctic Fishes (*Pisces*).—Several families and a considerable number of genera of freshwater fishes are native to this region only, but their names would convey little meaning to average European readers.

Nearctic Freshwater Molluscs (*Mollusca*).—Wallace states that the Nearctic region is richer in characteristic forms than any other part of the world.

Fauna of the Ethiopian Region.—We have seen that the approximation in high latitudes of the great land-masses of the Northern Hemisphere has led to a great deal in common between the faunas of the Palæarctic and Nearctic regions, and both of them are rather deficient as regards the presence of peculiar forms known to the lay reader. This renders it rather difficult to treat them in a popular manner; but there is no such difficulty with regard to the southern regions which remain for consideration, as all of them have well-marked characteristics, and their more typical animals are familiar to everyone. In varying degree they have been more or less isolated by physical barriers for very long periods of time, and this isolation has rendered possible the evolution of distinctive faunas.

Ethiopian Mammals (*Mammalia*).—There is no lack of Apes and Monkeys (*Primates*) belonging to genera not represented elsewhere. Among the higher or man-like Apes the Gorilla (*Gorilla*) and Chimpanzee (*Anthropopithecus*) are typical, while of lower forms may be mentioned the Colobi (*Colobus*) with reduced thumbs, the Guenons (*Cercopithecus*), and a number of

Baboons (*Papio* or *Cynocephalus*). The majority of Lemurs (*Lemuroidea*) are African. The peculiar Ethiopian Insect-Eaters (*Insectivora*) include the Golden Moles (*Chrysochloris*), and an otter-like West African form (*Potamogale*), among many other characteristic types. There are also Flesh-Eaters (*Carnivora*) belonging to purely Ethiopian genera, *e.g.* the Foussa (*Cryptoprocta*) of Madagascar, the Aard-Wolf (*Proteles*), and the Cape Hunting-Dog (*Lycaon*). Though Lion (*Felis leo*)

Fig. 1289.—Wart-Hog (*Phacochærus*)

and Leopard (*F. leopardus*) are both very characteristic, the former ranges into Asia (and has only become extinct in Europe during historic times), while the latter so closely resembles the Asiatic Panther (*F. panthera*) that the two animals are often considered as belonging to the same species. A curious negative feature is found in the complete absence of animals of the Bear kind. Of Hoofed Mammals (*Ungulata*) many remarkable forms are limited to the Ethiopian region. They include Zebras (species of *Equus*), characteristic species of Rhinoceros, Wart-Hog (*Phacochærus*, fig. 1289), Red River-Hog (*Potamochærus*), Hippopotamus (*Hippopotamus*), the Giraffe (*Giraffa*), Okapi (*Okapia*), a number of Antelopes, and the little Water-Chevrotain (*Dorca-*

therium). Deer and wild Oxen are absent. Gnawers (*Rodentia*) are represented by a number of peculiar forms, of which may be mentioned the Cape Jumping-Hare (*Pedetes*) and the African "Flying"-Squirrels (*Anomalurus*). The archaic order of Mammals Poor in Teeth (*Edentata*) is represented by the Cape Ant-Eater or Aard-Vark (*Orycteropus*), and Pangolins (*Manis*), though the latter are shared with the Oriental region.

Ethiopian Birds (*Aves*).—Among the many peculiar forms it may suffice to mention Plantain-Eaters (*Musophaga*), Colies (*Colius*), Whydah Finches (*Vidua*), Ox-Peckers (*Buphaga*), many of the beautiful little Sun-Birds (*Nectariniidæ*), the Secretary-Bird (*Serpentarius*), and the African Ostrich (*Struthio*).

Ethiopian Reptiles (*Reptilia*).—Crocodiles are abundant but not peculiar, while among Lizards (*Lacertilia*) the large majority of the Chameleons are limited to the region. Among the innumerable Serpents (*Ophidia*) the Egg-eating Snake (*Dasypeltis*) and deadly Puff-Adders (*Bitis*) are purely Ethiopian.

Ethiopian Amphibians (*Amphibia*).—The Clawed Toads (*Xenopus*) are limited to Africa, while, on the other hand, not only are Tailed Amphibians (*Urodela*) entirely absent, but also several families of Tailless Amphibians (*Anura*), *e.g.* the Tree-Frogs (*Hylidæ*).

Ethiopian Freshwater Fishes (*Pisces*).—Some of the most archaic types are limited to the region, *e.g.* one of the Lung-Fishes (*Protopterus*), the Bichir (*Polypterus*), and the Reed-Fish (*Calamoichthys*), the last two being Ganoids.

Ethiopian Land and Freshwater Molluscs (*Mollusca*).—One of the large Land-Snails (*Achatina*) is very characteristic, though not limited to Africa, while Land-Slugs are comparatively scarce, and freshwater molluscs are less abundant than in some other regions. The fauna of Lake Tanganyika presents some remarkable features. As we have seen elsewhere (see p. 313) the Caspian Sea and Lake Baikal were once continuous with the Arctic Ocean, the fact that each is inhabited by a peculiar species of Seal being accounted for in this way. It appears that in remote geological times Tanganyika was also part of a sea area, and was converted into a lake as one of the results of a series of land-upheavals. Some of the marine molluscs and other animals living in the sea of which it formed a part proved able to accommodate themselves to the altered conditions, and these "halolimnic" forms, some to all appearance closely resembling ancient extinct types, are now found in the fresh waters of this lake, side by side with ordinary freshwater species.

Ethiopian Insects (*Insecta*).—The region is very rich in insect life, but it is not possible here to enter into details regarding the many interesting and beautiful species. Wallace mentions the large and handsome Goliath-Beetles as being especially characteristic, and some of the complex societies of African Termites have been spoken of elsewhere (see p. 124).

FAUNA OF MADAGASCAR.—This subdivision of the Ethiopian region calls for a few remarks, since it is one of the best existing examples of an ancient continental island connected in remote times with the adjacent continent. There can be no doubt that a large part of the Mascarene fauna has been derived from the mainland of Africa, but Madagascar became isolated at a time when that continent did not include among its inhabitants many of the animals by which it is now characterized. Long-standing isolation has also resulted in the evolution of many peculiar species, some of highly remarkable kind. Both the positive and the negative characters of the Mascarene fauna are best illustrated by reference to the Mammals and Birds.

Mascarene Mammals (*Mammalia*).—Of the sixty-six species of Mammals native to Madagascar about half are Lemurs (*Lemuroidea*), representing no less than nine peculiar genera (*Lemur*, *Chirogaleus*, &c.), of which one (*Chiromys*) includes the remarkable Aye-Aye. Except for about fourteen small species shared between the continent of Africa and the Oriental region, these ill-defended creatures are found nowhere else, and their abundance in Madagascar is no doubt to be attributed to the scarcity of carnivores in that island. The case is on a par with that of the Pouched Mammals of Australia. With the single exception of a Shrew, all the Insect-Eaters (*Insectivora*) of Madagascar belong to the peculiar family of Tanrecs (*Centetidæ*), while the few Gnawers (*Rodentia*) are rats and mice, all belonging to distinctive genera. Flesh-Eaters (*Carnivora*) are only represented by the Foussa (*Cryptoprocta*) and eight kinds of Civet-Cat. Of Hoofed Mammals (*Ungulata*) there is only a species of River-Hog (*Potamochærus*), although the Hippopotamus is known to have been once indigenous. The characteristic Apes and Monkeys, most of the Flesh-Eaters and Hoofed

CHARACTERISTIC ANIMALS OF THE ISLAND OF MADAGASCAR

Madagascar is a good type of "ancient continental islands" that in remote times were connected with the adjacent continents, which they broadly resemble in the nature of their fauna, though the separation has been long enough to render possible the evolution of peculiar species. The Mascarene animals find their nearest allies on the mainland of Africa, the characteristic monkeys, carnivores, ungulates (with one exception), elephants, and ostriches of which are, however, absent. Half the Mammals (33) of the island are Lemurs, one of the most remarkable of which is the Aye-aye (*Chiromys Madagascariensis*, 1), formerly mistaken for a Rodent. A Mouse-Lemur (*Chirogaleus pusillus*) is represented at 2. Most of the Insectivores, of which the Tenrec (*Centetes ecaudatus*, 3) is best known, belong to a family (*Centetidæ*) represented nowhere else.

Of about 150 species of land-birds no less than 127 are peculiar. The two figured are a Fruit-Pigeon (*Alectorœnas pulcherrima*, 4), native to the Seychelles (which belong to the Mascarene sub-region), and a form (*Philepitta jala*, male, 5) related to the so-called "Ground-Thrushes" or Pittas, but constituting with another Mascarene species a special family (*Philepittidæ*).

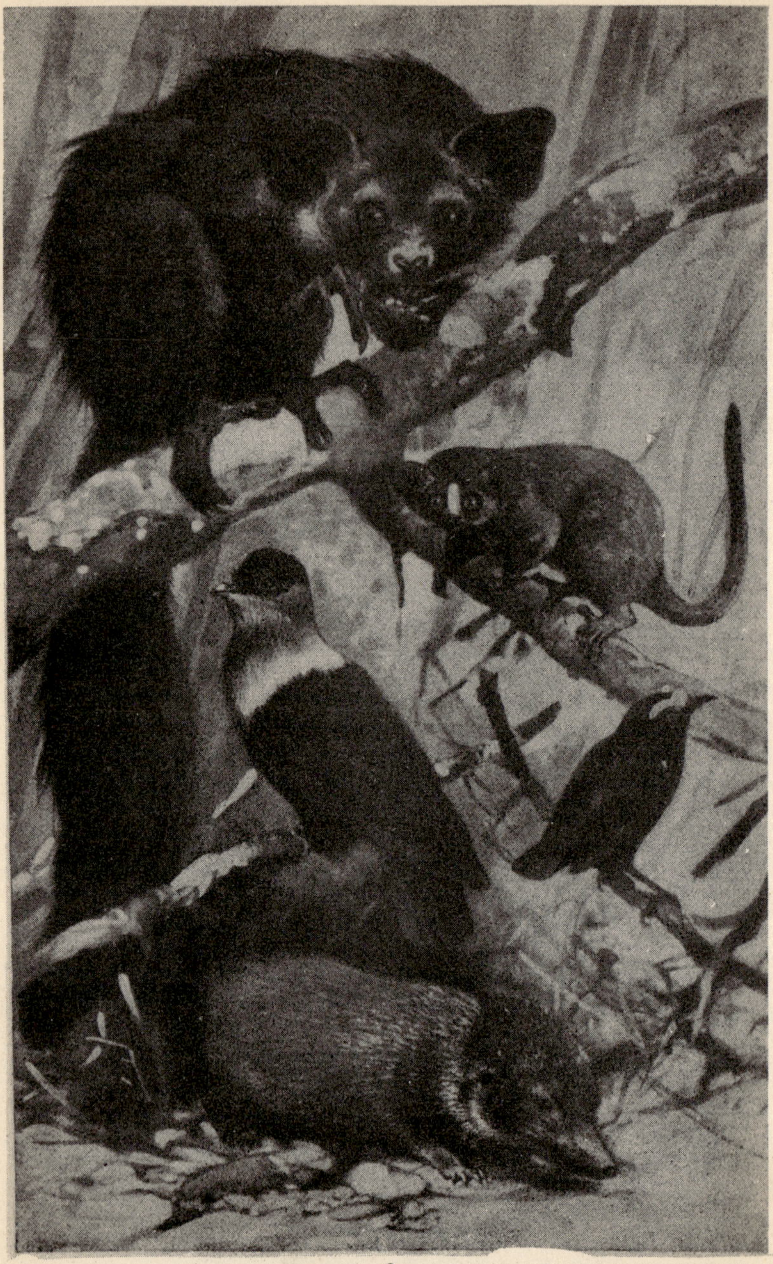

3

CHARACTERISTIC ANIMALS OF THE ISLAND OF MADAGASCAR

1. -aye. 2. Mouse-Lemur. 3. Tenrec. 4. Fruit-Pigeon. 5. Philepitta.

Mammals, and also the Elephants of the African continent are conspicuous by their absence.

Mascarene Birds (*Aves*).—The power of flight possessed by most members of this class to a large extent prevents the evolution of peculiar species by isolation, and we must not therefore expect the land-birds of Madagascar to be so characteristic as the mammals, though it is sufficiently striking to find that out of 238 species no less than 129 are limited to the island, and these include representatives of 35 peculiar genera. We may take as examples two species (of *Philepitta*) of great beauty, allied to the Ground-Thrushes, though constituting a distinct family, and four kinds of Fruit-Pigeon belonging to a genus (*Alectoroœnas*) only represented in Madagascar and some of the smaller islands of the sub-region.

FAUNA OF ST. HELENA.—This typical oceanic island, 1100 miles distant from Africa and 1800 miles from South America, may be taken here as a good illustration of its class. Never having formed part of a continent its indigenous fauna naturally presents a strong contrast with that of Madagascar, being entirely made up of such forms of life as have been able to reach it by natural agencies. And since a broad stretch of sea is an insuperable barrier to animals of many kinds, the faunistic characters of St. Helena are largely negative, as in all other such cases. On the other hand, the effect of isolation has been very great, and a large proportion of the species are peculiar.

St. Helena possesses no native Mammals, Land Birds, Reptiles, Freshwater Fishes, or Freshwater Molluscs. There is, however, one peculiar species of Plover (*Ægialitis Sanctæ-Helenæ*) allied to one native to South Africa. Of Land-Snails twenty appear to be indigenous, if we include thirteen that have become extinct in recent times. The Beetles (*Coleoptera*) of the island have been studied with greater care than any other group of insects, and 129 species are native to the island, to which all except one of them are absolutely restricted. More than two-thirds of these beetles are weevils, and, considering the boring habits of such creatures, it is highly probable that the remote ancestors of many of them were conveyed to St. Helena by the agency of drift-wood.

There can be no doubt that many of the animals originally native to this island have become extinct as the result of human occupation, the introduction of goats having had much to do with this (see p. 346).

Fauna of the Oriental Region.—The boundaries between this region and the Palæarctic area are in part ill-defined, which naturally means the possession of a number of species in common. The south-eastern boundary, marking it off from the Australian region, is usually known as "Wallace's line", which runs between Bali and Lombok, and thence northwards between Borneo and Celebes. Bali and Borneo thus mark the limit of the Oriental region in this direction.

Oriental Mammals (*Mammalia*).—Taking first the Apes and Monkeys (*Primates*), we find that the higher or man-like Apes are shared between this and the Ethiopian region, for while the Gorilla and Chimpanzee are peculiar to the latter, the Orang-utan (*Simia*) and Gibbons (*Hylobates* and *Siamanga*) are purely oriental. The Proboscis Monkey (*Nasalis*) is restricted to Borneo, while Entellus Monkeys, &c. (*Semnopithecus*), with Bonnet Monkeys and their immediate allies (*Macacus*), mostly belong to this region. It is also the home of three species of Lemur, two of the Loris (or "Slow" Lemurs), and the little Spectre Tarsier. Of the first, one (*Loris*) is restricted to South India and Ceylon, while the other (*Nycticebus*) ranges into the Philippines. The Spectre Tarsier (*Tarsius spectrum*), though chiefly oriental, is also found in Celebes. Two peculiar families of Insect-Eaters (*Insectivora*) are purely oriental, one including the Banxrings or Tree-Shrews (*Tupaiidæ*, fig. 1290), while the only representative of the other is the remarkable Flying-"Lemur" (*Galeopithecus*). There are also two peculiar genera (*Hylomys* and *Gymnura*) of the hedgehog kind. Among Bats (*Chiroptera*) the large Fruit-Bats (*Pteropus*) are characteristic, though not peculiar. Among Flesh-Eaters (*Carnivora*) the Tiger (*Felis tigris*), though very typical, also ranges into North China; but there are a number of peculiar genera belonging to various carnivorous families, while Bears are not absent, as in the Ethiopian region. The Hoofed Mammals (*Ungulata*) are abundantly represented, and some of them are found nowhere else, *e.g.* the little Chevrotains (*Tragulus*, represented in West Africa by *Dorcatherium*), the small Deer known as Muntjacs (*Cervulus*), and certain Antelopes (*Antilope* and the four-horned *Tetraceros*). Rhinoceroses and Elephants (*Proboscidea*) are shared between this region and Africa. Tapirs (*Tapirus*) are only to be found here and in the Neotropical area. Of Gnawers (*Rodentia*) the most notable are perhaps the Asiatic Flying-Squirrels (*Pteromys*). Mammals Poor in Teeth (*Edentata*) are represented by some of the Pangolins (*Manis*), though some of these are also native to Africa.

Oriental Birds (*Aves*).—Two families of Perching Birds are confined to the region, *i.e.* the Green Bulbuls (*Phyllornithidæ*) and the Broadbills (*Eurylæmidæ*); while some of the many peculiar genera include such better-known forms as the Tailor-Birds (*Orthotomus*), typical Hornbills (*Buceros*), Peacocks (*Pavo*), Peacock-Pheasants (*Polyplectron*), Silver Pheasants (*Gennæus*) and related species, and the Water-Pheasant (*Hydrophasianus*). Highly characteristic, though not entirely limited to this region, are the Jungle-Fowl (*Gallus*).

Fig. 1290.—Tree-Shrew (*Tupaia*)

Oriental Reptiles (*Reptilia*).—Crocodiles (*Crocodilus*) are abundant in the region, and the long-snouted Garials (*Garialis* and *Rhynchosuchus*) are limited to it. Of the numerous Lizards (*Lacertilia*) the pretty little Flying Dragons (*Draco*) are purely oriental. The burrowing Shield-tailed Snakes (*Uropeltidæ*) are found in no other region; and the same is true for one genus (*Bungarus*) of poisonous serpents, including the Krait, which is supposed to work more havoc among the natives of India than any other creature of its kind.

Oriental Amphibians (*Amphibia*).—Though tailed forms (*Urodela*) are represented they are vastly outnumbered by the tailless ones (*Anura*), but none of these call for special mention.

Oriental Freshwater Fishes (*Pisces*).—Most of the Snake-headed Fishes (*Ophiocephalidæ*), which are able to live during the dry season in liquid mud, are limited to the region, and the same is true of the members of a small family (*Mastacembelidæ*) of eel-like forms, which, however, have nothing to do with the true eels.

Oriental Insects (*Insecta*).—Regarding these Wallace remarks (in *Island Life*):—"Among insects we may notice the magnificent golden and green Papilionidæ [*i.e.* Swallow-tail Butterflies] of various genera as being unequalled in the world; while the great Atlas Moth is probably the most gigantic of Lepidoptera, being sometimes 10 inches across the wings, which are also very broad. Among the beetles the strange flat-bodied Malayan Mormolyce is the largest of all the Carabidæ [*i.e.* predaceous ground-beetles], while the Catoxantha is equally a giant among the Buprestidæ. [The beautiful wing-covers of various species of this family are largely used in India for ornamental purposes.] On the whole, the insects of this region probably surpass those of any other part of the world, except South America, in size, variety, and beauty."

FAUNA OF THE AUSTRALIAN REGION.—"Wallace's line" (see p. 413), which divides this region from that last considered, is not the sharply-marked boundary that was at one time supposed, for a considerable number of oriental forms range to the east of it, and Australian forms to the west of it. Some authorities consider that the line should be drawn to the east of Celebes, which would then belong to the oriental region. Wallace's line, if thus amended, would be a somewhat sharper boundary than it is now. New Zealand, too, possesses such well-marked positive and negative features that it should possibly be considered as a distinct (Novo-Zelanian) region, instead of being ranked merely as a sub-region. A few of its peculiarities will be indicated in the following brief sketch.

Australian Mammals (*Mammalia*).—Among the animals found in Celebes are three belonging to peculiar genera, *i.e.* a Black Ape (*Cynopithecus*), a Dwarf Ox (*Anoa*), and the Babirussa (*Porcus* or *Babirussa*, fig. 1291), a curious pig-like form with long curled tusks in the upper jaw. It is also inhabited by a species of Deer, a Civet-Cat, and five kinds of Squirrel, while the Spectre Tarsier (*Tarsus spectrum*) is said to be found on a small adjacent island. The Deer and Civet-Cat have possibly been introduced. Typical Pigs (*Sus*) range as far east as New Guinea, but with this exception, various Bats, a number of rats and mice, and the doubtfully indigenous Dingo (*Canis dingo*) of the Australian continent, the mammalian fauna of the region (excluding Celebes) is made up of Marsupials (represented in Celebes) and Egg-

Fig. 1291.—Babirussa (*Babirussa*)

laying Mammals (*Monotremata*). The last, which include the Duck-Bill (*Ornithorhynchus*) and Spiny Ant-eaters (*Echidna* and *Proechidna*), are found in no other part of the world, though Marsupials are scantily represented in America. New Zealand is singularly devoid of indigenous mammals, there only being two peculiar species of bat, a doubtful rat, and a problematical otter-like creature.

Australian Birds (*Aves*).—Among the most typical Australian groups are the beautiful Honey-Suckers (*Musiphagidæ*), many distinctive kinds of Parrot and Cockatoo, Birds of Paradise,

Crowned Pigeons, the land Kingfisher (*Dacelo*) familiarly known as the "Laughing Jackass", the "More-Pork" birds (*Podargus*), the Mound-Builders, Cassowaries, and Emus. All these, except Honey-Suckers, Parrots (not Cockatoos), and Pigeons, are represented in New Zealand, but the other birds named are absent. There are, however, some highly peculiar Novo-Zelanian forms, found in no other area. These include the Kea and Kaka Parrots (*Nestor*), the ground-dwelling Owl-Parrot (*Stringops*), and the Kiwi (*Apteryx*), which is the smallest existing representative of the Running Birds (*Ratitæ*). But within the period of human occupation a number of large species of the last-named group existed in the islands, *i.e.* the "Moas" (*Dinornithidæ*), some of which were over 10 feet in height.

Australian Reptiles (*Reptilia*).—Crocodiles range across the northern part of the region as far east as the Solomon and Fiji Islands. Among the numerous Lizards two peculiar to the Australian continent deserve mention, *i.e.* the Frilled Lizard (*Chlamydosaurus*), which can run for some distance on its hind-legs, and the spiny Mountain Devil (*Moloch*). Snakes are found in abundance, but details are unnecessary. New Zealand possesses a number of Lizards (*Geckoes* and *Skinks*), but neither Crocodiles nor terrestrial Snakes. Some small islands in the Bay of Plenty are, however, of peculiar interest, for they are the home of the Tuatara (*Hatteria*), which is the last surviving member of an exceedingly ancient and once widely distributed reptilian order (*Rhynchocephala*), that was very probably ancestral to all the other known groups.

Australian Amphibians (*Amphibia*).—Tailless forms (*Anura*) are well represented in the region, but New Zealand has only one indigenous species of amphibian, a sort of Toad (*Liopelma*).

Australian Fishes (*Pisces*).—The most interesting species native to this region is Ceratodus, a Lung-Fish (*Dipnoi*) now limited to Queensland.

Fauna of the Neotropical Region.—Although the results of isolation are not here quite so well marked as in the case of Australia, to say nothing of New Zealand, the fauna of the region presents many well-marked characteristics, both positive and negative. It affords a refuge to certain archaic forms, which have been able to prolong the tenure of their existence in the absence of large numbers of carnivores, and, for the same reason, may be regarded as the head-quarters of some other animals which, though not decadent, are comparatively defenceless. On the other hand, the region stands unsurpassed for variety and wealth of life, which is partly due to its unparalleled range in latitude and diversity in altitude. Every kind of climate and environment are exemplified, from the tropical forests of Brazil to the rigour of the high Andes or Tierra del Fuego, from the grassy pampas of the Argentine to the Patagonian desert.

Neotropical Mammals (*Mammalia*).—To this region are absolutely confined the American Monkeys (*Cebidæ*) and the Marmosets (*Hapalidæ*), both (especially the latter) of lower grade than their Old World cousins. Lemurs (*Lemuroidea*) are entirely absent, as from America in general. There are no fruit-eating Bats (*Pteropidæ*), but a number of genera are peculiar to the region, especially those including the blood-sucking Vampires (*Desmodus* and *Diphylla*). A somewhat remarkable negative feature of the Neotropical fauna is the almost complete absence of Insect-Eaters (*Insectivora*). The widely distributed Shrews (*Soricidæ*) are, however, represented in Central America, while the Agoutas (*Solenodon*) of Cuba and Hayti constitute a distinct family.

Of the most predaceous Flesh-Eaters (*Carnivora*), *i.e.* the members of the Cat Family (*Felidæ*), there is a decided scarcity, the three largest indigenous species—Puma (*Felis concolor*), Jaguar (*F. onca*), and Ocelot (*F. pardalis*)—also ranging into North America. The Civet Cat Family (*Viverridæ*) is entirely unrepresented; while of Bears (*Ursidæ*) there is only the Spectacled Bear (*Ursus ornatus*) of Peru and Chili. Weasels (*Mustelidæ*) and creatures of the Dog Family (*Canidæ*) are fairly abundant. On the other hand, the Neotropical region is the head-quarters of the almost purely American family of Raccoons (*Procyonidæ*) and their allies. The Kinkajou (*Cercoleptes*) is limited to the region, the long-snouted Coatimundis (*Nasua*) range as far north as Texas, while the Raccoons (*Procyon*) have a wide distribution in the New World. One member of this family is native to the Old World, *i.e.* the Panda (*Ælurus*) of the south-eastern Himalayas, and we have here therefore a good example of discontinuous distribution.

The positive and negative characteristics of the region as regards Hoofed Mammals (*Ungulata*) are both well marked.

The Odd-toed Ungulates (*Perissodactyla*) are only represented by the archaic Tapirs (*Tapirus*) of South and Central America. They are one of the stock examples of discontinuous distribution, being also found in south-east Asia. As in many similar cases they are the last surviving representatives of a once widely distributed group (compare p. 410). There is also a scarcity of Even-toed Ungulates (*Artiodactyla*), for of non-ruminants there are only the little Peccaries (*Dicotyles*), which differ in many ways from the Swine of the Old World. They also range into the south of the Nearctic region. Among the Ruminants or Cud-Chewers (*Ruminantia*) the Deer Family (*Cervidæ*) is represented by a number of species belonging to two genera exclusively American. One of these (*Padus*) only includes a very small form (*P. humilis*), native to the Chilian Andes, and of which the male possesses tiny spikes by way of antlers. Most of the species belonging to the other genus (*Cariacus*) are restricted to the Neotropical region, but the largest forms, *e.g.* Virginian and Mule Deer, which also have the most complex antlers, are Nearctic. The large family (*Bovidæ*) embracing Sheep, Goats, Antelopes, and Oxen, which has but few representatives in the Nearctic region, here has none at all. The Camels of the Old World are also absent, but the Guanaco (*Lama guanacus*) and Vicuñia (*L. vicunia*) belong to the same family (*Camelidæ*), and furnish another typical example of discontinuous distribution.

Gnawers (*Rodentia*) are extremely numerous in the Neotropical region, and among peculiar forms may be noted the Cavies (*Caviidæ*), which include the largest existing Rodent (*Hydrochœrus capybara*), the Agoutis (*Dasyproctidæ*), and the Chinchillas (*Chinchillidæ*). The archaic and decadent order of Mammals Poor in Teeth (*Edentata*) is also better represented here than anywhere else, for typical Ant-eaters (*Myrmecophagidæ*), Sloths (*Bradypodidæ*), and Armadilloes (*Dasypodidæ*) are only to be found in South America. As to Pouched Mammals (*Marsupialia*), the Opossums (*Didelphyidæ*) are native to both Americas, while the Opossum Rats (*Cœnolestes*) belong to Colombia and Ecuador.

Neotropical Birds (*Aves*).—The region stands unsurpassed for the richness and variety of its avifauna, while a great many families and genera are represented nowhere else, and some of the most distinctive forms are only shared with the Nearctic area.

THE GREAT ANT-EATER (*Myrmecophaga jubata*)

The southern land-masses constitute the last refuge of a number of archaic groups, among which are the Mammals poor in Teeth (*Edentata*), that are most abundantly represented in South America. The plate represents the Great Ant-eater (*Myrmecophaga jubata*), one of the most remarkable Edentates native to that continent. If the long tail is included, its total length may be over 7 feet. The digits of the inwardly turned fore-feet are armed with long sharp claws, well adapted for tearing open ant-hills, and also serving as formidable defensive weapons. The small mouth is placed at the end of a long narrow snout, and the jaws are toothless. Ants are secured by means of the long protrusible tongue, which is made sticky by the abundant secretion of enormous salivary glands. The Great Ant-eater is a ground-animal, but some of its immediate relatives are small arboreal creatures.

THE GREAT ANT-EATER (MYRMECOPHAGA JUBATA)

ONE OF THE MOST REMARKABLE ANIMALS OF SOUTH AMERICA

Of Perching Birds (*Passeres*) a number of families are peculiar, and of these the following are among the most typical:—Manakins (*Pipridæ*), small birds which resemble the Tits in appearance and habits. The large family of Chatterers (*Cotingidæ*), which include the Umbrella-Bird (*Cephalopterus ornatus*), so named from its large overhanging crest of feathers, and the clear-toned Bell-Bird (*Chasmorhynchus*). The Tree-Creepers or Picucules (*Dendrocolaptidæ*) vary remarkably in appearance and in the nature of their nests (see vol. iii, p. 463), while some of the insectivorous Ant-Thrushes (*Formicariidæ*) give notice by their twittering of the approach of armies of Foraging Ants (*Ecitons*). We have also the American "Orioles" (*Icteridæ*), among which are the Cow-Birds (*Molobrus*), some of which, like Cuckoos, lay their eggs in the nests of other species (see p. 186). The true "singing birds" (*Oscines*) of the Old World are comparatively ill represented in this region, the feathered inhabitants of which appeal more to the eye than the ear. Thrushes, however, are abundant.

Among Picarian Birds (*Picariæ*) the brilliantly coloured large-billed Toucans (*Rhamphastidæ*) constitute a family peculiar to the region. A well-known and remarkable family common to South and North America is that of the Humming-Birds (*Trochilidæ*), which for beauty of form and plumage have few serious rivals. Though they range as far north as Alaska, their head-quarters are in the Neotropical region, which is the home of some 400 species, about four-fifths of the total number.

Of Parrots (*Psittaci*) there are a number of genera not represented elsewhere, and the gorgeous long-tailed Macaws (*Conuridæ*) make up a family widely distributed through the region, though also ranging into the Nearctic area.

Among true Game-Birds (*Gallinæ*) the large and handsome Curassows and their allies, which are related to the Mound-Builders of the Australian region, constitute a family (*Cracidæ*) which is almost entirely neotropical. The remarkable Hoatzin (*Opisthocomus cristatus*), native to the northern part of South America (see vol. iii, p. 472), may perhaps be regarded as an aberrant game-bird, but it possesses so many structural peculiarities that it is placed in a distinct family (*Opisthocomidæ*), while some authorities even consider that it is entitled to an order (*Opisthocomi*) of its own.

The South American forms known as Tinamous, sufficiently like game-birds to have earned the local name of "partridges", are in reality very primitive forms, which constitute a distinct order (*Crypturi*). One of the South American Birds of Prey (*Accipitres*), the huge Condor (*Sarcorhampus gryphus*) of the Andes, a kind of Vulture, is the largest existing flying bird, its spread of wing being as much as 9 feet.

The only Running Birds (*Ratitæ*) native to the New World are the Rheas (*Rhea*) or South American Ostriches, which are smaller and less specialized than their African cousins.

Neotropical Reptiles (*Reptilia*).—The warmer parts of the region are inhabited by Crocodiles (*Crocodilus*), and forms known as Caimans (*Caiman*), which are pretty closely related to the Alligators. Among the many Lizards (*Lacertilia*) members of the Iguana Family (*Iguanidæ*) are conspicuous, though the group is shared with North America, and there are outlying forms in Madagascar and the Fiji Islands. The type-genus (*Iguana*) is only represented in tropical America and the West Indies, while the curious Basilisks (*Basiliscus*) are limited to the former area. The Sea-Lizard (*Amblyrhynchus cristatus*) of the Galapagos Islands is remarkable from its habit of browsing on seaweeds which grow on the sea-floor in shallow water.

Snakes (*Ophidia*) are well represented in the Neotropical region. They include most of the species of Boa, and the gigantic Anaconda (*Euneces murinus*), which is the largest known serpent. The harmless Coral-Snake (*Ilysia scytale*), coral-red with black rings, is native to tropical South America. Of this species Gadow remarks (in *The Cambridge Natural History*) that, "On account of its beauty, perfectly harmless nature, and for 'cooling purposes', this snake which grows to nearly a yard in length, is sometimes worn as a necklace by native ladies". The name Coral Snake is also applied to a virulently poisonous species (*Elaps corallinus*) native to the same area and also to the Lesser Antilles. It is related to the Cobras and Kraits of India, and the Death-Adders of Australia.

Amphibians (*Amphibia*).—Though tailed forms (*Urodela*) just get into the northern part of the region, the vast majority of its Amphibians are Frogs and Toads (*Anura*). The tongueless and toothless Surinam Toad (*Pipa Americana*), native to the north of South America, is one of the most interesting species, which has been spoken about elsewhere, as also have some other neotropical forms (see vol. iii, p. 437).

Neotropical Freshwater Fishes (*Pisces*).—A large eel-shaped Lung-Fish (*Lepidosiren*) is peculiar to South America, and the order (*Dipnoi*) to which it belongs is only elsewhere represented in Africa and Queensland (see p. 411).

In ordinary Bony Fishes (*Teleostei*) the region is extremely rich, and a few peculiar forms require mention. One family (*Osteoglossidæ*) is remarkable in the fact that its geographical range closely corresponds with that of the Lung-Fishes, except that it also includes Borneo and Sumatra. One of the neotropical species (*Arapaima gigas*), abundant in the great rivers of Brazil and the Guianas, is the largest freshwater representative of the order, for it may grow to a length of over 15 feet, and attain a weight of more than 400 lbs. Some of the neotropical members of the widely distributed Cat-Fish Family (*Siluridæ*) are small forms distinguished by their armoured skins. The Electric Eels (*Gymnotidæ*) are characteristic of tropical America.

Most Sharks and Rays (*Elasmobranchii*) are typically marine, yet some of the Sting-Rays (*Trygonidæ*) are at home in the great rivers of South America, though the Indian Ocean is the headquarters of the family.

Neotropical Land-Molluscs (*Mollusca*).—The Neotropical region is particularly rich in members of this group, the West Indies being especially so, but it is unnecessary to enter into details. One curious negative feature is the complete absence of all members of the family (*Limacidæ*) that includes the ordinary Land-Slugs of the Old World, these being replaced by other types.

Neotropical Insects (*Insecta*).—Regarding these Wallace makes the following remarks (in *The Geographical Distribution of Animals*):—"The Neotropical region is so excessively rich in insect life, it so abounds in peculiar groups, in forms of exquisite beauty, and in an endless profusion of species, that no adequate idea of this branch of its fauna can be conveyed by the mere enumeration of peculiar and characteristic groups. . . . The Butterflies of South America surpass those of all other regions in numbers, variety, and beauty; and we find here, not only more peculiar genera and families than elsewhere, but, what is more remarkable, a fuller representation of the whole series of families."

It is very interesting to note that in the tropical forests of South America the carnivorous beetles, which in countries like our own live upon the ground, have taken to an arboreal life. They are, in fact, driven from their natural domain by predaceous Ants, the habits of some of which have elsewhere been mentioned (see vol. ii, p. 104).

CHAPTER LXXVI

LIFE IN DIFFERENT SURROUNDINGS—SHALLOW WATER, DEEP WATER, AND SURFACE FAUNAS OF THE SEA

In writing this book an attempt has been made to illustrate some of the innumerable ways in which animals have become adapted to exist in various surroundings or environments. Occasion has been taken to consider pretty fully adaptations to various kinds of food, to the exigencies of life in water, on the ground, in the ground, among the trees, and in the air. It may therefore perhaps suffice here to deal with a few facts having reference to the adaptations which have been evolved in relation to existence in the sea, especially as the last chapter has been mainly devoted to land animals.

In dealing with marine forms it is found convenient to divide the oceans into three zones which pass into one another, the Neritic, the Abysmal, and the Pelagic, each of which is characterized, broadly speaking, by a special fauna. The Pelagic zone includes the surface waters so far as penetrated by light to any marked extent; the Neritic zone extends from high-tide mark to a depth of 500 fathoms; and the Abysmal zone stretches from this into the deepest and gloomiest ocean abysses.

It is further the practice to divide marine animals into the three groups of Benthos, Nekton, and Plankton, according to their locomotor possibilities. In the Benthos are included fixed forms, and animals which creep upon the sea-floor, or burrow in stone, sand, or mud. Adult corals, for instance, possess no power of moving from place to place, most crabs and sea-snails live on the sea-floor, while many annelids and most bivalves burrow. The Nekton is made up of animals, *e.g.* cetaceans and fishes, which are powerful swimmers and easily range from place to place of their own free-will. The Plankton fauna consist of weaker creatures, and numerous larvæ, which float or drift with the currents, against which the swimming powers that many of them possess can make no headway, though useful in a minor degree. Such are various animalcules, small crustaceans, jelly-fishes, and salps. Floating eggs and innumerable larvæ also belong to the Plankton.

THE NERITIC ZONE—LIFE IN SHALLOW WATER

The Neritic Zone embraces the area between tide-marks, *i.e.* the littoral sub-zone and the shallow waters adjacent. There being abundant light a great variety of colours and patterns are exhibited by the animals, many of these being useful to their possessors in one way or another. And, as might be anticipated, neritic animals mostly possess well-developed eyes, unless they happen to have become adapted to a burrowing mode of life. The fauna of this zone is rich in the extreme, its character varying with climate and the nature of the sea-floor, among other determining circumstances. The intertidal area is of particular interest, for, being exposed to the action of the air at periodic intervals, it is intermediate in character between sea and land, presenting an environment which has rendered possible the evolution of certain terrestrial forms (see vol. ii, p. 459), some of which have again more or less reverted to the ancient aquatic existence. Land-Crabs, for instance, have sprung from purely marine forms, while Cetaceans have undergone a secondary adaptation to the original mode of life that characterized their exceedingly remote fish-like ancestors.

Neritic Mammals (*Mammalia*).—A number of forms which partly belong to the land have more or less claim to be included in the fauna of this zone, though some of them also spend more or less of their time in the Pelagic area. Such in particular are the Sea-Lions or Eared Seals (*Otaridæ*), Walruses (*Trichechidæ*), and Seals (*Phocidæ*), which make up a special group (*Pinnipedia*) of the Flesh-Eaters. The Sea-Cows (*Sirenia*), including the Dugong (*Halicore*) and Manatee (*Manatus*), have deserted the land entirely, though the latter pass up into rivers and are therefore, in part, members of the freshwater fauna.

Neritic Birds (*Aves*).—The nature of the development of birds prevents them from deserting the land altogether, but many species spend so large a part of their lives on the shore or in shallow water that some allusion to them is necessary here. Among forms which still make considerable use of the land, other than for nesting purposes, the Gulls (*Laridæ*) may be particularly mentioned, and many others have been dealt with in earlier sections, while the Penguins (*Impennes*) are as neritic as it is possible for members of the class to be.

Neritic Reptiles.—The only case requiring mention is that presented by the Sea-Lizard (*Amblyrhynchus cristatus*), which spends a large part of its time feeding on the sea-weeds that grow in the shallow water.

Neritic Fishes (*Pisces*).—These are immensely numerous, and many of them have been dealt with in other sections. The majority of food-fishes, for instance, are neritic, though those of the herring and mackerel kind furnish important exceptions, yet many of these pelagic species favour the zone of shallow water for spawning purposes. The beautiful forms which abound in the neighbourhood of coral-reefs would alone require considerable space to do them justice. The effect produced upon the imagination by the coral-fauna is vividly summarized by Alcock (in *A Naturalist in Indian Seas*) in the following impressionist sentences:—"Looking back after thirteen years, I can only remember visions of fairy groves and glades, lit by a strange ethereal light, half moon half sun, where, among Christmas-trees of purple and blue and golden green, fishes painted like butterflies flitted and hovered". Those who desire to get some notion of the colour-schemes presented by such a fauna are referred to the magnificent plates in Saville Kent's *Great Barrier Reef of Australia*. There are naturally a large number of interesting adaptations to be found among reef-animals, one of which has elsewhere been described (see p. 171). An interesting protective arrangement is found in a Coral-Fish (*Epinephelus hexagonatus*, fig. 1292) common in the Andaman Islands. The dark polygonal patches on its skin harmonize very well with the particular corals among which it feeds. A modification of different kind is presented by the Parrot-Fishes (*Scarus*), which owe their name to the strong curved jaws that enable them to browse upon the branches of various sorts of coral.

Many British fishes of no economic value haunt the neighbourhood of the coast, or may be seen in tidal pools. Such are some of the Gobies (*Gobiidæ*), which include the beautiful Dragonets

(*Callionymus*), and, in warmer countries, the little Mud-Skippers (*Periophthalmus* and *Boleophthalmus*), the habits of which have already been noticed. Other families are those which include the Blennies (*Blenniidæ*), many of the Bull-Heads (*Cottidæ*), and the gorgeously tinted Wrasses (*Labridæ*). There are also the curious Pipe-Fishes (*Syngnathidæ*), remarkable for the brood-pouch possessed by the male, and among these are the Sea-Horses (*Hippocampus*, *Phyllopteryx*, &c.), which are not found in British seas.

Primitive Vertebrates (*Protochordata*) *of the Neritic Zone.*—Lancelets (*Amphioxus*) and Acorn-headed Worms (*Balanoglossus*)

Fig. 1292.—Coral-Fish (*Epinephelus hexagonatus*)

are widely distributed neritic forms, with burrowing habits. The zone is also inhabited by large numbers of Ascidians or Sea-Squirts (*Urochorda*), some solitary and some colonial, which in their adult stage are attached to various objects.

Neritic Molluscs (*Mollusca*).—Head-footed Molluscs (*Cephalopoda*) abound in shallow water, Squids and Cuttle-Fishes, for instance, being found in large numbers around our own coasts, while eight-armed forms, such as the Poulpe (*Octopus*) and its allies, belong as much to the Benthos as to the Nekton, of the Neritic region, for they crawl as much as they swim, or possibly more so.

Sea-Snails and Sea-Slugs (*Gastropoda*) simply swarm both in shallow water and between tide-marks, especially in the tropics. Among the commonest littoral forms on the British coasts are the Limpets (*Patella*), which adhere so closely to the rocks that they defy the wash of the tide, to which their conical shell affords but little purchase; the Purple-Shells (*Purpura lapillus*), well protected against the buffets of the waves when withdrawn into their thick white dwellings; and the Periwinkles (*Littorina*), including the edible species (*L. littorea*); a smaller, more rounded kind (*L. obtusata*), often of bright-orange hue, which crawls over brown sea-weeds; and a third sort (*L. rudis*), that dwells near high-water mark and has its breathing organs modified in consequence (see vol. ii, p. 459). Sea-Lemons (*Doris*) and other marine slugs are also common.

Among neritic Bivalves (*Lamellibranchia*) forms of economic importance may be mentioned, such as the Oysters (*Ostrea*), attached by the substance of one valve; the Edible Mussels (*Mytilus*), moored by silky byssus threads; the Scallops (*Pecten*), some of which can swim by opening and closing their shells; and the Cockles (*Cardium*), which burrow in the sand. Other delvers in sand or mud are the Gapers (*Mya*), the Razor-Shells (*Solen*), and many more; while Piddocks (*Pholas*) and Date-Shells (*Lithodomus*) are able to excavate dwellings in stone.

Of Primitive Molluscs (*Amphineura*) the flattened Mail-Shells (*Chiton*) live under stones or in rock-crevices.

Neritic Crustaceans (*Crustacea*).—Prominent among these are the Prawns, Shrimps, Lobsters, and Crabs, of many species. Some forms of the last kind which we commonly see on our own coasts are the Edible Crab (*Cancer pagurus*), the green Shore-Crab (*Carcinus mœnas*), and, near low-tide mark, the little flattened Porcelain Crabs (*Porcellana*).

Neritic Annelids (*Annelida*).—Of these there is a vast host. Of British forms may be mentioned the actively-creeping Sea-Centipedes (*Nereis*) and many related species; the Sea-Mice (*Aphrodite*), short plump worms with beautiful iridescent bristles; Scale-Worms (*Polynoe*); Lug-Worms (*Arenicola*), that burrow in sand or mud; Sand-Worms (*Sabellaria*), living in communities and gluing grains of sand into dwellings; and various species sheltered in white calcareous tubes, sometimes irregular in shape (*Serpula*), or coiled into small flat spirals (*Spirorbis*) attached to brown sea-weeds.

Other Worm-like Animals of the Neritic Zone.—Here may be mentioned, in passing, the colonial Moss-Polypes (*Polyzoa*), of which the branching skeletons are often taken for sea-weeds; Nemertine Worms (*Nemertea*), slimy unsegmented creatures often found coiled up under stones; Siphon-Worms (*Sipunculus*), that burrow in the sand; and Turbellarian Worms (*Turbellaria*), variously shaped flattened forms often seen adhering to stones or other objects.

Neritic Hedgehog-Skinned Animals (*Echinodermata*).—In warmer seas, and to some extent in our own, Feather-Stars (*Comatula*) climb or swim in shallow water. Ordinary Star-Fishes (*Asteroidea*) use their numerous tube-feet for creeping, and Brittle-Stars (*Ophiuroidea*) progress on the sea-floor by

Fig. 1293.—Section through part of a Coral Reef

means of their snake-like arms. Sea-Urchins (*Echinoidea*) creep slowly about after the fashion of star-fishes, and their tube-feet adhere so strongly to rock-surfaces that some of them can even withstand the surf of coral-reefs. The Sea-Cucumbers (*Holothuroidea*) of shallow water either creep or burrow.

Neritic Zoophytes (*Cœlenterata*).—On British coasts the solitary Sea-Anemones, often beautifully coloured, are the most noticeable of the Sea-Flowers (*Anthozoa*). The fauna of the Great Barrier Reef of Australia includes some creatures of this kind which are as much as 2 feet in diameter when fully expanded. In some of the warmer seas, where the water is sufficiently clear, reefs are built up from the dead skeletons of a bewildering variety of Corals, simple or colonial, and the animals to which they belong are closely related to the sea-anemones. Some Corals live on the floor of the deep sea, but the reef-builders, so far as we know, cannot exist in water deeper than about 40 fathoms. Since some reefs extend downwards into much greater depths (their foundations consisting of the skeletons of dead polypes, fig. 1293), Darwin came to the conclusion that such reefs had been formed in areas where the sea-floor was sinking, but at so slow a rate that upward growth kept pace with it. The theory affords a simple explanation of the ring-shaped reefs known as atolls, which might be supposed to have come into existence from the gradual sinking of islands fringed by reefs (figs. 1294, 1295). Borings recently made on coral islands lend strong support to the hypothesis.

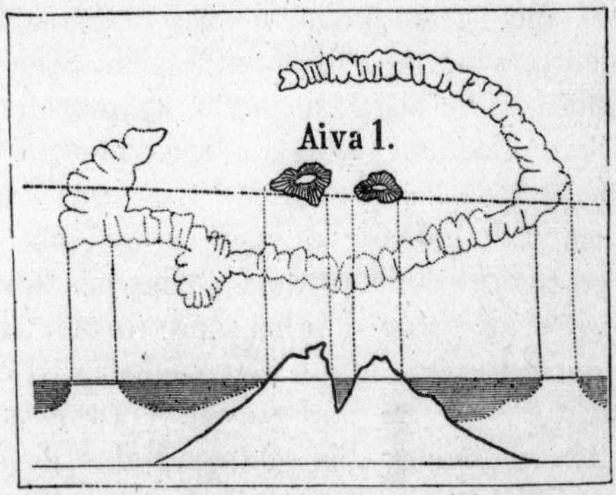

Fig. 1294.—An encircling Coral-Reef in Plan and Section. By gradual sinking of the island, with corresponding upgrowth of coral, an atoll (fig. 1295) might be formed.

Fig. 1295.—An Atoll

The population of the Neritic zone further includes large numbers of hydroid zoophytes and jelly-fishes (*Hydrozoa*), these being in some cases the fixed and free-swimming stages in the life-history of the same species.

THE ABYSMAL ZONE—LIFE IN DEEP WATER

The Abysmal Zone includes that part of the sea into which daylight penetrates but little, if at all. Even the average depth of the ocean, taken as a whole, is about 2100 fathoms (12,600 feet), while the profoundest abysses may be more than double this. The deepest patch at present known is off the coast of New Zealand, where a sounding of over 5000 fathoms (30,000 feet) has been obtained. It was long supposed that the deep sea was entirely devoid of life, but the numerous scientific investigations made during the last few decades have proved that even at great depths there is a rich and varied fauna, closely allied to that of the Neritic zone, but presenting many peculiar features in relation to the entirely different physical conditions. Except where this realm adjoins the Pelagic zone above it, it is probably in complete darkness so far as daylight is concerned, though it is more or less lit up by the phosphorescent glow given out by many of its inhabitants. The pressure is enormous, and the deep sea is also very cold, the temperature of its floor not being far removed from freezing-point. There is a complete absence of plants (except perhaps bacteria), and many of the animals are consequently predaceous in a marked degree. The requisite supply of food is maintained by the dead organisms which rain down from the Pelagic zone, or get washed in at the sides from the Neritic zone. Deep-sea animals present a great variety of colours, though no one tint can be said to characterize the fauna as a whole, and there is generally no blending of different hues in the same animal, nor any complex patterns or markings. It would seem that the utilitarian explanations that are more or less applicable to the colour-schemes of neritic forms fall short here. Certain other features will best be explained by briefly reviewing some of the chief groups of animals.

Deep-Sea Fishes (*Pisces*).—Most of the fishes of the deep sea are black or brown in colour, but some of them are purple, pink, or red, and since these brighter hues are most prevalent in the upper regions of the abyss, at depths of from 100 to 250 fathoms, it is not impossible that they may correspond to a dull kind of sunset illumination due to light which has filtered down from the surface. Many deep-sea fishes are also characterized by the possession of variously arranged phosphorescent organs on the head and body, but the use of these can only be conjectured in most cases. In some of the Deep-Sea Anglers (e.g. *Melanocetus Murrayi*) a luminous knob at the end of the "lure" almost certainly serves the purpose of attracting prey (see vol. ii, p. 85). The bodies of these abysmal forms are of great fragility, and there is a deficiency of lime in their skeletons. Huge mouths, provided with formidable teeth, associated with swallowing powers of no mean order, distinguish many species, giving them a hungry

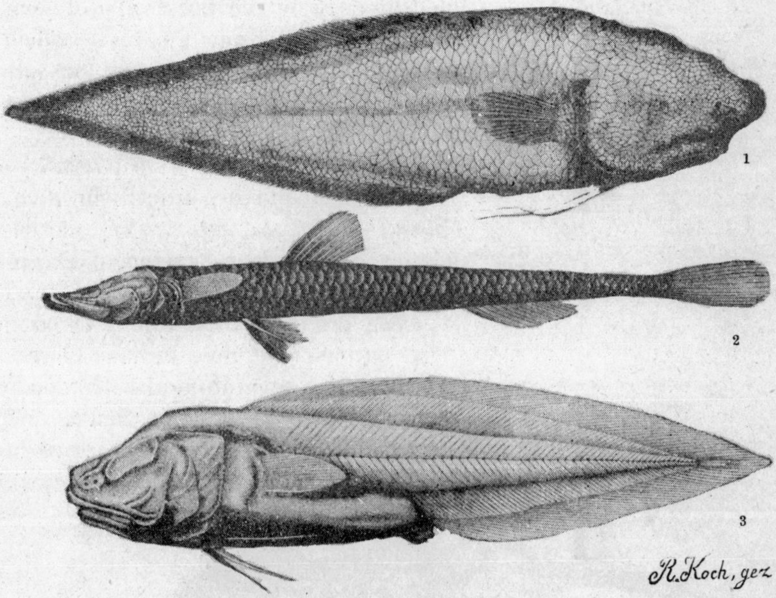

Fig. 1296.—Blind Deep-Sea Fishes. 1, Typhlonus nasus; 2, Ipnops Murrayi; 3, Aphyonus gelatinosus.

and ferocious appearance, and suggesting that no chance of a square meal is let slip. In the manner of sight there are startling differences which at first appear difficult to reconcile. In most cases the eyes are either large and owl-like, serving to catch the faintest rays of light, or else they are degenerate, sometimes, indeed, having entirely disappeared (fig. 1296). It is usually supposed that those fishes descended from ancestors which exchanged neritic for abysmal life with sufficiently plastic eyes, so to speak, to render their adaptation to the new conditions possible, have gradually acquired exaggerated positive characteristics, while the blind or purblind forms have taken origin from ancestors in which such plasticity was absent. It is also clear that species which spend more or less of their time in the uppermost part of the abyss (and even in the Pelagic zone) have a better chance of improving their organs of vision. But the matter is still in the conjectural stage.

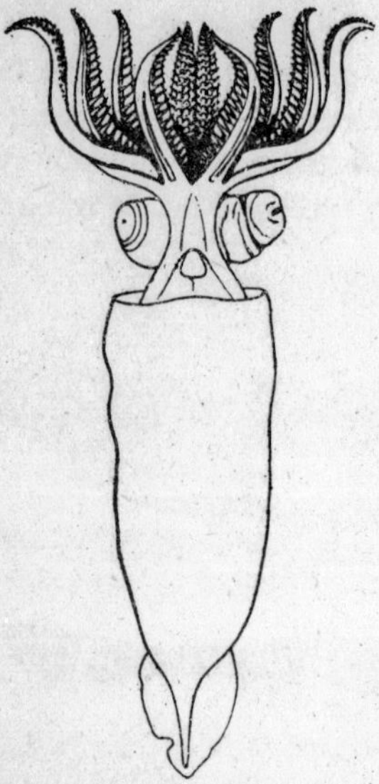

Fig. 1297.—Deep-Sea Cuttle-Fish (*Taonius abyssicola*) with large eyes

Some of the fishes which see indifferently or not at all partly make up for the deficiency by the possession of long feelers, derived from fin-rays, which serve as a means of exploring the surrounding area to some distance (see p. 28).

Deep-Sea Molluscs (*Mollusca*).—Some of the deep-sea Cuttle-Fishes (e.g. *Taonius abyssicola*, fig. 1297) are distinguished by the possession of exceptionally large eyes. The species figured has been dredged from depths of 902–1370 fathoms in the Indian Ocean. There are also several curious Octopods (see vol. iii, p. 33). The Snails and Bivalves possess unusually thin and fragile shells, while some of the former have lost the characteristic rasping-organ (*odontophore*).

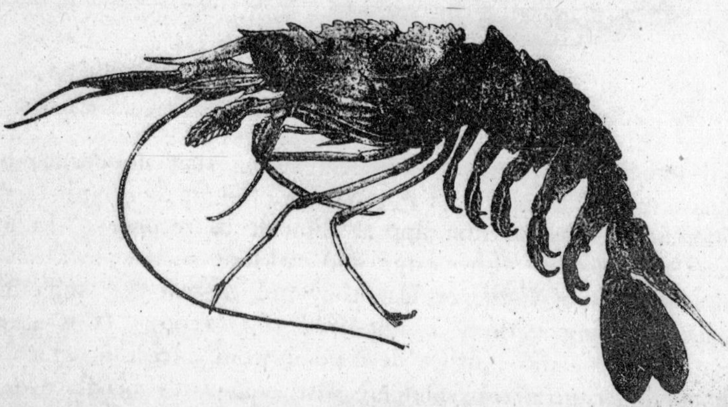

Fig. 1298.—Deep-Sea Prawn (*Glyphocrangon priononota*) with large eyes, and well-developed organs of smell

Deep-Sea Crustaceans (*Crustacea*).—Pink and red are here the prevailing colours, but some forms are purple, yellow, cream-colour, red, and even white, while others are spotted or striped in a simple manner. The hard investment of the body is comparatively thin and free from lime. As among Fishes, we find that the eyes are either greatly developed, or else more or less degenerate. We may take as an example of the former condition a kind of Prawn (*Glyphocrangon priononota*, fig. 1298) inhabiting the Indian Ocean at depths of 865–1022 fathoms. The figure illustrates two other interesting features. One branch of the first feelers (the thicker of the two filaments seen projecting in front) is of large size, and as this is the region which bears the olfactory organs the possession of a keen sense of smell may be inferred. There is, further, a sharp defensive spine at the end of the tail, which can be turned up and held in that position by a sort of "locking joint", acting as a bayonet to repel enemies at close quarters. It also appears that in some deep-sea crustaceans the fluid excreted from the renal organs gives out a phosphorescent light. In another kind

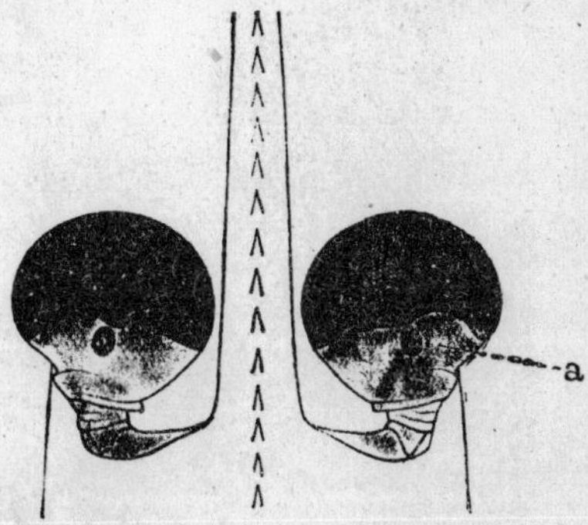

Fig. 1299.—Large Eyes of a Deep-Sea Prawn (*Parapandalus spinipes*), enlarged. *a*, Accessory eye (?) or luminous organ (?).

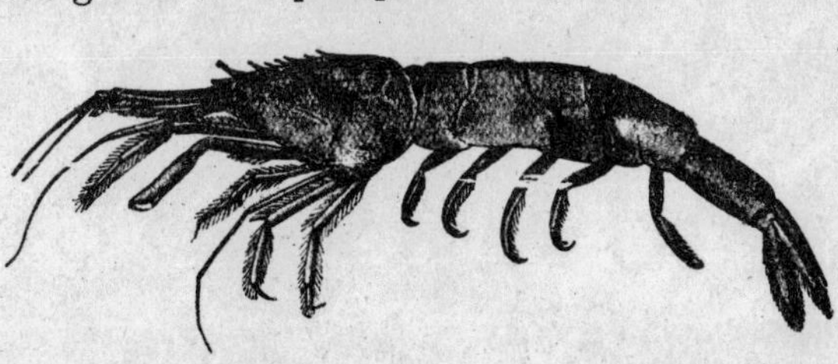

Fig. 1300.—A Blind Deep-Sea Shrimp (*Prionocrangon ommatosteres*)

of Prawn (*Parapandalus spinipes*, fig. 1299) there is what looks like a small accessory eye near the big one. If, however, this is really a luminous organ, as some think, the prawn provides its own eyes with light.

To illustrate blind crustaceans we may take one of the Shrimps (*Prionocrangon ommatosteres*, fig. 1300), which is absolutely destitute of eyes.

Fig. 1301.—Group of Deep-Sea Animals. In foreground—a Sea-Cucumber on left, and a Coral (*Lophohelia*) on right. At back—Venus' Flower-Basket (*Euplectella*) on right, two Sea-Lilies (*Rhizocrinus* and *Pentacrinus*) in centre, and on left. In the middle—a Pelican Fish (*Saccopharynx pelecanoides*).

The Stopper-Fisted Hermit-Crabs (*Pylocheles*) of the Indian Ocean and Caribbean Sea do not possess the twisted tails of our common native species, which live in cast-off snail-shells, nor is one of the pincers much larger than the other. These particular hermits are in all respects symmetrical, in adaptation to their dwellings, which consist of water-logged joints of mangrove or bamboo. The large pincers act as a front-door, but a loophole is left between them to serve as a means of observation.

Certain kinds of crustacean grow to a very much larger size in the deep sea than elsewhere. Among the Slaters (*Isopoda*), for example, of which the terrestrial wood-lice are the most familar types, we find one species (*Bathynomus giganteus*) which is a foot long.

Hedgehog-Skinned Animals (*Echinodermata*) *of the Deep Sea.*—Star-Fishes, Brittle-Stars, and Sea-Urchins are all abundantly represented in the abyss, while the beautiful Sea-Lilies (*Crinoidea*, fig. 1301), the representatives of a once dominant group, are found only in this zone. To this too are restricted the Elasipods, remarkable and apparently primitive types of the Sea-Cucumbers (*Holothuroidea*). They have a flattened under surface, and creep about like slugs on the soft deposits which cover the sea-floor (fig. 1301).

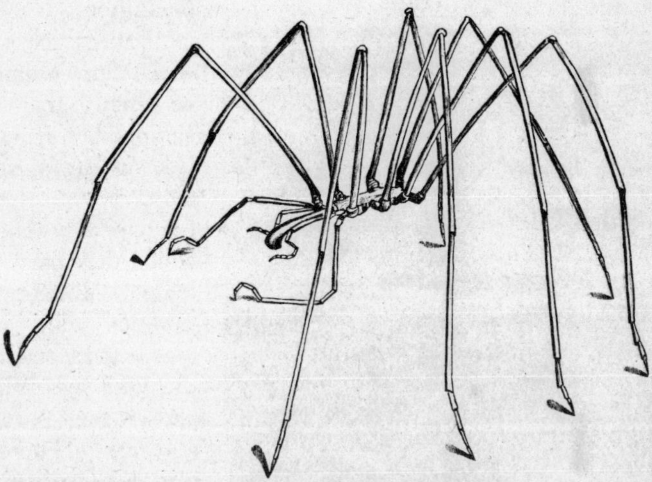

Fig. 1302.—Deep-Sea Pycnogonid (*Colossendeis*)

Abysmal Sea-"Spiders" (*Pycnogonida*).—These curious jointed-limbed animals, which in the Neritic zone are represented by comparatively small forms, attain relatively colossal proportions in the abyss. One of them (*Colossendeis*) is represented in fig. 1302.

Deep-Sea Corals (*Anthozoa*) *and Sponges* (*Porifera*).—Some very beautiful Corals and Sponges are found in the deep sea. Some of the latter resemble elegant vases in shape, with walls supported by glassy threads interwoven like lace (fig. 1301). Others are moored in the soft deposits of the sea-floor by long bundles of slender spicules of similar nature.

PELAGIC ZONE—SURFACE LIFE

It will here be convenient to consider separately animals which are powerful swimmers (Nekton) and those which float or drift (Plankton).

Fig. 1303.—Sun-Fish (*Orthagoriscus mola*)

PELAGIC NEKTON.—Among Mammals we find that the Pinnipede Carnivores (see p. 436) spend more or less of their time in this zone, to which they partly belong. More purely pelagic, and altogether independent of the land, are Whales, and their allies (*Cetacea*). There are also Birds which are pelagic, notably the Albatross (*Diomedea exulans*) and the Tropic Birds (*Phaëthon*); while the Sea-Snakes (*Hydrophinæ*) of the Indian Ocean and part of the Pacific belong here in the main. A number of Fishes are chiefly met with in the open sea, among them being the Blue Shark (*Carcharias glaucus*) and the Rondeletian Shark (*Carcharodon Rondeletii*). The Flying-Fish (*Exocœtus volitans*) and its enemy the Bonito (*Albicore bonito*) are also pelagic, and so is the remarkably-shaped Sun-Fish (*Orthagoriscus mola*, fig. 1303). Many of the best swimmers among the Cuttle-Fishes and Squids are also found at or near the surface of the sea, far away from land.

Pelagic Plankton.—The floating and drifting population of the sea possess a number of common characteristics related to their mode of life. They are typically translucent or transparent, a feature due to the large proportion of water in their tissues. By making some of them more or less difficult to see, this may serve to some extent as a means of protection (see vol. ii, p. 278), and by reducing the density of their bodies it must certainly

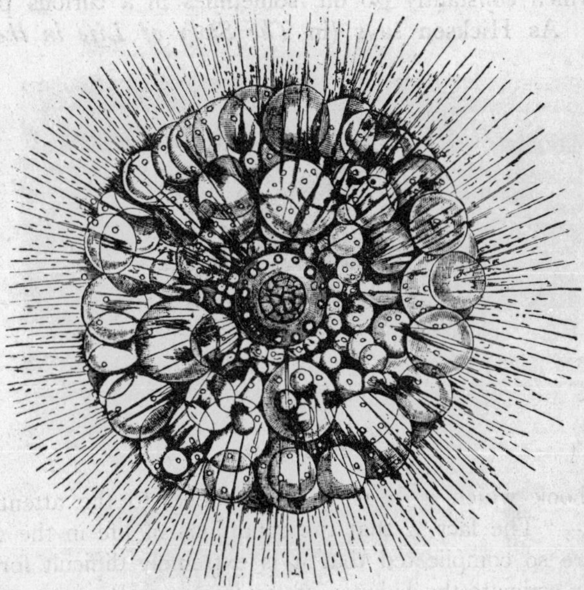

Fig. 1304.—A Ray-Animalcule (*Thalassicola pelagica*) with "bubbly" protoplasm, much enlarged.

render floating a comparatively easy matter. The latter purpose is also promoted by arrangements of other kind. In many of the minute crustaceans and crustacean larvæ, for example, there are numerous spines and hairs which must reduce the tendency to sink. Oil-globules are of common occurrence, both in adult animals and in some floating eggs, such as those of fishes. And there may also be gas-receptacles for buoying up the body. In some of the Animalcules, for example, the living substance (protoplasm) of the animal is of "bubbly" consistency, owing to the presence of minute spaces filled with liquid, or even gas (fig. 1304). In many of the Compound Jelly-Fishes (*Siphonophora*) there is a gas-filled float at the upper end of the colony, and sometimes (*Velella*, fig. 1305) a crest projecting from this may almost be said to serve as a sail.

It must not be supposed, however, that plankton animals are always found at the surface, for, on the contrary, they are able to withdraw themselves from it to a greater or less depth, and thus avoid the damaging effects of a rough sea or an excess of temperature. Our ignorance is at present too great to enable us to explain the reasons for all the upward or downward movements which constantly go on, sometimes in a curious periodic manner. As Hickson says (in *The Story of Life in the Seas*,

Fig. 1305.—Velella

a little book which is heartily commended to the attention of readers):—"The fact is, that the conditions of life in the surface waters are so complicated that it is extremely difficult for us to accurately estimate the balance of the forces which act upon these organisms. The direct heat of the sun, the light of both the sun and the moon, the tranquillity or roughness of the sea, the conditions of the tides and winds which cause changes in the surface temperature of the water, independently of the direct heat of the sun, all influence the delicate tissues of which these animals' bodies are composed, and cause them to change their position." Phosphorescence is another common property of plankton animals, and its meaning is in many cases difficult to understand. Planktons are of very various character. Some contain animals of many different species, others consist of a single form of life.

Vertebrates (*Vertebrata*) *of the Plankton.*—Among Fishes (*Pisces*) occasion has already been taken to note (see vol. iii,

p. 425) that a great many species lay floating eggs, and these, together with the transparent larvæ that hatch out of them, belong to the plankton fauna. Primitive Vertebrates (*Protochordata*) are abundantly represented by certain Sea-Squirts or Ascidians (*Urochorda*), including some little tadpole-shaped forms (*Appendicularia*, &c.), Barrel Ascidians (*Doliolum*), Salps (*Salpa*), and Fire-Cylinders (*Pyrosoma*), all of which have received notice

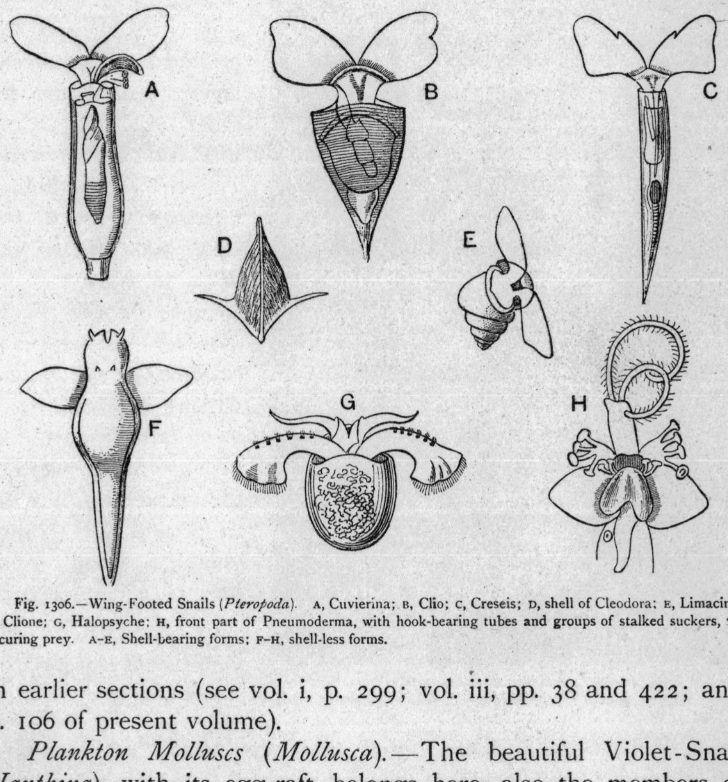

Fig. 1306.—Wing-Footed Snails (*Pteropoda*). A, Cuvierina; B, Clio; C, Creseis; D, shell of Cleodora; E, Limacin F, Clione; G, Halopsyche; H, front part of Pneumoderma, with hook-bearing tubes and groups of stalked suckers, securing prey. A–E, Shell-bearing forms; F–H, shell-less forms.

in earlier sections (see vol. i, p. 299; vol. iii, pp. 38 and 422; an p. 106 of present volume).

Plankton Molluscs (*Mollusca*).—The beautiful Violet-Sna (*Ianthina*), with its egg-raft, belongs here, also the members c the remarkable and diversified group of Fin-Footed Snails (*Hetero poda*), and a curious little Sea-Slug (*Phyllirhoë*), which is flattene from side to side (see vol. iii, pp. 34 and 36). Far mo characteristic than these, however, are the little Wing-Foot Snails (*Pteropoda*, fig. 1306), which are often found associat in vast shoals, affording an important contribution to the bill fare of animals so large as Whales.

The larvæ of numerous Molluscs simply swarm in the surface waters of the sea.

Plankton Insects (*Insecta*).—Although Insects are essentially land-forms, a few Bugs (e.g. *Halobates*) live on the surface of the open sea.

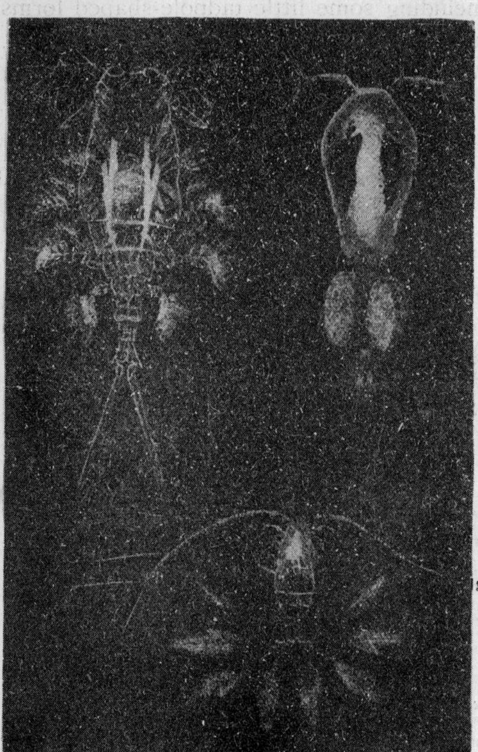

Fig. 1307.—Fork-Footed Crustaceans (*Copepoda*) with well-developed limbs. 1, Oncæa venusta; 2, Copilia vitrea; 3, Calocalanus pavo.

Plankton Crustaceans (*Crustacea*).—Many members of this group, and innumerable crustacean larvæ, are among the most important plankton animals. Some, as the Swimming-Crabs, may be of fair size, but by far the most dominant order is that of the Fork-Footed Crustaceans (*Copepoda*, fig. 1307), which are of great economic importance, because they constitute the staple diet of Herrings and some other valuable food-fishes (see p. 283).

Plankton Annelids (*Annelida*). — Some members of this group are specially adapted to a life in the surface waters, and one remarkable example (*Tomopteris*) has elsewhere been described (see vol. iii, p. 22).

Plankton Echinoderms (*Echinodermata*).—The curious larvæ of all sorts of Echinoderms are abundantly found in plankton at certain times of the year, but the adult members of the group seem little suited for this kind of life. A kind of Sea-Cucumber (*Pelagothuria*), however, has acquired the necessary adaptations for the purpose (see vol. iii, p. 24).

Nemertine Worms (*Nemertea*) *of the Plankton.*—The larvæ

of these curious Worms, like those of the last-named group, are well represented in the surface waters of the sea, and some adult Nemertines have given up creeping and taken to a pelagic life. One of the most remarkable (*Pelagonemertes*) is represented in fig. 1308.

Plankton Thread-Worms (*Nemathelmia*). — Among the commonest inhabitants of the surface waters are the curious little fish-shaped Arrow-Worms (*Sagitta*, *Spadella*, &c.), which constitute a special group (*Chætognatha*) that is generally supposed to be an outlying constituency of the Thread-Worms (see vol. iii, p. 21), though its affinities are doubtful.

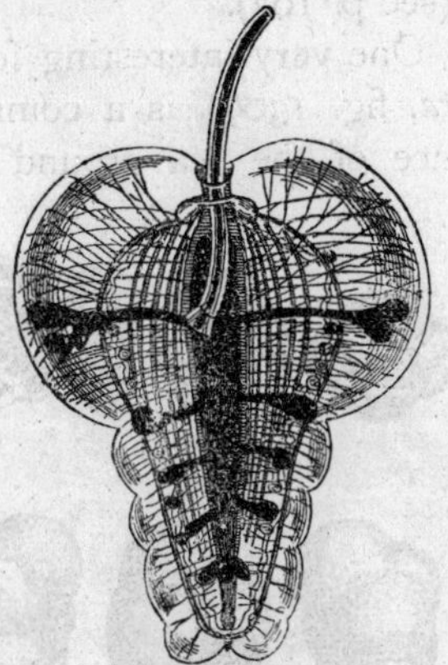

Fig. 1308.—Pelagic Nemertine Worm (*Pelagonemertes*), reduced

Fig. 1309.—Night-Light Animalcules (*Noctiluca*), enlarged

Fig. 1310.—Shells of Ray-Animalcules (*Radiolaria*), imbedded in the fibrous skeleton of a sponge

Plankton Zoophytes (*Cœlenterata*).—A bewildering variety of jelly-fishes, belonging to all sorts of groups, abound in the surface waters. Many of them have abandoned altogether the fixed zoophyte-stage that is found in the life-history of many such creatures (see vol. iii, p. 349). Perhaps the most interesting among them are the Compound Jelly-Fishes (*Siphonophora*), which are floating colonies, often of very complicated nature, as the members of the colony are modified in many various ways in order to fit them for diverse functions (see p. 103).

Plankton Animalcules (*Protozoa*).—One very interesting form, the Night-Light Animalcule (*Noctiluca*, fig. 1309), is a common cause of the phosphorescent appearance of the sea around our

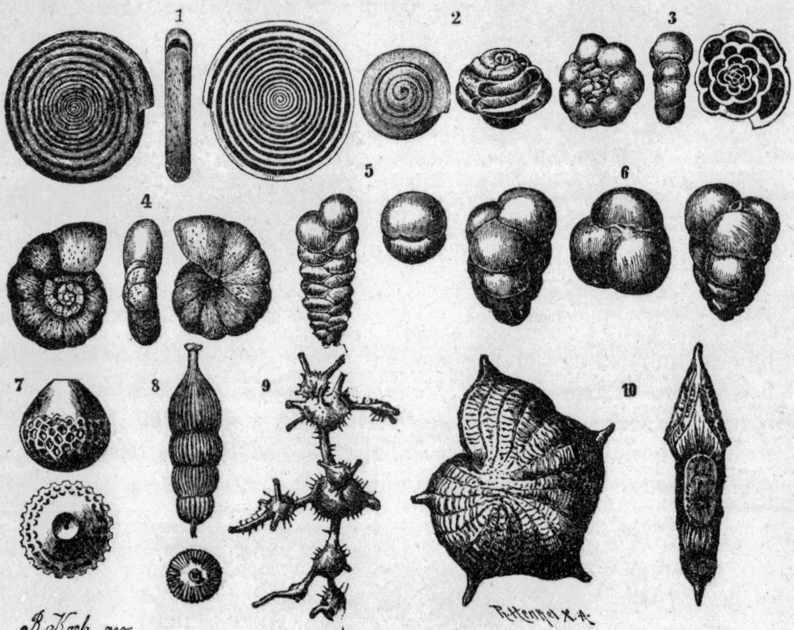

Fig. 1311.—Group of Foraminifera. 1, Ammodiscus incertus; 2, A. charoides; 3, Trochammina coronata; 4, T. nitida; 5, Textularia agglutinans; 6, Verneuilina pygmæa; 7, Lagena seminuda; 8, Nodosaria scalaris; 9, Ramulina globulifera; 10, Polystomella imperatrix.

coasts. Two groups are very dominant in the plankton, the Ray-Animalcules (*Radiolaria*, fig. 1310) and the Forams (*Foraminifera*, fig. 1311). The former possess a flinty skeleton, often of great complexity and beauty, while the latter are provided with elegant calcareous shells of the most various shapes. Vast areas of the sea-floor are covered by soft "oozes", which are largely composed of the hard parts of deceased members of these two groups that are being continually rained down from the surface waters. There also appear to be some few species of both groups that actually live on the floor of the abysmal zone.

Besides the typical plankton fauna which has just been briefly dealt with, the Pelagic zone is also inhabited by another assemblage of animals associated with various drifting objects, and particularly with the vast accumulations of sea-weeds that are found in the Sargasso Sea and elsewhere. Details would here be out of place, but it may be remarked that fixed forms of life, such as hydroid zoophytes, by attaching themselves to floating sea-weed, are enabled to maintain a foothold in the Pelagic zone. It is a matter of common knowledge that one of the most curious of fixed Crustaceans, the Ship-Barnacle (*Lepas*), is commonly found adhering to drifting objects.

The skins of Whales and Fishes also afford a home to quite a number of attached species, some of which are external parasites belonging to various groups. And many pelagic animals are also the unwilling hosts of numerous internal parasites, from which no zone affords escape.

Large bodies of fresh water may also be divided into zones, inhabited by characteristic faunas. The plankton of lakes is of particular interest, and also of some economic importance, as its population augments the food-supply available for freshwater fishes.

CHAPTER LXXVII

DISTRIBUTION IN TIME—THE GEOLOGICAL RECORD

If a large and complicated tree were submerged in water except the ends of some of its branches, these ends, projecting above the surface, would have the same sort of relationship to one another as existing groups of animals. To sketch the submerged tree on the evidence of the parts seen above water would prove a hopeless task, and to determine the mutual affinities of existing groups of animals without knowledge of their past history is also a difficult matter, though structure and development give many clues. Geology, however, furnishes us with a great deal of material from which to reconstruct the ancient life-history of the earth. It deals with periods of which the oldest date back to immensely remote times, if measured by the ordinary human standards of years and centuries, and the history of mankind occupies only the last page of the chronicle.

The Geological Record.—At the present time deposits of sand, mud, and limestone are being formed in the sea, in bodies of fresh water, and some other places, and these enclose the remains of dead animals, such as are well provided with hard parts standing the best chance of preservation. These deposits are arranged in successive layers, of which the uppermost are necessarily the youngest, and contain the remains of such animals as have most recently deceased. Examination of the hard framework of the land shows that a large part of it is made up of rocks, such as clay, slate, sandstone, and limestone, which are similarly arranged in layers, *i.e.* are *stratified*, each such layer being known as a *stratum* (fig. 1312). Imbedded in these strata are *fossils*, which are no other than the remains of animals (and plants) which once existed, or markings, *e.g.* footprints and other impressions, that prove the existence of certain forms of life at the time when the rocks containing them were formed. These stratified rocks, the pages of the geological record, are the deposits formed in ancient seas and ancient lakes, or more rarely on old land-surfaces, in the same way that sand, or mud, or ooze is now accumulating on the floor of the existing ocean, in existing bodies of fresh water, or, it may be, on land. Such old deposits, however, have usually undergone more or less consolidation, and those which we now find above-water owe their present position to movements of elevation, such as are even yet in progress in certain parts of the world. But as these movements are generally extremely slow, they usually produce no obvious result in the brief span of a human lifetime. Remembering that a particular stratum or layer of rock (and of necessity its fossils) is older than those which rest upon it, and younger than those which underlie it, geologists have been able to arrange the different strata in their proper chronological sequence, and thus to construct a continuous geological record, often picturesquely known as the "record of the rocks". The fossils of the record obviously afford some idea, though necessarily an imperfect one, of the successive faunas of the globe for many millions of years, how many can only be conjectured. A hundred millions is a common estimate, based on many different kinds of evidence.

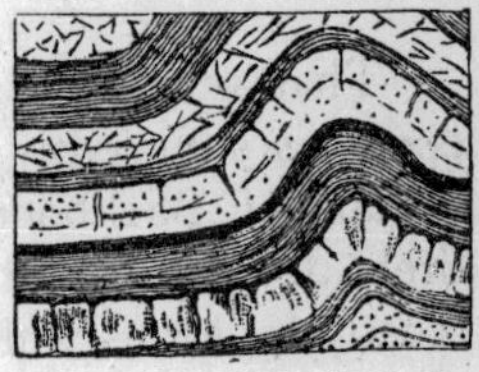
Fig. 1312.—Strata in Vertical Section

GEOLOGICAL PERIODS.—Without entering into details which may be found in any text-book of geology, it may be stated that the geological record can be divided into four great epochs, which are, beginning with the youngest:

KAINOZOIC EPOCH (Gk. *kainos*, recent; *zoē*, life).—Age of Birds and Mammals.

MESOZOIC EPOCH (Gk. *mesos*, middle; *zoē*).—Age of Reptiles.

PALÆOZOIC EPOCH (Gk. *palaios*, ancient; *zoē*).—Age of Amphibians, Fishes, and Invertebrates.

EOZOIC EPOCH (Gk. *eos*, dawn; *zoē*).—Age of Unknown Life.

The time represented by these four epochs is of very unequal length, but the Kainozoic, in which we live, has endured for a much shorter period than the Mesozoic, which in its turn was briefer than the Palæozoic, while possibly the Eozoic was longer than the other three put together. The entire geological record includes stratified rocks to a thickness of over 100,000 feet, a sufficiently bulky volume in which to study the evolutionary history (phylogeny) of animal groups. As will be seen from the above indication of the types dominant in the successive epochs, there has been a successive progress from low to high, in conformity with the doctrine of evolution; but the record is very imperfect, and that part of it belonging to the Eozoic is made up of pages which so far have turned out to be practically blank. Many parts of the world, however, are as yet unexplored, so far as their geology is concerned, and during the last few decades the additions to our knowledge have been so great that much is to be hoped for in the future.

LIFE IN THE PALÆOZOIC EPOCH

That animal life existed long before the commencement of this epoch is sufficiently shown that in its earliest stage all the great groups of Backboneless Animals (Invertebrata), save those entirely devoid of hard parts capable of preservation, are represented, mostly by forms which we are able to classify with some approach to certainty. And before the epoch came to an end all the classes of Backboned Animals (Vertebrata), except Primitive Vertebrates (of the past history of which, owing to the soft nature of their bodies, we can never hope to learn much), Birds, and Mammals, had come into existence, as testified by numerous fossils.

PALÆOZOIC ANIMALCULES (PROTOZOA).—The Ray-Animalcules (*Radiolaria*) and Forams (*Foraminifera*) are here and there abundant. The flinty shells of the former make up hard siliceous bands (cherts) which were certainly deposited in very deep water, and correspond to the Radiolarian oozes which now cover parts of the ocean floor. Some of the limestones (*e.g.* the Fusulina limestone) belonging to that part of the epoch when our coal-fields were formed are made up mainly of the shells of Foraminifera, and these may be compared to the wide-spread foraminiferal oozes of the present day.

It may be remarked, in passing, that some of the rocks of the Eozoic epoch (in Brittany) contain the remains of Ray-Animalcules.

PALÆOZOIC ZOOPHYTES (CŒLENTERATA).—The variously-shaped colonial forms known as Graptolites (*Rhabdophora*, fig. 1313) are largely represented in some of the older Palæozoic rocks, and the group died out entirely before the end of the epoch. They were very probably related to the existing Hydroid Zoophytes, and most of them belonged to the plankton of their time, and were most likely attached to drifting masses of sea-weed. In fact, Sargasso conditions were probably then more widely spread than now.

Corals were extremely abundant, and some of them were reef-builders, but they were mostly of a more primitive type than those now existing, and chiefly belonged to the extinct group of Four-Rayed Sea-Flowers (*Tetractinia* or *Rugosa*).

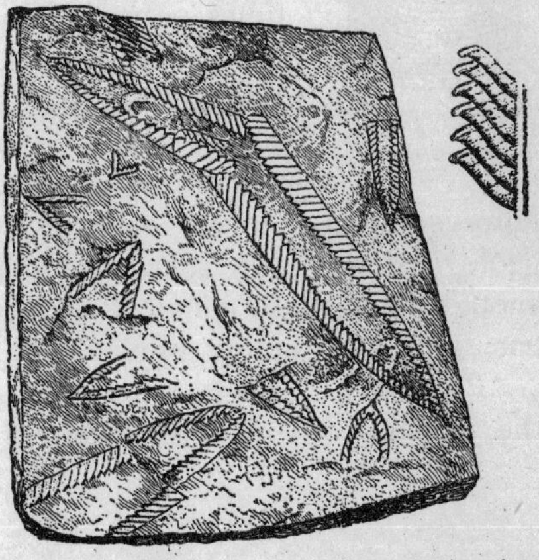

Fig. 1313.—Forked Graptolites (*Didymograptus*) on the surface of a piece of rock. A small part of one is drawn to a larger scale.

PALÆOZOIC HEDGEHOG-SKINNED ANIMALS (ECHINODERMATA).—Sea-Lilies (*Crinoidea*), now a declining group, were extremely abundant, and some of the Palæozoic limestones are mainly composed of their remains. Two other classes of fixed Crinoids are limited to this epoch, and one of them (*Cystoidea*) is of particular interest, because it probably represents the stock from which all other echinoderm groups have been derived, directly or indirectly. The other order (*Blastoidea*) was a sterile side-branch. Star-Fishes (*Asteroidea*) and Brittle-Stars (*Ophiuroidea*) were both represented, and one of the former (*Palæodiscus*) possessed a biting apparatus like that of many Sea-Urchins. The class (*Echinoidea*) to which creatures of the last-named kind belong was represented by a number of primitive types, with more numerous plates than later species, and (on the evidence of Palæodiscus) it has been suggested that Sea-Urchins are descended from Star-Fishes.

PALÆOZOIC LAMP-SHELLS (BRACHIOPODA).—This group of greatly specialized worms, distinguished by the possession of a bivalve shell, at the present time contributes but little to the fauna of the sea. In the Palæozoic epoch it was extremely dominant, and embraced a great variety of species, mostly belonging to extinct types. It is notable, however, that some of the lowlier forms which lived at the beginning of the period, *e.g.* the Tongue-Shells (*Lingula*, &c., fig. 1314), have persisted to the present day with but slight modification, so far as can be judged from the shell alone. That these and other "persistent types" should remain unmodified for vast periods of time has been brought forward as an argument against the doctrine of evolution. It is, on the contrary, what might be expected to sometimes occur in animals devoid of relatively complex adaptations to their surroundings. It was also at one time positively stated that Lamp-Shells, taken as a whole, afford no instance of modification on evolutionary lines. Of late years, however, thanks to the brilliant work of the American school of geologists, we know that the evidence afforded by this group is enough in itself to convince any candid naturalist that evolution has been the guiding principle in the animal world.

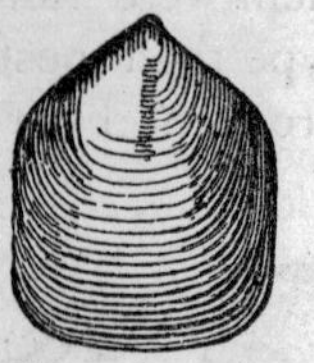

Fig. 1314. — A fossil Tongue-Shell (*Lingulella*), somewhat enlarged

PALÆOZOIC JOINTED-LIMBED ANIMALS (ARTHROPODA).—All the existing orders of *Crustaceans* (*Crustacea*) were represented

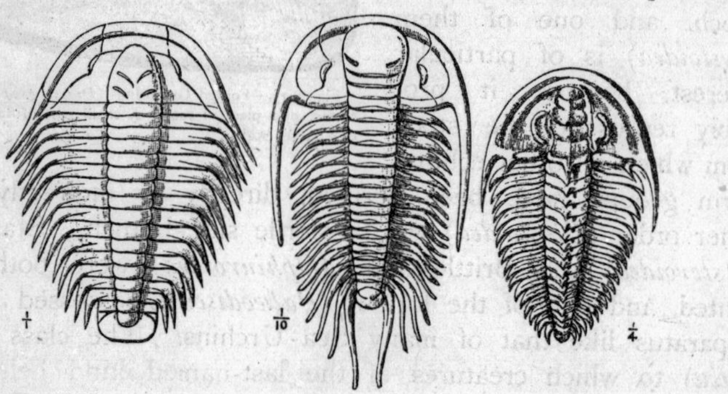

Fig. 1315.—Upper Surfaces of three Trilobites. Olenus (left), Paradoxides (centre), Olenellus (right). Actual size indicated by the fractions.

in the fauna of this epoch, except the Fork-footed Crustaceans (*Copepoda*), which are of too delicate a nature to be preserved as fossil, though they no doubt existed. It is noticeable that some of the more primitive types made their appearance very early, the contrary being true for the more specialized ones, such as creatures of the prawn and crab kind.

The curious *Trilobites* (*Trilobita*, fig. 1315), which constituted a closely allied class, were dominant in the older Palæozoic periods, but became entirely extinct before the end of the epoch. In these creatures the upper side of the body was covered by a firm investment divided into a head-shield, a varying number of thoracic segments, and a tail-shield. There was also, as a rule, a longitudinal division into three regions, and this is the origin of the name "trilobite". The numerous species exhibited a great range of characters, both as regards size, shape, and other features. The upper side of the head-shield often bore a pair of eyes, frequently large and facetted, but visual organs were sometimes entirely absent. Our knowledge of the under surface and limbs of trilobites was very incomplete till comparatively recently, partly on account of the delicacy of these parts, but now, chiefly owing to the investigations of American geologists on certain well-preserved species, many points relating to them have been elucidated. The head carried a pair of slender feelers, and there were numerous pairs of forked limbs used for crawling and swimming, while some of those in the region of the mouth acted as jaws (fig. 1316). Many of the stages in growth have been observed, and it may be said that trilobites which, when adult, are of simple structure, resemble the early stages of those which attain to greater complexity. This is precisely what the doctrine of evolution would lead us to expect. It may be added that many trilobites were able to roll up like hedgehogs, and this was no doubt a means of protection.

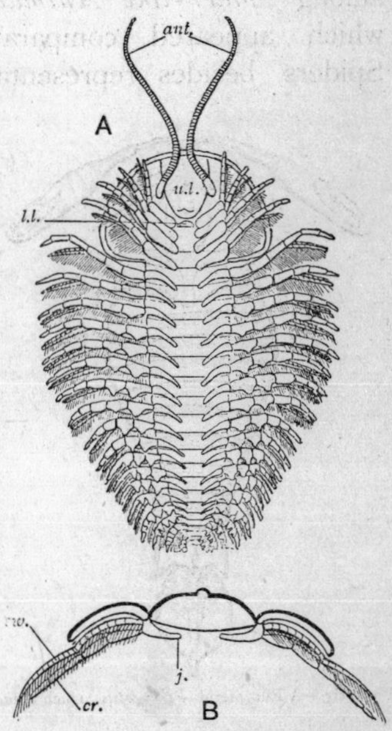

Fig. 1316.—A, Under side of a Trilobite (*Triarthrus*) restored, showing the numerous jointed limbs. *ant.*, antennæ; *u.l.*, upper lip; *l.l.*, lower lip. B, Diagrammatic cross-section through same, showing limb-regions. *j*, Projection serving as a jaw; *sw.* and *cr.*, swimming and creeping branches.

Appearing rather later in time than the Trilobites, which they to some extent supplanted, we find *Eurypterids* (e.g. *Pterygotus*, fig. 1317), some of which attained a length of about 5 feet. They died out before the end of the epoch, and appear to have been related to the Crustaceans. The *King-Crabs* (*Xiphosura*), now represented by a single genus (*Limulus*), first made their appearance in Palæozoic times. They are sometimes included with the Eurypterids in a special group (*Merostomata*).

Centipedes and *Millipedes* (*Myriapoda*) were represented by several palæozoic forms with somewhat primitive characters, while among *Spider-like Animals* (*Arachnida*) there were Scorpions, which appeared comparatively early, Whip-Scorpions, and Spiders, besides representatives (e.g. *Eophrynus*, fig. 1318) of

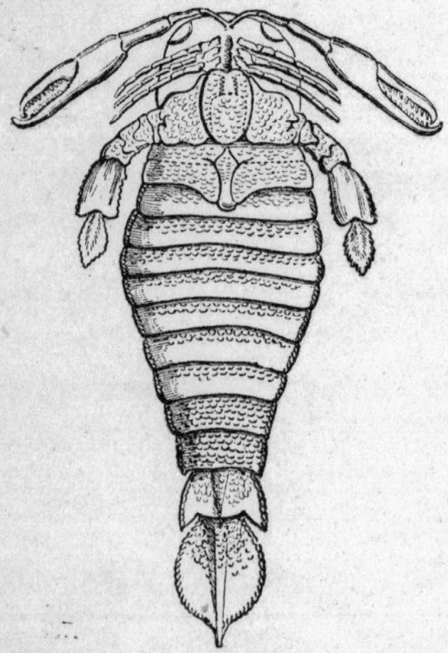

Fig. 1317.—A Eurypterid (*Pterygotus*), much reduced

Fig. 1318.—An extinct Arachnid (*Eophrynus*)

an order limited to the epoch. Four orders of *Insects* (*Insecta*) had palæozoic representatives, *i.e.* Primitive Wingless Insects (*Aptera*), Straight-Wings (*Orthoptera*), Net-Wings (*Neuroptera*), and Bugs (*Hemiptera*). Some of them were of considerable size, and it is by no means certain that the older types really belonged to existing orders.

PALÆOZOIC MOLLUSCS (MOLLUSCA).—Among *Head-Footed Molluscs* (*Cephalopoda*) now existing, only the Pearly Nautilus (*Nautilus*) possesses an external shell, of which the part not occupied by the animal is divided by partitions into a series of gas-filled chambers. But in the palæozoic rocks we find the remains of a great many species thus characterized. Their shells were straight, curved, open spirals, or closed spirals, like that of Nautilus, which dates back to the middle of the epoch. It seems probable that the straight-chambered shell was first evolved, and that this gradually underwent a process of coiling up, as a means of facilitating locomotion.

Marine *Snails* (*Gastropoda*) are abundantly represented among the palæozoic fossils, and it may be said generally that they belonged to the more primitive families, and were mostly of vegetarian habit. We also know that Land-Snails existed. The *Tusk-Shells* (*Scaphopoda*) date back to this epoch, and *Bivalves* (*Lamellibranchia*), the older ones of primitive type, were abundant. *Primitive Molluscs* (*Amphineura*) were represented by Mail-Shells (*Chiton*, &c.) of various kind.

PALÆOZOIC FISHES (PISCES).—There is no clear proof of the existence of fishes in the earlier rocks of the epoch, but later on they became abundant. The teeth and spines of *Sharks*, &c. (*Elasmobranchii*), are common fossils, and the armour-plated marine ancestors of *Ganoids* (*Ganoidei*) were abundantly represented, as also forms in all probability ancestral to the *Lung-Fishes* (*Dipnoi*). Many palæozoic fishes also belonged to orders that are now extinct. Some of the oldest of the fish-like forms, distinguished by a covering of shelly plates on the front part of the body, also by the absence of lower jaws and paired fins, were probably not really fishes at all, and have been placed in a special group (*Ostracodermata*, fig. 1319) of lower rank.

Fig. 1319.—An Ostracoderm (Cephalaspis), much reduced

PALÆOZOIC AMPHIBIANS (AMPHIBIA).—These are represented in the second half of the epoch by numerous species, all belonging to an extinct order (*Stegocephala*), distinguished by the possession of skins which were more or less armour-plated, especially on the head. While some of these creatures were small, others attained considerable dimensions. The footprints of some of them have been preserved. The chief interest attaching to the order lies in the fact that it was probably ancestral to Reptiles. It is also worth while noting that some few members of the order (e.g. *Dolichosoma*) were limbless and snake-like, suggesting a comparison with the recent Cæcilians (*Gymnophiona*), a widely distributed and in some respects primitive group, *e.g.* in the possession of little bony plates in the skin.

PALÆOZOIC REPTILES (REPTILIA).—A few fossil types from

the last stage in the Palæozoic epoch, formerly placed in the Stegocephala, are now referred to an extinct order of Reptiles (*Proreptilia*), which furnishes the nearest approach to the original reptilian stock. A further stage in evolution was represented by a second order (*Rhynchocephala*), from which the remaining groups of reptiles have probably sprung. There is a single existing species, the Tuatara (*Hatteria punctata*) of New Zealand. There were some other palæozoic reptiles, but these will be mentioned in dealing with the succeeding epoch.

LIFE IN THE MESOZOIC EPOCH

The animals of this epoch approached more nearly those of the present day than did their palæozoic predecessors. They included, however, a number of remarkable extinct groups, some of which were extremely dominant, while other classes, *e.g.* Birds and Mammals, which now play leading parts, were but feebly represented.

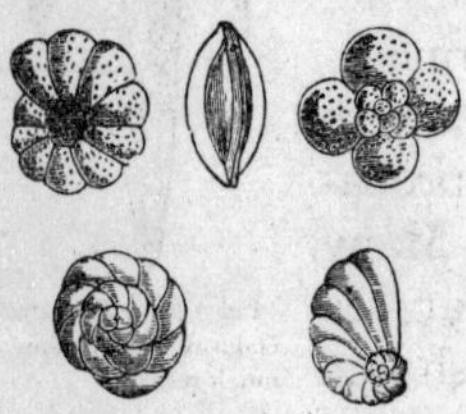

Fig. 1320.—Foraminifera from the Chalk

MESOZOIC ANIMALCULES (PROTOZOA).—The familiar chalk, which makes up the "white cliffs of Albion", and ranges east far into Asia, was deposited in the later part of the epoch. It is very largely made up of the remains of Foraminifera (fig. 1320), and before compacted and upheaved must have borne a close resemblance to the foraminiferal oozes which are now spread over a large part of the ocean floor.

MESOZOIC SPONGES (PORIFERA).—During the chalk period a large number of Sponges possessed of siliceous skeletons existed in the moderately deep sea, and it is their remains which chiefly furnished material for the large flint nodules that abound in part of the chalk, and which have a very particular interest for students of the evolution of human civilization, since from them many of the stone implements and weapons of prehistoric European races were fashioned.

MESOZOIC ZOOPHYTES (CŒLENTERATA).—Corals were extremely abundant during the epoch, and many of them were reef-builders. They belonged to the same great group (*Hexactinia*) that includes the most typical recent forms, being, like them, distinguished by a six-rayed symmetry.

Mesozoic Hedgehog-Skinned Animals (Echinodermata).—Sea-Lilies (*Crinoidea*) were far less dominant than during the Palæozoic epoch, and were represented by types of different kind, some of them (e.g. *Pentacrinus*) being closely allied to forms now living in the deep sea. Feather-Stars, belonging to the same class, but distinguished by the fact that when adult they abandon their stalks and take to a free life, first made their appearance during this epoch.

Ordinary Star-Fishes (*Asteroidea*) and Brittle-Stars (*Ophiuroidea*) were of increasing importance, and very numerous Sea-Urchins (*Echinoidea*) existed, many of them resembling recent forms, and differing greatly from the primitive palæozoic types.

Mesozoic Lamp-Shells (Brachiopoda).—These lost their dominance during this epoch, and the most important species belonged to genera which are represented at the present day (e.g. *Terebratula* and *Rhynchonella*).

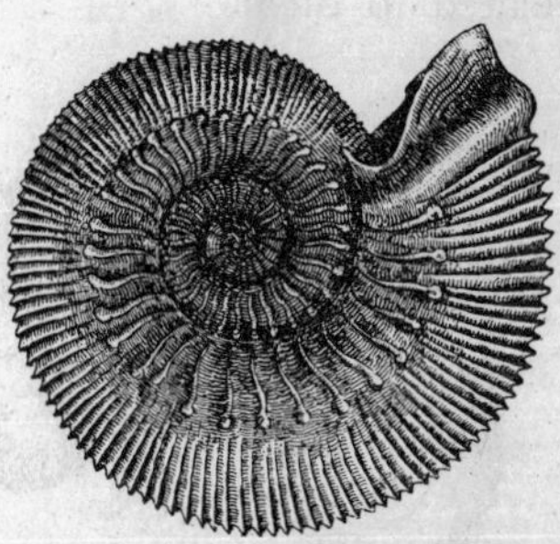
Fig. 1321.—Shell of an Ammonite (reduced)

Mesozoic Jointed-Limbed Animals (Arthropoda).—The Trilobites and Eurypterids of the Palæozoic epoch were entirely unrepresented, but undoubted *Crustaceans* (*Crustacea*) were common. These included numerous species belonging to the highest order (*Decapoda*), and more or less resembling the Lobsters, Prawns, Shrimps, and Crabs of the present day.

Among the air-breathing forms *Insects* (*Insecta*) were gradually acquiring a dominant position. Of orders for the first time represented may be mentioned Beetles (*Coleoptera*), Flies (*Diptera*), and Membrane-Wings (*Hymenoptera*). Ants are the most ancient members of the last order, so far as the evidence goes.

Mesozoic Molluscs (Mollusca).—*Head-Footed Molluscs* (*Cephalopoda*) took a leading place in the marine fauna. Two important types, *i.e.* Ammonites and Belemnites, were practically limited to the epoch. The former (fig. 1321) possessed spiral chambered shells, with the turns in one plane, and the edges of the partitions between the successive chambers elaborately folded. Towards the end of the epoch, however, we find more or less unrolled species (fig. 1322), some even that were perfectly straight. Such types may perhaps be regarded as unsuccessful attempts at adaptation to changing surroundings. The Belemnites (fig. 1323) possessed internal shells, and in this and some other respects, *e.g.* the possession of an ink-bag, resembled recent Cuttle-Fishes, though they belonged to a distinct group. Cuttle-Fishes and Squids, which are now dominant members of their class, were feebly represented in Mesozoic times, but as they alone proved able, mainly by acquiring a rapid mode of swimming, to fully adapt themselves to their environment, they finally succeeded in almost entirely supplanting the more ancient types related to them.

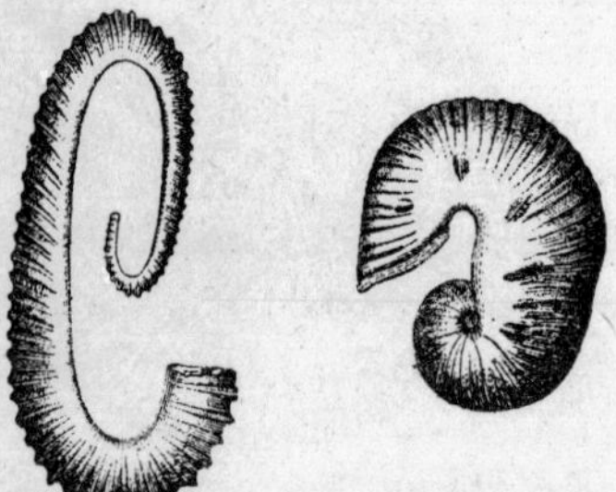

Fig. 1322.—Unrolled Cephalopods related to Ammonites (*Hamites* left, *Scaphites* right), reduced

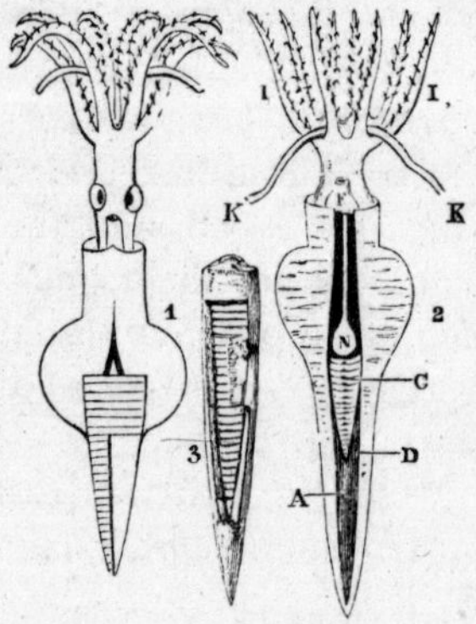

Fig. 1323.—Belemnites (reduced). 1 and 2, Restorations; A D C, internal shell; F, funnel; I I, short arms; K K, long arms; N, ink-bag; 3, shell.

Although many of the primitive palæozoic types of marine *Snails* (*Gastropoda*) were able to maintain their foothold during this epoch, the leading place was taken by specialized carnivorous forms, which became more numerous and varied as time went on.

Bivalves (*Lamellibranchia*) played a much more important part than in the preceding epoch, many new and more advanced types coming into existence. The families now represented by Oysters, Cockles, Mussels, and Razor-Shells, among many others, first made their appearance.

Mesozoic Fishes (Pisces).—The last marine representatives of existing *Lung-Fishes* (*Dipnoi*) existed in the earlier part of the epoch, and some of the fossil teeth are so like those of the Queensland Lung-Fish (*Ceratodus*) as to suggest a close relationship with that form. There were many mesozoic *Sharks*, &c. (*Elasmobranchii*), and we can trace the gradual specialization of their flattened relatives, the Skates and Rays. *Ganoids* (*Ganoidei*) abounded, and some of them appear to have been ancestral to Sturgeons.

Ordinary Bony Fishes (*Teleostei*) are the dominant members of their class at the present day, and date back to the later stages of the Mesozoic epoch. Some of the older types, less well adapted than they to an aquatic life, have gradually declined since the time of their first appearance.

MESOSOIC AMPHIBIANS (AMPHIBIA).—The armoured Amphibians (*Stegocephala*) of the palæozoic lived on into the earlier part of this epoch, to which belonged the largest known member of the order (*Mastodonsaurus*), the head of which was about four feet long. The teeth and footprints (fig. 1324) of this and related forms were characteristic, and have been known to geologists for a comparatively long time. The former were conical, and exhibit in cross-section very elaborate folds of enamel, which suggested the name of "Labyrinthodon" (*i.e.* labyrinth tooth). The footprints look something like the impressions of clumsy hands, hence the old name "Cheirotherium" (*i.e.* hand-animal).

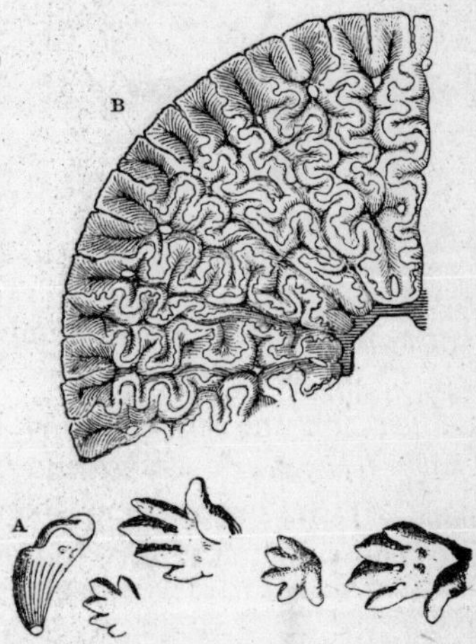

Fig. 1324.—Labyrinthodon. A, Tooth and footprints (reduced); B, part of cross-section of tooth (enlarged).

MESOZOIC REPTILES (REPTILIA).—The ancient order (*Rhynchocephala*), of which the Tuatara (*Hatteria*) is the only living representative, includes a number of species which were widely distributed in the early part of this epoch. Some of them were as much as 6 feet in length.

One of the most interesting extinct orders of the class, the *Varied-Toothed Reptiles* (*Anomodontia*) includes characteristic land-forms which lived during the later part of the Palæozoic epoch and the earlier part of the Mesozoic. The interest attaching to them lies in the fact that in certain respects they were intermediate in structure between the Armoured Amphibians and the lower Mammals, so that they probably represent the stock from which the last class has taken origin. Among mesozoic types may be mentioned the following:—Pareiasaurus (fig. 1325), a particularly clumsy-looking creature some 8 feet long and between 2 and 3 feet high; Cynognathus, with skull and teeth not unlike those of a dog; and Dicynodon, possessing large tusk-like upper canines.

The five extinct orders of Reptiles now to be mentioned were

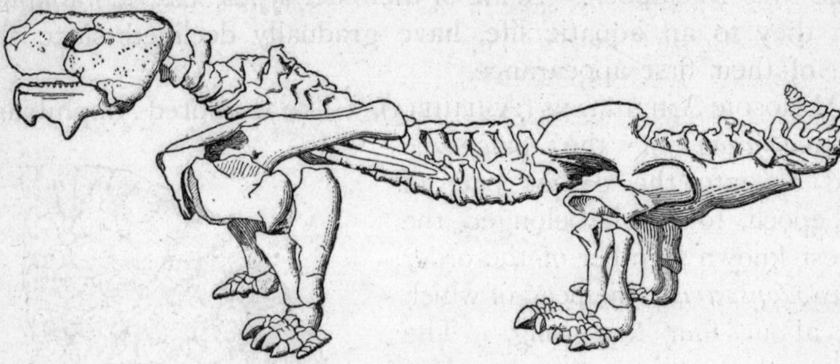

Fig. 1325.—Pareiasaurus (much reduced)

represented by a large number of forms peculiar to the epoch, and severally adapted to the most various conditions of life, in the sea, on the land, and even in the air.

Fish-Lizards (*Ichthyosauria*).—These were large rapacious marine forms, something like whales in shape, and with paddle-like limbs (fig. 1326). Judging from their enormous eyes they

Fig. 1326.—Restoration of Fish-Lizard (*Ichthyosaurus*), much reduced

were of nocturnal habit. Another interesting feature was the unsymmetrical tail, with the larger lobe below. The shape of this would facilitate return to the surface after diving (see vol. iii, p. 289).

Sea-Lizards (*Plesiosauria*).—These also were marine reptiles with large paddles, and the most familiar types (e.g. *Plesiosaurus* fig. 1327) possessed a long almost swan-like neck. The earlier members of the order appear only to have been semi-aquatic.

Sea-Serpents (*Pythonomorpha*).—During the later part of the epoch the marine reptiles belonging to the last two orders diminished in numbers and importance. They were to some extent replaced by the snake-shaped creatures of the present group, with small short paddles. Some of the largest forms (*Mosasaurus*) seem to have been as much as 49 feet in length.

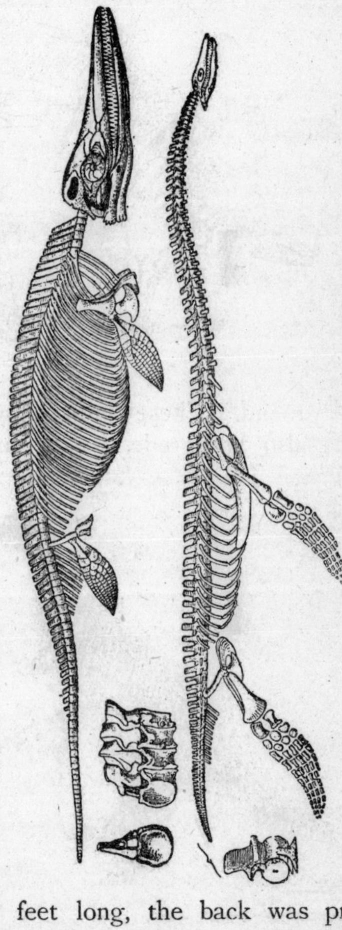

Fig. 1327. Skeletons of Fish-Lizard (*Ichthyosaurus*) and Sea-Lizard (*Plesiosaurus*), much reduced

Terrible Reptiles or Dinosaurs (*Dinosauria*).—The members of this varied group were the dominant land-reptiles of the epoch, and were represented by a great variety of remarkable species. The Reptile-Footed Dinosaurs (*Sauropoda*) were herbivorous forms with hoof-bearing plantigrade extremities. Some of them attained a very large size, the most gigantic (*Atlantosaurus*) is even believed to have been as much as 115 feet long. The Beast-footed Dinosaurs (*Theropoda*) were of carnivorous habit, and distinguished by the great proportionate length of their hind-limbs, which suggests that hopping was their typical mode of locomotion. They included species of greatly differing size, from that of a cat to that of an elephant. The Armoured Dinosaurs (*Stegosauria*) were herbivorous creatures, and in the type-genus (*Stegosaurus*, fig. 1328), which included species some 28 feet long, the back was protected by a series of large flattened bony plates, passing into spines on the upper side of the tail. The head was of relatively small size, and the brain so tiny that the intelligence must have been small. The herbivorous Bird-Footed Dinosaurs (*Ornithopoda*) are so-called because the structure of their hind-limbs presents some points of resemblance to birds, probably due to their having been adapted to the same kind of locomotion on

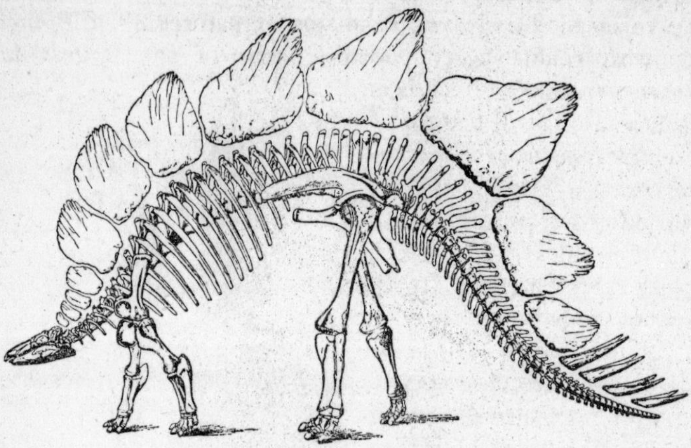

Fig. 1328.—Stegosaurus (much reduced)

the ground. These limbs were relatively very long, and they were also digitigrade, *i.e.* the animals possessing them walked on tiptoe. The best-known member of the group (*Iguanodon*, fig. 1329) inhabited England, Belgium, and Germany during the second half of the Mesozoic epoch, and the larger of the two known species was nearly 30 feet in length. The Horned Dinosaurs (*Ceratopsia*), which were among the later forms of the epoch, included a remarkable herbivorous creature (*Triceratops*) over 20 feet in length, with three horns on the head, and a curious bony shield covering the neck.

Fig. 1329.—Iguanodon (much reduced). *sc*, Scapula; *co*, coracoid; I and V (in fore-limb), thumb and little finger; *p*, pubis produced back into post-pubis (*pp*); *is*, ischium; I–IV (in hind-limb), 1st to 4th toes.

Flying Reptiles (*Pterosauria*).—The organs of flight of these extraordinary animals have elsewhere been described (see vol. iii, p. 308). Some were of small size, and of these the Pterodactyles (*Pterodactylus*, fig. 1330) were short-tailed. But one of the later types (*Pteranodon*) was a toothless reptile with a spread of wing not far short of 20 feet.

Crocodiles (*Crocodilia*) and *Turtles* (*Chelonia*) were numerous during the Mesozoic epoch, and in the later part of it both *Lizards* (*Lacertilia*) and *Snakes* (*Ophidia*) are known to have existed.

MESOZOIC BIRDS (AVES).—The few mesozoic birds which have so far been discovered have certain characters, *e.g.* the possession of teeth, which suggest reptilian descent. In the oldest known form (*Archæopteryx*), which has elsewhere been described (see vol. iii, p. 296), the tail was long, and bore pairs of quill-feathers at regular intervals.

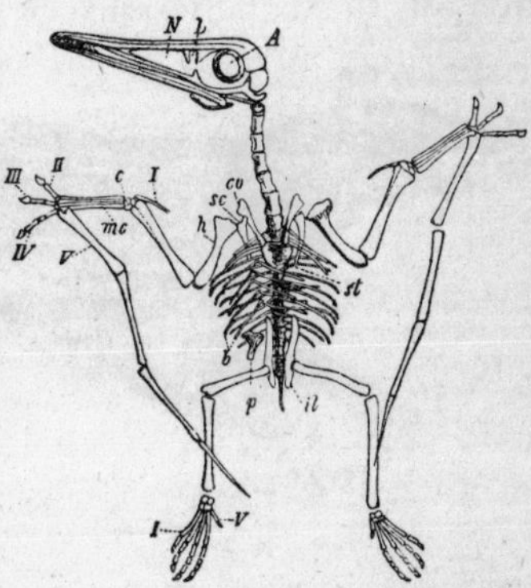

Fig. 1330.—Pterodactyle (*Pterodactylus*), reduced. A, Eye; L, lachrymal bone; *sc*, scapula; *co*, coracoid; *h*, humerus; *c*, carpus; *mc*, metacarpus; I–V (in fore-limb), thumb and fingers; *st*, sternum; *b*, abdominal ribs; *p*, pubis; *il*, ilium; I–V (in hind-limb), toes.

MESOZOIC MAMMALS (MAMMALIA).—That a certain number of small mammals lived during the Mesozoic epoch is known from the discovery of fossil lower jaws in several localities. Some of these suggest affinity with Egg-laying Mammals (*Monotremata*), while others probably belonged to small Pouched Mammals (*Marsupialia*). It has been suggested that Mammals evolved from some of the Varied-Toothed Reptiles (*Anomodontia*) on a land-area in the southern hemisphere, which there is some reason to believe once existed (see p. 411). Smith Woodward (in *Vertebrate Palæontology*) states that in Jurassic (*i.e.* mid-mesozoic) times—" . . . it is extremely probable that on some continent in that part of the globe the Anomodontia were gradually being transformed into Mammalia. At least, in the Jurassic formations both of Europe and North America there are occasional remains of small mammals as large as rats; and the most plausible explanation of these is, that they were accidental escapes from some other region with a more advanced fauna, just as are the rats and mice of the present day in the comparatively antique realm of Australia."

LIFE IN THE KAINOZOIC EPOCH

Even in the earlier stages of the Kainozoic epoch we find that the fauna had a comparatively modern aspect, and the later stages ultimately merge into the present. Among backboned land-animals Mammals and Birds were dominant, and it will be as well to confine our attention to a few interesting facts concerning these groups.

KAINOZOIC MAMMALS (MAMMALIA).—The fossil remains which have so far been examined enable us to trace the gradual evolution of the subdivisions of several mammalian orders, notably

Fig. 1331.—Restoration of Phenacodus (reduced)

so as regards *Hoofed Mammals* (*Ungulata*) and *Flesh-Eaters* (*Carnivora*). In the earliest stage of the epoch we find the ancestors of the hoofed forms represented by small primitive swamp-dwellers, constituting an extinct group (*Condylarthra*), of which a well-known type (*Phenacodus*) is represented in figs. 1331 and 1332. By increasing complications of structure, affecting limbs, teeth, brain, &c., the various odd-toed and even-toed ungulates have sprung from creatures of the kind, as also *Conies* (*Hyracoidea*), and, most probably, *Elephants* (*Proboscidea*). The nature of some of the specializations which took place have been briefly explained in a previous section (see vol. iii, p. 137).

What is true for Hoofed Mammals as regards one primitive group is also true for Flesh-Eaters with reference to another such group (*Creodonta*). Indeed there is not a great deal

AN EXTINCT GROUND-SLOTH (*Megatherium*)

It is a remarkable fact that certain groups of land-animals were in part represented, in comparatively late geological times, by gigantic forms which have since become extinct. This is the case, for example, with the Mammals poor in Teeth (*Edentata*), to which belongs the South American Ground-Sloth (*Megatherium*) represented in the plate, which is taken from a photograph of a restoration in the British Museum. In size it was nearly as large as an elephant, and is believed to have fed on leaves, as do the relatively insignificant Sloths which now live in the trees of the South American forests. The plate represents the Ground-Sloth in the position it assumed for the purpose of pulling down branches, or uprooting small trees, in order to obtain its food.

EXTINCT SOUTH AMERICAN GROUND-SLOTH (MEGATHERIUM)

of difference between the early kainozoic ancestors of Ungulates and Carnivores, both of which undoubtedly sprang from the same mesozoic stock, though this is as yet unknown. In similar fashion we find that the lines of descent of recent *Insect-Eaters* (*Insectivora*), *Lemurs* (*Lemuroidea*), and *Monkeys* (*Primates*) converge as we trace them back to the beginning of the epoch. The branches of the genealogical tree of mammals corresponding to the last two groups actually meet, and on this account some experts would place the Lemurs in the same order as Monkeys (*Primates*). We further find that the lines of descent of Insectivores, Lemurs, and Monkeys converge towards those of the Ungulates and Carnivores, and this appears to be also true for the *Mammals Poor in Teeth* (*Edentata*). Some day, perhaps, we may be able to trace back all these six orders, together with Conies and Elephants, to common mesozoic ancestors.

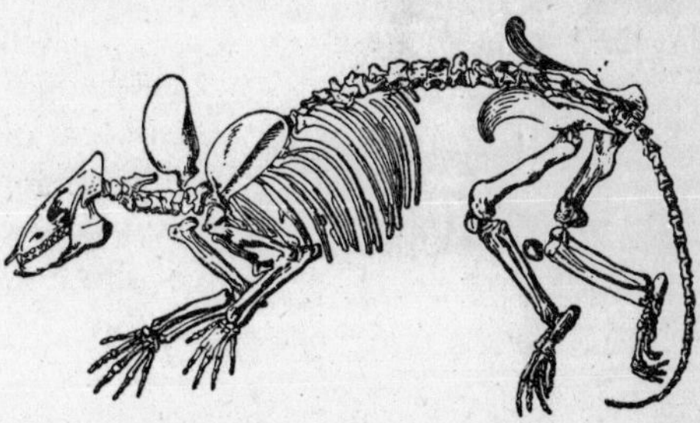

Fig. 1332.—Skeleton of Phenacodus (reduced)

Whales, &c. (*Cetacea*), *Sea-Cows* (*Sirenia*), *Gnawers* (*Rodentia*), and *Bats* (*Chiroptera*) seem to have acquired their typical characters before the Kainozoic epoch began, and we are not yet able to trace them back to the main line of mammalian descent. The two first groups, and creatures of the seal kind, replaced the marine reptiles of Mesozoic time in the life of the sea, and the Flying Reptiles proved unable to maintain their supremacy against the competition of Bats and Birds.

In the later part of the Kainozoic epoch certain orders of mammals were represented by relatively gigantic forms. A good instance of this is afforded by certain extinct American representatives of the *Mammals Poor in Teeth* (*Edentata*). At this time South America and the southern part of the sister continent were inhabited by huge Ground-Sloths, of which one typical form (*Megatherium*) was at least as large as an elephant. It and its allies combined some of the structural features of existing Sloths and American Ant-Eaters. That so large an animal as the one mentioned was not a climber is sufficiently obvious.

It is supposed to have been a leaf-eater, pulling off branches, or even uprooting small trees. A related form (*Mylodon*), which attained the size of a rhinoceros, possessed an external skeleton consisting of small bony plates imbedded in the skin. Remains of the skin, &c., of an allied type (*Neomylodon*) were not long since discovered in a South American cave, and in so fresh a state as to warrant a belief in the animal's recent extinction, while some naturalists, partly on the strength of native traditions, believe (or at any rate hope) that the creature still lives in the desert regions of Patagonia. Gigantic Armadilloes, of which one type (*Glyptodon*) was about 16 feet in length, inhabited America in comparatively late Kainozoic times.

Fig. 1333.—Irish Elk (*Cervus Hibernicus*), much reduced

Turning to Australia, we find that some of the immediate predecessors of the *Pouched Mammals* (*Marsupialia*) of that continent attained large dimensions. The skull of the Pouched "Lion" (*Thylacoleo*), a form related to the existing Phalangers, was about 9 inches long. Its name is rather unfortunate, for it was probably of vegetarian habit. Very much larger than this was a gigantic animal (*Diprotodon*) related both to the Phalangers and Kangaroos, for it was about as large as a rhinoceros, its skull alone being over 3 feet in length. Its limbs were adapted for walking.

Three large extinct Mammals have a special interest as being contemporaneous with prehistoric Man in Western Europe, including Britain. One was the Irish "Elk" (*Cervus Hibernicus*, fig. 1333), remains of which are not uncommon in the peat-bogs of Ireland. The female possessed no antlers, but the male was well-endowed in this respect, for in him these weapons sometimes had a spread of about 10 feet. The Sabre-Toothed Tiger (*Machairodus*) belonged to a group of Flesh-Eaters now extinct, and possessed enormous upper tusks, which are responsible for its name. The lower tusks were quite small. It seems that the huge weapons of creatures of the kind were too well developed to be of much use, probably indeed acting as encum-

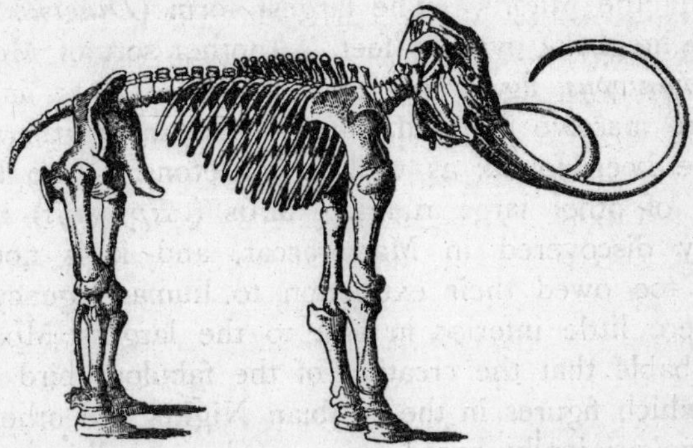

Fig. 1334.—Mammoth (*Elephas primigenius*), much reduced

brances which in the end brought about extinction. Here, as in many other cases, over-specialization proved fatal. The last extinct Mammal to be mentioned is the Mammoth (*Elephas primigenius*, fig. 1334), a sort of Elephant which had a very wide geographical range in the northern hemisphere, especially in the colder parts of this. The frozen bodies of Mammoths are now and then discovered in the iron-bound soil of the Siberian tundras, and these prove the existence of a thick coat of long black over-hair, together with reddish wool, a character no doubt to be regarded as a climatal adaptation. One of the prehistoric drawings made by the men of the Stone Age (see p. 233) gives a rough outline of one of these animals, and indicates the shaggy coat. It was found in a French cavern, and executed upon a piece of mammoth tusk. The Siberian variety has long been known as a source of fossil ivory.

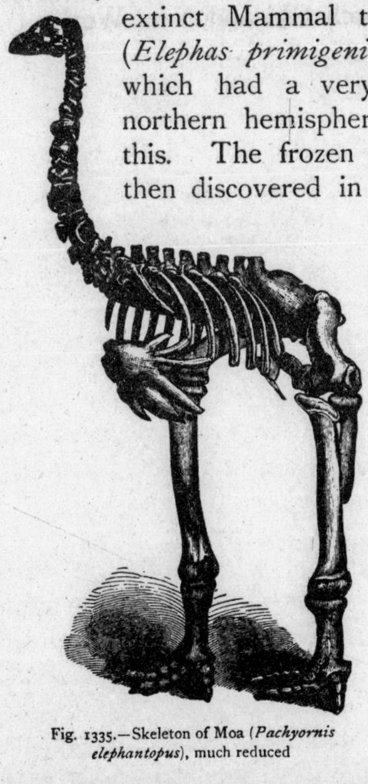

Fig. 1335.—Skeleton of Moa (*Pachyornis elephantopus*), much reduced

Kainozoic Birds (*Aves*).—Some of the extinct *Running Birds* (*Ratitæ*) are perhaps the most interesting. In New Zealand, for example, the Moas existed during the period of human occupation, and were finally exterminated by the Maoris. The largest form (*Dinornis maximus*) attained a height of over 11 feet. Another sort of Moa (*Pachyornis elephantopus*, fig. 1335), though not so large as this, was much more massive in build. Egg-shells and feathers of these birds have been found, as well as skeletons. The bones and egg-shells of other large running birds (*Æpyornis*) have been abundantly discovered in Madagascar, and it is not unlikely that they too owed their extinction to human agency. Some species were little inferior in size to the largest Moas. It is not improbable that the creation of the fabulous bird known as a "roc", which figures in the Arabian Nights and other Eastern stories, was originally based upon ancient traditions regarding some of the extinct running birds.

At the present time such birds are limited to the soutnern hemisphere, but we know that during early Kainozoic times they also existed in the northern half of both Old and New Worlds.

PHILOSOPHIC ZOOLOGY

CHAPTER LXXVIII

PHILOSOPHIC ZOOLOGY—THE THEORY OF EVOLUTION —EVOLUTION AS A FACT

Having now considered at some length the relations of animals to their surroundings (or environment), in which, of course, other organisms are included, and having also reviewed the life-cycles or life-histories of certain typical forms, this work may be fitly concluded by a brief survey of the Theory of Evolution, which at the present day not only dominates the realm of Natural History, but has also had a far-reaching influence upon almost every branch of learning.

The kinds or *species* of animal at present existing are almost innumerable, and we know from the geological record that a host of others once lived which are now extinct, some having become so within the historic period, while others died out millions of years ago. Until the second half of last century it was commonly believed that all these species came into existence by "special creation", and to ask "why?" any kind of animal had a particular structure, developed after a special fashion, exemplified certain habits, or lived in a definite area, was considered undesirable or even impious. The only answer to such questions given by the doctrine of special creation was that these things were so because they had been designed to be so, according to a plan into which the human mind was forbidden to pry. Now and then, however, from the time of Aristotle onwards, this paralyzing dogma failed to satisfy the minds of certain naturalists who were ahead of their times. Among these perhaps the most notable was the eminent French zoologist Lamarck, who in 1801 expressed the view that all existing species have descended from, *i.e.* been evolved from, pre-existing species. He further propounded a Theory of Evolution, which attempted to explain *how* species have originated from those which preceded them. But comparatively little attention was paid to the evolutionary views of Lamarck and some other naturalists till the year 1858. In that year a new Theory of Evolution (now commonly known as Darwinism) was simultaneously propounded by Charles Darwin and Alfred Russel Wallace, who, working independently on facts collected in entirely different parts of the world, had reached practically the same conclusions regarding the manner in which organisms of different kind have come into existence. The publication of Darwin's epoch-making book, *The Origin of Species*, followed in 1859, and since that date the doctrine of evolution has made steady headway, at first against strong and even embittered opposition, until now the doctrine of special creation is almost entirely held by those who have had no scientific training worthy the name, together with some few others who cling tenaciously to the old and once popular view.

This chapter is concerned with the *fact* of Evolution, and not with the various theories associated with the names of Darwin and many others which attempt an explanation of that fact. The distinction between the fact and its explanation is of importance in a popular work like this. Botanists and zoologists, after the manner of their kind, are constantly engaged in polemics about all sorts of evolutionary problems, their controversies being often not a little acrimonious, and sometimes even taking a personal turn. These things, however, are not unknown among the votaries of other studies. But in such cases it is not the fact of evolution that is in question, but this or that difficult question as to the way in which it has come about. All are agreed that evolution and not special creation has been and is the primary law of organic nature, probably, indeed, of nature in general.

Since the whole of this book has been written from the evolutionary stand-point, much has already been adduced in support of the fact of evolution, and it will therefore suffice to summarize some of the chief arguments in its favour, following the order adopted by Romanes (in *Darwin and After Darwin*).

THE ARGUMENT FROM CLASSIFICATION.—If the various kinds or species of animal were absolutely separate creations we should expect to find them clearly distinguishable from one another, but this is by no means universally the case. Indeed, it is by no means easy to exactly state what a species is. Some such definition may be given, for example, as the one by Swainson:—"A species, in the usual acceptation of the term, is an animal which, in a state of nature, is distinguished by certain peculiarities of form, size, colour, or other circumstances, from another animal. It propagates, 'after its kind', individuals perfectly resembling the parent; its peculiarities, therefore, are permanent." But unfortunately there are such things as *varieties* or *races*, which are subdivisions of species, and might be taken for such if seen in a museum. In the case of the Field Snail (*Helix hortensis*), for example, there are many such races, distinguished by variously coloured and banded shells. But in cases like this we usually find that the different varieties, when crossed, produce offspring (mongrels) which are perfectly fertile as regards one another and the parent varieties. On the other hand, the offspring (hybrids) produced by crossing two undoubted species are usually, but not always, infertile. A notable instance is seen in mules, which are obtained by crossing horses (*Equus caballus*) with asses (*E. asinus*). We further find that two or more apparently distinct species may be connected by a series of intermediate varieties. This is beautifully seen in some of the extinct Lamp-Shells and Snails, while the early turns of the spiral in some Ammonites (see p. 465) may resemble one adult species, though the later turns may correspond to another adult species. Facts of the kind cited, while only susceptible of interpretation in a mystical manner by the doctrine of special creation, harmonize very well with the evolution theory, according to which organisms are constantly being adapted to changing surroundings, and new specializations are continually coming into existence. On this hypothesis we may regard varieties as species "in the making".

Species are aggregated into larger groups known as genera, these into families, and so on, to orders, classes, and phyla or sub-kingdoms, respectively marked out by agreements and differences of increasingly broader and more general kind. If these various groups of, *e.g.*, Backboned Animals, are diagrammatically arranged so as to best express their mutual arrangements, a tree-like arrangement results (see vol. i, p. 111), the phylum corresponding to a main branch. This was perceived in pre-evolutionary days, and the only rational explanation so far given of it is that such a tree is really a genealogical one. The conclusion is fully confirmed by the geological record.

We also find a number of existing animals which, though on the whole susceptible of classification in one group, also show points of marked agreement with members of one or more other groups. A notable instance is afforded by Peripatus (see vol. i, p. 398), which, though an undoubted Arthropod, is singularly like a segmented Worm or Annelid in some respects. If the classification tree is a genealogical one, the existence of such animals is readily intelligible. Such cases are otherwise inexplicable, unless some unintelligible and dogmatic statement offered by the believer in special creation can be so regarded.

THE ARGUMENT FROM FORM AND STRUCTURE (MORPHOLOGY). —A very large number of examples might be brought forward to show that many organs can only be rationally interpreted on an evolutionary basis. A particularly good instance is afforded by the lungs of air-breathing vertebrates, which appear to be modifications of the swim-bladders possessed by fishes (see vol. ii, p. 421). And it may be added that there are many other structural characters of these air-breathing forms which point to an aquatic ancestry. That this should be so, is only intelligible from the stand-point of evolution.

If we take a particular group of animals, say Mammals, we shall find that they are constructed on a particular plan, modified in a great variety of ways to suit the exigencies of various modes of life. This is very well illustrated by the structure of the limbs, in reference to different kinds of locomotion, *e.g.* swift progression by running on a firm surface, swimming, climbing, and burrowing, as set out in detail in the section on Locomotion (vol. iii). We have here, it would appear, a gradual Adaptation by a process of evolution to conditions of different kind.

The strongest argument from structure in favour of the doctrine of evolution is that derived from those parts of animals which are known as *vestiges* (rudimentary organs). The human body, for example, is in itself quite a museum of such structures. Indeed, one may say that it is an archæological museum, for vestiges can only be reasonably explained as the remains of organs which were of greater importance in ancestral forms. The lower end of the backbone (coccyx), for instance, looks uncommonly like the remains of what was once a tail, and the same explanation can be given of the tailless condition of the man-like or anthropoid apes (Gorilla, &c.). The troublesome little outgrowth from the intestine familiarly known as the "appendix", which when diseased leads to appendicitis, corresponds to what is a large and useful structure in some other Mammals; and a little red fold (semilunar fold) in the inner corner of the eye appears to be the remnant of a third eyelid. And so on, almost indefinitely. Among Mammals other than

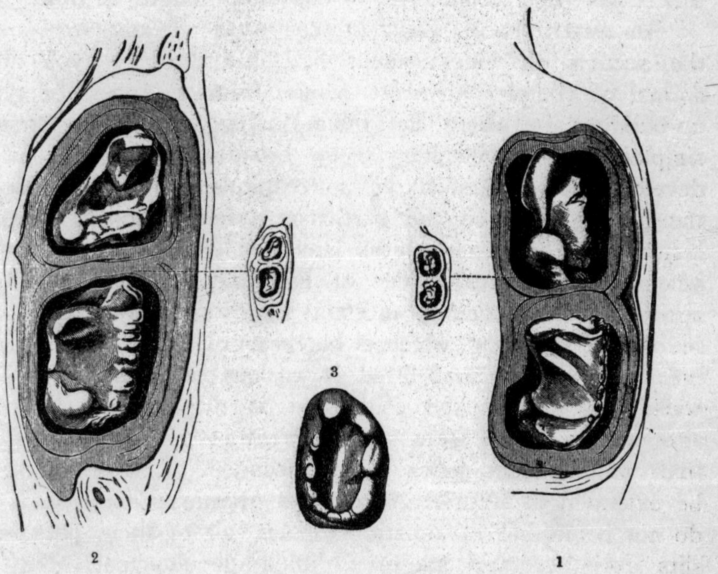

Fig. 1336.—(1) and (2), Upper and lower grinding-teeth of a young Duck-Bill (*Ornithorhynchus*), natural size and enlarged; (3) grinding tooth (enlarged) of an extinct Mesozoic mammal (*Microlestes*).

ourselves we find a great variety of vestiges. Whalebone Whales, to take a well-known case, possess neither teeth nor externally visible hind-limbs. But traces of teeth are found in the jaws of very young individuals, although they are never cut. And vestigial hind-limbs are found even in adults, imbedded in the muscles of the hinder part of the body, exactly where hind-limbs should be were they fully developed. Unless we simply accept these things as inexplicable facts, we must fall back on the doctrine of evolution, and consider such structures as dwindled heritages, reminiscent of earlier conditions.

Passing from the higher Mammals to their lowest existing

relatives, we find in the Australian Duck-Bill (*Ornithorhynchus*) that the adult animal possesses four horny plates in place of teeth. But these are preceded by small molars (fig. 1336) which last for a short time only. The conclusion may be drawn that the Duck-Bill is descended from ancestors which possessed teeth when adult. And, in connection with this, it is interesting and significant that the transitory teeth of this creature are singularly like those possessed by an extremely ancient Mesozoic mammal, which has been extinct for an enormous length of time.

Argument from Development.—As already explained in the section on Development and Life-History (vol. iii), an animal of complex structure results from a process of gradual up-building, in which the ovum or egg-cell is the first and simplest stage. Speaking very broadly, the course of this development is taken to be a recapitulation of the history of the group to which the particular animal belongs. The life-history of a particular form may, for example, include stages adapted to different modes of life, and in some cases these apparently correspond to ancestral stages similarly adapted. We see this in the Frog, which is hatched out as an aquatic tadpole, breathing by gills and fitted in various other ways for life in water. From this the conclusion is drawn that the remote ancestors of Frogs were aquatic creatures, related to the stock from which recent fishes have descended. The argument may be extended to Reptiles, Birds, and Mammals, for though these do not begin life as aquatic tadpoles, all of them possess gill-slits during certain stages in their development. But these slits have nothing to do with breathing, apparently serving no useful purpose, and ultimately close up. One result of their presence in the embryo is that some of the blood-vessels develop in a somewhat roundabout manner (see vol. i, p. 244). These vessels begin in conformity to what may be called the "fish-plan", abandoning this later on for the arrangement characterizing the air-breathing adult. Such a peculiar method of development is quite unintelligible unless it is explained by reference to ancestry.

The Feather-Star (*Comatula*) furnishes a striking example of recapitulation in its life-history. It is for some time fixed to some firm object by means of a stalk, which is later on abandoned. This may very reasonably be taken to mean that

Feather-Stars have descended from fixed forms resembling the related Sea-Lilies, some of which still live in the deep sea.

The Argument from the Geological Record.—Although our knowledge of the successive faunas which have existed in the course of the earth's history is lamentably incomplete, all the facts with which we are acquainted harmonize with the doctrine of evolution (see p. 456). There has been a general progress from low to high, and many animal pedigrees have been worked out in considerable detail. Taking Hoofed Mammals and Flesh-Eaters, for instance, the geological record shows that the existing subdivisions of these orders can be traced back, respectively, to common ancestors (see p. 472). The most ancient birds known possess characters which are strong evidence of reptilian descent, and Reptiles, in their turn, are in all probability an offshoot from an amphibian stock. Similar evolutionary conclusions can be drawn in all cases where sufficiently abundant evidence is available.

The Argument from Geographical Distribution.—The way in which animals are at the present time distributed over the face of the globe is susceptible of no satisfactory explanation unless we have recourse to the theory of evolution. Admitting this, and at the same time making full use of the evidence afforded by the geological record, many things which would otherwise be entirely unintelligible find an easy solution, as has already been sufficiently indicated (see p. 409). We are able in this way to understand why Tapirs are at the present time only to be found in south-east Asia and tropical America, Pouched Mammals in the Australian region and America, and similarly for many other apparent anomalies.

CHAPTER LXXIX

THE THEORY OF EVOLUTION—THE ORIGIN OF SPECIES

If we admit that the existing kinds or species of animals have arisen by a process of evolution from pre-existing species, the pertinent question "How?" demands an answer. Our ignorance is here so profound that we have so far only been able to frame working hypotheses to account for the facts. And every theory from time to time propounded leads to endless controversy, though, on the whole, we are constantly getting nearer to the heart of things. Everything depends upon the properties and possibilities of the living substance (protoplasm) which is the essential part of every organism, but it is precisely here that the gaps in our knowledge are most painfully obvious. The history of every science presents us with regularly alternating phases of fact-collection, and generalization upon facts. At the present time we badly need more facts, upon which to base further speculations as to the methods of evolution. And this is more particularly true regarding experiments on heredity and related matters, upon which satisfactory answers to evolutionary questions must necessarily depend.

We are here only concerned with a brief statement of the leading theories and principles which have so far been brought forward, commencing with the doctrine of Natural Selection, simultaneously advanced by Darwin and Wallace, and which has had a quite unprecedented influence upon the methods of human thought.

NATURAL SELECTION (DARWINISM)

This theory of evolution, which is essentially of utilitarian character, marshals together a large number of indisputable facts, suggests their mutual relations, and builds up, step by step, a very convincing hypothesis as to how and why new species have come into existence during the countless ages for which life has existed on the earth.

It is, to begin with, sufficiently obvious that the available living space on the earth is, after all, restricted, and there must therefore be a limit to the number of plants and animals that can exist at the same time. We know, however, that all organisms tend to increase in a more or less rapid manner, yet, in a given locality, the numbers of individuals belonging to a particular species remain fairly steady. There must, therefore, be various checks preventing indefinite increase—a constant fight for life, a Struggle for Existence. Every plant and every animal is engaged in a keen competition with other forms of life, and has also to battle with the constantly-changing physical conditions which collectively constitute climate. Individuals that for any reason surpass others in this constant warfare with their surroundings are, so to speak, *selected* by Nature to carry on their race, while their less fortunate fellows go to the wall. We have, in short, the active principle of Natural Selection or Survival of the Fittest.

We have further to consider how and why it is that given individuals are thus favoured in the universal struggle for existence. The classes of facts which give us some insight into this matter may be conveniently arranged in the following tabular statement, followed by a brief discussion of the principles involved.

PROVED FACTS	NECESSARY CONSEQUENCES
Limited Surface of Globe and Rapid Increase in Numbers	Struggle for Existence
Struggle for Existence and Variation	Natural Selection or Survival of the Fittest
Natural Selection and Heredity ...	Origin of New Species

Rapid Increase in Numbers.—Darwin takes the elephant as an example of an animal of which the numbers increase with minimum rapidity, a family of six within the space of 60 years being the average, while individuals live for about a century. Supposing all the offspring to survive for the full tenure of existence, this gives a total of about 19,000,000 elephants descended from a single pair after the lapse of from 740 to 750 years.

As an example of a species which increases with great rapidity we may take the Field Vole (*Arvicola arvalis*), which produces several broods during the same summer, some of these propagating in their turn before winter. Crampe has calculated that, if there were no checks to increase, a single pair of these animals, supposing their first brood to be born on April 15 of a given year, would be represented by the very respectable total of 198 on the following 8th of October. Continental agriculturists sometimes have a very unpleasant object-lesson as to these possibilities, for in certain "vole years" the ordinary checks to increase are inefficient, the result being that enormous numbers of field-voles make their appearance, and do an immense amount of damage to crops.

It not infrequently happens that when particular species of animals are introduced into a new country, where the checks that keep down their numbers in their native countries cease to operate, they increase in a phenomenal way. The result of introducing rabbits into Australia affords one of the best examples of this.

VARIATION AND HEREDITY.—It is a well-known fact that no two individuals of the same species are precisely alike. There is, in other words, a tendency to vary. The fact of Variation enables us to understand why certain individuals, rather than others, have a better chance of surviving in the struggle for existence. For in any given environment variations in some directions must more or less favour the animals which possess them. They are, in fact, *useful* variations, tending to greater *fitness* as regards some particular set of surroundings. In many herbivorous animals, for example, in regions where carnivorous enemies abound, it is clear that an individual varying in such a way that its locomotor powers are somewhat better than those of its fellows, will have a better chance of escaping from enemies, and also of securing an abundant supply of food. Other things being equal, it will also be more likely to perpetuate its species than more slowly moving individuals of the same species.

Next comes the question of Heredity. No one disputes the possibility of certain characters being transmitted from one generation to another. The doctrine of Natural Selection involves the view that favourable variations are thus perpetuated, and as, in each successive generation, individuals which continue to vary in favourable directions will have the best chance of surviving, we can suppose such variations to gradually accumulate until their amount is so large as to constitute a new species.

Darwin's conclusions as to the joint result of variation and heredity were largely based on observations made upon domes-

Fig. 1337.—Blue Rock and some of the domesticated varieties of Pigeon: (1), Blue Rock (*Columba livia*); (2), Tumbler; (3), Owl; (4), Jacobin; (5), Fantail; (6), Pouter

ticated animals. We know, for example, that all the numerous breeds of pigeons (fig. 1337), such as Pouters, Fantails, Carriers, Tumblers, &c. &c., are descended from one original species, *i.e.* the Blue Rock (*Columba livia*), as the result of artificial selection by human agency. That is to say, individuals varying in some particular direction have been selected by man with a view to producing offspring presenting the special character or characters in an increased degree.

Objections to the Theory of Natural Selection.—At various times a number of objections have been made to the theory, some being of a very trifling and quibbling sort, others of more serious nature. It is no part of the plan of this book to enter into all the difficulties that require or have required to be met, and it may suffice to mention one of the most formidable objections, derived from the supposed "swamping effects of intercrossing". That is to say, supposing a favourable variation to have arisen, it seems at first sight that it is just as likely to gradually disappear again by intercrossing as to be emphasized by heredity, indeed more likely. Fleeming Jenkin, the first propounder of this difficulty, illustrated it by the possible case of a white man becoming king of a black island population, his whiteness typifying a favourable variation. His immediate descendants would not be white, but yellow, and in the course of several generations the royal house would probably be just as black as their subjects.

It may be added that if a number of domesticated races of, say, pigeons, are allowed to cross freely together, their peculiar characteristics gradually disappear, and the features possessed by the original wild stock are reacquired. This is generally explained as a case of reversion or atavism, or in more popular language, a "throw back" to the ancestral type.

The objection has been often met by supposing that the particular variation occurred not in one, but in a number of individuals, thus giving a better start for the formation of a new species, but such an idea requires proof. Even if we admit the probability of the occurrence, the factor of Isolation must be emphasized, as has been done by Romanes and others. Isolation of individuals presenting a certain kind of variation would certainly prevent the swamping effect of intercrossing from operating, and pigeon-fanciers, for example, could never succeed in producing new breeds if they did not sort out and keep their birds separate, according to their special requirements. Such isolation actually occurs in nature when a small number of individuals belonging to a particular species reach, say, an oceanic island, where adaptations to a new set of surroundings become necessary, and where they are separated from the original home of their kind. And it is particularly significant to note, in this connection, that such islands are peculiarly rich in distinct species. Isolation is also exemplified by the area between tide-marks, as in some of the periwinkles. Some of these creatures are gradually becoming adapted to breathing damp air, those which are best off in this respect living near high-water mark. It is pretty clear that individuals varying so as to breathe damp air better than their fellows would naturally take to living further from the sea, and would be thus to some extent isolated.

Isolation may also be of a physiological nature, as emphasized by Romanes in his theory of *physiological selection.* We know that, as a rule, the crosses between allied species, *i.e.* hybrids, are infertile, and it is largely owing to this fact that animal species remain distinct. It seems, therefore, a plausible assumption that the rise of new species has partly been rendered possible by an increasing tendency for the crosses between them and their parent stocks to be infertile. In other words, there has been a physiological variation in the direction indicated, alongside of other variations in shape, proportion, colour, &c. &c.

SUPPLEMENTARY FACTORS OF EVOLUTION

Admitting the importance of Natural Selection, it by no means follows that it has been the only evolutionary factor determining the origin of new species.

Courtship Selection.—Darwin believed that some of the characters of male animals have been brought about by selection exercised on the part of their mates. The possibilities in this direction have already been discussed at some length (see p. 143) in dealing with the Law of Battle and the Law of Beauty. It is, after all, a special kind of Natural Selection, which may have determined the evolution of certain weapons and of æsthetic characters.

Lamarckism.—Under this head may be included the pre-Darwinian views of the French naturalists Lamarck and Buffon, to which Darwin himself was inclined to attach some importance. These views turn upon the inheritance of "acquired characters", regarding which there has been an interminable amount of discussion. It must be premised that the body of an animal higher in the scale than an Animalcule is related to (1) the existence of the individual, and (2) the existence of the species. The greater part of the body, having more particularly to do with (1), is conveniently termed the "soma" (Gk. *soma*, body), and this is the bearer of germ-cells, some of which are destined to grow into fresh individuals, and are therefore concerned with (2). An "acquired" character is one which comes into existence in the soma, as an accommodation to its mode of life, *i.e.* as an individual adjustment to surroundings. Here have to be considered the results of "use and disuse" of organs possessed by the individual. Let us take, for example, some of the sea-snails which live between tide-marks, and are accommodating themselves to breathing damp air as against air dissolved in water. The gill or gills which are specially concerned with the latter kind of breathing have less work to do than in purely aquatic forms, and there is no reason to doubt that they may therefore (as the result of partial "disuse") be slightly diminished in size in the lifetime of an individual which is migrating towards high-tide mark. On the other hand, the roof of the gill-chamber (see vol. ii, p. 460) has to do with breathing damp air, and in the lifetime of the individual supposed, may well (by "use") acquire increased specialization in connection with that duty.

According to the Lamarckian view, these two acquired characters of the soma, *i.e.* dwindling gill and specializing roof to gill-chamber, would be transmitted to the offspring. Were this so, use and disuse might ultimately lead to the evolution of a race of land-snails well adapted for air-breathing, but with gills shrunk to mere vestiges or absent altogether.

Lamarckism also involves the view that the surroundings of an animal, by their *direct* action, bring about acquired characters, positive or negative, as the case may be. We have, in other words, a direct action of the environment. Considering once more the case of a sea-snail living between tide-marks, it may be regarded as alternately subject to two influences so far as breathing is concerned, *i.e.* the action of the water which covers it for part of its existence, and the action of the damp air which surrounds it during the other part. The former favours gill-retention, the latter gill-reduction, and conversely as regards the arrangement for breathing ordinary air. Near low-tide mark the influence of water is obviously predominant, and near high-tide mark the action of air is more felt.

Some further remarks will be made about acquired characters in the sequel.

NEO-LAMARCKISM.—It is difficult to sum up in a few words the beliefs of the Neo-Lamarckian school. They essentially involve the view that there are general Laws of Growth, leading to progress in definite directions, by means of successive variations of the same kind. The action of Natural Selection is largely discounted.

This chapter may perhaps best be concluded by the addition of a few remarks on Variation and Heredity.

VARIATION

Beyond the fact that living matter *does* vary, we know very little. No clear answer can as yet be given to the questions *why* this should be so, and *how* variations of a given kind are brought about. There can be no doubt, however, that the individuals of any particular species differ from one another in a great variety of ways, and often to a very considerable amount. There is, in fact, an illimitable field for the action of selected principles. Many variations, too, are sudden or *discontinuous*, and probably new species have been often evolved at a much more rapid rate than supposed by Darwin, who believed in the selection and accumulation of *small* variations. Since his time our knowledge of variational possibilities has been largely increased.

There can be no doubt that a large majority of the characters of animals are *adaptations* to the environment, *i.e.* fit them to live in relation to certain surroundings. The origin of such adaptations must naturally be sought in variations. Here it is necessary to clearly distinguish between variations of the soma and variations of the germ, *i.e.* somatic and germinal variation. As we have seen, the Lamarckians believe that the former (acquired characters) can be transmitted. According to the school of Weismann, on the other hand, it is only the germinal variations which are capable of transmission. As, of course, the development of a germ-cell into an individual means the production of a new soma as well as more germ-cells, this new soma will have been influenced by variations which have taken place in the germ from which it has been developed. That is to say, the character of a soma mainly depends upon the characters of the germ from which it has been developed, but the soma has no direct influence upon the germs of which it is the bearer.

Organic Selection.—Lloyd Morgan, Baldwin, and Osborn have elaborated a view (of which Weismann himself suggested the possibility) as to the possibility of co-operation between germinal and somatic variations in the interests of the species. Even if we admit that the latter (acquired characters) are non-transmissible, it by no means follows that they have no evolutionary import. However unimportant the soma may be as to the provision of variations that can be inherited and so help in the making of new species, it is at least the bearer of germ-cells, to which its survival and well-being are of the first importance. If, therefore, it is able to accommodate itself to its surroundings so as to survive and leave offspring, it will give variations which have arisen in its germ-cells a chance of being preserved. Accommodation, *i.e.* the rise of acquired characters, is consequently intimately bound up with the adaptation of the species.

It must not be regarded as definitely settled that acquired characters are never transmitted, although many supposed instances have been explained away. A vast amount of observation and experiment is still necessary, and dogmatism is at present quite out of place.

The question still remains as to whether variations are independent of the action of the environment, directly due to its action, or to some extent dependent upon it. There are probably perhaps several possibilities. The germ-cells, for instance, are in many cases so sheltered from the action of surroundings that some of their variations may well be inherent. It is also well-nigh certain that there is such a thing as environmental variation. But here there are two possibilities. The action of the surroundings may directly set up variations, or it may simply act in such a way as to favour variational possibilities, *i.e.* it may direct and further, but not absolutely initiate. Nor is its action necessarily limited to either alternative.

HEREDITY

In cases of egg-development it is necessarily the germ-cells that are the means of transmitting characters from one generation to the next. Innumerable investigations upon such cells also render it practically certain that the part concerned with heredity is the *nucleus*, *i.e.* the specialized particle of protoplasm which every germ-cell contains. Weismann limits the field still further, and considers that the nucleus is in part composed of "germ plasma", a protoplasmic material specially concerned with the transmission of characters. In typical egg-propagation (see vol. iii, p. 335) germ-cells from the two parents fuse together, and the essential point about the process seems to be the union of the two nuclei. This has undoubtedly an important bearing on the question of heredity, but precisely what bearing is still a matter of doubt. It is perhaps the most remarkable fact in the whole realm of knowledge that the fusion of two microscopic particles of protoplasm should carry with it so vast a range of possibilities as regards inheritance.

There are some clear cases which prove that the germ-cells are influenced by some of the factors in the surroundings. Yung, for example, by bringing up tadpoles on specially nutritious food, was able to produce with certainty an abnormal proportion of females (90 per cent or even more), and we have elsewhere seen (see p. 256) that a fertilized bee's egg may give rise to either a worker or queen, according to the nature of the food received by the larva. Even more remarkable is the case of certain lowly crustaceans upon which Schmankewitsch experimented. In the course of several generations he was able to convert a species (*Artemia Milhausenii*) living in saltish water into another species (*A. salina*), by gradually increasing the amount of salt. He also found it possible to conduct the experiment in the reverse order, and in this instance was able to go a step further, obtaining a third species of a distinct genus (*Branchipus stagnalis*), characteristic of perfectly fresh water. In the light of such facts it seems difficult to believe that there is no possibility of acquired somatic characters being transmissible, for we can scarcely maintain that in all the cases cited the germ-cells were directly influenced by modification in the surroundings.

Galton has formulated a law (since modified by Karl Pearson) expressing numerically the influence of parents and remoter ancestors upon the characters of offspring, and the application of mathematical methods to biological statistics is likely to yield important results in the immediate future, as regards heredity, variation, and many other problems. On the botanical side very remarkable results bearing on the theory of heredity have been obtained by applying the principles of Mendel, but these cannot be discussed here, especially as there are difficulties in the way of conducting similar experiments on animals.

Readers who wish to acquire further knowledge in matters relating to biological theory would do well to consult the works of Darwin, Wallace (especially *Darwinism*), Romanes (*Darwin and After Darwin*), Weismann, Lloyd Morgan, Verworn (*General Physiology*), E. B. Wilson (*The Cell in Development and Inheritance*), T. Hunt Morgan (*Evolution and Adaptation*), and Mendel (*Principles of Heredity*). A good preliminary acquaintance with the subject may be obtained by reading Arthur Thomson's *Science of Life*.

GLOSSARY

Abomasum, in the stomach of Ruminants, the fourth compartment (chemical stomach).

Abysmal zone (Gk. *abyssŏs*, very deep), the deepest part of the sea.

Accommodation, adjustment of the individual to its surroundings.

Acetabulum (L. for vinegar cup), the socket in the hip into which the thigh-bone fits.

Acquired character, a character acquired by an individual in relation to its surroundings.

Adaptation, the adjustment of species to their surroundings.

Adductor muscles (L. *adduco*, I lead to), muscles which by their contraction close the shells of Bivalve Molluscs, Lamp-Shells, and Mussel-Shrimps.

Adipose fin, the small, fatty second dorsal fin of members of the Salmon Family.

Æsthetic or **Æsthetics** (Gk. *aisthētikŏs*, sensitive), the philosophy of the beautiful.

Afferent branchial vessels (L. *affĕrō*, I carry to; Gk. *branchia*, gills), blood-vessels which carry impure blood to gills to be purified.

Afferent nerve-fibre (L. *affĕrō*, I carry to), a nerve-fibre in which the impulse travels towards the central organs.

Air-bladder. See *Swim-bladder.*

Ala spuria. See *Bastard-wing.*

Albinism (L. *albus*, white or pale), exceptional whiteness or paleness in hue of some members of a species.

Albino, an individual exhibiting albinism.

Albumen, or **Albumin**, the complex albuminoid (which see) of which the white of an egg is made up.

Albuminoids, complex compounds, chiefly made up of carbon, hydrogen, oxygen, sulphur, and (in some cases) phosphorus.

Alima, pl. **-æ**, in Mantis-Shrimps, an attenuated kind of larva.

Ambergris, concretions formed in the intestine of the sperm-whale. Used in perfumery.

Ambulacral, relating to an ambulacrum; Ambulacral area, a band or zone bearing tube-feet; Ambulacral ossicle, one of the calcareous plates roofing an ambulacrum.

Ambulacrum, pl. **-a** (L. for pleasure grove), in Star-Fishes, one of the grooves in which the tube-feet are lodged.

Ammocætes, the larva of a Lamprey.

Amœboid movement, irregular flowing or creeping movements, performed by naked masses of protoplasm, *e.g.* in the Proteus Animalcule (Amœba).

Amphibious (Gk. *amphi*, both ways; *biŏs*, life): (1) able to breathe both ordinary air and air dissolved in water; (2) breathing dissolved air during the early part of life and ordinary air afterwards.

Ampulla (L. *ampulla*, a flask): (1) in the internal ear of Vertebrates, the swollen part of a semicircular canal; (2) in Echinoderms, a small sac connected with a tube-foot.

Anabolic, relating to anabolism.

Anabolism (Gk. *anabŏlē*, an ascent), the up-building chemical processes that take place within the body.

Analogous, displaying analogy.

Analogy (Gk. *analŏgŏs*, in agreement with), applied to parts which do the same physiological work irrespective of relative position and mode of development. See also *Homology.*

Anatomy (Gk. *anatomē*, dissection), the study of structure.

Anbury, in turnips, a disease due to the presence of a fungus-animal (*Plasmodiophora brassicæ*).

Antenna (L. for yard-arm): (1) one of the feelers of an Insect, or Myriapod; (2) one of the second feelers of a Crustacean; (3) one of the head-feelers of a Bristle-Worm.

Antennary gland, in higher Crustaceans, one of a pair of excretory organs by which nitrogenous waste is removed from the body. They open at the bases of the antennæ.

Antennule, in Crustaceans, one of the small first pair of feelers.

Anthrax, in cattle, &c., a bacterial disease, often set up by insect bites.

Anthropoid (Gk. *anthrōpŏs*, man; *eidŏs*, appearance), man-like.

Anti-toxin (Gk. *anti*, against; L. *toxicum*, poison), a complex organic substance (defensive proteid) conferring immunity against disease-germs.

Antler, in Deer, a bony outgrowth from the skull, which is shed annually.

Antler-royal, the third branch of a Red Deer's antler (counting from its base).

Aorta (Gk. *aeirō*, I carry), the chief artery of the body.

Aortic arches, the arteries which traverse the visceral arches of Vertebrates.

Apical disc, in Echinoderms (especially sea-urchins), a double circlet of plates on the upper surface of the body.

Apiculture (L. *apis*, a bee), bee-culture.

Apteria (Gk. *a*, without; *pterylŏn* a feather), featherless patches of a Bird's skin.

Arch, of a vertebra (or joint of the backbone), the dorsal part which forms the roof and sides of the hole traversed by the spinal cord.

Archenteron (Gk. *archē*, a beginning; *enteron*, an intestine), the digestive cavity of the Gastrula (which see).

Area of distribution, area inhabited by a species or other animal group. It is *discontinuous* if consisting of two or more isolated portions.

Artery, a blood-vessel which carries blood from the heart.

Articular processes, projections on the arches of vertebræ, by which these are connected together.

Artificial selection, the production of breeds of domesticated animals by human agency.

Assimilation (L. *adsimilo*, I make like), the conversion of digested food into body-substance.

Atavism (L. *atavus*, an ancestor). See *Reversion*.

Atlas, the ring-shaped first vertebra of the neck-region.

Atoll, a ring-shaped coral island.

Atrial cavity (L. *atrium*, a hall), a space surrounding most of the pharynx in Lancelets and Ascidians.

Atriopore, the opening of the Atrial cavity (which see).

Auricle (L. *auricula*, a little ear), a relatively thin-walled heart-chamber, into which veins pour blood.

Auricularia, pl. -æ (L. for lobe of the ear), in Sea-Cucumbers, a bilateral larva, provided with a sinuous ciliated band, suggesting the appearance of an ear in side-view.

Australian region, Australia and adjacent islands, with eastern part of East Indies, New Zealand, and Polynesia.

Axis, the second neck-vertebra.

Balancers (halteres), small club-shaped structures representing the reduced hind-wings in Flies.

Baleen ("whalebone"), in toothless Whales, elastic plates hanging down from the roof of the mouth.

Barb, one of the flattened branches borne by the axis of a feather.

Barbel, one of the sensitive filaments with which the mouth-region is provided in some Fishes, *e.g.* Cat-Fishes.

Barbule, one of the small branches borne by the barbs of a feather.

Bastard-wing (ala spuria), a tuft of feathers borne by the thumb of a bird.

Bêche-de-mer, Trepang (which see).

Bedeguar, a tufted gall on the rose, produced by the attack of a Gall-Fly.

Beneficials, those wild animals that by their habits promote the welfare of mankind.

Benthos (Gk. *bĕnthŏs*, depth), the assemblage of animals inhabiting deep water.

Bez-tine, the second branch of a Red Deer's antler (counting from its base).

Biconcave, hollow on both sides, *e.g.* the vertebra of a Fish.

Bicuspid. See *Premolar*.

Bilateral Symmetry. See *Symmetry*.

Bile, or **Gall**, the secretion of the liver.

Bile-duct, a tube through which bile passes into the intestine.

Biology (Gk. *biŏs*, life; *lŏgŏs*, a discourse), the science of life.

Bipinnaria, pl. -æ, in Star-Fishes, the bilateral larva, which is provided with pairs of soft ciliated arms.

Bivalve, applied to the shell of a Mollusc when made up of two pieces or valves, *e.g.* in a Mussel. Lamp-shells (Brachiopoda) are also bivalve, and Mussel-Shrimps (Ostracoda) possess a bivalve shield or shell.

Blastopore (Gk. *blastŏs*, a germ; *pŏra*, a passage), the mouth of a Gastrula (which see).

Blastosphere (Gk. *blastŏs*, a germ; *sphaira*, a sphere), a hollow and spheroidal kind of Blastula (which see).

Blastula (Gk. dim. of *blastŏs*, a germ), the embryonic stage resulting from Cleavage (which see).

Blight, a disease of plants, often due to the presence of aphides.

Blubber, in marine Mammals, a thick layer of fat below the skin.

Body-cavity, in animals higher than Zoophytes, a space or series of spaces between the internal organs and body-wall.

Botany (Gk. *botanē*, a plant), the science dealing with plants.

Bouchot, in mussel-culture, a collector made of stakes with interwoven twigs.

Brachiolaria, pl. -æ, a variety of the Bipinnaria (which see).

Bronchus, pl. -i, one of the two main branches of the wind-pipe.

Brood-parasitism, used of animals (*e.g.* the Cuckoo) which evade the responsibility of bringing up their own young.

Brow-tine, the lowest branch of a Red Deer's antler, projecting over the forehead.

Byssus (Gk. *byssos*), adhesive threads by which some Bivalve Molluscs attach themselves.

Cæcum, pl. **-a** (L. *cæcus*, blind), a blindly ending tube.

Calcaneum (L. for heel), the heel-bone.

Calcar (L. for spur), a small pointed projection on the inner side of a Frog's hind-foot.

Calcareous (L. *calx*, *calcis*, lime), of a limy nature.

Callosity, a hardened patch of skin.

Calyx (Gk. *kalyx*, a cup), the outer investing leaves of a flower.

Canine, one of the four "eye-teeth" in a Mammal. Situated outside the Incisors (which see), and well developed in carnivorous forms.

Cannon-bone: (1) in Horse, &c., the large metacarpal or metatarsal of the single digit; (2) in Ruminants, the compound bone formed by fusion of third and fourth metacarpals or metatarsals.

Capillaries (L. *capillus*, hair), microscopic blood-vessels with exceedingly thin walls. The name is misleading, since they are much smaller than the finest hairs.

Carapace, a firm protective shield covering the upper side and flanks in some animals.

Cardia (the Greek name), the opening between gullet and stomach.

Cardo (L. for hinge), the basal joint of an Insect's second jaw.

Carinate (L. *carina*, a keel): (1) with a keel-like projection; (2) applied to flying birds, in which the breast-bone possesses such a projection, for the attachment of the muscles of flight.

Carnassials (L. *carnosus*, relating to flesh), or **Flesh-teeth**, in Carnivores, four cutting cheek-teeth which act like scissors.

Carnivorous, flesh-eating.

Carotid (Gk. *kărā*, the head), a term applied to arteries which carry blood to the head and neck.

Carpale, pl. **-ia** (Gk. *karpŏs*, the wrist), the distal elements of the carpus.

Carpel (Gk. *karpŏs*, fruit), a modified flower-leaf that bears ovules. The Pistil (which see) consists of one or more carpels.

Carpus (Gk. *karpŏs*, the wrist), the skeleton of the wrist.

Cartilage, gristle.

Caste, in social Insects, a set of similar individuals.

Caval veins, in air-breathing Vertebrates, the great veins which return impure blood to the heart.

Caviare, the preserved hard roes (ovaries) of the sturgeon.

Cell, a nucleated mass of protoplasm, generally microscopic, and usually regarded as the unit of structure.

Centrale, a central element of the carpus or tarsus.

Centrum, pl. **-a**, of a vertebra, the relatively massive ventral part, flooring the hole traversed by the spinal cord.

Cephalo-thorax (Gk. *kĕphalē*, the head; *thōrax*, the chest), in some Arthropods, the front region of the body, formed by fusion of the head with part or all of the thorax.

Cerata (Gk. *kĕrata*, horns), in Sea-slugs (Nudibranchs), club-shaped outgrowths springing from the back.

Cercaria, pl. **-æ** (Gk. *kĕrkŏs*, a tail), in Flukes, a tadpole-shaped stage in the life-history. Produced by the Redia (which see), and immediately preceding the adult stage.

Cerci (Gk. *kĕrkŏs*, a tail), jointed rods projecting from the hinder end of an Insect's abdomen.

Cere (L. *cera*, wax), a bare patch of skin at the base of a Bird's beak.

Cerebellum (L. dim. of *cerebrum*, the brain), an unpaired dorsal outgrowth from the hinder part of the brain of a Vertebrate.

Cerebral hemispheres (L. *cerebrum*, the brain), the highest part of the brain in Vertebrates, usually consisting of a pair of outgrowths from near its front end.

Cervical (L. *cervix*, the neck), relating to the neck.

Chalaza (Gk. for hail), in a Bird's egg, a twisted cord-like structure traversing the albumen ("white") at either end.

Cheek-teeth, the back-teeth.

Chelicera, pl. **-æ**, (Gk. *chēlē*, a claw; *kĕras*, a horn), one of the first pair of head-limbs in Spider-like animals (Arachnida).

Chlorophyll (Gk. *chlōrŏs*, grass green; *phyllŏn*, a leaf), or **Leaf-green**, the characteristic pigment of green plants. It also occurs in a few lower animals.

Chordotonal organ (Gk. *chŏrdē*, a string; *tonaios*, stretched), in some Insects, a kind of sense-organ related to balance, or hearing, or both.

Choroid (Gk. *chŏriŏn*, skin; *eidŏs*, appearance), the middle coat of the eyeball. It is pigmented and vascular, and externally forms the iris (which see).

Chromatophore (Gk. *chrōma*, colouring matter; *phĕrō*, I bear), a small or minute body containing pigment, and situated in the skin. Colour-changes are due to the alteration in size of such bodies.

Chrysalis, pl. **-ides** (the Greek name), the pupa of a Moth or Butterfly.

Ciliary action, the movement of cilia.

Cilium, pl. **cilia** (L. *cilium*, eyelash), a microscopic thread of protoplasm, possessing the power of alternately bending and straightening. Numerous cilia are usually associated together. The derivation is misleading.

Circulatory organs, the structures concerned with distributing blood and lymph throughout the body.

Cirrus, pl. **-i** (L. *cirrus*, a tentacle): (1) one of the slender-jointed appendages of a Barnacle; (2) one of the sensory filaments borne by the segments of Bristle-Worms; (3) in Sea-Lilies, one of the jointed threads of which numerous circlets are borne by the stalk.

Claire, in French oyster culture, a muddy salt pond in which oysters are 'greened' by feeding on minute algæ.

Clavicle, the collar-bone.

Cleavage, the early divisions of the fertilized egg-cell, resulting in a Blastula (which see).

Clitellum (L. *clitellæ*, a pack-saddle), in Earth-Worms and Leeches, a glandular region of the skin, which secretes the material for the cocoon.

Cloaca (L. *cloaca*, a sewer), a chamber into which, *e.g.* in a Frog, intestine, excretory organs, and reproductive organs open.

Coccyx (Gk. for cuckoo), the reduced tail-region of the backbone in Man and the man-like Apes.

Cochineal, a red pigment extracted from the dried bodies of Cochineal Insects.

Cochlea (L. *cochlea*, a snail-shell), in Mammals, a spirally-coiled part of the membranous labyrinth.

Cocoon, a variously shaped case in which the eggs or other inactive stages in the life-history of various animals are enclosed.

Cœlom (Gk. *koilŏs*, hollow), a Body-cavity (which see) containing lymph-like fluid and communicating with the exterior by excretory tubes.

Cœnosarc (Gk. *koinŏs*, common; *sarx*, *sarcos*, flesh), in colonial Zoophytes, the common body by which the individuals are united.

Collar-cell, in Sponges, a cell bearing a single flagellum with a collar-like projection at its base.

Collector, in oyster- and mussel-culture, an arrangement of twigs, boards, or tiles, to which the larvæ or fry attach themselves.

Colonial, relating to a Colony (which see).

Colony, an assemblage of lower animals, in which the bodies of all the individuals are continuous. The condition is a result of vegetative propagation.

Columella (L. *columella*, a little pillar), a small rod which stretches across the drum of the ear in Birds, some Reptiles, and some Amphibians.

Columnar epithelium, epithelium composed of cells elongated at right angles to the surface.

Commensalism (L. *con-*, together; *mensa*, a dining-table), the association of two organisms as messmates, or commensals, to the benefit of one or both.

Compound eye, an eye made up of more or less numerous optically distinct elements each with an external facet. Possessed by many Arthropods.

Concha (L. *concha*, a shell) the ear-flap of a Mammal.

Condyle (Gk. *condylos*, a tubercle), a rounded projection on a bone or cartilage, where it helps to form a movable joint. Mandibular condyles, at back of lower jaw, where it unites with skull. Occipital condyle (or condyles), on back of skull, where it joins the backbone.

Conjugation (L. *conjugato*, *conjugatum*, to bind together), in some Animalcules, the temporary or permanent fusion of two individuals, accompanied by union of nuclear material, and having an invigorating effect, shown by active vegetative propagation.

Continental island, an island that was at one time part of an existing continent.

Contractile, endowed with contractility.

Contractility, the power possessed by protoplasm of changing its shape with no or slight change in volume.

Coracoid bone (Gk. *kŏrax*, a raven), a ventral element in the shoulder-skeleton of lower Vertebrates. Coracoid process, a projection (compared in Man to a raven's beak) on the shoulder-blade of Mammals, equivalent to the coracoid bone.

Cornea (L. *corneus*, horny), a transparent area of the sclerotic coat through which light enters the eye.

Corolla (L. for little crown), the inner investing leaves of a flower. Usually brightly coloured.

Corpus callosum (L. for hard body), a band of nerve-fibres which in most Mammals connects the cerebral hemispheres.

Corpuscles (L. dim. of *corpus*, a body), microscopic bodies floating in blood or lymph. White or Colourless Corpuscles, nucleated cells, able to change their shape, found in both blood and lymph. Red Corpuscles, round or oval discs present in the blood of many animals.

Cortex (L. *cortex*, bark), the external layer of the cerebral hemispheres and cerebellum.

Costal (L. *costa*, a rib), relating to the ribs.

Courtship coloration, beautiful colours displayed (usually by the male) as a courtship accessory.

Courtship selection, preferential mating, as determined by combat, or by the possession of æsthetic characters.

Cranial flexure, a bend in the brain.

Cranial nerves, the nerves which arise from the brain.

Cranium (Gk. *krāniŏn*, the skull), the brain-case.

Crop, in the gut of various animals, a dilated part of the gullet, or enlarged region following the gullet. It serves for temporary storage of food.

Cross-fertilization, fertilization of an egg-cell by a sperm (or its equivalent) derived from another organism.

Cross-pollination, transfer of pollen from the stamens of one flower to the stigma of another flower.

Coxa (L. *coxa*, a hip), the basal joint of an Insect's leg.

Cul de mulet, Sea-anemones used as an article of food in parts of southern Europe.

Cultch, in oyster-culture, empty shells, broken tiles, &c., upon which oysters are grown.

Cuticle, an elastic exoskeleton of horny consistency external to the epidermis, by which it is secreted.

Cysticercus, pl. -i (Gk. *cystis*, a bladder; *kĕrkŏs*, a tail), in most Tape-Worms, the bladder-worm stage.

Darwinism. See *Natural selection.*

Degeneration, a process of simplification whereby some forms adapt themselves to a parasitic or to a fixed mode of life.

Denitrifying, used of bacteria which liberate nitrogen from organic matter.

Dental formula, a numerical expression, showing the number and kinds of teeth present in a given species of Mammal.

Dentine (L. *dens*, *dentis*, a tooth), a hard substance of which teeth are chiefly composed.

Dermatoptic vision (Gk. *dĕrma*, *-atŏs*, a skin; *optikŏs*, pertaining to sight), seeing by means of the skin.

Dermis (Gk. *dĕrma*, a skin), the inner layer of the skin.

Diaphragm (the Greek name), the midriff.

Didactyle (Gk. *di-*, two; *daktylŏs*, a finger or toe), possessing two digits.

Digitigrade (L. *digitus*, the toe of an animal; *grado*, I walk), walking upon the digits.

Diphycercal (Gk. *diphyēs*, double; *kĕrkŏs*, a tail). See *Protocercal.*

Diploblastic (Gk. *diplous*, double; *blastŏs*, a germ), applied to animals in which the body is essentially composed of two cellular layers.

Dispersal, the spreading of a species from the area where it was first evolved.

Dorsal (L. *dorsum*, the back), applied to the upper side of an animal.

Ductless glands, a name applied to a number of small structures, of various use, which do not possess ducts or tubes for carrying off a liquid secretion. See *Lymphatic glands*, *Thymus*, *Thyroid*, *Spleen.*

Ectoderm (Gk. *ĕktŏs*, outside; *dĕrma*, a skin), the external cellular layer of the body.

Ectoparasite. See *Parasite.*

Eder-fold, one of the nesting-grounds of the eider-duck.

Efferent branchial vessels (L. *effĕrō*, I carry from; Gk. *branchia*, gills), blood-vessels which carry off purified blood from gills.

Efferent nerve-fibre (L. *effĕrō*, I carry from), a nerve-fibre in which the impulse travels outwards from the central organs.

Élevage, in French oyster-culture, the rearing of young oysters to a marketable size.

Éleveur, a French oyster-culturalist concerned with élevage.

Elytron, pl. -a, (Greek name for (1)): (1) in Insects, a fore-wing modified into a hard cover for the delicate hind-wing; (2) in some marine Bristle-Worms, a breathing-scale.

Embryology (Gk. *ĕmbryŏn*, an embryo; *lŏgŏs*, a discourse), the study of the development of animals.

Endoderm (Gk. *ĕndŏn*, within; *dĕrmă*, a skin), the internal cellular layer of the body.

Endoparasite. See *Parasite.*

Endoskeleton, internal hard parts serving for support, &c.

Entomophilous (Gk. *ĕntŏmŏs*, an insect; *phileō*, I love), of flowers, pollinated by insects.

Environment, the sum total of an animal's surroundings.

Eozoic epoch (Gk. *eos*, dawn; *zoē*, life), the most ancient geological era.

Ephippium (Gk. *ĕphippiŏn*, a saddle-cloth), in Water-"Fleas", a saddle-shaped thickening of the parent-shell, serving to enclose and protect the winter-eggs.

Ephyra, pl. -æ, a young jelly-fish of flattened form, produced by transverse fission of a fixed Zoophyte.

Epidermis (the Greek name), the protective outer layer of the skin.

Epigenesis (Gk. *ĕpi*, after; *gennaŏ*, I produce), the accepted view that development of animals is a process involving a gradual up-building from simple to complex. See *Preformation.*

Epiglottis (the Greek name), in Mammals, an elastic flap which prevents food from entering the wind-pipe.

Epipodium, pl. -ia (Gk. *epi*, upon; *pous*, *pŏdŏs*, a foot), in some Molluscs, a muscular flap arising high up either side of the foot.

Epipubic, connected with the front end of the Pubis (which see).

Epithelium, pl. -a, layers of cells covering external and lining internal surfaces.

Ethiopian region, south Arabia with Africa south of the Sahara.

Euglenoid movement, a wriggling mode of creeping effected by altering the shape of the body, as in Euglena, a sort of Animalcule.

Eustachian tube, a passage connecting the drum of the ear with the pharynx in air-breathing Vertebrates.

Evolution (L. *evolutio*, an unfolding), the development of species by modification of pre-existing species. See also *Special creation.*

Excretion, the getting rid of waste products.

Exhalent. See *Siphon.*

Exoskeleton, external hard parts serving for support, &c.

Extensor, applied to muscles which straighten or extend a limb, or region of the body.

Fascine, in oyster-culture, a bundle of twigs used as a spat-collector.

Femoral, relating to the thigh.

Femur (L. for thigh): (1) the thigh-bone of Vertebrates; (2) a part of the leg in Insects, &c.

Fenestra ovalis (L. for oval window), in Vertebrates, a membrane-filled vacuity in the outer wall of the firm capsule containing the essential organs of hearing.

Fertilization, the fusion of two nuclear masses, commonly derived from different individuals.

Fetlock, in limbs of Horse, &c.: (1) the knuckle-joint of the single digit; (2) the tuft of hair attached to this joint.

Fibula (L. for bodkin), the bone of the lower leg which is on the little-toe side.

Fibulare, a proximal element of the tarsus, situated on the side next the little toe.

Filoplume, a small and imperfect feather, of downy texture.

Finger-and-Toe. See *Anbury*.

Fin-rays, in Fishes, skeletal rods which support the fins.

Fins, in various aquatic animals, flat expansions of the body used in swimming.

Fission (L. *findo*, *fissum*, to split), vegetative propagation by splitting of the parent body.

Flagellum, pl. -a (L. for whip-lash), an elongated thread of protoplasm, capable of executing lashing movements. A single cell bears but one or a few. See *Cilium*.

Flexor, applied to muscles which bend or flex a limb, or region of the body.

Fluke, in Cetaceans, one of the tail-lobes.

Fly-sickness, a fatal disease of horses, &c., set up by the attacks of the tsetse-fly.

Food-vacuole, in Animalcules, a food-containing space within the body.

Food-yolk, nutritive material stored up in (or outside) the egg-cell, for use during development.

Foot: (1) in broad sense, the extremity of any limb used for locomotion; (2) more strictly, the extremity of a hind-limb in Vertebrates; (3) an unpaired muscular projection from the under side of a Mollusc, used in locomotion.

Foot-stump. See *Parapod*.

Foramen, pl. -ina (L. for hole), a hole through which (usually) a nerve or blood-vessel passes. Foramen magnum, the large opening in the back of the brain-case, where brain and spinal cord are continuous.

Foramina repugnatoria, in Millipedes, small pores on the sides of the body, by which the stink-glands open.

Fore-gut, the front part of the digestive tube, developed as an inpushing from the exterior.

Fossils (L. *fossilis*, dug out), the remains of organisms, or proofs of their existence, which have been naturally imbedded in rocks.

Frenulum (L. dim. of *frenum*, a bridle), in Moths, one or more bristles projecting from the front of the hind-wing, and attaching this to the fore-wing by interlocking with the Retinaculum (which see).

Funicle (L. *funiculus*, a cord), in Moss-Polypes, a fibrous band connecting the stomach with the body-wall.

Funnel, a muscular tube through which Cuttle-fishes, &c., eject water from the gill-cavity, and are enabled to swim.

Furcula (L. for a prop), the "merry-thought" of a Bird, consisting of the two collar-bones united together.

Galea (L. for a helmet), in Insects, the outer branch of the second or third jaw.

Gall: (1) bile; (2) an abnormal external growth resulting from the attack of a parasite.

Gall-bladder, a membranous bag in which bile is temporarily stored.

Ganglion, pl. ganglia (Gk. for a small tumour), an aggregation of nerve-cells.

Ganglion-cell. See *Nerve-cell*.

Ganoid (Gk. *ganos*, brilliancy; *eidos*, appearance), applied to the regularly arranged bony plates (ganoid scales) covering the bodies of some Fishes.

Gapes, in Birds, a disease due to the presence of parasitic worms (*Syngamus trachealis*) in the air-passages.

Gastric glands, minute tubes imbedded in the lining of the stomach, and secreting gastric juice.

Gastric juice, a digestive fluid secreted or elaborated by the gastric glands. It acts on albuminoids, converting them into soluble diffusible peptones.

Gastric mill, in Crustaceans, a chewing apparatus with which the stomach is provided.

Gastrula (L. dim. from *gaster*, a stomach), a double-layered embryo possessing mouth and digestive cavity (archenteron).

Gemmation (L. *gemma*, a bud), production of new individuals by budding.

General aggressive resemblance, applied to predaceous forms which harmonize in appearance with their surroundings, and are thus rendered inconspicuous.

Genus, pl. genera (L. for a race or family), a classificatory group including one or more species.

Germinal disc, that part of the egg which, *e.g.* in a Bird, develops into the embryo.

Germinal variation, variation of germ-cells (ova and sperms).

Germ Plasma, that part of the nucleus of a germ-cell concerned (according to Weismann) with heredity.

Gill arches and clefts, in Fishes, &c., those visceral arches and clefts (which see) related to the gills.

Gill-cover, or **Operculum**, (pl. -a), in many Fishes, &c., a flap which covers the gill-slits.

Gill-rakers, in some Fishes, filaments projecting from the edges of the inner openings of the gill-pouches, and serving as a straining-apparatus.

Gizzard, in various animals, a thick-walled part of the digestive tube in which food is broken up.

Glenoid cavity (Gk. *glēnē*, a shallow socket), the socket into which the bone of the upper arm fits.

Glochidium, pl. **-a**, the larva of a Fresh-water Mussel.

Glottis (the Greek name), the opening of the windpipe in the floor of the pharynx.

Gonophore (Gk. *gŏnŏs*, offspring; *phĕrō*, I bear), in Zoophytes, a bud in which egg-cells or sperms are produced.

Green glands. See *Antennary gland.*

Grey matter, that part of the central nervous system made up largely of nerve-cells.

Ground-Pearl, in some Scale-Insects, the encysted underground pupa.

Gular (L. *gula*, the throat), near the throat.

Gut, the digestive tube or alimentary canal.

Hæmoglobin (Gk. *haima*, blood; *globin*, a kind of albuminoid), a complex substance to which red corpuscles owe their colour, and which in some animals may be dissolved in the blood-plasma. Acts as an oxygen-carrier.

Halteres (L. for club-shaped weights used by gymnasts). See *Balancers.*

Haptic (Gk. *haptikŏs*, endowed with the sense of touch), used of sensations of contact.

Herbivorous, plant-eating.

Heredity, the transmission of characters from one generation to another.

Heterocercal (Gk. *hĕtĕros*, diverse; *kĕrkŏs*, tail), unsymmetrical. Used of the tail-fin of certain Fishes, *e.g.* Sharks.

Heterodactylous (Gk. *hĕtĕrŏs*, different; *daktylŏs*, a toe), in the feet of some climbing Birds, with the first and second toes turned back, while the third and fourth are directed forwards.

Hind-gut, the hinder part of the digestive tube, developed as an inpushing from the exterior.

Hip-girdle, the skeleton of the hip-region.

Histology (Gk. *histŏs*, a texture; *lŏgŏs*, a discourse), or **Minute anatomy**, the study of structure by means of the compound microscope.

Hock, in hind-limb of Horse, &c., the ankle.

Holarctic (Gk. *hŏlŏs*, all; *arktŏs*, the north), native to the colder parts of the Northern Hemisphere.

Homocercal (Gk. *hŏmŏs*, like; *kĕrkŏs*, a tail), applied to the lobed and externally symmetrical tail of ordinary Fishes.

Homologous, displaying homology.

Homology (Gk. *hŏmŏlŏgŏs*, agreeing), applied to parts which resemble one another as regards relative position and mode of development, irrespective of use or function. Serial homology, agreement between structures forming a series, *e.g.* spinal nerves. See also *Analogy.*

Honey-comb stomach. See *Reticulum.*

Host, an organism on which a parasite preys. See *Parasitism.*

Humeral, related to the upper arm.

Humerus (the Latin name), the upper-arm bone.

Hybernation, the habit of passing into a torpid state during the cold or dry season.

Hybrid (L. *hybrida*, a cross-bred animal), a cross between two distinct species. Hybrids are usually sterile.

Hydroid Zoophytes, colonial Cœlenterates which in fixed stage superficially resemble sea-weeds.

Hyoid bone, supports root of tongue in higher Vertebrates.

Hyomandibular, related to the first two visceral arches (which see), respectively known as mandibular and hyoid.

Ilium, the dorsal element of the hip-girdle.

Imago, pl. **-ines** (L. for figure, portrait, or statue), in Insects, the adult stage.

Incisor, one of the front teeth of a Mammal. Next to these are the Canines. See *Canine.*

Inhalent. See *Siphon.*

Insertion of a muscle, the end attached to a relatively movable part.

Instinct, the power of performing complex actions, subserving adjustment to surroundings, independently of experience or instruction.

Integropalliate, in the shell of a Bivalve Mollusc, with continuous pallial line.

Intelligence, the ability to profit by experience in adjusting behaviour to changing surroundings.

Interambulacral area, in Echinoderms, a band or zone which does not bear tube-feet.

Inter-clavicle, a skeletal element situated between the clavicles in some animals.

Intermedium, a proximal median element in the carpus or tarsus.

Interradial, in radially symmetrical animals, relating to an interradius.

Interradius, in radially symmetrical animals, a region of the body coming between two of the radii.

Invertebrate, devoid of a backbone or its equivalent.

Iris (L. for rainbow), the coloured part of the eye, serving as a diaphragm external to the lens. Its opening is the pupil.

Ischium, the ventral and posterior element of the hip-girdle.

Isinglass, a fine kind of gelatine, prepared from the swim-bladders of fishes, especially sturgeons.

Joint-gill, in Crustaceans, a gill attached to the joint at the base of a limb.

Kainozoic epoch, (Gk. *kainŏs*, recent; *zoē*, life), the latest geological era.

Katabolic, relating to katabolism.

Katabolism (Gk. *katabolē*, a casting down),

the down-breaking chemical processes that take place within the body.

Knee, in fore-limb of Horse, &c., the wrist.

Kungu cake, an edible substance prepared on the shores of Lake Nyassa, by collecting and compressing the aquatic larvæ of Insects.

Labellum (L. for little lip), the large lower petal of an Orchid.

Labium (L. for a lip), the lower lip of an Insect, formed by the more or less complete fusion of the third jaws (second maxillæ).

Labrum (L. for lip), the upper lip of an Arthropod.

Laceration, in Sea-Anemones, production of new individuals by the separation of small fragments of the base.

Lacinia (L. for a small part), in Insects, the inner branch of the second or third jaw.

Lacteals (L. *lac*, milk), the lymphatics of the intestine, so called on account of the milky appearance of their contents (digested fat) after a meal.

Lagena (L. for earthen jar), a curved tubular part of the membranous labyrinth in Birds, &c., equivalent to the Cochlea (which see) of Mammals.

Land-bridge, a submerged area that once united two tracts of land now separated by the sea.

Larva, pl. **-æ** (L. *larva*, a kind of actor's mask), in many life-histories, an early free-living stage (*e.g.* a Tadpole or a Caterpillar) which is more or less unlike the adult.

Larynx (the Greek name), the voice-box.

Licked beef, diseased flesh in the neighbourhood of Warbles (which see).

Ligament: (1) a fibrous band running between two skeletal elements; (2) an elastic band (external ligament) or pad (internal ligament) by which the shell of a Bivalve Mollusc is opened.

Limb-gill, in Crustaceans, a gill attached to a limb.

Littoral (L. *litus*, *littoris*, a shore), belonging to the shore.

Liver-rot, in Sheep, &c., a disease caused by the presence of Liver-Flukes.

Lophophore (Gk. *lŏphŏs*, tuft or crest; *phĕrō*, I bear), in Moss-Polypes, the crown of tentacles.

Louping-ill, in Sheep, a bacterial disease caused by the attacks of Ticks.

Lung-books, in Scorpions and Spiders, breathing organs consisting of depressions into which numerous leaf-like folds project.

Luring, the attraction of farm-pests from the plants they attack.

Lymph, clear fluid containing colourless corpuscles.

Lymphatic glands, swellings in the course of lymphatics, in which new colourless corpuscles are developed.

Lymph-system, a series of spaces and tubes containing Lymph (which see).

Macronucleus (Gk. *makrŏs*, large), in Animalcules, the large nucleus.

Madreporite, in Echinoderms, a perforated calcareous plate, through which fluid enters the water-vascular system.

Maggot, in Insects, a limbless worm-shaped larva.

Malpighian tubes, in Insects, excretory tubes opening into the hinder part of the gut.

Mandible: (1) in Vertebrates, the lower jaw; (2) in Arthropods, one of the first pair of jaws.

Manna, a sweet substance (honey-dew) secreted by a species of Scale-insect.

Mantle, in Molluscs and Lamp-Shells, a flap of the body-wall, on the outer side of which shell-substance is formed.

Mantle-cavity, in Molluscs and Lamp-shells, a space between the body and Mantle (which see). It contains the gill or gills (in aquatic Molluscs), and the intestine, excretory organs, &c., usually open into it.

Manyplies. See *Omasum*.

Masking, inconspicuousness produced by a covering of foreign objects, *e.g.* stones and bits of sea-weed.

Mastax (Gk. for the mouth), the gizzard-like pharynx of Rotifers.

Maxilla, pl. **-æ** (L. *maxilla*, a jaw): (1) in Vertebrates, a bone of the jaw; (2) in Arthropods, one of the second or third pair of jaws.

Medusa, in Jelly-Fishes, the egg-producing stage, which is usually free-swimming.

Megalopa, pl. **-æ** (Gk. *megălŏpŏus*, having large feet), in Crabs, the larval stage succeeding the Zoæa. The legs are well-developed and the tail large.

Melanic, exhibiting melanism.

Melanism (Gk. *mĕlas*, *-anŏs*, dark), exceptional darkness in hue of some members of a species.

Membranous labyrinth, in Vertebrates, the complex bag constituting the essential part of the internal ear.

Mentum (L. for the chin), the part of an Insect's lower lip that succeeds the Submentum (which see).

Mesentery (Gk. *mĕsĕntĕriŏn*, same meaning as (1)): (1) in Vertebrates, a membrane by which the digestive tube is held in place; (2) in Bristle-Worms, one of the transverse partitions marking off the segments internally; (3) in Sea-Anemones, &c., one of the partitions connecting the gullet with the body-wall.

Mesoderm (Gk. *mĕsŏs*, middle; *dĕrma*, a skin), the middle cellular layer of the body.

Mesoglœa (Gk. *mĕsŏs*, middle; *glŏiŏs*, a jelly-like substance), in Zoophytes, the middle often jelly-like layer of the body.

Mesotarsal, in the middle of the tarsus, *e.g.* a Bird's ankle-joint.

Mesozoic epoch (Gk. *mesos*, middle; *zoē*, life), the latest geological era but one.

Metabolic, relating to metabolism.

Metabolism (Gk. *mĕtabolē*, change), the cycle of chemical changes taking place within the body.

Metacarpale, pl. -ia, one of the skeletal elements supporting the palm.

Metacarpus (Gk. *mĕtakarpiŏn*, the palm of the hand), skeleton of palm of hand.

Metamorphosis (Gk. for transformation), the series of changes by which the adult stage is attained, in cases where the young animal differs markedly from its parents. See *Larva*.

Metatarsale, pl. -ia, one of the skeletal elements supporting the instep.

Metatarsus (Gk. *mĕta*, after; *tarsŏs*, the broad part of the foot), the skeleton of the instep-region of the foot.

Micronucleus (Gk. *mikrŏs*, small), in Animalcules, the small nucleus.

Microtome (Gk. *mikrŏs*, small; *tĕmnŏ*, I cut), an instrument for cutting thin slices for microscopic examination.

Mid-gut, the middle section of the digestive tube.

Migration (L. *migratio*, removal from one home to another), the wandering of species from one place to another, often in a periodic manner. See also *Dispersal*.

Milk dentition, in Mammals, the first set of teeth.

Milk molar, in Mammals, one of the cheek-teeth of the milk dentition.

Mimicry, or **Spurious warning**, the resemblance existing between certain innocuous forms and others exhibiting Warning coloration, &c. (which see). The mimicking species share in the relative immunity enjoyed by the mimicked forms.

Miners' anæmia, a dangerous intestinal disease, caused by a palisade-worm (*Dochmius duodenalis*).

Molar, one of the permanent cheek-teeth of a Mammal, belonging to the hinder part of the series, and without a predecessor in the first set of teeth (milk teeth).

Mongrel, a cross between two varieties or races of the same species. Mongrels are usually fertile.

Morphology, (Gk. *mŏrphē*, form; *lŏgŏs*, a discourse), the study of form and structure.

Morula (L. dim. of *morum*, a mulberry), a solid and spherical variety of Blastula (which see).

Mucous membrane, the soft membrane lining the digestive tube.

Mule, a cross between Horse and Ass.

Muscle: (1) the tissue which makes up flesh; (2) a definitely-shaped piece of flesh, concerned with some special movement or movements.

Mutualism, or **Symbiosis**, the intimate association of two organisms as mutualists, for the benefit of both.

Myrmecophilous (Gk. *myrmēx*, *-ēkŏs*, an ant; *phileō*, I love), of certain plants, protected by ants, which in return receive food and shelter.

Nagana, Fly-sickness (which see).

Natural selection, the survival of individuals which vary in favourable directions in relation to their surroundings.

Nauplius (Gk. *Naupliŏs*, a son of Neptune), in lower Crustaceans, an ovoid unsegmented larva possessing only the three first pair of head-appendages, by means of which it swims.

Nearctic region (Gk. *nĕŏs*, new; *arktŏs*, the north), the northern part of the New World.

Nectar (Gk. *nĕktăr*, the drink of the gods), a sweet fluid produced by a nectary.

Nectary, in plants, an organ secreting nectar.

Neo-Lamarckism, a theory of evolution which postulates the existence of definite Laws of Growth.

Neolithic period (Gk. *nĕŏs*, new; *lithŏs*, a stone), the later stages of the Stone Age.

Neotropical region (Gk. *nĕŏs*, new; *trŏpikŏs*, relating to the tropics), Central and South America, with the West Indies.

Nephridium, pl. -ia (dim. of Gk. *nĕphrŏs*, a kidney), in many groups of animals, excretory tubes by which nitrogenous waste is removed from the body. They place the Cœlom (which see) in communication with the exterior.

Neritic zone (*nĕritēs*, a sea-snail), the shallow waters of the sea.

Nerve-cell, the essential part of a Neuron (which see).

Nerve-fibre, the conducting thread into which a Neuron (which see) is produced.

Nerve-loop, in Molluscs, part of the central nervous system which gives off nerves to the gills and viscera.

Nerve-ring, in Annelids, Arthropods, Molluscs, &c., part of the central nervous system which surrounds the front portion of the gut.

Nervure, one of the linear thickenings supporting the wing of an Insect.

Nettling-cell, in Zoophytes (Cœlenterata), a stinging capsule.

Neural (Gk. *nĕurŏn*, a nerve), related to the central nervous system, or in the proximity of this.

Neuron (Gk. for a nerve), a nerve-unit, consisting of a nerve-cell with its prolongations.

Nictitating membrane, the translucent third eyelid of Birds, &c., which can be drawn over the eye as a protection.

Nidicolæ (L. *nidus*, a nest; *colo*, I inhabit), in Birds, helpless nestlings.

Nidifugæ (L. *nidus*, a nest; *fugio*, I run away), in Birds, young which run about and feed themselves almost immediately after hatching.

Nitrifying, used of bacteria, &c., which cause free nitrogen to enter into combination.

Notochord (Gk. *nōtŏn*, the back; *chŏrdē*, a string), an elastic supporting-rod which underlies the central nervous system of a Vertebrate embryo, and may persist throughout life. Usually more or less replaced by the backbone, of which it is the forerunner.

Nuchal (L. *nucha*, neck), relating to the neck.

Nucleus (L. for a kernel), a specialized particle of protoplasm within a cell.

Nymph, in Insects with incomplete metamorphosis, the stage which hatches from the egg.

Oceanic island, an island that has never formed part of any existing continent.

Ocellus, pl. -i, (L. for a little eye), in Arthropods, a small simple eye.

Ocular (L. *oculus*, an eye), bearing eyes, *e.g.* the ocular plates in the apical disc of a sea-urchin.

Odontophore (Gk. *ŏdous*, *ŏdŏntŏs*, a tooth; *phĕrō*, I bear), the rasping organ in the mouth-cavity of Snails, Cuttle-Fishes, &c.

Œsophagus, the gullet.

Omasum, in the stomach of Ruminants, the third compartment.

Omnivorous, of mixed diet.

Ontogeny (Gk. *ŏnta*, beings; *gĕnnaō*, I produce), the development of individual animals.

Operculum, pl. -a (L. for lid or cover): (1) the gill-cover of a Fish; (2) the horny or shelly plate with which the opening of the shell can be closed in some Sea-snails; (3) in Scorpions, King-Crabs, &c., a plate on the under side of the body, immediately behind the last pair of legs; (4) the plug with which some tube-dwelling Annelids can close the openings of their tubes.

Opisthobranch (Gk. *ŏpisthĕ*, behind; *branchia*, gills), applied to Sea-Snails with gills behind the heart.

Oral (L. *ōs*, the mouth), relating to the mouth.

Oral papillæ, in Peripatus, a pair of stump-like limbs near the mouth, upon which the slime-glands open.

Orbit, the cavity of the skull in which the eye-ball is lodged.

Organic selection, the co-operation of Accommodation and Adaptation (which see) in the production of new species.

Oriental region, south Asia, with the adjacent part of the East Indies, the Philippines, and Formosa.

Origin of a muscle, the end attached to a relatively fixed part.

Osculum (L. for a little mouth), in Sponges, an opening by which currents of water leave the body.

Osphradium, pl. -ia (dim. of Gk. *ŏsphra*, an odour), a sense-organ which probably tests the nature of the water entering the gill-cavity of aquatic Molluscs.

Ossicle (L. dim. of *ŏs*, a bone), a small irregular bone. Auditory ossicles, in drum of ear.

Otocyst (Gk. *ous*, *ōtŏs*, an ear; *cystis*, a bladder), a minute vesicle of sensory nature, containing one or more hard particles. Probably a balancing organ.

Otolith (Gk. *ous*, *ōtŏs*, an ear; *lithŏs*, a stone), a firm particle within an otocyst or internal auditory organ.

Ovary, an organ producing egg-cells.

Oviparous (L. *ovum*, an egg; *pario*, I produce), egg-laying.

Ovipositor, in Insects, a piercing arrangement at the hinder end of the body in the female, for making holes in plants, &c., and introducing eggs into them.

Ovule (L. dim. of *ovum*, an egg), in Flowering Plants, the small body which becomes a seed after the egg-cell it contains has been fertilized.

Ovum, pl. -a (L. for an egg), an egg-cell, the earliest stage in the development of an embryo.

Oyster-park, an enclosed area of shallow water in which oysters are grown.

Pacinian corpuscle, a minute ovoid laminated body, connected with a sensory nerve, and probably having to do with the pressure-sense.

Palæarctic region (Gk. *palaiŏs*, ancient; *arktŏs*, the north), the northern part of the old world.

Palæolithic period (Gk. *palaiŏs*, ancient; *lithŏs*, a stone), the earlier stages of the Stone Age.

Palæozoic epoch (Gk. *palaiŏs*, ancient; *zoē*, life), the most ancient geological era but one.

Pallial line, in Bivalve Molluscs, a mark on the inner side of each valve, corresponding to the attachment of the mantle or pallium.

Pallium (L. for a cloak). See *Mantle*.

Palmated (L. *palma*, a hand), divided like a hand.

Palp (L. *palpo*, I touch gently), a sensitive outgrowth, *e.g.* of some mouth-parts in Insects. Labial palp, one of four sensitive triangular flaps adjoining the mouth of a Bivalve Mollusc.

Pancreas (the Greek name), the sweet-bread. An abdominal gland, which pours its secretion (pancreatic juice) into the intestine.

Pancreatic juice, the secretion of the pancreas. It acts upon albuminoids, starch, and fats.

Papilla (L. for a nipple), a small projection.

Parapod, or **Parapodium**, pl. -ia (Gk. *para*, by the side of; *pous*, *pŏdŏs*, a foot): (1) in Bristle-Worms, one of the hollow conical unjointed foot-stumps; (2) in some Sea-Slugs, a muscular flap arising far down on each side of the foot.

Parasite (Gk. *parasītŏs*, a sycophant), an organism which lives on (ectoparasite) or in (endoparasite) a larger organism ("host"), feeding on its juices, substance, or digested food.

Parasitism (Gk. *parasītŏs*, a sycophant), the association of a parasite with a "host", the former preying upon the latter by feeding on its blood, &c., or the food it has digested.

Parotid glands, the hindermost pair of salivary glands.

Patella (the Latin name), the knee-pan

Paunch. See *Rumen*.

Pearl, in Molluscs, a disease product, formed by deposit of calcareous layers round a foreign body, *e.g.* a dead parasite or a grain of sand. See also *Ground-Pearl*.

Pecten (L. for a comb), a vascular folded structure that projects into the eye of a Bird, behind the lens.

Pectines (L. for combs), in Scorpions, a pair of comb-shaped organs situated immediately behind the operculum (which see).

Pectoral (L. *pectus*, *pectoris*, the chest), applied to structures, *e.g.* the fore-limbs of a dog, connected with the chest or thorax.

Pectoralis major, the great muscle of the breast, by which the fore-limbs are drawn towards one another.

Pedicellaria, pl. **-æ** (dim. of L. *pedica*, a trap), in Star-Fishes and Sea-Urchins, a pincer-like spine.

Pedipalp, in Spider-like animals (Arachnida), one of the second pair of head-limbs.

Pelagic (Gk. *pĕlagikŏs*, marine), living in the open sea, at or near the surface.

Pelagic zone, the surface waters of the sea.

Pelvic, applied to structures, *e.g.* the hinder pair of fins in a shark, connected with the Pelvis (which see).

Pelvis (L. *pelvis*, a basin), applied to that part of the skeleton to which the hind-limbs are attached.

Pemmican, sun-dried meat.

Pentadactyle (Gk. *pĕntĕ*, five; *daktylŏs*, a finger or toe), possessing five digits.

Pepsin, an albumen-digesting ferment contained in gastric juice.

Peptic glands. See *Gastric glands*.

Peptone, a soluble and diffusible form of albuminoid. It is produced by the action of gastric juice and pancreatic juice upon the albuminous part of the food.

Pericardial, relating to the pericardium.

Pericardium (Gk. *peri*, around; *cardia*, the heart), the cavity in which the heart is contained.

Peristaltic (the Greek word), applied to the wave-like contractions of the intestines and (in lower forms) blood-vessels.

Permanent dentition, the second set of teeth in a Mammal.

Persistent type, an animal species or genus persisting for a long period of geological time, without obvious modification.

Petal (Gk. *pĕtalŏn*, a flower-leaf), one of the inner set (corolla) of investing flower-leaves.

Phagocyte (Gk. *phagein*, to eat; *cytŏs*, a small box, hence a cell), a colourless corpuscle.

Phalanges, sing. **Phalanx** (Gk. *phalanx*, a finger- or toe-bone), bones of fingers and toes.

Pharyngeal, relating to the Pharynx (which see).

Pharynx (the Greek name), that region of the digestive tube which follows the mouth-cavity.

Phylogeny (Gk. *phylŏn*, a tribe; *gĕnnaō*, I produce), the evolutionary history of animals.

Phylum, **-a** (Gk. *phylŏn*, a race or tribe), one of the main subdivisions of the animal kingdom, *e.g.* Vertebrata, Mollusca, Protozoa.

Physiological selection, the theory that the isolation necessary for the origin of new species is due to partial or complete sterility of varying forms with the parent stock.

Physiology (Gk. *physis*, nature; *lŏgŏs*, a discourse), the study of the uses or functions of the parts (organs) of plants and animals. It was formerly used in a much wider sense.

Pilidium, pl. **-a** (Gk. *pilidiŏn*, a little cap), in some Nemertine worms, a ciliated larva resembling a cap or helmet with rounded side-flaps.

Pineal body, a problematic structure connected with the roof of the brain in Vertebrates, and probably representing the remains of a Pineal eye (which see).

Pineal eye, an unpaired dorsal eye present in some Reptiles. See *Pineal body*.

Pinna, the ear-flap of a Mammal.

Pinnule (dim. of L. *pinna*, a feather), in Feather-stars, one of the small branches of the ten arms.

Pisciculture (L. *piscis*, a fish), the artificial culture of Fishes, *e.g.* carp in ponds.

Pisiform bone (L. *pisum*, a pea), a small rounded bone present in the carpus of some animals, external to the ulnare (which see).

Pistil (L. *pistillum*, pestle), the central part of a flower, in which seeds are produced.

Pituitary body, a problematic structure attached to the under side of the brain in a Vertebrate. Possibly the vestige of a sense organ (cp. *Pineal body*).

Placoid (Gk. *plakous*, a cake; *eidŏs*, appearance), used of the thick rounded bony scales of Sharks and Rays.

Placula (Gk. dim. of *plakous*, a flat cake), a plate-shaped Blastula (which see).

Plankton (Gk. *planktos*, wandering), the floating and drifting population of the sea and lakes.

Plantigrade (L. *planta*, the sole of the foot; *gradior*, I walk), walking upon the palms of the hands and soles of the feet.

Planula (L. dim. of *planus*, a vagrant), in Sponges and Zoophytes, an ovoid ciliated larva.

Plasma (Gk. *plasma*, that which has been formed), the fluid part of the blood and lymph. See also *Corpuscles*.

Plastron, (Fr. for a breastplate), the under part of the exoskeleton in a Tortoise or Turtle.

Ploughshare-bone: (1) in Birds, the bone which supports the tail-quills; (2) in the Mole, a flat curved bone on the inner side of the hand.

Pluteus, pl. **-ei** (L. for a roof made of hurdles), in Brittle-Stars and Sea-Urchins, the bilateral larva, which is provided with pairs of ciliated arms, and supported by an internal calcareous skeleton.

Pneumatic duct, in Fishes, a tube which (temporarily or permanently) connects the swim-bladder with the gullet.

Polar bodies, in the maturation of the egg-cell (ovum), two small cells resulting from the last two cell-divisions.

Pollen (L. for fine flour), in flowers, the fertilizing substance produced by the stamens, and consisting of minute pollen-grains.

Pollen-tube, a delicate tube growing from a pollen-grain, and effecting the fertilization of the egg-cell.

Pollination, in flowers, transfer of pollen to the stigma.

Pollinium, pl. **-ia,** an agglutinated mass of pollen.

Polype, in Zoophytes (Cœlenterata), an individual animal.

Portal veins, veins which carry impure blood to the liver (hepatic portal vein) or to the kidneys (renal portal veins).

Post-axial, behind the axis of a limb.

Posterior nares, the opening or openings by which in air-breathing Vertebrates the cavities of the nose open into the mouth-cavity or pharynx.

Pre-axial, in front of the axis of a limb.

Precoracoid, a skeletal element present in front of the coracoid in some animals.

Preformation, the obsolete theory that the development of an animal results from simple increase in size of parts already present in miniature.

Prehensile (L. *prehenso*, I seize), grasping.

Premolar, one of the permanent cheek-teeth of a Mammal, belonging to the front part of the series, and often preceded by a Milk molar (which see).

Primary, inherited from remote ancestors.

Proboscis (the Greek name), an elongated structure at the front end of certain animals, *e.g.* the trunk of an elephant or the sucking mouth-parts of a butterfly.

Process, a projecting part, *e.g.* of a bone.

Procœlous (Gk. *prŏ-*, in front; *koilŏs*, hollow), applied to vertebræ of which the bodies are concave in front and convex behind.

Producteur, a French oyster-culturalist concerned with production.

Production, in French oyster-culture, the collection and rearing of spat.

Proglottis, pl. **-ides** (Gk. *proglŏssis*, the tip of the tongue), in Tape-Worms, one of the egg-producing joints of the body.

Pro-legs, in Insect-larvæ, temporary sucker-like legs.

Pronation (L. *pronus*, prone), position of the fore-arm when back of hand is directed upwards.

Prosobranch (Gk. *prŏ-*, in front of; *branchia*, gills), applied to Sea-snails with gill or gills in front of the heart.

Prostomium (Gk. *prŏ-*, before; *stŏma*, a mouth), the head-lobe.

Proteids. See *Albuminoids*.

Protocercal (Gk. *prōtŏs*, first; *kĕrkŏs*, tail), applied to the symmetrical unlobed tail of some fishes.

Protoplasm (Gk. *prōtŏs*, first; *plasma*, that which has been formed), the complex substance which makes up the living part of the bodies of all organisms.

Proventriculus (Gk. *prŏ-*, in front of; L. *ventriculus*, the stomach), the first or chemical stomach of a Bird.

Proximal, at or near the attached end.

Psalter. See *Omasum*.

Pseudobranch (Gk. *pseudēs*, false; *branchia*, gills), a gill which has been reduced to a Vestige (which see).

Pseudopodium, pl. **-ia** (Gk. *pseudēs*, false; *pous*, *pŏdŏs*, a foot), in naked Animalcules, one of the blunt lobes which can be protruded by the protoplasm.

Psychology (Gk. *psychē*, the mind; *lŏgŏs*, a discourse), the study of mind.

Pteryla, pl. **-æ** (Gk. *pterŏn*, a plume), a feather-covered tract of skin.

Pubis, the ventral and anterior element of the hip-girdle.

Pulmonary (L. *pulmo*, a lung), relating to the lungs.

Pulvillus, pl. **-i** (L. *pulvillus*, a little pillow), in the feet of some Insects, an adhesive end-flap.

Pupa (L. for a doll), in Insects, a motionless stage in the life-history.

Pupil (L. *pupilla*, same meaning), the opening in the Iris (which see).

Pygal (Gk. *pygē*, the rump), related to the hinder part of the body.

Pyloric, applied to that end of the stomach which adjoins the intestine. See *Pylorus*.

Pylorus (Gk. *pylaōrŏs*, having charge of a gate), the opening between stomach and intestine.

Quadrate bone and **Quadrate cartilage,** a bone (or cartilage) by which the lower jaw is attached to the skull in most Vertebrates except Mammals.

Quarter-evil. See *Anthrax*.

Rachis (Gk. *rhachis*, the backbone), the axis of a feather.

Radial, in radially symmetrical animals, relating to a radius.

Radiale, a proximal element in the carpus, situated on the side next the thumb.

Radial symmetry. See *Symmetry.*

Radius: (1) (L. *radius*, a ray), in radially symmetrical animals, one of the axes of symmetry which radiate from a central point, as the spokes of a wheel do from the hub; (2) (the Latin meaning), the bone of the fore-arm which is on the thumb-side.

Radula (L. *radula*, a scraper), the horny tooth-studded ribbon that constitutes the rasping part of the Odontophore (which see).

Raphides (Gk. *rhaphis*, *-idŏs*, a needle), in plants, bundles of needle-shaped crystals of oxalate of lime.

Ratite (L. *rates*, a raft): (1) shaped like a raft, *i.e.* devoid of a keel-like projection; (2) applied to running birds, in which the breast-bone is so shaped.

Recapitulation, repetition of ancestral stages in the life-history.

Recognition-markings, in Birds and Mammals, colour-arrangements which aid in rapid recognition by members of the same species.

Rectrices (L. for female rulers), quill-feathers of the tail.

Redia, pl. -æ (after the Italian naturalist *Redi*), in Flukes, a cylindrical stage in the life-history, produced by the Sporocyst (which see).

Reed. See *Abomasum.*

Regeneration, the power of repairing injuries.

Rejuvenescence (L. *rejuvenesco*, I become young again), the invigoration produced by nuclear fusion. See *Fertilization.*

Remiges (L. for rowers), quill-feathers of the wing.

Rennet stomach. See *Abomasum.*

Rennin, a milk-curdling ferment contained in gastric juice.

Resemblance, General, a harmonizing with surroundings producing inconspicuousness. It may be protective, aggressive, or both. When capable of adjustment it is said to be *variable.*

Resemblance, Special, a resemblance to some specific object in the surroundings, by which inconspicuousness is produced. It may be protective, aggressive, or both. When capable of adjustment it is said to be *variable.*

Reticulum (L. for a little net), in the stomach of Ruminants, the second compartment.

Retina (L. *rete*, a net), the sensitive internal layer of the eye.

Retinaculum (L. for a rope or bond), in Moths, a tuft of scales or flap on the posterior part of the fore-wing. The Frenulum (which see) interlocks with it.

Retractile (L. *retractum*, drawn back), capable of being drawn back.

Reversion, the appearance of characters unlike those of the preceding generation, but resembling those of remoter ancestors.

Rhabdites (Gk. *rhabdŏs*, a rod), in Planarian Worms (Turbellaria), microscopic rods discharged from the skin as a means of defence and probably of irritant nature.

Rhopalion, pl. -a (Gk. *rhŏpalŏn*, a club), in some Jelly-fishes, a specialized club-shaped tentacle bearing various sense-organs.

Rods and Cones, the sensitive cells of the eye in Vertebrates.

Rostellum (L. for little beak), a sticky knob connected with the pollinia of an orchid.

Rudimentary organ. See *Vestige.*

Rumen (L. *ruminatio*, chewing the cud), in the stomach of Ruminants, the first compartment.

Rumination (L. *ruminatio*), chewing the cud.

Sacrum, in the backbone, the part connected with the supports (hip-girdles) of the hind-limbs.

Saliva (the Latin name), spittle.

Salivary gland, a gland which secretes or elaborates saliva (spittle).

Scaly epithelium, epithelium composed of flat cells.

Scapula (the Latin name), the shoulder-blade.

Sclerotic (Gk. *sklērŏs*, hard), the tough external coat of the eyeball.

Sebaceous (L. *sebum*, grease), of a greasy or oily nature.

Secondary: (1) acquired within the limits of a group; (2) replacing some earlier structure.

Segmentation: (1) the division of the adult body into successive rings, segments, or somites; (2) the early stages of division in the egg-cell.

Self-fertilization, fertilization of an egg-cell by a sperm (or its equivalent) derived from the same organism.

Self-pollination, transfer of pollen to the stigma of a flower from its own stamens.

Semi-plantigrade, with palms and soles partly resting on the ground.

Sepal (Gk. *skĕpē*, a covering), one of the outer set (calyx) of investing flower-leaves.

Sessile (L. *sessilis*, sitting), without a stalk.

Seta, pl. -æ (the Latin name), a bristle.

Shagreen, the skins of certain Sharks and Dog-Fishes, containing numerous hard scales.

Shell-cameos, carvings made on certain shells which are composed of differently coloured layers.

Shell-gland, in lower Crustaceans, one of a pair of excretory organs removing nitrogenous waste from the body. They open at the bases of the third jaws (2nd maxillæ).

Shell-muscle, the muscle by which a snail is attached to its shell.

Shoulder-girdle, skeleton of shoulder.

Side-gill, in Crustaceans, a gill attached to the side of the body.

Signalling coloration, conspicuous patches of colour, *e.g.* the white tail of a Rabbit, displayed during rapid movement. The approach of danger is thus communicated to other members of the community.

Simple epithelium, epithelium only one cell thick.

Sinupalliate (L. *sinus*, a bay), in Bivalve Molluscs, with a posterior indentation in the pallial line, caused by the attachment of a muscle for drawing back the siphons.

Siphon (L. *sipho*, a siphon), in aquatic Molluscs, a tubular prolongation of the mantle by which water enters (inhalent siphon) or leaves (exhalent siphon) the gill-chamber.

Siphuncle (L. *siphunculus*, a small pipe), in the Pearly Nautilus and many extinct Cephalopods, a sort of tube that runs through the chambers of the shell.

Society, an association of gregarious animals.

Soma (Gk. for body), the body of an animal exclusive of the germ-cells.

Somatic variation, variation of the soma (which see).

Spat, the free-swimming larvæ or fry of Oysters, Mussels, &c.

Special creation, applied to the almost obsolete view that all species or kinds of organism have been independently created. See *Evolution*.

Sperm (Gk. *spĕrma*, seed), a small and usually motile propagative cell, which fertilizes an egg-cell (ovum) by fusing with it.

Spermaceti, in the Sperm-Whale, liquid fat contained in a deep depression on the upper side of the skull.

Spermary, an organ producing sperms.

Spicule, (L. *spiculum*, a sharp point), in some Zoophytes (Cœlenterata), Sponges, and Animalcules (Protozoa), an element of the skeleton, of varied shape and chemical composition.

Spinal cord, or **Spinal marrow**, a cylindrical nerve-mass, constituting the hinder part of the central nervous system in a vertebrate animal.

Spinal nerve, a nerve taking origin in the spinal cord.

Spinnerets, in Spiders, small rounded projections on the under side of the abdomen, on which the silk glands open.

Spiracle, (L. *spīro*, I breathe): (1) the external opening of the Spiracular cleft (which see); (2) the blow-hole (nostril) of a whale.

Spiracular cleft, the front gill-cleft of some Fishes (*e.g.* Sharks), which is losing or beginning to lose its original function.

Spleen (the Greek name), a large abdominal ductless gland in Vertebrates, of doubtful function. It is richly provided with blood-vessels.

Splenic fever. See *Anthrax*.

Splint-bones, in the Horse, &c., the dwindled remains of 2nd and 4th metacarpals or metatarsals.

Spore (L. *spŏra*, seed), in some Animalcules, one of the minute parts into which the body breaks up during vegetative propagation of a particular kind.

Spore-formation, in some Animalcules, vegetative propagation by means of spores.

Sporocyst (Gk. *spŏra*, seed; *cystis*, a bladder), in Flukes, a shapeless bag-like stage in the life-history.

Sporoduct, in some Gregarines, one of the tubes by which the spores pass out of the firm case (cyst) in which they are produced.

Sporosac (Gk. *spŏra*, seed), in Zoophytes, a degenerate Gonophore (which see).

Staggers, in Sheep, a disease due to the presence of tape-worm cysts on the brain.

Stamen (Gk. *stēmōn*, a thread), a slender modified flower-leaf, which produces pollen.

Statoblast (Gk. *statŏs*, resting; *blastŏs*, a bud), in fresh-water Moss-Polypes, an internally formed winter-bud.

Sternal: (1) in Vertebrates, relating to the breast-bone or sternum; (2) in Arthropods, near the sternal or under side of the body.

Sternum, pl. **-a** (Gk. *stĕrnŏn*, the breast or breast-bone): (1) in Vertebrates, the breast-bone; (2) in Arthropods, that part of the exoskeleton covering the ventral surface of a segment.

Stigma, pl. **-ata** (Gk. for a mark): (1) the opening of an air-tube in Insects, &c.; (2) in Plants, the receptive surface to which pollen-grains adhere.

Stimulus, pl. **-i** (L. for an ox-goad), any physical or chemical agent by which a sense-organ is thrown into activity.

Sting, a piercing weapon that inflicts a poisoned wound. The name is not applied to parts connected with the mouth, such as the poison-fangs of a Viper.

Stipes (L. for a branch, or stump), in Insects, the second joint of the second jaw.

Stratified: (1) of epithelium, more than one cell thick; (2) of rocks, arranged in layers.

Stratum, pl. **-a** (L. for pavement), a layer of rock.

Struggle for existence, a metaphorical way of expressing the strenuous nature of Accommodation (which see).

Sturdy. See *Staggers*.

Subclavius, in Birds, the muscle which raises the wing.

Sublingual glands, a pair of salivary glands situated under the tongue.

Submaxillary glands, a pair of salivary glands situated between the halves of the lower jaw.

Submentum (L. *sub*, under; *mentum*, the chin), in Insects, the basal part of the lower lip.

Supination (L. *supinus*, lying on the back), position of forearm when palm of hand is directed upwards.

Supra-scapula, a skeletal element present above the scapula in some animals.

Sur-royal, the fourth branch of a Red Deer's antler (counting from its base).

Survival of the fittest. See *Natural selection*.

Swim-bladder, or **Air-bladder**, a gas-containing outgrowth from the digestive tube of some Fishes, which serves as a hydrostatic organ.

Symbiosis (Gk. *syn*, together; *biŏsis*, life). See *Mutualism.*

Symmetry (the Greek name), regularity of build. In Radial Symmetry the parts of the body are arranged with reference to a centre of symmetry, *e.g.* in a coral polype. In Bilateral Symmetry, as seen, *e.g.*, in a Fish, we can distinguish right and left sides, anterior and posterior ends, upper and lower surfaces.

Sympathetic nervous system, a part of the nervous system concerned with the regulation of the blood-vessels and internal organs.

Syndactylous (Gk. *syn*, together; *daktylŏs*, a finger or toe), with some of the digits bound closely together.

Syrinx (Gk. for reed-pipe), the vocal organ or voice-box of a Bird, situated where the wind-pipe divides into a branch (*bronchus*) for each lung.

Systemic, applied to a heart which contains pure blood only.

Tail-coverts, feathers covering the tail-quills.

Tarsale, pl. **-ia**, one of the distal elements of the tarsus.

Tarso-metatarsus, a bone in the leg of a Bird, formed by the fusion of part of the ankle-skeleton (tarsus) with three of the instep-bones (metatarsus).

Tarsus (Gk. *tarsŏs*, the broadest part of the foot): (1) in Vertebrates, the skeleton of the ankle; (2) in Insects, the foot.

Teeth: (1) in Vertebrates, hard structures used for securing prey, or for breaking up food; (2) hard projections with which the radula (which see) of Molluscs is studded; (3) small projections usually present in the "hinge" of a bivalve shell: they fit into corresponding sockets, and prevent shifting when the shell opens or closes.

Telson (Gk. for a termination), in higher Crustaceans, the last segment of the abdomen. It bears no limbs, and is the middle part of the tail-fin.

Tendon, a fibrous inelastic band by which a muscle is attached to a part of a skeleton.

Tensor muscles (L. *tendo*, *tentum*, *tensum*, to stretch), in Birds, muscles which keep the wing-membranes on the stretch.

Tentacle (L. *tento*, I feel). a soft feeler, *e.g.* one of the "horns" of a Snail, or one of the numerous fleshy filaments surrounding the mouth-end of a Sea-Anemone.

Tentaculocyst (tentacle; Gk. *cystis*, a bladder), in some Jelly-Fishes, a short specialized tentacle serving as a balancing organ.

Tergum, pl. **-a** (L. for the back), in Arthropods, that part of the exoskeleton covering the dorsal surface of a segment.

Test (L. *testa*, a shell), the firm investment of Ascidians, Echinoderms, and some other lower animals.

Tetradactyle (Gk. *tetra*, four; *daktylŏs*, a finger or toe), possessing four digits.

Thoracic duct, a narrow tube lying immediately ventral to the backbone. It receives most of the lymphatics, and opens into the great veins at the base of the neck.

Thread-cell. See *Nettling-cell.*

Thymus gland (Gk. *thymŏs*, the heart), a fatty-looking ductless gland situated (in Mammals) near the base of the heart.

Thyroid gland (Gk. *thyreŏs*, a shield; *eidŏs*, resemblance), a ductless gland in the neck-region, having something to do with regulating the nutrition of the body.

Tibia (the Latin name for (1)): (1) the shin-bone of Vertebrates; (2) that region of the leg in Insects, &c., which adjoins the foot.

Tibiale, in the tarsus, a proximal element situated on the side next the great toe.

Tibio-tarsus, in Birds, a bone formed by fusion of the shin-bone (tibia) with part of the ankle-skeleton (tarsus).

Tissue, an aggregate of cells specialized for the performance of some particular kind of physiological work.

Tornaria, pl. **-æ** (Gk. *tŏrnŏō*, I make round), the ciliated larva of some species of acorn-headed worm.

Tortoise-shell, an ornamental product prepared from the horny epidermic plates of certain Turtles.

Trachea (Gk. *trachēliaiŏs*, relating to the neck), the wind-pipe.

Tracheæ. See *Tracheal tubes.*

Tracheal gill, in some aquatic Insects, a gill traversed by air-tubes (*tracheæ*).

Tracheal tubes, the air-tubes of air-breathing Arthropods.

Tragus, a pointed projection ("earlet") within the ear of a true Bat.

Trepang, dried Sea-Cucumbers, an important article of food in the Far East.

Trez-tine. See *Antler-royal.*

Trichinosis, a disease due to the attacks of minute thread-worms (Trichinæ).

Trichocysts (Gk. *thrix*, *trichŏs*, a hair; *cystis*, a bladder), in some Animalcules, microscopic rods discharged from the outer layer of the body as a means of defence, and probably of irritant nature.

Tridactyle (Gk. *tri*, three; *daktylos*, a finger or toe), possessing three digits.

Triploblastic (Gk. *triplŏŏs*, threefold; *blastŏs*, a bud), applied to animals in which the body essentially consists of three cellular layers.

Trochanter (Gk. for a process of the thigh-bone), in Insects, the small second joint of the leg.

Trochosphere (Gk. *trŏchŏs*, a wheel; *sphaira*, a sphere), in various Invertebrates, a bilateral ovoid larva, with a well-marked head-lobe, at the base of which is a circlet of large cilia.

Tubercle, a rounded projection, *e.g.* on the crown of a tooth.

Tuberculated, possessing tubercles.

Tympanic (L. *tympanum*, a drum), connected with the drum of the ear in air-breathing Mammals.

Tympanum (L. *tympanum*, a drum): (1) the drum of the ear; (2) the cavity of the song-box (syrinx) of a bird.

Ulna (L. for the elbow), the bone of the fore-arm which is on the little finger side.

Ulnare, a proximal element of the carpus, situated on the side next the little finger.

Umbo (L. *umbo*, the boss of a shield), the projecting beak commonly possessed by each half of a bivalve shell, and which is the oldest part.

Uncinate (L. *uncinatus*, hooked), hook-like.

Unidactyle (L. *unus*, one; *daktylŏs*, a finger or toe), possessing one digit.

Univalve, applied to the shell of a Mollusc, when made up of only one piece or valve, as, *e.g.*, in a Snail.

Ureter, a tube by which the urine is carried off from a kidney.

Urostyle (Gk. *oura*, a tail; *stylŏs*, a pillar), the bony rod which forms the hinder part of a Frog's backbone.

Vacuole (L. dim. of *vacuum*, an empty space), in cells, a small space filled with liquid or gas. Pulsating vacuole, in Animalcules, a vacuole which alternately empties and fills in a regular manner.

Vagus nerves (L. *vagus*, wandering), the tenth pair of cranial nerves, which run back into the abdominal region.

Valve (L. *valva*, a folding-door): (1) an arrangement of one or more projecting flaps by means of which food in the gut, blood in the heart, &c., are obliged to move forward; (2) a distinct piece of shell. See *Bivalve and Univalve*.

Vane, the projecting flat part of a feather.

Variable aggressive coloration, in predaceous forms, coloration which changes with the surroundings so as to produce inconspicuousness.

Variation, the appearance of new characters with the result that no two individuals of the same species are exactly alike.

Vegetative propagation, increase by methods other than egg-production, *e.g.* by Gemmation, Fission, and Spore-formation (which see).

Vein, a blood-vessel which carries blood to or towards the heart.

Veliger (L. *velum*, a sail; *gero*, I carry), in Molluscs, a shell-bearing larva with a large ciliated head-flap by means of which swimming is effected.

Velum (L. for sail or veil), in some Jelly-fishes, an inwardly projecting shelf at the edge of the umbrella.

Ventral (L. for the belly), applied to the under side of an animal.

Ventricle (the Latin name), a relatively thick-walled and muscular heart-chamber, which pumps blood into arteries.

Vertebra, pl. **vertebræ** (the Latin name), one of the joints of the backbone.

Vertebral column, the backbone, or (in some Fishes) its gristly equivalent.

Vertebrate, applied to animals possessing a backbone or its equivalent.

Vestige, or **Rudimentary organ**, a structure which has undergone reduction, as the result of adaptation to surroundings.

Vestigial, reduced to a Vestige (which see).

Visceral, relating to the viscera. See *Viscus*.

Visceral arches and clefts, thickenings and slit-like openings on each side of the throat, which are possessed by every Vertebrate for at least part of its life. The clefts place the pharynx in communication with the exterior.

Visceral hump, the projecting upper part of many Molluscs, containing many of the chief internal organs.

Viscus, pl. **-era**, one of the internal organs contained in the chest or abdomen.

Vitelline membrane, the membrane surrounding an egg-cell.

Viviparous (L. *vivus*, alive; *pario*, I produce), giving birth to more or less well-developed young, as opposed to egg-laying.

Vocal chords, in Mammals, &c.; two elastic folds in the voice-box. A sound is emitted when their edges are brought parallel and thrown into vibration by an air-current.

Wallace's Line, the boundary between the Oriental and Australian regions.

Wampum, the shell-money and ornaments of North American Indians.

Warbles, swellings on the backs of cattle, caused by the presence of larval bot-flies.

Warning coloration, crude colours and patterns possessed by many inedible or well-armed forms, and producing conspicuousness. By advertising unpleasant properties it reduces the chance of attacks by enemies. Some forms are also protected by emitting warning sounds, or assuming warning (or terrifying) attitudes.

Water-vascular system, in Echinoderms, a system of tubes into which sea-water enters. It is concerned with locomotion and respiration.

White matter, that part of the central nervous system made up of nerve-fibres.

Wing coverts, feathers covering the wing-quills.

Zebra-mule, a cross between Zebra and Horse.

Zoæa, pl. **-æ** (Gk. *zōia*, life), in higher Crustaceans, a large-headed larva, swimming by its foot-jaws, and possessing a limbless abdomen.

Zoögeography (Gk. *zōŏn*, an animal), distribution of animals in space.

Zooid, in Moss-Polypes, one of the individuals of a colony.

Zoology (Gk. *zōŏn*, an animal), the science dealing with animals.

Zoophilous (Gk. *zōŏn*, an animal; *phileō*, I love), of flowers, pollinated by animals.

Zoophyte (Gk. *zōŏn*, an animal; *phyton*, a plant), a popular and rather vague word applied to various colonial lower animals, *e.g.* many Corals, which were at one time regarded as intermediate between plants and animals.

Zygodactylous (Gk. *zygŏn*, a yoke; *daktylŏs*, a toe), of the feet of some climbing Birds; with second and third toes turned to the front and first and fourth directed backwards.

INDEX

A

B

C

D

F

G

H

I

J

K

L

M

N

O

P

Q

R

S

T

W

X

Y

Z